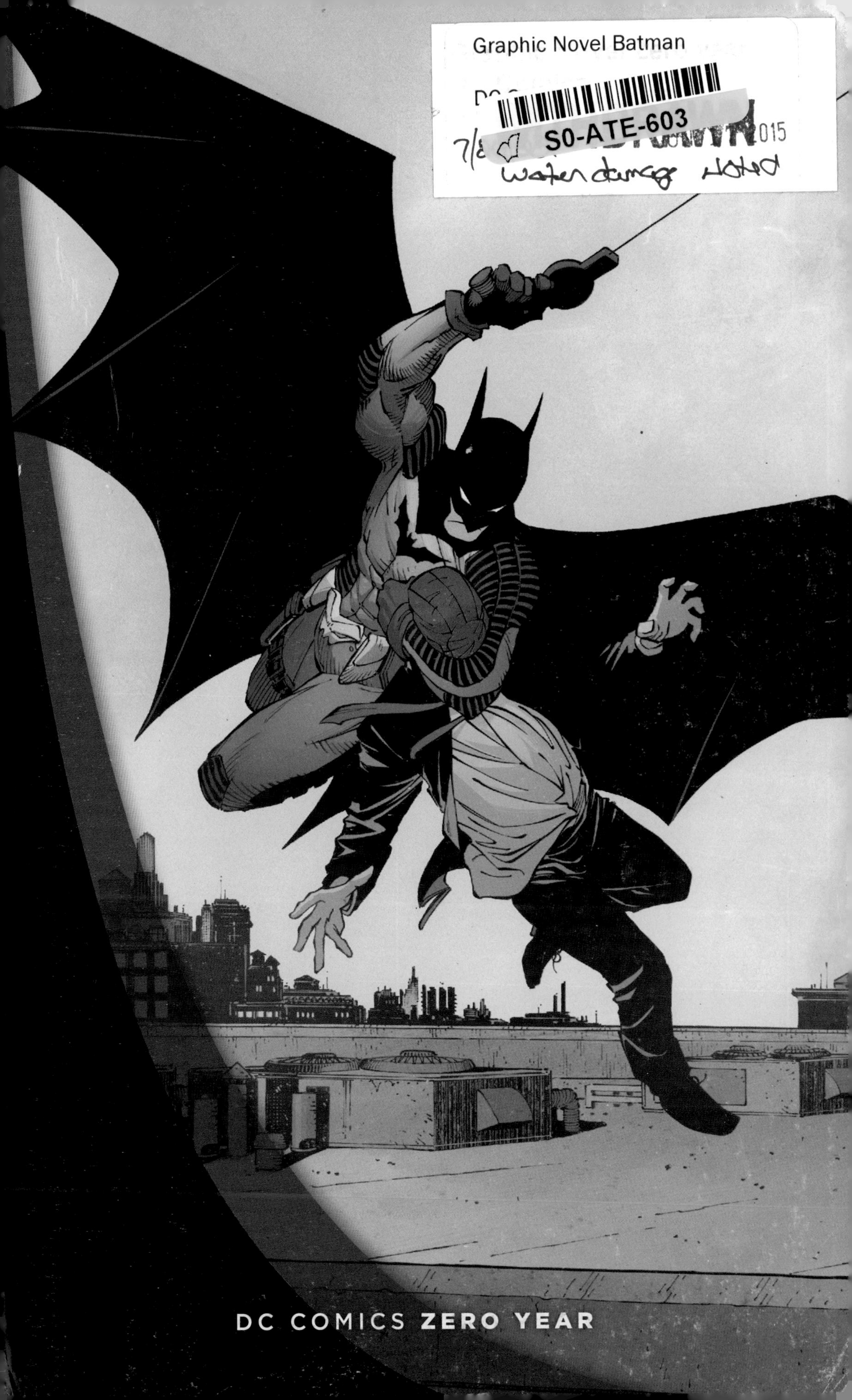
DC COMICS ZERO YEAR

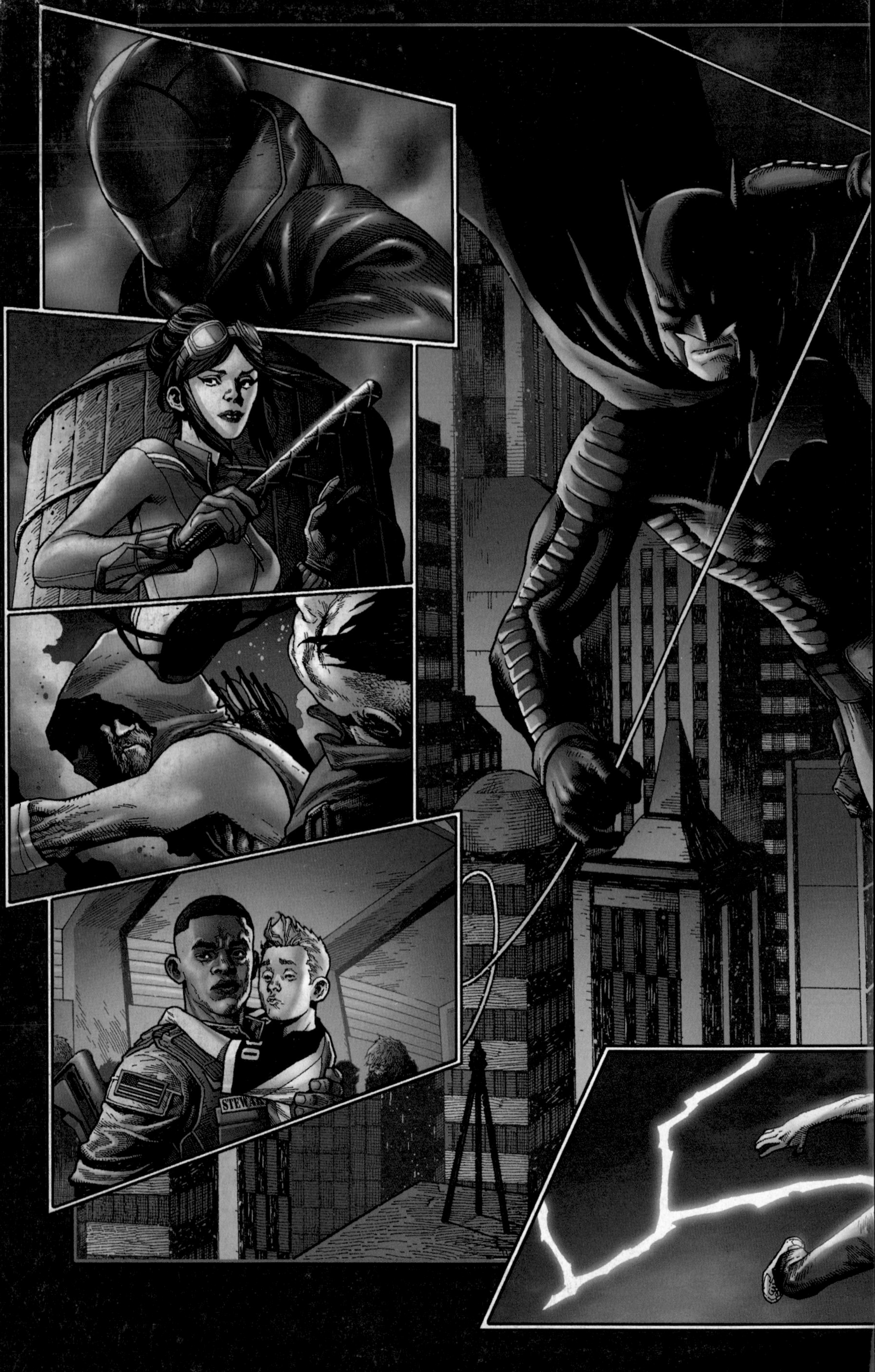

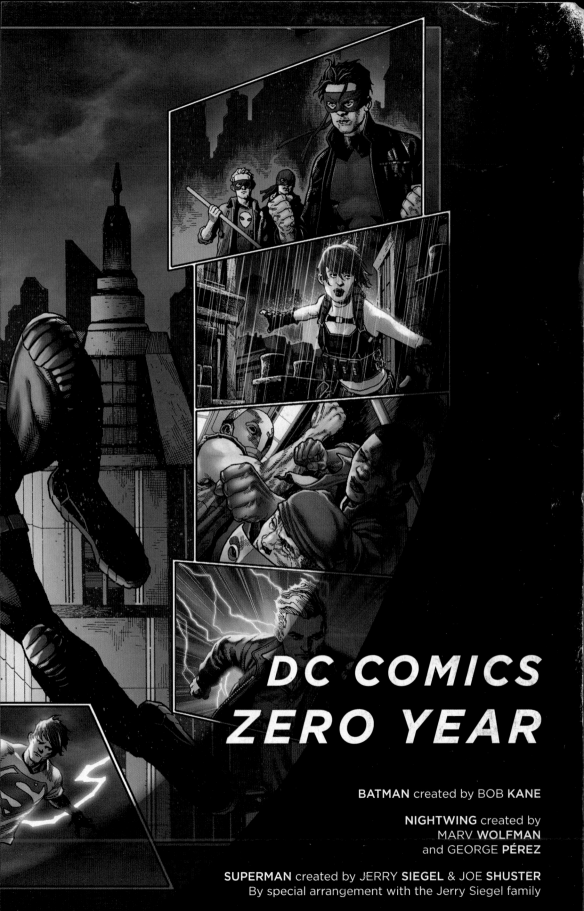

DC COMICS ZERO YEAR

BATMAN created by BOB KANE

NIGHTWING created by
MARV WOLFMAN
and GEORGE PÉREZ

SUPERMAN created by JERRY SIEGEL & JOE SHUSTER
By special arrangement with the Jerry Siegel family

MIKE MARTS EDDIE BERGANZA RACHEL GLUCKSTERN WIL MOSS MATT IDELSON Editors – Original Series
RICKEY PURDIN KATIE KUBERT HARVEY RICHARDS CHRIS CONROY Associate Editors – Original Series
ANTHONY MARQUES DARREN SHAN Assistant Editors – Original Series ROBIN WILDMAN Editor
ROBBIN BROSTERMAN Design Director – Books ROBBIE BIEDERMAN Publication Design

BOB HARRAS Senior VP – Editor-in-Chief, DC Comics

DIANE NELSON President DAN DIDIO and JIM LEE Co-Publishers
GEOFF JOHNS Chief Creative Officer AMIT DESAI Senior VP – Marketing & Franchise Management
AMY GENKINS Senior VP – Business & Legal Affairs NAIRI GARDINER Senior VP – Finance
JEFF BOISON VP – Publishing Planning MARK CHIARELLO VP – Art Direction & Design JOHN CUNNINGHAM VP – Marketing
TERRI CUNNINGHAM VP – Editorial Administration LARRY GANEM VP – Talent Relations & Services
ALISON GILL Senior VP – Manufacturing & Operations HANK KANALZ Senior VP – Vertigo & Integrated Publishing
JAY KOGAN VP – Business & Legal Affairs, Publishing JACK MAHAN VP – Business Affairs, Talent
NICK NAPOLITANO VP – Manufacturing Administration SUE POHJA VP – Book Sales FRED RUIZ VP – Manufacturing Operations
COURTNEY SIMMONS Senior VP – Publicity BOB WAYNE Senior VP – Sales

DC COMICS: ZERO YEAR

Published by DC Comics. Cover and compilation Copyright © 2015 DC Comics. All Rights Reserved.
Originally published in single magazine form in BATMAN 24-25, ACTION COMICS 25, BATGIRL 25, BATWING 25, BATWOMAN 25,
BIRDS OF PREY 25, CATWOMAN 25, DETECTIVE COMICS 25, THE FLASH 25, GREEN ARROW 25, GREEN LANTERN CORPS 25,
NIGHTWING 25, RED HOOD AND THE OUTLAWS 25 © 2013, 2014 DC Comics. All Rights Reserved. All characters, their distinctive likenesses
and related elements featured in this publication are trademarks of DC Comics. The stories, characters and incidents featured in this
publication are entirely fictional. DC Comics does not read or accept unsolicited ideas, stories or artwork.

DC Comics, 1700 Broadway, New York, NY 10019
A Warner Bros. Entertainment Company
Printed by RR Donnelley, Salem, VA, USA. 2/27/15. First Printing.

ISBN: 978-1-4012-5337-0

SUSTAINABLE FORESTRY INITIATIVE
Certified Chain of Custody
20% Certified Forest Content,
80% Certified Sourcing
www.sfiprogram.org
SFI-01042
APPLIES TO TEXT STOCK ONLY

Snyder, Scott, author.
DC Comics : zero year / Scott Snyder, writer ; Greg Capullo, artist.
pages cm. — (The New 52!)
ISBN 978-1-4012-5337-0 (paperback)
1. Graphic novels. I. Capullo, Greg, illustrator. II. Title. III. Title: Zero year.

PN6727.S555D3 2014
741.5'973—dc23

2014027353

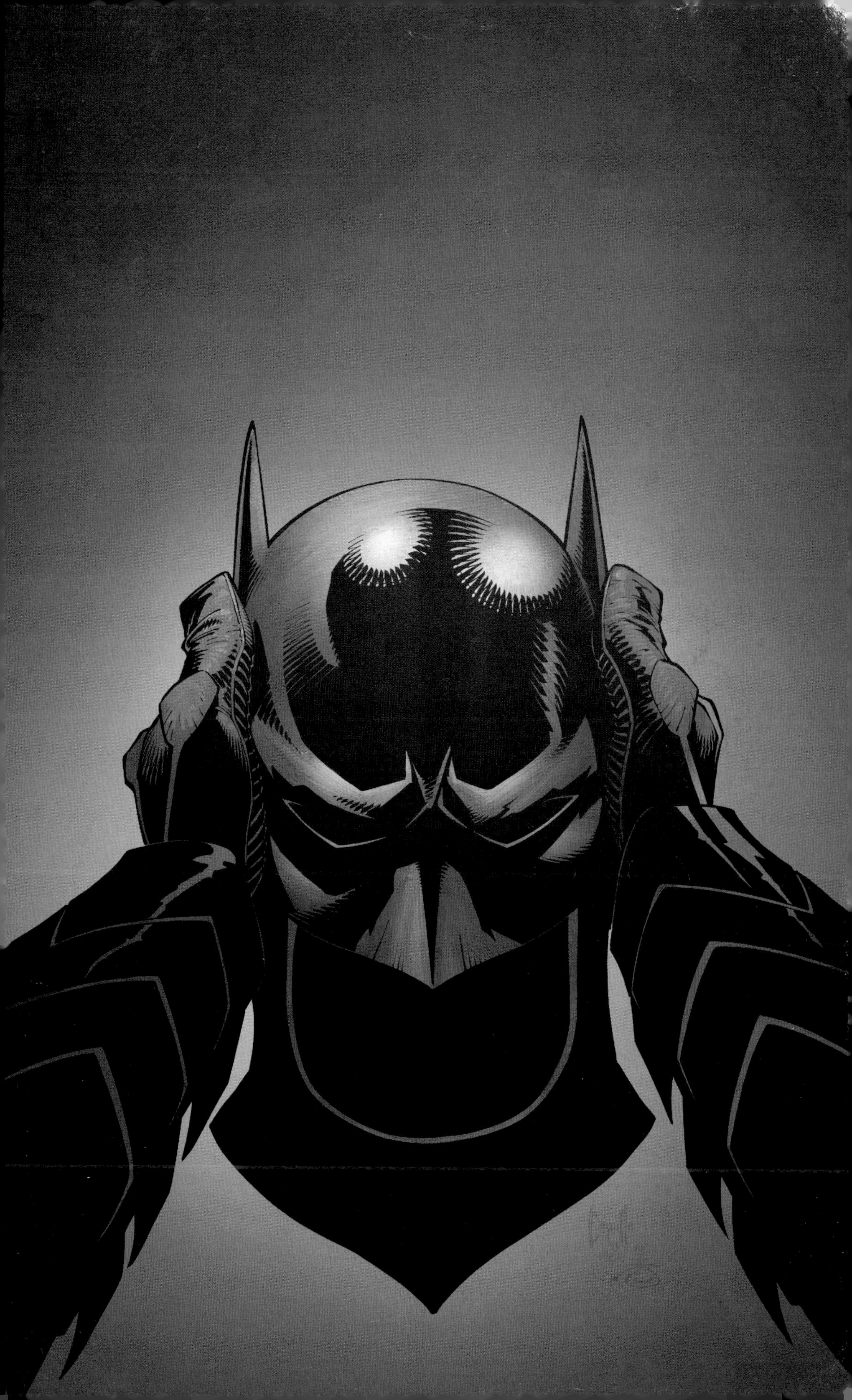

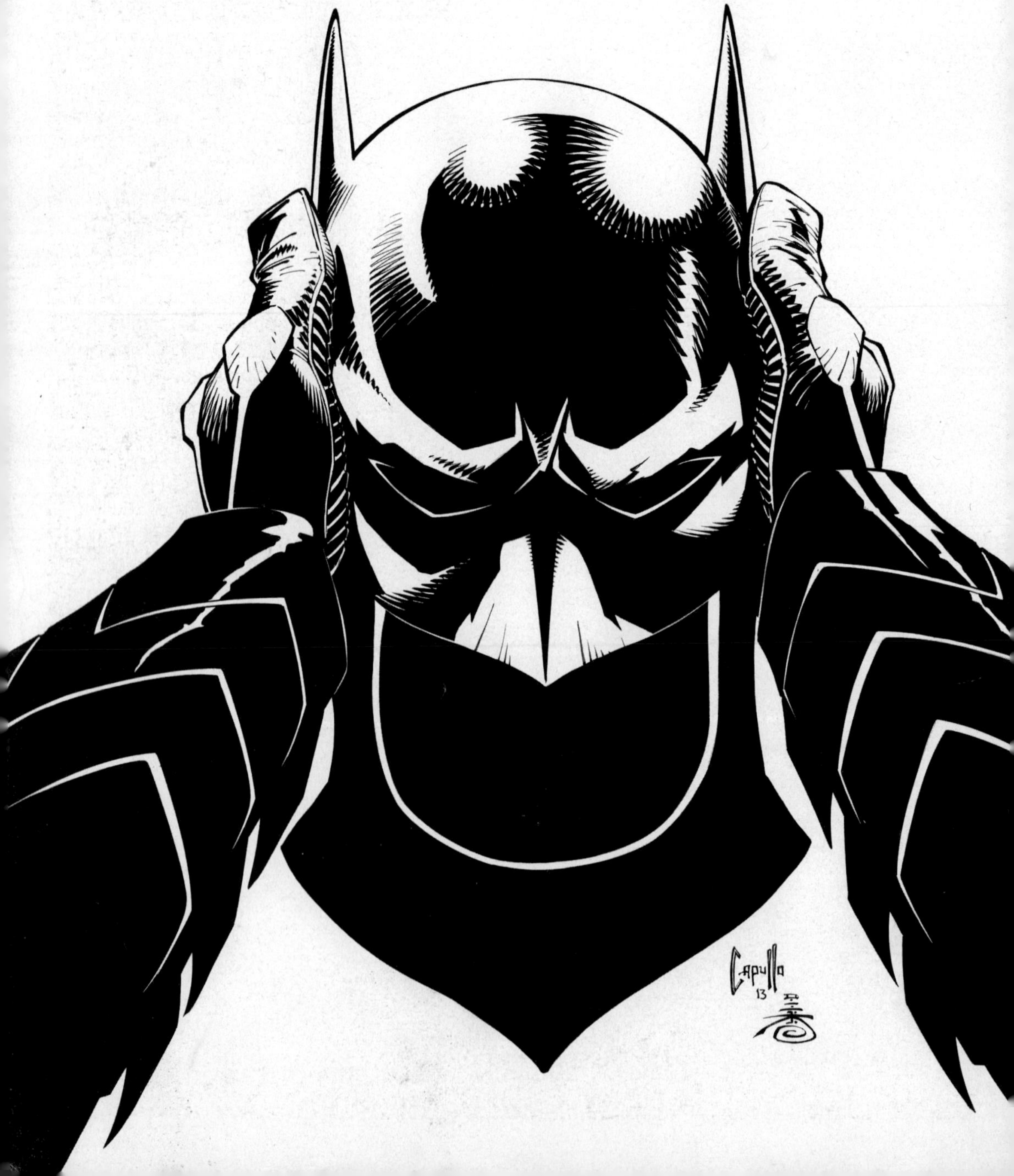
Capullo
13

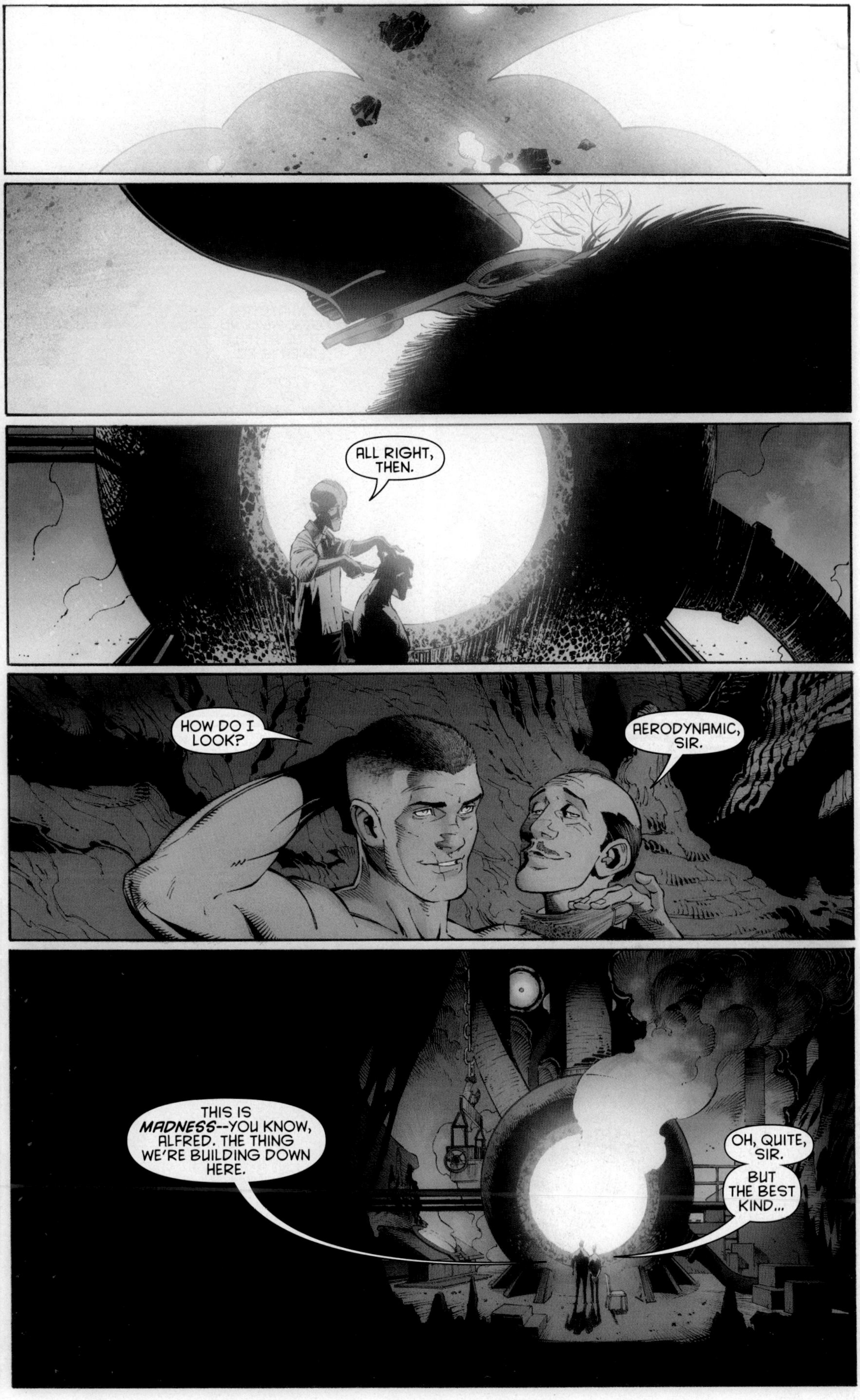
ALL RIGHT, THEN.
HOW DO I LOOK?
AERODYNAMIC, SIR.
THIS IS *MADNESS*--YOU KNOW, ALFRED. THE THING WE'RE BUILDING DOWN HERE.
OH, QUITE, SIR.
BUT THE BEST KIND...

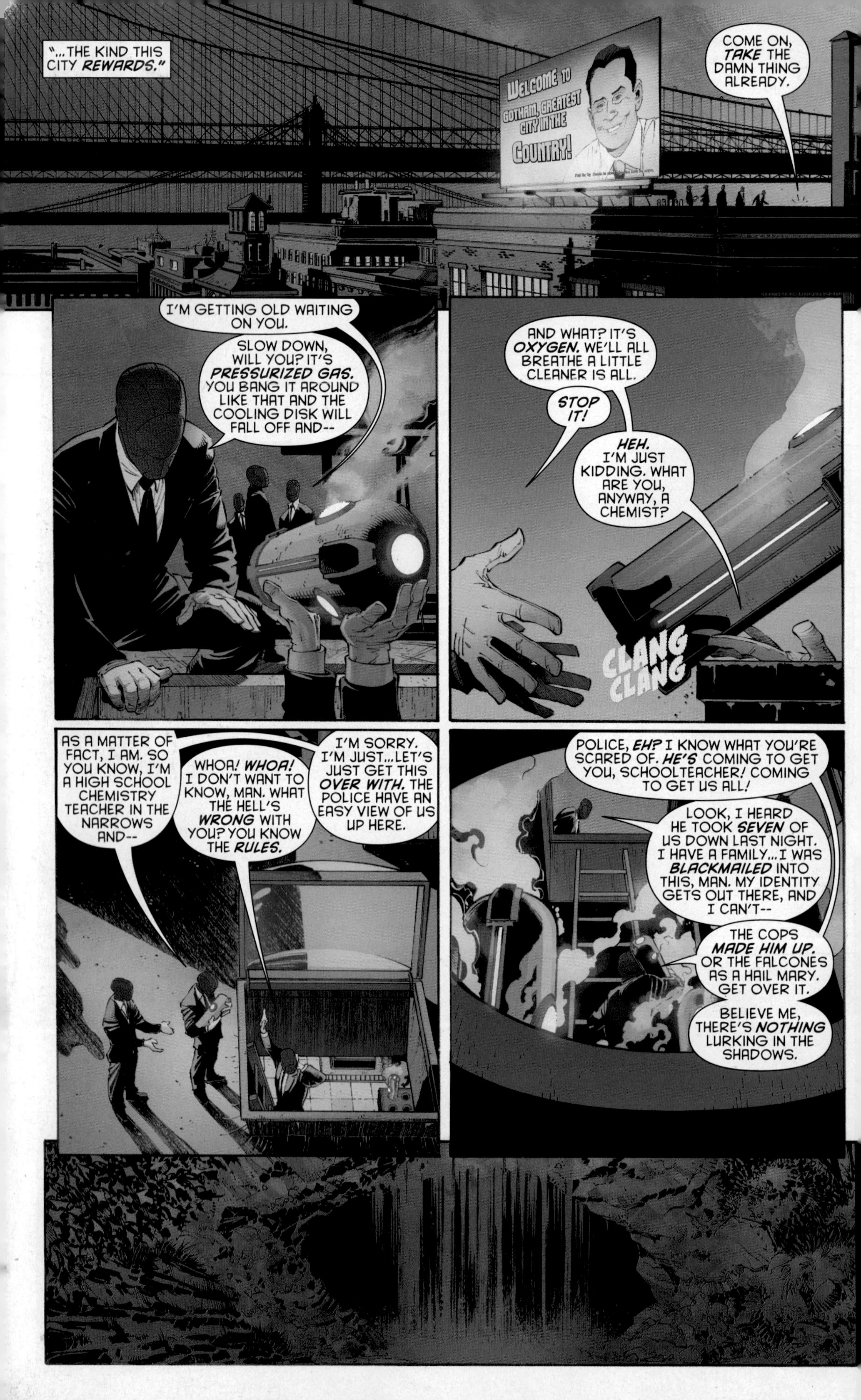
"...THE KIND THIS CITY REWARDS."
WELCOME TO GOTHAM, GREATEST CITY IN THE COUNTRY!
COME ON, TAKE THE DAMN THING ALREADY.
I'M GETTING OLD WAITING ON YOU.
SLOW DOWN, WILL YOU? IT'S PRESSURIZED GAS. YOU BANG IT AROUND LIKE THAT AND THE COOLING DISK WILL FALL OFF AND--
AND WHAT? IT'S OXYGEN. WE'LL ALL BREATHE A LITTLE CLEANER IS ALL.
STOP IT!
HEH. I'M JUST KIDDING. WHAT ARE YOU, ANYWAY, A CHEMIST?
CLANG CLANG
AS A MATTER OF FACT, I AM. SO YOU KNOW, I'M A HIGH SCHOOL CHEMISTRY TEACHER IN THE NARROWS AND--
WHOA! WHOA! I DON'T WANT TO KNOW, MAN. WHAT THE HELL'S WRONG WITH YOU? YOU KNOW THE RULES.
I'M SORRY. I'M JUST...LET'S JUST GET THIS OVER WITH. THE POLICE HAVE AN EASY VIEW OF US UP HERE.
POLICE, EH? I KNOW WHAT YOU'RE SCARED OF. HE'S COMING TO GET YOU, SCHOOLTEACHER! COMING TO GET US ALL!
LOOK, I HEARD HE TOOK SEVEN OF US DOWN LAST NIGHT. I HAVE A FAMILY...I WAS BLACKMAILED INTO THIS, MAN. MY IDENTITY GETS OUT THERE, AND I CAN'T--
THE COPS MADE HIM UP. OR THE FALCONES AS A HAIL MARY. GET OVER IT.
BELIEVE ME, THERE'S NOTHING LURKING IN THE SHADOWS.

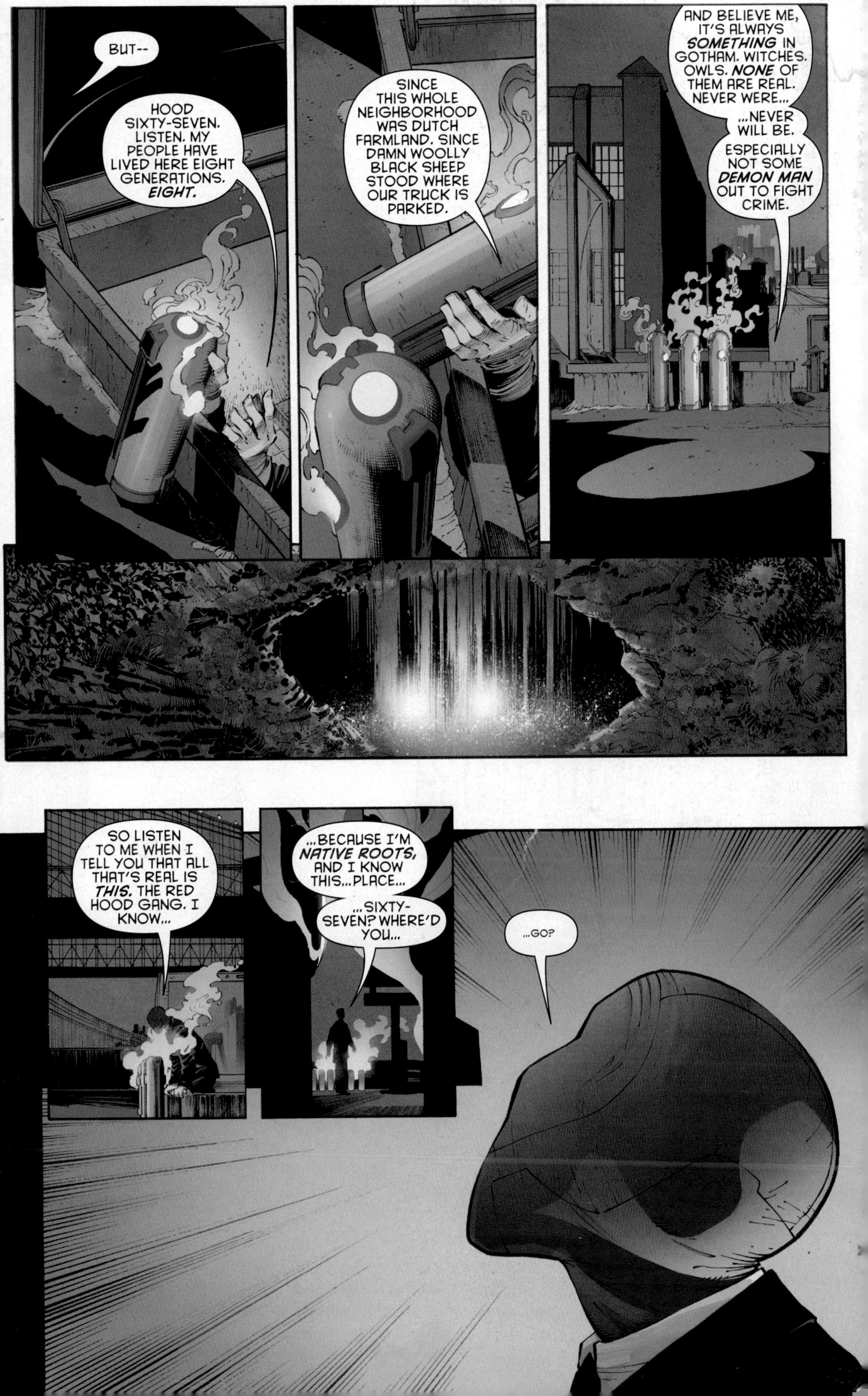
BUT--
HOOD SIXTY-SEVEN. LISTEN. MY PEOPLE HAVE LIVED HERE EIGHT GENERATIONS. EIGHT.
SINCE THIS WHOLE NEIGHBORHOOD WAS DUTCH FARMLAND. SINCE DAMN WOOLLY BLACK SHEEP STOOD WHERE OUR TRUCK IS PARKED.
AND BELIEVE ME, IT'S ALWAYS SOMETHING IN GOTHAM. WITCHES. OWLS. NONE OF THEM ARE REAL. NEVER WERE...
...NEVER WILL BE.
ESPECIALLY NOT SOME DEMON MAN OUT TO FIGHT CRIME.
SO LISTEN TO ME WHEN I TELL YOU THAT ALL THAT'S REAL IS THIS. THE RED HOOD GANG. I KNOW...
...BECAUSE I'M NATIVE ROOTS, AND I KNOW THIS...PLACE...
...SIXTY-SEVEN? WHERE'D YOU...
...GO?

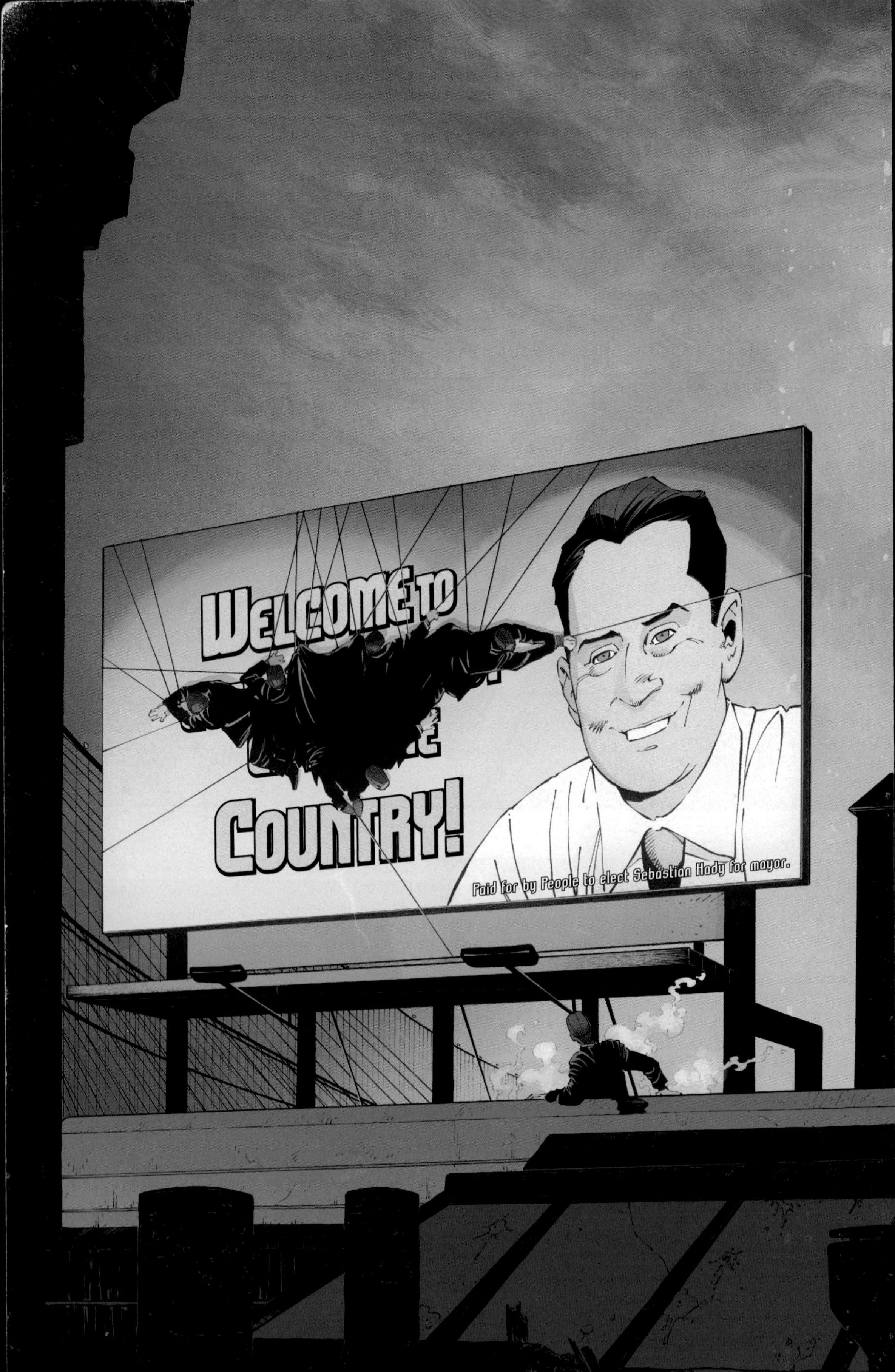
WELCOME TO
COUNTRY!
Paid for by People to elect Sebastian Hady for mayor.

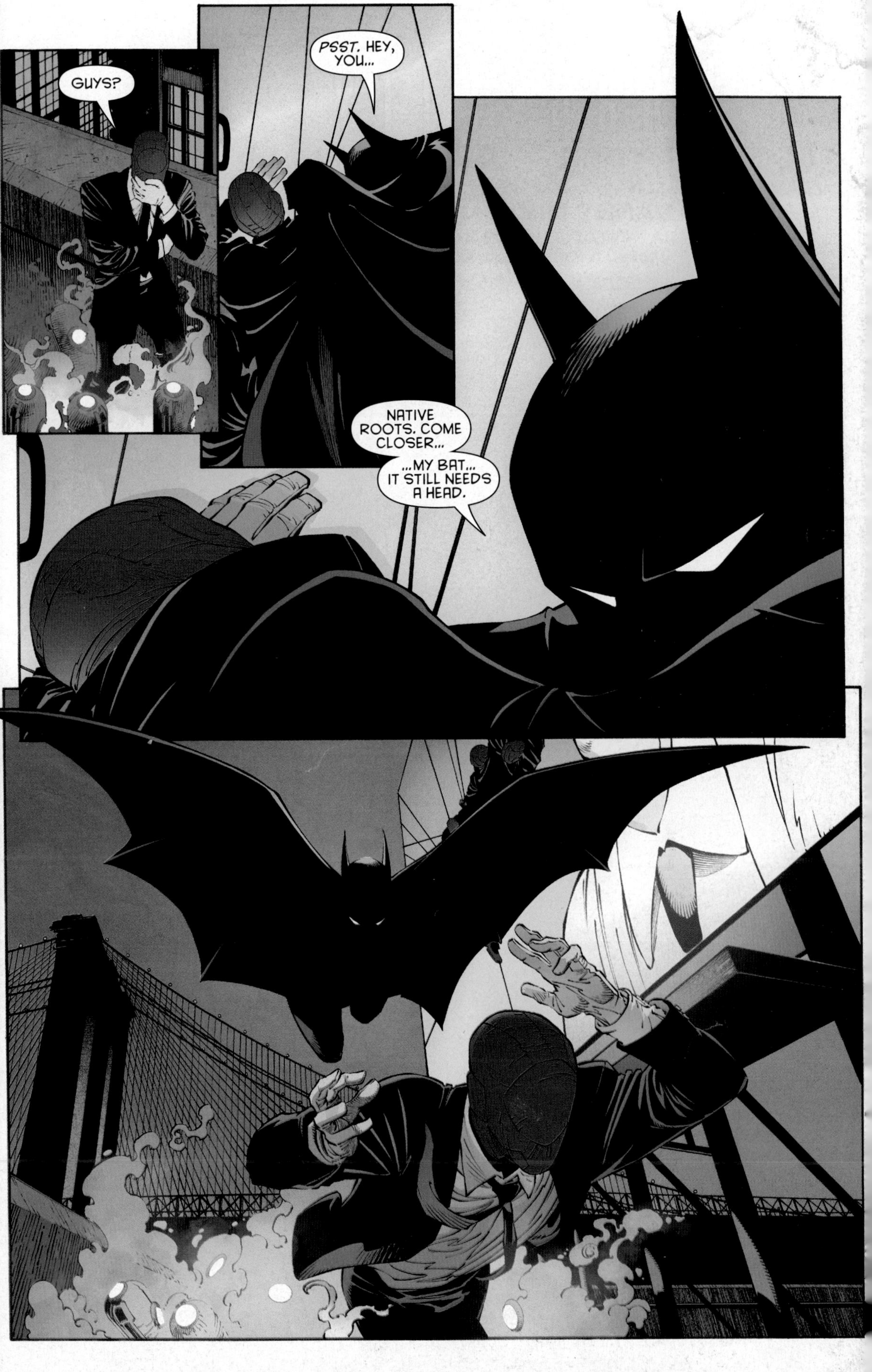
GUYS?
PSST. HEY, YOU...
NATIVE ROOTS. COME CLOSER...
...MY BAT... IT STILL NEEDS A HEAD.

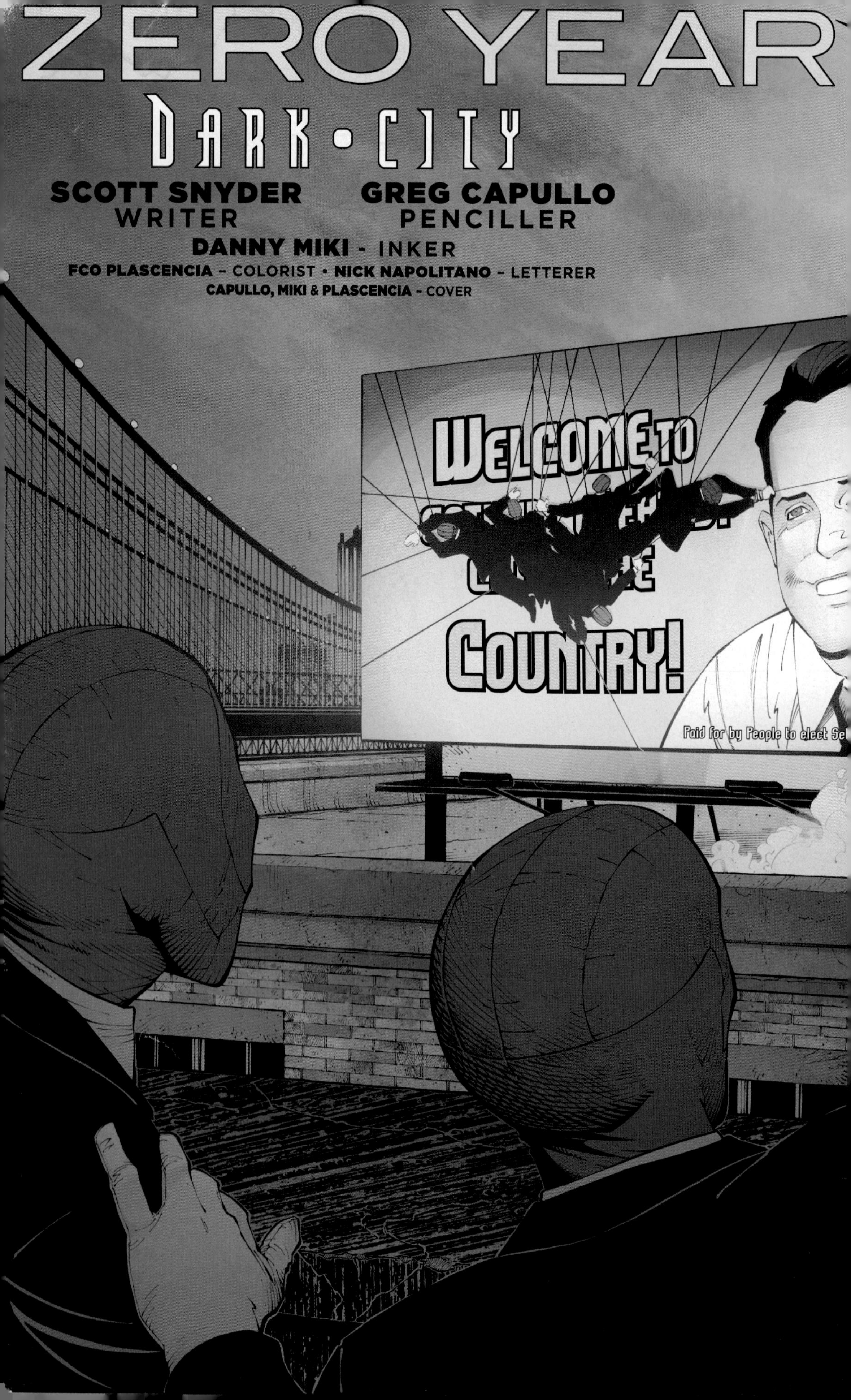
ZERO YEAR
DARK • CITY
SCOTT SNYDER WRITER
GREG CAPULLO PENCILLER
DANNY MIKI - INKER
FCO PLASCENCIA - COLORIST • NICK NAPOLITANO - LETTERER
CAPULLO, MIKI & PLASCENCIA - COVER
WELCOME TO
COUNTRY!
Paid for by People to elect

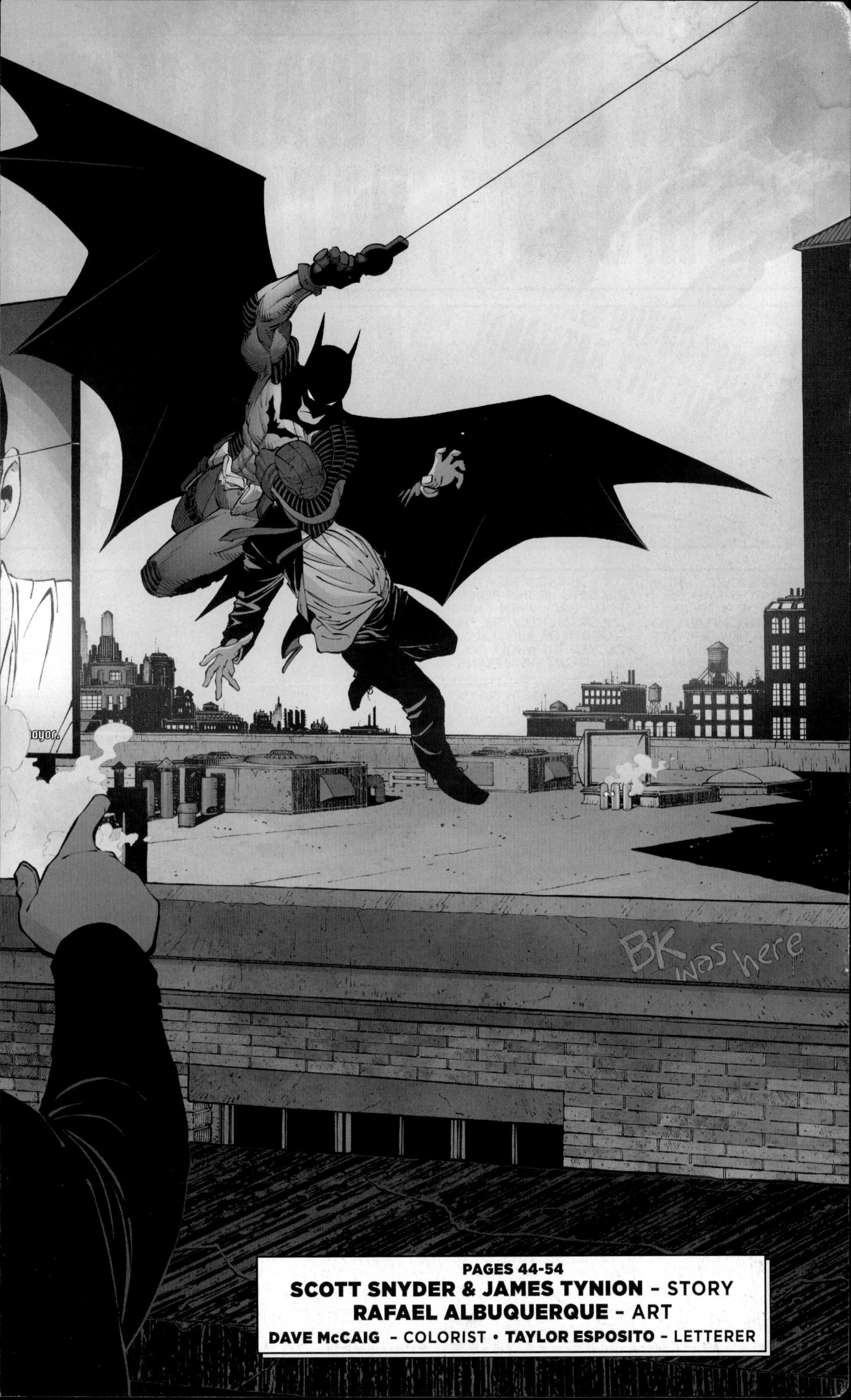
BK was here

PAGES 44-54
SCOTT SNYDER & JAMES TYNION - STORY
RAFAEL ALBUQUERQUE - ART
DAVE McCAIG - COLORIST • **TAYLOR ESPOSITO** - LETTERER

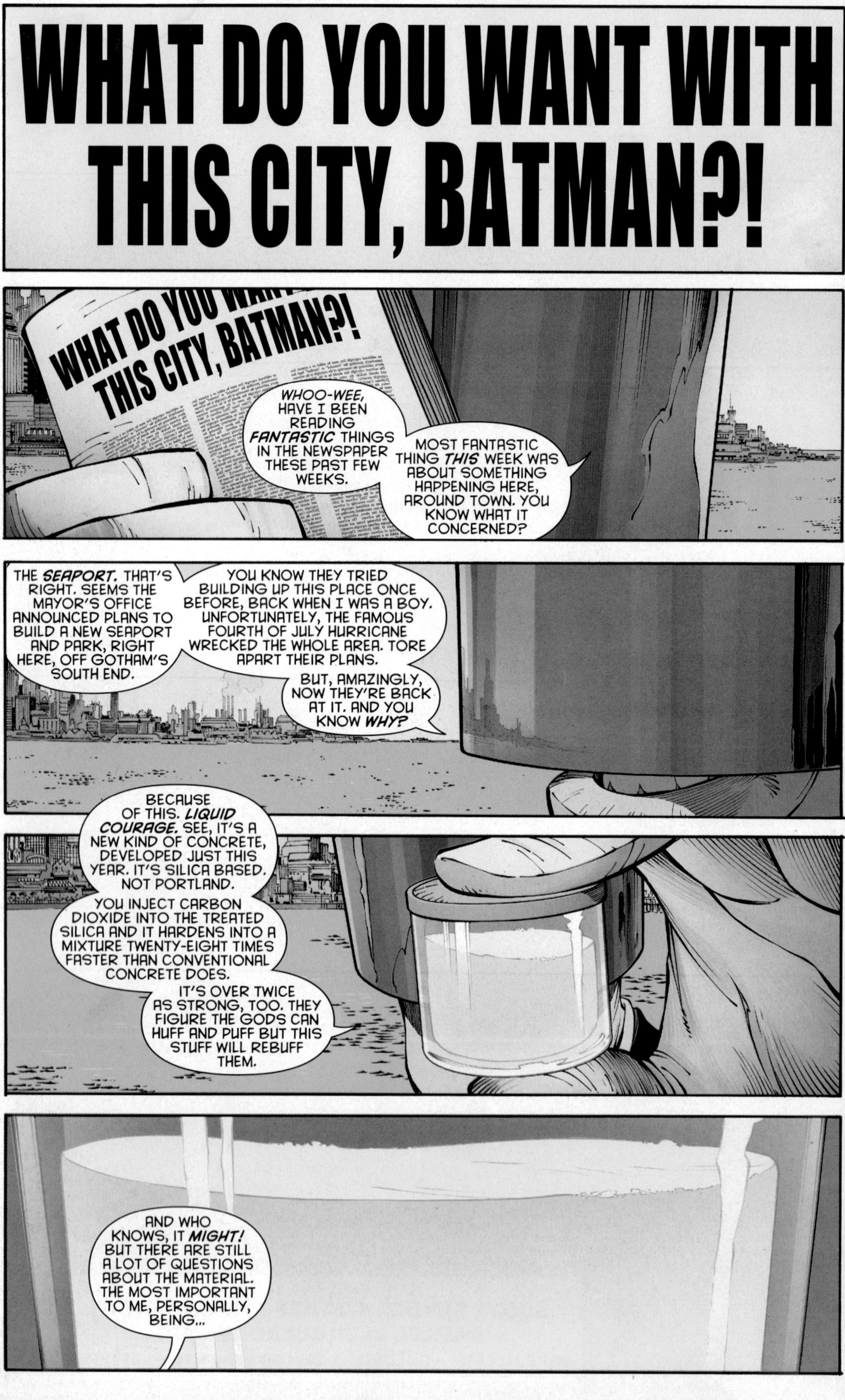
WHAT DO YOU WANT WITH THIS CITY, BATMAN?!
WHAT DO YOU
THIS CITY, BATMAN?!
WHOO-WEE, HAVE I BEEN READING *FANTASTIC* THINGS IN THE NEWSPAPER THESE PAST FEW WEEKS.
MOST FANTASTIC THING *THIS* WEEK WAS ABOUT SOMETHING HAPPENING HERE, AROUND TOWN. YOU KNOW WHAT IT CONCERNED?
THE *SEAPORT.* THAT'S RIGHT. SEEMS THE MAYOR'S OFFICE ANNOUNCED PLANS TO BUILD A NEW SEAPORT AND PARK, RIGHT HERE, OFF GOTHAM'S SOUTH END.
YOU KNOW THEY TRIED BUILDING UP THIS PLACE ONCE BEFORE, BACK WHEN I WAS A BOY. UNFORTUNATELY, THE FAMOUS FOURTH OF JULY HURRICANE WRECKED THE WHOLE AREA. TORE APART THEIR PLANS.
BUT, AMAZINGLY, NOW THEY'RE BACK AT IT. AND YOU KNOW *WHY?*
BECAUSE OF THIS. *LIQUID COURAGE.* SEE, IT'S A NEW KIND OF CONCRETE, DEVELOPED JUST THIS YEAR. IT'S SILICA BASED. NOT PORTLAND.
YOU INJECT CARBON DIOXIDE INTO THE TREATED SILICA AND IT HARDENS INTO A MIXTURE TWENTY-EIGHT TIMES FASTER THAN CONVENTIONAL CONCRETE DOES.
IT'S OVER TWICE AS STRONG, TOO. THEY FIGURE THE GODS CAN HUFF AND PUFF BUT THIS STUFF WILL REBUFF THEM.
AND WHO KNOWS, IT *MIGHT!* BUT THERE ARE STILL A LOT OF QUESTIONS ABOUT THE MATERIAL. THE MOST IMPORTANT TO ME, PERSONALLY, BEING...

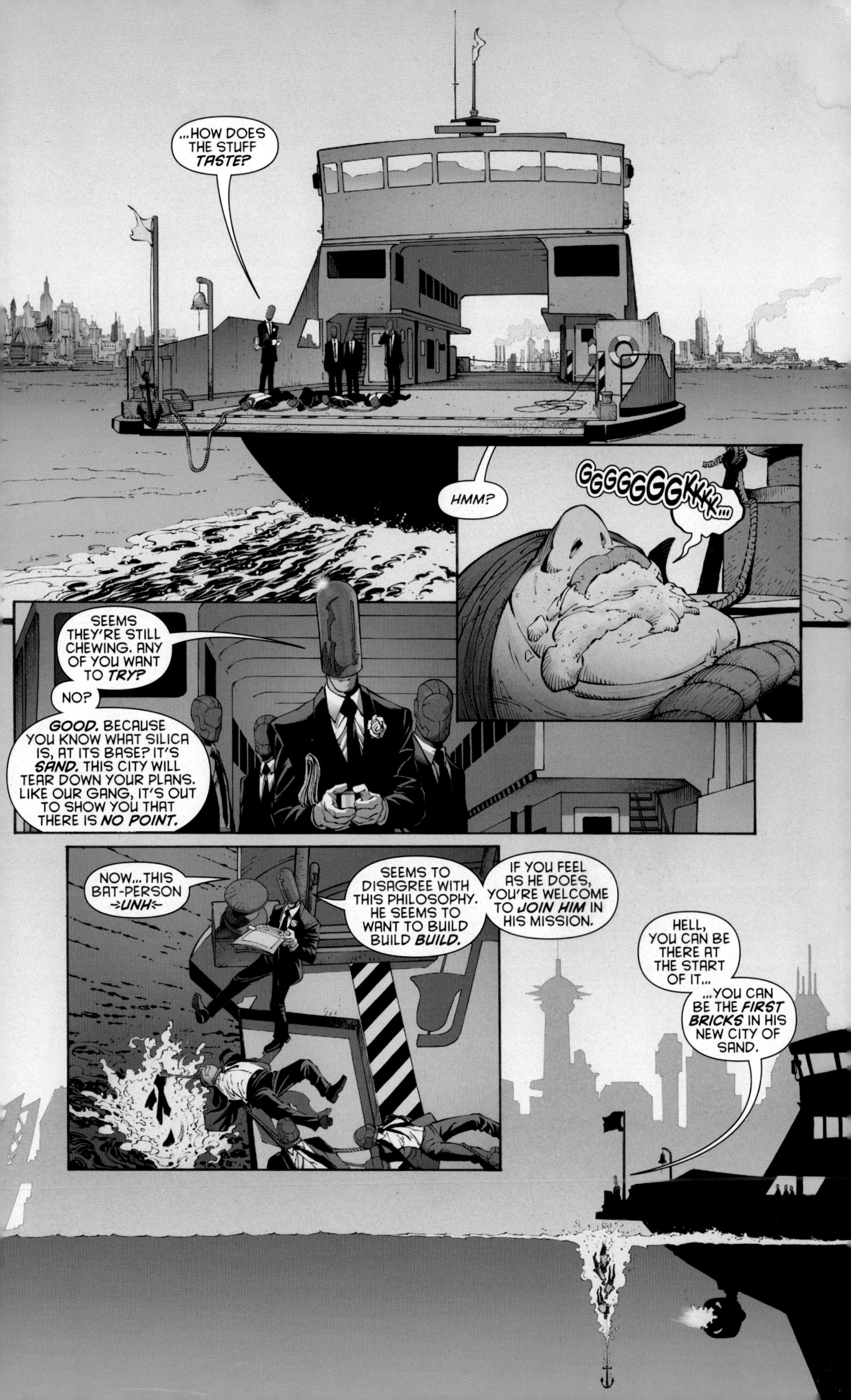
...HOW DOES THE STUFF *TASTE?*
HMM?
GGGGGGGKKKK...
SEEMS THEY'RE STILL CHEWING. ANY OF YOU WANT TO *TRY?*
NO?
GOOD. BECAUSE YOU KNOW WHAT SILICA IS, AT ITS BASE? IT'S *SAND.* THIS CITY WILL TEAR DOWN YOUR PLANS. LIKE OUR GANG, IT'S OUT TO SHOW YOU THAT THERE IS *NO POINT.*
NOW... THIS BAT-PERSON -*UNH*-
SEEMS TO DISAGREE WITH THIS PHILOSOPHY. HE SEEMS TO WANT TO BUILD BUILD *BUILD.*
IF YOU FEEL AS HE DOES, YOU'RE WELCOME TO *JOIN HIM* IN HIS MISSION.
HELL, YOU CAN BE THERE AT THE START OF IT...
...YOU CAN BE THE *FIRST BRICKS* IN HIS NEW CITY OF SAND.

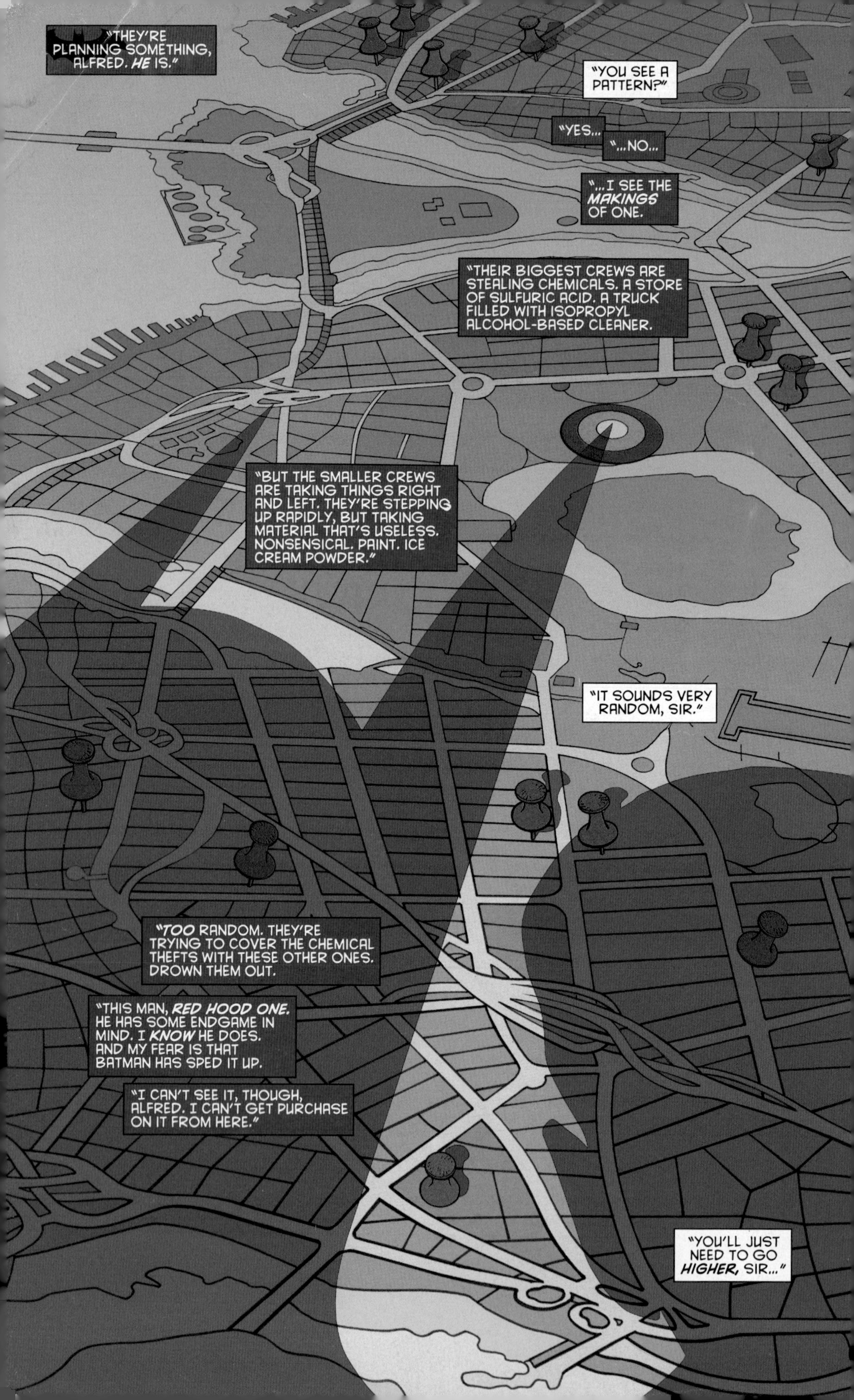
"THEY'RE PLANNING SOMETHING, ALFRED. HE IS."
"YOU SEE A PATTERN?"
"YES...
"...NO...
"...I SEE THE MAKINGS OF ONE.
"THEIR BIGGEST CREWS ARE STEALING CHEMICALS. A STORE OF SULFURIC ACID. A TRUCK FILLED WITH ISOPROPYL ALCOHOL-BASED CLEANER.
"BUT THE SMALLER CREWS ARE TAKING THINGS RIGHT AND LEFT. THEY'RE STEPPING UP RAPIDLY, BUT TAKING MATERIAL THAT'S USELESS. NONSENSICAL. PAINT. ICE CREAM POWDER."
"IT SOUNDS VERY RANDOM, SIR."
"TOO RANDOM. THEY'RE TRYING TO COVER THE CHEMICAL THEFTS WITH THESE OTHER ONES. DROWN THEM OUT.
"THIS MAN, RED HOOD ONE. HE HAS SOME ENDGAME IN MIND. I KNOW HE DOES. AND MY FEAR IS THAT BATMAN HAS SPED IT UP.
"I CAN'T SEE IT, THOUGH, ALFRED. I CAN'T GET PURCHASE ON IT FROM HERE."
"YOU'LL JUST NEED TO GO HIGHER, SIR..."

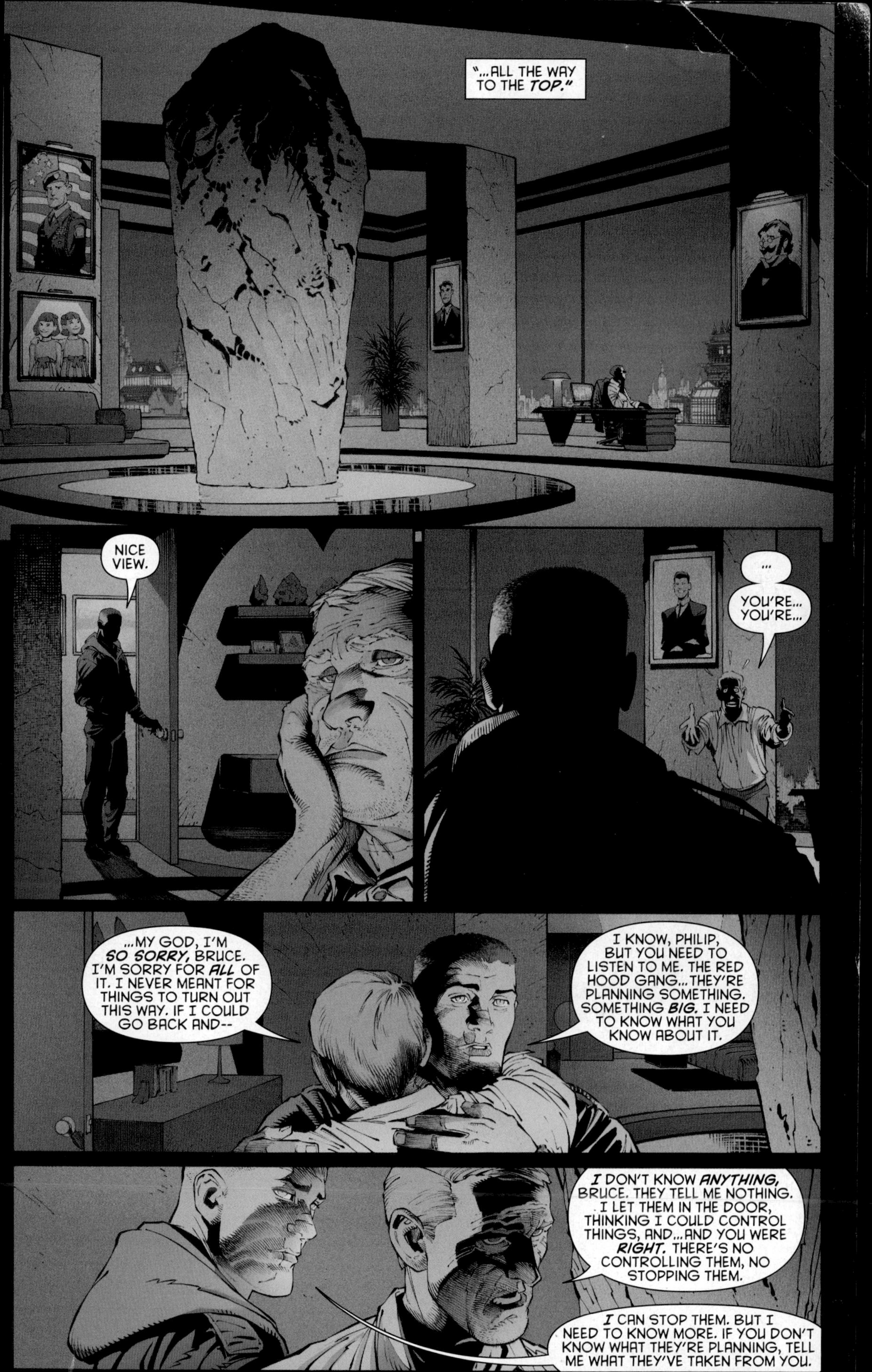
"...ALL THE WAY TO THE TOP."
NICE VIEW.
...
YOU'RE... YOU'RE...
...MY GOD, I'M SO SORRY, BRUCE. I'M SORRY FOR ALL OF IT. I NEVER MEANT FOR THINGS TO TURN OUT THIS WAY. IF I COULD GO BACK AND--
I KNOW, PHILIP, BUT YOU NEED TO LISTEN TO ME. THE RED HOOD GANG... THEY'RE PLANNING SOMETHING. SOMETHING BIG. I NEED TO KNOW WHAT YOU KNOW ABOUT IT.
I DON'T KNOW ANYTHING, BRUCE. THEY TELL ME NOTHING. I LET THEM IN THE DOOR, THINKING I COULD CONTROL THINGS, AND... AND YOU WERE RIGHT. THERE'S NO CONTROLLING THEM, NO STOPPING THEM.
I CAN STOP THEM. BUT I NEED TO KNOW MORE. IF YOU DON'T KNOW WHAT THEY'RE PLANNING, TELL ME WHAT THEY'VE TAKEN FROM YOU.

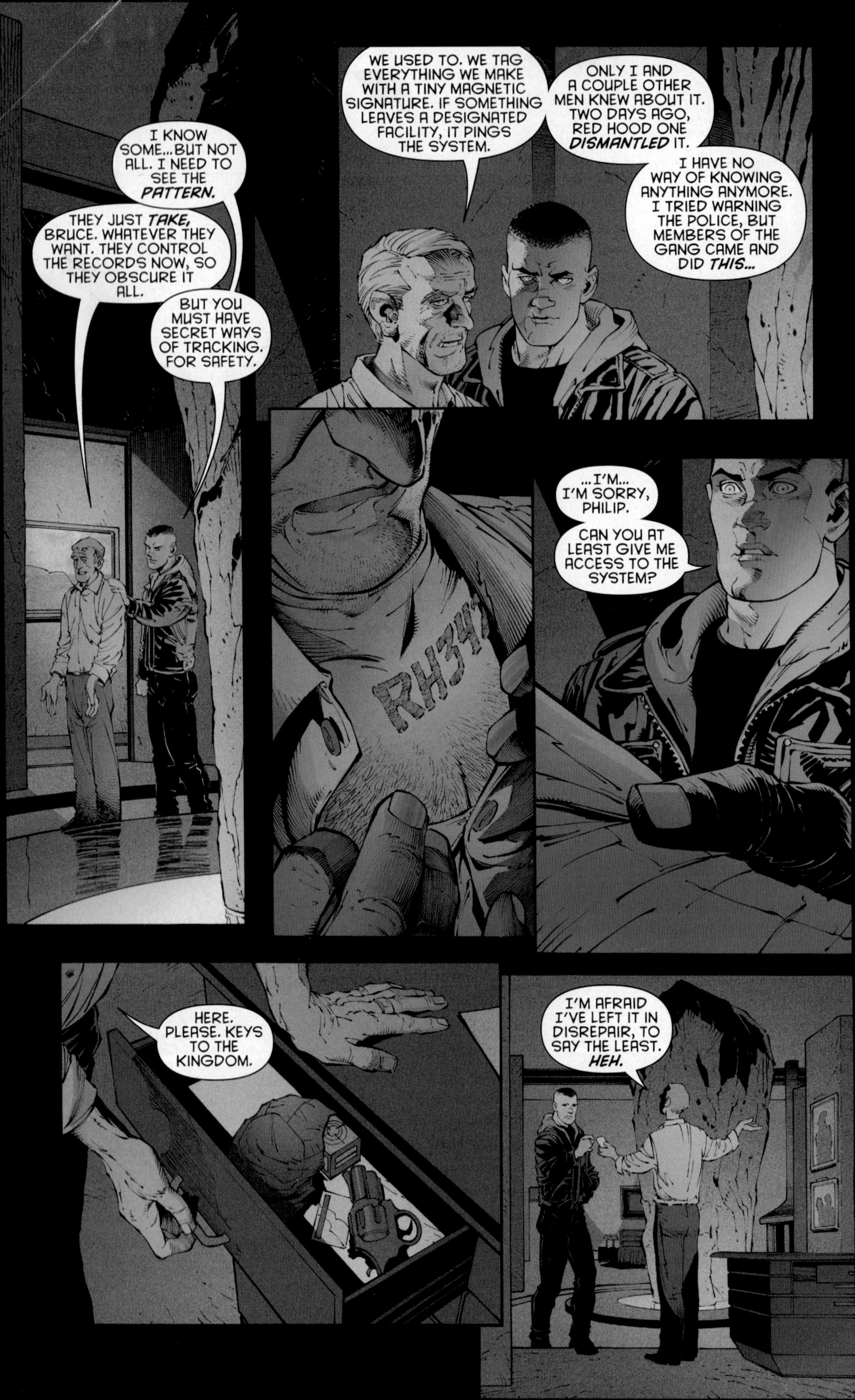
I KNOW SOME...BUT NOT ALL. I NEED TO SEE THE PATTERN.
THEY JUST TAKE, BRUCE. WHATEVER THEY WANT. THEY CONTROL THE RECORDS NOW, SO THEY OBSCURE IT ALL.
BUT YOU MUST HAVE SECRET WAYS OF TRACKING. FOR SAFETY.
WE USED TO. WE TAG EVERYTHING WE MAKE WITH A TINY MAGNETIC SIGNATURE. IF SOMETHING LEAVES A DESIGNATED FACILITY, IT PINGS THE SYSTEM.
ONLY I AND A COUPLE OTHER MEN KNEW ABOUT IT. TWO DAYS AGO, RED HOOD ONE DISMANTLED IT.
I HAVE NO WAY OF KNOWING ANYTHING ANYMORE. I TRIED WARNING THE POLICE, BUT MEMBERS OF THE GANG CAME AND DID THIS...
RH34
...I'M... I'M SORRY, PHILIP.
CAN YOU AT LEAST GIVE ME ACCESS TO THE SYSTEM?
HERE. PLEASE. KEYS TO THE KINGDOM.
I'M AFRAID I'VE LEFT IT IN DISREPAIR, TO SAY THE LEAST. HEH.

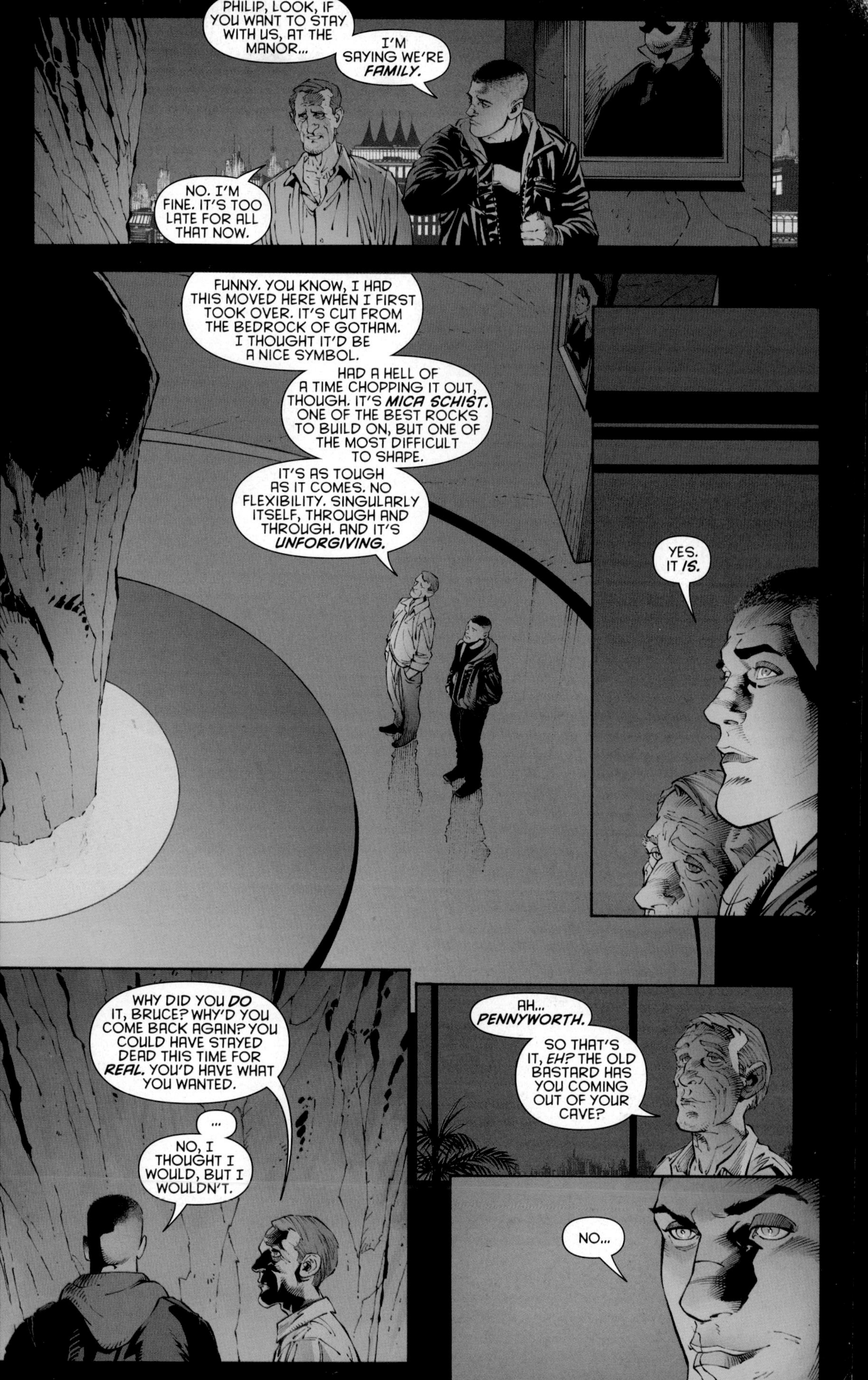
PHILIP, LOOK, IF YOU WANT TO STAY WITH US, AT THE MANOR...
I'M SAYING WE'RE FAMILY.
NO. I'M FINE. IT'S TOO LATE FOR ALL THAT NOW.
FUNNY. YOU KNOW, I HAD THIS MOVED HERE WHEN I FIRST TOOK OVER. IT'S CUT FROM THE BEDROCK OF GOTHAM. I THOUGHT IT'D BE A NICE SYMBOL.
HAD A HELL OF A TIME CHOPPING IT OUT, THOUGH. IT'S MICA SCHIST. ONE OF THE BEST ROCKS TO BUILD ON, BUT ONE OF THE MOST DIFFICULT TO SHAPE.
IT'S AS TOUGH AS IT COMES. NO FLEXIBILITY. SINGULARLY ITSELF, THROUGH AND THROUGH. AND IT'S UNFORGIVING.
YES. IT IS.
WHY DID YOU DO IT, BRUCE? WHY'D YOU COME BACK AGAIN? YOU COULD HAVE STAYED DEAD THIS TIME FOR REAL. YOU'D HAVE WHAT YOU WANTED.
...
NO, I THOUGHT I WOULD, BUT I WOULDN'T.
AH... PENNYWORTH.
SO THAT'S IT, EH? THE OLD BASTARD HAS YOU COMING OUT OF YOUR CAVE?
NO...

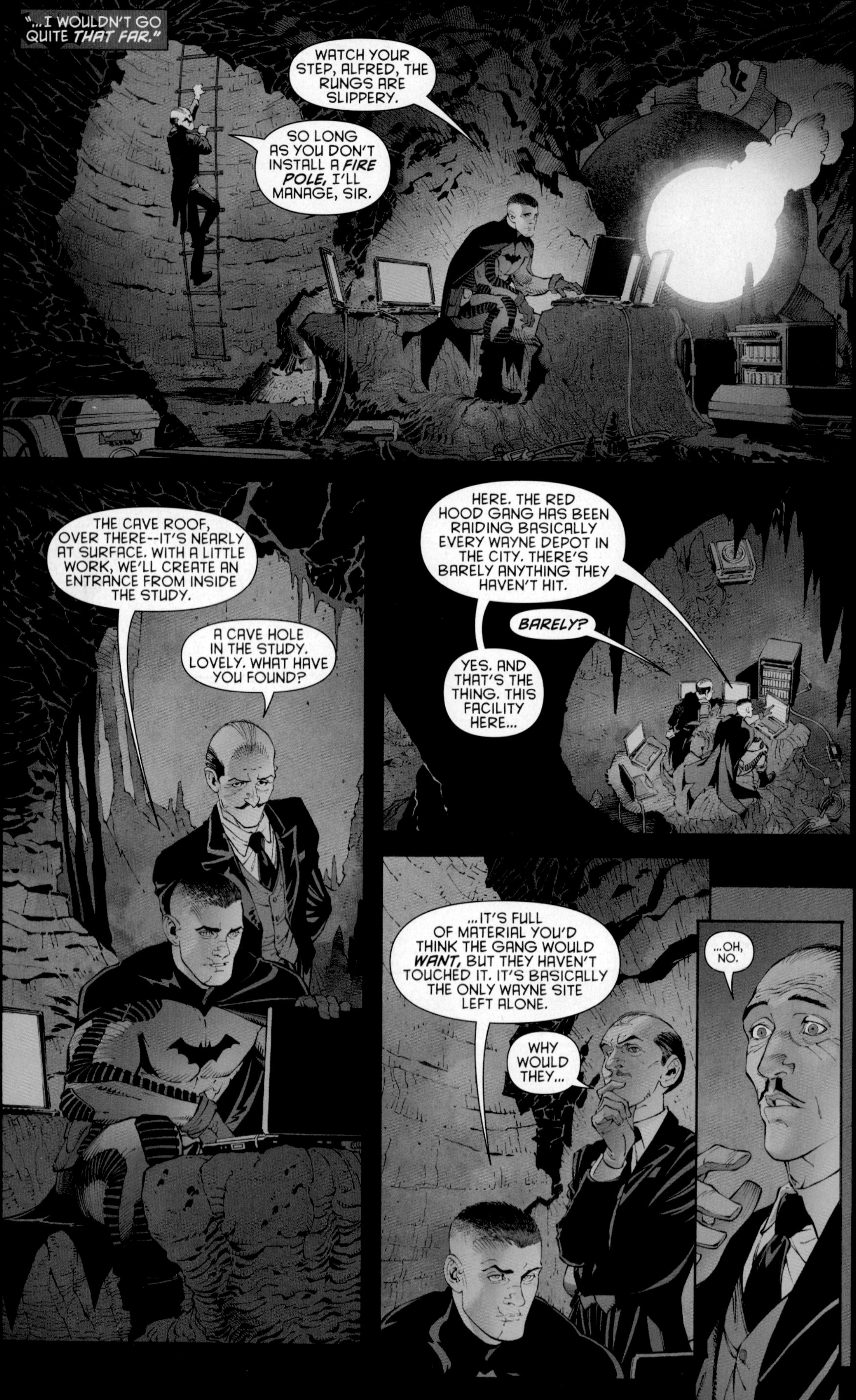
"...I WOULDN'T GO QUITE *THAT FAR.*"
WATCH YOUR STEP, ALFRED, THE RUNGS ARE SLIPPERY.
SO LONG AS YOU DON'T INSTALL A *FIRE POLE,* I'LL MANAGE, SIR.
THE CAVE ROOF, OVER THERE--IT'S NEARLY AT SURFACE. WITH A LITTLE WORK, WE'LL CREATE AN ENTRANCE FROM INSIDE THE STUDY.
A CAVE HOLE IN THE STUDY. LOVELY. WHAT HAVE YOU FOUND?
HERE. THE RED HOOD GANG HAS BEEN RAIDING BASICALLY EVERY WAYNE DEPOT IN THE CITY. THERE'S BARELY ANYTHING THEY HAVEN'T HIT.
BARELY?
YES. AND THAT'S THE THING. THIS FACILITY HERE...
...IT'S FULL OF MATERIAL YOU'D THINK THE GANG WOULD *WANT,* BUT THEY HAVEN'T TOUCHED IT. IT'S BASICALLY THE ONLY WAYNE SITE LEFT ALONE.
WHY WOULD THEY...
...OH, NO.

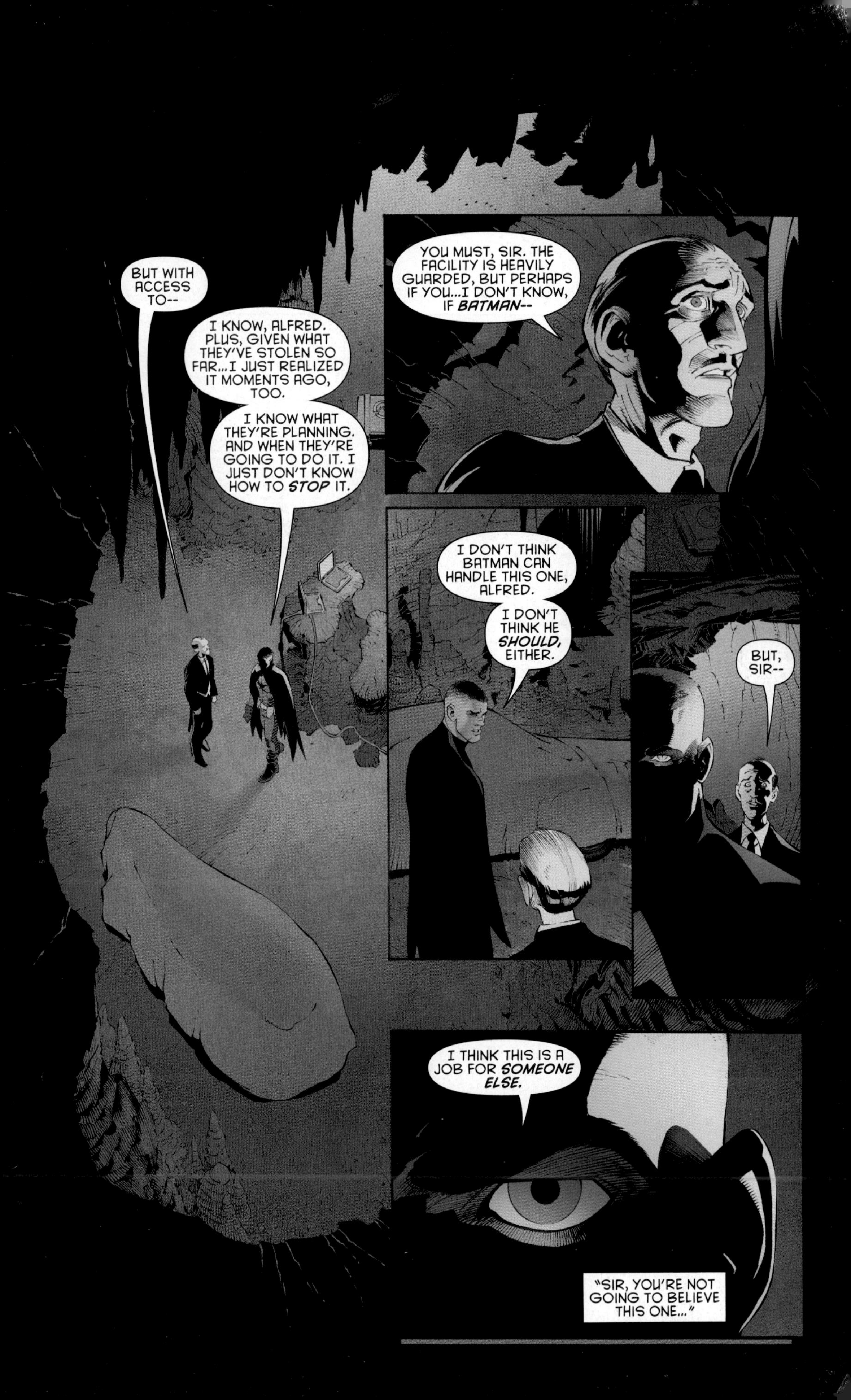
BUT WITH ACCESS TO--
I KNOW, ALFRED. PLUS, GIVEN WHAT THEY'VE STOLEN SO FAR...I JUST REALIZED IT MOMENTS AGO, TOO.
I KNOW WHAT THEY'RE PLANNING. AND WHEN THEY'RE GOING TO DO IT. I JUST DON'T KNOW HOW TO STOP IT.
YOU MUST, SIR. THE FACILITY IS HEAVILY GUARDED, BUT PERHAPS IF YOU...I DON'T KNOW, IF BATMAN--
I DON'T THINK BATMAN CAN HANDLE THIS ONE, ALFRED.
I DON'T THINK HE SHOULD, EITHER.
BUT, SIR--
I THINK THIS IS A JOB FOR SOMEONE ELSE.
"SIR, YOU'RE NOT GOING TO BELIEVE THIS ONE..."

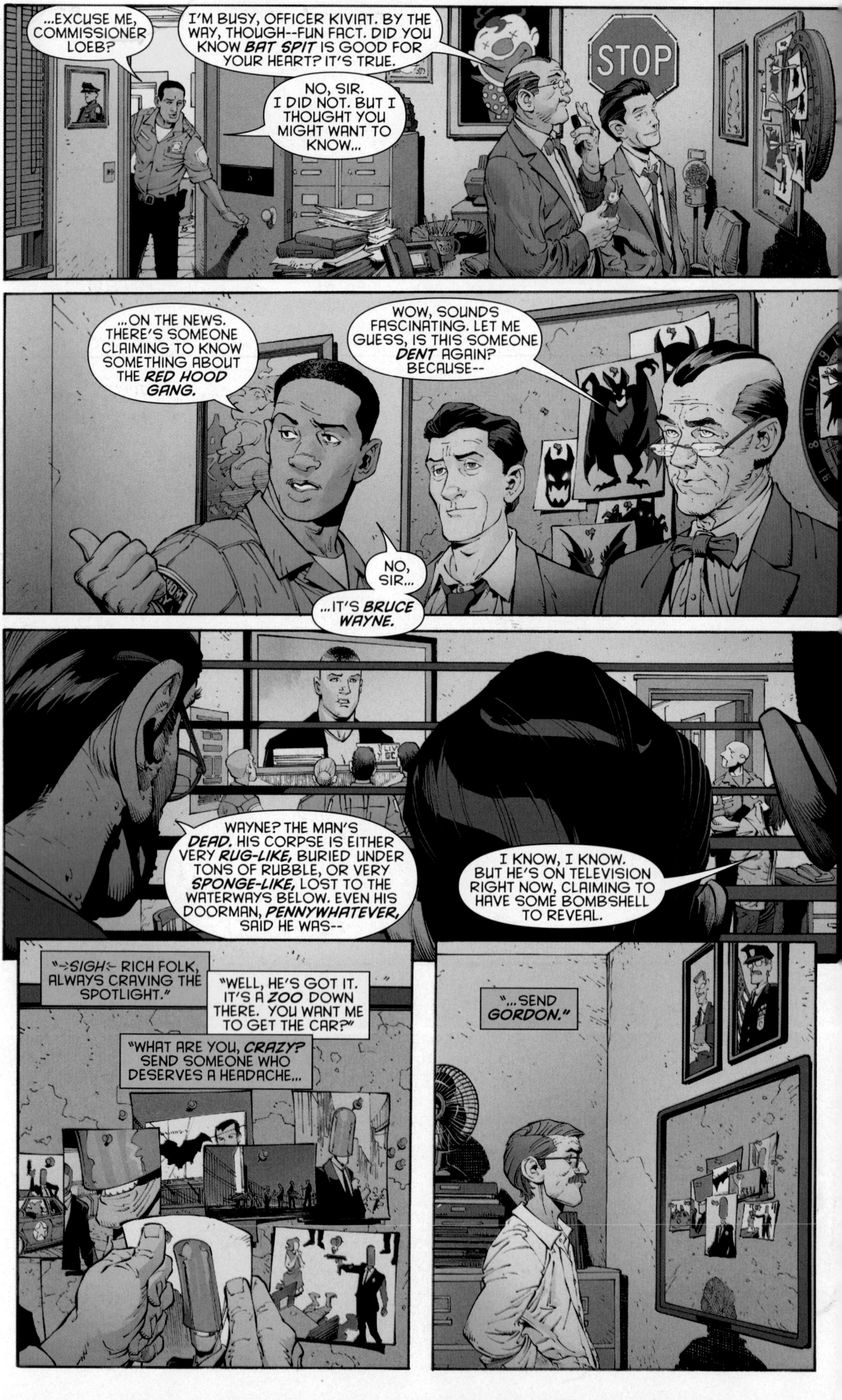
...EXCUSE ME, COMMISSIONER LOEB?
I'M BUSY, OFFICER KIVIAT. BY THE WAY, THOUGH--FUN FACT. DID YOU KNOW BAT SPIT IS GOOD FOR YOUR HEART? IT'S TRUE.
NO, SIR. I DID NOT. BUT I THOUGHT YOU MIGHT WANT TO KNOW...
STOP
...ON THE NEWS. THERE'S SOMEONE CLAIMING TO KNOW SOMETHING ABOUT THE RED HOOD GANG.
WOW, SOUNDS FASCINATING. LET ME GUESS, IS THIS SOMEONE DENT AGAIN? BECAUSE--
NO, SIR...
...IT'S BRUCE WAYNE.
WAYNE? THE MAN'S DEAD. HIS CORPSE IS EITHER VERY RUG-LIKE, BURIED UNDER TONS OF RUBBLE, OR VERY SPONGE-LIKE, LOST TO THE WATERWAYS BELOW. EVEN HIS DOORMAN, PENNYWHATEVER, SAID HE WAS--
I KNOW, I KNOW. BUT HE'S ON TELEVISION RIGHT NOW, CLAIMING TO HAVE SOME BOMBSHELL TO REVEAL.
"→SIGH← RICH FOLK, ALWAYS CRAVING THE SPOTLIGHT."
"WELL, HE'S GOT IT. IT'S A ZOO DOWN THERE. YOU WANT ME TO GET THE CAR?"
"WHAT ARE YOU, CRAZY? SEND SOMEONE WHO DESERVES A HEADACHE...
"...SEND GORDON."

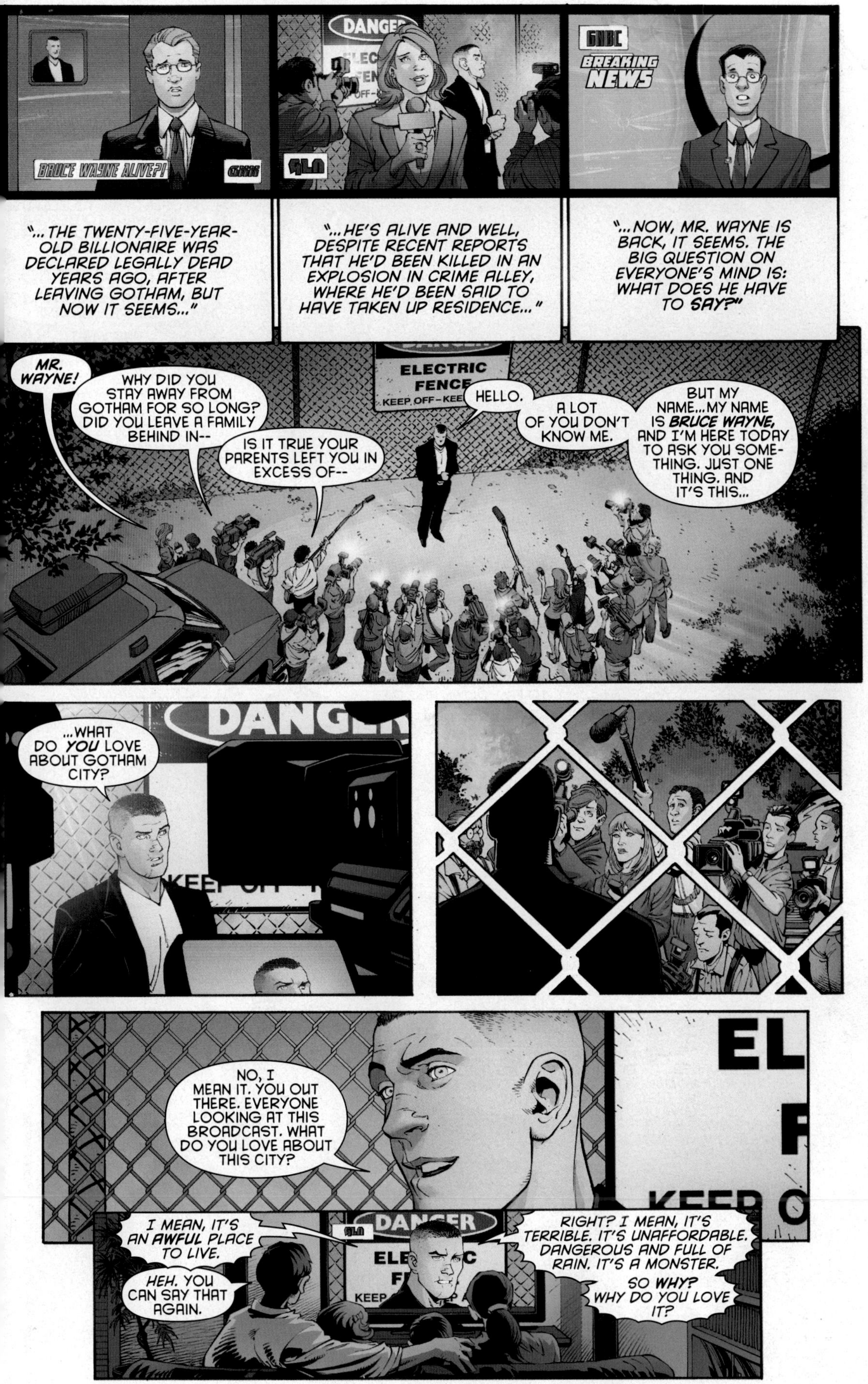

BRUCE WAYNE ALIVE?!
DANGER
GNBC
BREAKING NEWS
"...THE TWENTY-FIVE-YEAR-OLD BILLIONAIRE WAS DECLARED LEGALLY DEAD YEARS AGO, AFTER LEAVING GOTHAM, BUT NOW IT SEEMS..."
"...HE'S ALIVE AND WELL, DESPITE RECENT REPORTS THAT HE'D BEEN KILLED IN AN EXPLOSION IN CRIME ALLEY, WHERE HE'D BEEN SAID TO HAVE TAKEN UP RESIDENCE..."
"...NOW, MR. WAYNE IS BACK, IT SEEMS. THE BIG QUESTION ON EVERYONE'S MIND IS: WHAT DOES HE HAVE TO SAY?"
ELECTRIC FENCE
KEEP OFF-KEE
MR. WAYNE!
WHY DID YOU STAY AWAY FROM GOTHAM FOR SO LONG? DID YOU LEAVE A FAMILY BEHIND IN--
IS IT TRUE YOUR PARENTS LEFT YOU IN EXCESS OF--
HELLO.
A LOT OF YOU DON'T KNOW ME.
BUT MY NAME...MY NAME IS BRUCE WAYNE, AND I'M HERE TODAY TO ASK YOU SOMETHING. JUST ONE THING. AND IT'S THIS...
DANGER
...WHAT DO YOU LOVE ABOUT GOTHAM CITY?
NO, I MEAN IT. YOU OUT THERE. EVERYONE LOOKING AT THIS BROADCAST. WHAT DO YOU LOVE ABOUT THIS CITY?
I MEAN, IT'S AN AWFUL PLACE TO LIVE.
HEH. YOU CAN SAY THAT AGAIN.
RIGHT? I MEAN, IT'S TERRIBLE. IT'S UNAFFORDABLE. DANGEROUS AND FULL OF RAIN. IT'S A MONSTER.
SO WHY? WHY DO YOU LOVE IT?

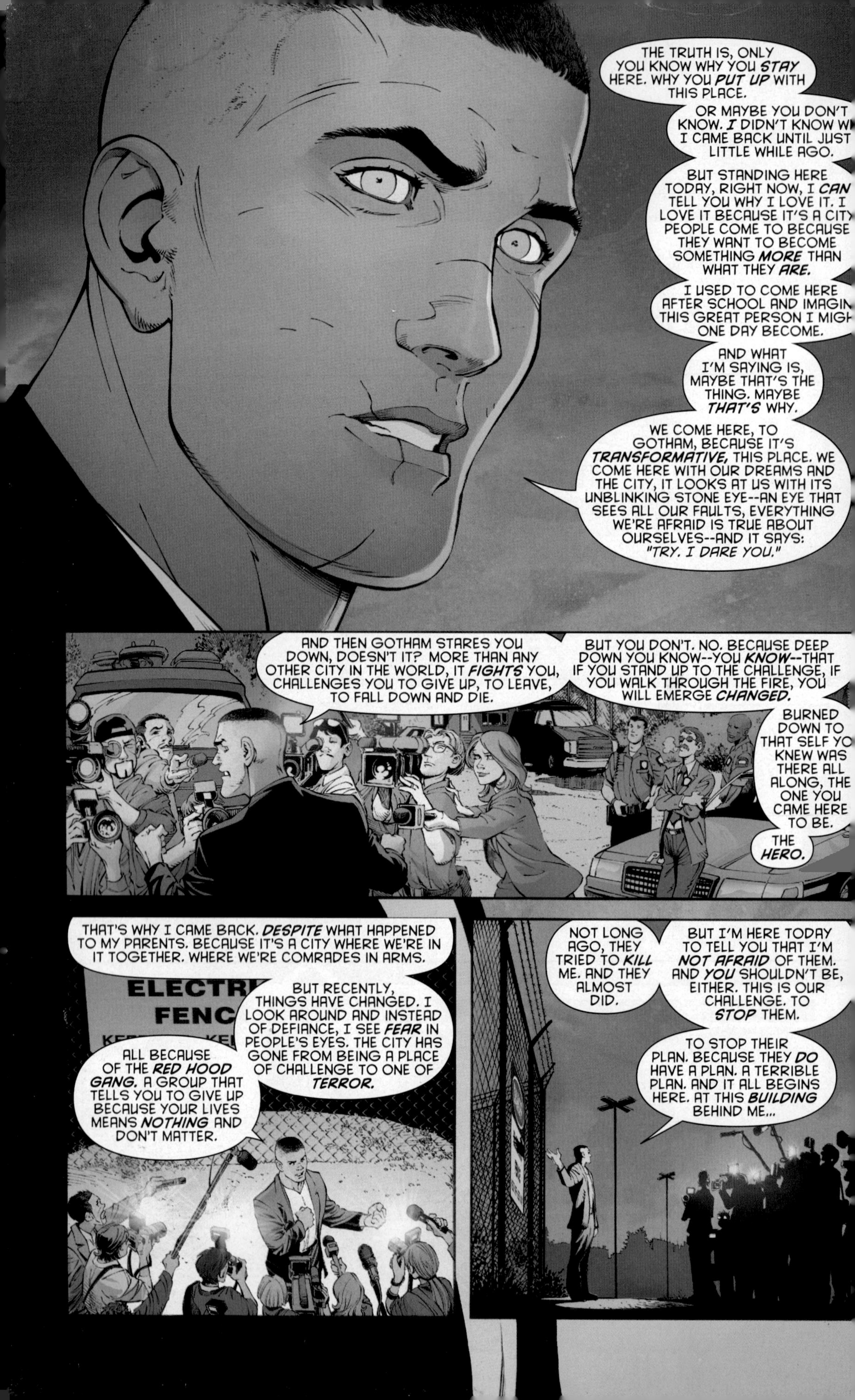
THE TRUTH IS, ONLY YOU KNOW WHY YOU *STAY* HERE. WHY YOU *PUT UP* WITH THIS PLACE.
OR MAYBE YOU DON'T KNOW. *I* DIDN'T KNOW WH I CAME BACK UNTIL JUST LITTLE WHILE AGO.
BUT STANDING HERE TODAY, RIGHT NOW, I *CAN* TELL YOU WHY I LOVE IT. I LOVE IT BECAUSE IT'S A CITY PEOPLE COME TO BECAUSE THEY WANT TO BECOME SOMETHING *MORE* THAN WHAT THEY *ARE.*
I USED TO COME HERE AFTER SCHOOL AND IMAGIN THIS GREAT PERSON I MIGH ONE DAY BECOME.
AND WHAT I'M SAYING IS, MAYBE THAT'S THE THING. MAYBE *THAT'S* WHY.
WE COME HERE, TO GOTHAM, BECAUSE IT'S *TRANSFORMATIVE,* THIS PLACE. WE COME HERE WITH OUR DREAMS AND THE CITY, IT LOOKS AT US WITH ITS UNBLINKING STONE EYE--AN EYE THAT SEES ALL OUR FAULTS, EVERYTHING WE'RE AFRAID IS TRUE ABOUT OURSELVES--AND IT SAYS: *"TRY. I DARE YOU."*
AND THEN GOTHAM STARES YOU DOWN, DOESN'T IT? MORE THAN ANY OTHER CITY IN THE WORLD, IT *FIGHTS* YOU, CHALLENGES YOU TO GIVE UP, TO LEAVE, TO FALL DOWN AND DIE.
BUT YOU DON'T. NO. BECAUSE DEEP DOWN YOU KNOW--YOU *KNOW*--THAT IF YOU STAND UP TO THE CHALLENGE, IF YOU WALK THROUGH THE FIRE, YOU WILL EMERGE *CHANGED.*
BURNED DOWN TO THAT SELF YO KNEW WAS THERE ALL ALONG, THE ONE YOU CAME HERE TO BE.
THE *HERO.*
THAT'S WHY I CAME BACK. *DESPITE* WHAT HAPPENED TO MY PARENTS. BECAUSE IT'S A CITY WHERE WE'RE IN IT TOGETHER. WHERE WE'RE COMRADES IN ARMS.
BUT RECENTLY, THINGS HAVE CHANGED. I LOOK AROUND AND INSTEAD OF DEFIANCE, I SEE *FEAR* IN PEOPLE'S EYES. THE CITY HAS GONE FROM BEING A PLACE OF CHALLENGE TO ONE OF *TERROR.*
ALL BECAUSE OF THE *RED HOOD GANG.* A GROUP THAT TELLS YOU TO GIVE UP BECAUSE YOUR LIVES MEANS *NOTHING* AND DON'T MATTER.
NOT LONG AGO, THEY TRIED TO *KILL* ME. AND THEY ALMOST DID.
BUT I'M HERE TODAY TO TELL YOU THAT I'M *NOT AFRAID* OF THEM. AND *YOU* SHOULDN'T BE, EITHER. THIS IS OUR CHALLENGE. TO *STOP* THEM.
TO STOP THEIR PLAN. BECAUSE THEY *DO* HAVE A PLAN. A TERRIBLE PLAN. AND IT ALL BEGINS HERE. AT THIS *BUILDING* BEHIND ME...

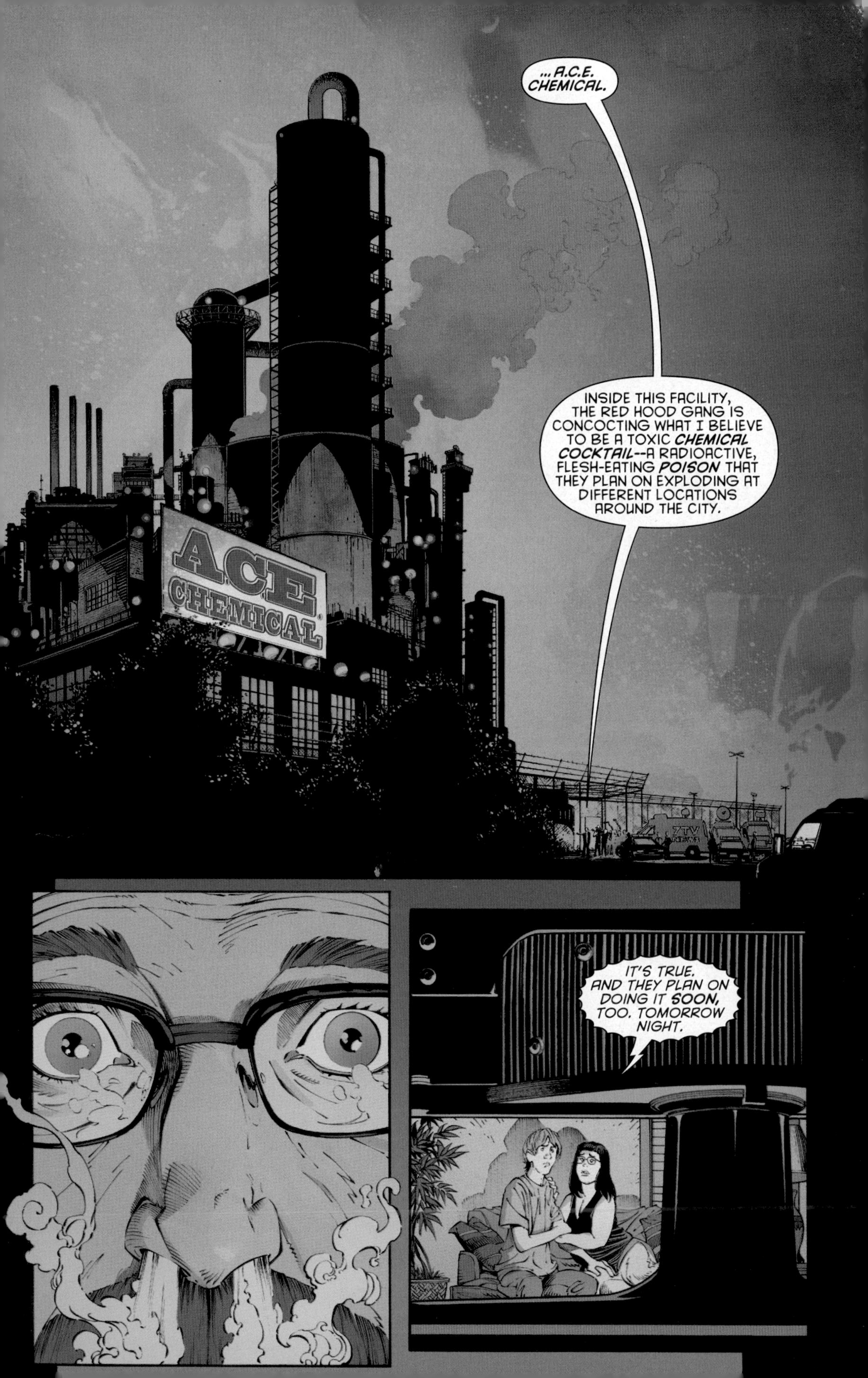
...A.C.E. CHEMICAL.
INSIDE THIS FACILITY, THE RED HOOD GANG IS CONCOCTING WHAT I BELIEVE TO BE A TOXIC CHEMICAL COCKTAIL--A RADIOACTIVE, FLESH-EATING POISON THAT THEY PLAN ON EXPLODING AT DIFFERENT LOCATIONS AROUND THE CITY.
A.C.E. CHEMICAL
7TV NEWS
IT'S TRUE. AND THEY PLAN ON DOING IT SOON, TOO. TOMORROW NIGHT.

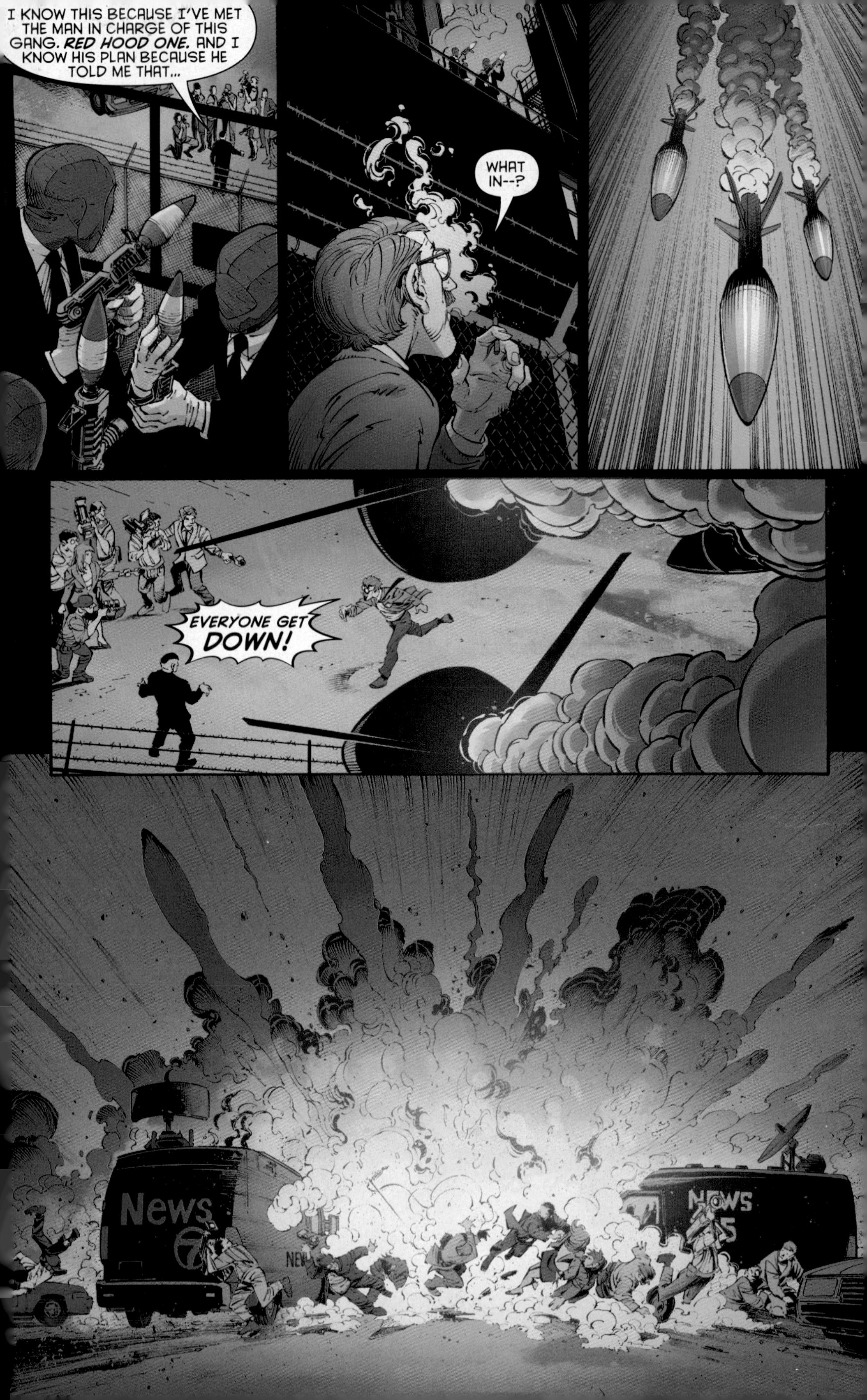
I KNOW THIS BECAUSE I'VE MET THE MAN IN CHARGE OF THIS GANG. *RED HOOD ONE.* AND I KNOW HIS PLAN BECAUSE HE TOLD ME THAT...
WHAT IN--?
EVERYONE GET DOWN!
News
NEWS
NEWS 5

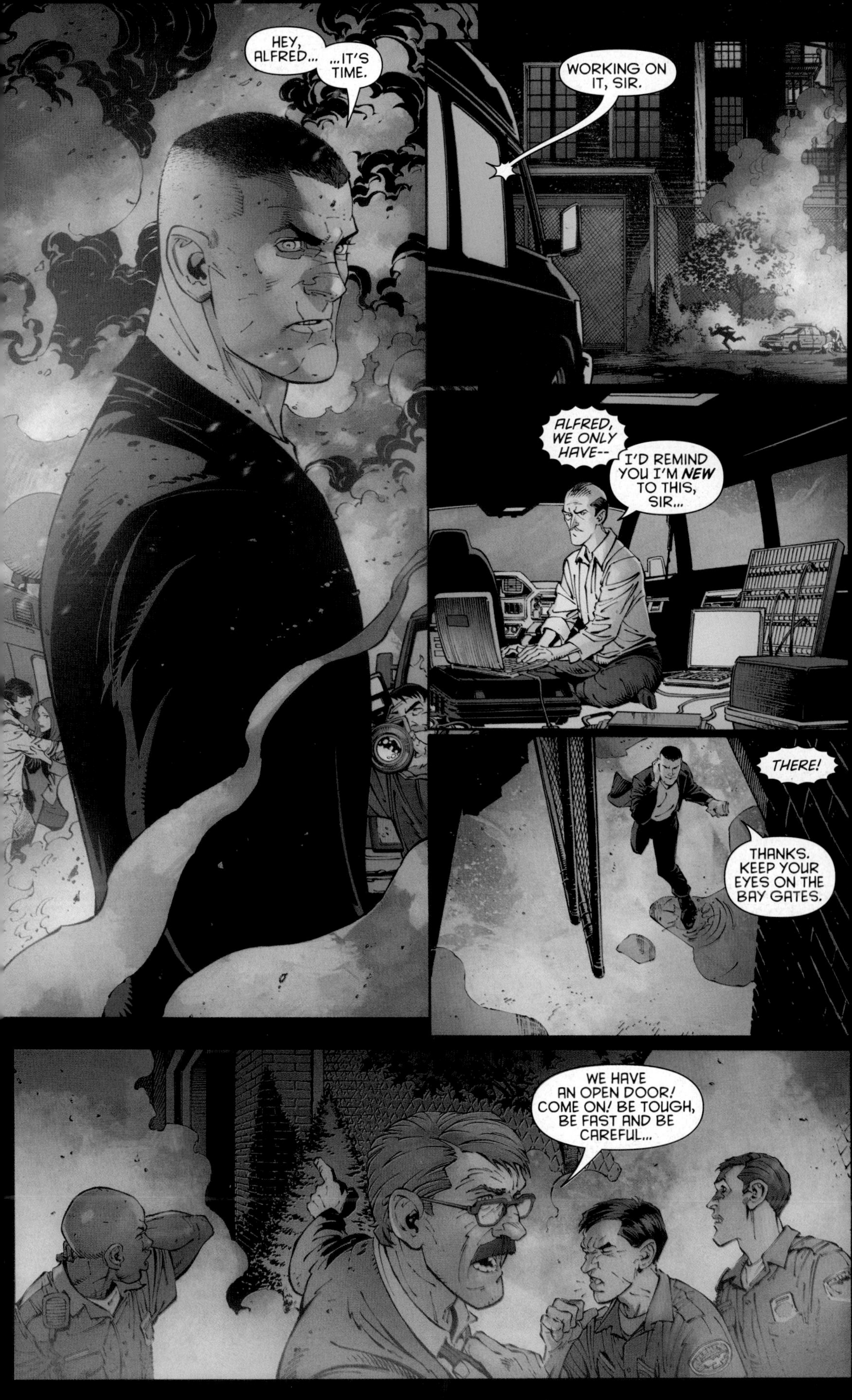
HEY, ALFRED...
...IT'S TIME.
WORKING ON IT, SIR.
ALFRED, WE ONLY HAVE--
I'D REMIND YOU I'M NEW TO THIS, SIR...
THERE!
THANKS. KEEP YOUR EYES ON THE BAY GATES.
WE HAVE AN OPEN DOOR! COME ON! BE TOUGH, BE FAST AND BE CAREFUL...

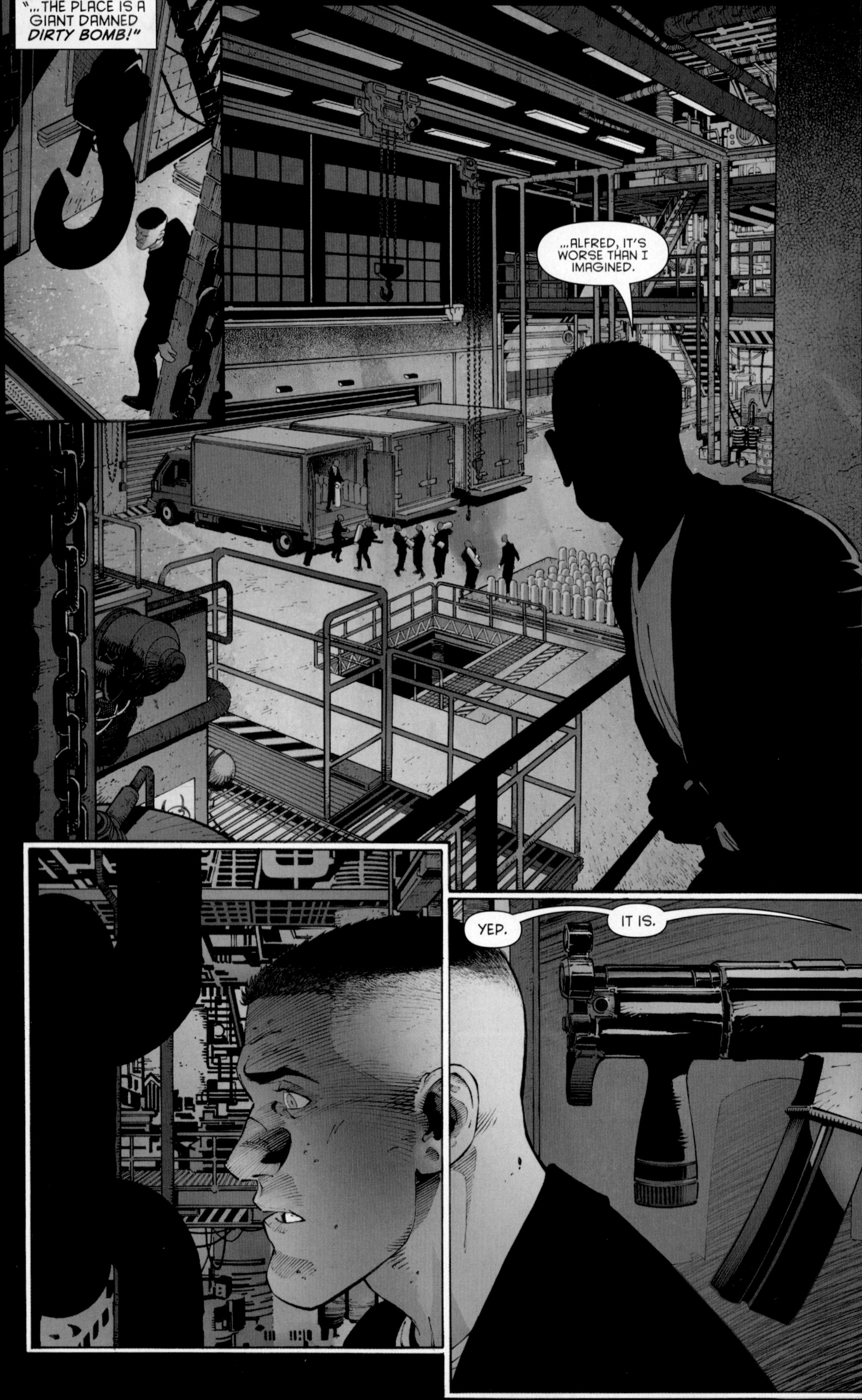
"...THE PLACE IS A GIANT DAMNED *DIRTY BOMB!*"
...ALFRED, IT'S WORSE THAN I IMAGINED.
YEP.
IT IS.

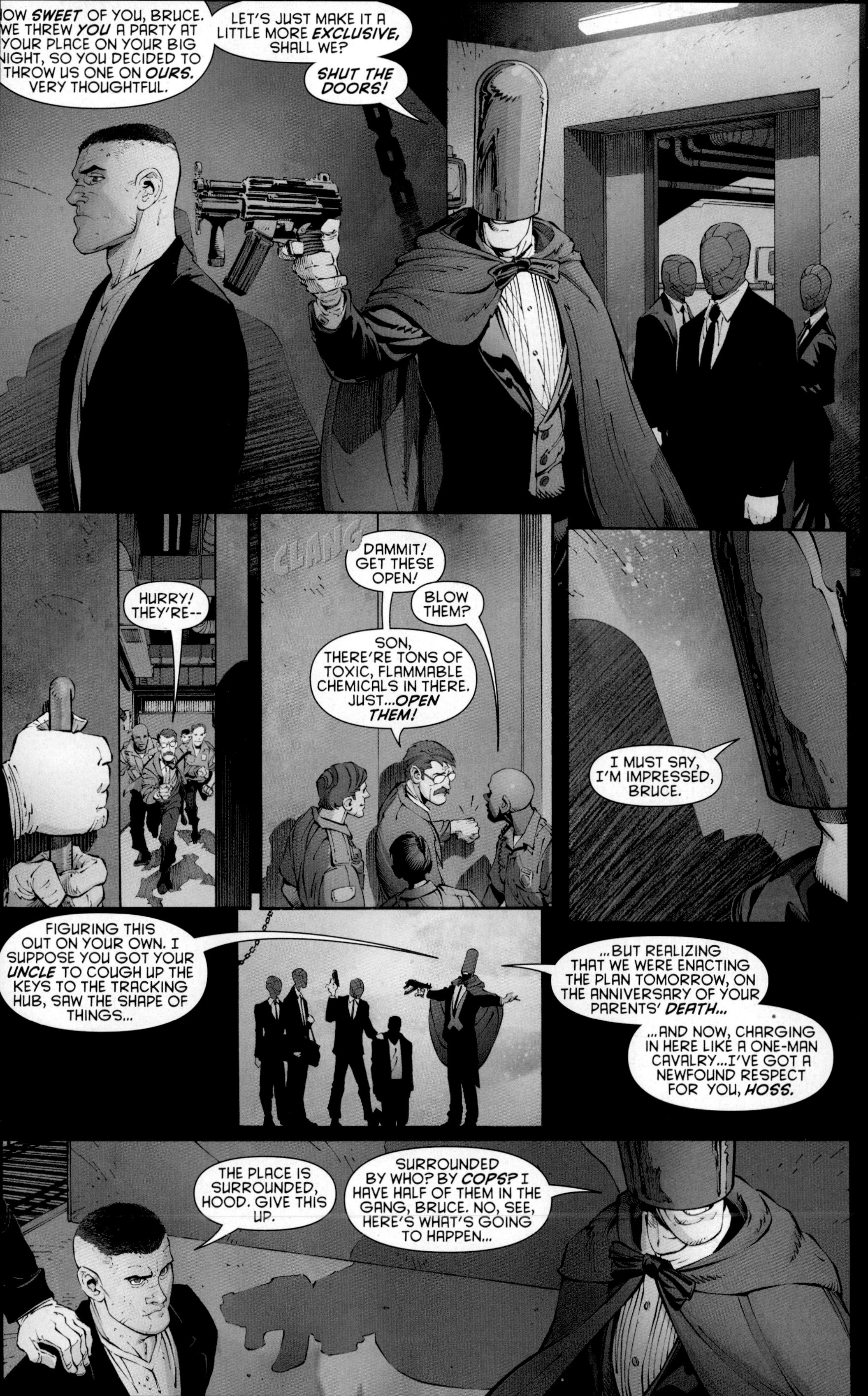

HOW SWEET OF YOU, BRUCE. WE THREW YOU A PARTY AT YOUR PLACE ON YOUR BIG NIGHT, SO YOU DECIDED TO THROW US ONE ON OURS. VERY THOUGHTFUL.
LET'S JUST MAKE IT A LITTLE MORE EXCLUSIVE, SHALL WE?
SHUT THE DOORS!
HURRY! THEY'RE--
CLANG
DAMMIT! GET THESE OPEN!
BLOW THEM?
SON, THERE'RE TONS OF TOXIC, FLAMMABLE CHEMICALS IN THERE. JUST...OPEN THEM!
I MUST SAY, I'M IMPRESSED, BRUCE.
FIGURING THIS OUT ON YOUR OWN. I SUPPOSE YOU GOT YOUR UNCLE TO COUGH UP THE KEYS TO THE TRACKING HUB, SAW THE SHAPE OF THINGS...
...BUT REALIZING THAT WE WERE ENACTING THE PLAN TOMORROW, ON THE ANNIVERSARY OF YOUR PARENTS' DEATH...
...AND NOW, CHARGING IN HERE LIKE A ONE-MAN CAVALRY...I'VE GOT A NEWFOUND RESPECT FOR YOU, HOSS.
THE PLACE IS SURROUNDED, HOOD. GIVE THIS UP.
SURROUNDED BY WHO? BY COPS? I HAVE HALF OF THEM IN THE GANG, BRUCE. NO, SEE, HERE'S WHAT'S GOING TO HAPPEN...

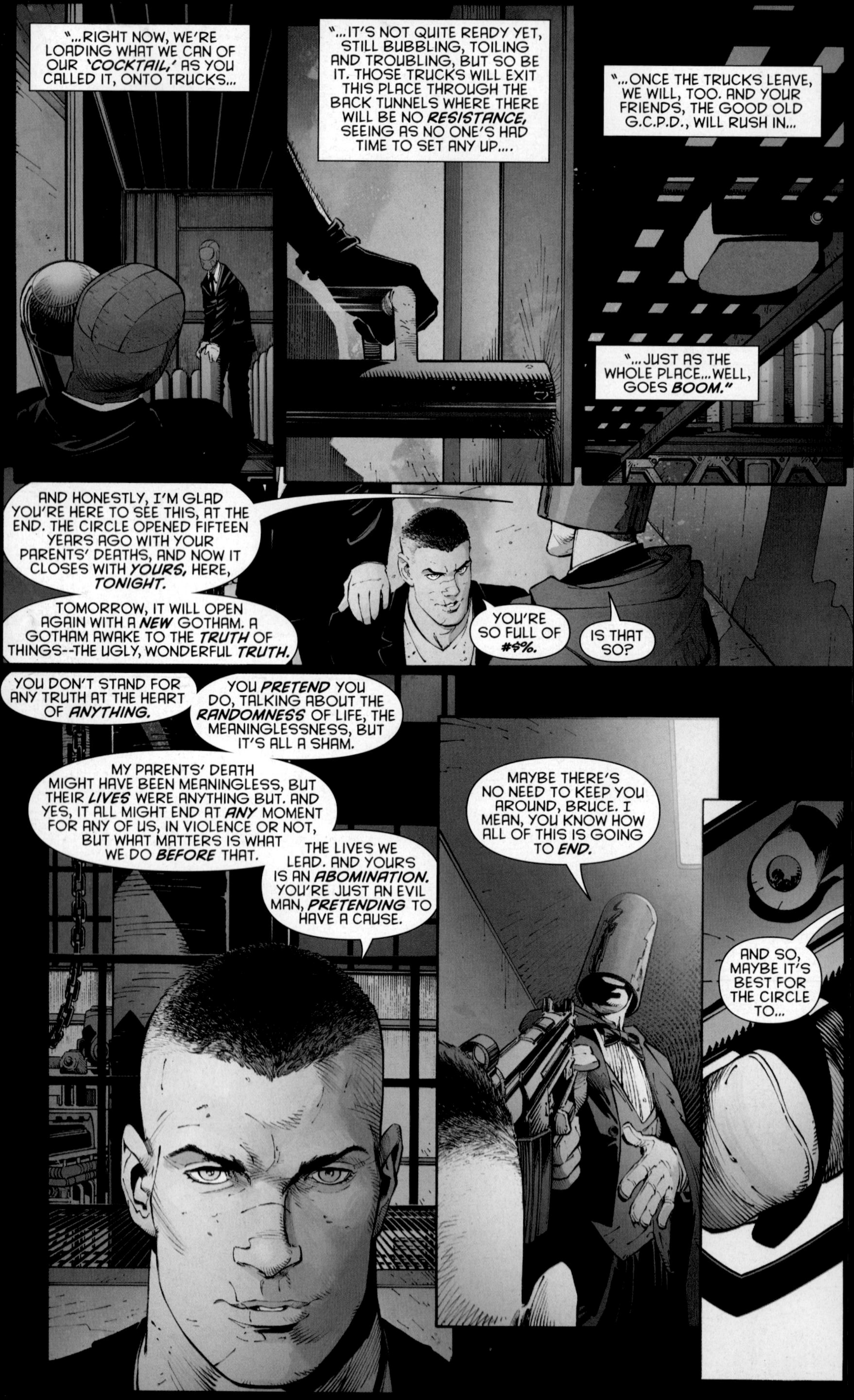
"...RIGHT NOW, WE'RE LOADING WHAT WE CAN OF OUR 'COCKTAIL,' AS YOU CALLED IT, ONTO TRUCKS...
"...IT'S NOT QUITE READY YET, STILL BUBBLING, TOILING AND TROUBLING, BUT SO BE IT. THOSE TRUCKS WILL EXIT THIS PLACE THROUGH THE BACK TUNNELS WHERE THERE WILL BE NO RESISTANCE, SEEING AS NO ONE'S HAD TIME TO SET ANY UP....
"...ONCE THE TRUCKS LEAVE, WE WILL, TOO. AND YOUR FRIENDS, THE GOOD OLD G.C.P.D., WILL RUSH IN...
"...JUST AS THE WHOLE PLACE...WELL, GOES BOOM."
AND HONESTLY, I'M GLAD YOU'RE HERE TO SEE THIS, AT THE END. THE CIRCLE OPENED FIFTEEN YEARS AGO WITH YOUR PARENTS' DEATHS, AND NOW IT CLOSES WITH YOURS, HERE, TONIGHT.
TOMORROW, IT WILL OPEN AGAIN WITH A NEW GOTHAM. A GOTHAM AWAKE TO THE TRUTH OF THINGS--THE UGLY, WONDERFUL TRUTH.
YOU'RE SO FULL OF #$%.
IS THAT SO?
YOU DON'T STAND FOR ANY TRUTH AT THE HEART OF ANYTHING.
YOU PRETEND YOU DO, TALKING ABOUT THE RANDOMNESS OF LIFE, THE MEANINGLESSNESS, BUT IT'S ALL A SHAM.
MY PARENTS' DEATH MIGHT HAVE BEEN MEANINGLESS, BUT THEIR LIVES WERE ANYTHING BUT. AND YES, IT ALL MIGHT END AT ANY MOMENT FOR ANY OF US, IN VIOLENCE OR NOT, BUT WHAT MATTERS IS WHAT WE DO BEFORE THAT.
THE LIVES WE LEAD. AND YOURS IS AN ABOMINATION. YOU'RE JUST AN EVIL MAN, PRETENDING TO HAVE A CAUSE.
MAYBE THERE'S NO NEED TO KEEP YOU AROUND, BRUCE. I MEAN, YOU KNOW HOW ALL OF THIS IS GOING TO END.
AND SO, MAYBE IT'S BEST FOR THE CIRCLE TO...

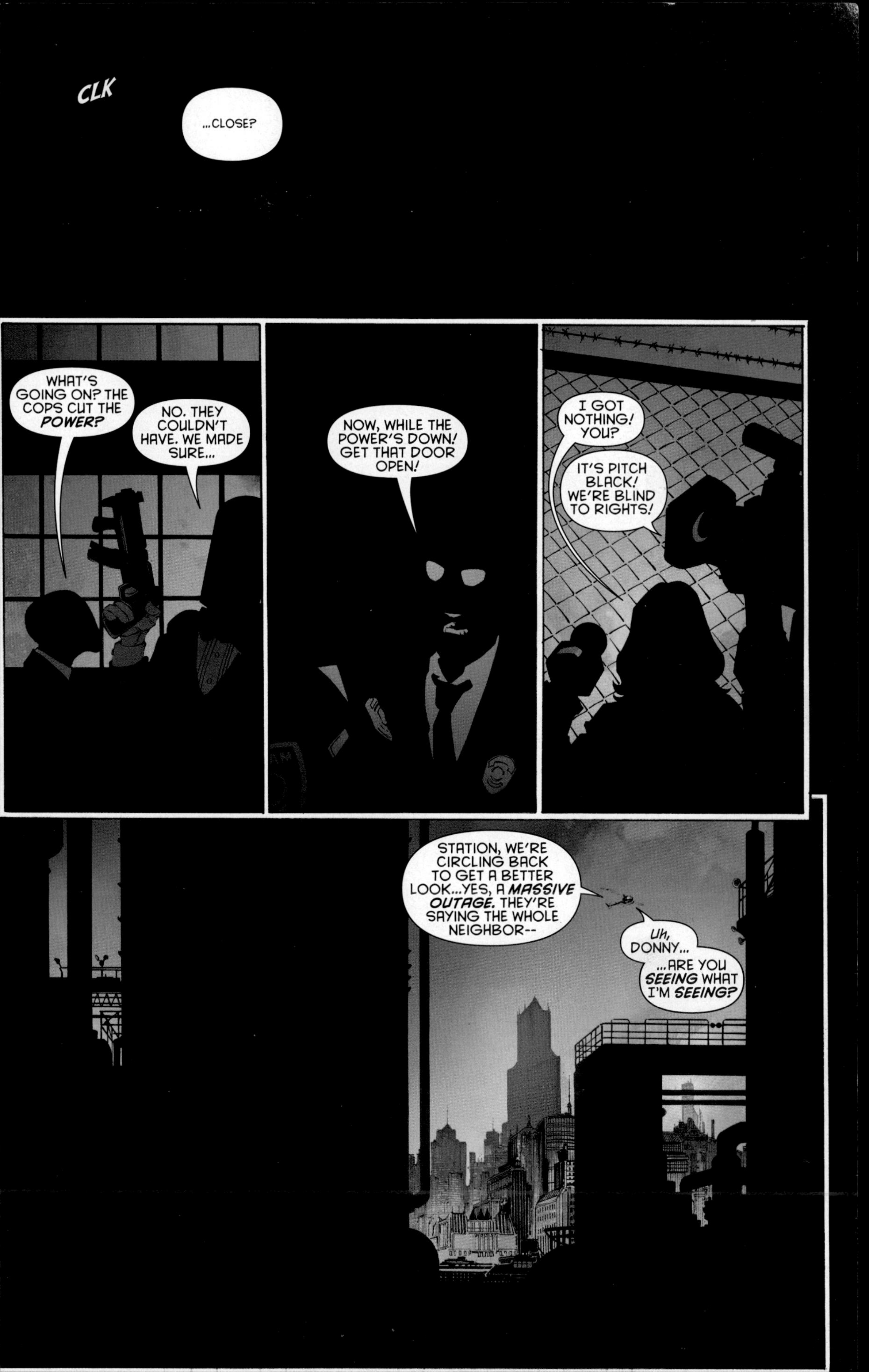

CLK
...CLOSE?
WHAT'S GOING ON? THE COPS CUT THE *POWER?*
NO. THEY COULDN'T HAVE. WE MADE SURE...
NOW, WHILE THE POWER'S DOWN! GET THAT DOOR OPEN!
I GOT NOTHING! YOU?
IT'S PITCH BLACK! WE'RE BLIND TO RIGHTS!
STATION, WE'RE CIRCLING BACK TO GET A BETTER LOOK...YES, A *MASSIVE OUTAGE.* THEY'RE SAYING THE WHOLE NEIGHBOR--
UH, DONNY...
...ARE YOU *SEEING* WHAT I'M *SEEING?*

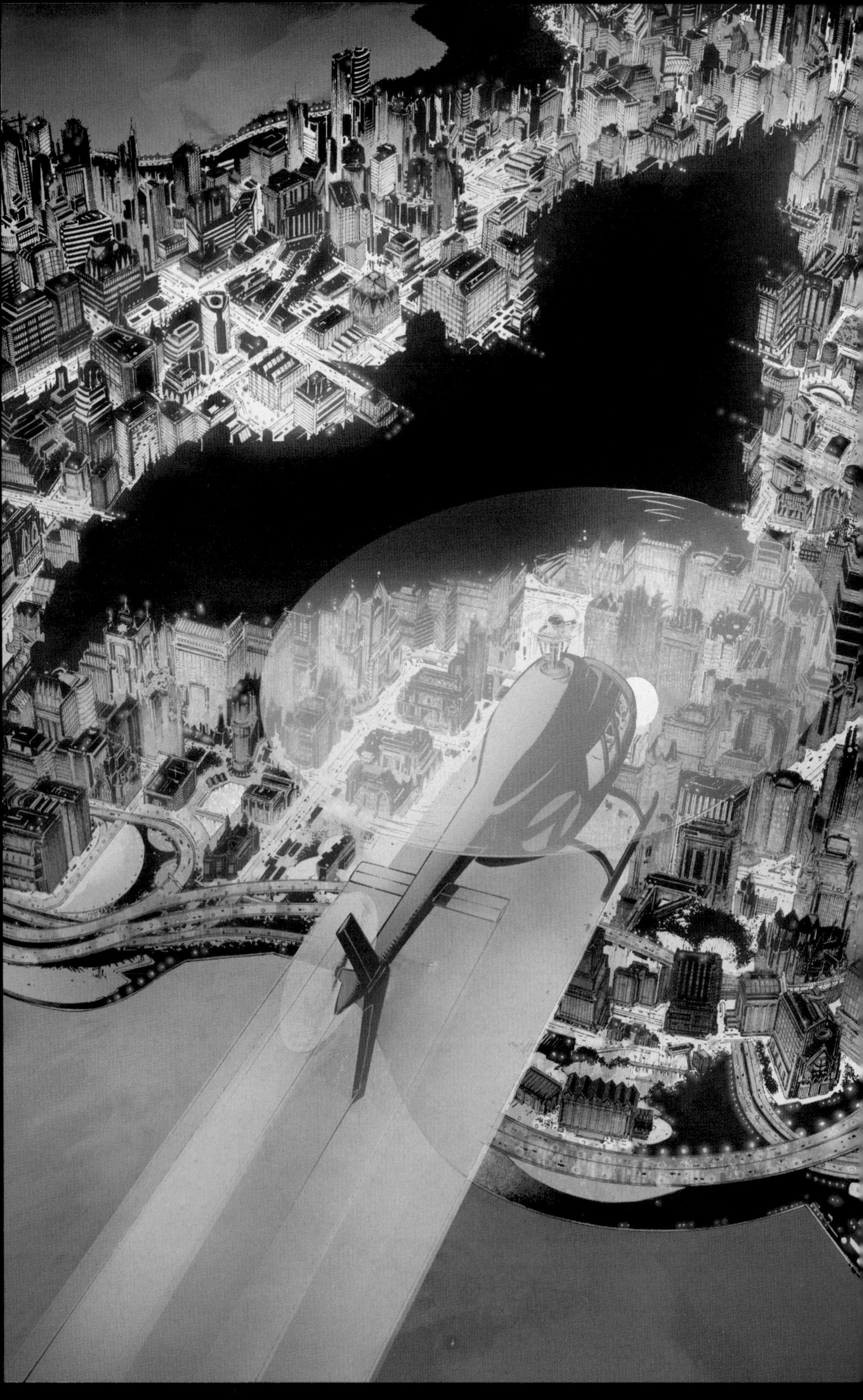

FIFTY-FOUR. YOU HAVE THE BAG WITH THE NIGHT-VISION GOGGLES.

GOT 'EM. COMING YOUR WAY.

I LOST WAYNE! I CAN'T FIND HIM!

GOT HIM. COME HERE, YOU--

ALL RIGHT, BRUCE, WHERE'D YOU RUN OFF TO?

AH... HE'S THERE, ON THE CATWALK. GET HIM.

AAGH!

WHAT IN...?

COME, MR. WAYNE.

DID YOU SEE THAT?! SOMETHING TOOK HIM!

BOSS, THERE'S SOMETHING IN HERE WITH US! BOSS!

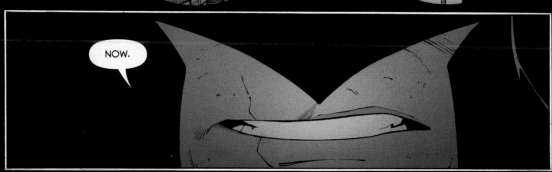

NOW.

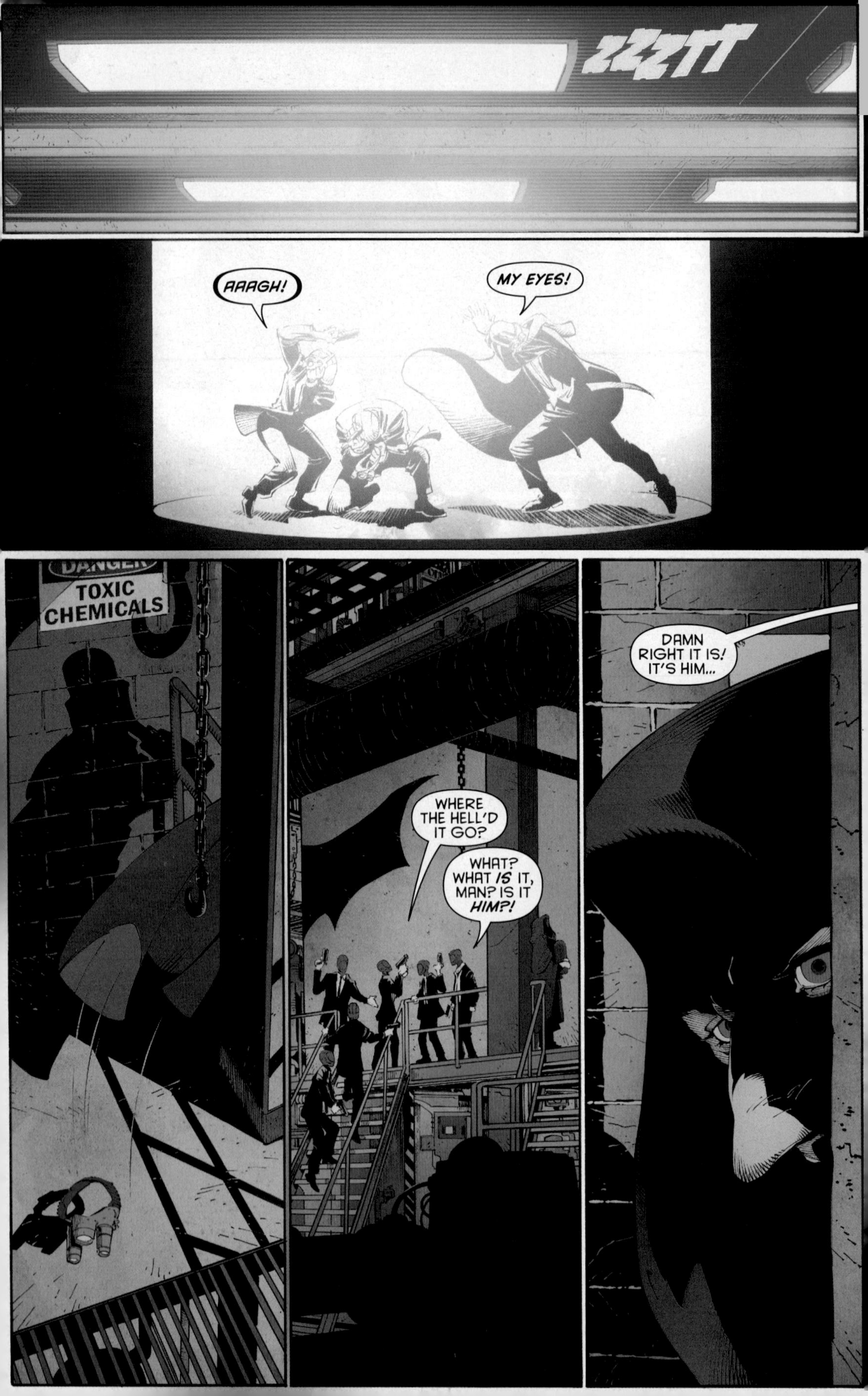
ZZZTT
AAAGH!
MY EYES!
DANGER
TOXIC CHEMICALS
WHERE THE HELL'D IT GO?
WHAT? WHAT IS IT, MAN? IS IT HIM?!
DAMN RIGHT IT IS! IT'S HIM...

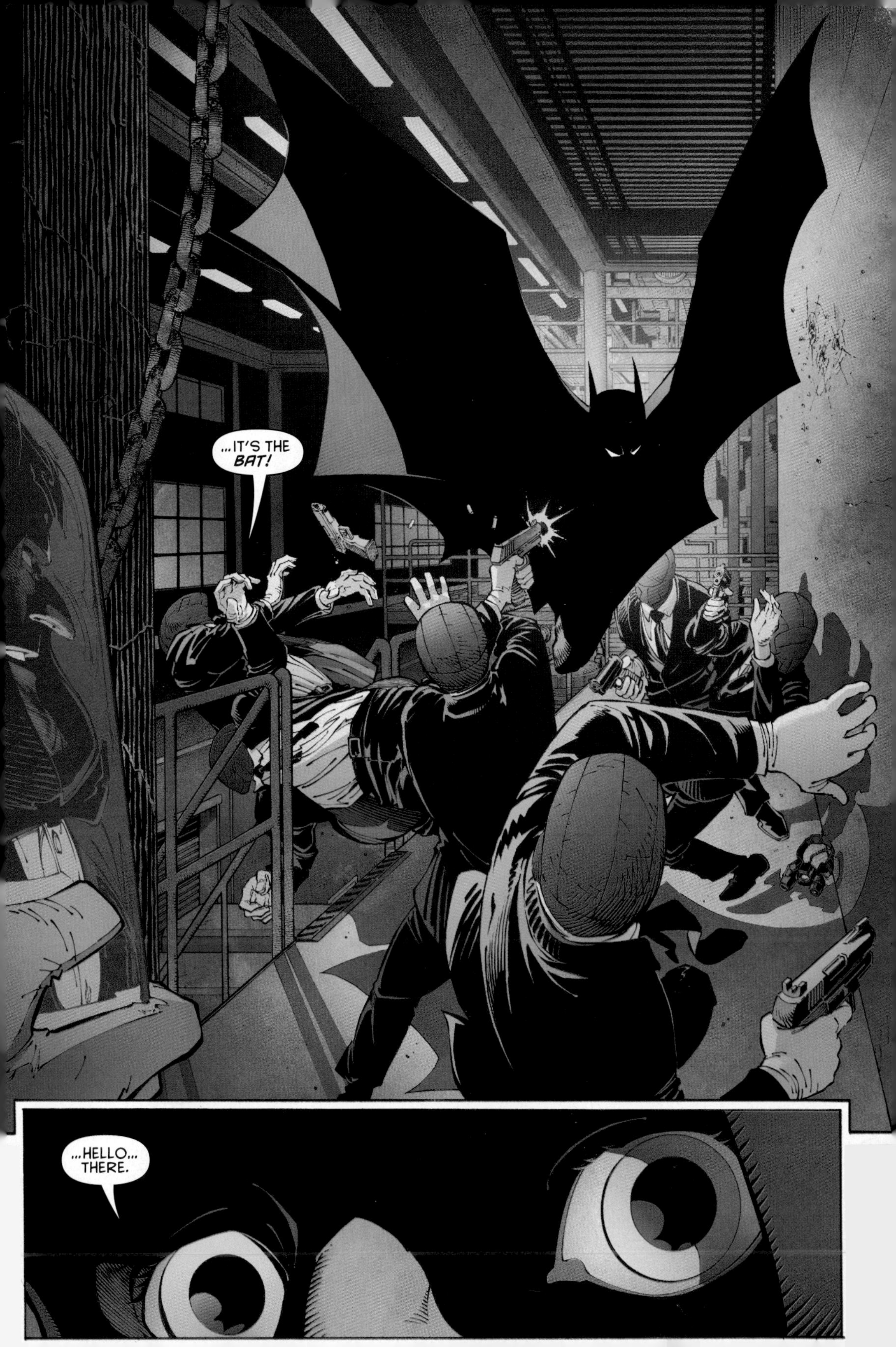
...IT'S THE BAT!
...HELLO... THERE.

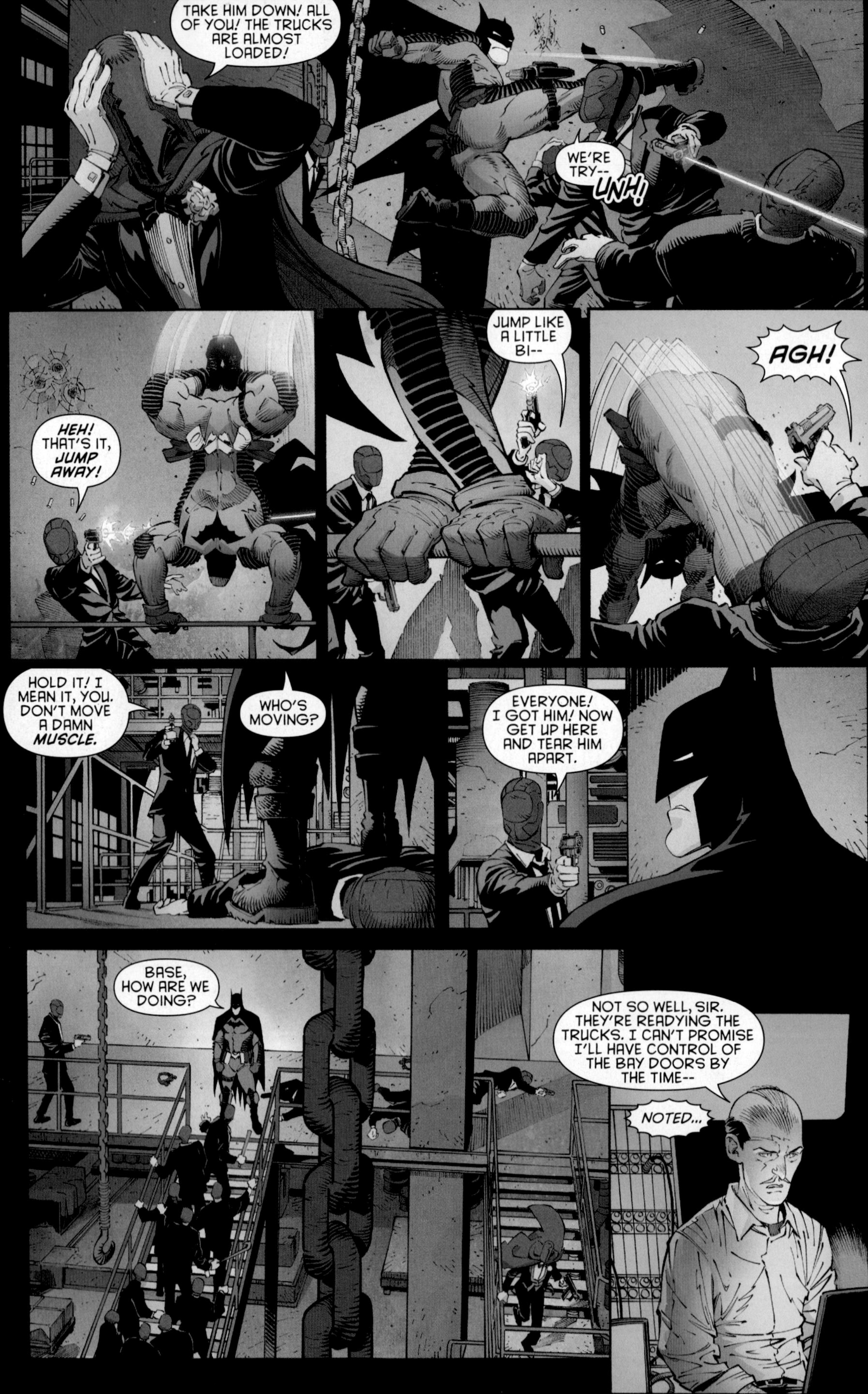
TAKE HIM DOWN! ALL OF YOU! THE TRUCKS ARE ALMOST LOADED!
WE'RE TRY--
UNH!
HEH! THAT'S IT, JUMP AWAY!
JUMP LIKE A LITTLE BI--
AGH!
HOLD IT! I MEAN IT, YOU. DON'T MOVE A DAMN MUSCLE.
WHO'S MOVING?
EVERYONE! I GOT HIM! NOW GET UP HERE AND TEAR HIM APART.
BASE, HOW ARE WE DOING?
NOT SO WELL, SIR. THEY'RE READYING THE TRUCKS. I CAN'T PROMISE I'LL HAVE CONTROL OF THE BAY DOORS BY THE TIME--
NOTED...

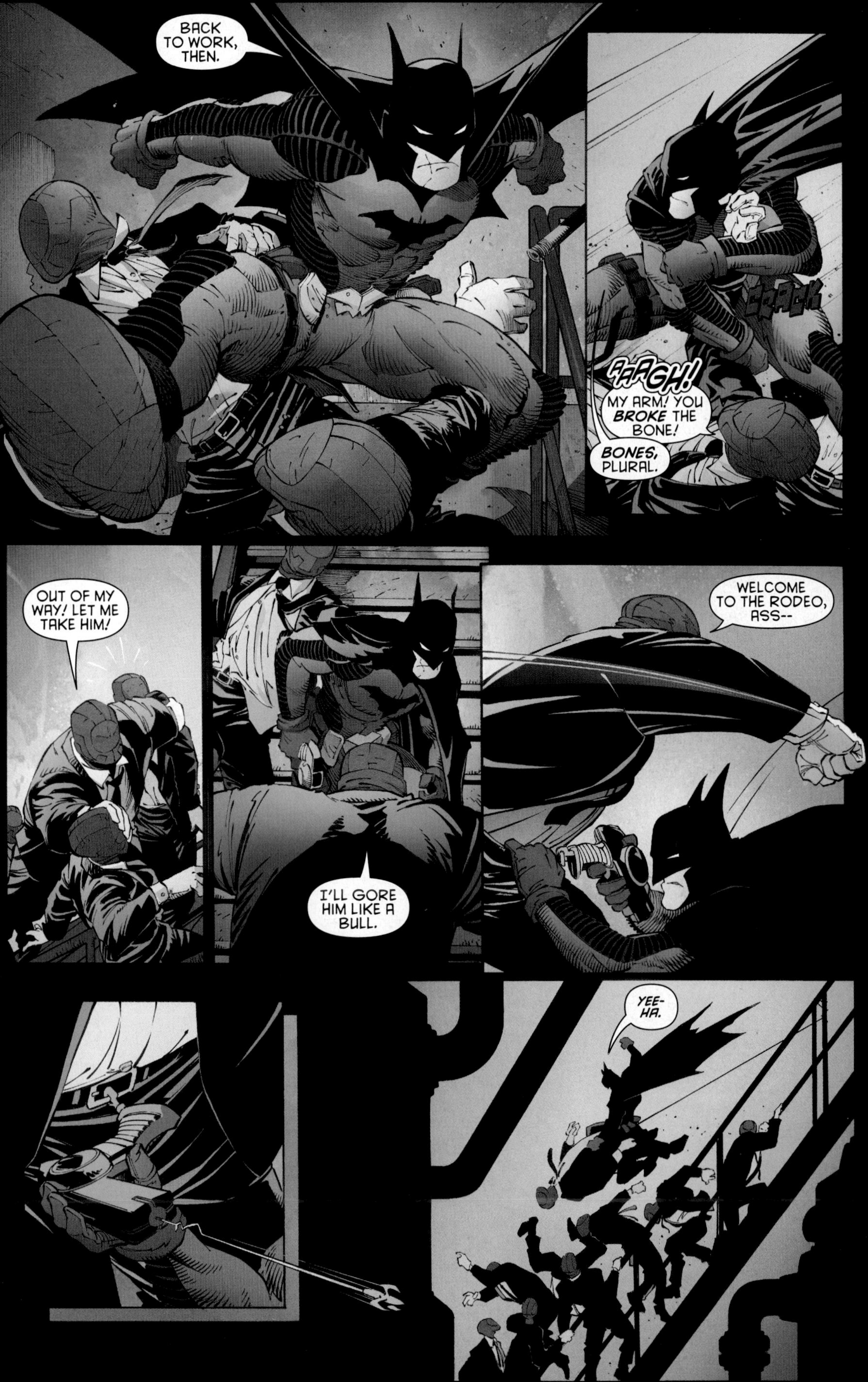
BACK TO WORK, THEN.
AAAGH!
MY ARM! YOU *BROKE* THE BONE!
BONES, PLURAL.
OUT OF MY WAY! LET ME TAKE HIM!
I'LL GORE HIM LIKE A BULL.
WELCOME TO THE RODEO, ASS--
YEE-HA.

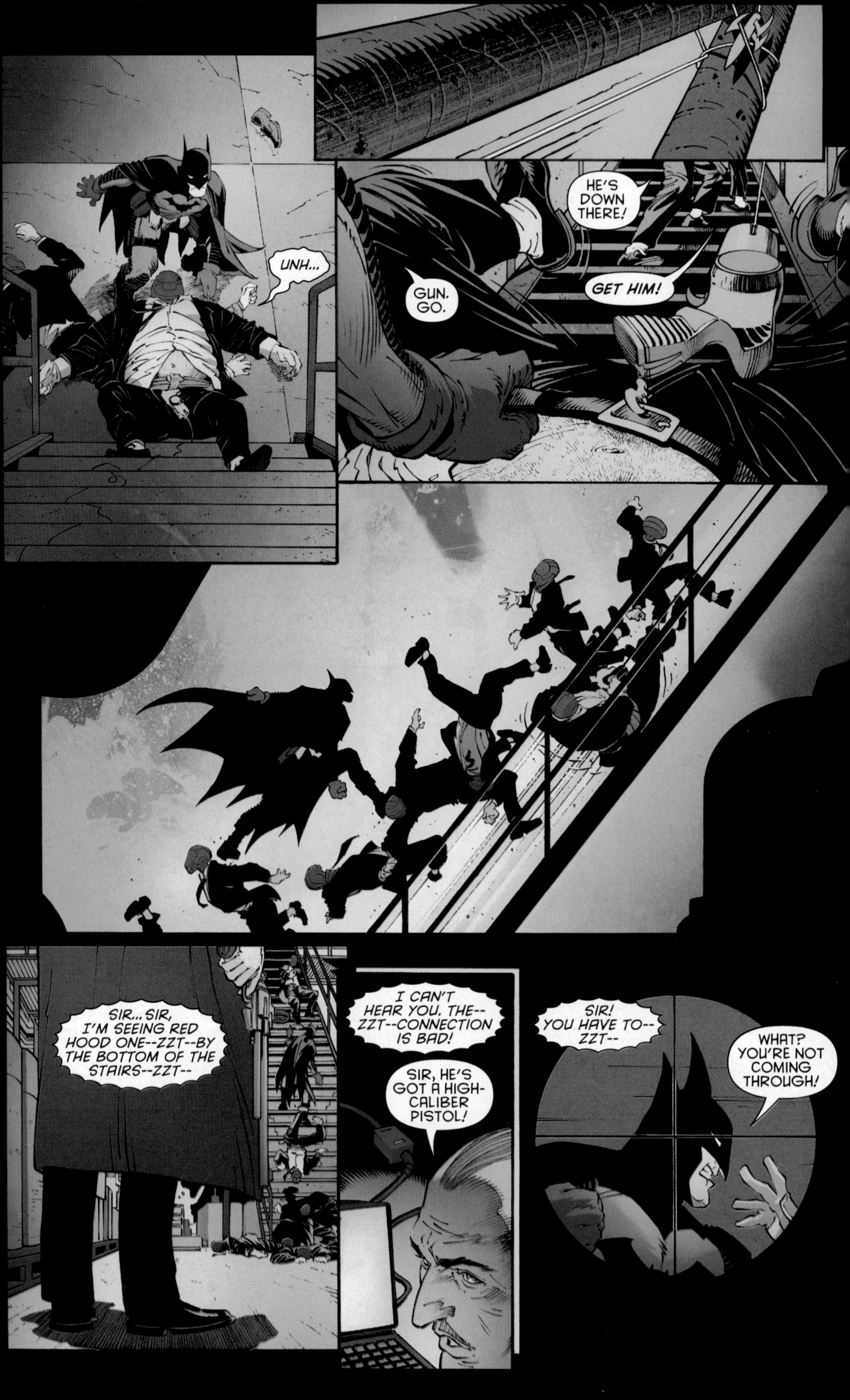
UNH...
HE'S DOWN THERE!
GUN. GO.
GET HIM!
SIR... SIR, I'M SEEING RED HOOD ONE--ZZT--BY THE BOTTOM OF THE STAIRS--ZZT--
I CAN'T HEAR YOU. THE--ZZT--CONNECTION IS BAD!
SIR, HE'S GOT A HIGH-CALIBER PISTOL!
SIR! YOU HAVE TO--ZZT--
WHAT? YOU'RE NOT COMING THROUGH!

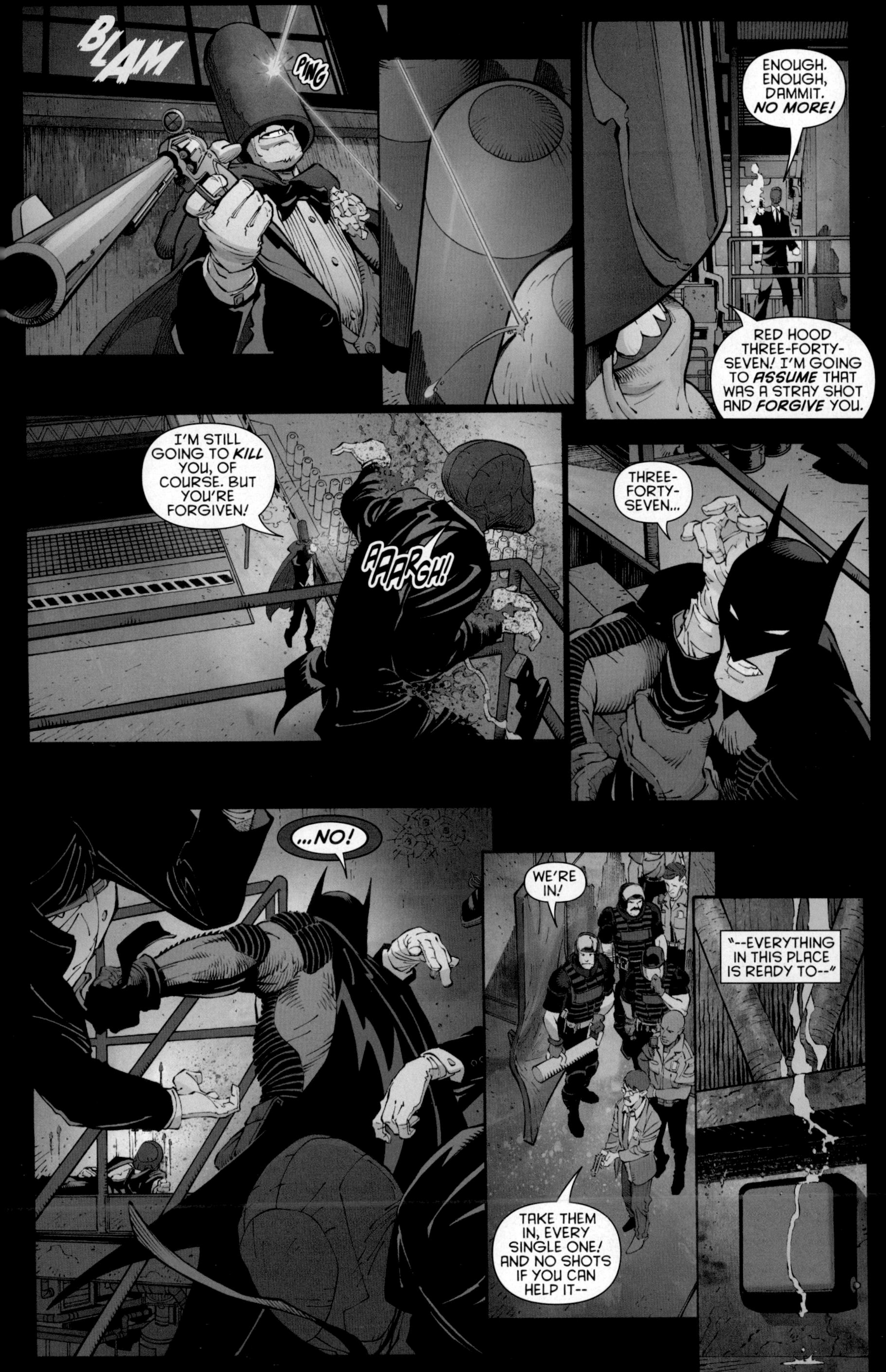
BLAM
PING
ENOUGH. ENOUGH, DAMMIT. NO MORE!
RED HOOD THREE-FORTY-SEVEN! I'M GOING TO ASSUME THAT WAS A STRAY SHOT AND FORGIVE YOU.
I'M STILL GOING TO KILL YOU, OF COURSE. BUT YOU'RE FORGIVEN!
AAARGH!
THREE-FORTY-SEVEN...
...NO!
WE'RE IN!
TAKE THEM IN, EVERY SINGLE ONE! AND NO SHOTS IF YOU CAN HELP IT--
"--EVERYTHING IN THIS PLACE IS READY TO--"

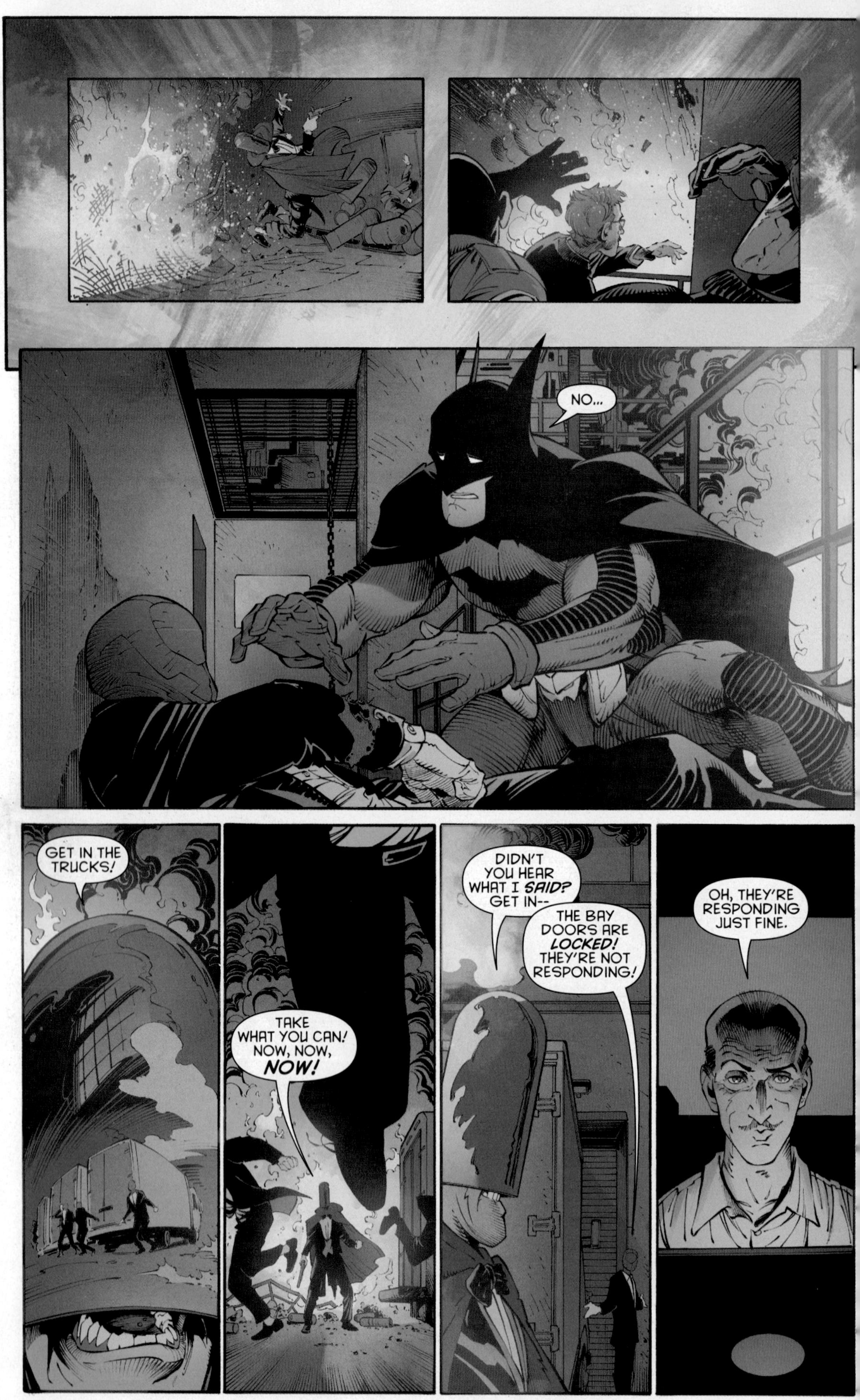
NO...
GET IN THE TRUCKS!
TAKE WHAT YOU CAN! NOW, NOW, NOW!
DIDN'T YOU HEAR WHAT I SAID? GET IN--
THE BAY DOORS ARE LOCKED! THEY'RE NOT RESPONDING!
OH, THEY'RE RESPONDING JUST FINE.

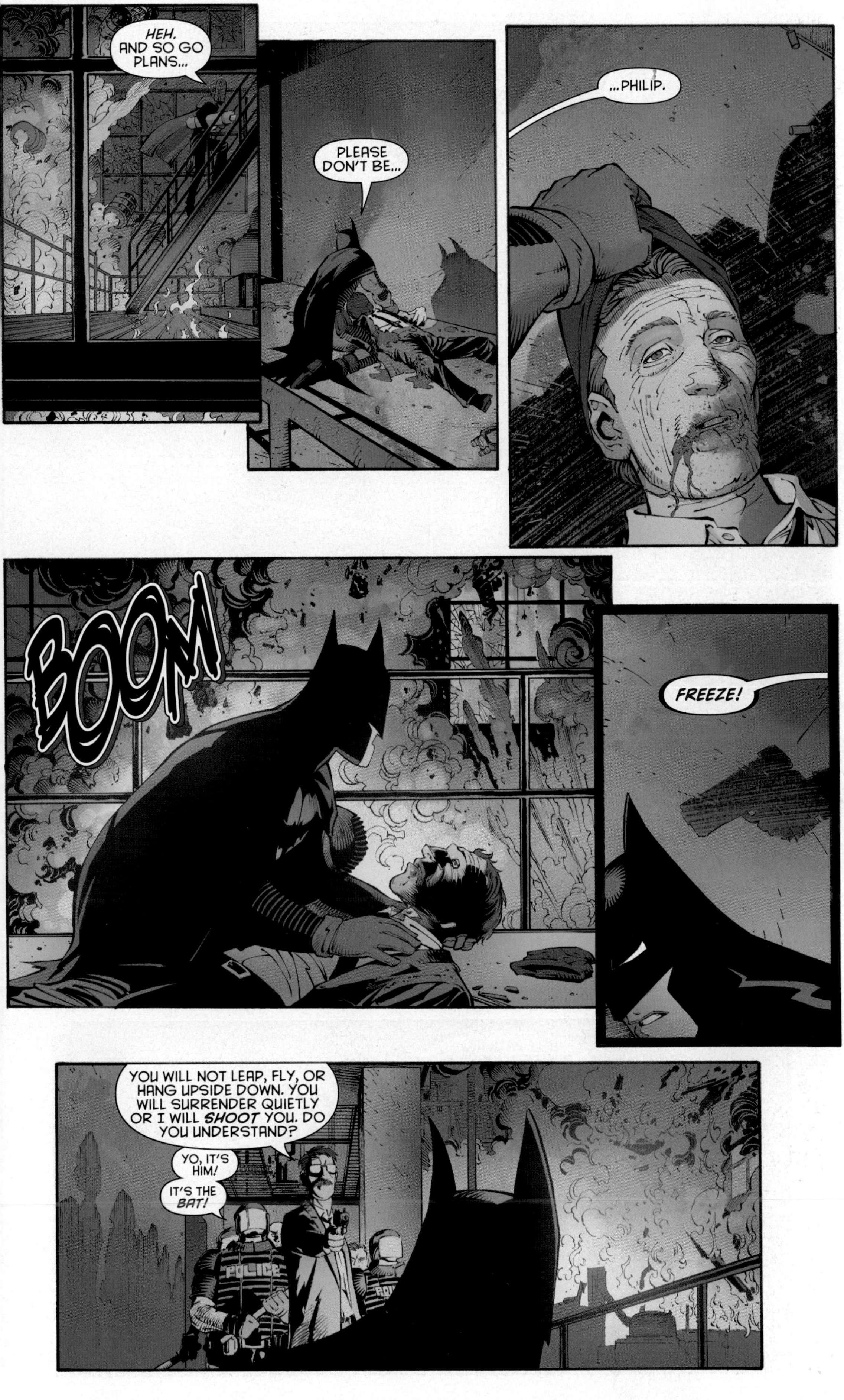
HEH. AND SO GO PLANS...
PLEASE DON'T BE...
...PHILIP.
BOOM
FREEZE!
YOU WILL NOT LEAP, FLY, OR HANG UPSIDE DOWN. YOU WILL SURRENDER QUIETLY OR I WILL SHOOT YOU. DO YOU UNDERSTAND?
YO, IT'S HIM!
IT'S THE BAT!
POLICE

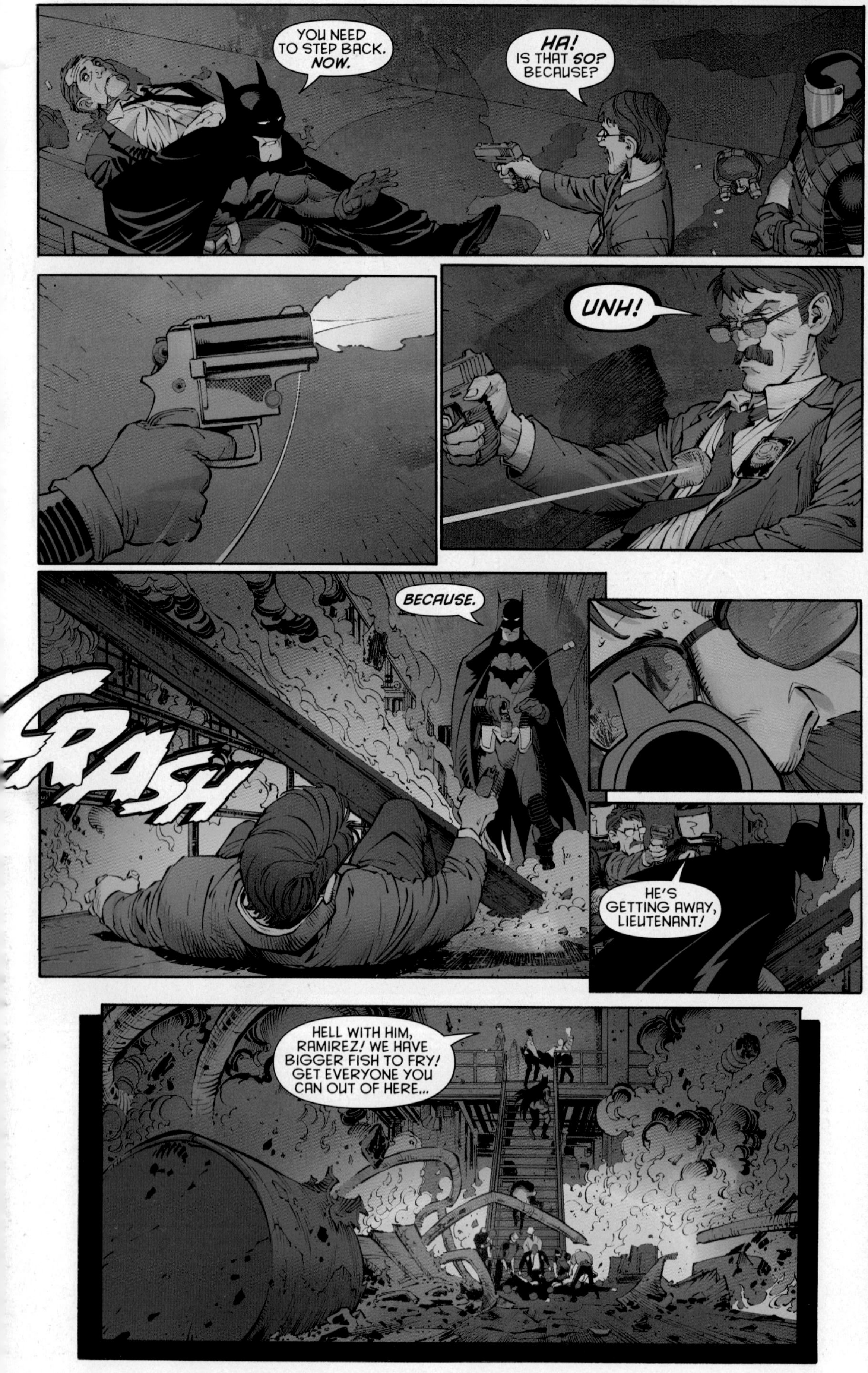
YOU NEED TO STEP BACK. NOW.
HA! IS THAT SO? BECAUSE?
UNH!
BECAUSE.
RASH
HE'S GETTING AWAY, LIEUTENANT!
HELL WITH HIM, RAMIREZ! WE HAVE BIGGER FISH TO FRY! GET EVERYONE YOU CAN OUT OF HERE...

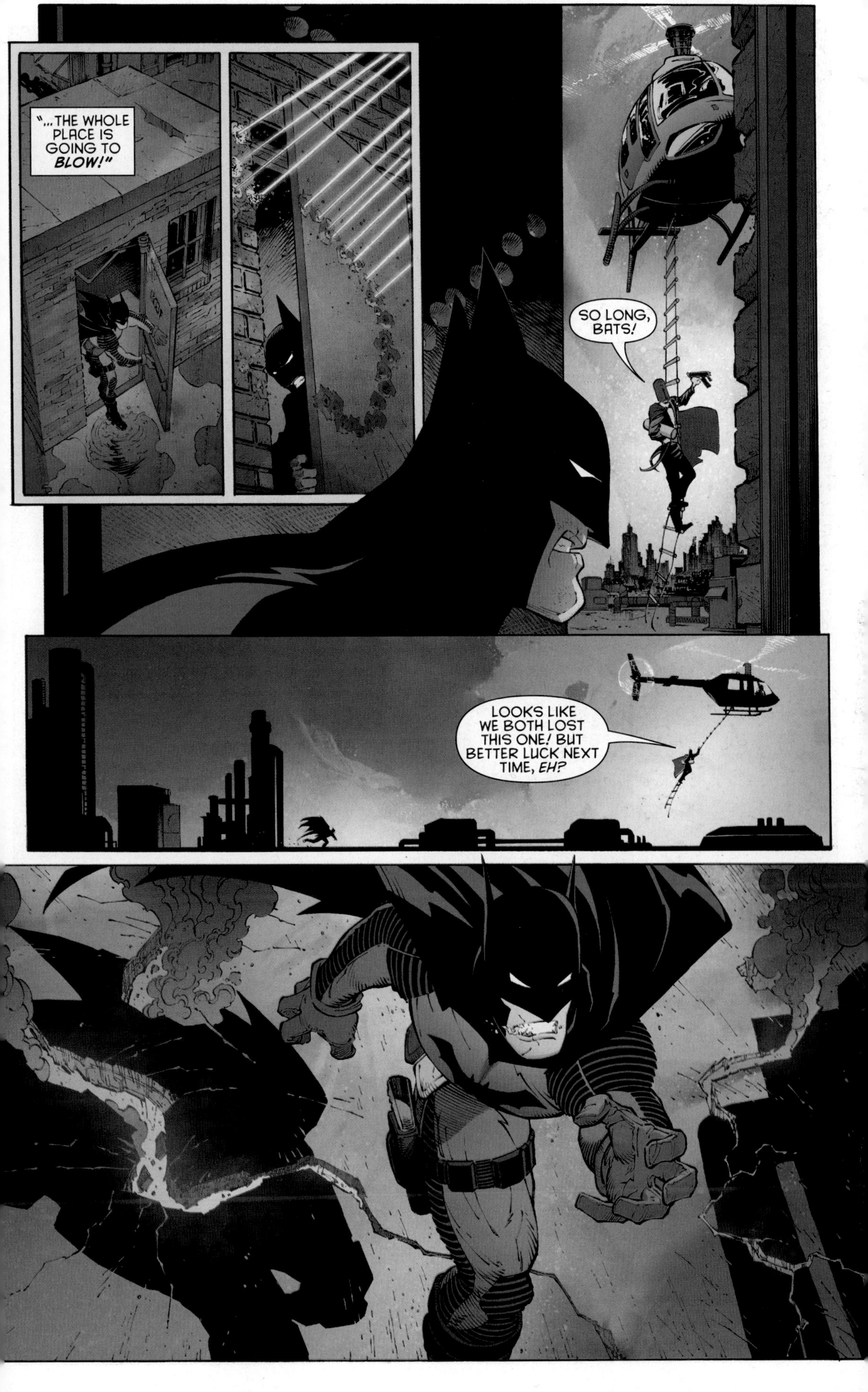
"...THE WHOLE PLACE IS GOING TO *BLOW!*"
SO LONG, BATS!
LOOKS LIKE WE BOTH LOST THIS ONE! BUT BETTER LUCK NEXT TIME, *EH?*

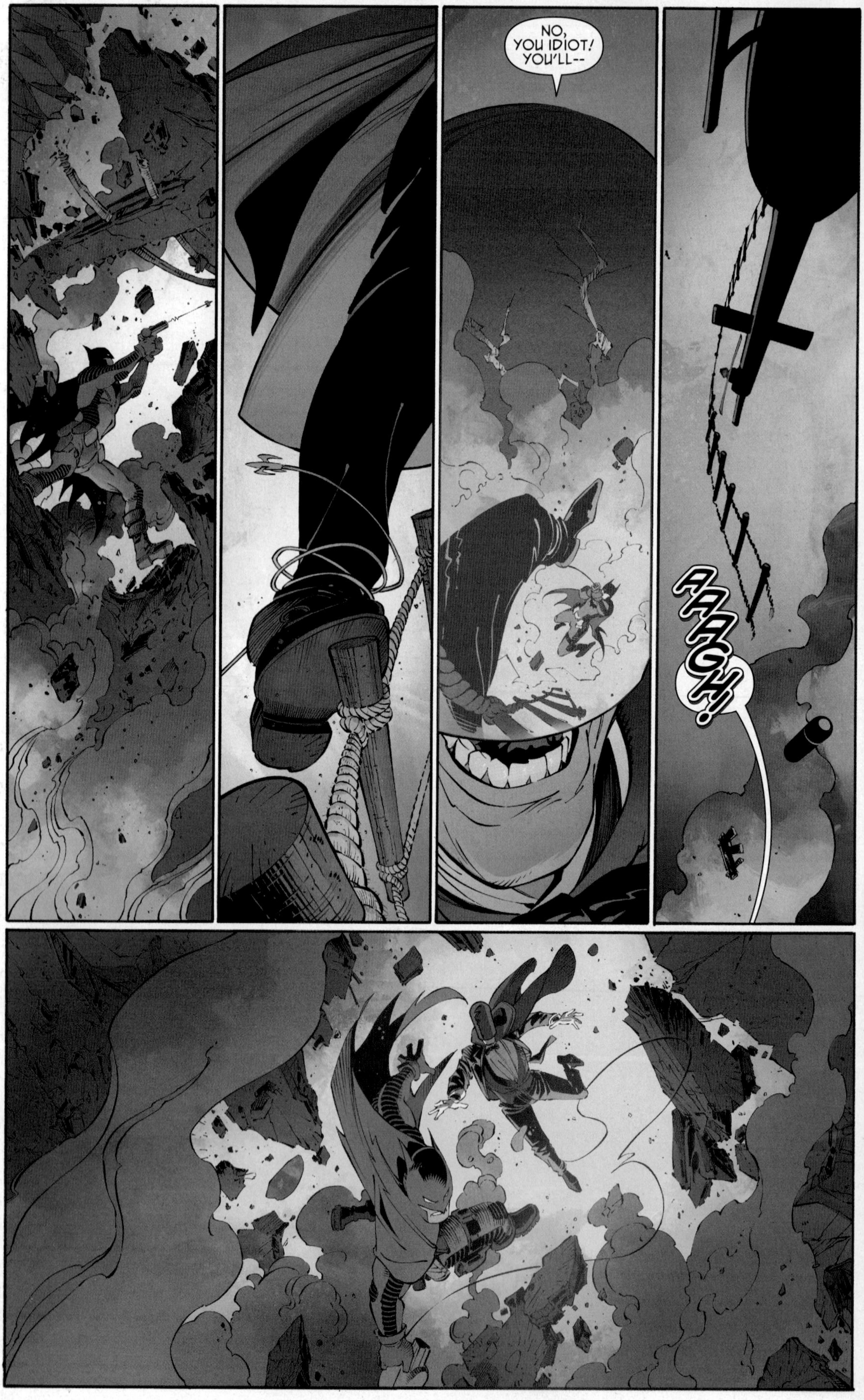
NO, YOU IDIOT! YOU'LL--
AAAGH!

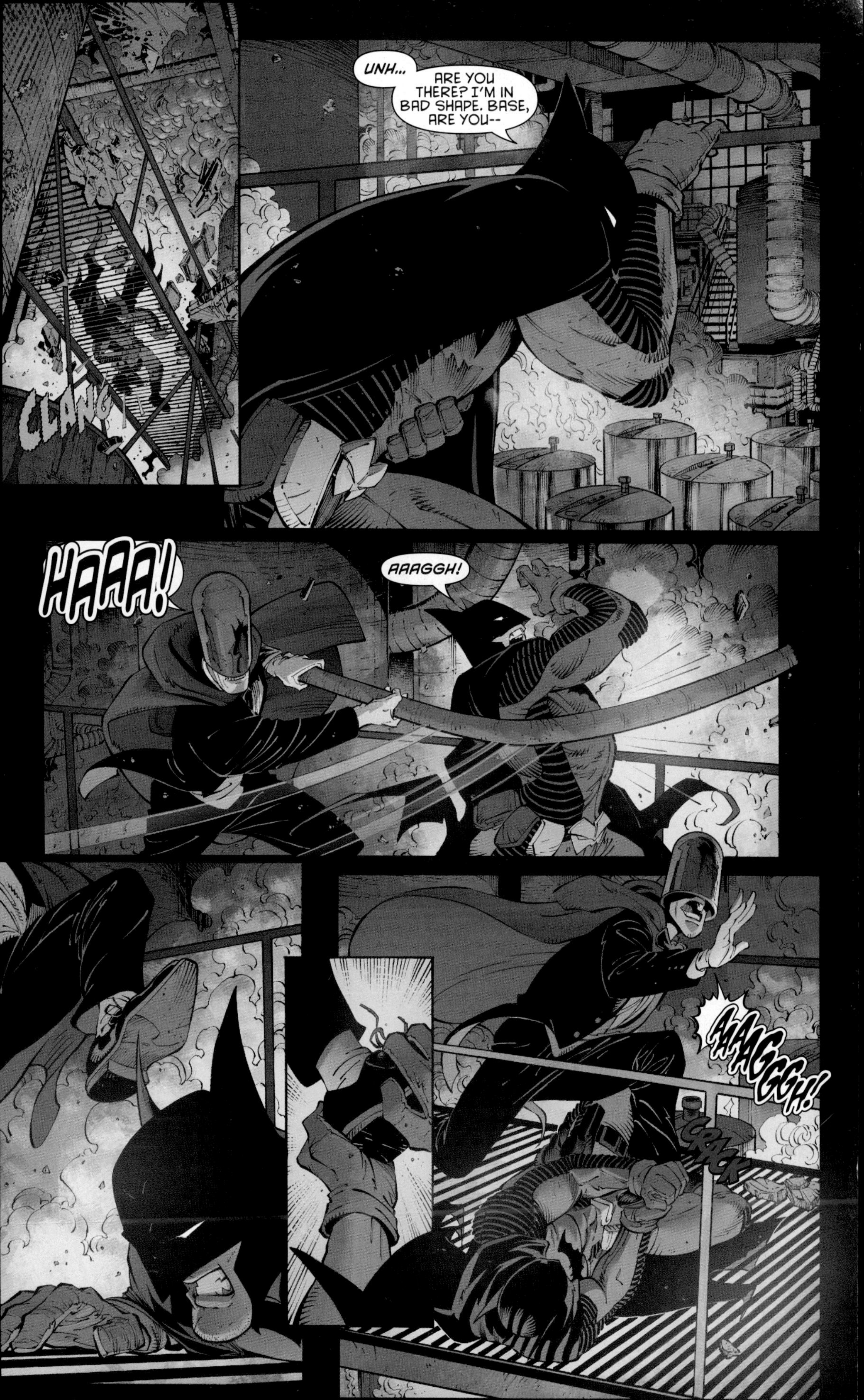
CLANG!
UNH...
ARE YOU THERE? I'M IN BAD SHAPE. BASE, ARE YOU--
HAAA!
AAAAGGH!
AAAAAGGGH!
CRACK

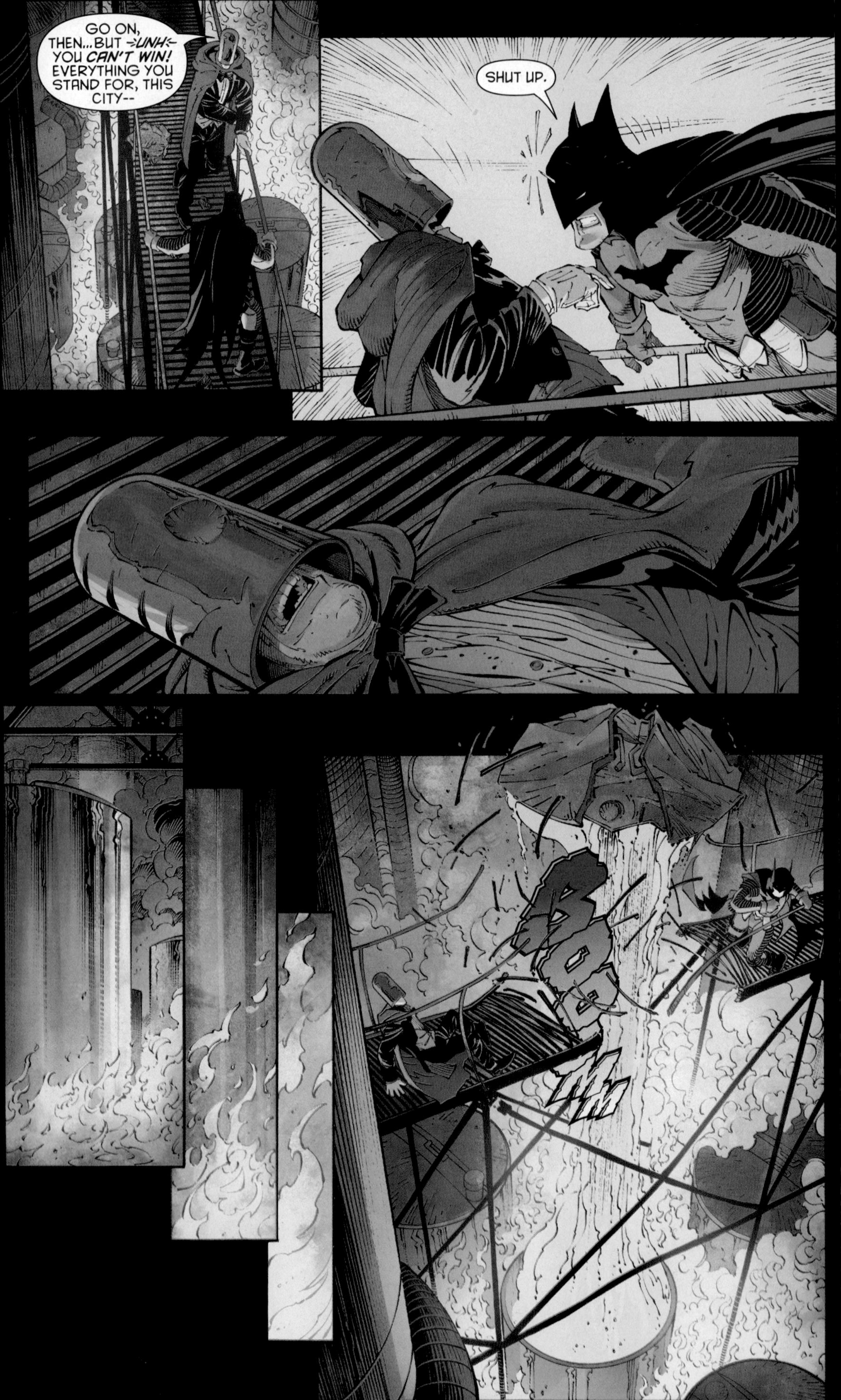
GO ON, THEN...BUT ⇒UNH⇐ YOU CAN'T WIN! EVERYTHING YOU STAND FOR, THIS CITY--
SHUT UP.
BOOM

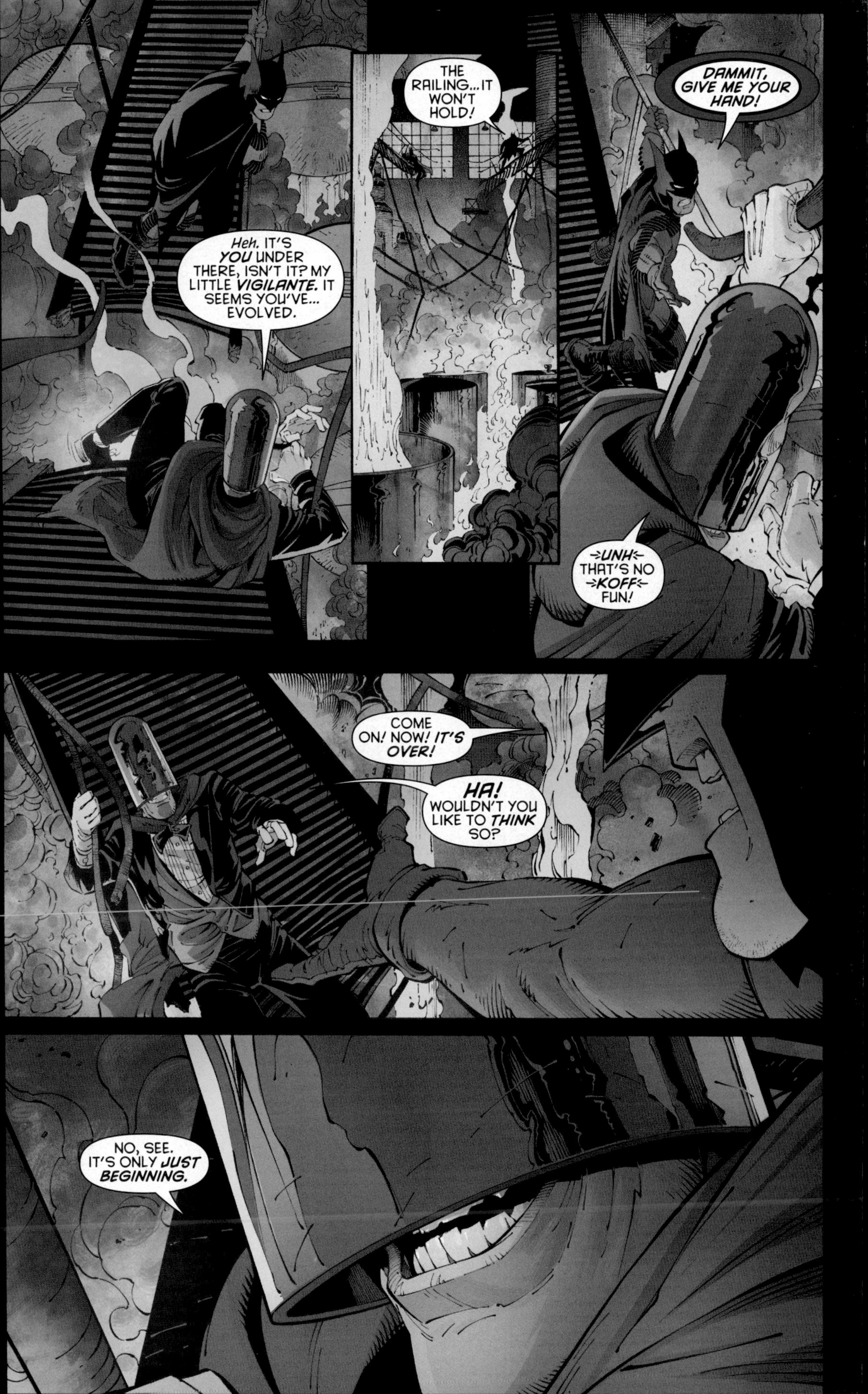

Heh. IT'S YOU UNDER THERE, ISN'T IT? MY LITTLE VIGILANTE. IT SEEMS YOU'VE... EVOLVED.
THE RAILING...IT WON'T HOLD!
DAMMIT, GIVE ME YOUR HAND!
UNH THAT'S NO KOFF FUN!
COME ON! NOW! IT'S OVER!
HA! WOULDN'T YOU LIKE TO THINK SO?
NO, SEE. IT'S ONLY JUST BEGINNING.

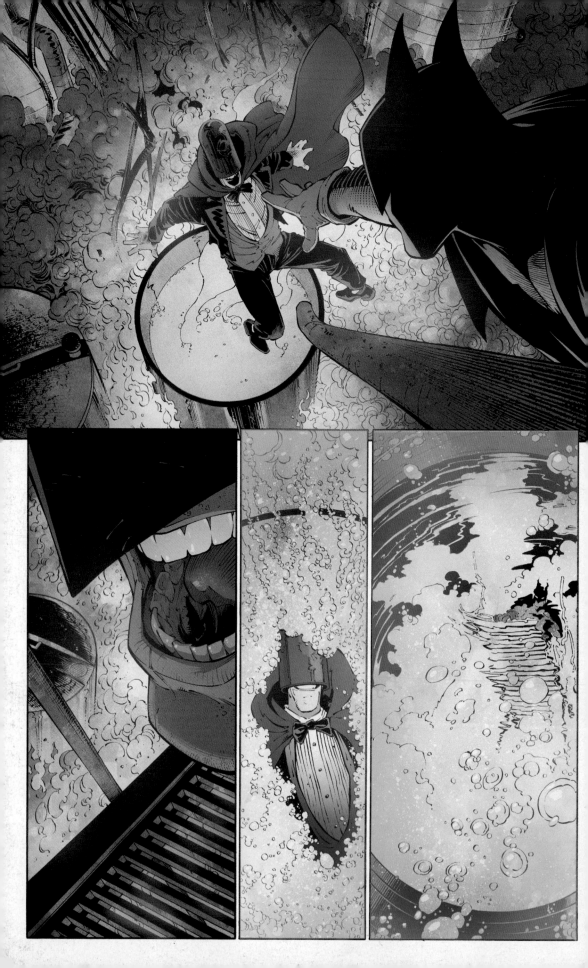

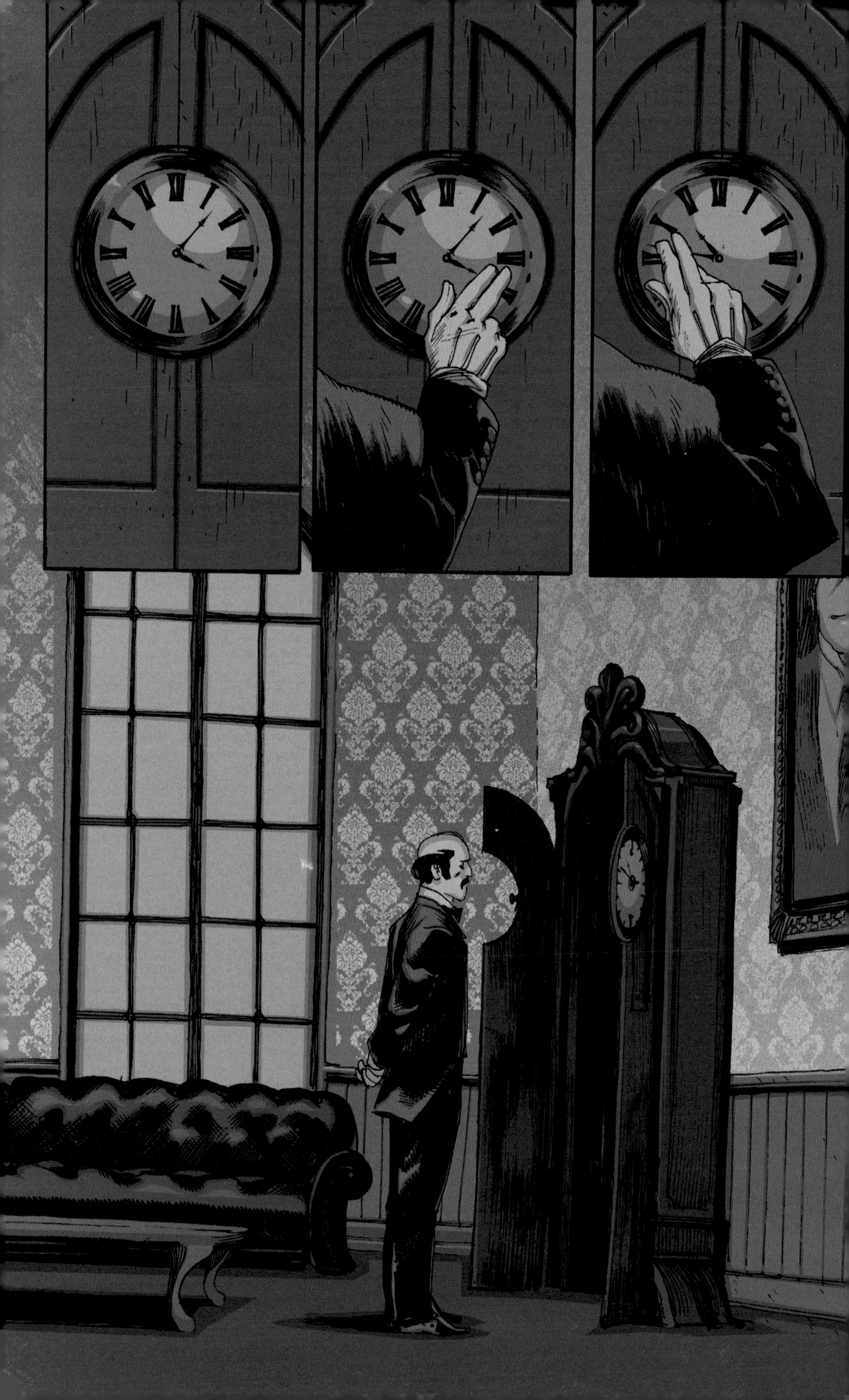

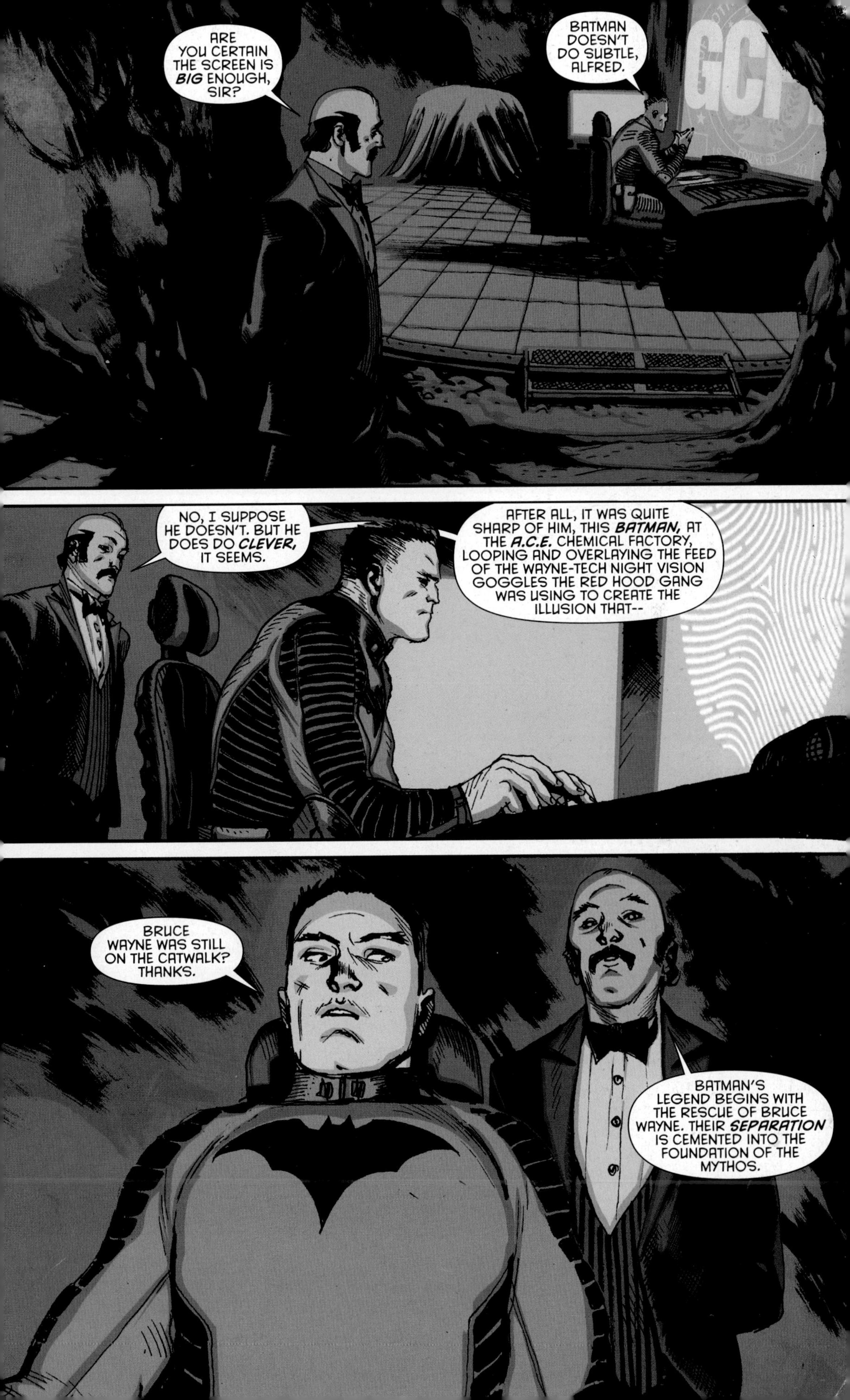
ARE YOU CERTAIN THE SCREEN IS *BIG* ENOUGH, SIR?
BATMAN DOESN'T DO SUBTLE, ALFRED.
GC
NO, I SUPPOSE HE DOESN'T. BUT HE DOES DO *CLEVER,* IT SEEMS.
AFTER ALL, IT WAS QUITE SHARP OF HIM, THIS *BATMAN,* AT THE *A.C.E.* CHEMICAL FACTORY, LOOPING AND OVERLAYING THE FEED OF THE WAYNE-TECH NIGHT VISION GOGGLES THE RED HOOD GANG WAS USING TO CREATE THE ILLUSION THAT--
BRUCE WAYNE WAS STILL ON THE CATWALK? THANKS.
BATMAN'S LEGEND BEGINS WITH THE RESCUE OF BRUCE WAYNE. THEIR *SEPARATION* IS CEMENTED INTO THE FOUNDATION OF THE MYTHOS.

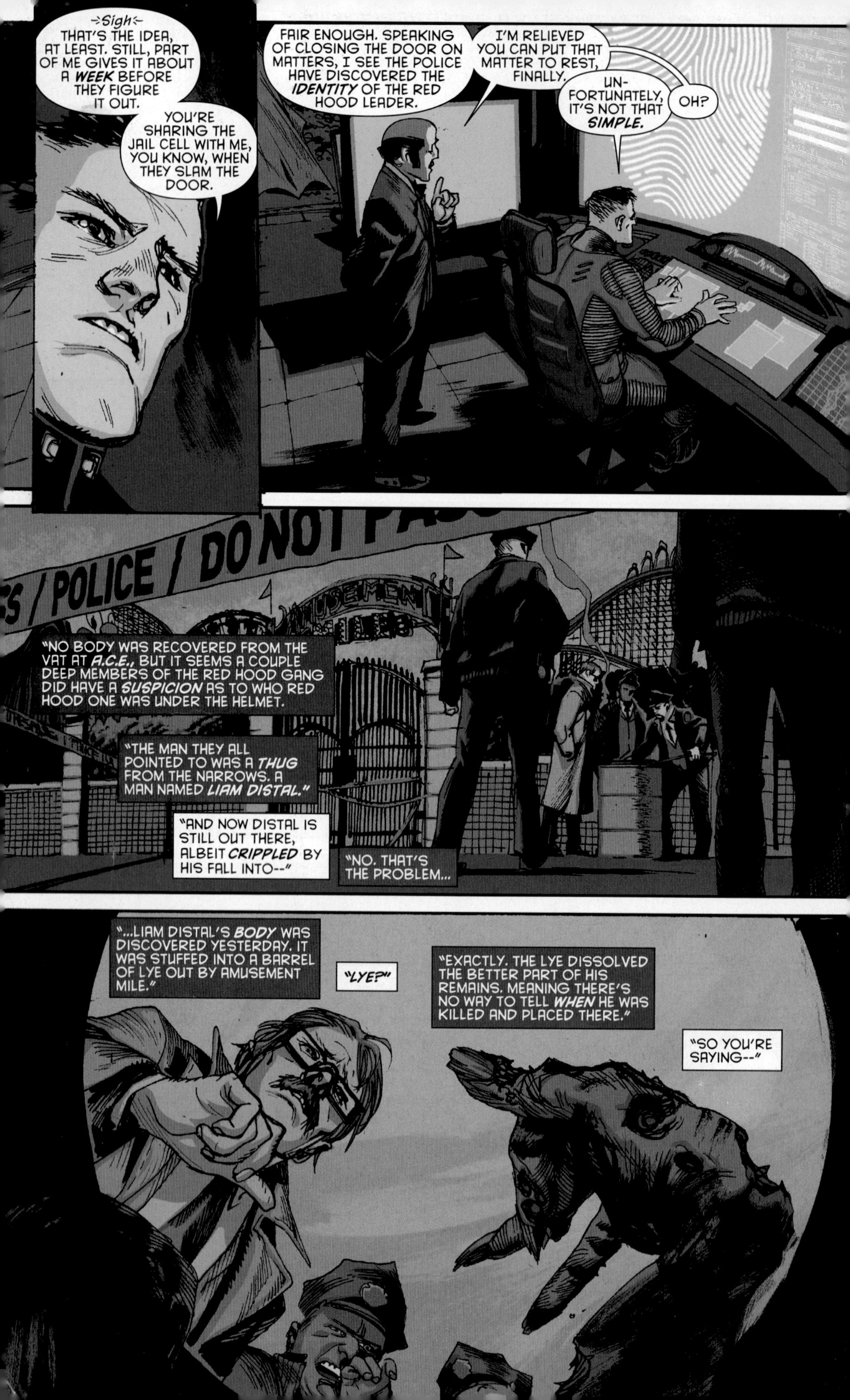

-Sigh-
THAT'S THE IDEA, AT LEAST. STILL, PART OF ME GIVES IT ABOUT A *WEEK* BEFORE THEY FIGURE IT OUT.
YOU'RE SHARING THE JAIL CELL WITH ME, YOU KNOW, WHEN THEY SLAM THE DOOR.
FAIR ENOUGH. SPEAKING OF CLOSING THE DOOR ON MATTERS, I SEE THE POLICE HAVE DISCOVERED THE *IDENTITY* OF THE RED HOOD LEADER.
I'M RELIEVED YOU CAN PUT THAT MATTER TO REST, FINALLY.
UN-FORTUNATELY, IT'S NOT THAT *SIMPLE.*
OH?
POLICE / DO NOT PASS
"NO BODY WAS RECOVERED FROM THE VAT AT *A.C.E.,* BUT IT SEEMS A COUPLE DEEP MEMBERS OF THE RED HOOD GANG DID HAVE A *SUSPICION* AS TO WHO RED HOOD ONE WAS UNDER THE HELMET.
"THE MAN THEY ALL POINTED TO WAS A *THUG* FROM THE NARROWS. A MAN NAMED *LIAM DISTAL.*"
"AND NOW DISTAL IS STILL OUT THERE, ALBEIT *CRIPPLED* BY HIS FALL INTO--"
"NO. THAT'S THE PROBLEM...
"...LIAM DISTAL'S *BODY* WAS DISCOVERED YESTERDAY. IT WAS STUFFED INTO A BARREL OF LYE OUT BY AMUSEMENT MILE."
"LYE?"
"EXACTLY. THE LYE DISSOLVED THE BETTER PART OF HIS REMAINS. MEANING THERE'S NO WAY TO TELL *WHEN* HE WAS KILLED AND PLACED THERE."
"SO YOU'RE SAYING--"

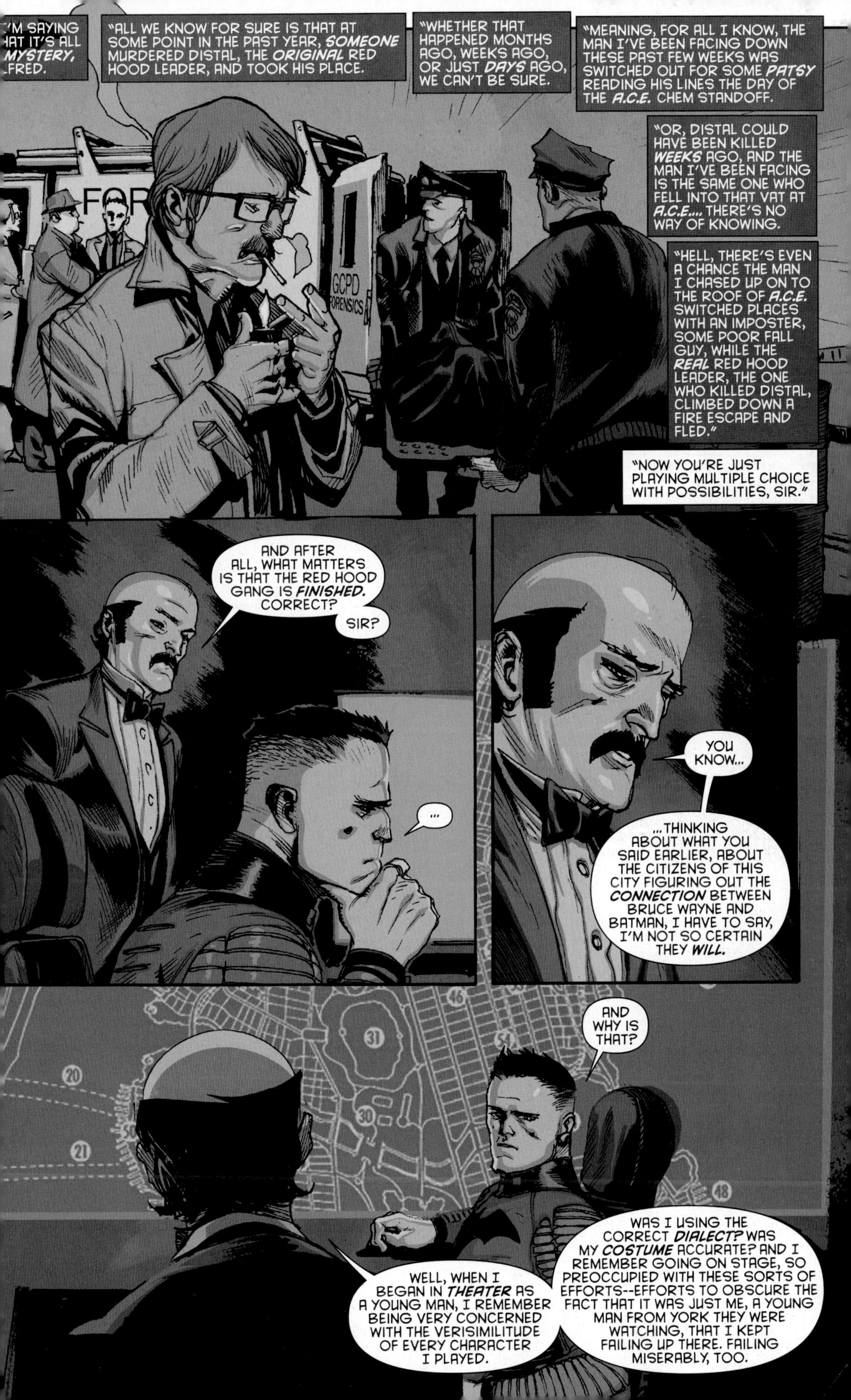

'M SAYING
HAT IT'S ALL
MYSTERY,
LFRED.
"ALL WE KNOW FOR SURE IS THAT AT SOME POINT IN THE PAST YEAR, SOMEONE MURDERED DISTAL, THE ORIGINAL RED HOOD LEADER, AND TOOK HIS PLACE.
"WHETHER THAT HAPPENED MONTHS AGO, WEEKS AGO, OR JUST DAYS AGO, WE CAN'T BE SURE.
"MEANING, FOR ALL I KNOW, THE MAN I'VE BEEN FACING DOWN THESE PAST FEW WEEKS WAS SWITCHED OUT FOR SOME PATSY READING HIS LINES THE DAY OF THE A.C.E. CHEM STANDOFF.
"OR, DISTAL COULD HAVE BEEN KILLED WEEKS AGO, AND THE MAN I'VE BEEN FACING IS THE SAME ONE WHO FELL INTO THAT VAT AT A.C.E.... THERE'S NO WAY OF KNOWING.
"HELL, THERE'S EVEN A CHANCE THE MAN I CHASED UP ON TO THE ROOF OF A.C.E. SWITCHED PLACES WITH AN IMPOSTER, SOME POOR FALL GUY, WHILE THE REAL RED HOOD LEADER, THE ONE WHO KILLED DISTAL, CLIMBED DOWN A FIRE ESCAPE AND FLED."
"NOW YOU'RE JUST PLAYING MULTIPLE CHOICE WITH POSSIBILITIES, SIR."
FOR
GCPD FORENSICS
AND AFTER ALL, WHAT MATTERS IS THAT THE RED HOOD GANG IS FINISHED. CORRECT?
SIR?
...
YOU KNOW...
...THINKING ABOUT WHAT YOU SAID EARLIER, ABOUT THE CITIZENS OF THIS CITY FIGURING OUT THE CONNECTION BETWEEN BRUCE WAYNE AND BATMAN, I HAVE TO SAY, I'M NOT SO CERTAIN THEY WILL.
AND WHY IS THAT?
WELL, WHEN I BEGAN IN THEATER AS A YOUNG MAN, I REMEMBER BEING VERY CONCERNED WITH THE VERISIMILITUDE OF EVERY CHARACTER I PLAYED.
WAS I USING THE CORRECT DIALECT? WAS MY COSTUME ACCURATE? AND I REMEMBER GOING ON STAGE, SO PREOCCUPIED WITH THESE SORTS OF EFFORTS--EFFORTS TO OBSCURE THE FACT THAT IT WAS JUST ME, A YOUNG MAN FROM YORK THEY WERE WATCHING, THAT I KEPT FAILING UP THERE. FAILING MISERABLY, TOO.

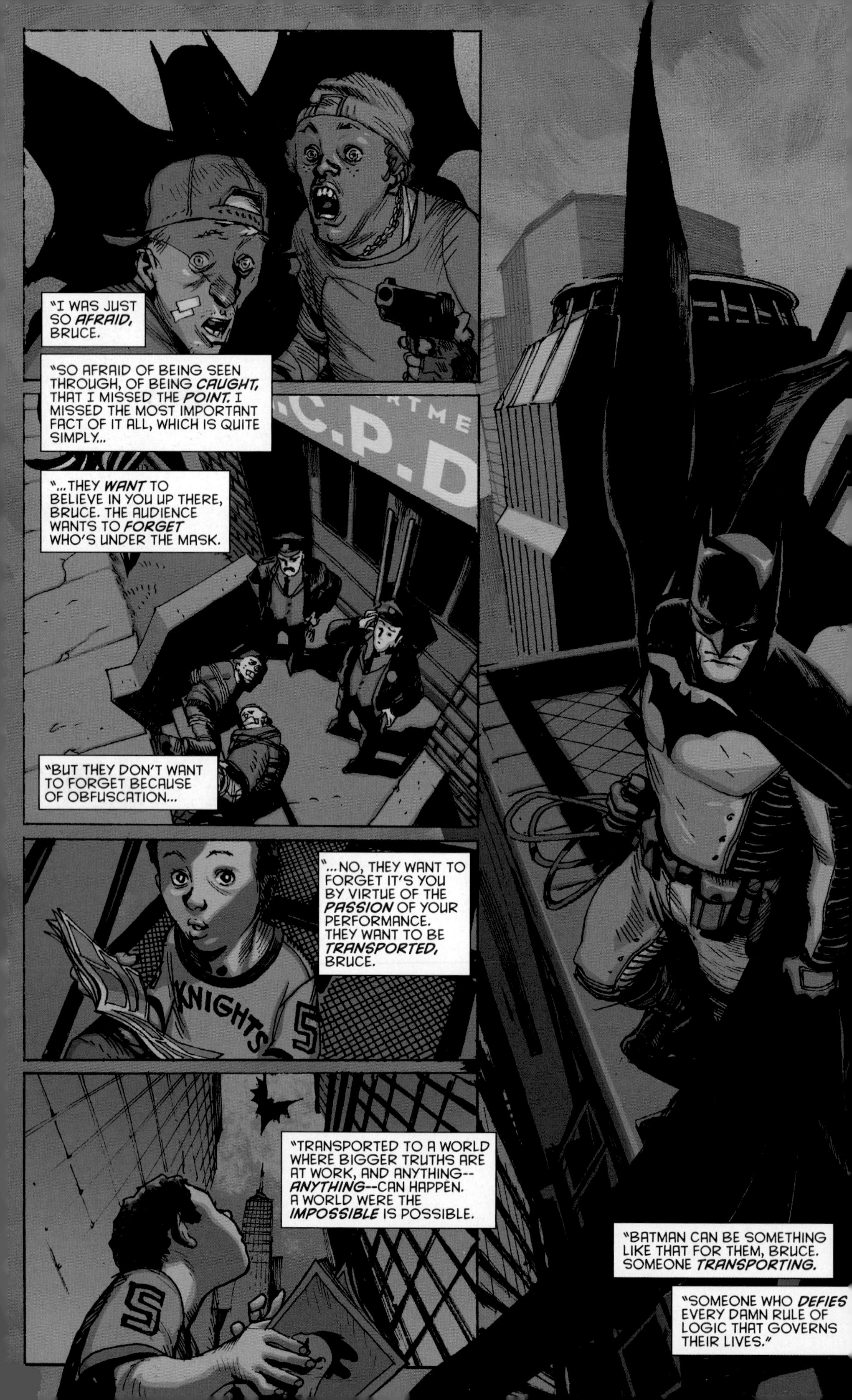
"I WAS JUST SO *AFRAID,* BRUCE.
"SO AFRAID OF BEING SEEN THROUGH, OF BEING *CAUGHT,* THAT I MISSED THE *POINT.* I MISSED THE MOST IMPORTANT FACT OF IT ALL, WHICH IS QUITE SIMPLY...
"...THEY *WANT* TO BELIEVE IN YOU UP THERE, BRUCE. THE AUDIENCE WANTS TO *FORGET* WHO'S UNDER THE MASK.
"BUT THEY DON'T WANT TO FORGET BECAUSE OF OBFUSCATION...
"...NO, THEY WANT TO FORGET IT'S YOU BY VIRTUE OF THE *PASSION* OF YOUR PERFORMANCE. THEY WANT TO BE *TRANSPORTED,* BRUCE.
KNIGHTS
5
"TRANSPORTED TO A WORLD WHERE BIGGER TRUTHS ARE AT WORK, AND ANYTHING-- *ANYTHING*--CAN HAPPEN. A WORLD WERE THE *IMPOSSIBLE* IS POSSIBLE.
"BATMAN CAN BE SOMETHING LIKE THAT FOR THEM, BRUCE. SOMEONE *TRANSPORTING.*
"SOMEONE WHO *DEFIES* EVERY DAMN RULE OF LOGIC THAT GOVERNS THEIR LIVES."

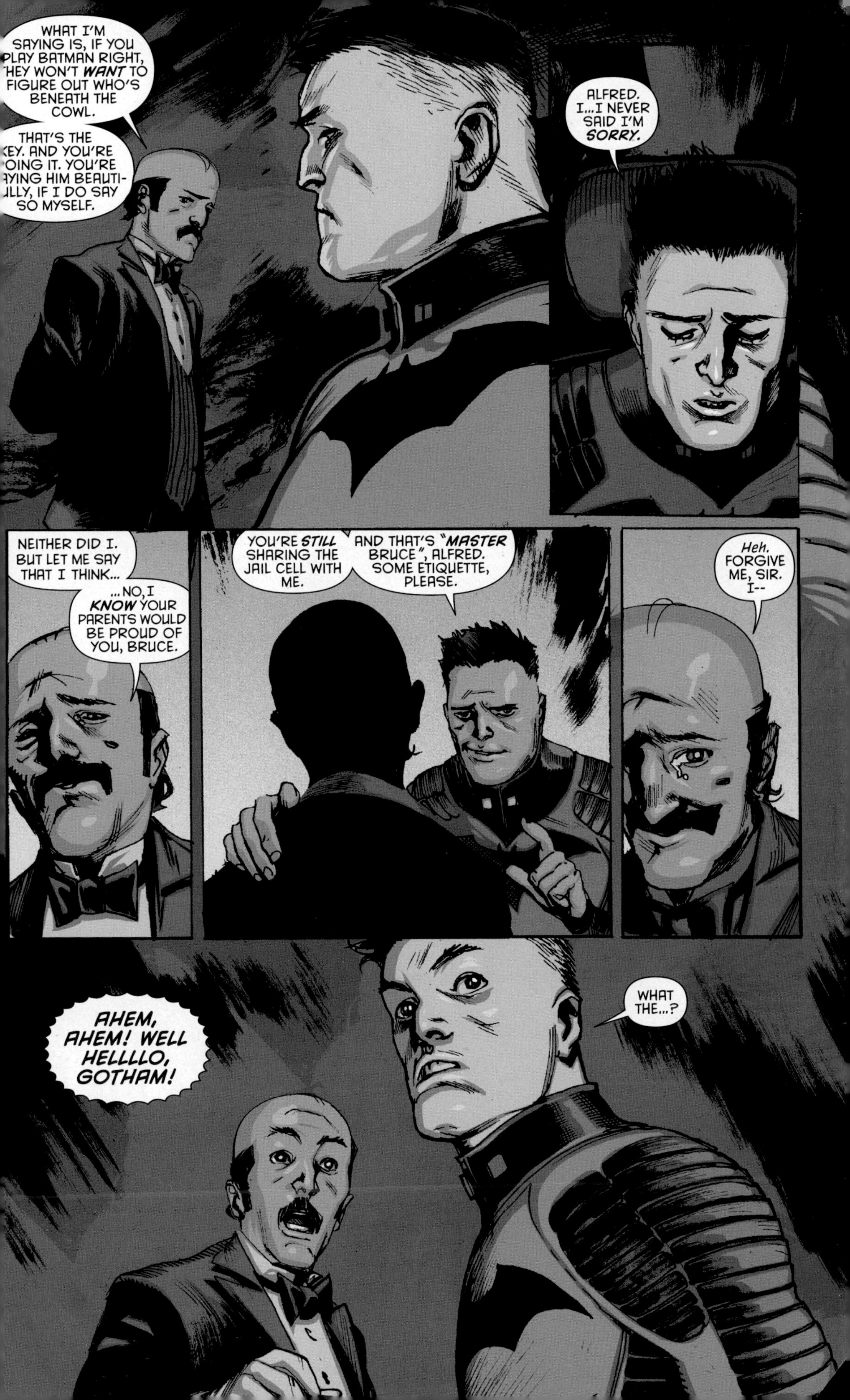
WHAT I'M SAYING IS, IF YOU LAY BATMAN RIGHT, HEY WON'T *WANT* TO FIGURE OUT WHO'S BENEATH THE COWL.
THAT'S THE EY. AND YOU'RE OING IT. YOU'RE YING HIM BEAUTI- LLY, IF I DO SAY SO MYSELF.
ALFRED. I...I NEVER SAID I'M *SORRY.*
NEITHER DID I. BUT LET ME SAY THAT I THINK...
...NO, I *KNOW* YOUR PARENTS WOULD BE PROUD OF YOU, BRUCE.
YOU'RE *STILL* SHARING THE JAIL CELL WITH ME.
AND THAT'S "*MASTER* BRUCE", ALFRED. SOME ETIQUETTE, PLEASE.
Heh. FORGIVE ME, SIR. I--
AHEM, AHEM! WELL HELLLLO, GOTHAM!
WHAT THE...?

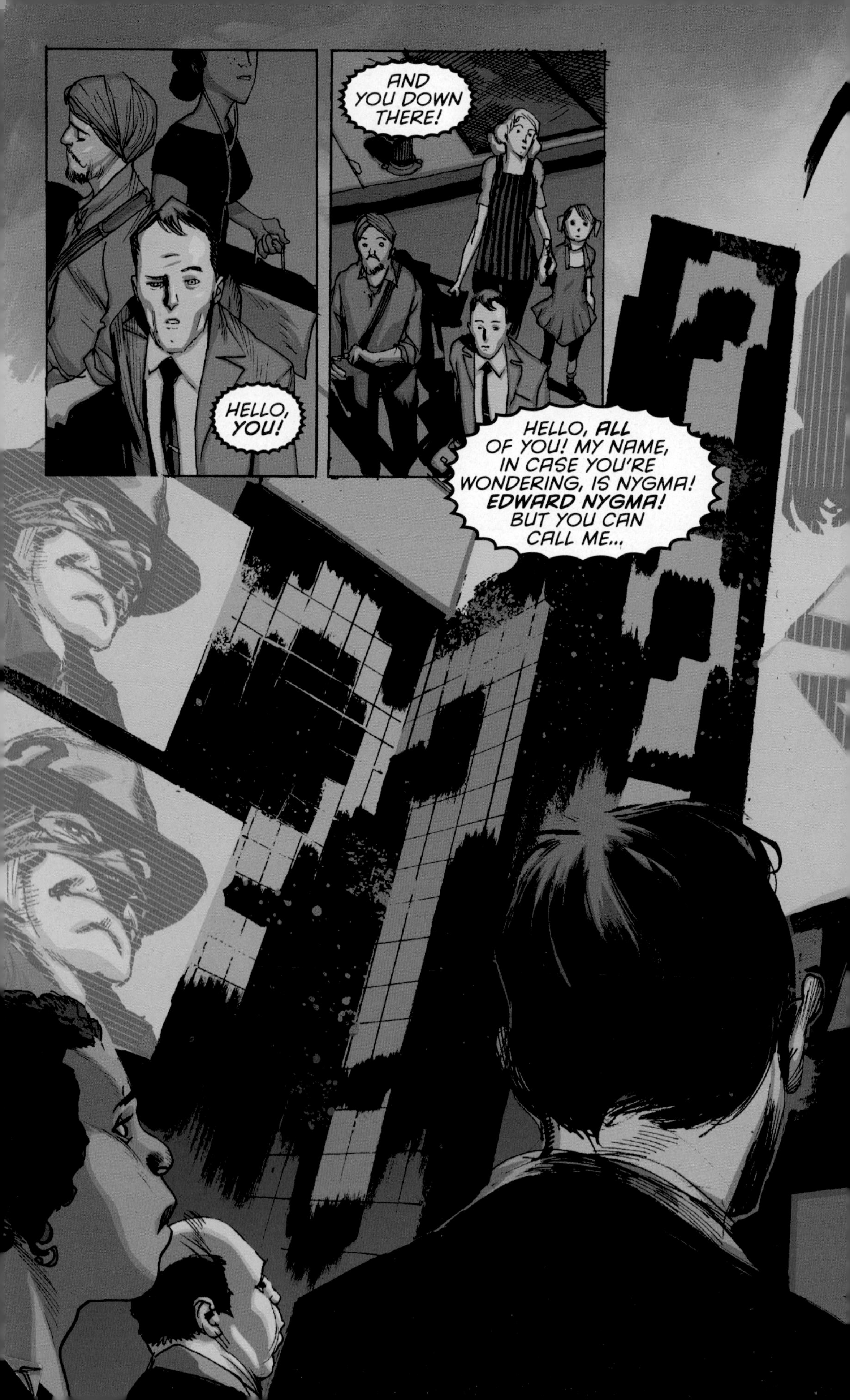
HELLO, YOU!
AND YOU DOWN THERE!
HELLO, ALL OF YOU! MY NAME, IN CASE YOU'RE WONDERING, IS NYGMA! EDWARD NYGMA! BUT YOU CAN CALL ME...

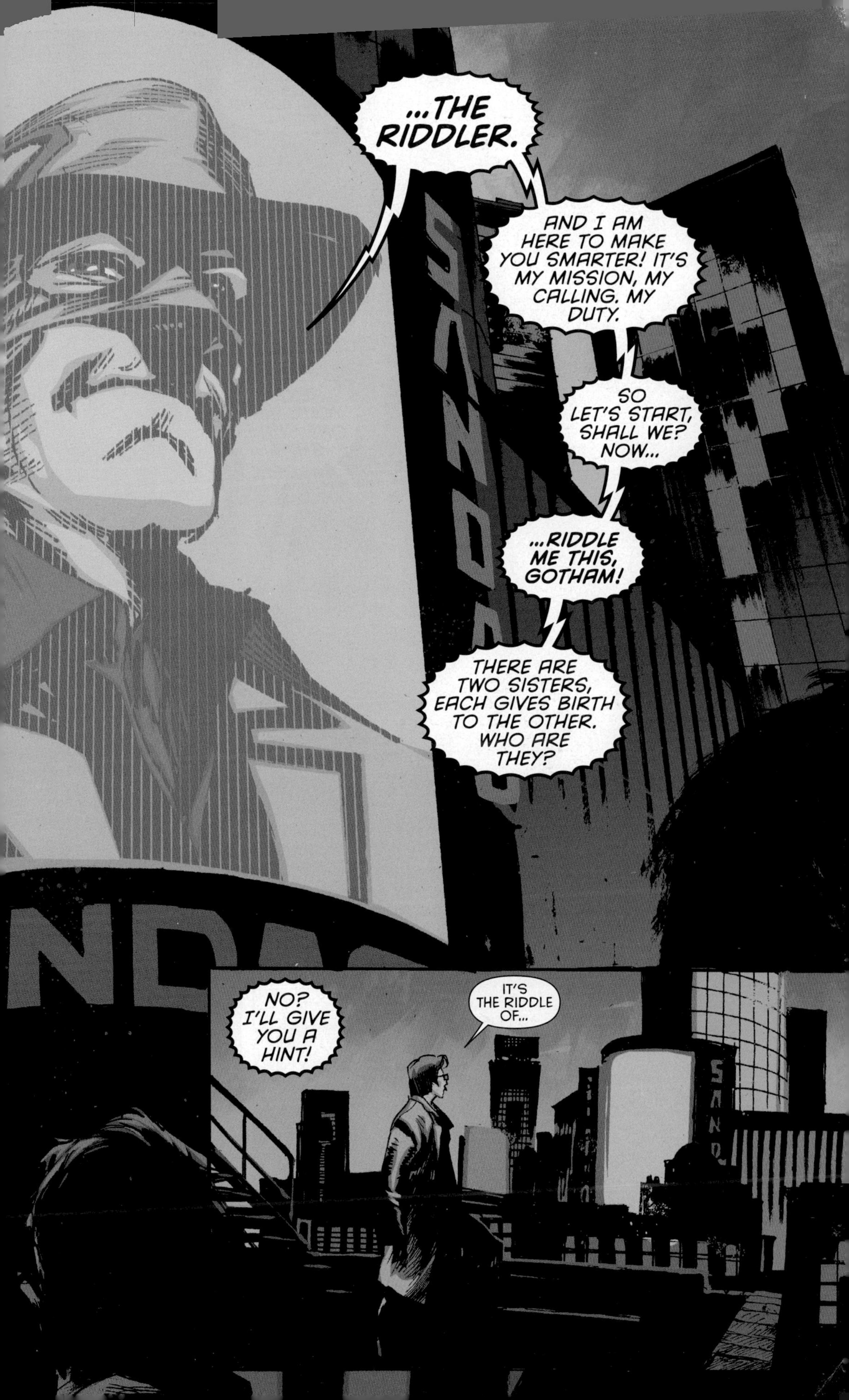
...THE RIDDLER.
AND I AM HERE TO MAKE YOU SMARTER! IT'S MY MISSION, MY CALLING. MY DUTY.
SO LET'S START, SHALL WE? NOW...
...RIDDLE ME THIS, GOTHAM!
THERE ARE TWO SISTERS, EACH GIVES BIRTH TO THE OTHER. WHO ARE THEY?
NO? I'LL GIVE YOU A HINT!
IT'S THE RIDDLE OF...

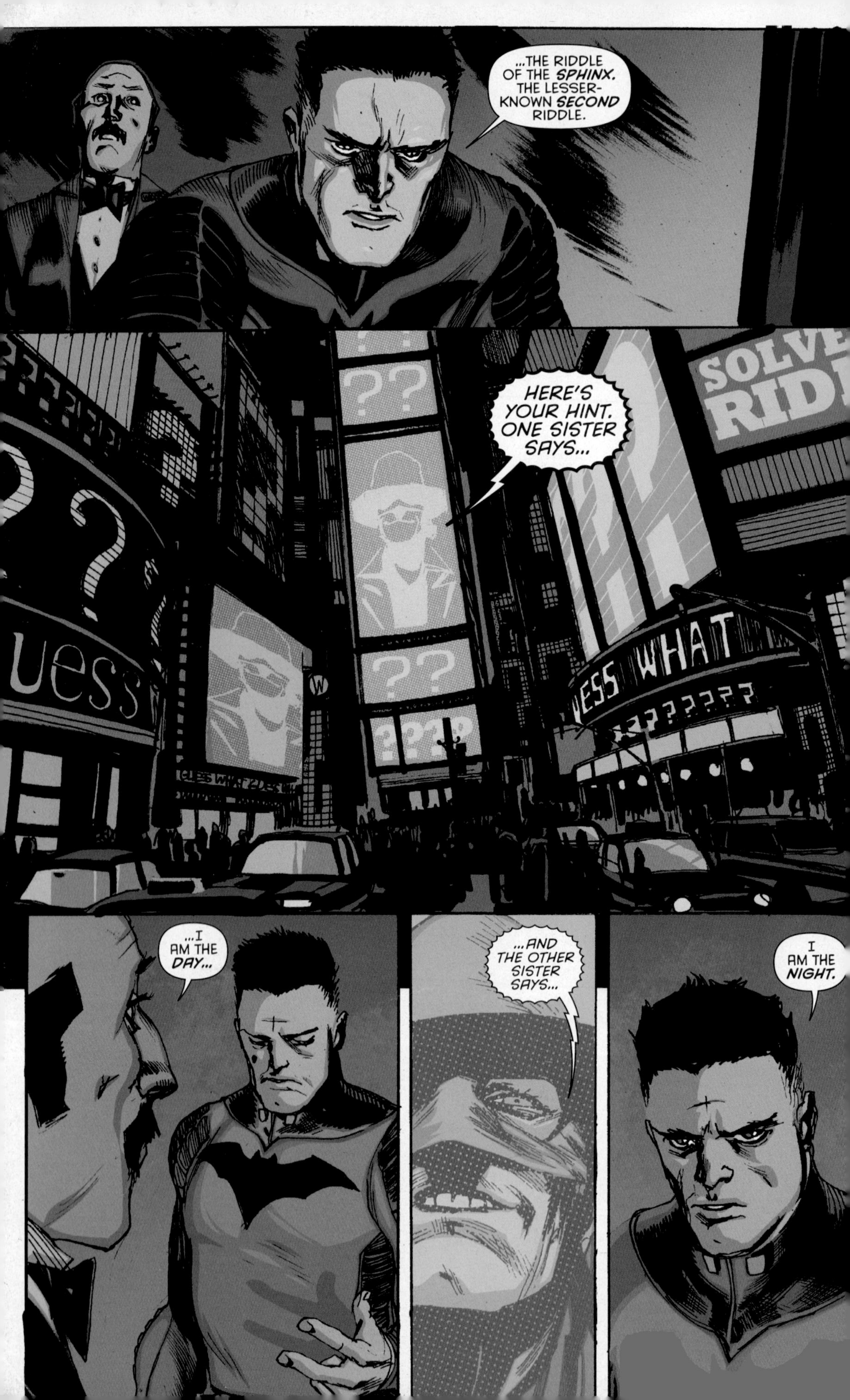
...THE RIDDLE OF THE *SPHINX.* THE LESSER-KNOWN *SECOND* RIDDLE.
SOLVE RIDD
??
HERE'S YOUR HINT. ONE SISTER SAYS...
GUESS
GUESS WHAT
?????
...I AM THE *DAY*...
...AND THE OTHER SISTER SAYS...
I AM THE *NIGHT.*

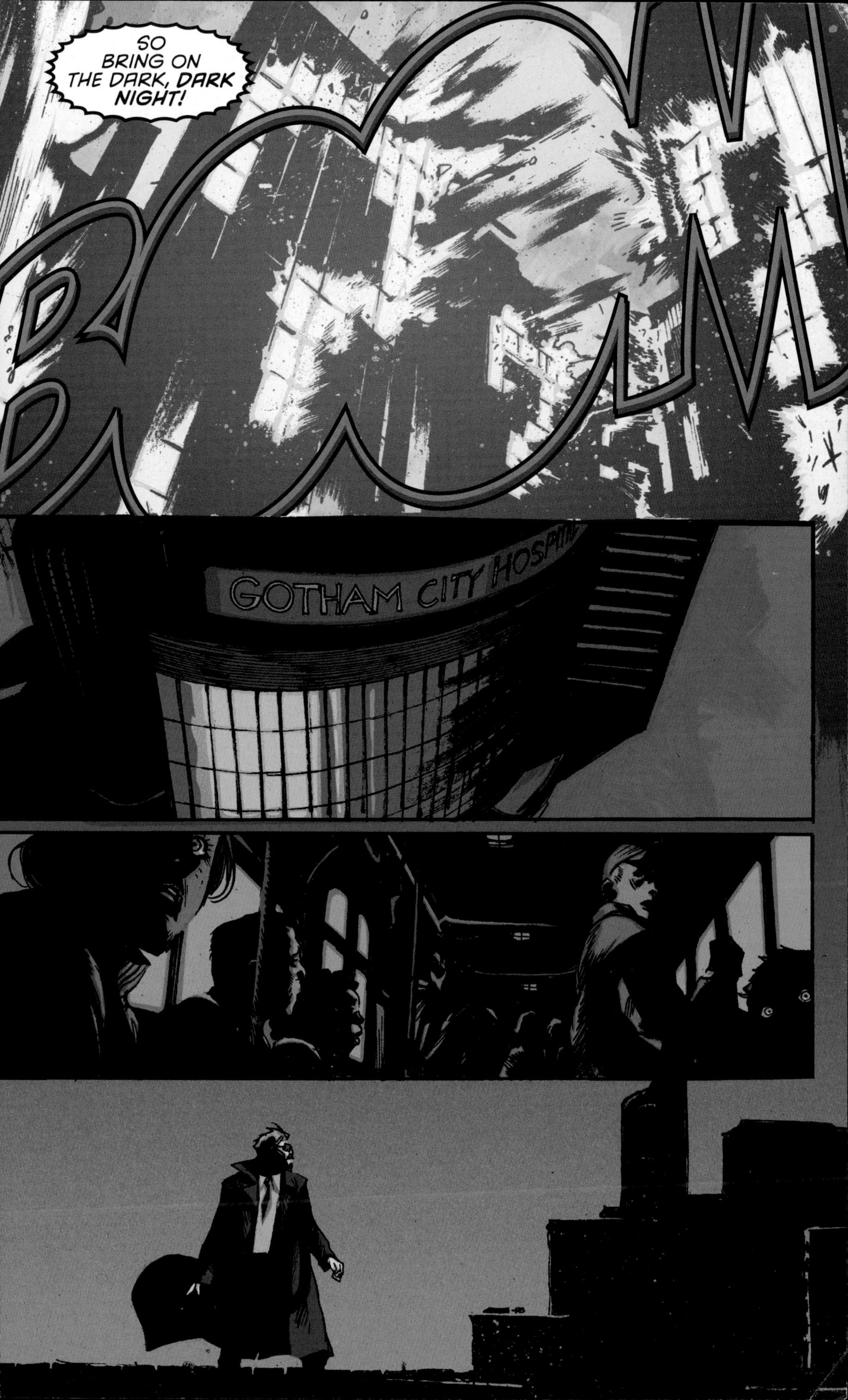
SO BRING ON THE DARK, DARK NIGHT!
BOOOM
GOTHAM CITY HOSPI

ALL RIGHT, GOTHAM, TIME TO GET SMART!

YOU'RE GOING TO HAVE TO DO BETTER THAN THAT...OR THE CITY **DIES** FOR REAL!

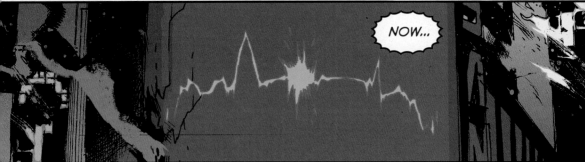

NOW...

...LET THE **GAMES** BEGIN!

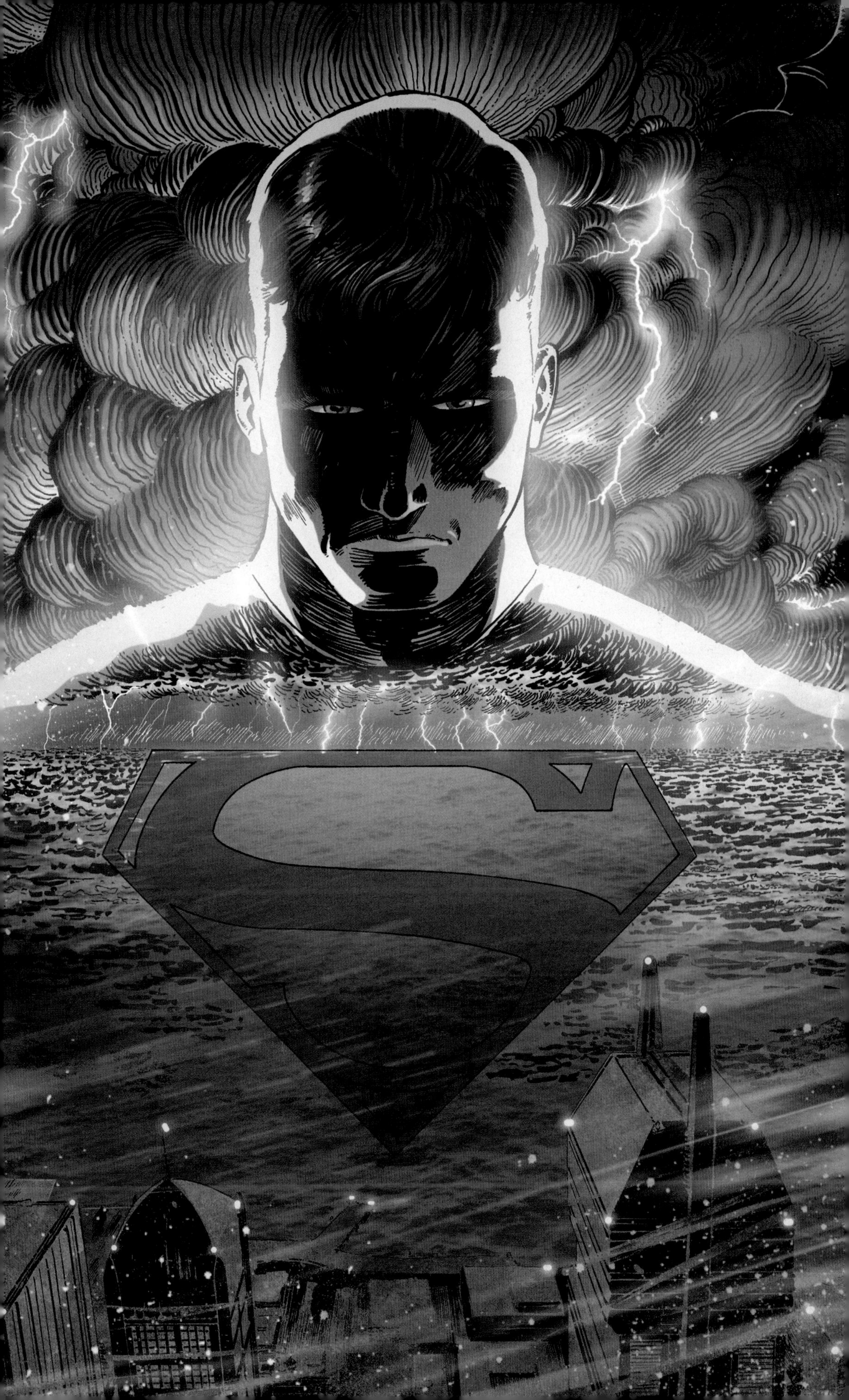

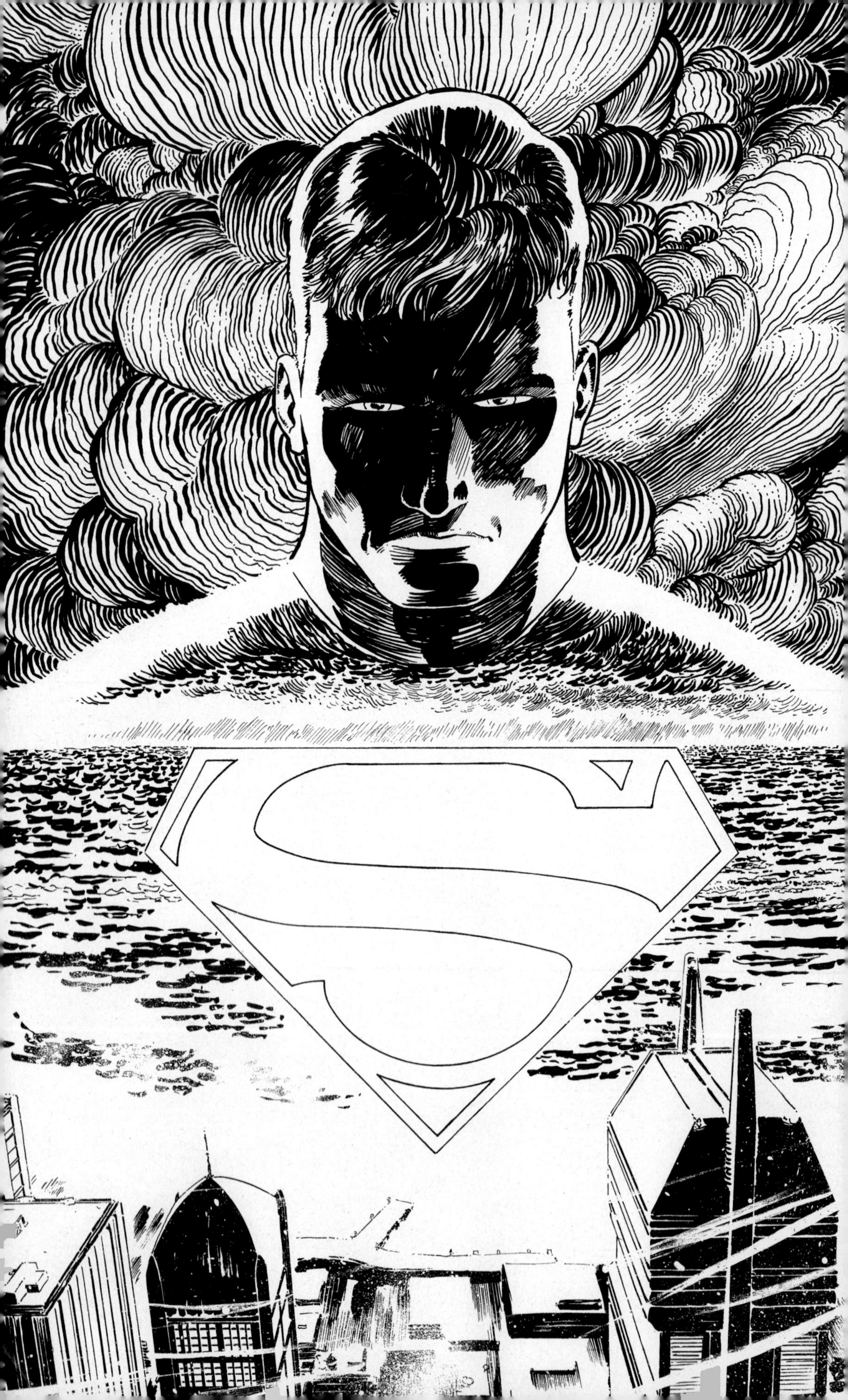

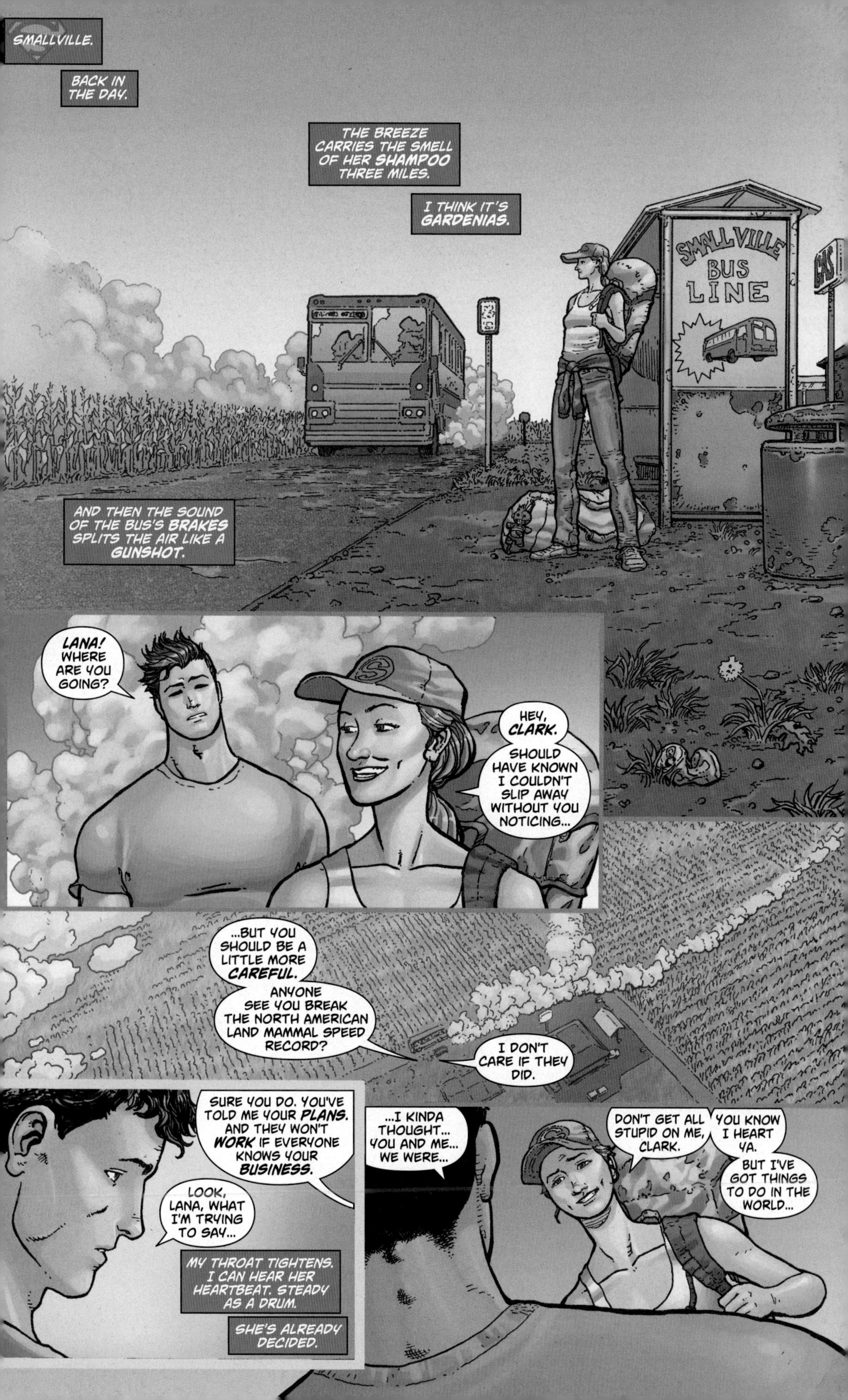
SMALLVILLE.
BACK IN THE DAY.
THE BREEZE CARRIES THE SMELL OF HER SHAMPOO THREE MILES.
I THINK IT'S GARDENIAS.
SMALLVILLE BUS LINE
AND THEN THE SOUND OF THE BUS'S BRAKES SPLITS THE AIR LIKE A GUNSHOT.
LANA! WHERE ARE YOU GOING?
HEY, CLARK.
SHOULD HAVE KNOWN I COULDN'T SLIP AWAY WITHOUT YOU NOTICING...
...BUT YOU SHOULD BE A LITTLE MORE CAREFUL.
ANYONE SEE YOU BREAK THE NORTH AMERICAN LAND MAMMAL SPEED RECORD?
I DON'T CARE IF THEY DID.
SURE YOU DO. YOU'VE TOLD ME YOUR PLANS. AND THEY WON'T WORK IF EVERYONE KNOWS YOUR BUSINESS.
LOOK, LANA, WHAT I'M TRYING TO SAY...
MY THROAT TIGHTENS. I CAN HEAR HER HEARTBEAT. STEADY AS A DRUM.
SHE'S ALREADY DECIDED.
...I KINDA THOUGHT... YOU AND ME... WE WERE...
DON'T GET ALL STUPID ON ME, CLARK.
YOU KNOW I HEART YA.
BUT I'VE GOT THINGS TO DO IN THE WORLD...

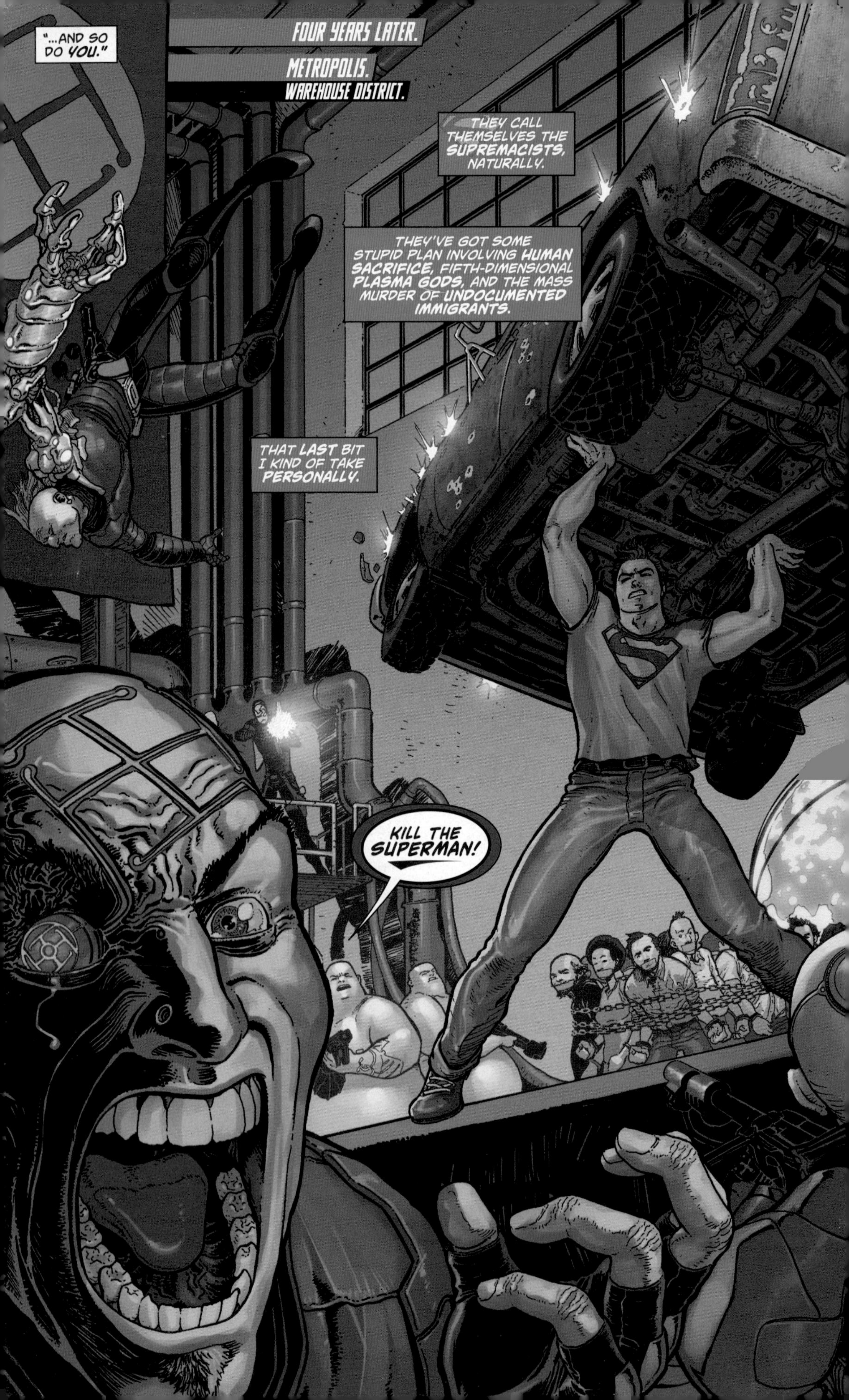
"...AND SO DO YOU."
FOUR YEARS LATER.
METROPOLIS.
WAREHOUSE DISTRICT.
THEY CALL THEMSELVES THE SUPREMACISTS, NATURALLY.
THEY'VE GOT SOME STUPID PLAN INVOLVING HUMAN SACRIFICE, FIFTH-DIMENSIONAL PLASMA GODS, AND THE MASS MURDER OF UNDOCUMENTED IMMIGRANTS.
THAT LAST BIT I KIND OF TAKE PERSONALLY.
KILL THE SUPERMAN!

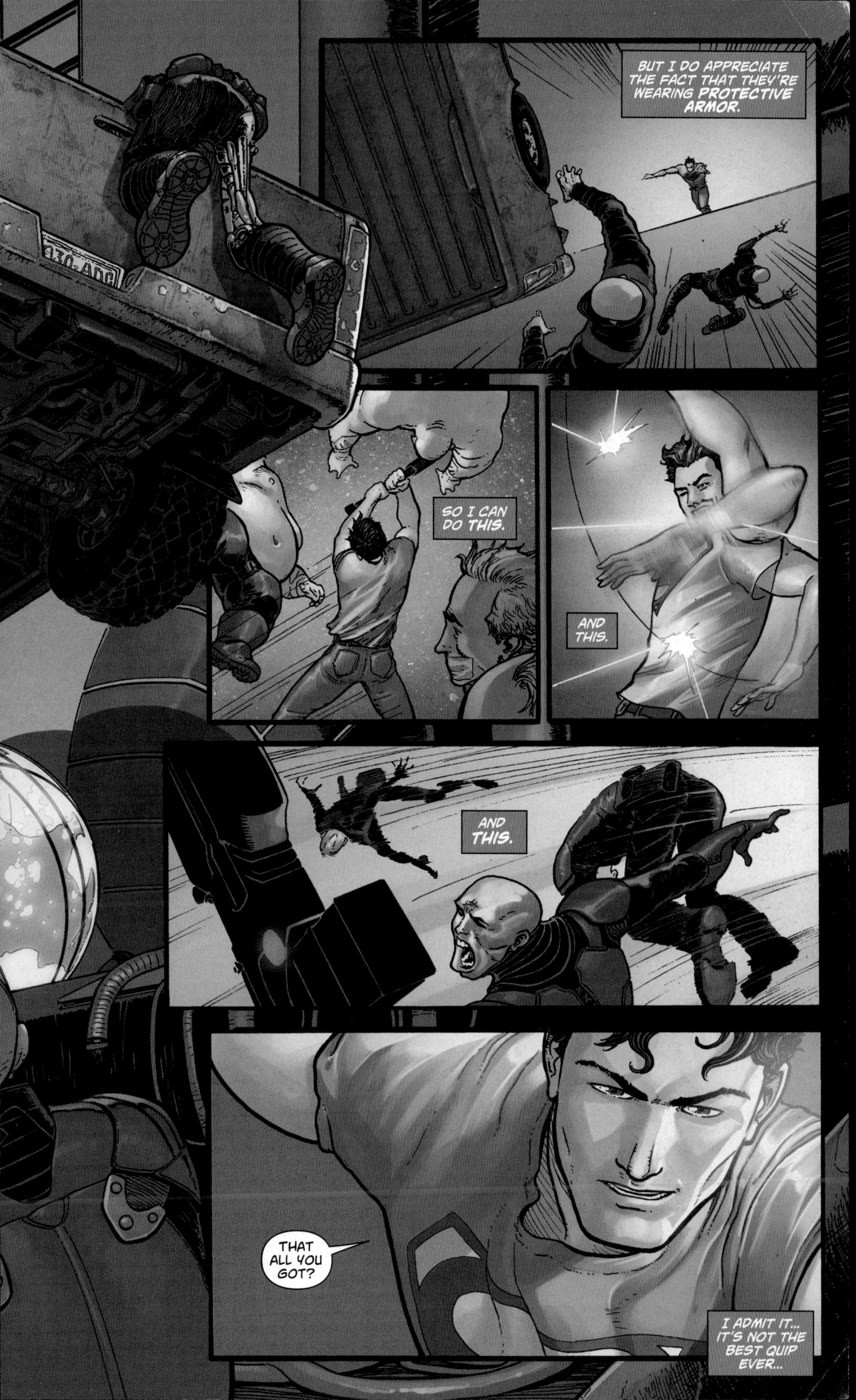

930-ADC
BUT I DO APPRECIATE THE FACT THAT THEY'RE WEARING PROTECTIVE ARMOR.
SO I CAN DO THIS.
AND THIS.
AND THIS.
THAT ALL YOU GOT?
I ADMIT IT... IT'S NOT THE BEST QUIP EVER...

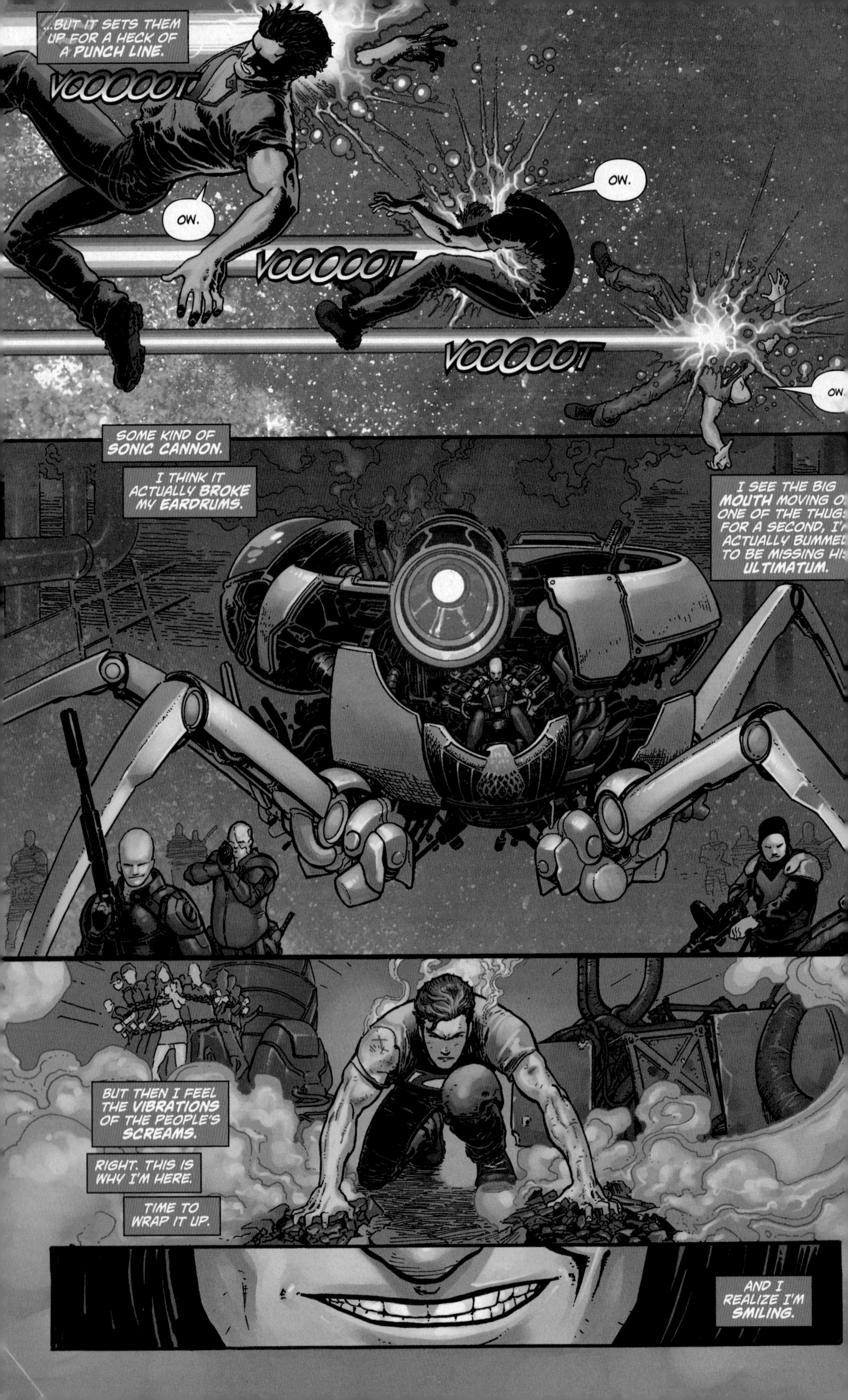

...BUT IT SETS THEM UP FOR A HECK OF A PUNCH LINE.
VOOOOOT
OW.
VOOOOOT
OW.
VOOOOOT
OW
SOME KIND OF SONIC CANNON.
I THINK IT ACTUALLY BROKE MY EARDRUMS.
I SEE THE BIG MOUTH MOVING O ONE OF THE THUG FOR A SECOND, I' ACTUALLY BUMME TO BE MISSING HI ULTIMATUM.
BUT THEN I FEEL THE VIBRATIONS OF THE PEOPLE'S SCREAMS.
RIGHT. THIS IS WHY I'M HERE.
TIME TO WRAP IT UP.
AND I REALIZE I'M SMILING.

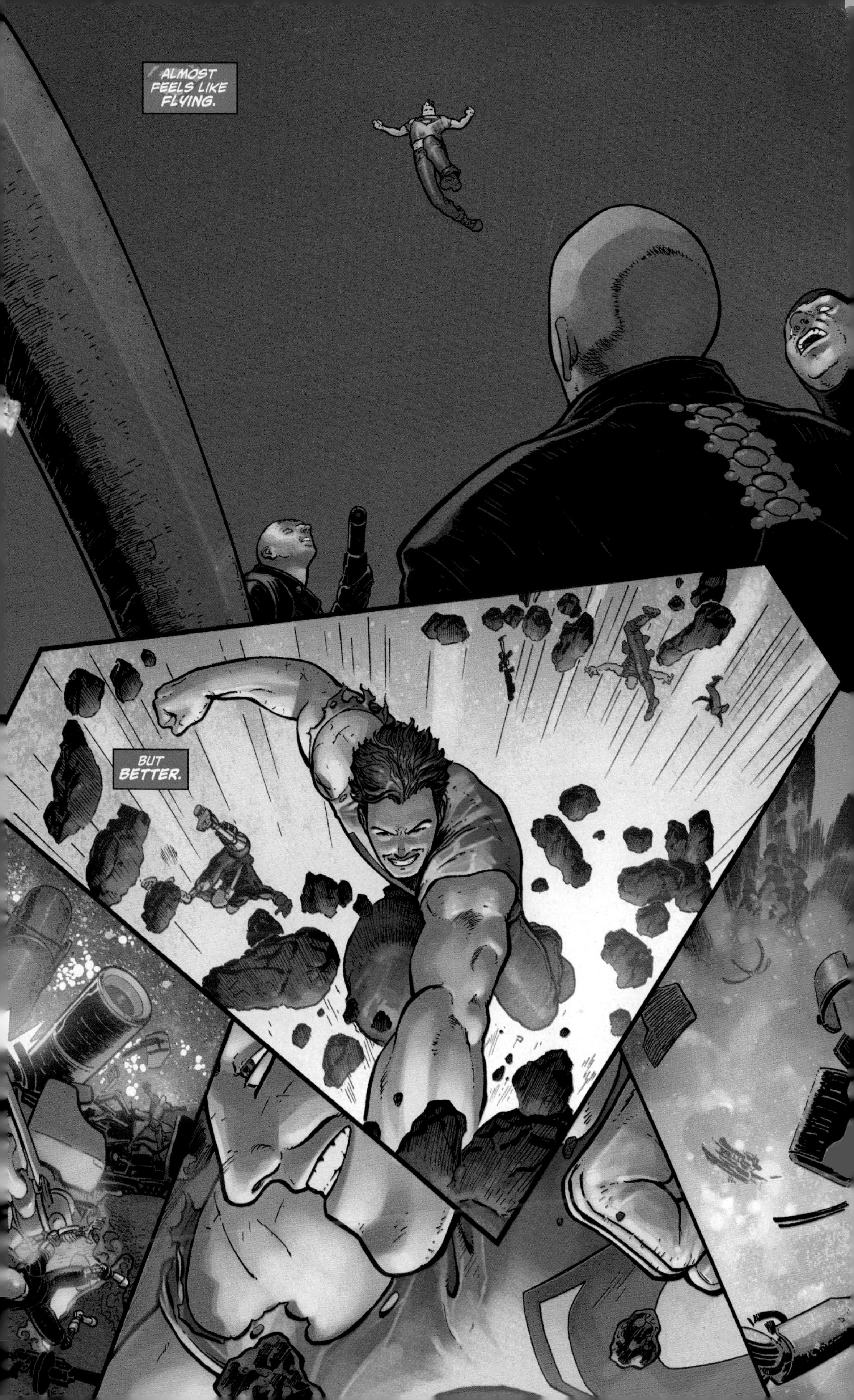
ALMOST FEELS LIKE FLYING.
BUT BETTER.

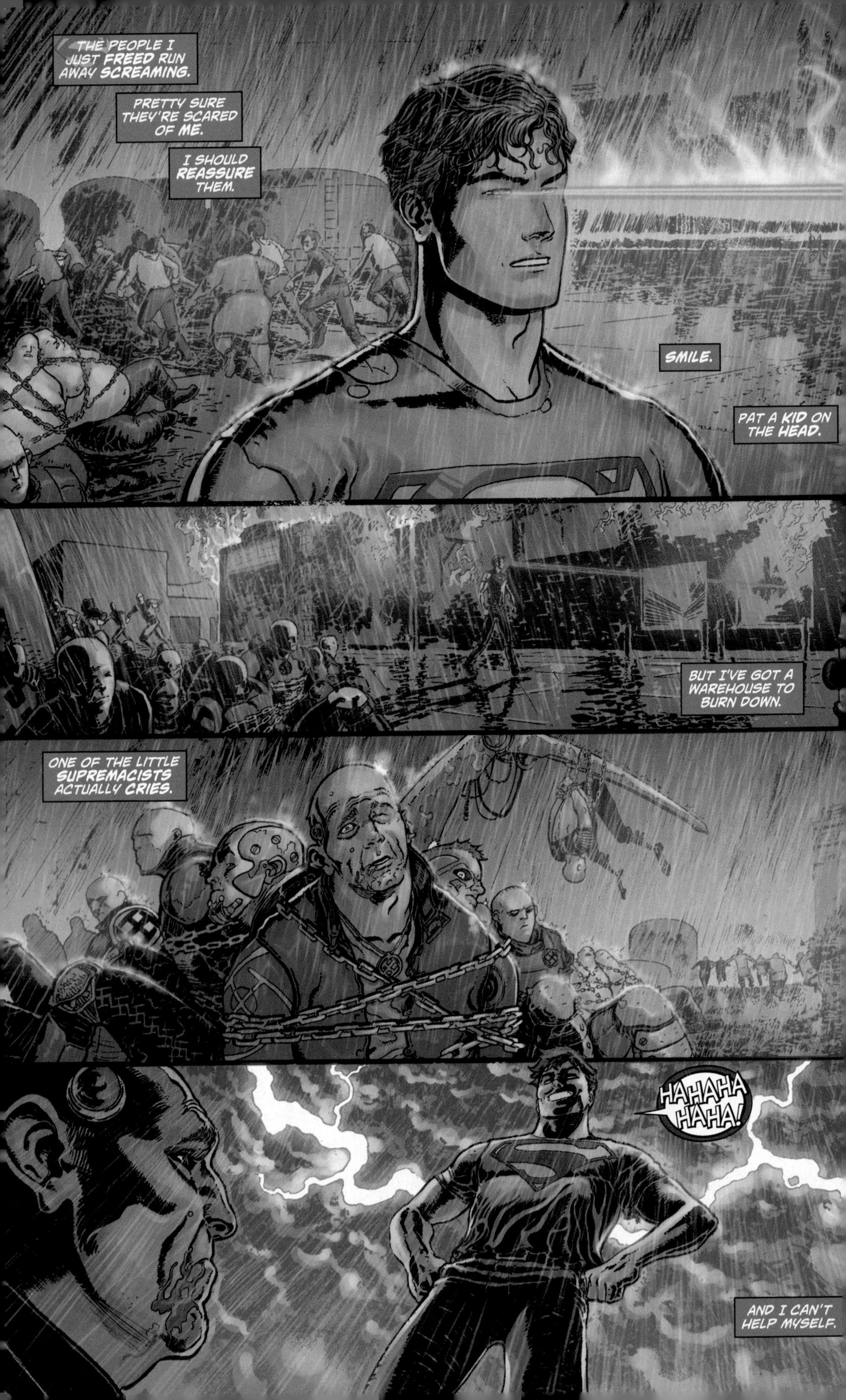
THE PEOPLE I JUST FREED RUN AWAY SCREAMING.
PRETTY SURE THEY'RE SCARED OF ME.
I SHOULD REASSURE THEM.
SMILE.
PAT A KID ON THE HEAD.
BUT I'VE GOT A WAREHOUSE TO BURN DOWN.
ONE OF THE LITTLE SUPREMACISTS ACTUALLY CRIES.
HAHAHA HAHA!
AND I CAN'T HELP MYSELF.

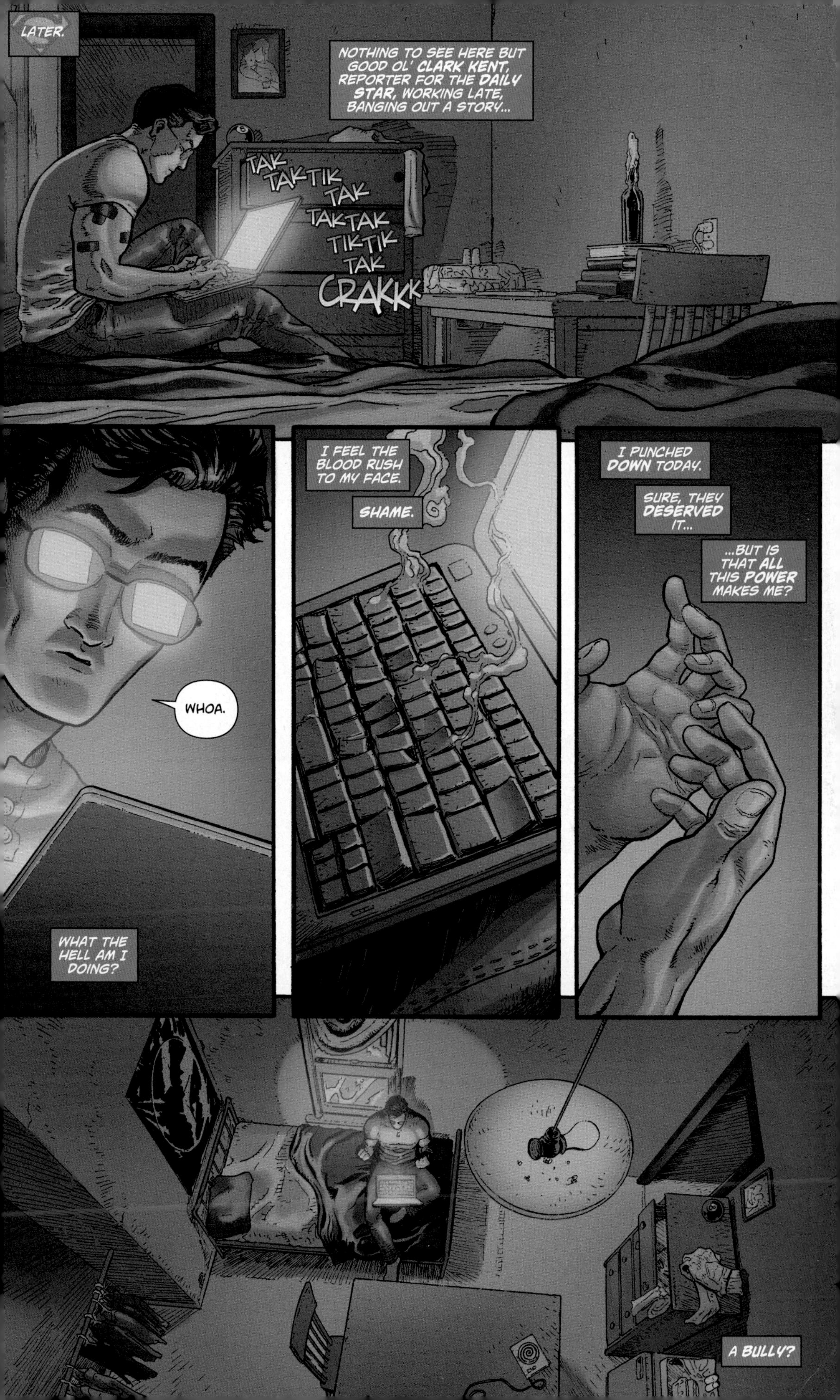
LATER.
NOTHING TO SEE HERE BUT GOOD OL' CLARK KENT, REPORTER FOR THE DAILY STAR, WORKING LATE, BANGING OUT A STORY...
TAK TAKTIK TAK TAKTAK TIKTIK TAK
CRAKKK
WHOA.
WHAT THE HELL AM I DOING?
I FEEL THE BLOOD RUSH TO MY FACE.
SHAME.
I PUNCHED DOWN TODAY.
SURE, THEY DESERVED IT...
...BUT IS THAT ALL THIS POWER MAKES ME?
A BULLY?

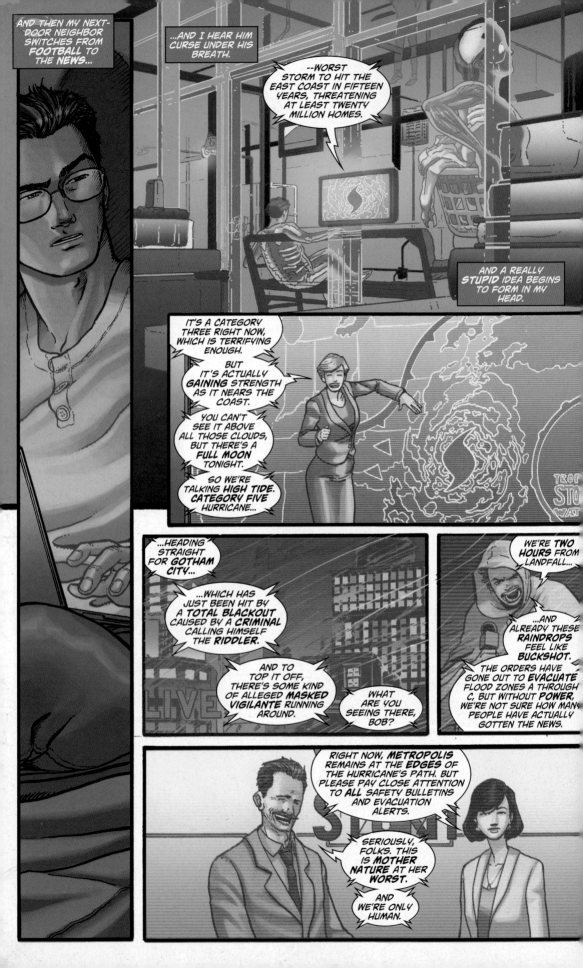

AND THEN MY NEXT-DOOR NEIGHBOR SWITCHES FROM *FOOTBALL* TO THE *NEWS*...

...AND I HEAR HIM CURSE UNDER HIS BREATH.

--WORST STORM TO HIT THE EAST COAST IN FIFTEEN YEARS, THREATENING AT LEAST TWENTY MILLION HOMES.

AND A REALLY *STUPID* IDEA BEGINS TO FORM IN MY HEAD.

IT'S A CATEGORY THREE RIGHT NOW, WHICH IS TERRIFYING ENOUGH.

BUT IT'S ACTUALLY *GAINING* STRENGTH AS IT NEARS THE COAST.

YOU CAN'T SEE IT ABOVE ALL THOSE CLOUDS, BUT THERE'S A *FULL MOON* TONIGHT.

SO WE'RE TALKING *HIGH TIDE. CATEGORY FIVE* HURRICANE...

...HEADING STRAIGHT FOR *GOTHAM CITY*...

...WHICH HAS JUST BEEN HIT BY A *TOTAL BLACKOUT* CAUSED BY A *CRIMINAL* CALLING HIMSELF THE *RIDDLER.*

AND TO *TOP IT OFF,* THERE'S SOME KIND OF ALLEGED *MASKED VIGILANTE* RUNNING AROUND.

WHAT ARE YOU *SEEING* THERE, BOB?

WE'RE *TWO HOURS* FROM LANDFALL...

...AND ALREADY THESE *RAINDROPS* FEEL LIKE *BUCKSHOT.*

THE ORDERS HAVE GONE OUT TO *EVACUATE* FLOOD ZONES A THROUGH C, BUT WITHOUT *POWER,* WE'RE NOT SURE HOW MANY PEOPLE HAVE ACTUALLY GOTTEN THE NEWS.

RIGHT NOW, *METROPOLIS* REMAINS AT THE *EDGES* OF THE HURRICANE'S PATH. BUT PLEASE PAY CLOSE ATTENTION TO *ALL* SAFETY BULLETINS AND EVACUATION ALERTS.

SERIOUSLY, FOLKS. THIS IS *MOTHER NATURE* AT HER *WORST.*

AND WE'RE ONLY *HUMAN.*

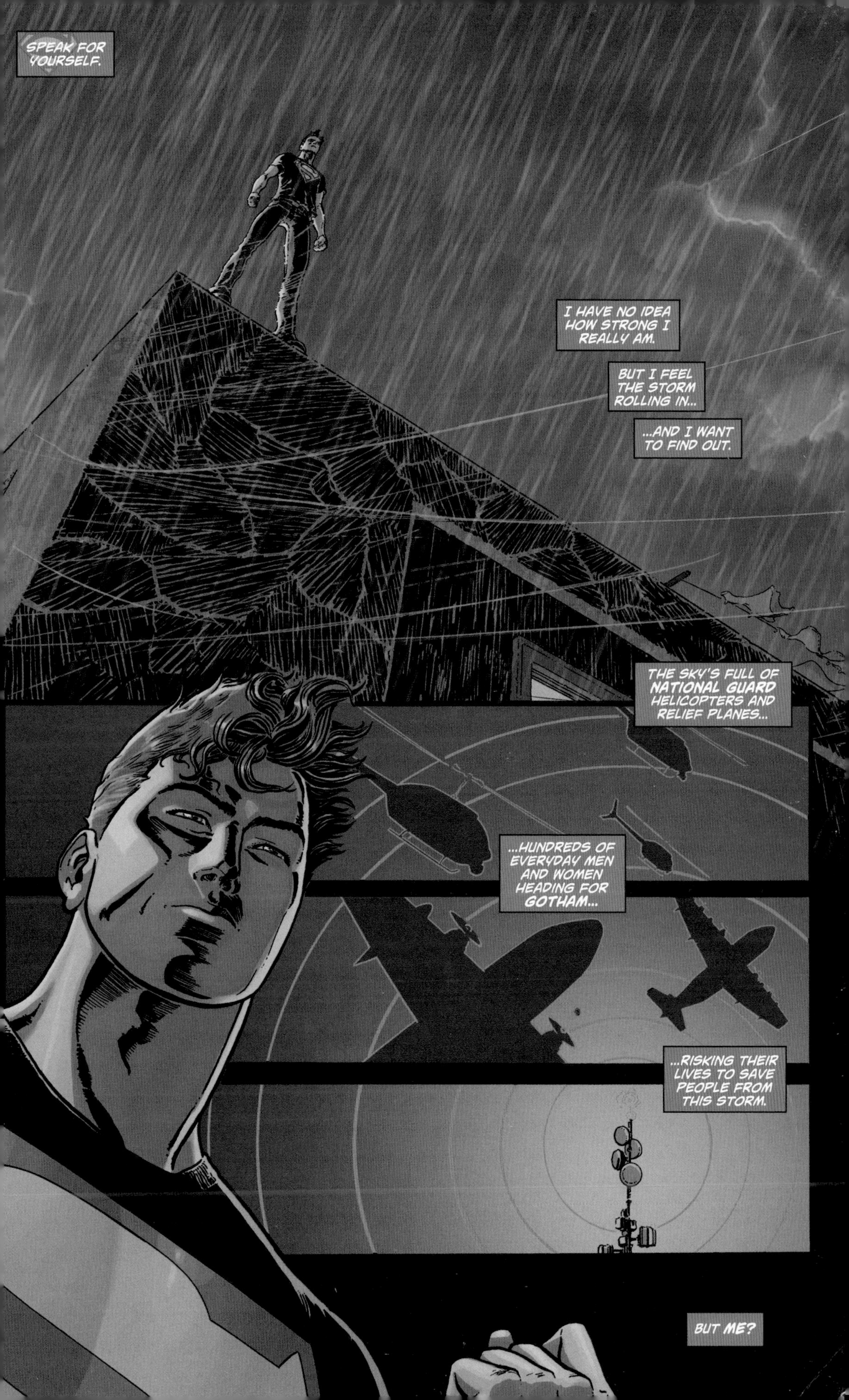
SPEAK FOR YOURSELF.
I HAVE NO IDEA HOW STRONG I REALLY AM.
BUT I FEEL THE STORM ROLLING IN...
...AND I WANT TO FIND OUT.
THE SKY'S FULL OF NATIONAL GUARD HELICOPTERS AND RELIEF PLANES...
...HUNDREDS OF EVERYDAY MEN AND WOMEN HEADING FOR GOTHAM...
...RISKING THEIR LIVES TO SAVE PEOPLE FROM THIS STORM.
BUT ME?

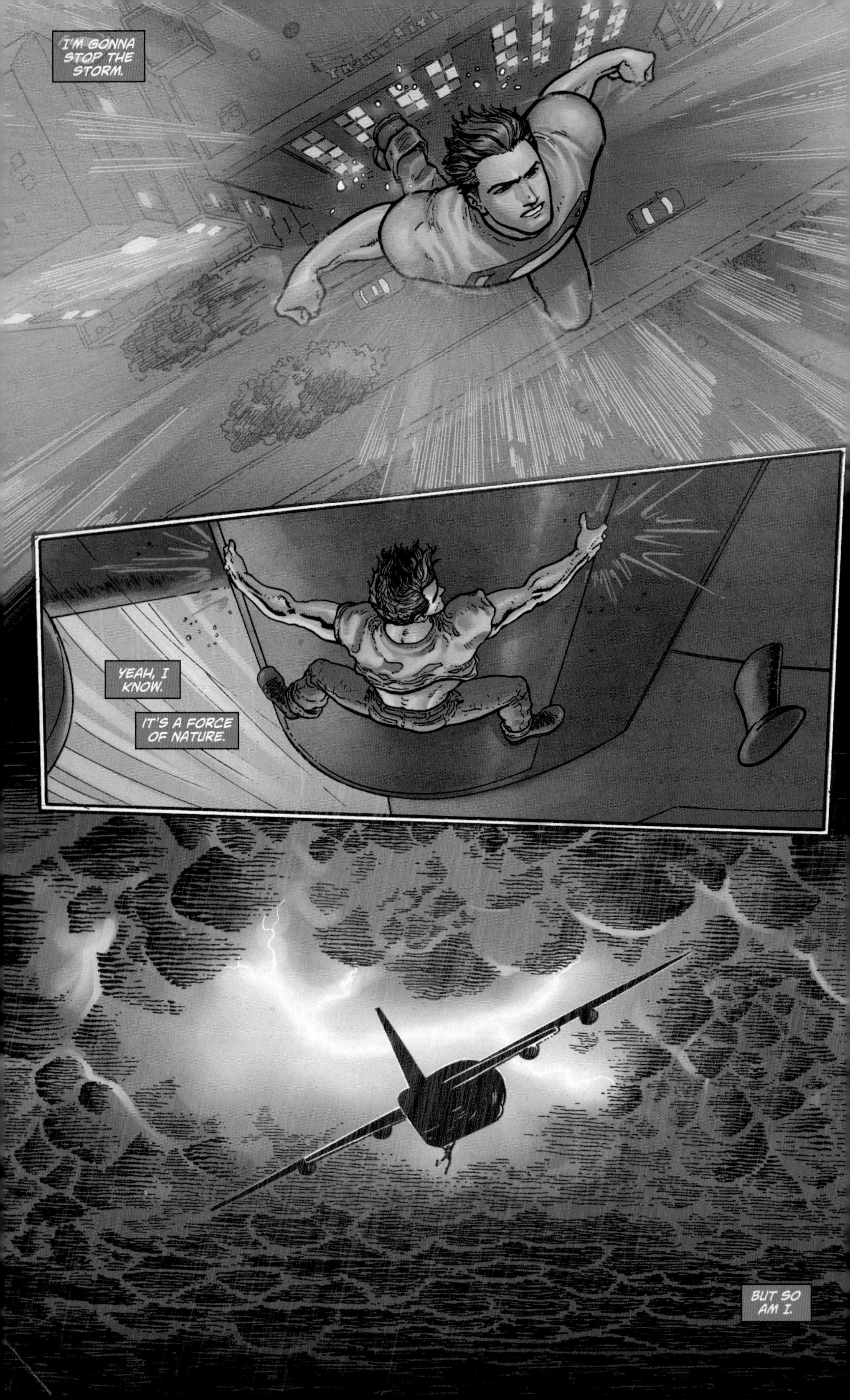
I'M GONNA STOP THE STORM.
YEAH, I KNOW.
IT'S A FORCE OF NATURE.
BUT SO AM I.

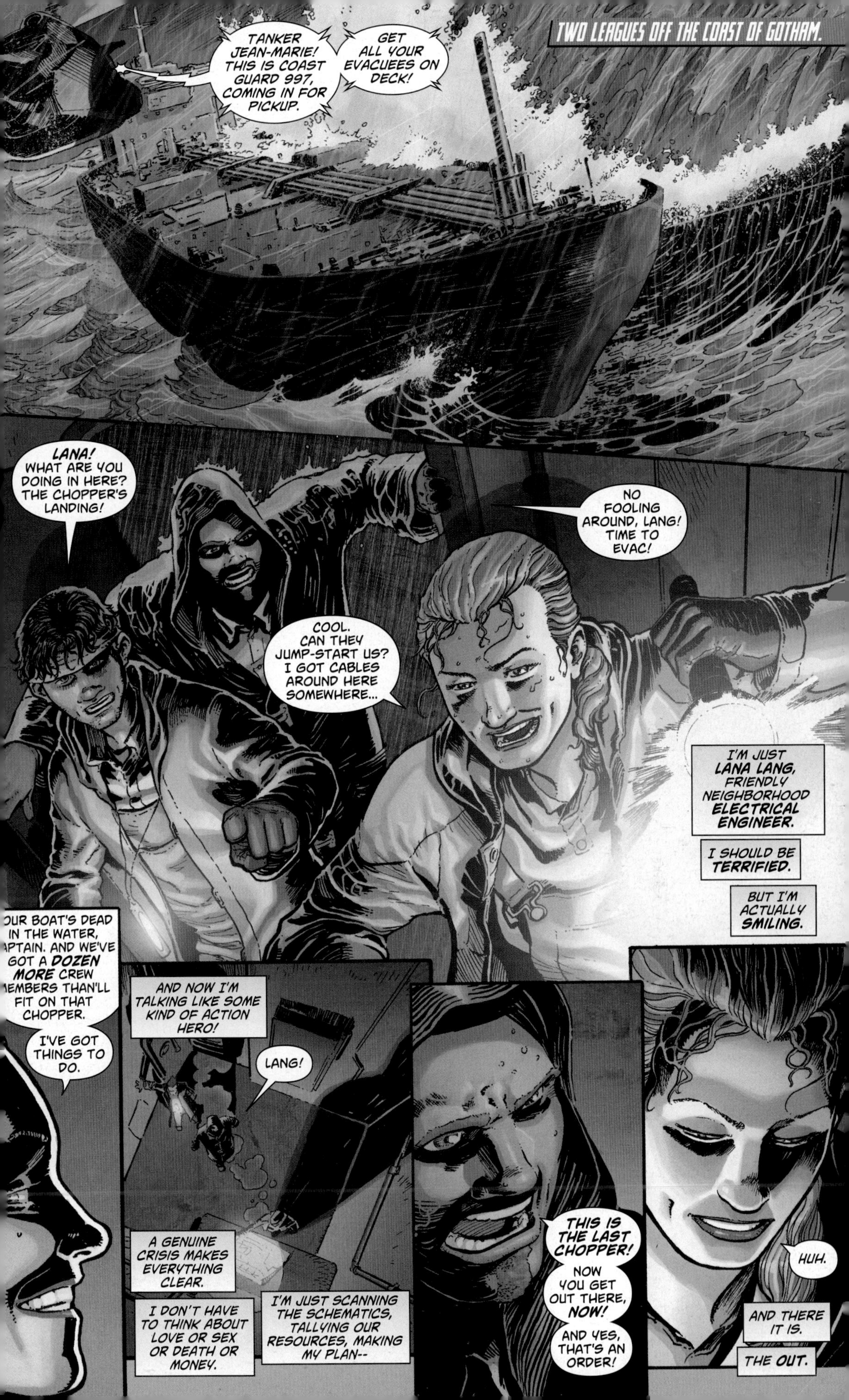
TWO LEAGUES OFF THE COAST OF GOTHAM.
TANKER JEAN-MARIE! THIS IS COAST GUARD 997, COMING IN FOR PICKUP.
GET ALL YOUR EVACUEES ON DECK!
LANA! WHAT ARE YOU DOING IN HERE? THE CHOPPER'S LANDING!
NO FOOLING AROUND, LANG! TIME TO EVAC!
COOL. CAN THEY JUMP-START US? I GOT CABLES AROUND HERE SOMEWHERE...
I'M JUST LANA LANG, FRIENDLY NEIGHBORHOOD ELECTRICAL ENGINEER.
I SHOULD BE TERRIFIED.
BUT I'M ACTUALLY SMILING.
OUR BOAT'S DEAD IN THE WATER, APTAIN. AND WE'VE GOT A DOZEN MORE CREW EMBERS THAN'LL FIT ON THAT CHOPPER.
I'VE GOT THINGS TO DO.
AND NOW I'M TALKING LIKE SOME KIND OF ACTION HERO!
LANG!
A GENUINE CRISIS MAKES EVERYTHING CLEAR.
I DON'T HAVE TO THINK ABOUT LOVE OR SEX OR DEATH OR MONEY.
I'M JUST SCANNING THE SCHEMATICS, TALLYING OUR RESOURCES, MAKING MY PLAN--
THIS IS THE LAST CHOPPER!
NOW YOU GET OUT THERE, NOW!
AND YES, THAT'S AN ORDER!
HUH.
AND THERE IT IS.
THE OUT.

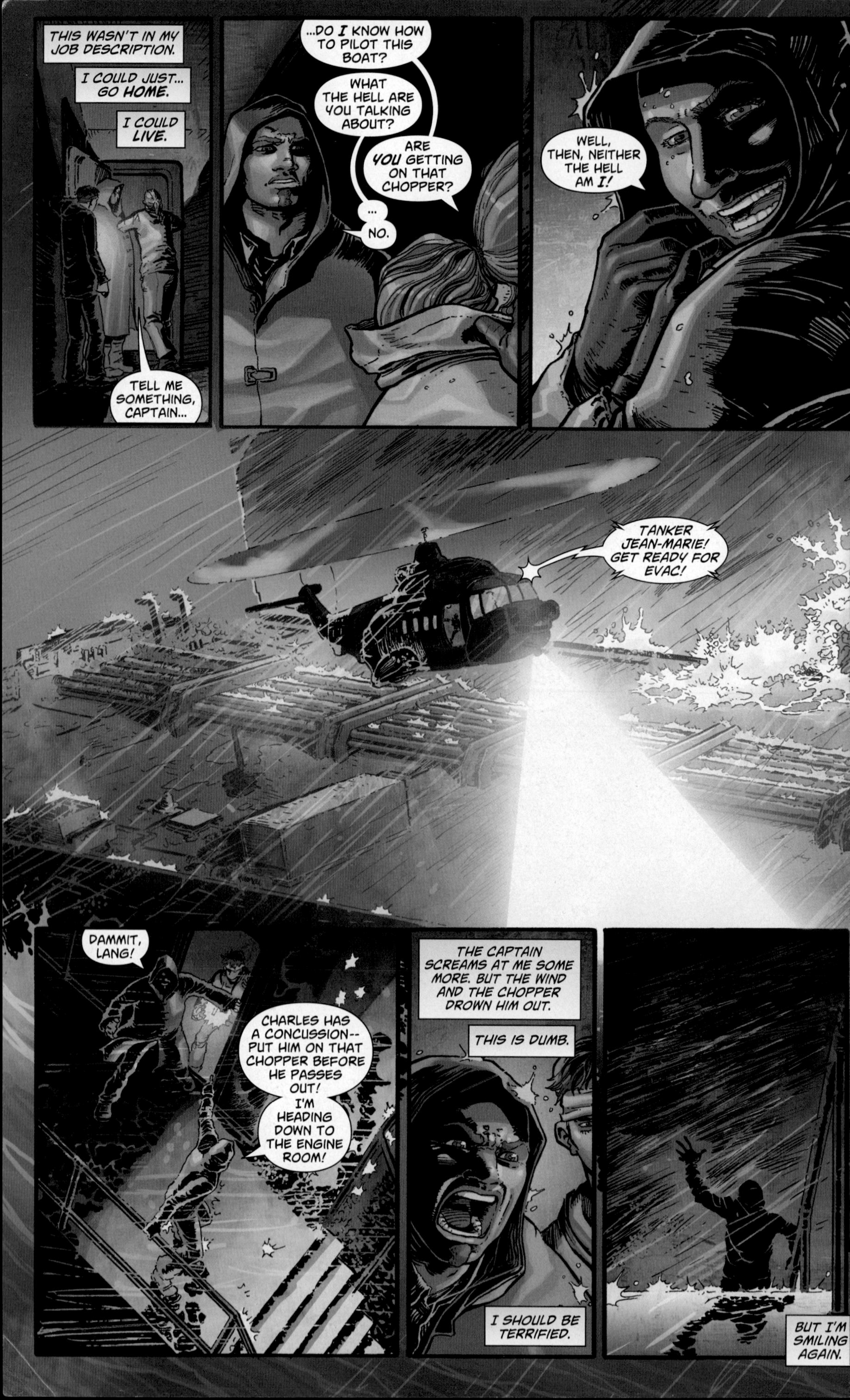
THIS WASN'T IN MY JOB DESCRIPTION.
I COULD JUST... GO HOME.
I COULD LIVE.
TELL ME SOMETHING, CAPTAIN...
...DO I KNOW HOW TO PILOT THIS BOAT?
WHAT THE HELL ARE YOU TALKING ABOUT?
ARE YOU GETTING ON THAT CHOPPER?
... NO.
WELL, THEN, NEITHER THE HELL AM I!
TANKER JEAN-MARIE! GET READY FOR EVAC!
DAMMIT, LANG!
CHARLES HAS A CONCUSSION-- PUT HIM ON THAT CHOPPER BEFORE HE PASSES OUT!
I'M HEADING DOWN TO THE ENGINE ROOM!
THE CAPTAIN SCREAMS AT ME SOME MORE. BUT THE WIND AND THE CHOPPER DROWN HIM OUT.
THIS IS DUMB.
I SHOULD BE TERRIFIED.
BUT I'M SMILING AGAIN.

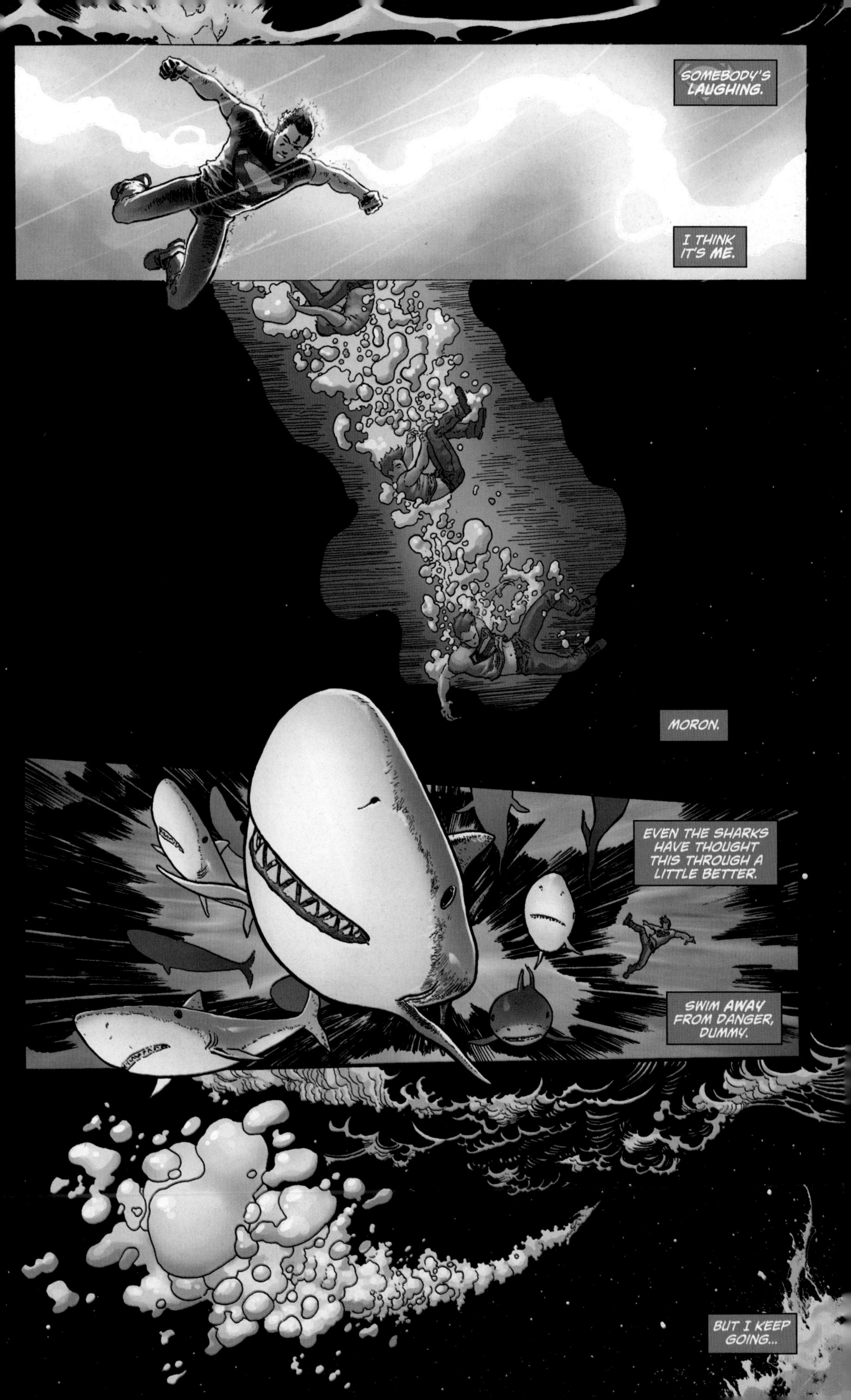
SOMEBODY'S LAUGHING.
I THINK IT'S ME.
MORON.
EVEN THE SHARKS HAVE THOUGHT THIS THROUGH A LITTLE BETTER.
SWIM AWAY FROM DANGER, DUMMY.
BUT I KEEP GOING...

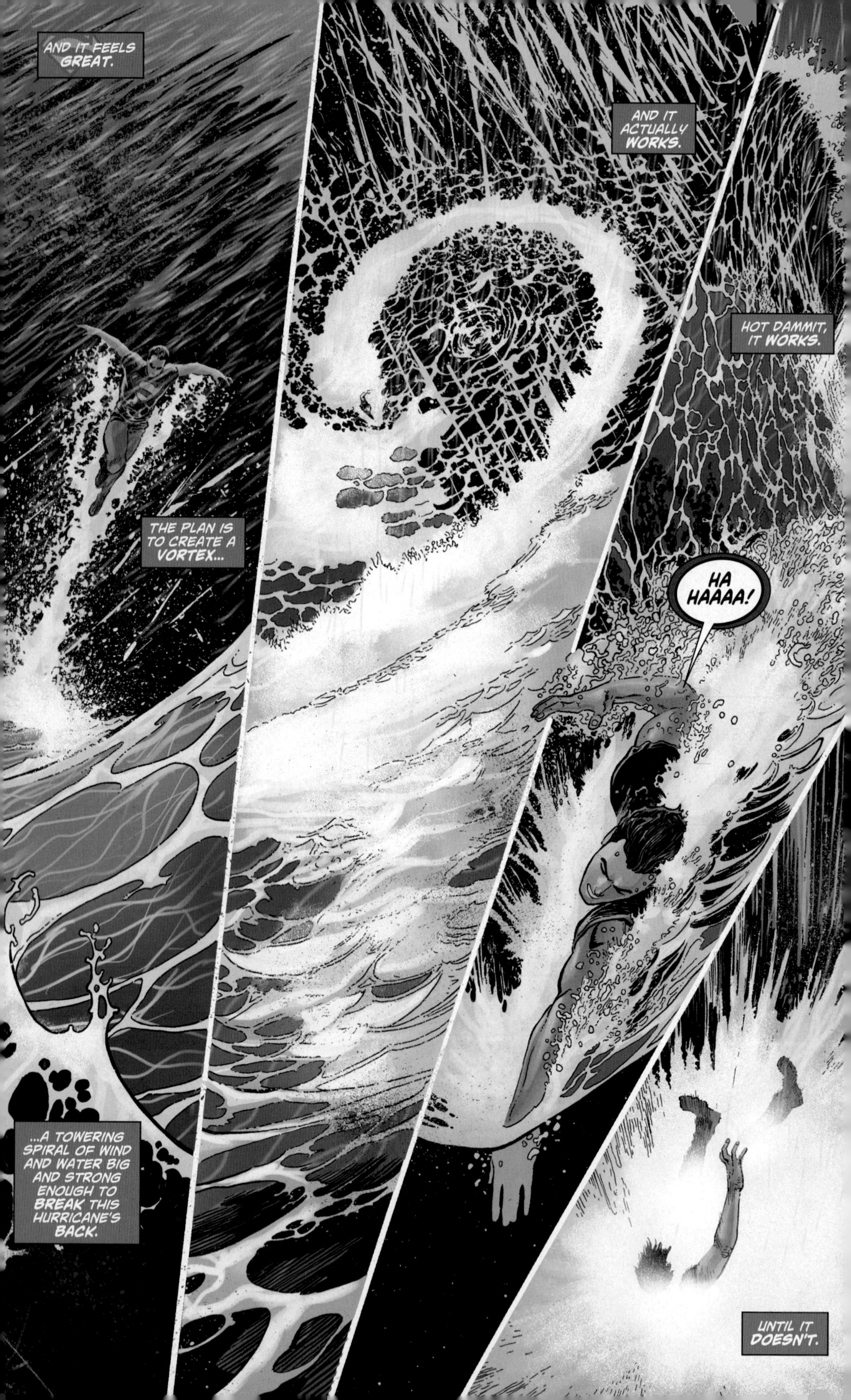
AND IT FEELS GREAT.
THE PLAN IS TO CREATE A VORTEX...
...A TOWERING SPIRAL OF WIND AND WATER BIG AND STRONG ENOUGH TO BREAK THIS HURRICANE'S BACK.
AND IT ACTUALLY WORKS.
HOT DAMMIT, IT WORKS.
HA HAAAA!
UNTIL IT DOESN'T.

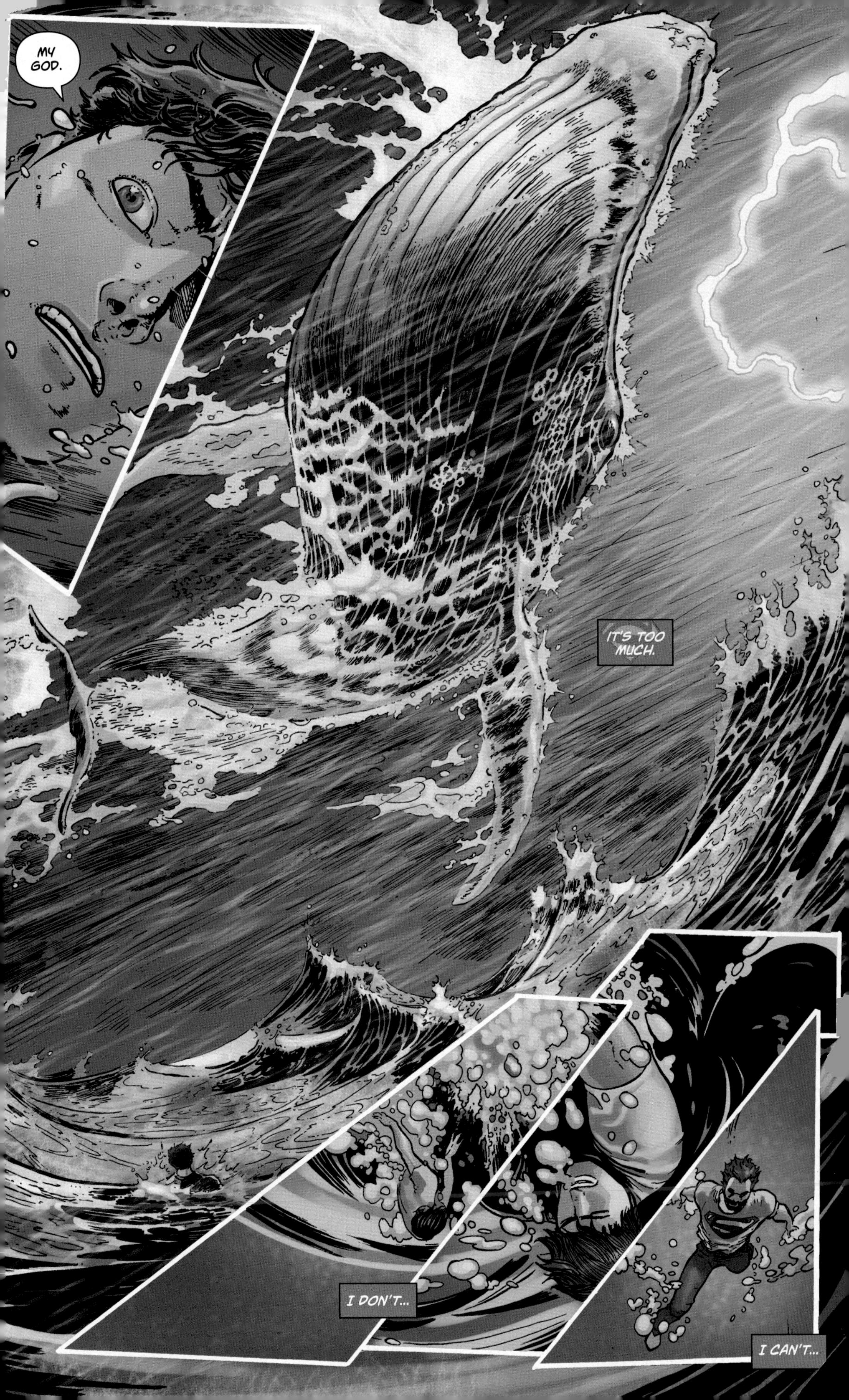
MY GOD.
IT'S TOO MUCH.
I DON'T...
I CAN'T...

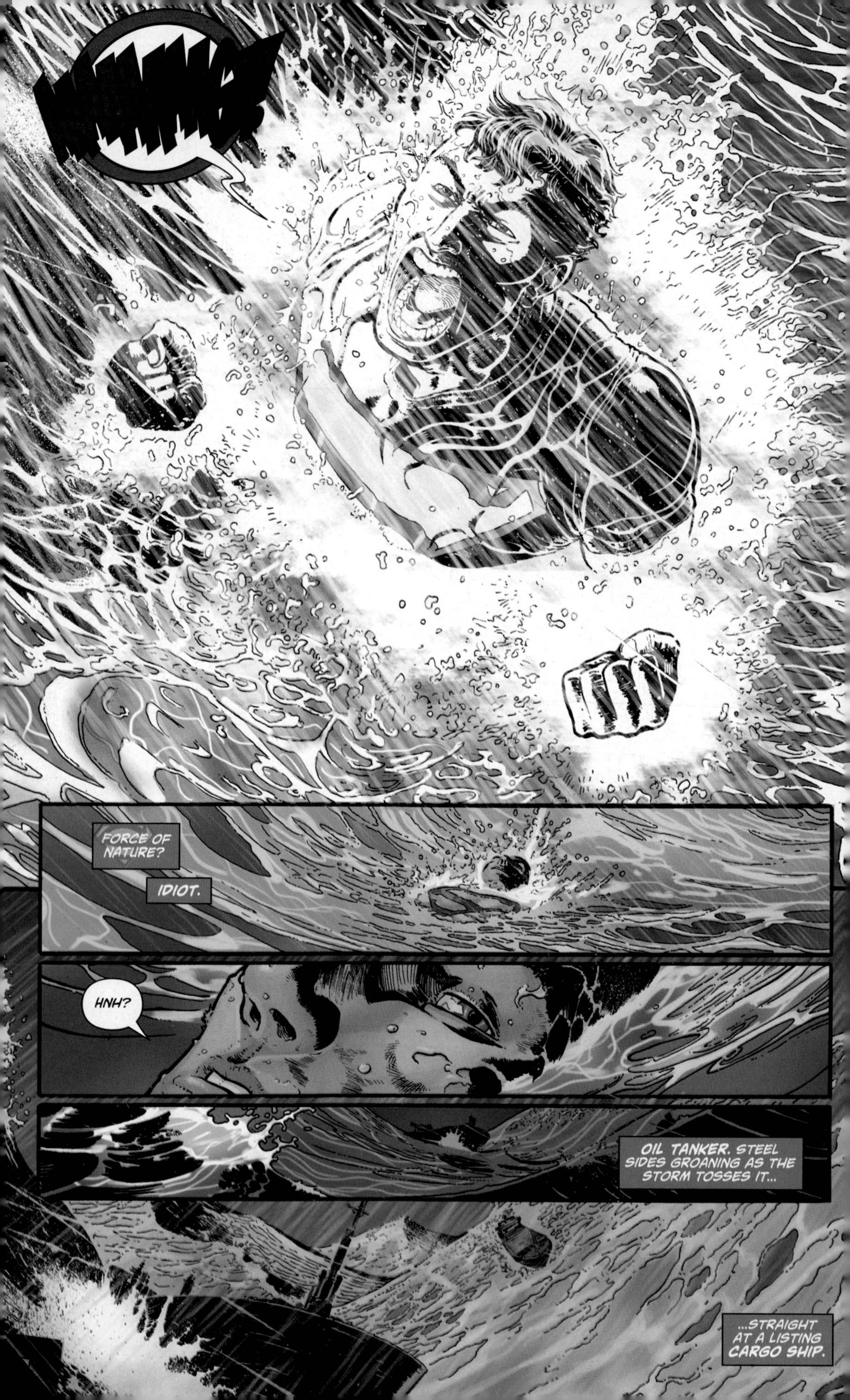
FORCE OF NATURE?
IDIOT.
HNH?
OIL TANKER. STEEL SIDES GROANING AS THE STORM TOSSES IT...
...STRAIGHT AT A LISTING CARGO SHIP.

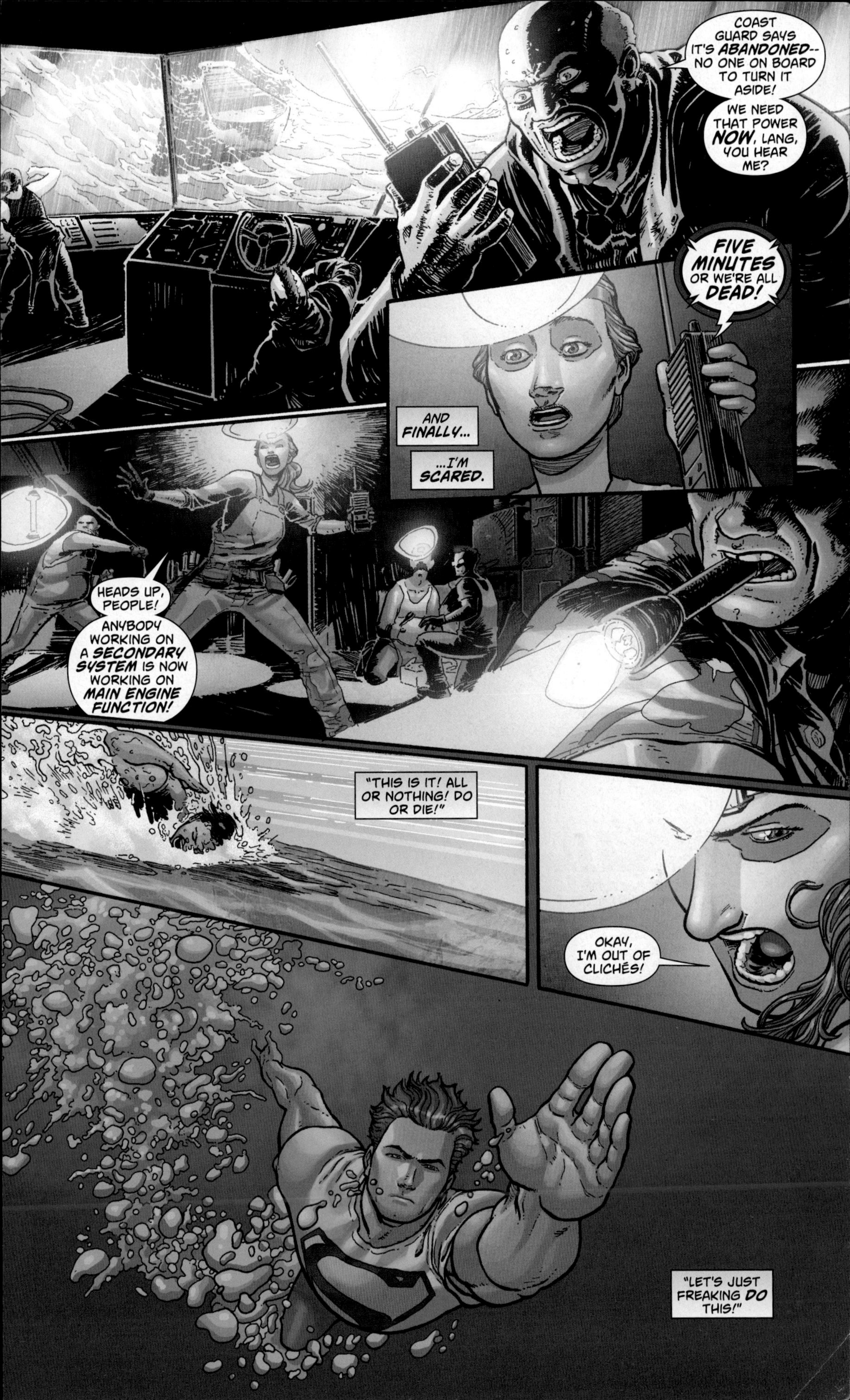
COAST GUARD SAYS IT'S ABANDONED-- NO ONE ON BOARD TO TURN IT ASIDE!
WE NEED THAT POWER NOW, LANG, YOU HEAR ME?
FIVE MINUTES OR WE'RE ALL DEAD!
AND FINALLY...
...I'M SCARED.
HEADS UP, PEOPLE!
ANYBODY WORKING ON A SECONDARY SYSTEM IS NOW WORKING ON MAIN ENGINE FUNCTION!
"THIS IS IT! ALL OR NOTHING! DO OR DIE!"
OKAY, I'M OUT OF CLICHÉS!
"LET'S JUST FREAKING DO THIS!"

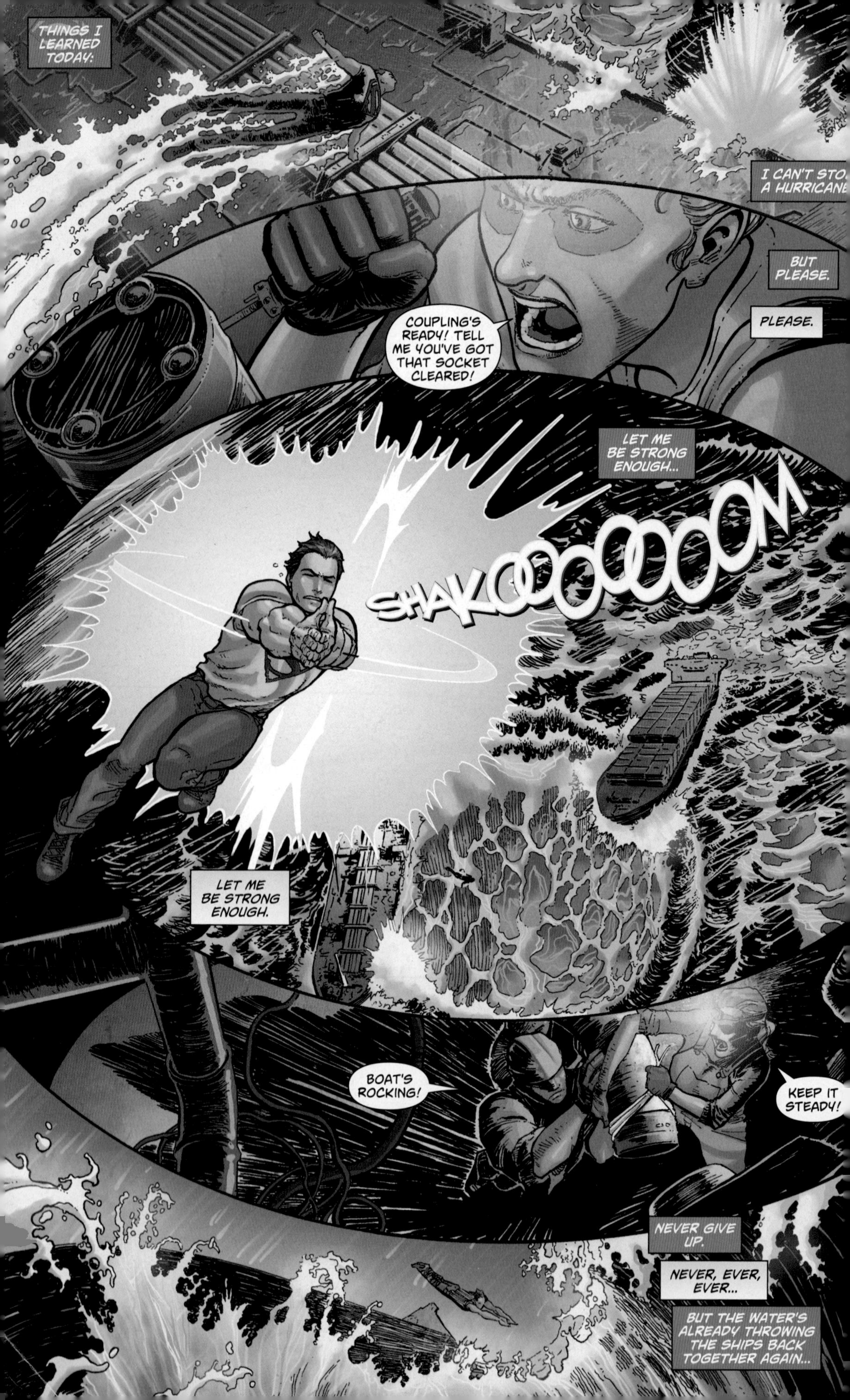
THINGS I LEARNED TODAY:
I CAN'T STO
A HURRICANE
BUT PLEASE.
PLEASE.
COUPLING'S READY! TELL ME YOU'VE GOT THAT SOCKET CLEARED!
LET ME BE STRONG ENOUGH...
SHAKOOOOOOOOM
LET ME BE STRONG ENOUGH.
BOAT'S ROCKING!
KEEP IT STEADY!
NEVER GIVE UP.
NEVER, EVER, EVER...
BUT THE WATER'S ALREADY THROWING THE SHIPS BACK TOGETHER AGAIN...

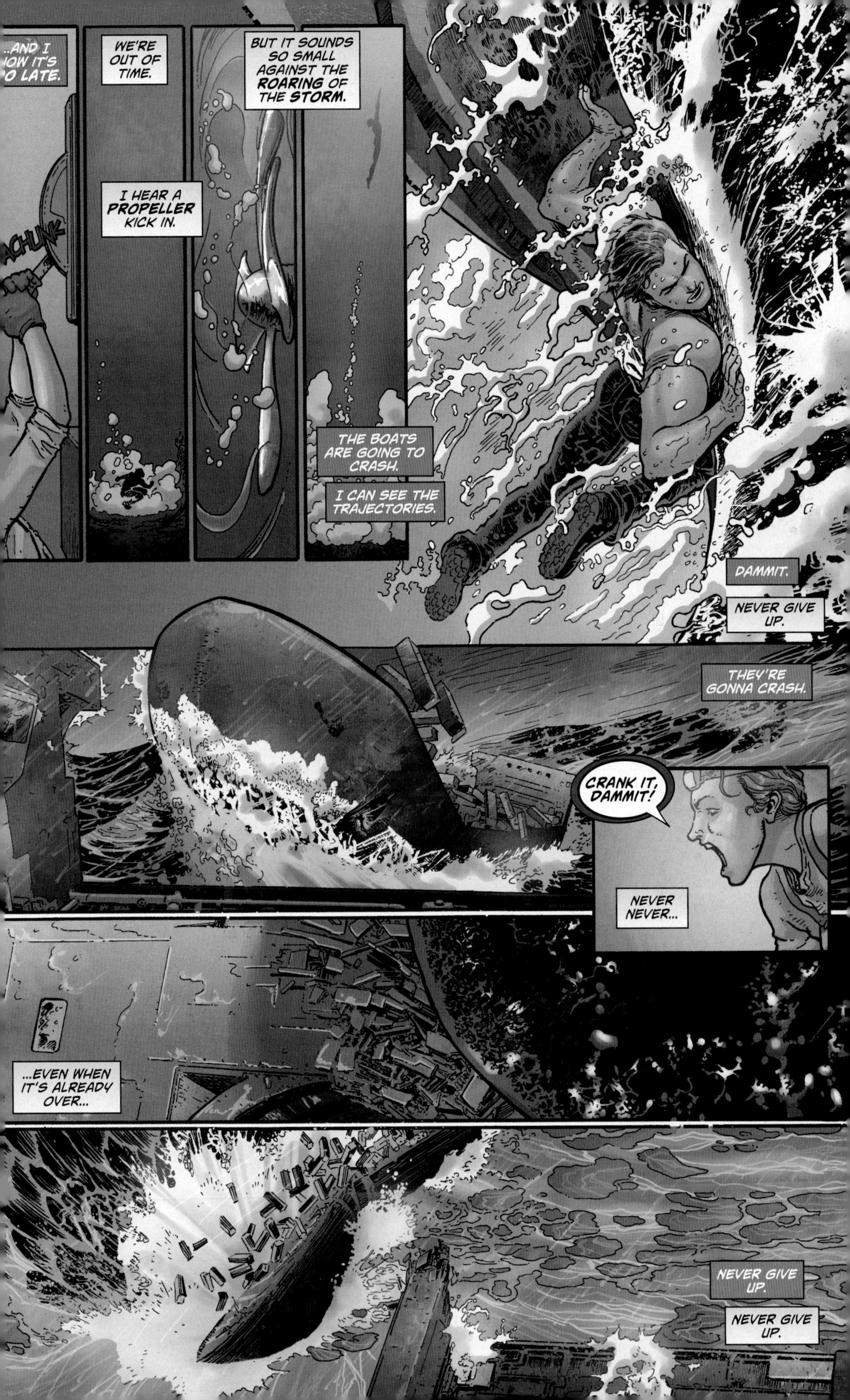
...AND I
OW IT'S
O LATE.
ACHUNK
WE'RE OUT OF TIME.
I HEAR A PROPELLER KICK IN.
BUT IT SOUNDS SO SMALL AGAINST THE ROARING OF THE STORM.
THE BOATS ARE GOING TO CRASH.
I CAN SEE THE TRAJECTORIES.
DAMMIT.
NEVER GIVE UP.
THEY'RE GONNA CRASH.
CRANK IT, DAMMIT!
NEVER NEVER...
...EVEN WHEN IT'S ALREADY OVER...
NEVER GIVE UP.
NEVER GIVE UP.

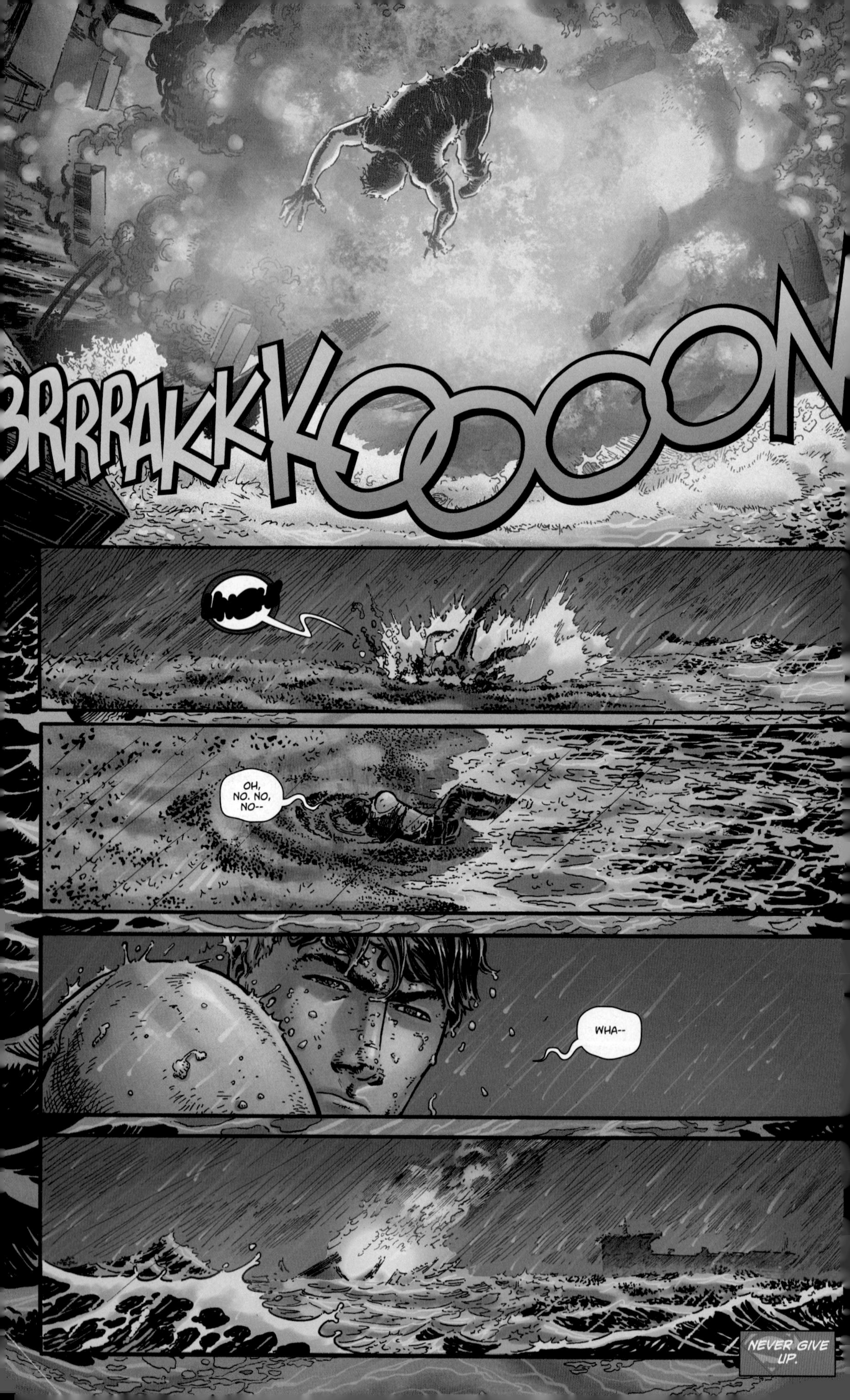
BRRRAKKKOOOON
OH, NO. NO, NO--
WHA--
NEVER GIVE UP.

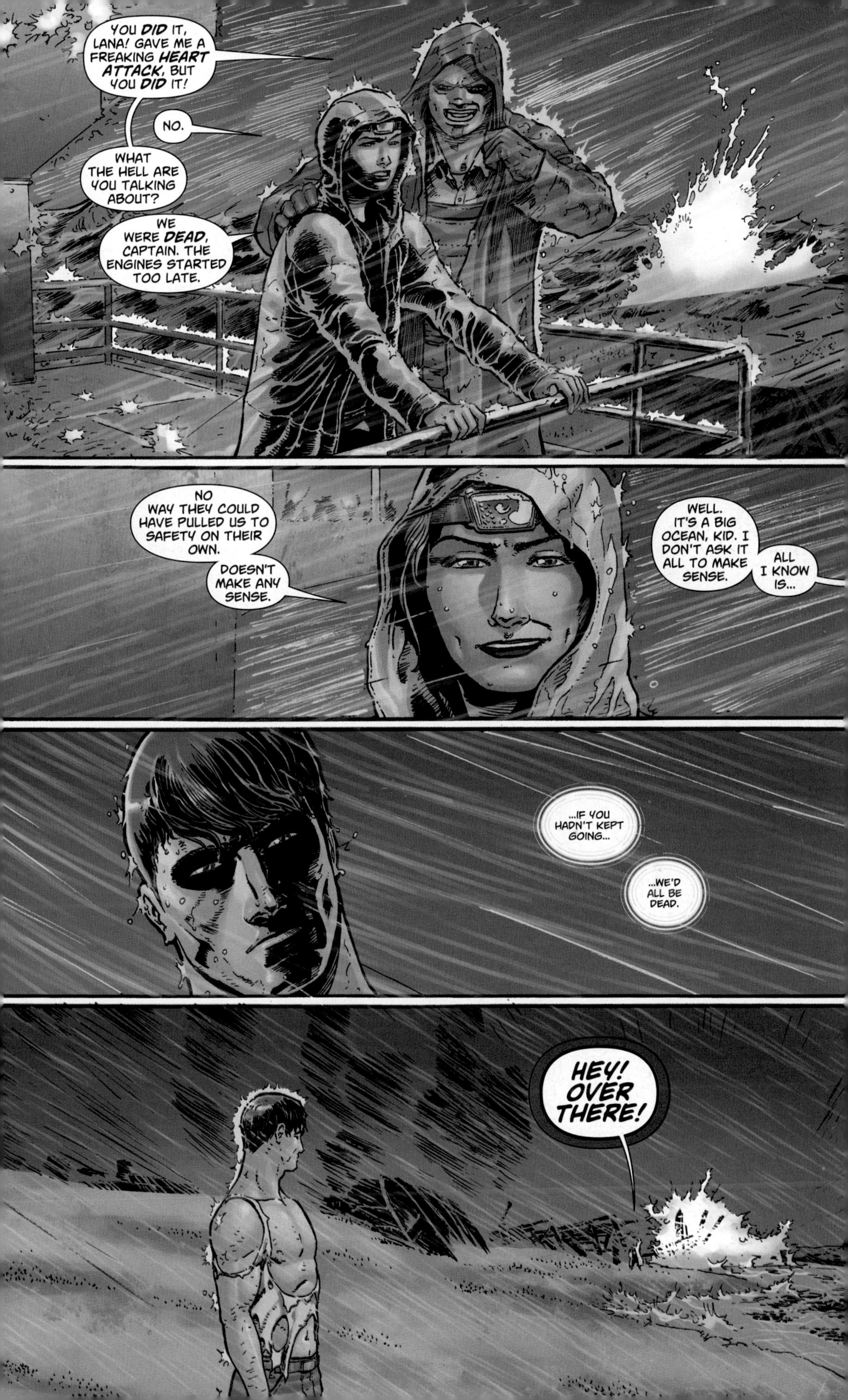
YOU **DID** IT, LANA! GAVE ME A FREAKING **HEART ATTACK**, BUT YOU **DID** IT!
NO.
WHAT THE HELL ARE YOU TALKING ABOUT?
WE WERE **DEAD**, CAPTAIN. THE ENGINES STARTED TOO LATE.
NO WAY THEY COULD HAVE PULLED US TO SAFETY ON THEIR OWN.
DOESN'T MAKE ANY SENSE.
WELL. IT'S A BIG OCEAN, KID. I DON'T ASK IT ALL TO MAKE SENSE.
ALL I KNOW IS...
...IF YOU HADN'T KEPT GOING...
...WE'D ALL BE DEAD.
HEY! OVER THERE!

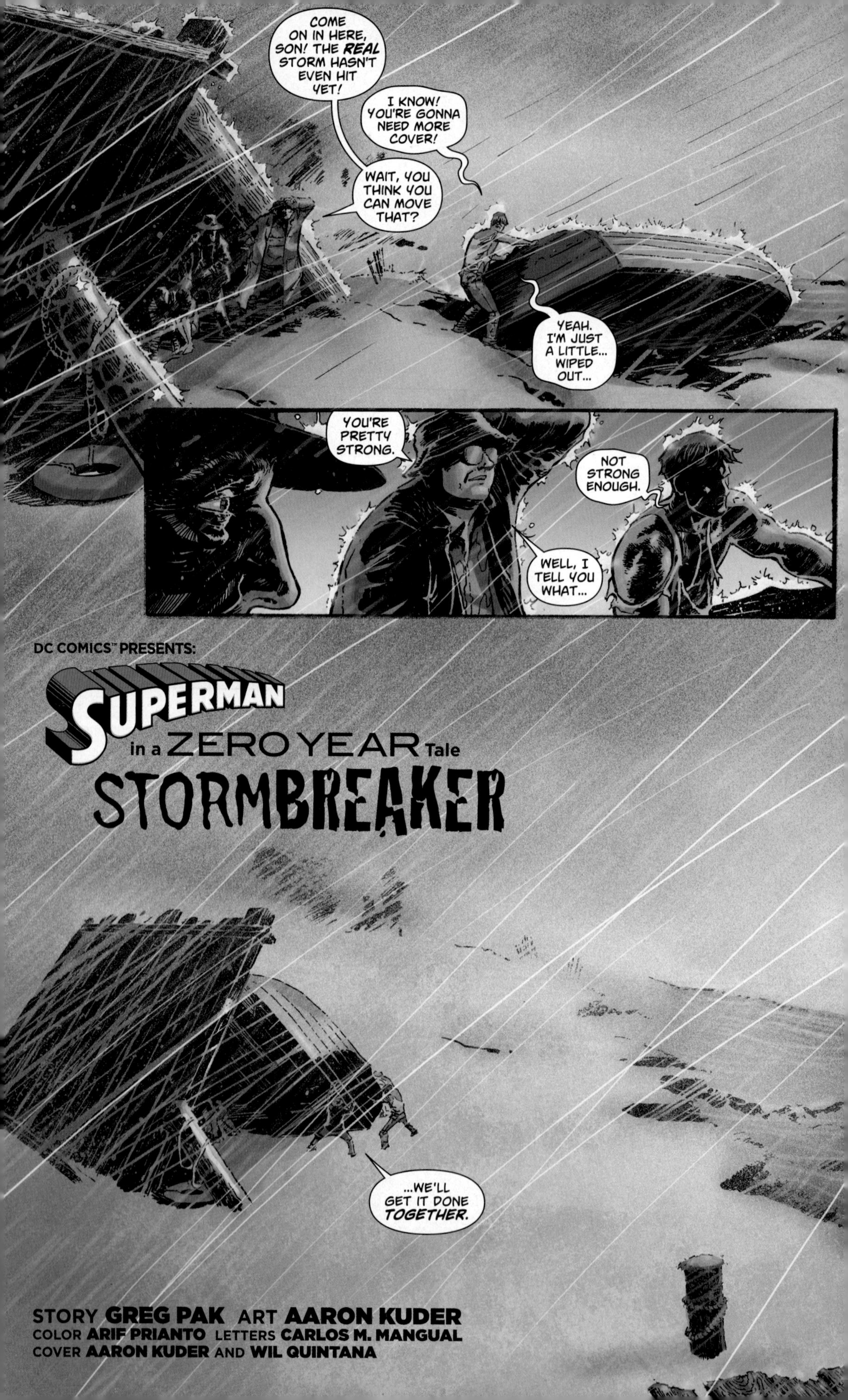
COME ON IN HERE, SON! THE REAL STORM HASN'T EVEN HIT YET!
I KNOW! YOU'RE GONNA NEED MORE COVER!
WAIT, YOU THINK YOU CAN MOVE THAT?
YEAH. I'M JUST A LITTLE... WIPED OUT...
YOU'RE PRETTY STRONG.
NOT STRONG ENOUGH.
WELL, I TELL YOU WHAT...
DC COMICS™ PRESENTS:
SUPERMAN
in a ZERO YEAR Tale
STORMBREAKER
...WE'LL GET IT DONE TOGETHER.
STORY GREG PAK ART AARON KUDER
COLOR ARIF PRIANTO LETTERS CARLOS M. MANGUAL
COVER AARON KUDER AND WIL QUINTANA

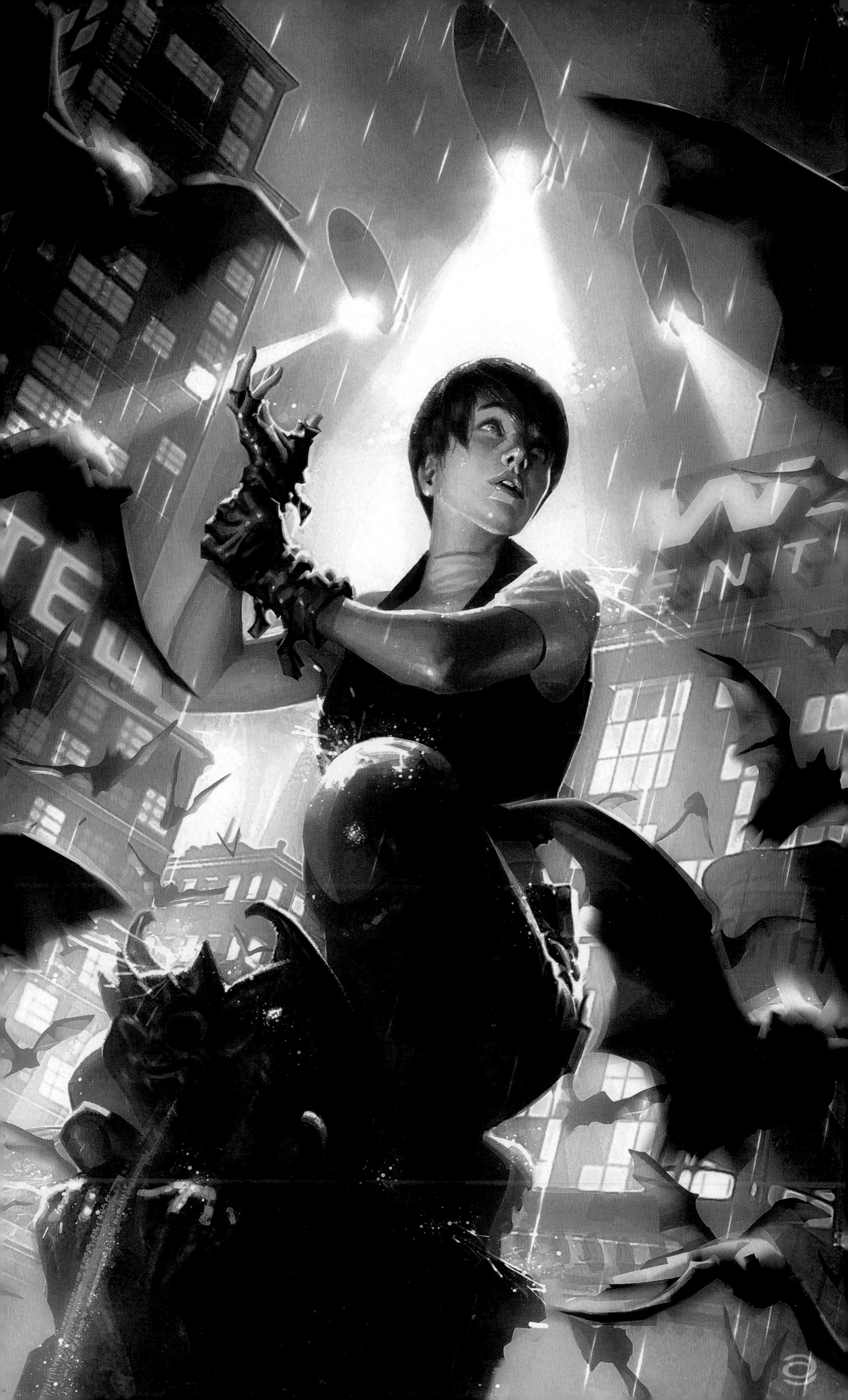

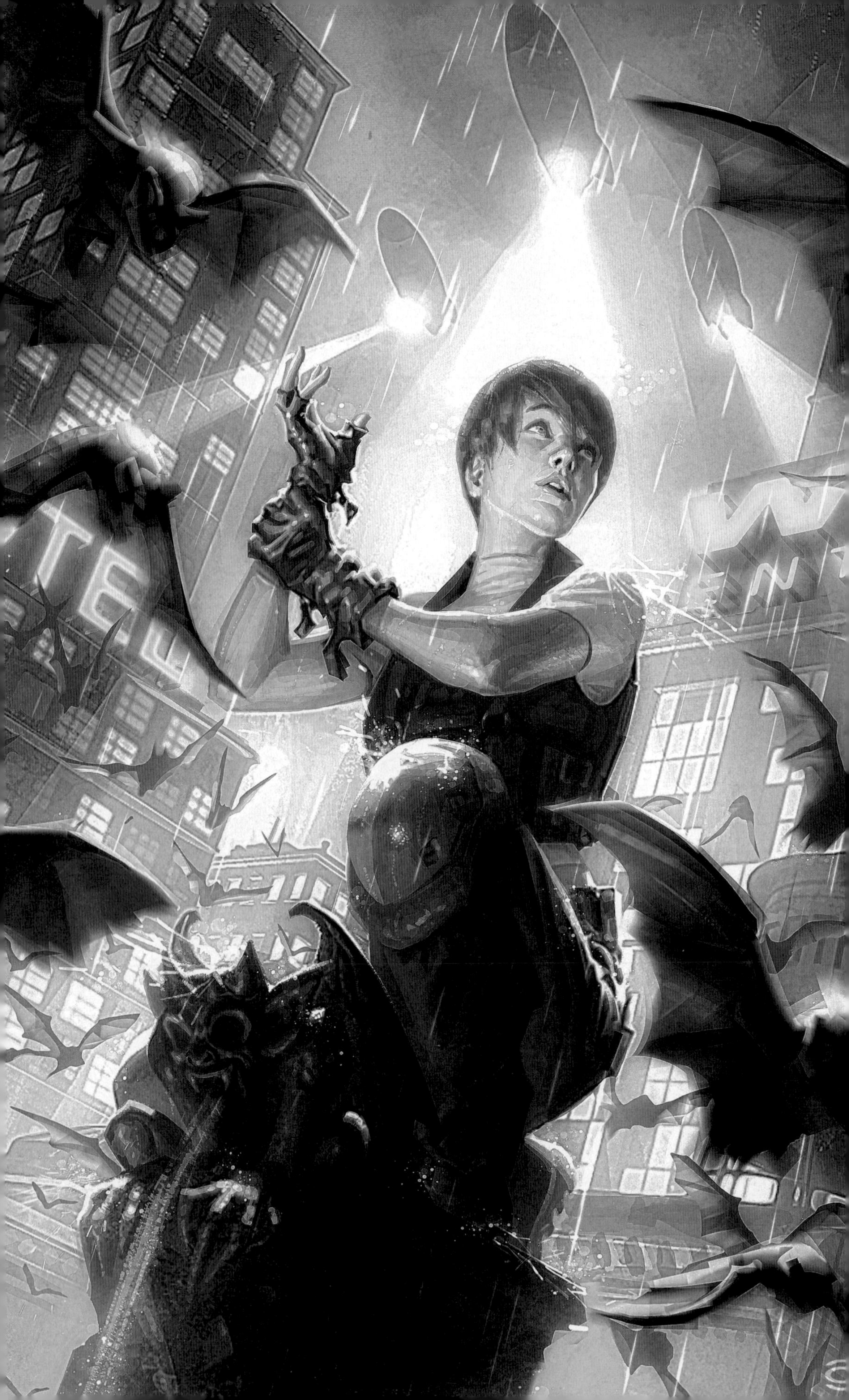

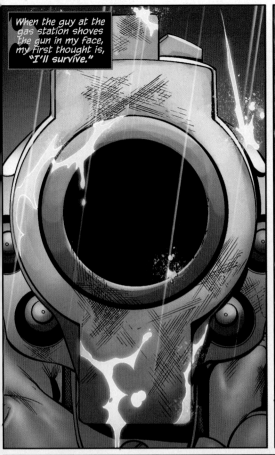

When the guy at the gas station shoves the gun in my face, my first thought is, "I'll survive."

You see, at school, all my friends have these *contingency plans* for disaster.

Coley's

Gasoline Snack Shop
Service Center

Regular
Plus 4.9
Premium 25.45
26.90

I mean, it's pretty much just action movie disaster scenarios--alien invasion, cars turning into robots, the zombie apocalypse.

You know.

The *usual*.

--BZZZT--EMERGENCY BROADCAST! FORCED EVACUATION FROM COLDLIGHT ISLAND--BZZZT--WE'RE GETTING WORD FROM THE G.C.P.D. OF RIOTS AS FOOD, BLANKETS, AND BATTERIES VANISH FROM THE SHELVES--BZZZT--DEVASTATING WIND AND RAIN TO COME--

BASE CAMP

The plans are all pretty much the same.

Hit the grocery store, hit the gun store, hit the superstore, and hole up.

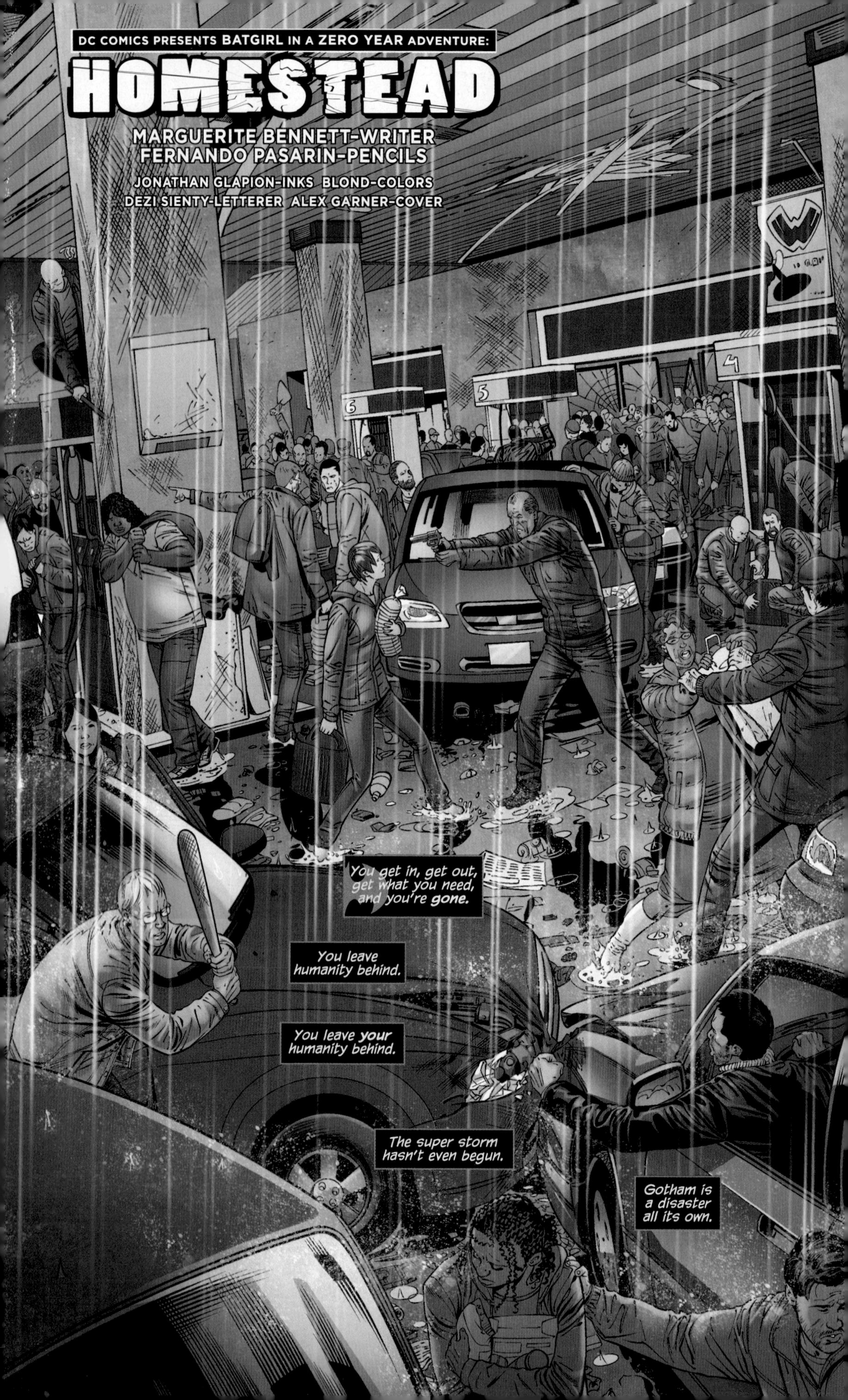
DC COMICS PRESENTS BATGIRL IN A ZERO YEAR ADVENTURE:
HOMESTEAD
MARGUERITE BENNETT-WRITER
FERNANDO PASARIN-PENCILS
JONATHAN GLAPION-INKS BLOND-COLORS
DEZI SIENTY-LETTERER ALEX GARNER-COVER
6
5
4
You get in, get out, get what you need, and you're gone.
You leave humanity behind.
You leave your humanity behind.
The super storm hasn't even begun.
Gotham is a disaster all its own.

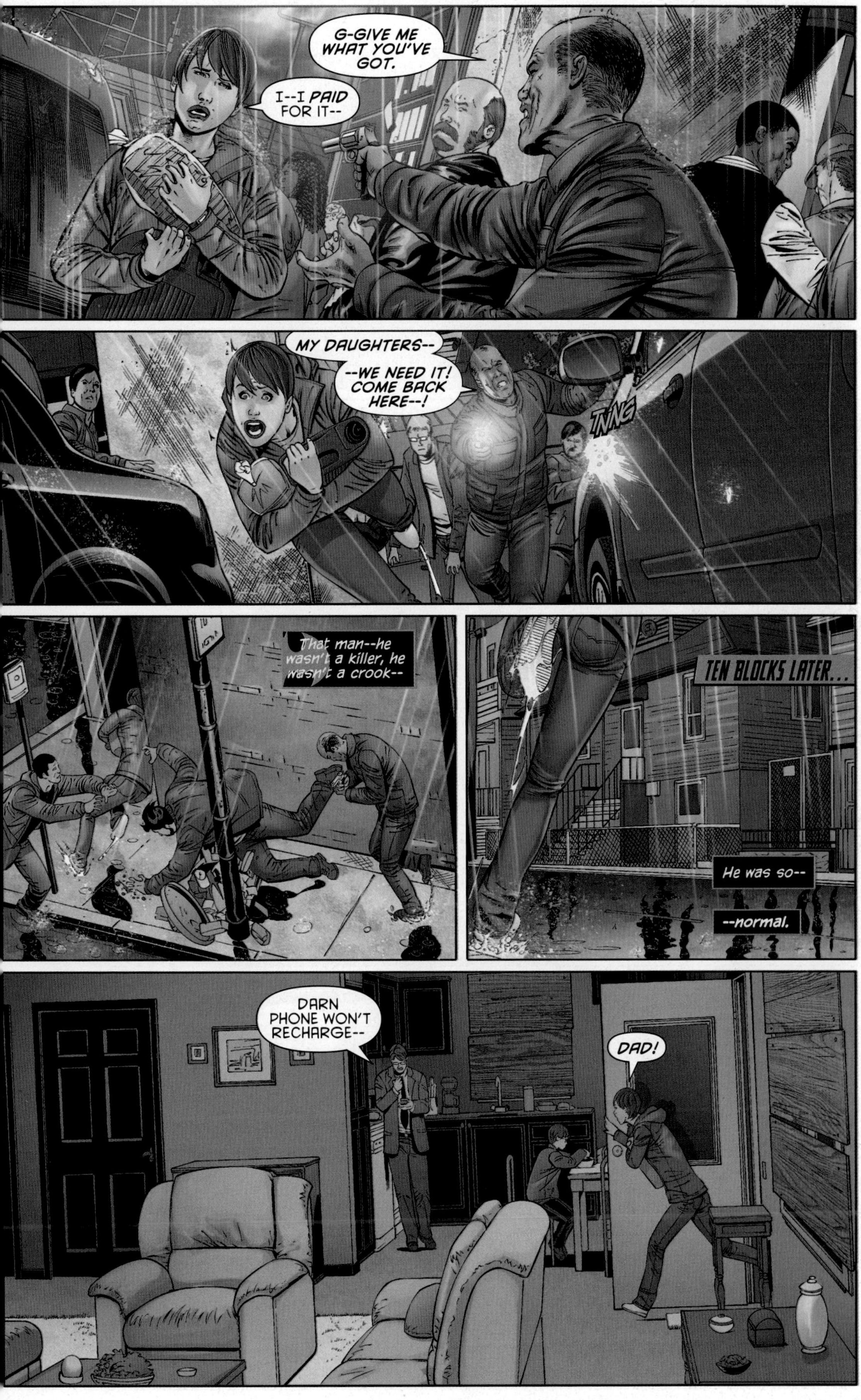
G-GIVE ME WHAT YOU'VE GOT.
I--I PAID FOR IT--
MY DAUGHTERS--
--WE NEED IT! COME BACK HERE--!
TNNG
That man--he wasn't a killer, he wasn't a crook--
TEN BLOCKS LATER...
He was so--
--normal.
DARN PHONE WON'T RECHARGE--
DAD!

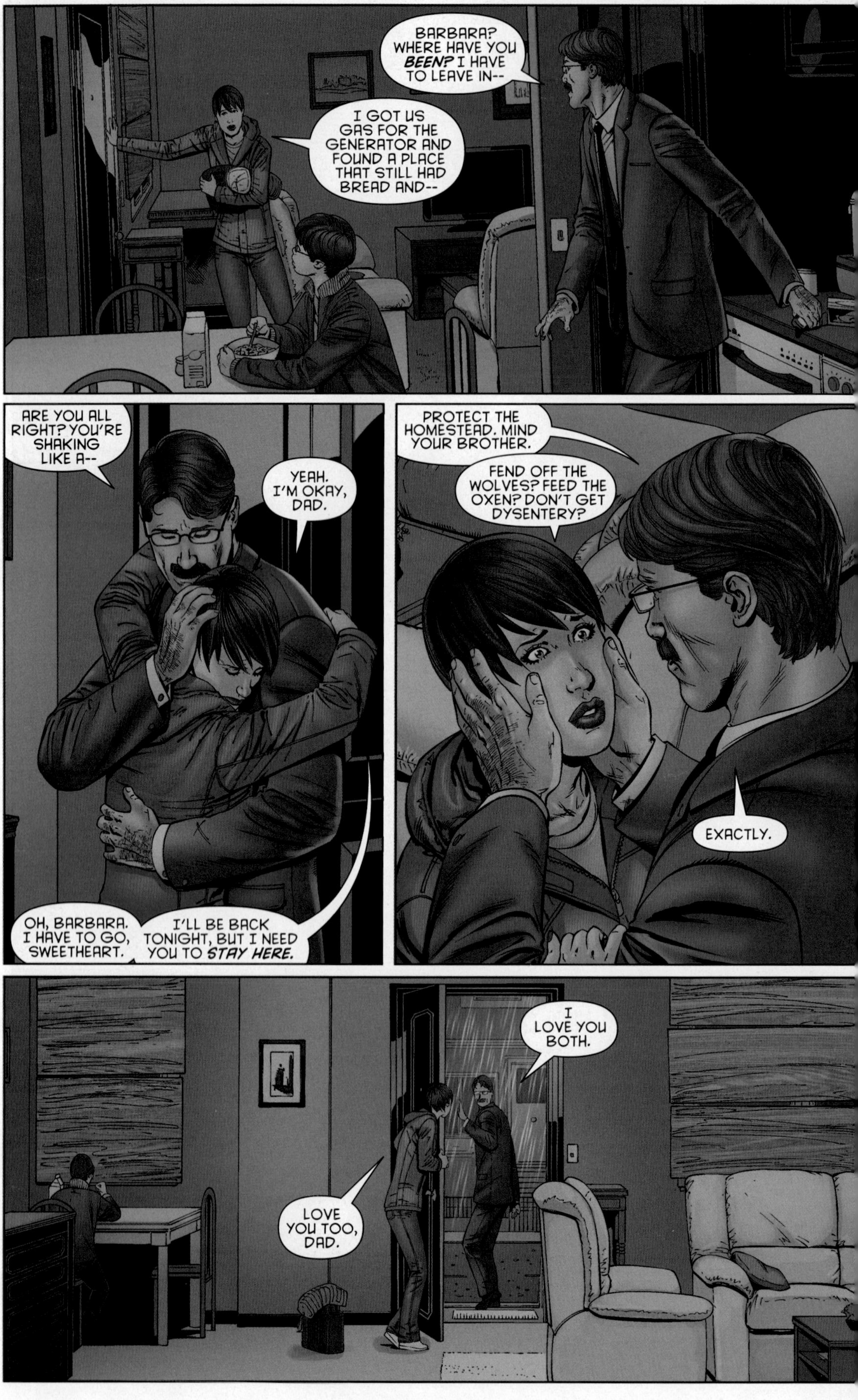
BARBARA? WHERE HAVE YOU BEEN? I HAVE TO LEAVE IN--
I GOT US GAS FOR THE GENERATOR AND FOUND A PLACE THAT STILL HAD BREAD AND--
ARE YOU ALL RIGHT? YOU'RE SHAKING LIKE A--
YEAH. I'M OKAY, DAD.
OH, BARBARA. I HAVE TO GO, SWEETHEART.
I'LL BE BACK TONIGHT, BUT I NEED YOU TO STAY HERE.
PROTECT THE HOMESTEAD. MIND YOUR BROTHER.
FEND OFF THE WOLVES? FEED THE OXEN? DON'T GET DYSENTERY?
EXACTLY.
I LOVE YOU BOTH.
LOVE YOU TOO, DAD.

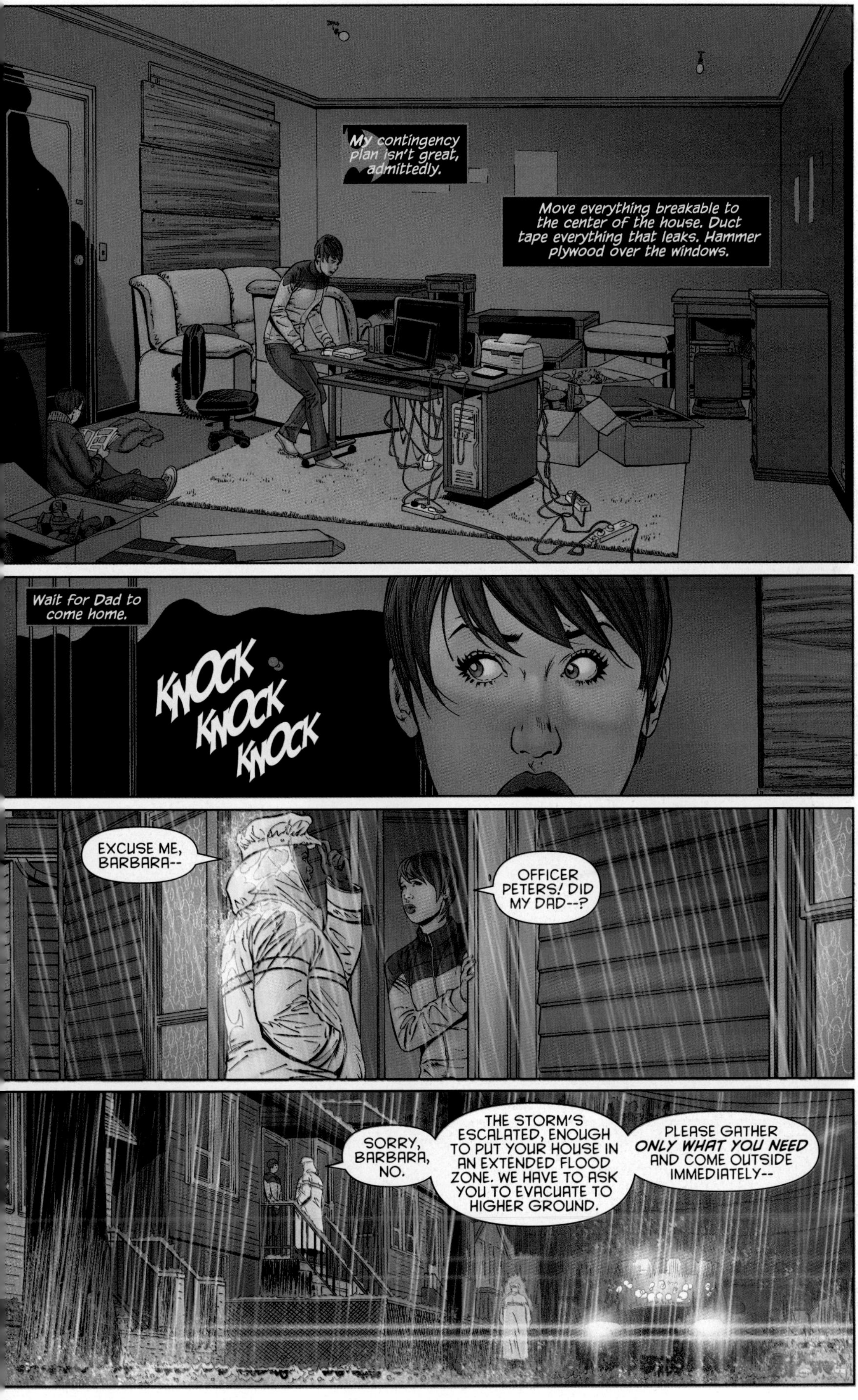

My contingency plan isn't great, admittedly.
Move everything breakable to the center of the house. Duct tape everything that leaks. Hammer plywood over the windows.
Wait for Dad to come home.
KNOCK KNOCK KNOCK
EXCUSE ME, BARBARA--
OFFICER PETERS! DID MY DAD--?
SORRY, BARBARA, NO.
THE STORM'S ESCALATED, ENOUGH TO PUT YOUR HOUSE IN AN EXTENDED FLOOD ZONE. WE HAVE TO ASK YOU TO EVACUATE TO HIGHER GROUND.
PLEASE GATHER ONLY WHAT YOU NEED AND COME OUTSIDE IMMEDIATELY--

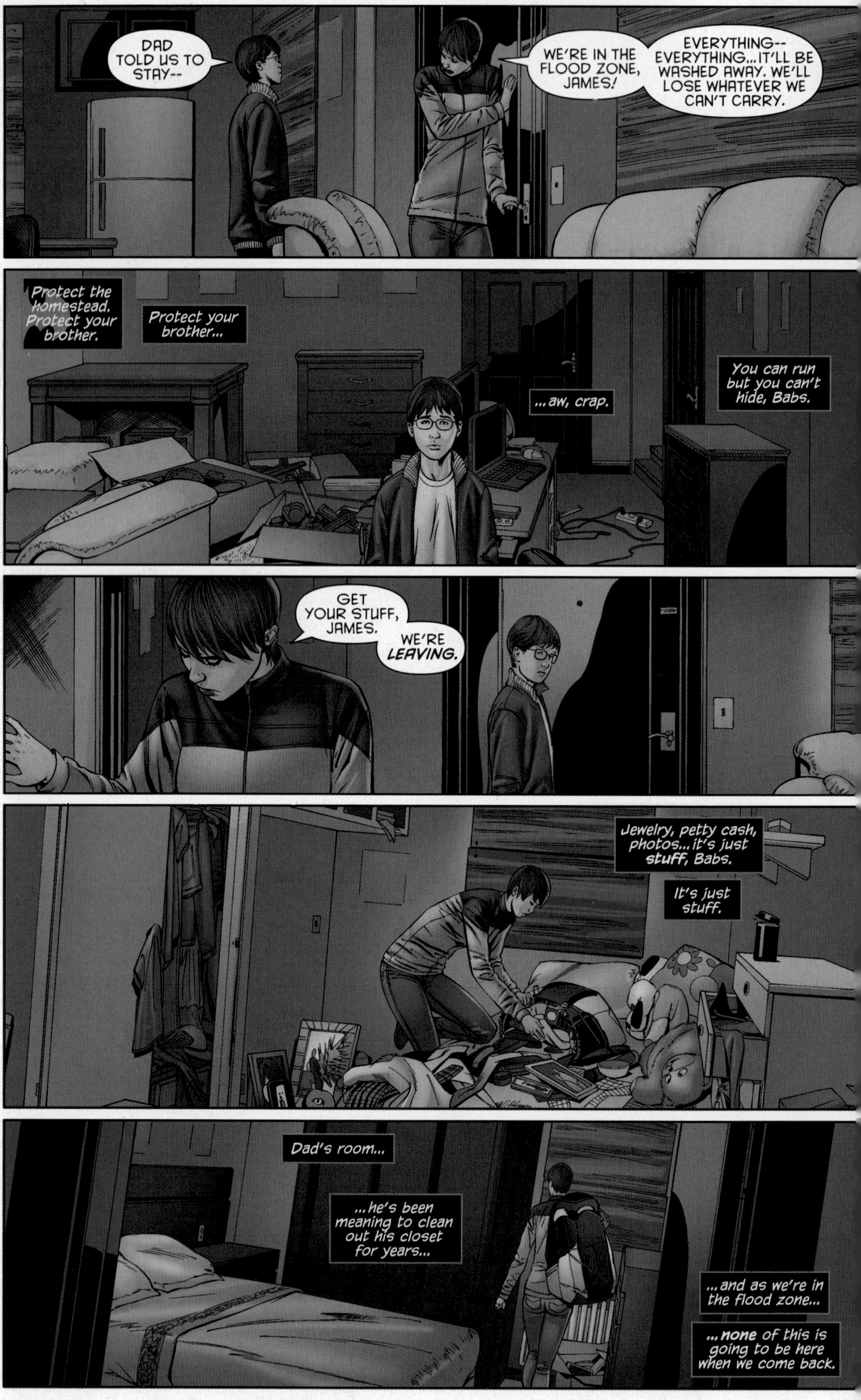
DAD TOLD US TO STAY--
WE'RE IN THE FLOOD ZONE, JAMES!
EVERYTHING-- EVERYTHING...IT'LL BE WASHED AWAY. WE'LL LOSE WHATEVER WE CAN'T CARRY.
Protect the homestead. Protect your brother.
Protect your brother...
...aw, crap.
You can run but you can't hide, Babs.
GET YOUR STUFF, JAMES.
WE'RE LEAVING.
Jewelry, petty cash, photos... it's just stuff, Babs.
It's just stuff.
Dad's room...
...he's been meaning to clean out his closet for years...
...and as we're in the flood zone...
...none of this is going to be here when we come back.

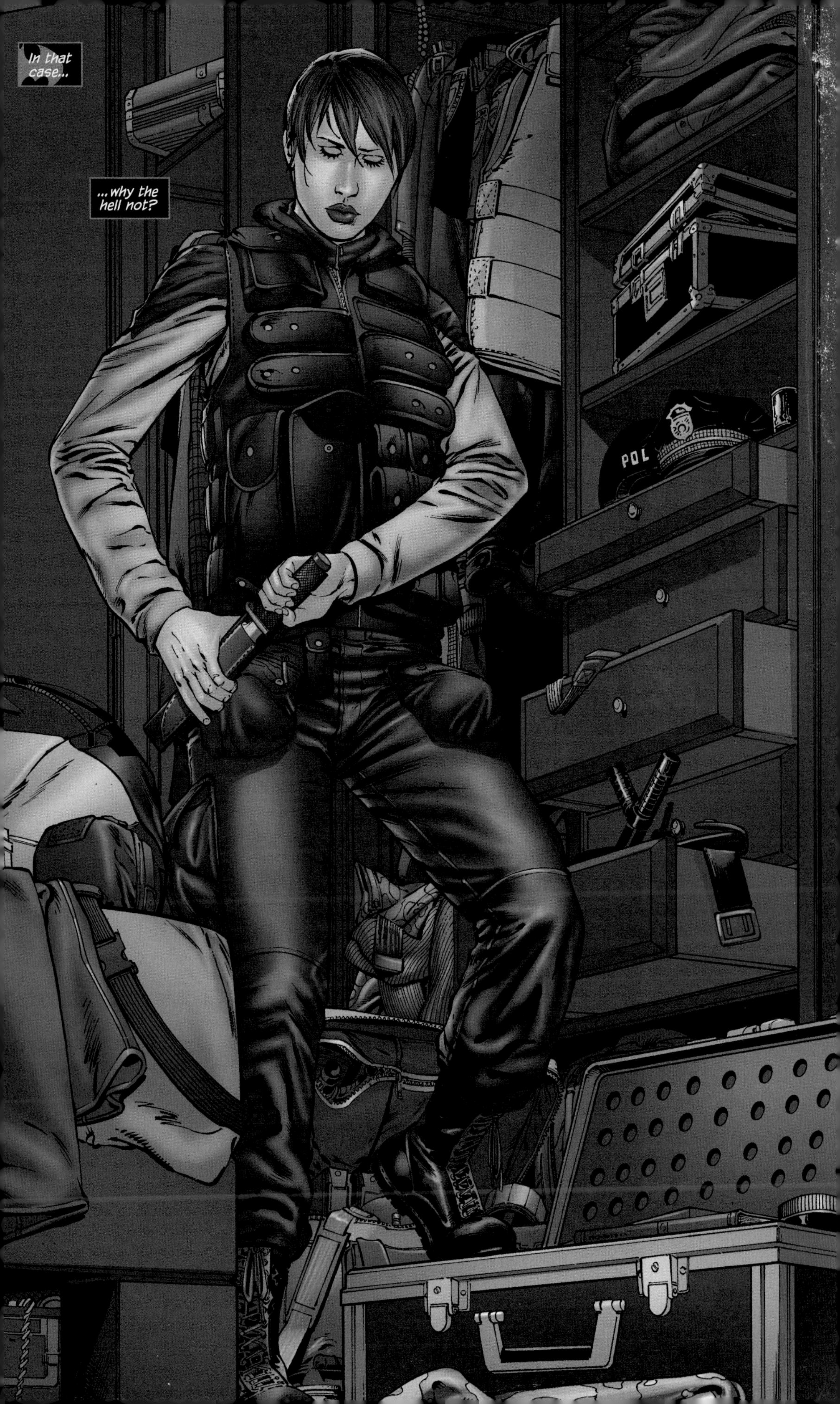
In that case...
...why the hell not?
POL

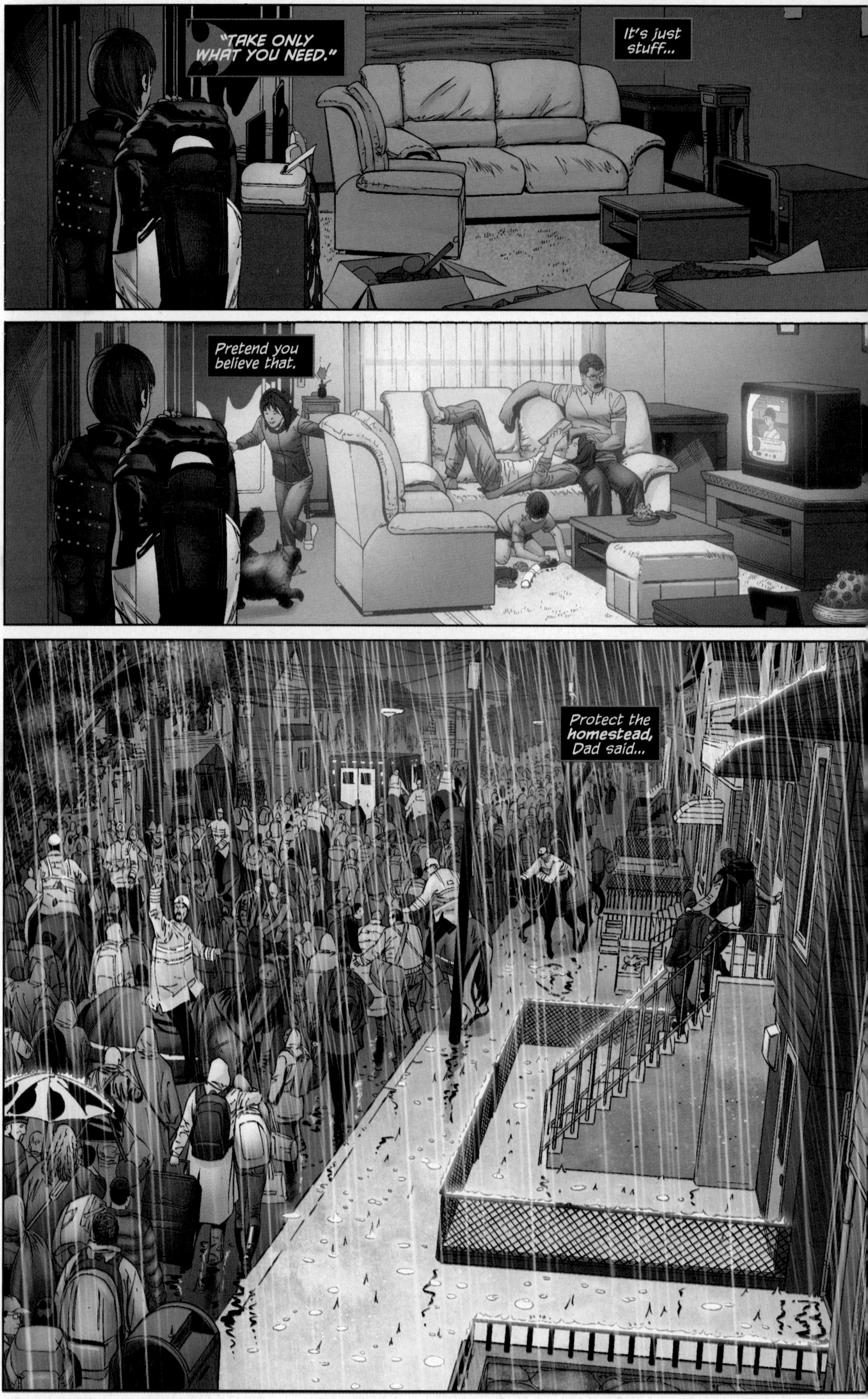
"TAKE ONLY WHAT YOU NEED."
It's just stuff...
Pretend you believe that.
Protect the homestead, Dad said...

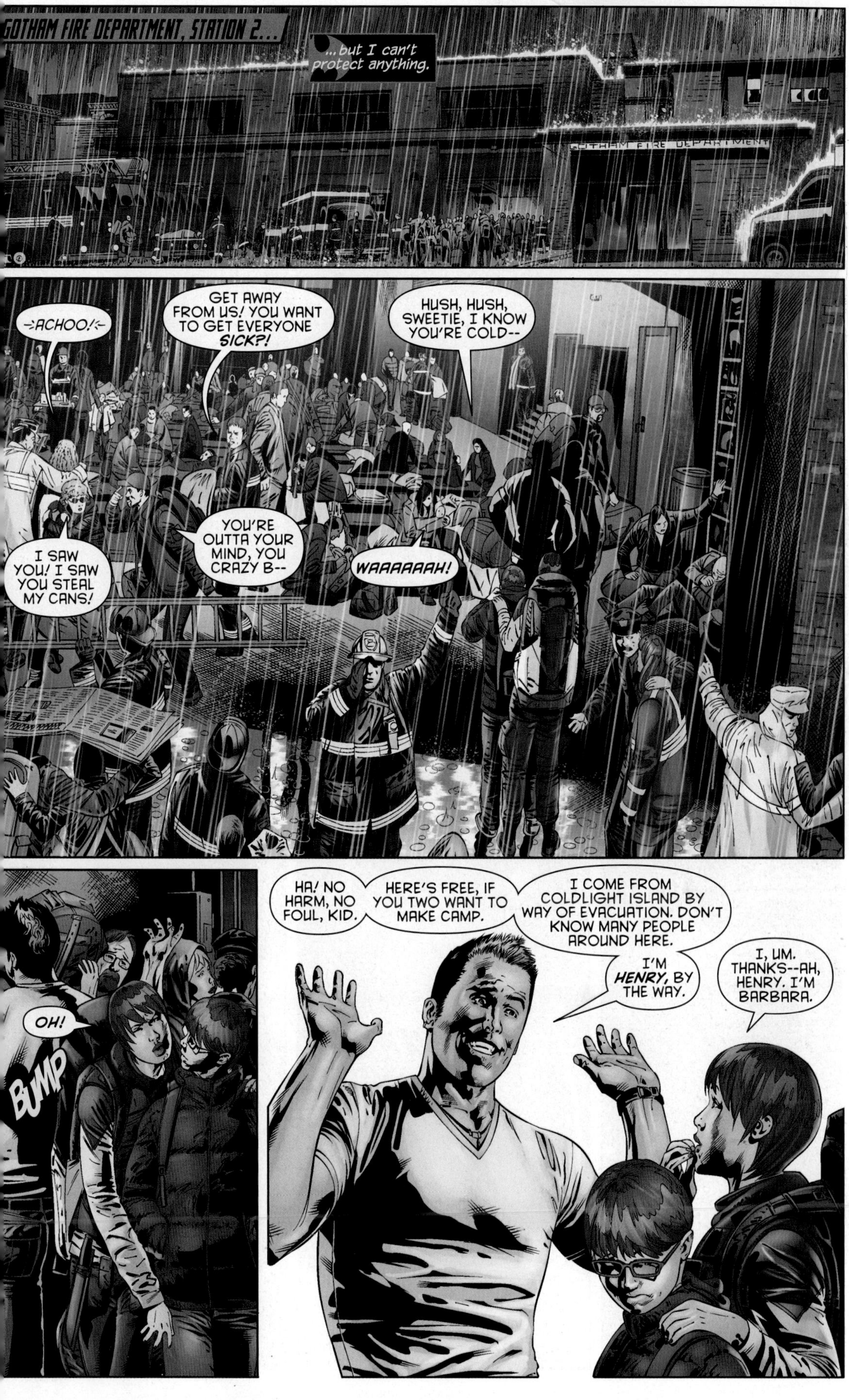
GOTHAM FIRE DEPARTMENT, STATION 2...
...but I can't protect anything.
GOTHAM FIRE DEPARTMENT
-ACHOO!-
GET AWAY FROM US! YOU WANT TO GET EVERYONE SICK?!
HUSH, HUSH, SWEETIE, I KNOW YOU'RE COLD--
I SAW YOU! I SAW YOU STEAL MY CANS!
YOU'RE OUTTA YOUR MIND, YOU CRAZY B--
WAAAAAAAH!
OH!
BUMP
HA! NO HARM, NO FOUL, KID.
HERE'S FREE, IF YOU TWO WANT TO MAKE CAMP.
I COME FROM COLDLIGHT ISLAND BY WAY OF EVACUATION. DON'T KNOW MANY PEOPLE AROUND HERE.
I'M HENRY, BY THE WAY.
I, UM. THANKS--AH, HENRY. I'M BARBARA.

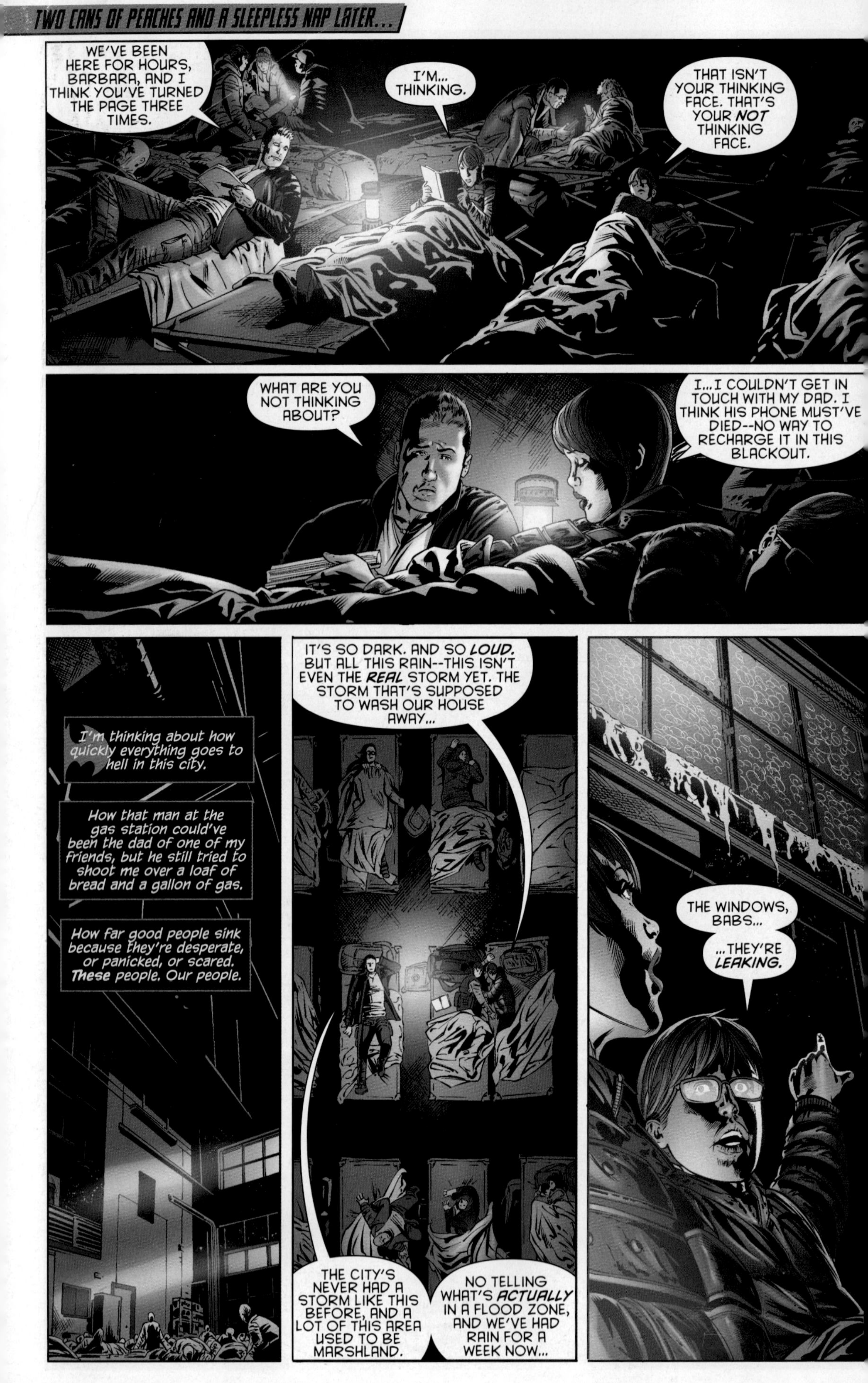
TWO CANS OF PEACHES AND A SLEEPLESS NAP LATER...
WE'VE BEEN HERE FOR HOURS, BARBARA, AND I THINK YOU'VE TURNED THE PAGE THREE TIMES.
I'M... THINKING.
THAT ISN'T YOUR THINKING FACE. THAT'S YOUR NOT THINKING FACE.
WHAT ARE YOU NOT THINKING ABOUT?
I... I COULDN'T GET IN TOUCH WITH MY DAD. I THINK HIS PHONE MUST'VE DIED--NO WAY TO RECHARGE IT IN THIS BLACKOUT.
I'm thinking about how quickly everything goes to hell in this city.
How that man at the gas station could've been the dad of one of my friends, but he still tried to shoot me over a loaf of bread and a gallon of gas.
How far good people sink because they're desperate, or panicked, or scared. These people. Our people.
IT'S SO DARK. AND SO LOUD. BUT ALL THIS RAIN--THIS ISN'T EVEN THE REAL STORM YET. THE STORM THAT'S SUPPOSED TO WASH OUR HOUSE AWAY...
THE CITY'S NEVER HAD A STORM LIKE THIS BEFORE, AND A LOT OF THIS AREA USED TO BE MARSHLAND.
NO TELLING WHAT'S ACTUALLY IN A FLOOD ZONE, AND WE'VE HAD RAIN FOR A WEEK NOW...
THE WINDOWS, BABS...
...THEY'RE LEAKING.

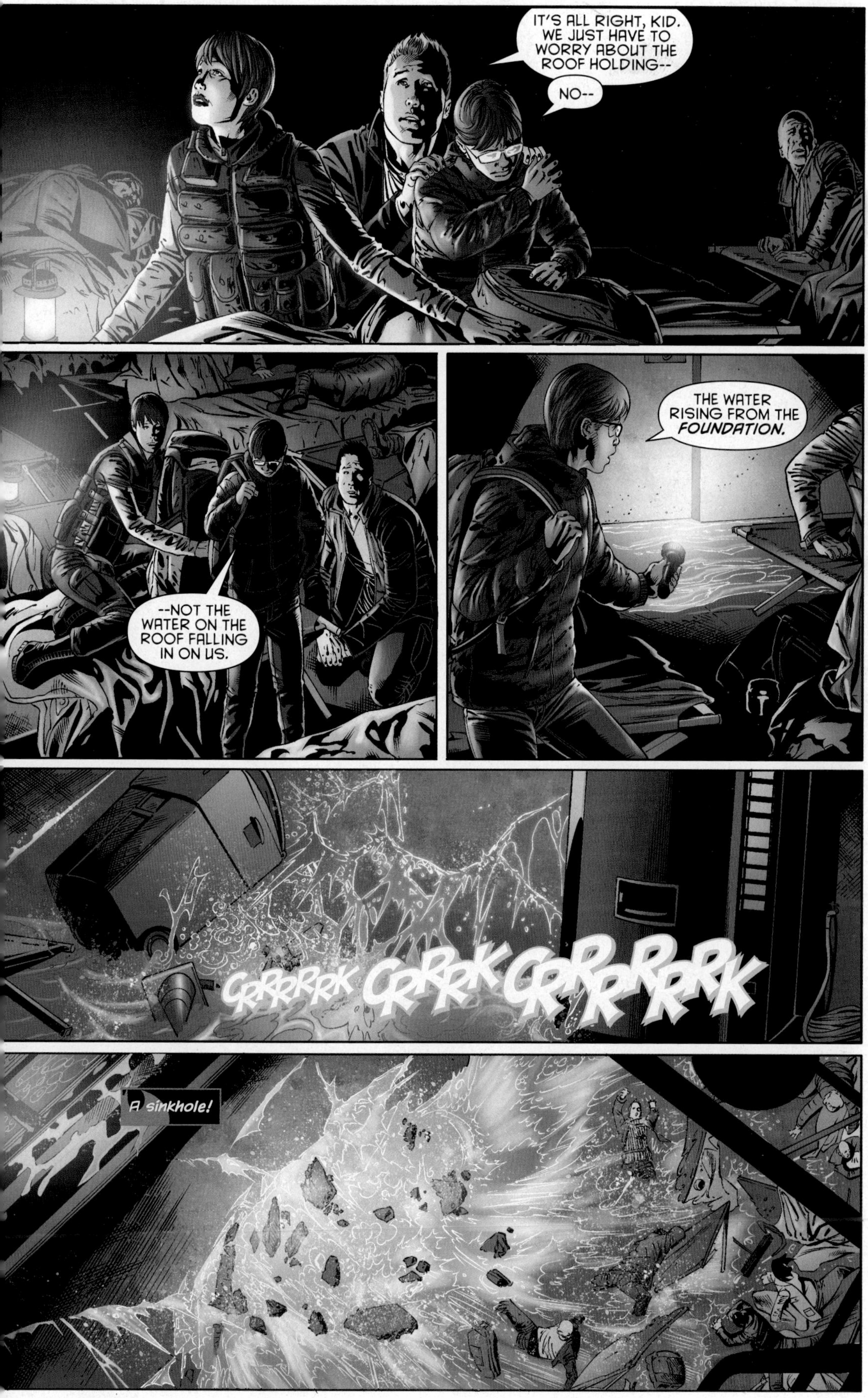
IT'S ALL RIGHT, KID. WE JUST HAVE TO WORRY ABOUT THE ROOF HOLDING--
NO--
--NOT THE WATER ON THE ROOF FALLING IN ON US.
THE WATER RISING FROM THE *FOUNDATION.*
CRRRRRK CRRRRK CRRRRRRRK
A sinkhole!

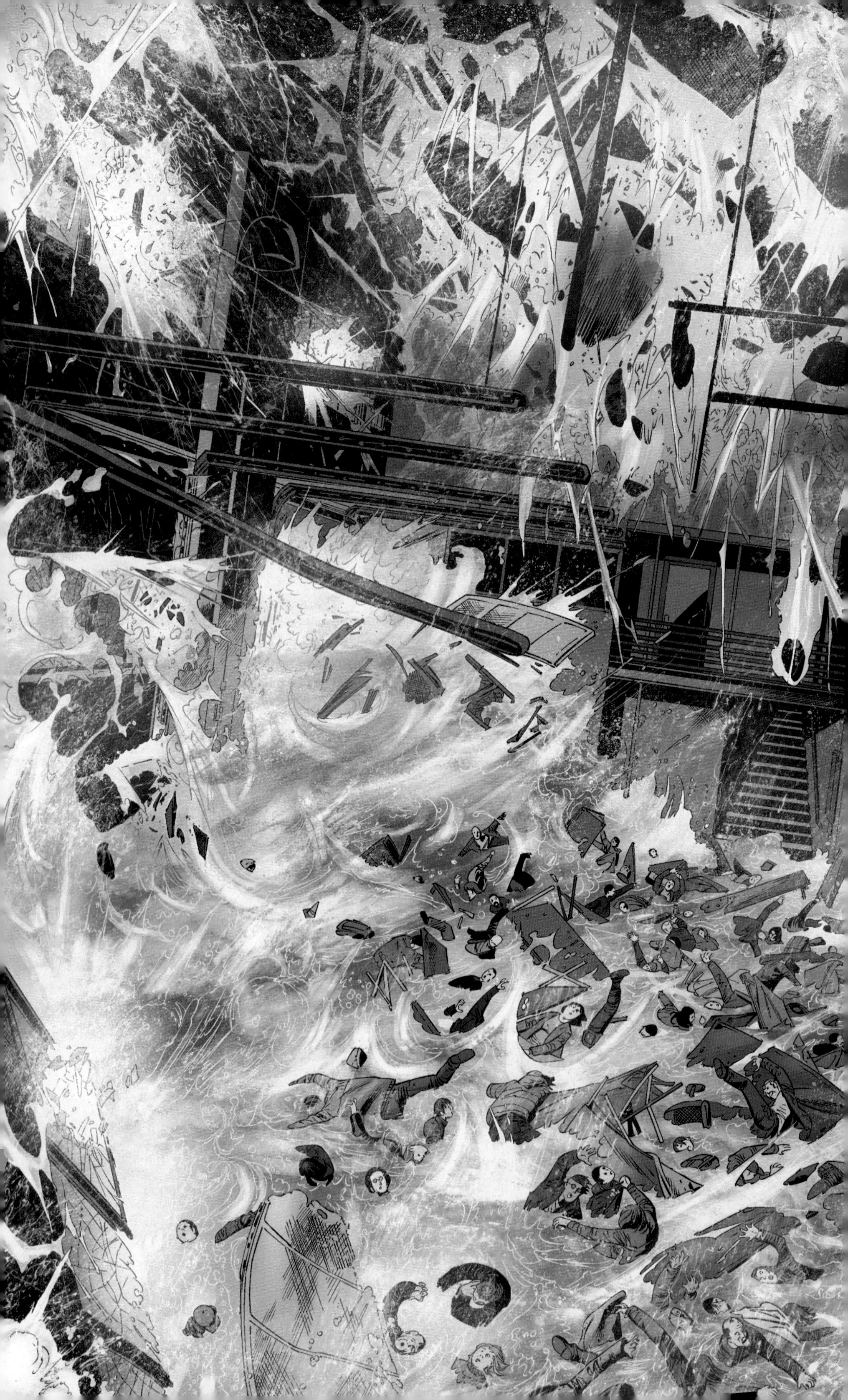

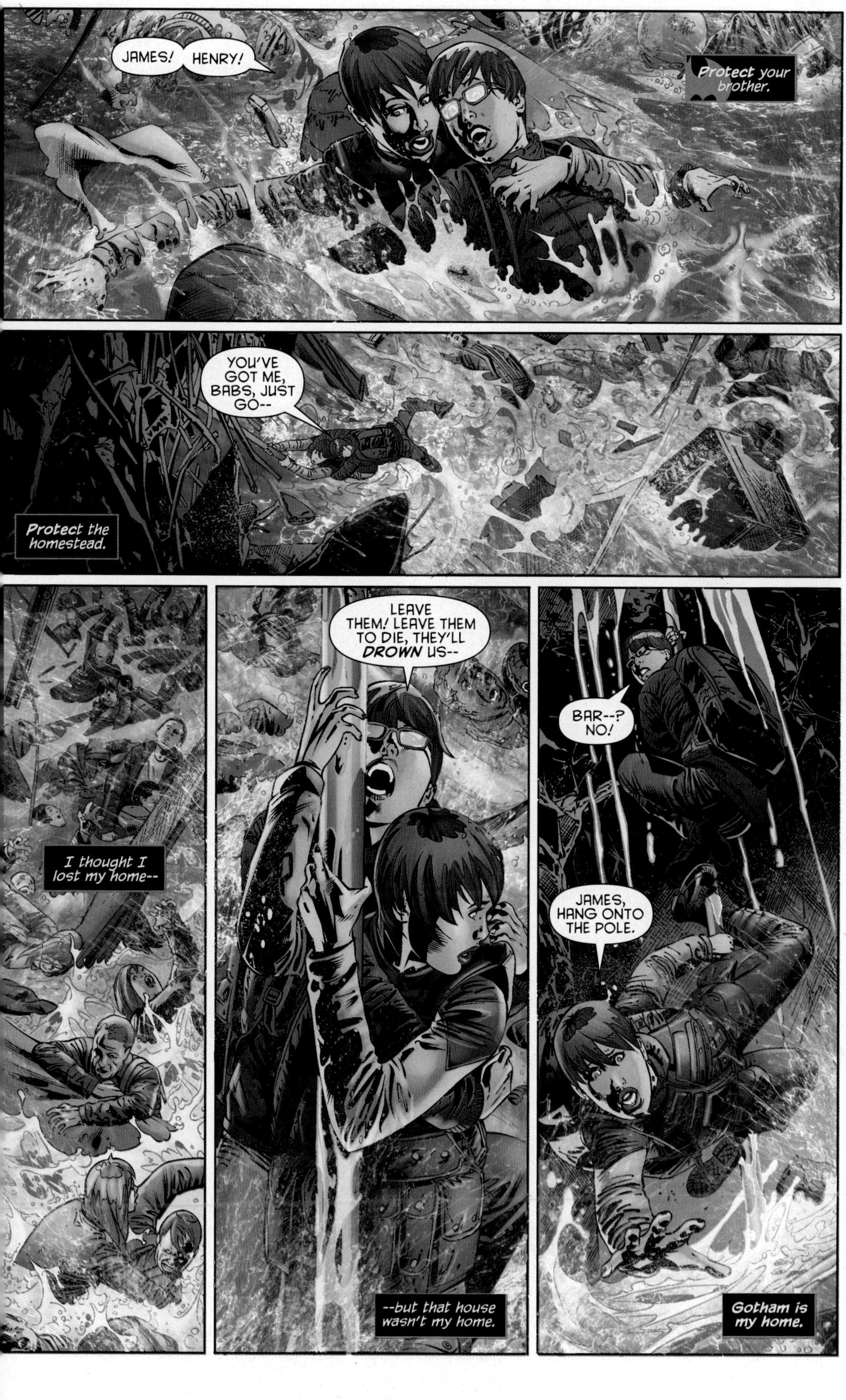
JAMES!
HENRY!
Protect your brother.
YOU'VE GOT ME, BABS, JUST GO--
Protect the homestead.
I thought I lost my home--
LEAVE THEM! LEAVE THEM TO DIE, THEY'LL DROWN US--
--but that house wasn't my home.
BAR--? NO!
JAMES, HANG ONTO THE POLE.
Gotham is my home.

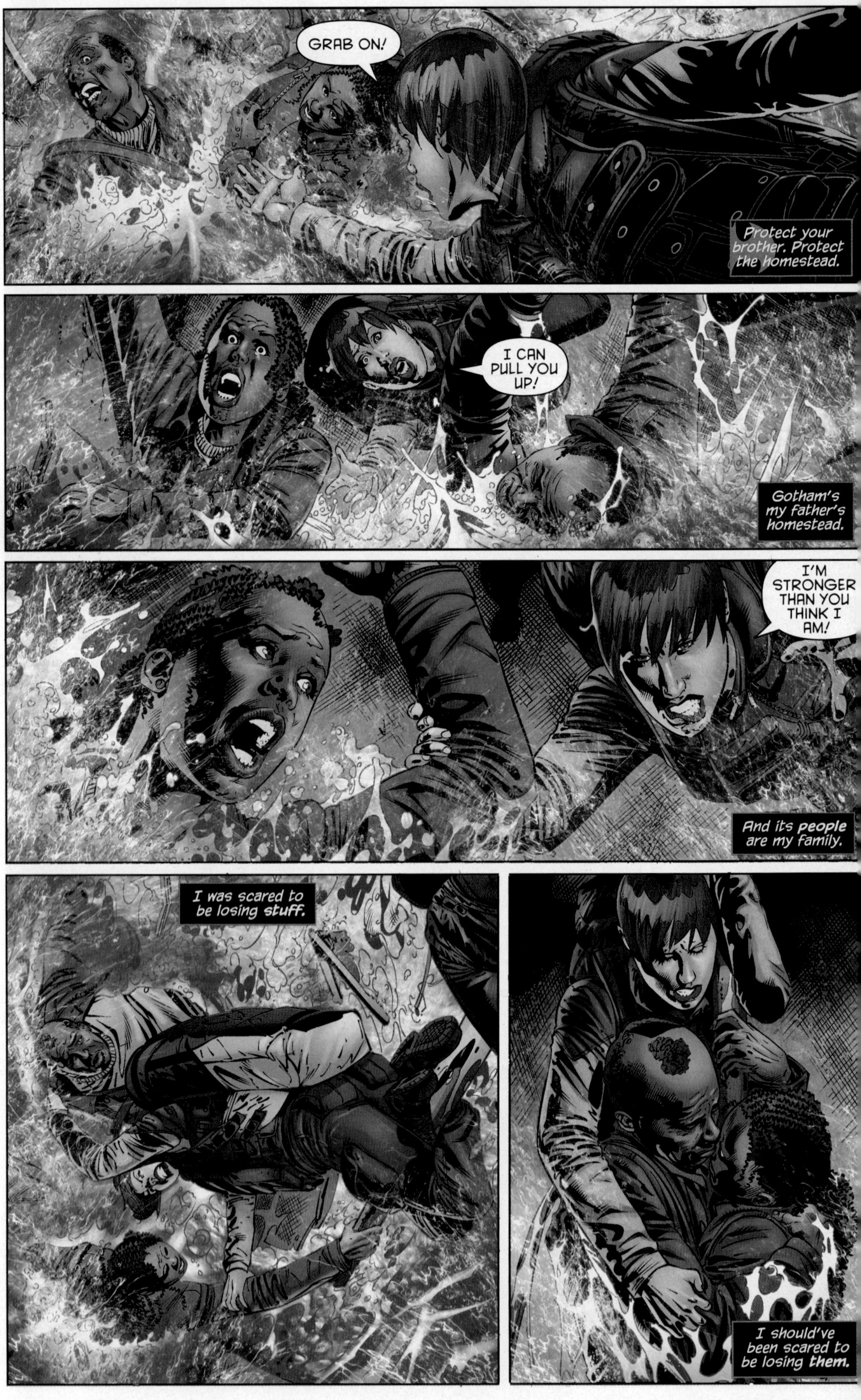
GRAB ON!
Protect your brother. Protect the homestead.
I CAN PULL YOU UP!
Gotham's my father's homestead.
I'M STRONGER THAN YOU THINK I AM!
And its **people** are my family.
I was scared to be losing **stuff**.
I should've been scared to be losing **them**.

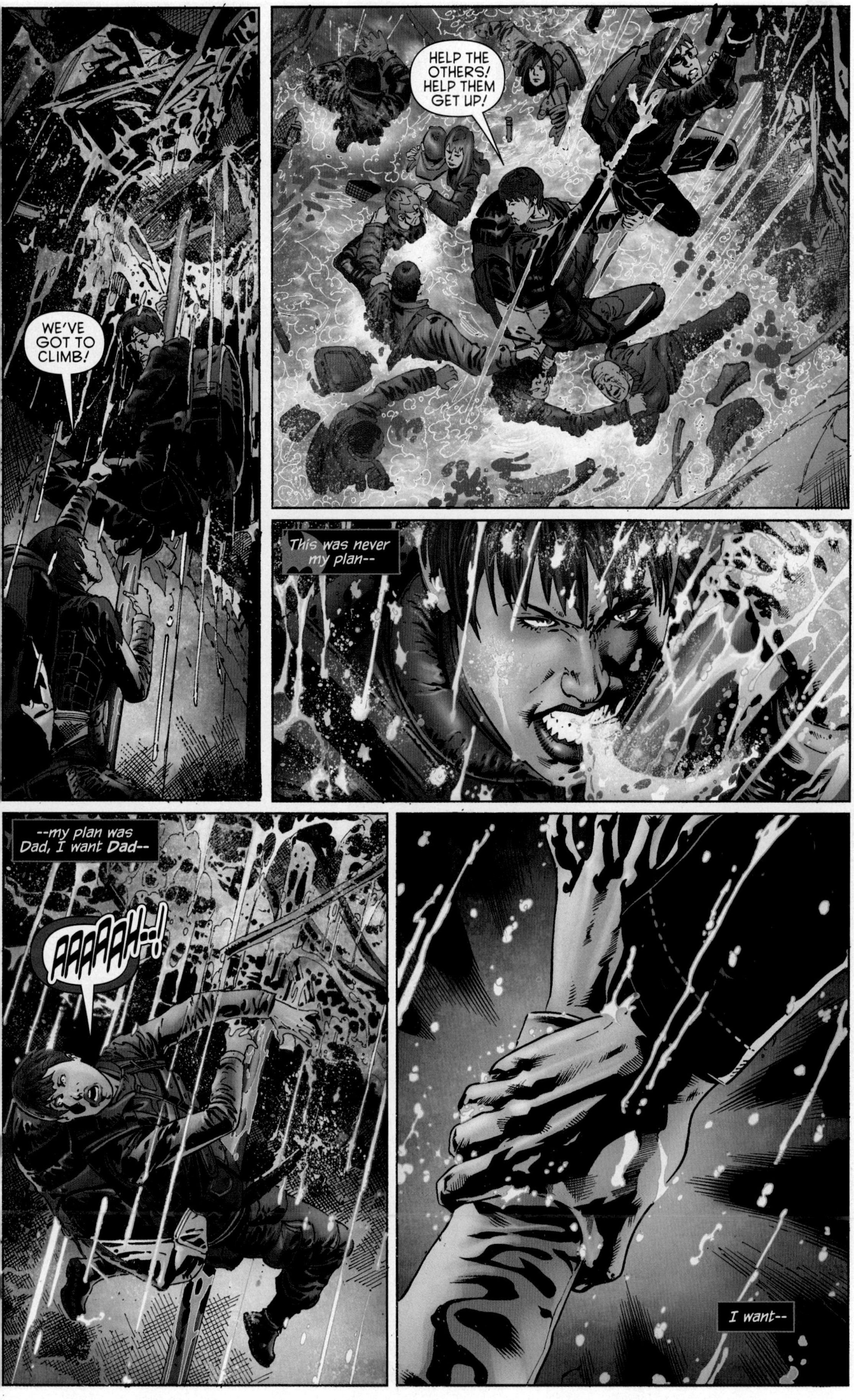
WE'VE GOT TO CLIMB!
HELP THE OTHERS! HELP THEM GET UP!
This was never my plan--
--my plan was Dad, I want Dad--
AAAAAAH--!
I want--

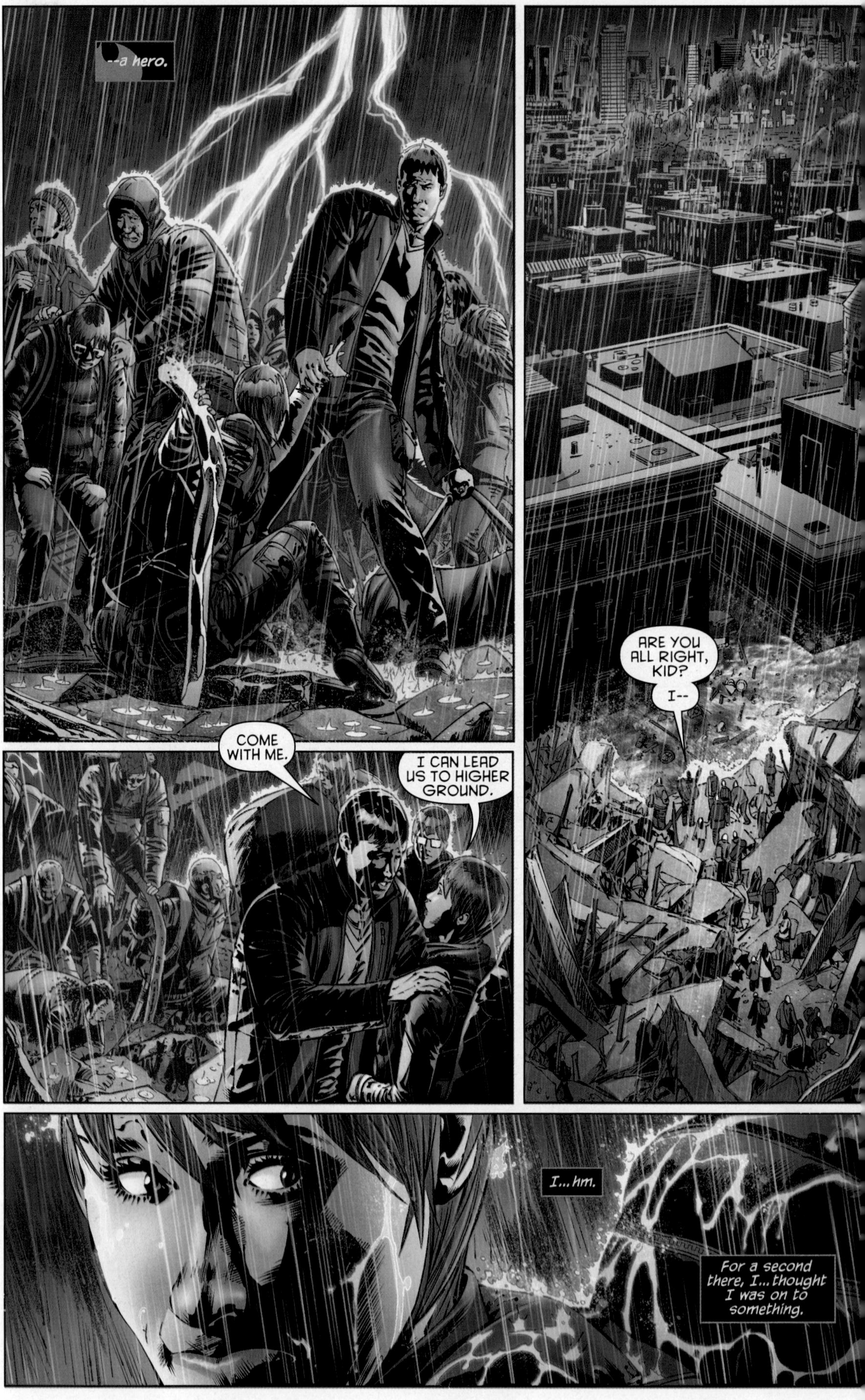
--a hero.
COME WITH ME.
I CAN LEAD US TO HIGHER GROUND.
ARE YOU ALL RIGHT, KID?
I--
I...hm.
For a second there, I...thought I was on to something.

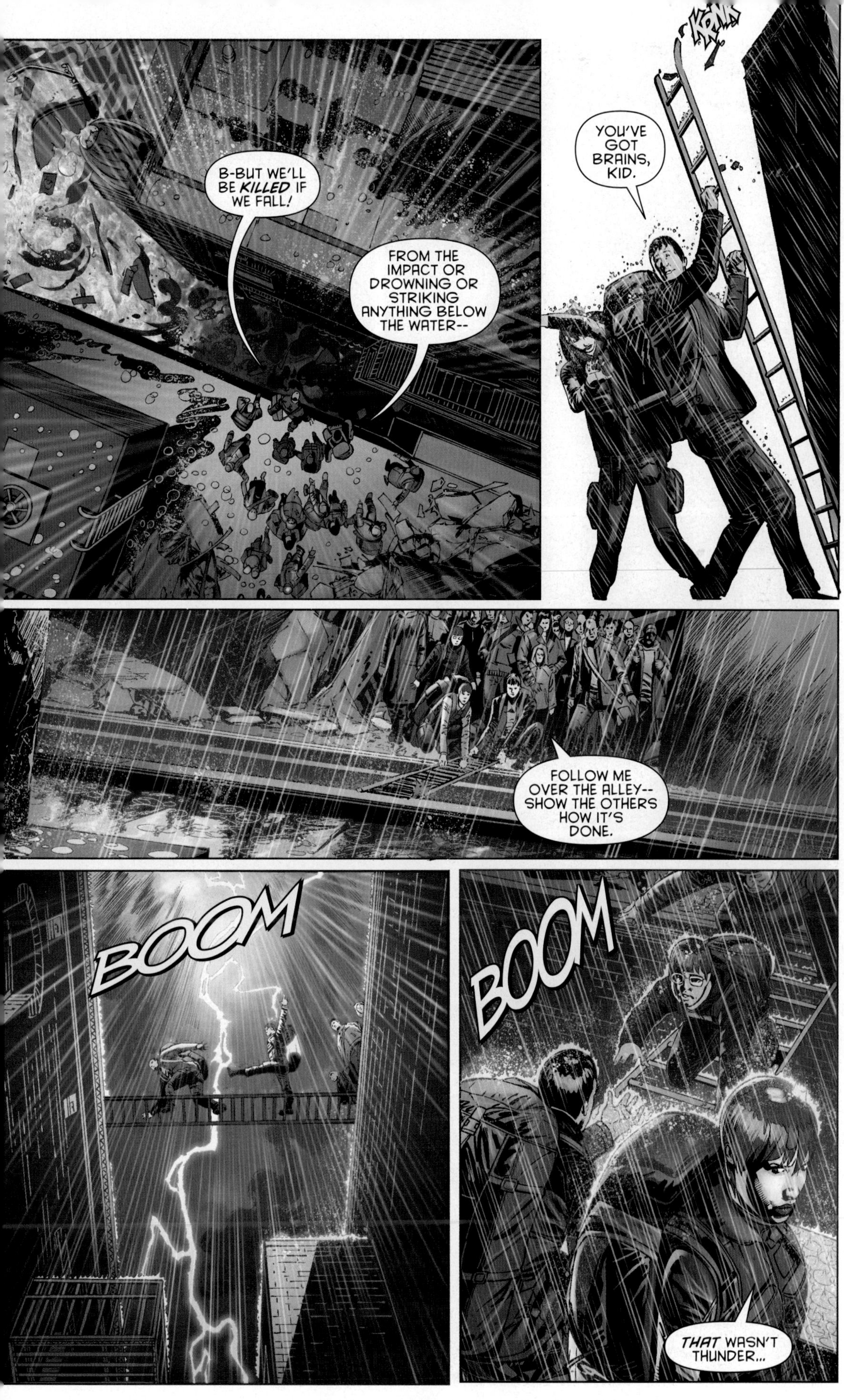
B-BUT WE'LL BE *KILLED* IF WE FALL!
FROM THE IMPACT OR DROWNING OR STRIKING ANYTHING BELOW THE WATER--
KONK
YOU'VE GOT BRAINS, KID.
FOLLOW ME OVER THE ALLEY-- SHOW THE OTHERS HOW IT'S DONE.
BOOM
BOOM
THAT WASN'T THUNDER...

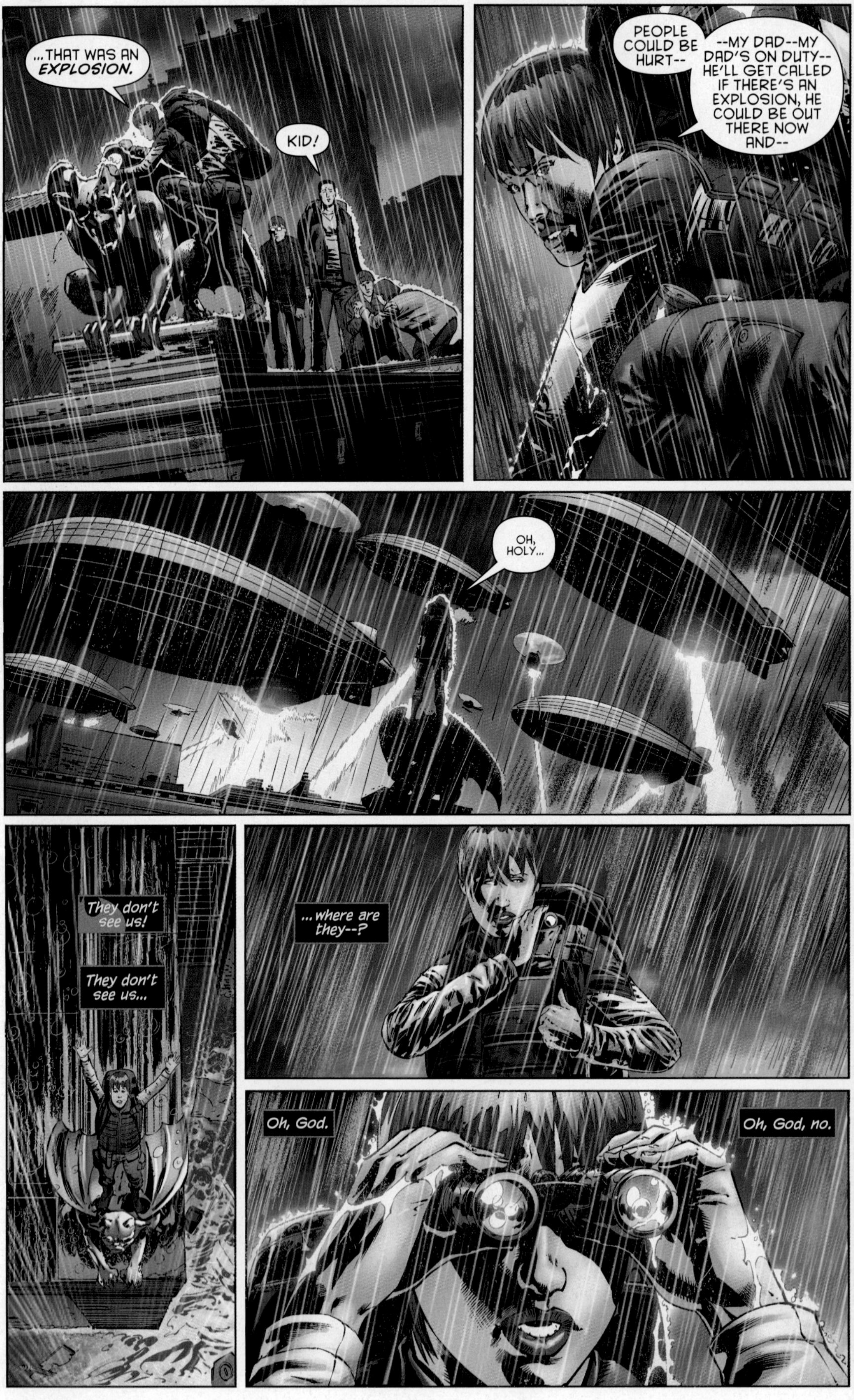
...THAT WAS AN *EXPLOSION.*
KID!
PEOPLE COULD BE HURT--
--MY DAD--MY DAD'S ON DUTY--HE'LL GET CALLED IF THERE'S AN EXPLOSION, HE COULD BE OUT THERE NOW AND--
OH, HOLY...
They don't see us!
They don't see us...
...where are they--?
Oh, God.
Oh, God, no.

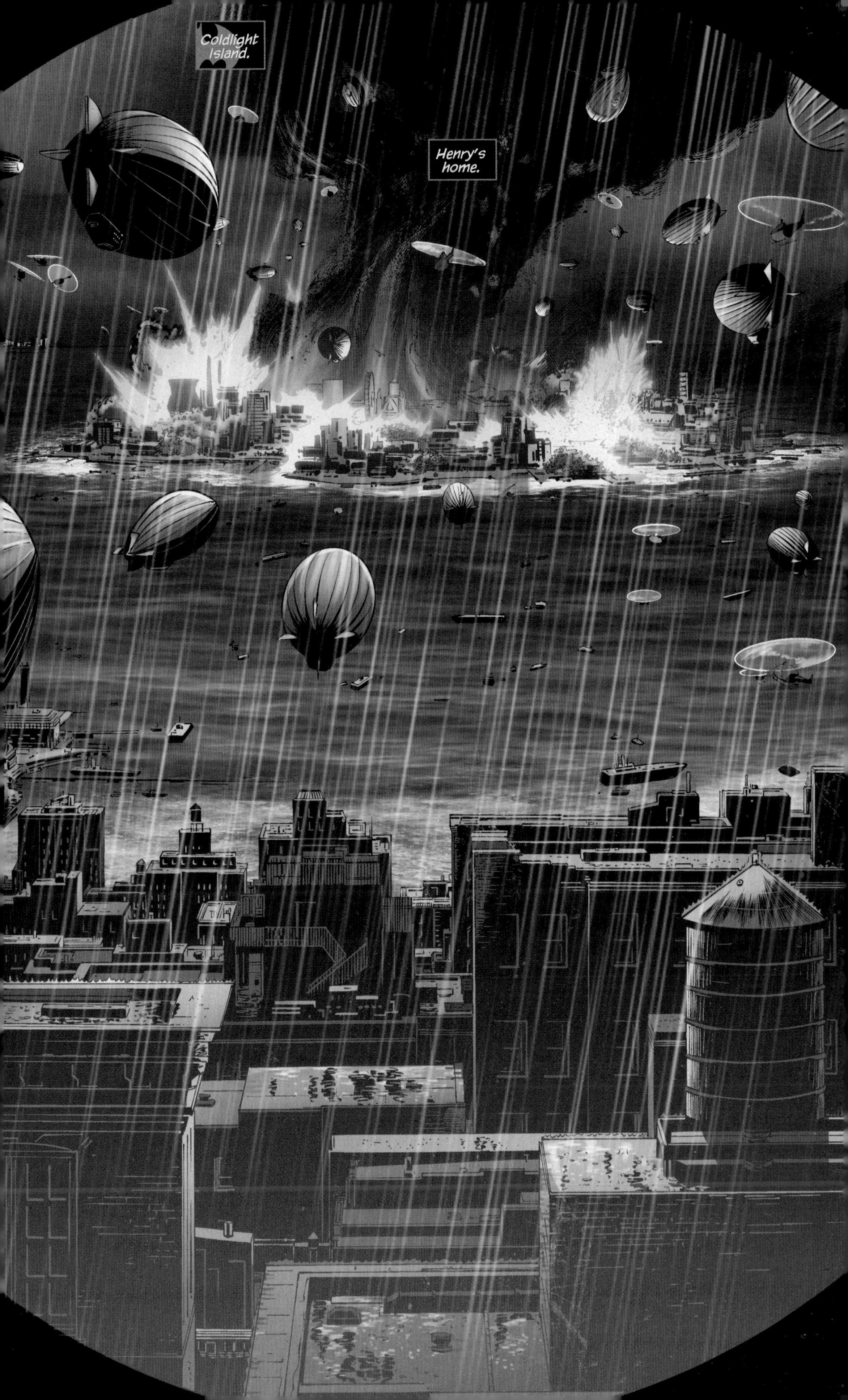
Coldlight Island.
Henry's home.

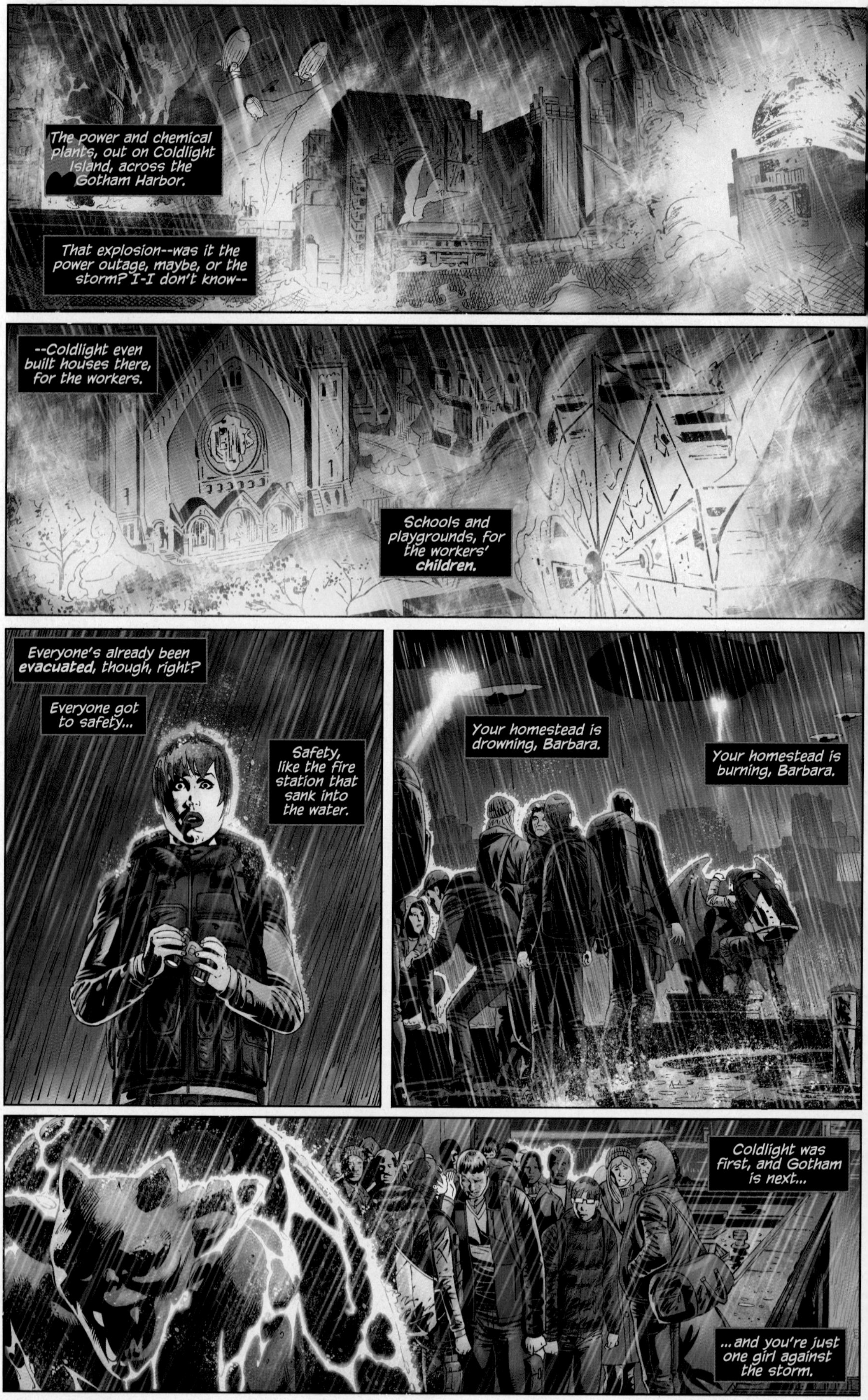
The power and chemical plants, out on Coldlight Island, across the Gotham Harbor.
That explosion--was it the power outage, maybe, or the storm? I-I don't know--
--Coldlight even built houses there, for the workers.
Schools and playgrounds, for the workers' **children.**
Everyone's already been **evacuated,** though, right?
Everyone got to safety...
Safety, like the fire station that sank into the water.
Your homestead is drowning, Barbara.
Your homestead is burning, Barbara.
Coldlight was first, and Gotham is next...
...and you're just one girl against the storm.

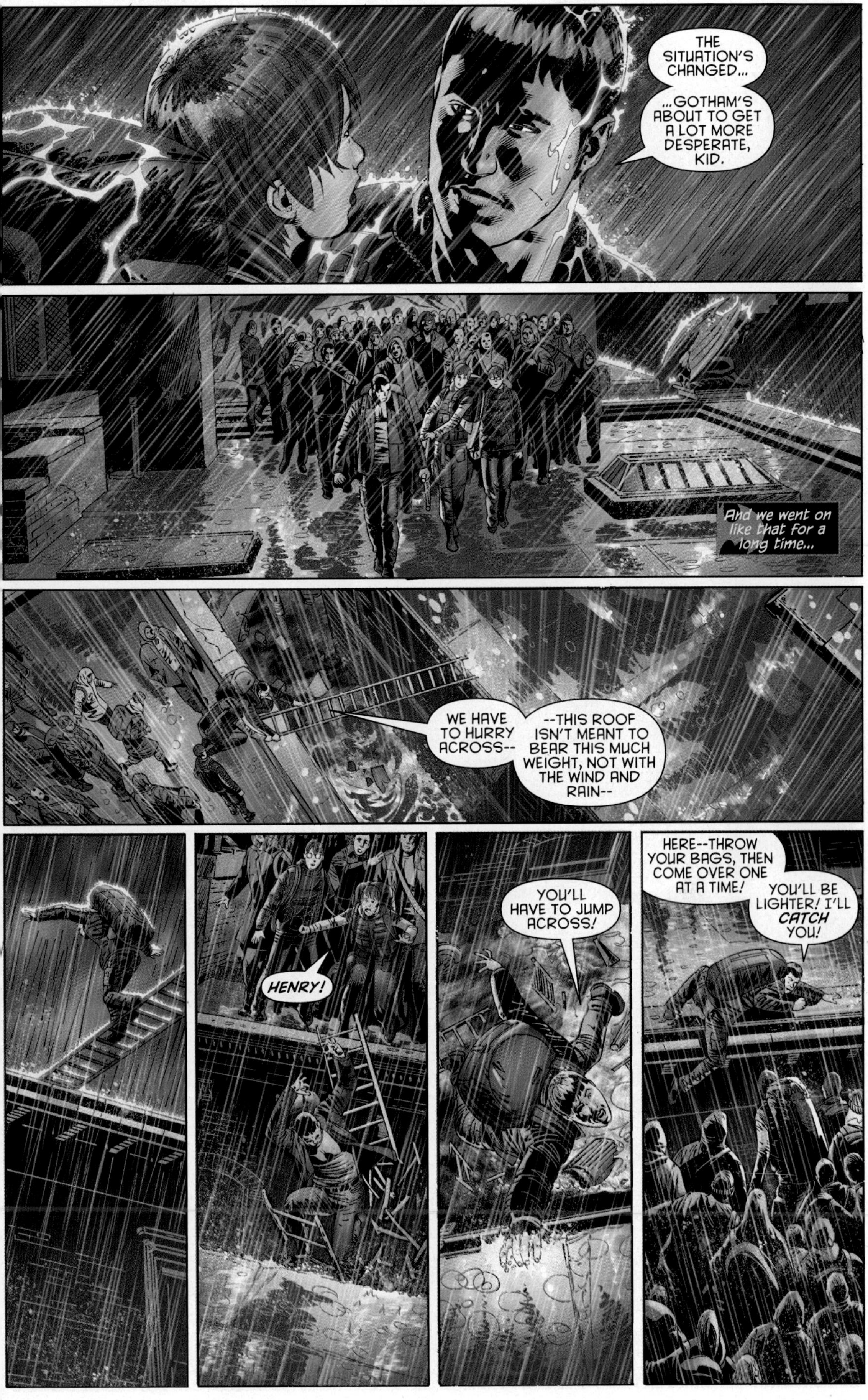
THE SITUATION'S CHANGED...
...GOTHAM'S ABOUT TO GET A LOT MORE DESPERATE, KID.
And we went on like that for a long time...
WE HAVE TO HURRY ACROSS--
--THIS ROOF ISN'T MEANT TO BEAR THIS MUCH WEIGHT, NOT WITH THE WIND AND RAIN--
HENRY!
YOU'LL HAVE TO JUMP ACROSS!
HERE--THROW YOUR BAGS, THEN COME OVER ONE AT A TIME!
YOU'LL BE LIGHTER! I'LL CATCH YOU!

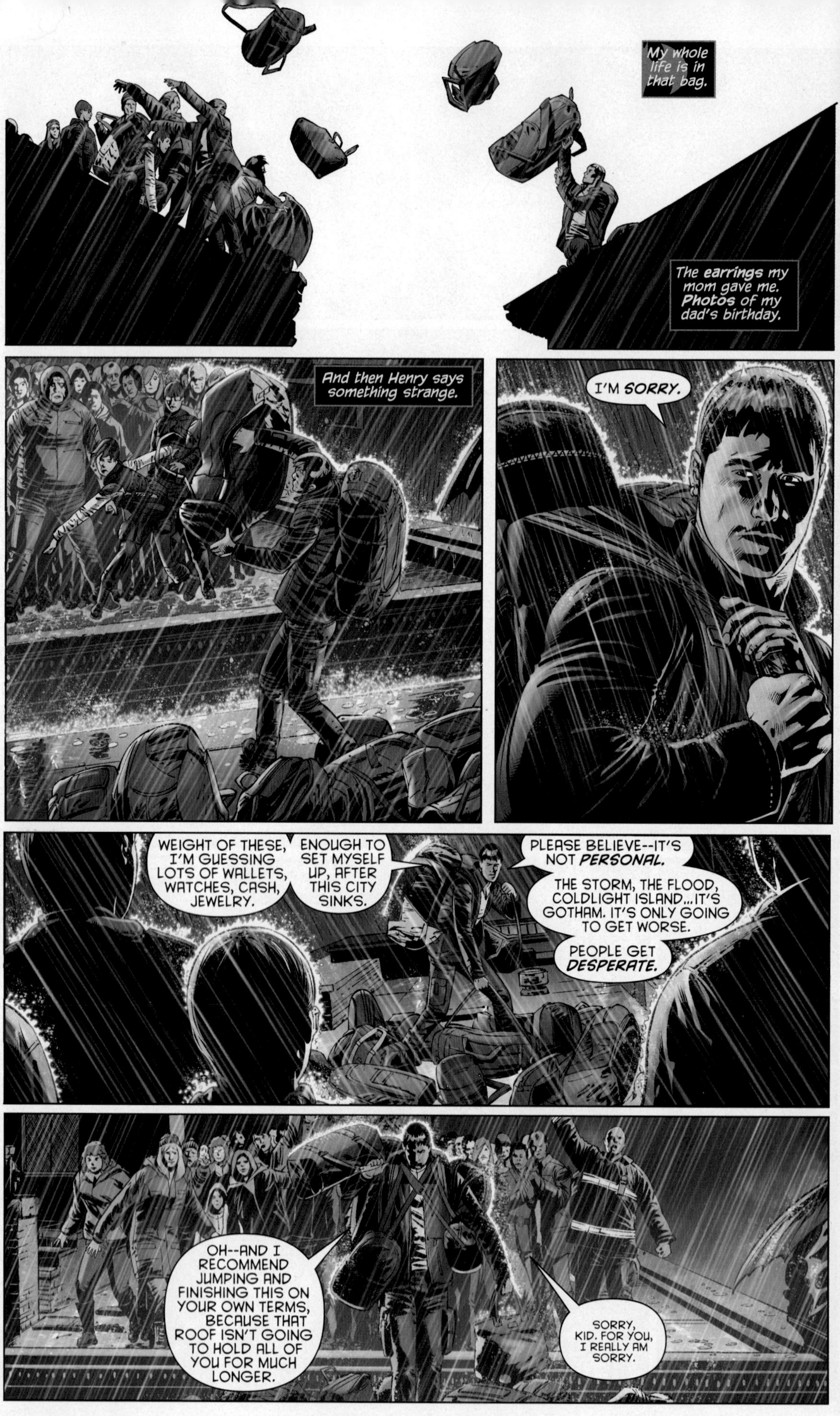
My whole life is in that bag.
The earrings my mom gave me. Photos of my dad's birthday.
And then Henry says something strange.
I'M SORRY.
WEIGHT OF THESE, I'M GUESSING LOTS OF WALLETS, WATCHES, CASH, JEWELRY.
ENOUGH TO SET MYSELF UP, AFTER THIS CITY SINKS.
PLEASE BELIEVE--IT'S NOT PERSONAL.
THE STORM, THE FLOOD, COLDLIGHT ISLAND...IT'S GOTHAM. IT'S ONLY GOING TO GET WORSE.
PEOPLE GET DESPERATE.
OH--AND I RECOMMEND JUMPING AND FINISHING THIS ON YOUR OWN TERMS, BECAUSE THAT ROOF ISN'T GOING TO HOLD ALL OF YOU FOR MUCH LONGER.
SORRY, KID. FOR YOU, I REALLY AM SORRY.

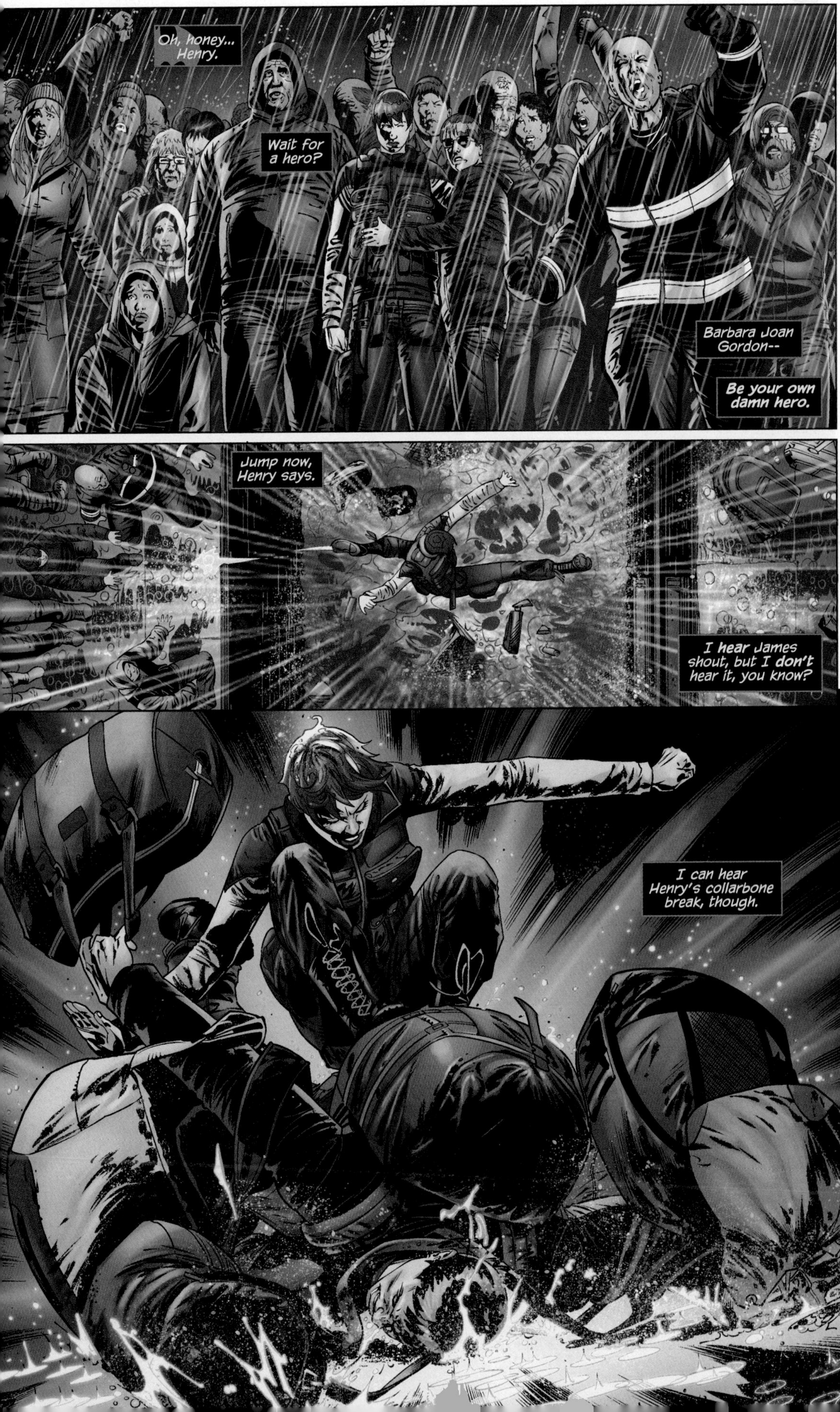

Oh, honey... Henry.
Wait for a hero?
Barbara Joan Gordon--
Be your own damn hero.
Jump now, Henry says.
I hear James shout, but I don't hear it, you know?
I can hear Henry's collarbone break, though.

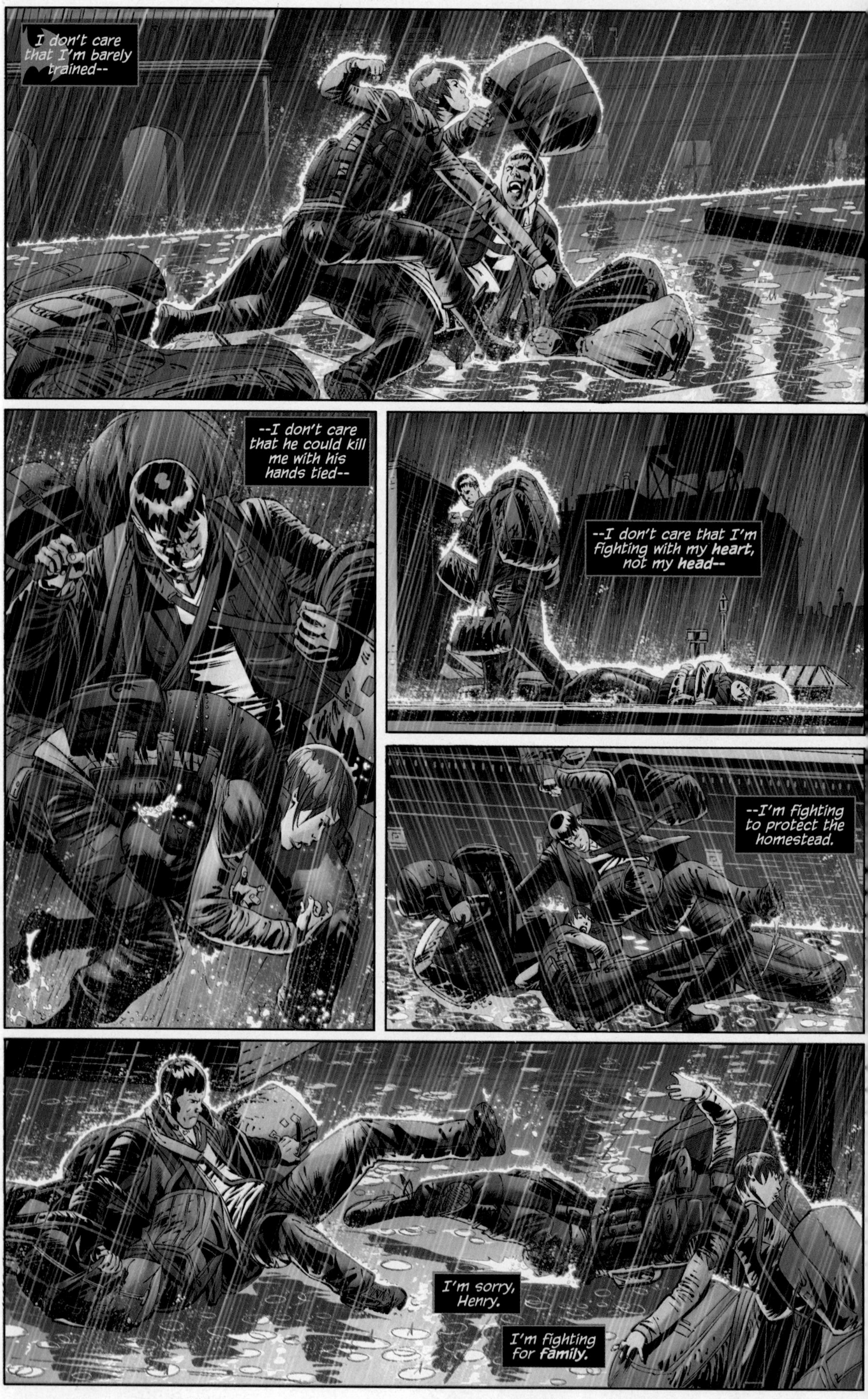
I don't care that I'm barely trained--
--I don't care that he could kill me with his hands tied--
--I don't care that I'm fighting with my heart, not my head--
--I'm fighting to protect the homestead.
I'm sorry, Henry.
I'm fighting for family.

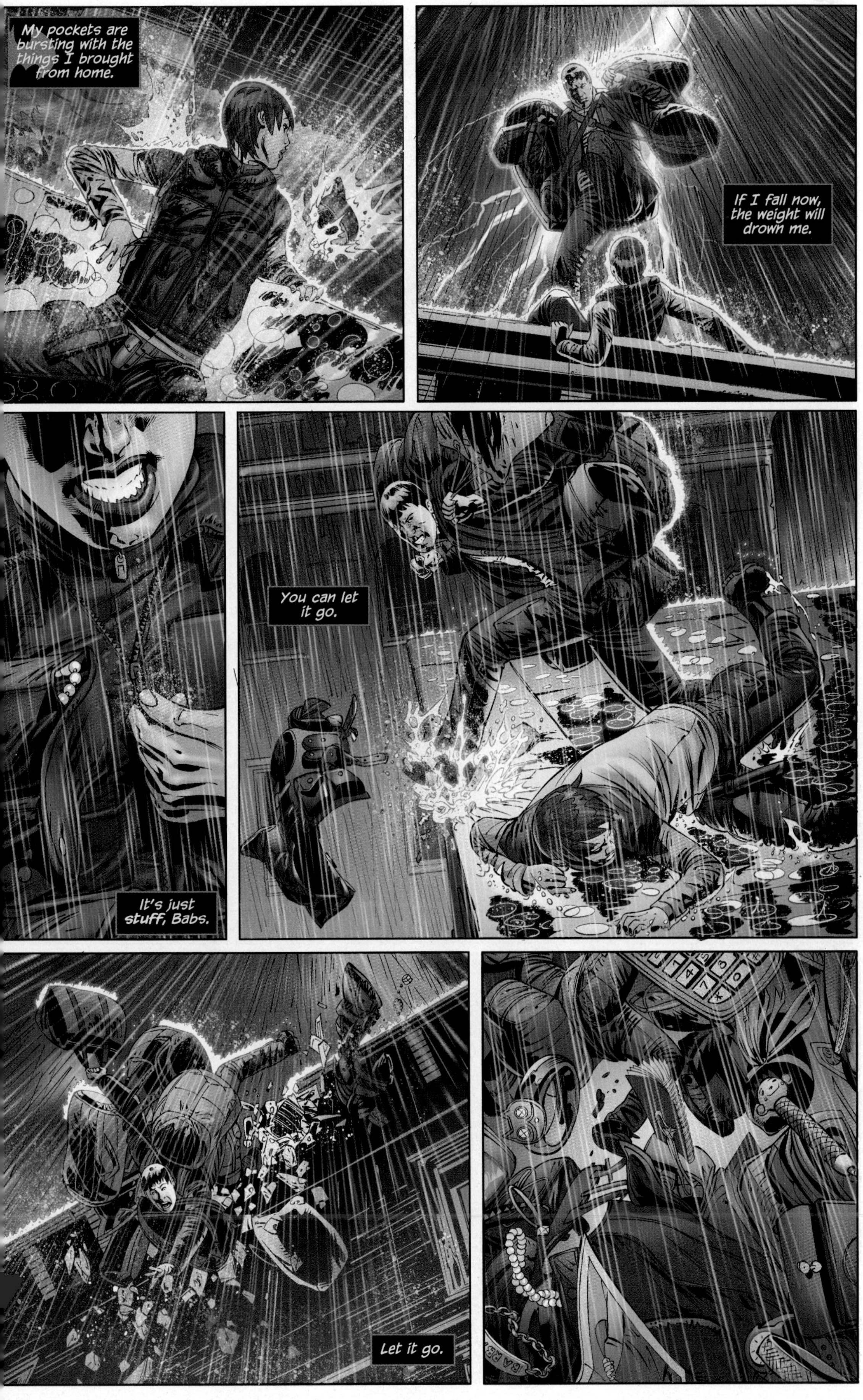
My pockets are bursting with the things I brought from home.
If I fall now, the weight will drown me.
It's just stuff, Babs.
You can let it go.
Let it go.

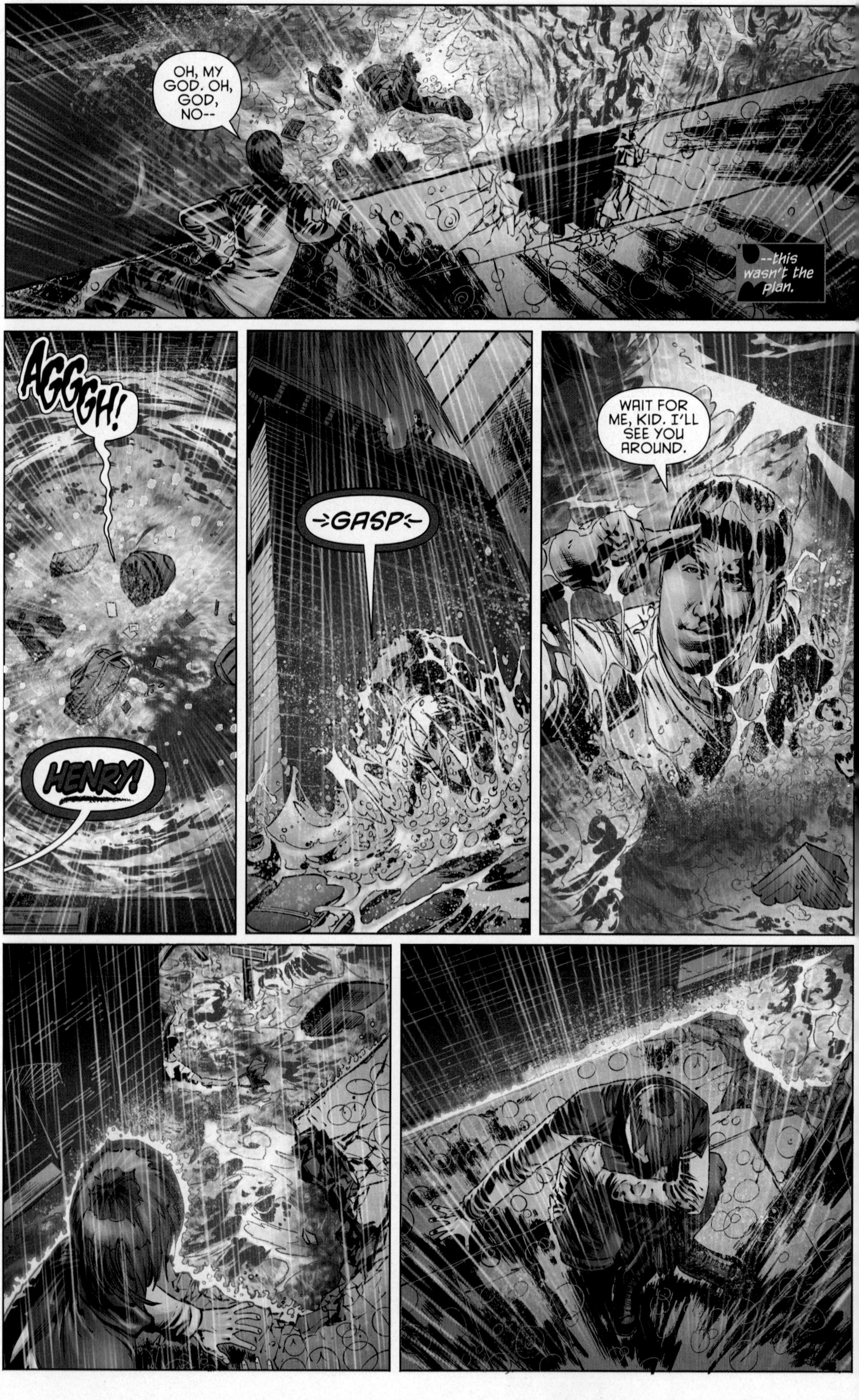
OH, MY GOD. OH, GOD, NO--
--this wasn't the plan.
AGGGH!
HENRY!
GASP
WAIT FOR ME, KID. I'LL SEE YOU AROUND.

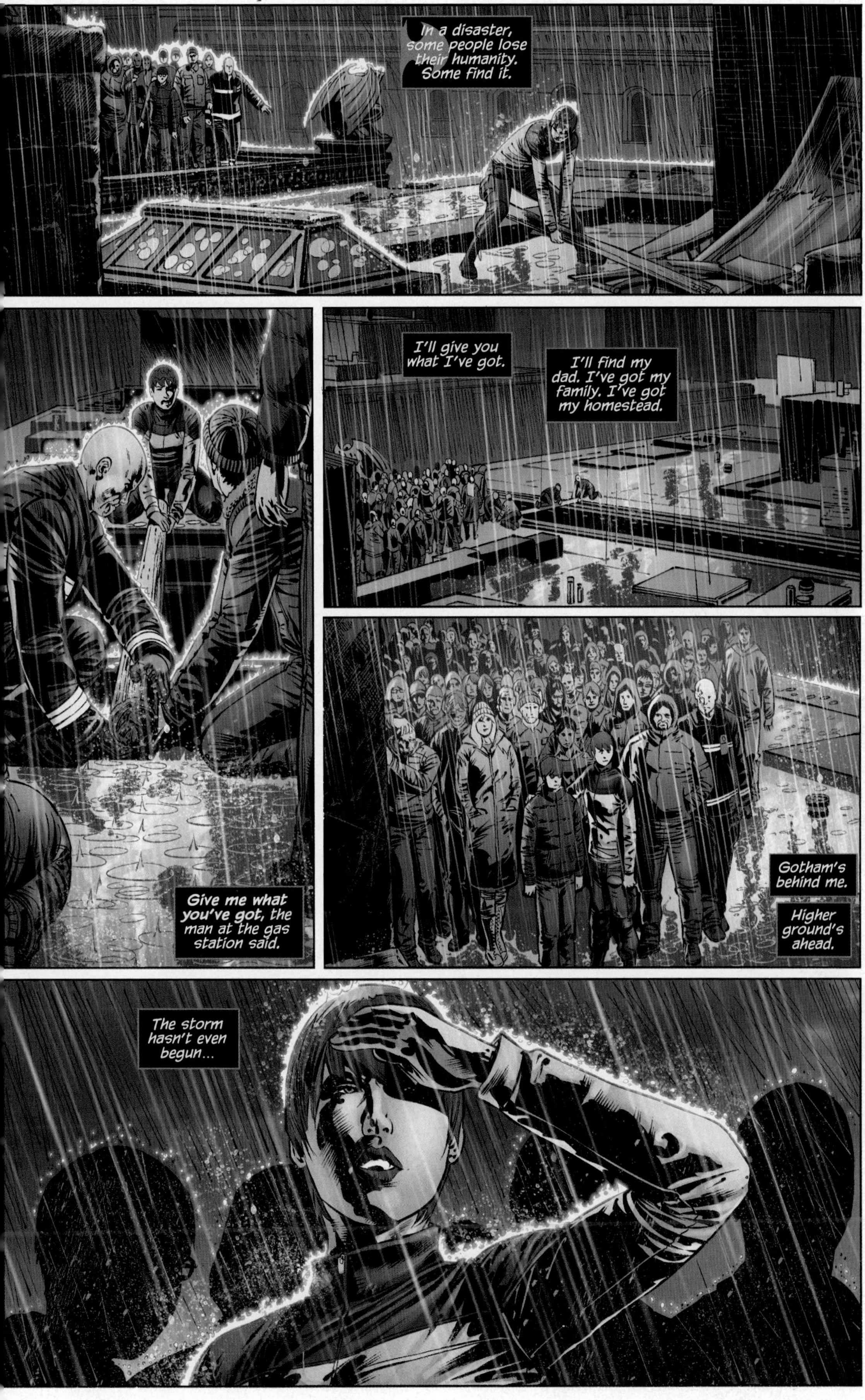
In a disaster, some people lose their humanity. Some find it.
Give me what you've got, the man at the gas station said.
I'll give you what I've got.
I'll find my dad. I've got my family. I've got my homestead.
Gotham's behind me.
Higher ground's ahead.
The storm hasn't even begun...

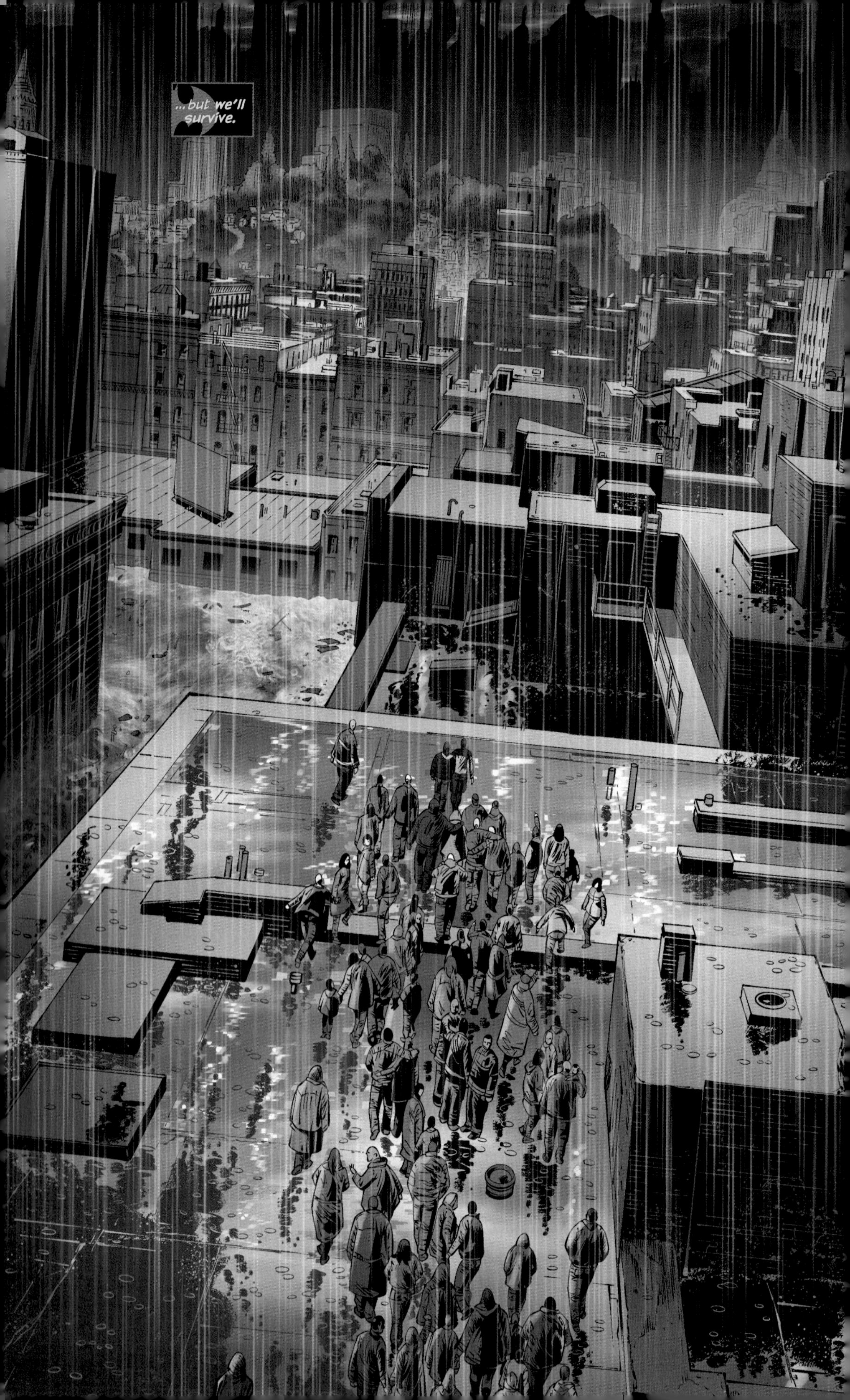
...but we'll survive.

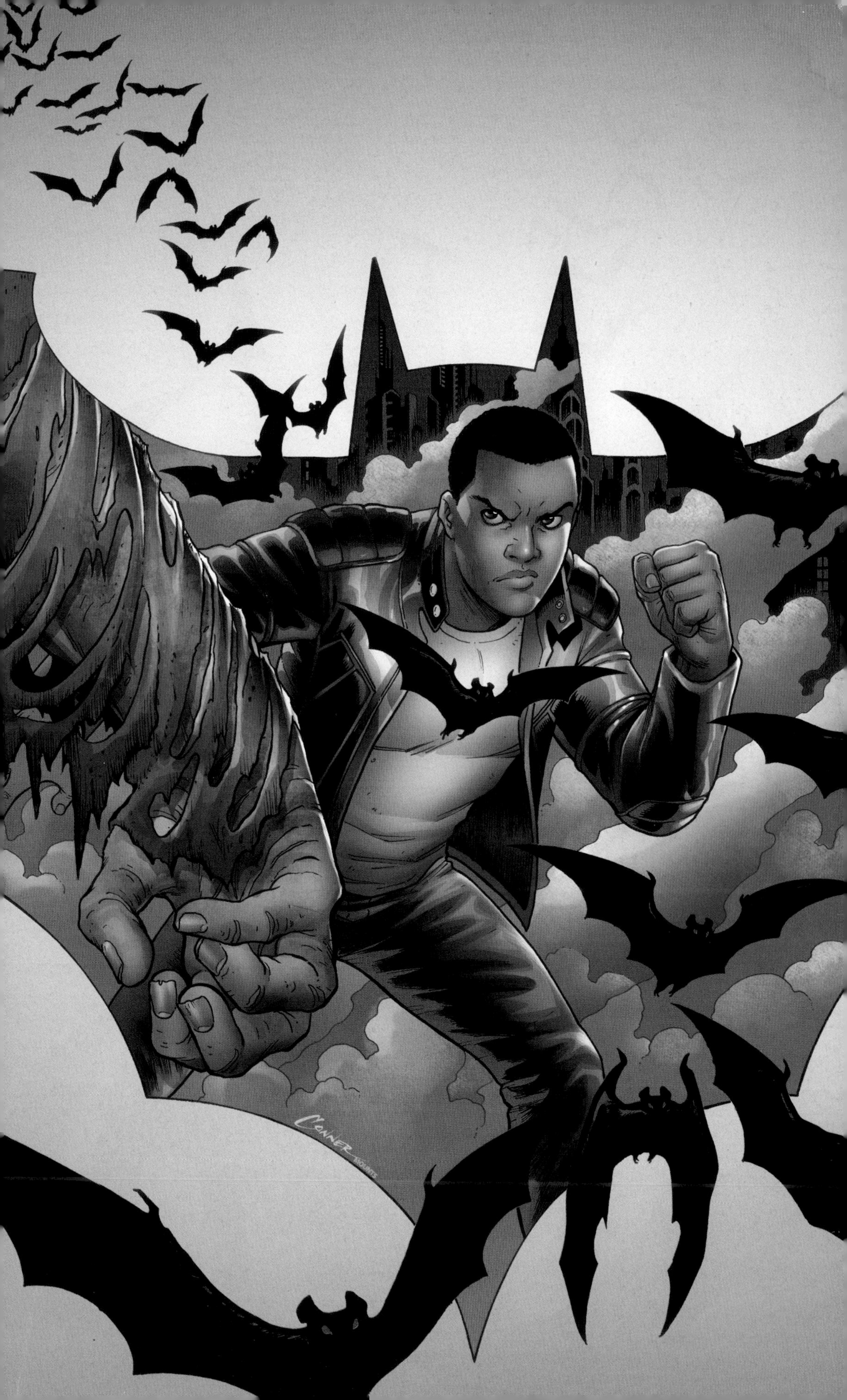

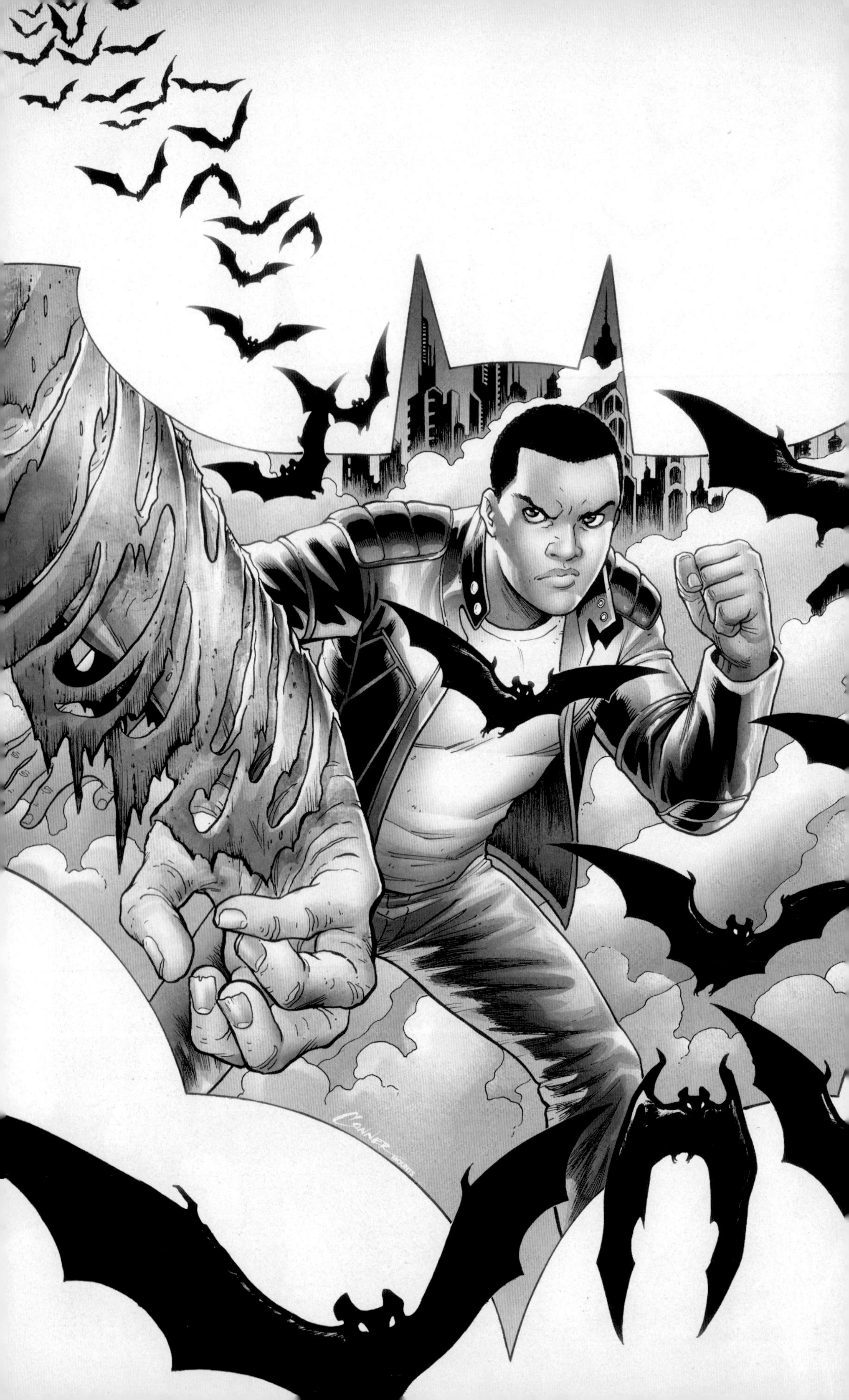

Most of us are taught at a very young age that life is fair.

We're taught to share, to take turns and to treat everyone fairly and equally.

They say there are no winners or losers.

They say all that matters is that you tried your best.

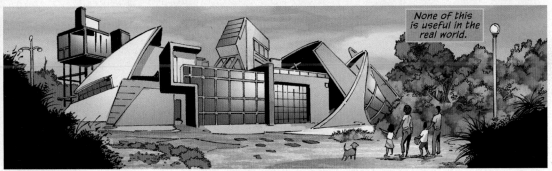

None of this is useful in the real world.

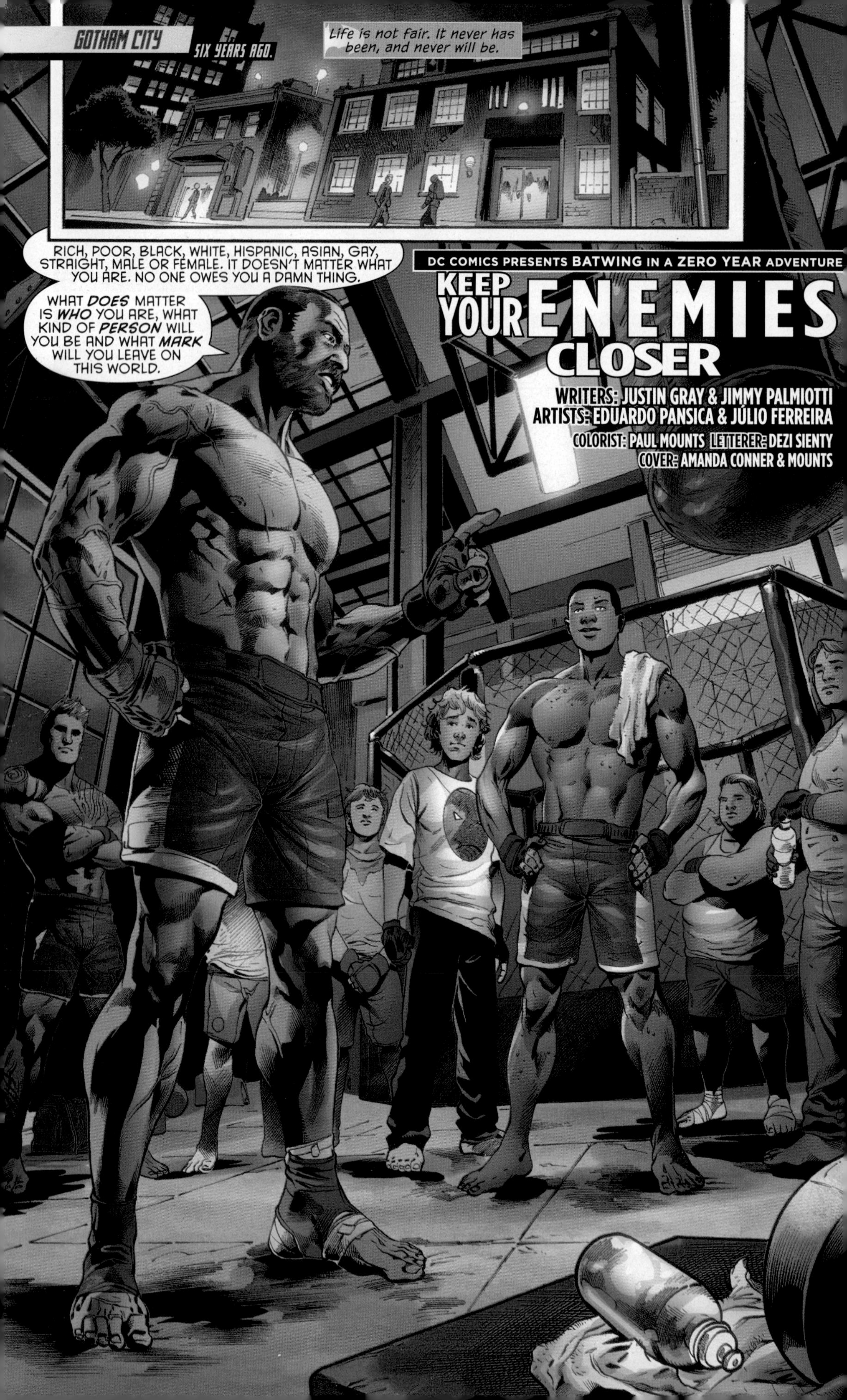

GOTHAM CITY
SIX YEARS AGO.
Life is not fair. It never has been, and never will be.
RICH, POOR, BLACK, WHITE, HISPANIC, ASIAN, GAY, STRAIGHT, MALE OR FEMALE. IT DOESN'T MATTER WHAT YOU ARE. NO ONE OWES YOU A DAMN THING.
WHAT DOES MATTER IS WHO YOU ARE, WHAT KIND OF PERSON WILL YOU BE AND WHAT MARK WILL YOU LEAVE ON THIS WORLD.
DC COMICS PRESENTS BATWING IN A ZERO YEAR ADVENTURE
KEEP YOUR ENEMIES CLOSER
WRITERS: JUSTIN GRAY & JIMMY PALMIOTTI
ARTISTS: EDUARDO PANSICA & JÚLIO FERREIRA
COLORIST: PAUL MOUNTS LETTERER: DEZI SIENTY
COVER: AMANDA CONNER & MOUNTS

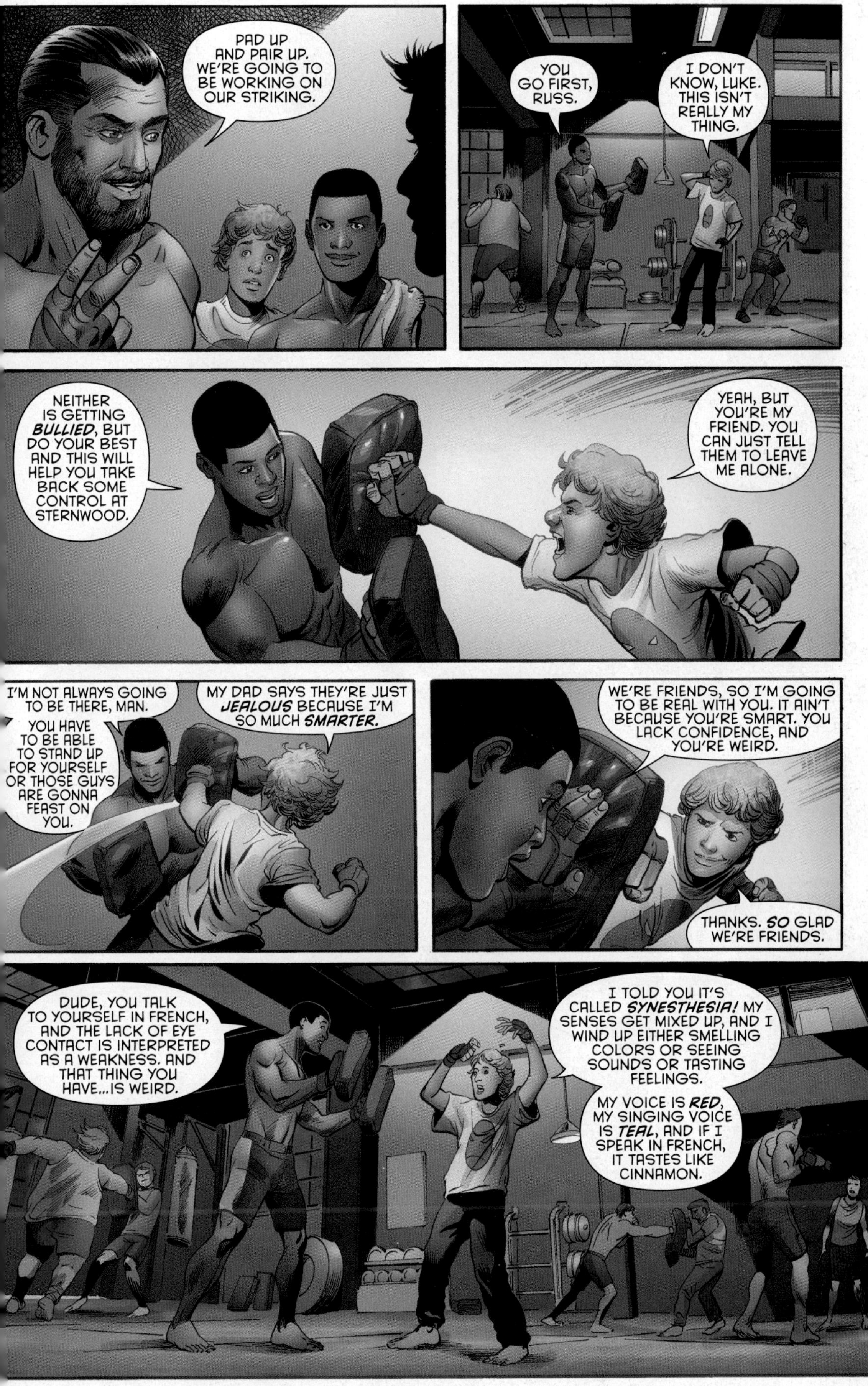
PAD UP AND PAIR UP. WE'RE GOING TO BE WORKING ON OUR STRIKING.
YOU GO FIRST, RUSS.
I DON'T KNOW, LUKE. THIS ISN'T REALLY MY THING.
NEITHER IS GETTING *BULLIED*, BUT DO YOUR BEST AND THIS WILL HELP YOU TAKE BACK SOME CONTROL AT STERNWOOD.
YEAH, BUT YOU'RE MY FRIEND. YOU CAN JUST TELL THEM TO LEAVE ME ALONE.
I'M NOT ALWAYS GOING TO BE THERE, MAN.
YOU HAVE TO BE ABLE TO STAND UP FOR YOURSELF OR THOSE GUYS ARE GONNA FEAST ON YOU.
MY DAD SAYS THEY'RE JUST *JEALOUS* BECAUSE I'M SO MUCH *SMARTER.*
WE'RE FRIENDS, SO I'M GOING TO BE REAL WITH YOU. IT AIN'T BECAUSE YOU'RE SMART. YOU LACK CONFIDENCE, AND YOU'RE WEIRD.
THANKS. *SO* GLAD WE'RE FRIENDS.
DUDE, YOU TALK TO YOURSELF IN FRENCH, AND THE LACK OF EYE CONTACT IS INTERPRETED AS A WEAKNESS. AND THAT THING YOU HAVE...IS WEIRD.
I TOLD YOU IT'S CALLED *SYNESTHESIA!* MY SENSES GET MIXED UP, AND I WIND UP EITHER SMELLING COLORS OR SEEING SOUNDS OR TASTING FEELINGS.
MY VOICE IS *RED*, MY SINGING VOICE IS *TEAL*, AND IF I SPEAK IN FRENCH, IT TASTES LIKE CINNAMON.

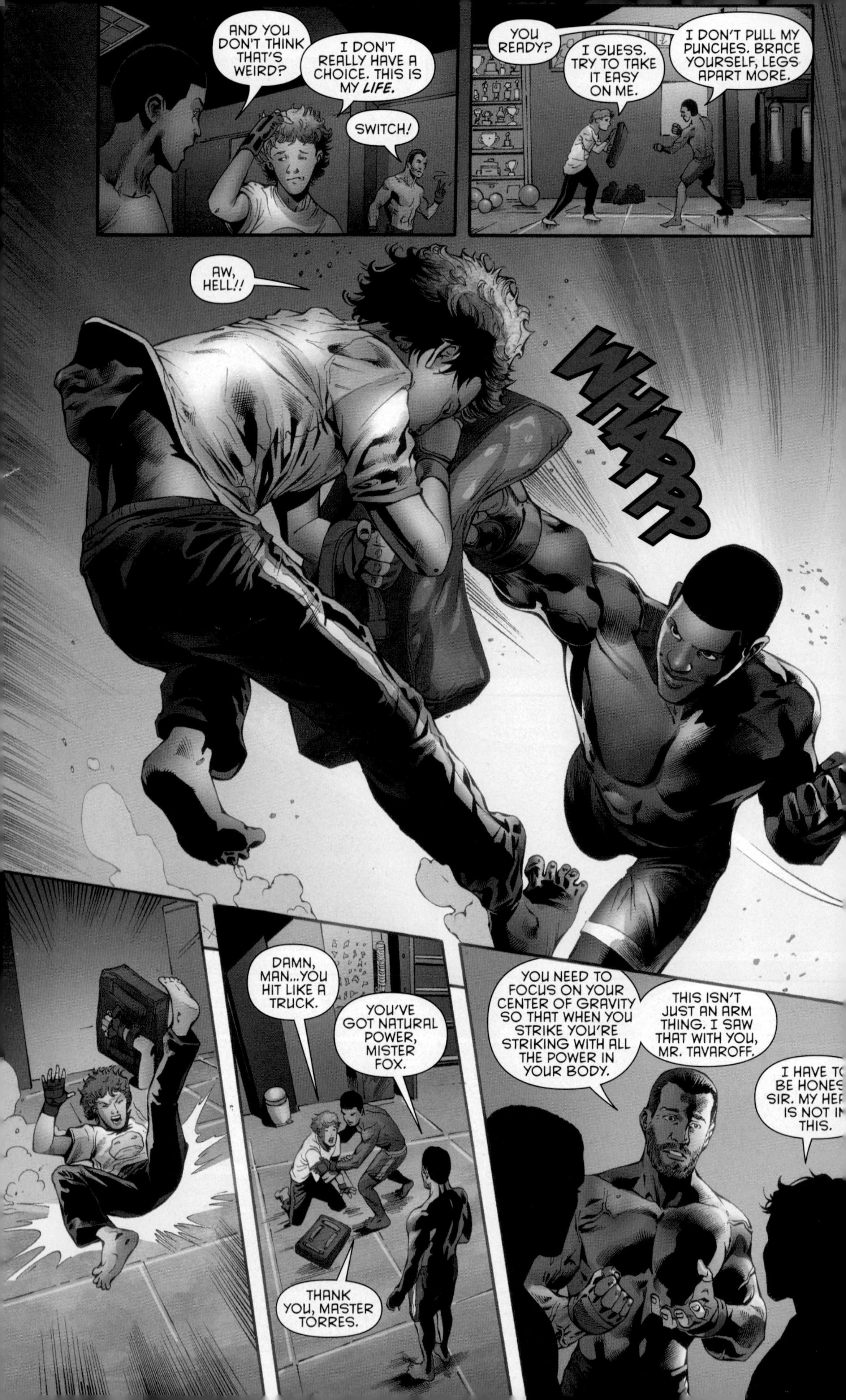

AND YOU DON'T THINK THAT'S WEIRD?
I DON'T REALLY HAVE A CHOICE. THIS IS MY LIFE.
SWITCH!
YOU READY?
I GUESS. TRY TO TAKE IT EASY ON ME.
I DON'T PULL MY PUNCHES. BRACE YOURSELF, LEGS APART MORE.
AW, HELL!!
WHAPPP
DAMN, MAN...YOU HIT LIKE A TRUCK.
YOU'VE GOT NATURAL POWER, MISTER FOX.
THANK YOU, MASTER TORRES.
YOU NEED TO FOCUS ON YOUR CENTER OF GRAVITY SO THAT WHEN YOU STRIKE YOU'RE STRIKING WITH ALL THE POWER IN YOUR BODY.
THIS ISN'T JUST AN ARM THING. I SAW THAT WITH YOU, MR. TAVAROFF.

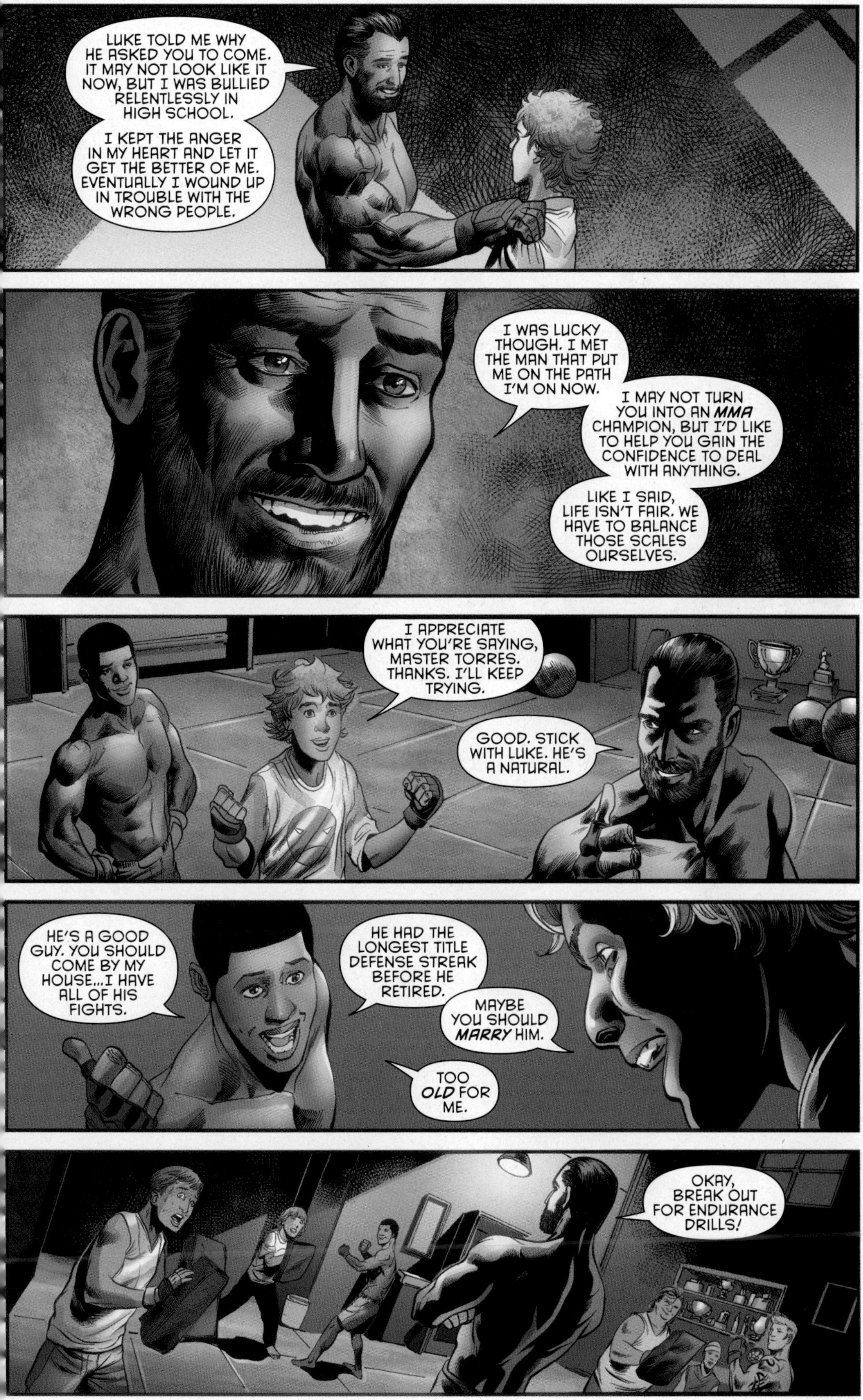
LUKE TOLD ME WHY HE ASKED YOU TO COME. IT MAY NOT LOOK LIKE IT NOW, BUT I WAS BULLIED RELENTLESSLY IN HIGH SCHOOL.
I KEPT THE ANGER IN MY HEART AND LET IT GET THE BETTER OF ME. EVENTUALLY I WOUND UP IN TROUBLE WITH THE WRONG PEOPLE.
I WAS LUCKY THOUGH. I MET THE MAN THAT PUT ME ON THE PATH I'M ON NOW.
I MAY NOT TURN YOU INTO AN MMA CHAMPION, BUT I'D LIKE TO HELP YOU GAIN THE CONFIDENCE TO DEAL WITH ANYTHING.
LIKE I SAID, LIFE ISN'T FAIR. WE HAVE TO BALANCE THOSE SCALES OURSELVES.
I APPRECIATE WHAT YOU'RE SAYING, MASTER TORRES. THANKS. I'LL KEEP TRYING.
GOOD. STICK WITH LUKE. HE'S A NATURAL.
HE'S A GOOD GUY. YOU SHOULD COME BY MY HOUSE...I HAVE ALL OF HIS FIGHTS.
HE HAD THE LONGEST TITLE DEFENSE STREAK BEFORE HE RETIRED.
MAYBE YOU SHOULD MARRY HIM.
TOO OLD FOR ME.
OKAY, BREAK OUT FOR ENDURANCE DRILLS!

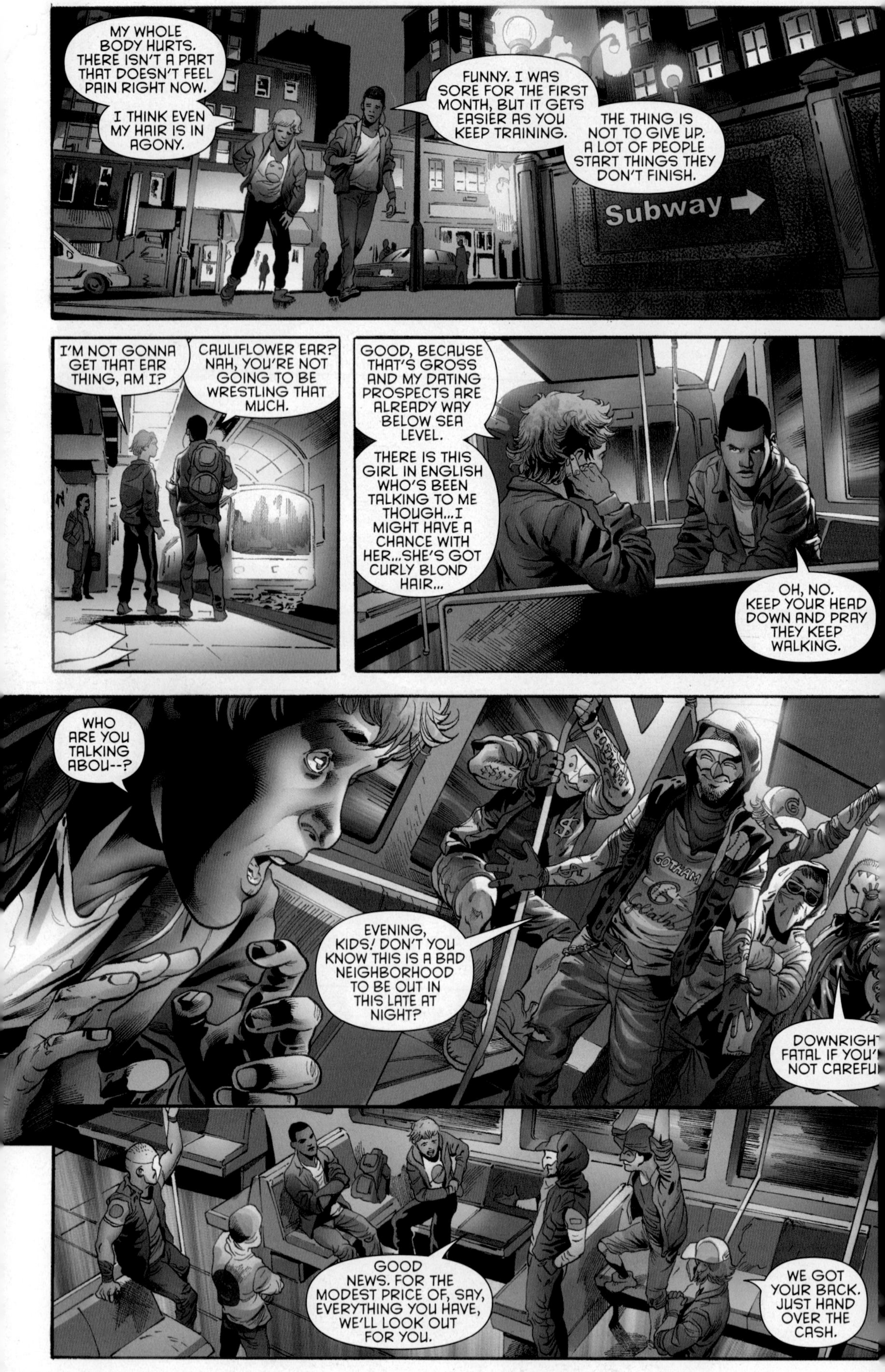
MY WHOLE BODY HURTS. THERE ISN'T A PART THAT DOESN'T FEEL PAIN RIGHT NOW.
I THINK EVEN MY HAIR IS IN AGONY.
FUNNY. I WAS SORE FOR THE FIRST MONTH, BUT IT GETS EASIER AS YOU KEEP TRAINING.
THE THING IS NOT TO GIVE UP. A LOT OF PEOPLE START THINGS THEY DON'T FINISH.
Subway
I'M NOT GONNA GET THAT EAR THING, AM I?
CAULIFLOWER EAR? NAH, YOU'RE NOT GOING TO BE WRESTLING THAT MUCH.
GOOD, BECAUSE THAT'S GROSS AND MY DATING PROSPECTS ARE ALREADY WAY BELOW SEA LEVEL.
THERE IS THIS GIRL IN ENGLISH WHO'S BEEN TALKING TO ME THOUGH...I MIGHT HAVE A CHANCE WITH HER...SHE'S GOT CURLY BLOND HAIR...
OH, NO. KEEP YOUR HEAD DOWN AND PRAY THEY KEEP WALKING.
WHO ARE YOU TALKING ABOU--?
EVENING, KIDS! DON'T YOU KNOW THIS IS A BAD NEIGHBORHOOD TO BE OUT IN THIS LATE AT NIGHT?
DOWNRIGHT FATAL IF YOU' NOT CAREFU
GOOD NEWS. FOR THE MODEST PRICE OF, SAY, EVERYTHING YOU HAVE, WE'LL LOOK OUT FOR YOU.
WE GOT YOUR BACK. JUST HAND OVER THE CASH.

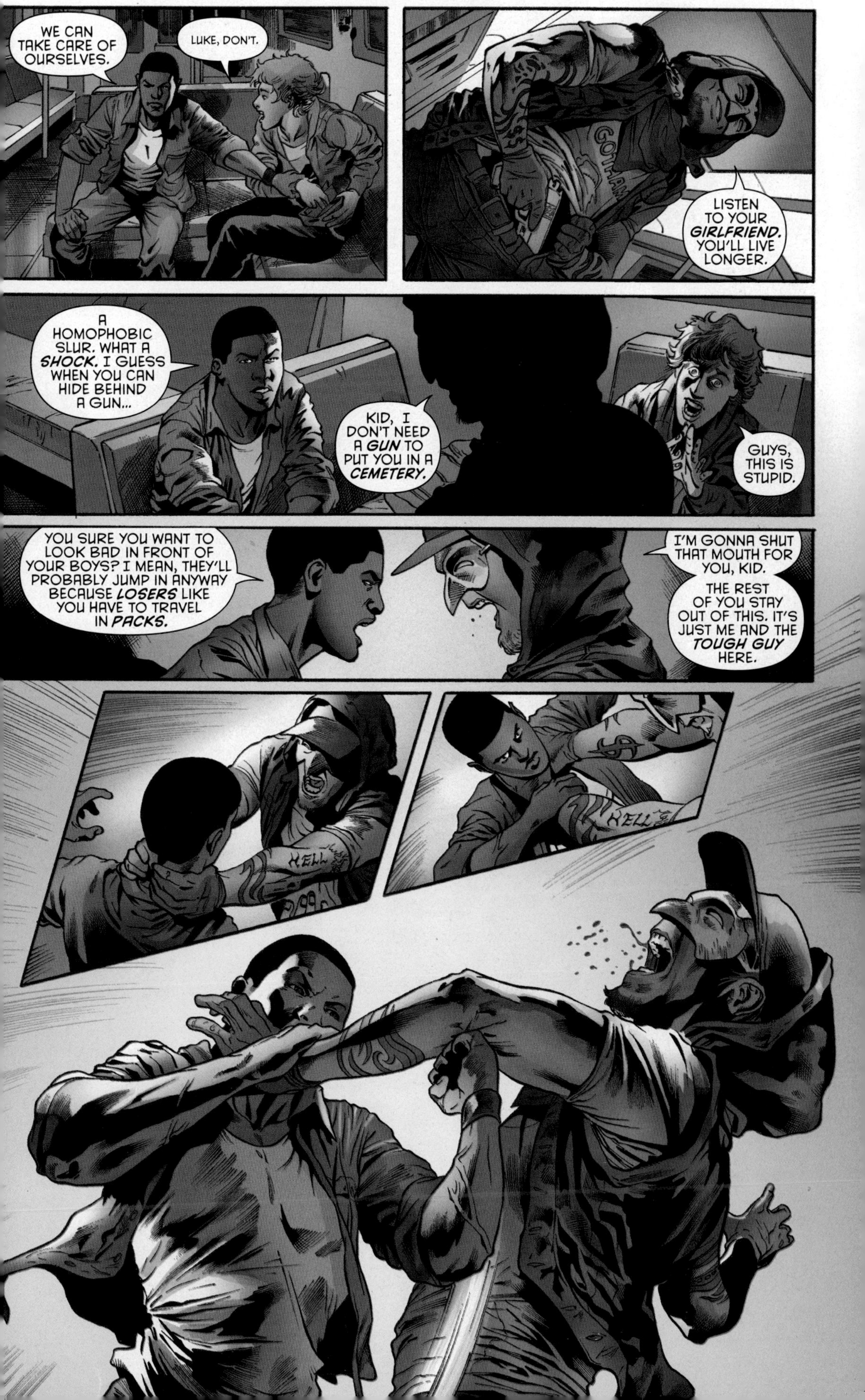
WE CAN TAKE CARE OF OURSELVES.
LUKE, DON'T.
LISTEN TO YOUR GIRLFRIEND. YOU'LL LIVE LONGER.
A HOMOPHOBIC SLUR. WHAT A SHOCK. I GUESS WHEN YOU CAN HIDE BEHIND A GUN...
KID, I DON'T NEED A GUN TO PUT YOU IN A CEMETERY.
GUYS, THIS IS STUPID.
YOU SURE YOU WANT TO LOOK BAD IN FRONT OF YOUR BOYS? I MEAN, THEY'LL PROBABLY JUMP IN ANYWAY BECAUSE LOSERS LIKE YOU HAVE TO TRAVEL IN PACKS.
I'M GONNA SHUT THAT MOUTH FOR YOU, KID.
THE REST OF YOU STAY OUT OF THIS. IT'S JUST ME AND THE TOUGH GUY HERE.

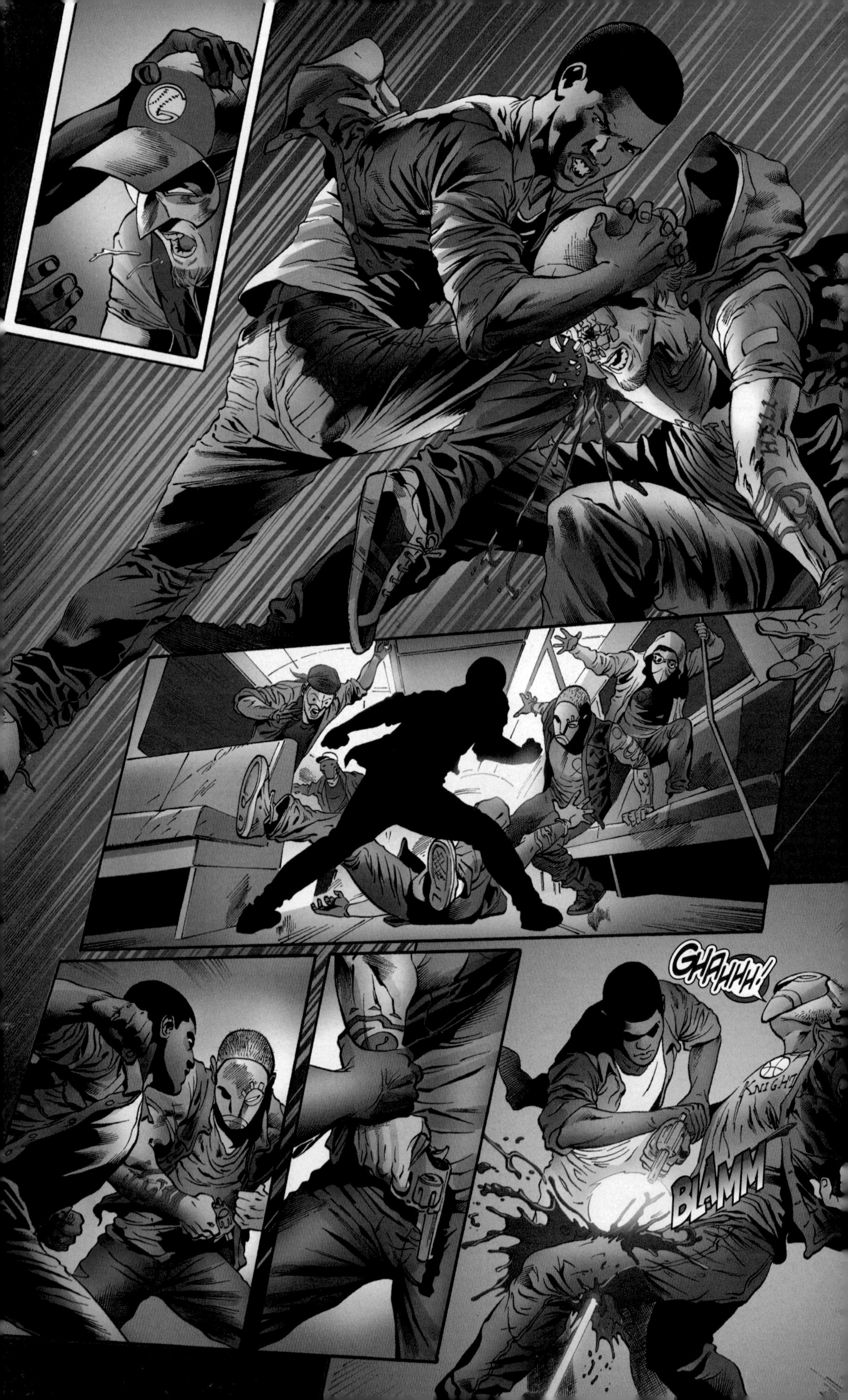
GHAHHH!
BLAMM

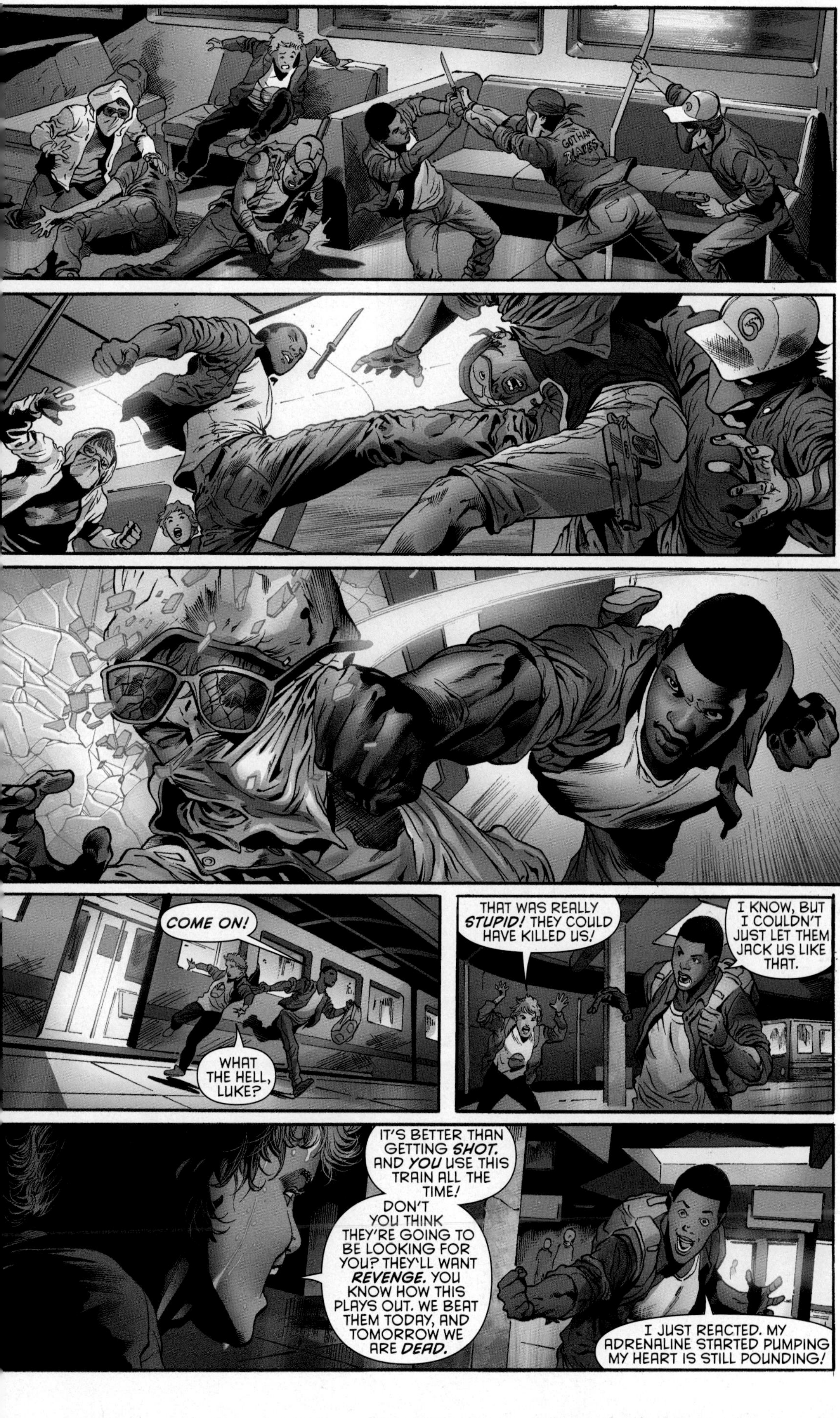
GOTHAM
COME ON!
WHAT THE HELL, LUKE?
THAT WAS REALLY STUPID! THEY COULD HAVE KILLED US!
I KNOW, BUT I COULDN'T JUST LET THEM JACK US LIKE THAT.
IT'S BETTER THAN GETTING SHOT. AND YOU USE THIS TRAIN ALL THE TIME!
DON'T YOU THINK THEY'RE GOING TO BE LOOKING FOR YOU? THEY'LL WANT REVENGE. YOU KNOW HOW THIS PLAYS OUT. WE BEAT THEM TODAY, AND TOMORROW WE ARE DEAD.
I JUST REACTED. MY ADRENALINE STARTED PUMPING. MY HEART IS STILL POUNDING!

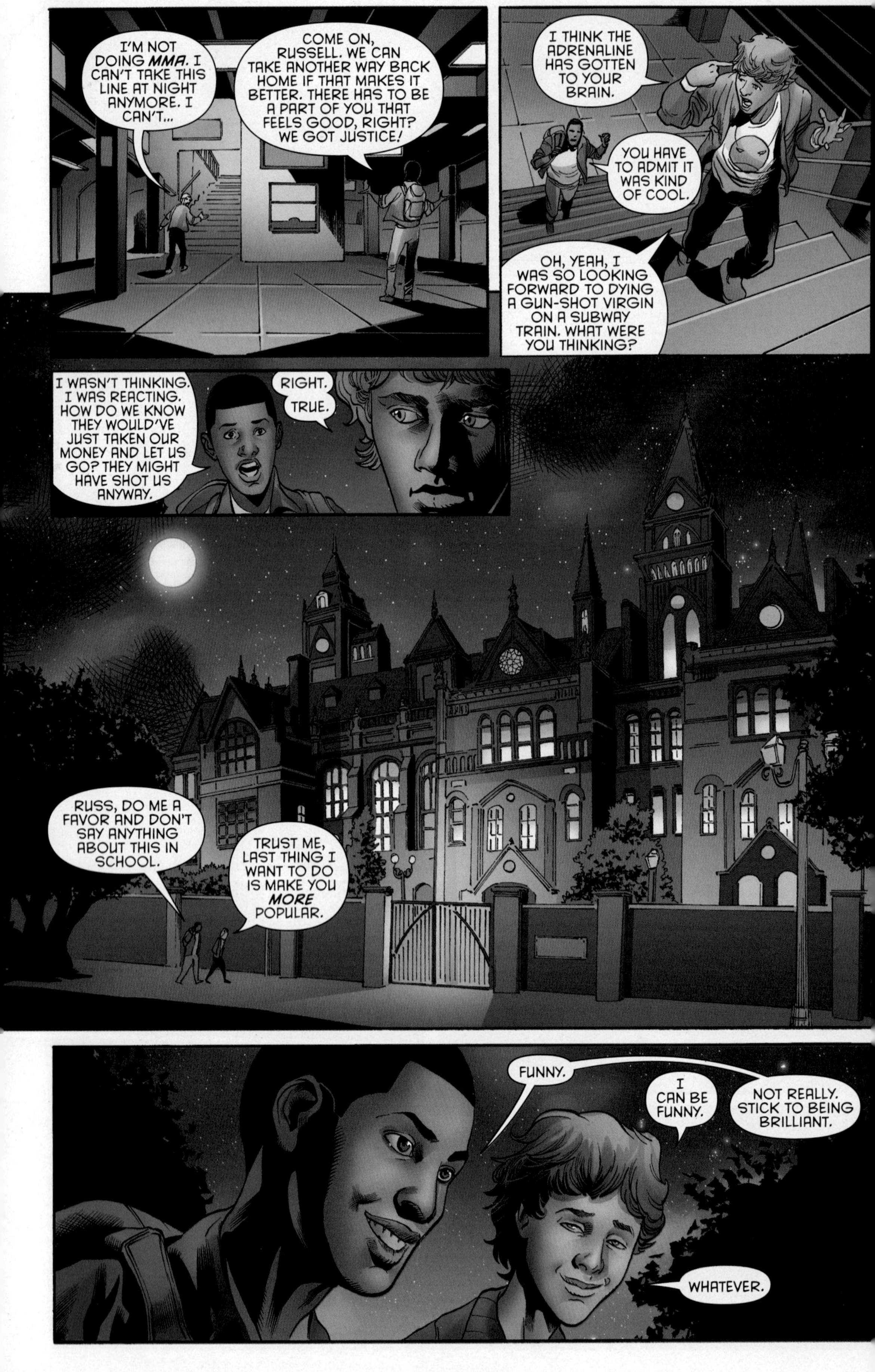
I'M NOT DOING *MMA*. I CAN'T TAKE THIS LINE AT NIGHT ANYMORE. I CAN'T...
COME ON, RUSSELL. WE CAN TAKE ANOTHER WAY BACK HOME IF THAT MAKES IT BETTER. THERE HAS TO BE A PART OF YOU THAT FEELS GOOD, RIGHT? WE GOT JUSTICE!
I THINK THE ADRENALINE HAS GOTTEN TO YOUR BRAIN.
YOU HAVE TO ADMIT IT WAS KIND OF COOL.
OH, YEAH, I WAS SO LOOKING FORWARD TO DYING A GUN-SHOT VIRGIN ON A SUBWAY TRAIN. WHAT WERE YOU THINKING?
I WASN'T THINKING. I WAS REACTING. HOW DO WE KNOW THEY WOULD'VE JUST TAKEN OUR MONEY AND LET US GO? THEY MIGHT HAVE SHOT US ANYWAY.
RIGHT. TRUE.
RUSS, DO ME A FAVOR AND DON'T SAY ANYTHING ABOUT THIS IN SCHOOL.
TRUST ME, LAST THING I WANT TO DO IS MAKE YOU *MORE* POPULAR.
FUNNY.
I CAN BE FUNNY.
NOT REALLY. STICK TO BEING BRILLIANT.
WHATEVER.

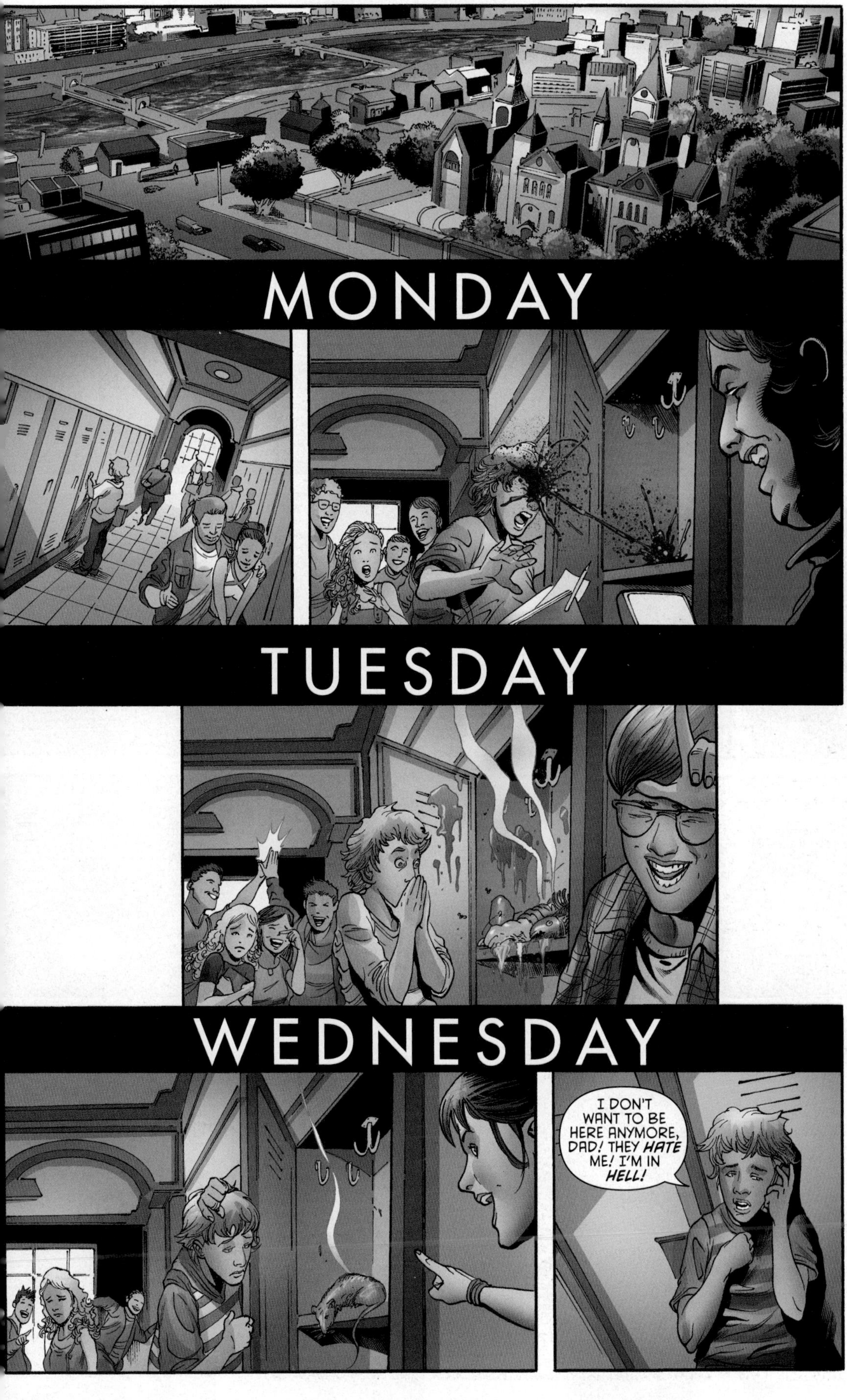
MONDAY
TUESDAY
WEDNESDAY
I DON'T WANT TO BE HERE ANYMORE, DAD! THEY *HATE* ME! I'M IN *HELL!*

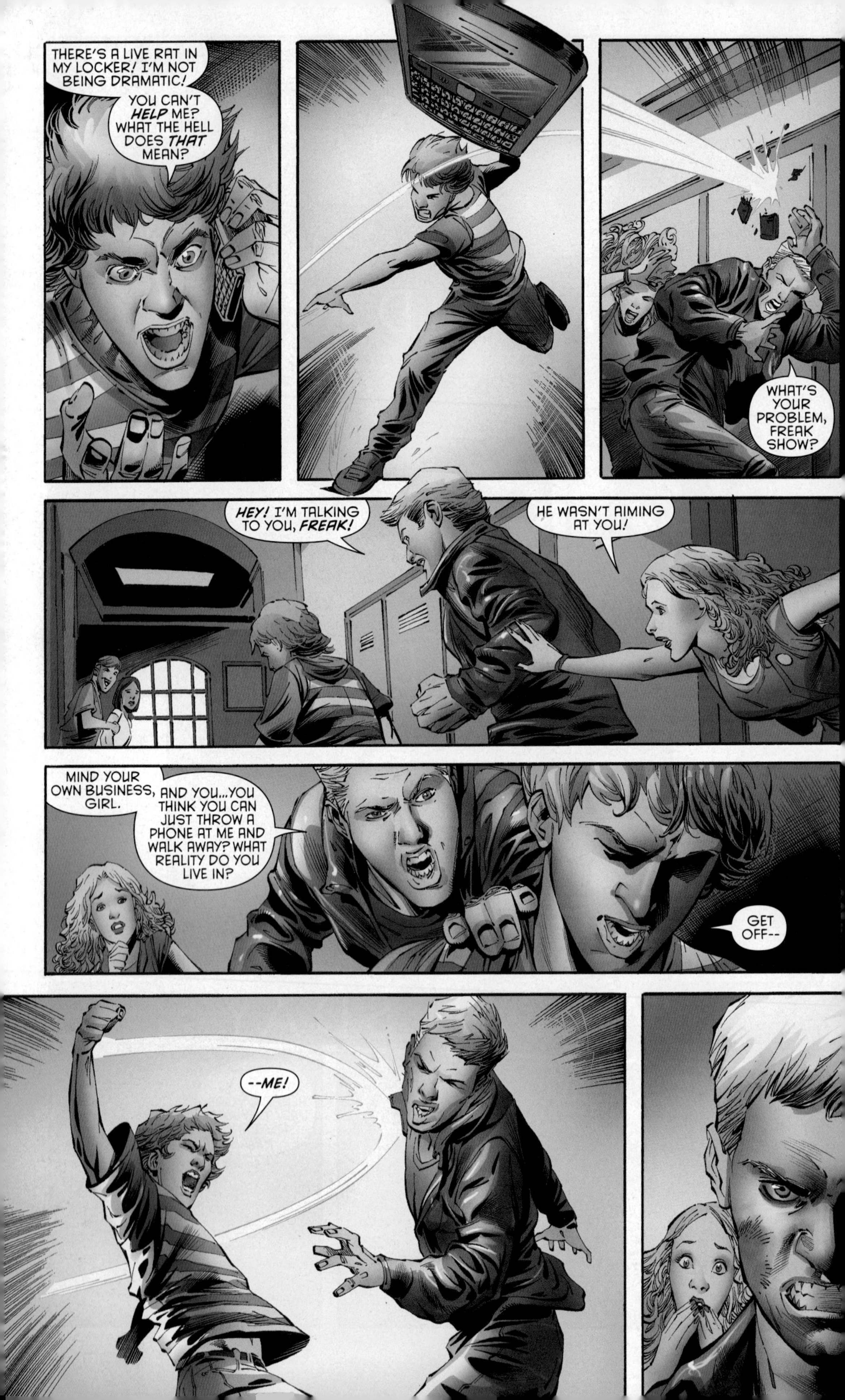

THERE'S A LIVE RAT IN MY LOCKER! I'M NOT BEING DRAMATIC!
YOU CAN'T *HELP* ME? WHAT THE HELL DOES *THAT* MEAN?
WHAT'S YOUR PROBLEM, FREAK SHOW?
HEY! I'M TALKING TO YOU, *FREAK!*
HE WASN'T AIMING AT YOU!
MIND YOUR OWN BUSINESS, GIRL.
AND YOU...YOU THINK YOU CAN JUST THROW A PHONE AT ME AND WALK AWAY? WHAT REALITY DO YOU LIVE IN?
GET OFF--
--*ME!*

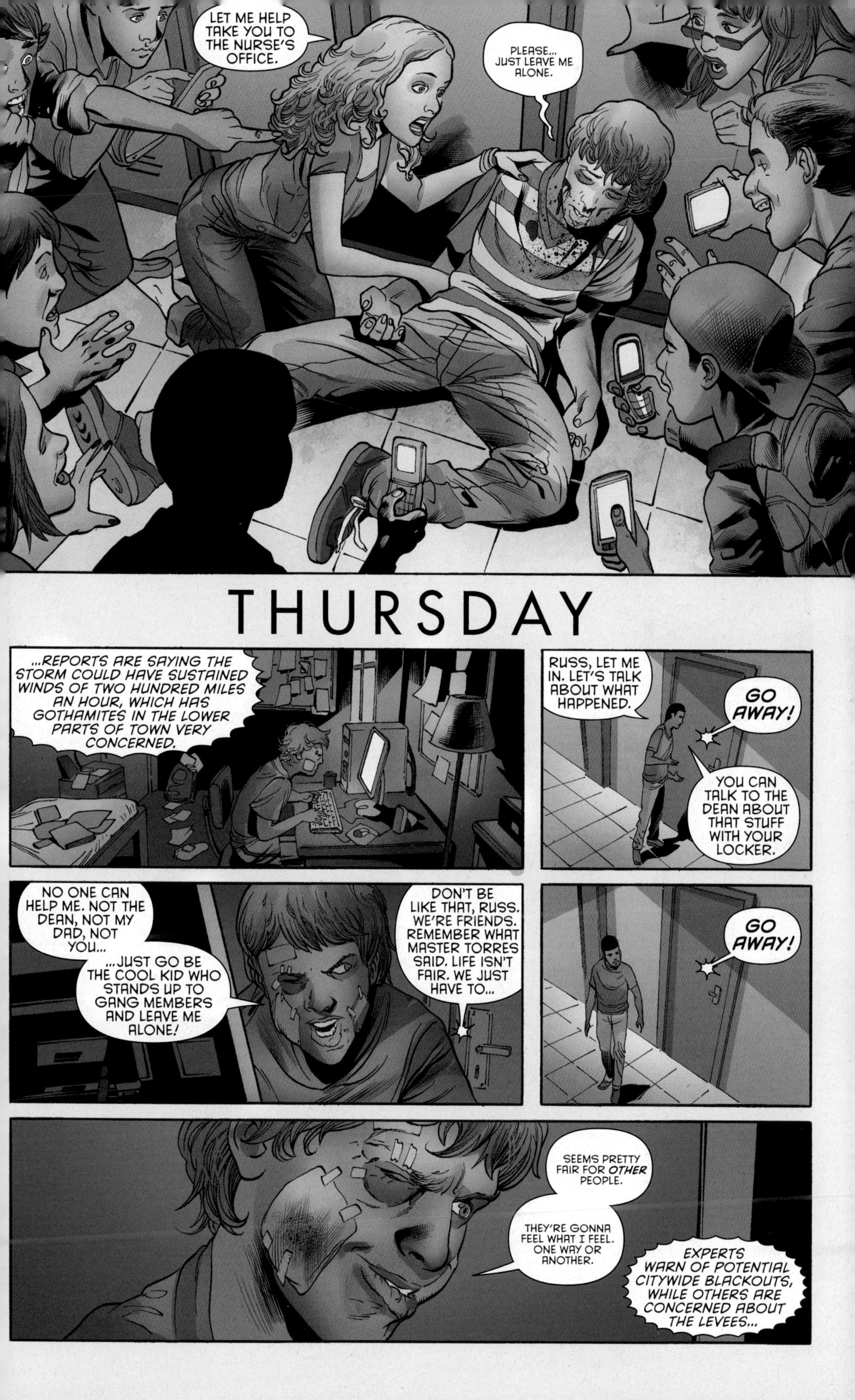
LET ME HELP TAKE YOU TO THE NURSE'S OFFICE.
PLEASE... JUST LEAVE ME ALONE.
THURSDAY
...REPORTS ARE SAYING THE STORM COULD HAVE SUSTAINED WINDS OF TWO HUNDRED MILES AN HOUR, WHICH HAS GOTHAMITES IN THE LOWER PARTS OF TOWN VERY CONCERNED.
RUSS, LET ME IN. LET'S TALK ABOUT WHAT HAPPENED.
GO AWAY!
YOU CAN TALK TO THE DEAN ABOUT THAT STUFF WITH YOUR LOCKER.
NO ONE CAN HELP ME. NOT THE DEAN, NOT MY DAD, NOT YOU...
...JUST GO BE THE COOL KID WHO STANDS UP TO GANG MEMBERS AND LEAVE ME ALONE!
DON'T BE LIKE THAT, RUSS. WE'RE FRIENDS. REMEMBER WHAT MASTER TORRES SAID. LIFE ISN'T FAIR. WE JUST HAVE TO...
GO AWAY!
SEEMS PRETTY FAIR FOR OTHER PEOPLE.
THEY'RE GONNA FEEL WHAT I FEEL. ONE WAY OR ANOTHER.
EXPERTS WARN OF POTENTIAL CITYWIDE BLACKOUTS, WHILE OTHERS ARE CONCERNED ABOUT THE LEVEES...

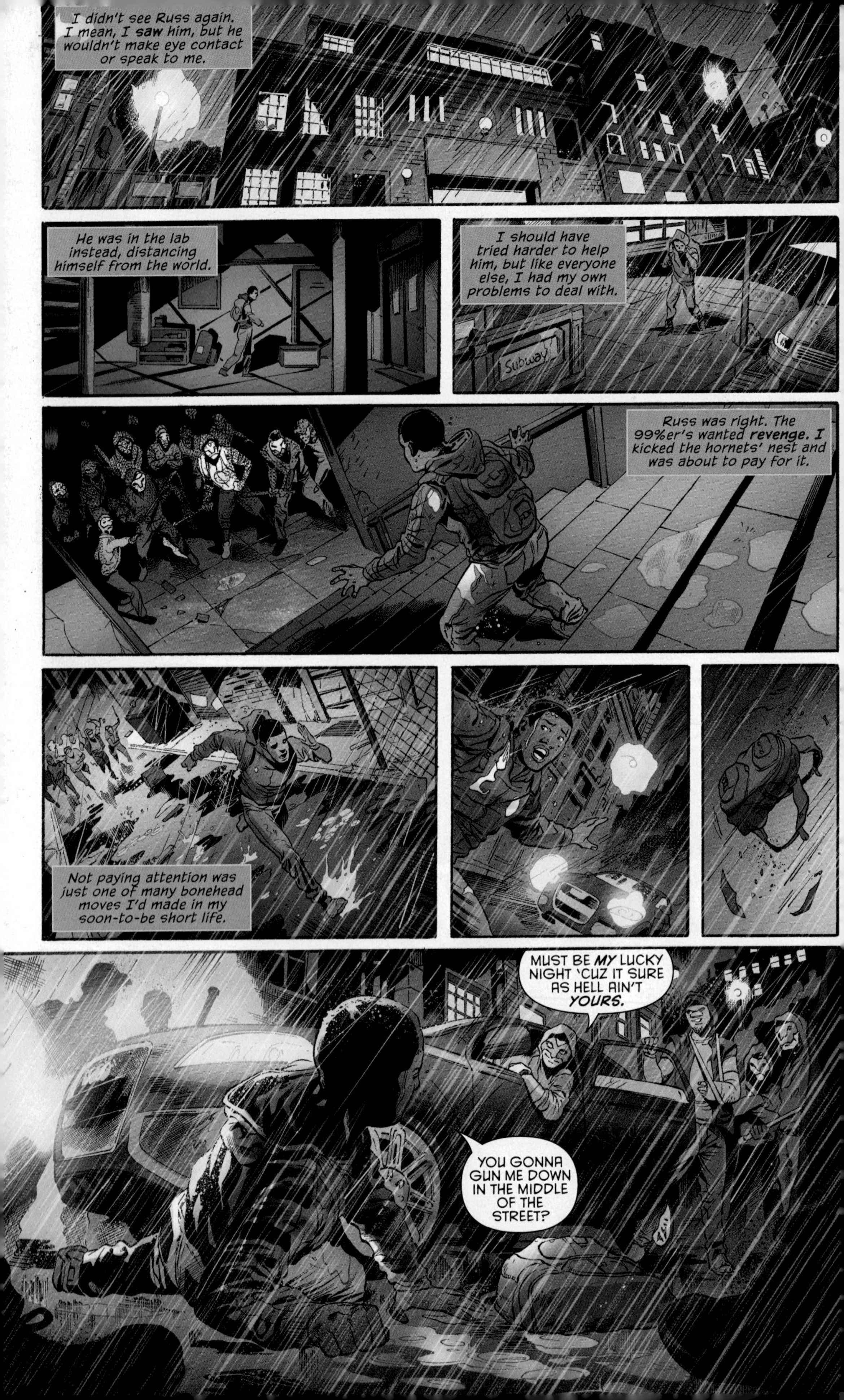
I didn't see Russ again. I mean, I saw him, but he wouldn't make eye contact or speak to me.
He was in the lab instead, distancing himself from the world.
I should have tried harder to help him, but like everyone else, I had my own problems to deal with.
Subway
Russ was right. The 99%er's wanted revenge. I kicked the hornets' nest and was about to pay for it.
Not paying attention was just one of many bonehead moves I'd made in my soon-to-be short life.
MUST BE MY LUCKY NIGHT 'CUZ IT SURE AS HELL AIN'T YOURS.
YOU GONNA GUN ME DOWN IN THE MIDDLE OF THE STREET?

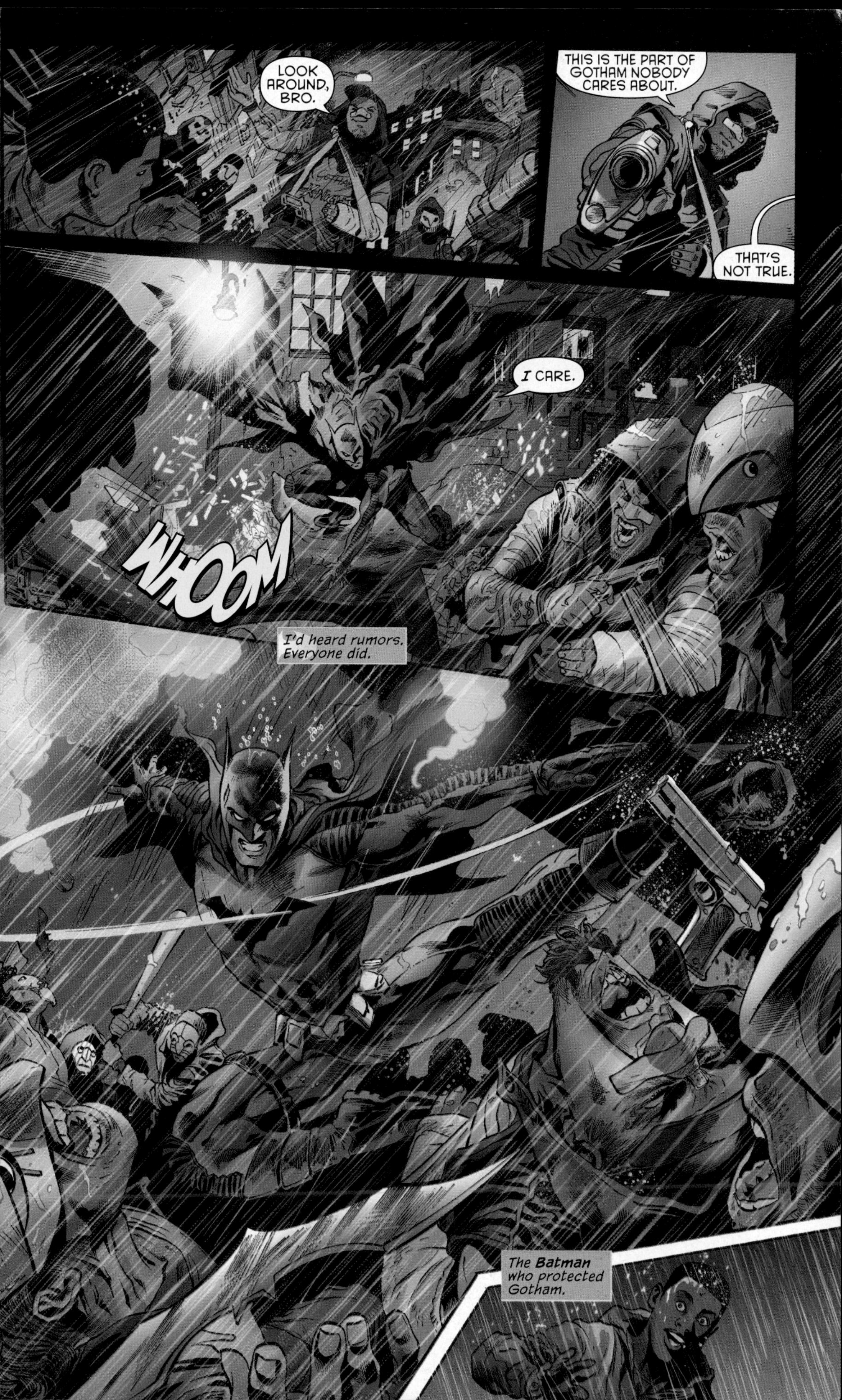
LOOK AROUND, BRO.
THIS IS THE PART OF GOTHAM NOBODY CARES ABOUT.
THAT'S NOT TRUE.
I CARE.
WHOOM
I'd heard rumors. Everyone did.
The Batman who protected Gotham.

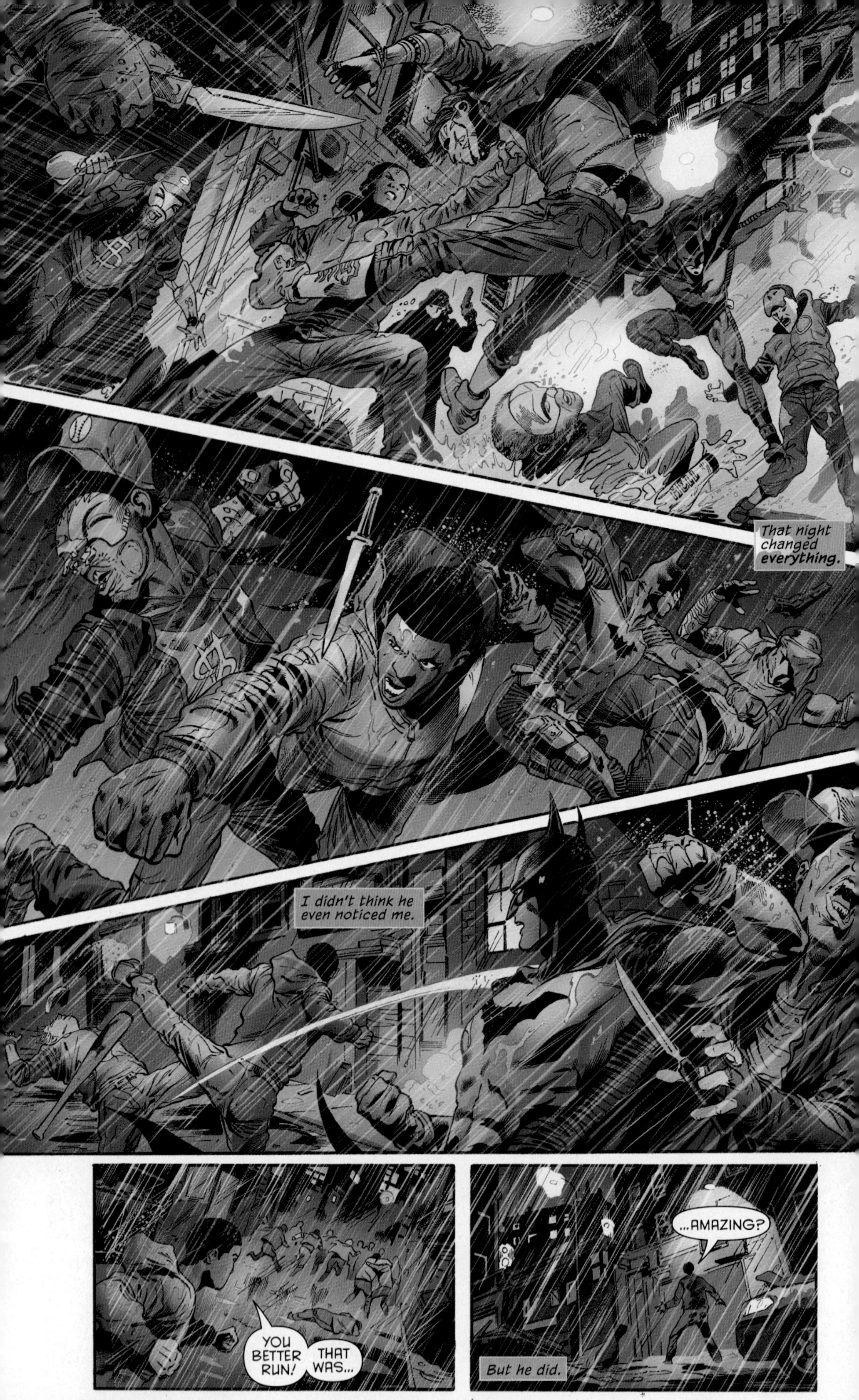
That night changed everything.
I didn't think he even noticed me.
YOU BETTER RUN!
THAT WAS...
...AMAZING?
But he did.

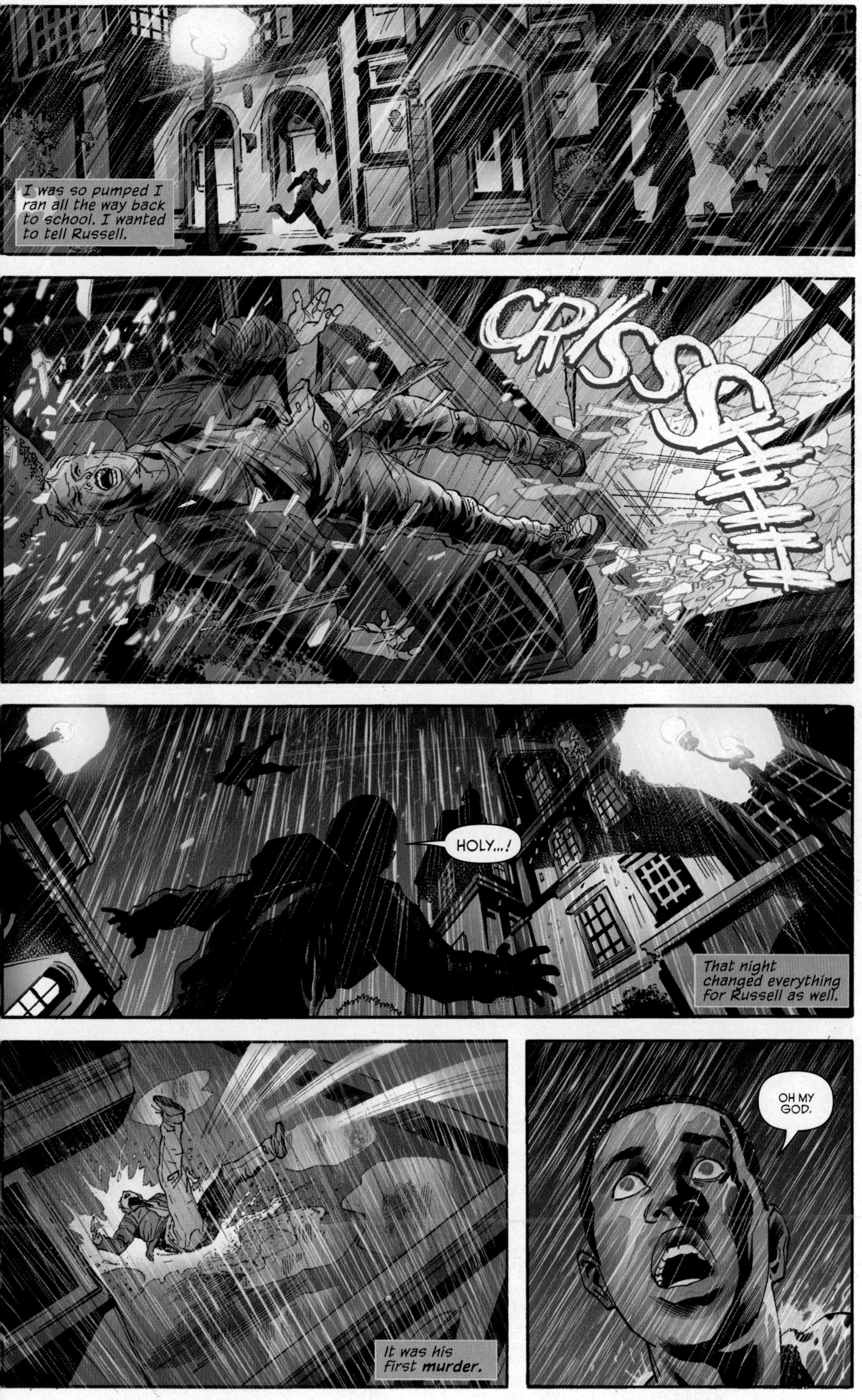
I was so pumped I ran all the way back to school. I wanted to tell Russell.
CRISSSHHHH
HOLY...!
That night changed everything for Russell as well.
It was his first murder.
OH MY GOD.

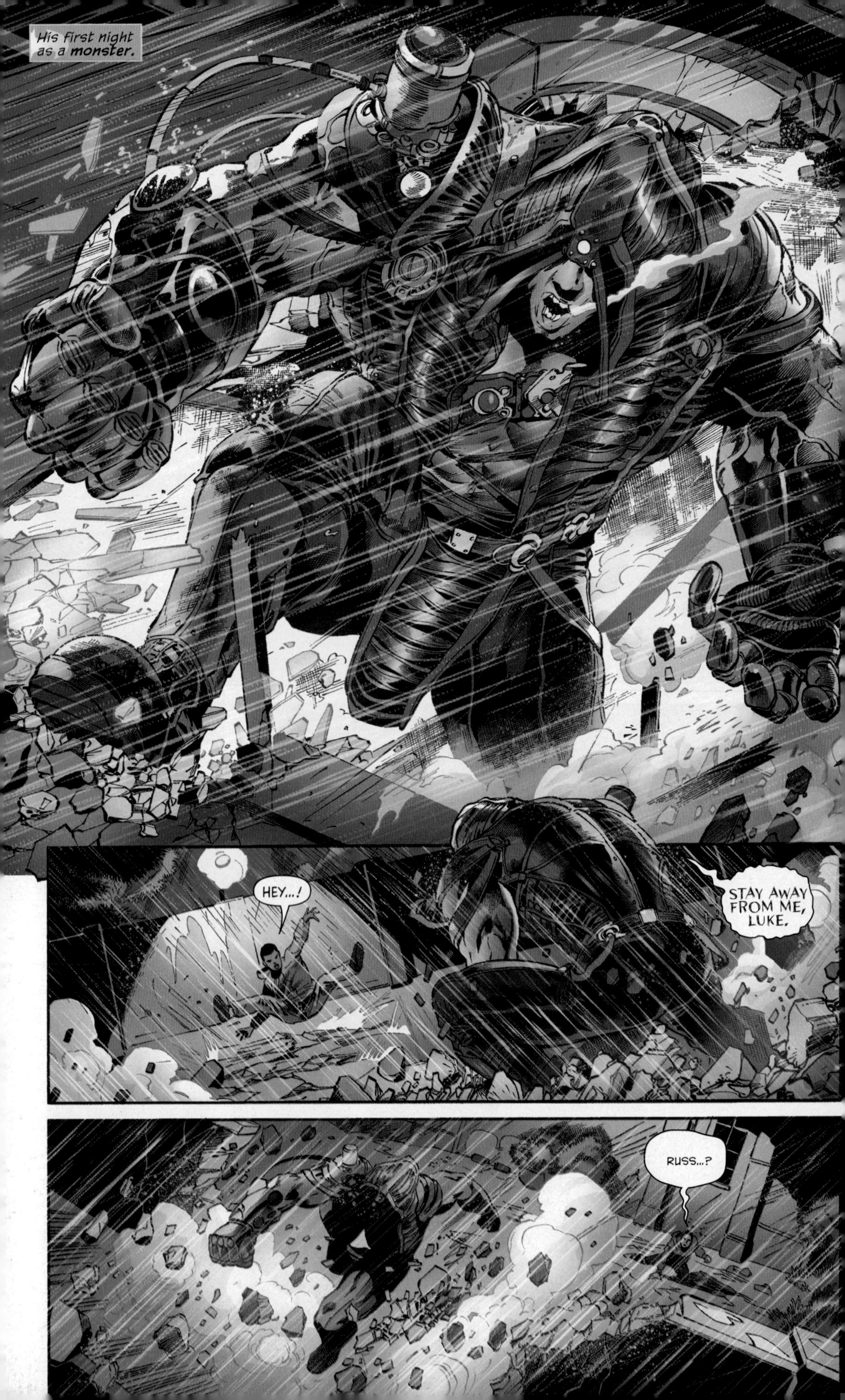

His first night as a monster.
HEY...!
STAY AWAY FROM ME, LUKE.
RUSS...?

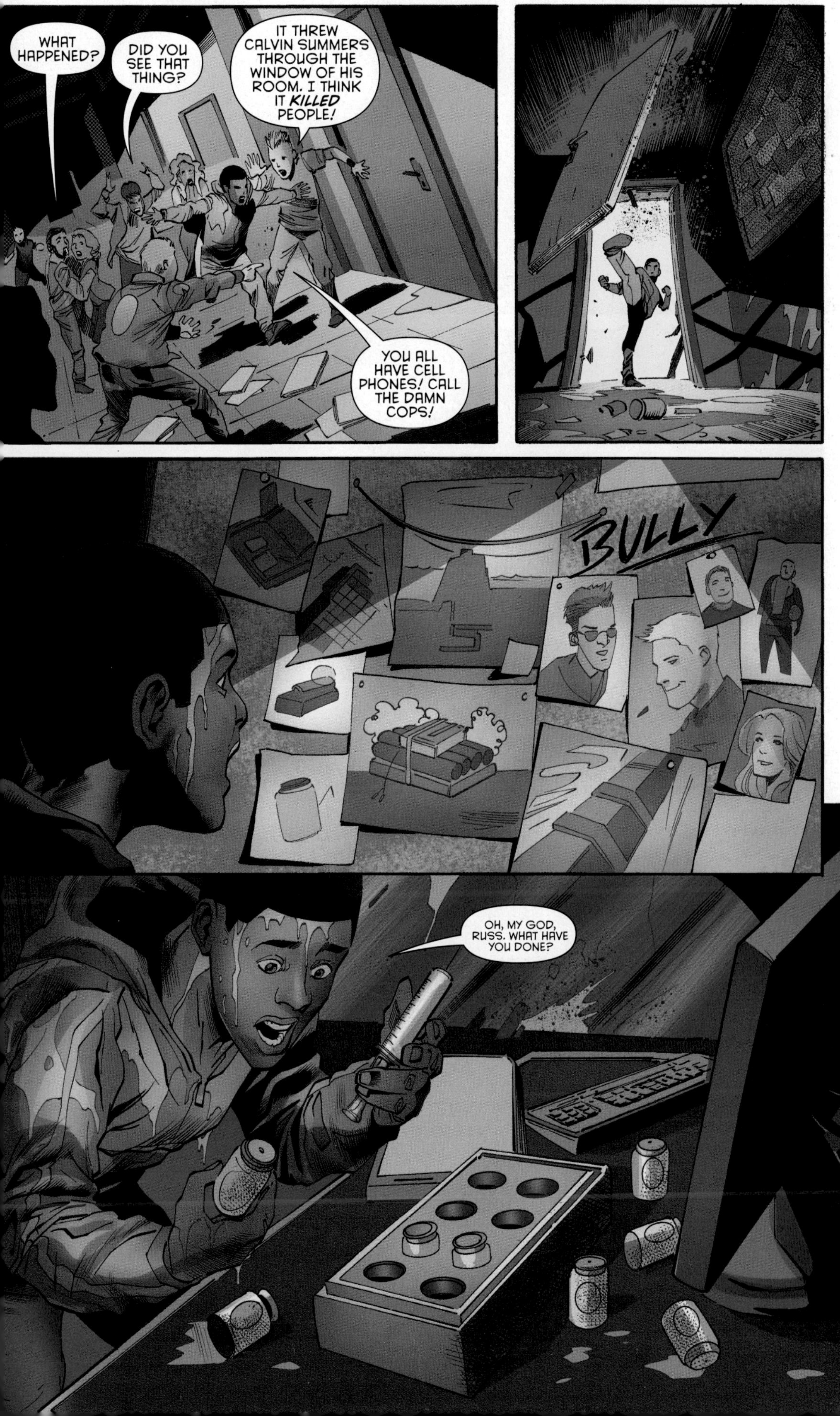
WHAT HAPPENED?
DID YOU SEE THAT THING?
IT THREW CALVIN SUMMERS THROUGH THE WINDOW OF HIS ROOM. I THINK IT *KILLED* PEOPLE!
YOU ALL HAVE CELL PHONES! CALL THE DAMN COPS!
BULLY
OH, MY GOD, RUSS. WHAT HAVE YOU DONE?

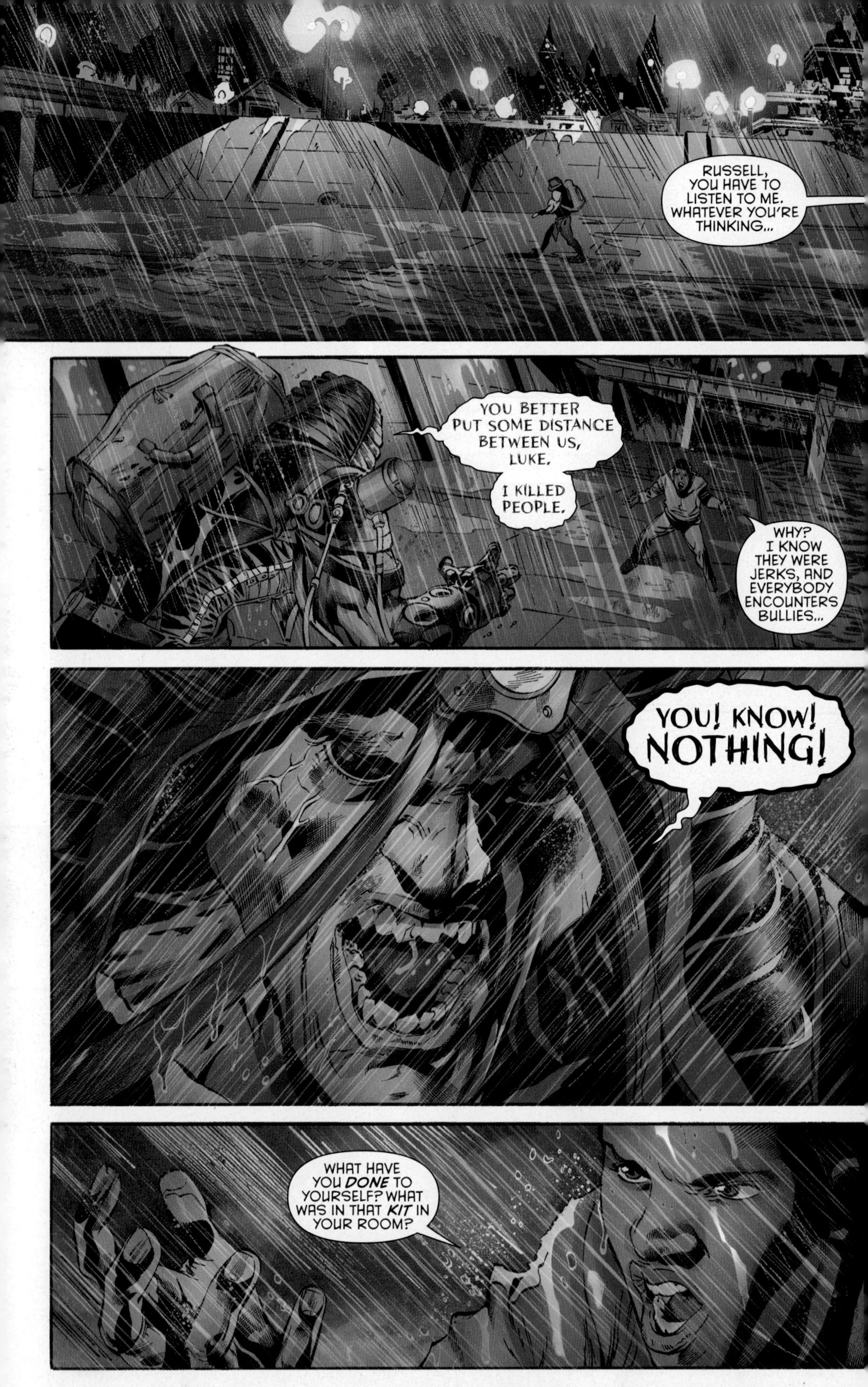
RUSSELL, YOU HAVE TO LISTEN TO ME. WHATEVER YOU'RE THINKING...
YOU BETTER PUT SOME DISTANCE BETWEEN US, LUKE.
I KILLED PEOPLE.
WHY? I KNOW THEY WERE JERKS, AND EVERYBODY ENCOUNTERS BULLIES...
YOU! KNOW! NOTHING!
WHAT HAVE YOU *DONE* TO YOURSELF? WHAT WAS IN THAT *KIT* IN YOUR ROOM?

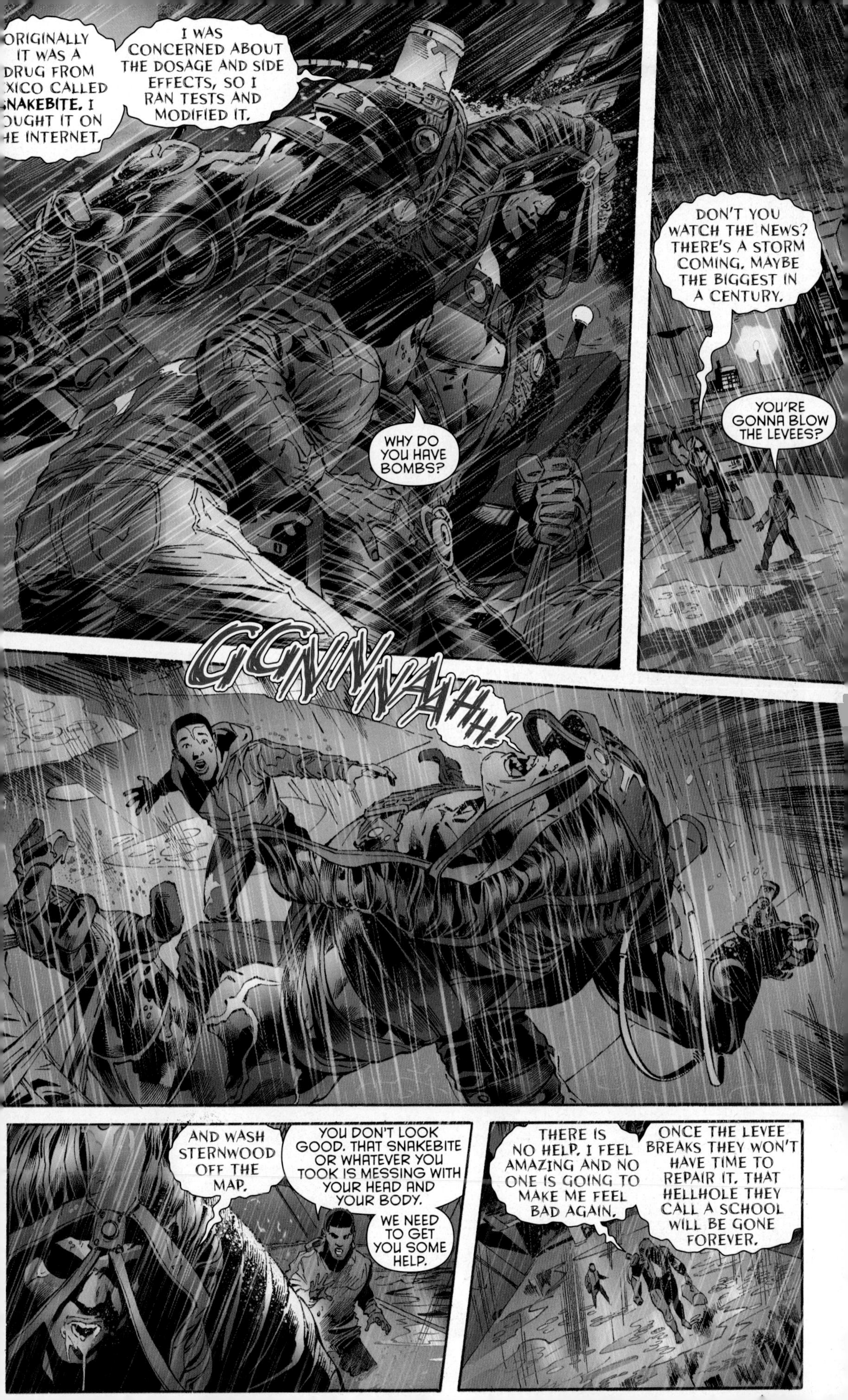
ORIGINALLY IT WAS A DRUG FROM XICO CALLED SNAKEBITE. I OUGHT IT ON HE INTERNET.
I WAS CONCERNED ABOUT THE DOSAGE AND SIDE EFFECTS, SO I RAN TESTS AND MODIFIED IT.
WHY DO YOU HAVE BOMBS?
DON'T YOU WATCH THE NEWS? THERE'S A STORM COMING, MAYBE THE BIGGEST IN A CENTURY.
YOU'RE GONNA BLOW THE LEVEES?
GGNNNAAHH!
AND WASH STERNWOOD OFF THE MAP.
YOU DON'T LOOK GOOD. THAT SNAKEBITE OR WHATEVER YOU TOOK IS MESSING WITH YOUR HEAD AND YOUR BODY.
WE NEED TO GET YOU SOME HELP.
THERE IS NO HELP. I FEEL AMAZING AND NO ONE IS GOING TO MAKE ME FEEL BAD AGAIN.
ONCE THE LEVEE BREAKS THEY WON'T HAVE TIME TO REPAIR IT. THAT HELLHOLE THEY CALL A SCHOOL WILL BE GONE FOREVER.

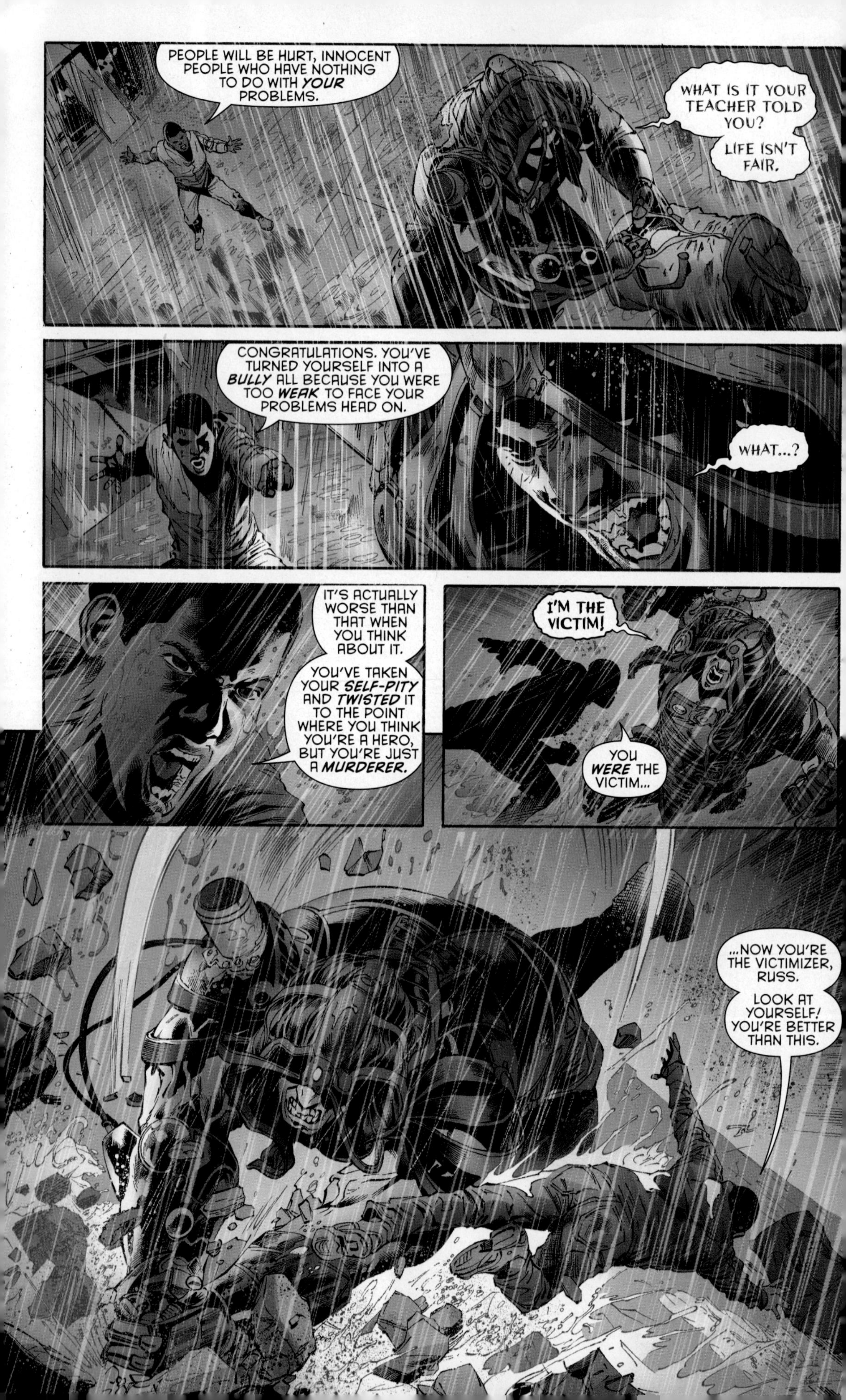

PEOPLE WILL BE HURT, INNOCENT PEOPLE WHO HAVE NOTHING TO DO WITH YOUR PROBLEMS.
WHAT IS IT YOUR TEACHER TOLD YOU?
LIFE ISN'T FAIR.
CONGRATULATIONS. YOU'VE TURNED YOURSELF INTO A BULLY ALL BECAUSE YOU WERE TOO WEAK TO FACE YOUR PROBLEMS HEAD ON.
WHAT...?
IT'S ACTUALLY WORSE THAN THAT WHEN YOU THINK ABOUT IT.
YOU'VE TAKEN YOUR SELF-PITY AND TWISTED IT TO THE POINT WHERE YOU THINK YOU'RE A HERO, BUT YOU'RE JUST A MURDERER.
I'M THE VICTIM!
YOU WERE THE VICTIM...
...NOW YOU'RE THE VICTIMIZER, RUSS.
LOOK AT YOURSELF! YOU'RE BETTER THAN THIS.

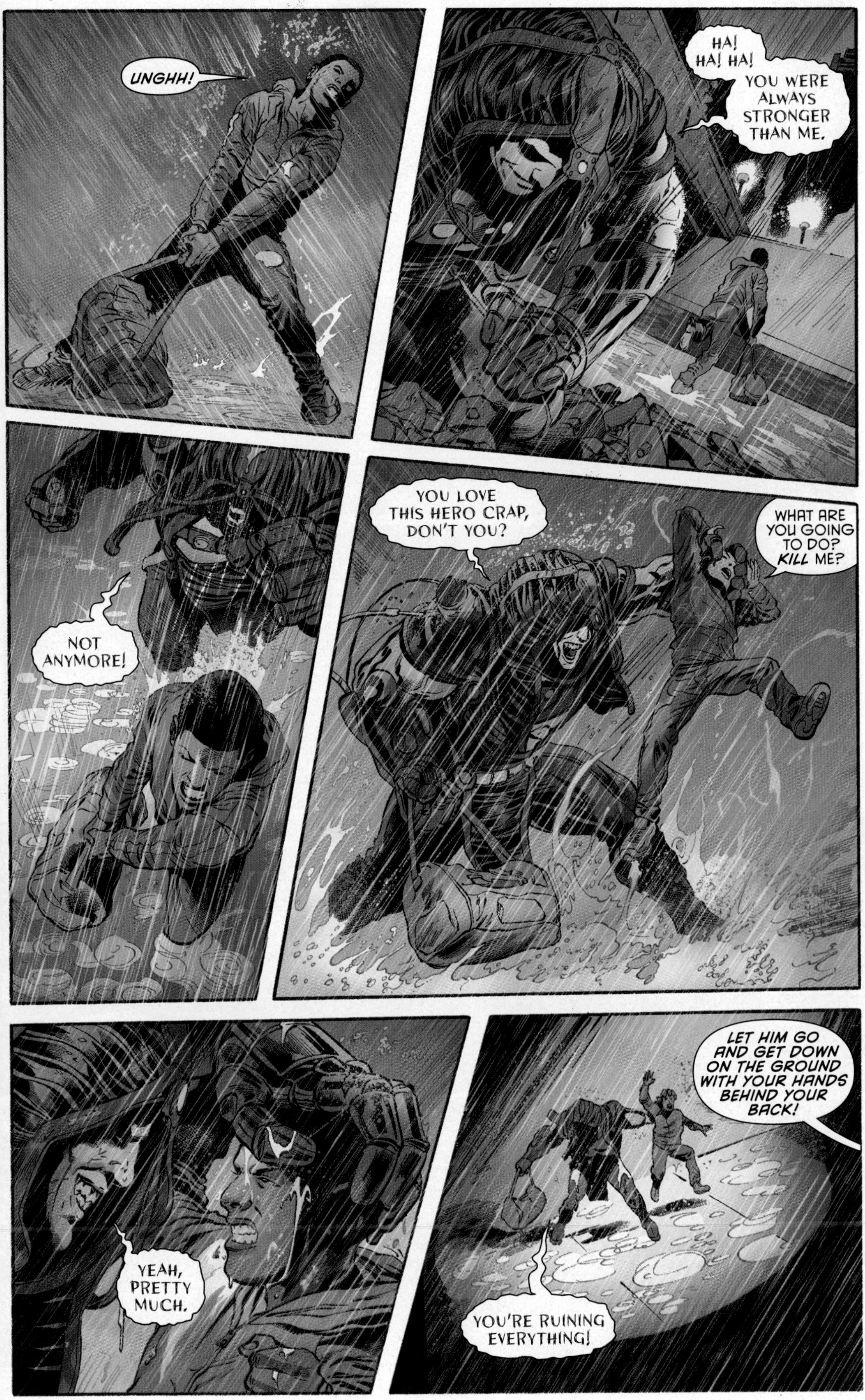
UNGHH!
HA! HA! HA!
YOU WERE ALWAYS STRONGER THAN ME.
NOT ANYMORE!
YOU LOVE THIS HERO CRAP, DON'T YOU?
WHAT ARE YOU GOING TO DO? *KILL* ME?
YEAH, PRETTY MUCH.
LET HIM GO AND GET DOWN ON THE GROUND WITH YOUR HANDS BEHIND YOUR BACK!
YOU'RE RUINING EVERYTHING!

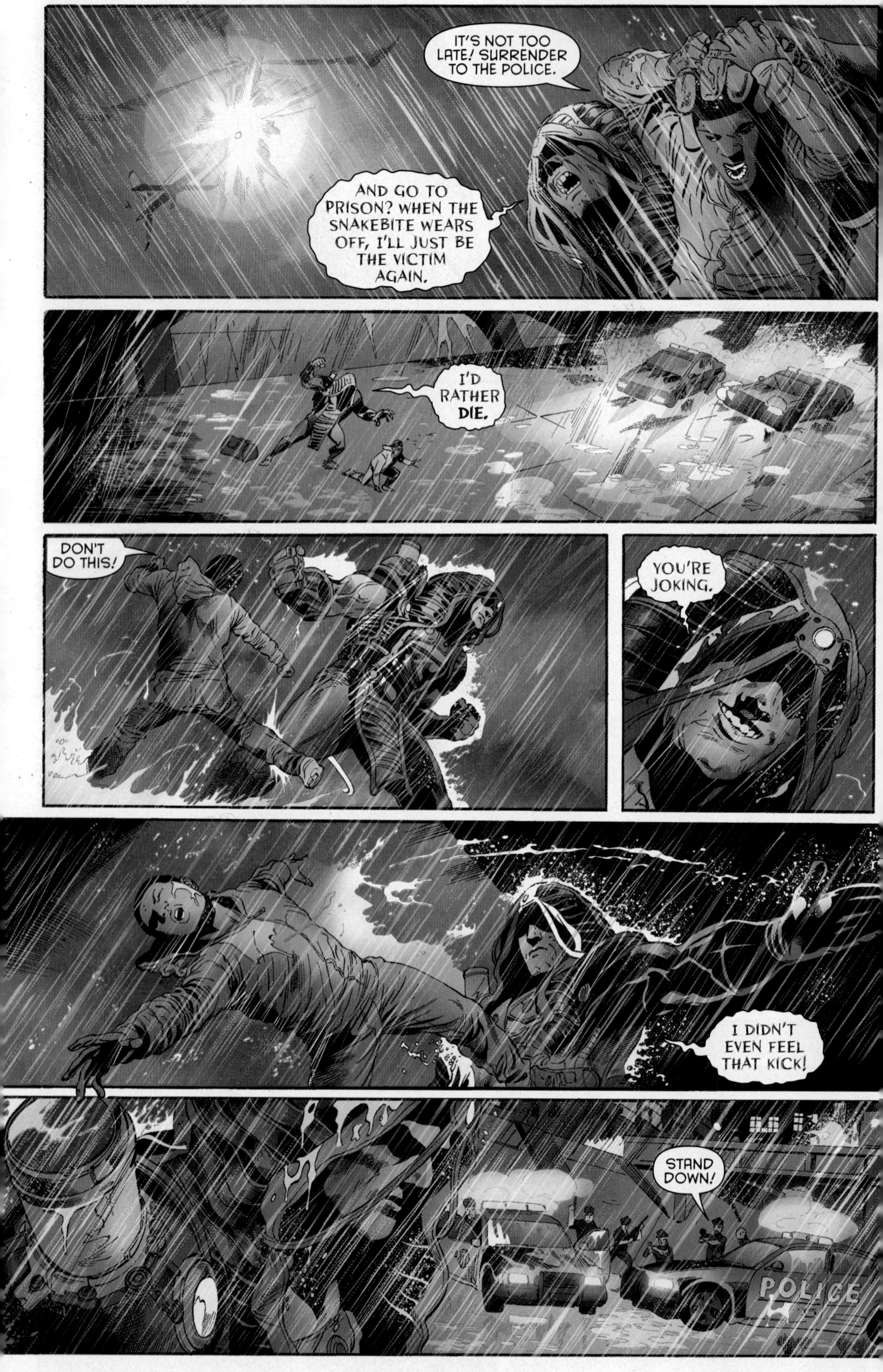
IT'S NOT TOO LATE! SURRENDER TO THE POLICE.
AND GO TO PRISON? WHEN THE SNAKEBITE WEARS OFF, I'LL JUST BE THE VICTIM AGAIN.
I'D RATHER DIE.
DON'T DO THIS!
YOU'RE JOKING.
I DIDN'T EVEN FEEL THAT KICK!
STAND DOWN!
POLICE

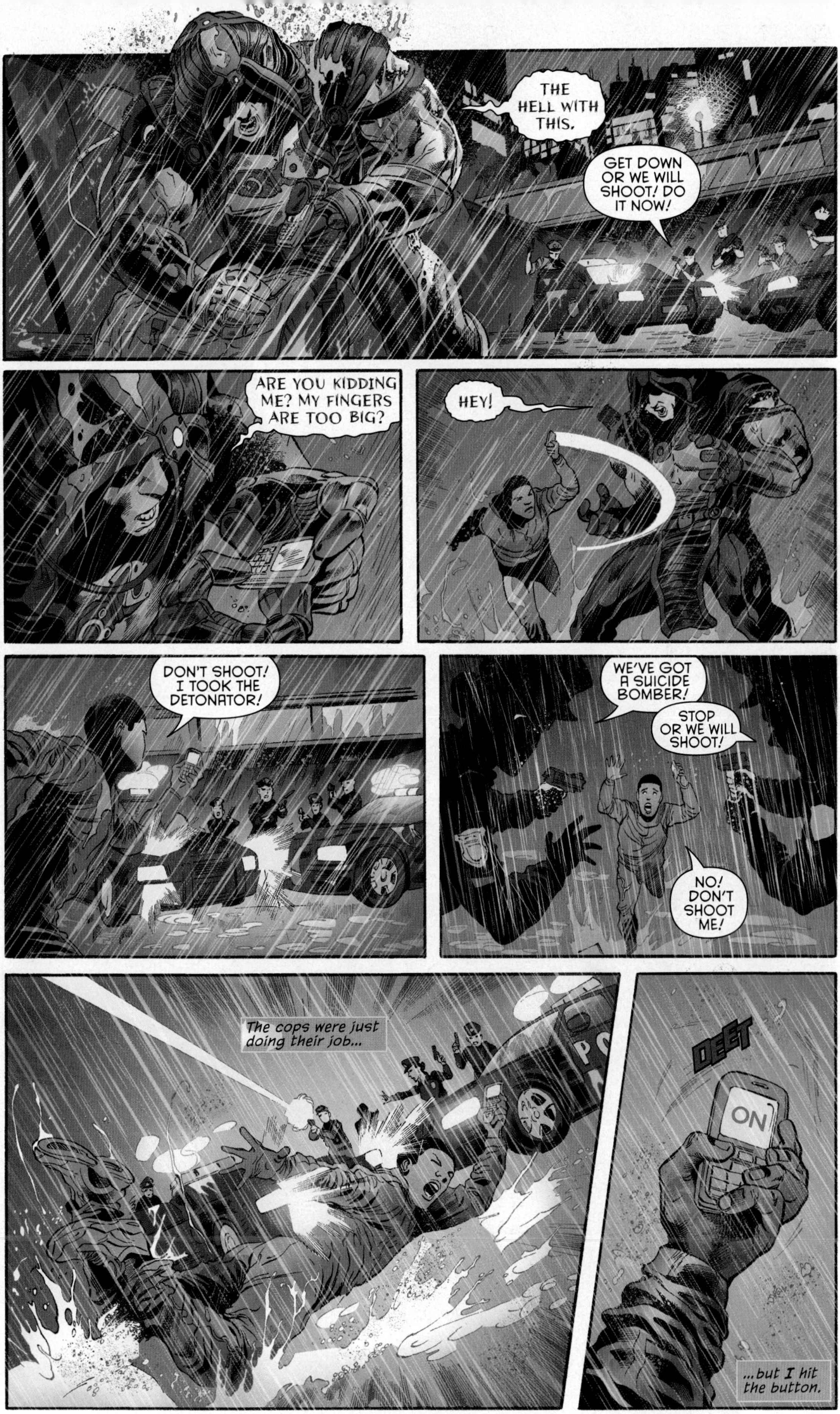
THE HELL WITH THIS.
GET DOWN OR WE WILL SHOOT! DO IT NOW!
ARE YOU KIDDING ME? MY FINGERS ARE TOO BIG?
HEY!
DON'T SHOOT! I TOOK THE DETONATOR!
WE'VE GOT A SUICIDE BOMBER!
STOP OR WE WILL SHOOT!
NO! DON'T SHOOT ME!
The cops were just doing their job...
DEET
ON
...but I hit the button.

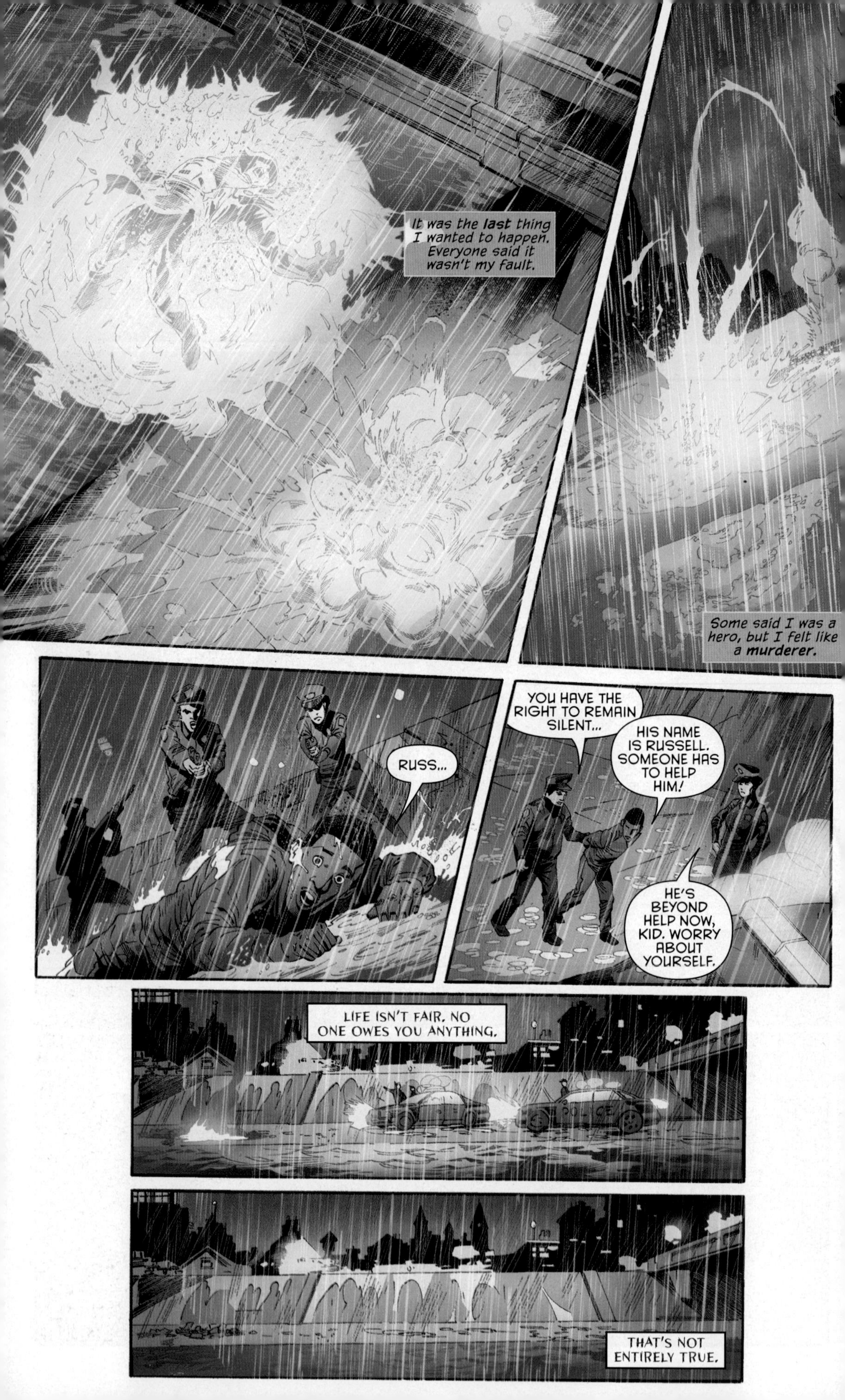
It was the last thing I wanted to happen. Everyone said it wasn't my fault.
Some said I was a hero, but I felt like a murderer.
RUSS...
YOU HAVE THE RIGHT TO REMAIN SILENT...
HIS NAME IS RUSSELL. SOMEONE HAS TO HELP HIM!
HE'S BEYOND HELP NOW, KID. WORRY ABOUT YOURSELF.
LIFE ISN'T FAIR. NO ONE OWES YOU ANYTHING.
POLICE
THAT'S NOT ENTIRELY TRUE.

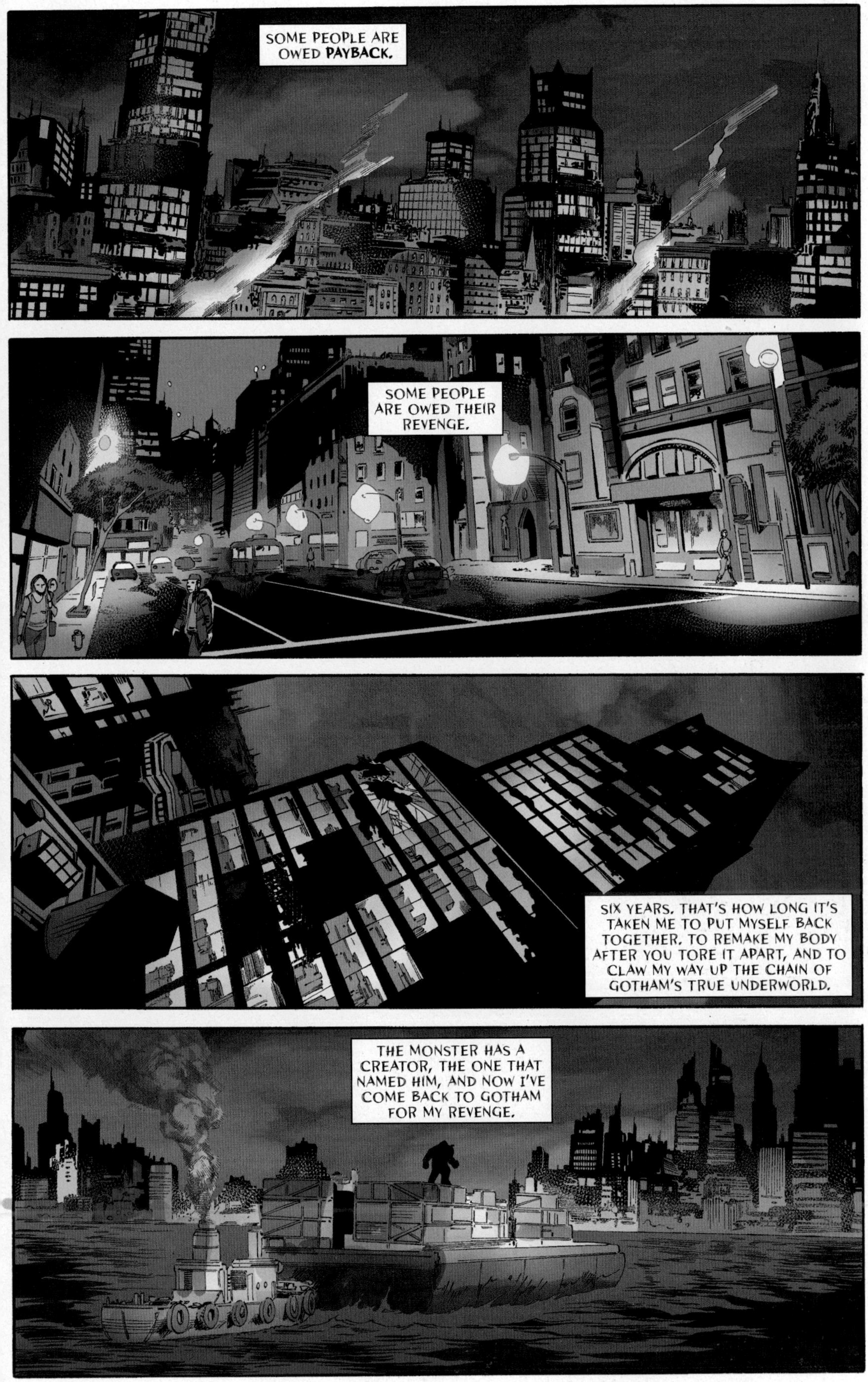
SOME PEOPLE ARE OWED PAYBACK.
SOME PEOPLE ARE OWED THEIR REVENGE.
SIX YEARS. THAT'S HOW LONG IT'S TAKEN ME TO PUT MYSELF BACK TOGETHER. TO REMAKE MY BODY AFTER YOU TORE IT APART, AND TO CLAW MY WAY UP THE CHAIN OF GOTHAM'S TRUE UNDERWORLD.
THE MONSTER HAS A CREATOR, THE ONE THAT NAMED HIM, AND NOW I'VE COME BACK TO GOTHAM FOR MY REVENGE.

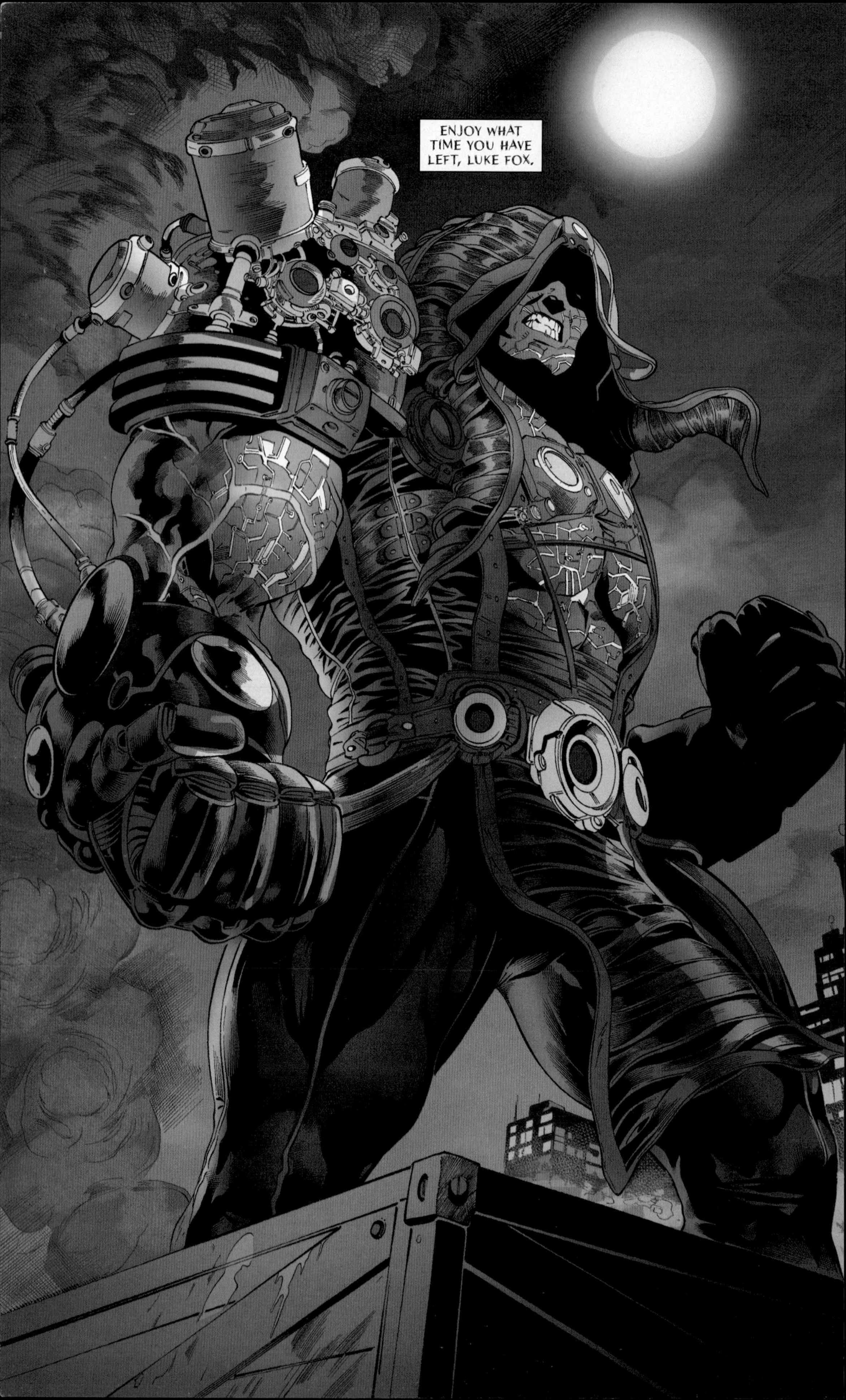
ENJOY WHAT TIME YOU HAVE LEFT, LUKE FOX.

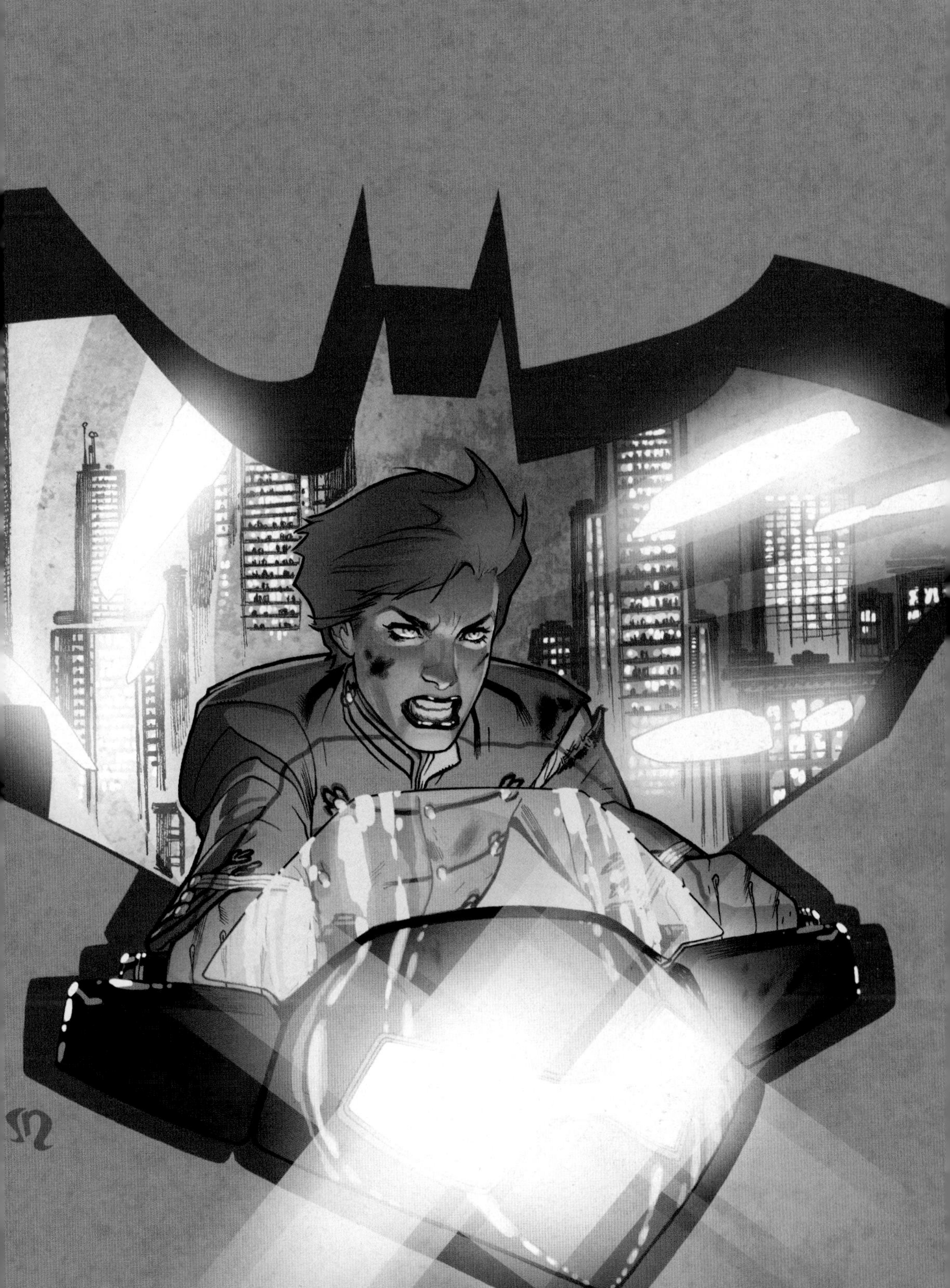

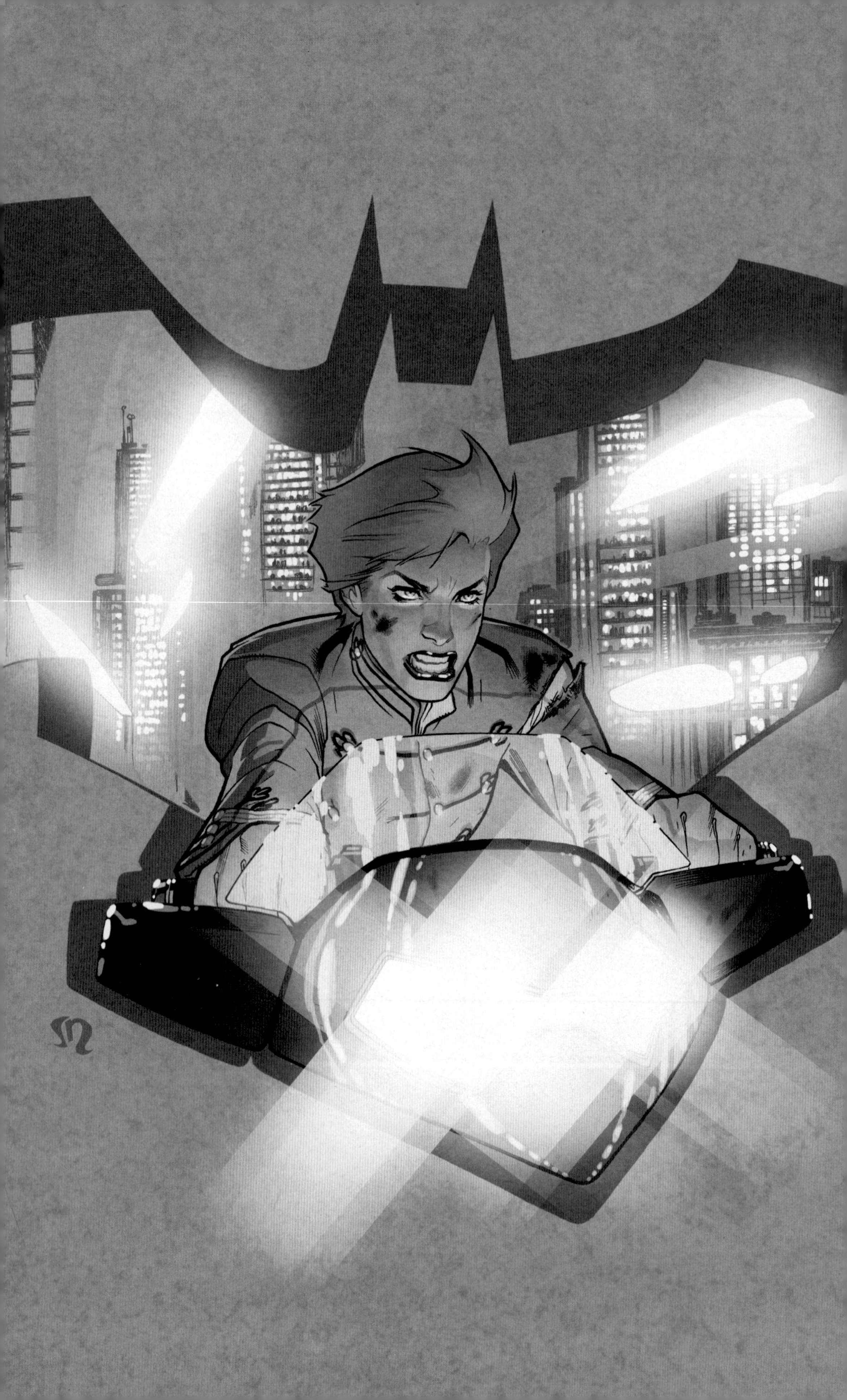

SUDDEN PHONE CALLS FROM HOME ARE NEVER GOOD, IT SEEMS.

DAD? WHAT *IS* IT?

KATIE, HON...IT'S UNCLE PHIL. HE'S BEEN *KILLED.*

EVEN IN MY YOUNG LIFE, I'VE HAD ENOUGH OF ATTENDING FUNERALS.

THE THING I MOST ASSOCIATE WITH MY HOMETOWN OF GOTHAM IS *DEATH.*

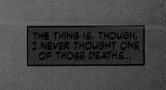

THE THING IS, THOUGH, I NEVER THOUGHT ONE OF THOSE DEATHS...

...WOULD BE MY OWN.
ZIP!
ZIP!
ZIP!
ZIP!
POK!
DC COMICS PRESENTS BATWOMAN IN A ZERO YEAR ADVENTURE:
...OR HIGH WATER
MARC ANDREYKO writer
TREVOR McCARTHY, ANDREA MUTTI, PAT OLLIFFE and JIM FERN artists
JAY LEISTEN and TOM NGUYEN inkers
GUY MAJOR colorist
TODD KLEIN letterer
STEPHANE ROUX cover

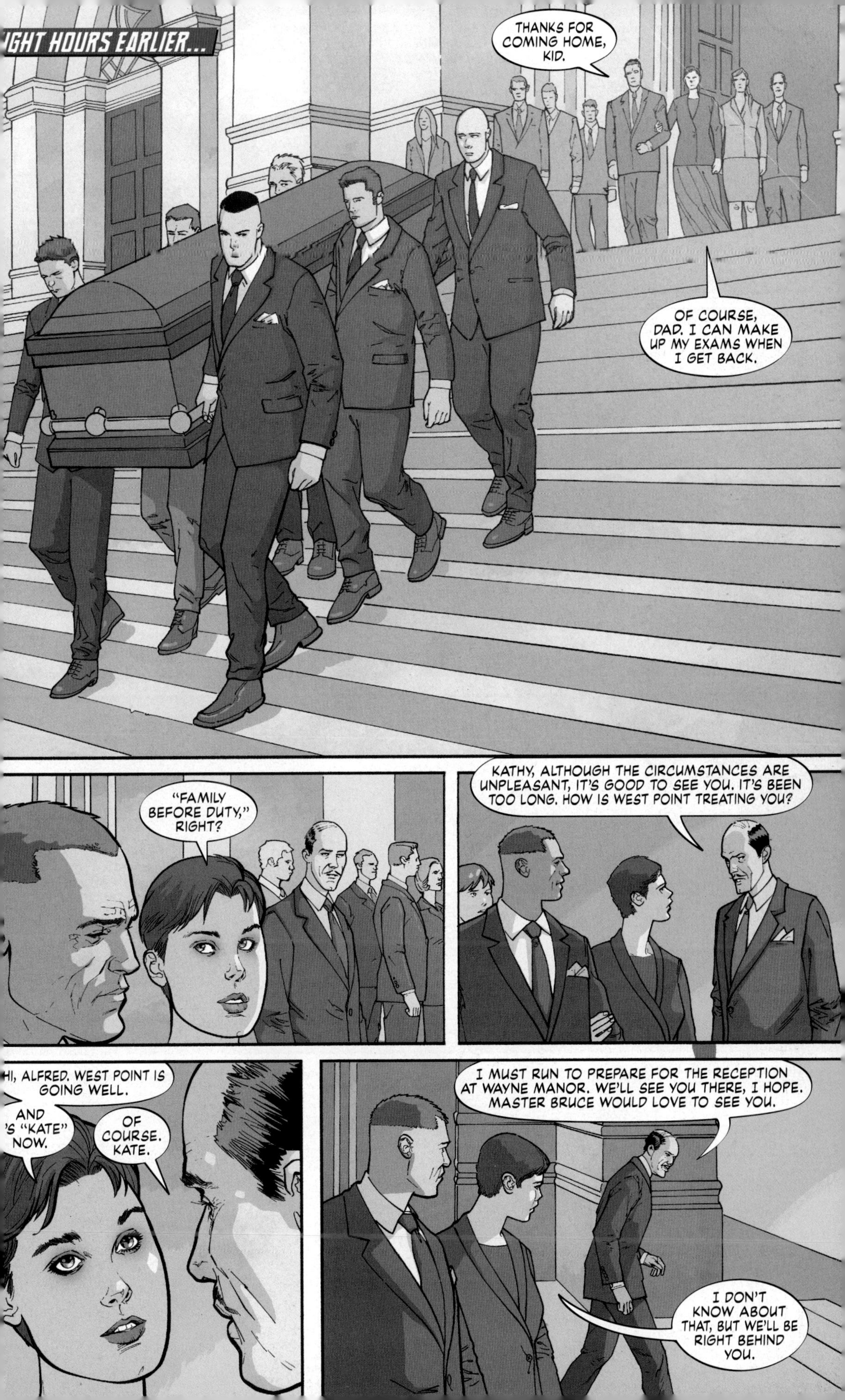
IGHT HOURS EARLIER...
THANKS FOR COMING HOME, KID.
OF COURSE, DAD. I CAN MAKE UP MY EXAMS WHEN I GET BACK.
"FAMILY BEFORE DUTY," RIGHT?
KATHY, ALTHOUGH THE CIRCUMSTANCES ARE UNPLEASANT, IT'S GOOD TO SEE YOU. IT'S BEEN TOO LONG. HOW IS WEST POINT TREATING YOU?
HI, ALFRED. WEST POINT IS GOING WELL.
AND 'S "KATE" NOW.
OF COURSE. KATE.
I MUST RUN TO PREPARE FOR THE RECEPTION AT WAYNE MANOR. WE'LL SEE YOU THERE, I HOPE. MASTER BRUCE WOULD LOVE TO SEE YOU.
I DON'T KNOW ABOUT THAT, BUT WE'LL BE RIGHT BEHIND YOU.

--AND THE NATIONAL WEATHER SERVICE HAS UPGRADED THE SYSTEM APPROACHING GOTHAM CITY TO A CATEGORY THREE TROPICAL STORM, DUBBING IT **RENE**--

THIS JUST IN! EDWARD NYGMA, NOW CALLING HIMSELF THE **"RIDDLER,"** HAS JUST RELEASED THIS BROADCAST. WE TAKE YOU TO IT LIVE.

--RIDDLE ME THIS, GOTHAM: THERE ARE TWO SISTERS. EACH GIVES BIRTH TO THE OTHER. WHO ARE THEY? NO? I'LL GIVE YOU A **HINT!** ONE SISTER SAYS, "I AM THE DAY." AND THE OTHER SISTER SAYS, "I AM THE NIGHT."

LOOKS LIKE I MIGHT HAVE YOU HERE LONGER THAN WE THOUGHT.

SO, BRING ON THE DARK, DARK NIGHT!

KA-POP! KA-POP!

ZZZZZT!

WHOA!

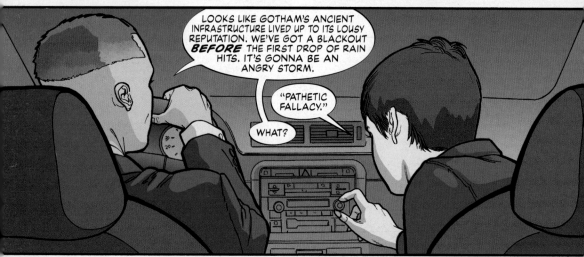

LOOKS LIKE GOTHAM'S ANCIENT INFRASTRUCTURE LIVED UP TO ITS LOUSY REPUTATION. WE'VE GOT A BLACKOUT **BEFORE** THE FIRST DROP OF RAIN HITS. IT'S GONNA BE AN ANGRY STORM.

"PATHETIC FALLACY."

WHAT?

"ANGRY STORM." IT'S AN EXAMPLE OF PATHETIC FALLACY--THE ATTRIBUTION OF HUMAN CHARACTERISTICS TO NATURE.

FANCY. AND HERE I THOUGHT YO WERE JUST LEARNING HO TO BE A GOO SOLDIER.

GOD, I HAT GOTHAM

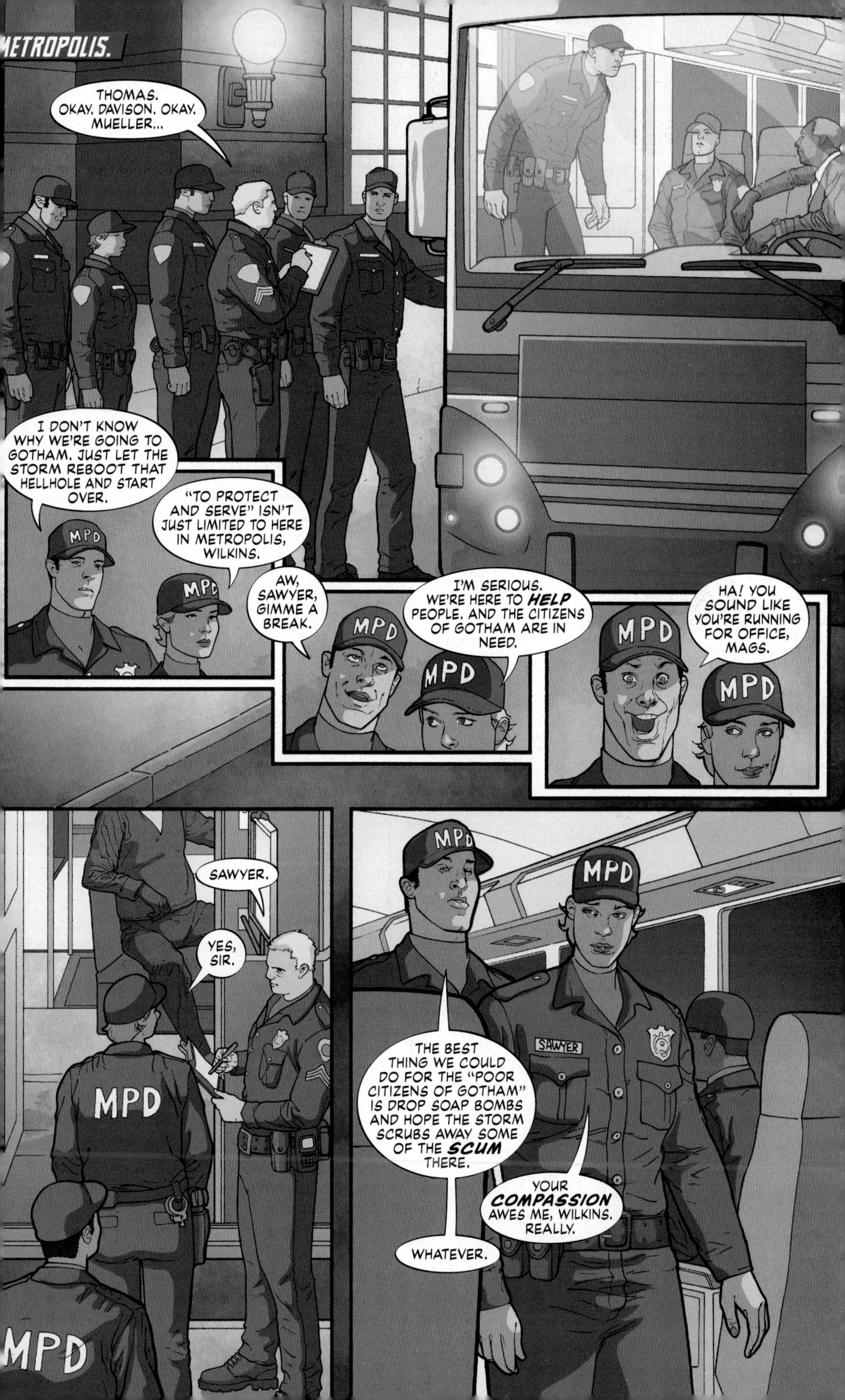
METROPOLIS.
THOMAS. OKAY. DAVISON. OKAY. MUELLER...
I DON'T KNOW WHY WE'RE GOING TO GOTHAM. JUST LET THE STORM REBOOT THAT HELLHOLE AND START OVER.
"TO PROTECT AND SERVE" ISN'T JUST LIMITED TO HERE IN METROPOLIS, WILKINS.
MPD
MPD
AW, SAWYER, GIMME A BREAK.
I'M SERIOUS. WE'RE HERE TO HELP PEOPLE. AND THE CITIZENS OF GOTHAM ARE IN NEED.
MPD
MPD
HA! YOU SOUND LIKE YOU'RE RUNNING FOR OFFICE, MAGS.
MPD
MPD
SAWYER.
YES, SIR.
MPD
MPD
MPD
MPD
SAWYER
THE BEST THING WE COULD DO FOR THE "POOR CITIZENS OF GOTHAM" IS DROP SOAP BOMBS AND HOPE THE STORM SCRUBS AWAY SOME OF THE SCUM THERE.
YOUR COMPASSION AWES ME, WILKINS. REALLY.
WHATEVER.

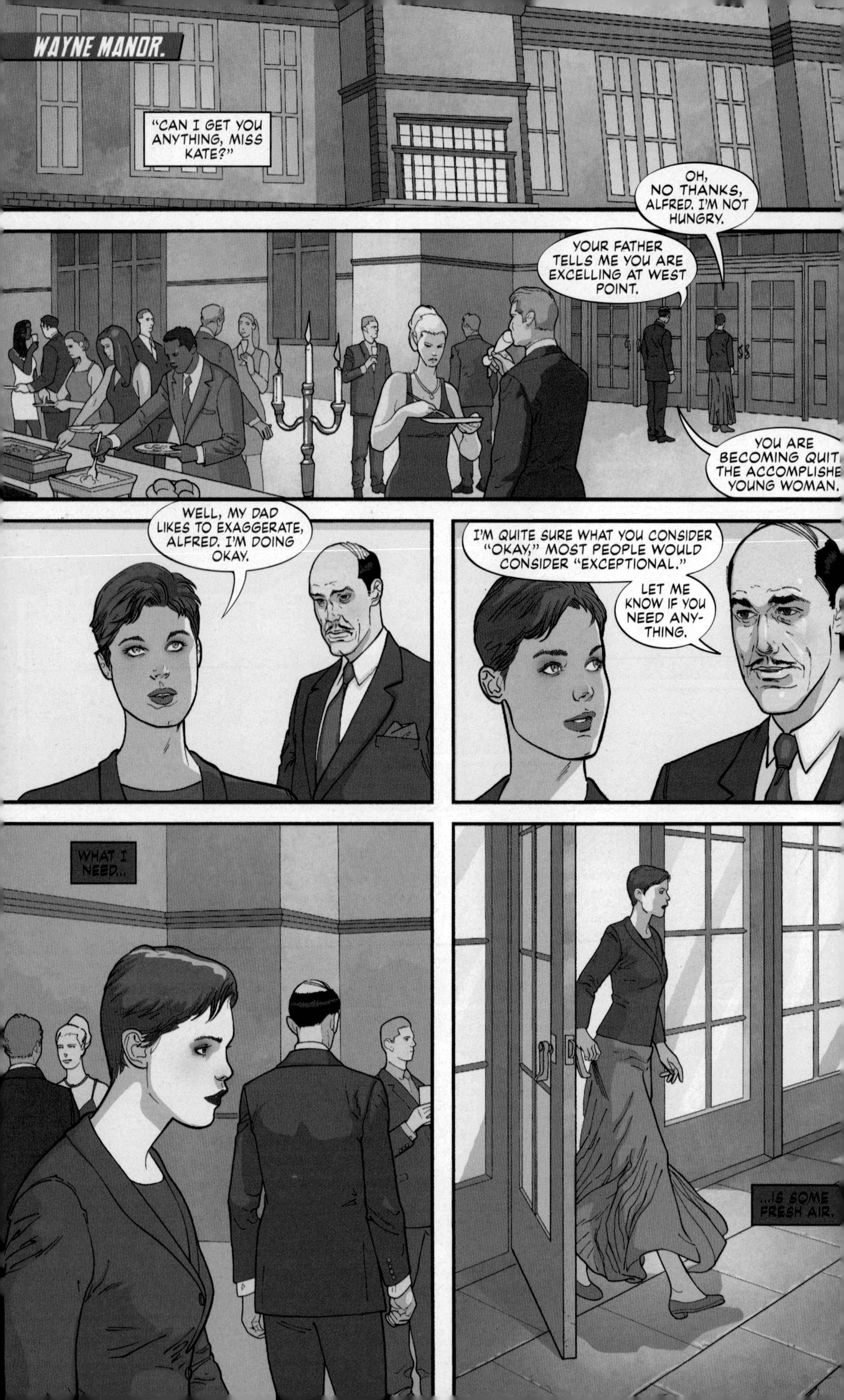
WAYNE MANOR.
"CAN I GET YOU ANYTHING, MISS KATE?"
OH, NO THANKS, ALFRED. I'M NOT HUNGRY.
YOUR FATHER TELLS ME YOU ARE EXCELLING AT WEST POINT.
YOU ARE BECOMING QUIT THE ACCOMPLISHE YOUNG WOMAN.
WELL, MY DAD LIKES TO EXAGGERATE, ALFRED. I'M DOING OKAY.
I'M QUITE SURE WHAT YOU CONSIDER "OKAY," MOST PEOPLE WOULD CONSIDER "EXCEPTIONAL."
LET ME KNOW IF YOU NEED ANY-THING.
WHAT I NEED...
...IS SOME FRESH AIR.

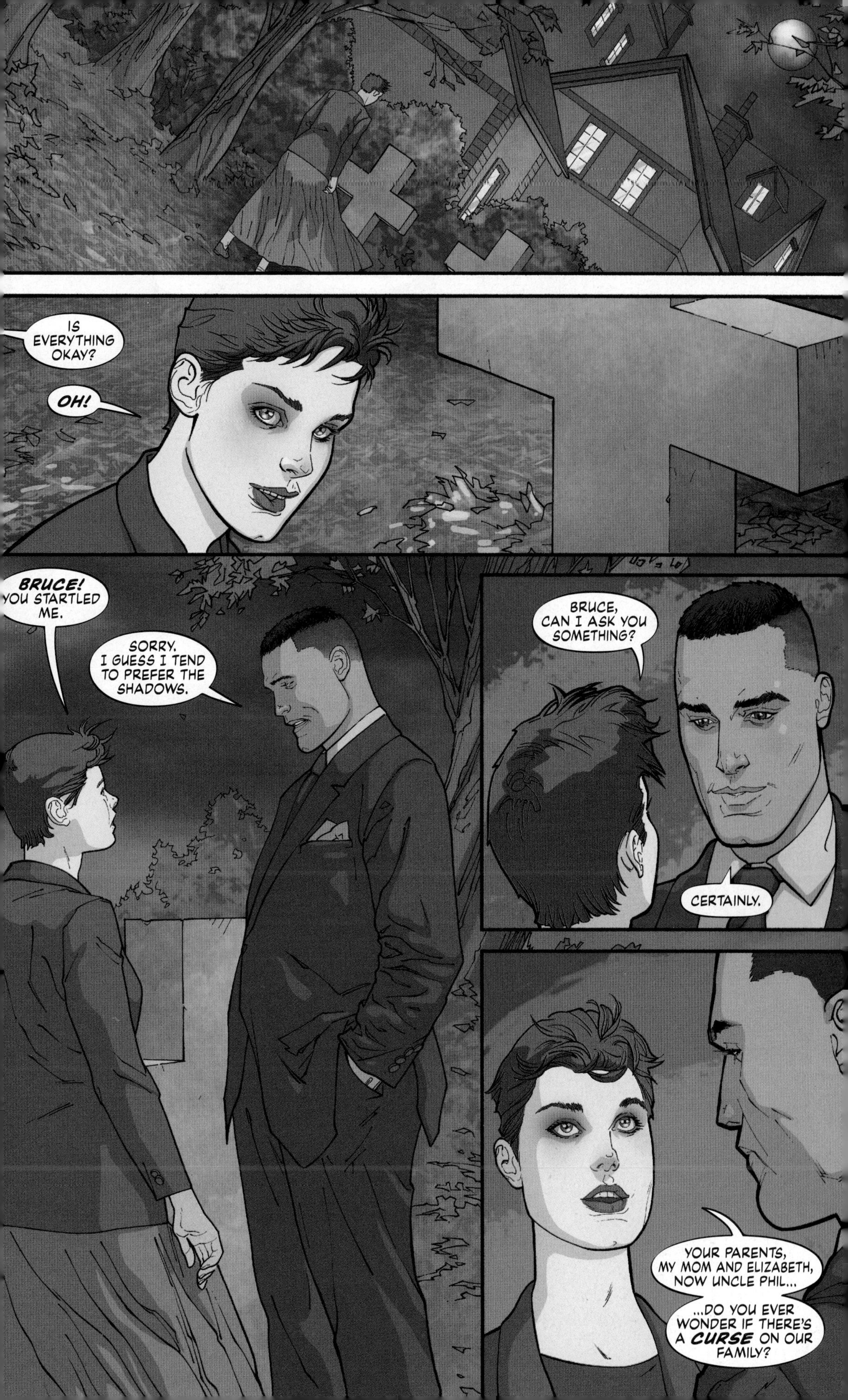
IS EVERYTHING OKAY?
OH!
BRUCE! YOU STARTLED ME.
SORRY. I GUESS I TEND TO PREFER THE SHADOWS.
BRUCE, CAN I ASK YOU SOMETHING?
CERTAINLY.
YOUR PARENTS, MY MOM AND ELIZABETH, NOW UNCLE PHIL...
...DO YOU EVER WONDER IF THERE'S A CURSE ON OUR FAMILY?

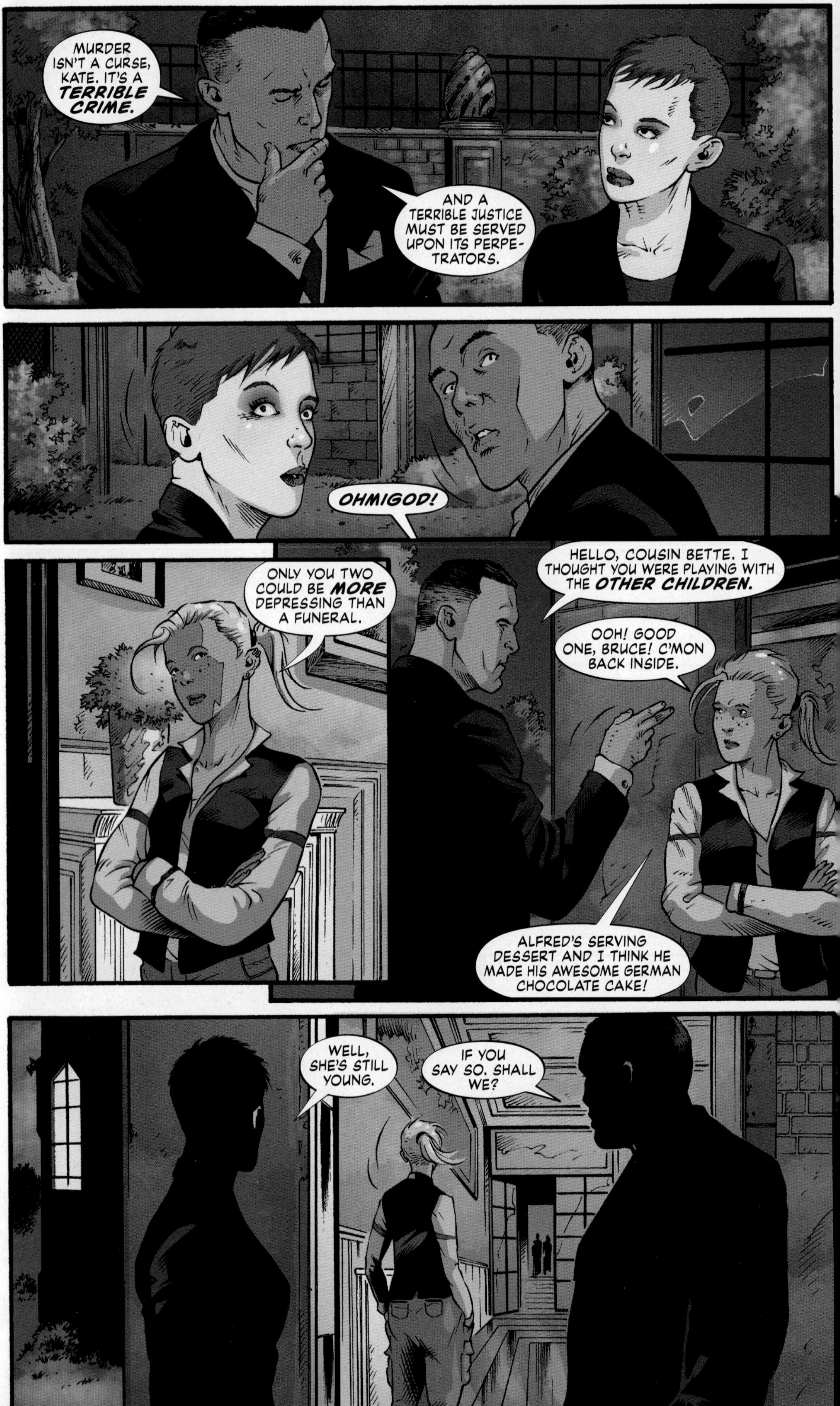
MURDER ISN'T A CURSE, KATE. IT'S A TERRIBLE CRIME.
AND A TERRIBLE JUSTICE MUST BE SERVED UPON ITS PERPE-TRATORS.
OHMIGOD!
ONLY YOU TWO COULD BE MORE DEPRESSING THAN A FUNERAL.
HELLO, COUSIN BETTE. I THOUGHT YOU WERE PLAYING WITH THE OTHER CHILDREN.
OOH! GOOD ONE, BRUCE! C'MON BACK INSIDE.
ALFRED'S SERVING DESSERT AND I THINK HE MADE HIS AWESOME GERMAN CHOCOLATE CAKE!
WELL, SHE'S STILL YOUNG.
IF YOU SAY SO. SHALL WE?

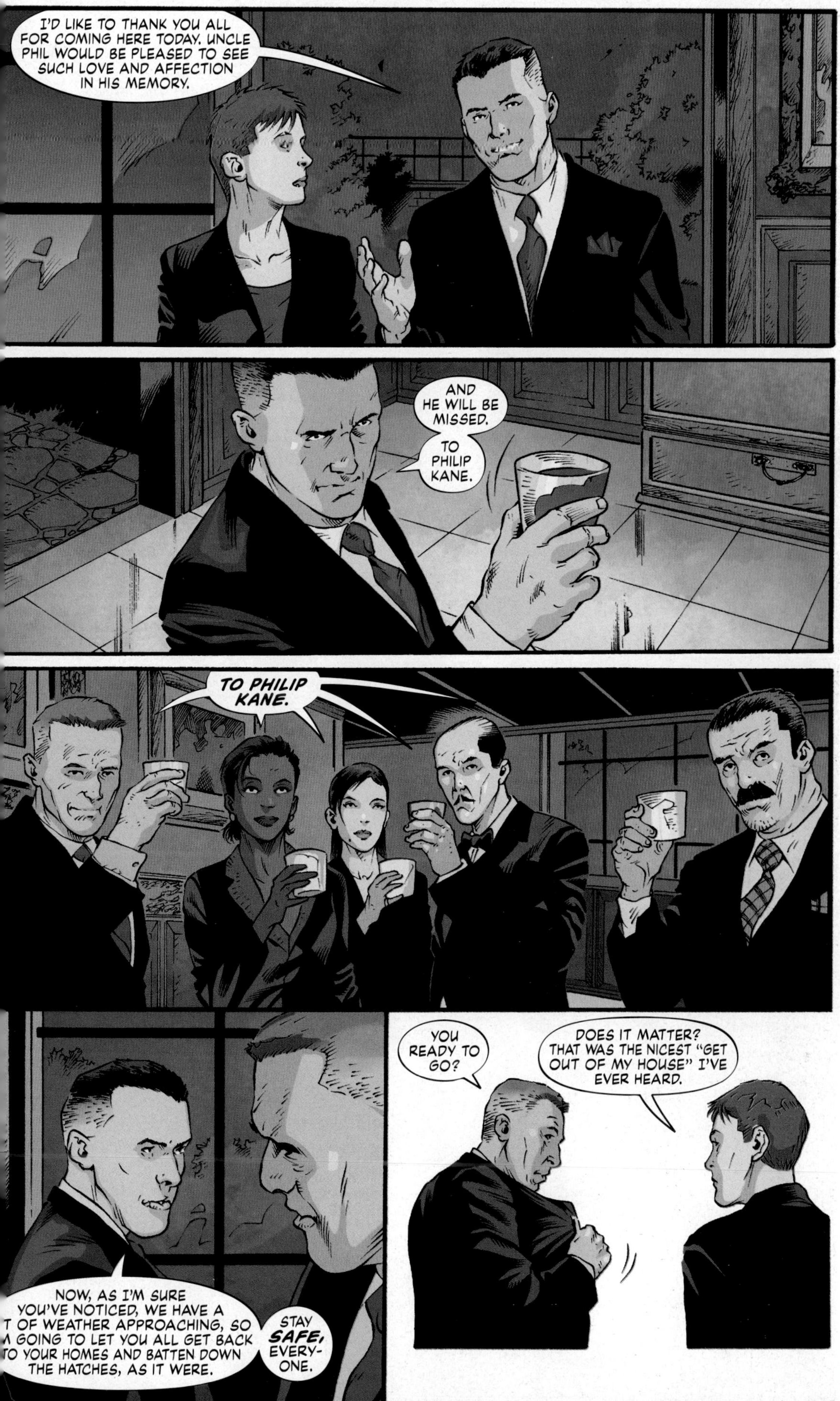
I'D LIKE TO THANK YOU ALL FOR COMING HERE TODAY. UNCLE PHIL WOULD BE PLEASED TO SEE SUCH LOVE AND AFFECTION IN HIS MEMORY.
AND HE WILL BE MISSED.
TO PHILIP KANE.
TO PHILIP KANE.
NOW, AS I'M SURE YOU'VE NOTICED, WE HAVE A T OF WEATHER APPROACHING, SO A GOING TO LET YOU ALL GET BACK TO YOUR HOMES AND BATTEN DOWN THE HATCHES, AS IT WERE.
STAY SAFE, EVERY-ONE.
YOU READY TO GO?
DOES IT MATTER? THAT WAS THE NICEST "GET OUT OF MY HOUSE" I'VE EVER HEARD.

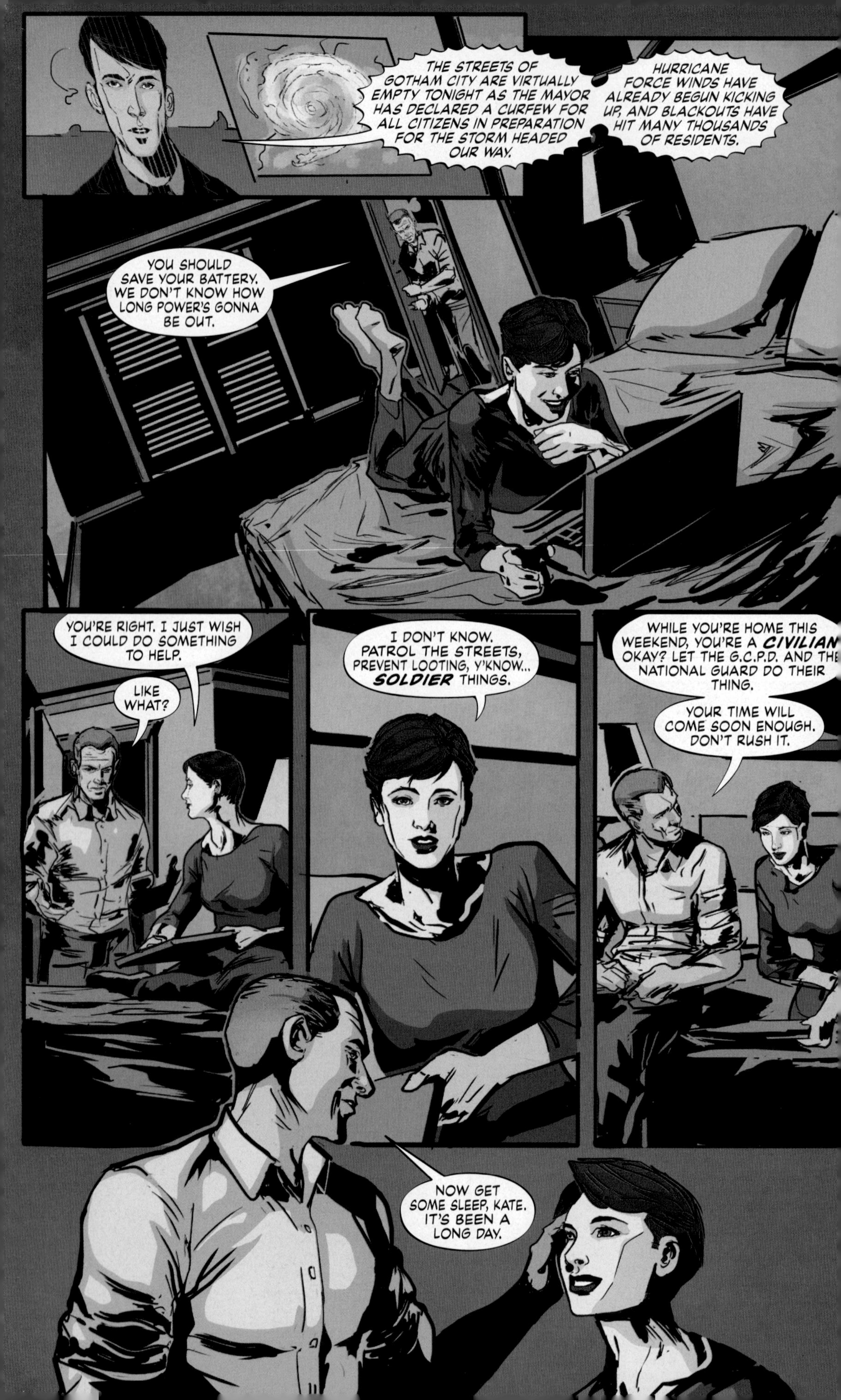
THE STREETS OF GOTHAM CITY ARE VIRTUALLY EMPTY TONIGHT AS THE MAYOR HAS DECLARED A CURFEW FOR ALL CITIZENS IN PREPARATION FOR THE STORM HEADED OUR WAY.
HURRICANE FORCE WINDS HAVE ALREADY BEGUN KICKING UP, AND BLACKOUTS HAVE HIT MANY THOUSANDS OF RESIDENTS.
YOU SHOULD SAVE YOUR BATTERY. WE DON'T KNOW HOW LONG POWER'S GONNA BE OUT.
YOU'RE RIGHT. I JUST WISH I COULD DO SOMETHING TO HELP.
LIKE WHAT?
I DON'T KNOW. PATROL THE STREETS, PREVENT LOOTING, Y'KNOW... SOLDIER THINGS.
WHILE YOU'RE HOME THIS WEEKEND, YOU'RE A CIVILIAN OKAY? LET THE G.C.P.D. AND THE NATIONAL GUARD DO THEIR THING.
YOUR TIME WILL COME SOON ENOUGH. DON'T RUSH IT.
NOW GET SOME SLEEP, KATE. IT'S BEEN A LONG DAY.

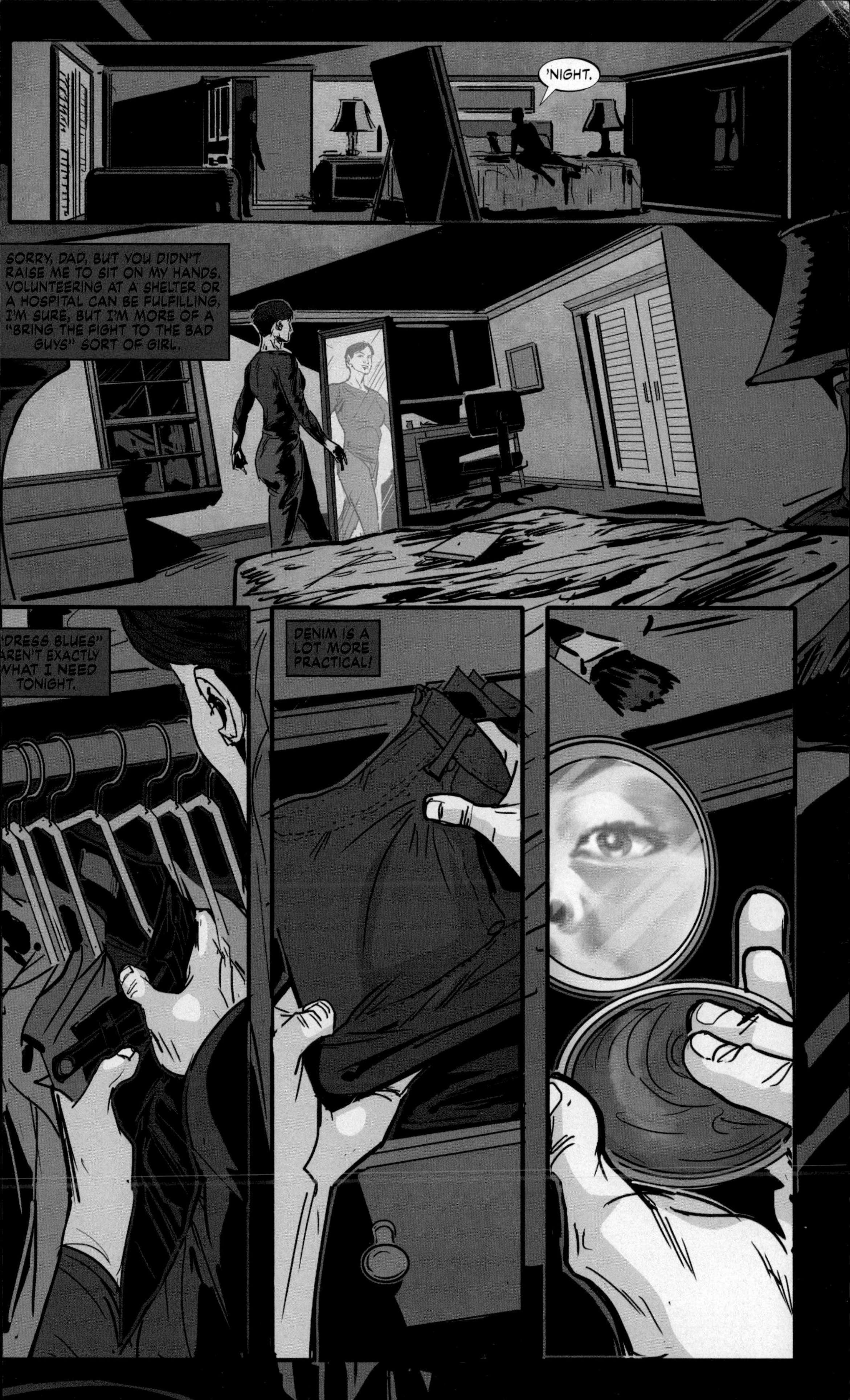
'NIGHT.
SORRY, DAD, BUT YOU DIDN'T RAISE ME TO SIT ON MY HANDS. VOLUNTEERING AT A SHELTER OR A HOSPITAL CAN BE FULFILLING, I'M SURE, BUT I'M MORE OF A "BRING THE FIGHT TO THE BAD GUYS" SORT OF GIRL.
"DRESS BLUES" AREN'T EXACTLY WHAT I NEED TONIGHT.
DENIM IS A LOT MORE PRACTICAL!

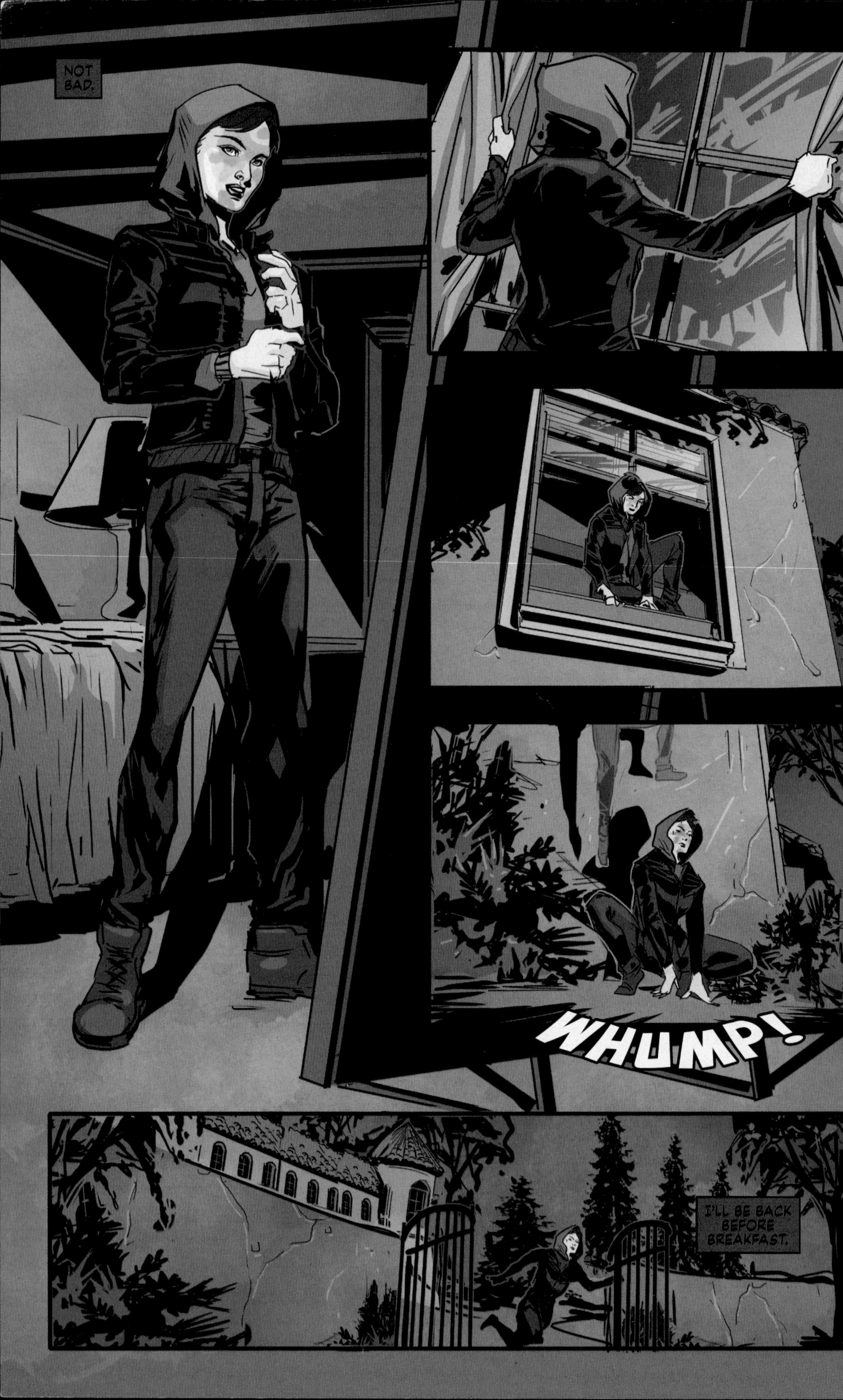
NOT BAD.
WHUMP!
I'LL BE BACK BEFORE BREAKFAST.

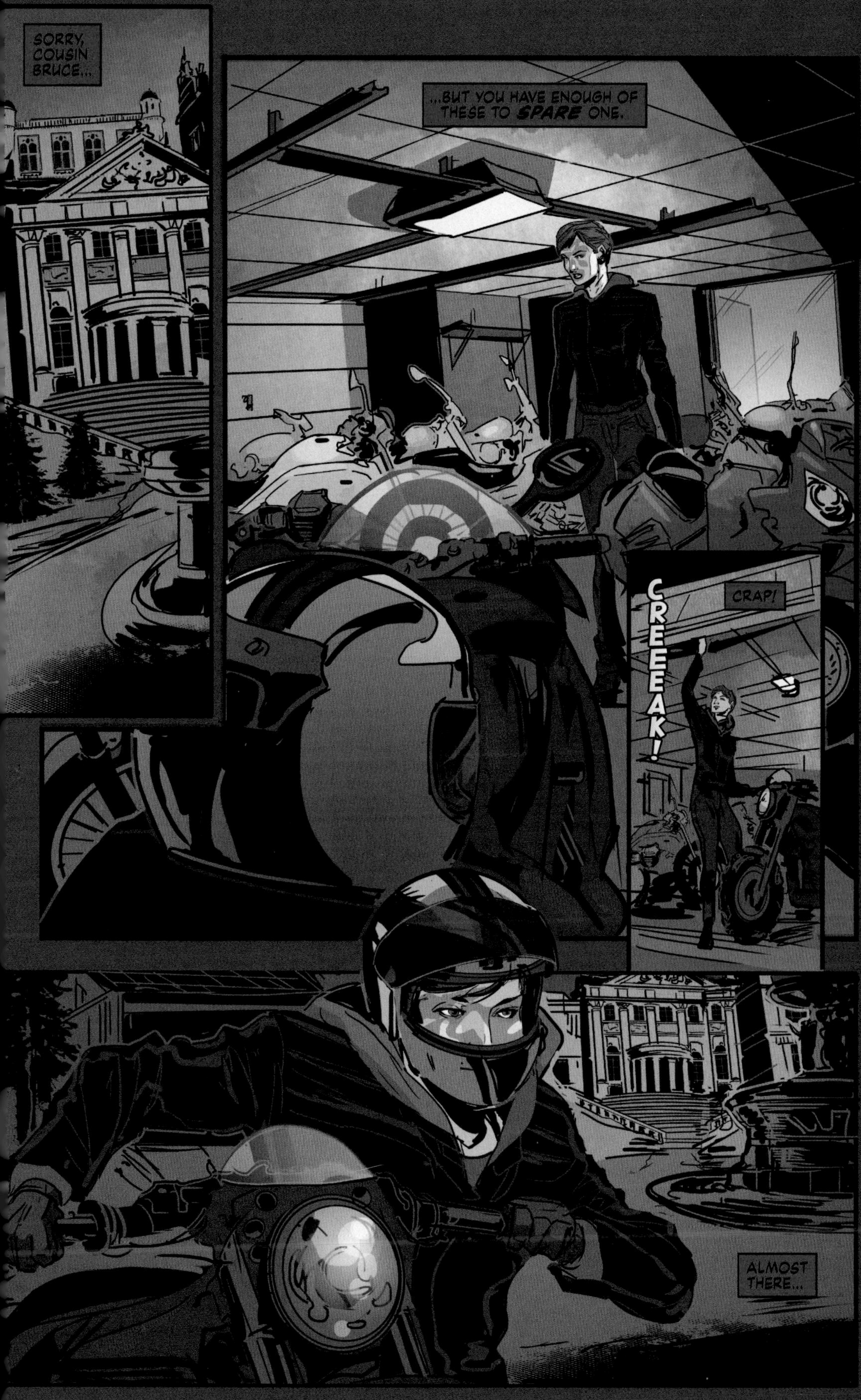
SORRY, COUSIN BRUCE...
...BUT YOU HAVE ENOUGH OF THESE TO SPARE ONE.
CREEEAK!
CRAP!
ALMOST THERE...

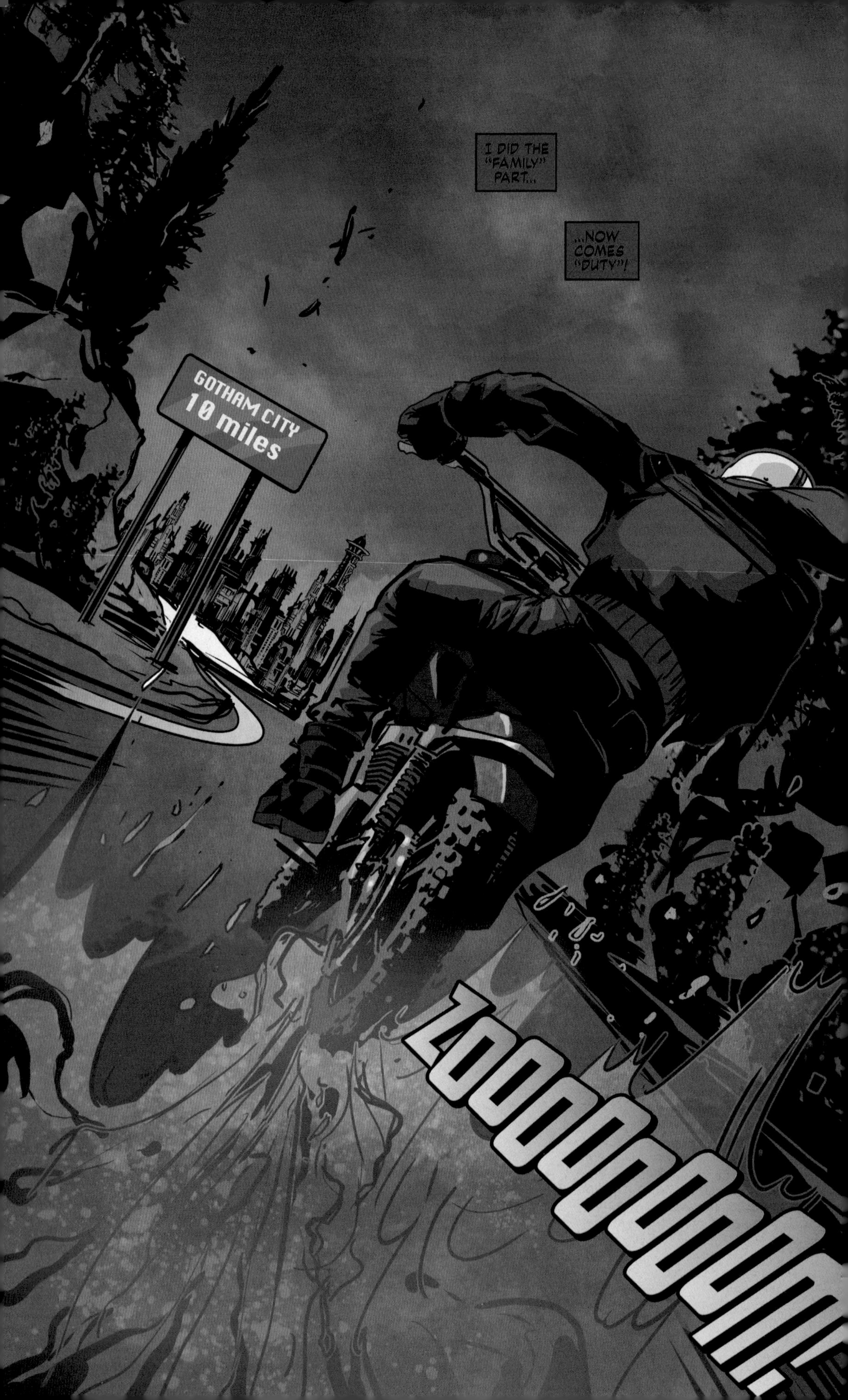
I DID THE "FAMILY" PART...
...NOW COMES "DUTY"!
GOTHAM CITY
10 miles
ZOOOOOOOM!

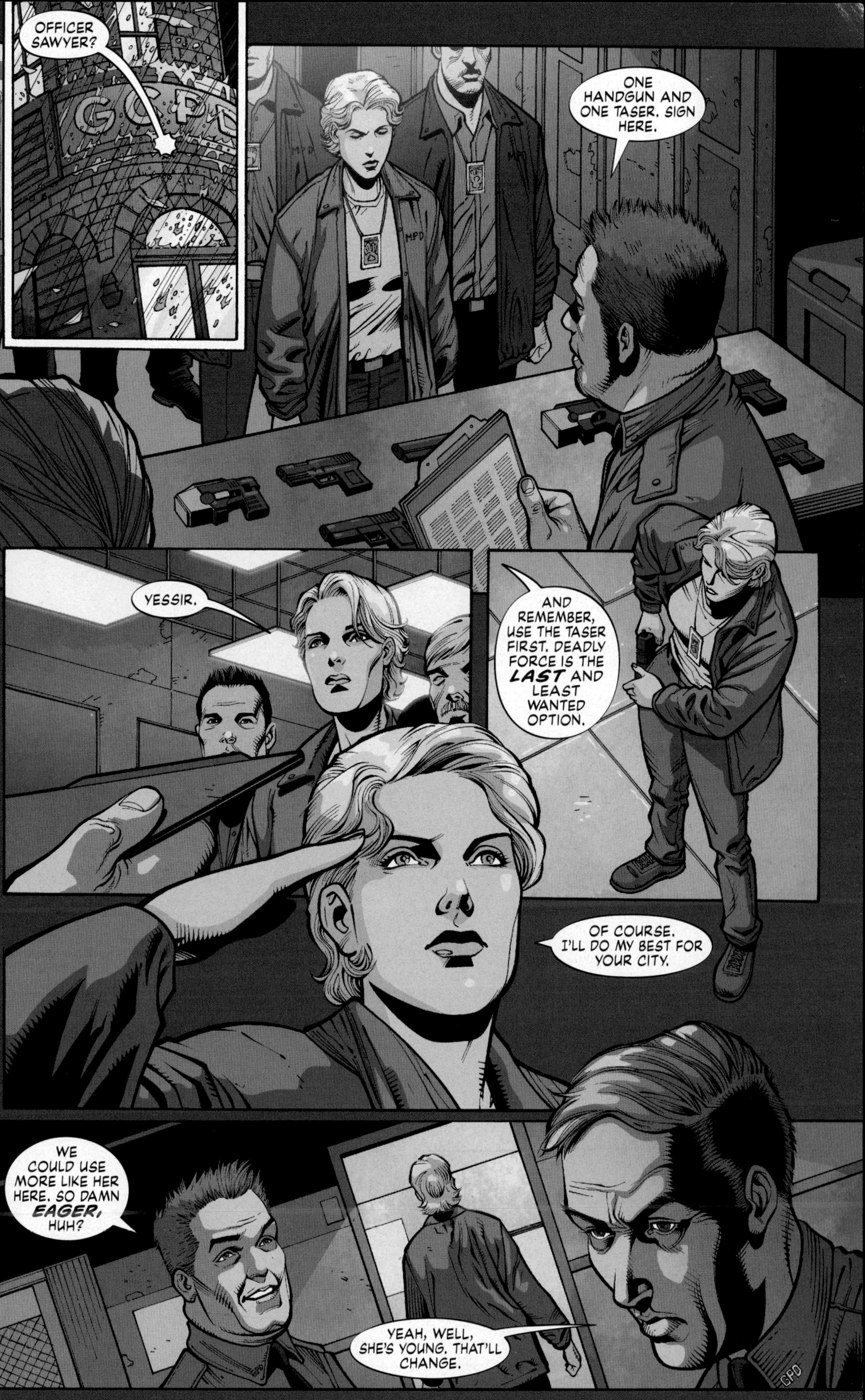
OFFICER SAWYER?
GCPD
ONE HANDGUN AND ONE TASER. SIGN HERE.
YESSIR.
AND REMEMBER, USE THE TASER FIRST. DEADLY FORCE IS THE *LAST* AND LEAST WANTED OPTION.
OF COURSE. I'LL DO MY BEST FOR YOUR CITY.
WE COULD USE MORE LIKE HER HERE. SO DAMN *EAGER,* HUH?
YEAH, WELL, SHE'S YOUNG. THAT'LL CHANGE.

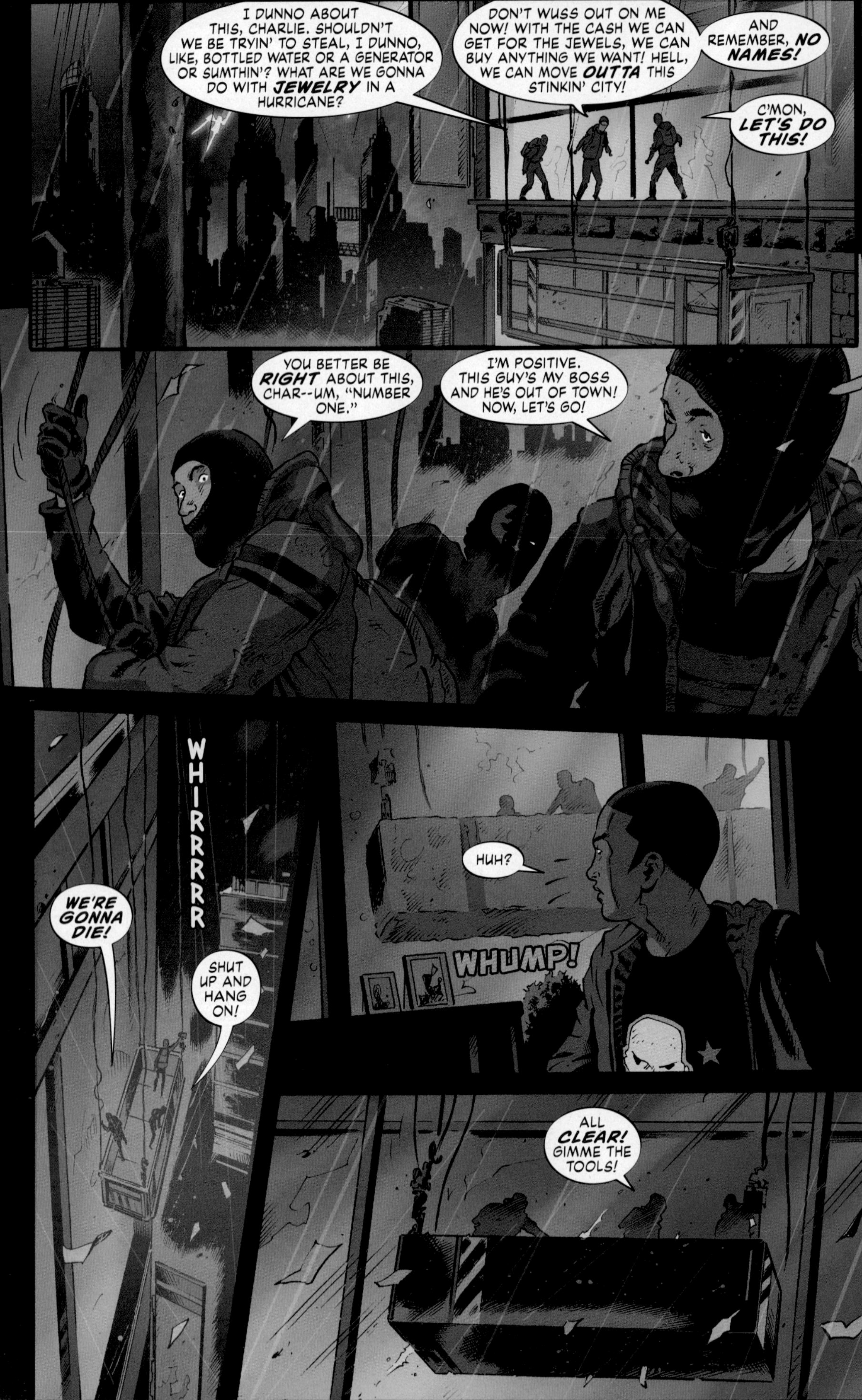
I DUNNO ABOUT THIS, CHARLIE. SHOULDN'T WE BE TRYIN' TO STEAL, I DUNNO, LIKE, BOTTLED WATER OR A GENERATOR OR SUMTHIN'? WHAT ARE WE GONNA DO WITH JEWELRY IN A HURRICANE?
DON'T WUSS OUT ON ME NOW! WITH THE CASH WE CAN GET FOR THE JEWELS, WE CAN BUY ANYTHING WE WANT! HELL, WE CAN MOVE OUTTA THIS STINKIN' CITY!
AND REMEMBER, NO NAMES!
C'MON, LET'S DO THIS!
YOU BETTER BE RIGHT ABOUT THIS, CHAR--UM, "NUMBER ONE."
I'M POSITIVE. THIS GUY'S MY BOSS AND HE'S OUT OF TOWN! NOW, LET'S GO!
WHIRRRRR
WE'RE GONNA DIE!
SHUT UP AND HANG ON!
HUH?
WHUMP!
ALL CLEAR! GIMME THE TOOLS!

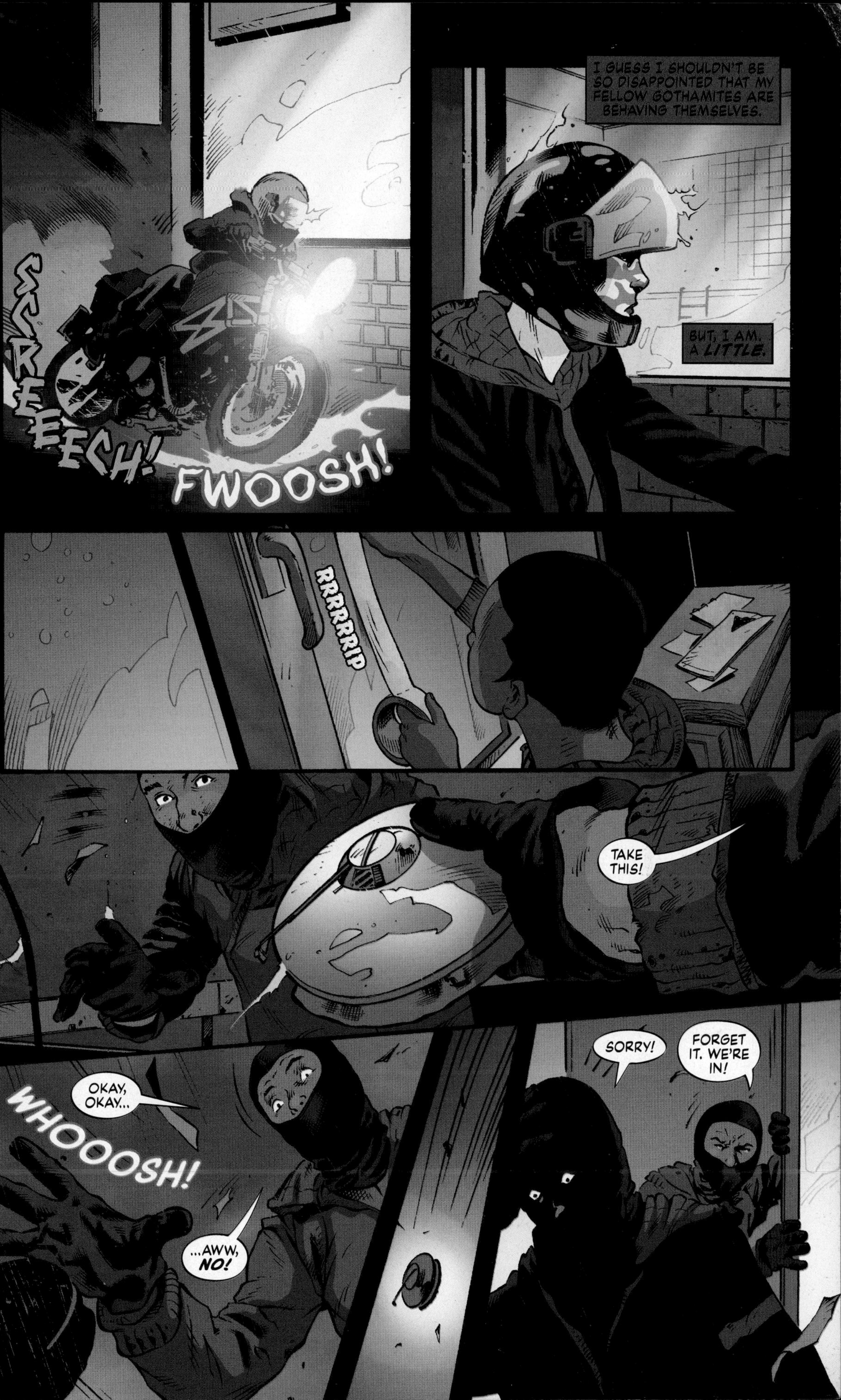
SCREEEECH!
FWOOSH!
I GUESS I SHOULDN'T BE SO DISAPPOINTED THAT MY FELLOW GOTHAMITES ARE BEHAVING THEMSELVES.
BUT, I AM. A LITTLE.
RRRRRRIP
TAKE THIS!
OKAY, OKAY...
WHOOOSH!
...AWW, NO!
SORRY!
FORGET IT. WE'RE IN!

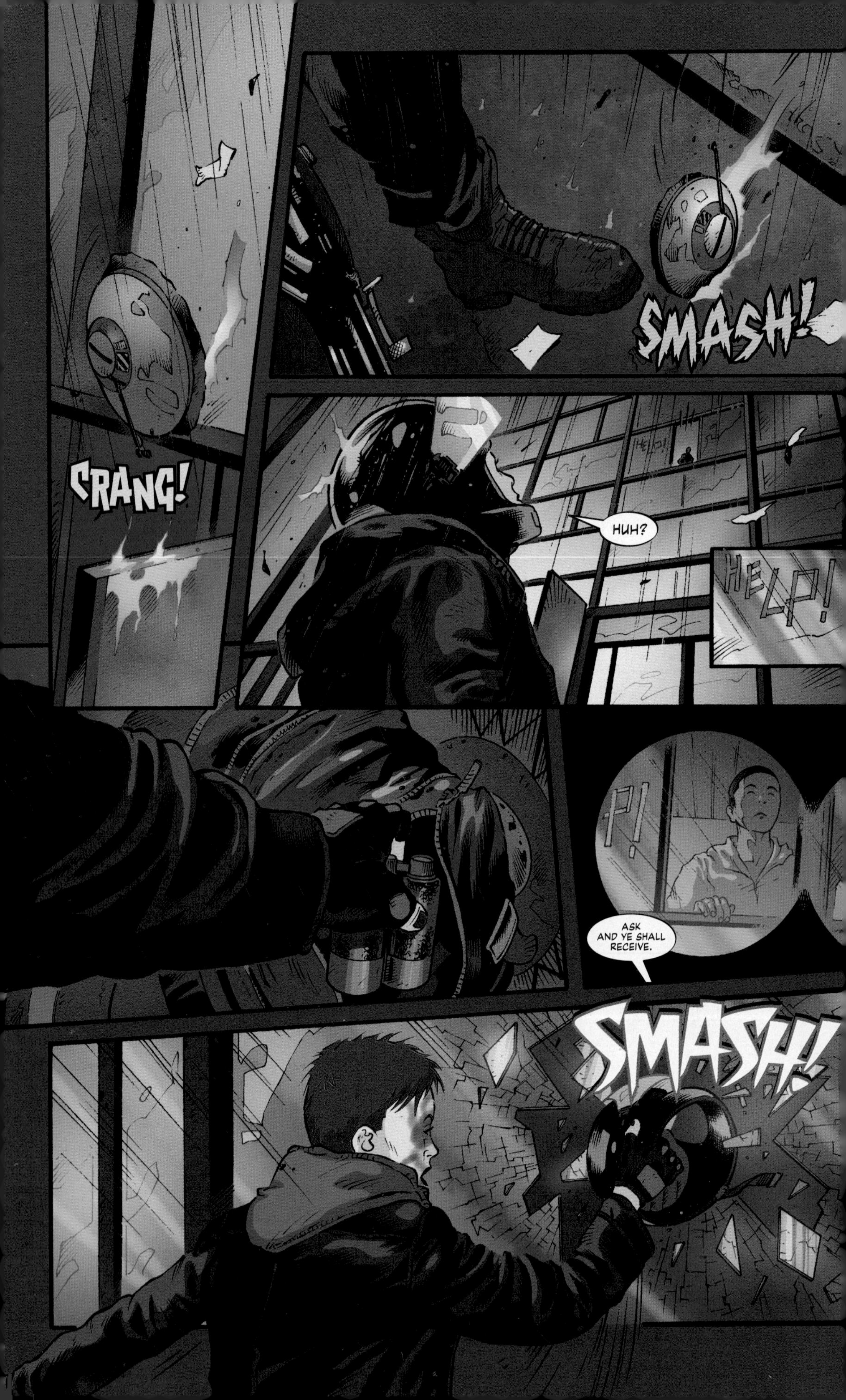
SMASH!
CRANG!
HUH?
HELP!
ASK AND YE SHALL RECEIVE.
SMASH!

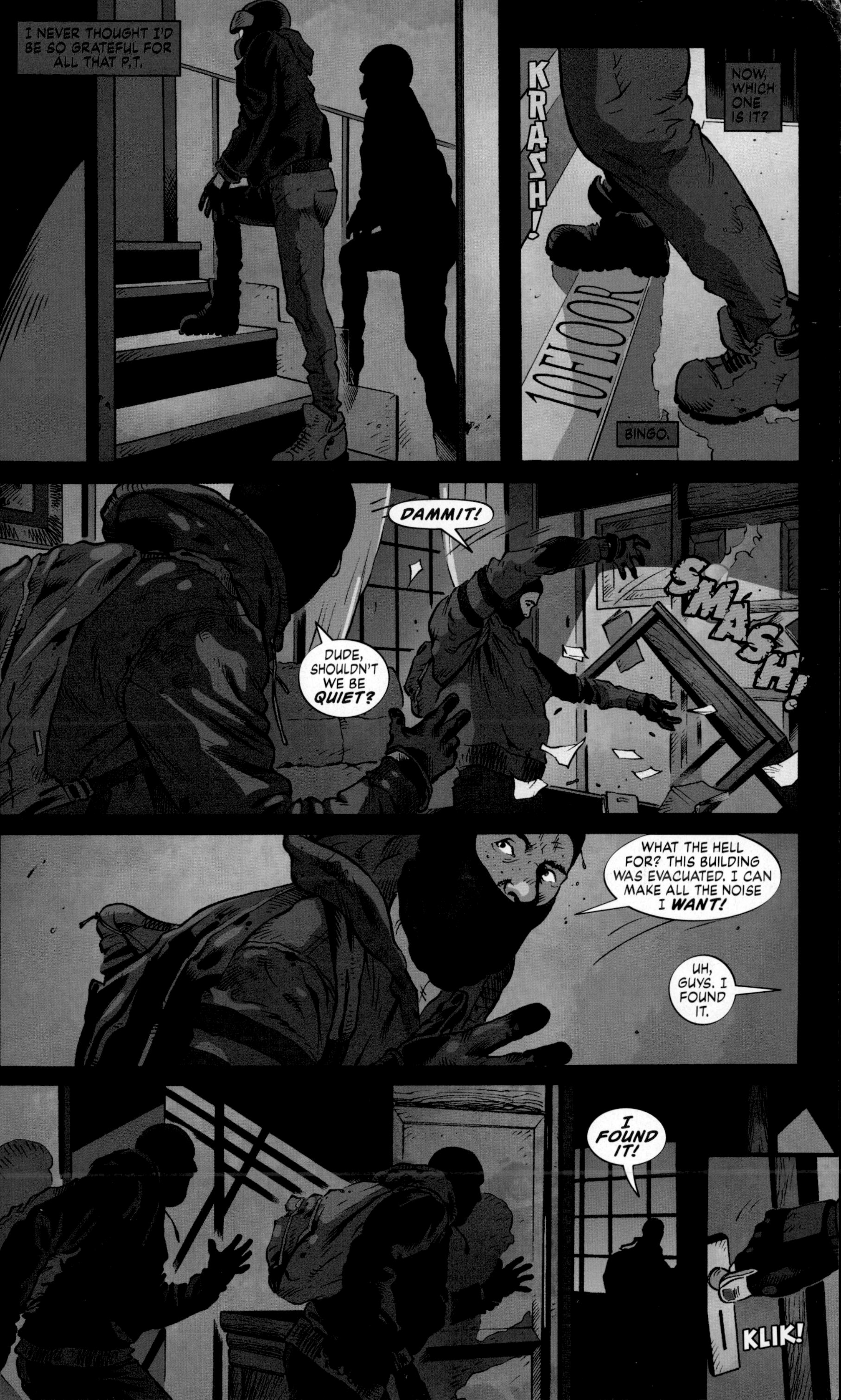
I NEVER THOUGHT I'D BE SO GRATEFUL FOR ALL THAT P.T.
KRASH!
NOW, WHICH ONE IS IT?
10 FLOOR
BINGO.
DAMMIT!
SMASH!
DUDE, SHOULDN'T WE BE QUIET?
WHAT THE HELL FOR? THIS BUILDING WAS EVACUATED. I CAN MAKE ALL THE NOISE I WANT!
UH, GUYS. I FOUND IT.
I FOUND IT!
KLIK!

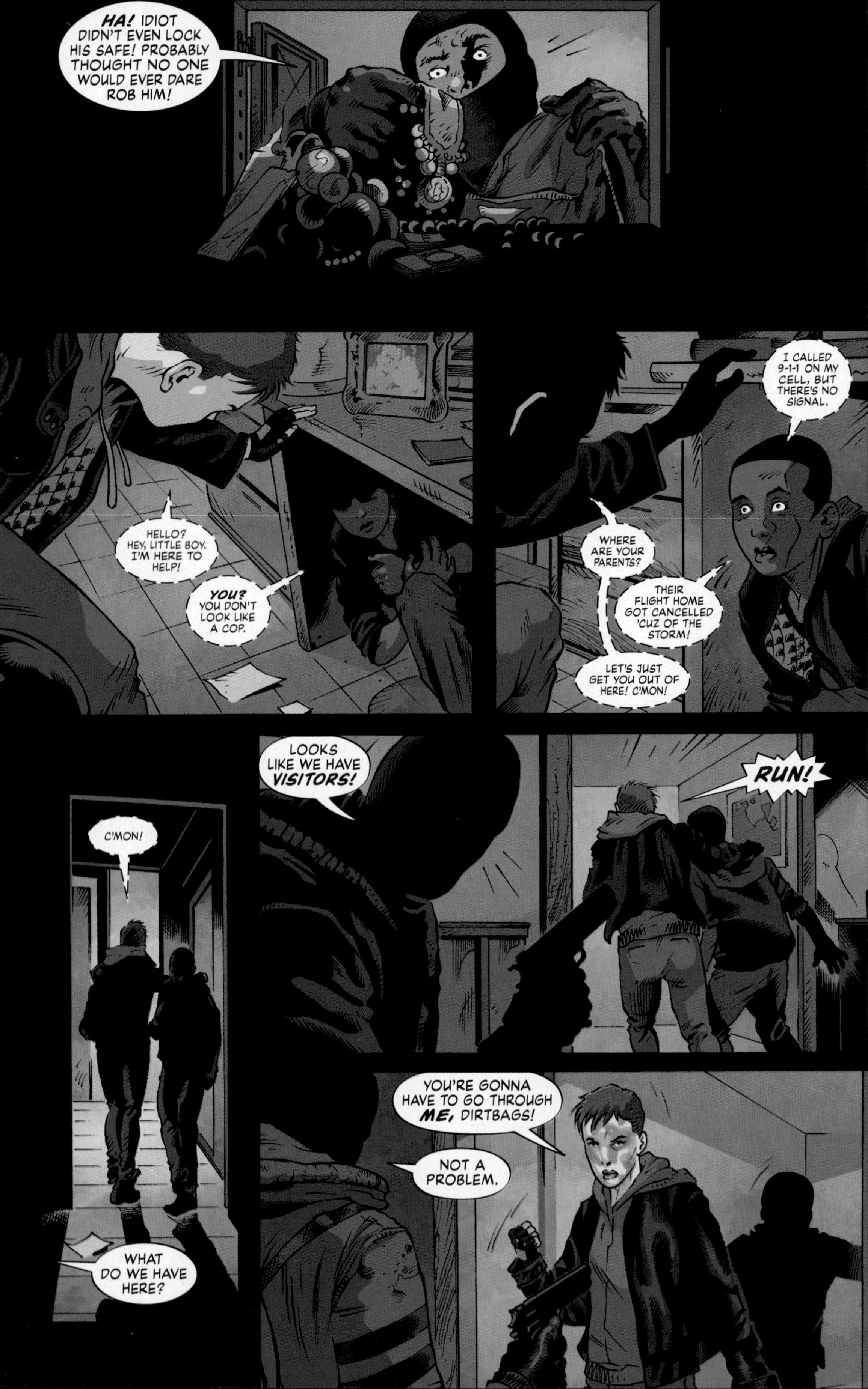
HA! IDIOT DIDN'T EVEN LOCK HIS SAFE! PROBABLY THOUGHT NO ONE WOULD EVER DARE ROB HIM!
HELLO? HEY, LITTLE BOY. I'M HERE TO HELP!
YOU? YOU DON'T LOOK LIKE A COP.
I CALLED 9-1-1 ON MY CELL, BUT THERE'S NO SIGNAL.
WHERE ARE YOUR PARENTS?
THEIR FLIGHT HOME GOT CANCELLED 'CUZ OF THE STORM!
LET'S JUST GET YOU OUT OF HERE! C'MON!
C'MON!
WHAT DO WE HAVE HERE?
LOOKS LIKE WE HAVE VISITORS!
RUN!
YOU'RE GONNA HAVE TO GO THROUGH ME, DIRTBAGS!
NOT A PROBLEM.

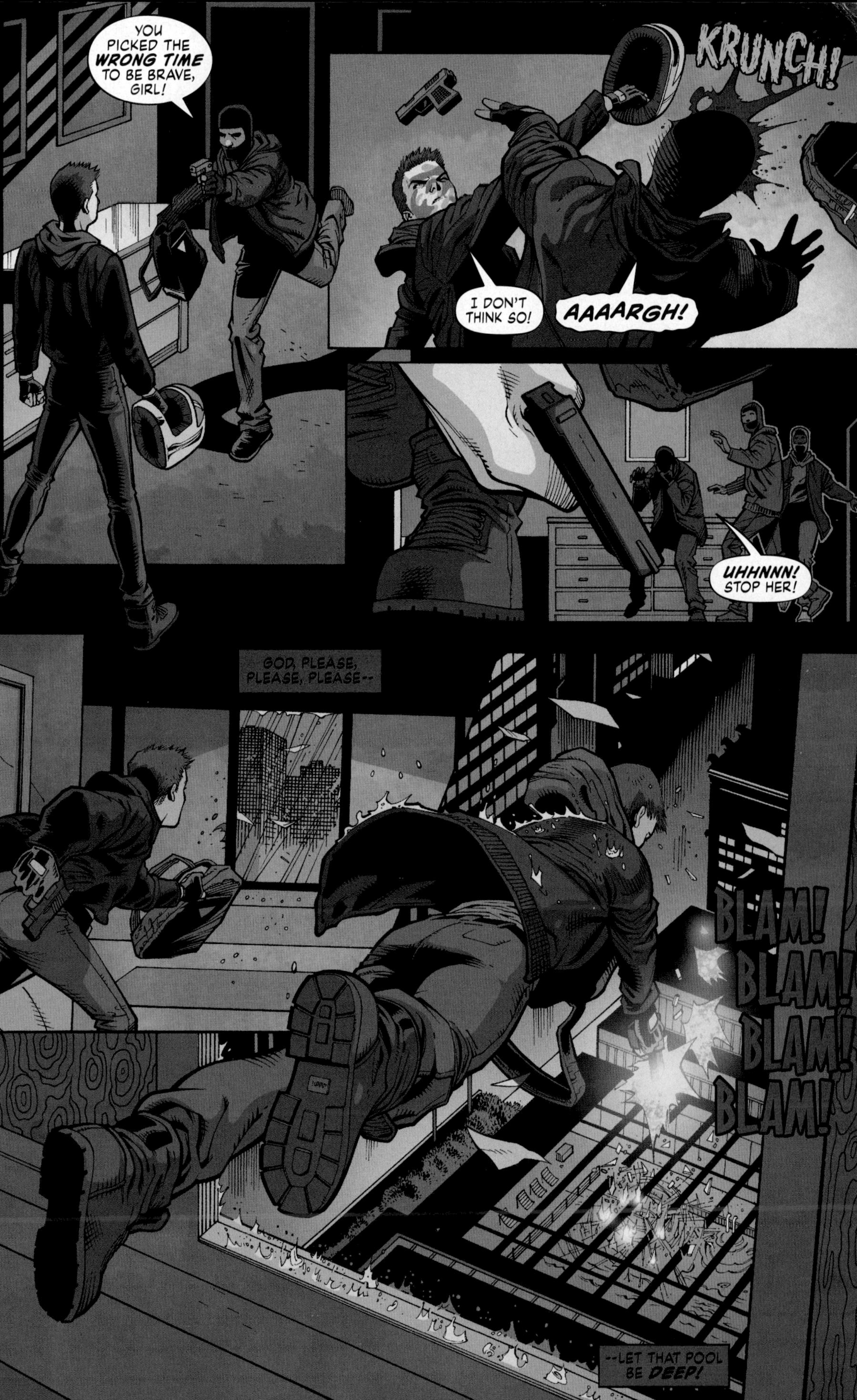
YOU PICKED THE WRONG TIME TO BE BRAVE, GIRL!
KRUNCH!
I DON'T THINK SO!
AAAARGH!
UHHNNN! STOP HER!
GOD, PLEASE, PLEASE, PLEASE--
BLAM! BLAM! BLAM! BLAM!
--LET THAT POOL BE DEEP!

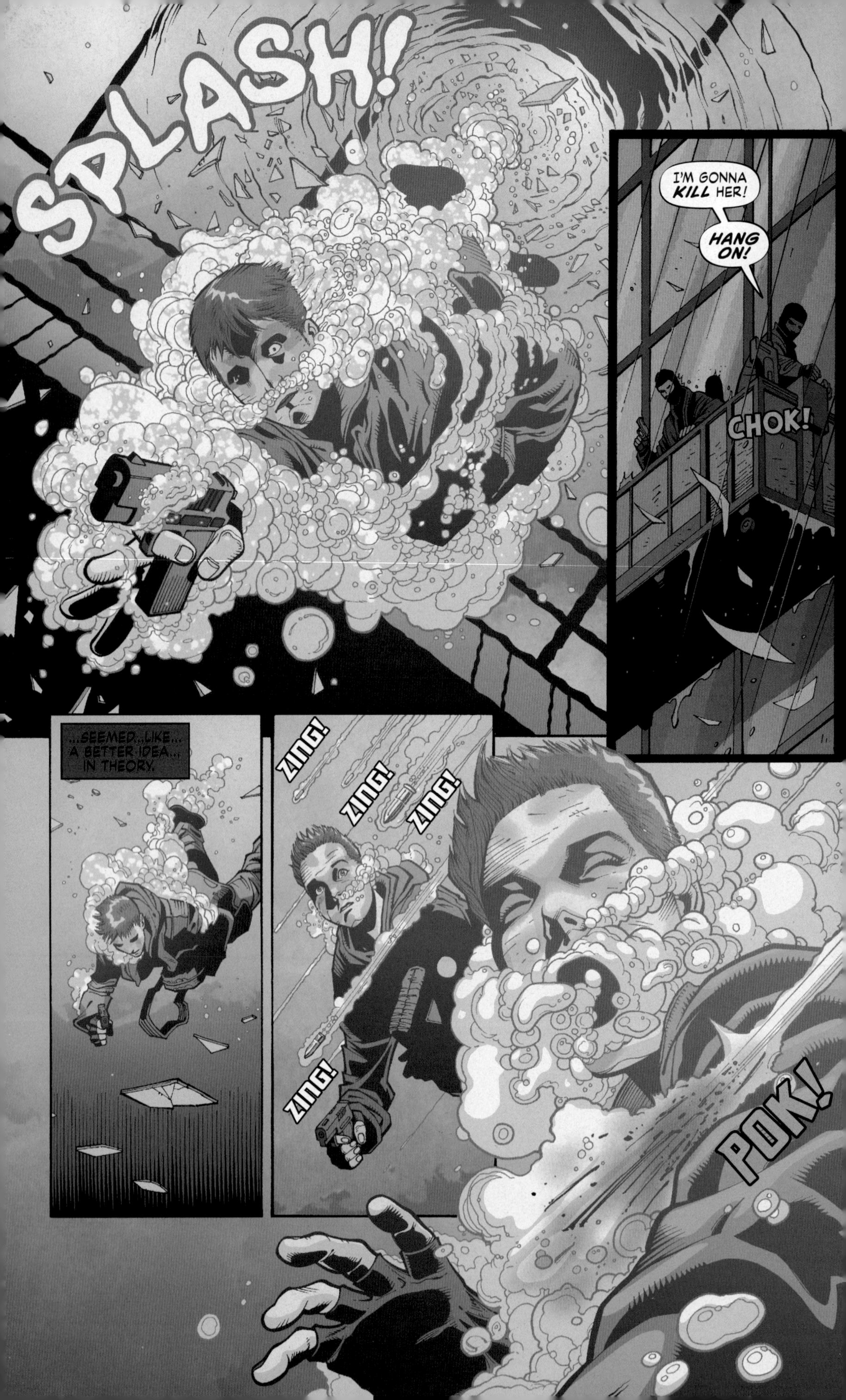
SPLASH!
I'M GONNA KILL HER!
HANG ON!
CHOK!
...SEEMED...LIKE... A BETTER IDEA... IN THEORY.
ZING!
ZING!
ZING!
ZING!
POK!

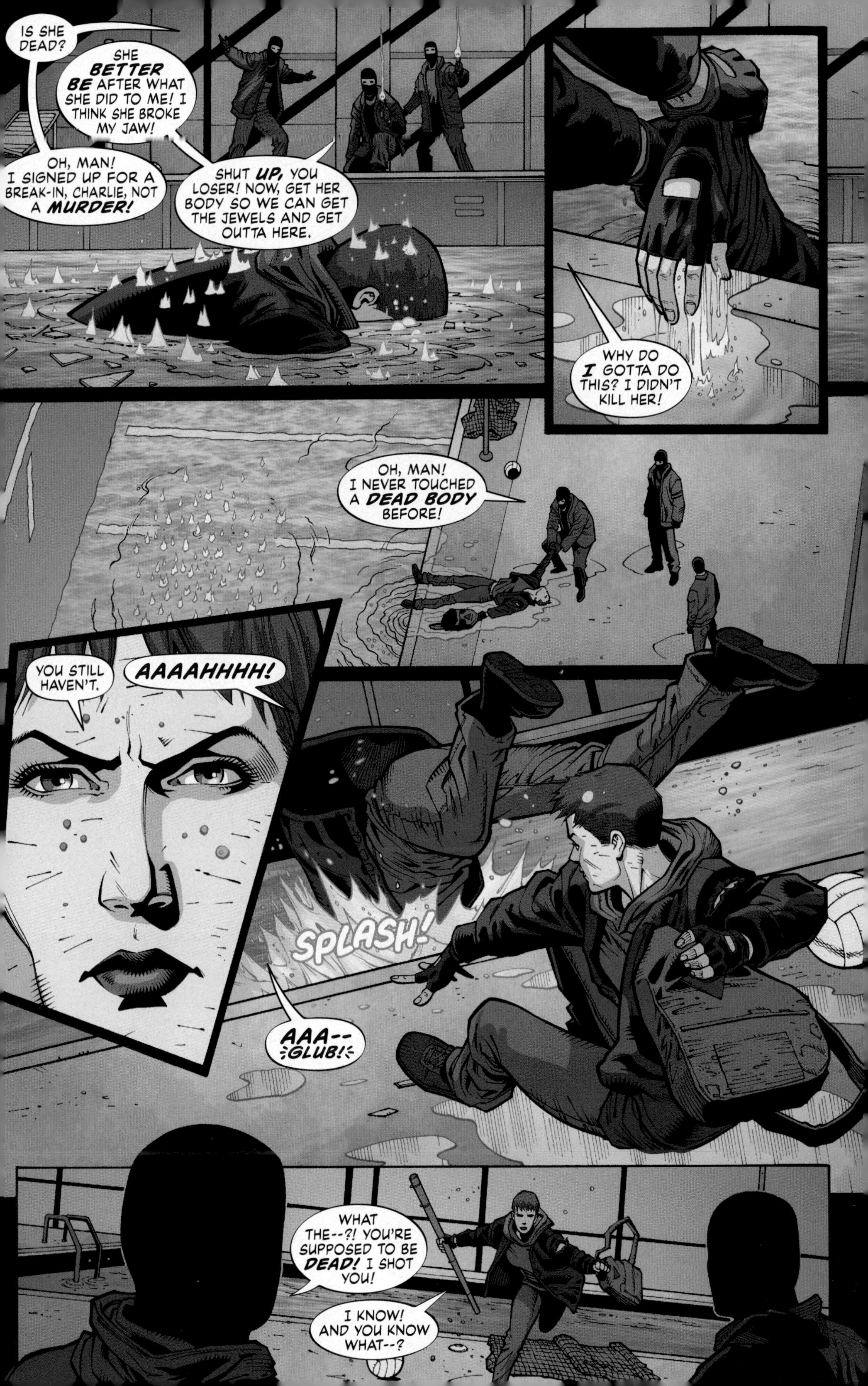
IS SHE DEAD?
SHE BETTER BE AFTER WHAT SHE DID TO ME! I THINK SHE BROKE MY JAW!
OH, MAN! I SIGNED UP FOR A BREAK-IN, CHARLIE, NOT A MURDER!
SHUT UP, YOU LOSER! NOW, GET HER BODY SO WE CAN GET THE JEWELS AND GET OUTTA HERE.
WHY DO I GOTTA DO THIS? I DIDN'T KILL HER!
OH, MAN! I NEVER TOUCHED A DEAD BODY BEFORE!
YOU STILL HAVEN'T.
AAAAHHHH!
SPLASH!
AAA-- GLUB!
WHAT THE--?! YOU'RE SUPPOSED TO BE DEAD! I SHOT YOU!
I KNOW! AND YOU KNOW WHAT--?

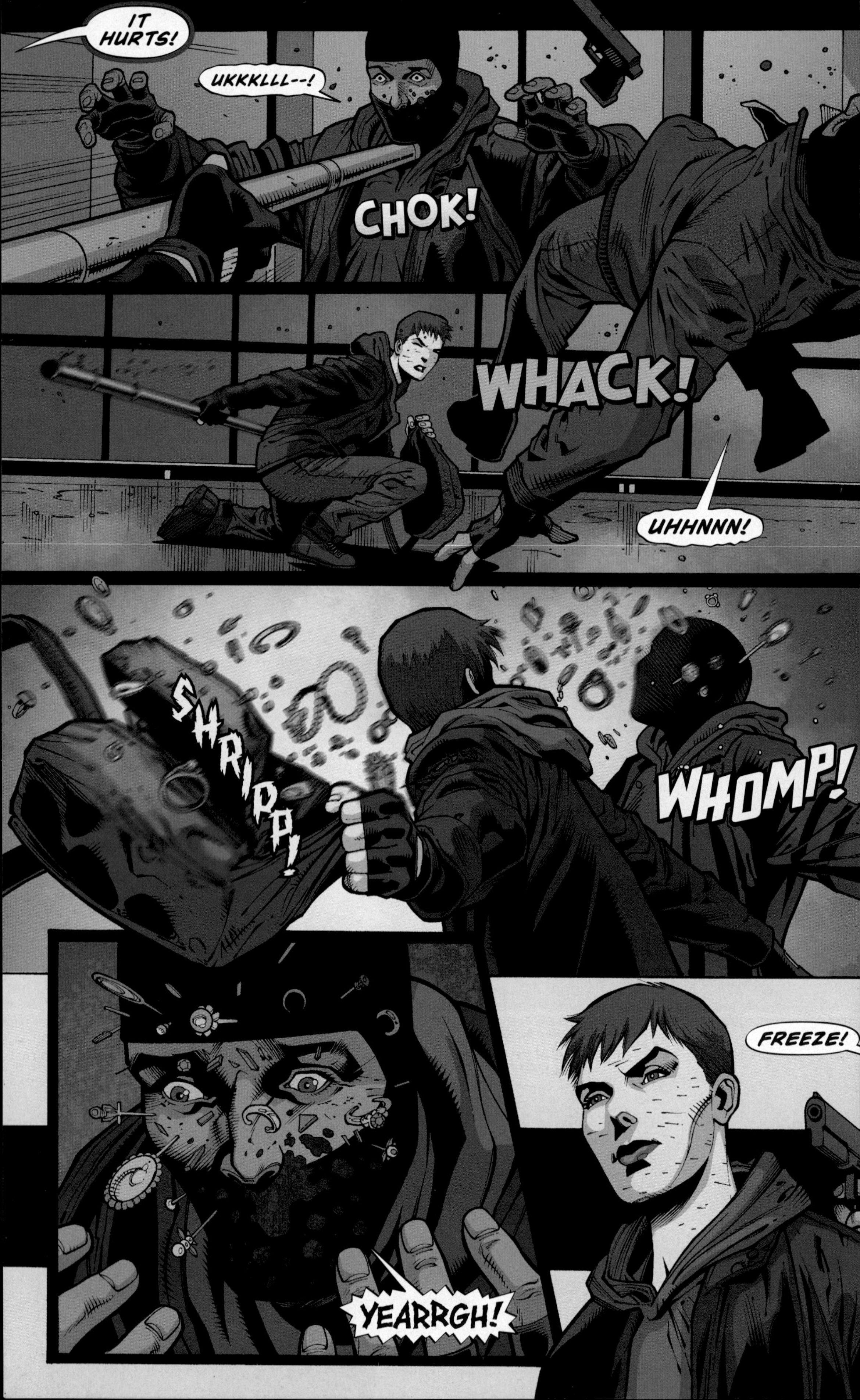
IT HURTS!
UKKKLLL--!
CHOK!
WHACK!
UHHNNN!
SHRIPP!
WHOMP!
YEARRGH!
FREEZE!

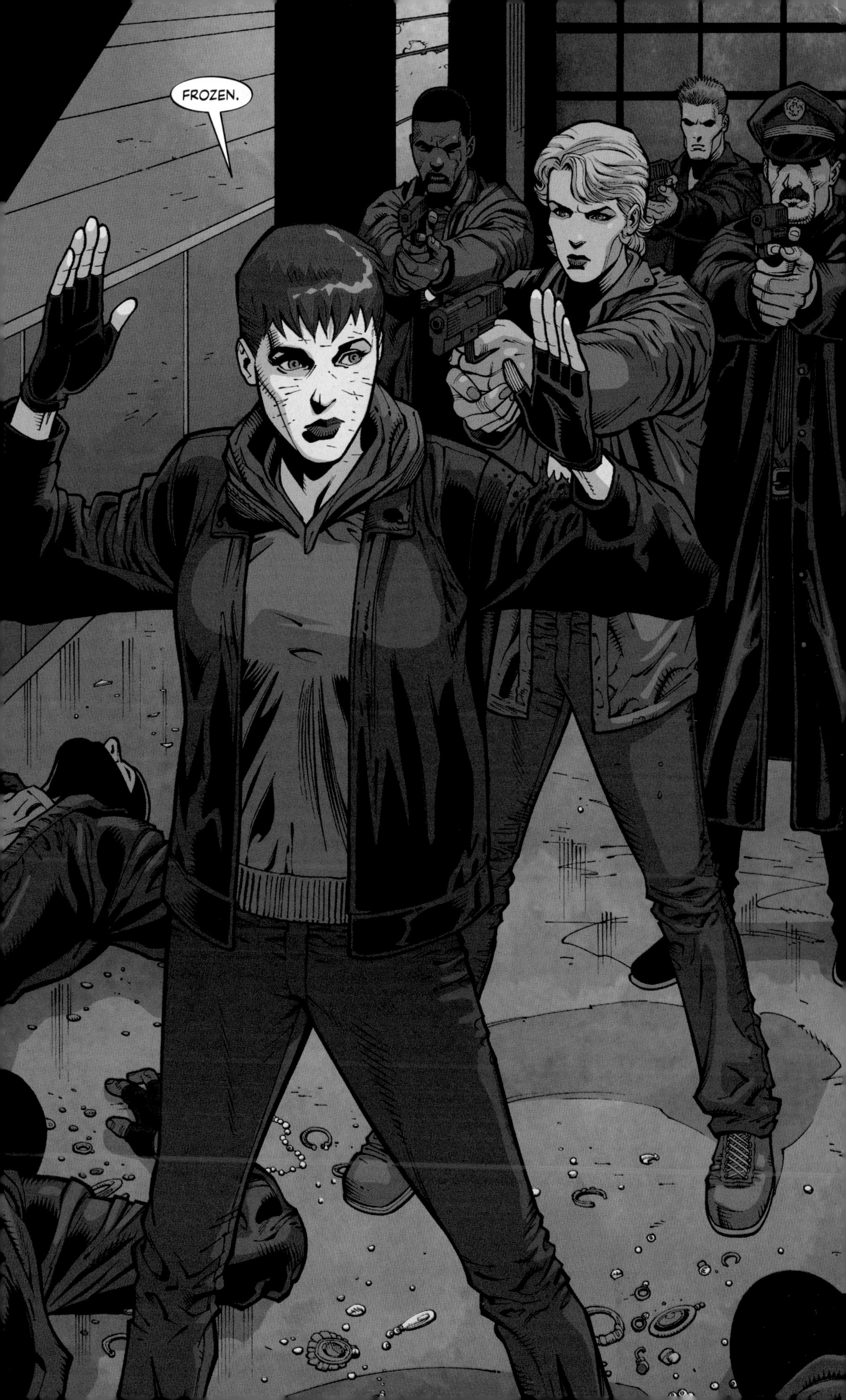
FROZEN.

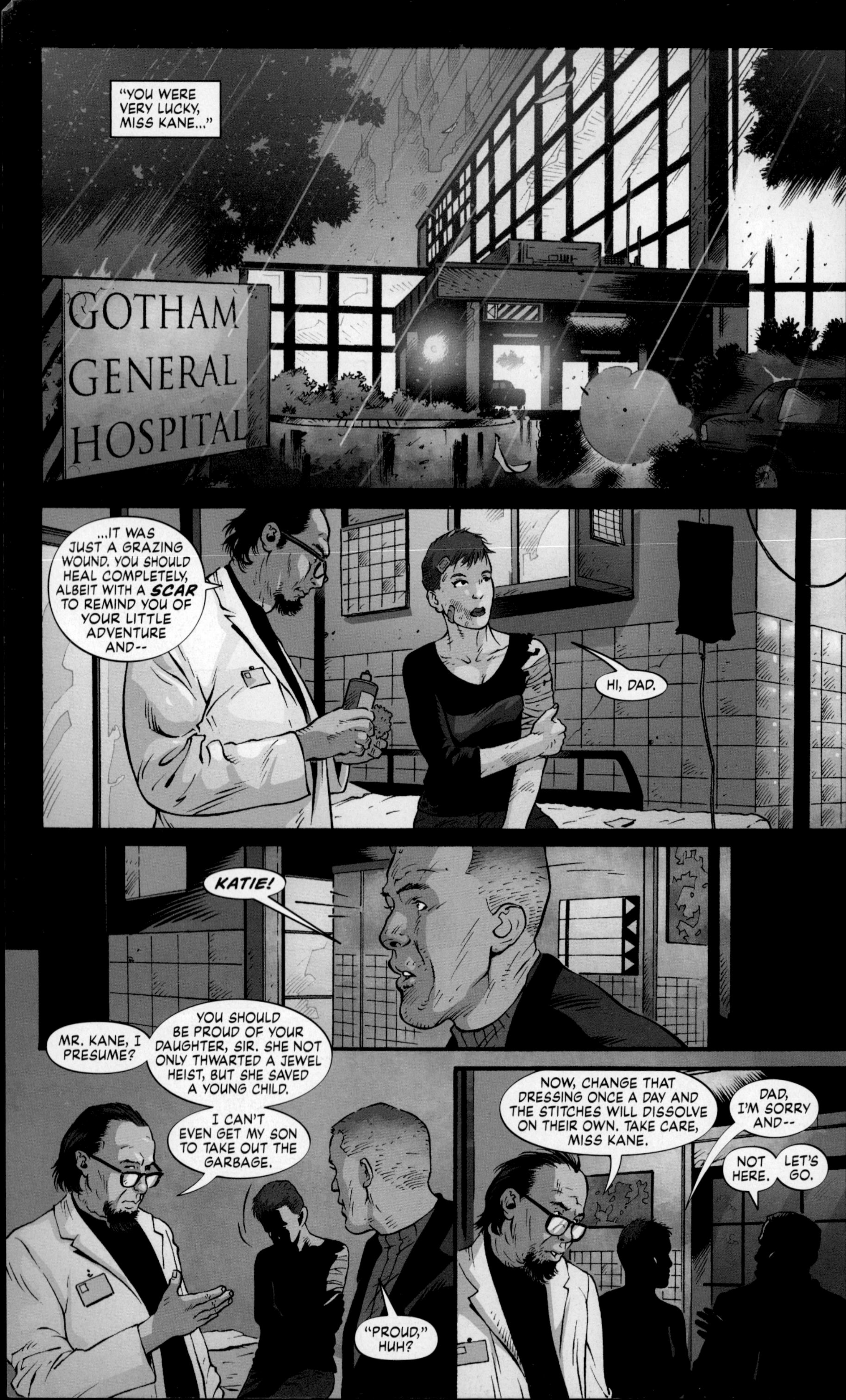
"YOU WERE VERY LUCKY, MISS KANE..."
GOTHAM GENERAL HOSPITAL
...IT WAS JUST A GRAZING WOUND. YOU SHOULD HEAL COMPLETELY, ALBEIT WITH A SCAR TO REMIND YOU OF YOUR LITTLE ADVENTURE AND--
HI, DAD.
KATIE!
MR. KANE, I PRESUME?
YOU SHOULD BE PROUD OF YOUR DAUGHTER, SIR. SHE NOT ONLY THWARTED A JEWEL HEIST, BUT SHE SAVED A YOUNG CHILD.
I CAN'T EVEN GET MY SON TO TAKE OUT THE GARBAGE.
"PROUD," HUH?
NOW, CHANGE THAT DRESSING ONCE A DAY AND THE STITCHES WILL DISSOLVE ON THEIR OWN. TAKE CARE, MISS KANE.
DAD, I'M SORRY AND--
NOT HERE.
LET'S GO.

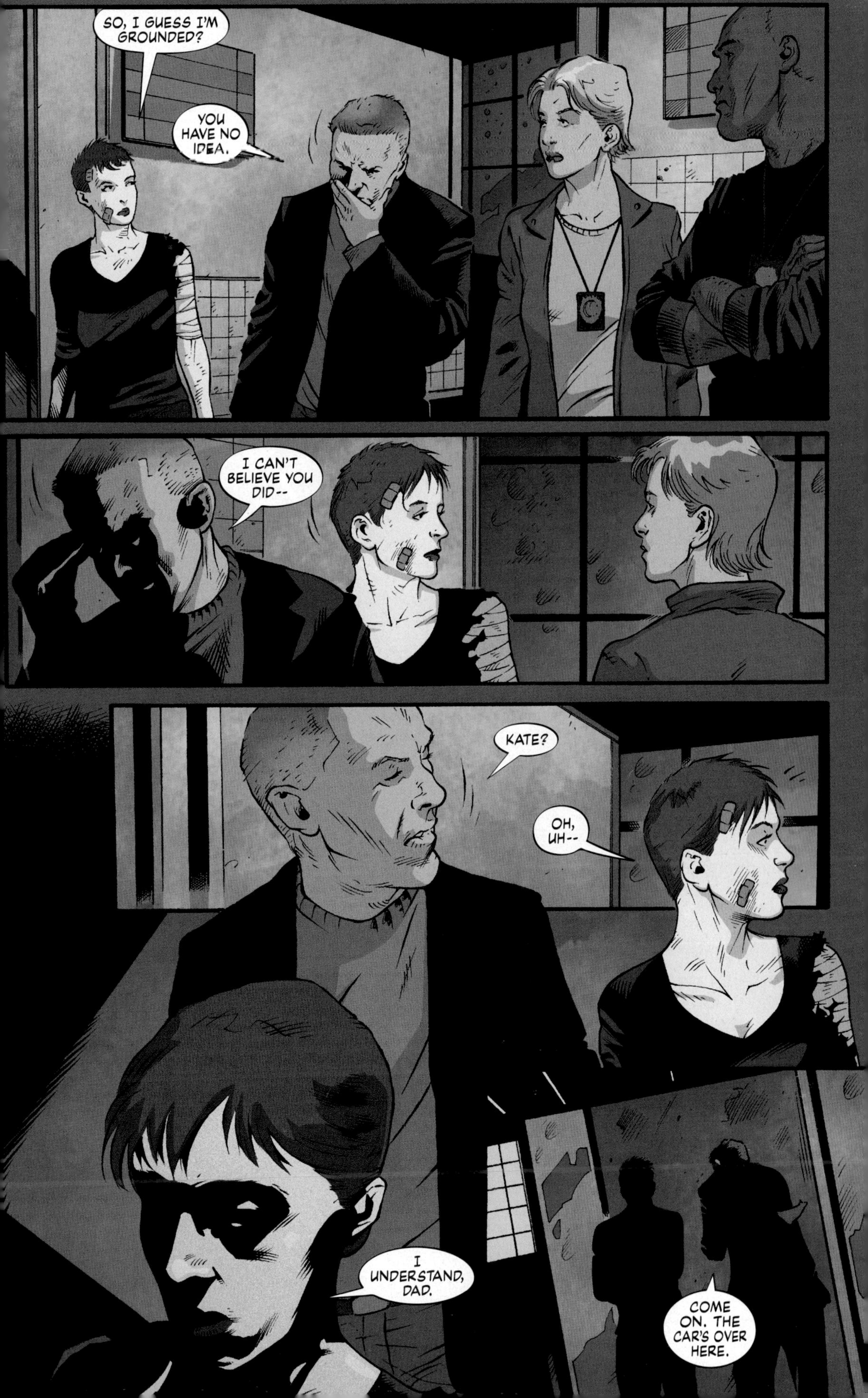
SO, I GUESS I'M GROUNDED?
YOU HAVE NO IDEA.
I CAN'T BELIEVE YOU DID--
KATE?
OH, UH--
I UNDERSTAND, DAD.
COME ON. THE CAR'S OVER HERE.

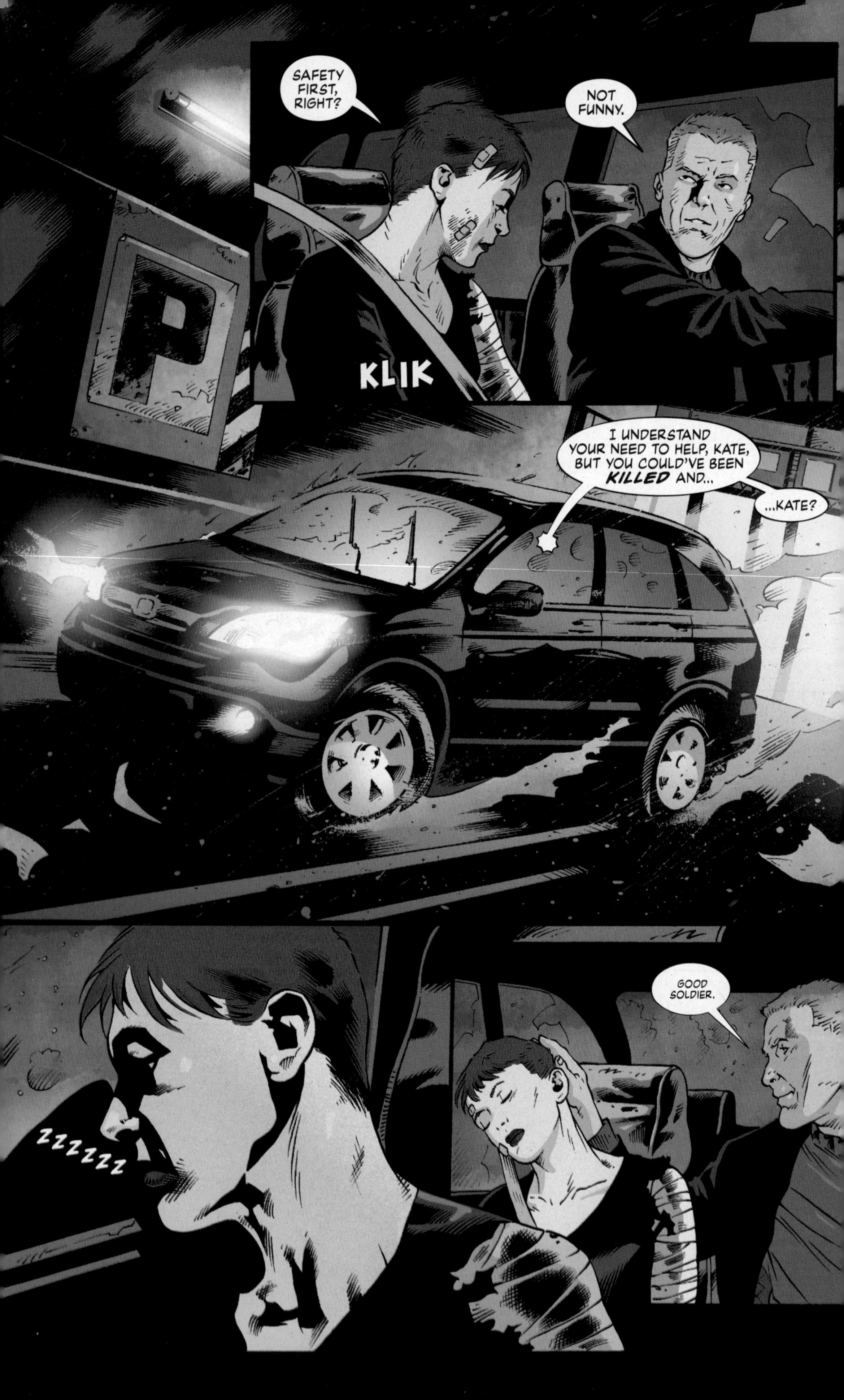
SAFETY FIRST, RIGHT?
NOT FUNNY.
KLIK
I UNDERSTAND YOUR NEED TO HELP, KATE, BUT YOU COULD'VE BEEN *KILLED* AND...
...KATE?
ZZZZZZ
GOOD SOLDIER.

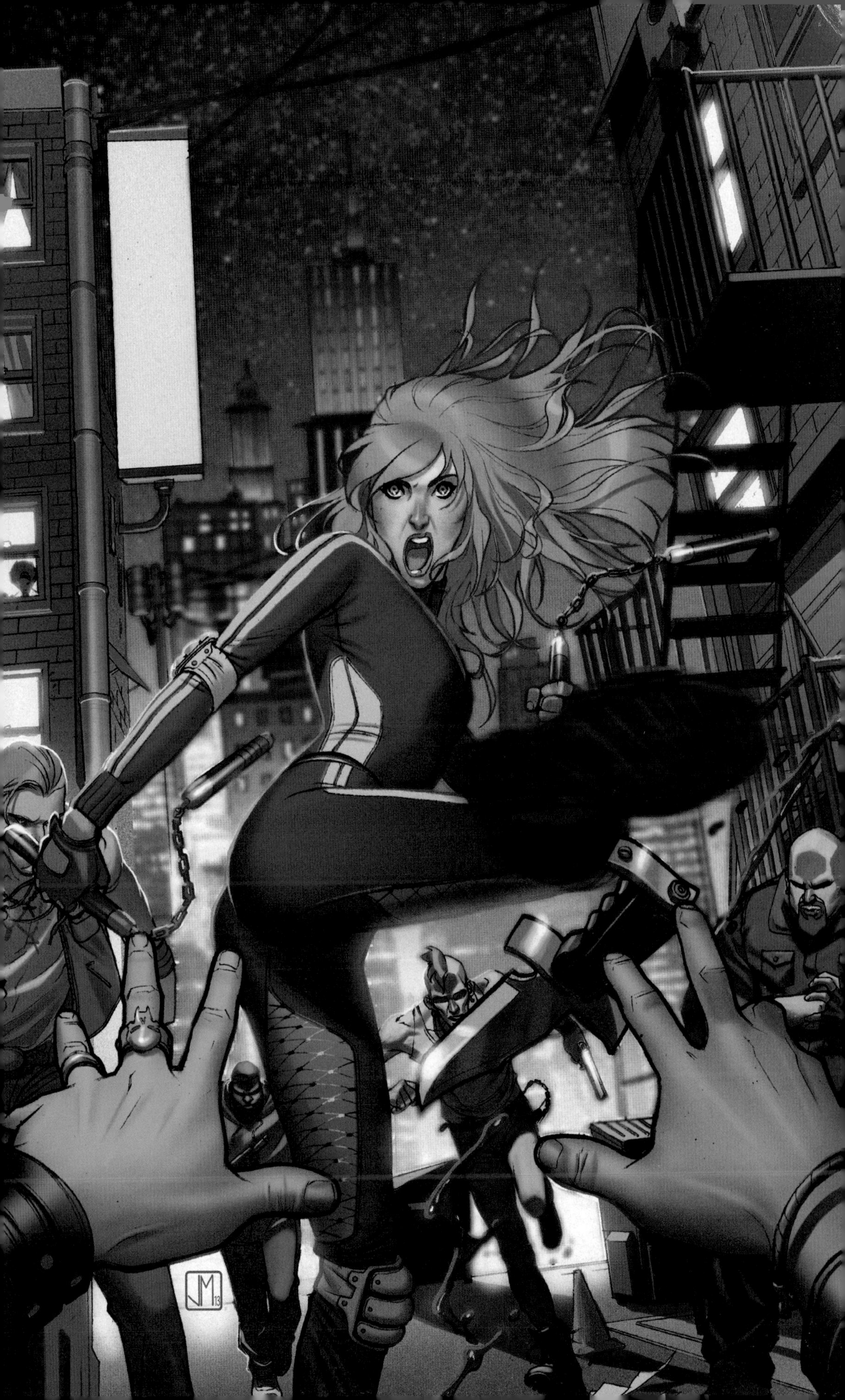

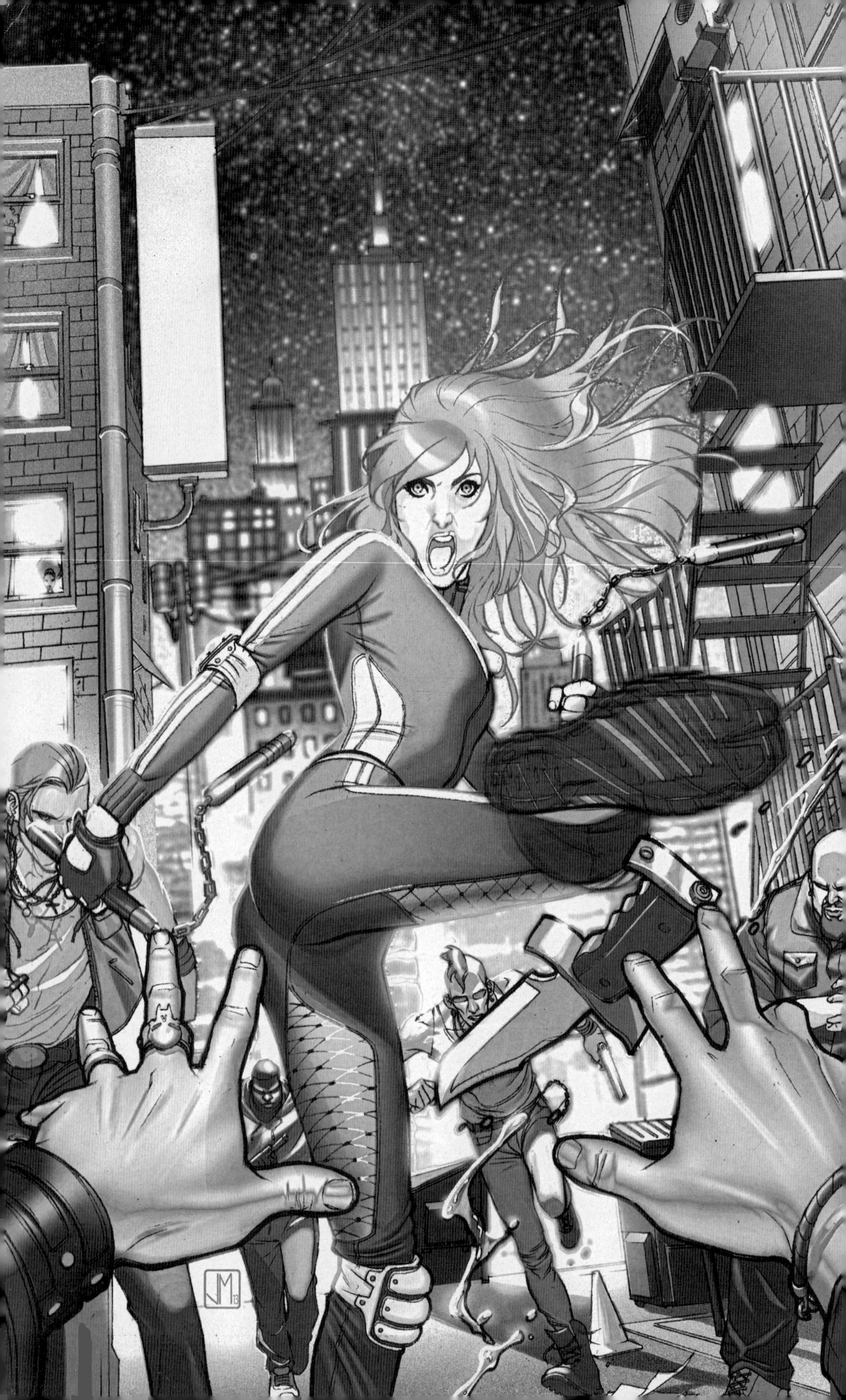

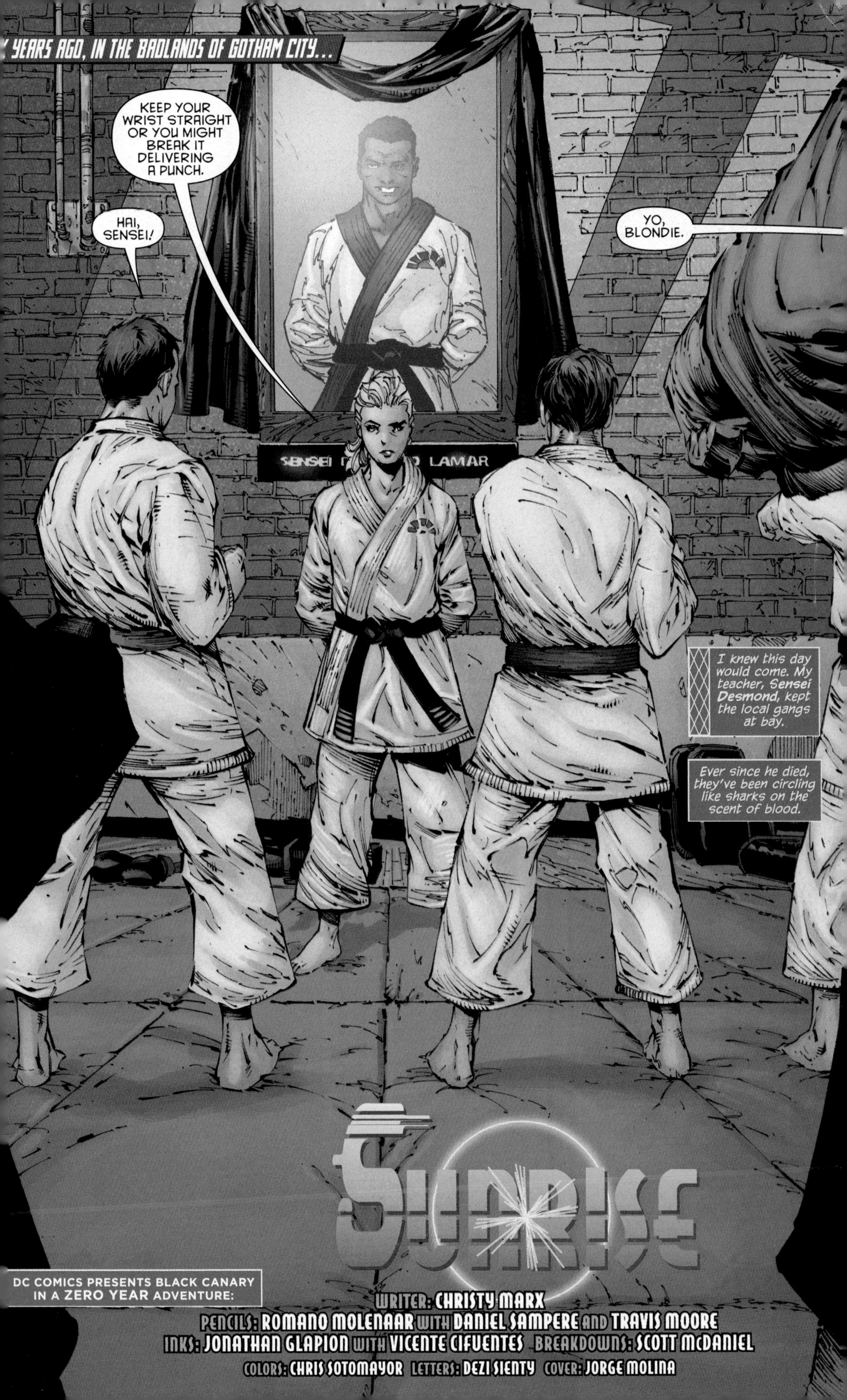
YEARS AGO, IN THE BADLANDS OF GOTHAM CITY...
KEEP YOUR WRIST STRAIGHT OR YOU MIGHT BREAK IT DELIVERING A PUNCH.
HAI, SENSEI!
SENSEI
LAMAR
YO, BLONDIE.
I knew this day would come. My teacher, Sensei Desmond, kept the local gangs at bay.
Ever since he died, they've been circling like sharks on the scent of blood.
SUNRISE
DC COMICS PRESENTS BLACK CANARY IN A ZERO YEAR ADVENTURE:
WRITER: CHRISTY MARX
PENCILS: ROMANO MOLENAAR WITH DANIEL SAMPERE AND TRAVIS MOORE
INKS: JONATHAN GLAPION WITH VICENTE CIFUENTES BREAKDOWNS: SCOTT McDANIEL
COLORS: CHRIS SOTOMAYOR LETTERS: DEZI SIENTY COVER: JORGE MOLINA

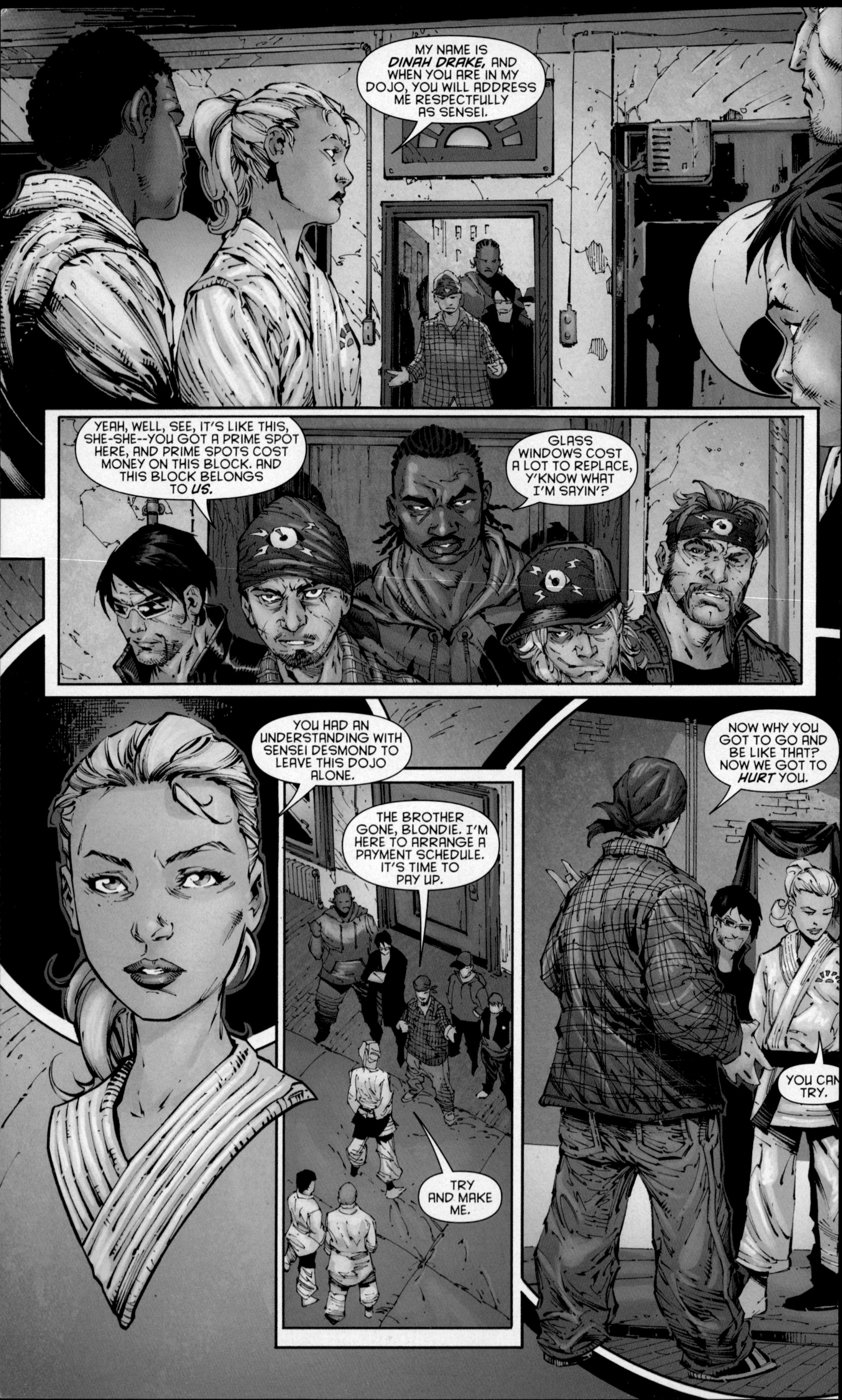

MY NAME IS DINAH DRAKE, AND WHEN YOU ARE IN MY DOJO, YOU WILL ADDRESS ME RESPECTFULLY AS SENSEI.
YEAH, WELL, SEE, IT'S LIKE THIS, SHE-SHE--YOU GOT A PRIME SPOT HERE, AND PRIME SPOTS COST MONEY ON THIS BLOCK. AND THIS BLOCK BELONGS TO US.
GLASS WINDOWS COST A LOT TO REPLACE, Y'KNOW WHAT I'M SAYIN'?
YOU HAD AN UNDERSTANDING WITH SENSEI DESMOND TO LEAVE THIS DOJO ALONE.
THE BROTHER GONE, BLONDIE. I'M HERE TO ARRANGE A PAYMENT SCHEDULE. IT'S TIME TO PAY UP.
TRY AND MAKE ME.
NOW WHY YOU GOT TO GO AND BE LIKE THAT? NOW WE GOT TO HURT YOU.
YOU CAN TRY.

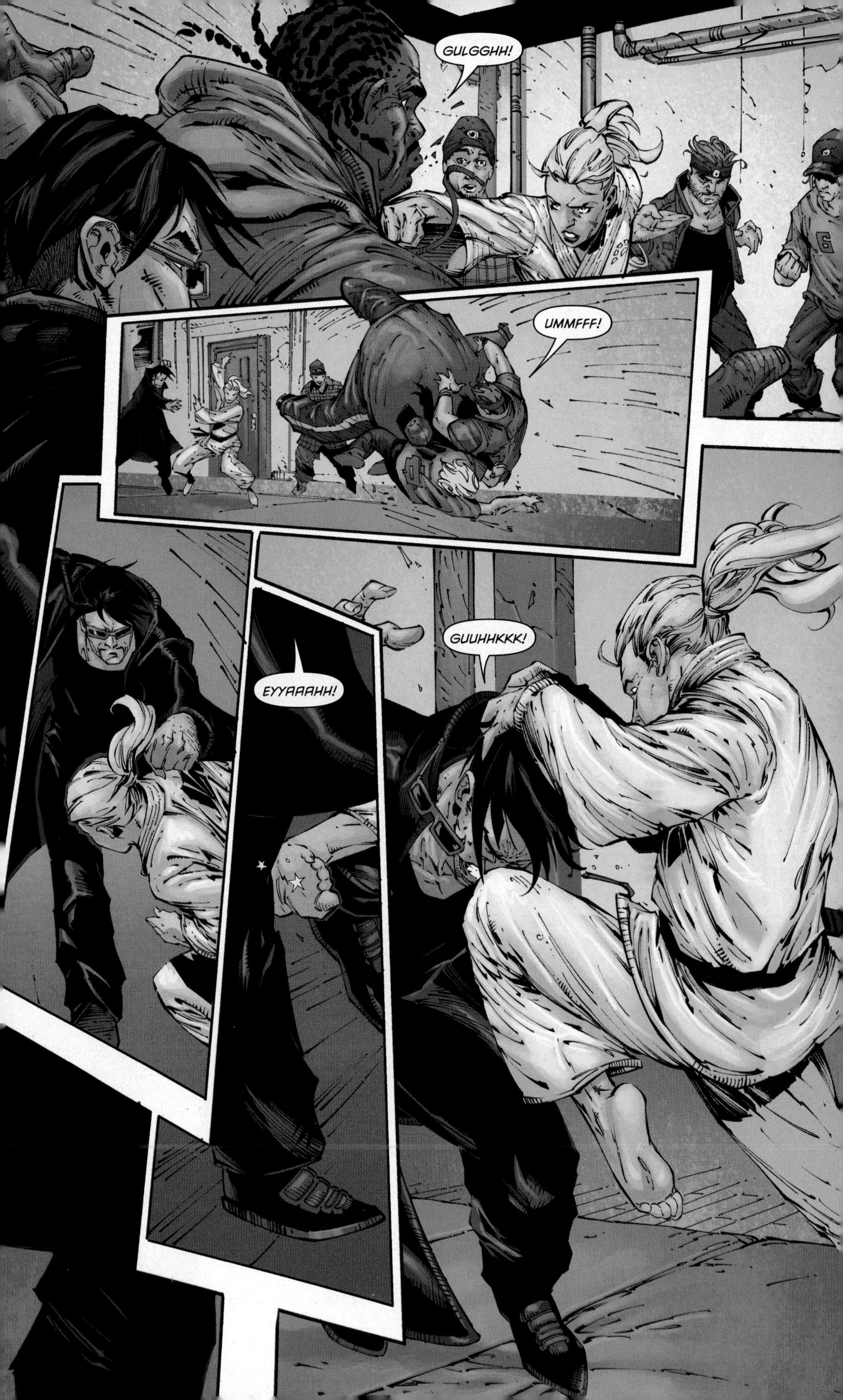
GULGGHH!
UMMFFF!
EYYAAAHH!
GUUHHKKK!

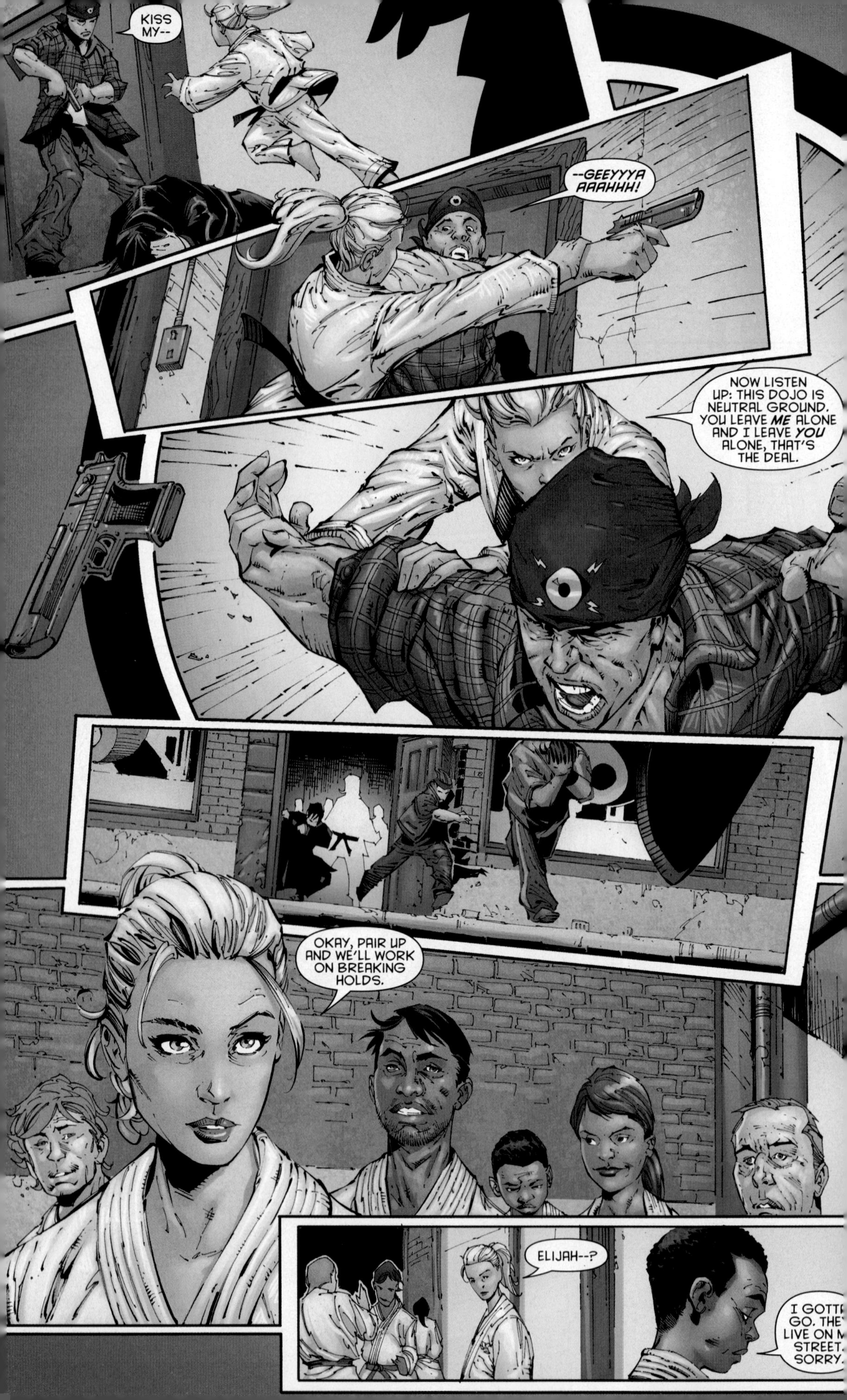
KISS MY--
--GEEYYYA AAAHHH!
NOW LISTEN UP: THIS DOJO IS NEUTRAL GROUND. YOU LEAVE *ME* ALONE AND I LEAVE *YOU* ALONE, THAT'S THE DEAL.
OKAY, PAIR UP AND WE'LL WORK ON BREAKING HOLDS.
ELIJAH--?

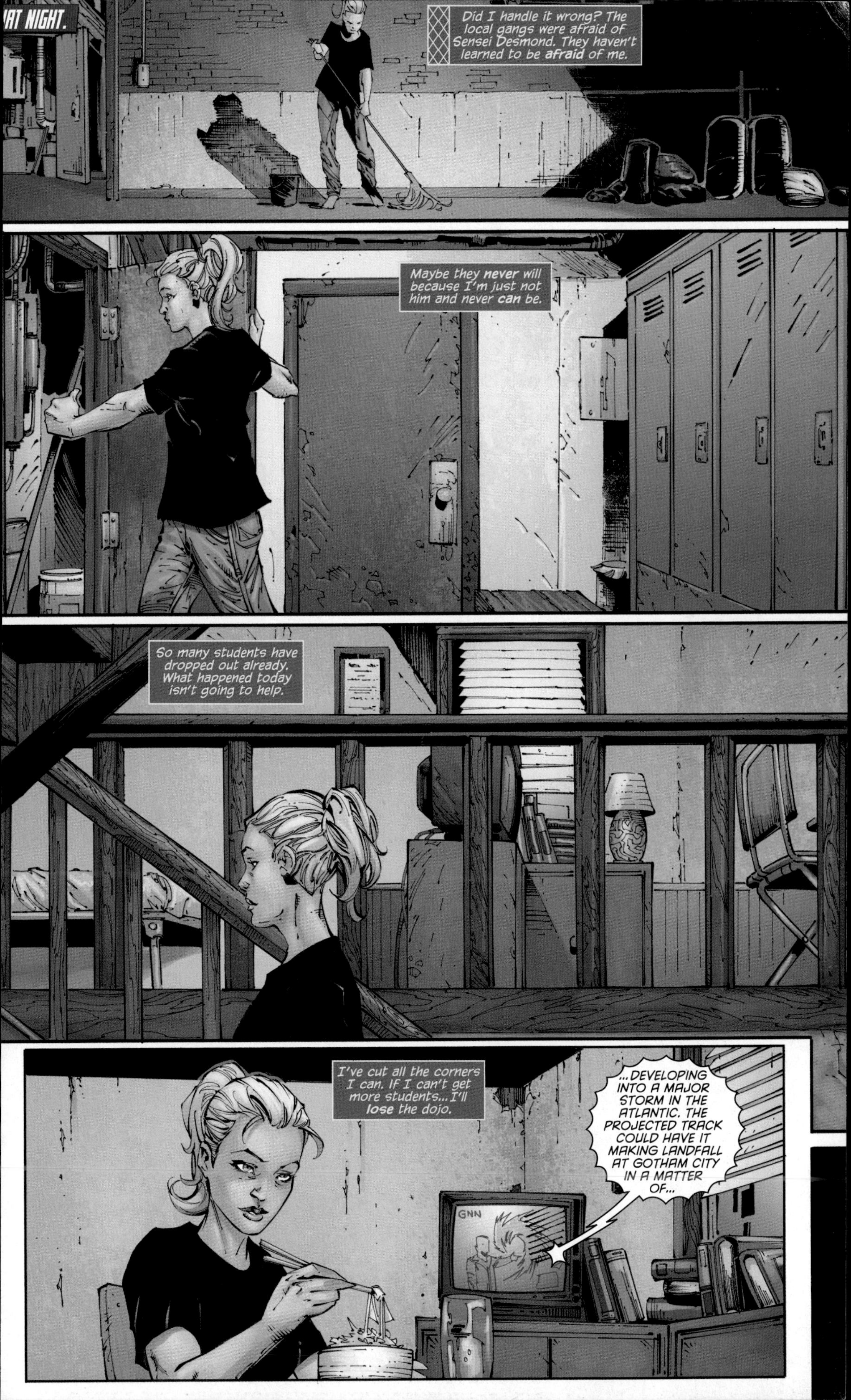
...AT NIGHT.
Did I handle it wrong? The local gangs were afraid of Sensei Desmond. They haven't learned to be afraid of me.
Maybe they never will because I'm just not him and never can be.
So many students have dropped out already. What happened today isn't going to help.
I've cut all the corners I can. If I can't get more students... I'll lose the dojo.
...DEVELOPING INTO A MAJOR STORM IN THE ATLANTIC. THE PROJECTED TRACK COULD HAVE IT MAKING LANDFALL AT GOTHAM CITY IN A MATTER OF...
GNN

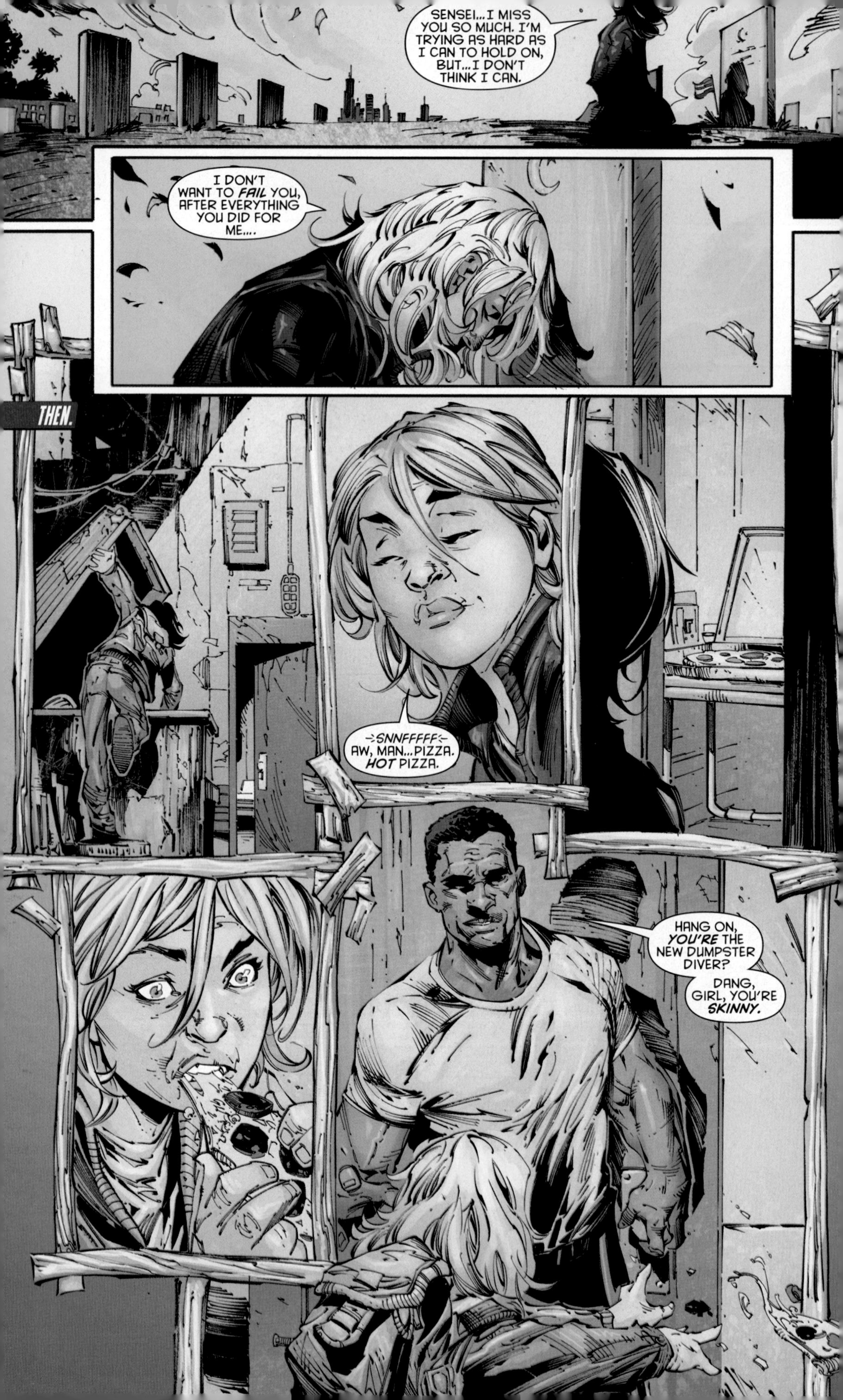

SENSEI...I MISS YOU SO MUCH. I'M TRYING AS HARD AS I CAN TO HOLD ON, BUT...I DON'T THINK I CAN.
I DON'T WANT TO FAIL YOU, AFTER EVERYTHING YOU DID FOR ME....
THEN.
-SNNFFFFF- AW, MAN...PIZZA. HOT PIZZA.
HANG ON, YOU'RE THE NEW DUMPSTER DIVER?
DANG, GIRL, YOU'RE SKINNY.

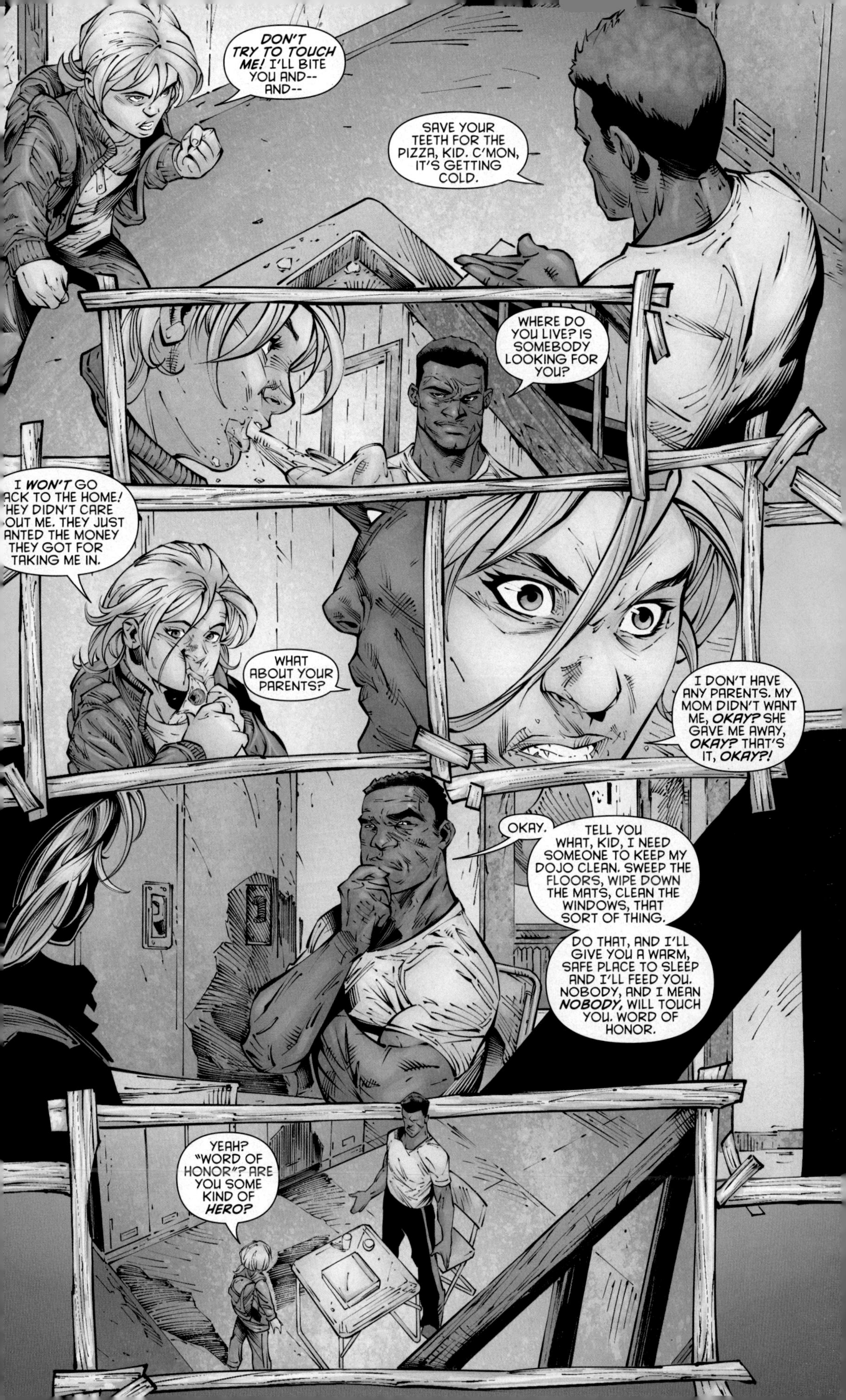

DON'T TRY TO TOUCH ME! I'LL BITE YOU AND-- AND--
SAVE YOUR TEETH FOR THE PIZZA, KID. C'MON, IT'S GETTING COLD.
WHERE DO YOU LIVE? IS SOMEBODY LOOKING FOR YOU?
I WON'T GO ACK TO THE HOME! HEY DIDN'T CARE OUT ME. THEY JUST ANTED THE MONEY THEY GOT FOR TAKING ME IN.
WHAT ABOUT YOUR PARENTS?
I DON'T HAVE ANY PARENTS. MY MOM DIDN'T WANT ME, OKAY? SHE GAVE ME AWAY, OKAY? THAT'S IT, OKAY?!
OKAY.
TELL YOU WHAT, KID, I NEED SOMEONE TO KEEP MY DOJO CLEAN. SWEEP THE FLOORS, WIPE DOWN THE MATS, CLEAN THE WINDOWS, THAT SORT OF THING.
DO THAT, AND I'LL GIVE YOU A WARM, SAFE PLACE TO SLEEP AND I'LL FEED YOU. NOBODY, AND I MEAN NOBODY, WILL TOUCH YOU. WORD OF HONOR.
YEAH? "WORD OF HONOR"? ARE YOU SOME KIND OF HERO?

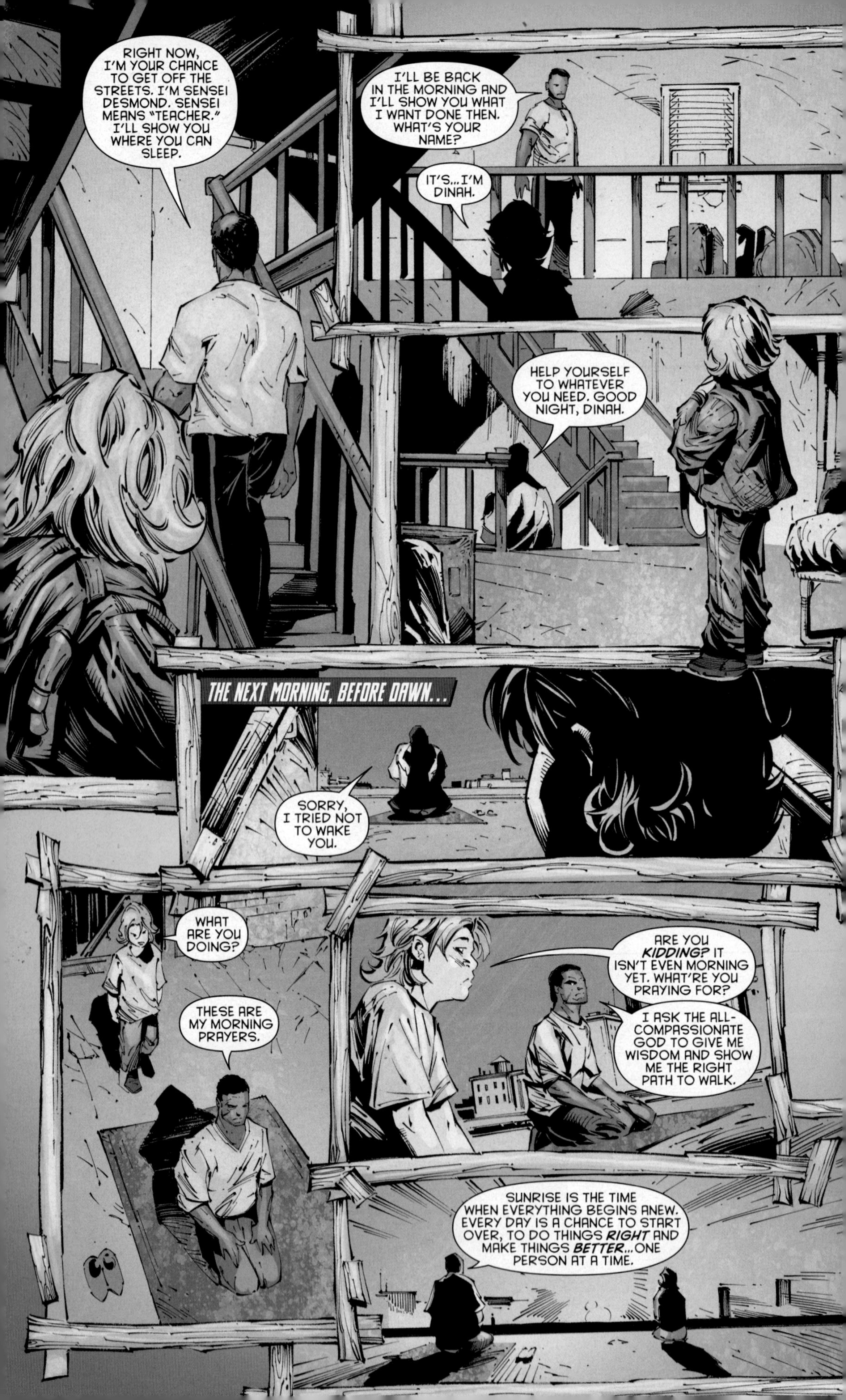
RIGHT NOW, I'M YOUR CHANCE TO GET OFF THE STREETS. I'M SENSEI DESMOND. SENSEI MEANS "TEACHER." I'LL SHOW YOU WHERE YOU CAN SLEEP.
I'LL BE BACK IN THE MORNING AND I'LL SHOW YOU WHAT I WANT DONE THEN. WHAT'S YOUR NAME?
IT'S...I'M DINAH.
HELP YOURSELF TO WHATEVER YOU NEED. GOOD NIGHT, DINAH.
THE NEXT MORNING, BEFORE DAWN...
SORRY, I TRIED NOT TO WAKE YOU.
WHAT ARE YOU DOING?
THESE ARE MY MORNING PRAYERS.
ARE YOU *KIDDING?* IT ISN'T EVEN MORNING YET. WHAT'RE YOU PRAYING FOR?
I ASK THE ALL-COMPASSIONATE GOD TO GIVE ME WISDOM AND SHOW ME THE RIGHT PATH TO WALK.
SUNRISE IS THE TIME WHEN EVERYTHING BEGINS ANEW. EVERY DAY IS A CHANCE TO START OVER, TO DO THINGS *RIGHT* AND MAKE THINGS *BETTER*...ONE PERSON AT A TIME.

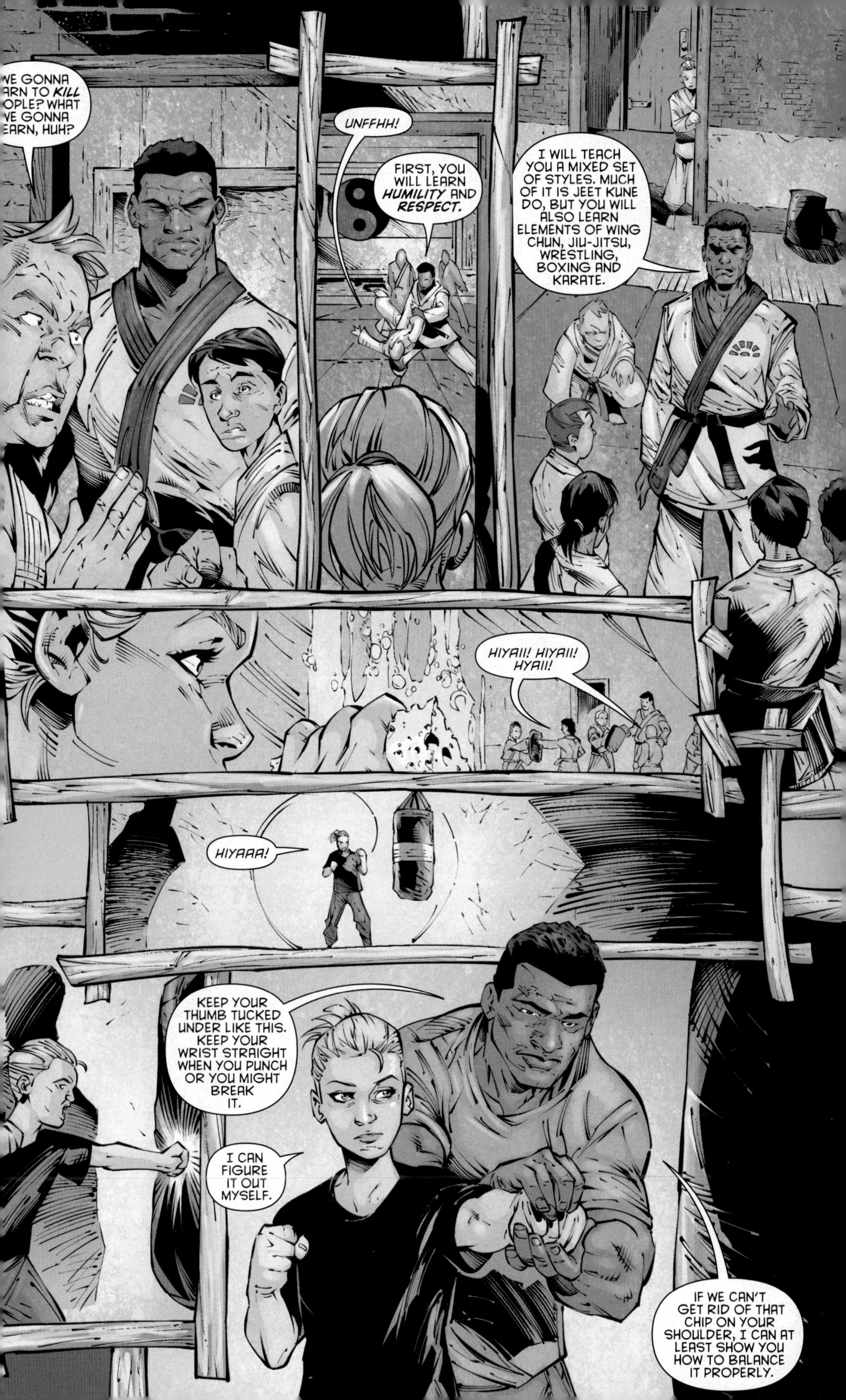
WE GONNA
ARN TO KILL
OPLE? WHAT
WE GONNA
EARN, HUH?
UNFFHH!
FIRST, YOU WILL LEARN HUMILITY AND RESPECT.
I WILL TEACH YOU A MIXED SET OF STYLES. MUCH OF IT IS JEET KUNE DO, BUT YOU WILL ALSO LEARN ELEMENTS OF WING CHUN, JIU-JITSU, WRESTLING, BOXING AND KARATE.
HIYAII! HIYAII! HYAII!
HIYAAA!
KEEP YOUR THUMB TUCKED UNDER LIKE THIS. KEEP YOUR WRIST STRAIGHT WHEN YOU PUNCH OR YOU MIGHT BREAK IT.
I CAN FIGURE IT OUT MYSELF.
IF WE CAN'T GET RID OF THAT CHIP ON YOUR SHOULDER, I CAN AT LEAST SHOW YOU HOW TO BALANCE IT PROPERLY.

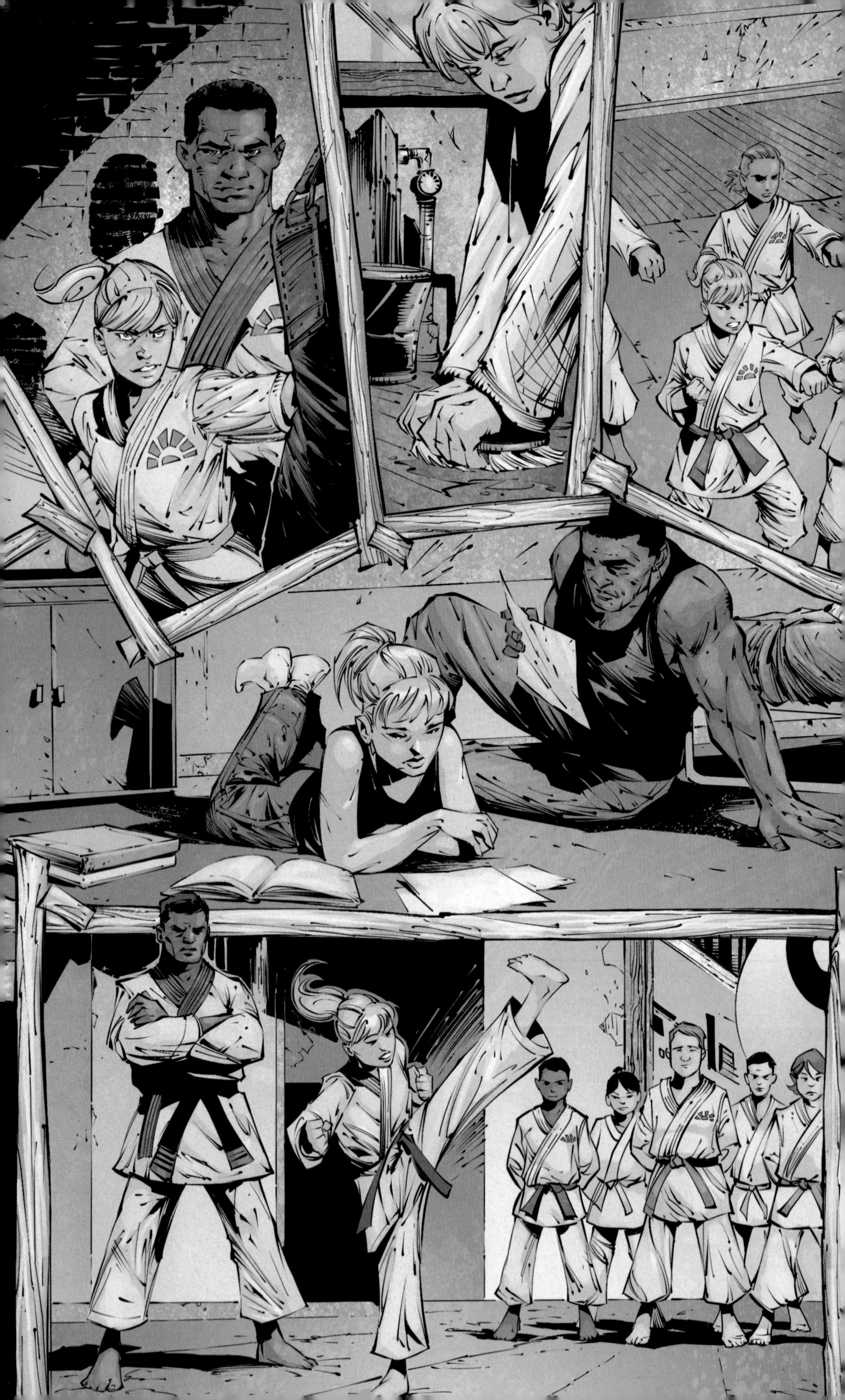

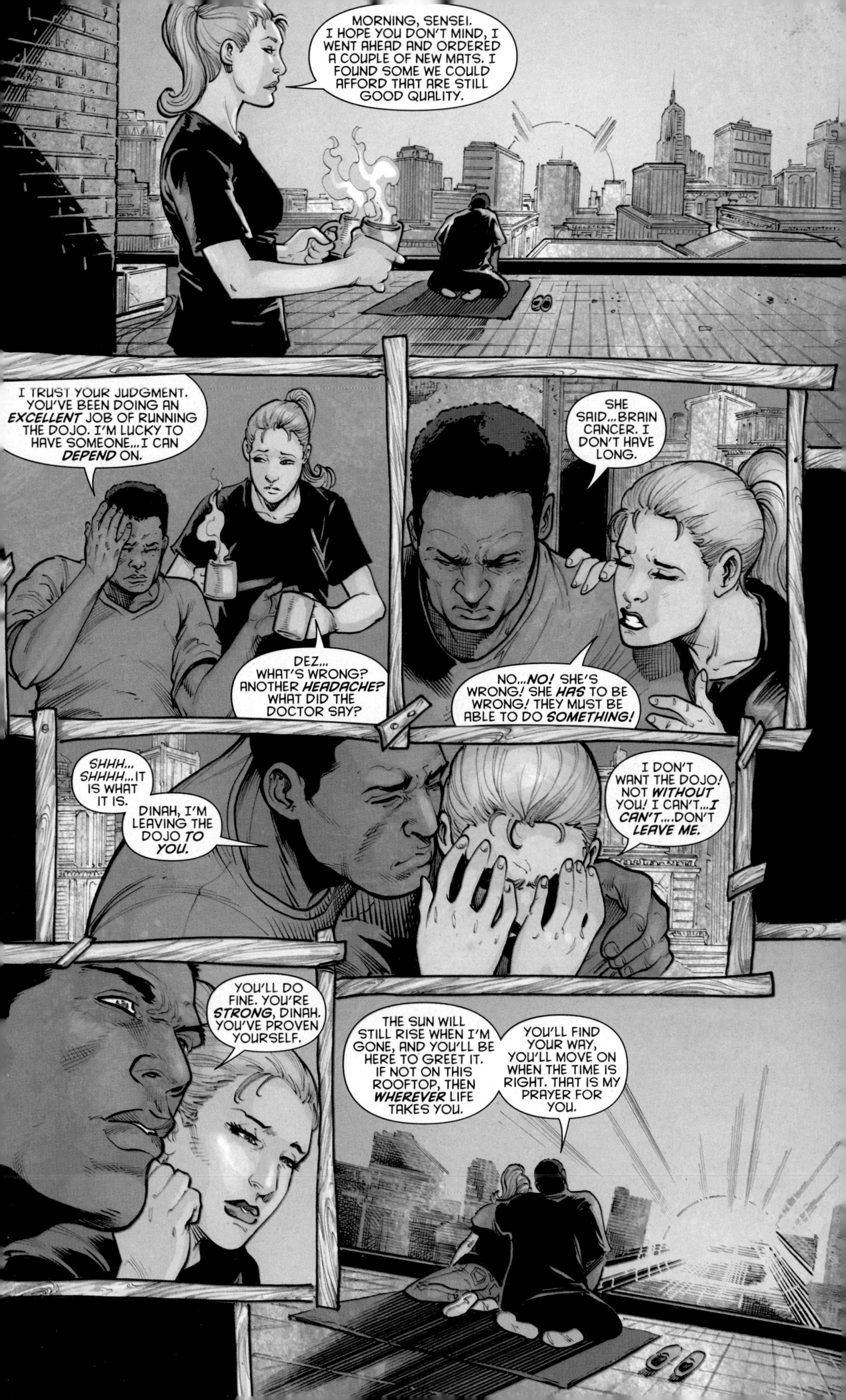
MORNING, SENSEI. I HOPE YOU DON'T MIND, I WENT AHEAD AND ORDERED A COUPLE OF NEW MATS. I FOUND SOME WE COULD AFFORD THAT ARE STILL GOOD QUALITY.
I TRUST YOUR JUDGMENT. YOU'VE BEEN DOING AN EXCELLENT JOB OF RUNNING THE DOJO. I'M LUCKY TO HAVE SOMEONE...I CAN DEPEND ON.
DEZ... WHAT'S WRONG? ANOTHER HEADACHE? WHAT DID THE DOCTOR SAY?
SHE SAID...BRAIN CANCER. I DON'T HAVE LONG.
NO...NO! SHE'S WRONG! SHE HAS TO BE WRONG! THEY MUST BE ABLE TO DO SOMETHING!
SHHH... SHHHH...IT IS WHAT IT IS.
DINAH, I'M LEAVING THE DOJO TO YOU.
I DON'T WANT THE DOJO! NOT WITHOUT YOU! I CAN'T...I CAN'T....DON'T LEAVE ME.
YOU'LL DO FINE. YOU'RE STRONG, DINAH. YOU'VE PROVEN YOURSELF.
THE SUN WILL STILL RISE WHEN I'M GONE, AND YOU'LL BE HERE TO GREET IT. IF NOT ON THIS ROOFTOP, THEN WHEREVER LIFE TAKES YOU.
YOU'LL FIND YOUR WAY, YOU'LL MOVE ON WHEN THE TIME IS RIGHT. THAT IS MY PRAYER FOR YOU.

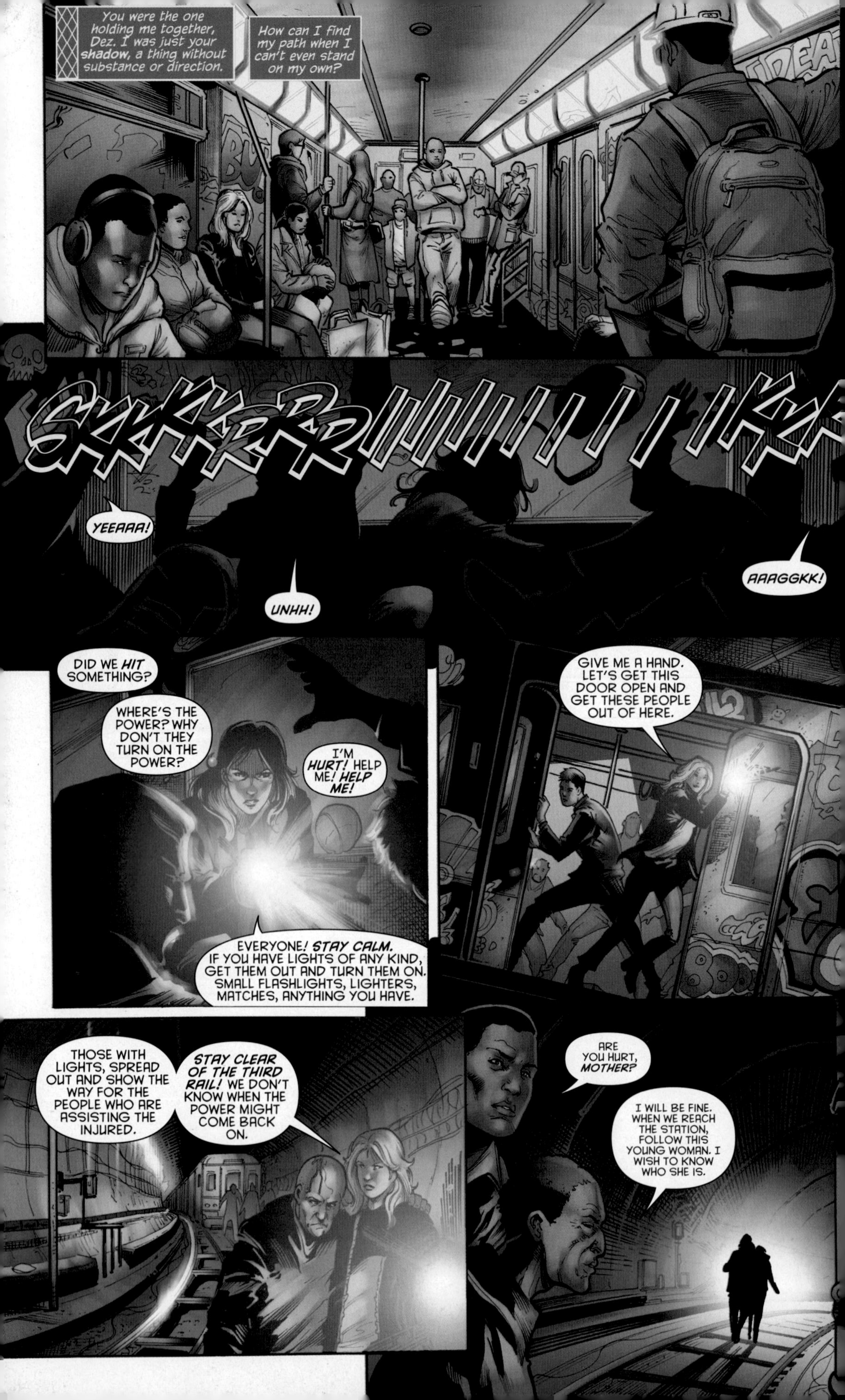

You were the one holding me together, Dez. I was just your shadow, a thing without substance or direction.
How can I find my path when I can't even stand on my own?
YEEAAA!
UNHH!
AAAGGKK!
DID WE HIT SOMETHING?
WHERE'S THE POWER? WHY DON'T THEY TURN ON THE POWER?
I'M HURT! HELP ME! HELP ME!
EVERYONE! STAY CALM. IF YOU HAVE LIGHTS OF ANY KIND, GET THEM OUT AND TURN THEM ON. SMALL FLASHLIGHTS, LIGHTERS, MATCHES, ANYTHING YOU HAVE.
GIVE ME A HAND. LET'S GET THIS DOOR OPEN AND GET THESE PEOPLE OUT OF HERE.
THOSE WITH LIGHTS, SPREAD OUT AND SHOW THE WAY FOR THE PEOPLE WHO ARE ASSISTING THE INJURED.
STAY CLEAR OF THE THIRD RAIL! WE DON'T KNOW WHEN THE POWER MIGHT COME BACK ON.
ARE YOU HURT, MOTHER?
I WILL BE FINE. WHEN WE REACH THE STATION, FOLLOW THIS YOUNG WOMAN. I WISH TO KNOW WHO SHE IS.

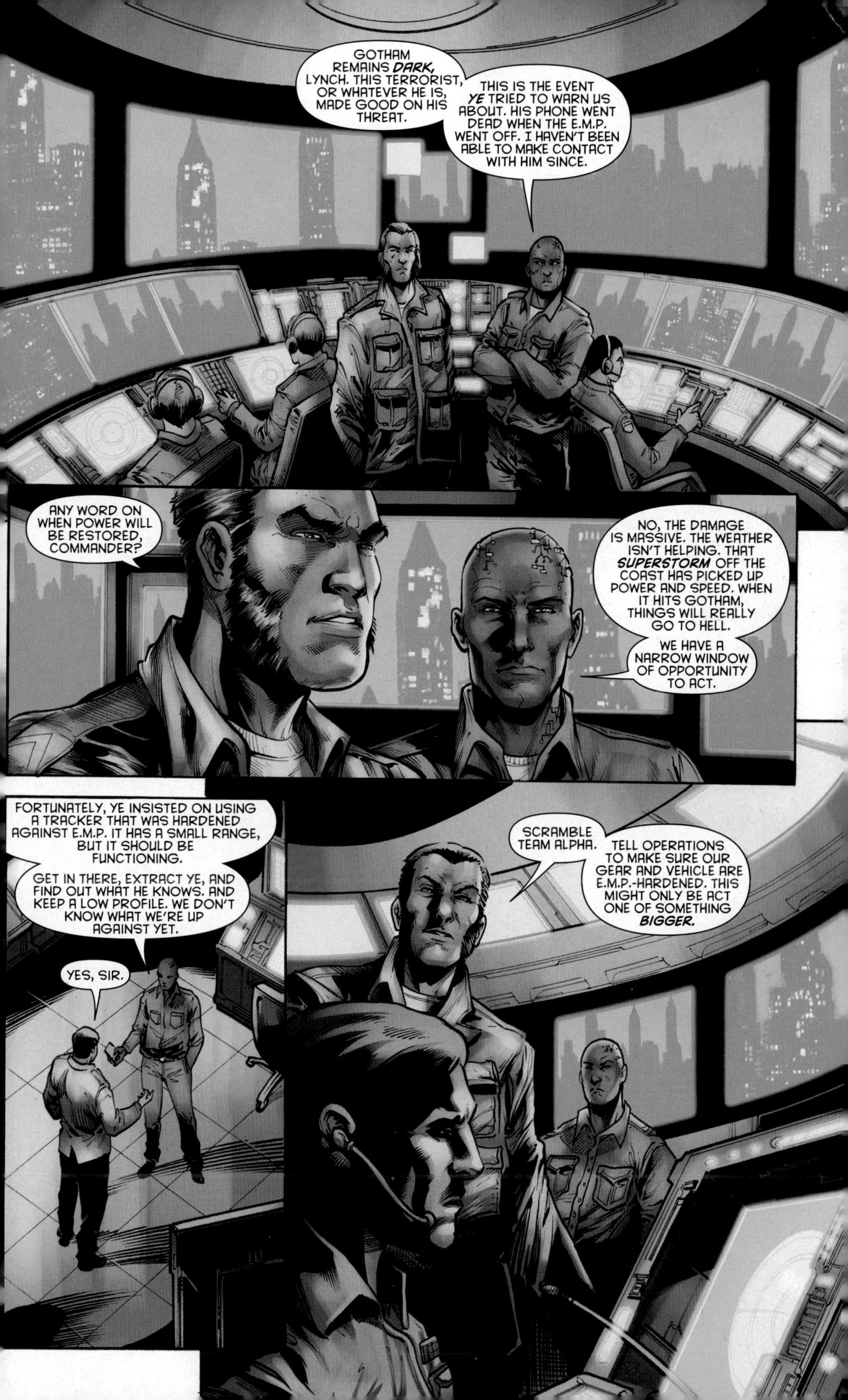
GOTHAM REMAINS DARK, LYNCH. THIS TERRORIST, OR WHATEVER HE IS, MADE GOOD ON HIS THREAT.
THIS IS THE EVENT YE TRIED TO WARN US ABOUT. HIS PHONE WENT DEAD WHEN THE E.M.P. WENT OFF. I HAVEN'T BEEN ABLE TO MAKE CONTACT WITH HIM SINCE.
ANY WORD ON WHEN POWER WILL BE RESTORED, COMMANDER?
NO, THE DAMAGE IS MASSIVE. THE WEATHER ISN'T HELPING. THAT SUPERSTORM OFF THE COAST HAS PICKED UP POWER AND SPEED. WHEN IT HITS GOTHAM, THINGS WILL REALLY GO TO HELL.
WE HAVE A NARROW WINDOW OF OPPORTUNITY TO ACT.
FORTUNATELY, YE INSISTED ON USING A TRACKER THAT WAS HARDENED AGAINST E.M.P. IT HAS A SMALL RANGE, BUT IT SHOULD BE FUNCTIONING.
GET IN THERE, EXTRACT YE, AND FIND OUT WHAT HE KNOWS. AND KEEP A LOW PROFILE. WE DON'T KNOW WHAT WE'RE UP AGAINST YET.
YES, SIR.
SCRAMBLE TEAM ALPHA.
TELL OPERATIONS TO MAKE SURE OUR GEAR AND VEHICLE ARE E.M.P.-HARDENED. THIS MIGHT ONLY BE ACT ONE OF SOMETHING BIGGER.

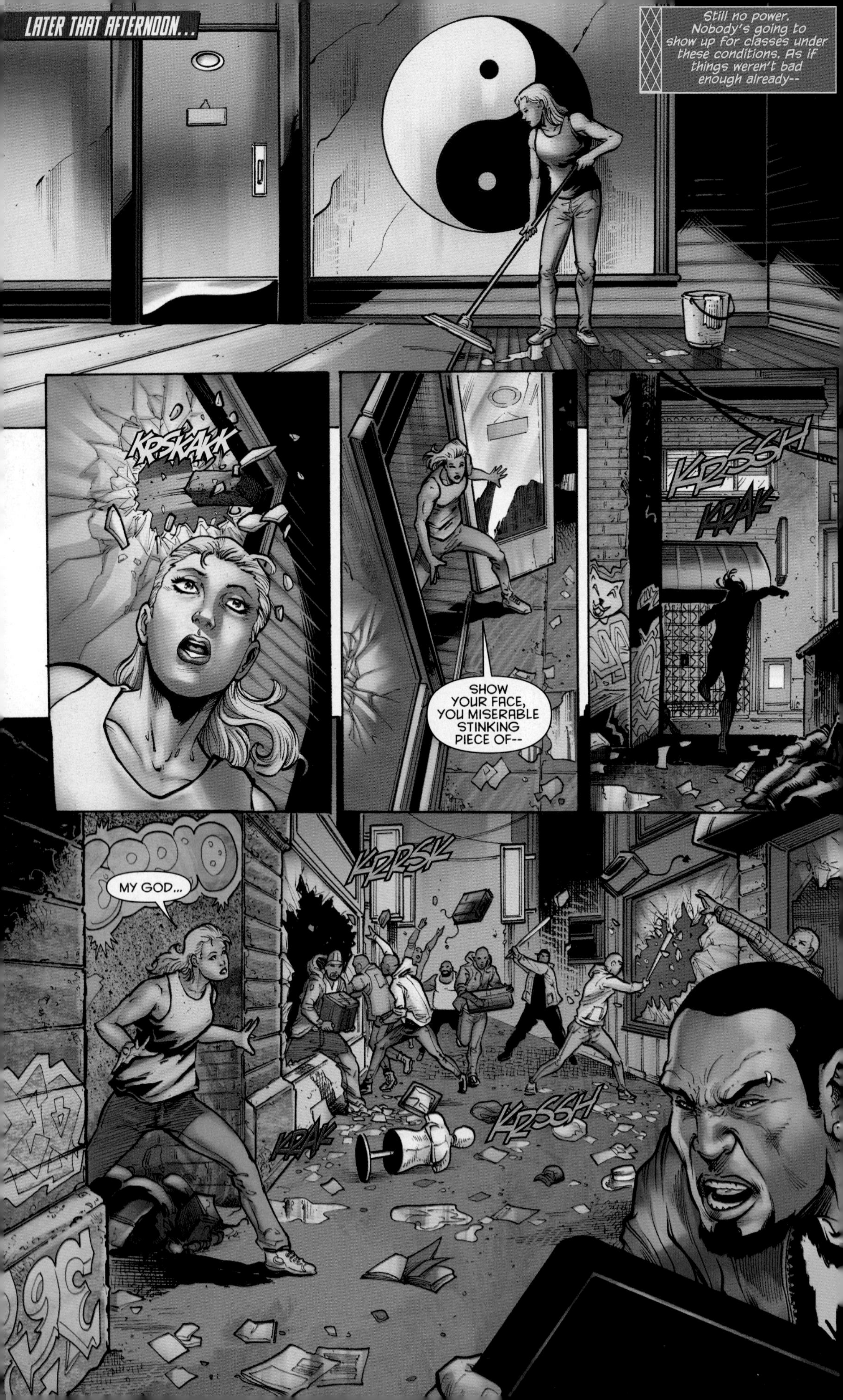
LATER THAT AFTERNOON...
Still no power. Nobody's going to show up for classes under these conditions. As if things weren't bad enough already--
KRSKAKK
SHOW YOUR FACE, YOU MISERABLE STINKING PIECE OF--
KRSSSH
KRAK
MY GOD...
KRRSK
KRSSSH
KRAK

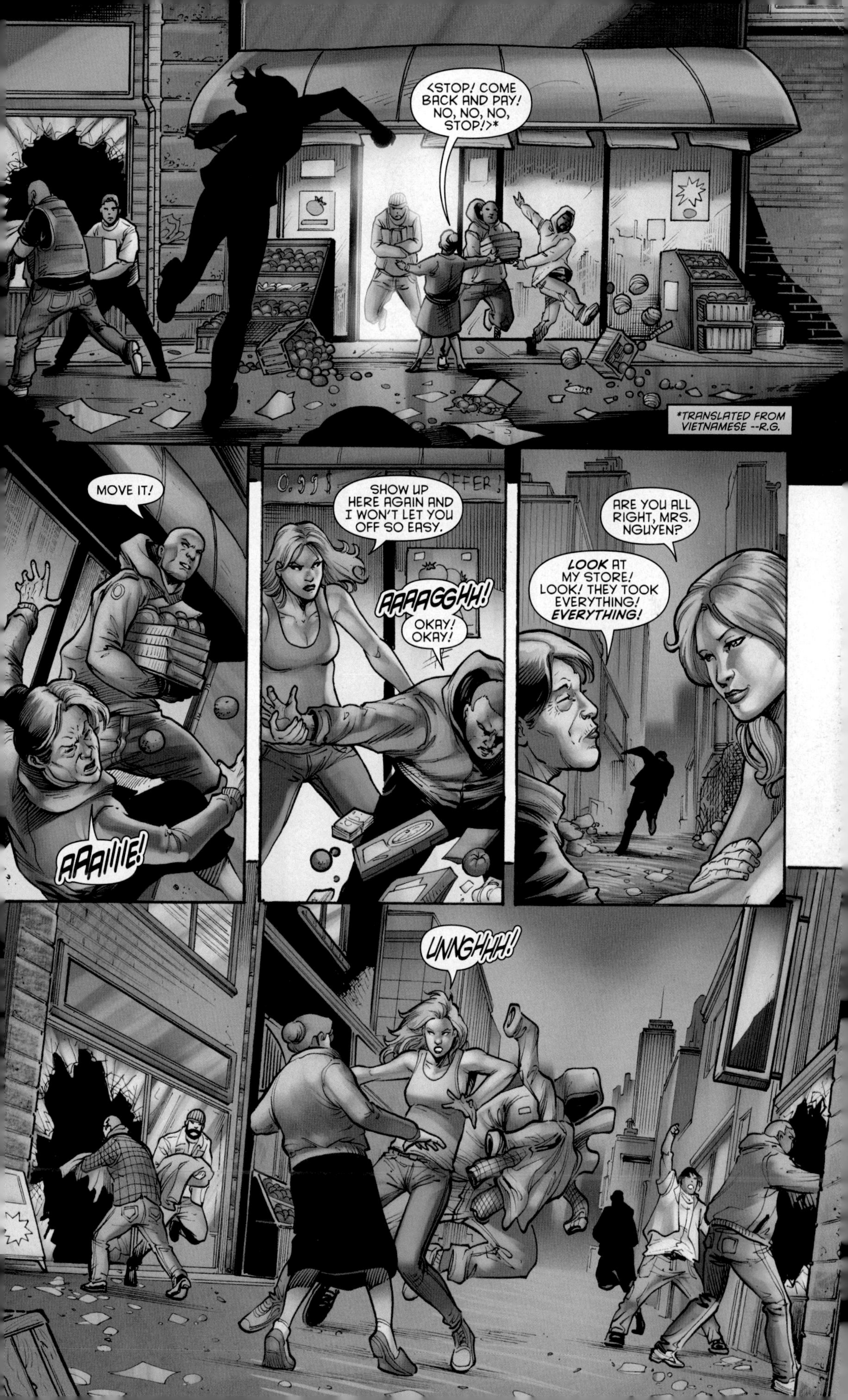

<STOP! COME BACK AND PAY! NO, NO, NO, STOP!>*
*TRANSLATED FROM VIETNAMESE --R.G.
MOVE IT!
AAAIIIE!
SHOW UP HERE AGAIN AND I WON'T LET YOU OFF SO EASY.
AAAAGGHH!
OKAY! OKAY!
ARE YOU ALL RIGHT, MRS. NGUYEN?
LOOK AT MY STORE! LOOK! THEY TOOK EVERYTHING! EVERYTHING!
UNNGHHH!

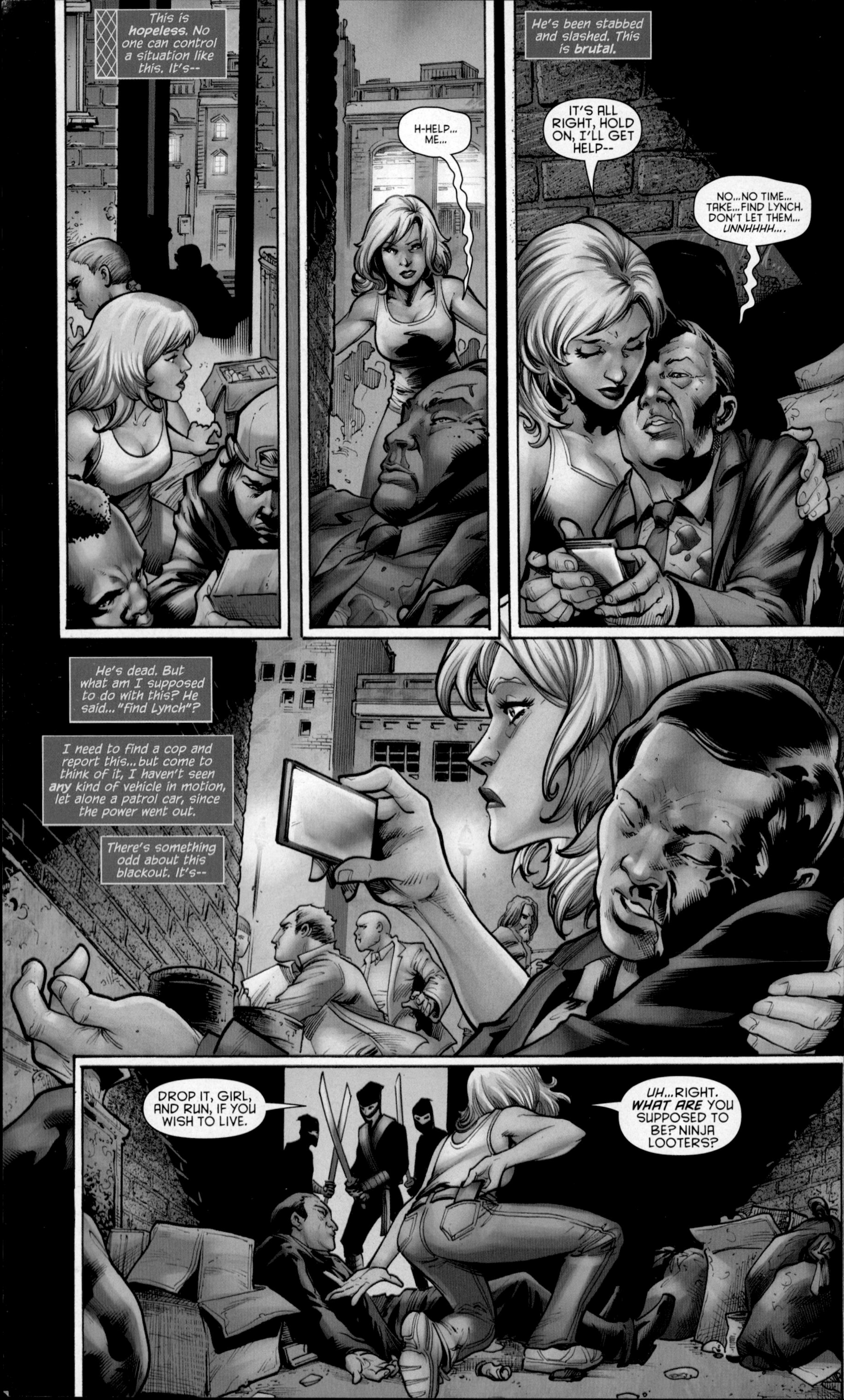
This is hopeless. No one can control a situation like this. It's--
H-HELP... ME...
He's been stabbed and slashed. This is brutal.
IT'S ALL RIGHT, HOLD ON, I'LL GET HELP--
NO...NO TIME... TAKE...FIND LYNCH. DON'T LET THEM... UNNHHHH....
He's dead. But what am I supposed to do with this? He said..."find Lynch"?
I need to find a cop and report this...but come to think of it, I haven't seen any kind of vehicle in motion, let alone a patrol car, since the power went out.
There's something odd about this blackout. It's--
DROP IT, GIRL, AND RUN, IF YOU WISH TO LIVE.
UH...RIGHT. WHAT ARE YOU SUPPOSED TO BE? NINJA LOOTERS?

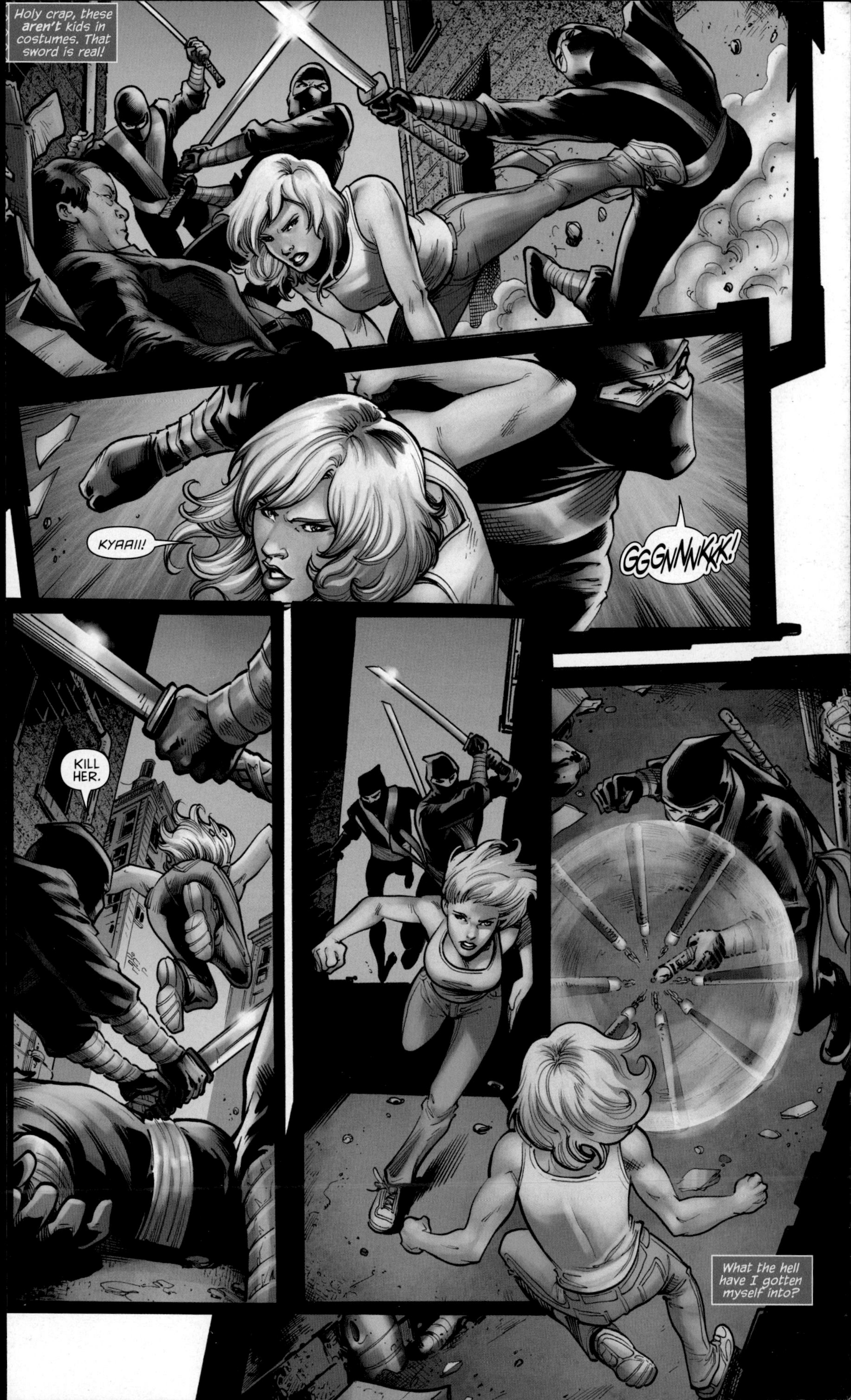
Holy crap, these aren't kids in costumes. That sword is real!
KYAAII!
GGGNNNKKK!
KILL HER.
What the hell have I gotten myself into?

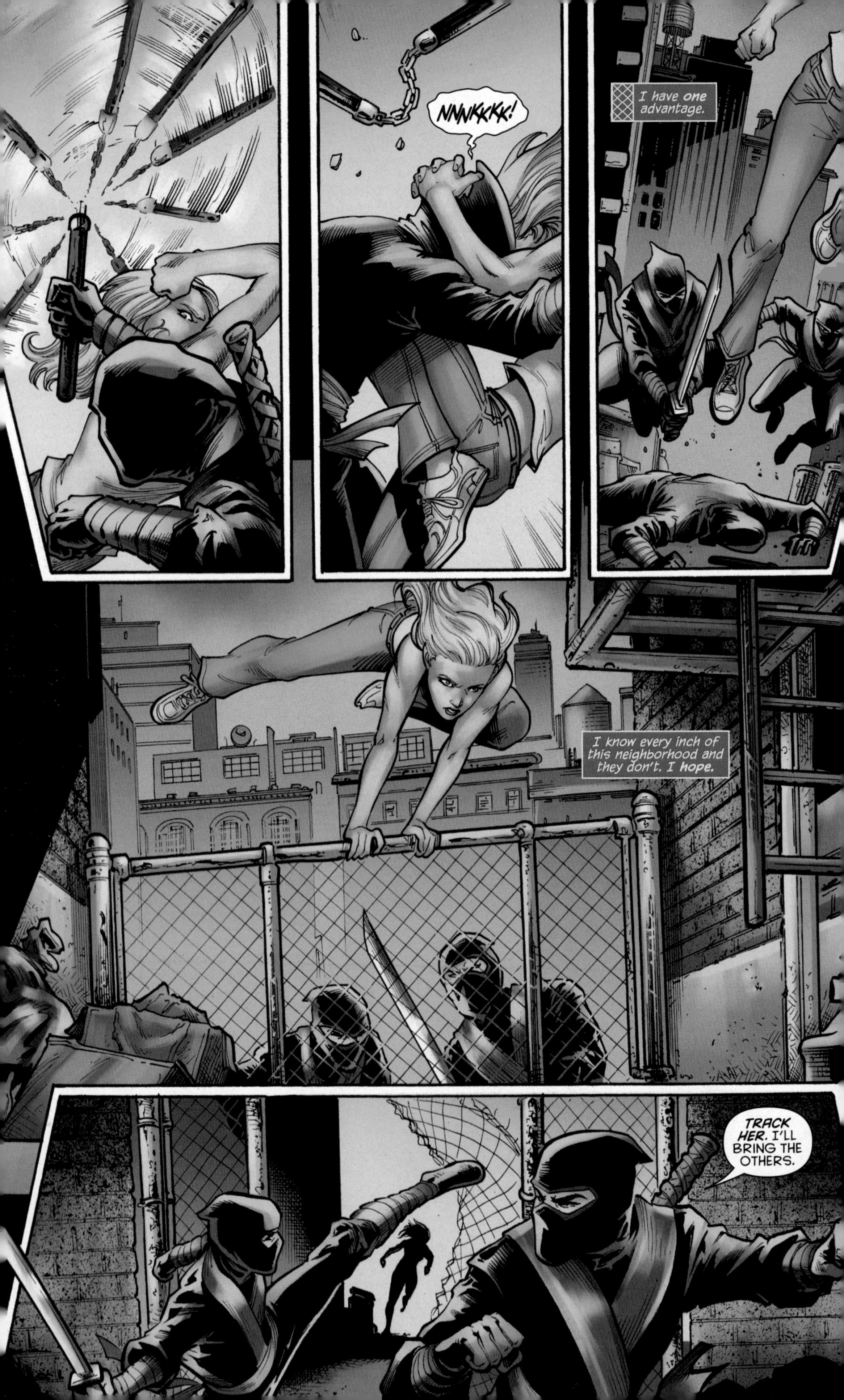
NNNKKKK!
I have one advantage.
I know every inch of this neighborhood and they don't. I hope.
TRACK HER. I'LL BRING THE OTHERS.

YE'S BEEN DEAD A COUPLE OF HOURS, AT LEAST. NO SIGN OF THE PACKAGE.

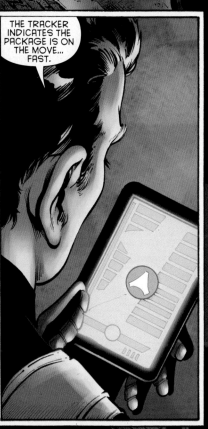

THE TRACKER INDICATES THE PACKAGE IS ON THE MOVE... FAST.

WHAT'S YOUR STORY? WHO DO YOU WORK FOR?

FAILURE... IS *DEATH*.

I DIE FOR THE *MASTER*.

GGGGHHHH...

DAMMIT, WHAT HAPPENED?

I DON'T KNOW, SIR. HE WASN'T THAT BADLY INJURED, BUT HE'S STONE DEAD NOW. HE MUST HAVE HAD POISON.

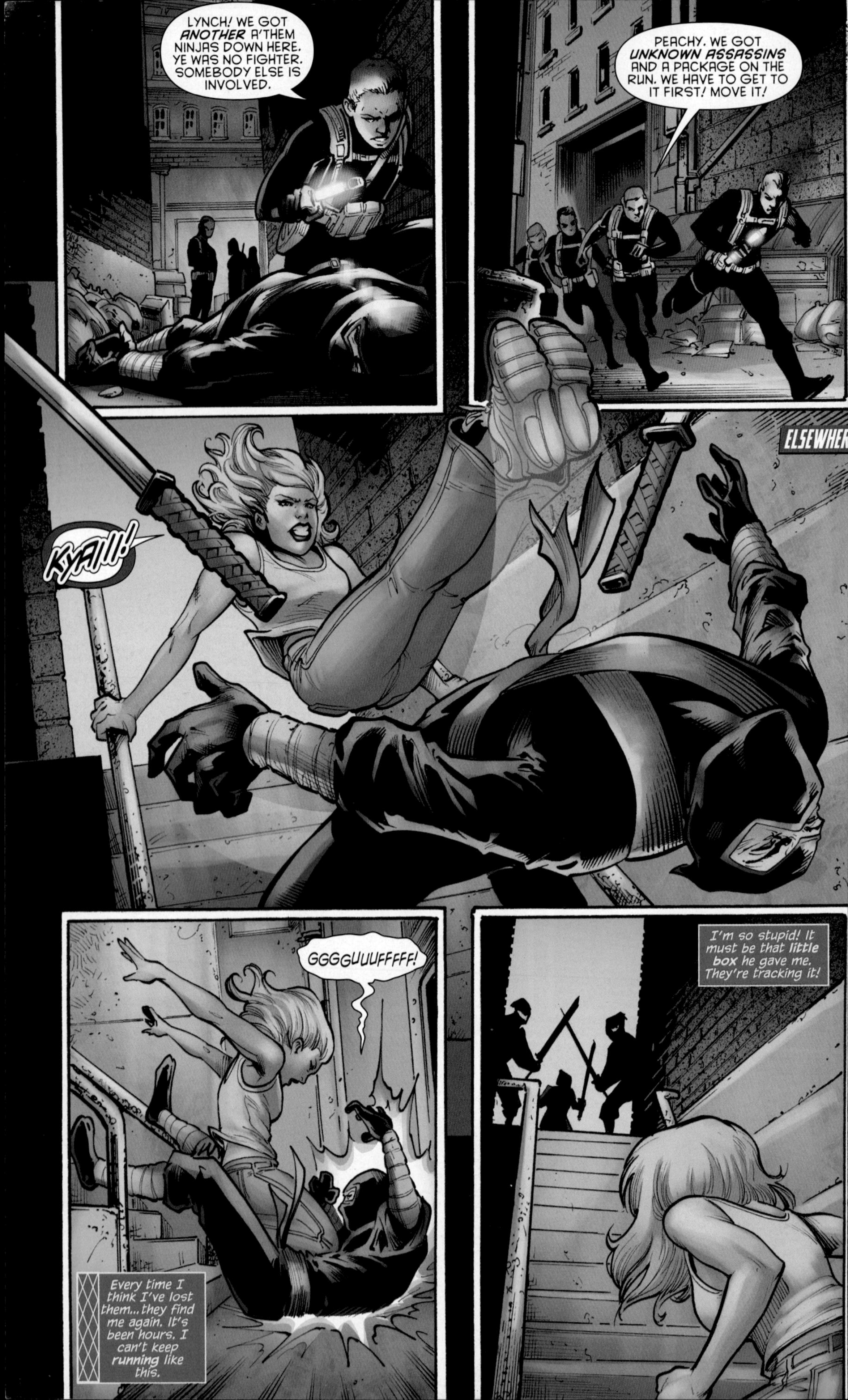
LYNCH! WE GOT ANOTHER A'THEM NINJAS DOWN HERE. YE WAS NO FIGHTER. SOMEBODY ELSE IS INVOLVED.
PEACHY. WE GOT UNKNOWN ASSASSINS AND A PACKAGE ON THE RUN. WE HAVE TO GET TO IT FIRST! MOVE IT!
ELSEWHER
KYAIII!
GGGGUUUFFFFF!
Every time I think I've lost them... they find me again. It's been hours. I can't keep running like this.
I'm so stupid! It must be that little box he gave me. They're tracking it!

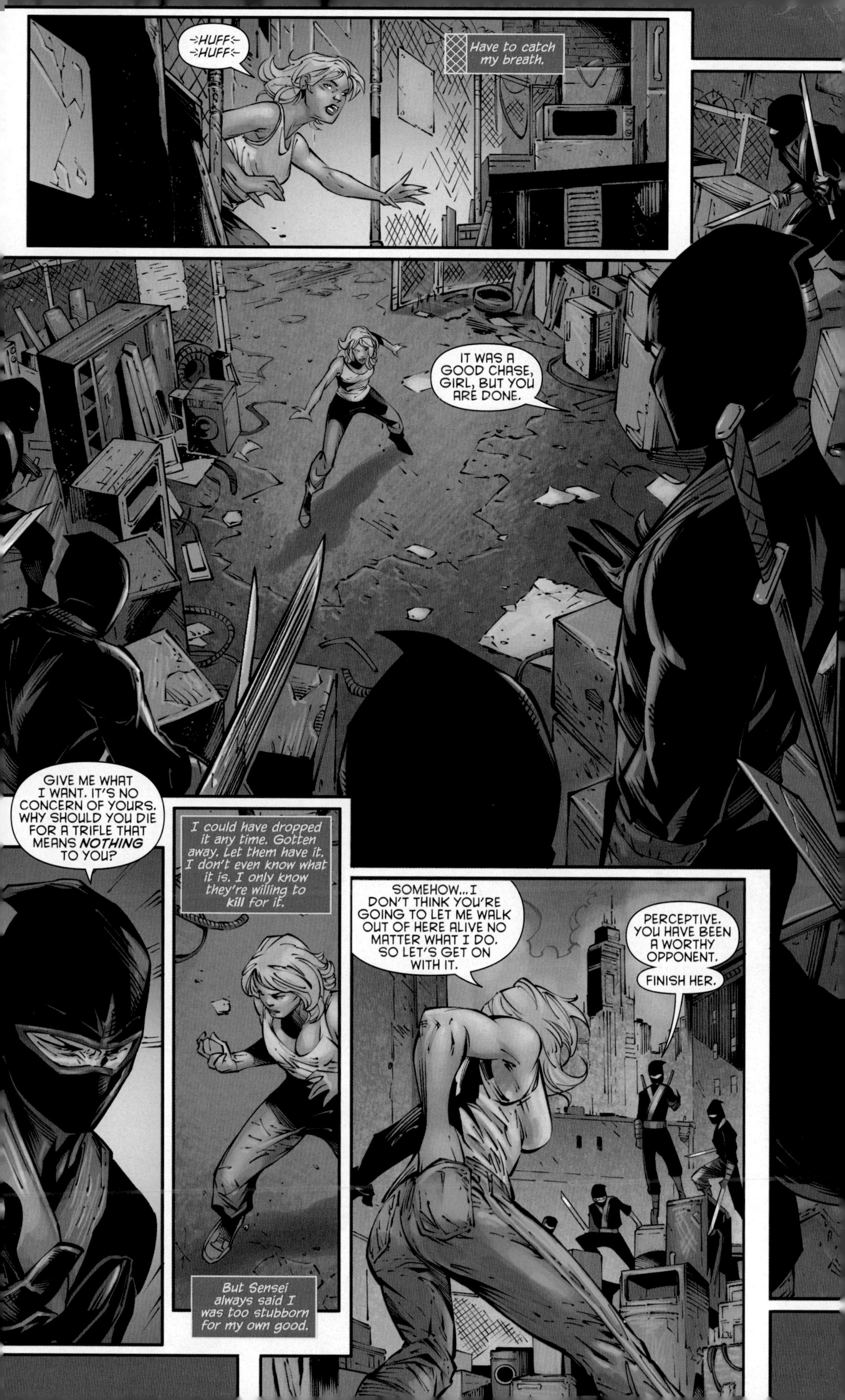
-HUFF-
-HUFF-
Have to catch my breath.
IT WAS A GOOD CHASE, GIRL, BUT YOU ARE DONE.
GIVE ME WHAT I WANT. IT'S NO CONCERN OF YOURS. WHY SHOULD YOU DIE FOR A TRIFLE THAT MEANS NOTHING TO YOU?
I could have dropped it any time. Gotten away. Let them have it. I don't even know what it is. I only know they're willing to kill for it.
But Sensei always said I was too stubborn for my own good.
SOMEHOW...I DON'T THINK YOU'RE GOING TO LET ME WALK OUT OF HERE ALIVE NO MATTER WHAT I DO. SO LET'S GET ON WITH IT.
PERCEPTIVE. YOU HAVE BEEN A WORTHY OPPONENT.
FINISH HER.

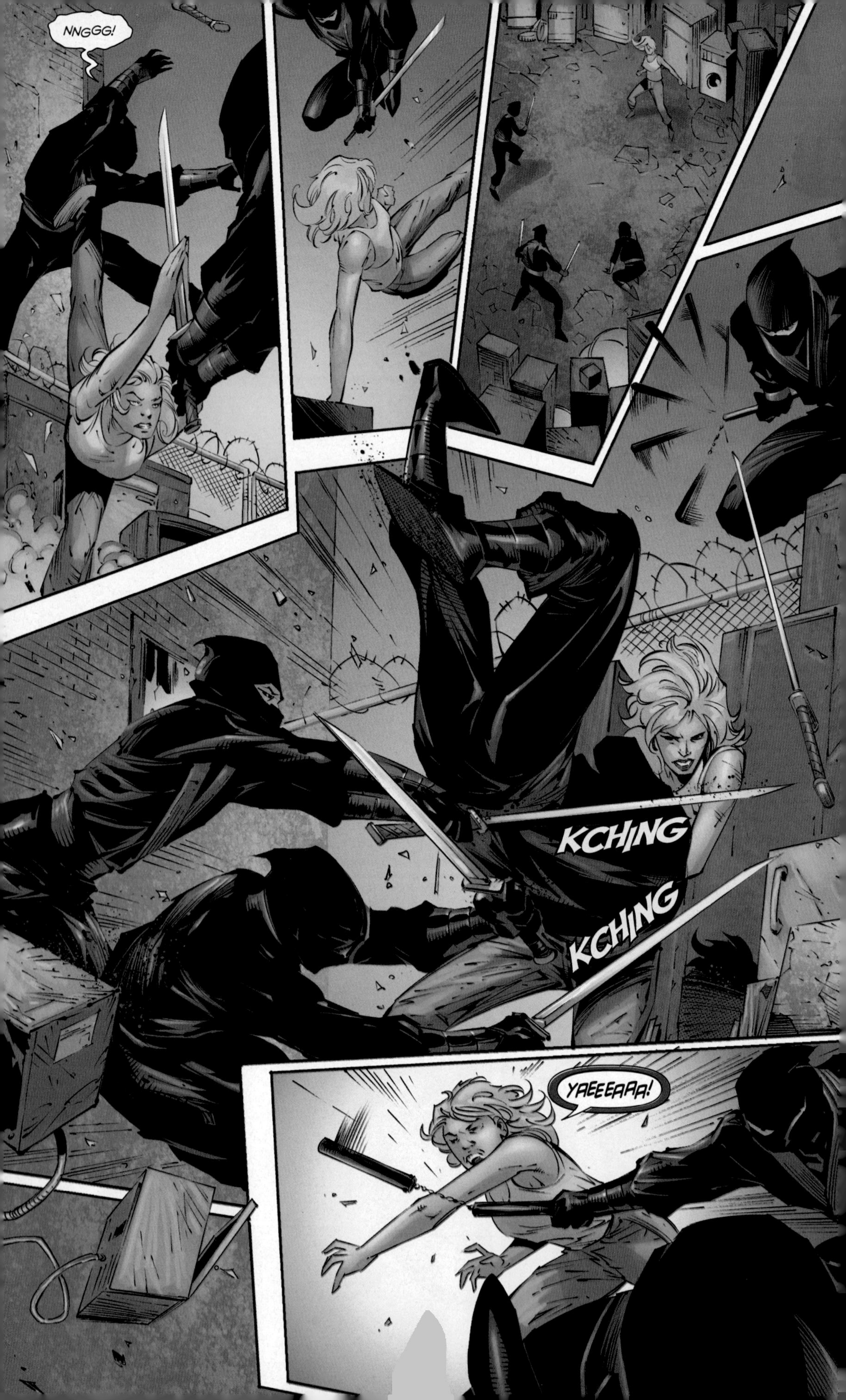
NNGGG!
KCHING
KCHING
YAEEEAAA!

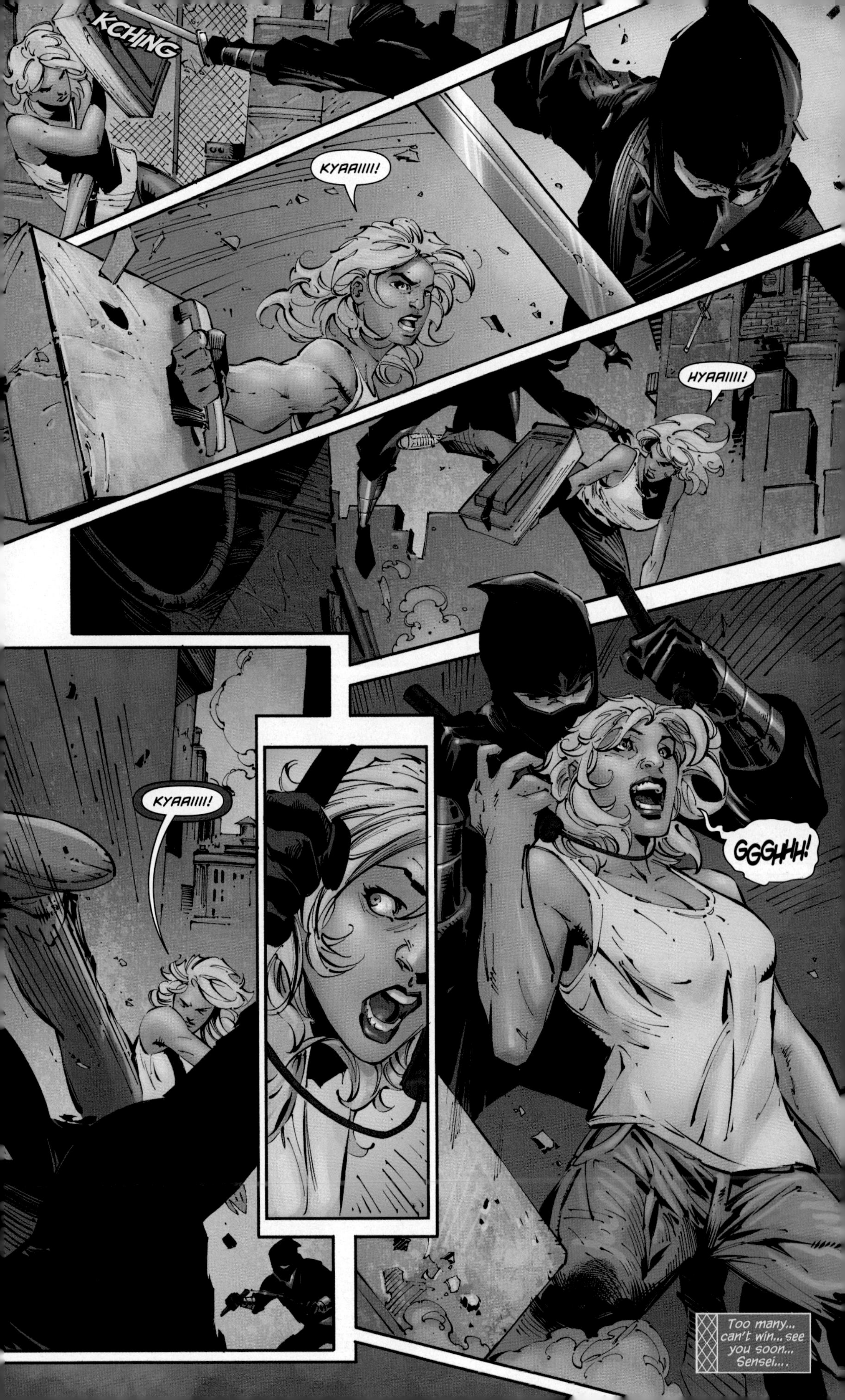
KCHING
KYAAIIII!
HYAAIIII!
KYAAIIII!
GGGHHH!
Too many... can't win... see you soon... Sensei...

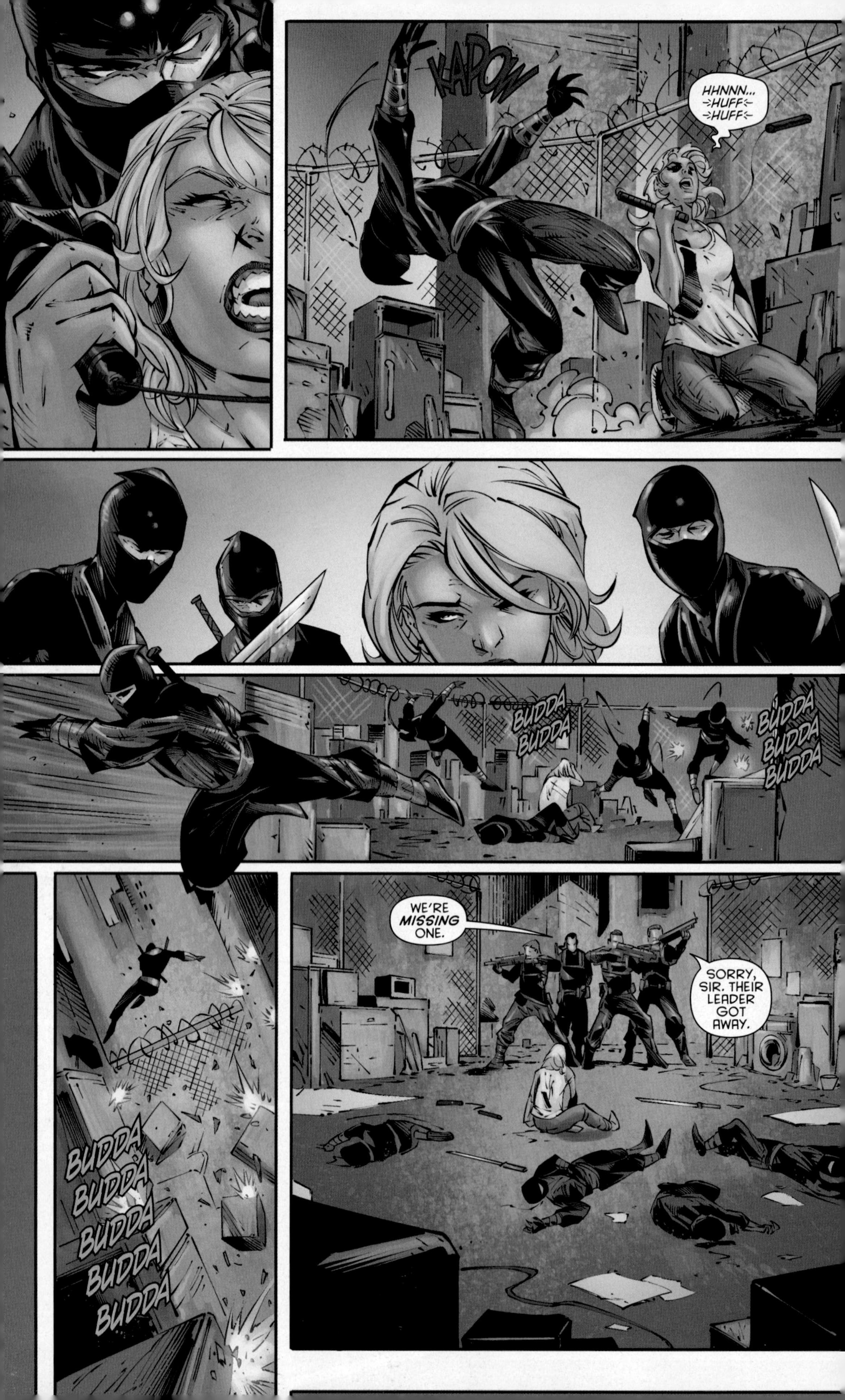
KAPOW
HHNNN... -HUFF- -HUFF-
BUDDA BUDDA
BUDDA BUDDA BUDDA
BUDDA BUDDA BUDDA BUDDA BUDDA
WE'RE MISSING ONE.
SORRY, SIR. THEIR LEADER GOT AWAY.

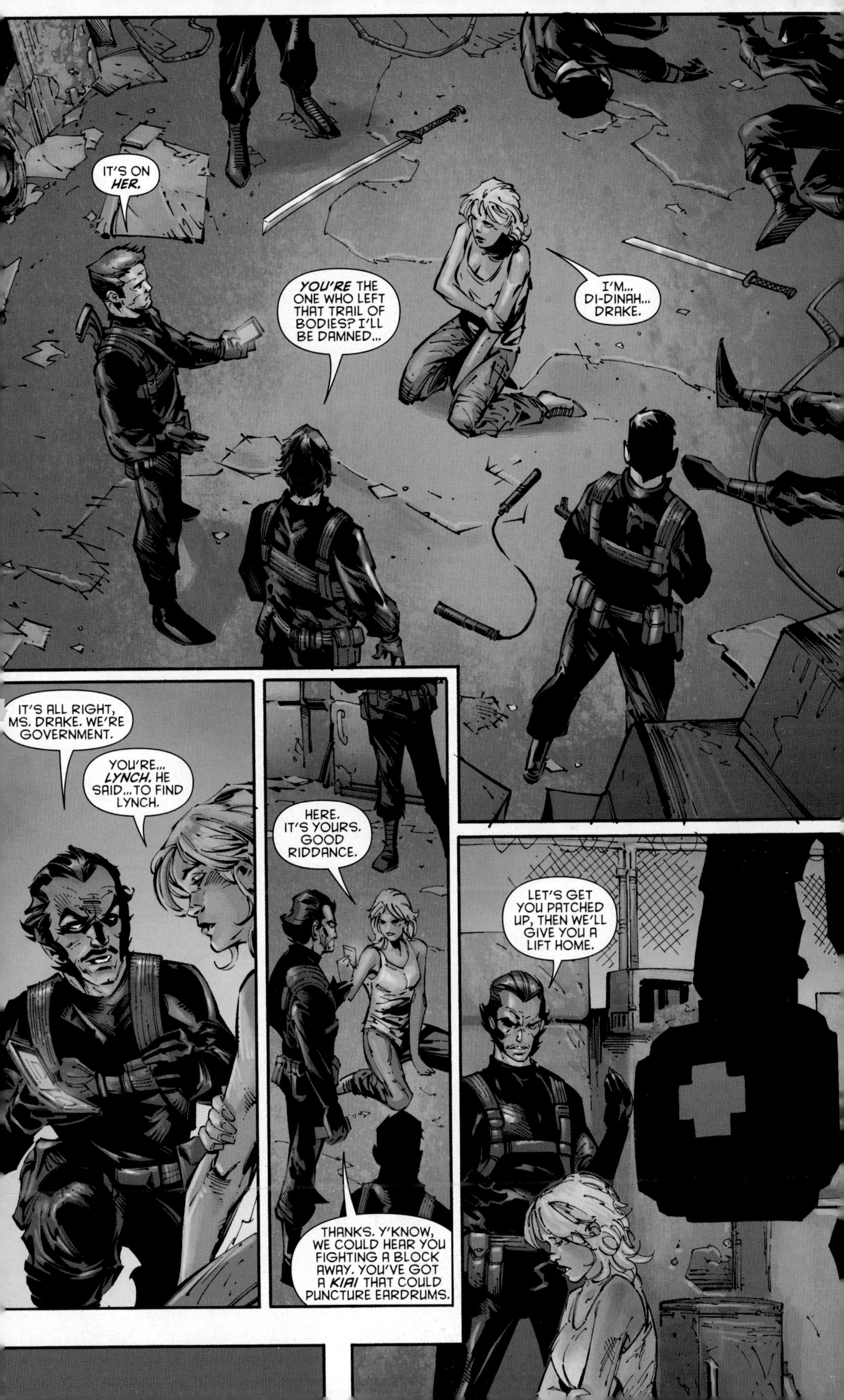

IT'S ON *HER.*
YOU'RE THE ONE WHO LEFT THAT TRAIL OF BODIES? I'LL BE DAMNED...
I'M... DI-DINAH... DRAKE.
IT'S ALL RIGHT, MS. DRAKE. WE'RE GOVERNMENT.
YOU'RE... *LYNCH.* HE SAID...TO FIND LYNCH.
HERE. IT'S YOURS. GOOD RIDDANCE.
THANKS. Y'KNOW, WE COULD HEAR YOU FIGHTING A BLOCK AWAY. YOU'VE GOT A *KIAI* THAT COULD PUNCTURE EARDRUMS.
LET'S GET YOU PATCHED UP, THEN WE'LL GIVE YOU A LIFT HOME.

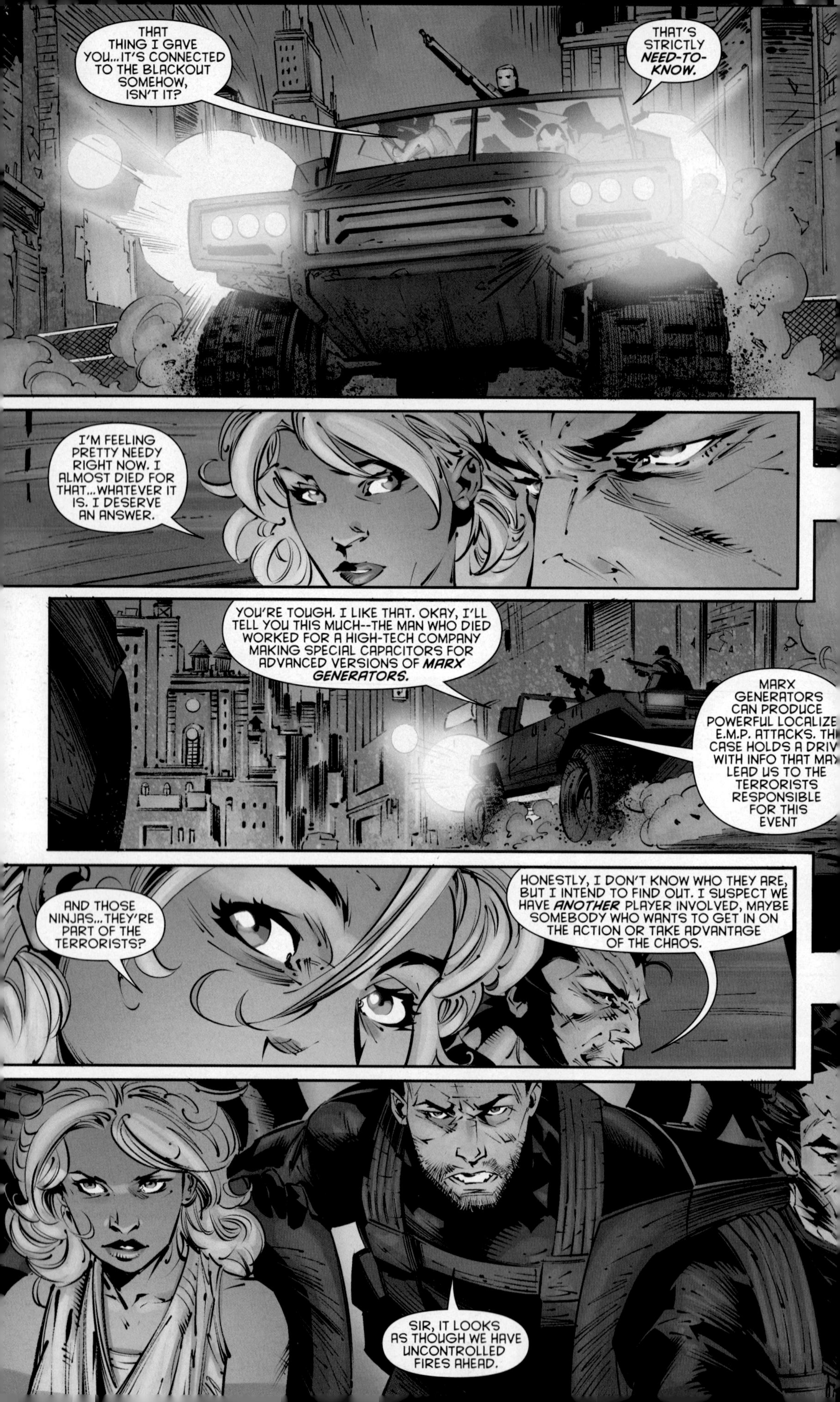

THAT THING I GAVE YOU...IT'S CONNECTED TO THE BLACKOUT SOMEHOW, ISN'T IT?
THAT'S STRICTLY NEED-TO-KNOW.
I'M FEELING PRETTY NEEDY RIGHT NOW. I ALMOST DIED FOR THAT...WHATEVER IT IS. I DESERVE AN ANSWER.
YOU'RE TOUGH. I LIKE THAT. OKAY, I'LL TELL YOU THIS MUCH--THE MAN WHO DIED WORKED FOR A HIGH-TECH COMPANY MAKING SPECIAL CAPACITORS FOR ADVANCED VERSIONS OF MARX GENERATORS.
MARX GENERATORS CAN PRODUCE POWERFUL LOCALIZE E.M.P. ATTACKS. TH CASE HOLDS A DRIV WITH INFO THAT MA LEAD US TO THE TERRORISTS RESPONSIBLE FOR THIS EVENT
AND THOSE NINJAS...THEY'RE PART OF THE TERRORISTS?
HONESTLY, I DON'T KNOW WHO THEY ARE, BUT I INTEND TO FIND OUT. I SUSPECT WE HAVE ANOTHER PLAYER INVOLVED, MAYBE SOMEBODY WHO WANTS TO GET IN ON THE ACTION OR TAKE ADVANTAGE OF THE CHAOS.
SIR, IT LOOKS AS THOUGH WE HAVE UNCONTROLLED FIRES AHEAD.

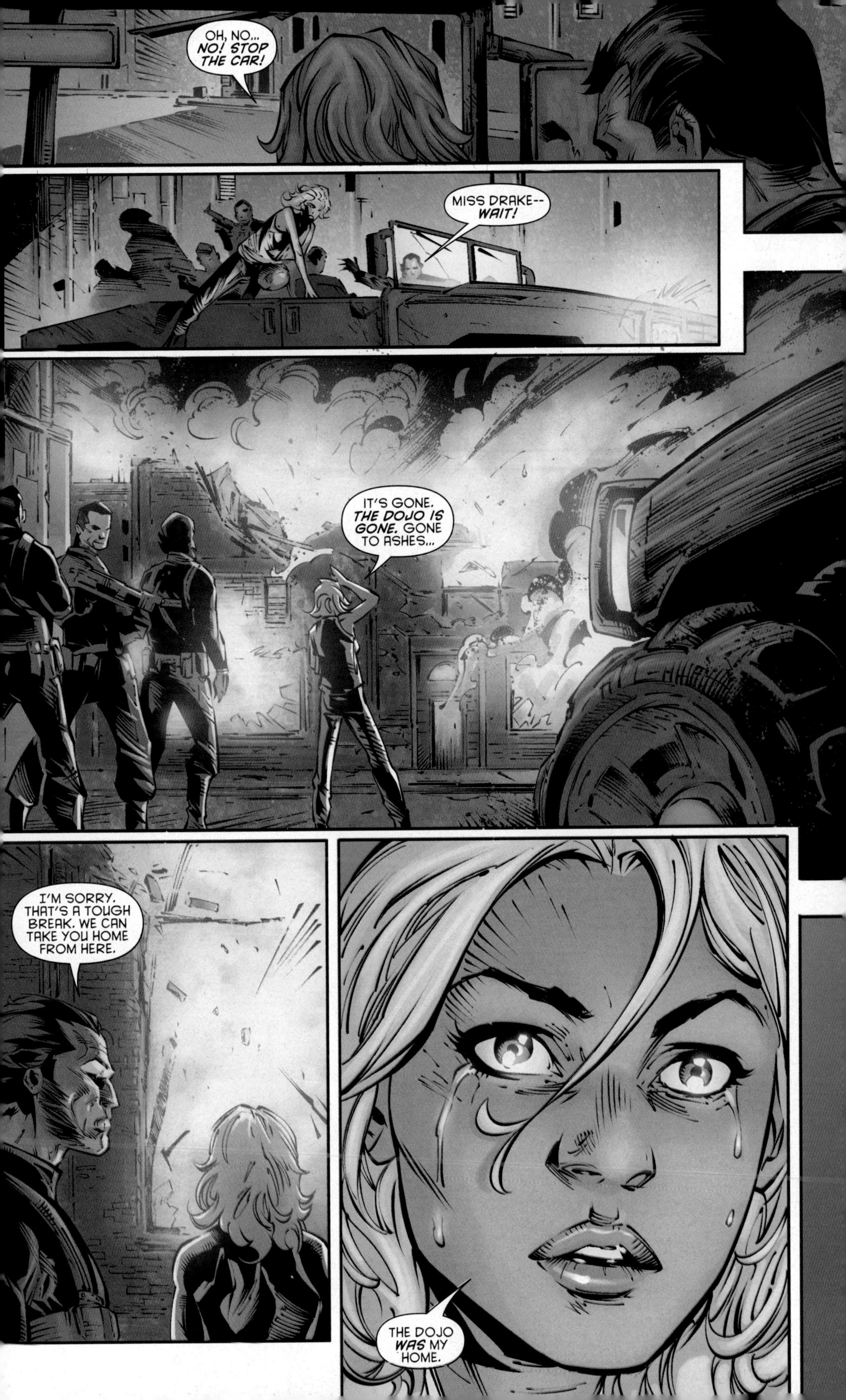
OH, NO... NO! STOP THE CAR!
MISS DRAKE-- WAIT!
IT'S GONE. THE DOJO IS GONE. GONE TO ASHES...
I'M SORRY. THAT'S A TOUGH BREAK. WE CAN TAKE YOU HOME FROM HERE.
THE DOJO WAS MY HOME.

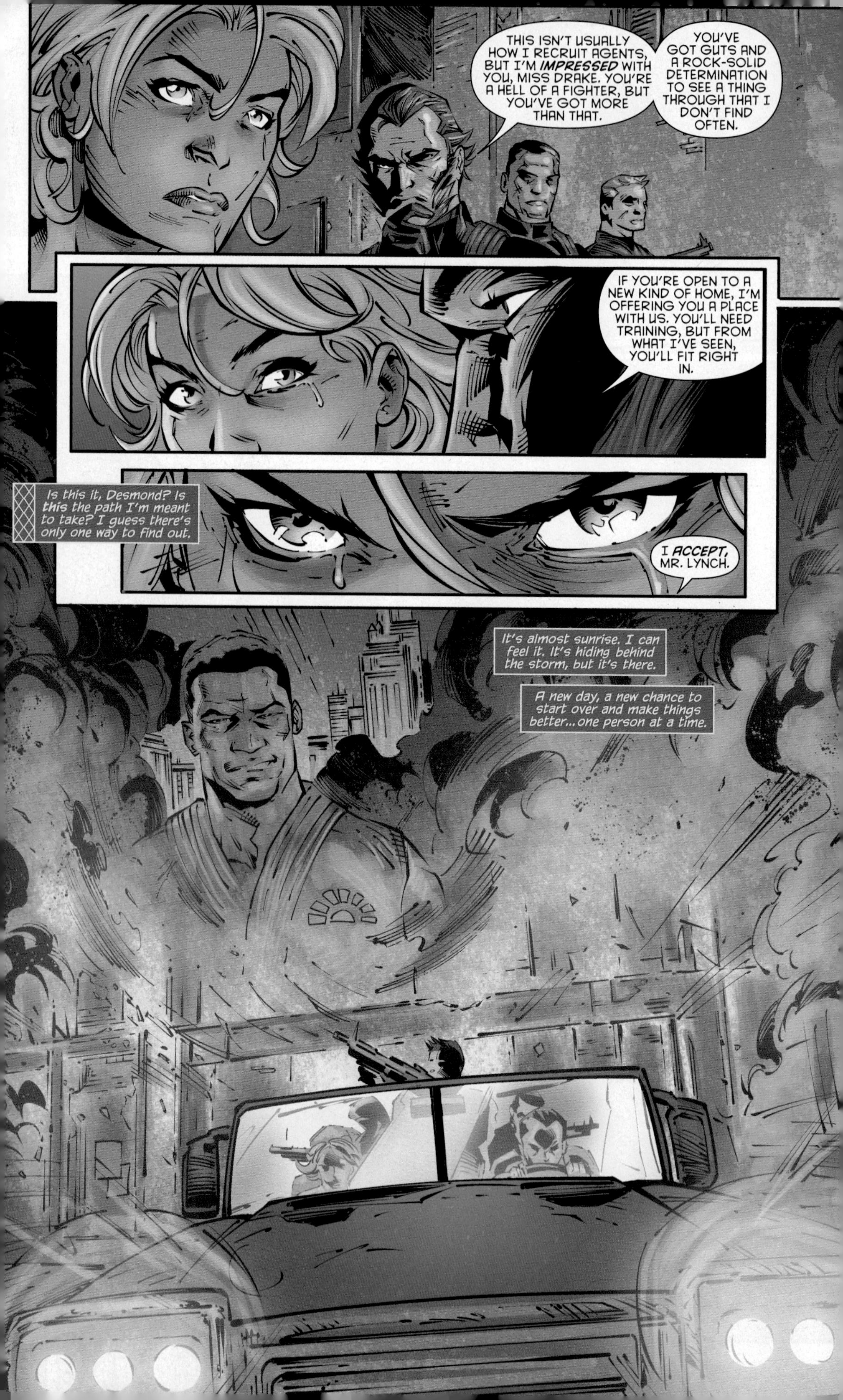
THIS ISN'T USUALLY HOW I RECRUIT AGENTS, BUT I'M *IMPRESSED* WITH YOU, MISS DRAKE. YOU'RE A HELL OF A FIGHTER, BUT YOU'VE GOT MORE THAN THAT.
YOU'VE GOT GUTS AND A ROCK-SOLID DETERMINATION TO SEE A THING THROUGH THAT I DON'T FIND OFTEN.
IF YOU'RE OPEN TO A NEW KIND OF HOME, I'M OFFERING YOU A PLACE WITH US. YOU'LL NEED TRAINING, BUT FROM WHAT I'VE SEEN, YOU'LL FIT RIGHT IN.
Is this it, Desmond? Is ***this*** *the path I'm meant to take? I guess there's only one way to find out.*
I *ACCEPT,* MR. LYNCH.
It's almost sunrise. I can feel it. It's hiding behind the storm, but it's there.
A new day, a new chance to start over and make things better...one person at a time.

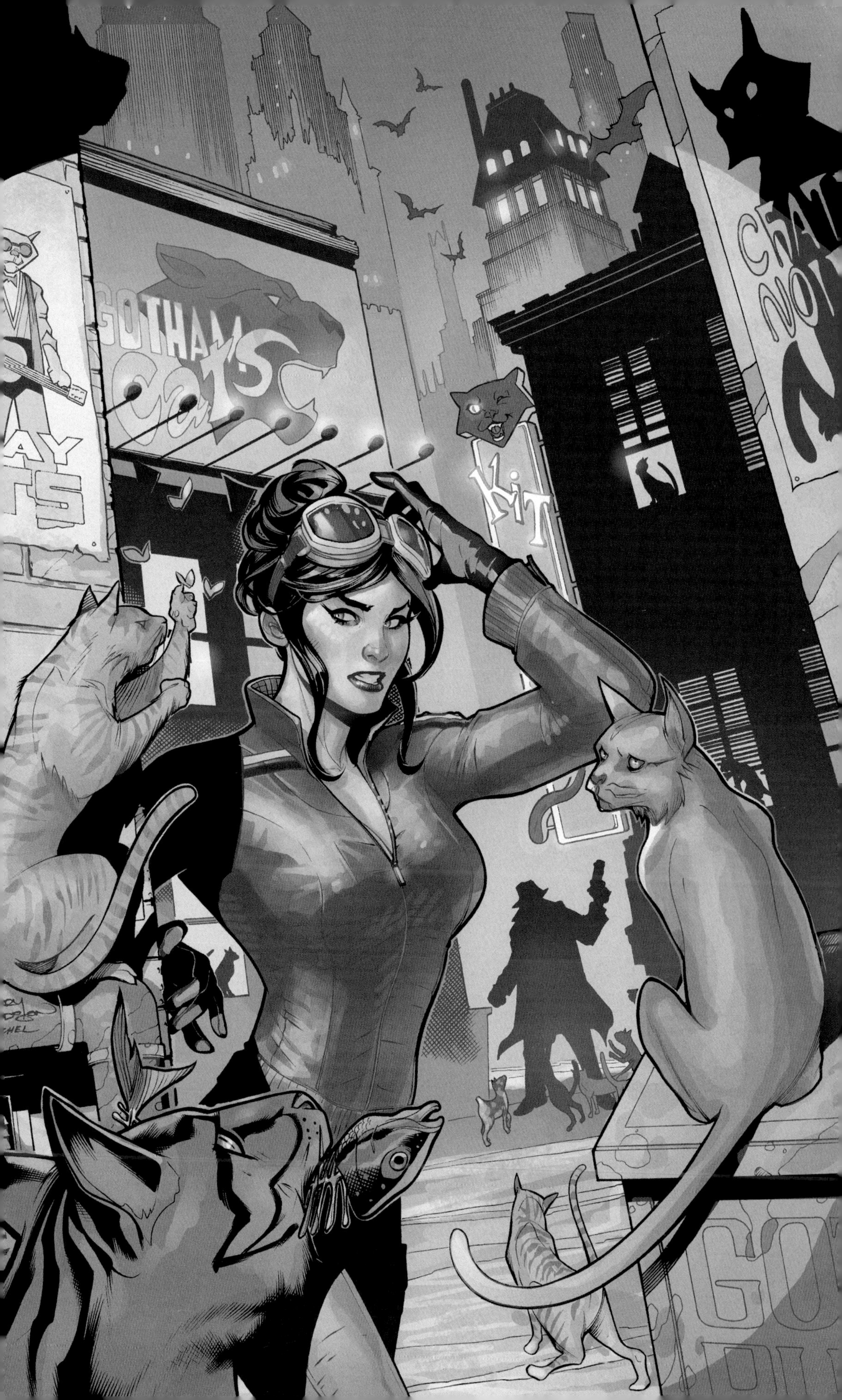
GOTHAM
Cats
Kit

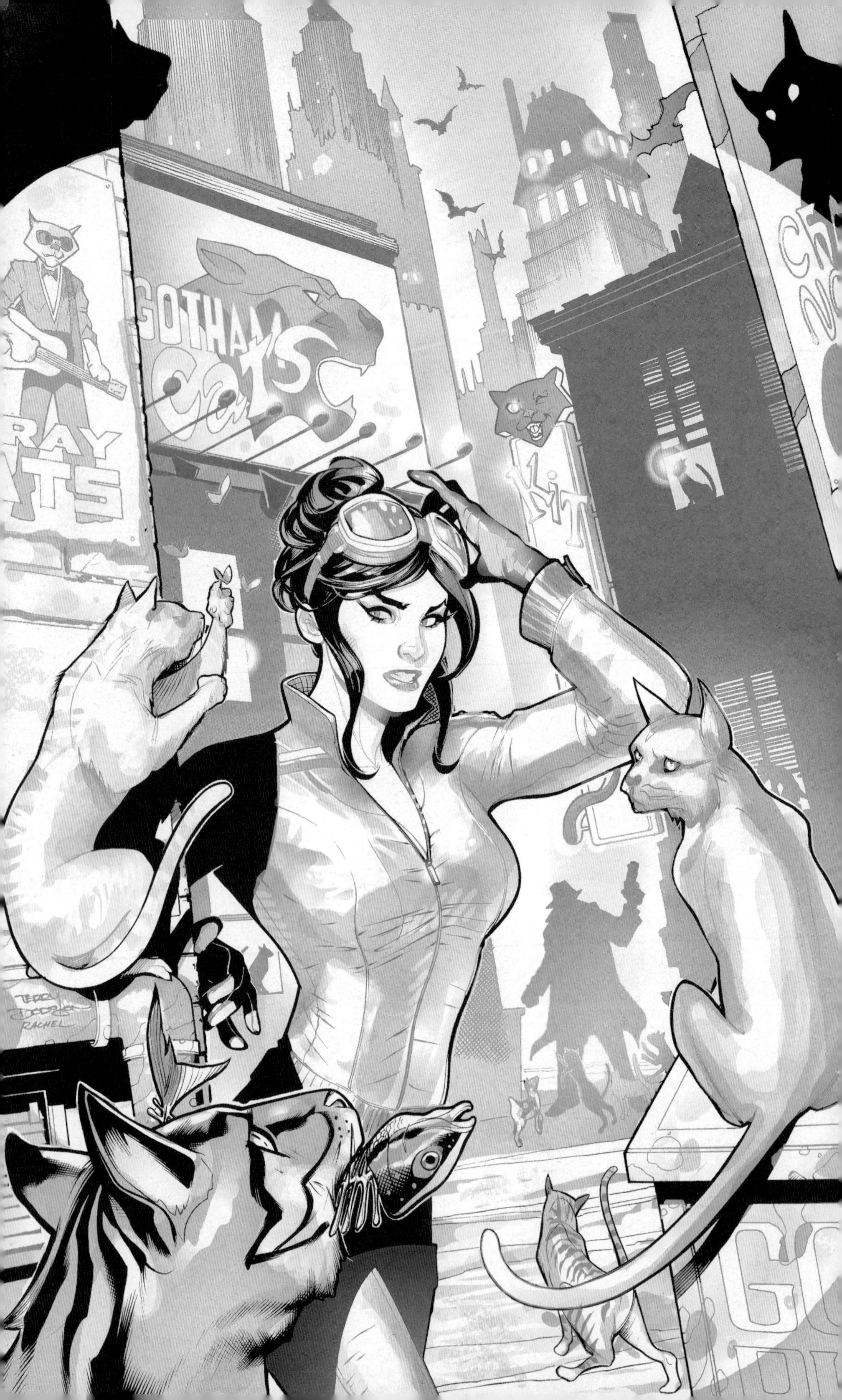
GOTHAM
Cats
TERRY DODSON
RACHEL

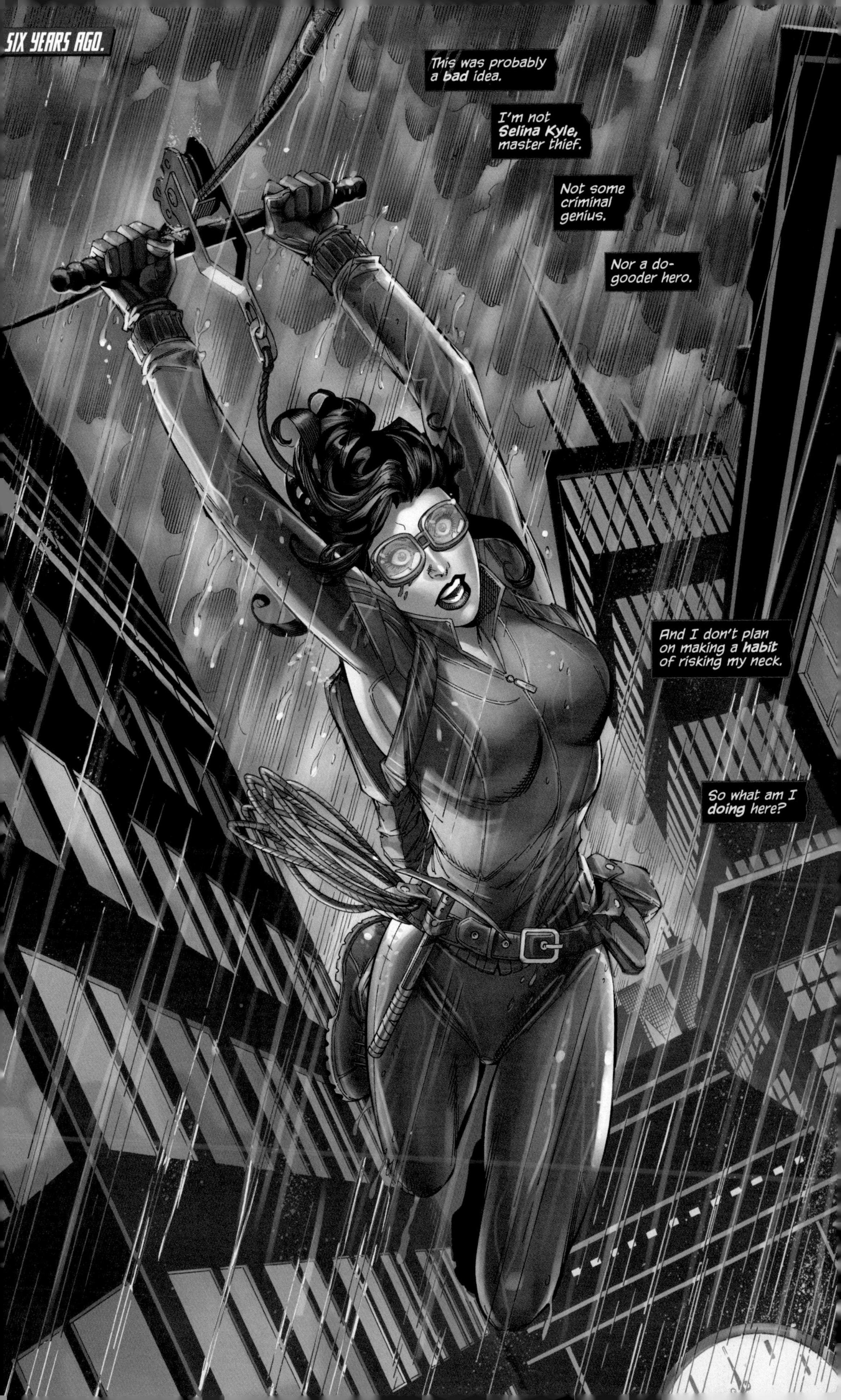
SIX YEARS AGO.
This was probably a **bad** idea.
I'm not **Selina Kyle,** master thief.
Not some criminal genius.
Nor a do-gooder hero.
And I don't plan on making a **habit** of risking my neck.
So what am I **doing** here?

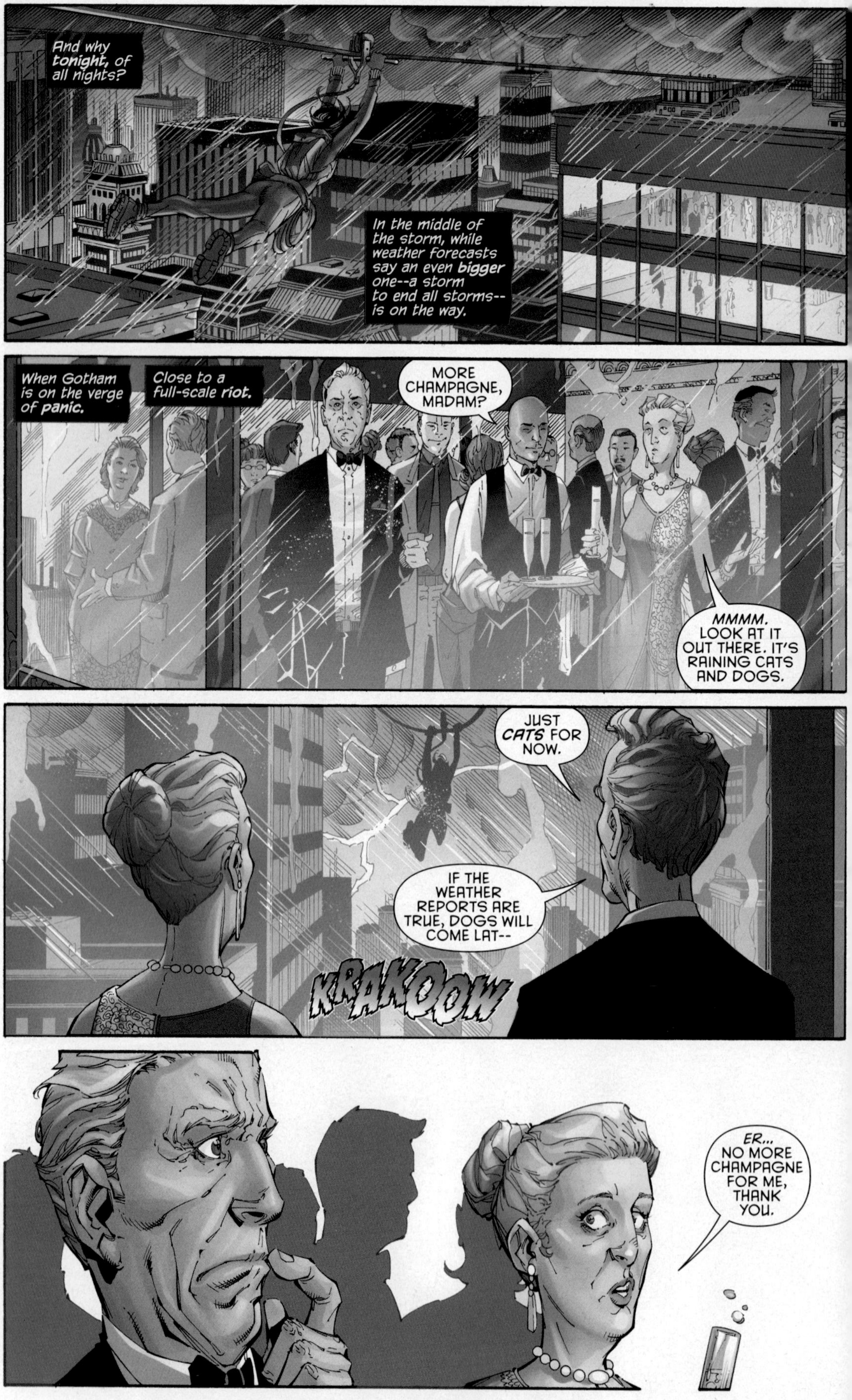
And why tonight, of all nights?
In the middle of the storm, while weather forecasts say an even bigger one--a storm to end all storms--is on the way.
When Gotham is on the verge of panic.
Close to a full-scale riot.
MORE CHAMPAGNE, MADAM?
MMMM. LOOK AT IT OUT THERE. IT'S RAINING CATS AND DOGS.
JUST CATS FOR NOW.
IF THE WEATHER REPORTS ARE TRUE, DOGS WILL COME LAT--
KRAKOOW
ER... NO MORE CHAMPAGNE FOR ME, THANK YOU.

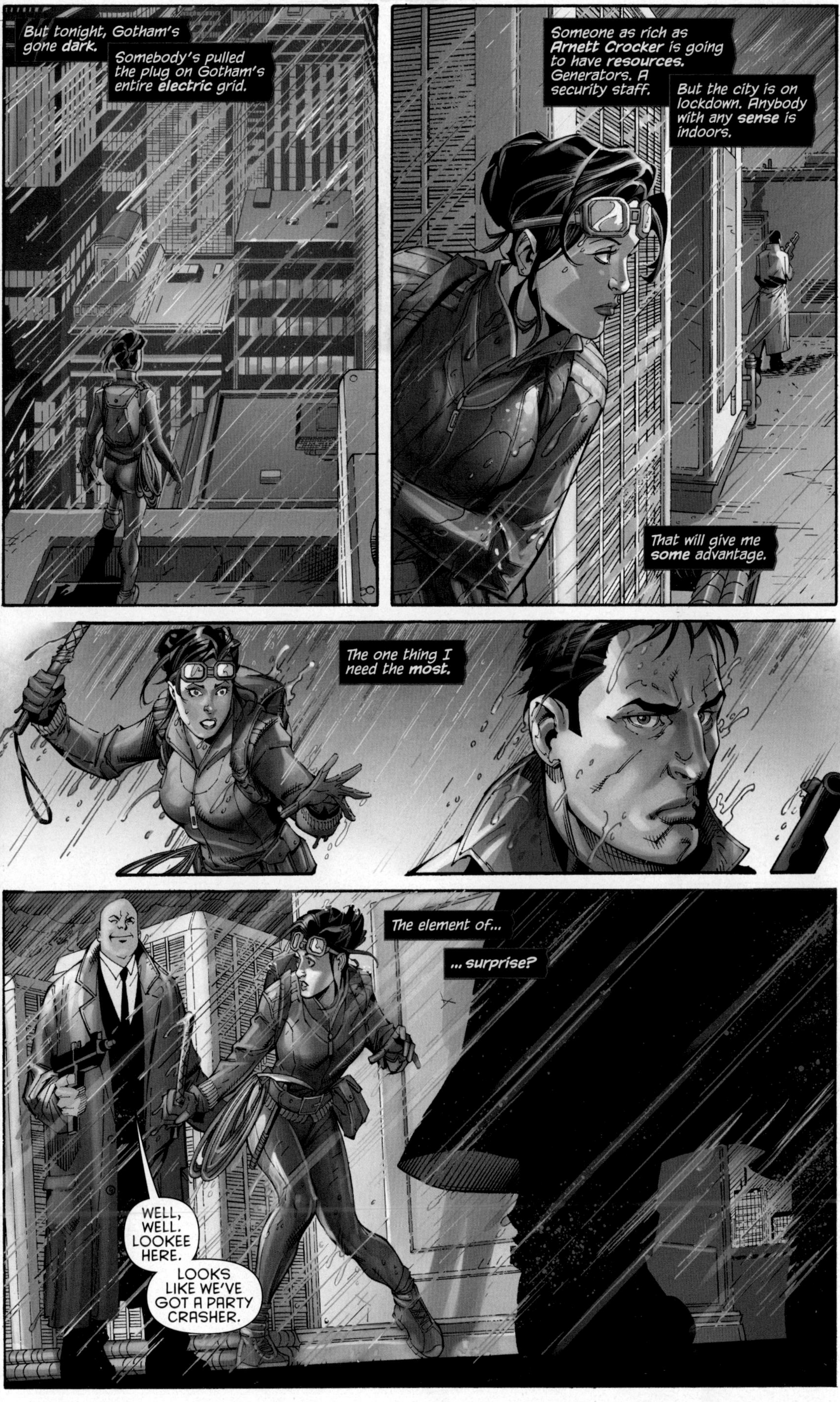

But tonight, Gotham's gone dark.
Somebody's pulled the plug on Gotham's entire electric grid.
Someone as rich as Arnett Crocker is going to have resources. Generators. A security staff.
But the city is on lockdown. Anybody with any sense is indoors.
That will give me some advantage.
The one thing I need the most.
The element of...
...surprise?
WELL, WELL. LOOKEE HERE.
LOOKS LIKE WE'VE GOT A PARTY CRASHER.

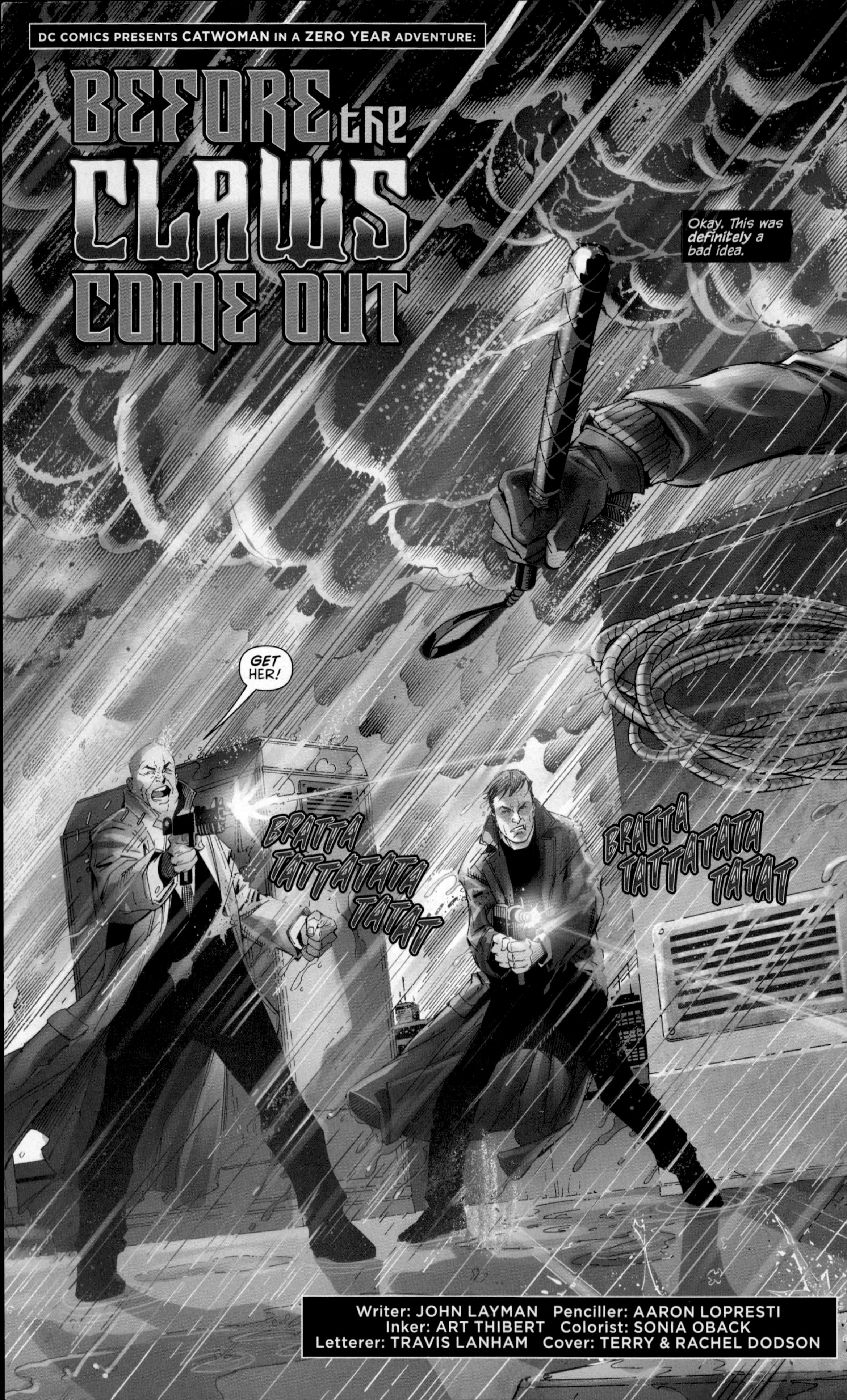
DC COMICS PRESENTS CATWOMAN IN A ZERO YEAR ADVENTURE:
BEFORE the CLAWS COME OUT
Okay. This was definitely a bad idea.
GET HER!
BRATTA TATTATATA TATAT
BRATTA TATTATATA TATAT
Writer: JOHN LAYMAN Penciller: AARON LOPRESTI
Inker: ART THIBERT Colorist: SONIA OBACK
Letterer: TRAVIS LANHAM Cover: TERRY & RACHEL DODSON

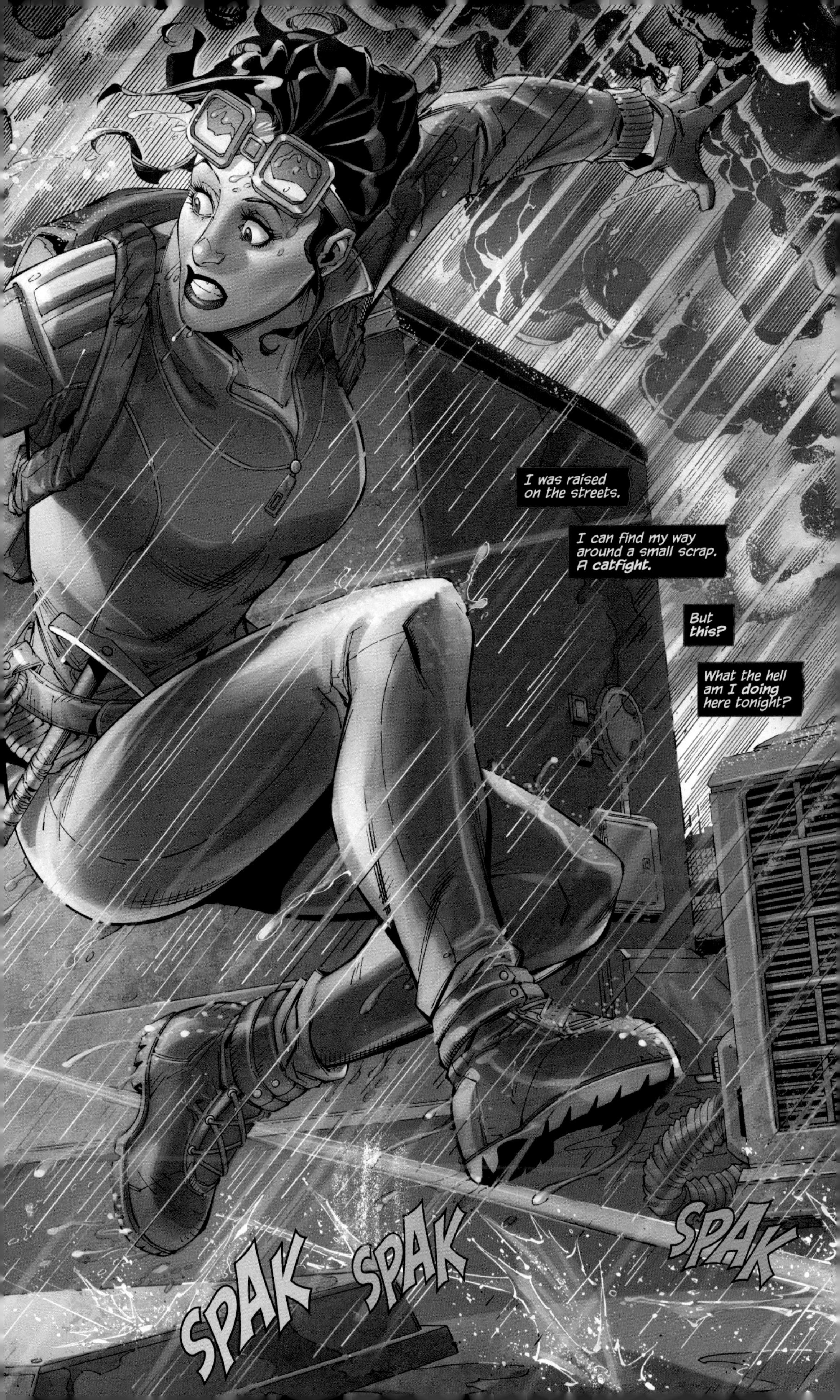
I was raised on the streets.
I can find my way around a small scrap. A **catfight**.
But **this?**
What the hell am I **doing** here tonight?
SPAK
SPAK
SPAK

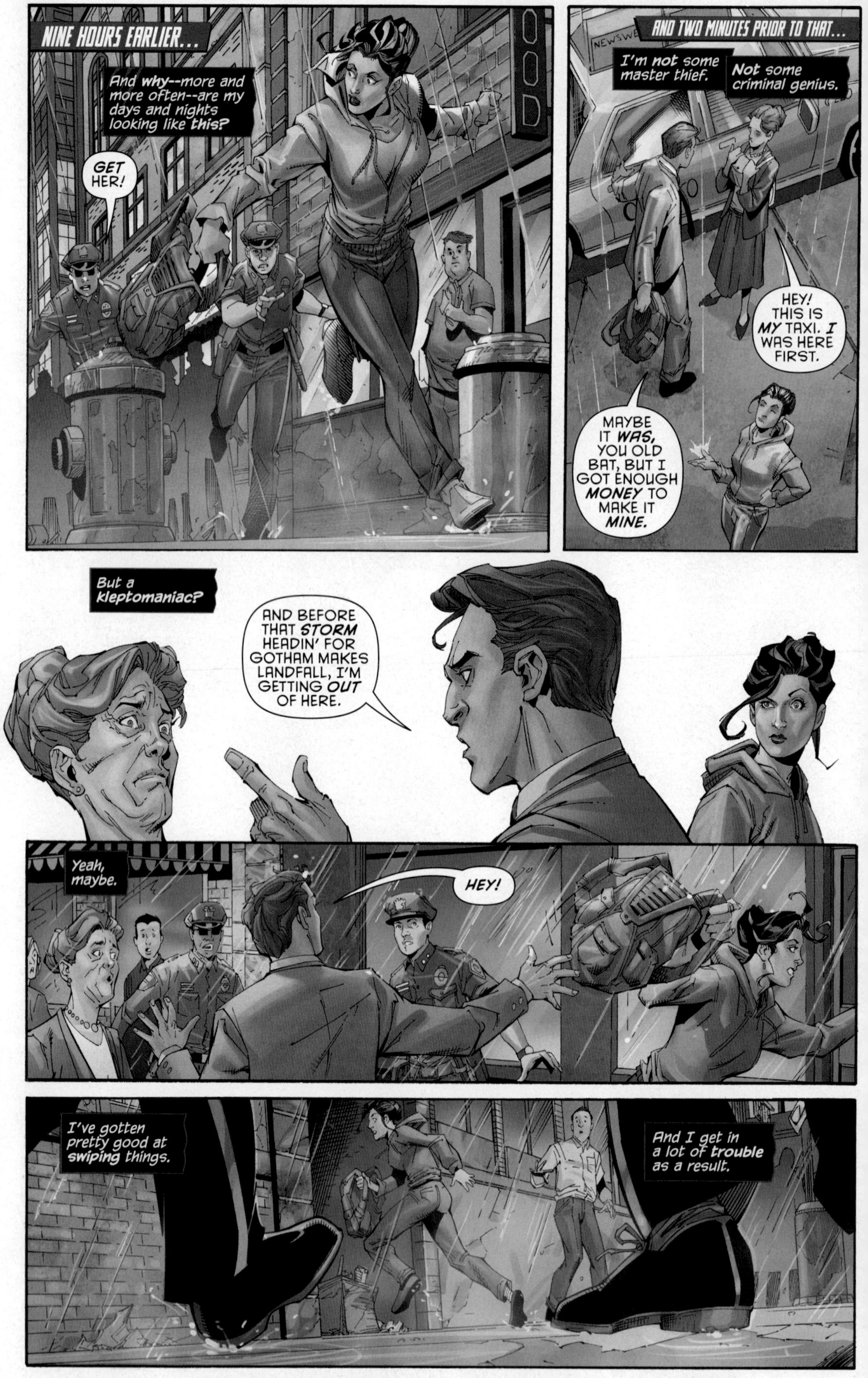
NINE HOURS EARLIER...
And why--more and more often--are my days and nights looking like this?
GET HER!
AND TWO MINUTES PRIOR TO THAT...
I'm not some master thief.
Not some criminal genius.
HEY! THIS IS MY TAXI. I WAS HERE FIRST.
MAYBE IT WAS, YOU OLD BAT, BUT I GOT ENOUGH MONEY TO MAKE IT MINE.
But a kleptomaniac?
AND BEFORE THAT STORM HEADIN' FOR GOTHAM MAKES LANDFALL, I'M GETTING OUT OF HERE.
Yeah, maybe.
HEY!
I've gotten pretty good at swiping things.
And I get in a lot of trouble as a result.

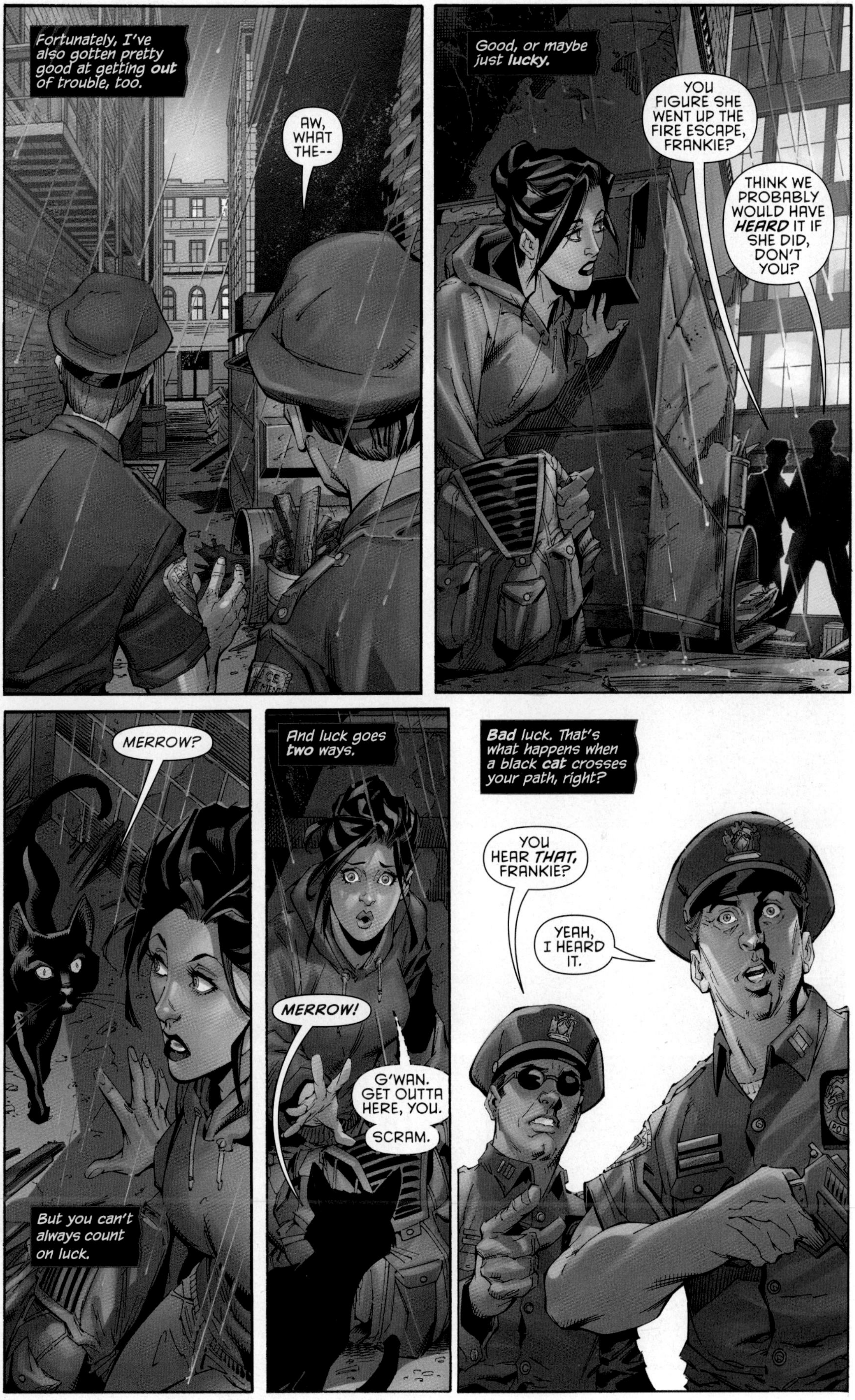
Fortunately, I've also gotten pretty good at getting out of trouble, too.
AW, WHAT THE--
Good, or maybe just lucky.
YOU FIGURE SHE WENT UP THE FIRE ESCAPE, FRANKIE?
THINK WE PROBABLY WOULD HAVE HEARD IT IF SHE DID, DON'T YOU?
MERROW?
But you can't always count on luck.
And luck goes two ways.
MERROW!
G'WAN. GET OUTTA HERE, YOU.
SCRAM.
Bad luck. That's what happens when a black cat crosses your path, right?
YOU HEAR THAT, FRANKIE?
YEAH, I HEARD IT.

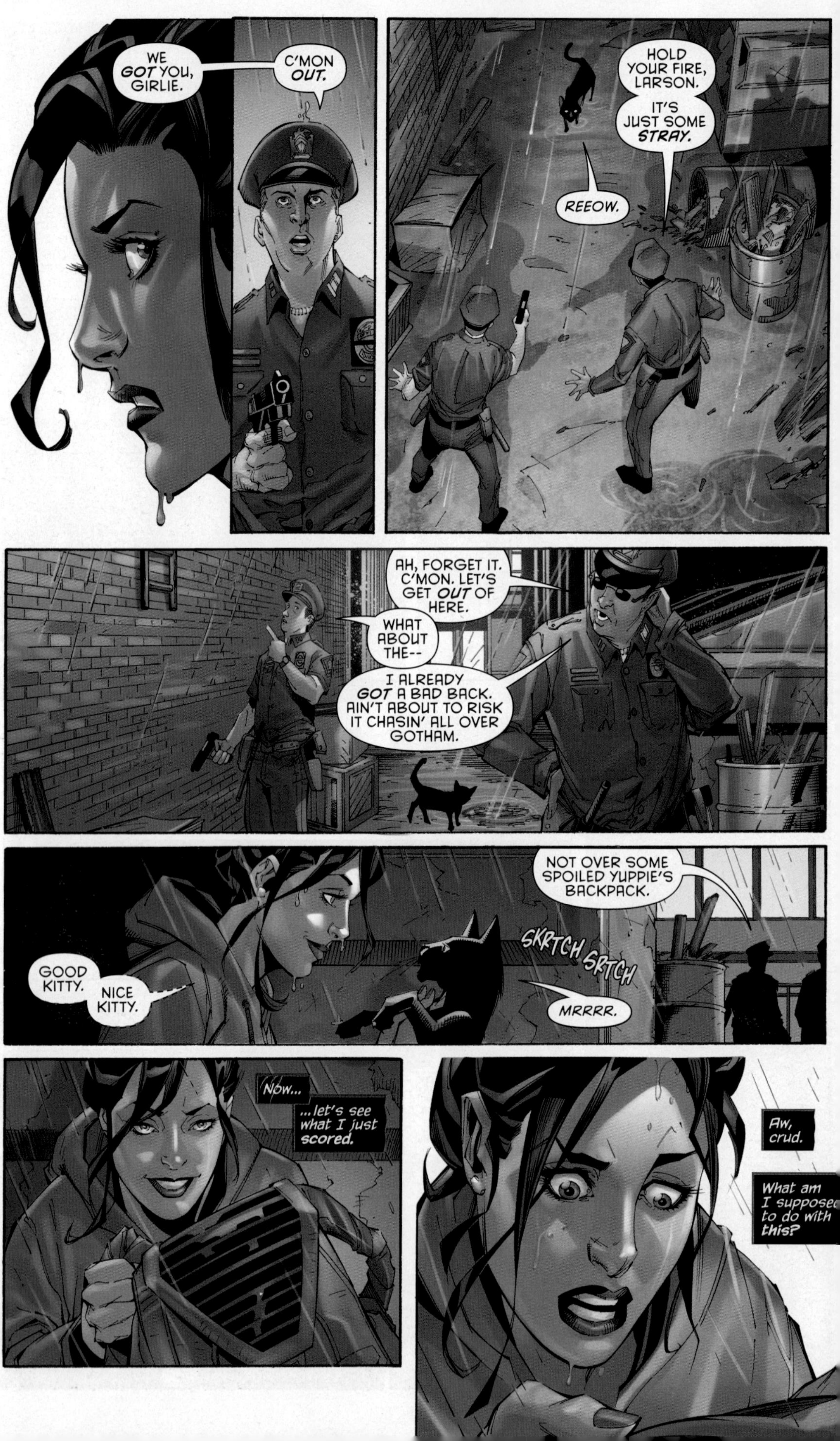
WE GOT YOU, GIRLIE.
C'MON OUT.
HOLD YOUR FIRE, LARSON.
IT'S JUST SOME STRAY.
REEOW.
AH, FORGET IT. C'MON. LET'S GET OUT OF HERE.
WHAT ABOUT THE--
I ALREADY GOT A BAD BACK. AIN'T ABOUT TO RISK IT CHASIN' ALL OVER GOTHAM.
NOT OVER SOME SPOILED YUPPIE'S BACKPACK.
GOOD KITTY.
NICE KITTY.
SKRTCH SRTCH
MRRRR.
Now...
...let's see what I just scored.
Aw, crud.
What am I supposed to do with this?

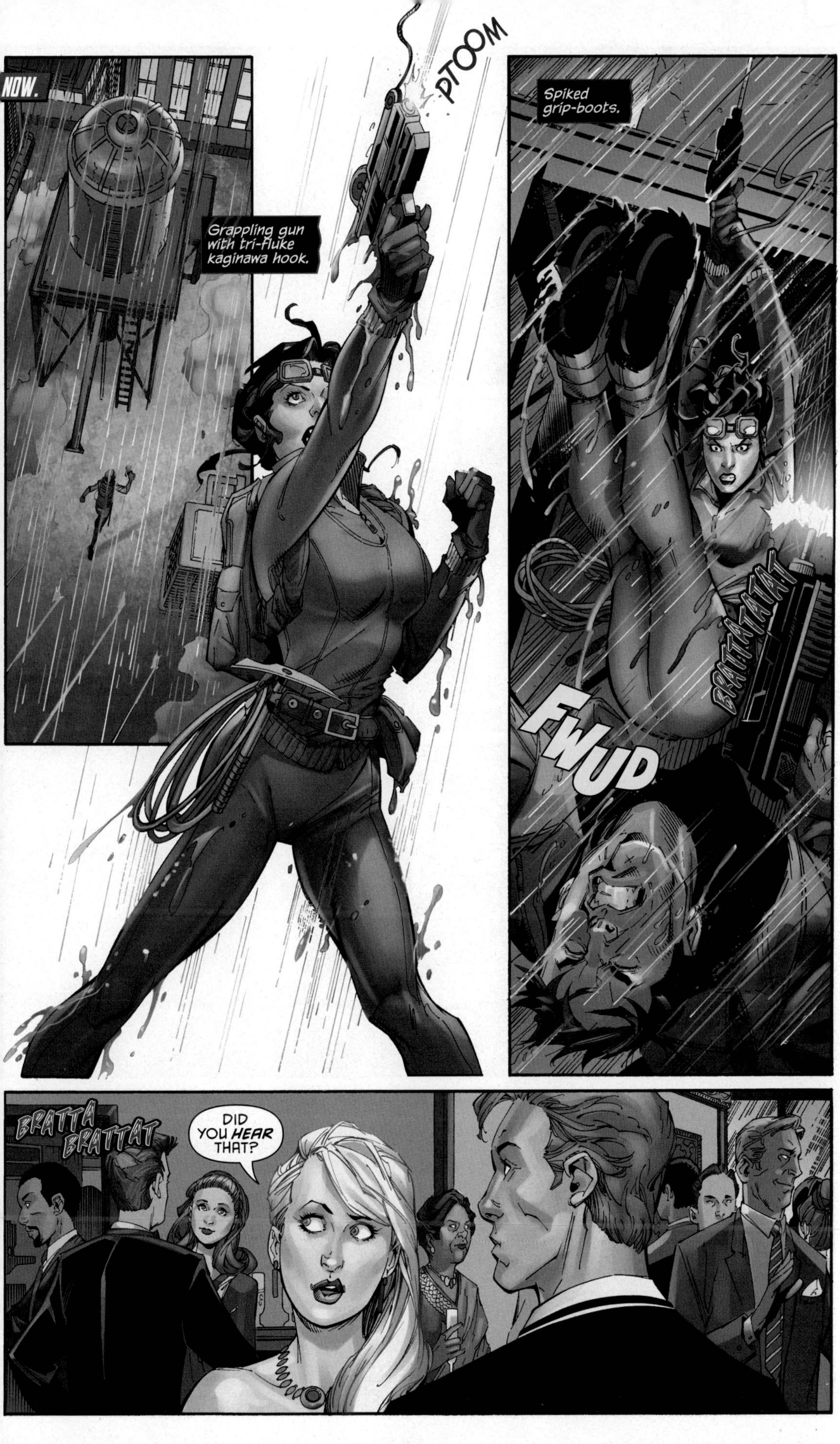
NOW.
PTOOM
Grappling gun with tri-fluke kaginawa hook.
Spiked grip-boots.
BRATTATATAT
FWUD
BRATTA BRATTAT
DID YOU HEAR THAT?

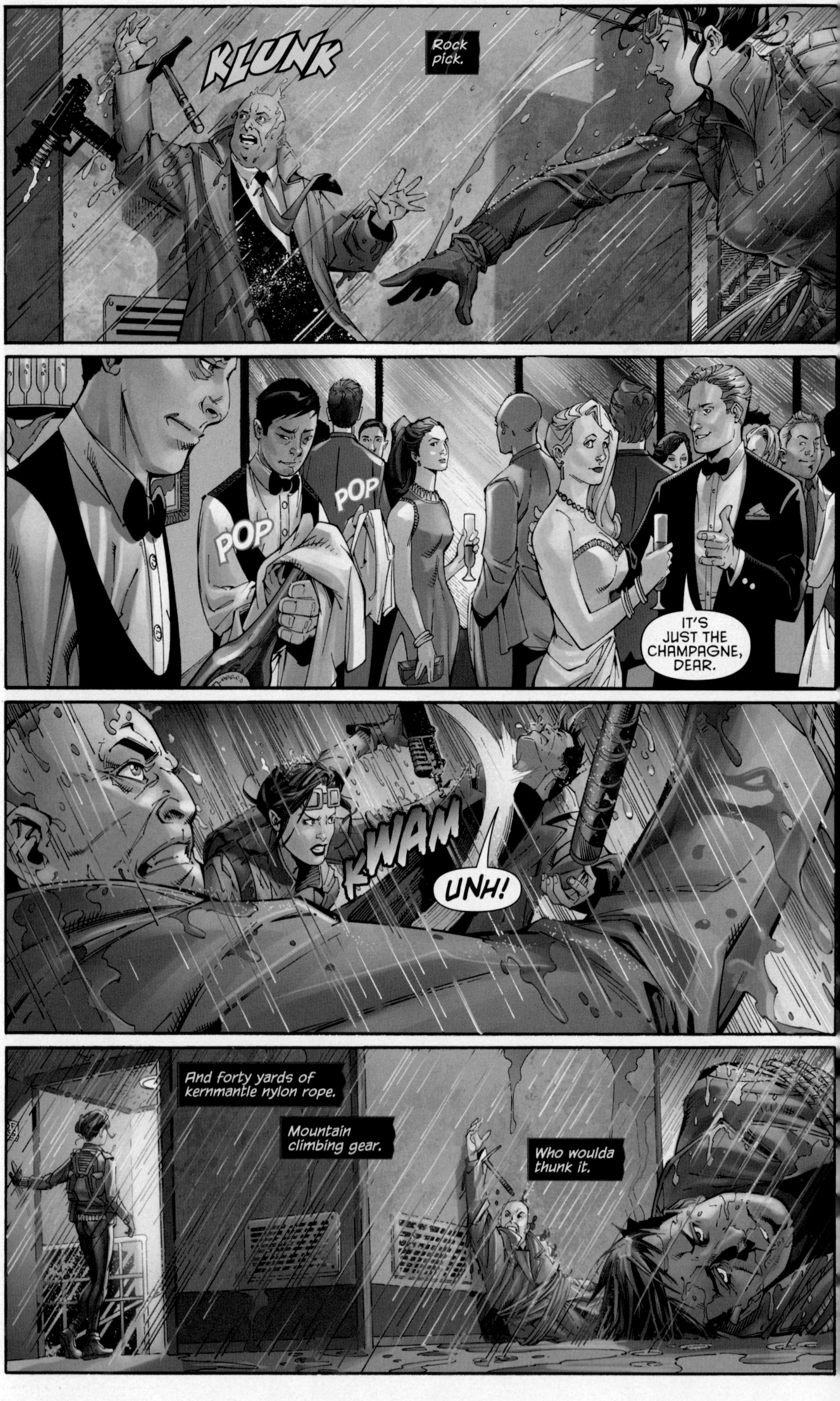
KLUNK
Rock pick.
POP
POP
IT'S JUST THE CHAMPAGNE, DEAR.
KWAM
UNH!
And forty yards of kernmantle nylon rope.
Mountain climbing gear.
Who woulda thunk it.

LOLA'S PAWN

24061

CLOSED
UNTIL FURTHER
NOTICE
DUE TO WEATHER

MOUNTAIN CLIMBING GEAR? I DON'T *THINK* SO, HONEY.

WHAT WAS HE DOING WITH *MOUNTAIN CLIMBING GEAR*, ANYWAY?

HOW SHOULD I KNOW, LOLA? BUT THIS IS *QUALITY* STUFF.

EXPENSIVE STUFF.

I FIGURE IT'S GOTTA BE WORTH EIGHT HUNDRED.

HA!

CLOSED
UNTIL FURTHER
NOTICE
DUE TO

WAM WAM WAM

MAYBE *THREE* HUNDRED ON A *GOOD* DAY, SELINA. AND THIS IS *NOT* A GOOD DAY.

"AND, SELINA, IF THIS STORM IS AS BAD AS EVERYBODY SAYS IT'S *GOING* TO BE--

NOBODY CARES ABOUT *SPORTING* EQUIPMENT RIGHT NOW.

LOOK OUT THERE. IT'S LIKE THE END OF THE WORLD IS COMING TO GOTHAM.

CLEAN WATER. MEDICINE. CANDLES. BATTERIES.

FOOD.

THAT'S WHAT EVERYBODY IN GOTHAM IS AFTER.

"--MAYBE THAT'S WHAT *YOU* SHOULD BE AFTER, TOO."

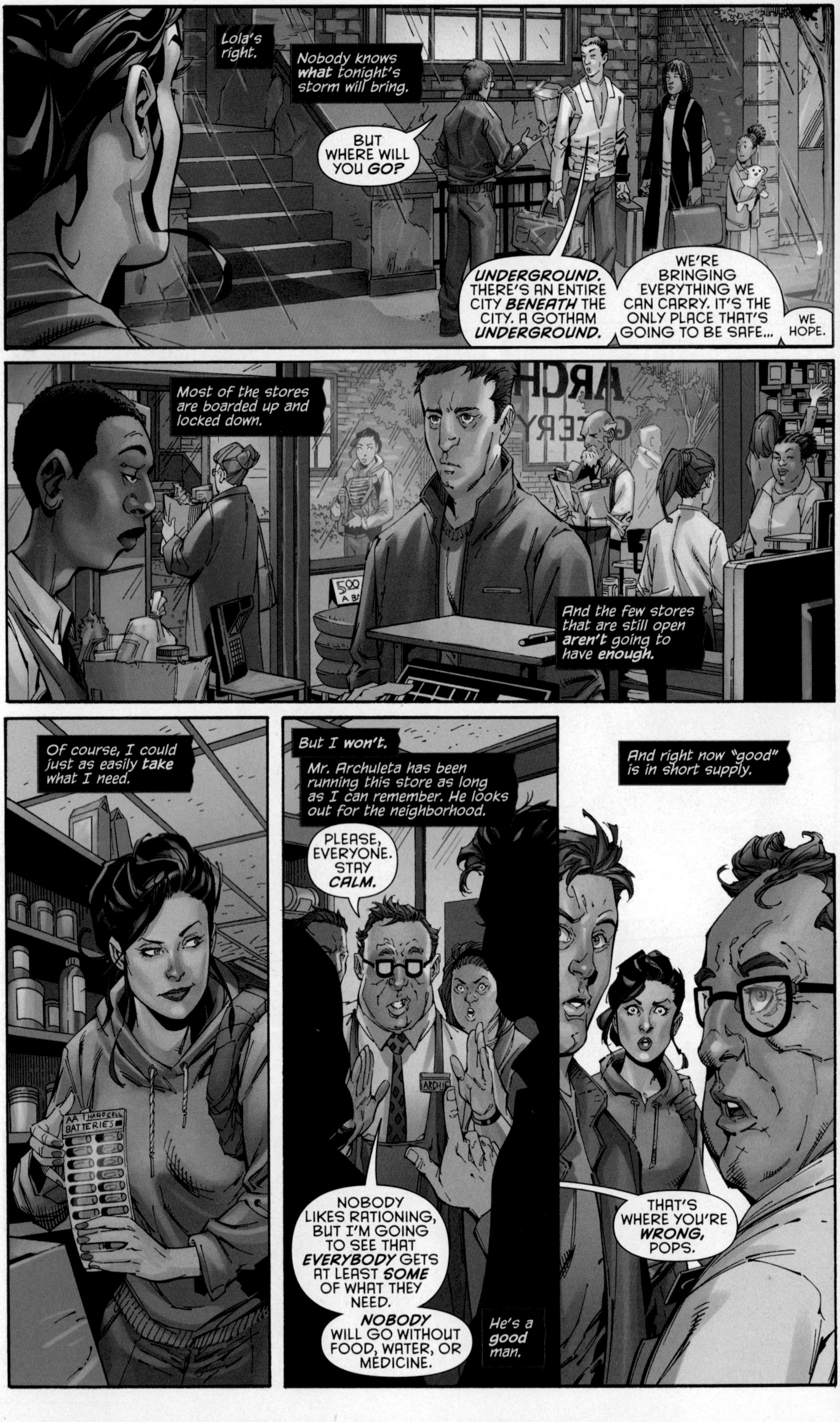
Lola's right.
Nobody knows what tonight's storm will bring.
BUT WHERE WILL YOU GO?
UNDERGROUND. THERE'S AN ENTIRE CITY BENEATH THE CITY. A GOTHAM UNDERGROUND.
WE'RE BRINGING EVERYTHING WE CAN CARRY. IT'S THE ONLY PLACE THAT'S GOING TO BE SAFE...
WE HOPE.
Most of the stores are boarded up and locked down.
And the few stores that are still open aren't going to have enough.
Of course, I could just as easily take what I need.
AA HARD CELL BATTERIES
But I won't.
Mr. Archuleta has been running this store as long as I can remember. He looks out for the neighborhood.
PLEASE, EVERYONE. STAY CALM.
NOBODY LIKES RATIONING, BUT I'M GOING TO SEE THAT EVERYBODY GETS AT LEAST SOME OF WHAT THEY NEED.
NOBODY WILL GO WITHOUT FOOD, WATER, OR MEDICINE.
He's a good man.
And right now "good" is in short supply.
THAT'S WHERE YOU'RE WRONG, POPS.

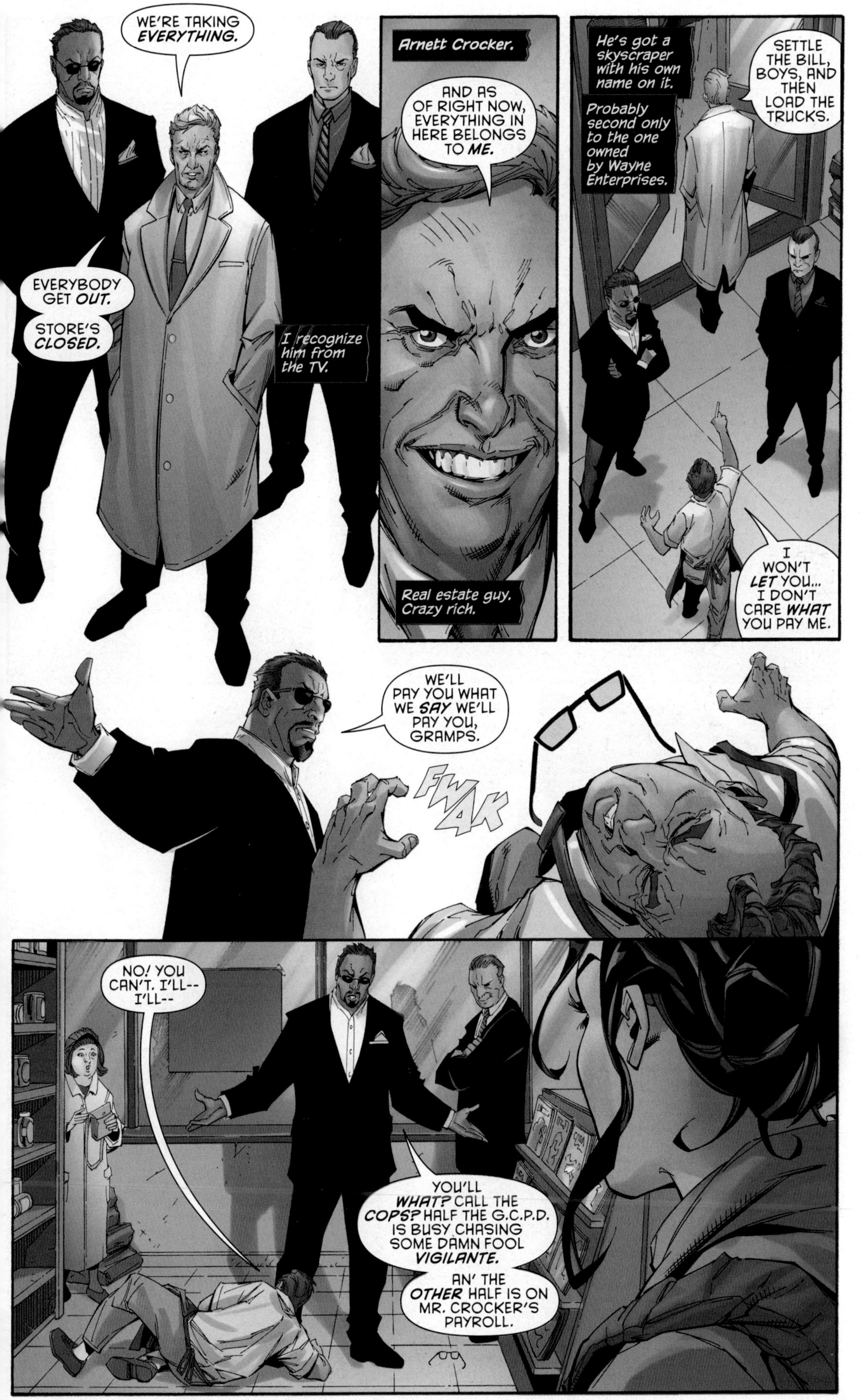
WE'RE TAKING EVERYTHING.
EVERYBODY GET OUT.
STORE'S CLOSED.
I recognize him from the TV.
Arnett Crocker.
AND AS OF RIGHT NOW, EVERYTHING IN HERE BELONGS TO ME.
Real estate guy. Crazy rich.
He's got a skyscraper with his own name on it.
Probably second only to the one owned by Wayne Enterprises.
SETTLE THE BILL, BOYS, AND THEN LOAD THE TRUCKS.
I WON'T LET YOU... I DON'T CARE WHAT YOU PAY ME.
WE'LL PAY YOU WHAT WE SAY WE'LL PAY YOU, GRAMPS.
FWAK
NO! YOU CAN'T. I'LL-- I'LL--
YOU'LL WHAT? CALL THE COPS? HALF THE G.C.P.D. IS BUSY CHASING SOME DAMN FOOL VIGILANTE.
AN' THE OTHER HALF IS ON MR. CROCKER'S PAYROLL.

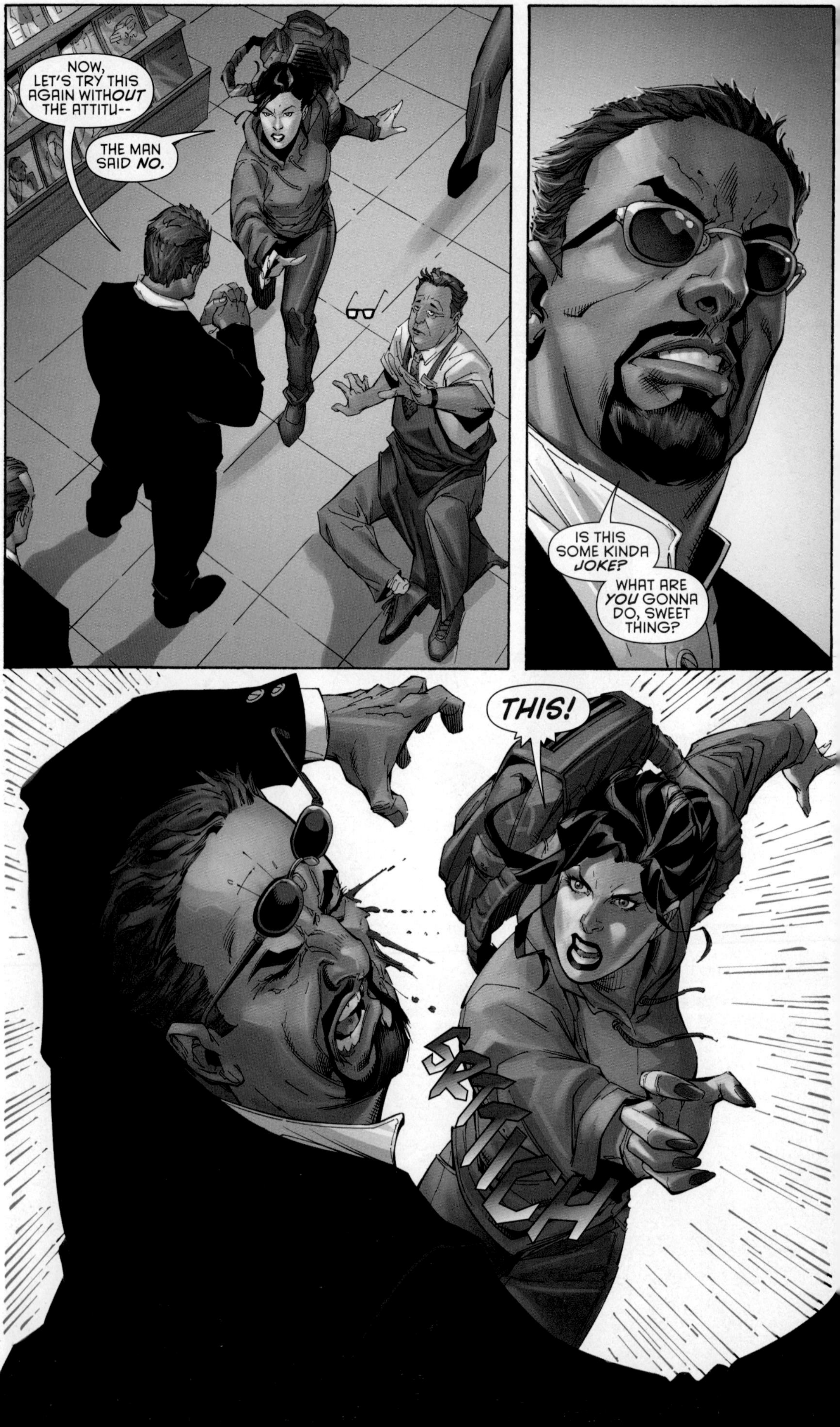
NOW, LET'S TRY THIS AGAIN WITHOUT THE ATTITU--
THE MAN SAID NO.
IS THIS SOME KINDA JOKE?
WHAT ARE YOU GONNA DO, SWEET THING?
THIS!
SKTTCH

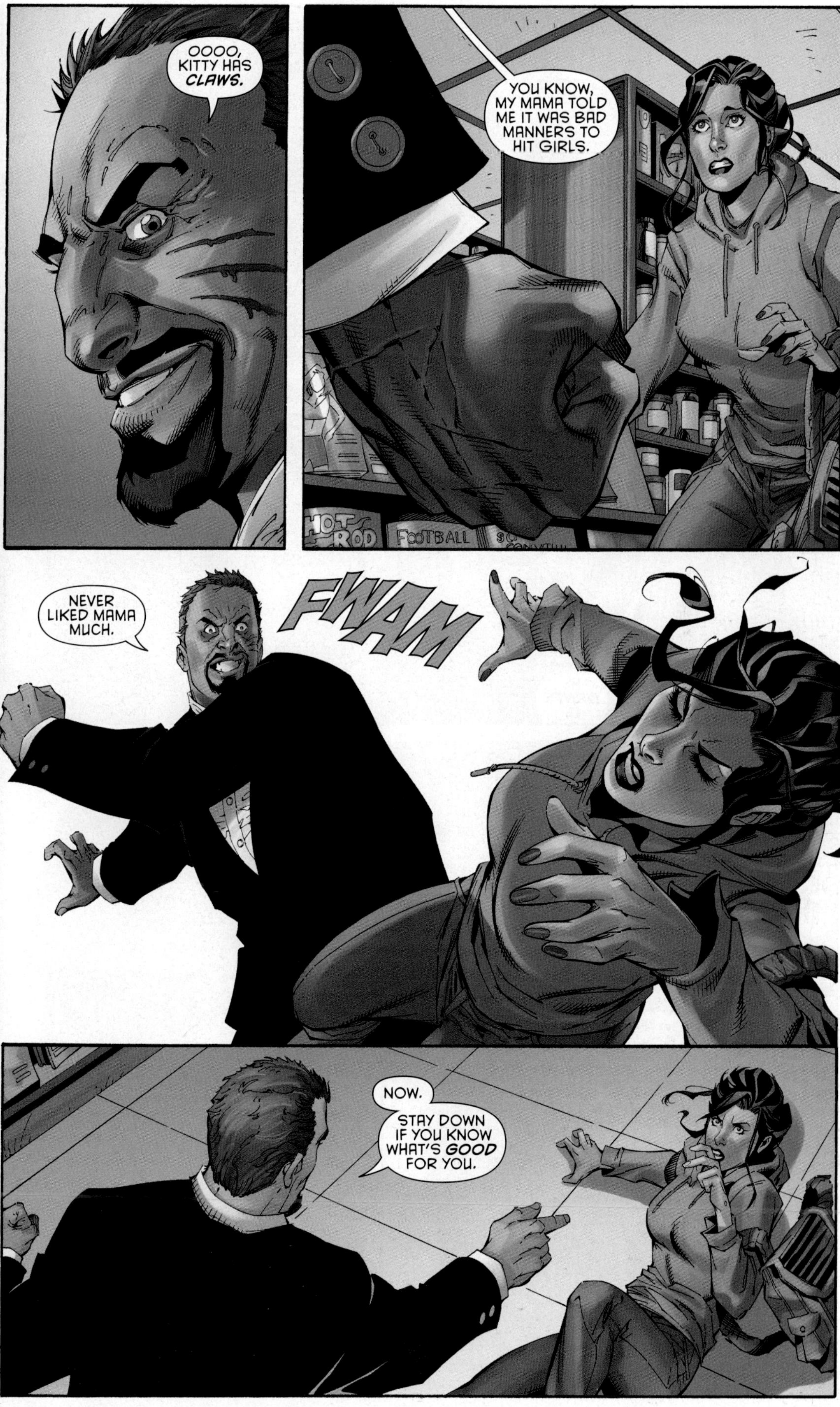
OOOO, KITTY HAS *CLAWS.*
YOU KNOW, MY MAMA TOLD ME IT WAS BAD MANNERS TO HIT GIRLS.
HOT ROD
FOOTBALL
NEVER LIKED MAMA MUCH.
FWAM
NOW.
STAY DOWN IF YOU KNOW WHAT'S *GOOD* FOR YOU.

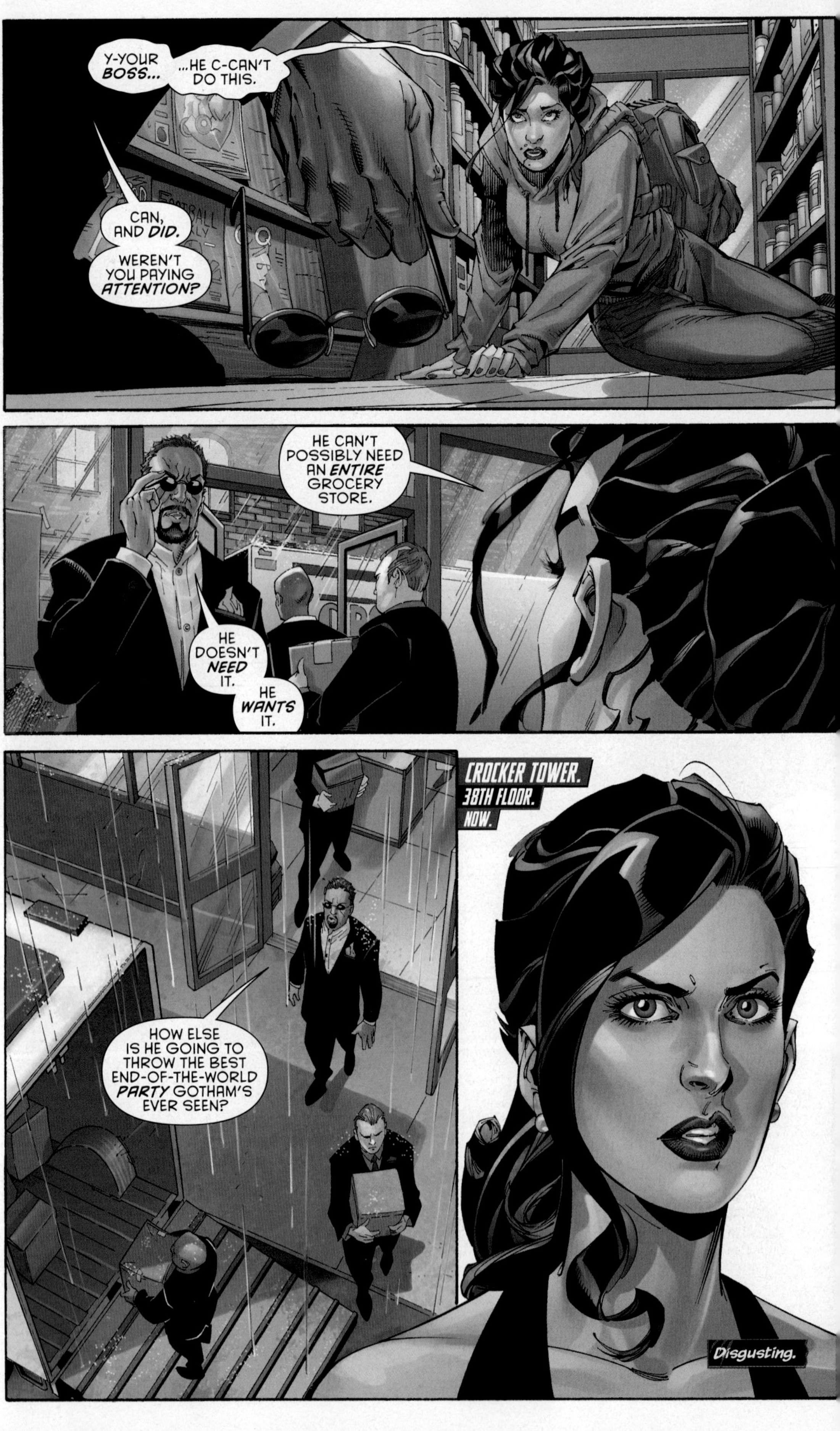

Y-YOUR BOSS...
...HE C-CAN'T DO THIS.
CAN, AND DID.
WEREN'T YOU PAYING ATTENTION?
HE CAN'T POSSIBLY NEED AN ENTIRE GROCERY STORE.
HE DOESN'T NEED IT.
HE WANTS IT.
CROCKER TOWER. 38TH FLOOR. NOW.
HOW ELSE IS HE GOING TO THROW THE BEST END-OF-THE-WORLD PARTY GOTHAM'S EVER SEEN?
Disgusting.

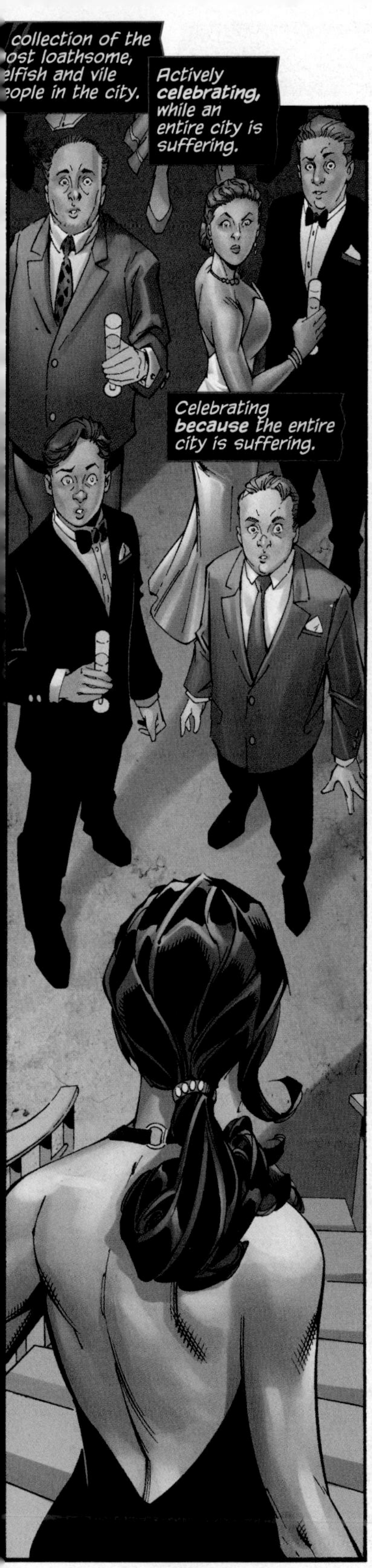
collection of the
ost loathsome,
elfish and vile
eople in the city.
Actively **celebrating,** while an entire city is suffering.
Celebrating **because** the entire city is suffering.

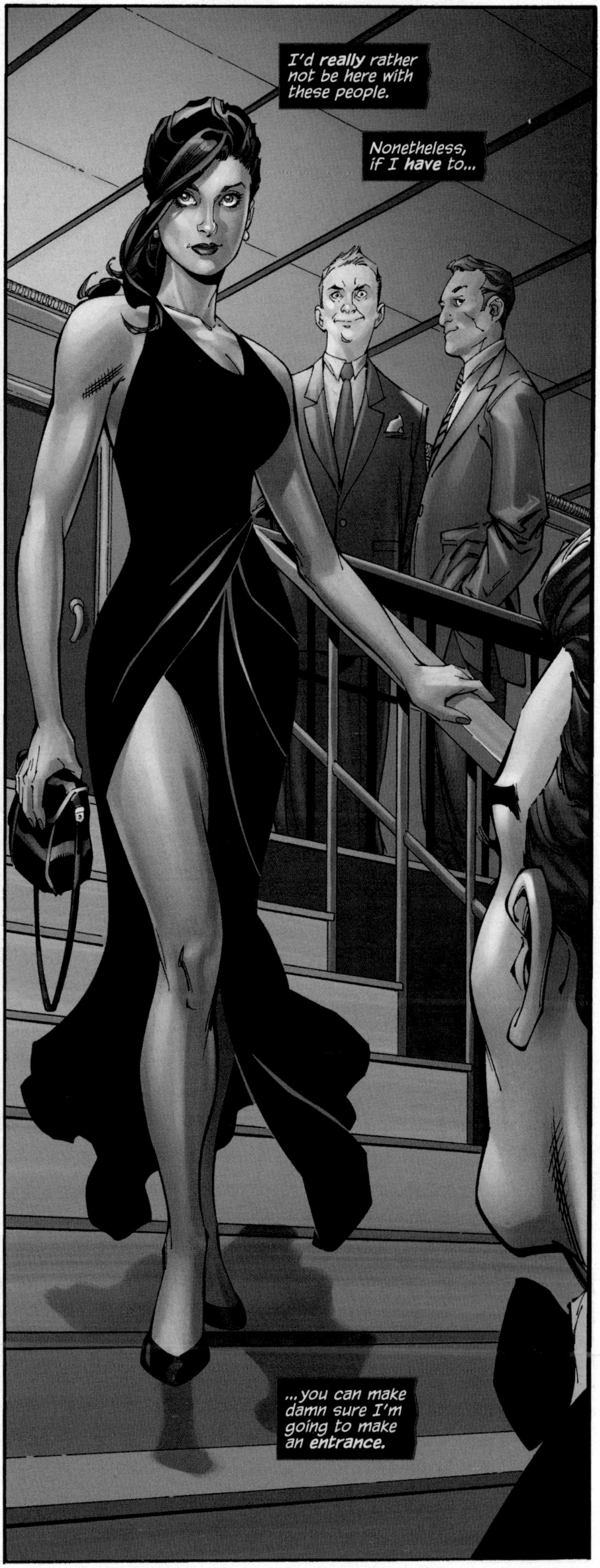
I'd **really** rather not be here with these people.
Nonetheless, if I **have** to...
...you can make damn sure I'm going to make an **entrance.**

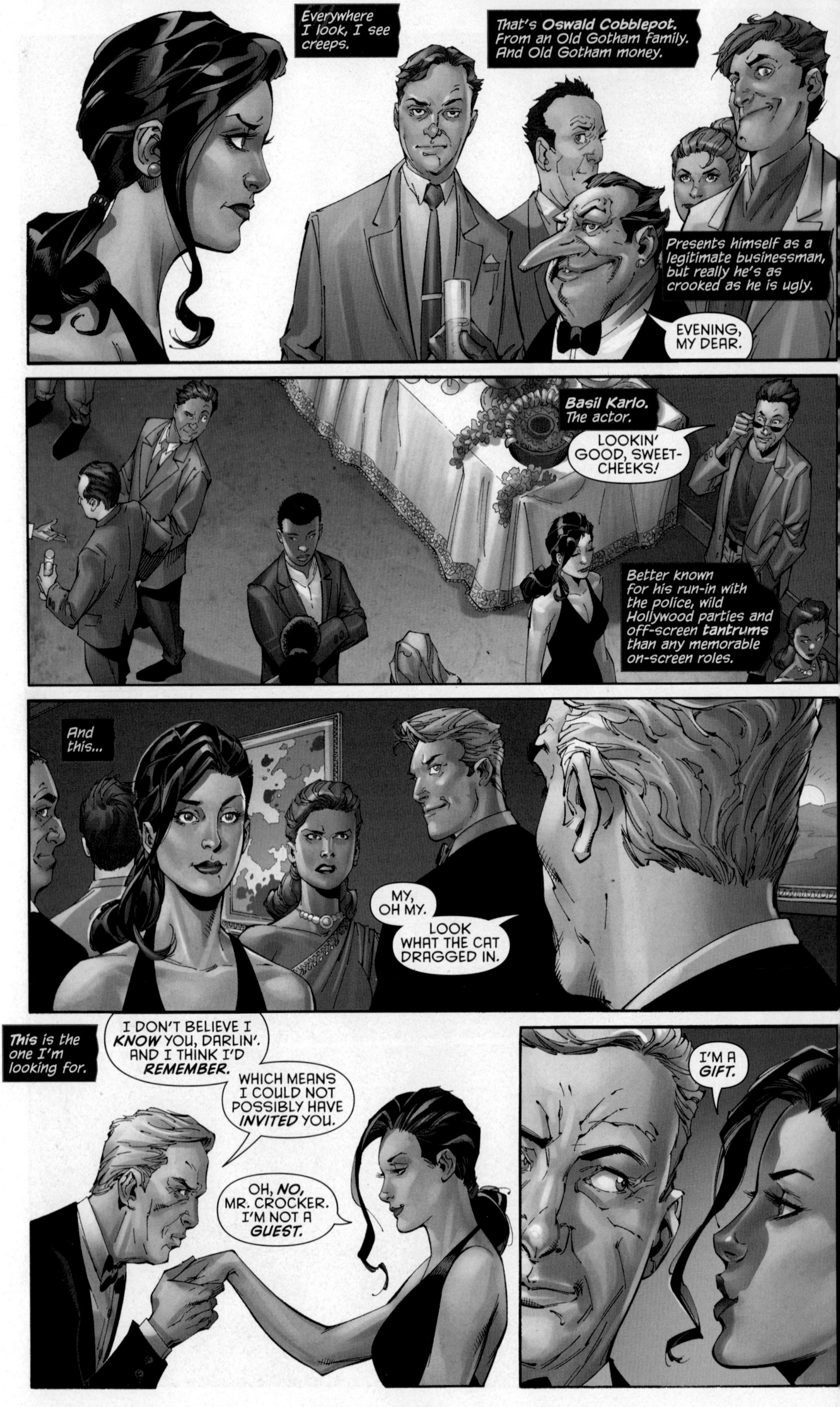
Everywhere I look, I see creeps.
That's Oswald Cobblepot. From an Old Gotham family. And Old Gotham money.
Presents himself as a legitimate businessman, but really he's as crooked as he is ugly.
EVENING, MY DEAR.
Basil Karlo. The actor.
LOOKIN' GOOD, SWEET-CHEEKS!
Better known for his run-in with the police, wild Hollywood parties and off-screen tantrums than any memorable on-screen roles.
And this...
MY, OH MY.
LOOK WHAT THE CAT DRAGGED IN.
This is the one I'm looking for.
I DON'T BELIEVE I KNOW YOU, DARLIN'. AND I THINK I'D REMEMBER.
WHICH MEANS I COULD NOT POSSIBLY HAVE INVITED YOU.
OH, NO, MR. CROCKER. I'M NOT A GUEST.
I'M A GIFT.

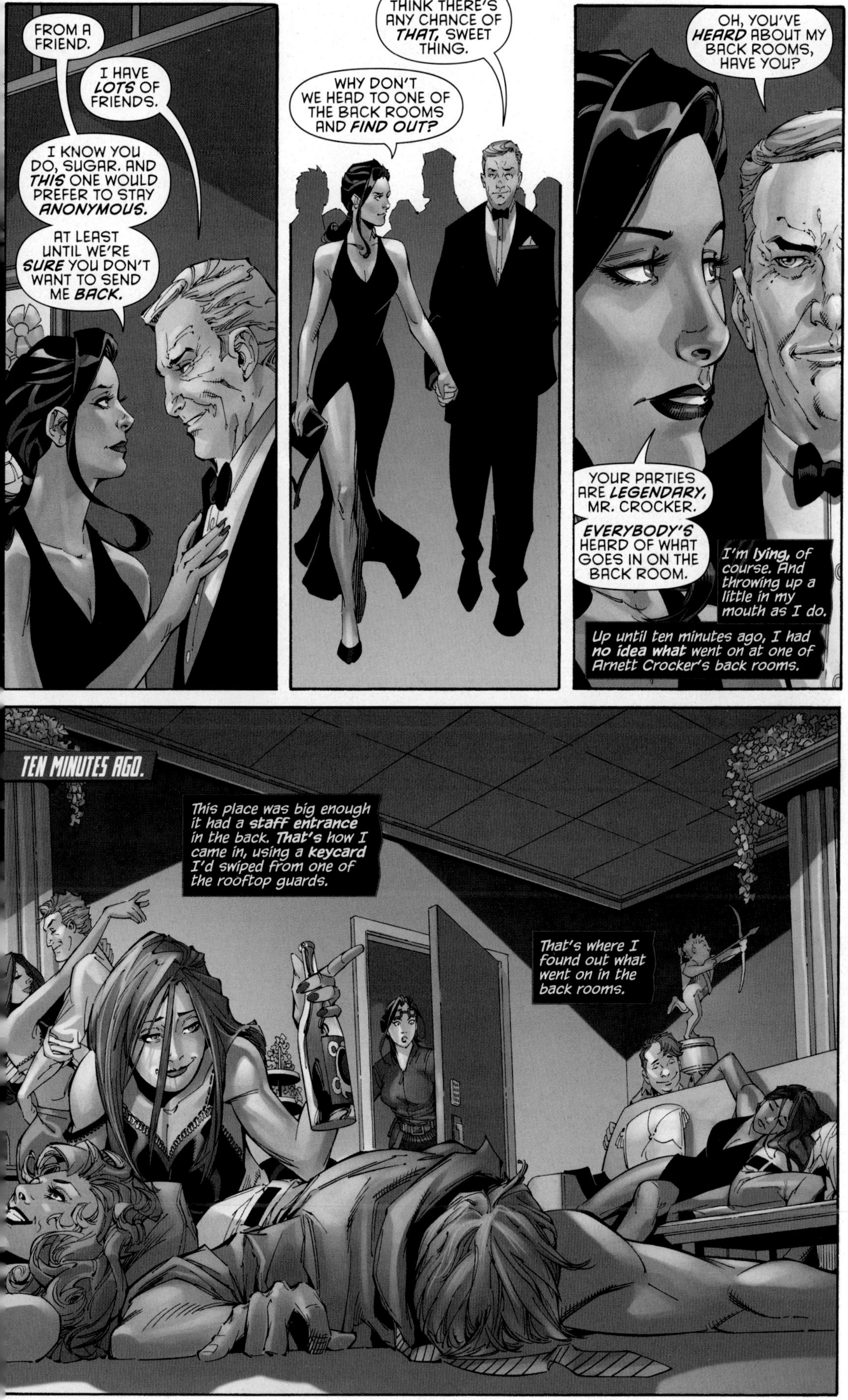

FROM A FRIEND.
I HAVE LOTS OF FRIENDS.
I KNOW YOU DO, SUGAR. AND THIS ONE WOULD PREFER TO STAY ANONYMOUS.
AT LEAST UNTIL WE'RE SURE YOU DON'T WANT TO SEND ME BACK.
DON'T THINK THERE'S ANY CHANCE OF THAT, SWEET THING.
WHY DON'T WE HEAD TO ONE OF THE BACK ROOMS AND FIND OUT?
OH, YOU'VE HEARD ABOUT MY BACK ROOMS, HAVE YOU?
YOUR PARTIES ARE LEGENDARY, MR. CROCKER.
EVERYBODY'S HEARD OF WHAT GOES IN ON THE BACK ROOM.
I'm lying, of course. And throwing up a little in my mouth as I do.
Up until ten minutes ago, I had no idea what went on at one of Arnett Crocker's back rooms.
TEN MINUTES AGO.
This place was big enough it had a staff entrance in the back. That's how I came in, using a keycard I'd swiped from one of the rooftop guards.
That's where I found out what went on in the back rooms.

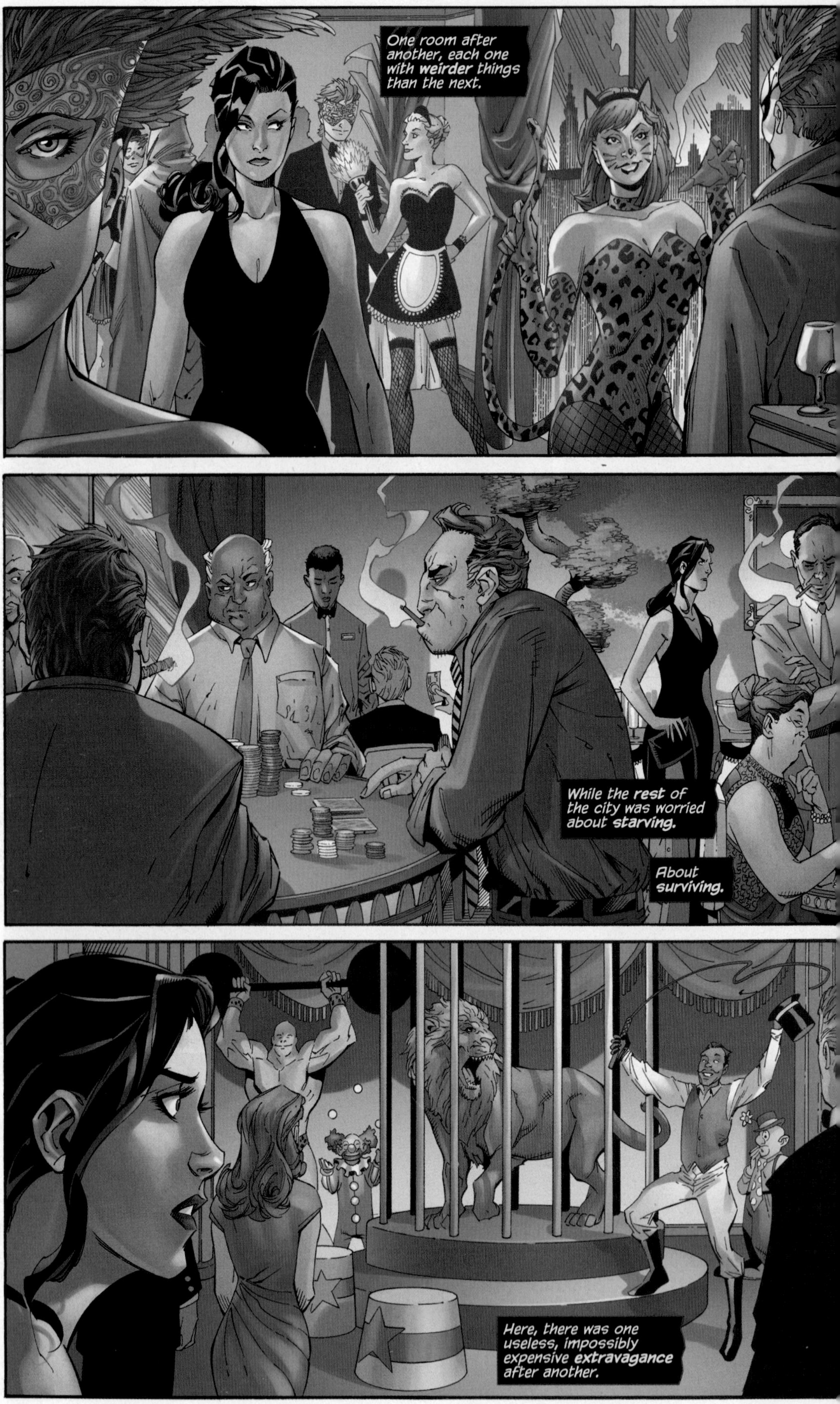
One room after another, each one with weirder things than the next.
While the rest of the city was worried about starving.
About surviving.
Here, there was one useless, impossibly expensive extravagance after another.

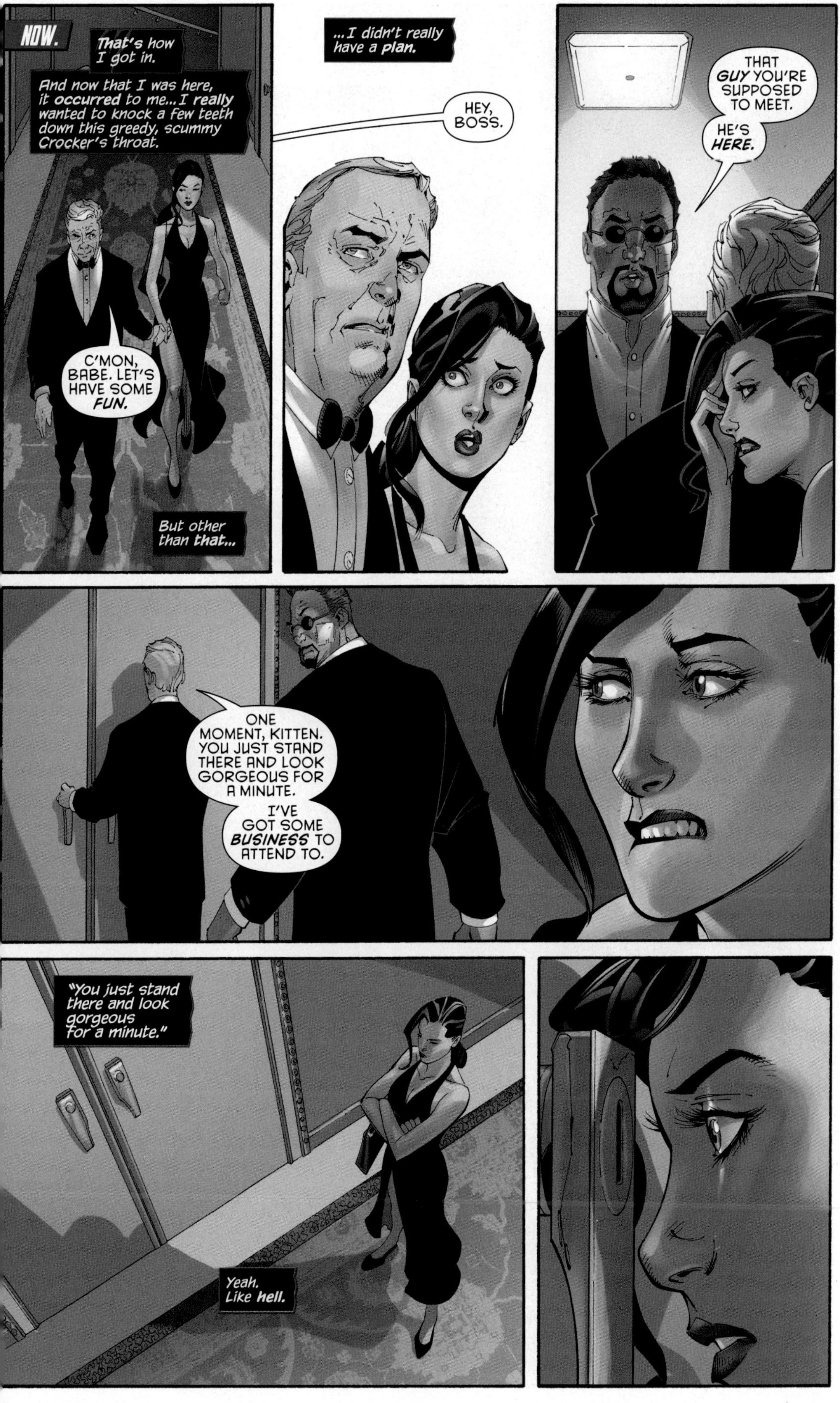

NOW.
That's how I got in.
And now that I was here, it occurred to me...I really wanted to knock a few teeth down this greedy, scummy Crocker's throat.
C'MON, BABE. LET'S HAVE SOME FUN.
But other than that...
...I didn't really have a plan.
HEY, BOSS.
THAT GUY YOU'RE SUPPOSED TO MEET.
HE'S HERE.
ONE MOMENT, KITTEN. YOU JUST STAND THERE AND LOOK GORGEOUS FOR A MINUTE.
I'VE GOT SOME BUSINESS TO ATTEND TO.
"You just stand there and look gorgeous for a minute."
Yeah. Like hell.

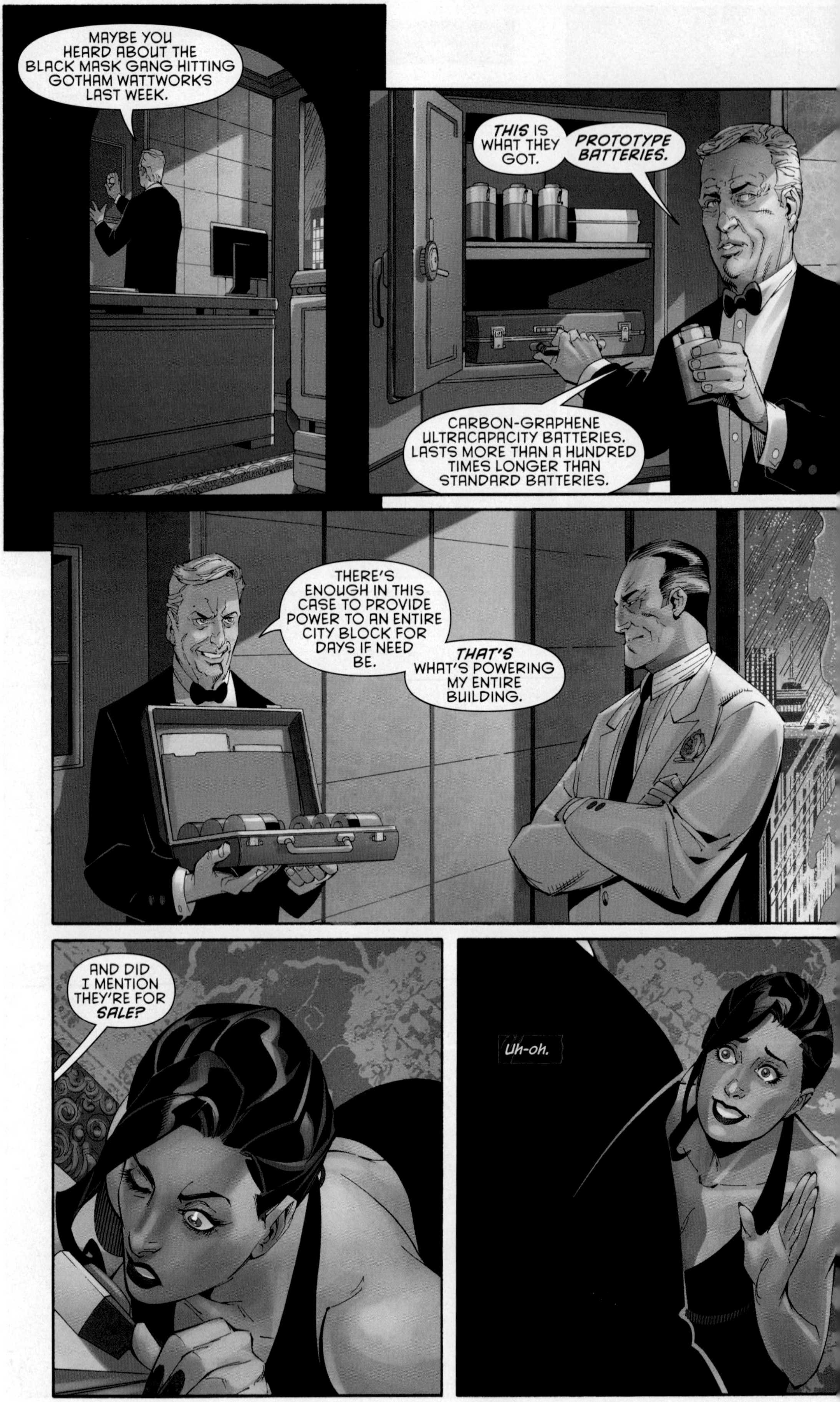
MAYBE YOU HEARD ABOUT THE BLACK MASK GANG HITTING GOTHAM WATTWORKS LAST WEEK.
THIS IS WHAT THEY GOT.
PROTOTYPE BATTERIES.
CARBON-GRAPHENE ULTRACAPACITY BATTERIES. LASTS MORE THAN A HUNDRED TIMES LONGER THAN STANDARD BATTERIES.
THERE'S ENOUGH IN THIS CASE TO PROVIDE POWER TO AN ENTIRE CITY BLOCK FOR DAYS IF NEED BE.
THAT'S WHAT'S POWERING MY ENTIRE BUILDING.
AND DID I MENTION THEY'RE FOR SALE?
Uh-oh.

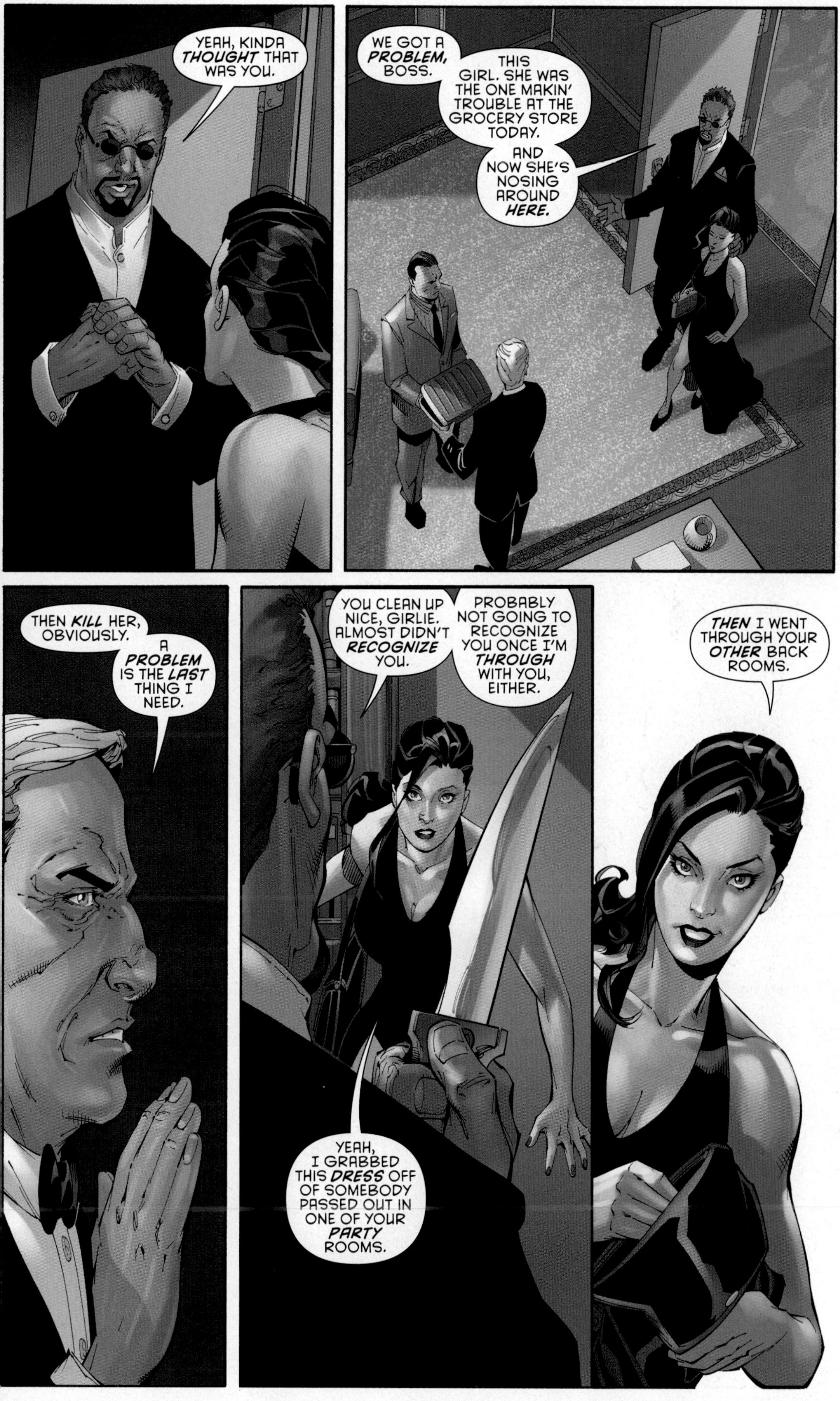
YEAH, KINDA THOUGHT THAT WAS YOU.
WE GOT A PROBLEM, BOSS.
THIS GIRL. SHE WAS THE ONE MAKIN' TROUBLE AT THE GROCERY STORE TODAY.
AND NOW SHE'S NOSING AROUND HERE.
THEN KILL HER, OBVIOUSLY.
A PROBLEM IS THE LAST THING I NEED.
YOU CLEAN UP NICE, GIRLIE. ALMOST DIDN'T RECOGNIZE YOU.
PROBABLY NOT GOING TO RECOGNIZE YOU ONCE I'M THROUGH WITH YOU, EITHER.
YEAH, I GRABBED THIS DRESS OFF OF SOMEBODY PASSED OUT IN ONE OF YOUR PARTY ROOMS.
THEN I WENT THROUGH YOUR OTHER BACK ROOMS.

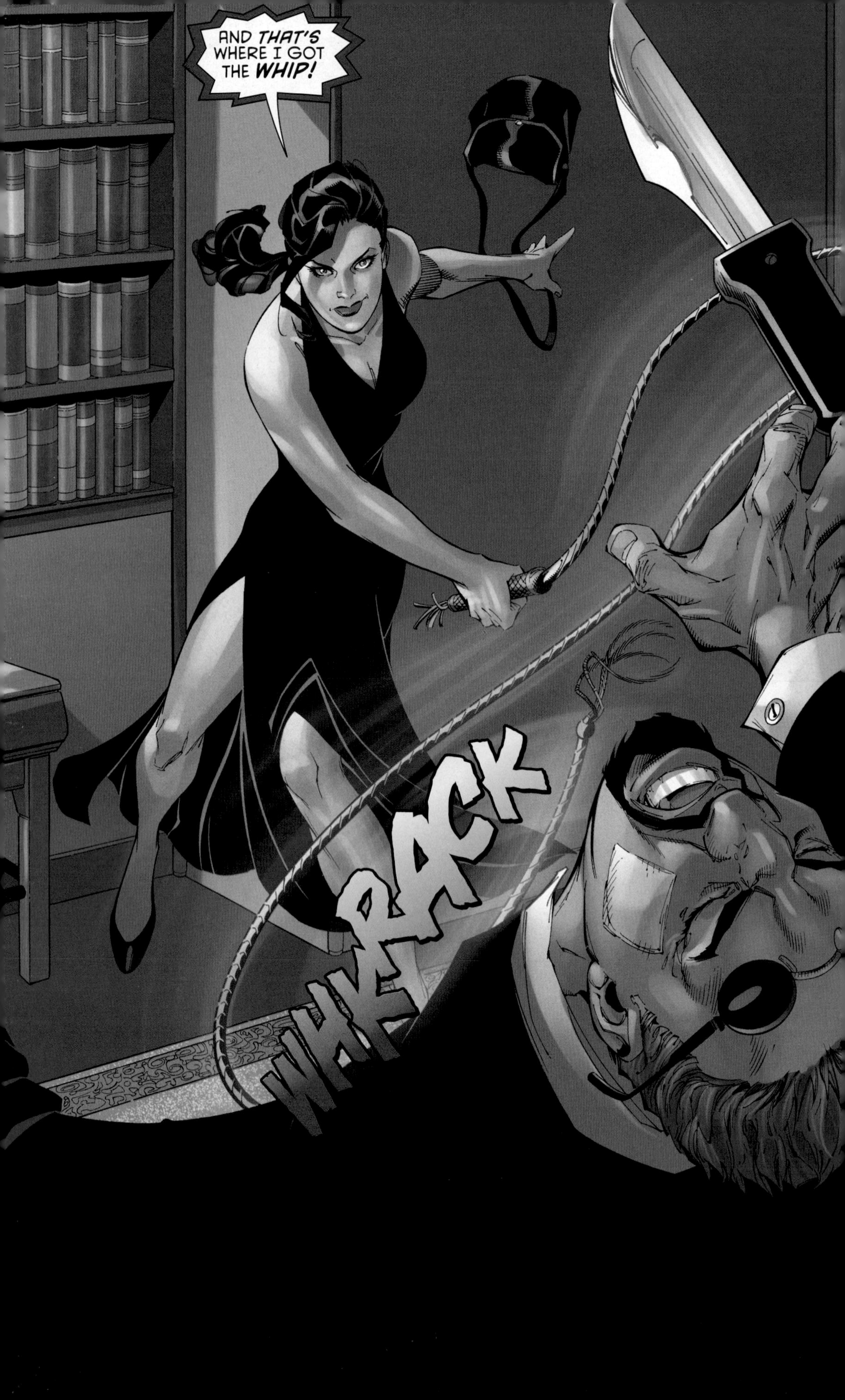
AND *THAT'S* WHERE I GOT THE *WHIP!*
WHKRACK

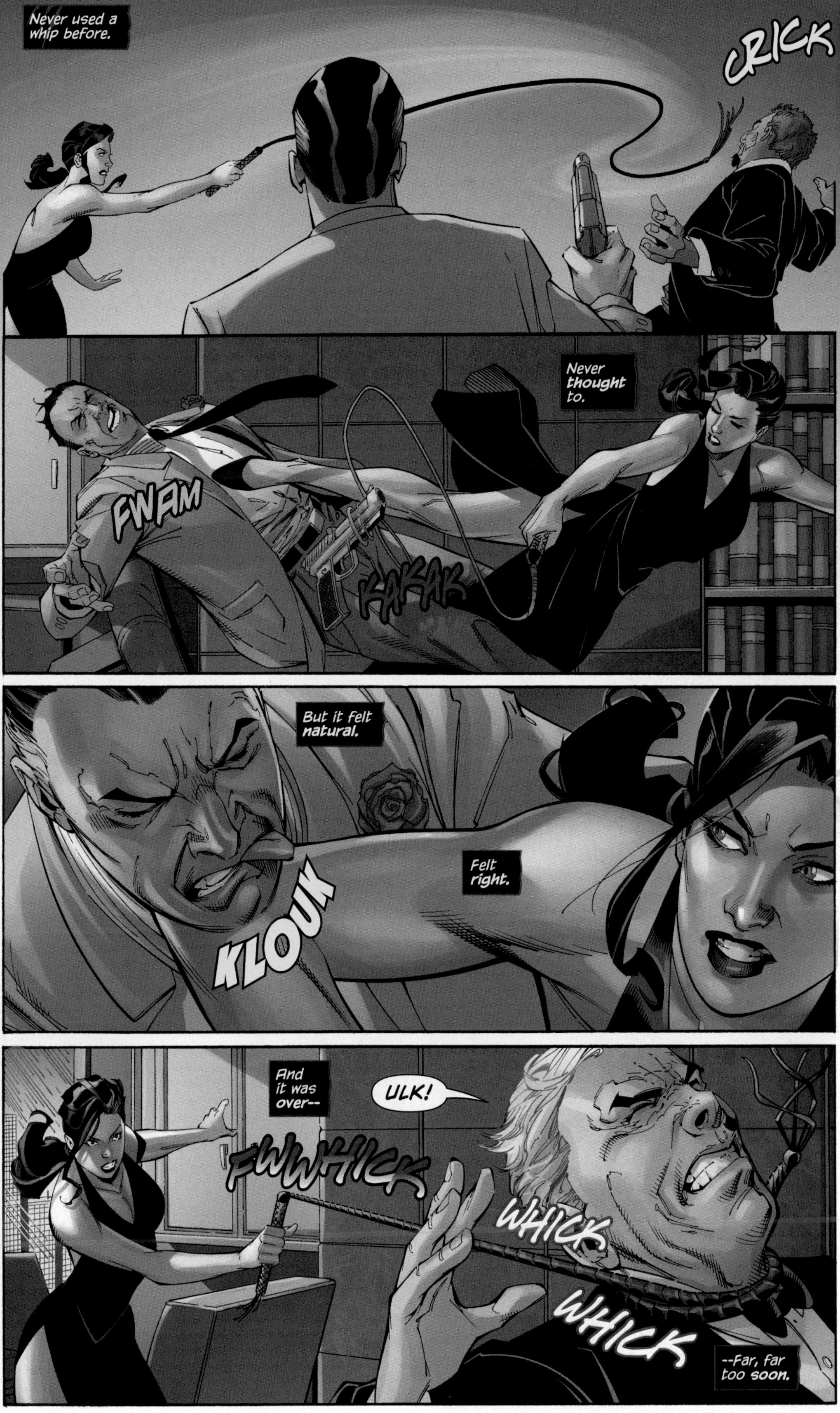
Never used a whip before.
CRICK
Never thought to.
FWAM
KAKAK
But it felt natural.
Felt right.
KLOUK
And it was over--
ULK!
FWWHICK
WHICK
WHICK
--Far, far too soon.

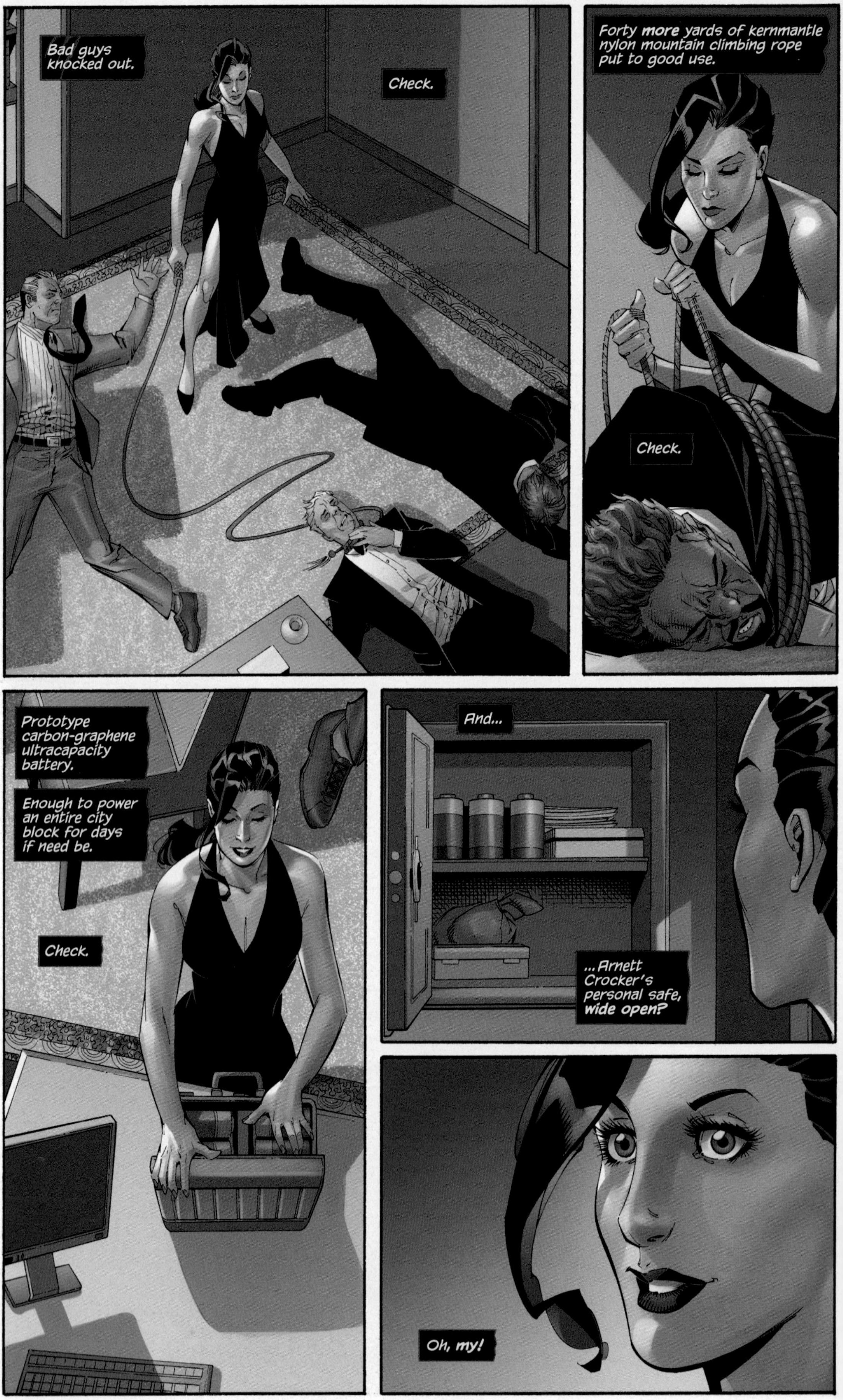

Bad guys knocked out.
Check.
Forty more yards of kernmantle nylon mountain climbing rope put to good use.
Check.
Prototype carbon-graphene ultracapacity battery.
Enough to power an entire city block for days if need be.
Check.
And...
...Arnett Crocker's personal safe, wide open?
Oh, my!

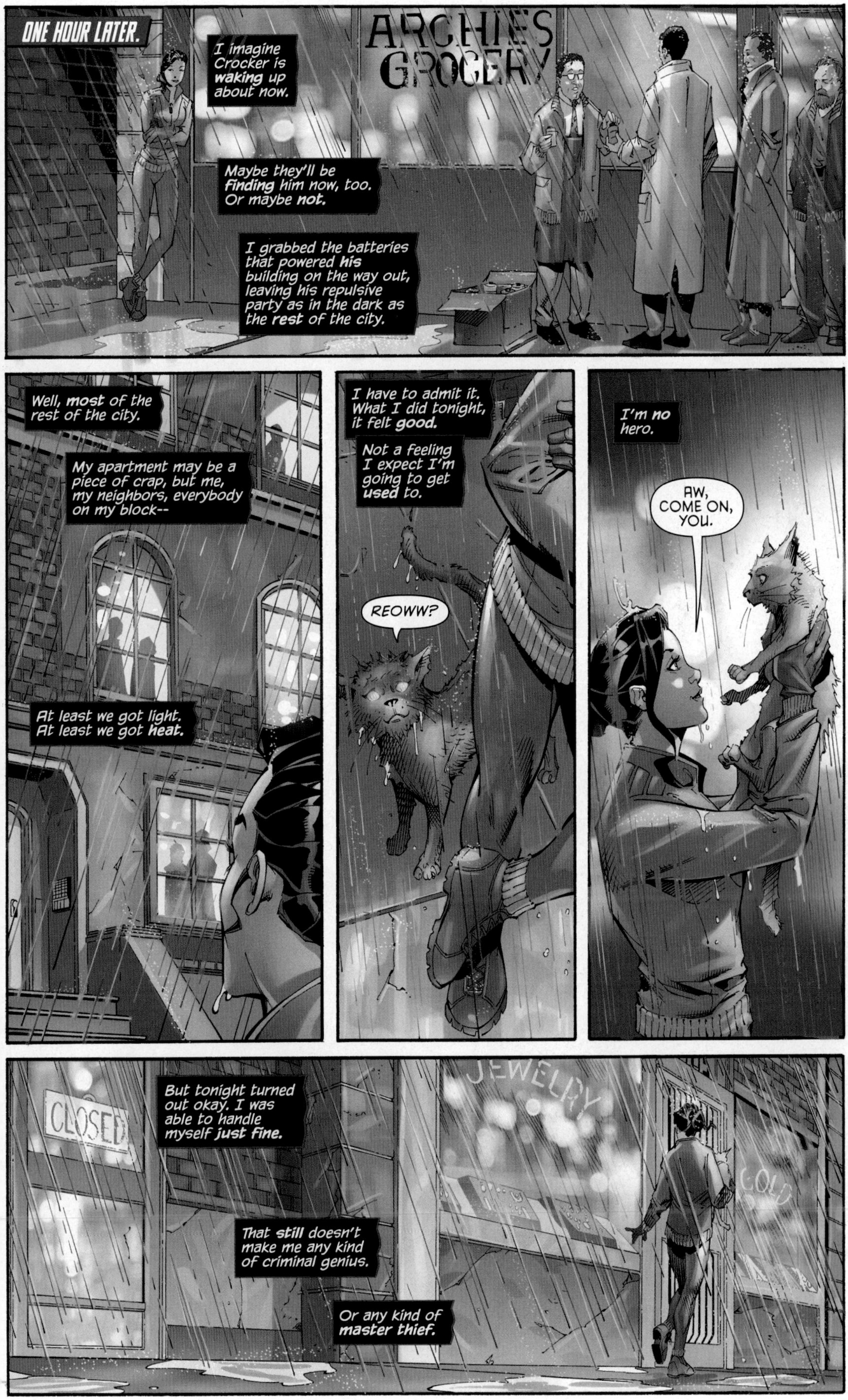
ONE HOUR LATER.
I imagine Crocker is waking up about now.
ARCHIES GROCERY
Maybe they'll be finding him now, too. Or maybe not.
I grabbed the batteries that powered his building on the way out, leaving his repulsive party as in the dark as the rest of the city.
Well, most of the rest of the city.
My apartment may be a piece of crap, but me, my neighbors, everybody on my block--
At least we got light. At least we got heat.
I have to admit it. What I did tonight, it felt good.
Not a feeling I expect I'm going to get used to.
REOWW?
I'm no hero.
AW, COME ON, YOU.
CLOSED
JEWELRY
But tonight turned out okay. I was able to handle myself just fine.
That still doesn't make me any kind of criminal genius.
Or any kind of master thief.

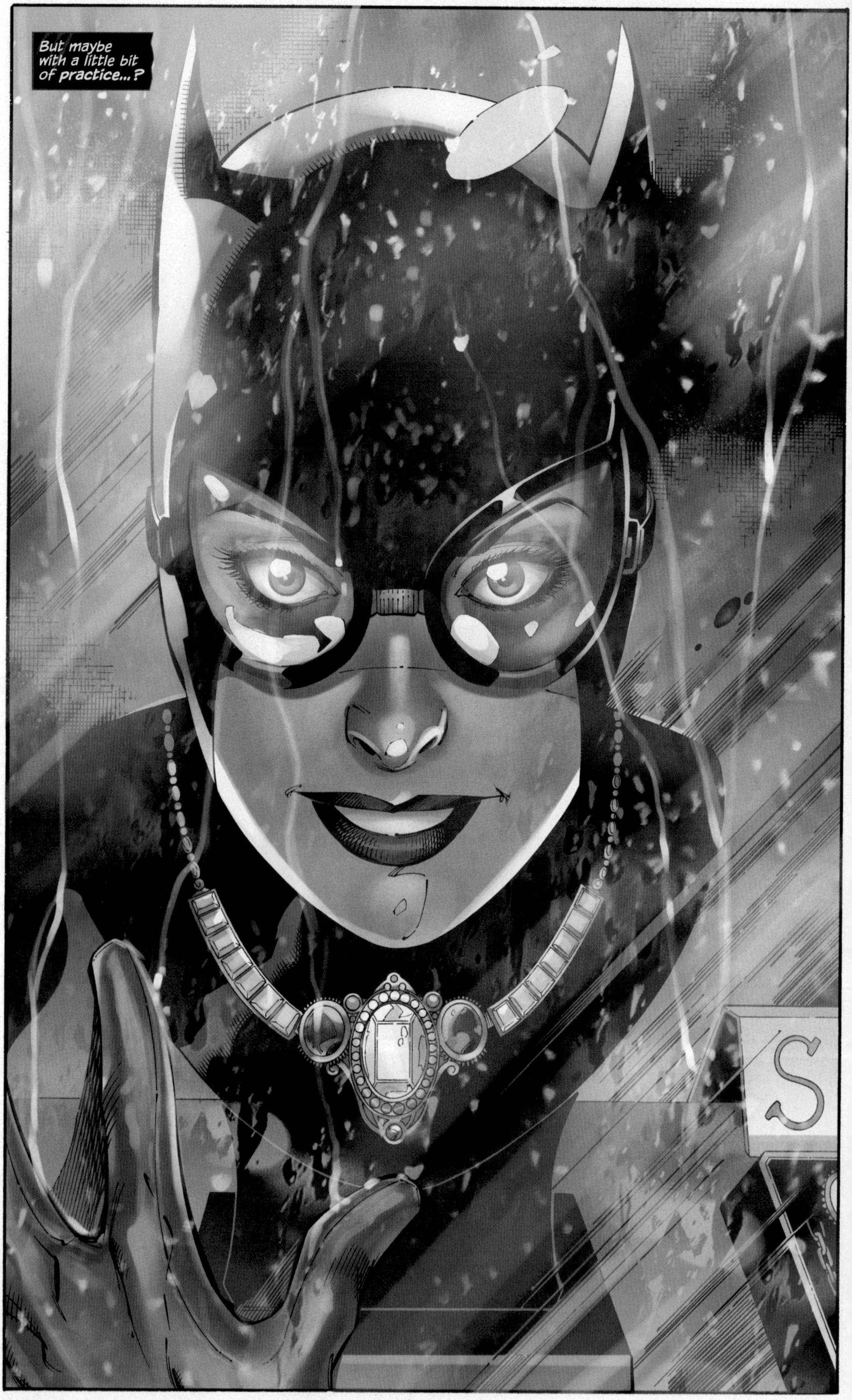
But maybe with a little bit of practice...?

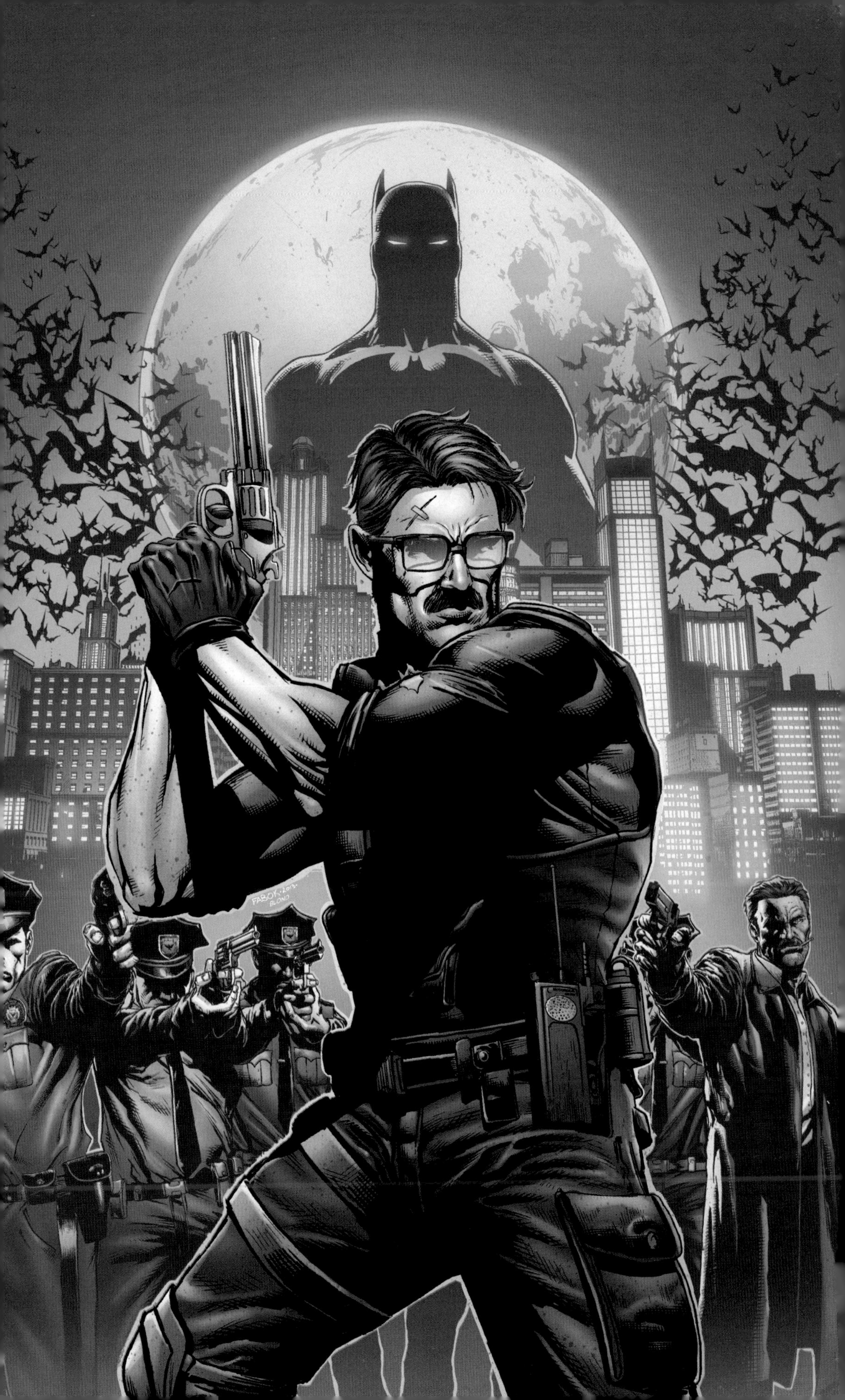
FABOK 2013
BLOND

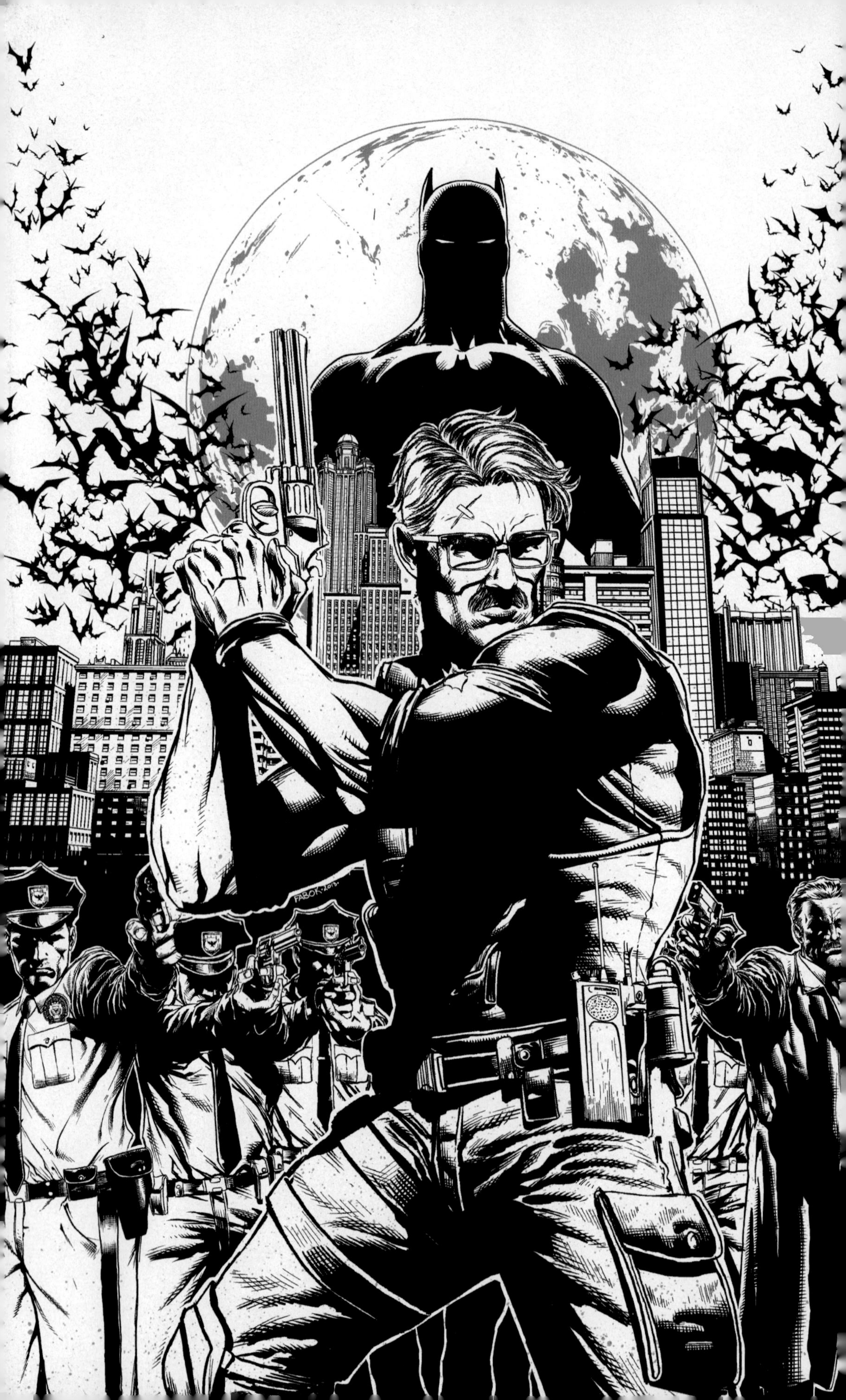
FABOK

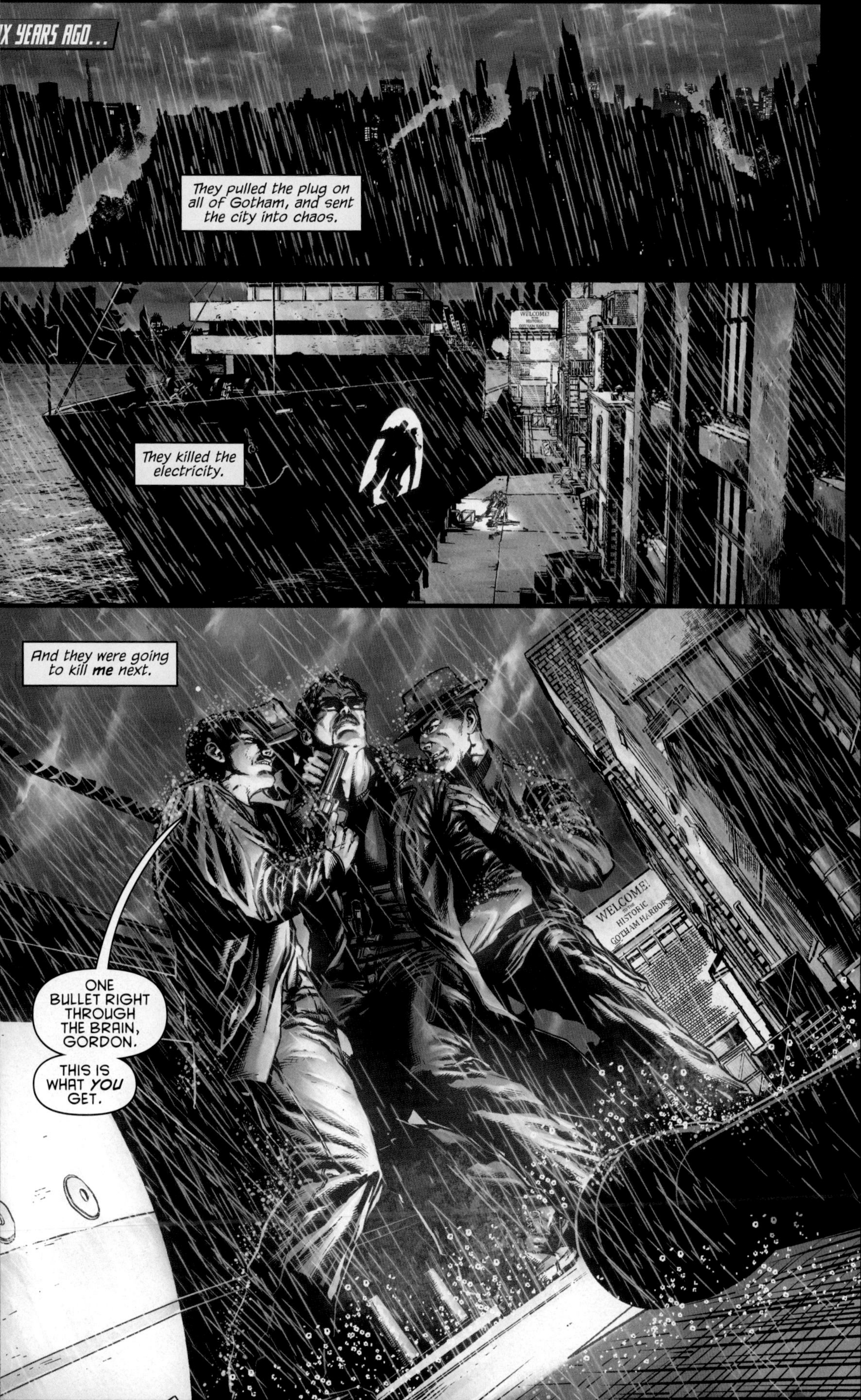

X YEARS AGO...
They pulled the plug on all of Gotham, and sent the city into chaos.
They killed the electricity.
And they were going to kill **me** next.
ONE BULLET RIGHT THROUGH THE BRAIN, GORDON.
THIS IS WHAT *YOU* GET.
WELCOME! HISTORIC GOTHAM HARBOR

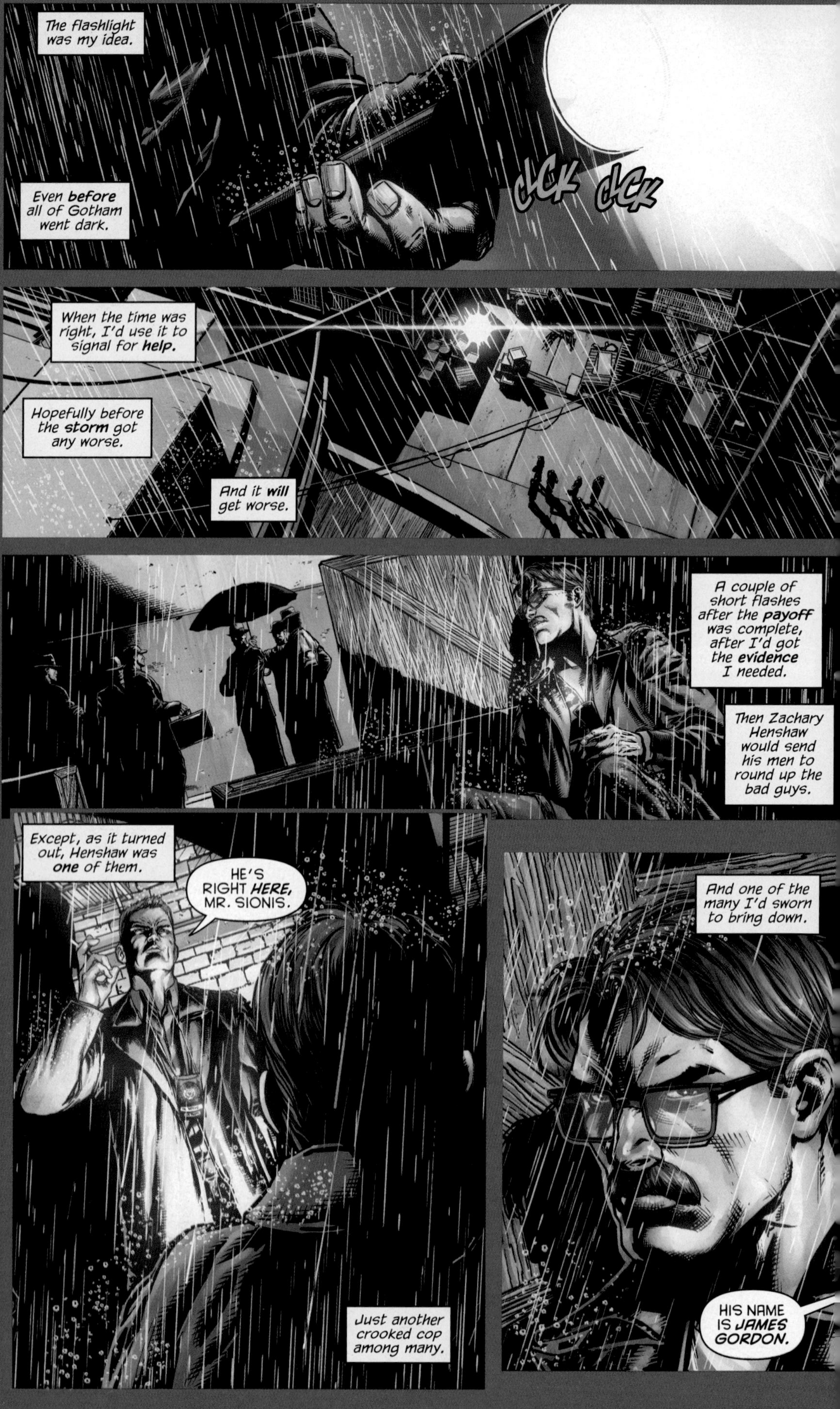
The flashlight was my idea.
Even before all of Gotham went dark.
CLICK CLICK
When the time was right, I'd use it to signal for help.
Hopefully before the storm got any worse.
And it will get worse.
A couple of short flashes after the payoff was complete, after I'd got the evidence I needed.
Then Zachary Henshaw would send his men to round up the bad guys.
Except, as it turned out, Henshaw was one of them.
HE'S RIGHT HERE, MR. SIONIS.
Just another crooked cop among many.
And one of the many I'd sworn to bring down.
HIS NAME IS JAMES GORDON.

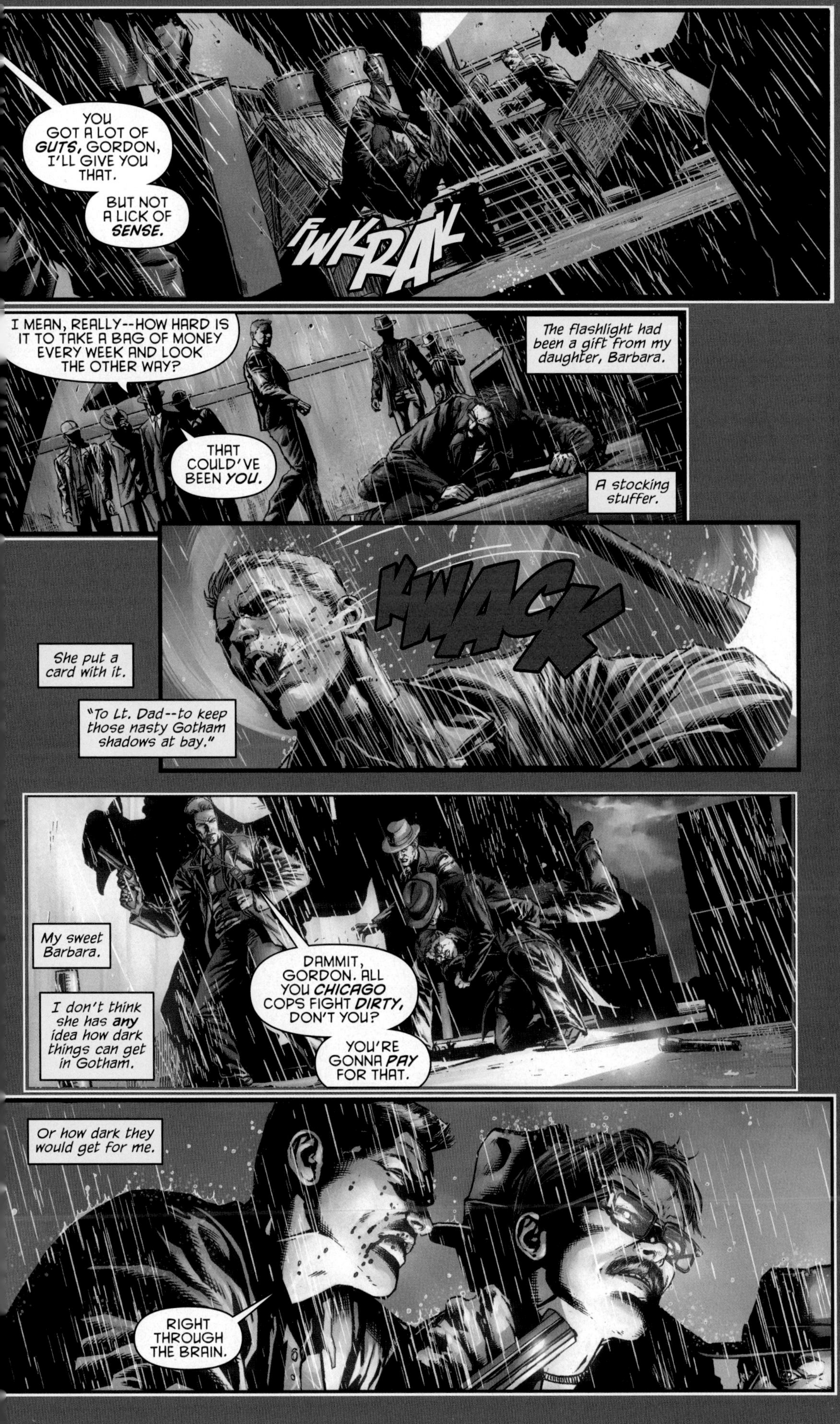
YOU GOT A LOT OF GUTS, GORDON, I'LL GIVE YOU THAT.
BUT NOT A LICK OF SENSE.
FWKRAK
I MEAN, REALLY--HOW HARD IS IT TO TAKE A BAG OF MONEY EVERY WEEK AND LOOK THE OTHER WAY?
The flashlight had been a gift from my daughter, Barbara.
THAT COULD'VE BEEN YOU.
A stocking stuffer.
KWACK
She put a card with it.
"To Lt. Dad--to keep those nasty Gotham shadows at bay."
My sweet Barbara.
I don't think she has any idea how dark things can get in Gotham.
DAMMIT, GORDON. ALL YOU CHICAGO COPS FIGHT DIRTY, DON'T YOU?
YOU'RE GONNA PAY FOR THAT.
Or how dark they would get for me.
RIGHT THROUGH THE BRAIN.

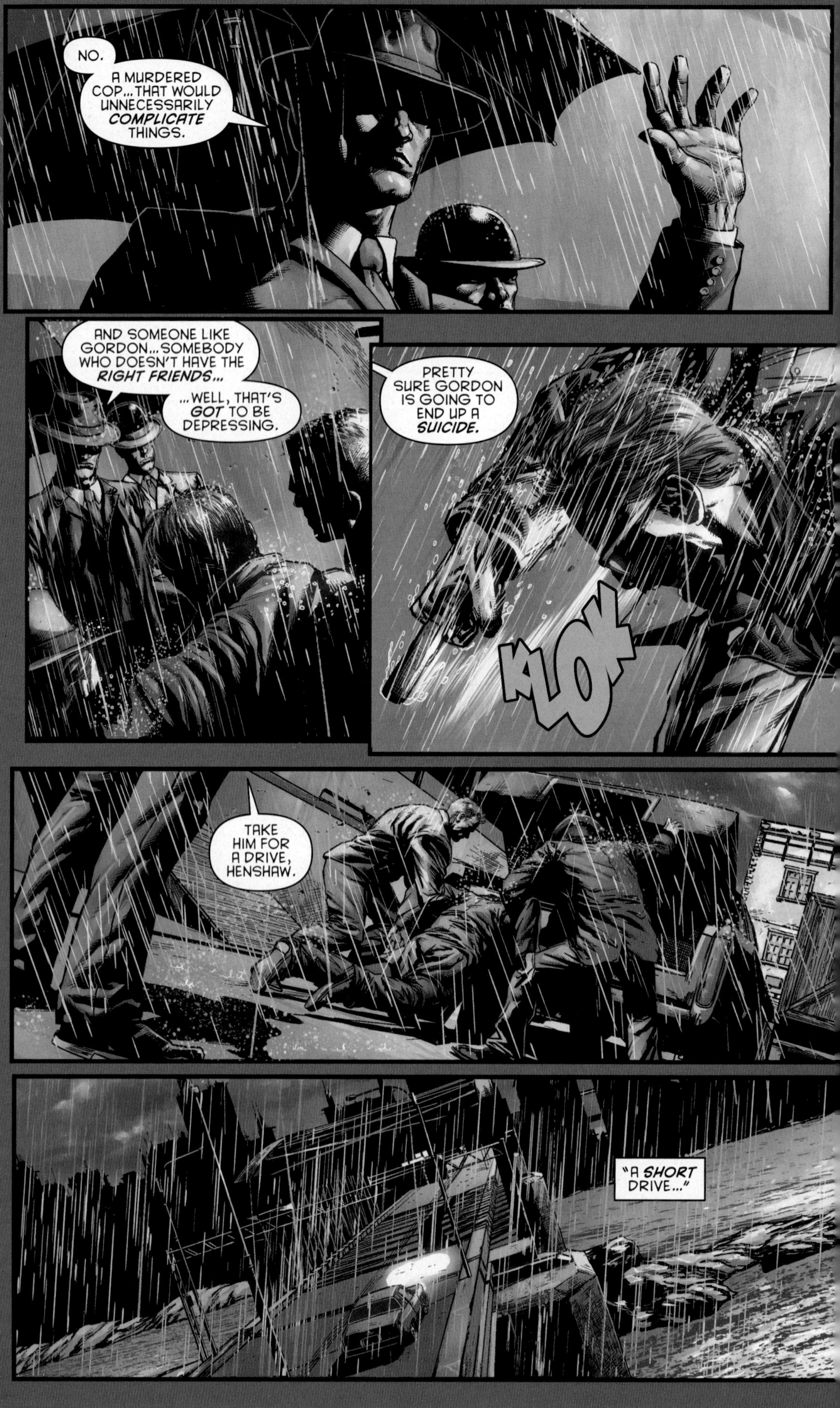
NO.
A MURDERED COP...THAT WOULD UNNECESSARILY *COMPLICATE* THINGS.
AND SOMEONE LIKE GORDON...SOMEBODY WHO DOESN'T HAVE THE *RIGHT FRIENDS*...
...WELL, THAT'S *GOT* TO BE DEPRESSING.
PRETTY SURE GORDON IS GOING TO END UP A *SUICIDE.*
KLOK
TAKE HIM FOR A DRIVE, HENSHAW.
"A *SHORT* DRIVE..."

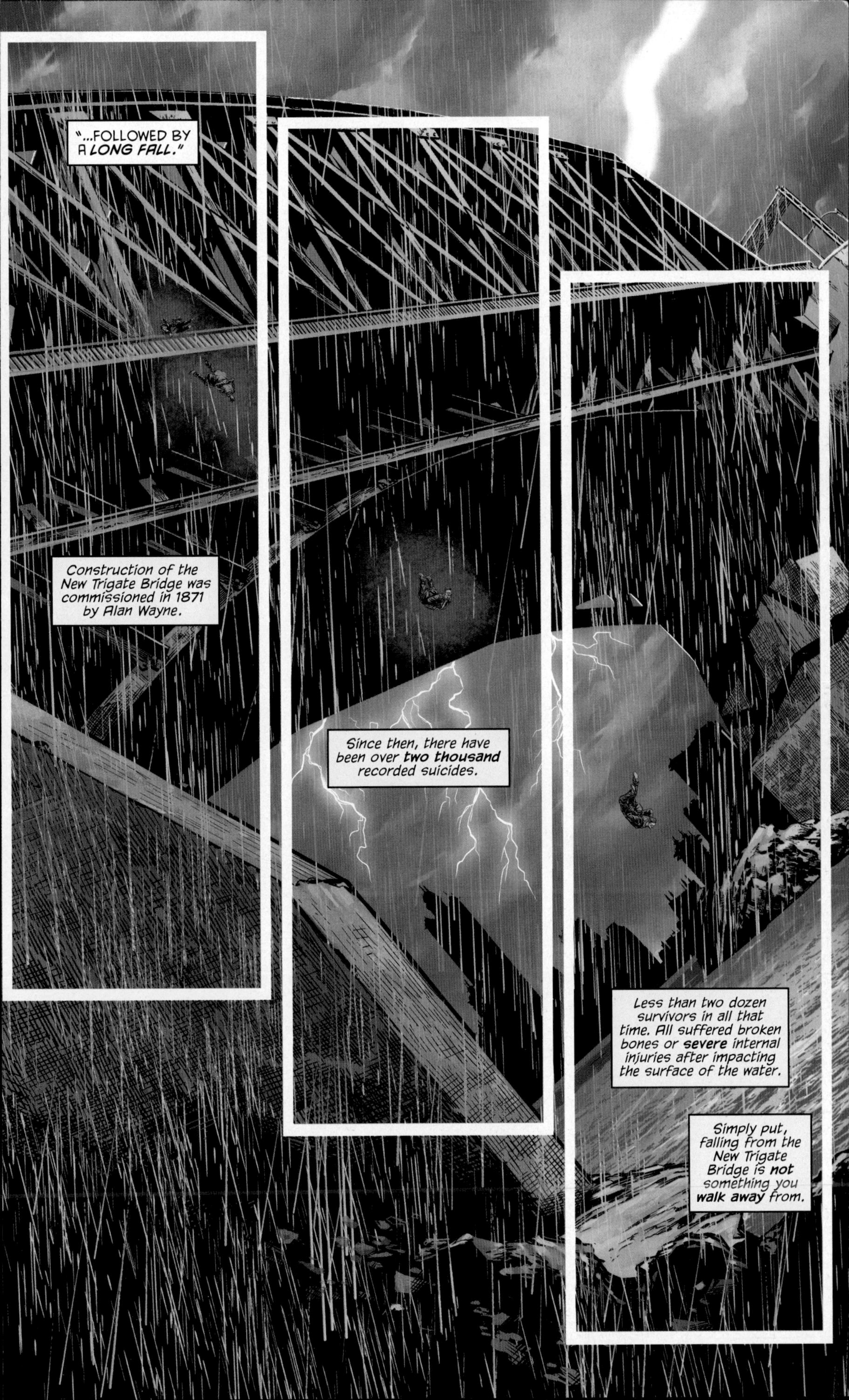
"...FOLLOWED BY A LONG FALL."
Construction of the New Trigate Bridge was commissioned in 1871 by Alan Wayne.
Since then, there have been over two thousand recorded suicides.
Less than two dozen survivors in all that time. All suffered broken bones or severe internal injuries after impacting the surface of the water.
Simply put, falling from the New Trigate Bridge is not something you walk away from.

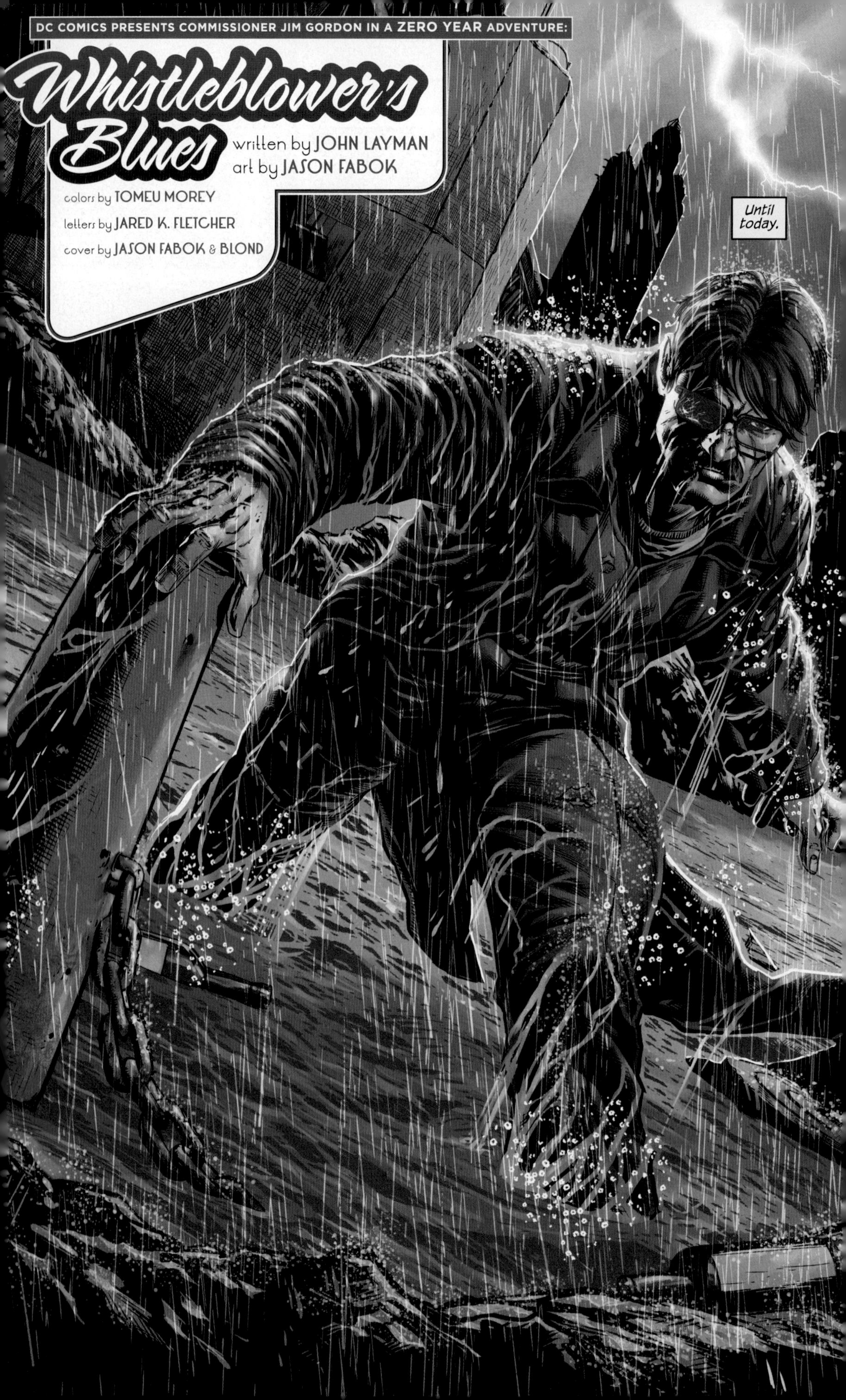
DC COMICS PRESENTS COMMISSIONER JIM GORDON IN A ZERO YEAR ADVENTURE:
Whistleblower's Blues
written by JOHN LAYMAN
art by JASON FABOK
colors by TOMEU MOREY
letters by JARED K. FLETCHER
cover by JASON FABOK & BLOND
Until today.

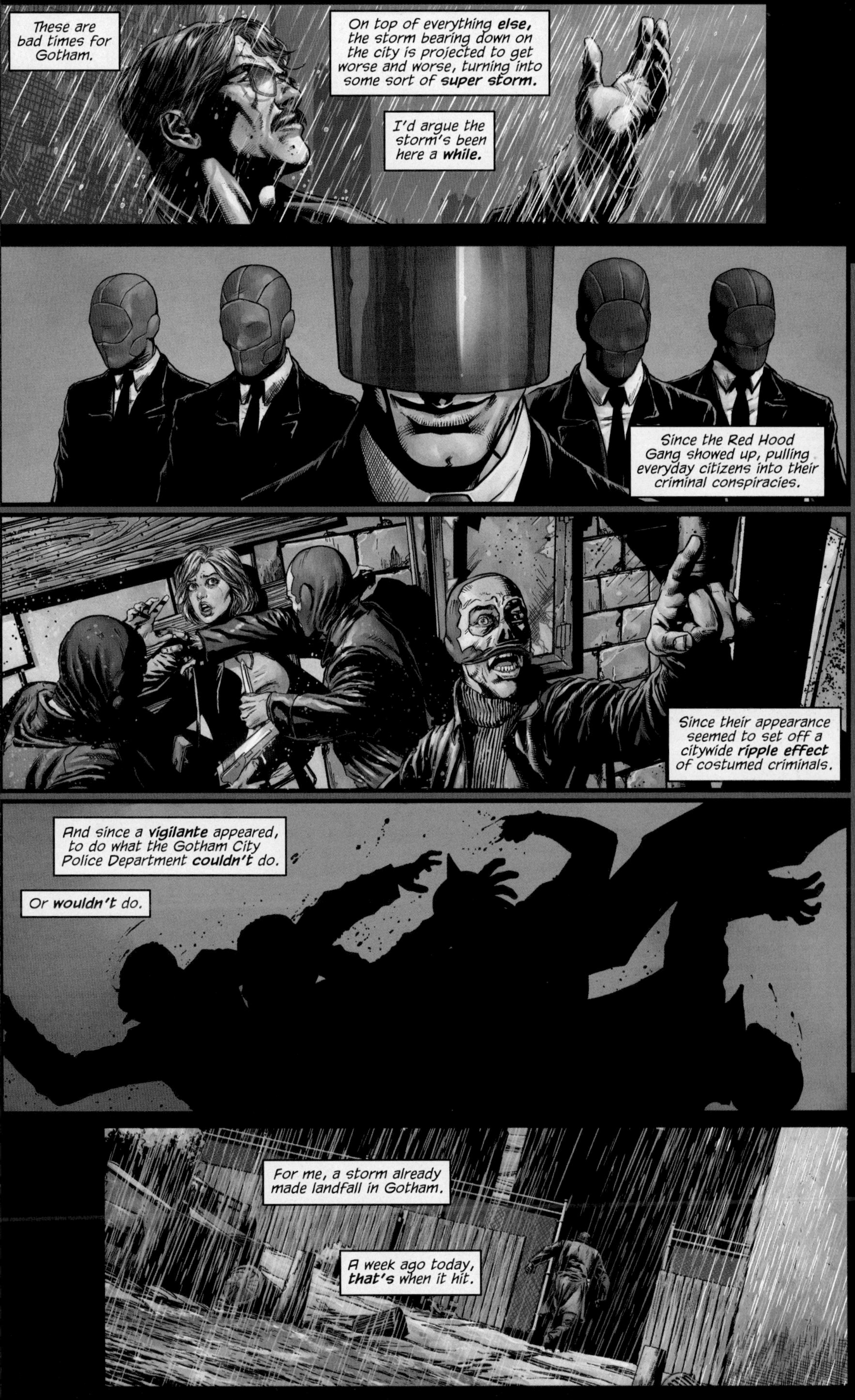
These are bad times for Gotham.
On top of everything else, the storm bearing down on the city is projected to get worse and worse, turning into some sort of super storm.
I'd argue the storm's been here a while.
Since the Red Hood Gang showed up, pulling everyday citizens into their criminal conspiracies.
Since their appearance seemed to set off a citywide ripple effect of costumed criminals.
And since a vigilante appeared, to do what the Gotham City Police Department couldn't do.
Or wouldn't do.
For me, a storm already made landfall in Gotham.
A week ago today, that's when it hit.

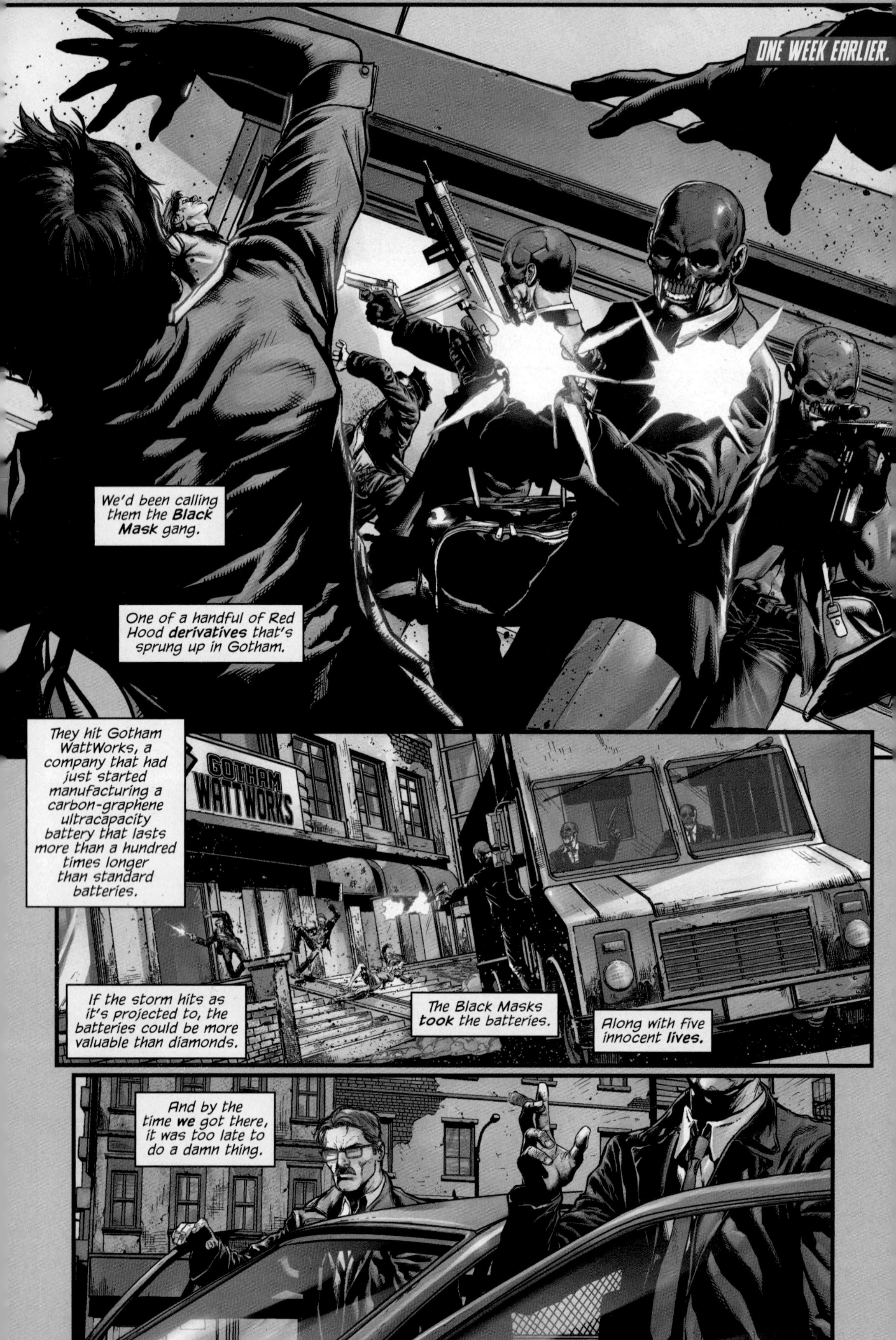
ONE WEEK EARLIER.
We'd been calling them the Black Mask gang.
One of a handful of Red Hood derivatives that's sprung up in Gotham.
They hit Gotham WattWorks, a company that had just started manufacturing a carbon-graphene ultracapacity battery that lasts more than a hundred times longer than standard batteries.
GOTHAM WATTWORKS
If the storm hits as it's projected to, the batteries could be more valuable than diamonds.
The Black Masks took the batteries.
Along with five innocent lives.
And by the time we got there, it was too late to do a damn thing.

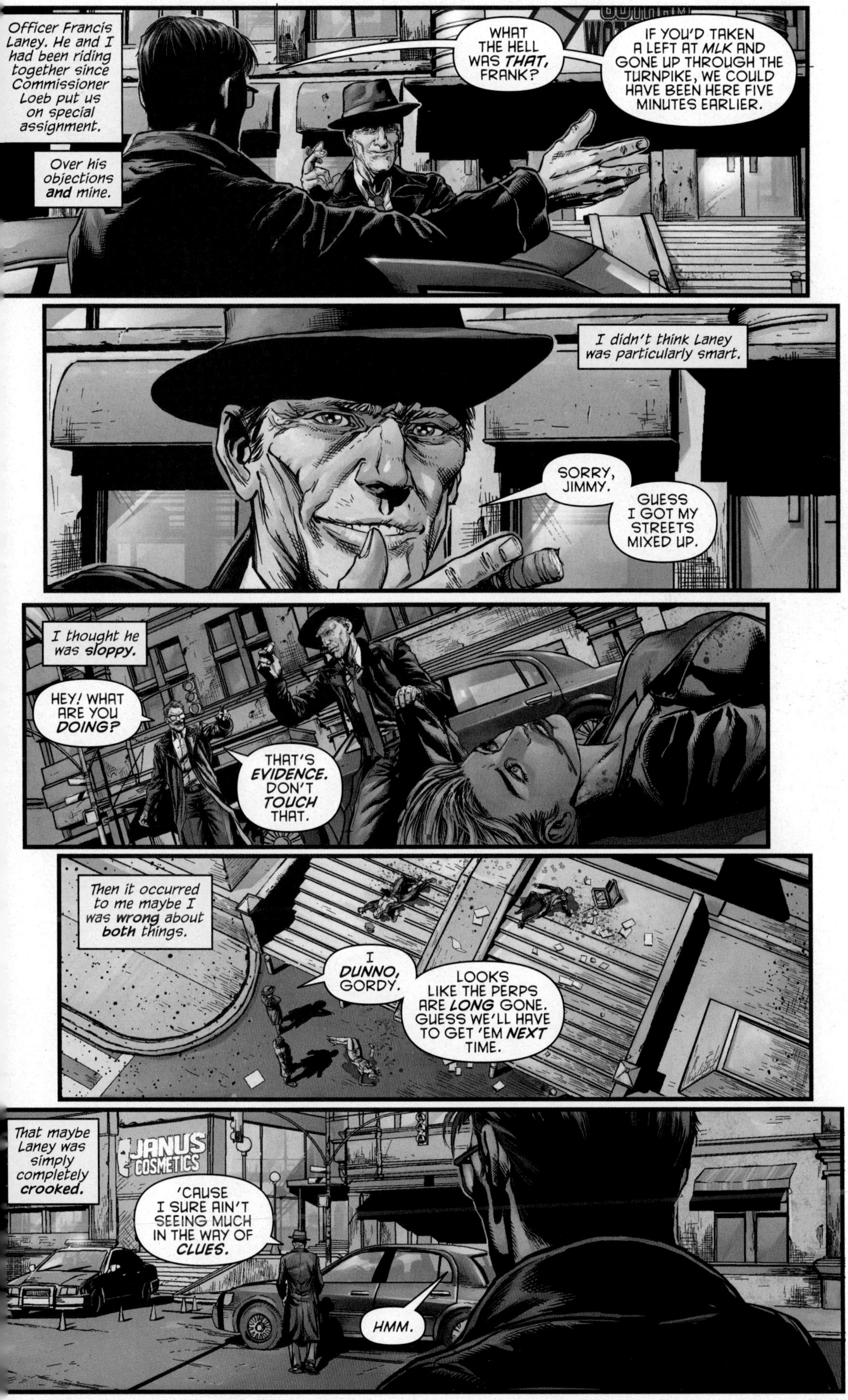

Officer Francis Laney. He and I had been riding together since Commissioner Loeb put us on special assignment.
Over his objections and mine.
WHAT THE HELL WAS THAT, FRANK?
IF YOU'D TAKEN A LEFT AT MLK AND GONE UP THROUGH THE TURNPIKE, WE COULD HAVE BEEN HERE FIVE MINUTES EARLIER.
I didn't think Laney was particularly smart.
SORRY, JIMMY.
GUESS I GOT MY STREETS MIXED UP.
I thought he was sloppy.
HEY! WHAT ARE YOU DOING?
THAT'S EVIDENCE. DON'T TOUCH THAT.
Then it occurred to me maybe I was wrong about both things.
I DUNNO, GORDY.
LOOKS LIKE THE PERPS ARE LONG GONE. GUESS WE'LL HAVE TO GET 'EM NEXT TIME.
That maybe Laney was simply completely crooked.
JANUS COSMETICS
'CAUSE I SURE AIN'T SEEING MUCH IN THE WAY OF CLUES.
HMM.

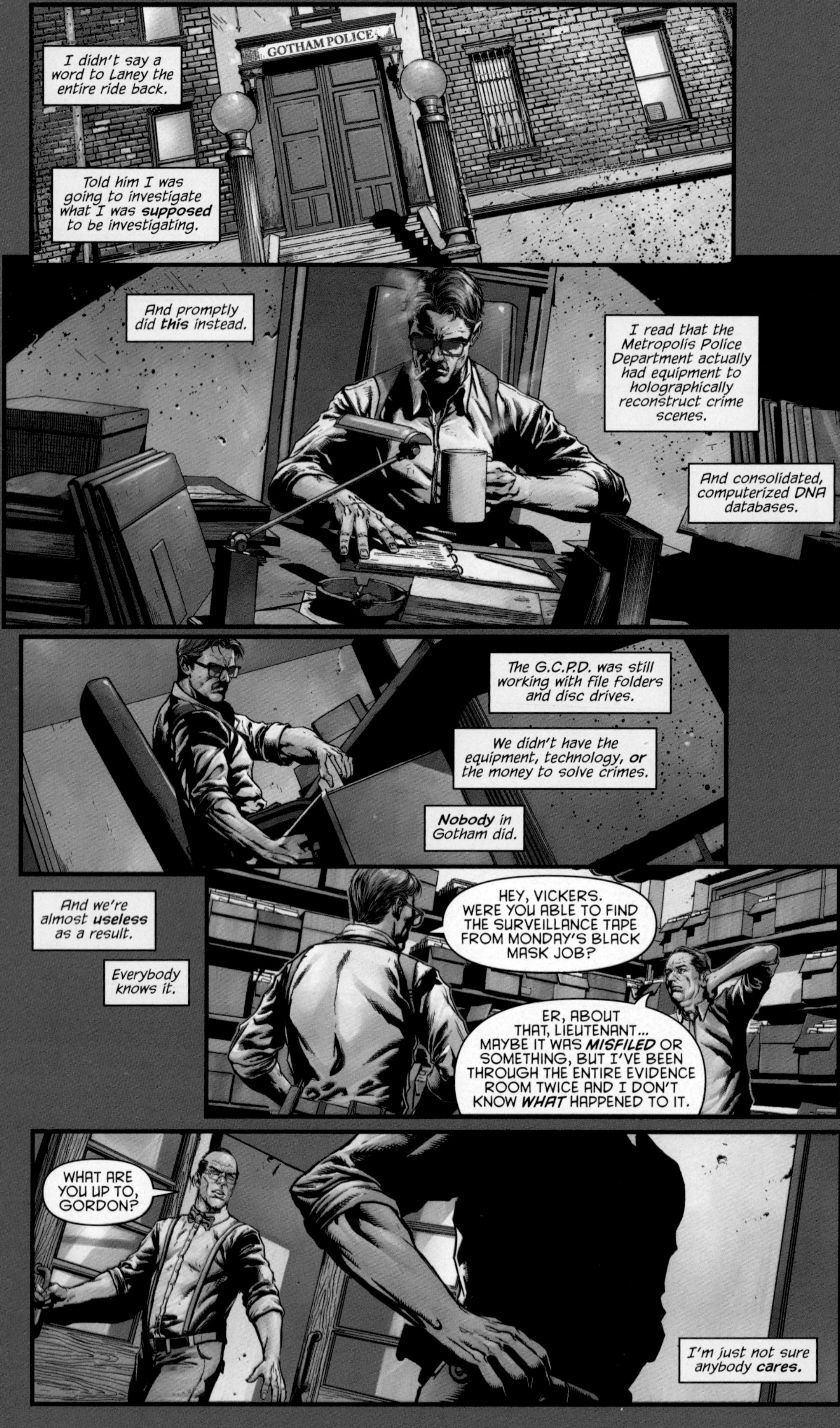

GOTHAM POLICE
I didn't say a word to Laney the entire ride back.
Told him I was going to investigate what I was **supposed** to be investigating.
And promptly did **this** instead.
I read that the Metropolis Police Department actually had equipment to holographically reconstruct crime scenes.
And consolidated, computerized DNA databases.
The G.C.P.D. was still working with file folders and disc drives.
We didn't have the equipment, technology, **or** the money to solve crimes.
Nobody in Gotham did.
And we're almost **useless** as a result.
Everybody knows it.
HEY, VICKERS. WERE YOU ABLE TO FIND THE SURVEILLANCE TAPE FROM MONDAY'S BLACK MASK JOB?
ER, ABOUT THAT, LIEUTENANT... MAYBE IT WAS ***MISFILED*** OR SOMETHING, BUT I'VE BEEN THROUGH THE ENTIRE EVIDENCE ROOM TWICE AND I DON'T KNOW ***WHAT*** HAPPENED TO IT.
WHAT ARE YOU UP TO, GORDON?
I'm just not sure anybody **cares.**

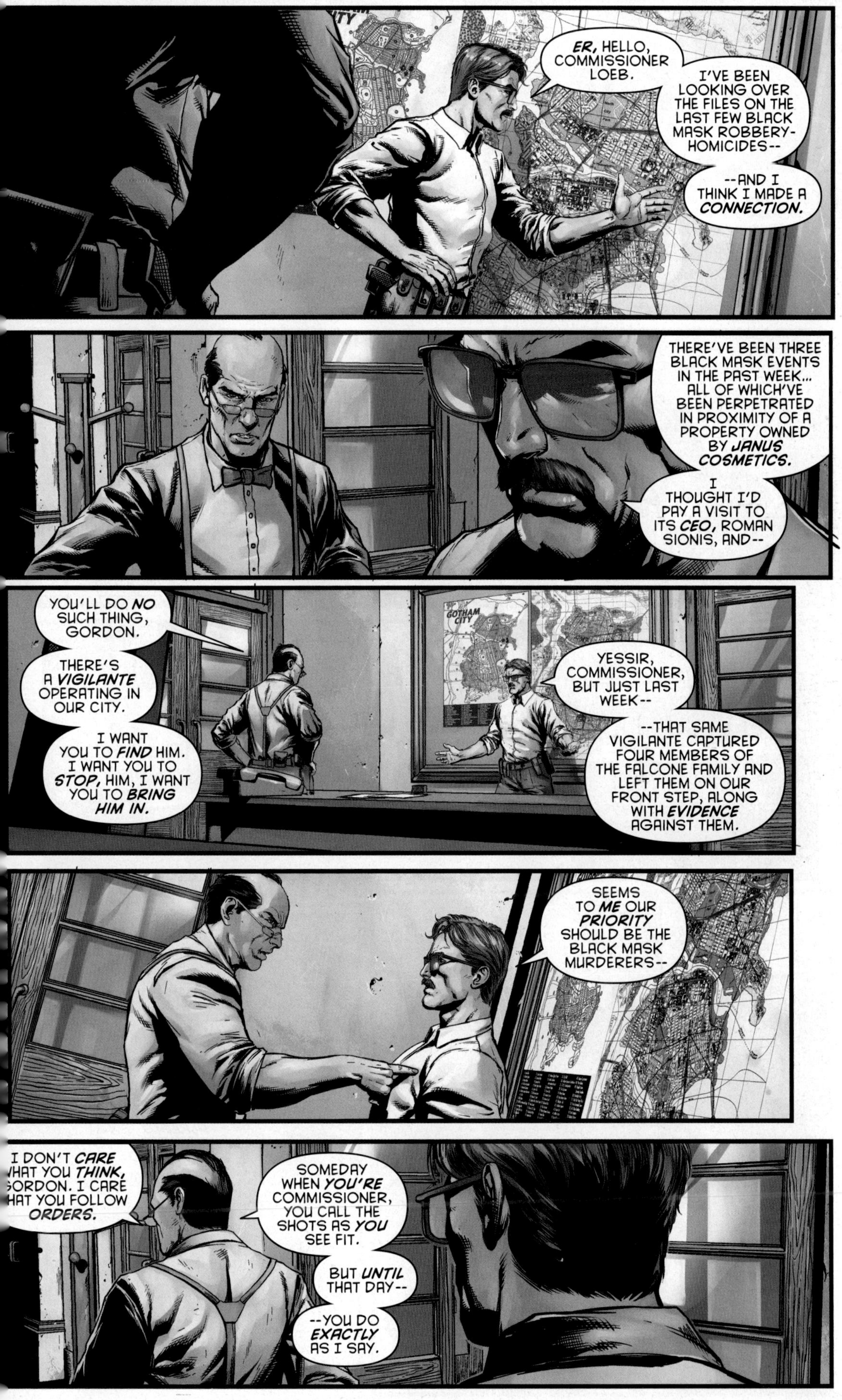
ER, HELLO, COMMISSIONER LOEB.
I'VE BEEN LOOKING OVER THE FILES ON THE LAST FEW BLACK MASK ROBBERY-HOMICIDES--
--AND I THINK I MADE A CONNECTION.
THERE'VE BEEN THREE BLACK MASK EVENTS IN THE PAST WEEK... ALL OF WHICH'VE BEEN PERPETRATED IN PROXIMITY OF A PROPERTY OWNED BY JANUS COSMETICS.
I THOUGHT I'D PAY A VISIT TO ITS CEO, ROMAN SIONIS, AND--
YOU'LL DO NO SUCH THING, GORDON.
THERE'S A VIGILANTE OPERATING IN OUR CITY.
I WANT YOU TO FIND HIM. I WANT YOU TO STOP, HIM, I WANT YOU TO BRING HIM IN.
YESSIR, COMMISSIONER, BUT JUST LAST WEEK--
--THAT SAME VIGILANTE CAPTURED FOUR MEMBERS OF THE FALCONE FAMILY AND LEFT THEM ON OUR FRONT STEP, ALONG WITH EVIDENCE AGAINST THEM.
SEEMS TO ME OUR PRIORITY SHOULD BE THE BLACK MASK MURDERERS--
I DON'T CARE WHAT YOU THINK, GORDON. I CARE THAT YOU FOLLOW ORDERS.
SOMEDAY WHEN YOU'RE COMMISSIONER, YOU CALL THE SHOTS AS YOU SEE FIT.
BUT UNTIL THAT DAY--
--YOU DO EXACTLY AS I SAY.

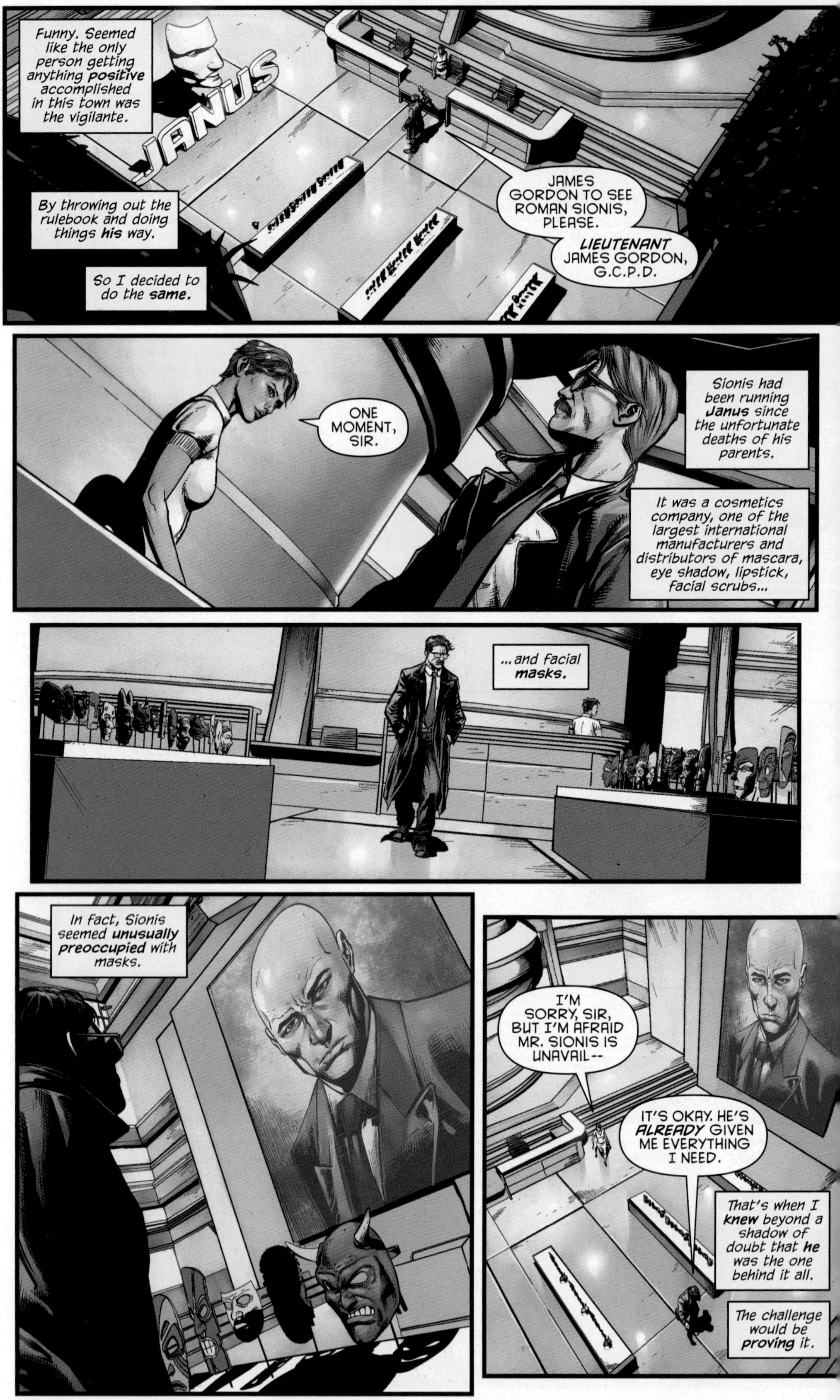

Funny. Seemed like the only person getting anything **positive** accomplished in this town was the vigilante.
JANUS
By throwing out the rulebook and doing things **his** way.
So I decided to do the **same.**
JAMES GORDON TO SEE ROMAN SIONIS, PLEASE.
LIEUTENANT JAMES GORDON, G.C.P.D.
ONE MOMENT, SIR.
Sionis had been running **Janus** since the unfortunate deaths of his parents.
It was a cosmetics company, one of the largest international manufacturers and distributors of mascara, eye shadow, lipstick, facial scrubs...
...and facial **masks.**
In fact, Sionis seemed **unusually preoccupied** with masks.
I'M SORRY, SIR, BUT I'M AFRAID MR. SIONIS IS UNAVAIL--
IT'S OKAY. HE'S ***ALREADY*** GIVEN ME EVERYTHING I NEED.
That's when I **knew** beyond a shadow of doubt that **he** was the one behind it all.
The challenge would be **proving** it.

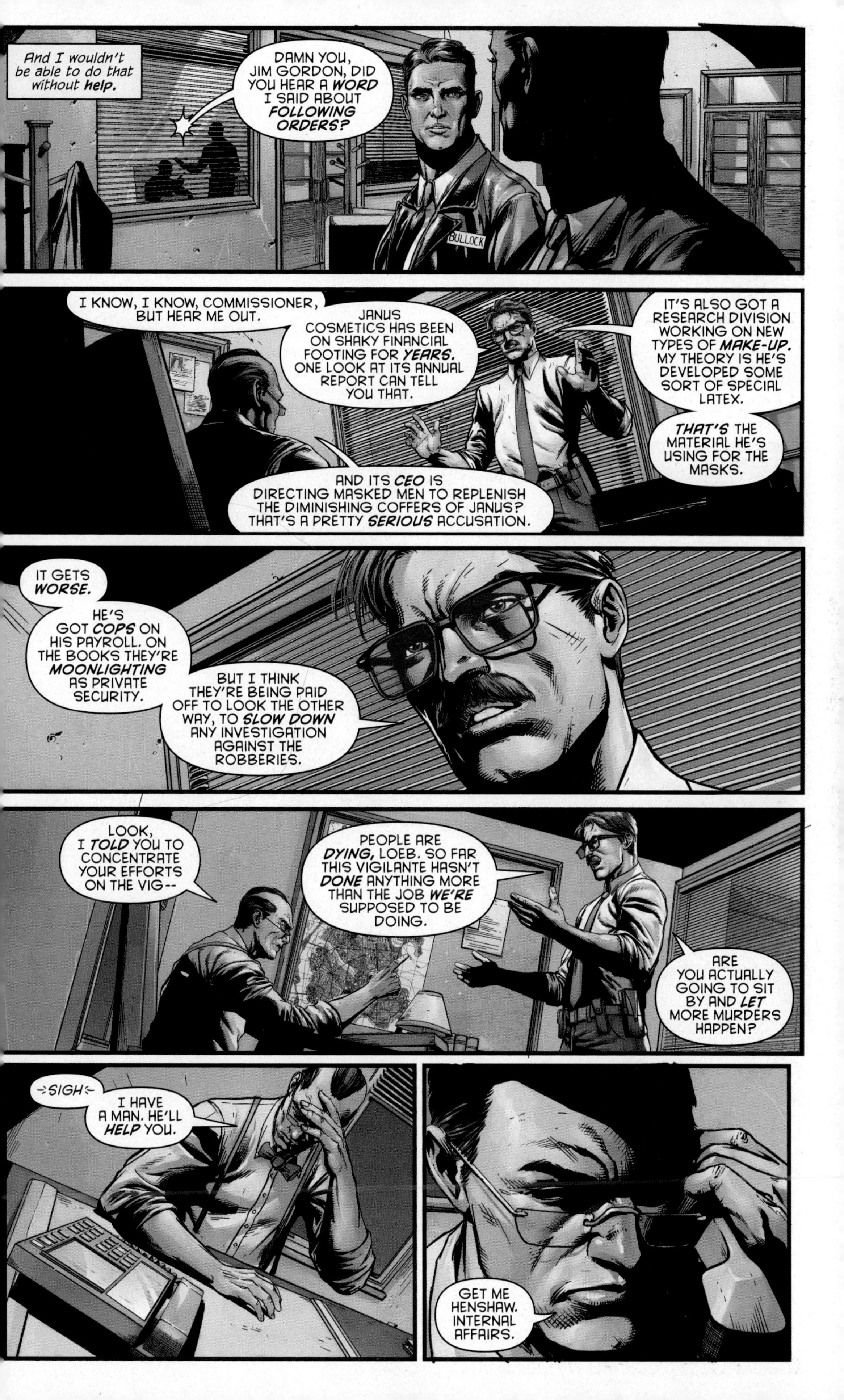
And I wouldn't be able to do that without help.
DAMN YOU, JIM GORDON, DID YOU HEAR A WORD I SAID ABOUT FOLLOWING ORDERS?
BULLOCK
I KNOW, I KNOW, COMMISSIONER, BUT HEAR ME OUT.
JANUS COSMETICS HAS BEEN ON SHAKY FINANCIAL FOOTING FOR YEARS. ONE LOOK AT ITS ANNUAL REPORT CAN TELL YOU THAT.
IT'S ALSO GOT A RESEARCH DIVISION WORKING ON NEW TYPES OF MAKE-UP. MY THEORY IS HE'S DEVELOPED SOME SORT OF SPECIAL LATEX.
THAT'S THE MATERIAL HE'S USING FOR THE MASKS.
AND ITS CEO IS DIRECTING MASKED MEN TO REPLENISH THE DIMINISHING COFFERS OF JANUS? THAT'S A PRETTY SERIOUS ACCUSATION.
IT GETS WORSE.
HE'S GOT COPS ON HIS PAYROLL. ON THE BOOKS THEY'RE MOONLIGHTING AS PRIVATE SECURITY.
BUT I THINK THEY'RE BEING PAID OFF TO LOOK THE OTHER WAY, TO SLOW DOWN ANY INVESTIGATION AGAINST THE ROBBERIES.
LOOK, I TOLD YOU TO CONCENTRATE YOUR EFFORTS ON THE VIG--
PEOPLE ARE DYING, LOEB. SO FAR THIS VIGILANTE HASN'T DONE ANYTHING MORE THAN THE JOB WE'RE SUPPOSED TO BE DOING.
ARE YOU ACTUALLY GOING TO SIT BY AND LET MORE MURDERS HAPPEN?
=SIGH=
I HAVE A MAN. HE'LL HELP YOU.
GET ME HENSHAW. INTERNAL AFFAIRS.

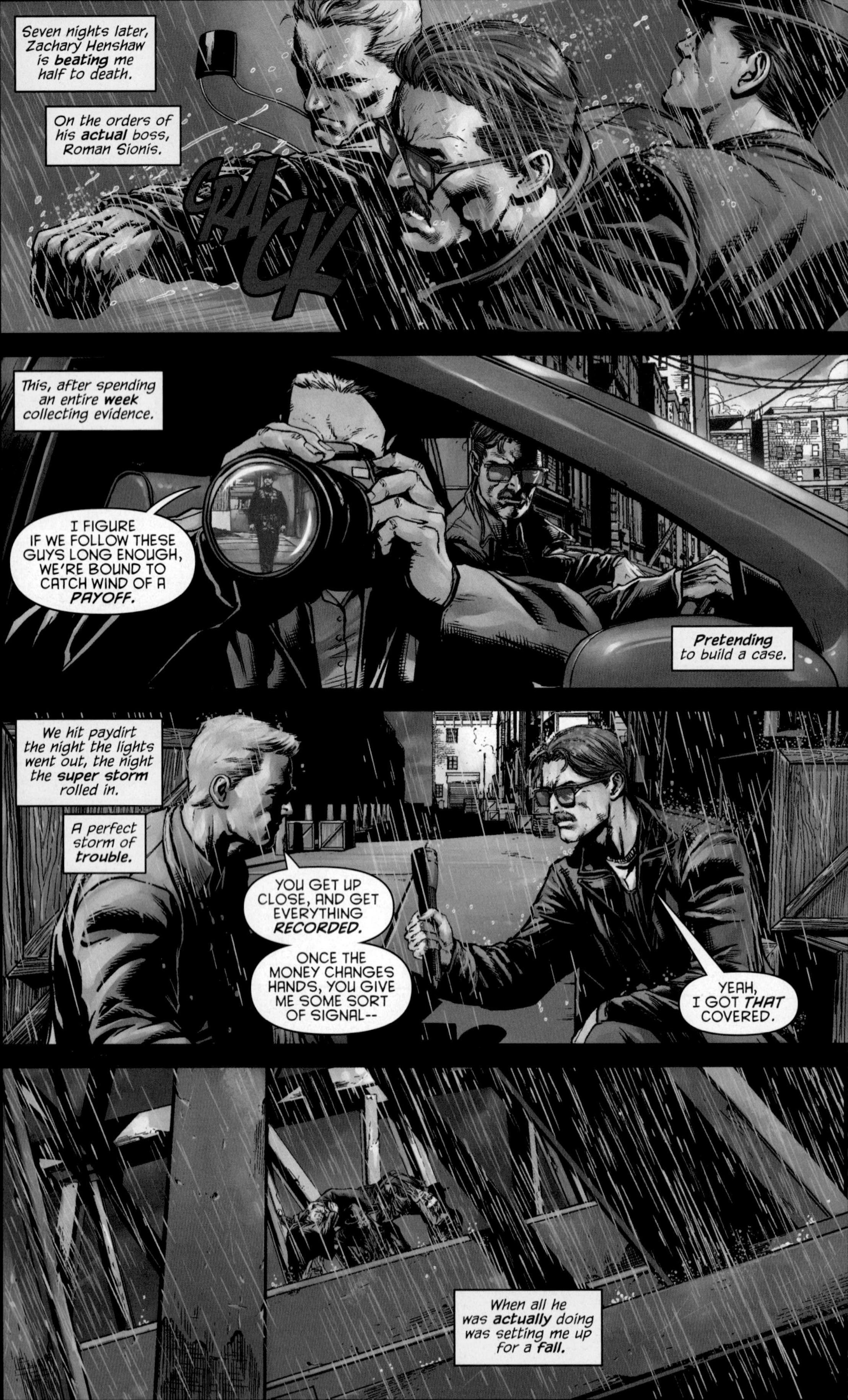

Seven nights later, Zachary Henshaw is **beating** me half to death.
On the orders of his **actual** boss, Roman Sionis.
CRACK
This, after spending an entire **week** collecting evidence.
I FIGURE IF WE FOLLOW THESE GUYS LONG ENOUGH, WE'RE BOUND TO CATCH WIND OF A **PAYOFF.**
Pretending to build a case.
We hit paydirt the night the lights went out, the night the **super storm** rolled in.
A perfect storm of **trouble.**
YOU GET UP CLOSE, AND GET EVERYTHING **RECORDED.**
ONCE THE MONEY CHANGES HANDS, YOU GIVE ME SOME SORT OF SIGNAL--
YEAH, I GOT **THAT** COVERED.
When all he was **actually** doing was setting me up for a **fall.**

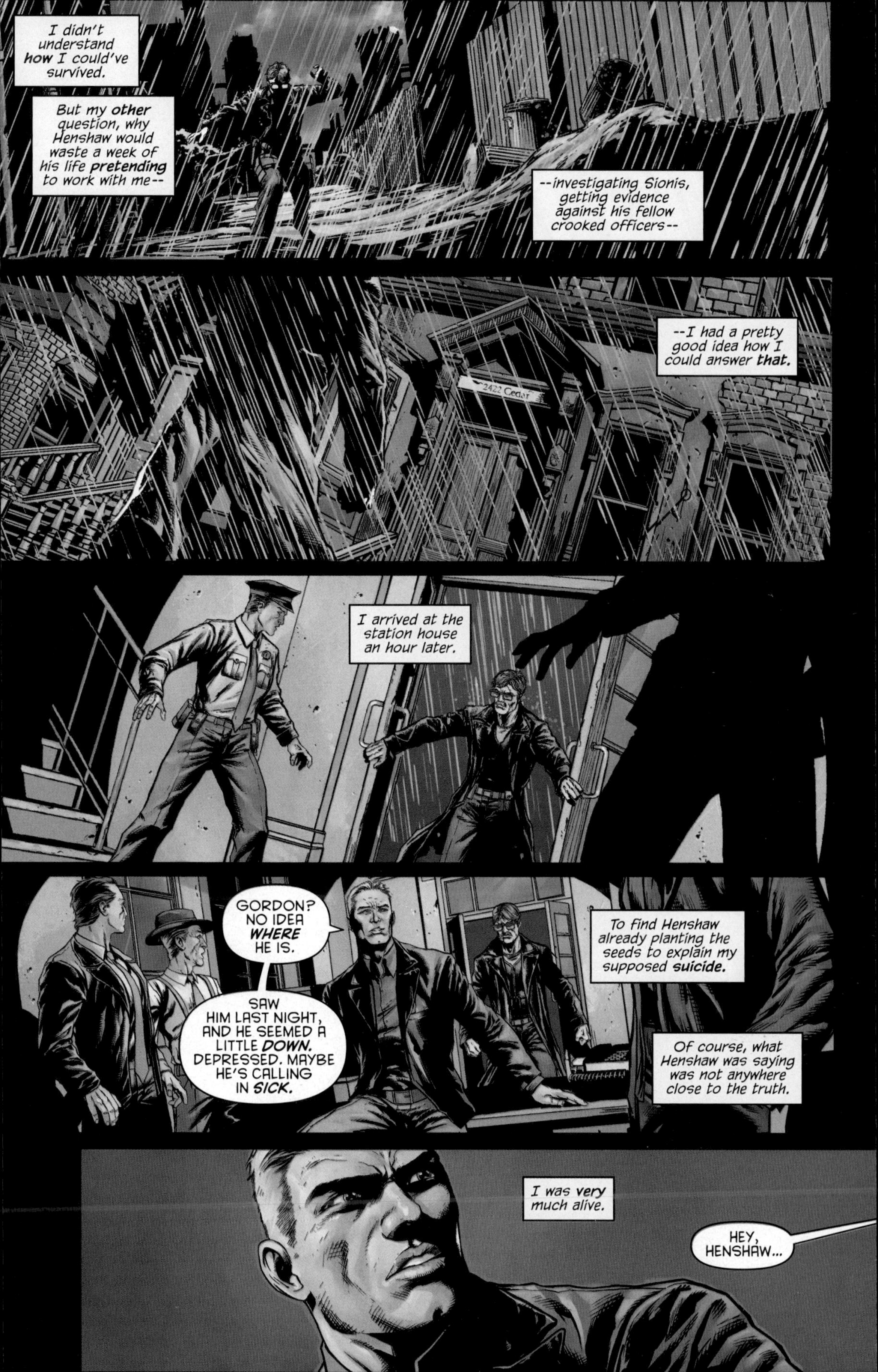
I didn't understand **how** I could've survived.
But my **other** question, why Henshaw would waste a week of his life **pretending** to work with me--
--investigating Sionis, getting evidence against his fellow crooked officers--
--I had a pretty good idea how I could answer **that.**
2422 Cedar
I arrived at the station house an hour later.
GORDON? NO IDEA ***WHERE*** HE IS.
SAW HIM LAST NIGHT, AND HE SEEMED A LITTLE ***DOWN.*** DEPRESSED. MAYBE HE'S CALLING IN ***SICK.***
To find Henshaw already planting the seeds to explain my supposed **suicide.**
Of course, what Henshaw was saying was not anywhere close to the truth.
I was **very** much alive.
HEY, HENSHAW...

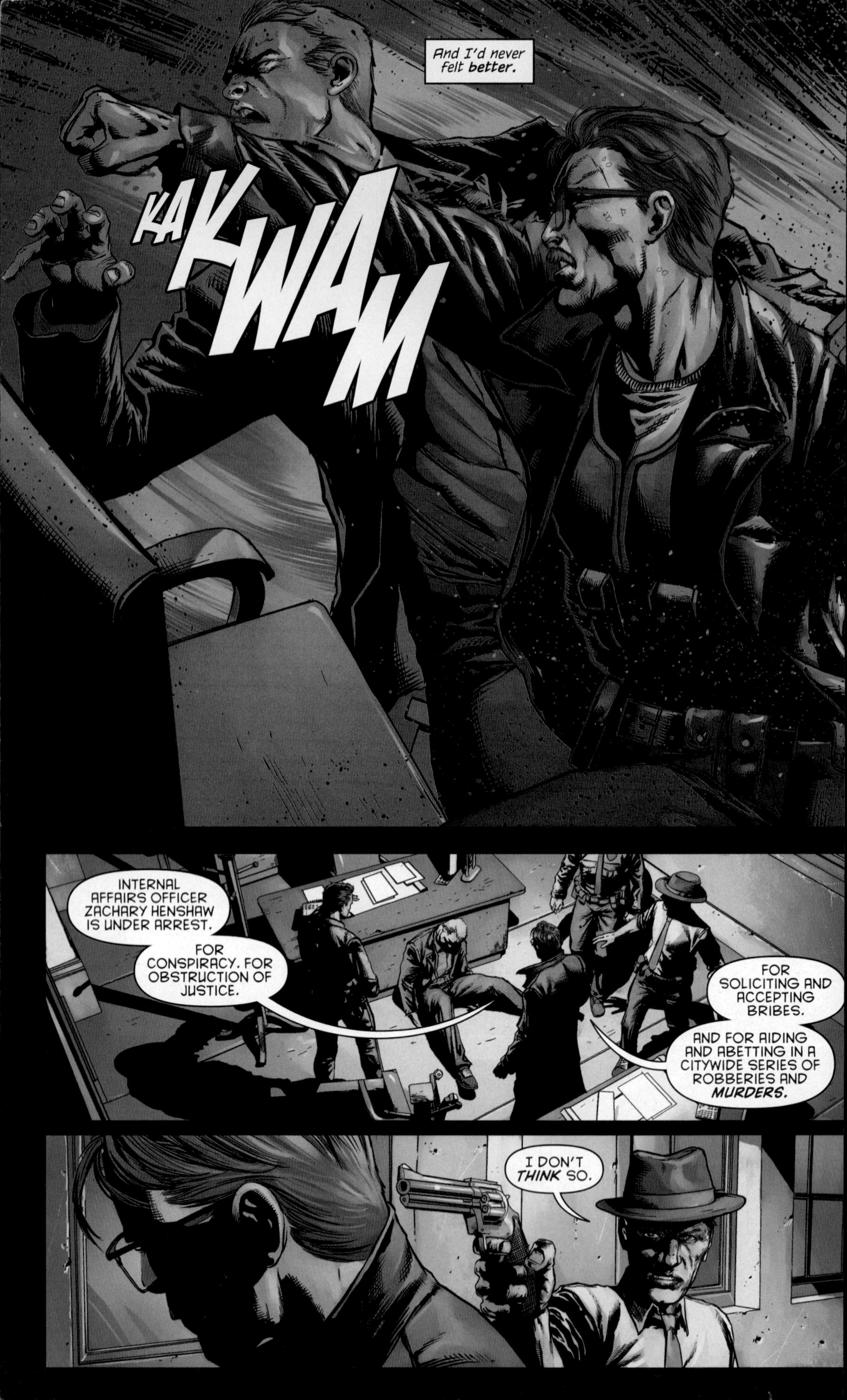
And I'd never felt better.
KAKWAM
INTERNAL AFFAIRS OFFICER ZACHARY HENSHAW IS UNDER ARREST.
FOR CONSPIRACY. FOR OBSTRUCTION OF JUSTICE.
FOR SOLICITING AND ACCEPTING BRIBES.
AND FOR AIDING AND ABETTING IN A CITYWIDE SERIES OF ROBBERIES AND MURDERS.
I DON'T THINK SO.

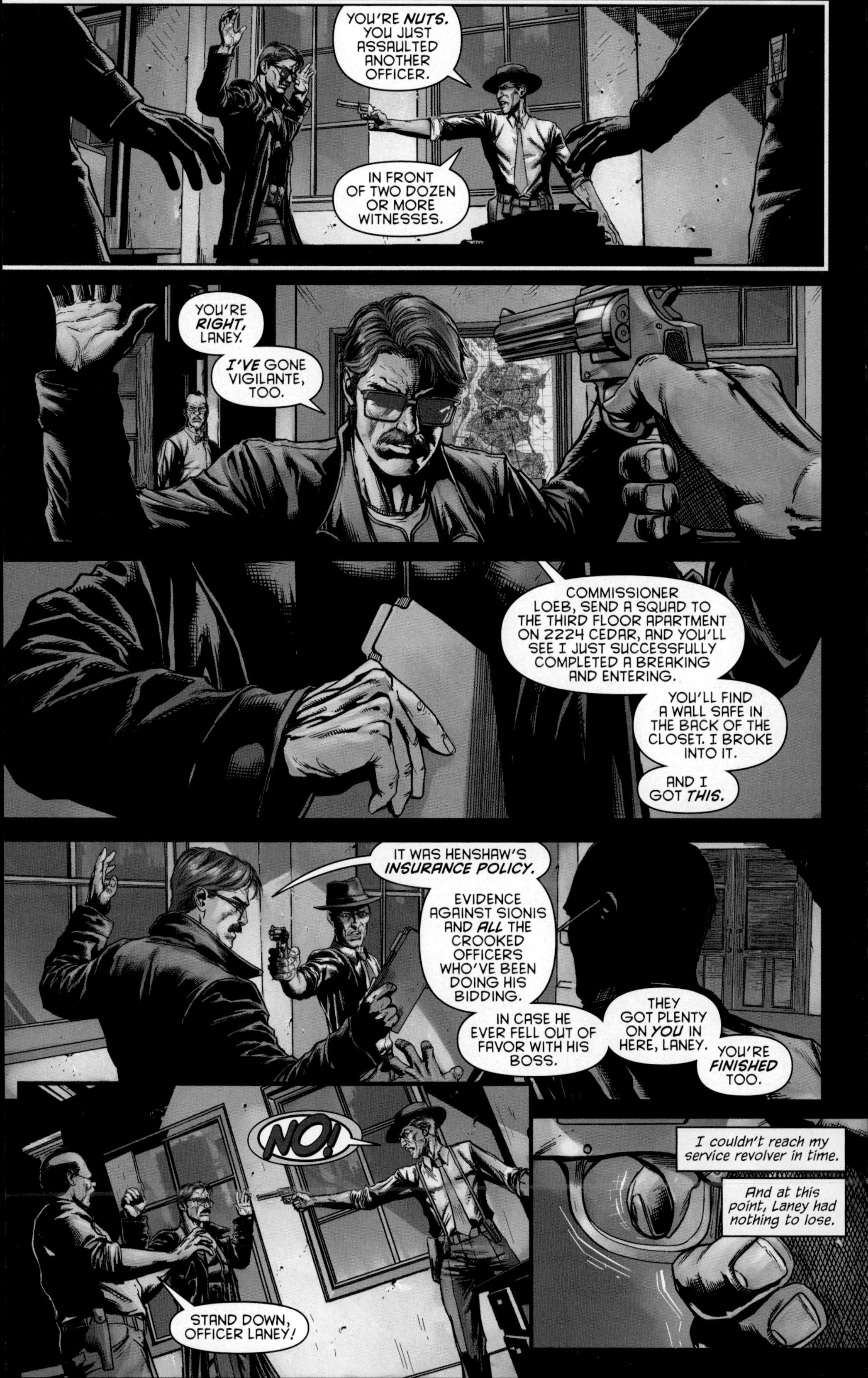
YOU'RE NUTS. YOU JUST ASSAULTED ANOTHER OFFICER.
IN FRONT OF TWO DOZEN OR MORE WITNESSES.
YOU'RE RIGHT, LANEY.
I'VE GONE VIGILANTE, TOO.
COMMISSIONER LOEB, SEND A SQUAD TO THE THIRD FLOOR APARTMENT ON 2224 CEDAR, AND YOU'LL SEE I JUST SUCCESSFULLY COMPLETED A BREAKING AND ENTERING.
YOU'LL FIND A WALL SAFE IN THE BACK OF THE CLOSET. I BROKE INTO IT.
AND I GOT THIS.
IT WAS HENSHAW'S INSURANCE POLICY.
EVIDENCE AGAINST SIONIS AND ALL THE CROOKED OFFICERS WHO'VE BEEN DOING HIS BIDDING.
IN CASE HE EVER FELL OUT OF FAVOR WITH HIS BOSS.
THEY GOT PLENTY ON YOU IN HERE, LANEY.
YOU'RE FINISHED TOO.
NO!
STAND DOWN, OFFICER LANEY!
I couldn't reach my service revolver in time.
And at this point, Laney had nothing to lose.

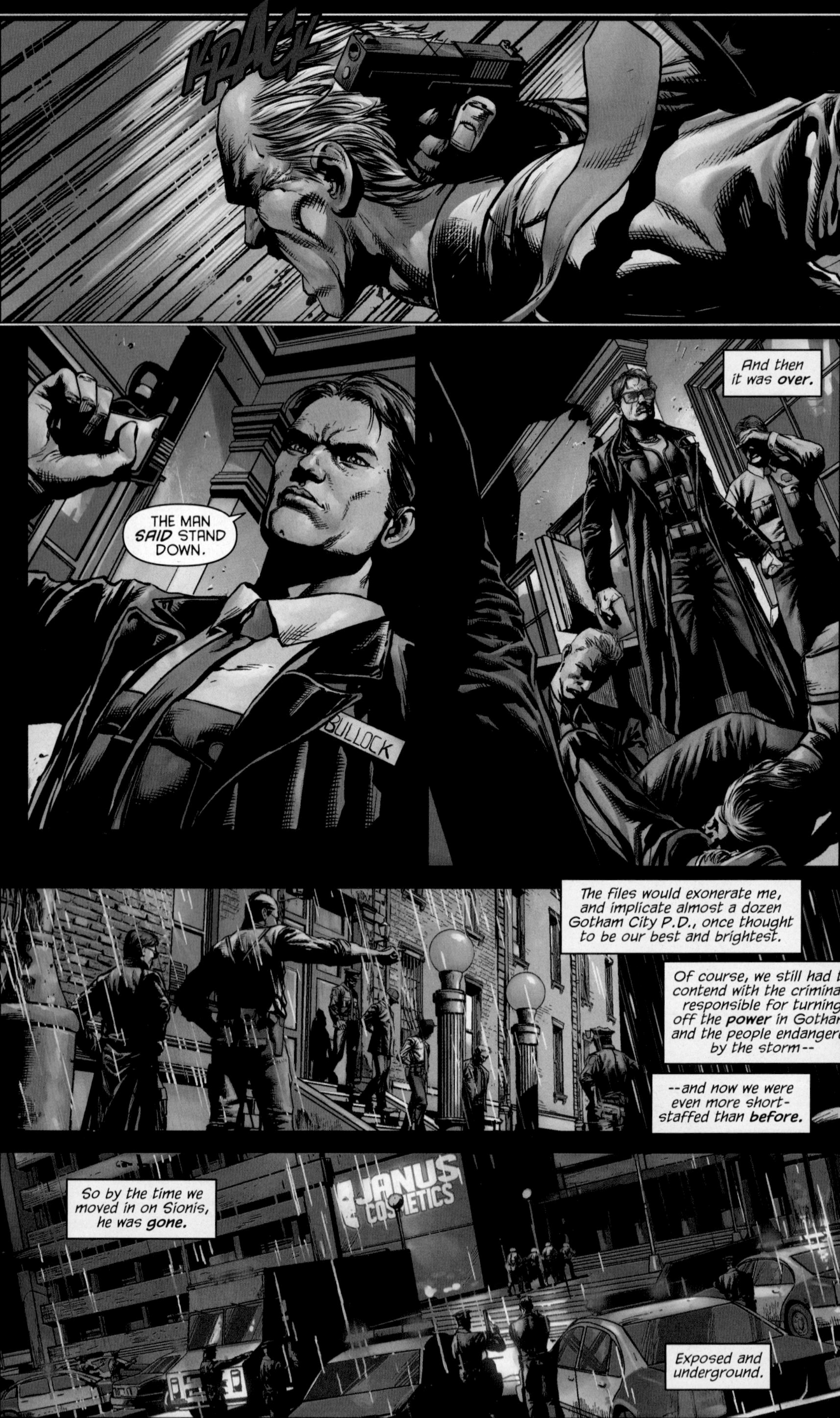
KRACK
THE MAN SAID STAND DOWN.
BULLOCK
And then it was over.
The files would exonerate me, and implicate almost a dozen Gotham City P.D., once thought to be our best and brightest.
Of course, we still had to contend with the criminal responsible for turning off the power in Gotham and the people endangered by the storm--
--and now we were even more short-staffed than before.
So by the time we moved in on Sionis, he was gone.
JANU$ COSMETICS
Exposed and underground.

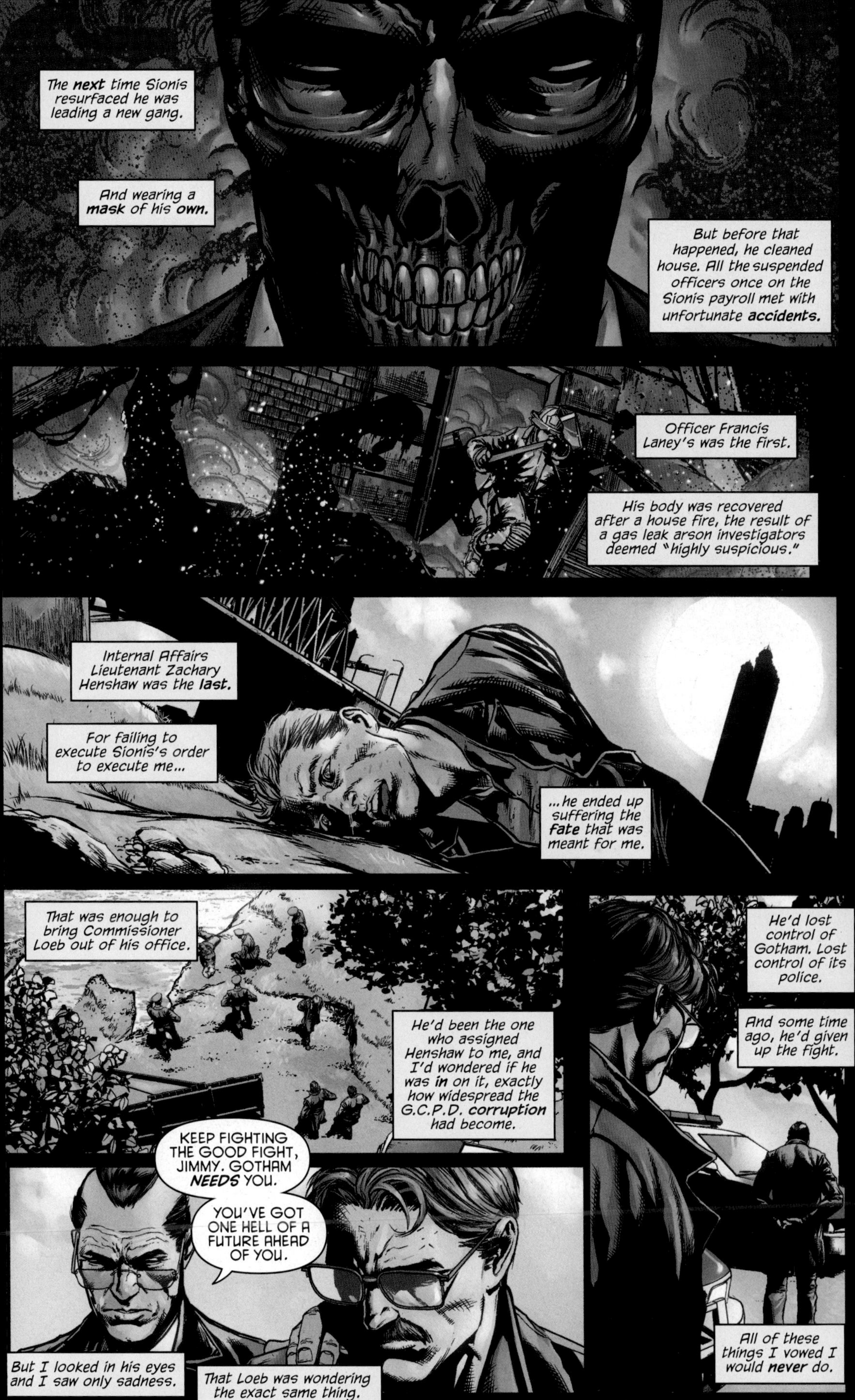
The next time Sionis resurfaced he was leading a new gang.
And wearing a mask of his own.
But before that happened, he cleaned house. All the suspended officers once on the Sionis payroll met with unfortunate accidents.
Officer Francis Laney's was the first.
His body was recovered after a house fire, the result of a gas leak arson investigators deemed "highly suspicious."
Internal Affairs Lieutenant Zachary Henshaw was the last.
For failing to execute Sionis's order to execute me...
...he ended up suffering the fate that was meant for me.
That was enough to bring Commissioner Loeb out of his office.
He'd been the one who assigned Henshaw to me, and I'd wondered if he was in on it, exactly how widespread the G.C.P.D. corruption had become.
KEEP FIGHTING THE GOOD FIGHT, JIMMY. GOTHAM NEEDS YOU.
YOU'VE GOT ONE HELL OF A FUTURE AHEAD OF YOU.
But I looked in his eyes and I saw only sadness.
That Loeb was wondering the exact same thing.
He'd lost control of Gotham. Lost control of its police.
And some time ago, he'd given up the fight.
All of these things I vowed I would never do.

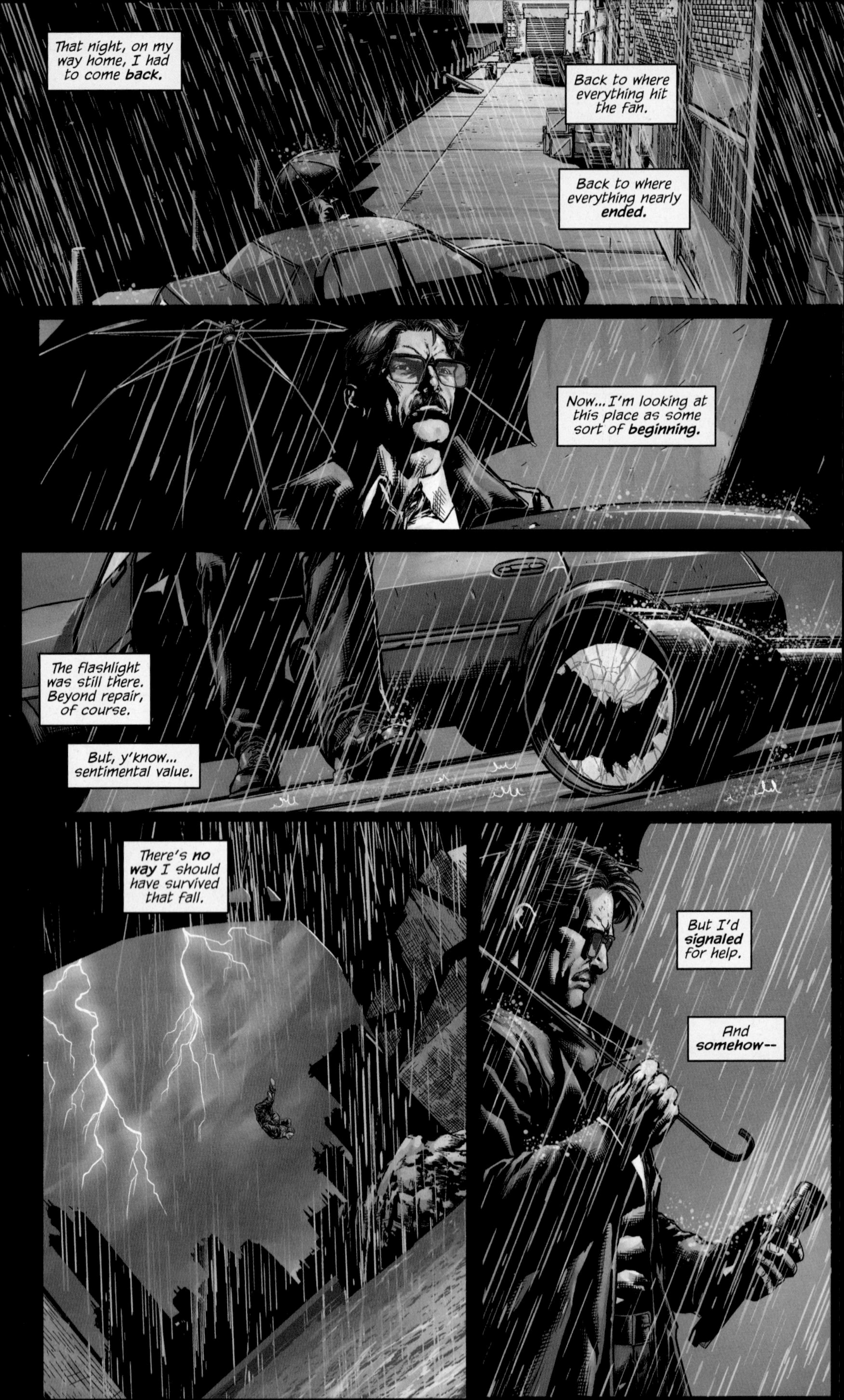
That night, on my way home, I had to come **back.**
Back to where everything hit the fan.
Back to where everything nearly **ended.**
Now...I'm looking at this place as some sort of **beginning.**
The flashlight was still there. Beyond repair, of course.
But, y'know... sentimental value.
There's **no way** I should have survived that fall.
But I'd **signaled** for help.
And **somehow--**

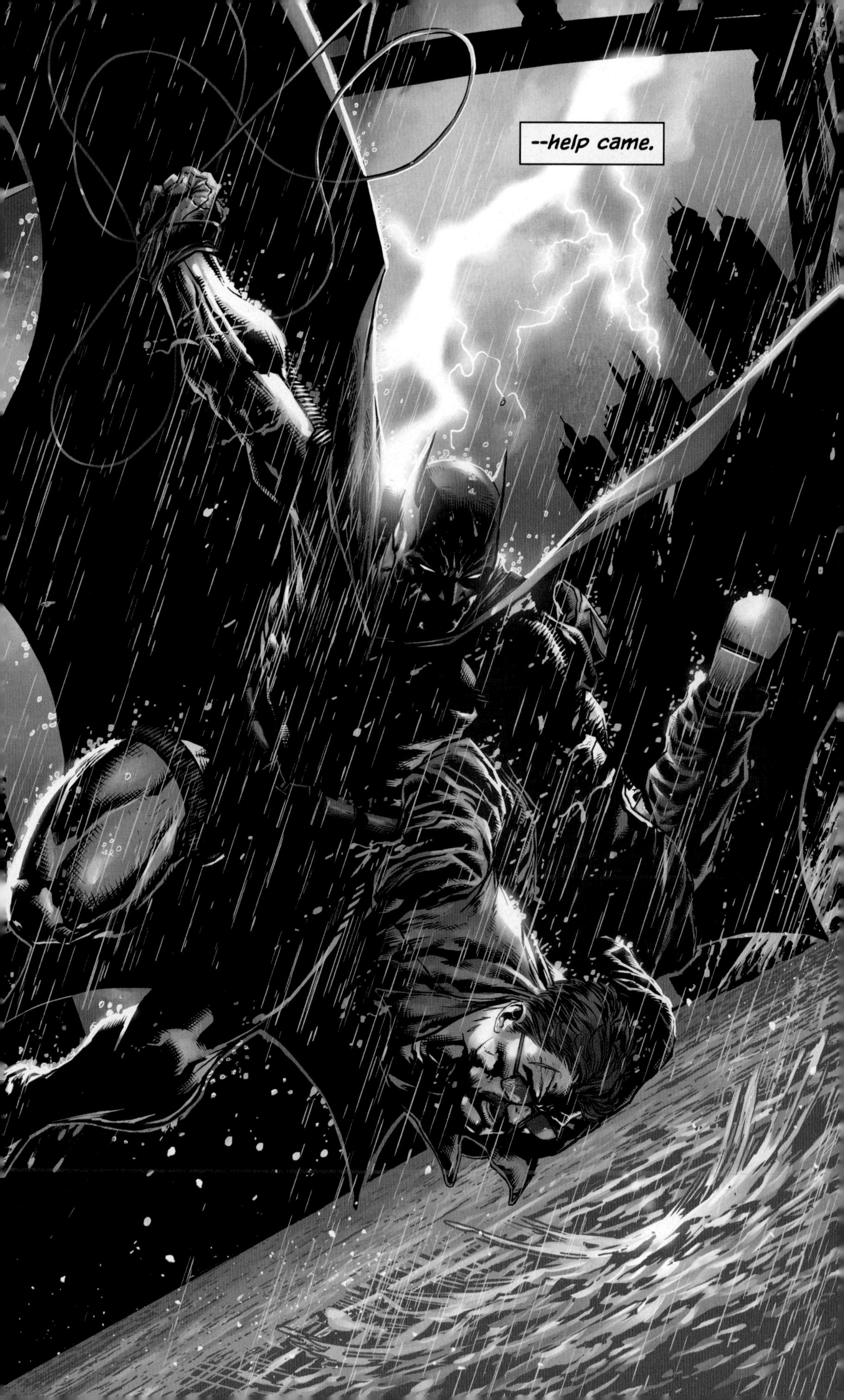
--help came.

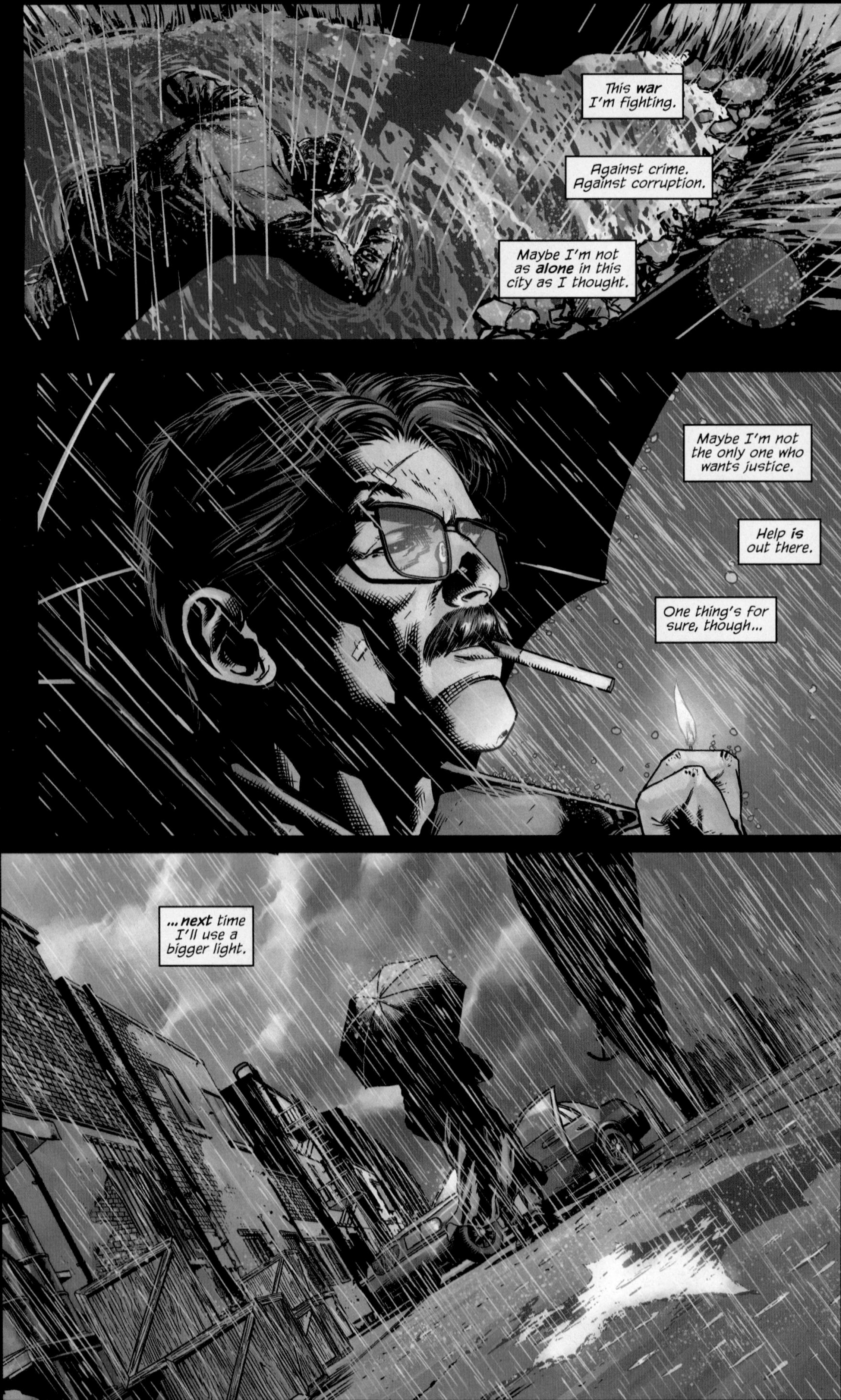
This war I'm fighting.
Against crime. Against corruption.
Maybe I'm not as alone in this city as I thought.
Maybe I'm not the only one who wants justice.
Help is out there.
One thing's for sure, though...
...next time I'll use a bigger light.

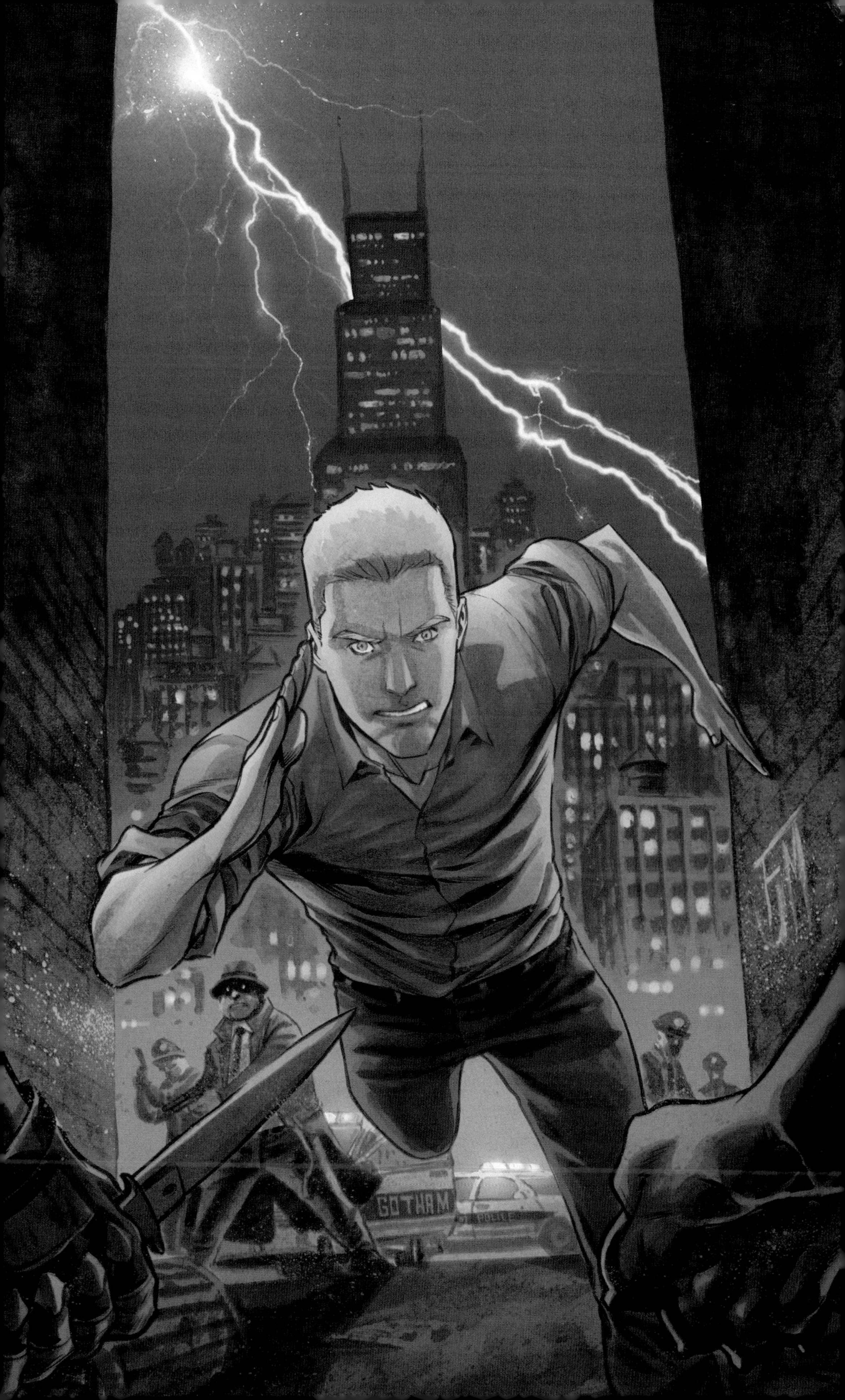
GOTHAM

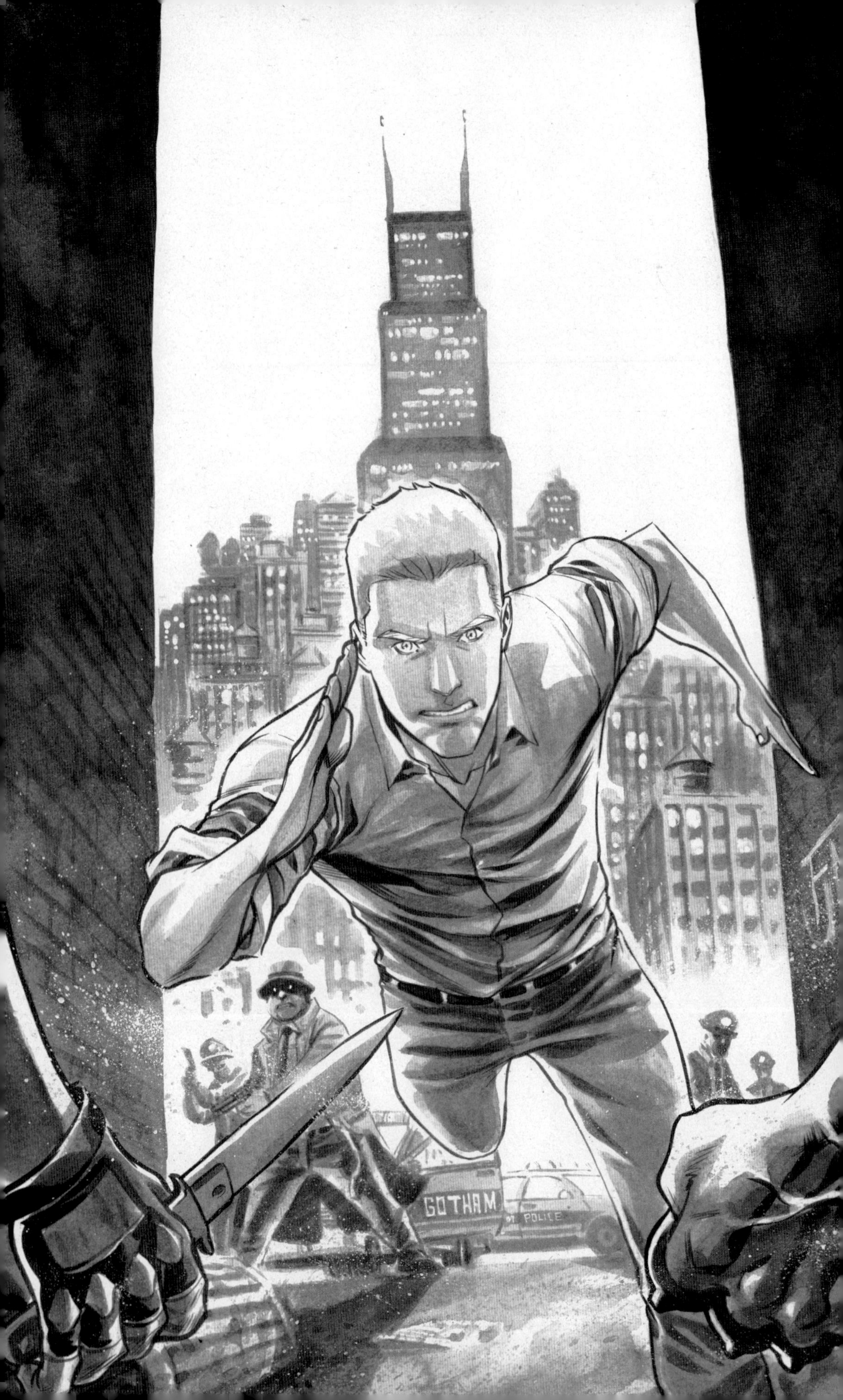
GOTHAM
POLICE

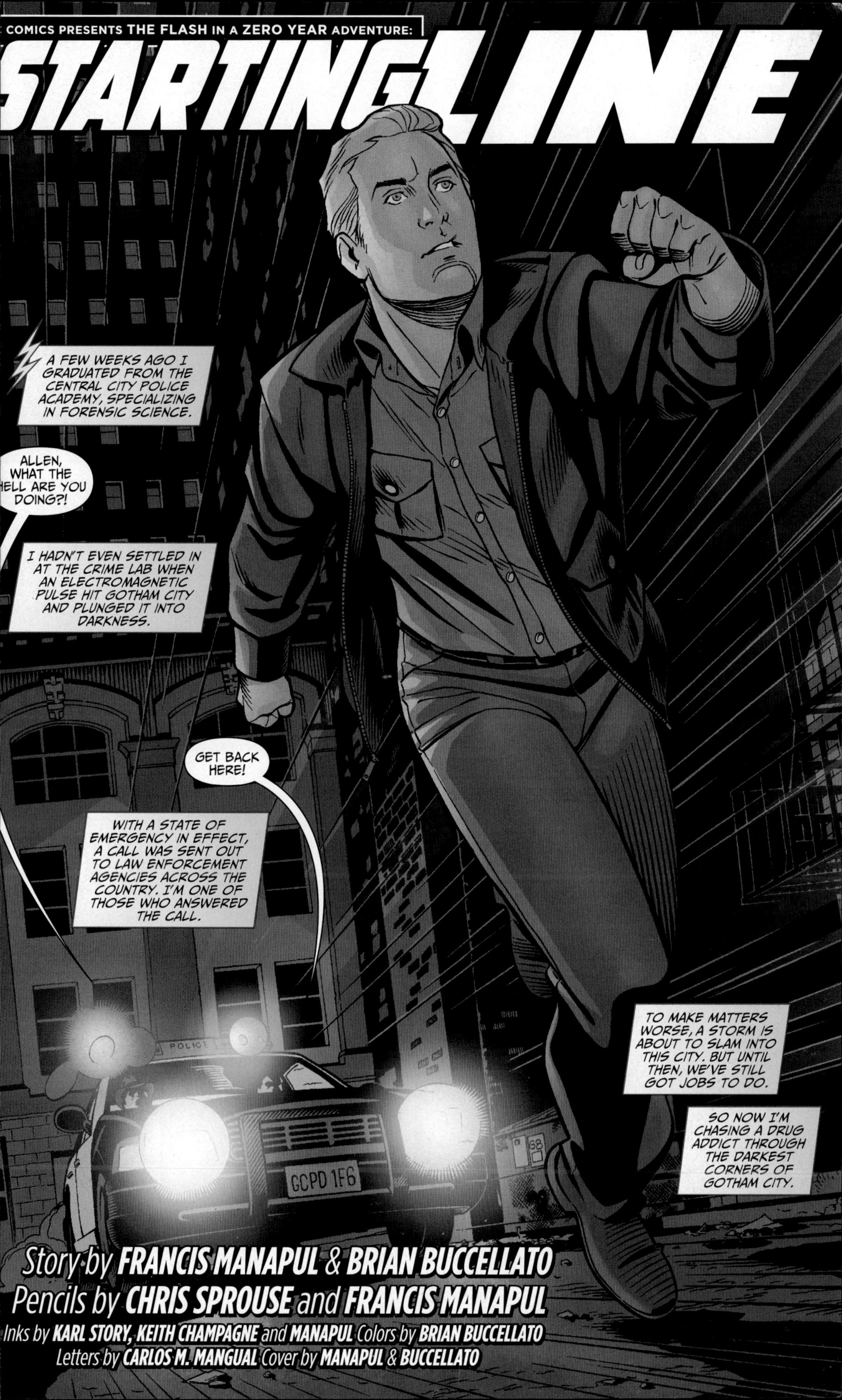
COMICS PRESENTS THE FLASH IN A ZERO YEAR ADVENTURE:
STARTING LINE
A FEW WEEKS AGO I GRADUATED FROM THE CENTRAL CITY POLICE ACADEMY, SPECIALIZING IN FORENSIC SCIENCE.
ALLEN, WHAT THE HELL ARE YOU DOING?!
I HADN'T EVEN SETTLED IN AT THE CRIME LAB WHEN AN ELECTROMAGNETIC PULSE HIT GOTHAM CITY AND PLUNGED IT INTO DARKNESS.
GET BACK HERE!
WITH A STATE OF EMERGENCY IN EFFECT, A CALL WAS SENT OUT TO LAW ENFORCEMENT AGENCIES ACROSS THE COUNTRY. I'M ONE OF THOSE WHO ANSWERED THE CALL.
TO MAKE MATTERS WORSE, A STORM IS ABOUT TO SLAM INTO THIS CITY. BUT UNTIL THEN, WE'VE STILL GOT JOBS TO DO.
SO NOW I'M CHASING A DRUG ADDICT THROUGH THE DARKEST CORNERS OF GOTHAM CITY.
POLICE
GCPD 1F6
68
Story by FRANCIS MANAPUL & BRIAN BUCCELLATO
Pencils by CHRIS SPROUSE and FRANCIS MANAPUL
Inks by KARL STORY, KEITH CHAMPAGNE and MANAPUL Colors by BRIAN BUCCELLATO
Letters by CARLOS M. MANGUAL Cover by MANAPUL & BUCCELLATO

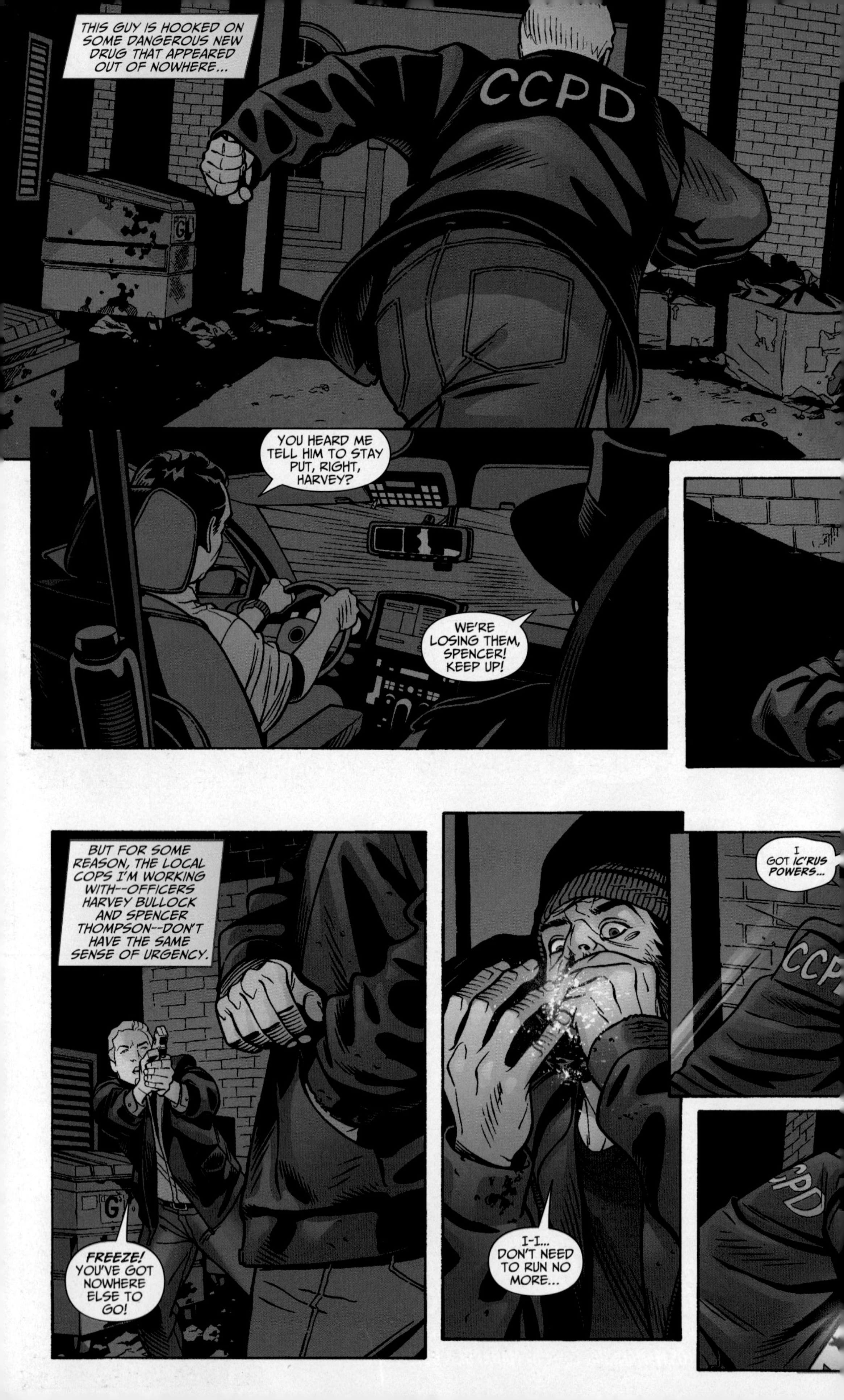
THIS GUY IS HOOKED ON SOME DANGEROUS NEW DRUG THAT APPEARED OUT OF NOWHERE...
CCPD
YOU HEARD ME TELL HIM TO STAY PUT, RIGHT, HARVEY?
WE'RE LOSING THEM, SPENCER! KEEP UP!
BUT FOR SOME REASON, THE LOCAL COPS I'M WORKING WITH--OFFICERS HARVEY BULLOCK AND SPENCER THOMPSON--DON'T HAVE THE SAME SENSE OF URGENCY.
FREEZE! YOU'VE GOT NOWHERE ELSE TO GO!
I-I... DON'T NEED TO RUN NO MORE...
I GOT IC'RUS POWERS...

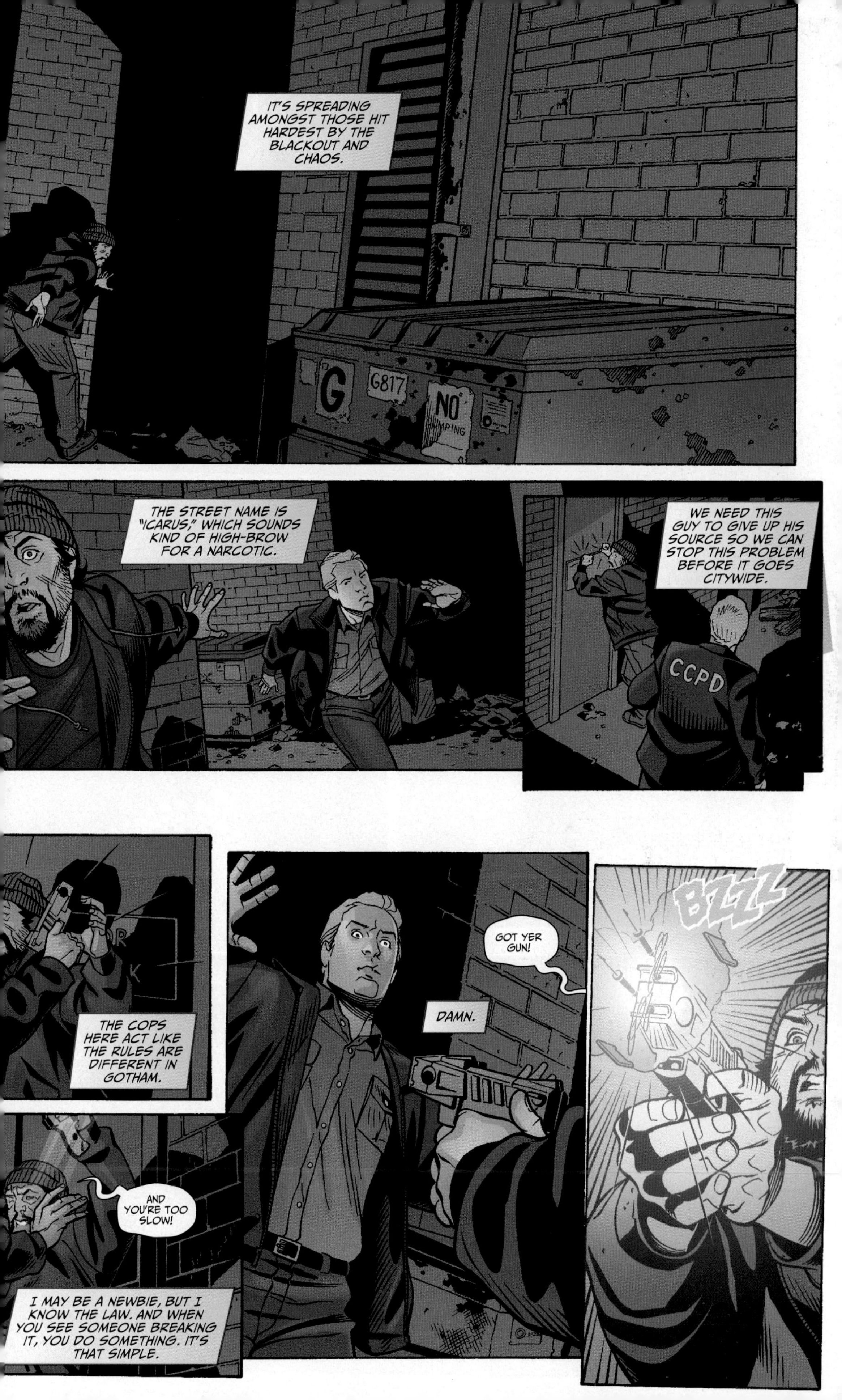
IT'S SPREADING AMONGST THOSE HIT HARDEST BY THE BLACKOUT AND CHAOS.
G
G817
NO DUMPING
THE STREET NAME IS "ICARUS," WHICH SOUNDS KIND OF HIGH-BROW FOR A NARCOTIC.
WE NEED THIS GUY TO GIVE UP HIS SOURCE SO WE CAN STOP THIS PROBLEM BEFORE IT GOES CITYWIDE.
CCPD
THE COPS HERE ACT LIKE THE RULES ARE DIFFERENT IN GOTHAM.
AND YOU'RE TOO SLOW!
I MAY BE A NEWBIE, BUT I KNOW THE LAW. AND WHEN YOU SEE SOMEONE BREAKING IT, YOU DO SOMETHING. IT'S THAT SIMPLE.
GOT YER GUN!
DAMN.
BZZZ

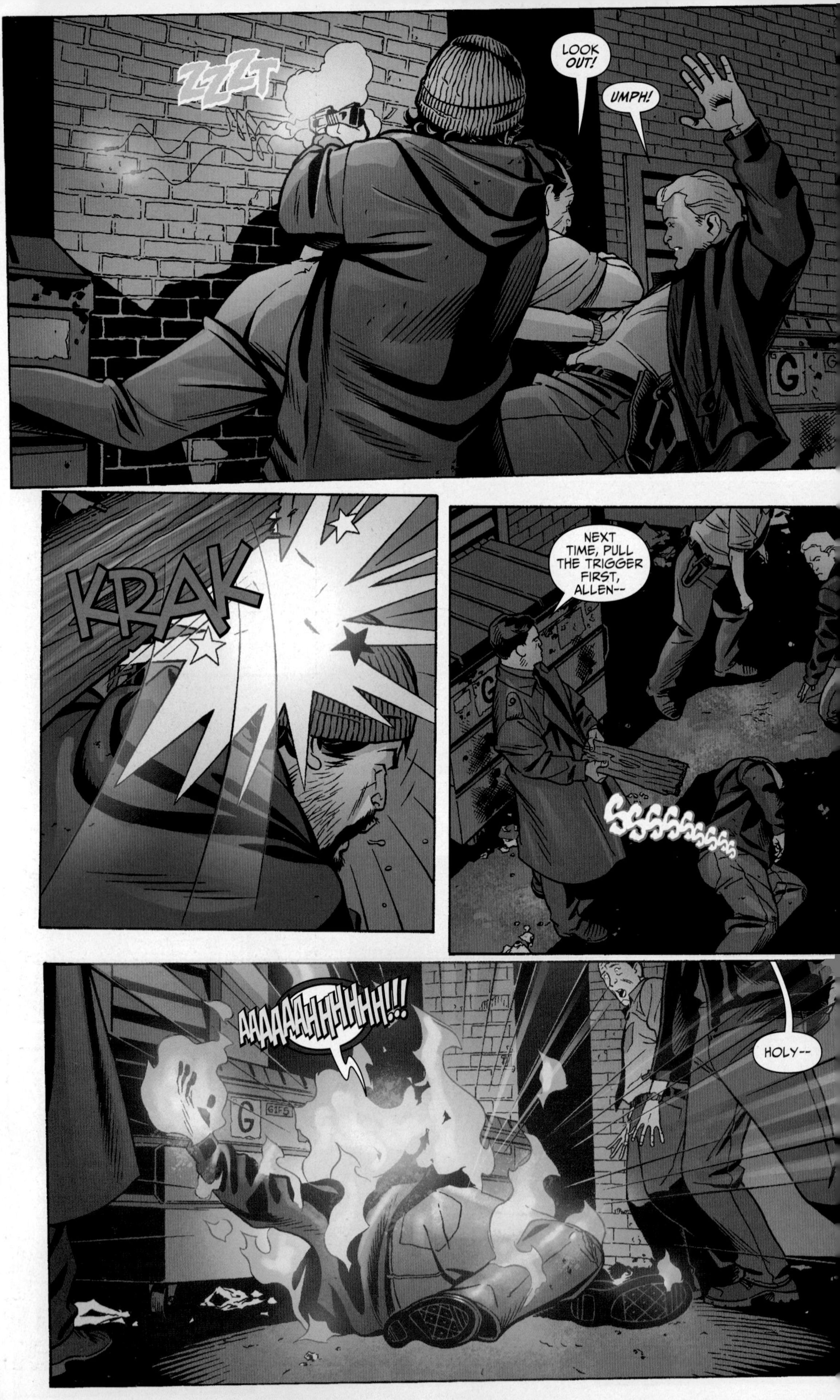
ZZZT
LOOK OUT!
UMPH!
KRAK
NEXT TIME, PULL THE TRIGGER FIRST, ALLEN--
SSSSSSSSSSSS
AAAAAAHHHHHH!!!
HOLY--

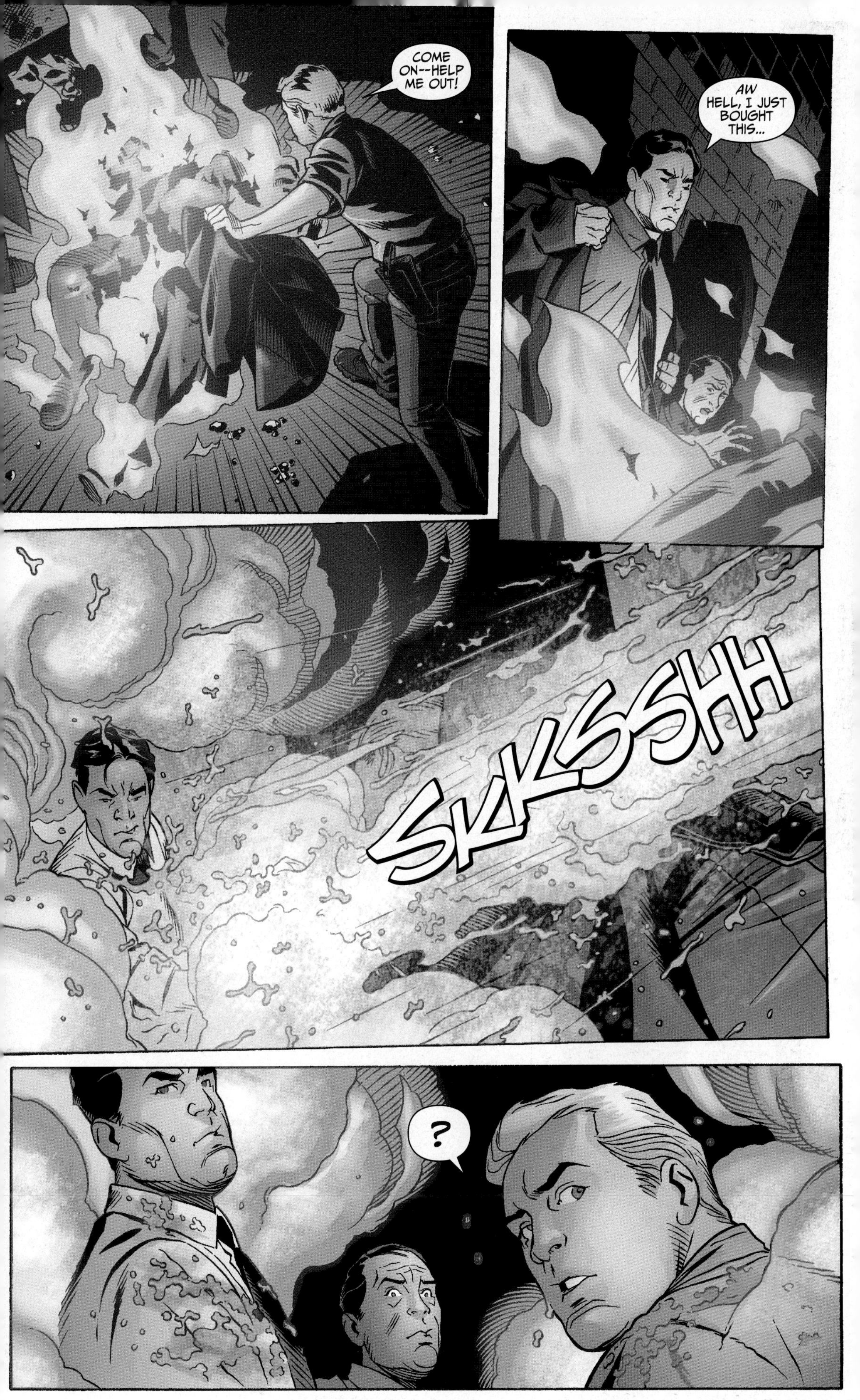
COME ON--HELP ME OUT!
AW HELL, I JUST BOUGHT THIS...
SKKSSHH
?

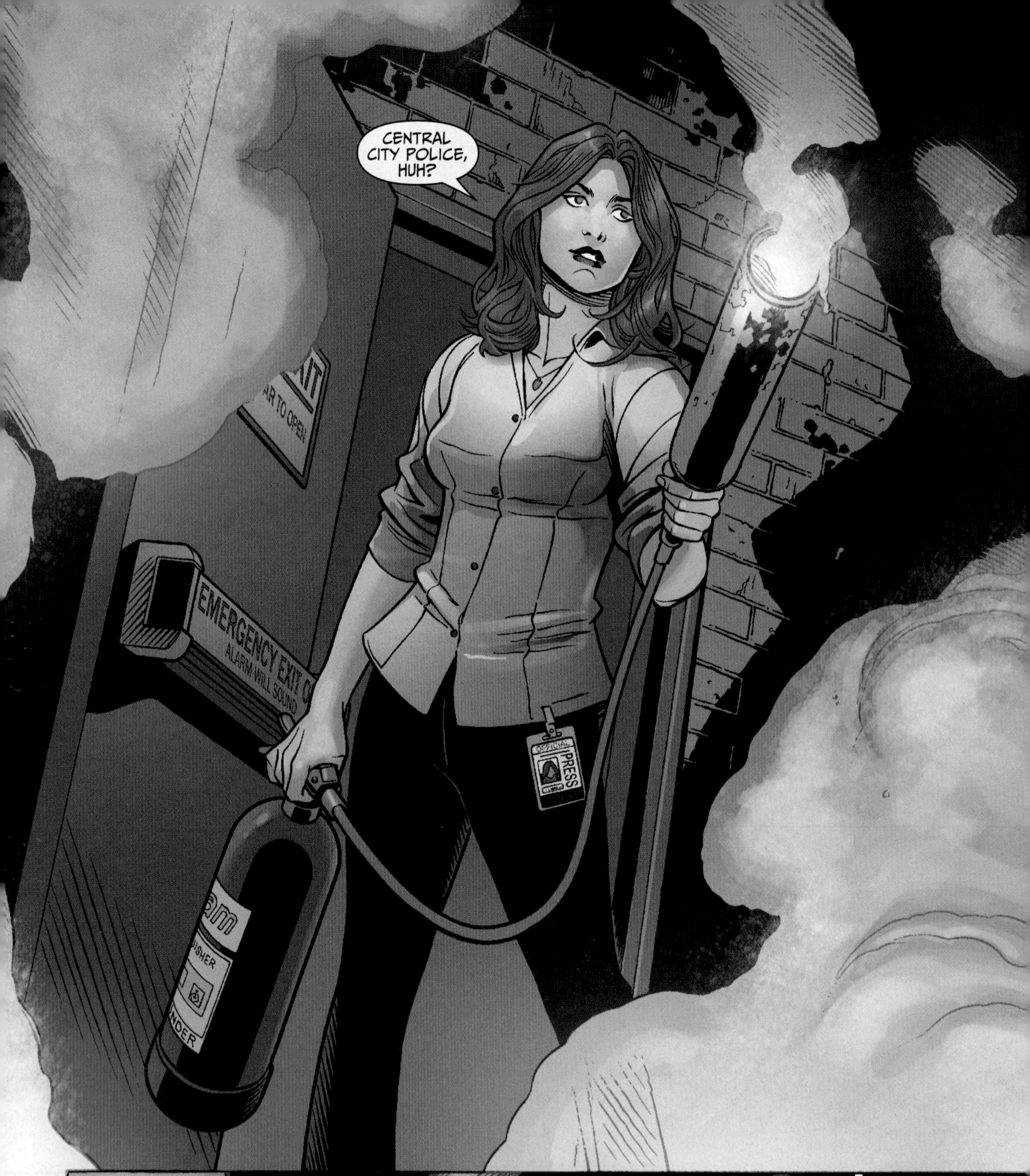
CENTRAL CITY POLICE, HUH?
EMERGENCY EXIT
ALARM WILL SOUND
PRESS

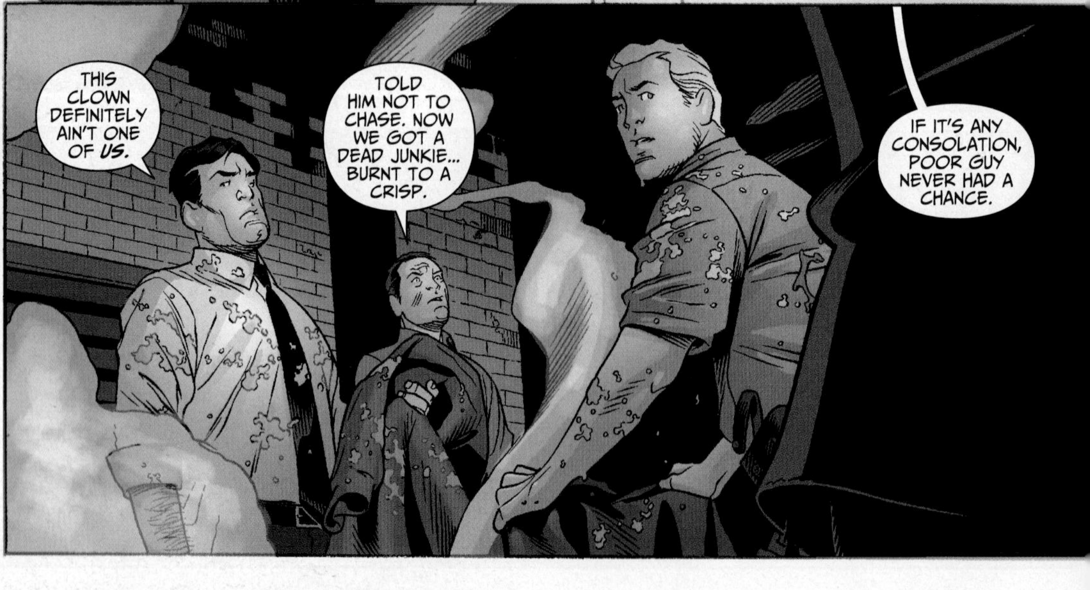
THIS CLOWN DEFINITELY AIN'T ONE OF *US*.
TOLD HIM NOT TO CHASE. NOW WE GOT A DEAD JUNKIE... BURNT TO A CRISP.
IF IT'S ANY CONSOLATION, POOR GUY NEVER HAD A CHANCE.

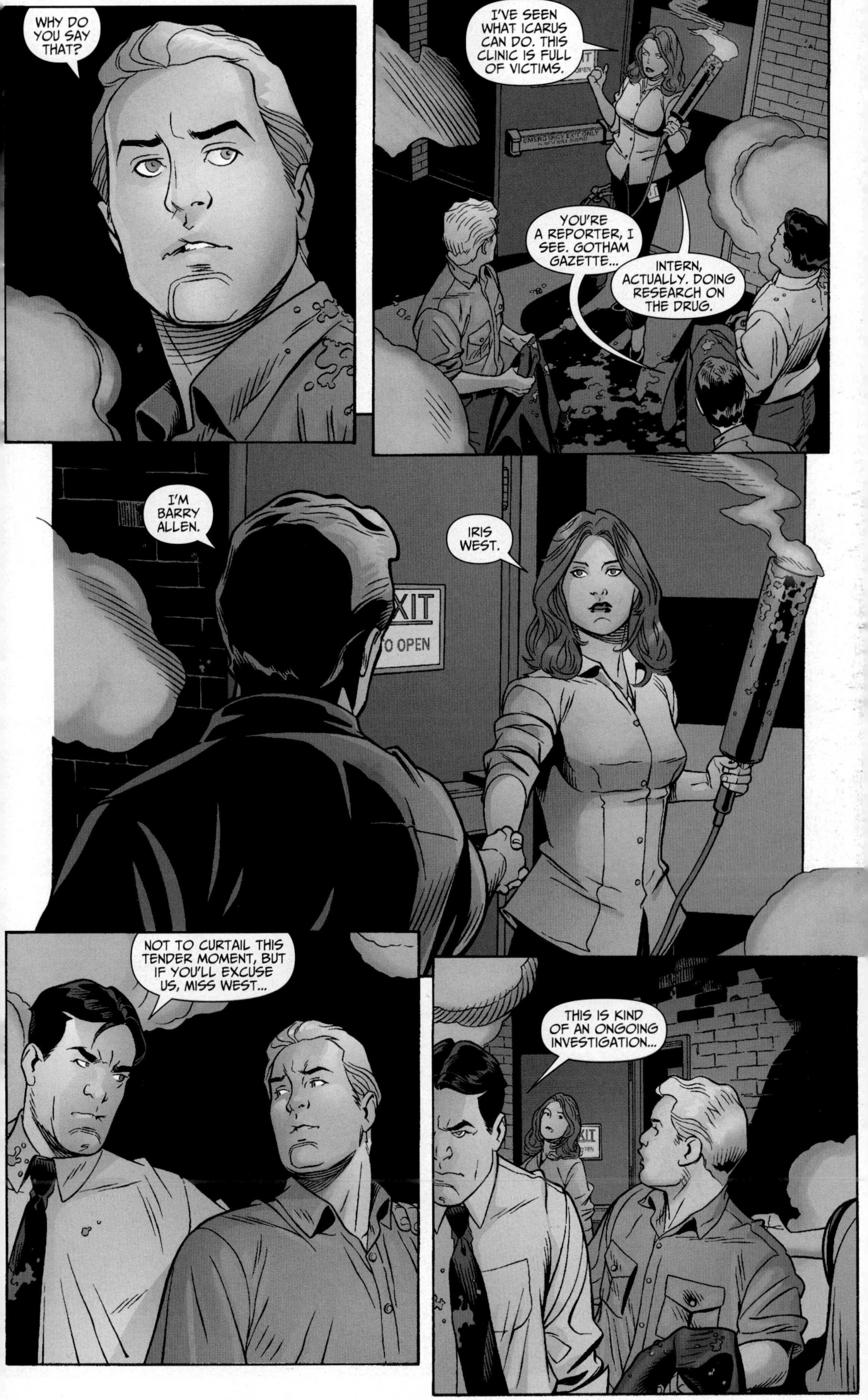
WHY DO YOU SAY THAT?
I'VE SEEN WHAT ICARUS CAN DO. THIS CLINIC IS FULL OF VICTIMS.
EMERGENCY EXIT ONLY
YOU'RE A REPORTER, I SEE. GOTHAM GAZETTE...
INTERN, ACTUALLY. DOING RESEARCH ON THE DRUG.
I'M BARRY ALLEN.
IRIS WEST.
XIT
O OPEN
NOT TO CURTAIL THIS TENDER MOMENT, BUT IF YOU'LL EXCUSE US, MISS WEST...
THIS IS KIND OF AN ONGOING INVESTIGATION...

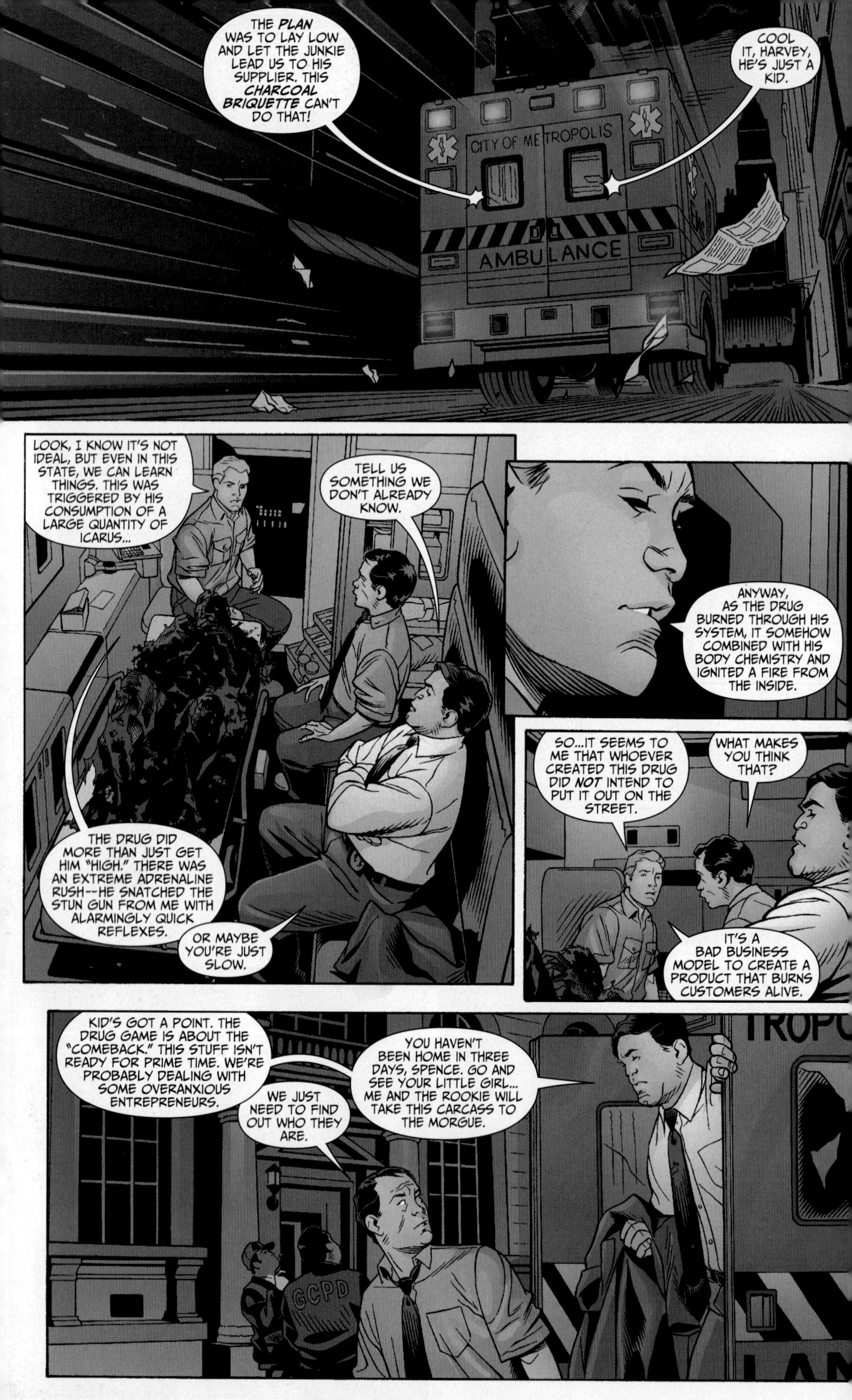
THE PLAN WAS TO LAY LOW AND LET THE JUNKIE LEAD US TO HIS SUPPLIER. THIS CHARCOAL BRIQUETTE CAN'T DO THAT!
COOL IT, HARVEY, HE'S JUST A KID.
CITY OF METROPOLIS
AMBULANCE
LOOK, I KNOW IT'S NOT IDEAL, BUT EVEN IN THIS STATE, WE CAN LEARN THINGS. THIS WAS TRIGGERED BY HIS CONSUMPTION OF A LARGE QUANTITY OF ICARUS...
TELL US SOMETHING WE DON'T ALREADY KNOW.
THE DRUG DID MORE THAN JUST GET HIM "HIGH." THERE WAS AN EXTREME ADRENALINE RUSH--HE SNATCHED THE STUN GUN FROM ME WITH ALARMINGLY QUICK REFLEXES.
OR MAYBE YOU'RE JUST SLOW.
ANYWAY, AS THE DRUG BURNED THROUGH HIS SYSTEM, IT SOMEHOW COMBINED WITH HIS BODY CHEMISTRY AND IGNITED A FIRE FROM THE INSIDE.
SO...IT SEEMS TO ME THAT WHOEVER CREATED THIS DRUG DID NOT INTEND TO PUT IT OUT ON THE STREET.
WHAT MAKES YOU THINK THAT?
IT'S A BAD BUSINESS MODEL TO CREATE A PRODUCT THAT BURNS CUSTOMERS ALIVE.
KID'S GOT A POINT. THE DRUG GAME IS ABOUT THE "COMEBACK." THIS STUFF ISN'T READY FOR PRIME TIME. WE'RE PROBABLY DEALING WITH SOME OVERANXIOUS ENTREPRENEURS.
WE JUST NEED TO FIND OUT WHO THEY ARE.
YOU HAVEN'T BEEN HOME IN THREE DAYS, SPENCE. GO AND SEE YOUR LITTLE GIRL... ME AND THE ROOKIE WILL TAKE THIS CARCASS TO THE MORGUE.
GCPD

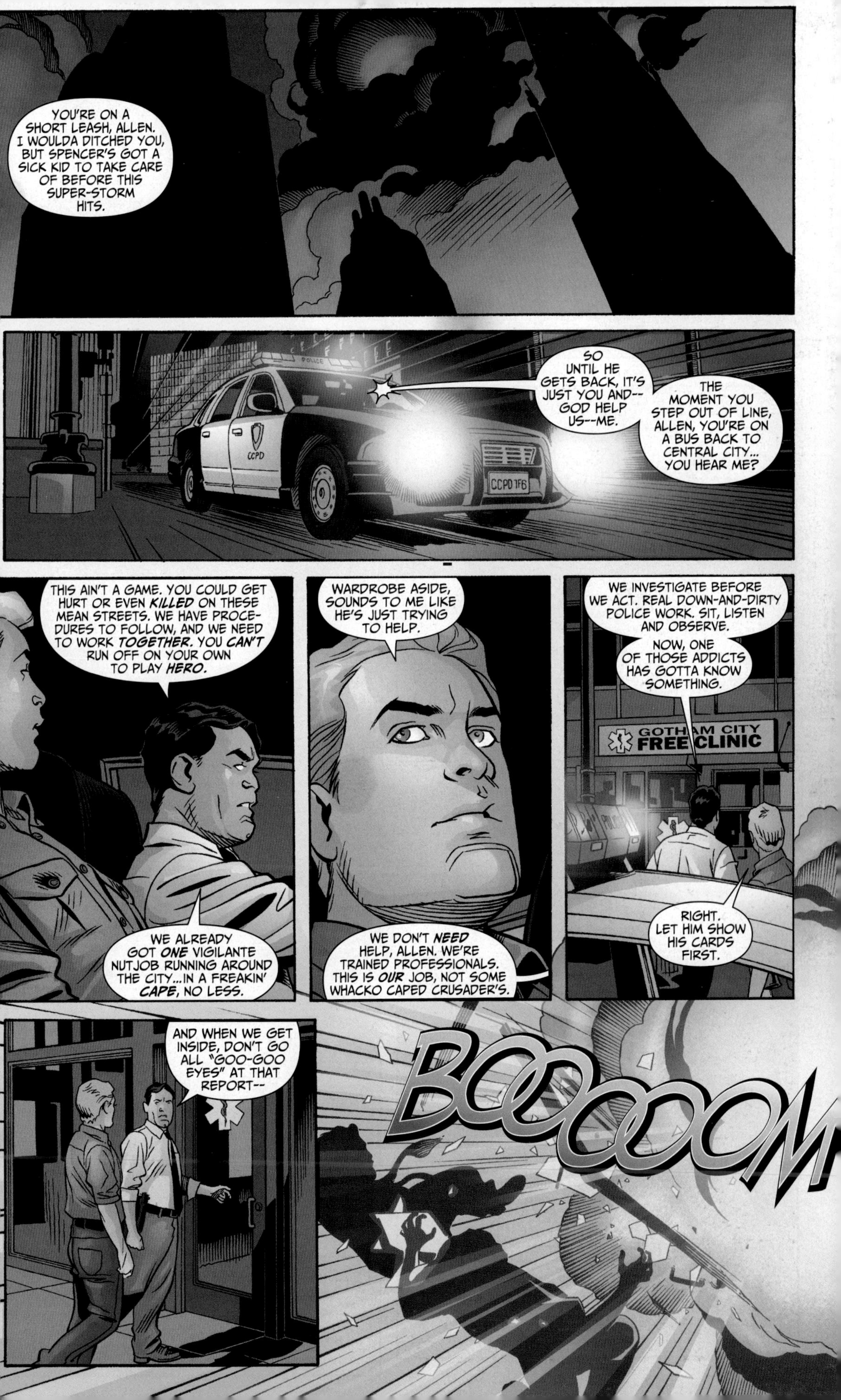

YOU'RE ON A SHORT LEASH, ALLEN. I WOULDA DITCHED YOU, BUT SPENCER'S GOT A SICK KID TO TAKE CARE OF BEFORE THIS SUPER-STORM HITS.
POLICE
SO UNTIL HE GETS BACK, IT'S JUST YOU AND-- GOD HELP US--ME.
THE MOMENT YOU STEP OUT OF LINE, ALLEN, YOU'RE ON A BUS BACK TO CENTRAL CITY... YOU HEAR ME?
CCPD
CCPD 1F6
THIS AIN'T A GAME. YOU COULD GET HURT OR EVEN *KILLED* ON THESE MEAN STREETS. WE HAVE PROCE-DURES TO FOLLOW, AND WE NEED TO WORK *TOGETHER.* YOU *CAN'T* RUN OFF ON YOUR OWN TO PLAY *HERO.*
WE ALREADY GOT *ONE* VIGILANTE NUTJOB RUNNING AROUND THE CITY...IN A FREAKIN' *CAPE*, NO LESS.
WARDROBE ASIDE, SOUNDS TO ME LIKE HE'S JUST TRYING TO HELP.
WE DON'T *NEED* HELP, ALLEN. WE'RE TRAINED PROFESSIONALS. THIS IS *OUR* JOB, NOT SOME WHACKO CAPED CRUSADER'S.
WE INVESTIGATE BEFORE WE ACT. REAL DOWN-AND-DIRTY POLICE WORK. SIT, LISTEN AND OBSERVE.
NOW, ONE OF THOSE ADDICTS HAS GOTTA KNOW SOMETHING.
GOTHAM CITY FREE CLINIC
RIGHT. LET HIM SHOW HIS CARDS FIRST.
AND WHEN WE GET INSIDE, DON'T GO ALL "GOO-GOO EYES" AT THAT REPORT--
BOOOOOOM

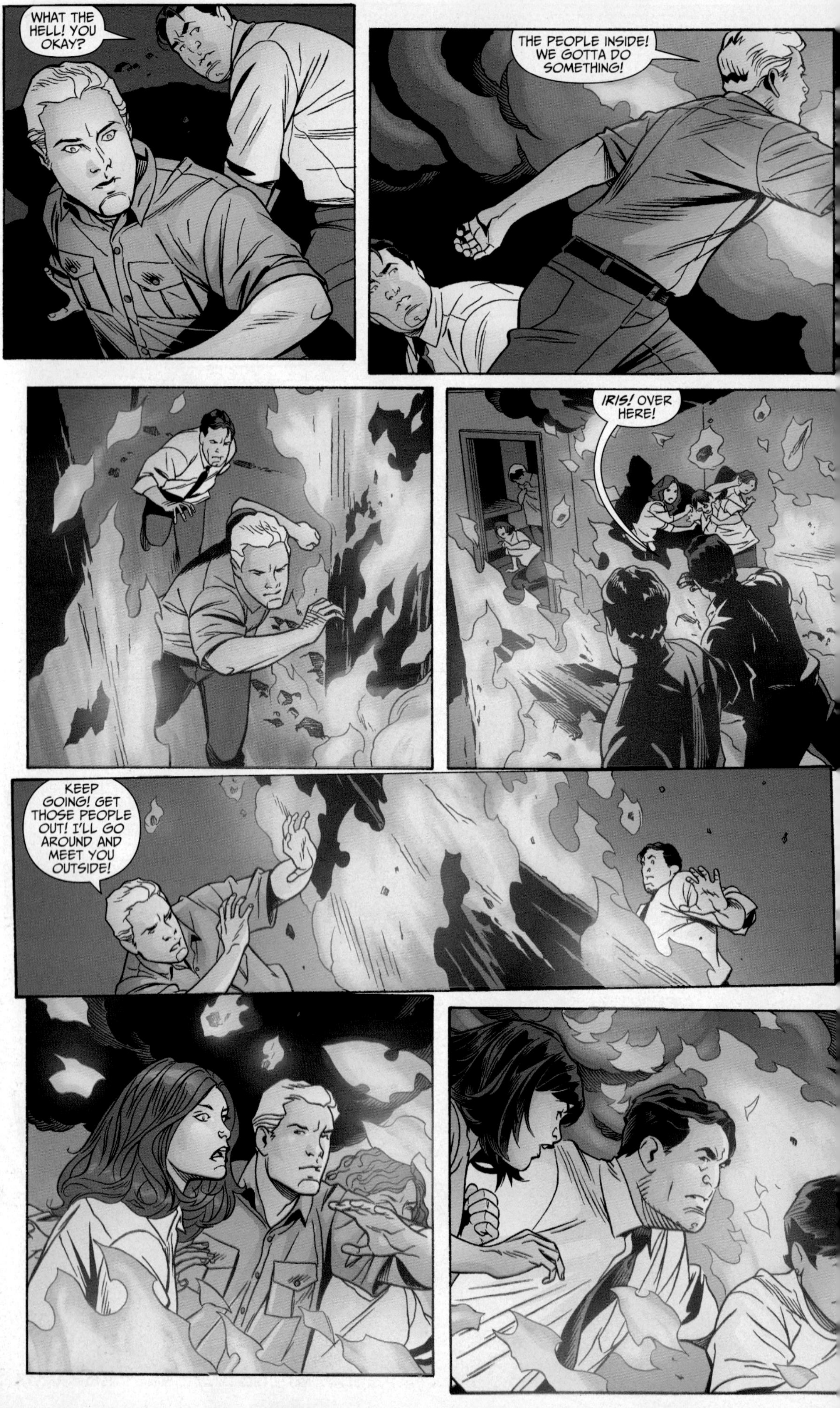
WHAT THE HELL! YOU OKAY?
THE PEOPLE INSIDE! WE GOTTA DO SOMETHING!
IRIS! OVER HERE!
KEEP GOING! GET THOSE PEOPLE OUT! I'LL GO AROUND AND MEET YOU OUTSIDE!

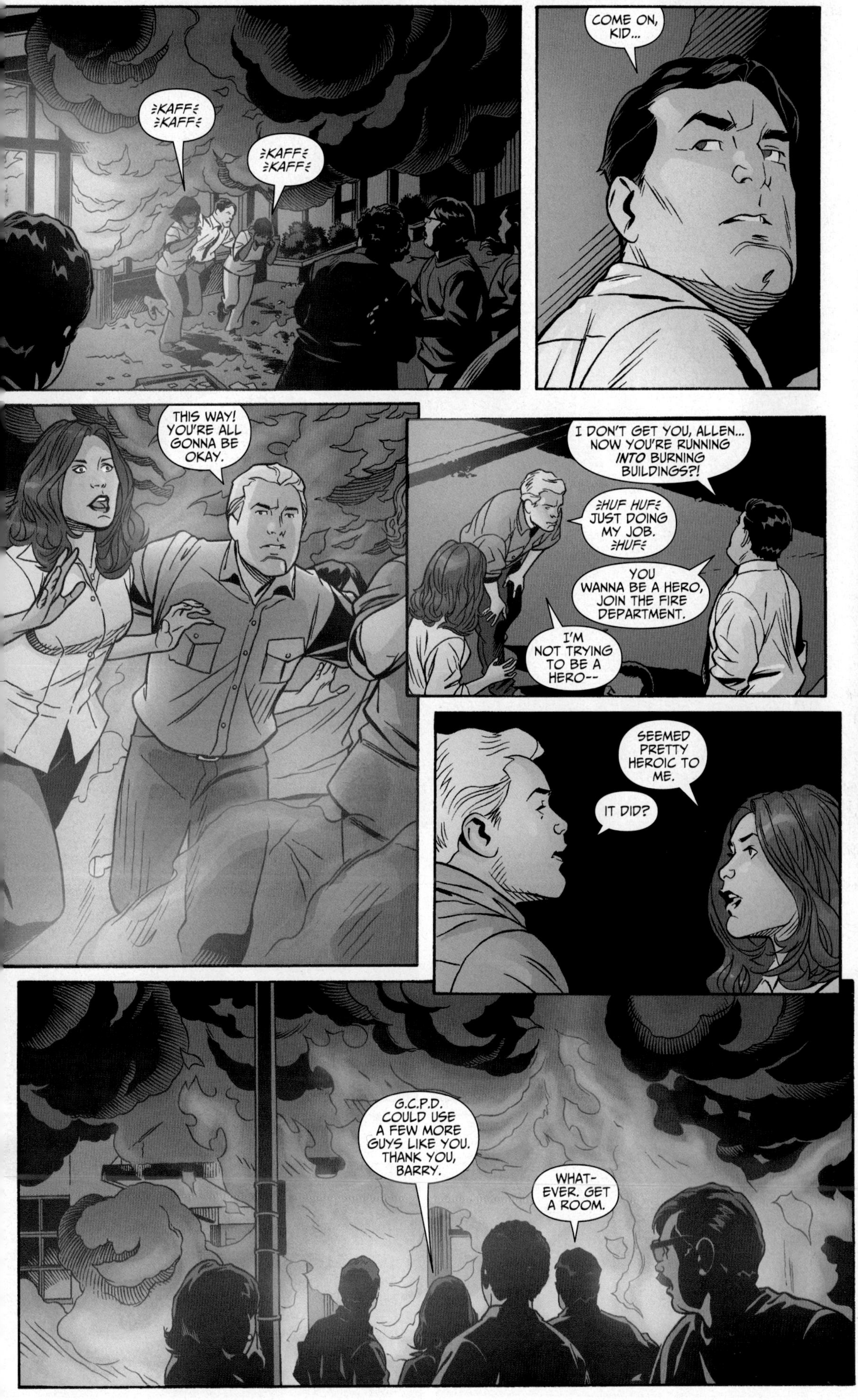

≡KAFF≡ ≡KAFF≡
≡KAFF≡ ≡KAFF≡
COME ON, KID...
THIS WAY! YOU'RE ALL GONNA BE OKAY.
I DON'T GET YOU, ALLEN... NOW YOU'RE RUNNING *INTO* BURNING BUILDINGS?!
≡HUF HUF≡ JUST DOING MY JOB. ≡HUF≡
YOU WANNA BE A HERO, JOIN THE FIRE DEPARTMENT.
I'M NOT TRYING TO BE A HERO--
SEEMED PRETTY HEROIC TO ME.
IT DID?
G.C.P.D. COULD USE A FEW MORE GUYS LIKE YOU. THANK YOU, BARRY.
WHAT-EVER. GET A ROOM.

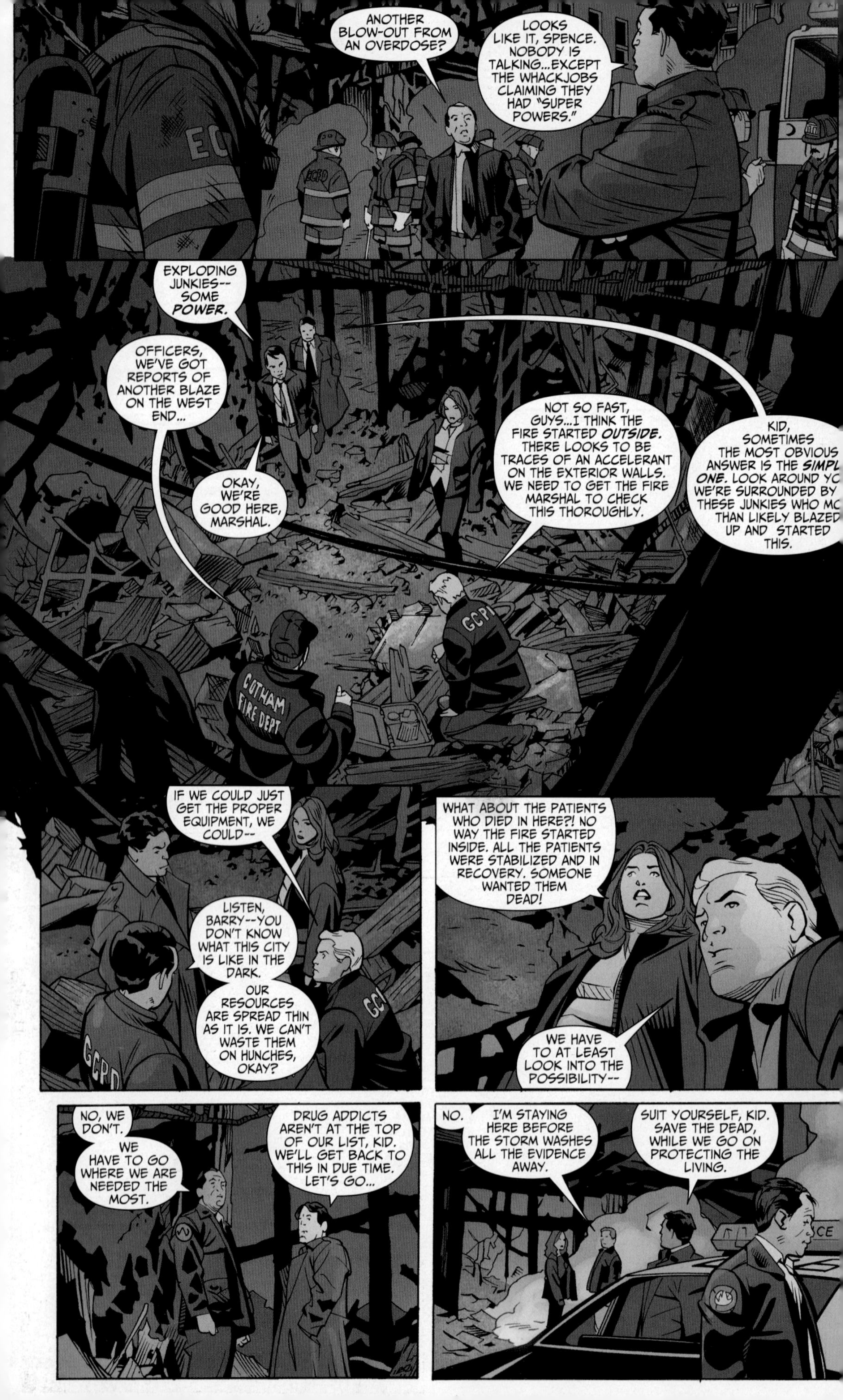
ANOTHER BLOW-OUT FROM AN OVERDOSE?
LOOKS LIKE IT, SPENCE. NOBODY IS TALKING...EXCEPT THE WHACKJOBS CLAIMING THEY HAD "SUPER POWERS."
EXPLODING JUNKIES-- SOME POWER.
OFFICERS, WE'VE GOT REPORTS OF ANOTHER BLAZE ON THE WEST END...
OKAY, WE'RE GOOD HERE, MARSHAL.
NOT SO FAST, GUYS...I THINK THE FIRE STARTED OUTSIDE. THERE LOOKS TO BE TRACES OF AN ACCELERANT ON THE EXTERIOR WALLS. WE NEED TO GET THE FIRE MARSHAL TO CHECK THIS THOROUGHLY.
KID, SOMETIMES THE MOST OBVIOUS ANSWER IS THE SIMPL ONE. LOOK AROUND YO WE'RE SURROUNDED BY THESE JUNKIES WHO MO THAN LIKELY BLAZED UP AND STARTED THIS.
IF WE COULD JUST GET THE PROPER EQUIPMENT, WE COULD--
LISTEN, BARRY--YOU DON'T KNOW WHAT THIS CITY IS LIKE IN THE DARK.
OUR RESOURCES ARE SPREAD THIN AS IT IS. WE CAN'T WASTE THEM ON HUNCHES, OKAY?
WHAT ABOUT THE PATIENTS WHO DIED IN HERE?! NO WAY THE FIRE STARTED INSIDE. ALL THE PATIENTS WERE STABILIZED AND IN RECOVERY. SOMEONE WANTED THEM DEAD!
WE HAVE TO AT LEAST LOOK INTO THE POSSIBILITY--
NO, WE DON'T.
WE HAVE TO GO WHERE WE ARE NEEDED THE MOST.
DRUG ADDICTS AREN'T AT THE TOP OF OUR LIST, KID. WE'LL GET BACK TO THIS IN DUE TIME. LET'S GO...
NO.
I'M STAYING HERE BEFORE THE STORM WASHES ALL THE EVIDENCE AWAY.
SUIT YOURSELF, KID. SAVE THE DEAD, WHILE WE GO ON PROTECTING THE LIVING.

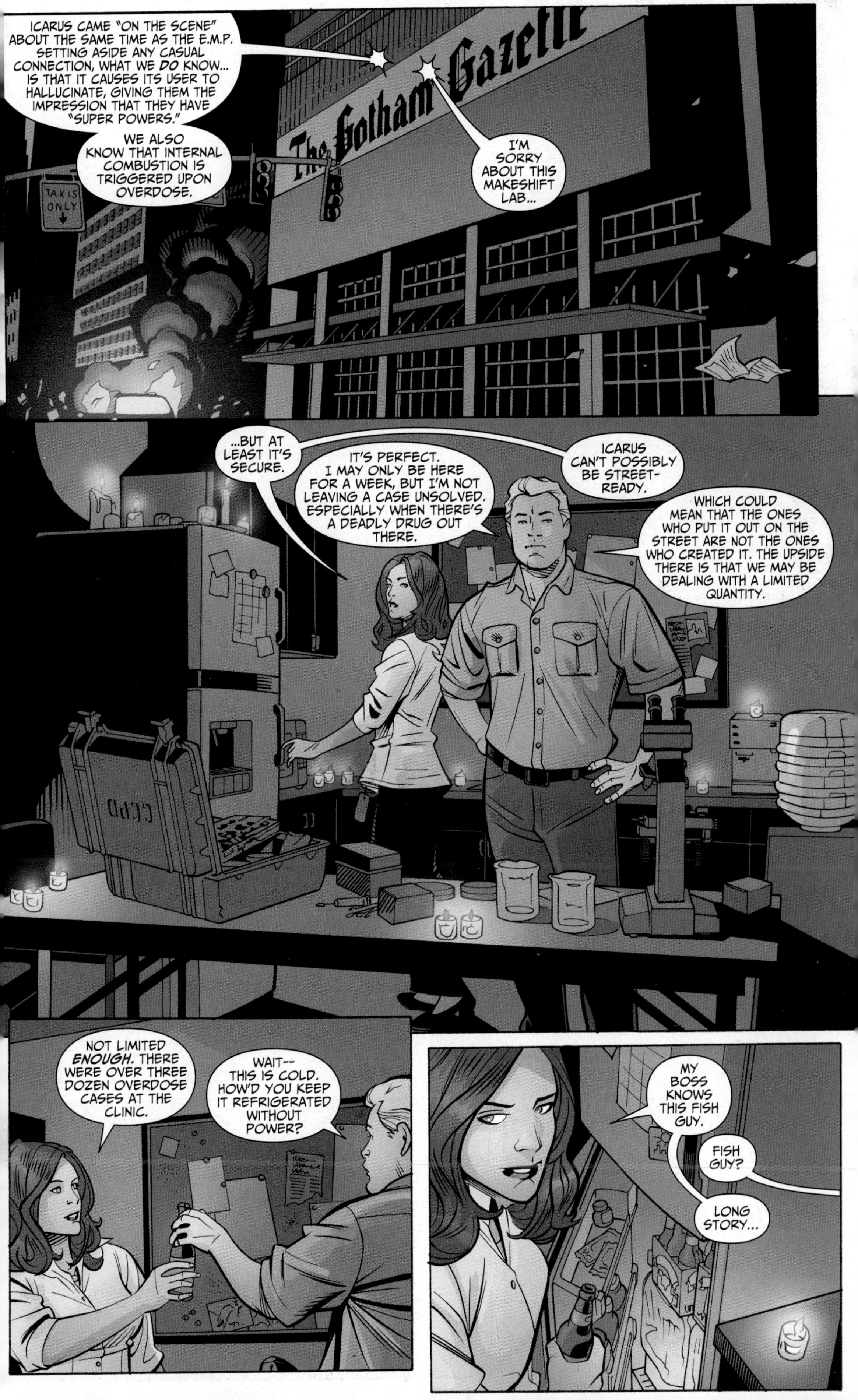

ICARUS CAME "ON THE SCENE" ABOUT THE SAME TIME AS THE E.M.P. SETTING ASIDE ANY CASUAL CONNECTION, WHAT WE *DO* KNOW... IS THAT IT CAUSES ITS USER TO HALLUCINATE, GIVING THEM THE IMPRESSION THAT THEY HAVE "SUPER POWERS."
WE ALSO KNOW THAT INTERNAL COMBUSTION IS TRIGGERED UPON OVERDOSE.
TAXIS ONLY
The Gotham Gazette
I'M SORRY ABOUT THIS MAKESHIFT LAB...
...BUT AT LEAST IT'S SECURE.
IT'S PERFECT. I MAY ONLY BE HERE FOR A WEEK, BUT I'M NOT LEAVING A CASE UNSOLVED. ESPECIALLY WHEN THERE'S A DEADLY DRUG OUT THERE.
ICARUS CAN'T POSSIBLY BE STREET-READY.
WHICH COULD MEAN THAT THE ONES WHO PUT IT OUT ON THE STREET ARE NOT THE ONES WHO CREATED IT. THE UPSIDE THERE IS THAT WE MAY BE DEALING WITH A LIMITED QUANTITY.
GCPD
NOT LIMITED *ENOUGH.* THERE WERE OVER THREE DOZEN OVERDOSE CASES AT THE CLINIC.
WAIT-- THIS IS COLD. HOW'D YOU KEEP IT REFRIGERATED WITHOUT POWER?
MY BOSS KNOWS THIS FISH GUY.
FISH GUY?
LONG STORY...

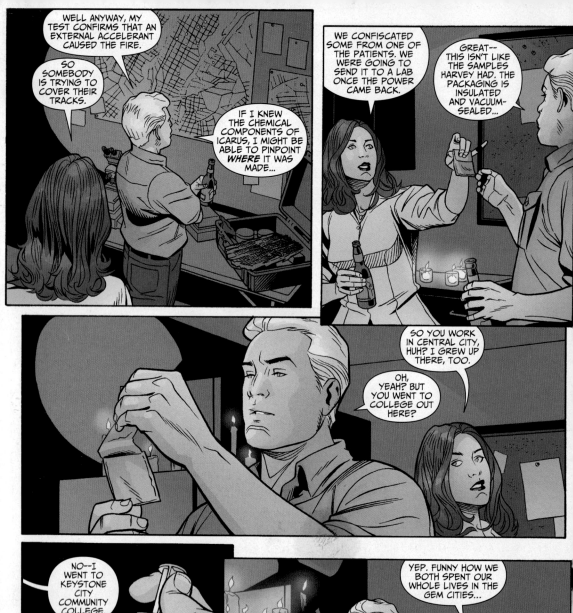

WELL ANYWAY, MY TEST CONFIRMS THAT AN EXTERNAL ACCELERANT CAUSED THE FIRE.

SO SOMEBODY IS TRYING TO COVER THEIR TRACKS.

IF I KNEW THE CHEMICAL COMPONENTS OF ICARUS, I MIGHT BE ABLE TO PINPOINT **WHERE** IT WAS MADE...

WE CONFISCATED SOME FROM ONE OF THE PATIENTS. WE WERE GOING TO SEND IT TO A LAB ONCE THE POWER CAME BACK.

GREAT-- THIS ISN'T LIKE THE SAMPLES HARVEY HAD. THE PACKAGING IS INSULATED AND VACUUM-SEALED...

SO YOU WORK IN CENTRAL CITY, HUH? I GREW UP THERE, TOO.

OH, YEAH? BUT YOU WENT TO COLLEGE OUT HERE?

NO--I WENT TO KEYSTONE CITY COMMUNITY COLLEGE.

WOW. CENTRAL AND KEYSTONE. SO YOU'RE TRULY A GEM CITIES CITIZEN.

YEP. FUNNY HOW WE BOTH SPENT OUR WHOLE LIVES IN THE GEM CITIES...

BUT IT TOOK A BLACKOUT IN GOTHAM FOR US MEET...

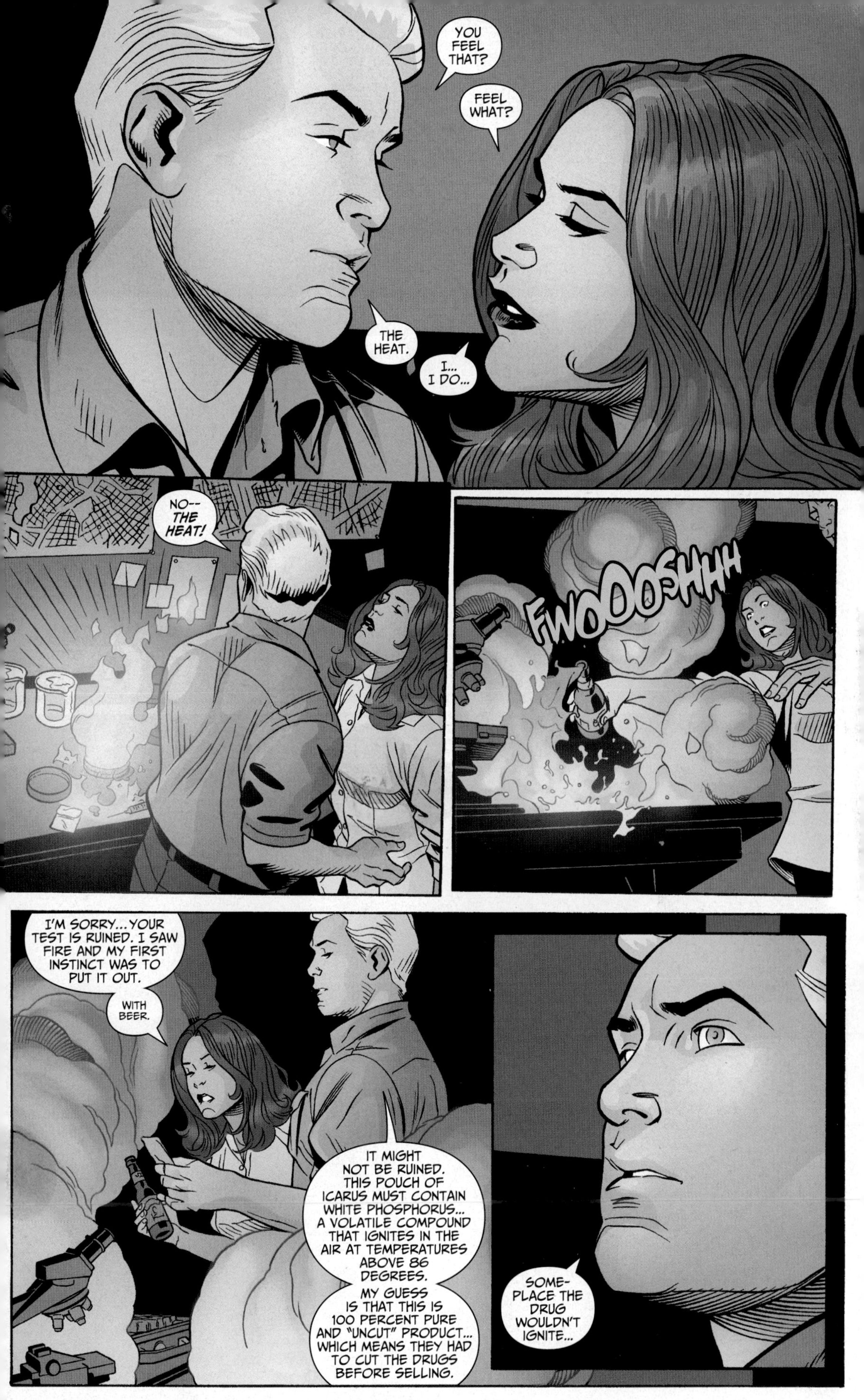
YOU FEEL THAT?
FEEL WHAT?
THE HEAT.
I... I DO...
NO-- THE HEAT!
FWOOOOSHHH
I'M SORRY... YOUR TEST IS RUINED. I SAW FIRE AND MY FIRST INSTINCT WAS TO PUT IT OUT.
WITH BEER.
IT MIGHT NOT BE RUINED. THIS POUCH OF ICARUS MUST CONTAIN WHITE PHOSPHORUS... A VOLATILE COMPOUND THAT IGNITES IN THE AIR AT TEMPERATURES ABOVE 86 DEGREES.
MY GUESS IS THAT THIS IS 100 PERCENT PURE AND "UNCUT" PRODUCT... WHICH MEANS THEY HAD TO CUT THE DRUGS BEFORE SELLING.
SOME-PLACE THE DRUG WOULDN'T IGNITE...

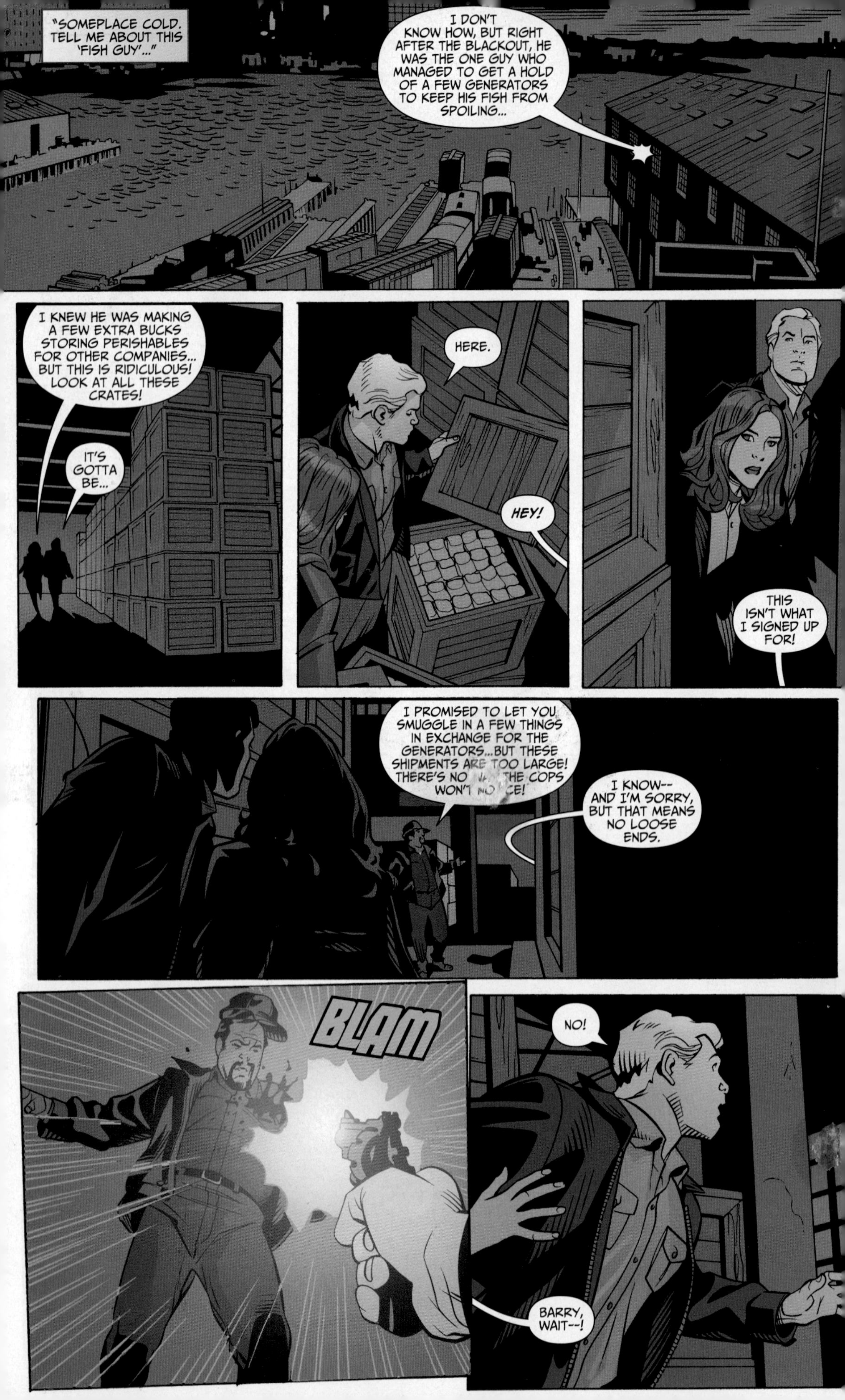
"SOMEPLACE COLD. TELL ME ABOUT THIS 'FISH GUY'..."
I DON'T KNOW HOW, BUT RIGHT AFTER THE BLACKOUT, HE WAS THE ONE GUY WHO MANAGED TO GET A HOLD OF A FEW GENERATORS TO KEEP HIS FISH FROM SPOILING...
I KNEW HE WAS MAKING A FEW EXTRA BUCKS STORING PERISHABLES FOR OTHER COMPANIES... BUT THIS IS RIDICULOUS! LOOK AT ALL THESE CRATES!
IT'S GOTTA BE...
HERE.
HEY!
THIS ISN'T WHAT I SIGNED UP FOR!
I PROMISED TO LET YOU SMUGGLE IN A FEW THINGS IN EXCHANGE FOR THE GENERATORS...BUT THESE SHIPMENTS ARE TOO LARGE! THERE'S NO WAY THE COPS WON'T NOTICE!
I KNOW-- AND I'M SORRY, BUT THAT MEANS NO LOOSE ENDS.
BLAM
NO!
BARRY, WAIT--!

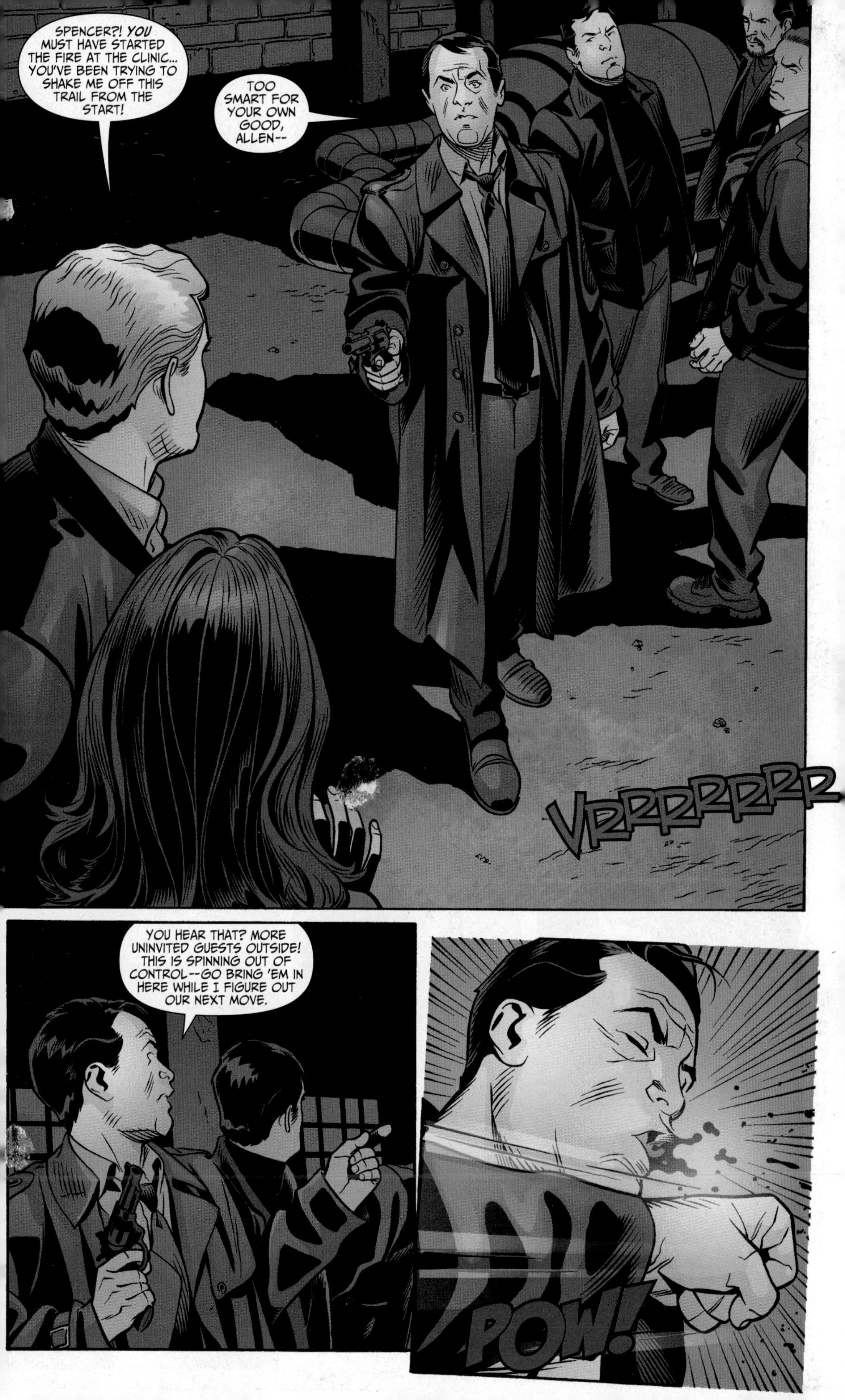
SPENCER?! *YOU* MUST HAVE STARTED THE FIRE AT THE CLINIC... YOU'VE BEEN TRYING TO SHAKE ME OFF THIS TRAIL FROM THE START!
TOO SMART FOR YOUR OWN GOOD, ALLEN--
VRRRRRRR
YOU HEAR THAT? MORE UNINVITED GUESTS OUTSIDE! THIS IS SPINNING OUT OF CONTROL--GO BRING 'EM IN HERE WHILE I FIGURE OUT OUR NEXT MOVE.
POW!

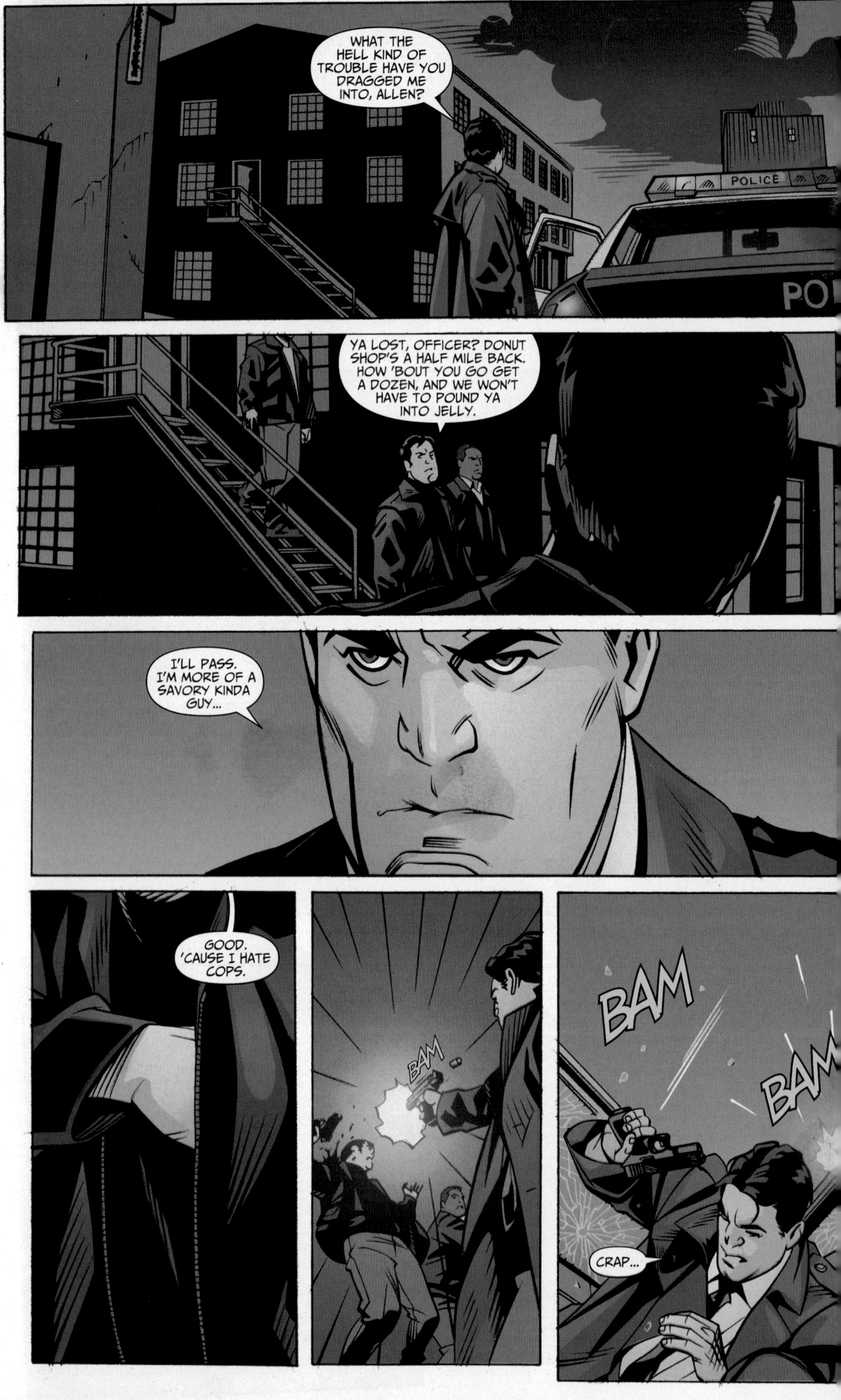
WHAT THE HELL KIND OF TROUBLE HAVE YOU DRAGGED ME INTO, ALLEN?
POLICE
PO
YA LOST, OFFICER? DONUT SHOP'S A HALF MILE BACK. HOW 'BOUT YOU GO GET A DOZEN, AND WE WON'T HAVE TO POUND YA INTO JELLY.
I'LL PASS. I'M MORE OF A SAVORY KINDA GUY...
GOOD. 'CAUSE I HATE COPS.
BAM
BAM
BAM
CRAP...

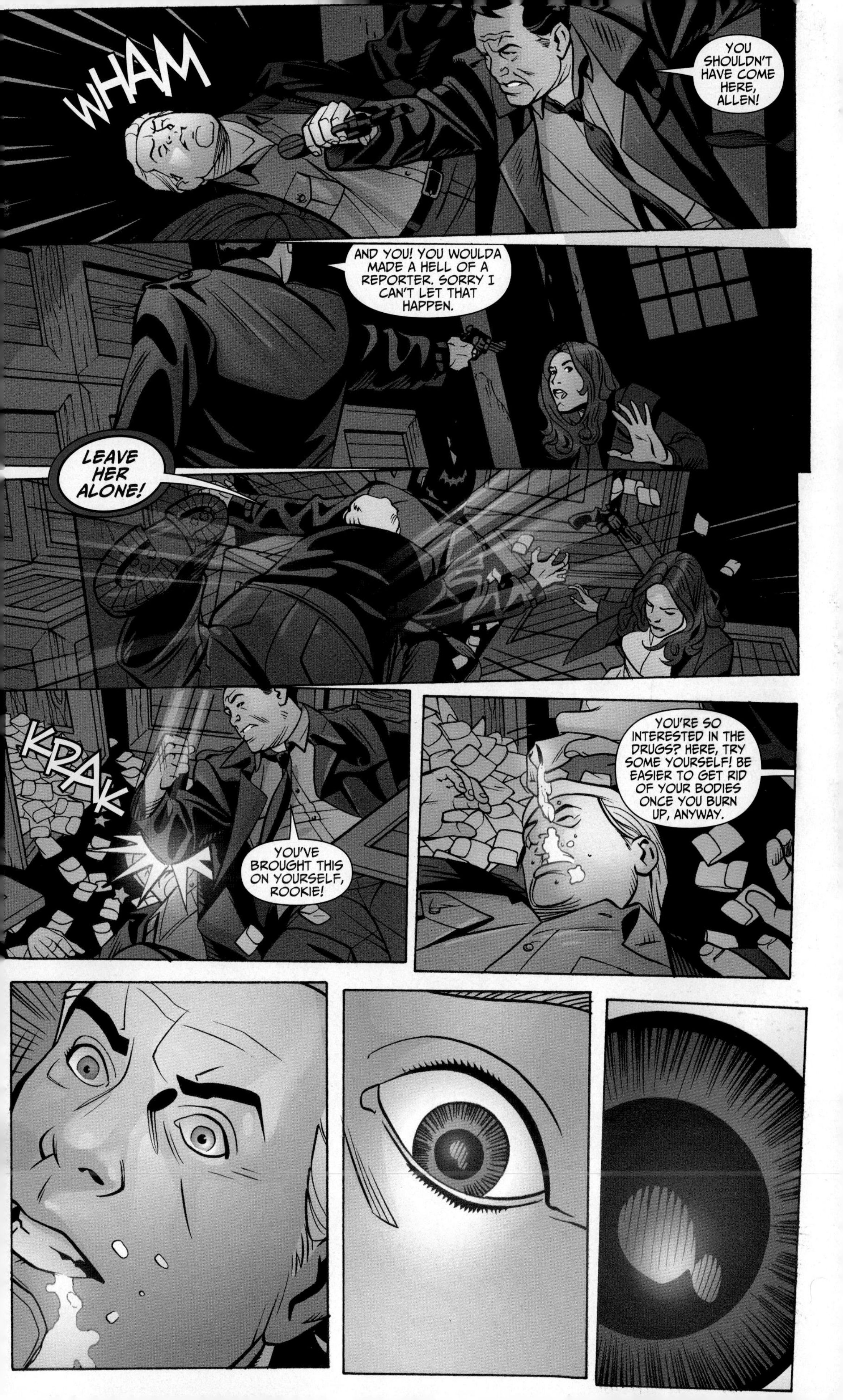
WHAM
YOU SHOULDN'T HAVE COME HERE, ALLEN!
AND YOU! YOU WOULDA MADE A HELL OF A REPORTER. SORRY I CAN'T LET THAT HAPPEN.
LEAVE HER ALONE!
KRAK
YOU'VE BROUGHT THIS ON YOURSELF, ROOKIE!
YOU'RE SO INTERESTED IN THE DRUGS? HERE, TRY SOME YOURSELF! BE EASIER TO GET RID OF YOUR BODIES ONCE YOU BURN UP, ANYWAY.

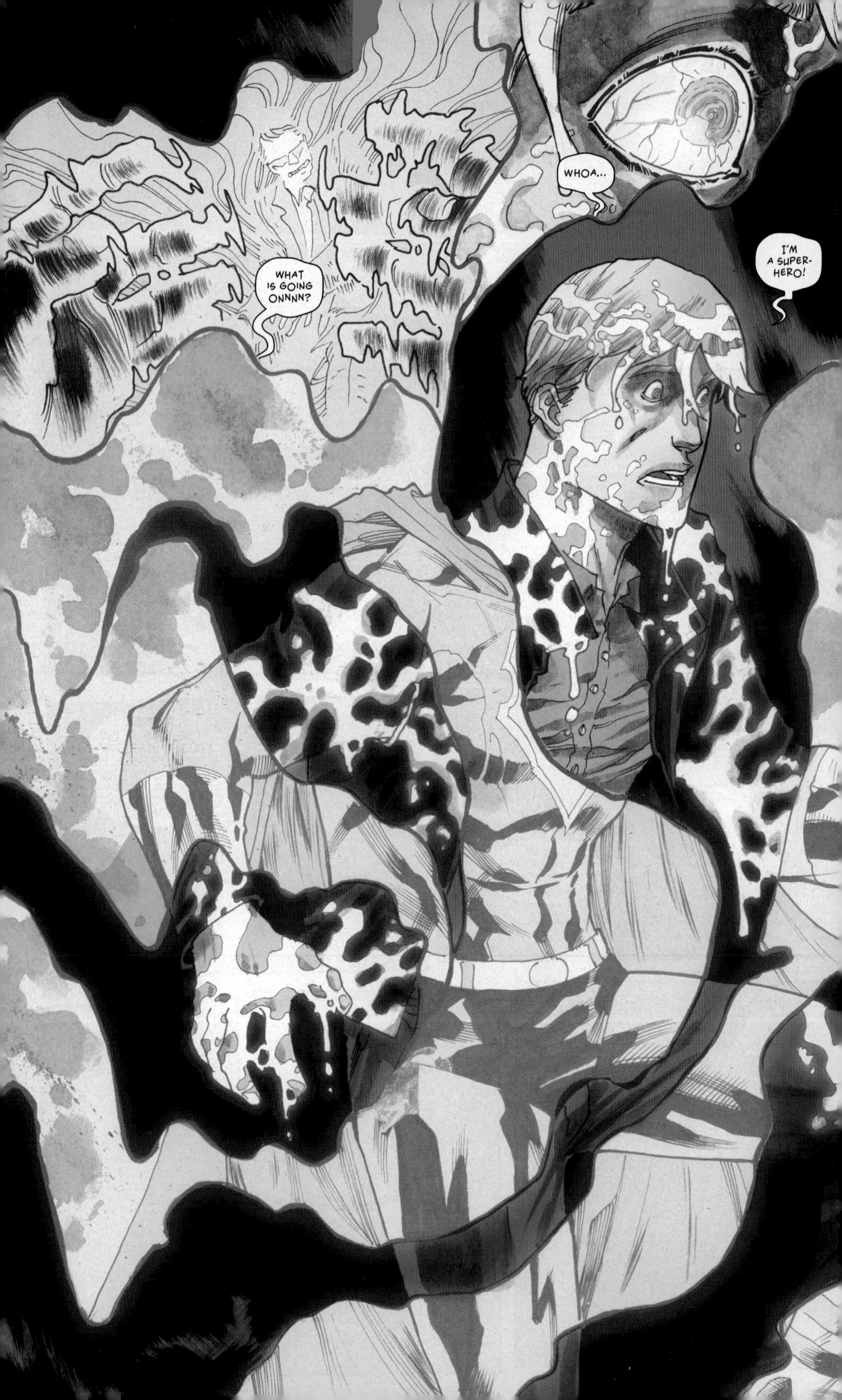
WHAT IS GOING ONNNN?
WHOA...
I'M A SUPER-HERO!

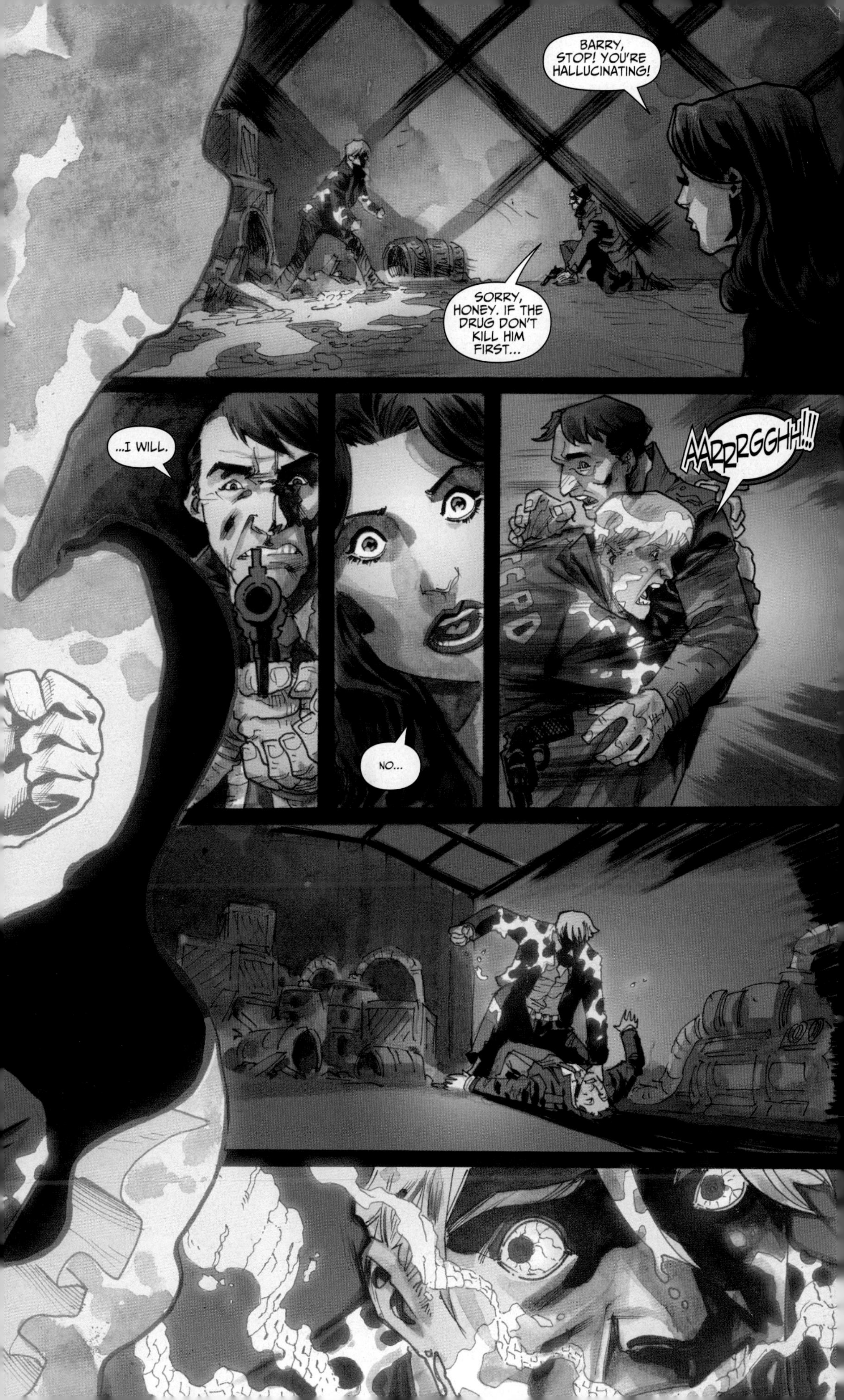
BARRY, STOP! YOU'RE HALLUCINATING!
SORRY, HONEY. IF THE DRUG DON'T KILL HIM FIRST...
...I WILL.
NO...
AARRRGGHH!!!

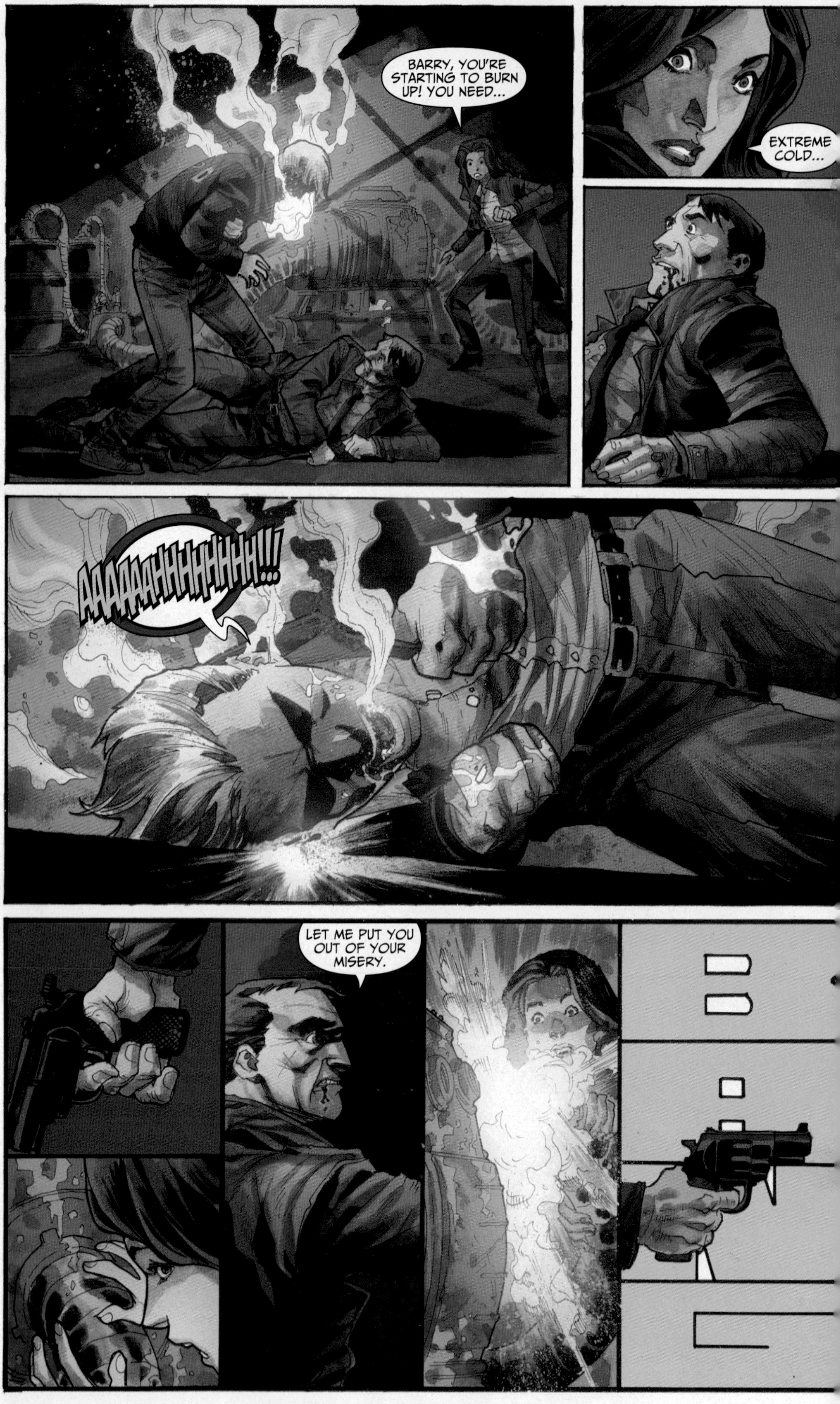
BARRY, YOU'RE STARTING TO BURN UP! YOU NEED...
EXTREME COLD...
AAAAAHHHHHHHH!!!
LET ME PUT YOU OUT OF YOUR MISERY.

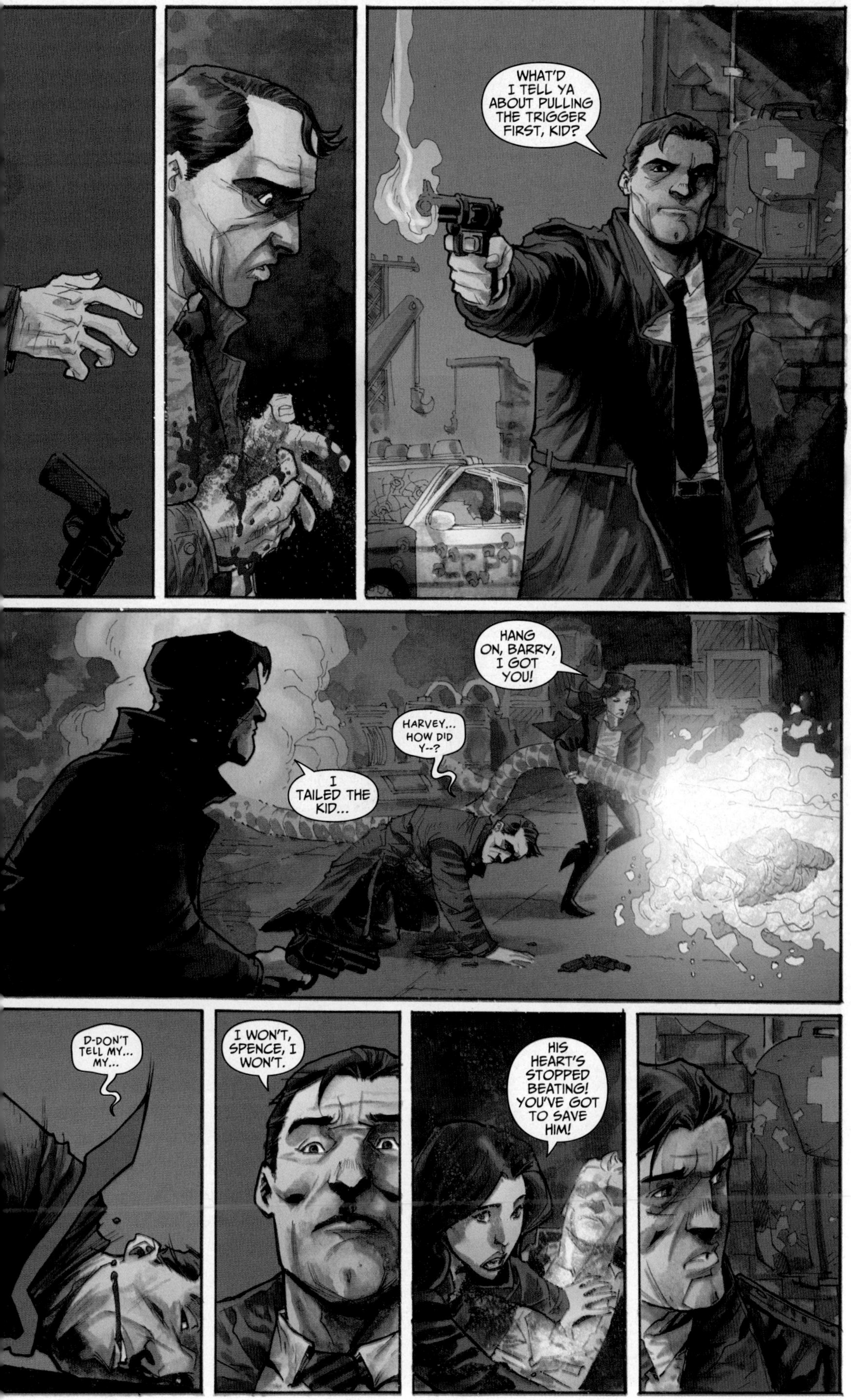
WHAT'D I TELL YA ABOUT PULLING THE TRIGGER FIRST, KID?
HANG ON, BARRY, I GOT YOU!
HARVEY... HOW DID Y--?
I TAILED THE KID...
D-DON'T TELL MY... MY...
I WON'T, SPENCE, I WON'T.
HIS HEART'S STOPPED BEATING! YOU'VE GOT TO SAVE HIM!

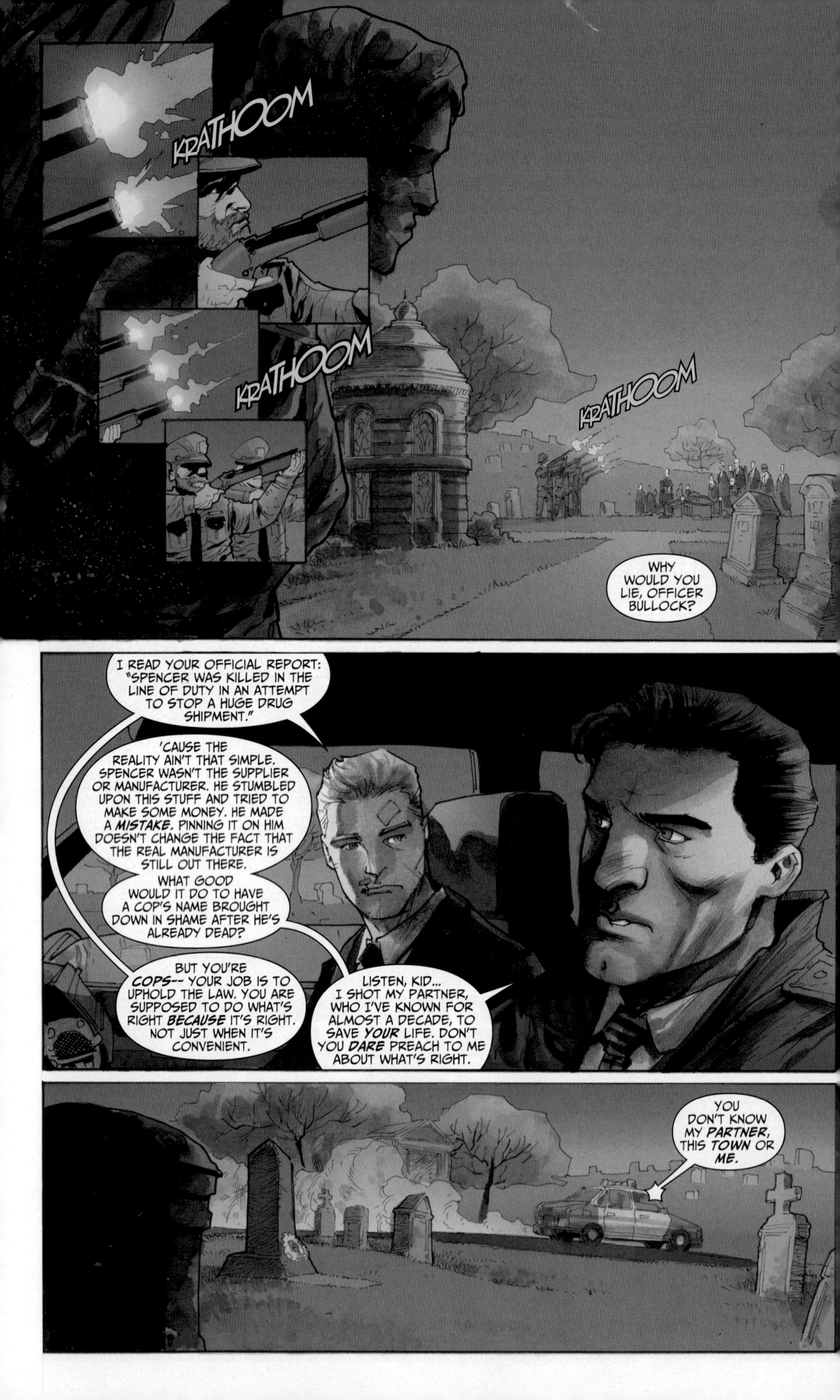
KRATHOOM
KRATHOOM
KRATHOOM
WHY WOULD YOU LIE, OFFICER BULLOCK?
I READ YOUR OFFICIAL REPORT: "SPENCER WAS KILLED IN THE LINE OF DUTY IN AN ATTEMPT TO STOP A HUGE DRUG SHIPMENT."
'CAUSE THE REALITY AIN'T THAT SIMPLE. SPENCER WASN'T THE SUPPLIER OR MANUFACTURER. HE STUMBLED UPON THIS STUFF AND TRIED TO MAKE SOME MONEY. HE MADE A MISTAKE. PINNING IT ON HIM DOESN'T CHANGE THE FACT THAT THE REAL MANUFACTURER IS STILL OUT THERE.
WHAT GOOD WOULD IT DO TO HAVE A COP'S NAME BROUGHT DOWN IN SHAME AFTER HE'S ALREADY DEAD?
BUT YOU'RE COPS-- YOUR JOB IS TO UPHOLD THE LAW. YOU ARE SUPPOSED TO DO WHAT'S RIGHT BECAUSE IT'S RIGHT. NOT JUST WHEN IT'S CONVENIENT.
LISTEN, KID... I SHOT MY PARTNER, WHO I'VE KNOWN FOR ALMOST A DECADE, TO SAVE YOUR LIFE. DON'T YOU DARE PREACH TO ME ABOUT WHAT'S RIGHT.
YOU DON'T KNOW MY PARTNER, THIS TOWN OR ME.

BEING AN OUTSIDER, IT'S EASY FOR YOU TO SIT IN JUDGMENT. TRY GETTING UP IN THE MORNING AND WORKING THE NARROWS, OR CRIME ALLEY.

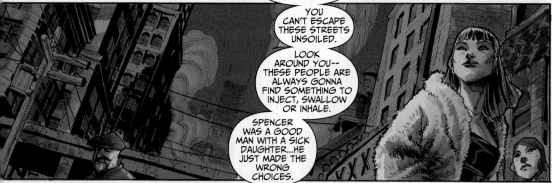

YOU CAN'T ESCAPE THESE STREETS UNSOILED.

LOOK AROUND YOU-- THESE PEOPLE ARE ALWAYS GONNA FIND SOMETHING TO INJECT, SWALLOW OR INHALE.

SPENCER WAS A GOOD MAN WITH A SICK DAUGHTER...HE JUST MADE THE WRONG CHOICES.

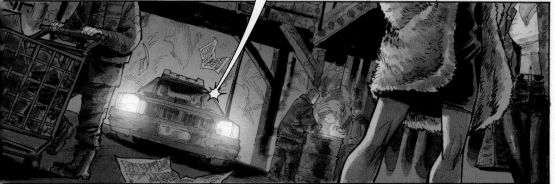

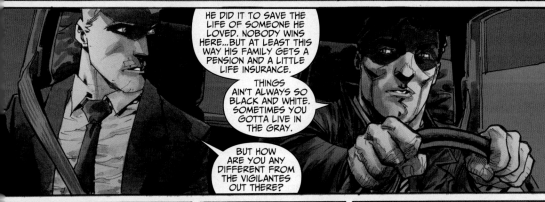

HE DID IT TO SAVE THE LIFE OF SOMEONE HE LOVED. NOBODY WINS HERE...BUT AT LEAST THIS WAY HIS FAMILY GETS A PENSION AND A LITTLE LIFE INSURANCE.

THINGS AIN'T ALWAYS SO BLACK AND WHITE. SOMETIMES YOU GOTTA LIVE IN THE GRAY.

BUT HOW ARE YOU ANY DIFFERENT FROM THE VIGILANTES OUT THERE?

TAP TAP

BETTER GO--DON'T WANT YOU TO MISS YOUR BUS.

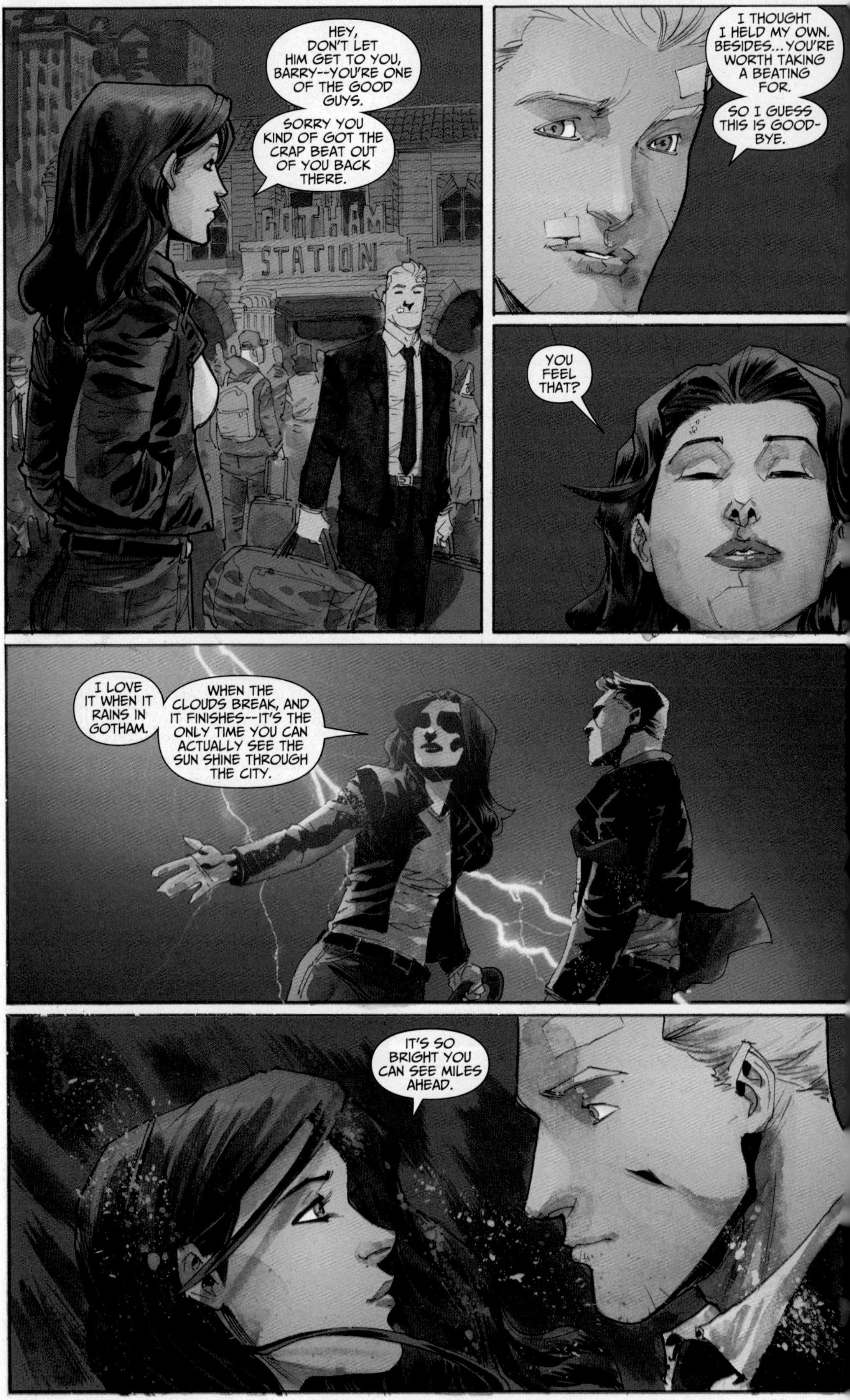
HEY, DON'T LET HIM GET TO YOU, BARRY--YOU'RE ONE OF THE GOOD GUYS.
SORRY YOU KIND OF GOT THE CRAP BEAT OUT OF YOU BACK THERE.
GOTHAM STATION
I THOUGHT I HELD MY OWN. BESIDES...YOU'RE WORTH TAKING A BEATING FOR.
SO I GUESS THIS IS GOOD-BYE.
YOU FEEL THAT?
I LOVE IT WHEN IT RAINS IN GOTHAM.
WHEN THE CLOUDS BREAK, AND IT FINISHES--IT'S THE ONLY TIME YOU CAN ACTUALLY SEE THE SUN SHINE THROUGH THE CITY.
IT'S SO BRIGHT YOU CAN SEE MILES AHEAD.

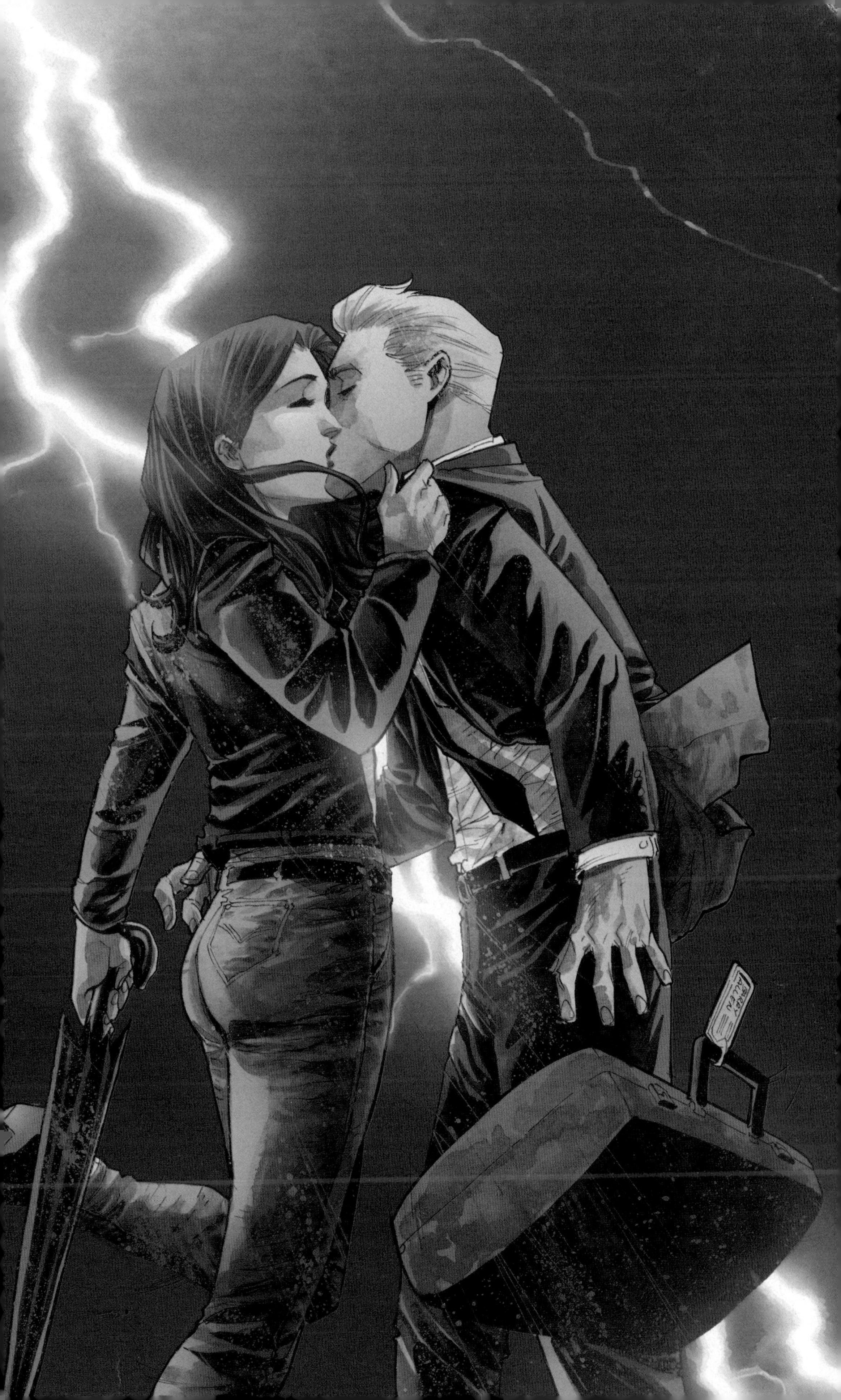
BARRY
ALLEN

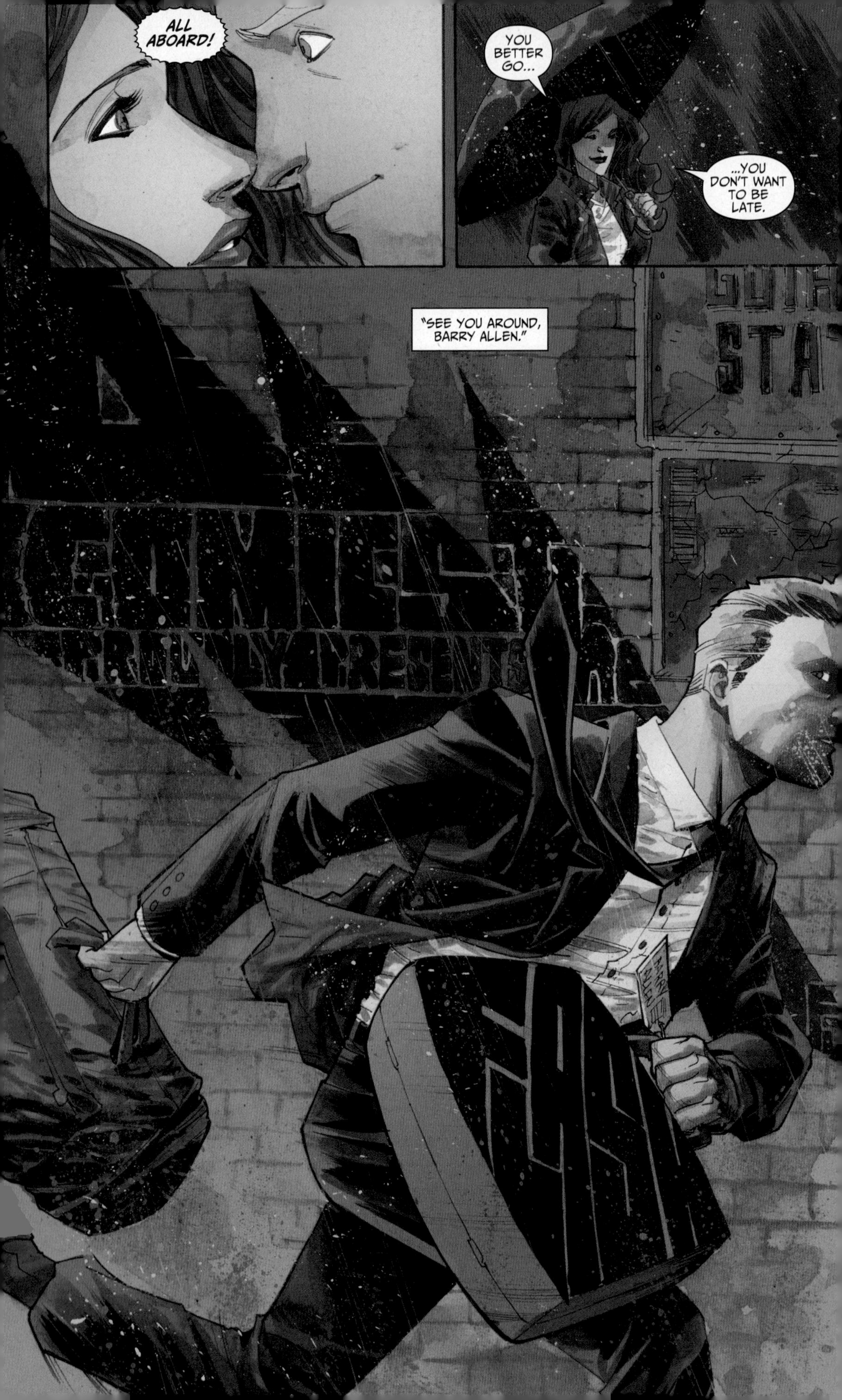
ALL ABOARD!
YOU BETTER GO...
...YOU DON'T WANT TO BE LATE.
"SEE YOU AROUND, BARRY ALLEN."

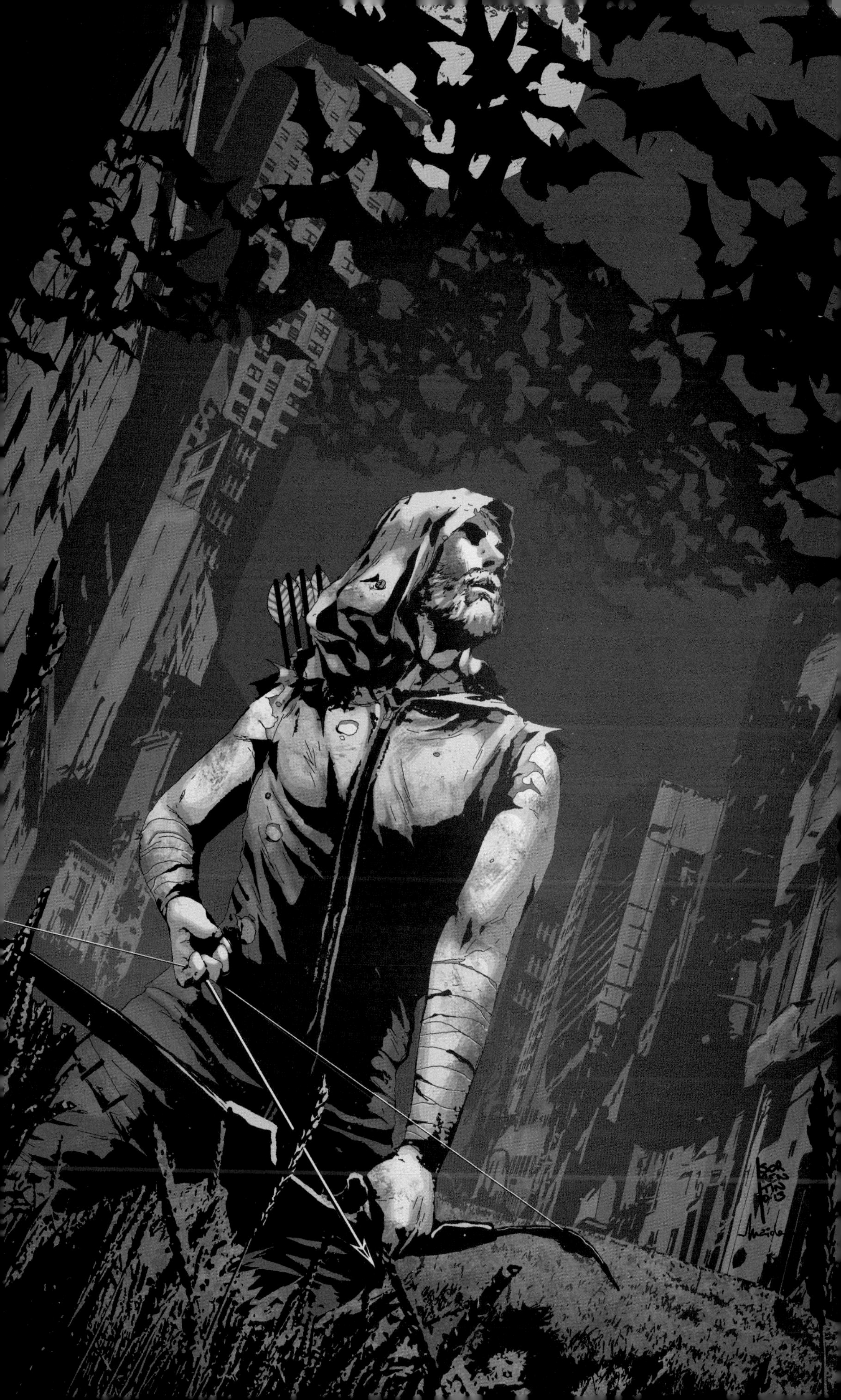

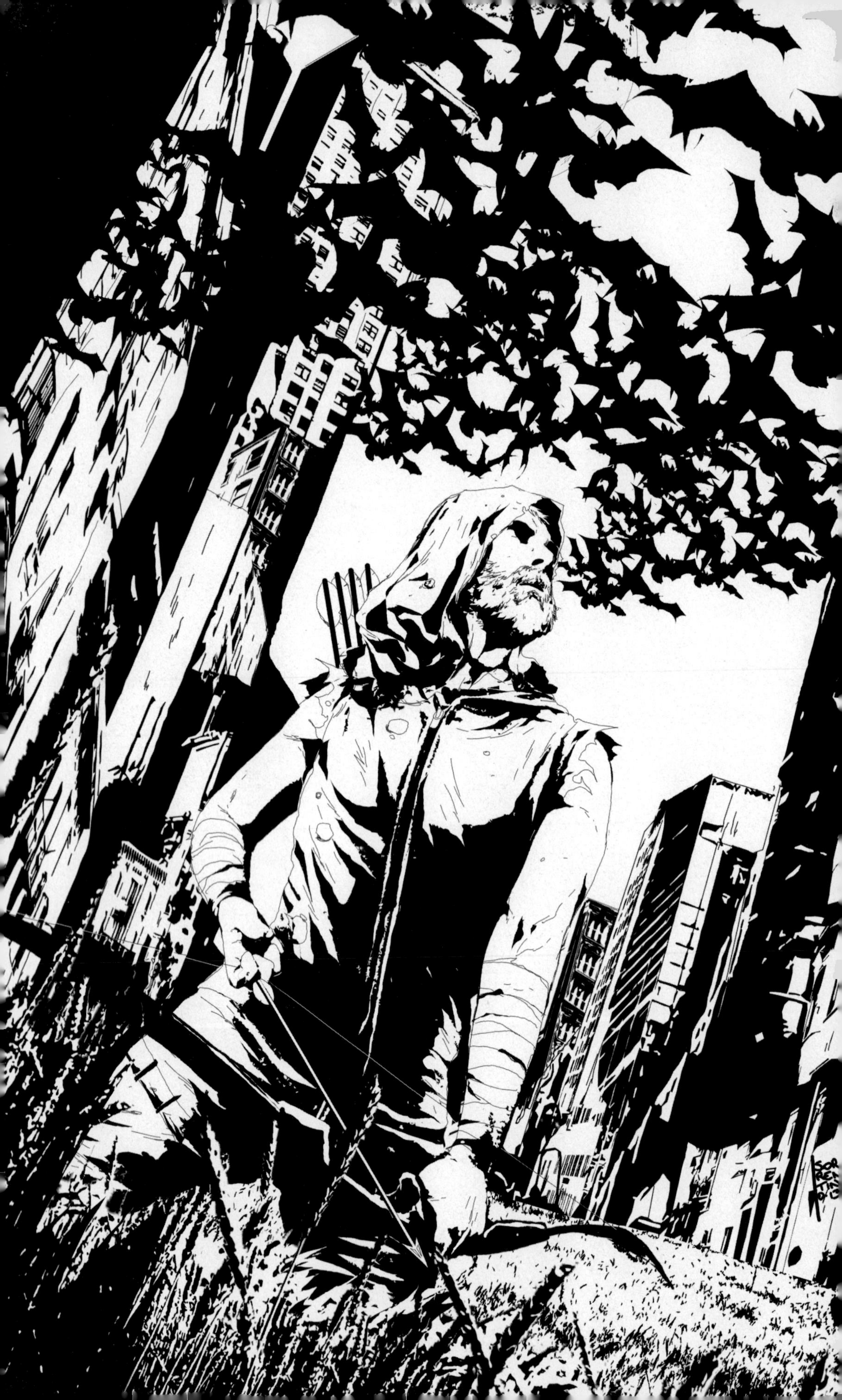

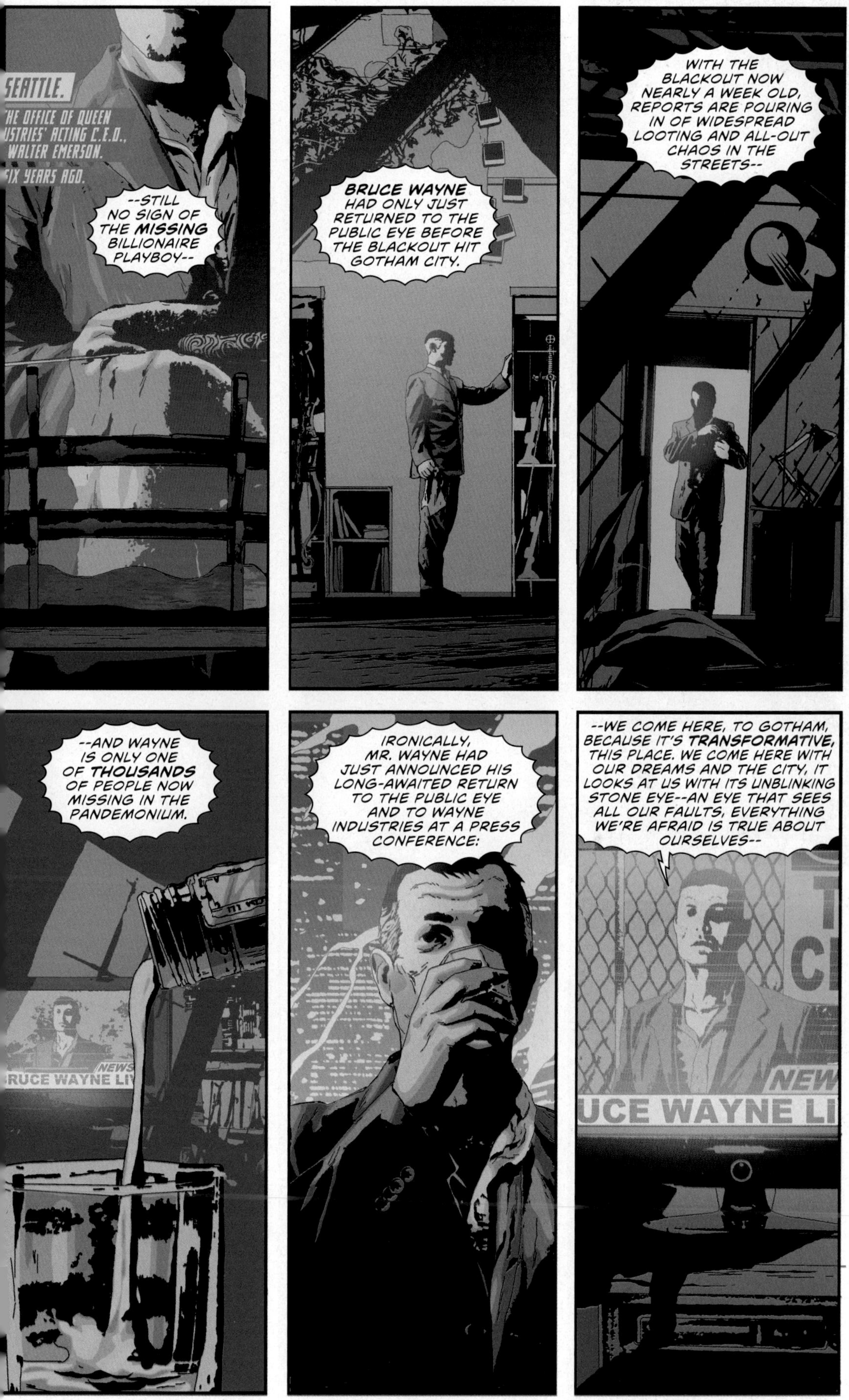
SEATTLE.
THE OFFICE OF QUEEN INDUSTRIES' ACTING C.E.O., WALTER EMERSON.
SIX YEARS AGO.
--STILL NO SIGN OF THE MISSING BILLIONAIRE PLAYBOY--
BRUCE WAYNE HAD ONLY JUST RETURNED TO THE PUBLIC EYE BEFORE THE BLACKOUT HIT GOTHAM CITY.
WITH THE BLACKOUT NOW NEARLY A WEEK OLD, REPORTS ARE POURING IN OF WIDESPREAD LOOTING AND ALL-OUT CHAOS IN THE STREETS--
--AND WAYNE IS ONLY ONE OF THOUSANDS OF PEOPLE NOW MISSING IN THE PANDEMONIUM.
NEWS
RUCE WAYNE LI
IRONICALLY, MR. WAYNE HAD JUST ANNOUNCED HIS LONG-AWAITED RETURN TO THE PUBLIC EYE AND TO WAYNE INDUSTRIES AT A PRESS CONFERENCE:
--WE COME HERE, TO GOTHAM, BECAUSE IT'S TRANSFORMATIVE, THIS PLACE. WE COME HERE WITH OUR DREAMS AND THE CITY, IT LOOKS AT US WITH ITS UNBLINKING STONE EYE--AN EYE THAT SEES ALL OUR FAULTS, EVERYTHING WE'RE AFRAID IS TRUE ABOUT OURSELVES--
NEWS
UCE WAYNE LI

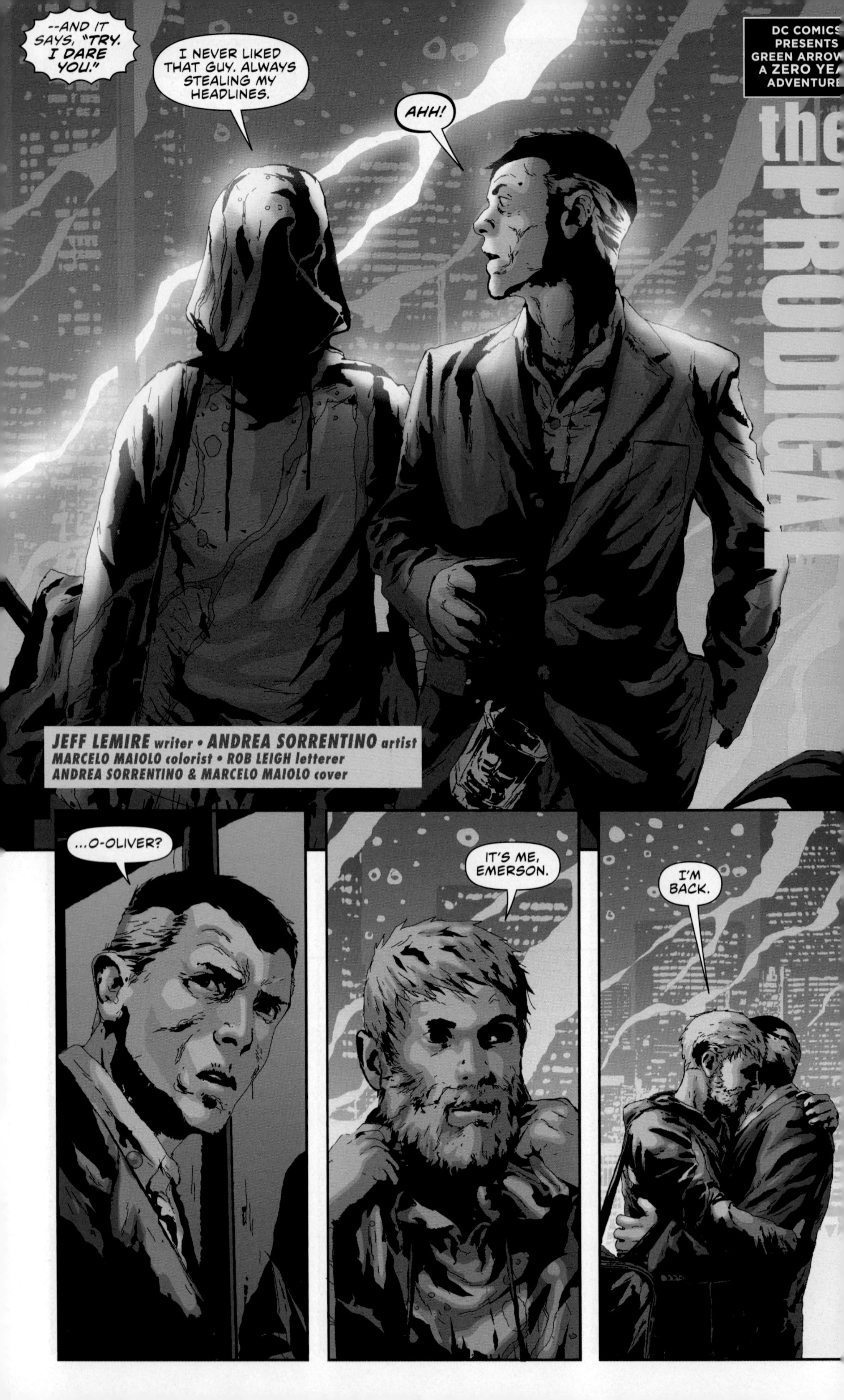
DC COMICS PRESENTS GREEN ARROW A ZERO YEA ADVENTURE
the PRODIGAL
--AND IT SAYS, "TRY. I DARE YOU."
I NEVER LIKED THAT GUY. ALWAYS STEALING MY HEADLINES.
AHH!
JEFF LEMIRE writer • ANDREA SORRENTINO artist
MARCELO MAIOLO colorist • ROB LEIGH letterer
ANDREA SORRENTINO & MARCELO MAIOLO cover
...O-OLIVER?
IT'S ME, EMERSON.
I'M BACK.

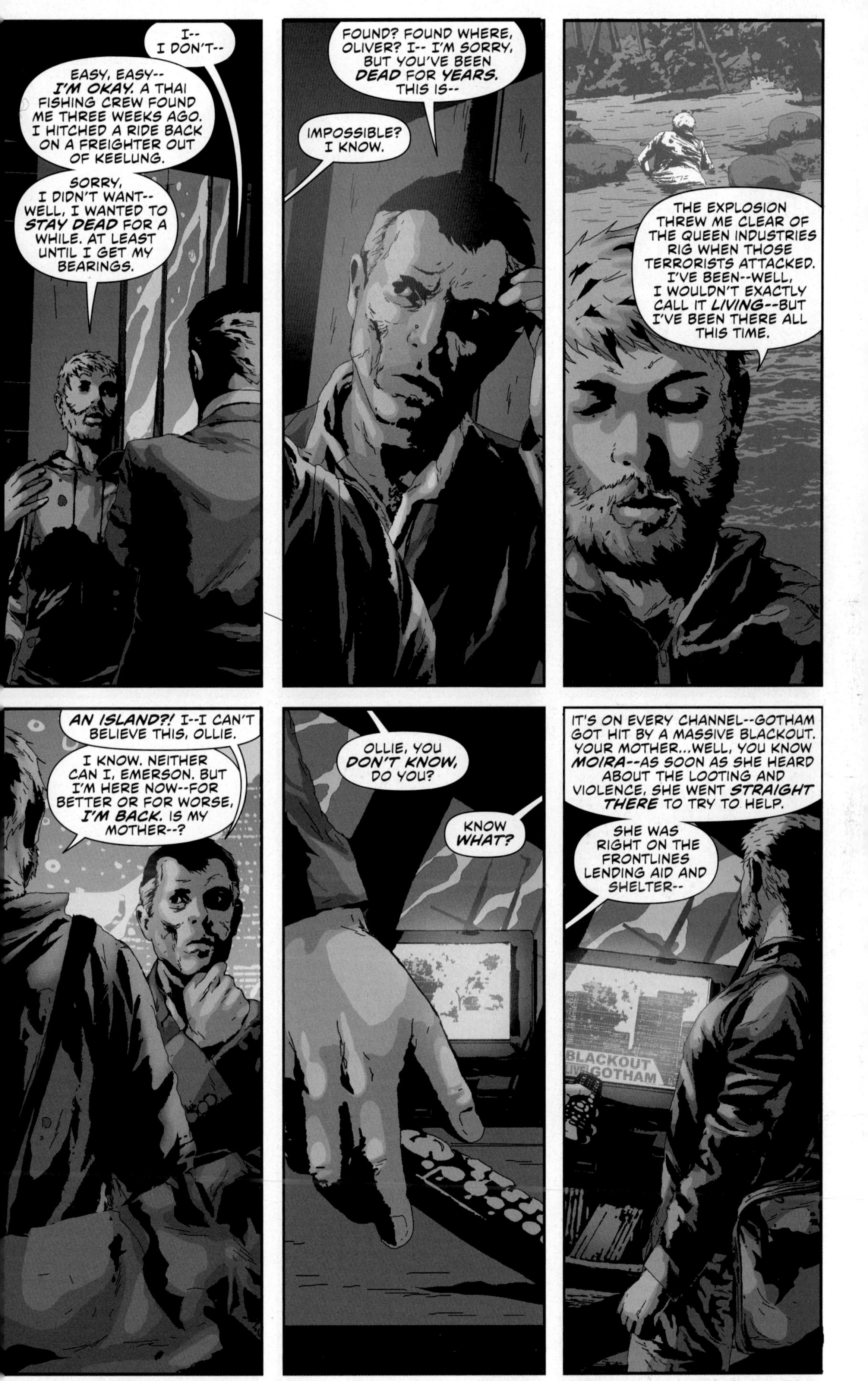

I-- I DON'T--
EASY, EASY-- I'M OKAY. A THAI FISHING CREW FOUND ME THREE WEEKS AGO. I HITCHED A RIDE BACK ON A FREIGHTER OUT OF KEELUNG.
SORRY, I DIDN'T WANT-- WELL, I WANTED TO STAY DEAD FOR A WHILE. AT LEAST UNTIL I GET MY BEARINGS.
FOUND? FOUND WHERE, OLIVER? I-- I'M SORRY, BUT YOU'VE BEEN DEAD FOR YEARS. THIS IS--
IMPOSSIBLE? I KNOW.
THE EXPLOSION THREW ME CLEAR OF THE QUEEN INDUSTRIES RIG WHEN THOSE TERRORISTS ATTACKED. I'VE BEEN--WELL, I WOULDN'T EXACTLY CALL IT LIVING--BUT I'VE BEEN THERE ALL THIS TIME.
AN ISLAND?! I--I CAN'T BELIEVE THIS, OLLIE.
I KNOW. NEITHER CAN I, EMERSON. BUT I'M HERE NOW--FOR BETTER OR FOR WORSE, I'M BACK. IS MY MOTHER--?
OLLIE, YOU DON'T KNOW, DO YOU?
KNOW WHAT?
BLACKOUT
LIVE GOTHAM
IT'S ON EVERY CHANNEL--GOTHAM GOT HIT BY A MASSIVE BLACKOUT. YOUR MOTHER...WELL, YOU KNOW MOIRA--AS SOON AS SHE HEARD ABOUT THE LOOTING AND VIOLENCE, SHE WENT STRAIGHT THERE TO TRY TO HELP.
SHE WAS RIGHT ON THE FRONTLINES LENDING AID AND SHELTER--

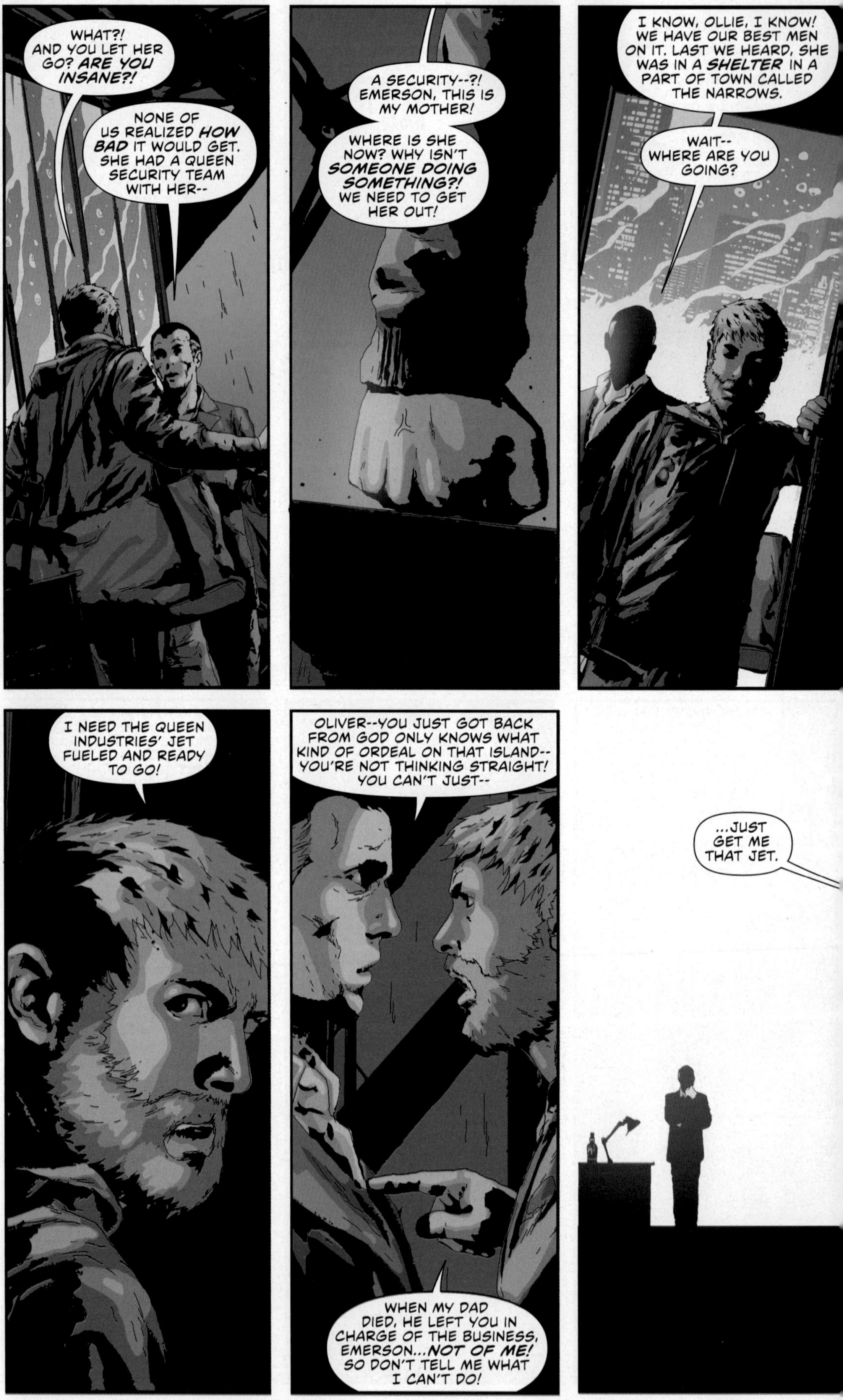
WHAT?! AND YOU LET HER GO? ARE YOU INSANE?!
NONE OF US REALIZED HOW BAD IT WOULD GET. SHE HAD A QUEEN SECURITY TEAM WITH HER--
A SECURITY--?! EMERSON, THIS IS MY MOTHER!
WHERE IS SHE NOW? WHY ISN'T SOMEONE DOING SOMETHING?! WE NEED TO GET HER OUT!
I KNOW, OLLIE, I KNOW! WE HAVE OUR BEST MEN ON IT. LAST WE HEARD, SHE WAS IN A SHELTER IN A PART OF TOWN CALLED THE NARROWS.
WAIT-- WHERE ARE YOU GOING?
I NEED THE QUEEN INDUSTRIES' JET FUELED AND READY TO GO!
OLIVER--YOU JUST GOT BACK FROM GOD ONLY KNOWS WHAT KIND OF ORDEAL ON THAT ISLAND--YOU'RE NOT THINKING STRAIGHT! YOU CAN'T JUST--
WHEN MY DAD DIED, HE LEFT YOU IN CHARGE OF THE BUSINESS, EMERSON...NOT OF ME! SO DON'T TELL ME WHAT I CAN'T DO!
...JUST GET ME THAT JET.

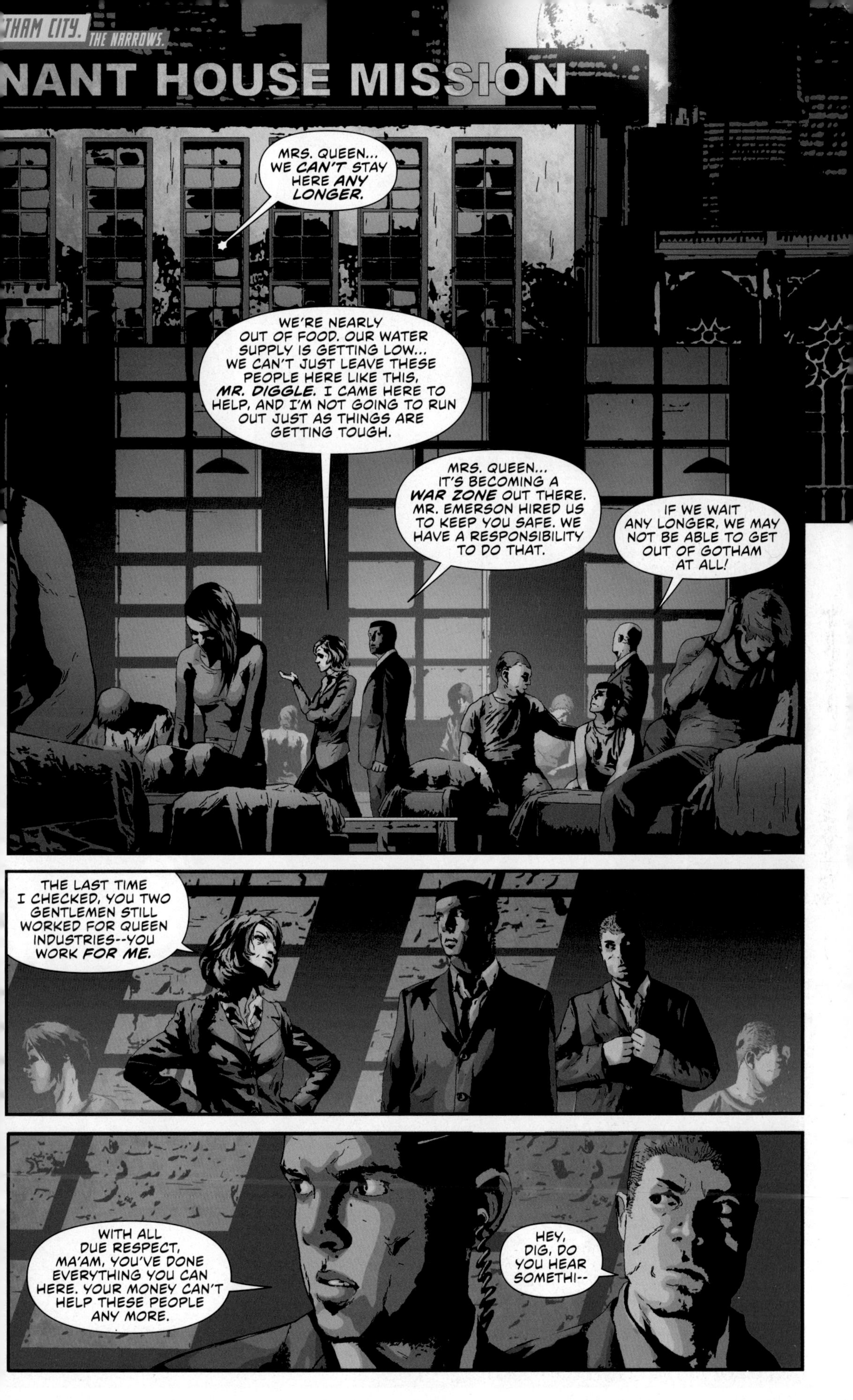
THAM CITY. THE NARROWS.
NANT HOUSE MISSION
MRS. QUEEN... WE CAN'T STAY HERE ANY LONGER.
WE'RE NEARLY OUT OF FOOD. OUR WATER SUPPLY IS GETTING LOW... WE CAN'T JUST LEAVE THESE PEOPLE HERE LIKE THIS, MR. DIGGLE. I CAME HERE TO HELP, AND I'M NOT GOING TO RUN OUT JUST AS THINGS ARE GETTING TOUGH.
MRS. QUEEN... IT'S BECOMING A WAR ZONE OUT THERE. MR. EMERSON HIRED US TO KEEP YOU SAFE. WE HAVE A RESPONSIBILITY TO DO THAT.
IF WE WAIT ANY LONGER, WE MAY NOT BE ABLE TO GET OUT OF GOTHAM AT ALL!
THE LAST TIME I CHECKED, YOU TWO GENTLEMEN STILL WORKED FOR QUEEN INDUSTRIES--YOU WORK FOR ME.
WITH ALL DUE RESPECT, MA'AM, YOU'VE DONE EVERYTHING YOU CAN HERE. YOUR MONEY CAN'T HELP THESE PEOPLE ANY MORE.
HEY, DIG, DO YOU HEAR SOMETHI--

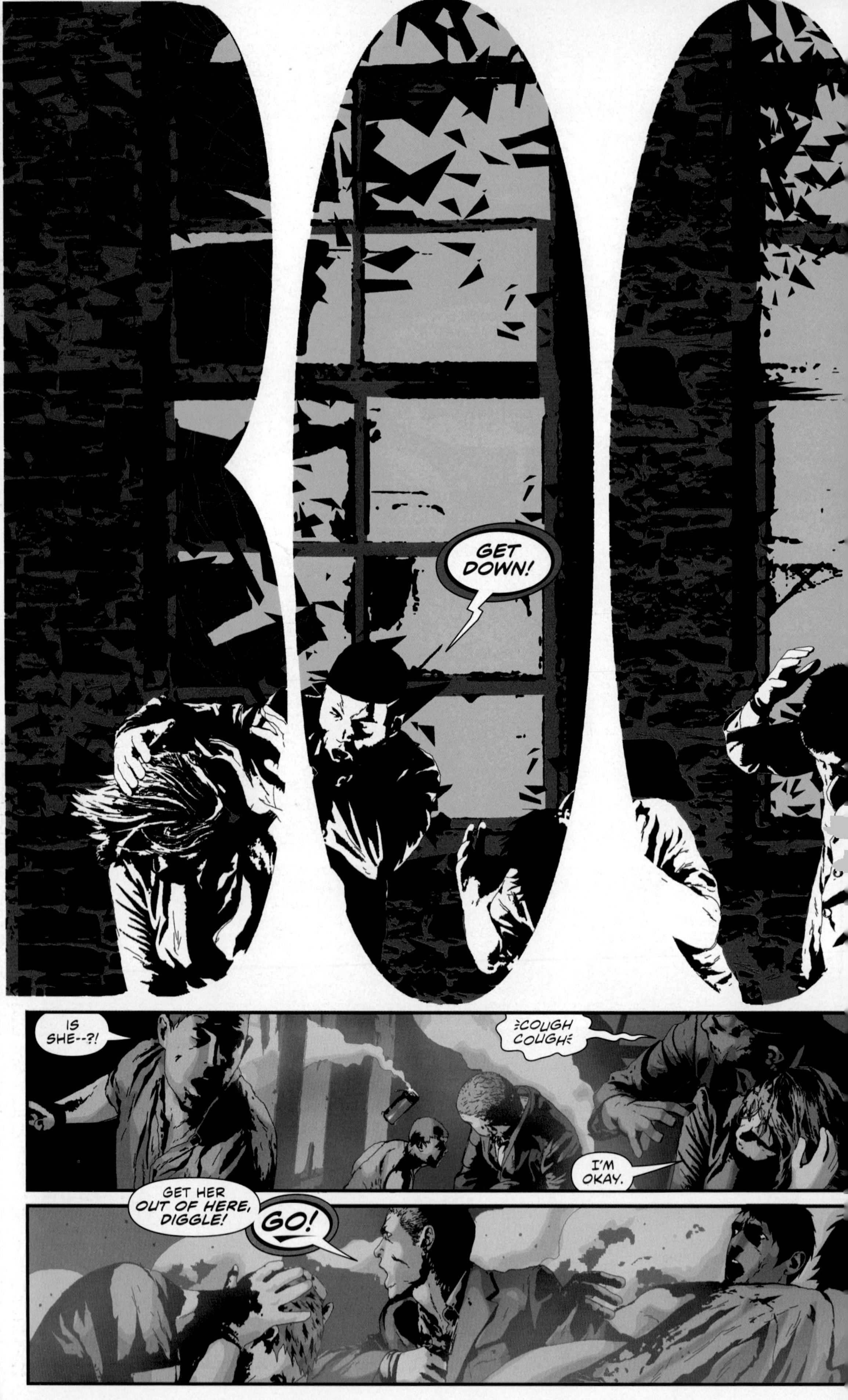
GET DOWN!
IS SHE--?!
COUGH COUGH
I'M OKAY.
GET HER OUT OF HERE, DIGGLE!
GO!

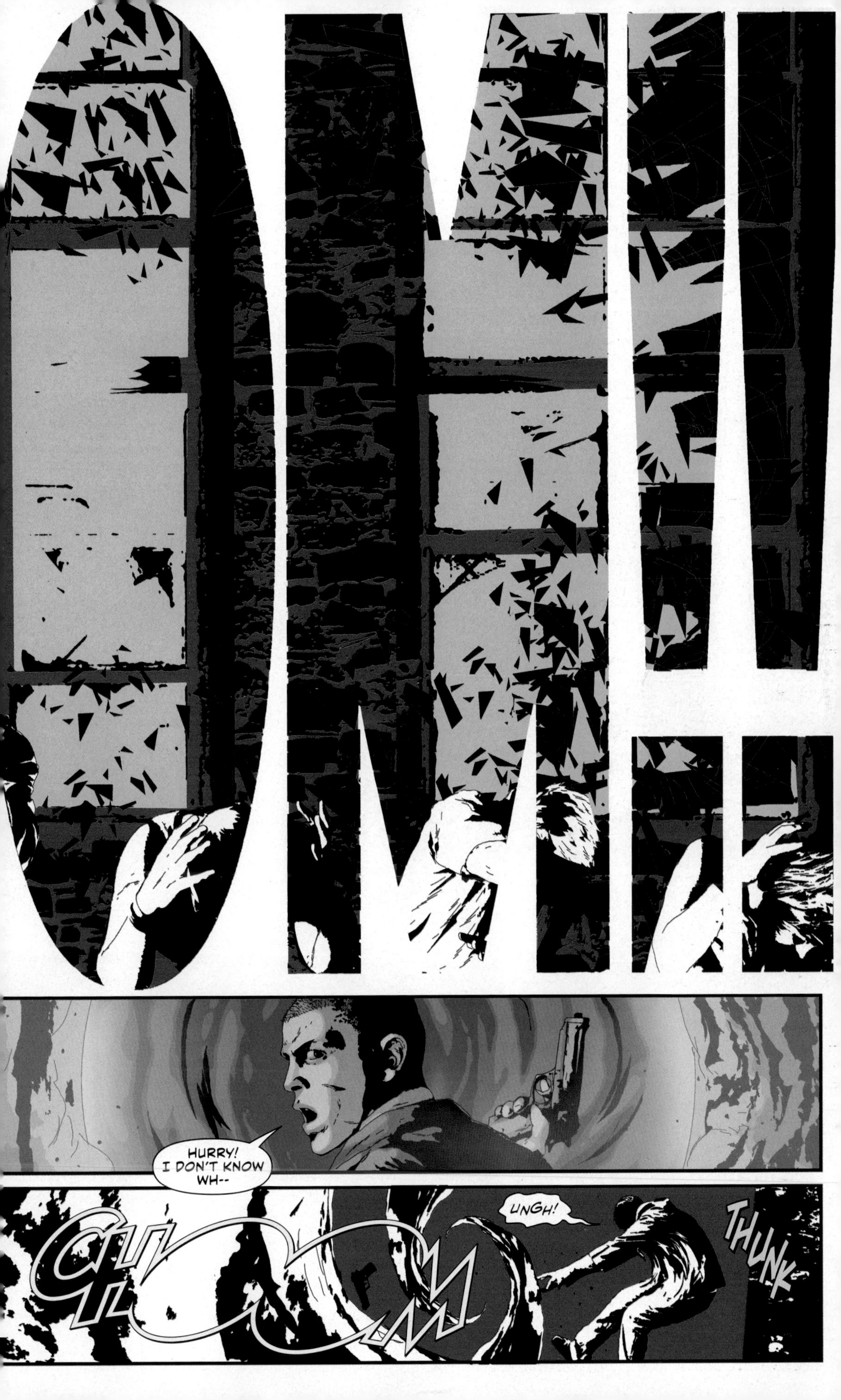
OM!!
HURRY! I DON'T KNOW WH--
UNGH!
THUNK

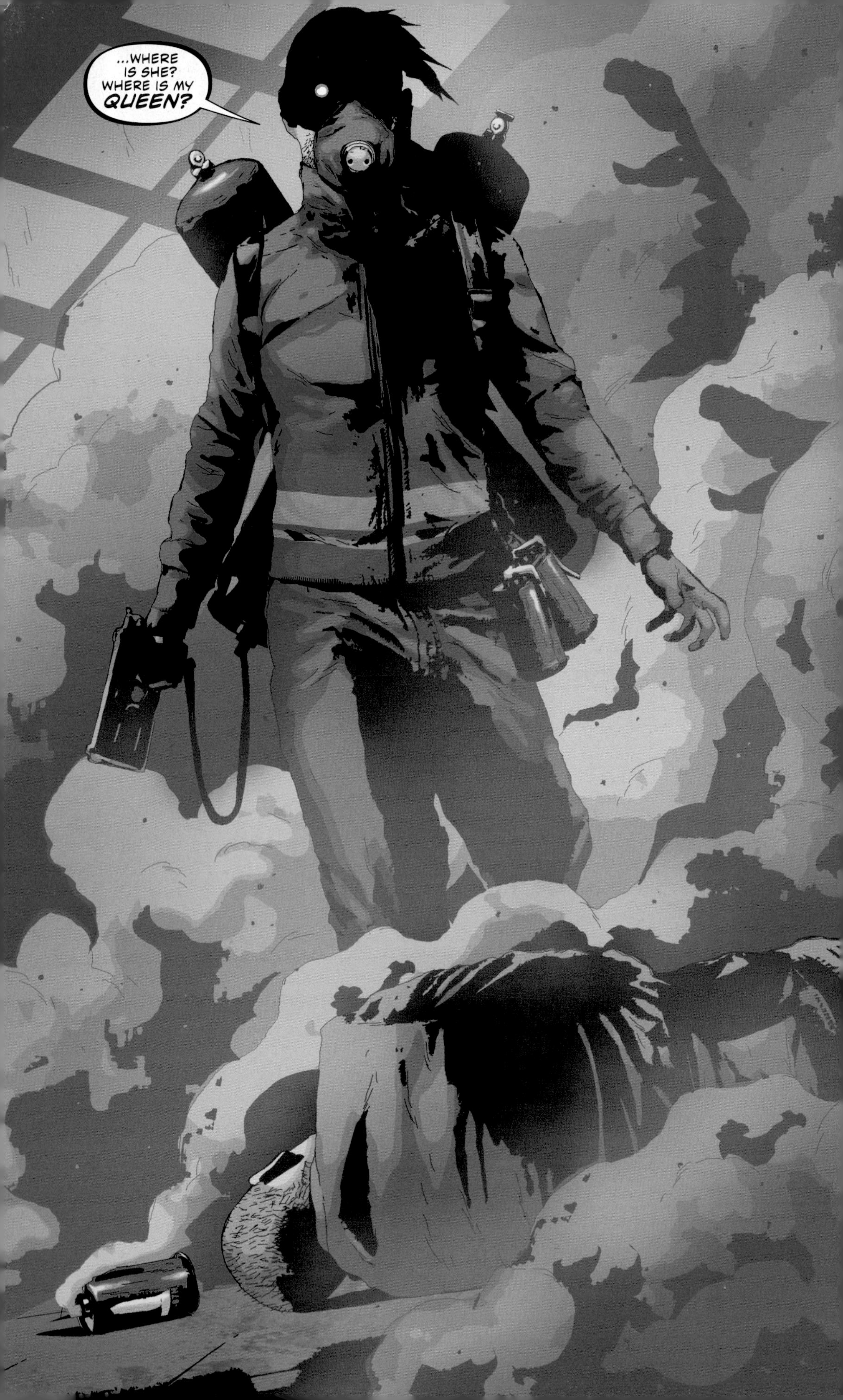
...WHERE IS SHE? WHERE IS MY QUEEN?

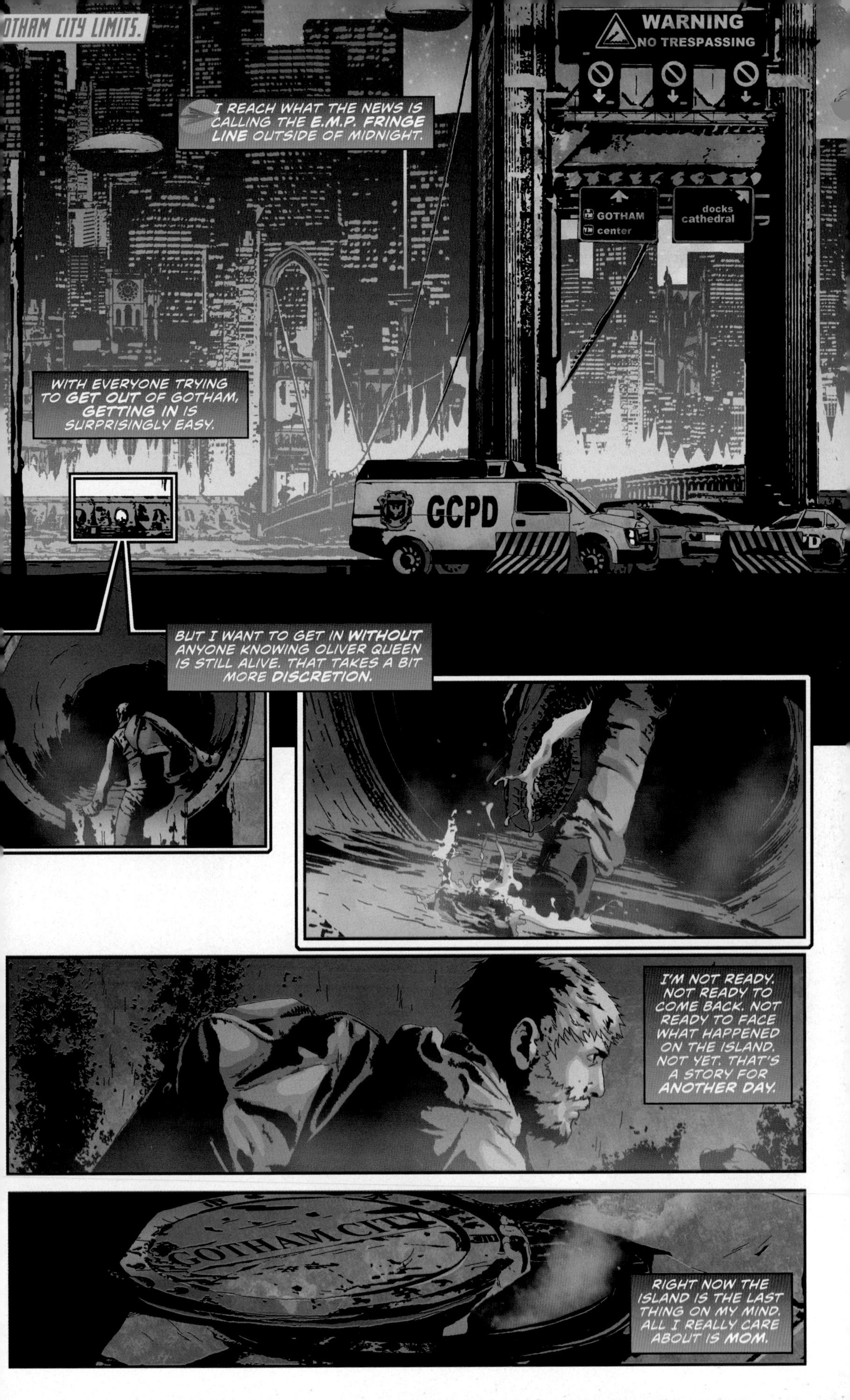

OTHAM CITY LIMITS.
WARNING
NO TRESPASSING
I REACH WHAT THE NEWS IS CALLING THE E.M.P. FRINGE LINE OUTSIDE OF MIDNIGHT.
GOTHAM center
docks cathedral
WITH EVERYONE TRYING TO GET OUT OF GOTHAM, GETTING IN IS SURPRISINGLY EASY.
GCPD
BUT I WANT TO GET IN WITHOUT ANYONE KNOWING OLIVER QUEEN IS STILL ALIVE. THAT TAKES A BIT MORE DISCRETION.
I'M NOT READY. NOT READY TO COME BACK. NOT READY TO FACE WHAT HAPPENED ON THE ISLAND. NOT YET. THAT'S A STORY FOR ANOTHER DAY.
GOTHAM CITY
RIGHT NOW THE ISLAND IS THE LAST THING ON MY MIND. ALL I REALLY CARE ABOUT IS MOM.

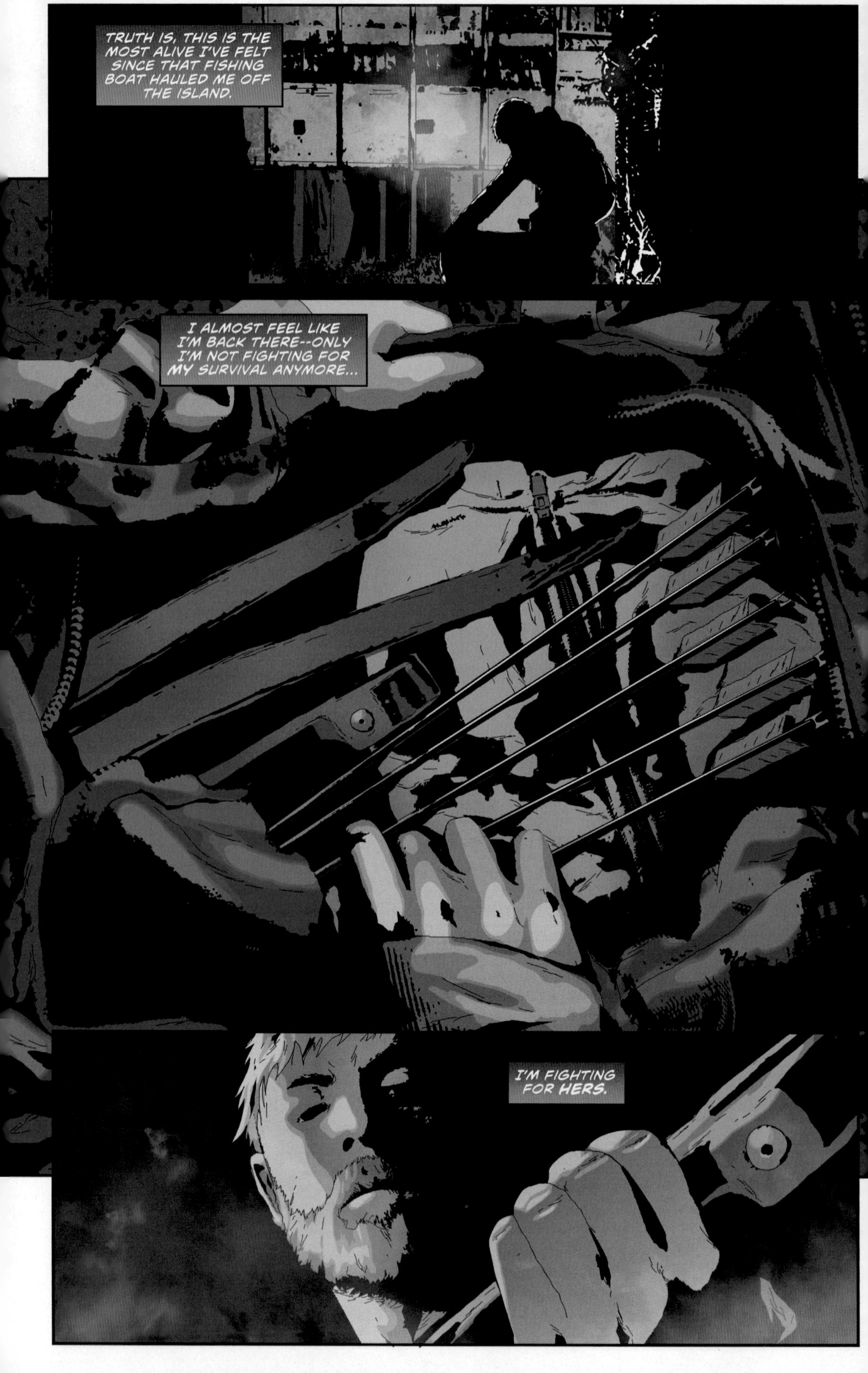
TRUTH IS, THIS IS THE MOST ALIVE I'VE FELT SINCE THAT FISHING BOAT HAULED ME OFF THE ISLAND.
I ALMOST FEEL LIKE I'M BACK THERE--ONLY I'M NOT FIGHTING FOR MY SURVIVAL ANYMORE...
I'M FIGHTING FOR HERS.

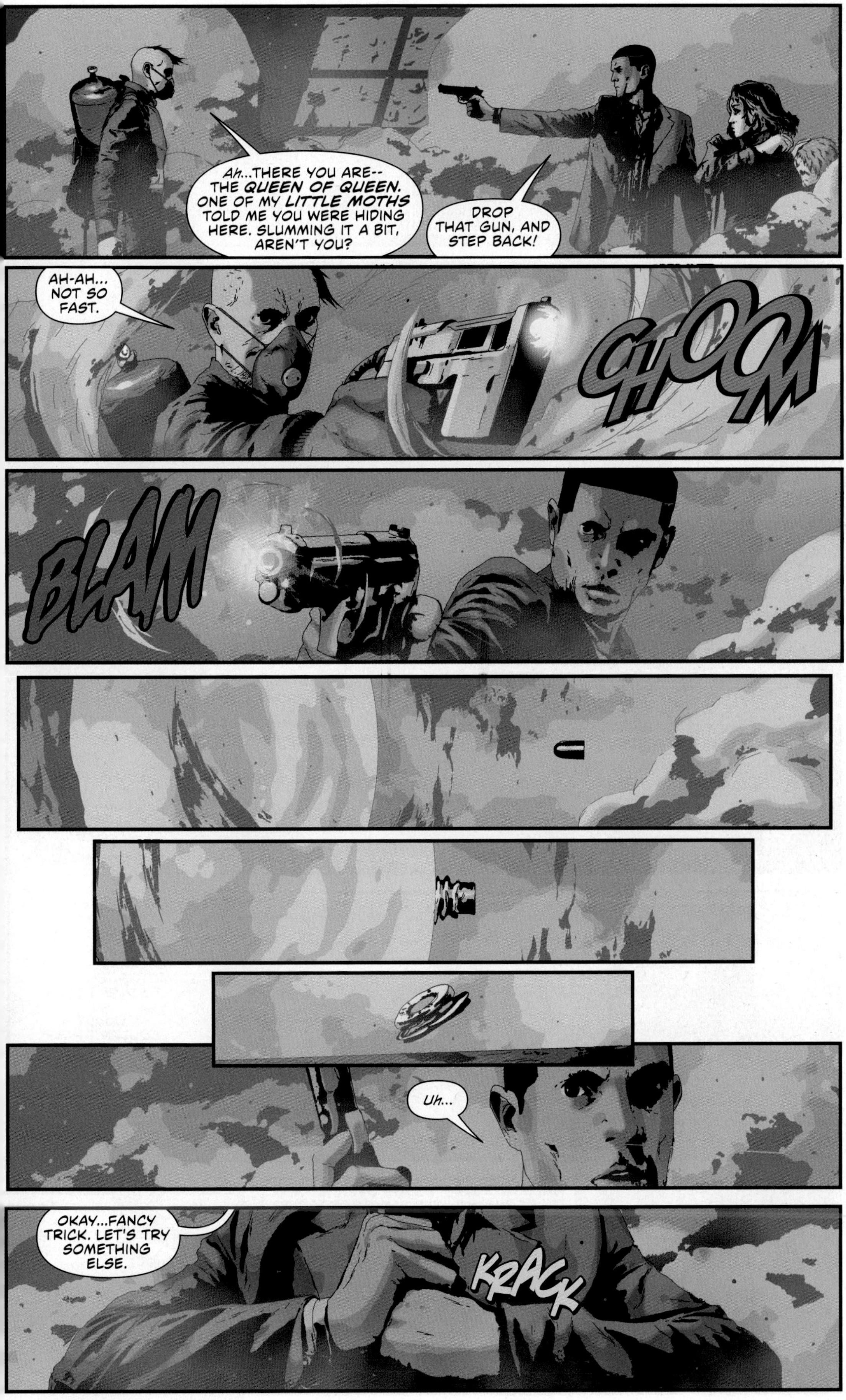
Ah...THERE YOU ARE-- THE QUEEN OF QUEEN. ONE OF MY LITTLE MOTHS TOLD ME YOU WERE HIDING HERE. SLUMMING IT A BIT, AREN'T YOU?
DROP THAT GUN, AND STEP BACK!
AH-AH... NOT SO FAST.
CHOOM
BLAM
Uh...
OKAY...FANCY TRICK. LET'S TRY SOMETHING ELSE.
KRACK

THE LADY AND I ARE *WALKING OUT OF HERE*, FREAK.

UNGH!

FREAK? YOU'RE IN *GOTHAM* NOW...EVERYONE'S A *FREAK!*

SO WHY DON'T YOU BUZZ OFF.

CHOOM

NGH!

MR. DIGGLE!

WH-WHO *ARE* YOU?!

I'M KIND OF THINKING "THE MOTH"...OR MAYBE "MOTHMAN"-- I CAN'T MAKE UP MY MIND. SOMETHING WITH MOTHS, THOUGH... I *LOVE* MOTHS.

I JUST COULDN'T HELP MYSELF...I WAS DRAWN TO *YOUR LIGHT.* OR YOUR BIG OLD *BANK ACCOUNT*...SAME THING REALLY.

WHEN *ALL THIS* BLOWS OVER, I THINK SOMEONE WOULD PAY A GREAT PRICE TO GET YOU BACK, *eh?* SO WHAT SAY WE GET OUT OF HERE?

UNGH!

WHAT SAY YO[U] PICK ON SOMEONE YOUR OWN SIZE?

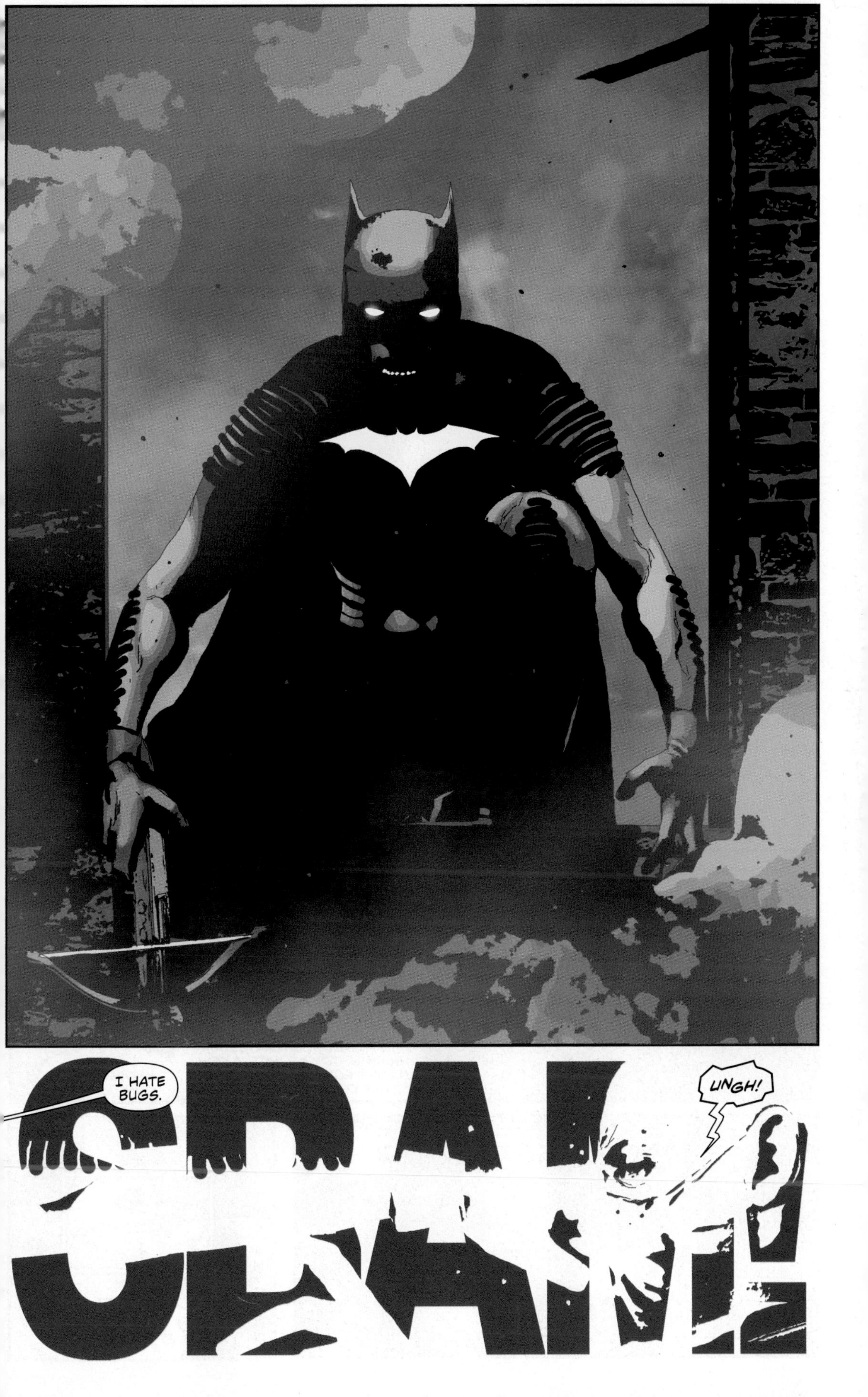
I HATE BUGS.
UNGH!

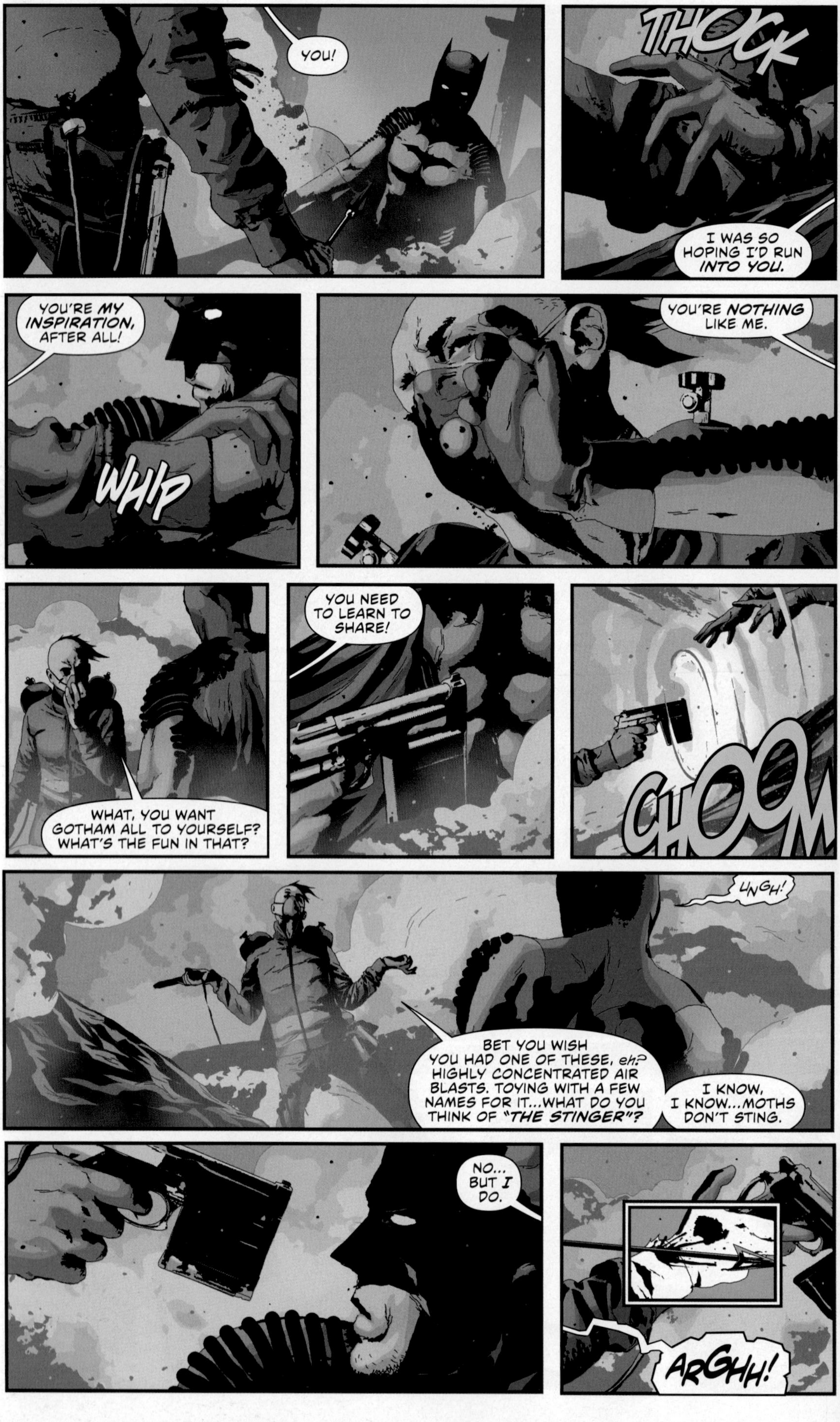
YOU!
THOCK
I WAS SO HOPING I'D RUN *INTO YOU.*
YOU'RE *MY INSPIRATION,* AFTER ALL!
WHIP
YOU'RE **NOTHING** LIKE ME.
WHAT, YOU WANT GOTHAM ALL TO YOURSELF? WHAT'S THE FUN IN THAT?
YOU NEED TO LEARN TO SHARE!
CHOOM
UNGH!
BET YOU WISH YOU HAD ONE OF THESE, *eh?* HIGHLY CONCENTRATED AIR BLASTS. TOYING WITH A FEW NAMES FOR IT...WHAT DO YOU THINK OF ***"THE STINGER"?***
I KNOW, I KNOW...MOTHS DON'T STING.
NO... BUT *I* DO.
ARGHH!

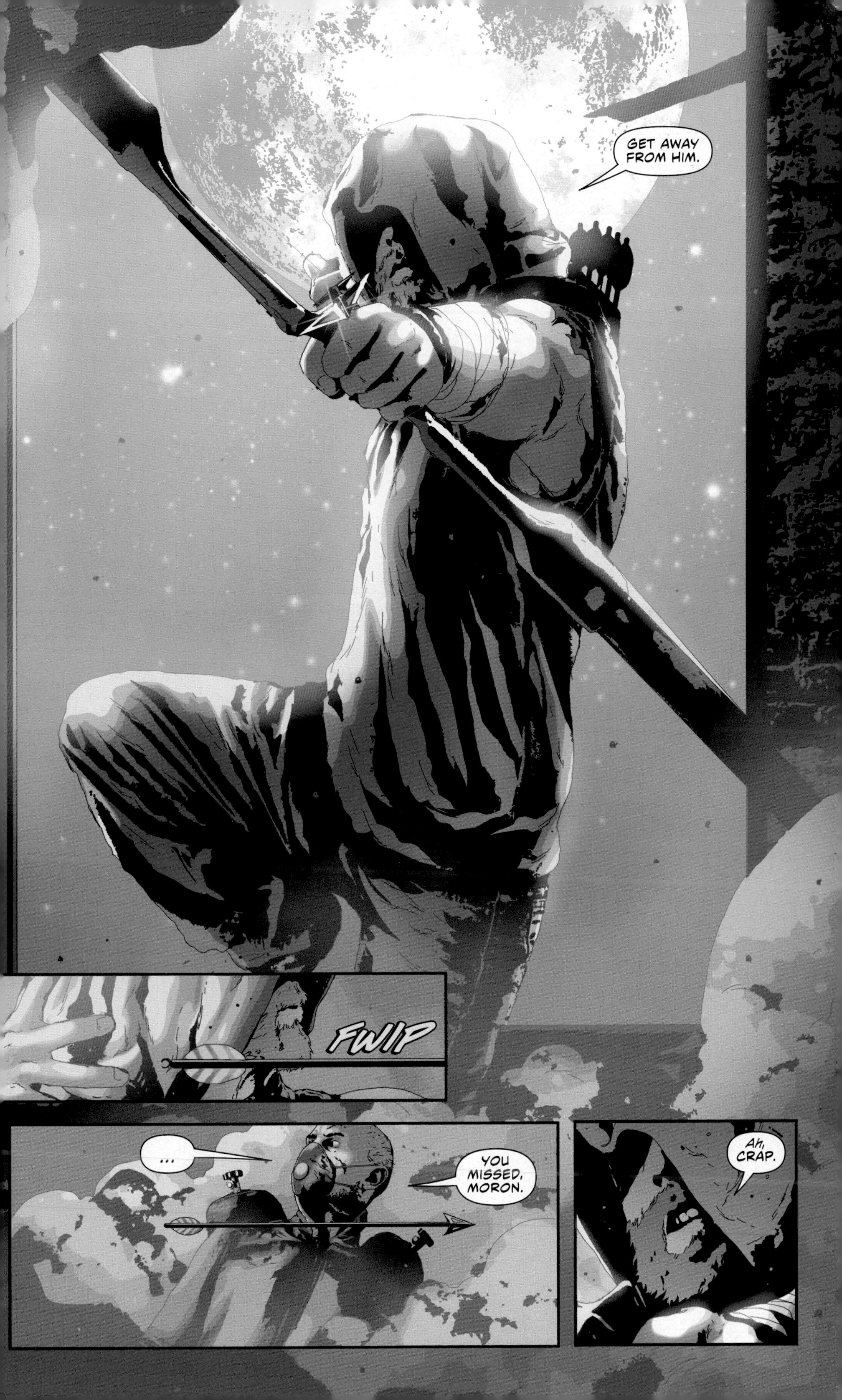

GET AWAY FROM HIM.
FWIP
...
YOU MISSED, MORON.
Ah, CRAP.

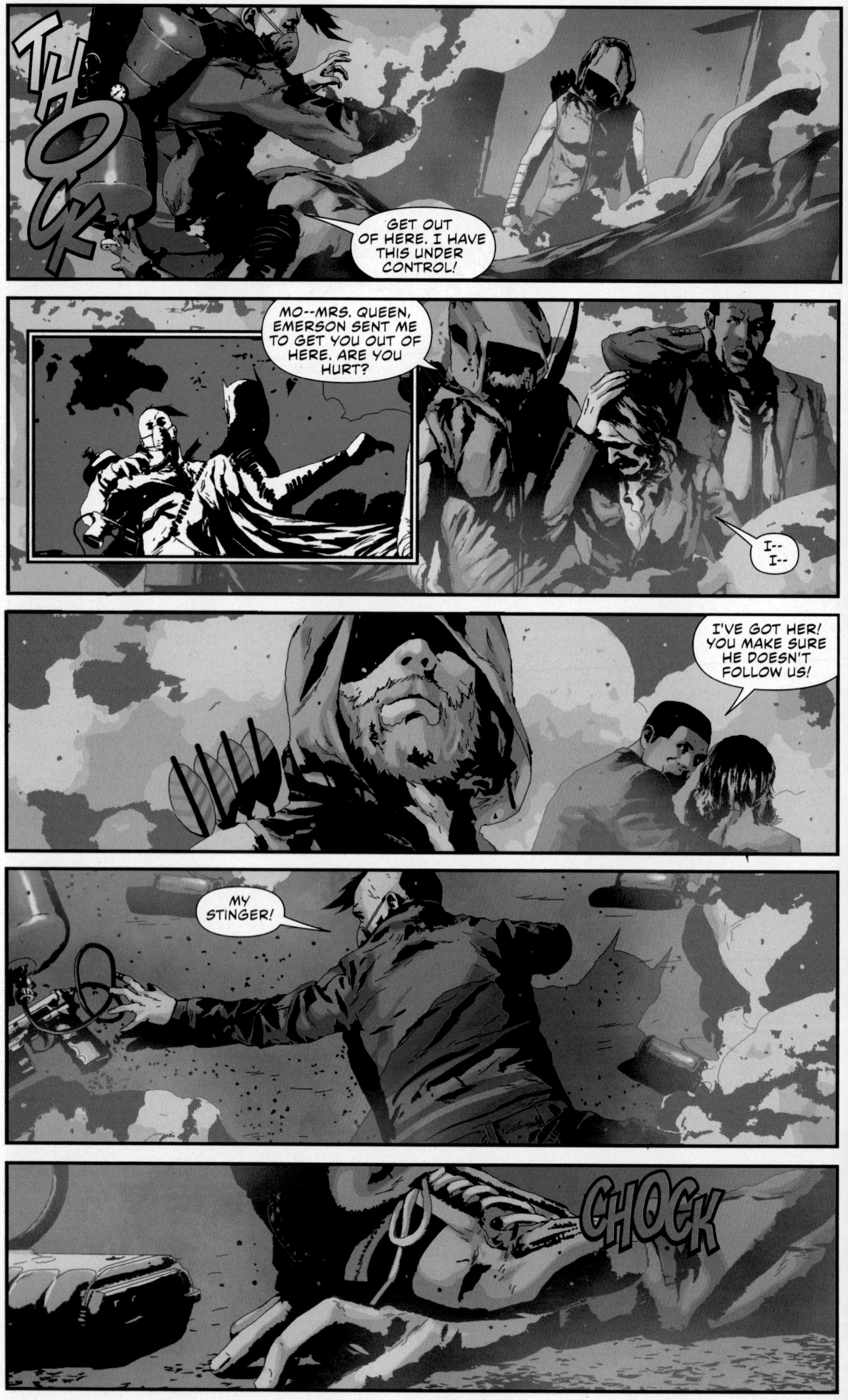
THOCK
GET OUT OF HERE. I HAVE THIS UNDER CONTROL!
MO--MRS. QUEEN, EMERSON SENT ME TO GET YOU OUT OF HERE. ARE YOU HURT?
I-- I--
I'VE GOT HER! YOU MAKE SURE HE DOESN'T FOLLOW US!
MY STINGER!
CHOCK

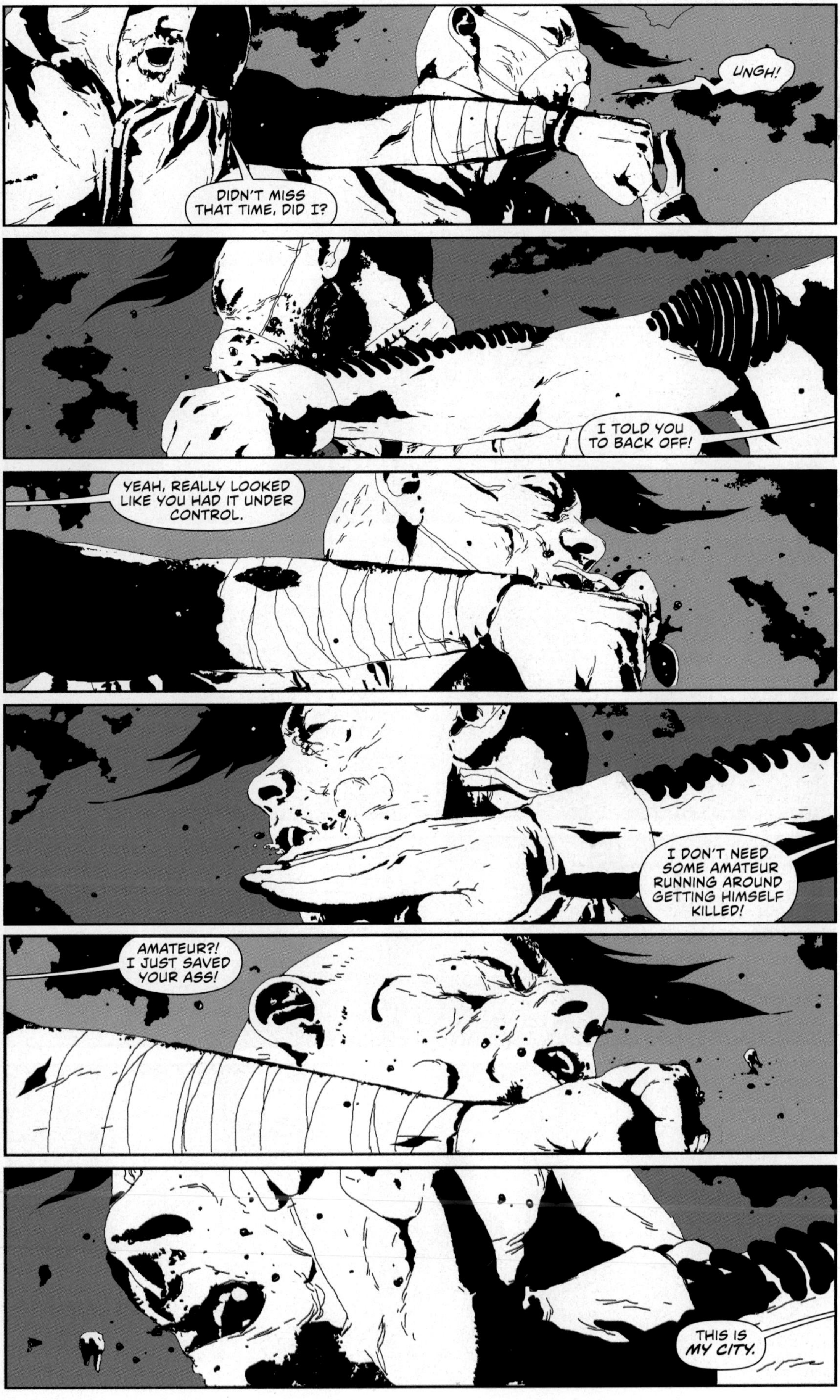
UNGH!
DIDN'T MISS THAT TIME, DID I?
I TOLD YOU TO BACK OFF!
YEAH, REALLY LOOKED LIKE YOU HAD IT UNDER CONTROL.
I DON'T NEED SOME AMATEUR RUNNING AROUND GETTING HIMSELF KILLED!
AMATEUR?! I JUST SAVED YOUR ASS!
THIS IS *MY CITY.*

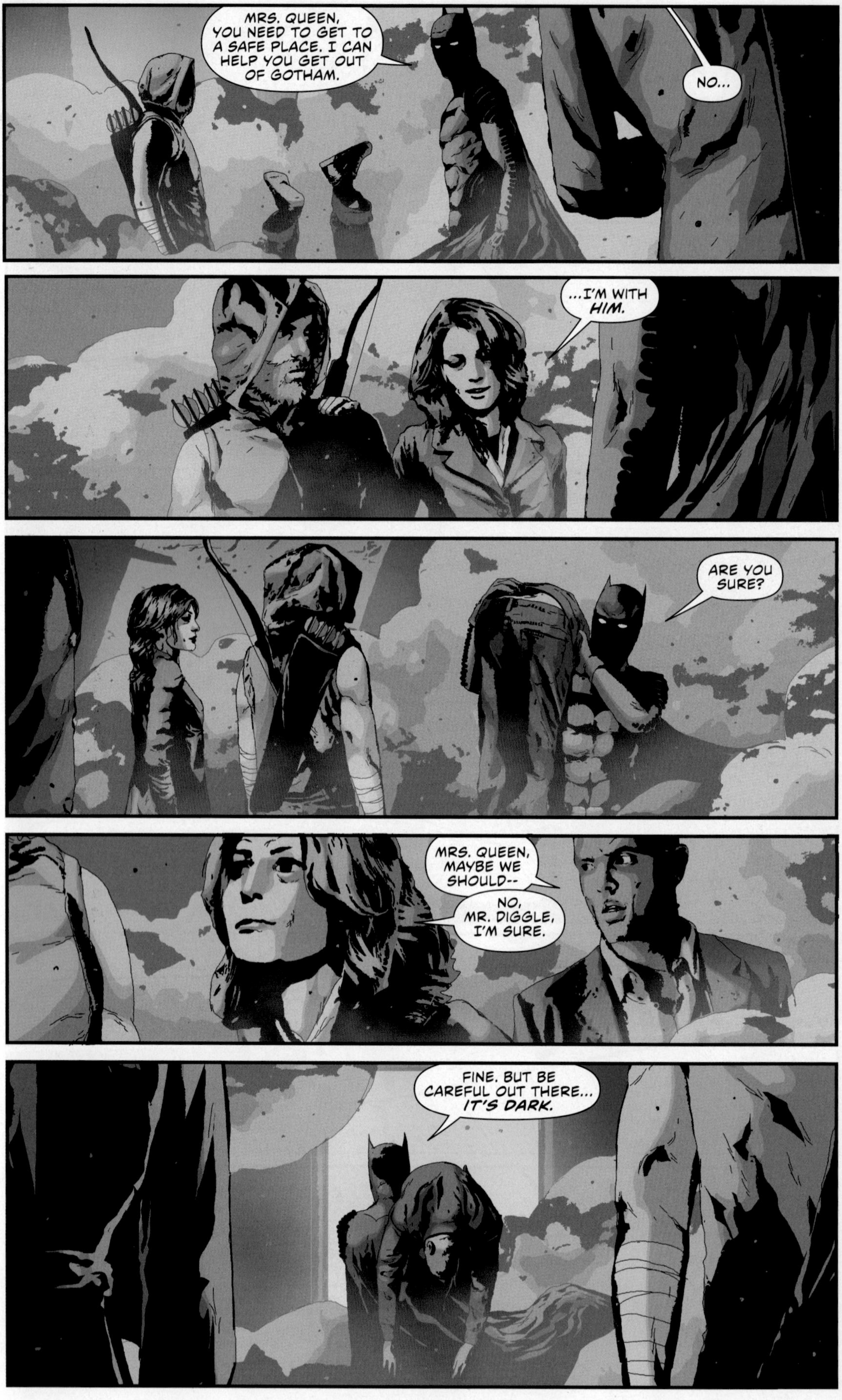

MRS. QUEEN, YOU NEED TO GET TO A SAFE PLACE. I CAN HELP YOU GET OUT OF GOTHAM.
NO...
...I'M WITH *HIM.*
ARE YOU SURE?
MRS. QUEEN, MAYBE WE SHOULD--
NO, MR. DIGGLE, I'M SURE.
FINE. BUT BE CAREFUL OUT THERE... *IT'S DARK.*

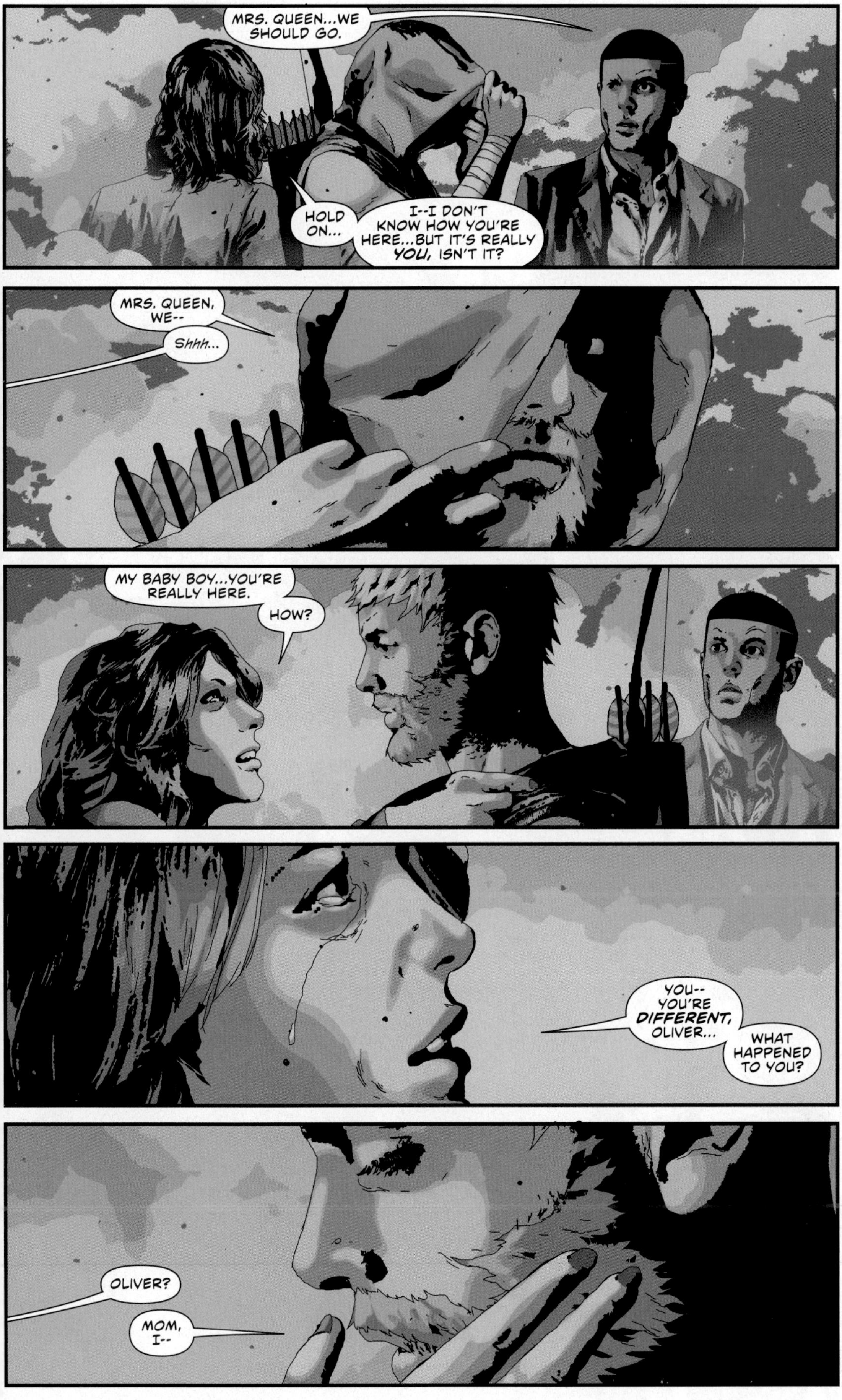
MRS. QUEEN...WE SHOULD GO.
HOLD ON...
I--I DON'T KNOW HOW YOU'RE HERE...BUT IT'S REALLY *YOU*, ISN'T IT?
MRS. QUEEN, WE--
Shhh...
MY BABY BOY...YOU'RE REALLY HERE.
HOW?
YOU--YOU'RE *DIFFERENT*, OLIVER...
WHAT HAPPENED TO YOU?
OLIVER?
MOM, I--

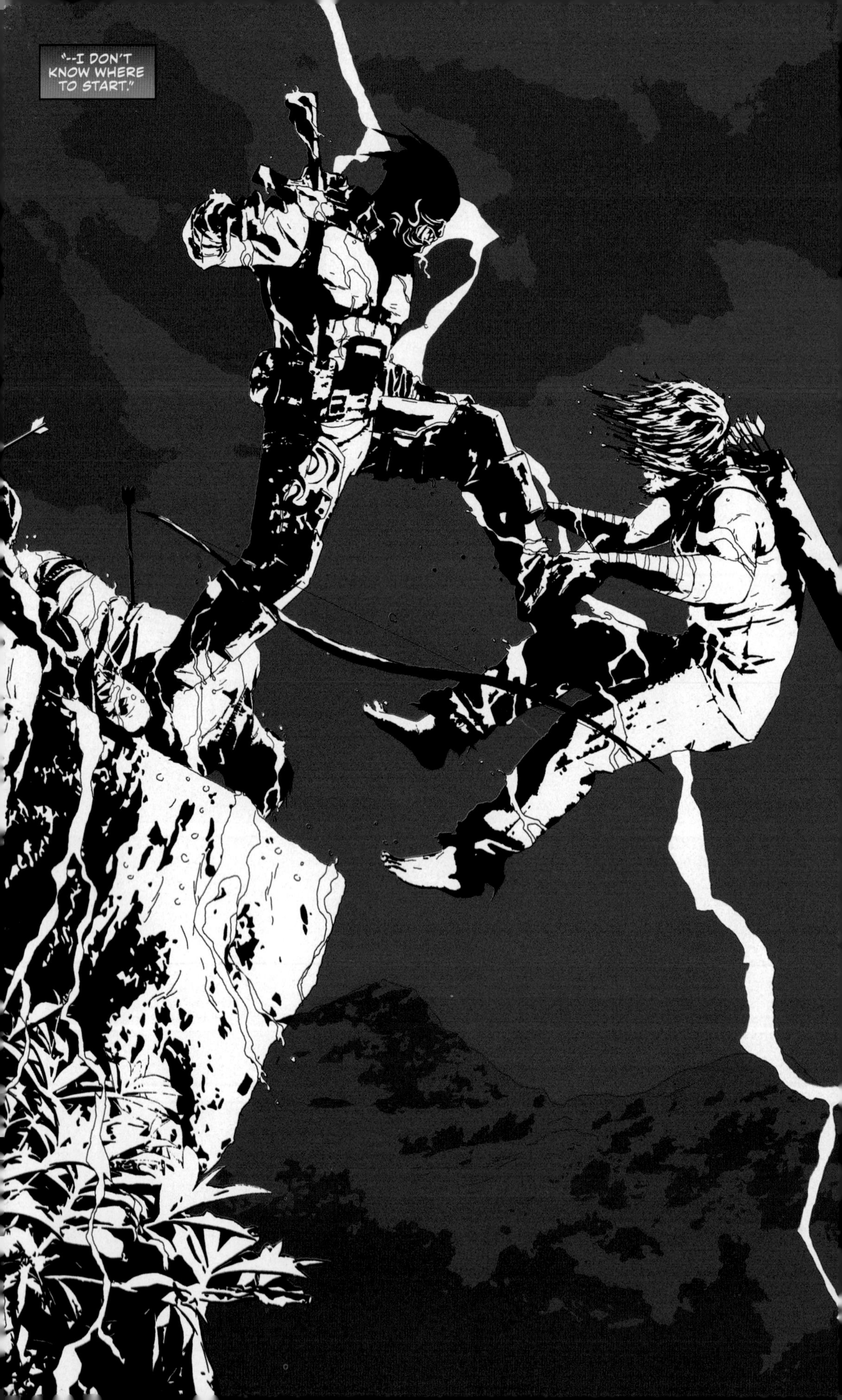
"--I DON'T KNOW WHERE TO START."

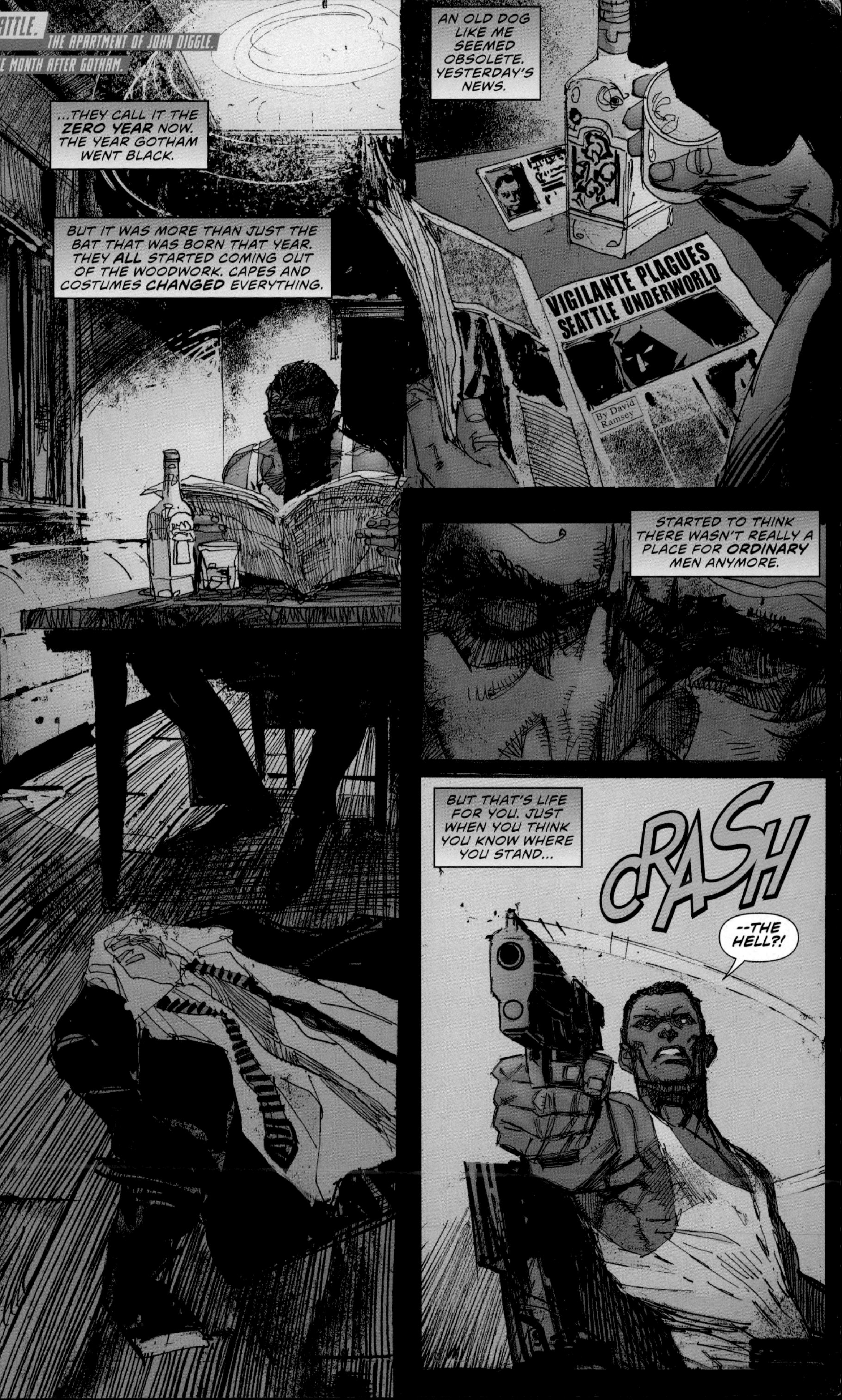

ATTLE. THE APARTMENT OF JOHN DIGGLE.
E MONTH AFTER GOTHAM.
...THEY CALL IT THE ZERO YEAR NOW. THE YEAR GOTHAM WENT BLACK.
BUT IT WAS MORE THAN JUST THE BAT THAT WAS BORN THAT YEAR. THEY ALL STARTED COMING OUT OF THE WOODWORK. CAPES AND COSTUMES CHANGED EVERYTHING.
AN OLD DOG LIKE ME SEEMED OBSOLETE. YESTERDAY'S NEWS.
VIGILANTE PLAGUES SEATTLE UNDERWORLD
By David Ramsey
STARTED TO THINK THERE WASN'T REALLY A PLACE FOR ORDINARY MEN ANYMORE.
BUT THAT'S LIFE FOR YOU. JUST WHEN YOU THINK YOU KNOW WHERE YOU STAND...
CRASH
--THE HELL?!

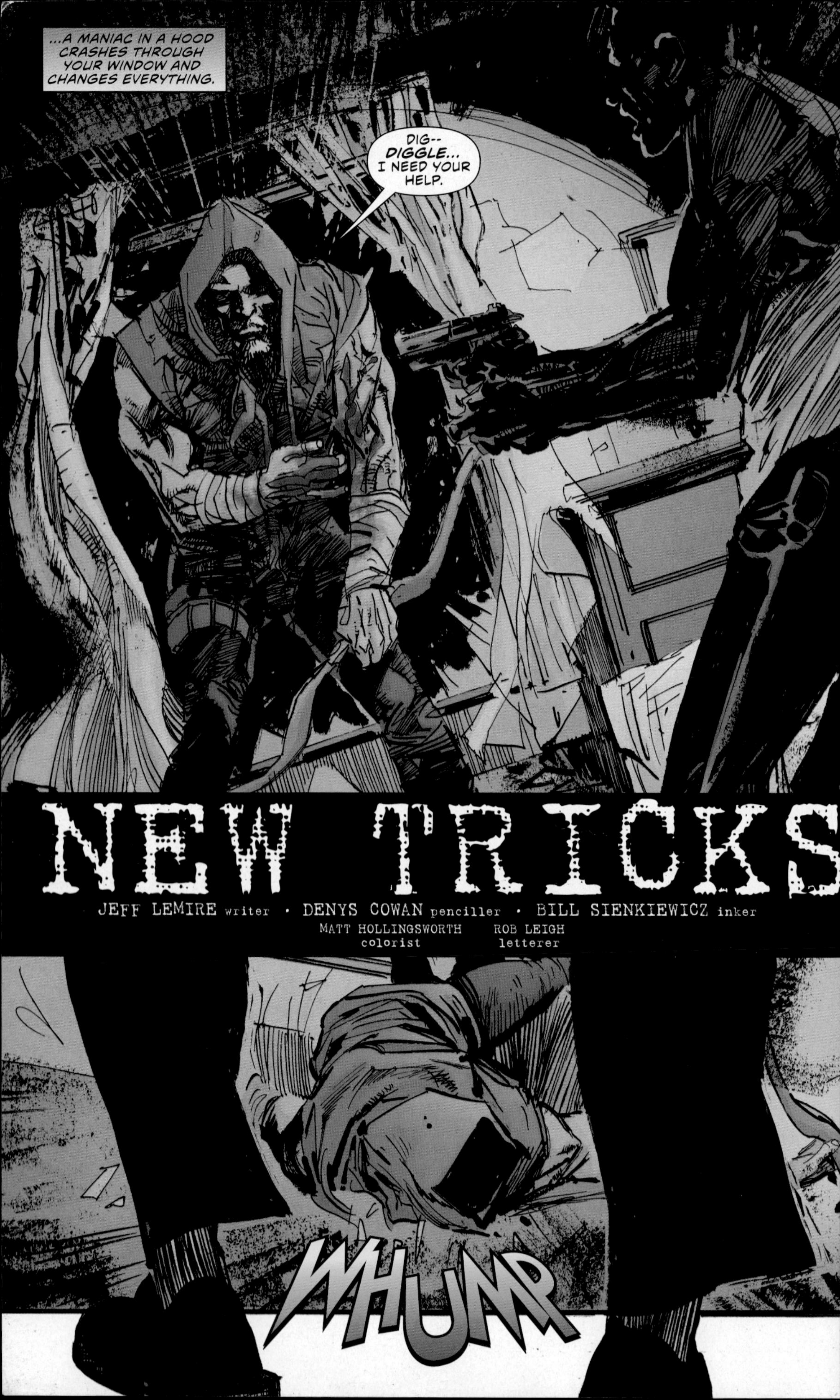
...A MANIAC IN A HOOD CRASHES THROUGH YOUR WINDOW AND CHANGES EVERYTHING.
DIG-- DIGGLE... I NEED YOUR HELP.
NEW TRICKS
JEFF LEMIRE writer • DENYS COWAN penciller • BILL SIENKIEWICZ inker
MATT HOLLINGSWORTH colorist
ROB LEIGH letterer
WHUMP

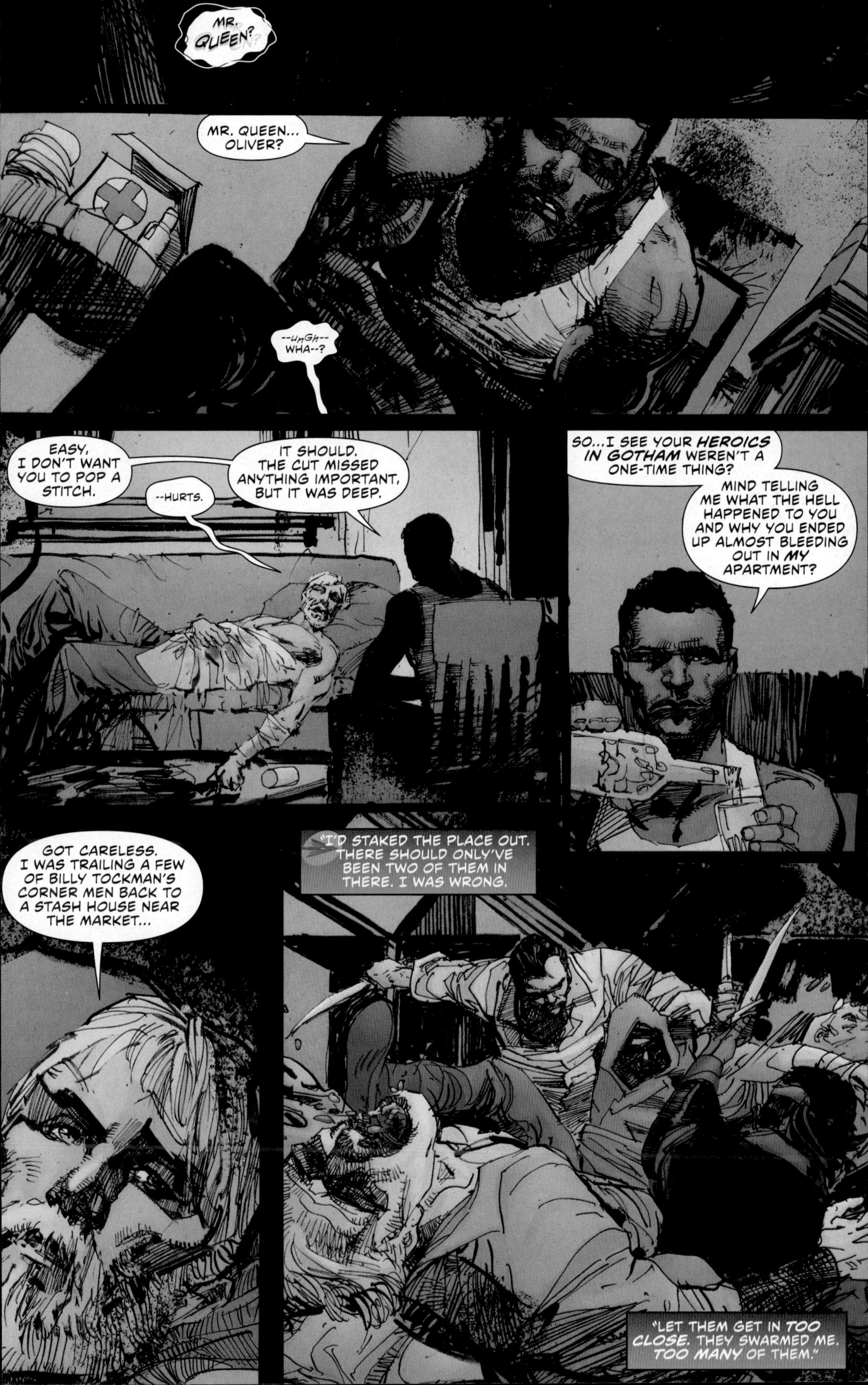

MR. QUEEN?
MR. QUEEN... OLIVER?
--UNGH-- WHA--?
EASY, I DON'T WANT YOU TO POP A STITCH.
--HURTS.
IT SHOULD. THE CUT MISSED ANYTHING IMPORTANT, BUT IT WAS DEEP.
SO...I SEE YOUR HEROICS IN GOTHAM WEREN'T A ONE-TIME THING?
MIND TELLING ME WHAT THE HELL HAPPENED TO YOU AND WHY YOU ENDED UP ALMOST BLEEDING OUT IN MY APARTMENT?
GOT CARELESS. I WAS TRAILING A FEW OF BILLY TOCKMAN'S CORNER MEN BACK TO A STASH HOUSE NEAR THE MARKET...
"I'D STAKED THE PLACE OUT. THERE SHOULD ONLY'VE BEEN TWO OF THEM IN THERE. I WAS WRONG.
"LET THEM GET IN TOO CLOSE. THEY SWARMED ME. TOO MANY OF THEM."

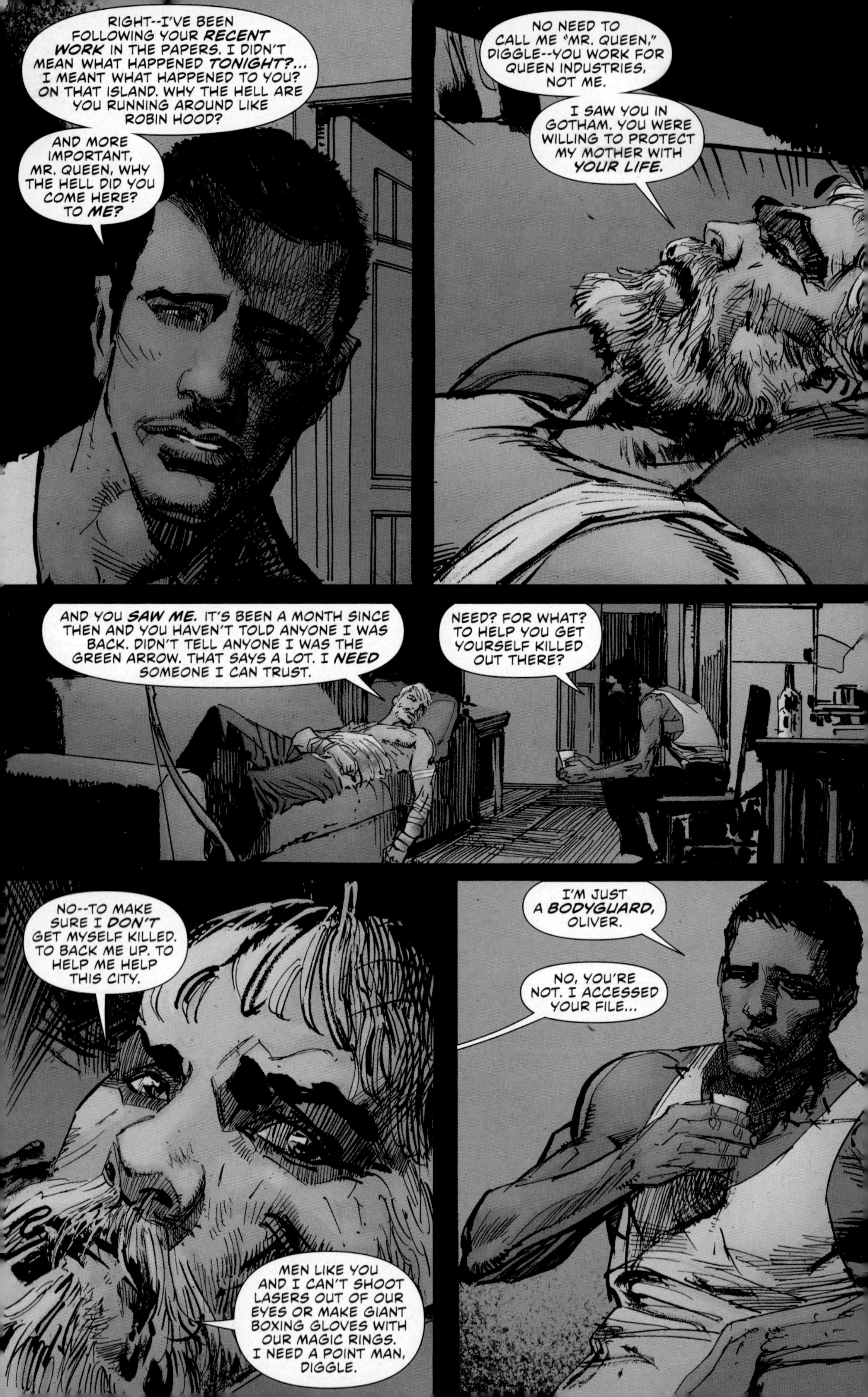

RIGHT--I'VE BEEN FOLLOWING YOUR RECENT WORK IN THE PAPERS. I DIDN'T MEAN WHAT HAPPENED TONIGHT?... I MEANT WHAT HAPPENED TO YOU? ON THAT ISLAND. WHY THE HELL ARE YOU RUNNING AROUND LIKE ROBIN HOOD?
AND MORE IMPORTANT, MR. QUEEN, WHY THE HELL DID YOU COME HERE? TO ME?
NO NEED TO CALL ME "MR. QUEEN," DIGGLE--YOU WORK FOR QUEEN INDUSTRIES, NOT ME.
I SAW YOU IN GOTHAM. YOU WERE WILLING TO PROTECT MY MOTHER WITH YOUR LIFE.
AND YOU SAW ME. IT'S BEEN A MONTH SINCE THEN AND YOU HAVEN'T TOLD ANYONE I WAS BACK. DIDN'T TELL ANYONE I WAS THE GREEN ARROW. THAT SAYS A LOT. I NEED SOMEONE I CAN TRUST.
NEED? FOR WHAT? TO HELP YOU GET YOURSELF KILLED OUT THERE?
NO--TO MAKE SURE I DON'T GET MYSELF KILLED. TO BACK ME UP. TO HELP ME HELP THIS CITY.
MEN LIKE YOU AND I CAN'T SHOOT LASERS OUT OF OUR EYES OR MAKE GIANT BOXING GLOVES WITH OUR MAGIC RINGS. I NEED A POINT MAN, DIGGLE.
I'M JUST A BODYGUARD, OLIVER.
NO, YOU'RE NOT. I ACCESSED YOUR FILE...

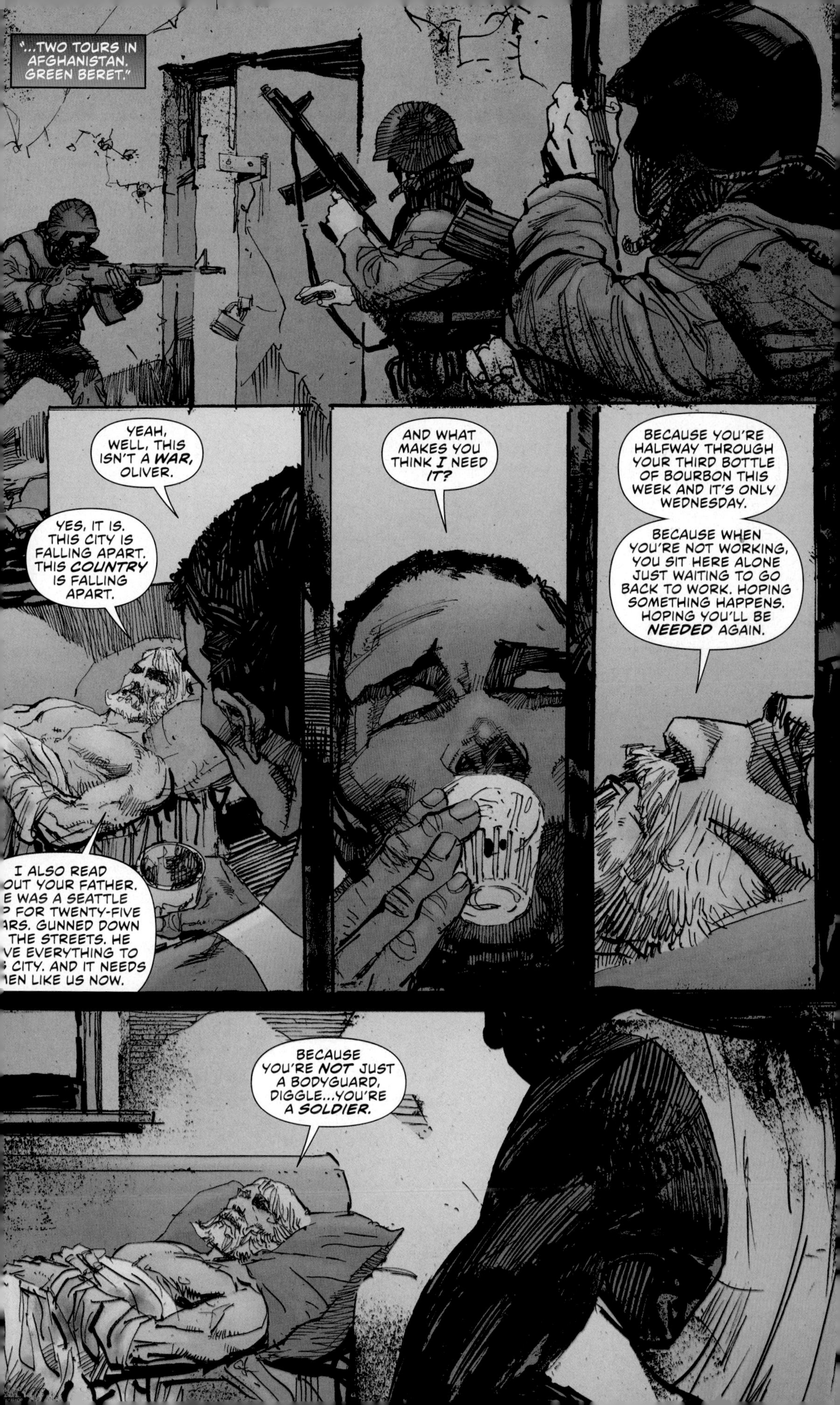

"...TWO TOURS IN AFGHANISTAN. GREEN BERET."
YEAH, WELL, THIS ISN'T A WAR, OLIVER.
YES, IT IS. THIS CITY IS FALLING APART. THIS COUNTRY IS FALLING APART.
I ALSO READ OUT YOUR FATHER. E WAS A SEATTLE FOR TWENTY-FIVE ARS. GUNNED DOWN THE STREETS. HE VE EVERYTHING TO CITY. AND IT NEEDS IEN LIKE US NOW.
AND WHAT MAKES YOU THINK I NEED IT?
BECAUSE YOU'RE HALFWAY THROUGH YOUR THIRD BOTTLE OF BOURBON THIS WEEK AND IT'S ONLY WEDNESDAY.
BECAUSE WHEN YOU'RE NOT WORKING, YOU SIT HERE ALONE JUST WAITING TO GO BACK TO WORK. HOPING SOMETHING HAPPENS. HOPING YOU'LL BE NEEDED AGAIN.
BECAUSE YOU'RE NOT JUST A BODYGUARD, DIGGLE...YOU'RE A SOLDIER.

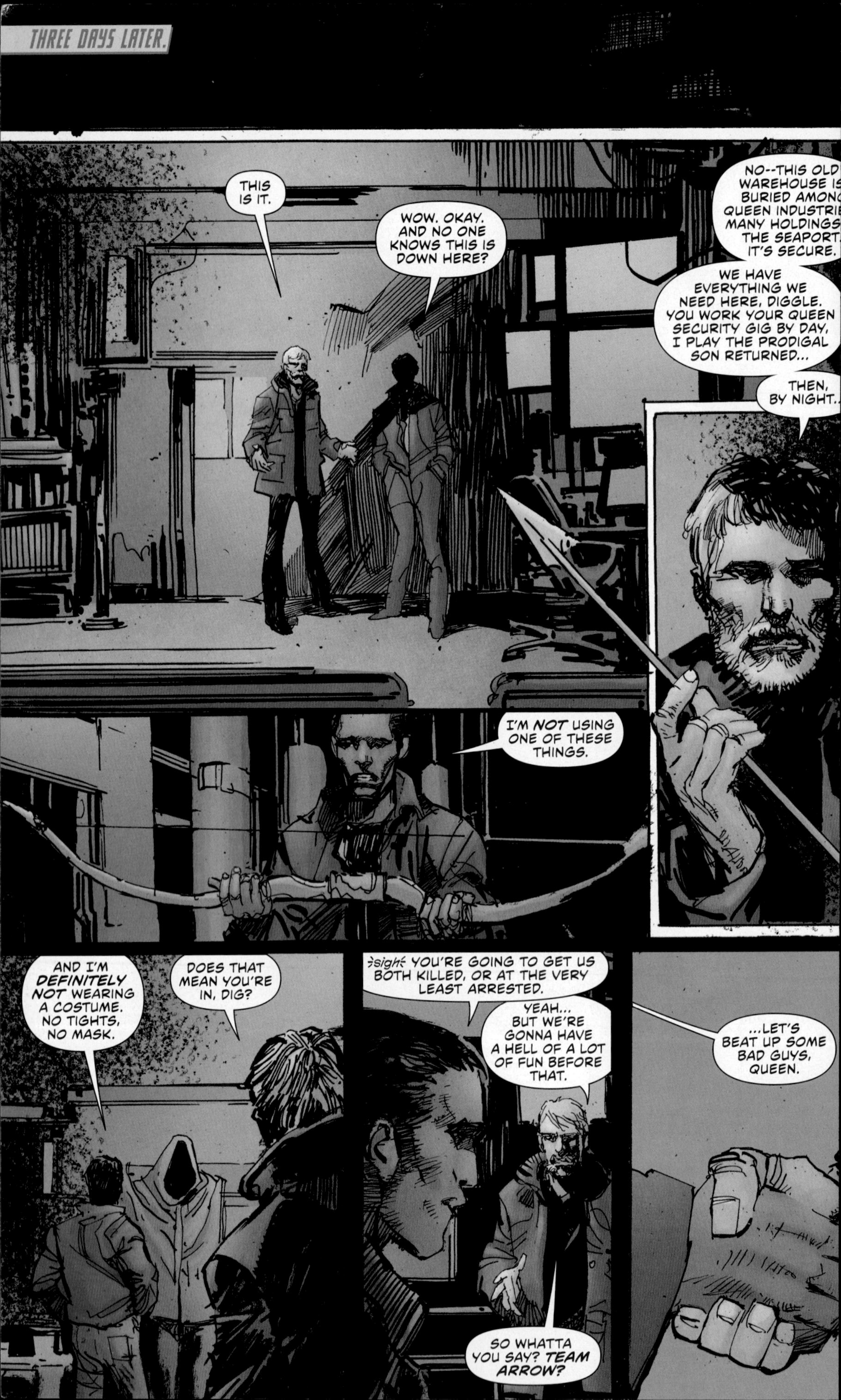
THREE DAYS LATER.
THIS IS IT.
WOW. OKAY. AND NO ONE KNOWS THIS IS DOWN HERE?
NO--THIS OLD WAREHOUSE IS BURIED AMONG QUEEN INDUSTRIES' MANY HOLDINGS AT THE SEAPORT. IT'S SECURE.
WE HAVE EVERYTHING WE NEED HERE, DIGGLE. YOU WORK YOUR QUEEN SECURITY GIG BY DAY, I PLAY THE PRODIGAL SON RETURNED...
THEN, BY NIGHT...
I'M NOT USING ONE OF THESE THINGS.
AND I'M DEFINITELY NOT WEARING A COSTUME. NO TIGHTS, NO MASK.
DOES THAT MEAN YOU'RE IN, DIG?
sigh YOU'RE GOING TO GET US BOTH KILLED, OR AT THE VERY LEAST ARRESTED.
YEAH... BUT WE'RE GONNA HAVE A HELL OF A LOT OF FUN BEFORE THAT.
SO WHATTA YOU SAY? TEAM ARROW?
...LET'S BEAT UP SOME BAD GUYS, QUEEN.

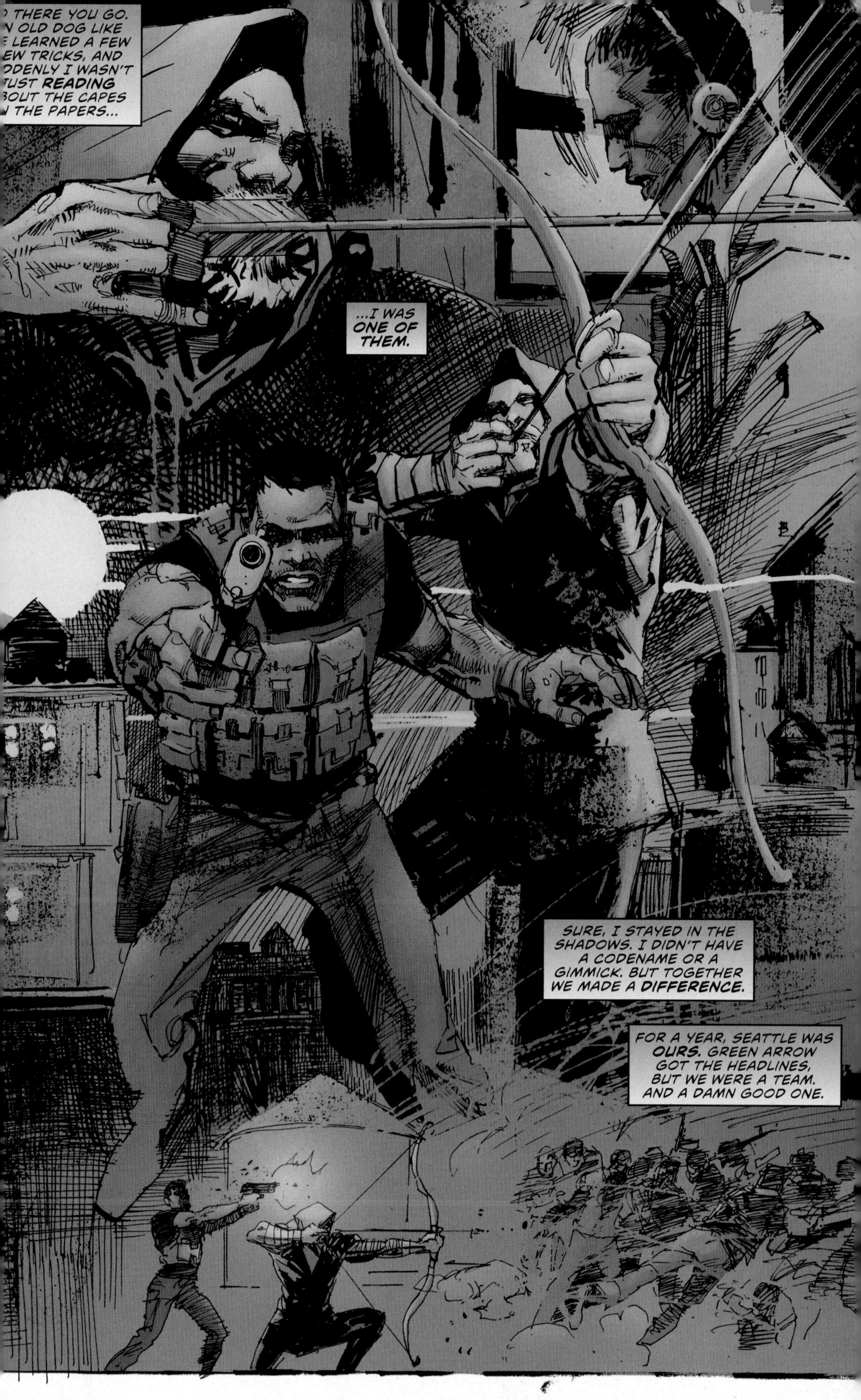

O THERE YOU GO. N OLD DOG LIKE E LEARNED A FEW EW TRICKS, AND DDENLY I WASN'T JUST READING BOUT THE CAPES N THE PAPERS...
...I WAS ONE OF THEM.
SURE, I STAYED IN THE SHADOWS. I DIDN'T HAVE A CODENAME OR A GIMMICK. BUT TOGETHER WE MADE A DIFFERENCE.
FOR A YEAR, SEATTLE WAS OURS. GREEN ARROW GOT THE HEADLINES, BUT WE WERE A TEAM. AND A DAMN GOOD ONE.

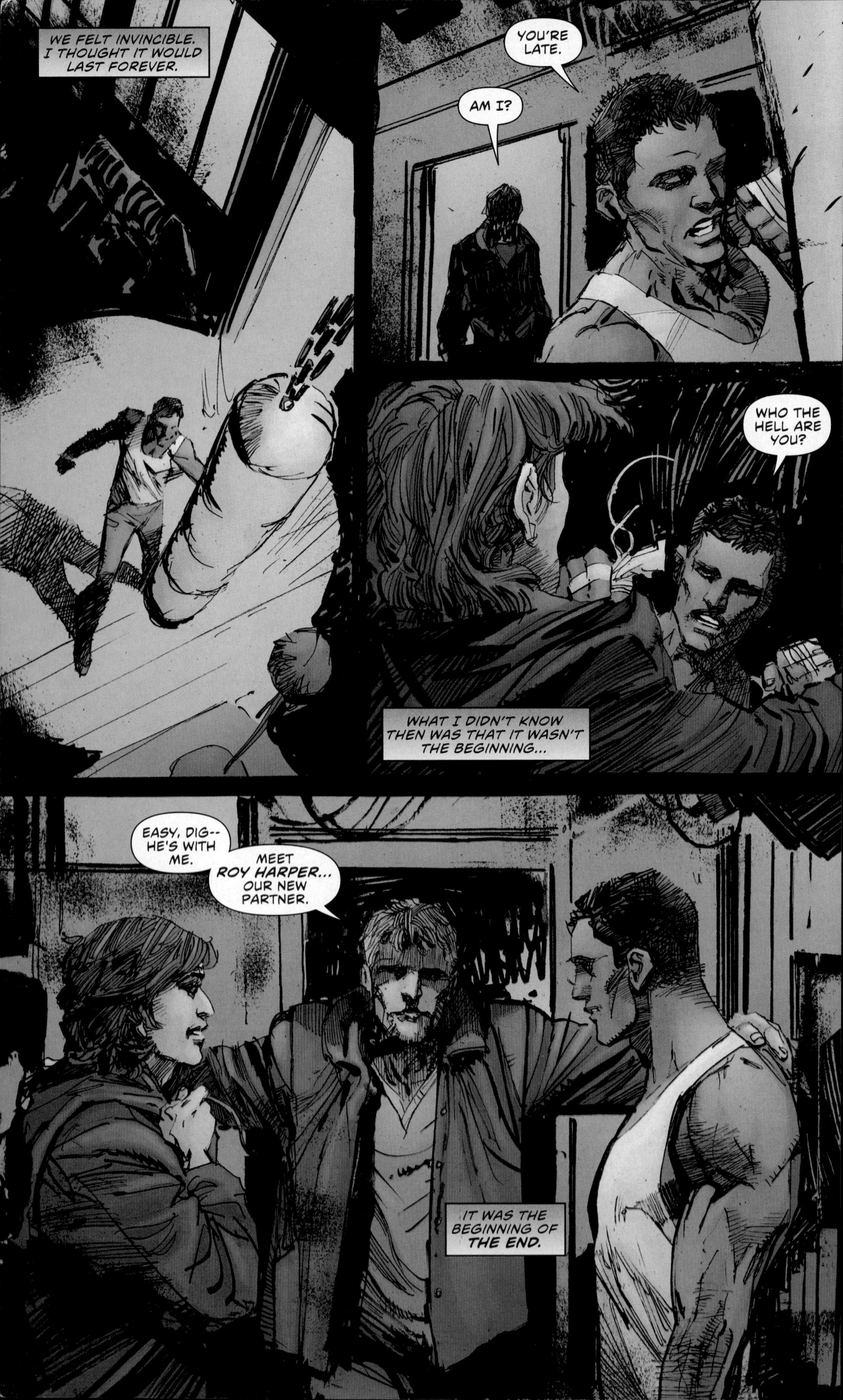
WE FELT INVINCIBLE. I THOUGHT IT WOULD LAST FOREVER.
YOU'RE LATE.
AM I?
WHO THE HELL ARE YOU?
WHAT I DIDN'T KNOW THEN WAS THAT IT WASN'T THE BEGINNING...
EASY, DIG-- HE'S WITH ME.
MEET ROY HARPER... OUR NEW PARTNER.
IT WAS THE BEGINNING OF THE END.

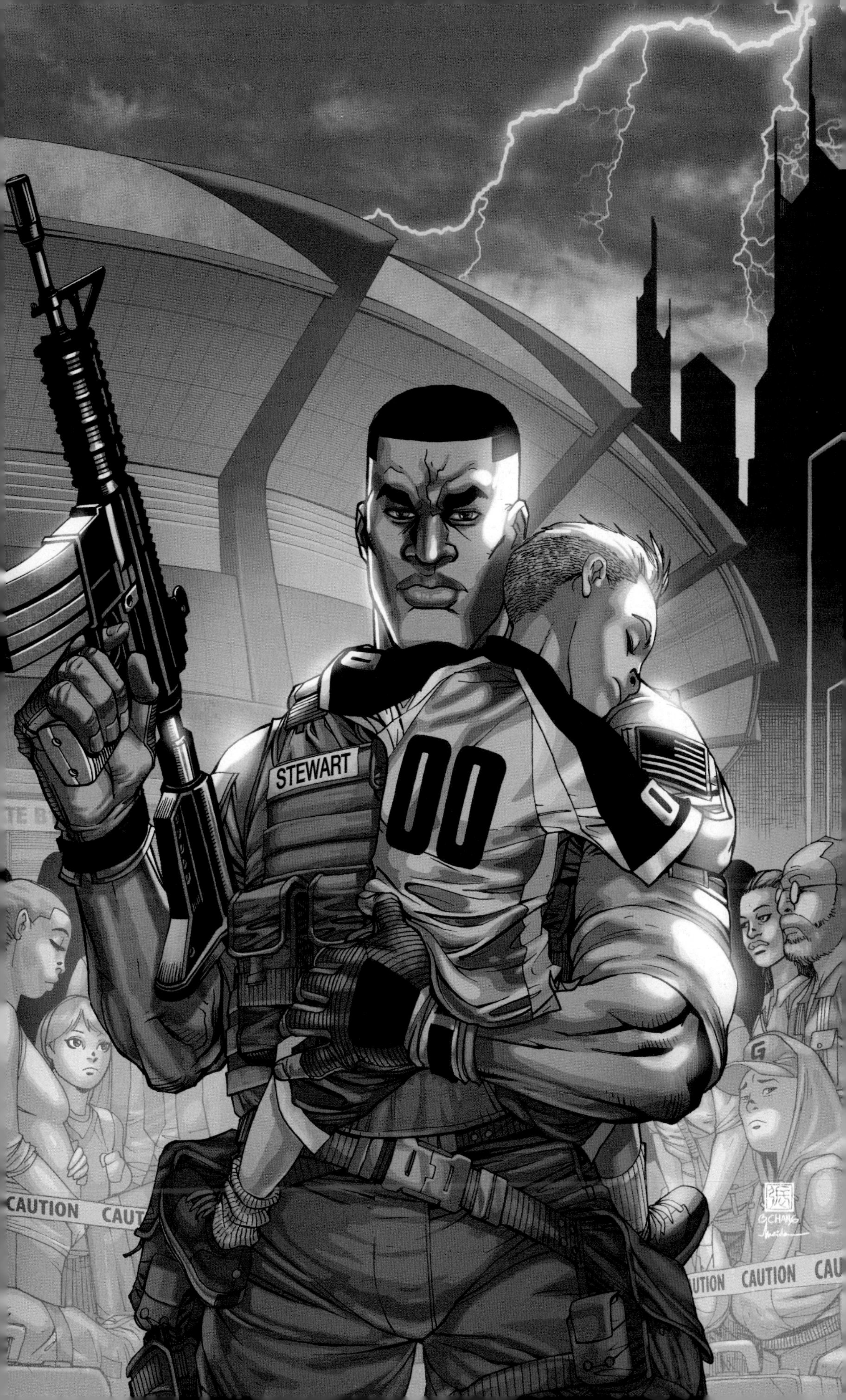
STEWART
00
CAUTION
CAUTION CAUTION
©CHANG

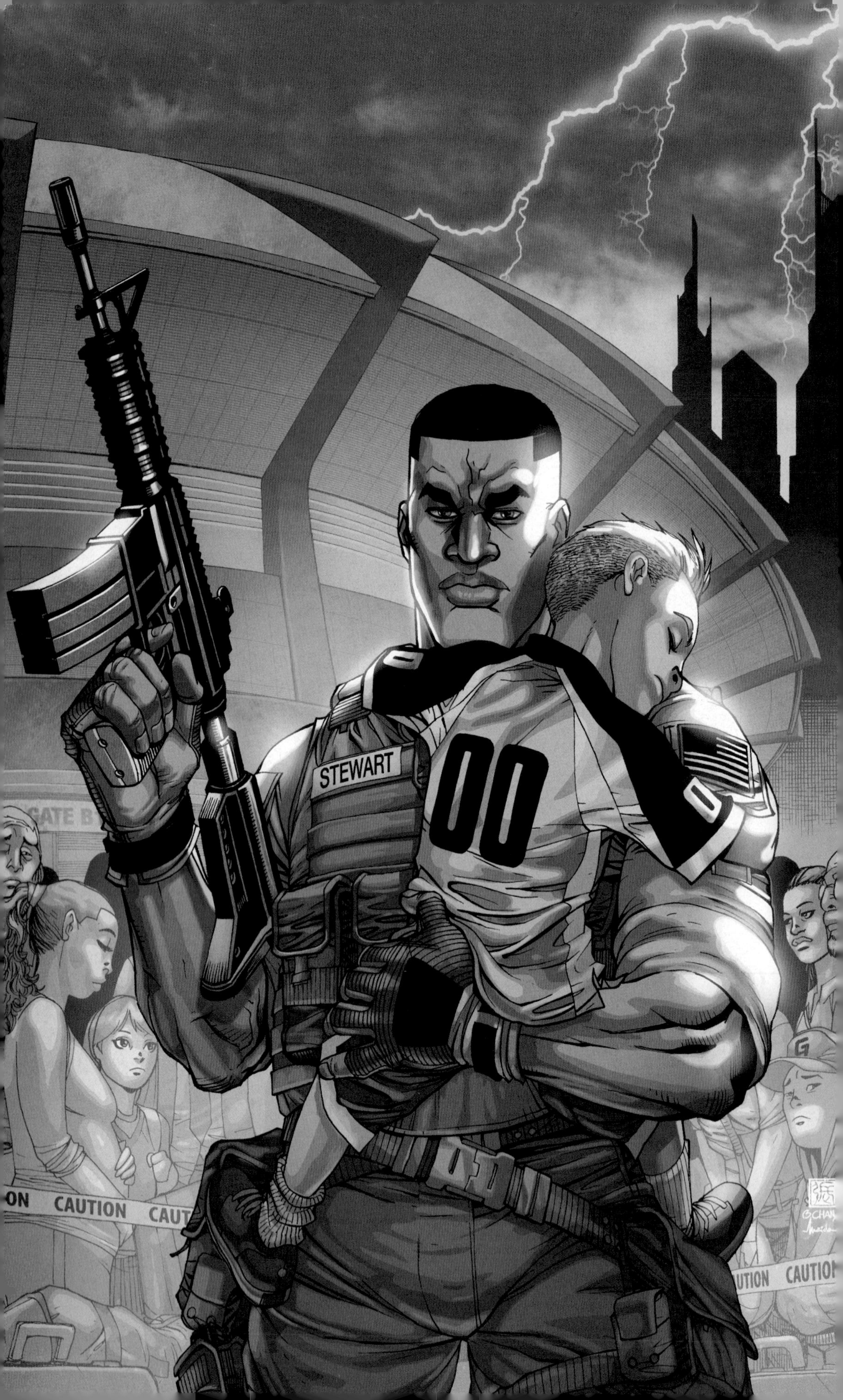
STEWART
00
CAUTION
CAUTION

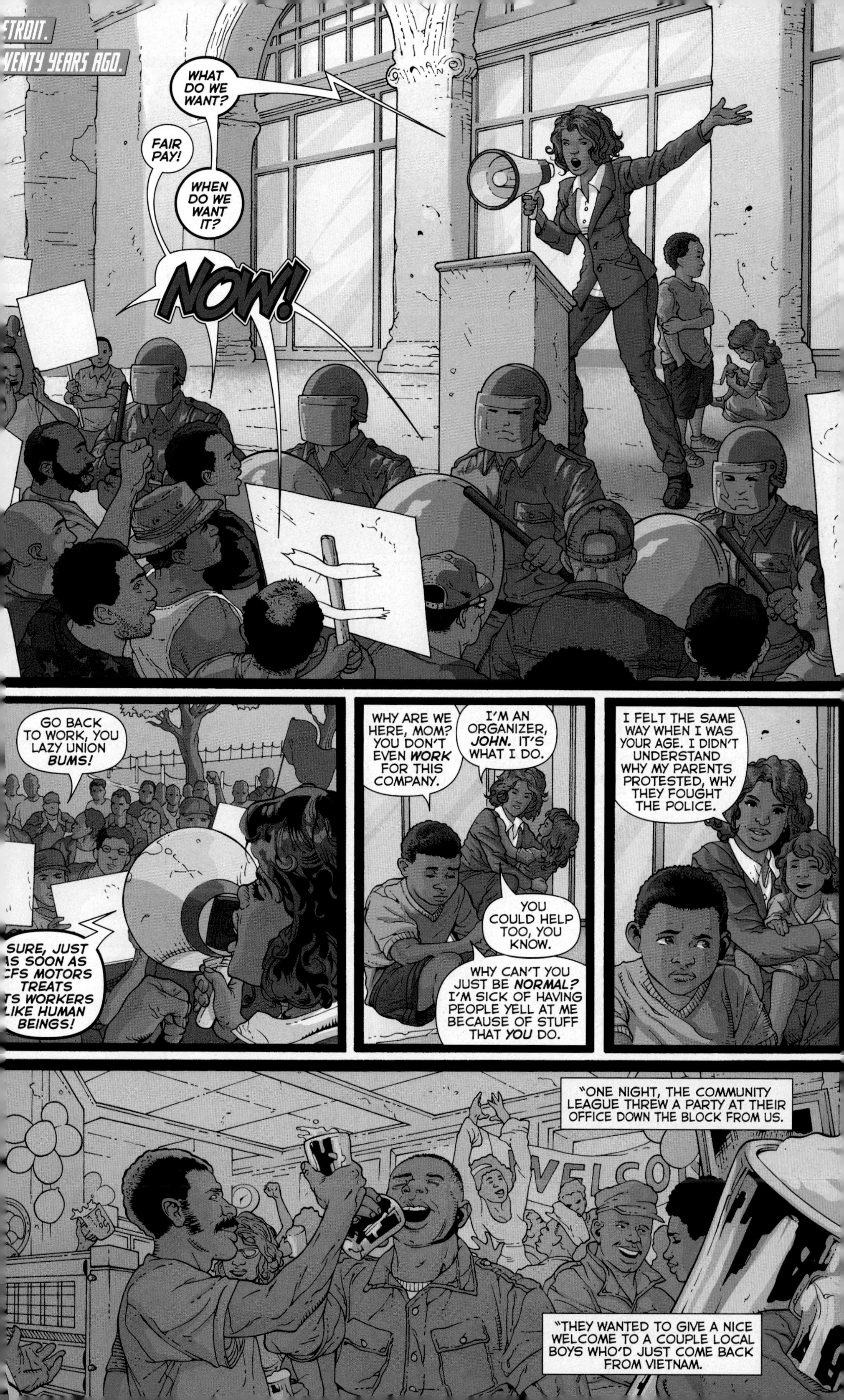

ETROIT.
VENTY YEARS AGO.
WHAT DO WE WANT?
FAIR PAY!
WHEN DO WE WANT IT?
NOW!
GO BACK TO WORK, YOU LAZY UNION BUMS!
SURE, JUST AS SOON AS CFS MOTORS TREATS TS WORKERS LIKE HUMAN BEINGS!
WHY ARE WE HERE, MOM? YOU DON'T EVEN WORK FOR THIS COMPANY.
I'M AN ORGANIZER, JOHN. IT'S WHAT I DO.
YOU COULD HELP TOO, YOU KNOW.
WHY CAN'T YOU JUST BE NORMAL? I'M SICK OF HAVING PEOPLE YELL AT ME BECAUSE OF STUFF THAT YOU DO.
I FELT THE SAME WAY WHEN I WAS YOUR AGE. I DIDN'T UNDERSTAND WHY MY PARENTS PROTESTED, WHY THEY FOUGHT THE POLICE.
"ONE NIGHT, THE COMMUNITY LEAGUE THREW A PARTY AT THEIR OFFICE DOWN THE BLOCK FROM US.
WELCO
"THEY WANTED TO GIVE A NICE WELCOME TO A COUPLE LOCAL BOYS WHO'D JUST COME BACK FROM VIETNAM.

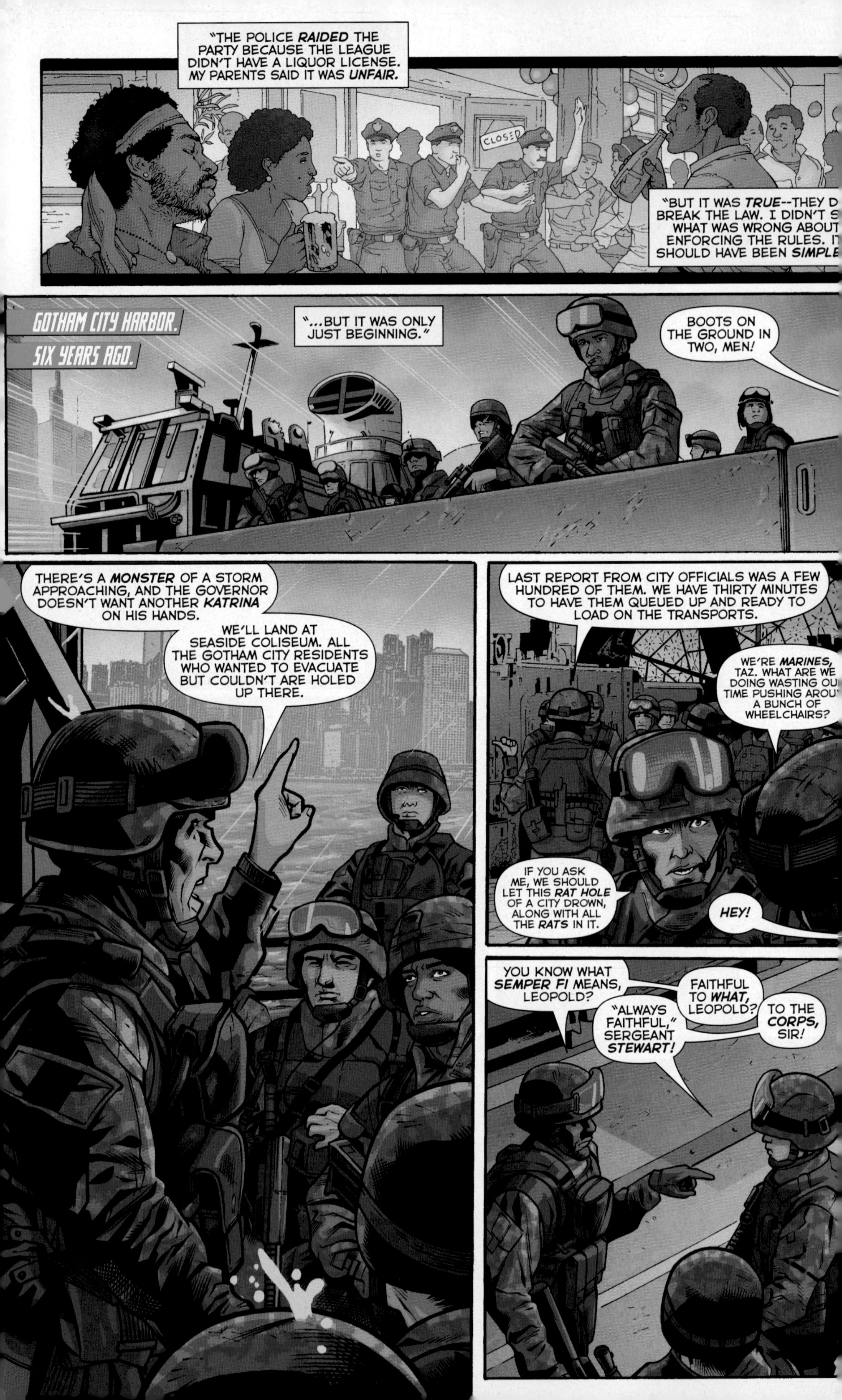

"THE POLICE RAIDED THE PARTY BECAUSE THE LEAGUE DIDN'T HAVE A LIQUOR LICENSE. MY PARENTS SAID IT WAS UNFAIR.
CLOSED
"BUT IT WAS TRUE--THEY D BREAK THE LAW. I DIDN'T S WHAT WAS WRONG ABOUT ENFORCING THE RULES. I SHOULD HAVE BEEN SIMPLE
GOTHAM CITY HARBOR.
SIX YEARS AGO.
"...BUT IT WAS ONLY JUST BEGINNING."
BOOTS ON THE GROUND IN TWO, MEN!
THERE'S A MONSTER OF A STORM APPROACHING, AND THE GOVERNOR DOESN'T WANT ANOTHER KATRINA ON HIS HANDS.
WE'LL LAND AT SEASIDE COLISEUM. ALL THE GOTHAM CITY RESIDENTS WHO WANTED TO EVACUATE BUT COULDN'T ARE HOLED UP THERE.
LAST REPORT FROM CITY OFFICIALS WAS A FEW HUNDRED OF THEM. WE HAVE THIRTY MINUTES TO HAVE THEM QUEUED UP AND READY TO LOAD ON THE TRANSPORTS.
WE'RE MARINES, TAZ. WHAT ARE WE DOING WASTING OU TIME PUSHING AROU A BUNCH OF WHEELCHAIRS?
IF YOU ASK ME, WE SHOULD LET THIS RAT HOLE OF A CITY DROWN, ALONG WITH ALL THE RATS IN IT.
HEY!
YOU KNOW WHAT SEMPER FI MEANS, LEOPOLD?
"ALWAYS FAITHFUL," SERGEANT STEWART!
FAITHFUL TO WHAT, LEOPOLD?
TO THE CORPS, SIR!

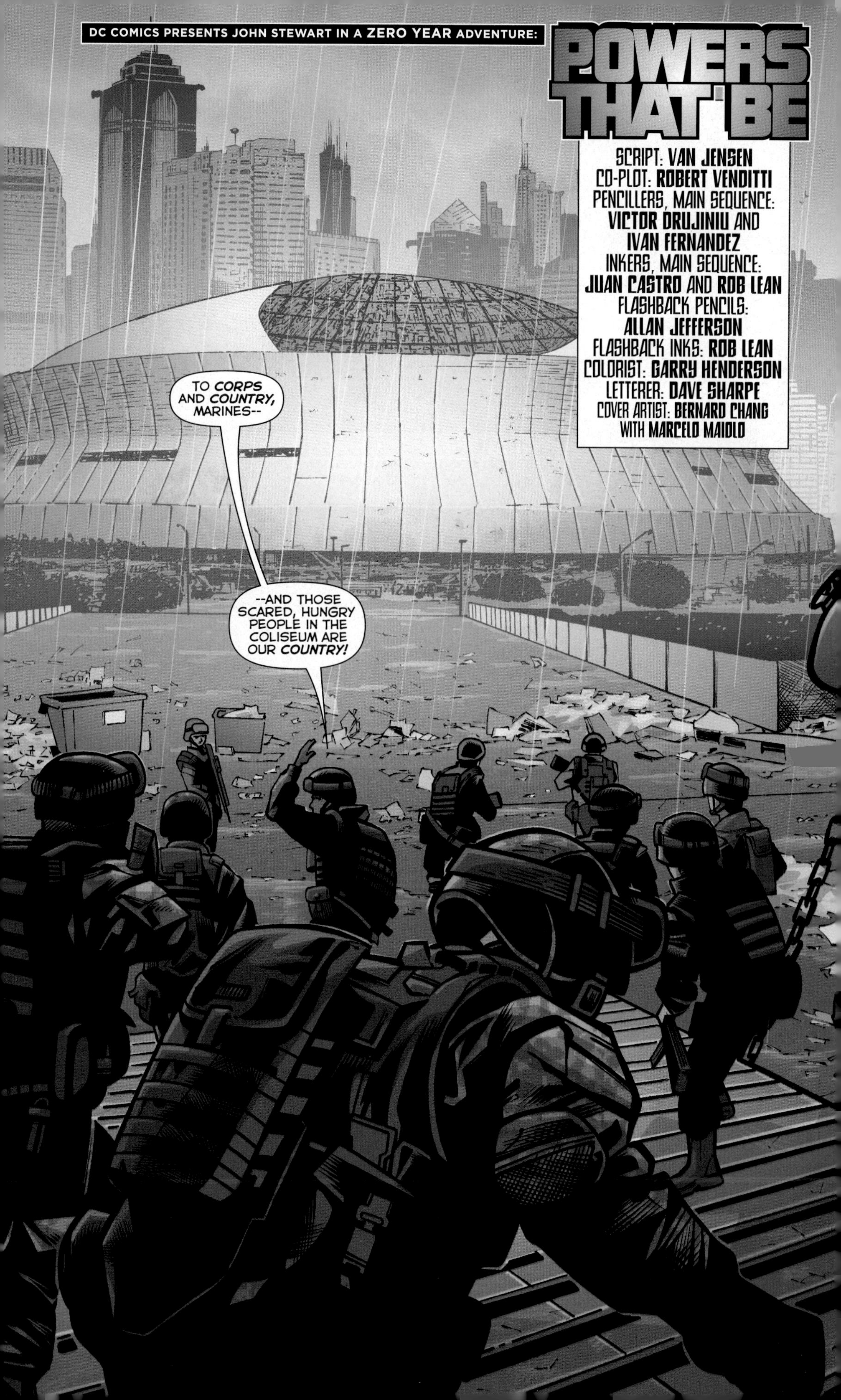

DC COMICS PRESENTS JOHN STEWART IN A ZERO YEAR ADVENTURE:
POWERS THAT BE
SCRIPT: VAN JENSEN
CO-PLOT: ROBERT VENDITTI
PENCILLERS, MAIN SEQUENCE: VICTOR DRUJINIU AND IVAN FERNANDEZ
INKERS, MAIN SEQUENCE: JUAN CASTRO AND ROB LEAN
FLASHBACK PENCILS: ALLAN JEFFERSON
FLASHBACK INKS: ROB LEAN
COLORIST: GARRY HENDERSON
LETTERER: DAVE SHARPE
COVER ARTIST: BERNARD CHANG WITH MARCELO MAIOLO
TO CORPS AND COUNTRY, MARINES--
--AND THOSE SCARED, HUNGRY PEOPLE IN THE COLISEUM ARE OUR COUNTRY!

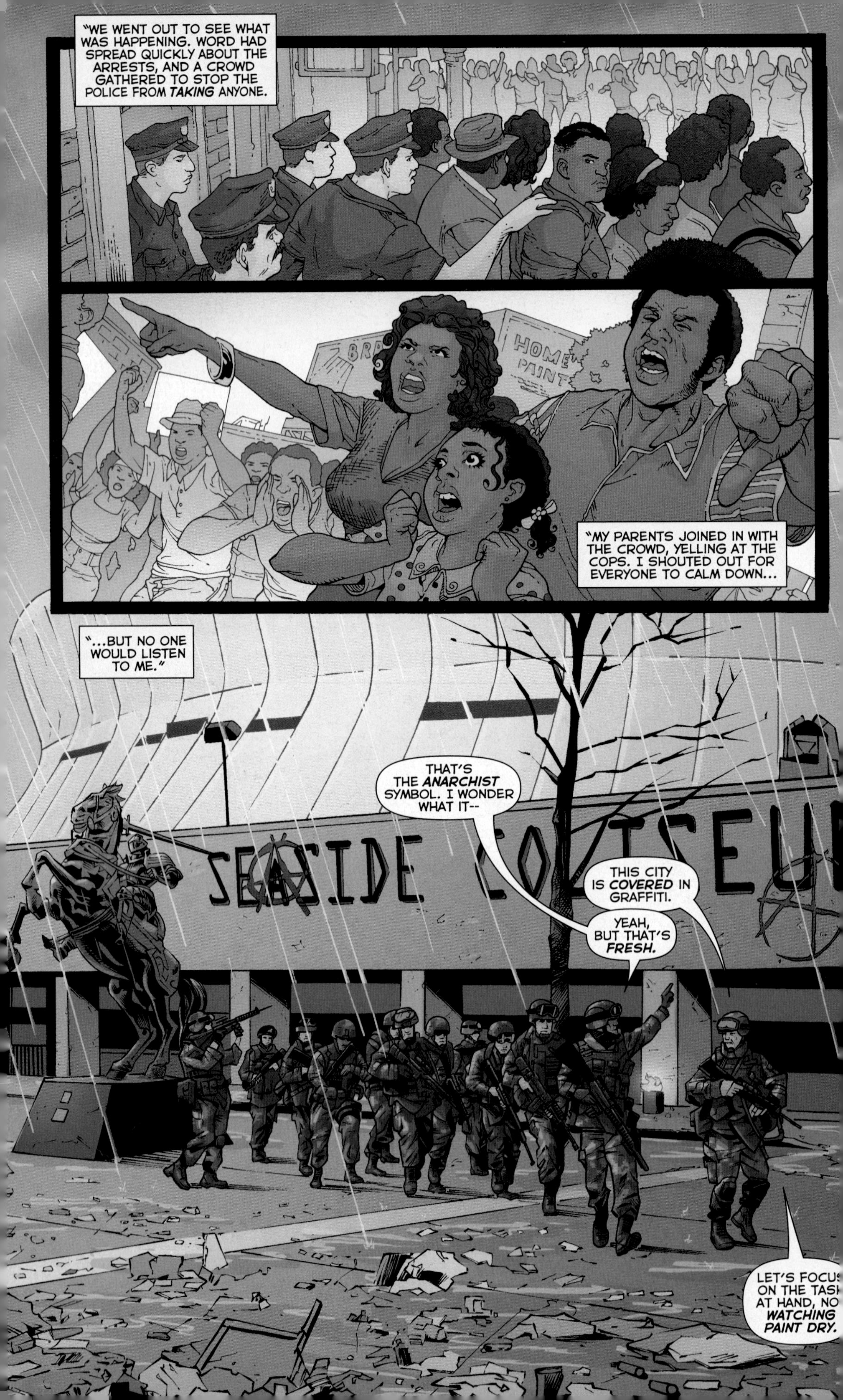
"WE WENT OUT TO SEE WHAT WAS HAPPENING. WORD HAD SPREAD QUICKLY ABOUT THE ARRESTS, AND A CROWD GATHERED TO STOP THE POLICE FROM *TAKING* ANYONE.
HOME PAINT
"MY PARENTS JOINED IN WITH THE CROWD, YELLING AT THE COPS. I SHOUTED OUT FOR EVERYONE TO CALM DOWN...
"...BUT NO ONE WOULD LISTEN TO ME."
SEASIDE COLISEUM
THAT'S THE *ANARCHIST* SYMBOL. I WONDER WHAT IT--
THIS CITY IS *COVERED* IN GRAFFITI.
YEAH, BUT THAT'S *FRESH.*
LET'S FOCUS ON THE TASK AT HAND, NOT *WATCHING PAINT DRY.*

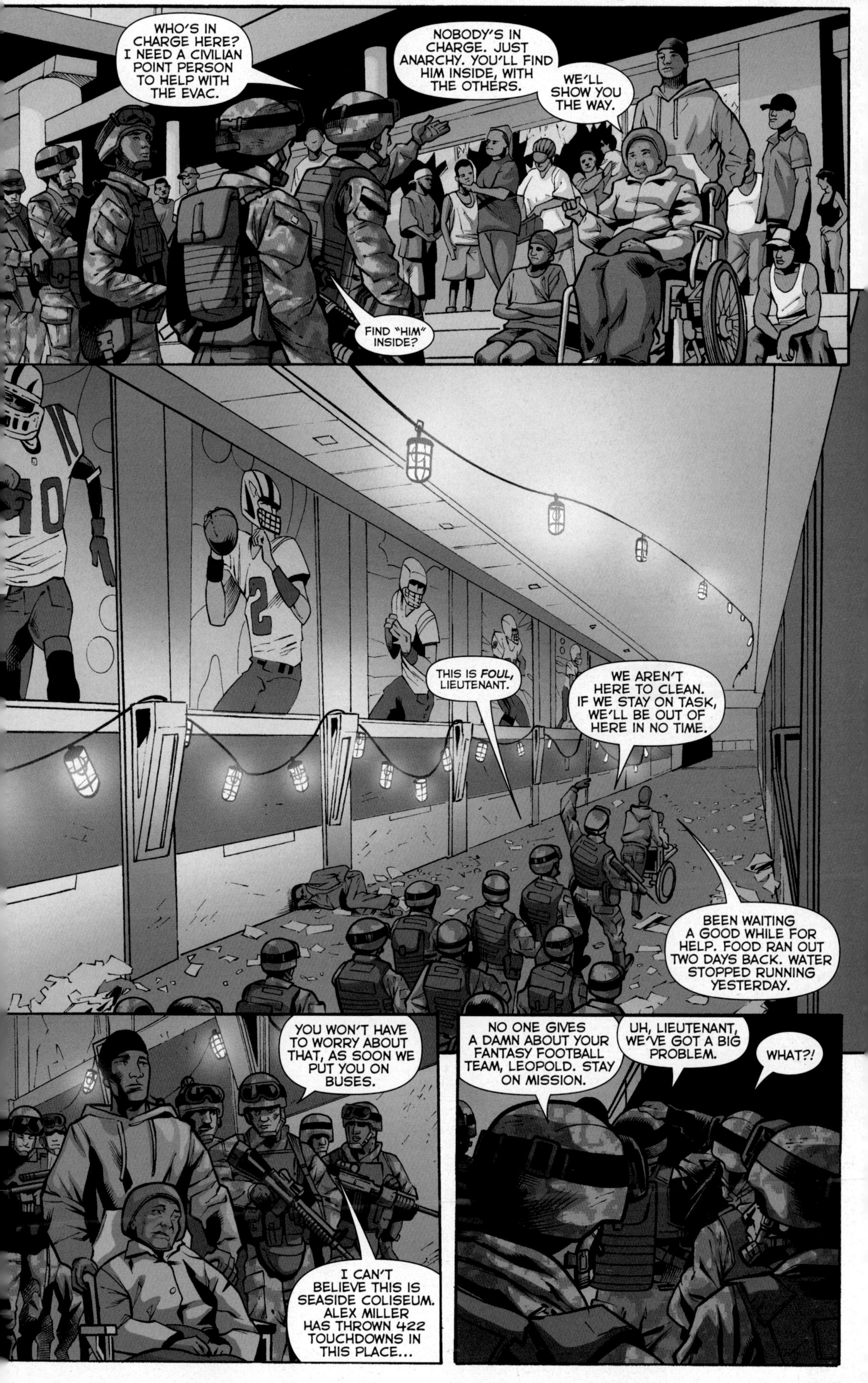
WHO'S IN CHARGE HERE? I NEED A CIVILIAN POINT PERSON TO HELP WITH THE EVAC.
NOBODY'S IN CHARGE. JUST ANARCHY. YOU'LL FIND HIM INSIDE, WITH THE OTHERS.
WE'LL SHOW YOU THE WAY.
FIND "HIM" INSIDE?
THIS IS *FOUL,* LIEUTENANT.
WE AREN'T HERE TO CLEAN. IF WE STAY ON TASK, WE'LL BE OUT OF HERE IN NO TIME.
BEEN WAITING A GOOD WHILE FOR HELP. FOOD RAN OUT TWO DAYS BACK. WATER STOPPED RUNNING YESTERDAY.
YOU WON'T HAVE TO WORRY ABOUT THAT, AS SOON WE PUT YOU ON BUSES.
I CAN'T BELIEVE THIS IS SEASIDE COLISEUM. ALEX MILLER HAS THROWN 422 TOUCHDOWNS IN THIS PLACE...
NO ONE GIVES A DAMN ABOUT YOUR FANTASY FOOTBALL TEAM, LEOPOLD. STAY ON MISSION.
UH, LIEUTENANT, WE'VE GOT A BIG PROBLEM.
WHAT?!

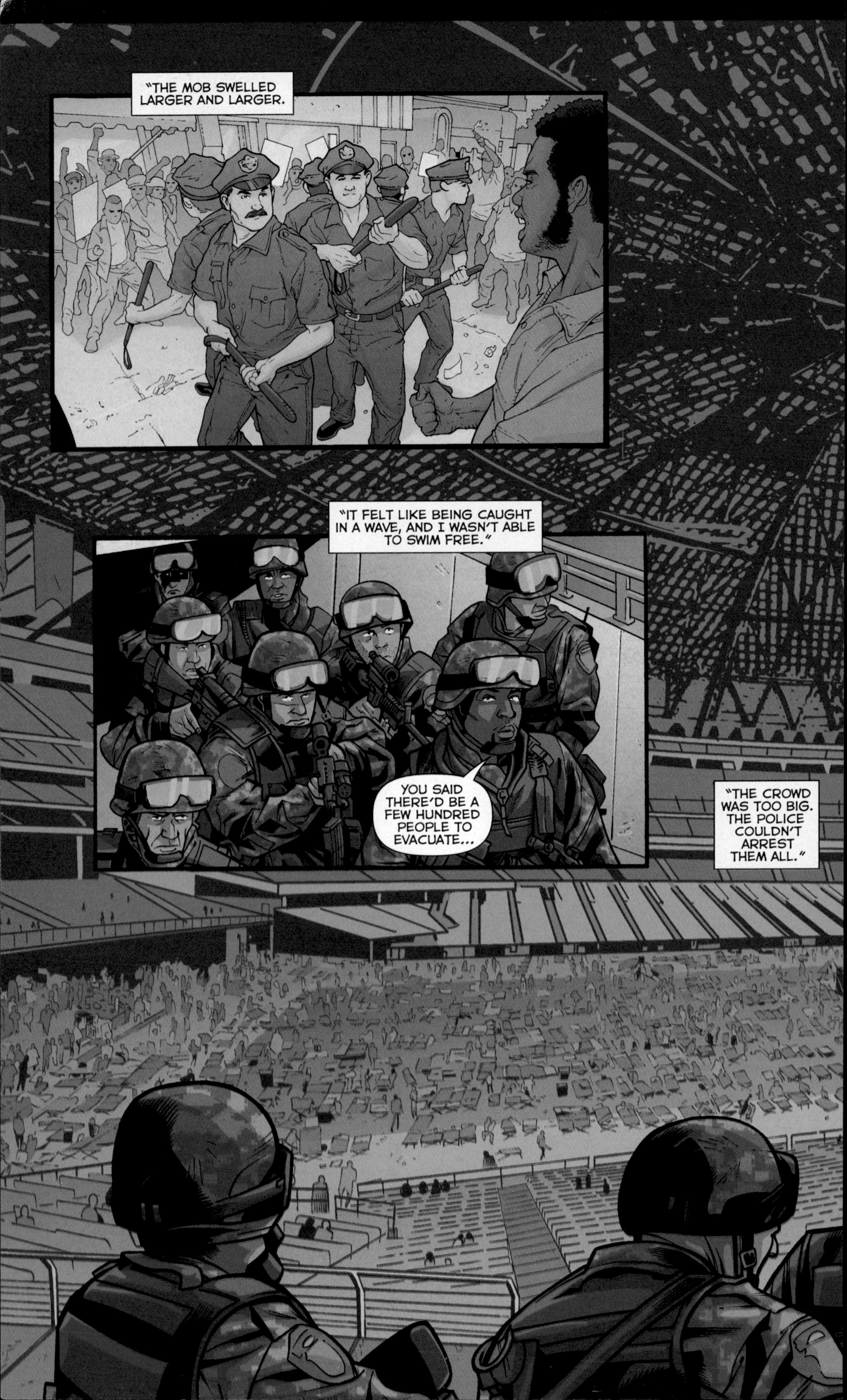
"THE MOB SWELLED LARGER AND LARGER.
"IT FELT LIKE BEING CAUGHT IN A WAVE, AND I WASN'T ABLE TO SWIM FREE."
YOU SAID THERE'D BE A FEW HUNDRED PEOPLE TO EVACUATE...
"THE CROWD WAS TOO BIG. THE POLICE COULDN'T ARREST THEM ALL."

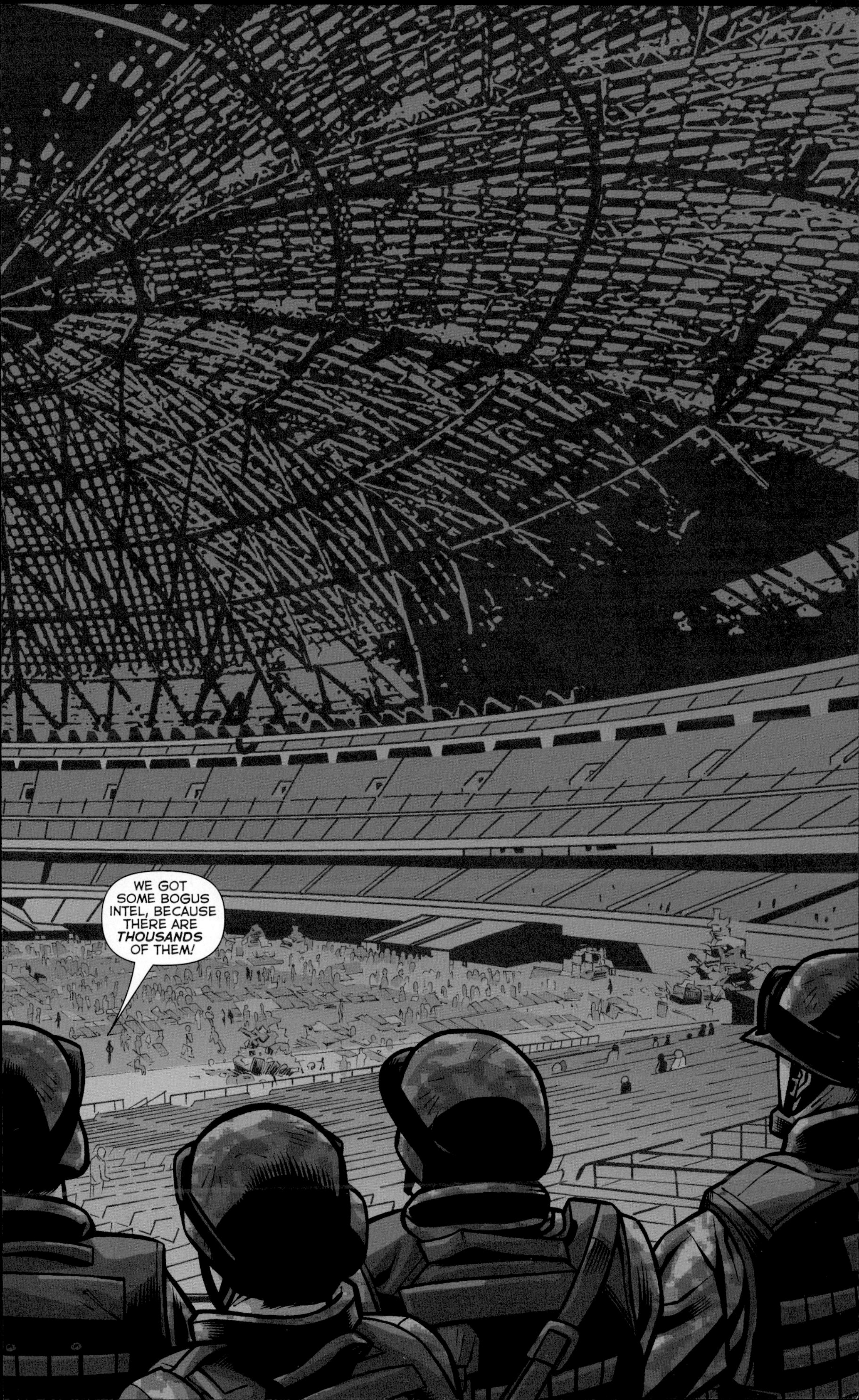
WE GOT SOME BOGUS INTEL, BECAUSE THERE ARE *THOUSANDS* OF THEM!

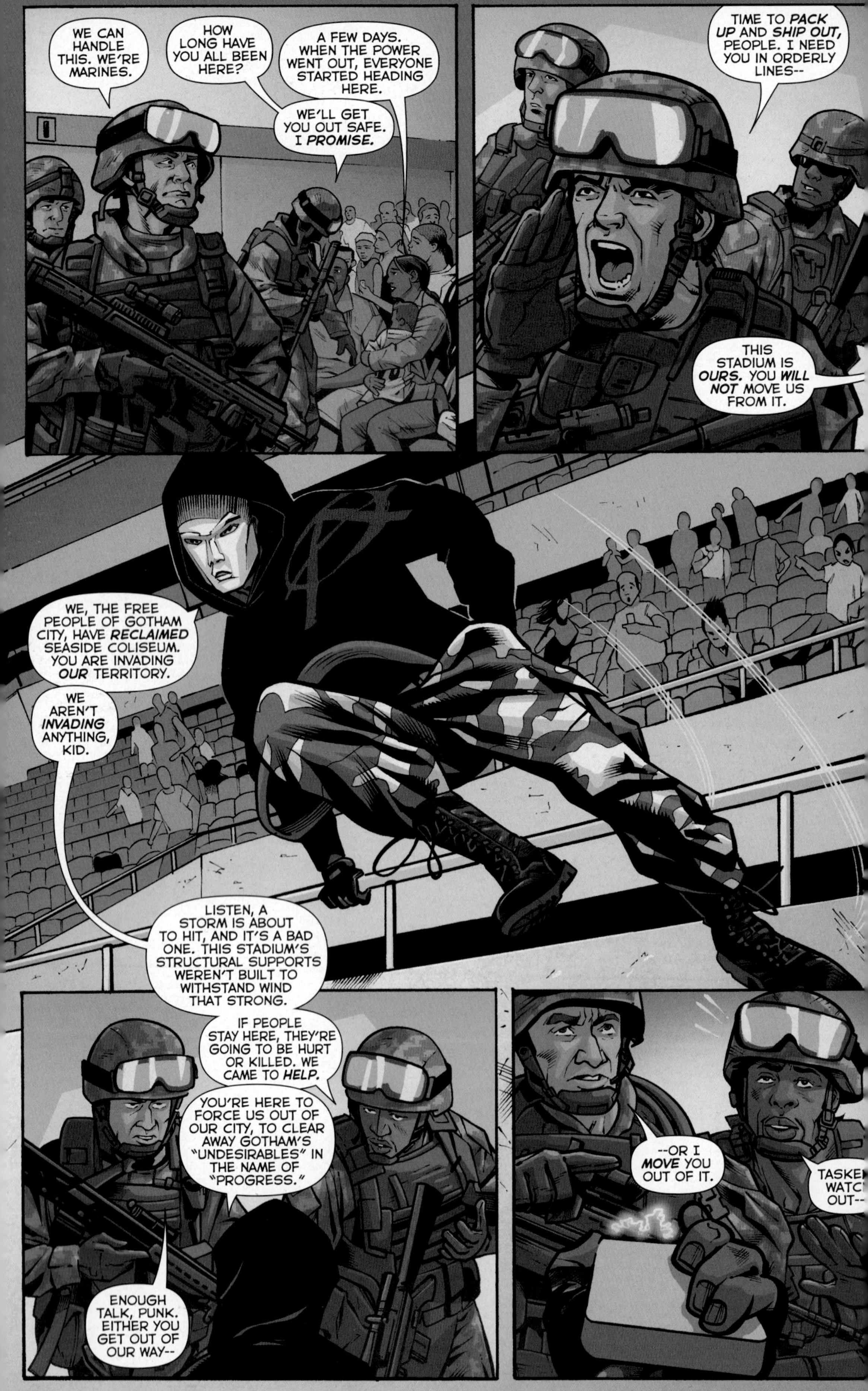
WE CAN HANDLE THIS. WE'RE MARINES.
HOW LONG HAVE YOU ALL BEEN HERE?
A FEW DAYS. WHEN THE POWER WENT OUT, EVERYONE STARTED HEADING HERE.
WE'LL GET YOU OUT SAFE. I PROMISE.
TIME TO PACK UP AND SHIP OUT, PEOPLE. I NEED YOU IN ORDERLY LINES--
THIS STADIUM IS OURS. YOU WILL NOT MOVE US FROM IT.
WE, THE FREE PEOPLE OF GOTHAM CITY, HAVE RECLAIMED SEASIDE COLISEUM. YOU ARE INVADING OUR TERRITORY.
WE AREN'T INVADING ANYTHING, KID.
LISTEN, A STORM IS ABOUT TO HIT, AND IT'S A BAD ONE. THIS STADIUM'S STRUCTURAL SUPPORTS WEREN'T BUILT TO WITHSTAND WIND THAT STRONG.
IF PEOPLE STAY HERE, THEY'RE GOING TO BE HURT OR KILLED. WE CAME TO HELP.
YOU'RE HERE TO FORCE US OUT OF OUR CITY, TO CLEAR AWAY GOTHAM'S "UNDESIRABLES" IN THE NAME OF "PROGRESS."
ENOUGH TALK, PUNK. EITHER YOU GET OUT OF OUR WAY--
--OR I MOVE YOU OUT OF IT.

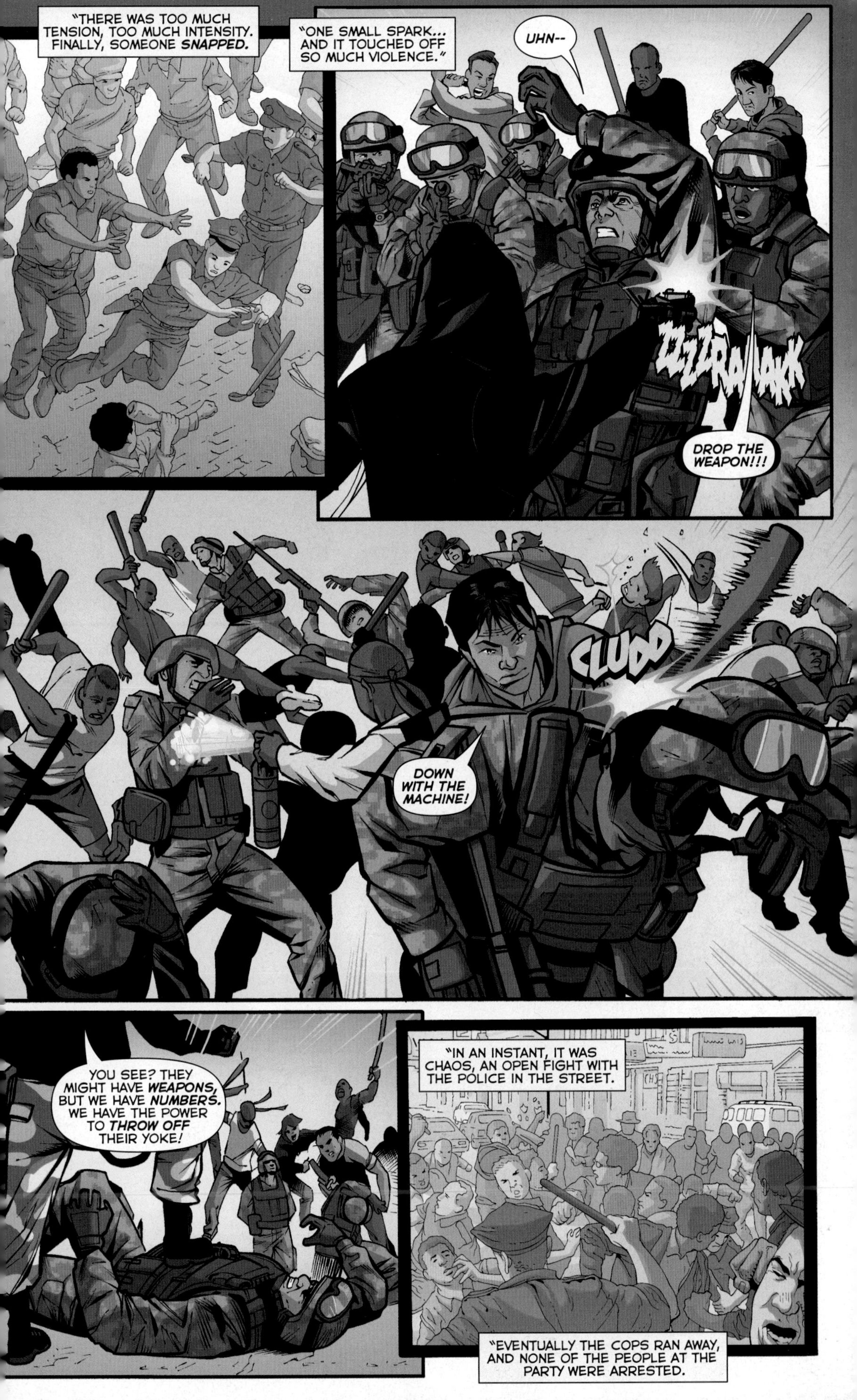

"THERE WAS TOO MUCH TENSION, TOO MUCH INTENSITY. FINALLY, SOMEONE SNAPPED.
"ONE SMALL SPARK... AND IT TOUCHED OFF SO MUCH VIOLENCE."
UHN--
DZZZRAAAKK
DROP THE WEAPON!!!
CLUDD
DOWN WITH THE MACHINE!
YOU SEE? THEY MIGHT HAVE WEAPONS, BUT WE HAVE NUMBERS. WE HAVE THE POWER TO THROW OFF THEIR YOKE!
"IN AN INSTANT, IT WAS CHAOS, AN OPEN FIGHT WITH THE POLICE IN THE STREET.
"EVENTUALLY THE COPS RAN AWAY, AND NONE OF THE PEOPLE AT THE PARTY WERE ARRESTED.

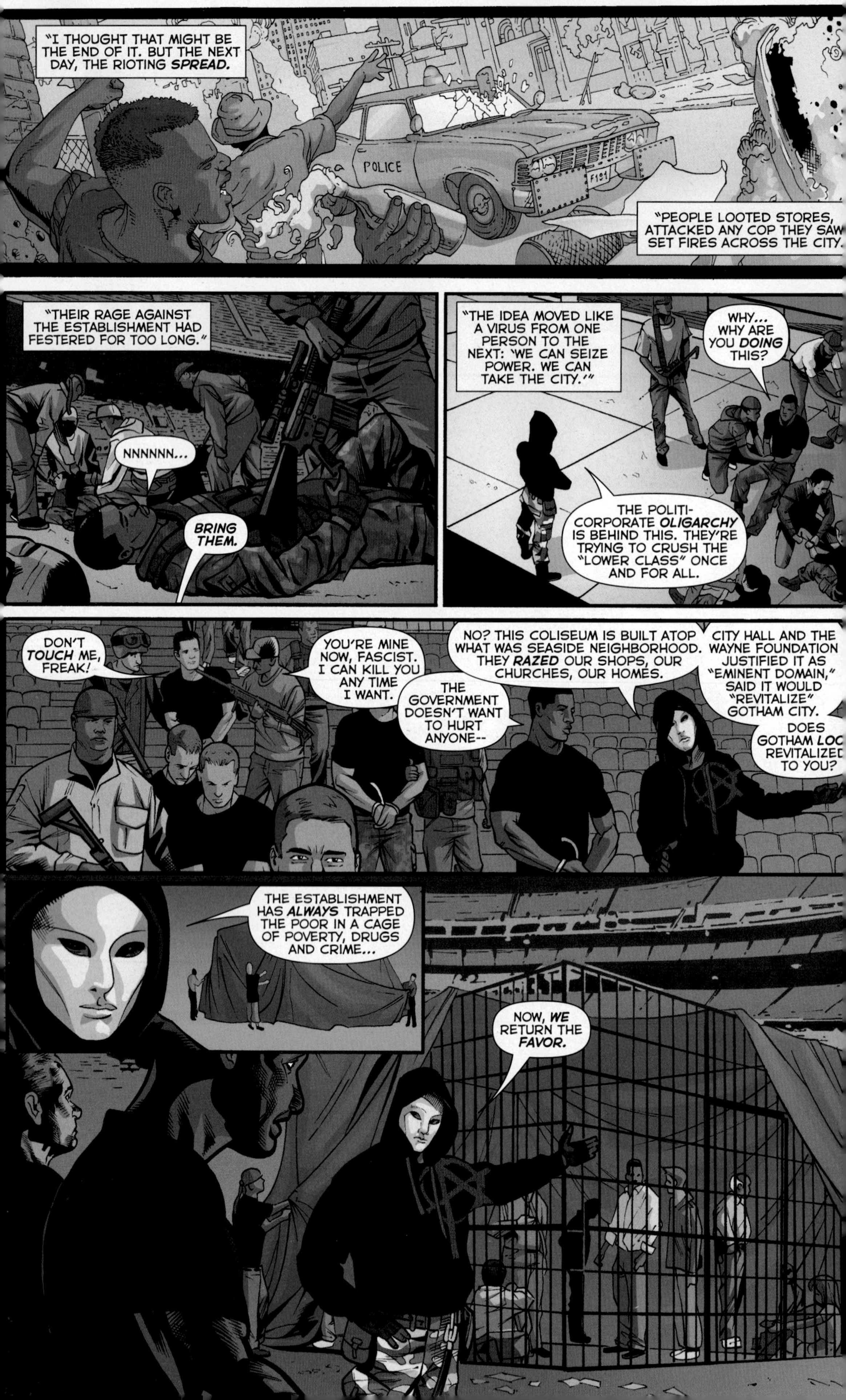
"I THOUGHT THAT MIGHT BE THE END OF IT. BUT THE NEXT DAY, THE RIOTING SPREAD.
POLICE
"PEOPLE LOOTED STORES, ATTACKED ANY COP THEY SAW SET FIRES ACROSS THE CITY.
"THEIR RAGE AGAINST THE ESTABLISHMENT HAD FESTERED FOR TOO LONG."
NNNNNN...
BRING THEM.
"THE IDEA MOVED LIKE A VIRUS FROM ONE PERSON TO THE NEXT: 'WE CAN SEIZE POWER. WE CAN TAKE THE CITY.'"
WHY... WHY ARE YOU DOING THIS?
THE POLITI-CORPORATE OLIGARCHY IS BEHIND THIS. THEY'RE TRYING TO CRUSH THE "LOWER CLASS" ONCE AND FOR ALL.
DON'T TOUCH ME, FREAK!
YOU'RE MINE NOW, FASCIST. I CAN KILL YOU ANY TIME I WANT.
THE GOVERNMENT DOESN'T WANT TO HURT ANYONE--
NO? THIS COLISEUM IS BUILT ATOP WHAT WAS SEASIDE NEIGHBORHOOD. THEY RAZED OUR SHOPS, OUR CHURCHES, OUR HOMES.
CITY HALL AND THE WAYNE FOUNDATION JUSTIFIED IT AS "EMINENT DOMAIN," SAID IT WOULD "REVITALIZE" GOTHAM CITY.
DOES GOTHAM LOO REVITALIZED TO YOU?
THE ESTABLISHMENT HAS ALWAYS TRAPPED THE POOR IN A CAGE OF POVERTY, DRUGS AND CRIME...
NOW, WE RETURN THE FAVOR.

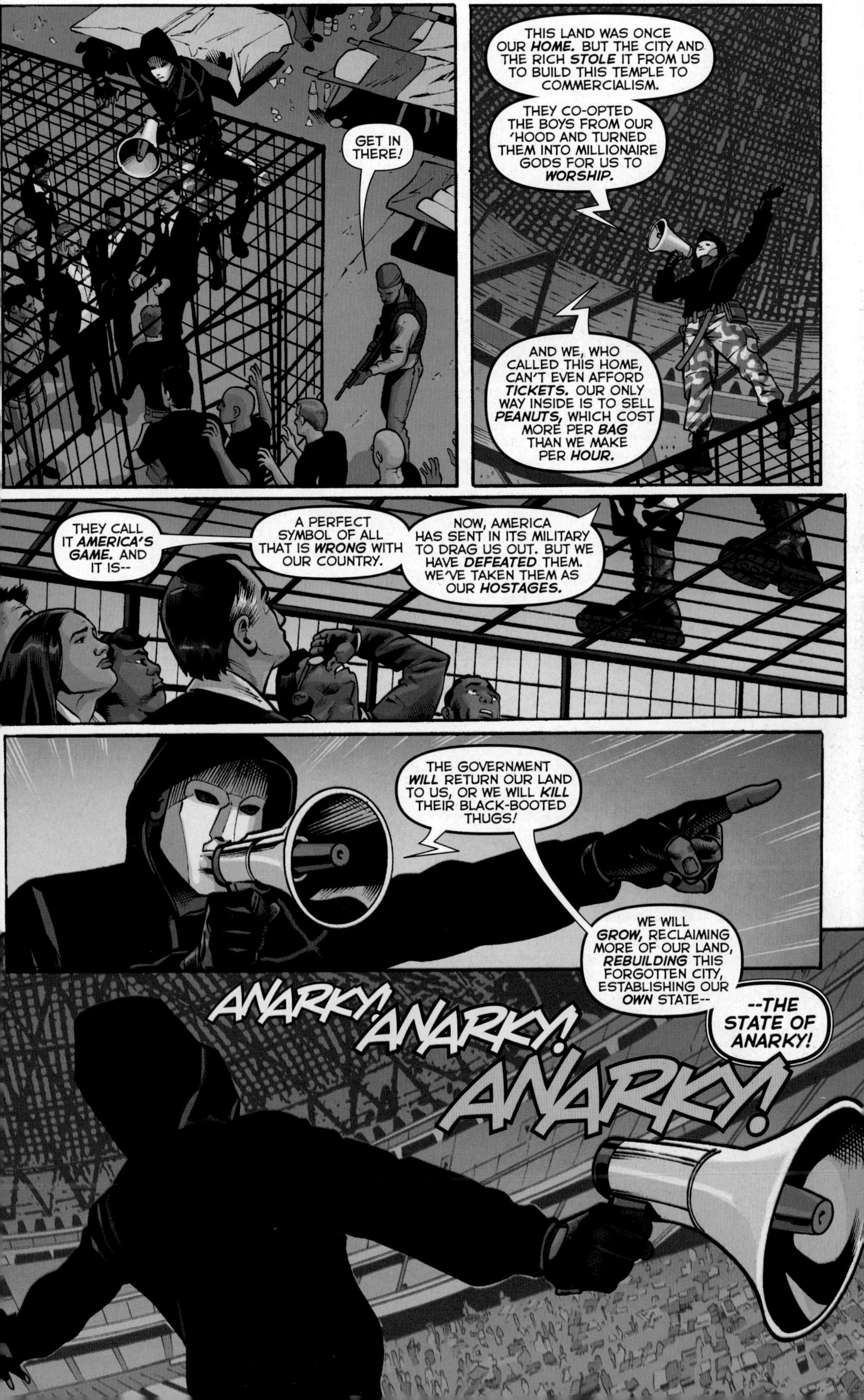

GET IN THERE!
THIS LAND WAS ONCE OUR HOME. BUT THE CITY AND THE RICH STOLE IT FROM US TO BUILD THIS TEMPLE TO COMMERCIALISM.
THEY CO-OPTED THE BOYS FROM OUR 'HOOD AND TURNED THEM INTO MILLIONAIRE GODS FOR US TO WORSHIP.
AND WE, WHO CALLED THIS HOME, CAN'T EVEN AFFORD TICKETS. OUR ONLY WAY INSIDE IS TO SELL PEANUTS, WHICH COST MORE PER BAG THAN WE MAKE PER HOUR.
THEY CALL IT AMERICA'S GAME. AND IT IS--
A PERFECT SYMBOL OF ALL THAT IS WRONG WITH OUR COUNTRY.
NOW, AMERICA HAS SENT IN ITS MILITARY TO DRAG US OUT. BUT WE HAVE DEFEATED THEM. WE'VE TAKEN THEM AS OUR HOSTAGES.
THE GOVERNMENT WILL RETURN OUR LAND TO US, OR WE WILL KILL THEIR BLACK-BOOTED THUGS!
WE WILL GROW, RECLAIMING MORE OF OUR LAND, REBUILDING THIS FORGOTTEN CITY, ESTABLISHING OUR OWN STATE--
--THE STATE OF ANARKY!
ANARKY! ANARKY! ANARKY!

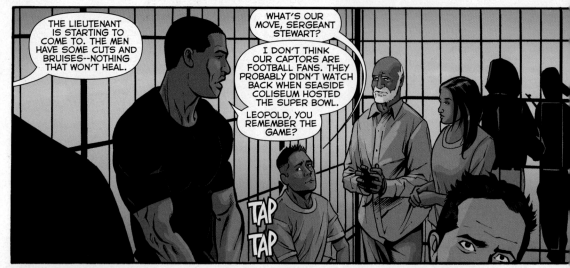

THE LIEUTENANT IS STARTING TO COME TO. THE MEN HAVE SOME CUTS AND BRUISES--NOTHING THAT WON'T HEAL.

WHAT'S OUR MOVE, SERGEANT STEWART?

I DON'T THINK OUR CAPTORS ARE FOOTBALL FANS. THEY PROBABLY DIDN'T WATCH BACK WHEN SEASIDE COLISEUM HOSTED THE SUPER BOWL.

LEOPOLD, YOU REMEMBER THE GAME?

TAP TAP

IT WAS A *CLASSIC!* ELI GRAHAM STOOD RIGHT ABOUT HERE WHEN HE THREW THE HAIL MARY TO BLAKE LEE--

THE *HALFTIME SHOW* ALSO HAPPENED RIGHT ON THIS SPOT.

TAP TAP

I LIKED WATCHING *BRITNEY* SHAKE IT AS MUCH AS THE NEXT GUY, BUT WHAT DOES THAT HAVE TO DO WITH ANYTHING?

AND WHY DO YOU KEEP *PACING* LIKE THAT?

THE THING I NOTICED WAS HOW THE HALFTIME SHOW STARTED.

THE TURF WAS EMPTY, AND THE LIGHTS WENT OFF FOR A SECOND, AND THEN, *POOF,* THERE SHE WAS--

--LIKE SHE'D APPEARED OUT OF THIN AIR.

TAP

TAP TAP

TONK

WHAT IS *THAT?*

WHAT THE HELL DOES THAT MEAN?

DEUS EX MACHINA.

"GOD FROM THE MACHINE."

IN GREEK THEATERS, THEY BUILT *TRAP DOORS* TO BRING IN ACTORS PLAYING GODS TO SURPRISE THE AUDIENCE.

GOOD WORK, SERGEANT. EVERYONE, BE READY TO MOVE...

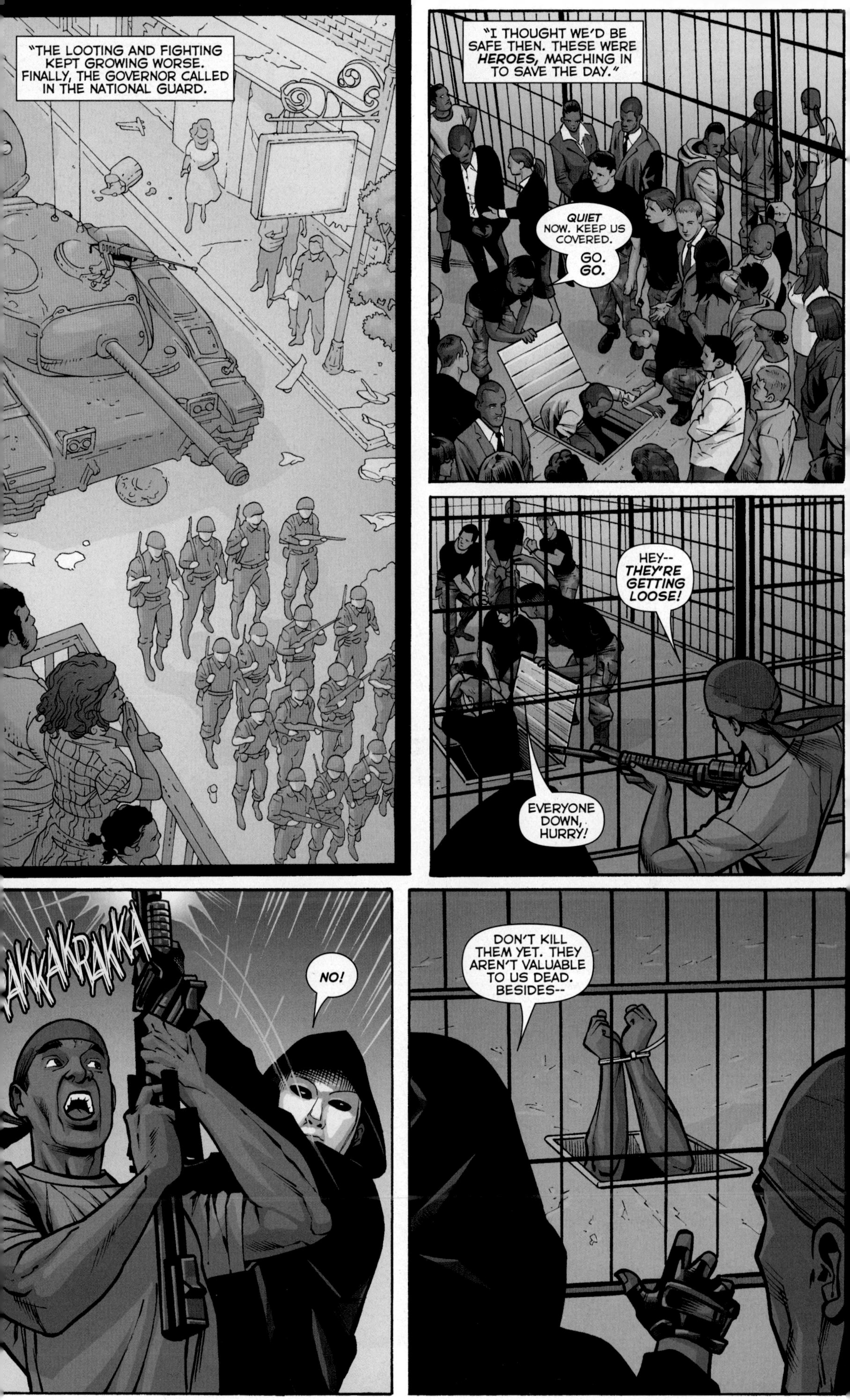
"THE LOOTING AND FIGHTING KEPT GROWING WORSE. FINALLY, THE GOVERNOR CALLED IN THE NATIONAL GUARD.
"I THOUGHT WE'D BE SAFE THEN. THESE WERE HEROES, MARCHING IN TO SAVE THE DAY."
QUIET NOW. KEEP US COVERED.
GO. GO.
HEY-- THEY'RE GETTING LOOSE!
EVERYONE DOWN, HURRY!
RAKKAKRAKKA
NO!
DON'T KILL THEM YET. THEY AREN'T VALUABLE TO US DEAD. BESIDES--

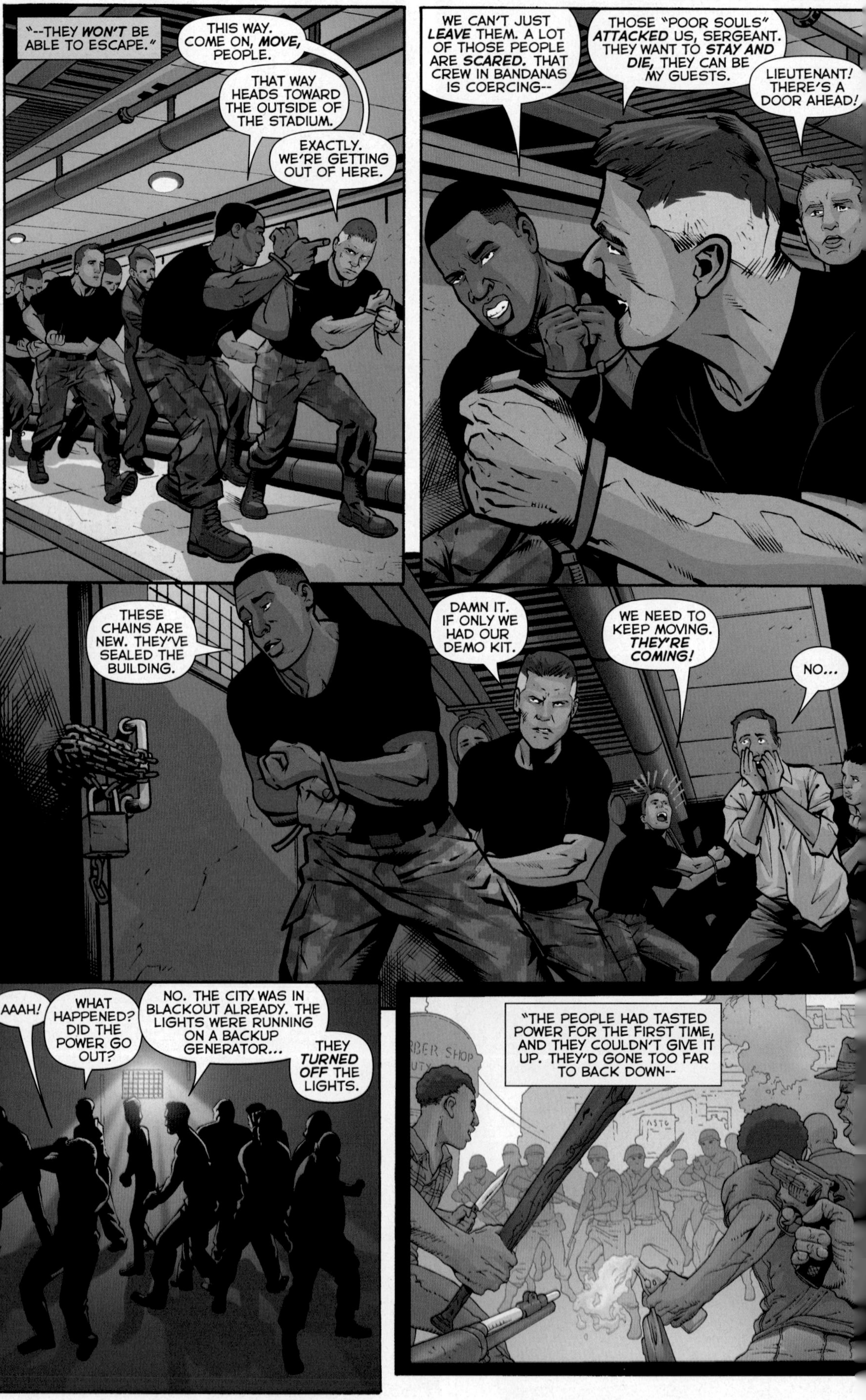
"--THEY WON'T BE ABLE TO ESCAPE."
THIS WAY. COME ON, MOVE, PEOPLE.
THAT WAY HEADS TOWARD THE OUTSIDE OF THE STADIUM.
EXACTLY. WE'RE GETTING OUT OF HERE.
WE CAN'T JUST LEAVE THEM. A LOT OF THOSE PEOPLE ARE SCARED. THAT CREW IN BANDANAS IS COERCING--
THOSE "POOR SOULS" ATTACKED US, SERGEANT. THEY WANT TO STAY AND DIE, THEY CAN BE MY GUESTS.
LIEUTENANT! THERE'S A DOOR AHEAD!
THESE CHAINS ARE NEW. THEY'VE SEALED THE BUILDING.
DAMN IT. IF ONLY WE HAD OUR DEMO KIT.
WE NEED TO KEEP MOVING. THEY'RE COMING!
NO...
AAAH!
WHAT HAPPENED? DID THE POWER GO OUT?
NO. THE CITY WAS IN BLACKOUT ALREADY. THE LIGHTS WERE RUNNING ON A BACKUP GENERATOR...
THEY TURNED OFF THE LIGHTS.
"THE PEOPLE HAD TASTED POWER FOR THE FIRST TIME, AND THEY COULDN'T GIVE IT UP. THEY'D GONE TOO FAR TO BACK DOWN--

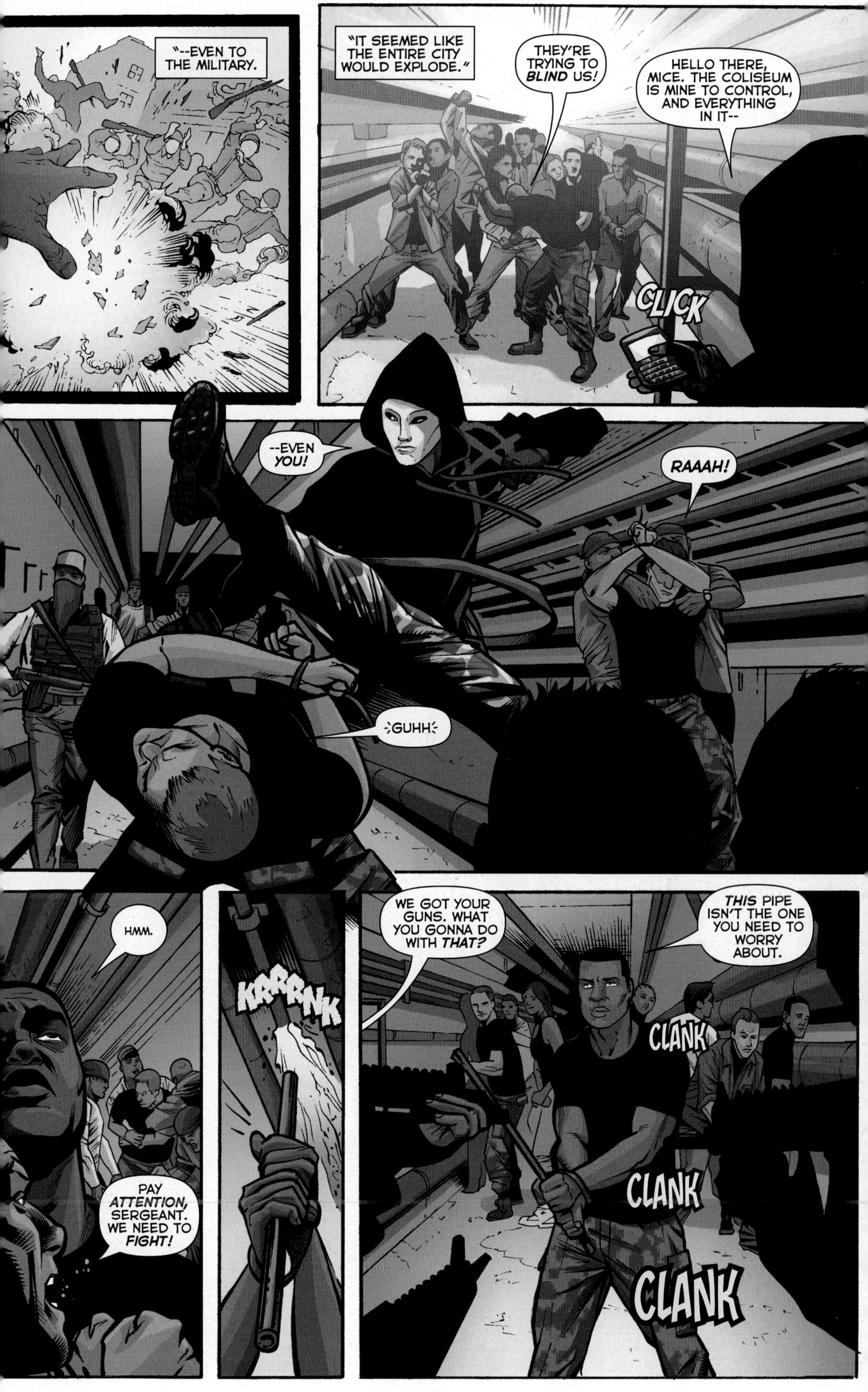

"--EVEN TO THE MILITARY.
"IT SEEMED LIKE THE ENTIRE CITY WOULD EXPLODE."
THEY'RE TRYING TO BLIND US!
HELLO THERE, MICE. THE COLISEUM IS MINE TO CONTROL, AND EVERYTHING IN IT--
CLICK
--EVEN YOU!
RAAAH!
GUHH
HMM.
PAY ATTENTION, SERGEANT. WE NEED TO FIGHT!
KRRRNK
WE GOT YOUR GUNS. WHAT YOU GONNA DO WITH THAT?
THIS PIPE ISN'T THE ONE YOU NEED TO WORRY ABOUT.
CLANK
CLANK
CLANK

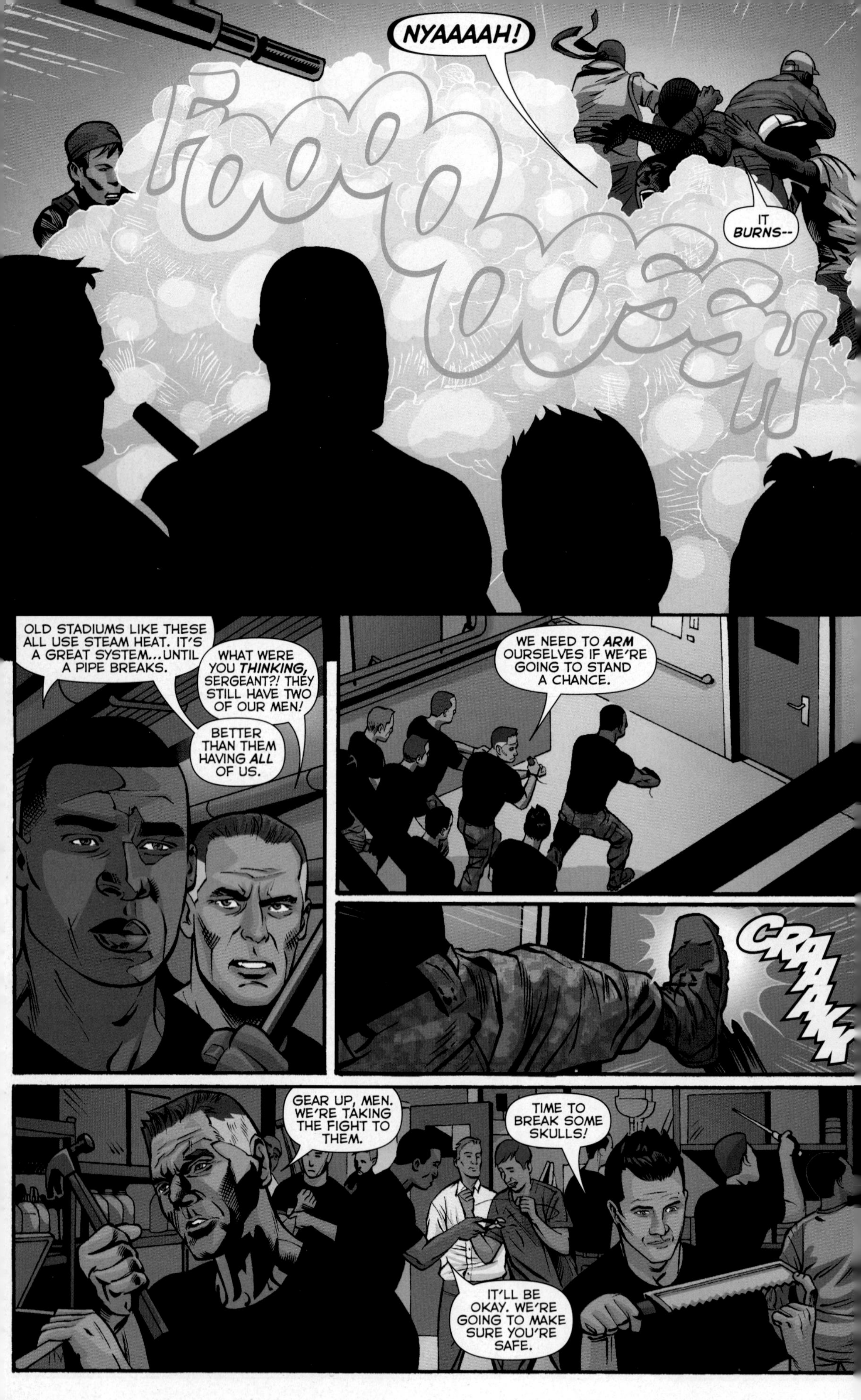
FOOOOOOSH
NYAAAAH!
IT BURNS--
OLD STADIUMS LIKE THESE ALL USE STEAM HEAT. IT'S A GREAT SYSTEM...UNTIL A PIPE BREAKS.
WHAT WERE YOU THINKING, SERGEANT?! THEY STILL HAVE TWO OF OUR MEN!
BETTER THAN THEM HAVING ALL OF US.
WE NEED TO ARM OURSELVES IF WE'RE GOING TO STAND A CHANCE.
CRAAAAK
GEAR UP, MEN. WE'RE TAKING THE FIGHT TO THEM.
TIME TO BREAK SOME SKULLS!
IT'LL BE OKAY. WE'RE GOING TO MAKE SURE YOU'RE SAFE.

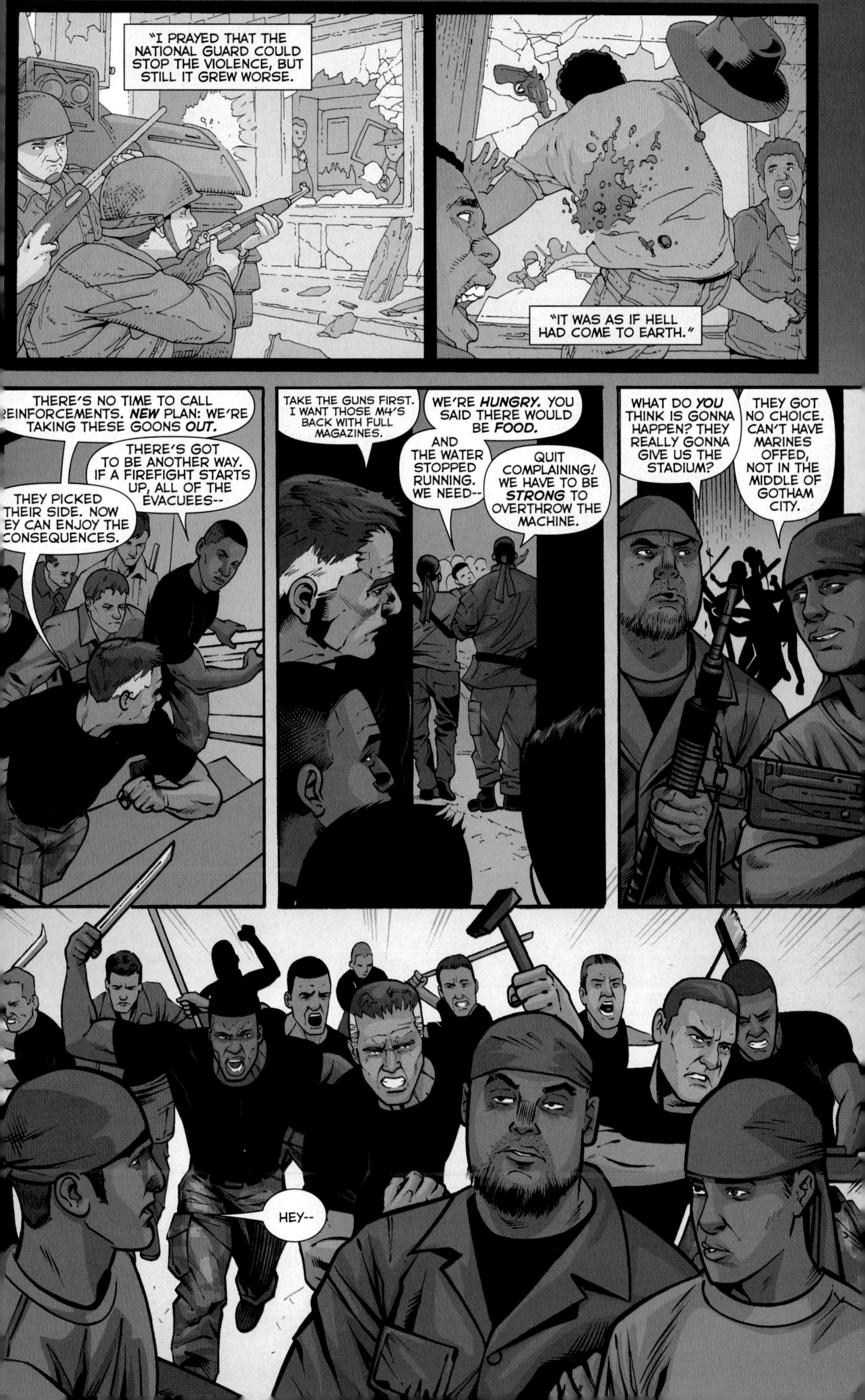
"I PRAYED THAT THE NATIONAL GUARD COULD STOP THE VIOLENCE, BUT STILL IT GREW WORSE.
"IT WAS AS IF HELL HAD COME TO EARTH."
THERE'S NO TIME TO CALL REINFORCEMENTS. NEW PLAN: WE'RE TAKING THESE GOONS OUT.
THERE'S GOT TO BE ANOTHER WAY. IF A FIREFIGHT STARTS UP, ALL OF THE EVACUEES--
THEY PICKED THEIR SIDE. NOW EY CAN ENJOY THE CONSEQUENCES.
TAKE THE GUNS FIRST. I WANT THOSE M4'S BACK WITH FULL MAGAZINES.
WE'RE HUNGRY. YOU SAID THERE WOULD BE FOOD.
AND THE WATER STOPPED RUNNING. WE NEED--
QUIT COMPLAINING! WE HAVE TO BE STRONG TO OVERTHROW THE MACHINE.
WHAT DO YOU THINK IS GONNA HAPPEN? THEY REALLY GONNA GIVE US THE STADIUM?
THEY GOT NO CHOICE. CAN'T HAVE MARINES OFFED, NOT IN THE MIDDLE OF GOTHAM CITY.
HEY--

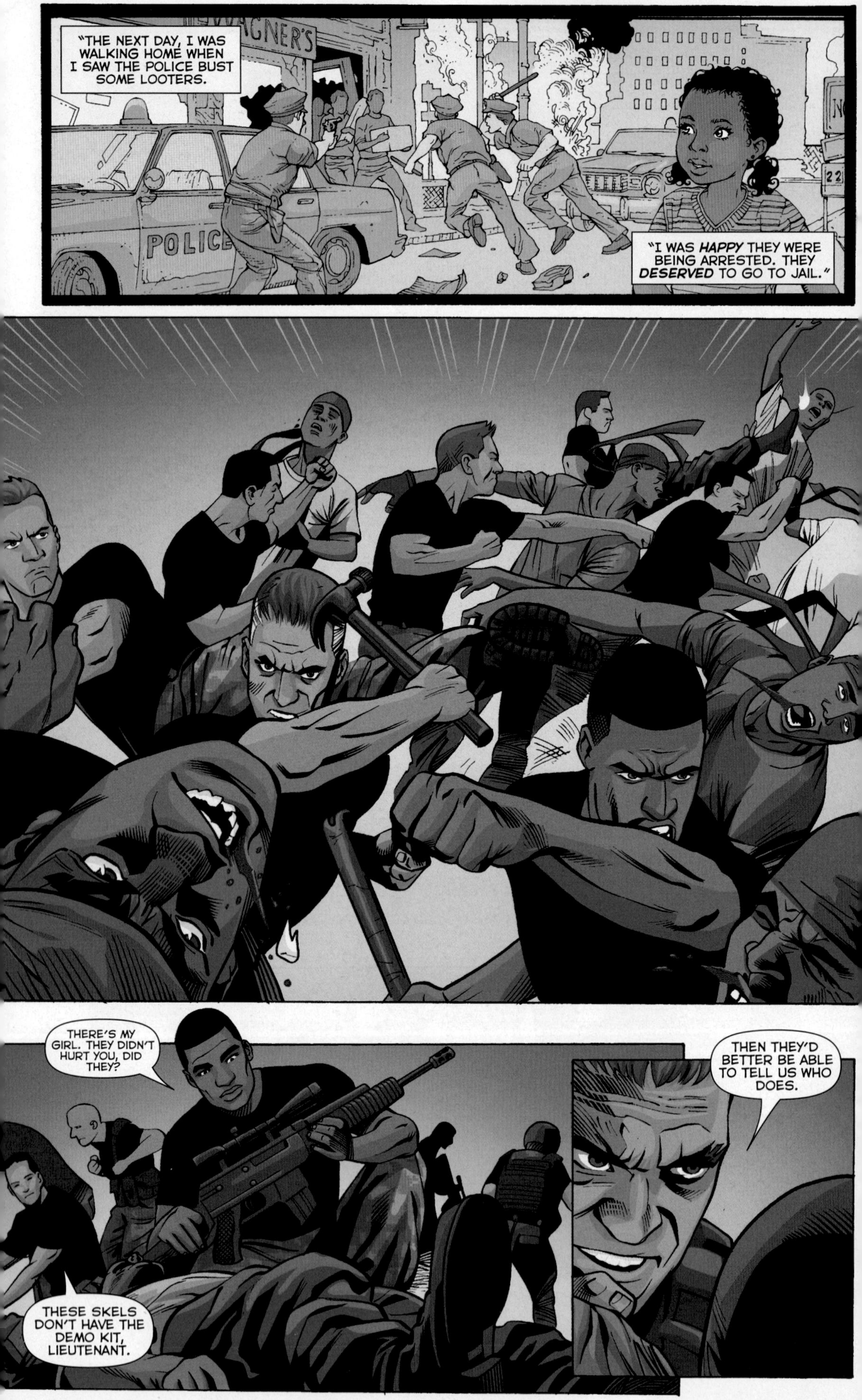
"THE NEXT DAY, I WAS WALKING HOME WHEN I SAW THE POLICE BUST SOME LOOTERS.
WAGNER'S
POLICE
"I WAS *HAPPY* THEY WERE BEING ARRESTED. THEY *DESERVED* TO GO TO JAIL."
THERE'S MY GIRL. THEY DIDN'T HURT YOU, DID THEY?
THESE SKELS DON'T HAVE THE DEMO KIT, LIEUTENANT.
THEN THEY'D BETTER BE ABLE TO TELL US WHO DOES.

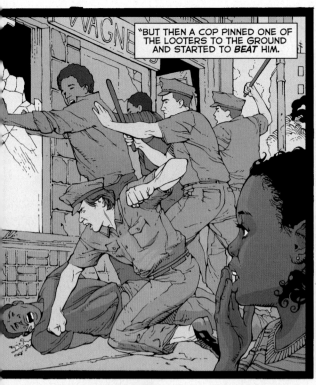

"BUT THEN A COP PINNED ONE OF THE LOOTERS TO THE GROUND AND STARTED TO *BEAT* HIM."

"THE COP HIT HIM SO HARD, I COULD TELL HE WAS KNOCKED OUT COLD."

WHERE ARE OUR EXPLOSIVES?

THEY'RE UP YOUR--

"STILL, HE JUST KEPT BEATING HIM... AND *BEATING* HIM."

"IT WASN'T *ABOUT* SAVING THE CITY. IT WASN'T *ABOUT* QUELLING THE RIOT."

WANT TO TRY THAT AGAIN? *WHERE* ARE OUR EXPLOSIVES?!

THERE'S NO ESCAPE FOR YOU, FASCIST--

"IT WAS *RAGE* AND *HATRED*, THE VERY WORST OF HUMANITY UNLEASHED."

CRUSH HIM, LIEUTENANT!

NOBODY MESSES WITH THE CORPS!

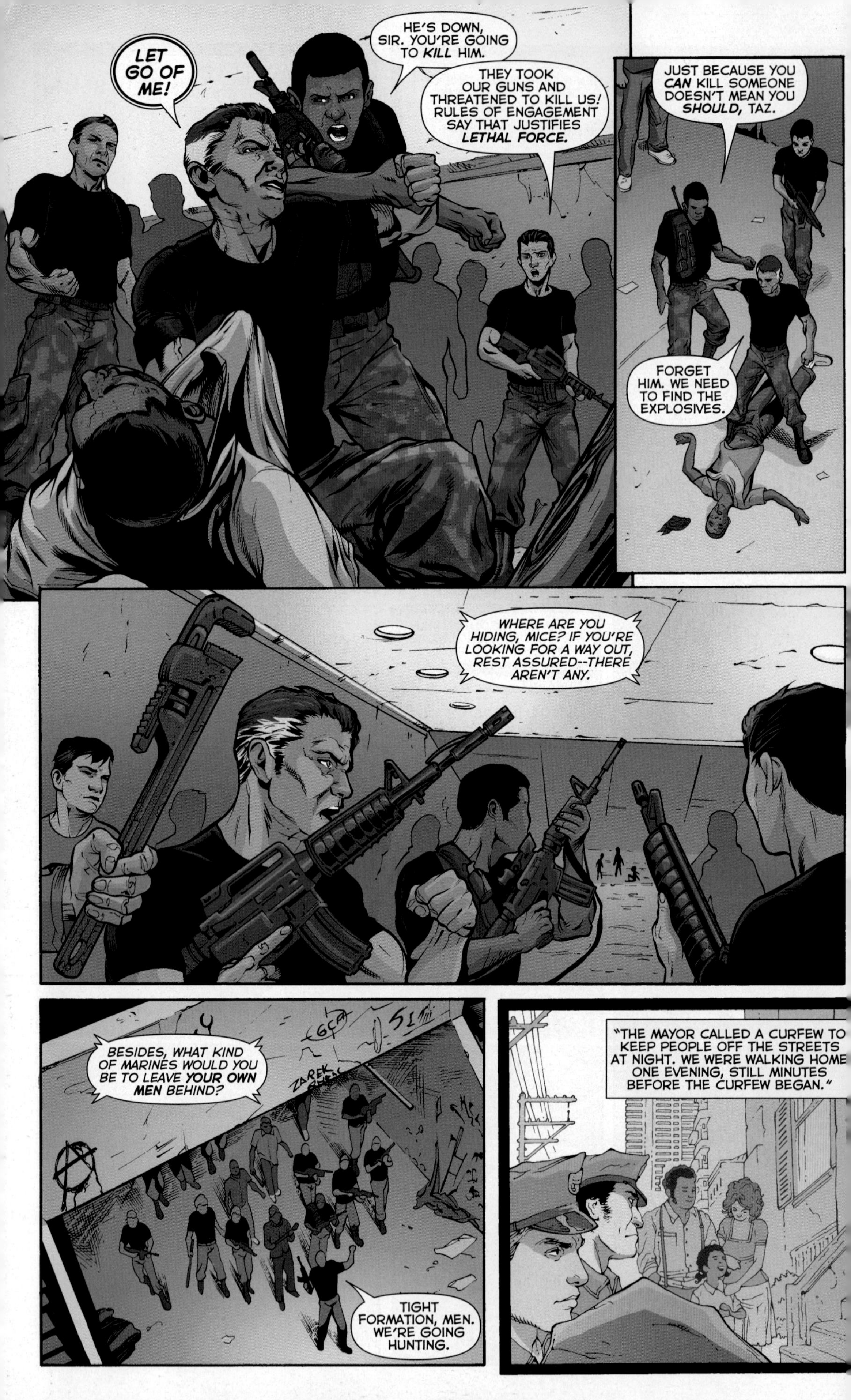
LET GO OF ME!
HE'S DOWN, SIR. YOU'RE GOING TO KILL HIM.
THEY TOOK OUR GUNS AND THREATENED TO KILL US! RULES OF ENGAGEMENT SAY THAT JUSTIFIES LETHAL FORCE.
JUST BECAUSE YOU CAN KILL SOMEONE DOESN'T MEAN YOU SHOULD, TAZ.
FORGET HIM. WE NEED TO FIND THE EXPLOSIVES.
WHERE ARE YOU HIDING, MICE? IF YOU'RE LOOKING FOR A WAY OUT, REST ASSURED--THERE AREN'T ANY.
BESIDES, WHAT KIND OF MARINES WOULD YOU BE TO LEAVE YOUR OWN MEN BEHIND?
TIGHT FORMATION, MEN. WE'RE GOING HUNTING.
"THE MAYOR CALLED A CURFEW TO KEEP PEOPLE OFF THE STREETS AT NIGHT. WE WERE WALKING HOME ONE EVENING, STILL MINUTES BEFORE THE CURFEW BEGAN."

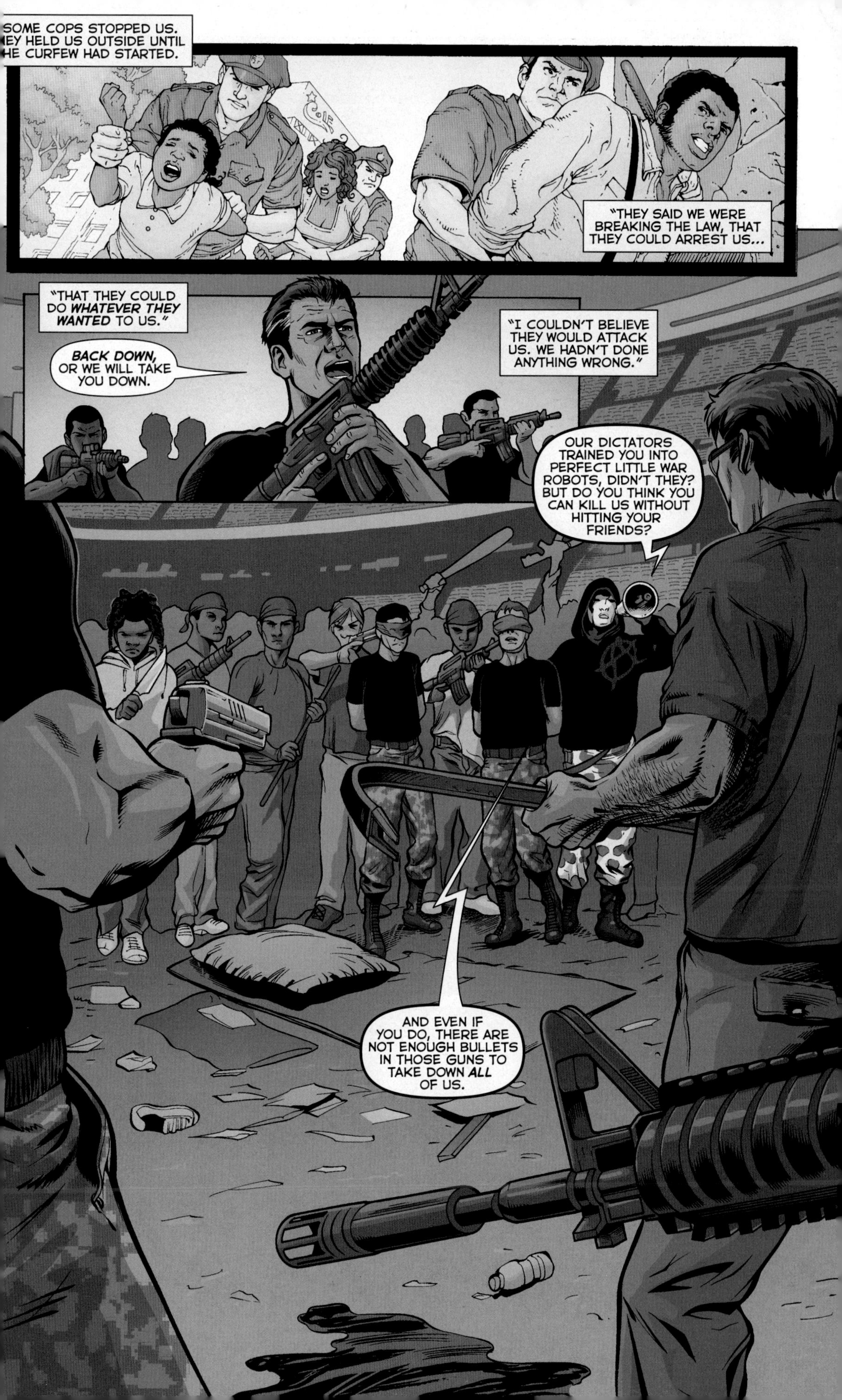
SOME COPS STOPPED US. EY HELD US OUTSIDE UNTIL HE CURFEW HAD STARTED.
"THEY SAID WE WERE BREAKING THE LAW, THAT THEY COULD ARREST US...
"THAT THEY COULD DO WHATEVER THEY WANTED TO US."
BACK DOWN, OR WE WILL TAKE YOU DOWN.
"I COULDN'T BELIEVE THEY WOULD ATTACK US. WE HADN'T DONE ANYTHING WRONG."
OUR DICTATORS TRAINED YOU INTO PERFECT LITTLE WAR ROBOTS, DIDN'T THEY? BUT DO YOU THINK YOU CAN KILL US WITHOUT HITTING YOUR FRIENDS?
AND EVEN IF YOU DO, THERE ARE NOT ENOUGH BULLETS IN THOSE GUNS TO TAKE DOWN ALL OF US.

"THERE COULD BE NO JUSTICE, NO FAIRNESS, NO *HOPE*."

BE READY TO *FIRE*, MEN!

THEY'RE BEING MANIPULATED. WE NEED TO TAKE OUT THE *LEADER*, NOT THE *FOLLOWERS*--

SHUT YOUR MOUTH AND *POINT YOUR RIFLE*, SERGEANT!

AIM FOR *CENTER MASS*!

IT...UH...LOOKS LIKE THEY'RE REALLY GOING TO SHOOT.

STAND STRONG! THOSE WHO FALL WILL BE MARTYRS TO OUR CAUSE!

ON MY MARK...

READY...

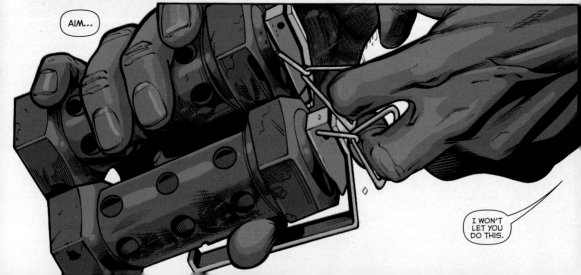

AIM...

I WON'T LET YOU DO THIS.

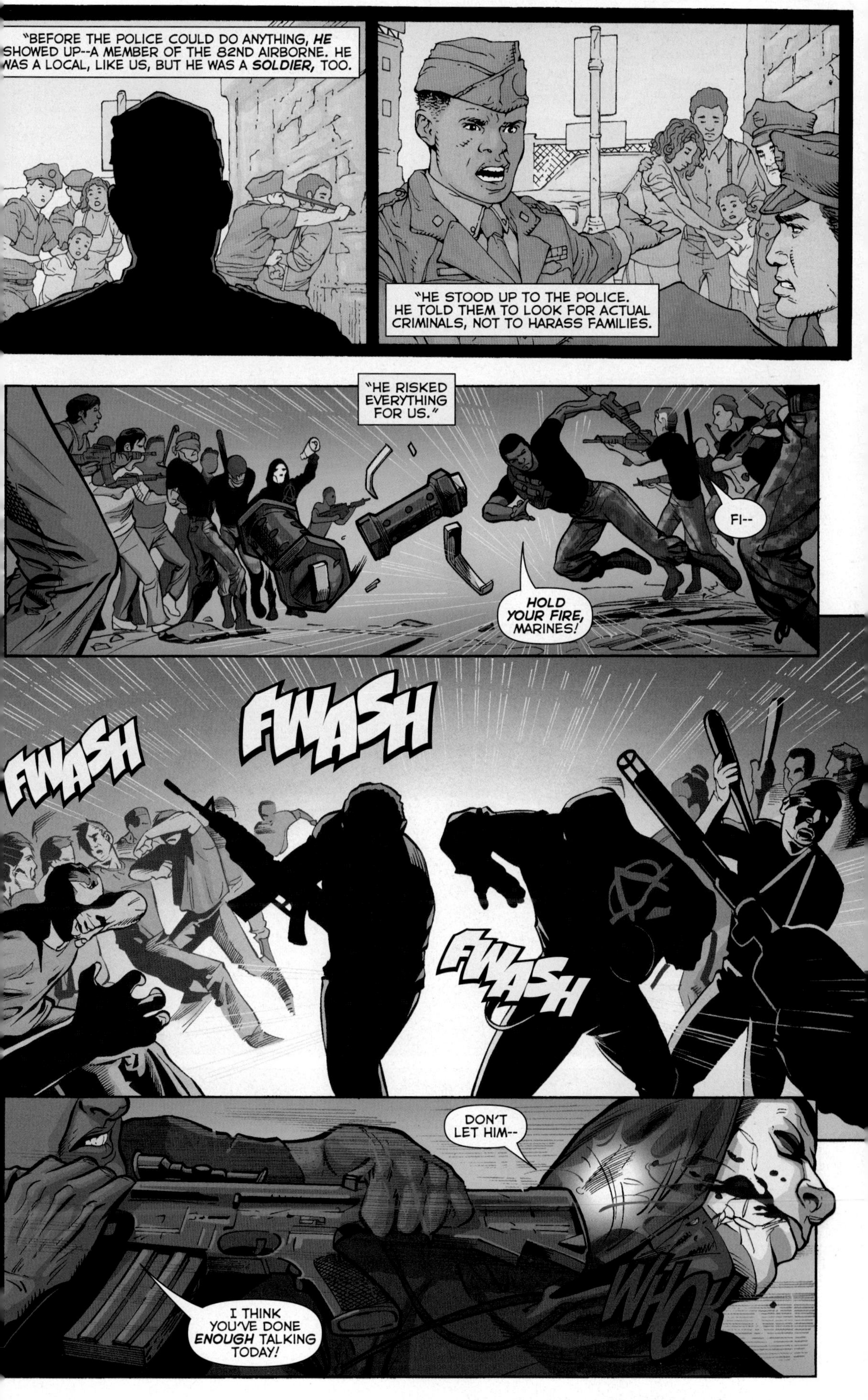
"BEFORE THE POLICE COULD DO ANYTHING, HE SHOWED UP--A MEMBER OF THE 82ND AIRBORNE. HE WAS A LOCAL, LIKE US, BUT HE WAS A SOLDIER, TOO.
"HE STOOD UP TO THE POLICE. HE TOLD THEM TO LOOK FOR ACTUAL CRIMINALS, NOT TO HARASS FAMILIES.
"HE RISKED EVERYTHING FOR US."
FI--
HOLD YOUR FIRE, MARINES!
FWASH
FWASH
FWASH
DON'T LET HIM--
I THINK YOU'VE DONE ENOUGH TALKING TODAY!
WHOK

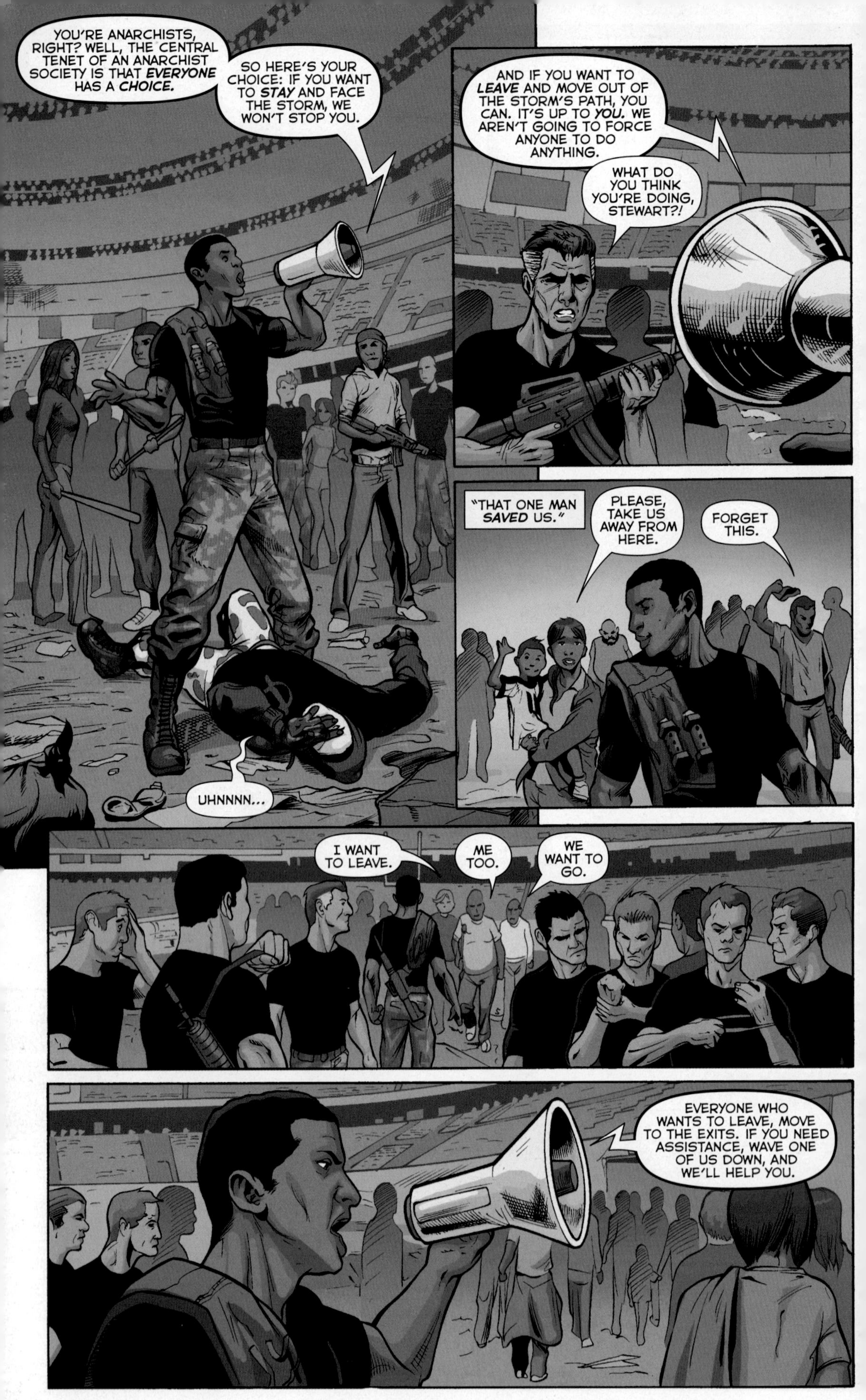

YOU'RE ANARCHISTS, RIGHT? WELL, THE CENTRAL TENET OF AN ANARCHIST SOCIETY IS THAT *EVERYONE* HAS A *CHOICE.*
SO HERE'S YOUR CHOICE: IF YOU WANT TO *STAY* AND FACE THE STORM, WE WON'T STOP YOU.
UHNNNN...
AND IF YOU WANT TO *LEAVE* AND MOVE OUT OF THE STORM'S PATH, YOU CAN. IT'S UP TO *YOU.* WE AREN'T GOING TO FORCE ANYONE TO DO ANYTHING.
WHAT DO YOU THINK YOU'RE DOING, STEWART?!
"THAT ONE *MAN SAVED* US."
PLEASE, TAKE US AWAY FROM HERE.
FORGET THIS.
I WANT TO LEAVE.
ME TOO.
WE WANT TO GO.
EVERYONE WHO WANTS TO LEAVE, MOVE TO THE EXITS. IF YOU NEED ASSISTANCE, WAVE ONE OF US DOWN, AND WE'LL HELP YOU.

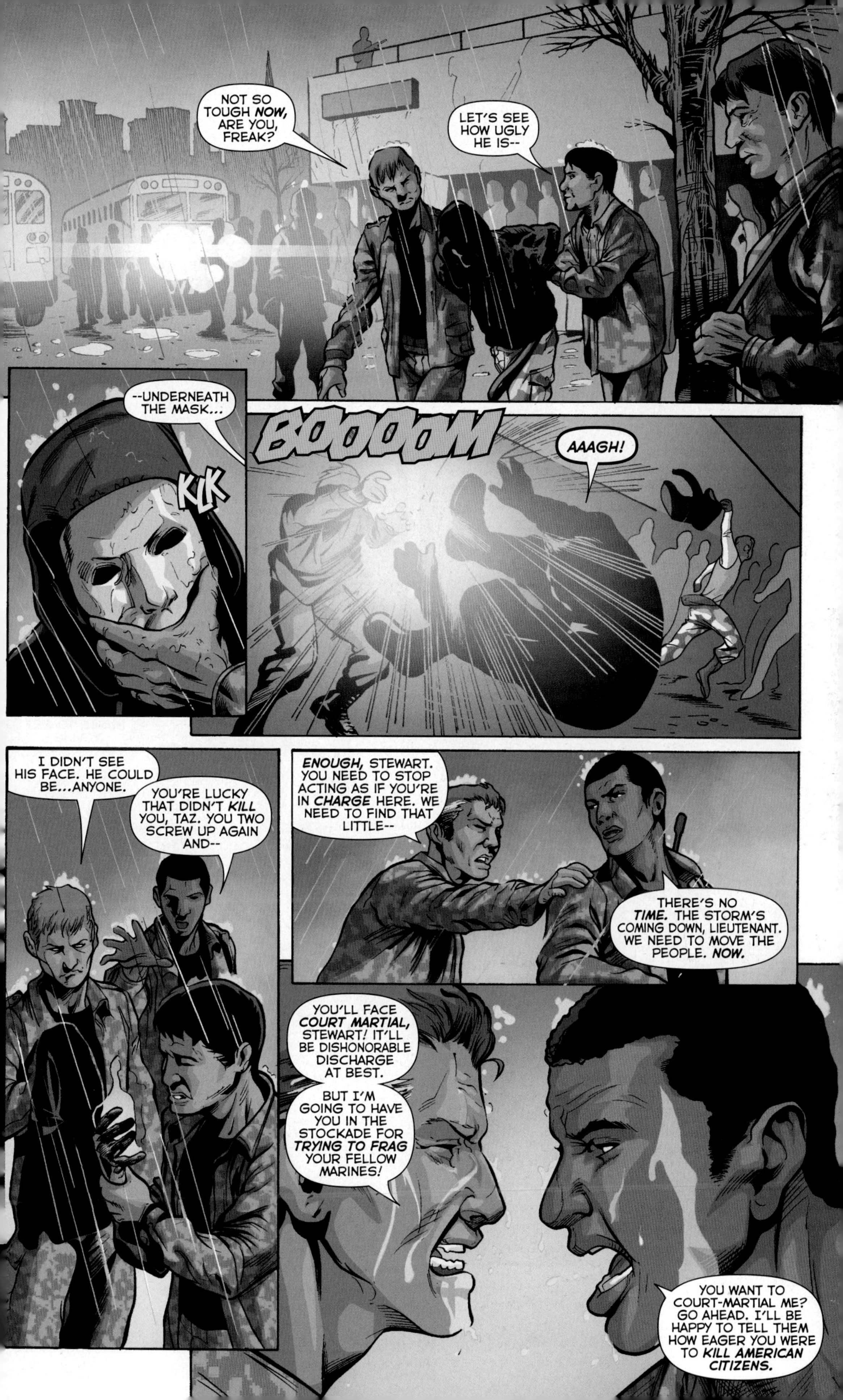
NOT SO TOUGH NOW, ARE YOU, FREAK?
LET'S SEE HOW UGLY HE IS--
--UNDERNEATH THE MASK...
KLK
BOOOOOM
AAAGH!
I DIDN'T SEE HIS FACE. HE COULD BE...ANYONE.
YOU'RE LUCKY THAT DIDN'T KILL YOU, TAZ. YOU TWO SCREW UP AGAIN AND--
ENOUGH, STEWART. YOU NEED TO STOP ACTING AS IF YOU'RE IN CHARGE HERE. WE NEED TO FIND THAT LITTLE--
THERE'S NO TIME. THE STORM'S COMING DOWN, LIEUTENANT. WE NEED TO MOVE THE PEOPLE. NOW.
YOU'LL FACE COURT MARTIAL, STEWART! IT'LL BE DISHONORABLE DISCHARGE AT BEST.
BUT I'M GOING TO HAVE YOU IN THE STOCKADE FOR TRYING TO FRAG YOUR FELLOW MARINES!
YOU WANT TO COURT-MARTIAL ME? GO AHEAD. I'LL BE HAPPY TO TELL THEM HOW EAGER YOU WERE TO KILL AMERICAN CITIZENS.

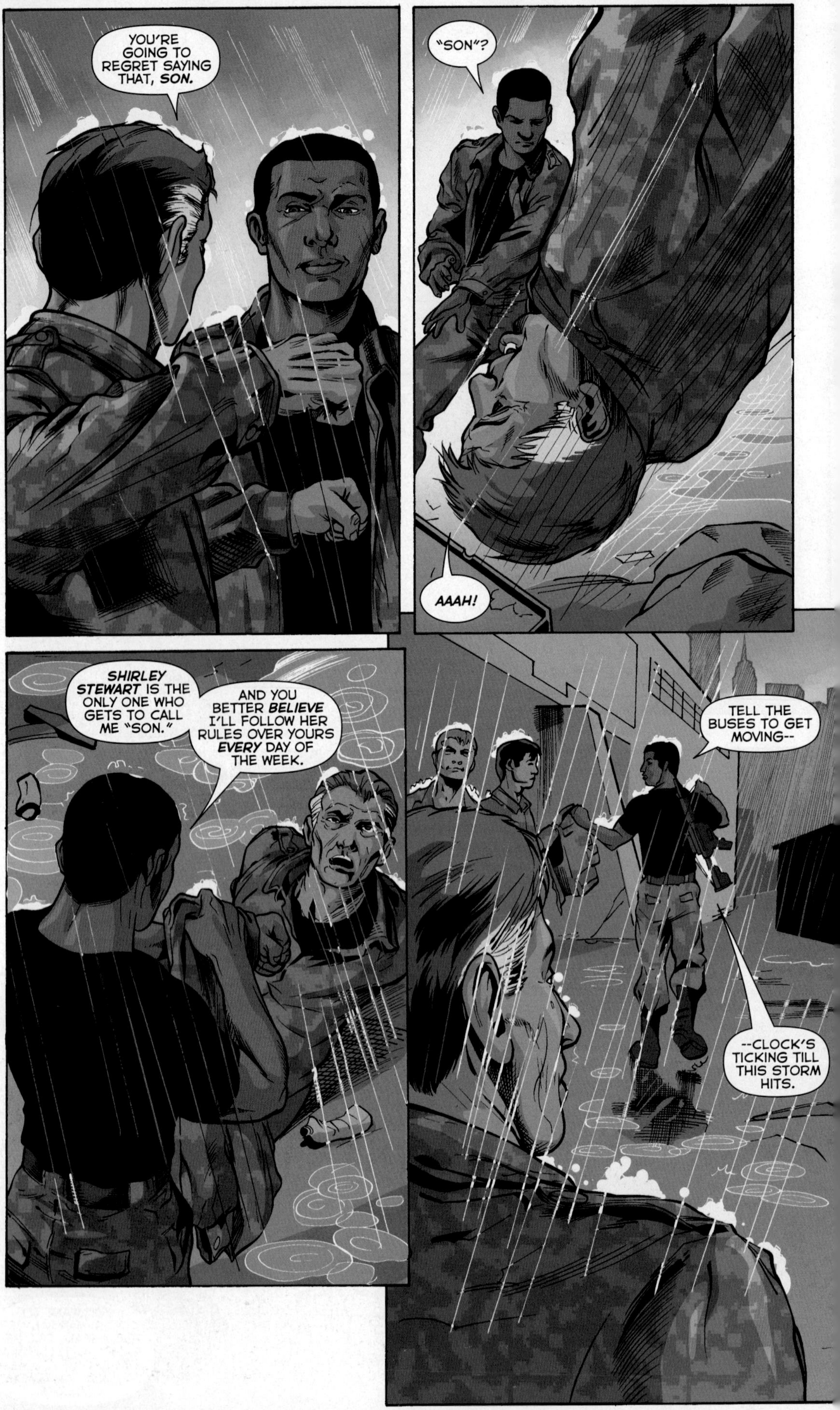
YOU'RE GOING TO REGRET SAYING THAT, SON.
"SON"?
AAAH!
SHIRLEY STEWART IS THE ONLY ONE WHO GETS TO CALL ME "SON."
AND YOU BETTER BELIEVE I'LL FOLLOW HER RULES OVER YOURS EVERY DAY OF THE WEEK.
TELL THE BUSES TO GET MOVING--
--CLOCK'S TICKING TILL THIS STORM HITS.

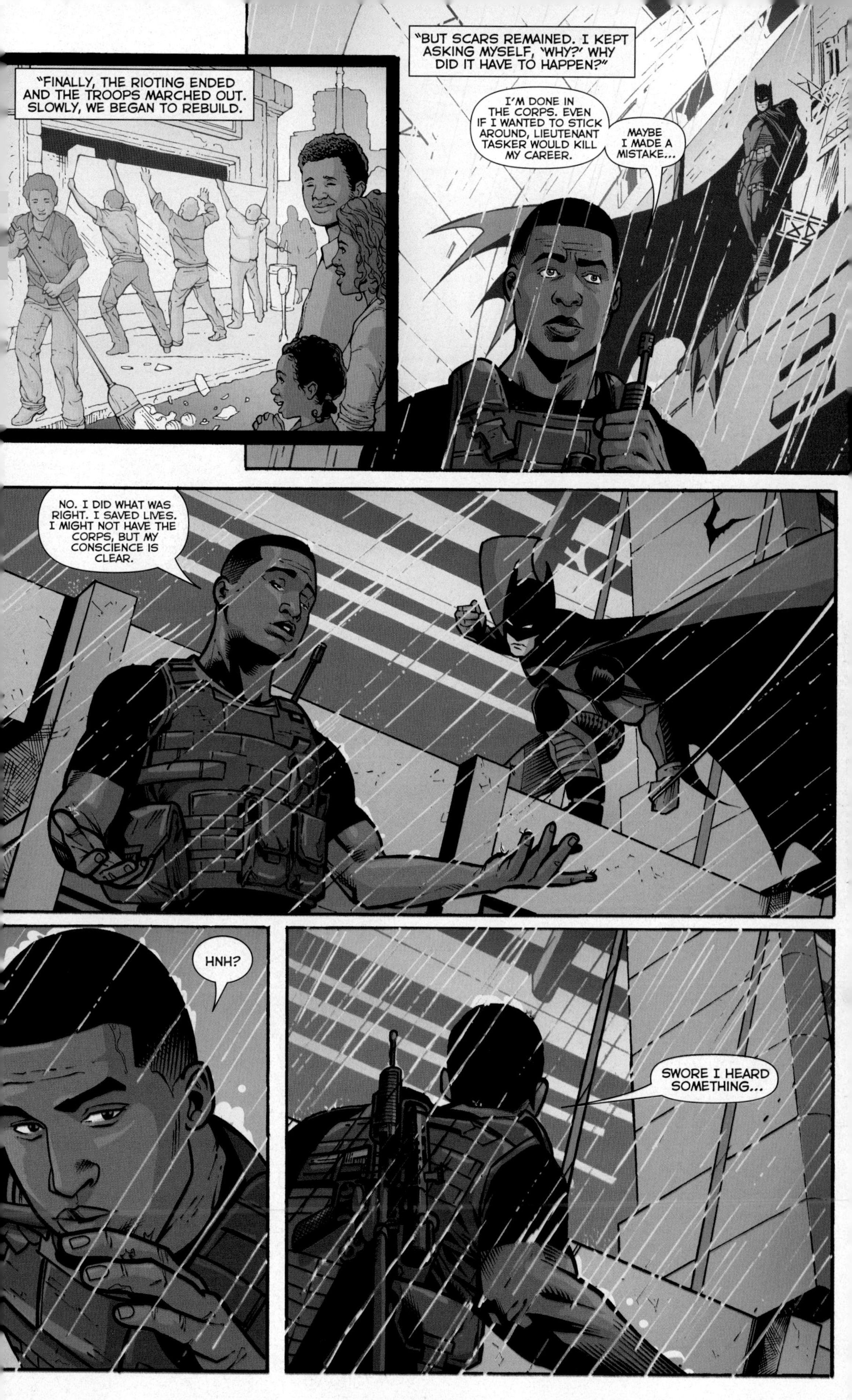
"FINALLY, THE RIOTING ENDED AND THE TROOPS MARCHED OUT. SLOWLY, WE BEGAN TO REBUILD.
"BUT SCARS REMAINED. I KEPT ASKING MYSELF, 'WHY?' WHY DID IT HAVE TO HAPPEN?"
I'M DONE IN THE CORPS. EVEN IF I WANTED TO STICK AROUND, LIEUTENANT TASKER WOULD KILL MY CAREER.
MAYBE I MADE A MISTAKE...
NO. I DID WHAT WAS RIGHT. I SAVED LIVES. I MIGHT NOT HAVE THE CORPS, BUT MY CONSCIENCE IS CLEAR.
HNH?
SWORE I HEARD SOMETHING...

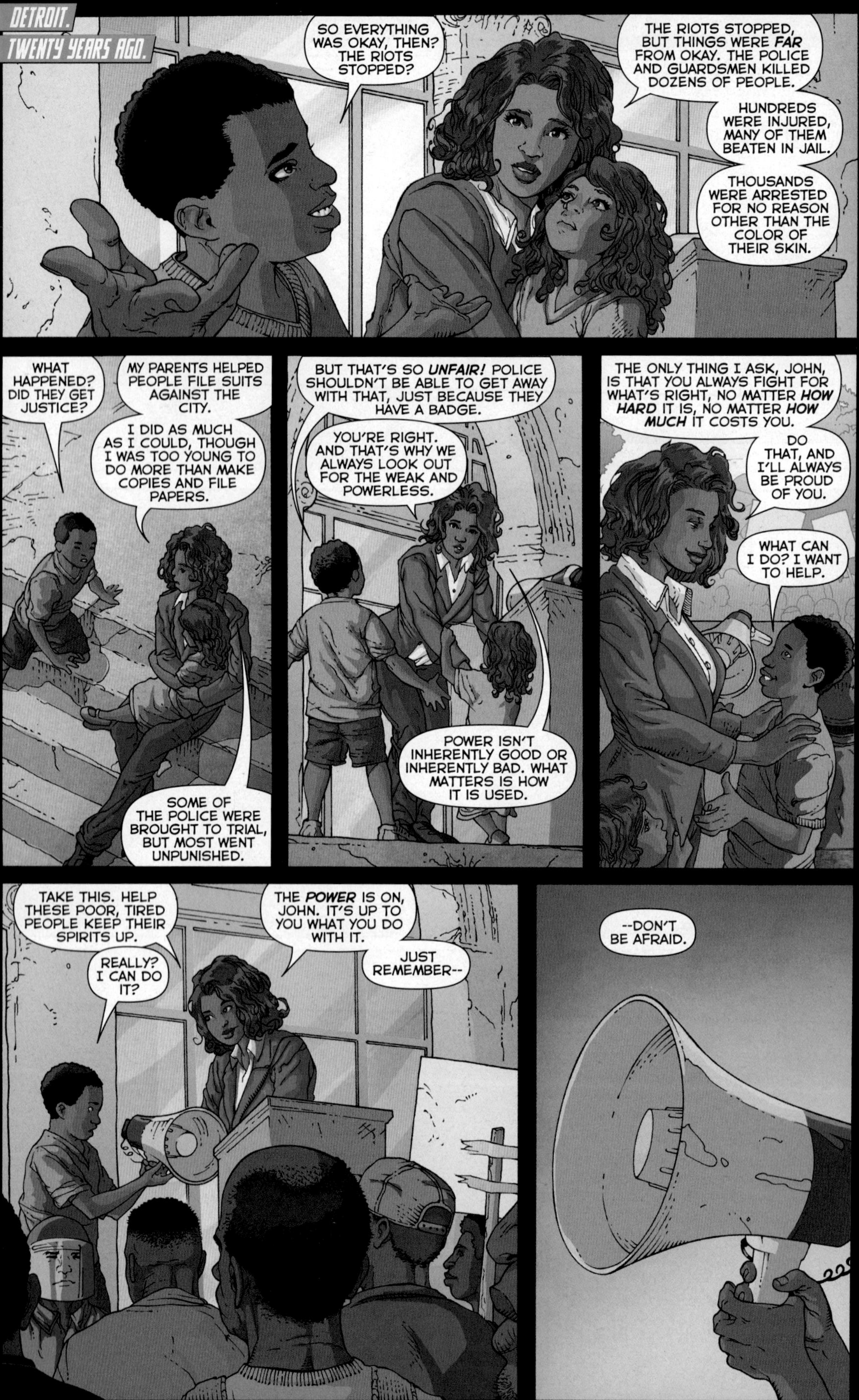
DETROIT.
TWENTY YEARS AGO.
SO EVERYTHING WAS OKAY, THEN? THE RIOTS STOPPED?
THE RIOTS STOPPED, BUT THINGS WERE FAR FROM OKAY. THE POLICE AND GUARDSMEN KILLED DOZENS OF PEOPLE.
HUNDREDS WERE INJURED, MANY OF THEM BEATEN IN JAIL.
THOUSANDS WERE ARRESTED FOR NO REASON OTHER THAN THE COLOR OF THEIR SKIN.
WHAT HAPPENED? DID THEY GET JUSTICE?
MY PARENTS HELPED PEOPLE FILE SUITS AGAINST THE CITY.
I DID AS MUCH AS I COULD, THOUGH I WAS TOO YOUNG TO DO MORE THAN MAKE COPIES AND FILE PAPERS.
SOME OF THE POLICE WERE BROUGHT TO TRIAL, BUT MOST WENT UNPUNISHED.
BUT THAT'S SO UNFAIR! POLICE SHOULDN'T BE ABLE TO GET AWAY WITH THAT, JUST BECAUSE THEY HAVE A BADGE.
YOU'RE RIGHT. AND THAT'S WHY WE ALWAYS LOOK OUT FOR THE WEAK AND POWERLESS.
POWER ISN'T INHERENTLY GOOD OR INHERENTLY BAD. WHAT MATTERS IS HOW IT IS USED.
THE ONLY THING I ASK, JOHN, IS THAT YOU ALWAYS FIGHT FOR WHAT'S RIGHT, NO MATTER HOW HARD IT IS, NO MATTER HOW MUCH IT COSTS YOU.
DO THAT, AND I'LL ALWAYS BE PROUD OF YOU.
WHAT CAN I DO? I WANT TO HELP.
TAKE THIS. HELP THESE POOR, TIRED PEOPLE KEEP THEIR SPIRITS UP.
REALLY? I CAN DO IT?
THE POWER IS ON, JOHN. IT'S UP TO YOU WHAT YOU DO WITH IT.
JUST REMEMBER--
--DON'T BE AFRAID.

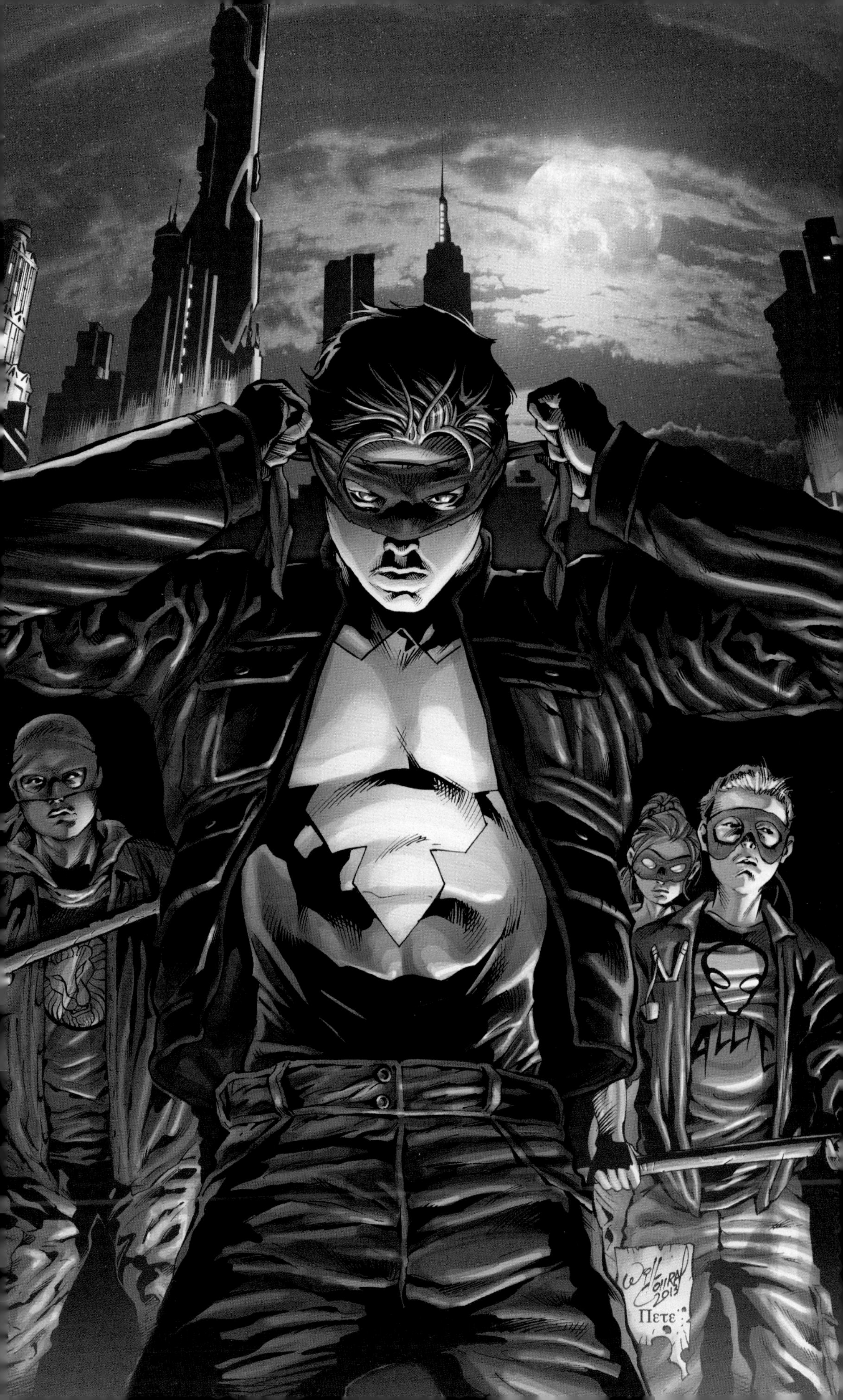

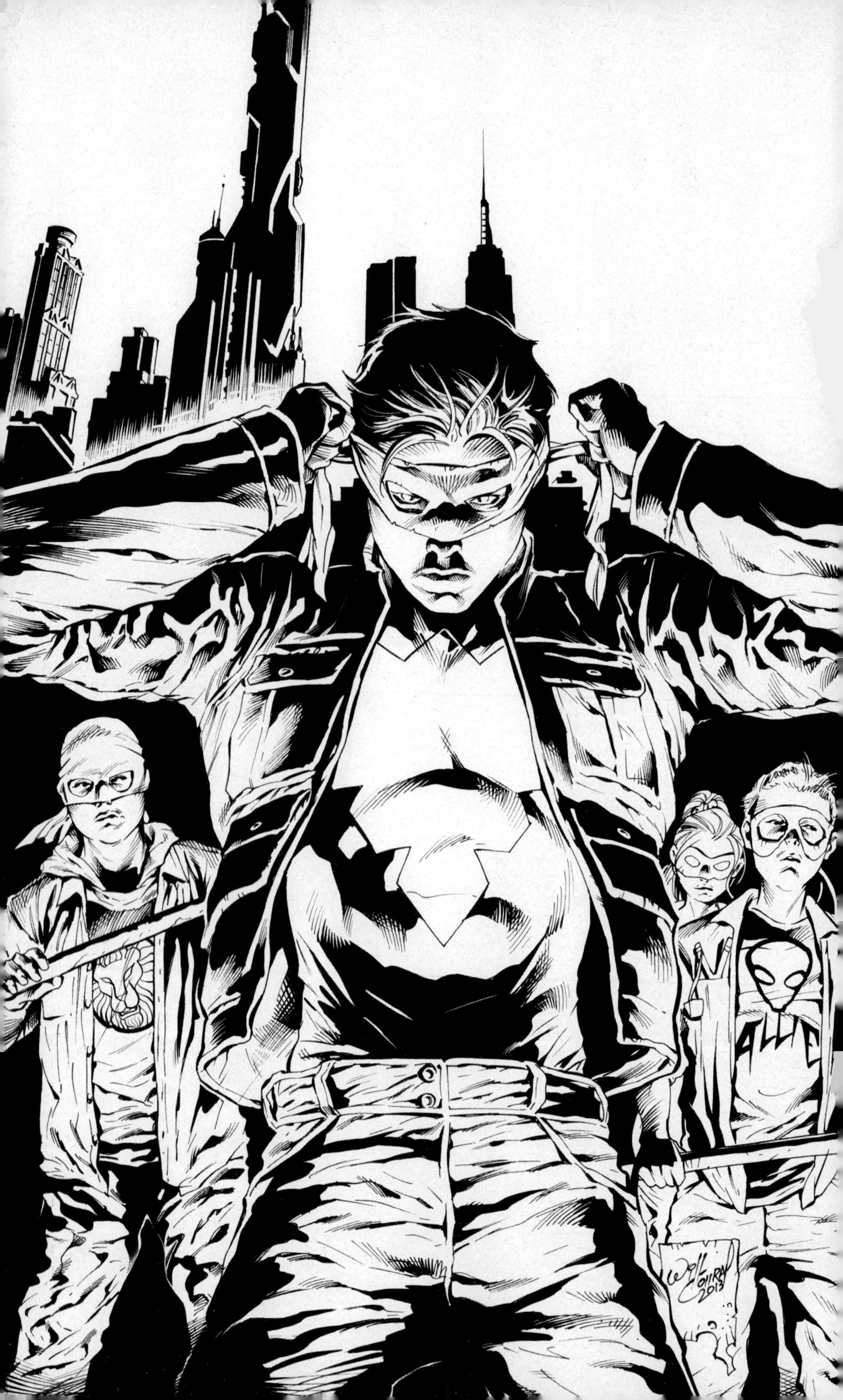

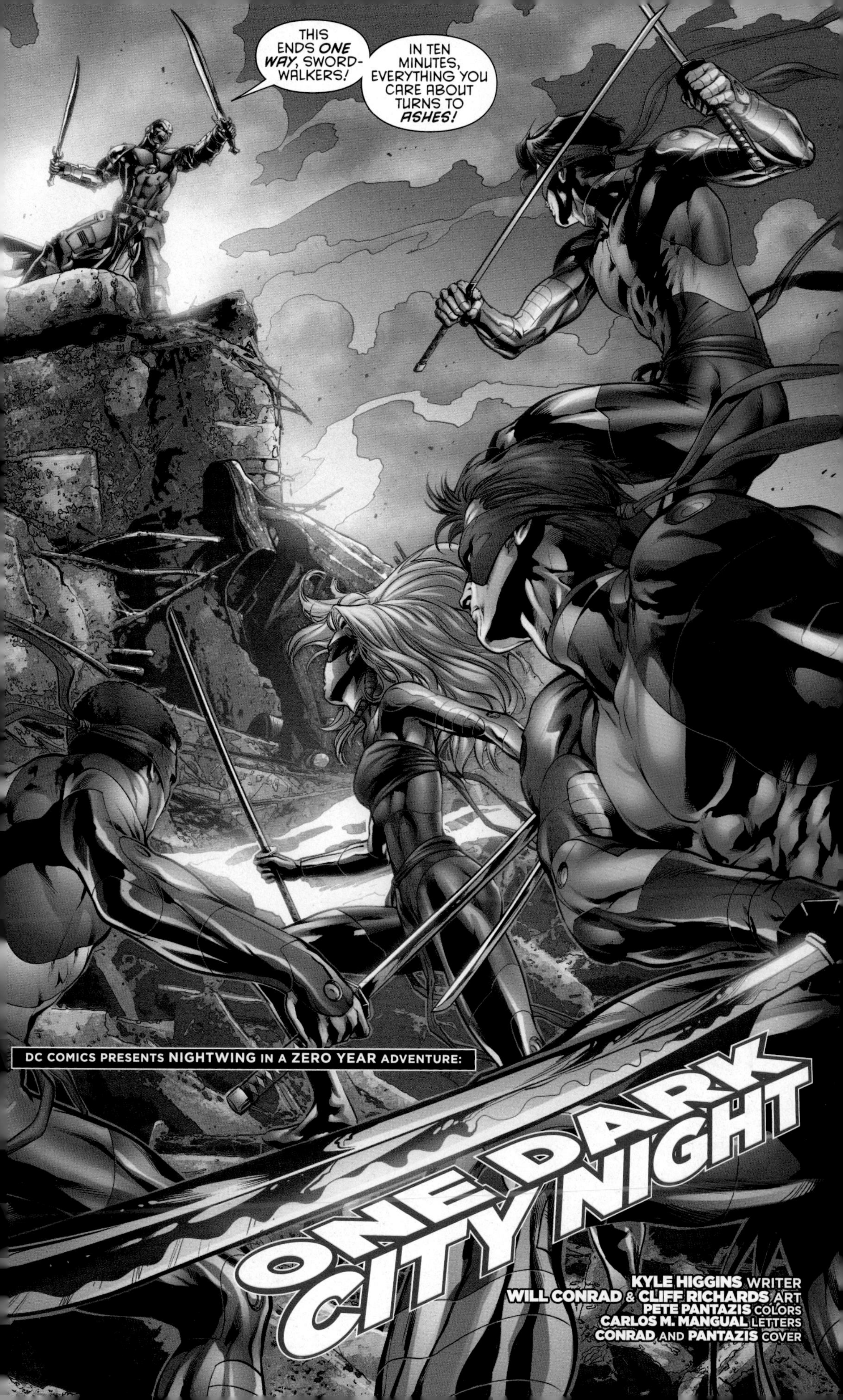

THIS ENDS *ONE WAY*, SWORD-WALKERS!
IN TEN MINUTES, EVERYTHING YOU CARE ABOUT TURNS TO *ASHES!*
DC COMICS PRESENTS NIGHTWING IN A ZERO YEAR ADVENTURE:
ONE DARK CITY NIGHT
KYLE HIGGINS WRITER
WILL CONRAD & CLIFF RICHARDS ART
PETE PANTAZIS COLORS
CARLOS M. MANGUAL LETTERS
CONRAD AND PANTAZIS COVER

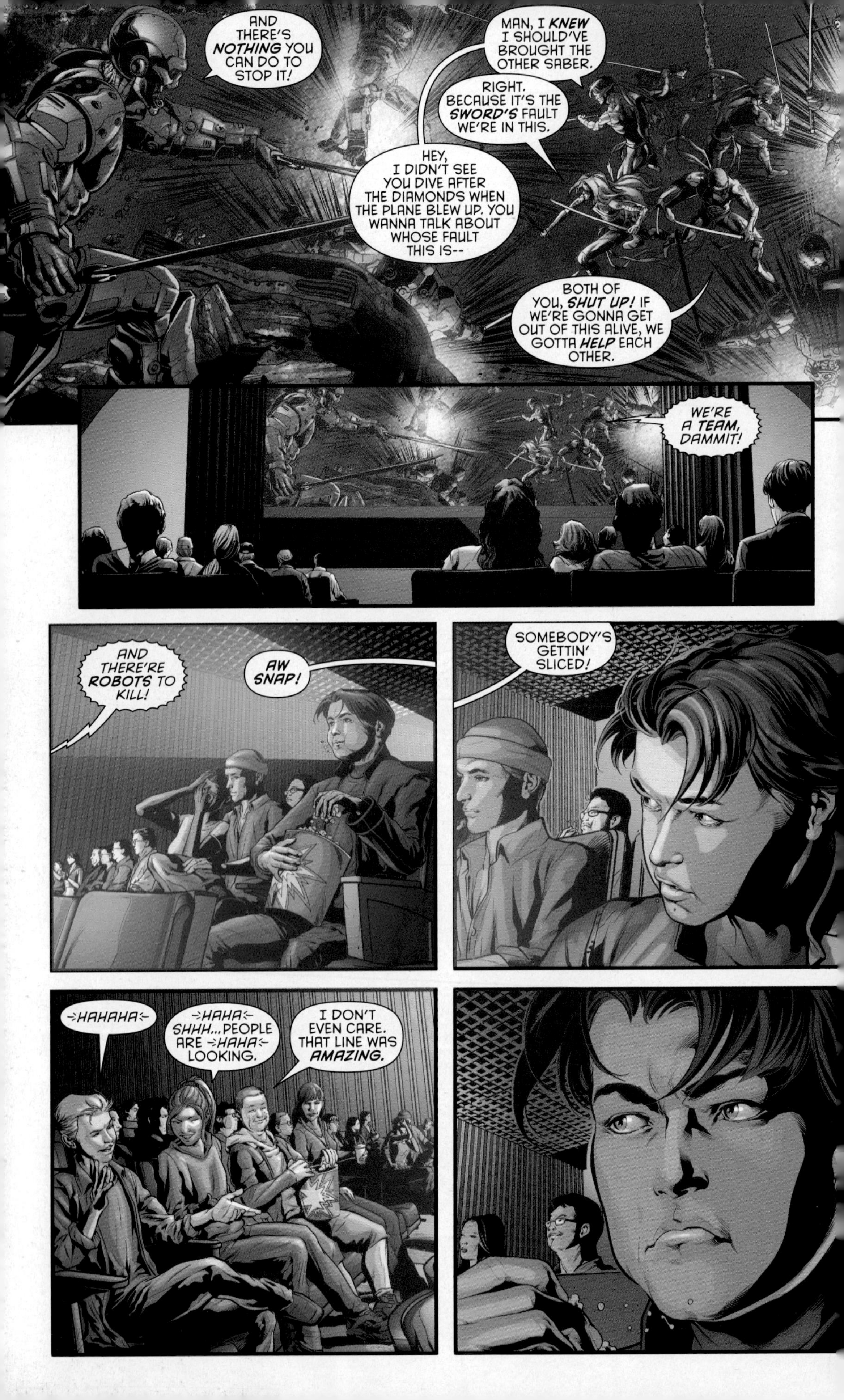
AND THERE'S NOTHING YOU CAN DO TO STOP IT!
MAN, I KNEW I SHOULD'VE BROUGHT THE OTHER SABER.
RIGHT. BECAUSE IT'S THE SWORD'S FAULT WE'RE IN THIS.
HEY, I DIDN'T SEE YOU DIVE AFTER THE DIAMONDS WHEN THE PLANE BLEW UP. YOU WANNA TALK ABOUT WHOSE FAULT THIS IS--
BOTH OF YOU, SHUT UP! IF WE'RE GONNA GET OUT OF THIS ALIVE, WE GOTTA HELP EACH OTHER.
WE'RE A TEAM, DAMMIT!
AND THERE'RE ROBOTS TO KILL!
AW SNAP!
SOMEBODY'S GETTIN' SLICED!
HAHAHA
HAHA SHHH... PEOPLE ARE HAHA LOOKING.
I DON'T EVEN CARE. THAT LINE WAS AMAZING.

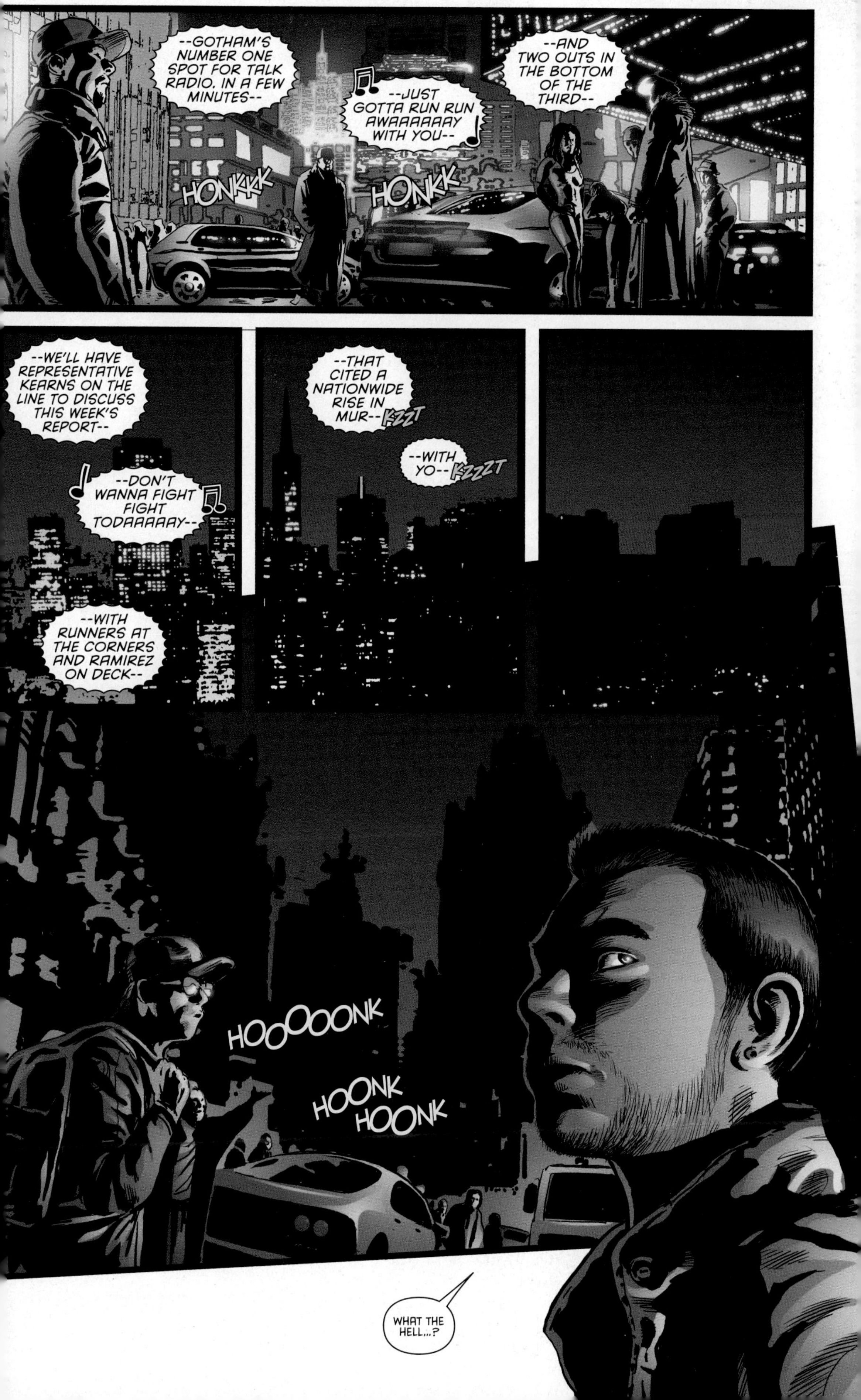
--GOTHAM'S NUMBER ONE SPOT FOR TALK RADIO. IN A FEW MINUTES--
--JUST GOTTA RUN RUN AWAAAAAAAY WITH YOU--
--AND TWO OUTS IN THE BOTTOM OF THE THIRD--
HONKKK
HONKK
--WE'LL HAVE REPRESENTATIVE KEARNS ON THE LINE TO DISCUSS THIS WEEK'S REPORT--
--DON'T WANNA FIGHT FIGHT TODAAAAAAY--
--WITH RUNNERS AT THE CORNERS AND RAMIREZ ON DECK--
--THAT CITED A NATIONWIDE RISE IN MUR--KZZT
--WITH YO--KZZZT
HOOOOONK
HOONK HOONK
WHAT THE HELL...?

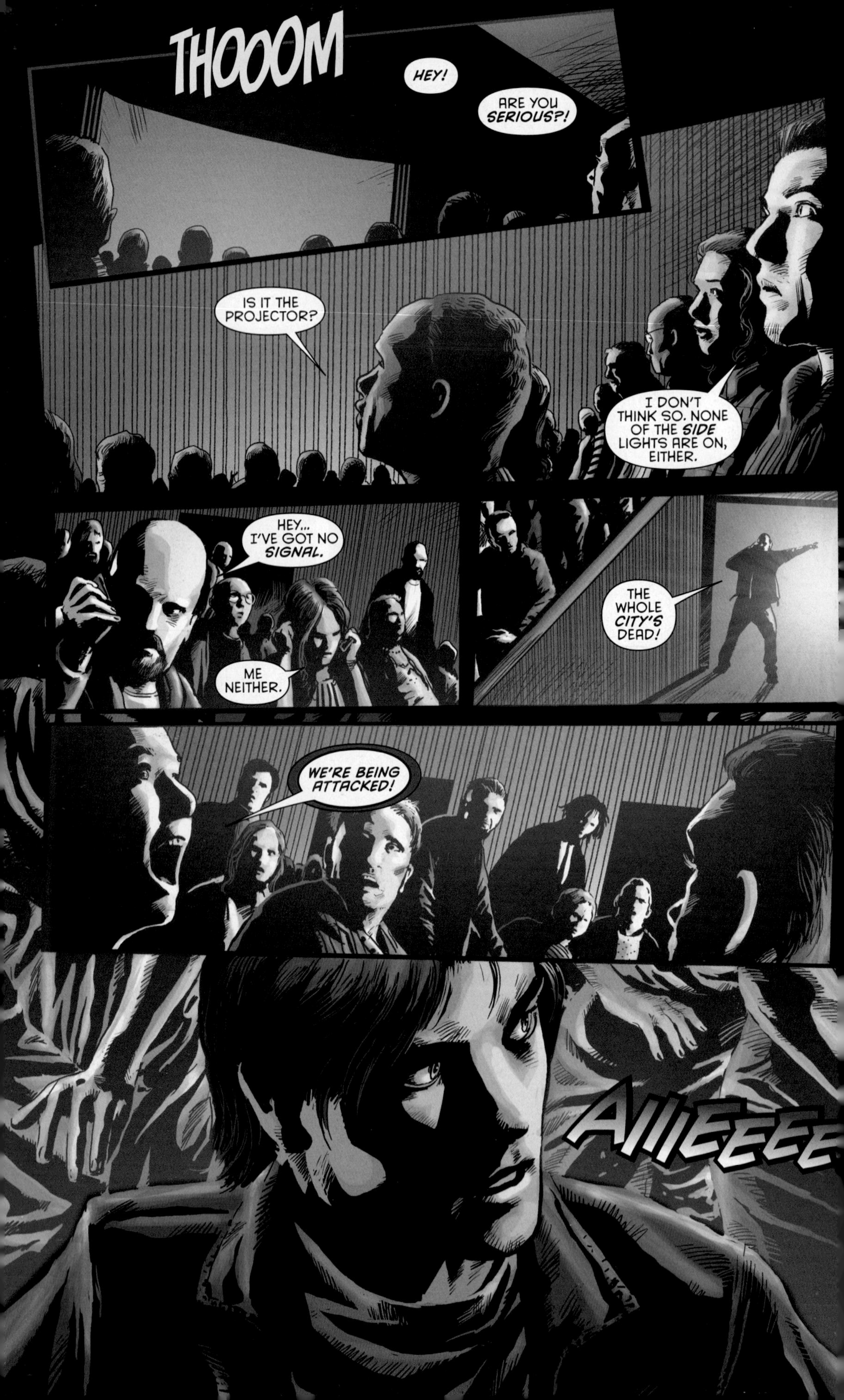
THOOOM
HEY!
ARE YOU SERIOUS?!
IS IT THE PROJECTOR?
I DON'T THINK SO. NONE OF THE SIDE LIGHTS ARE ON, EITHER.
HEY... I'VE GOT NO SIGNAL.
ME NEITHER.
THE WHOLE CITY'S DEAD!
WE'RE BEING ATTACKED!
AIIIEEEE

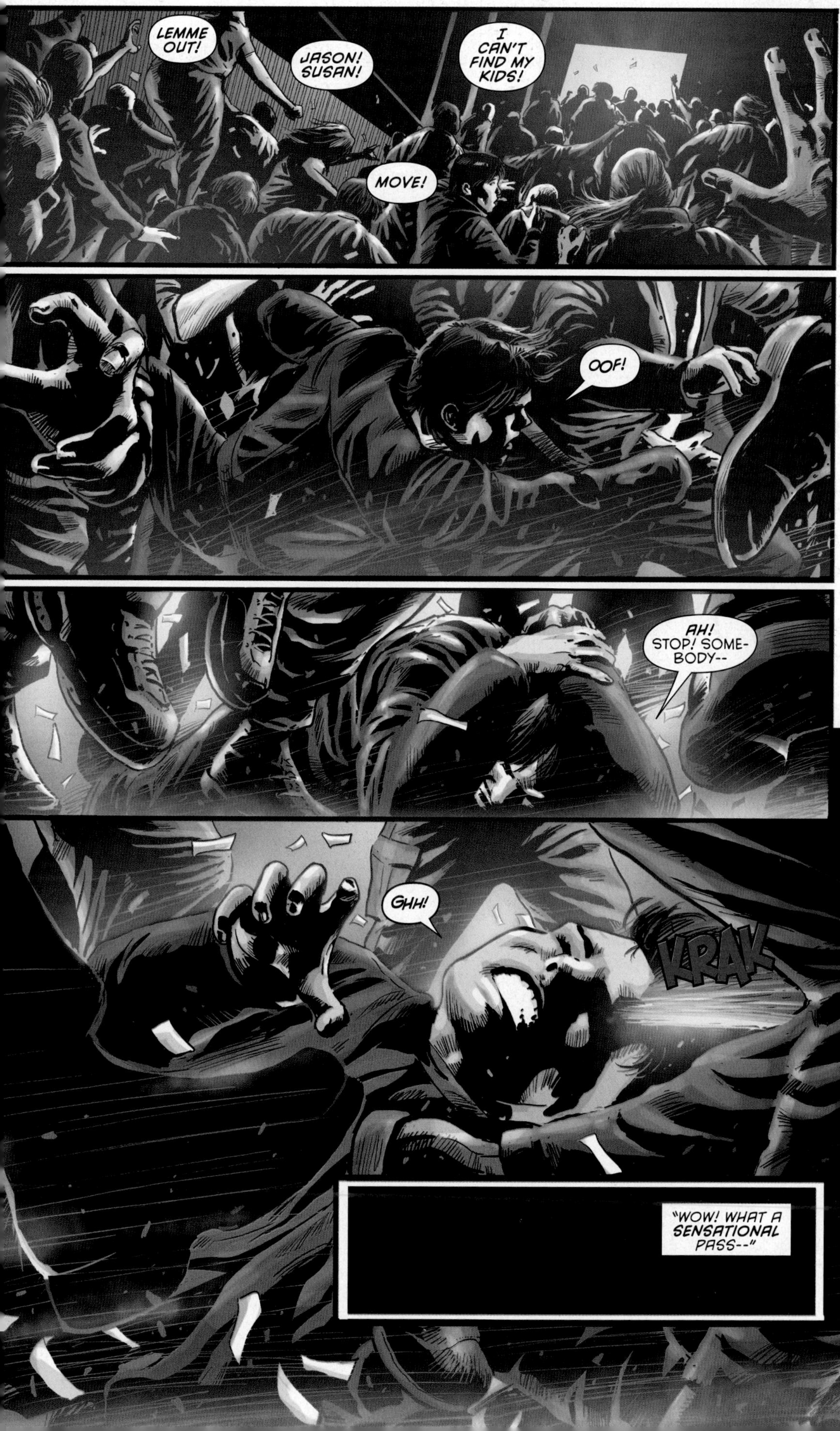
LEMME OUT!
JASON! SUSAN!
I CAN'T FIND MY KIDS!
MOVE!
OOF!
AH! STOP! SOME-BODY--
GHH!
KRAK
"WOW! WHAT A SENSATIONAL PASS--"

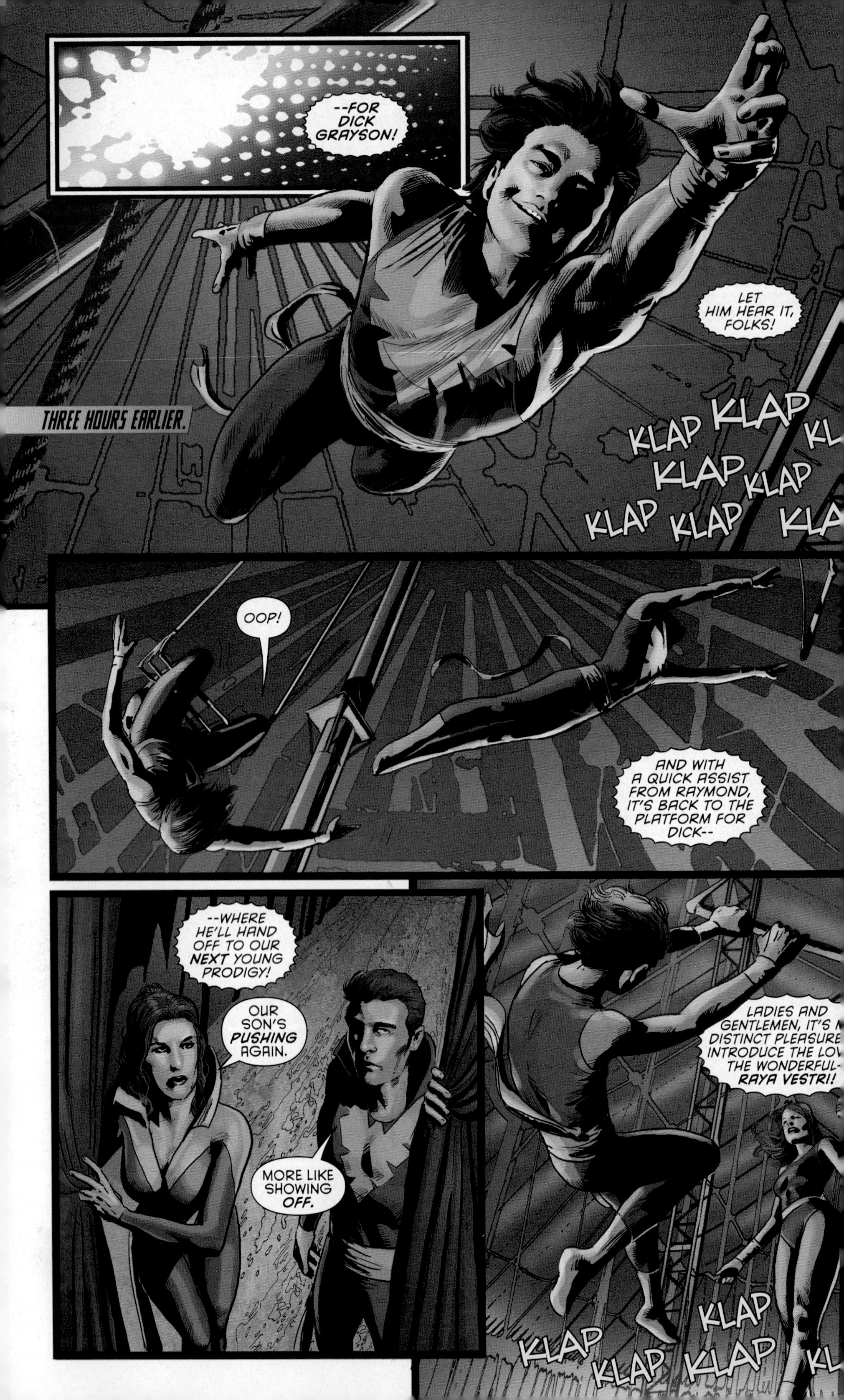

--FOR DICK GRAYSON!
LET HIM HEAR IT, FOLKS!
THREE HOURS EARLIER.
KLAP KLAP KLAP KLAP KLAP KLAP KLAP
OOP!
AND WITH A QUICK ASSIST FROM RAYMOND, IT'S BACK TO THE PLATFORM FOR DICK--
--WHERE HE'LL HAND OFF TO OUR NEXT YOUNG PRODIGY!
OUR SON'S PUSHING AGAIN.
MORE LIKE SHOWING OFF.
KLAP KLAP KLAP KLAP

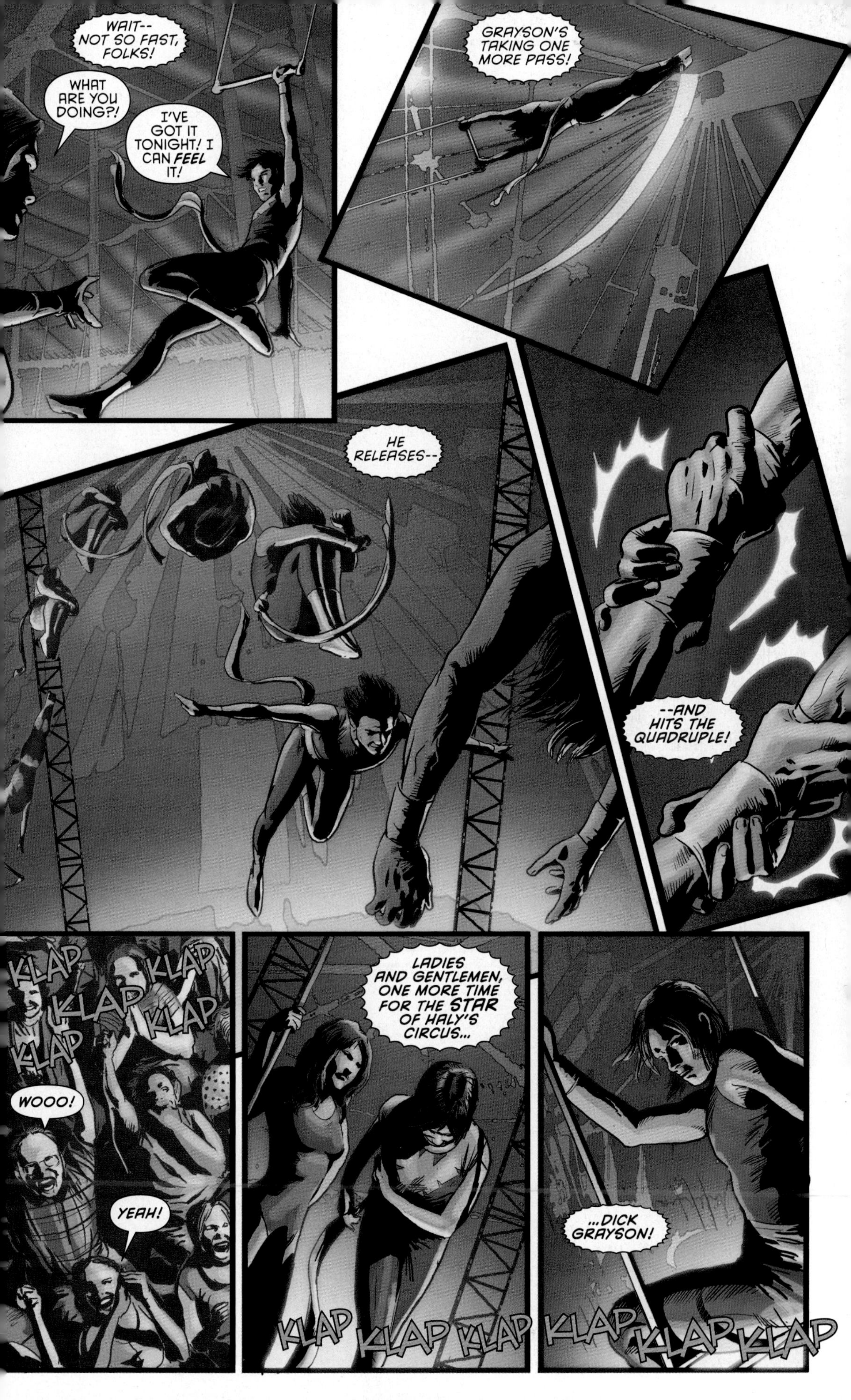
WAIT-- NOT SO FAST, FOLKS!
WHAT ARE YOU DOING?!
I'VE GOT IT TONIGHT! I CAN FEEL IT!
GRAYSON'S TAKING ONE MORE PASS!
HE RELEASES--
--AND HITS THE QUADRUPLE!
KLAP KLAP KLAP KLAP KLAP
WOOO!
YEAH!
LADIES AND GENTLEMEN, ONE MORE TIME FOR THE STAR OF HALY'S CIRCUS...
...DICK GRAYSON!
KLAP KLAP KLAP KLAP KLAP KLAP

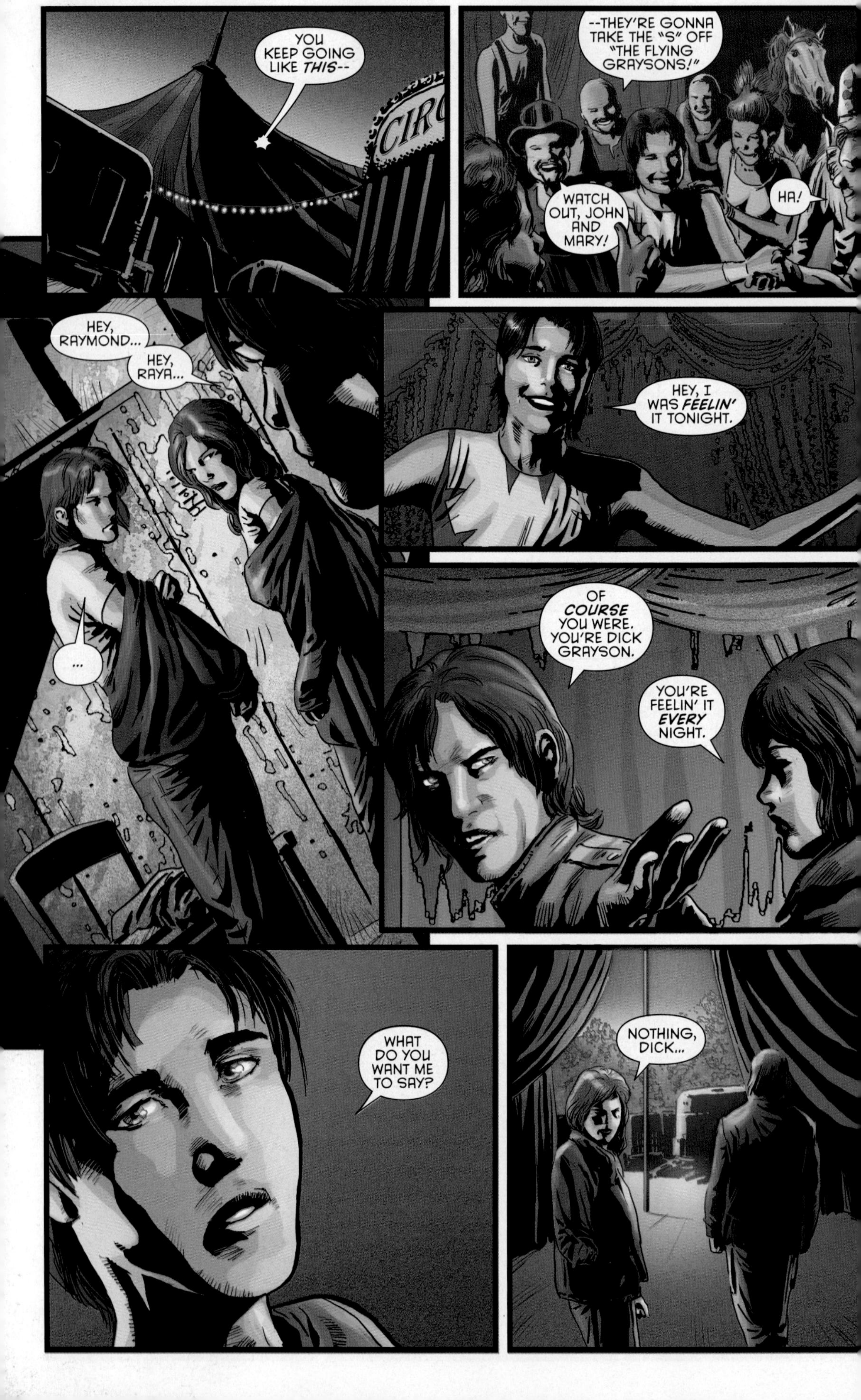
YOU KEEP GOING LIKE *THIS*--
--THEY'RE GONNA TAKE THE "S" OFF "THE FLYING GRAYSONS!"
WATCH OUT, JOHN AND MARY!
HA!
HEY, RAYMOND...
HEY, RAYA...
...
HEY, I WAS *FEELIN'* IT TONIGHT.
OF *COURSE* YOU WERE. YOU'RE DICK GRAYSON.
YOU'RE FEELIN' IT *EVERY* NIGHT.
WHAT DO YOU WANT ME TO SAY?
NOTHING, DICK...

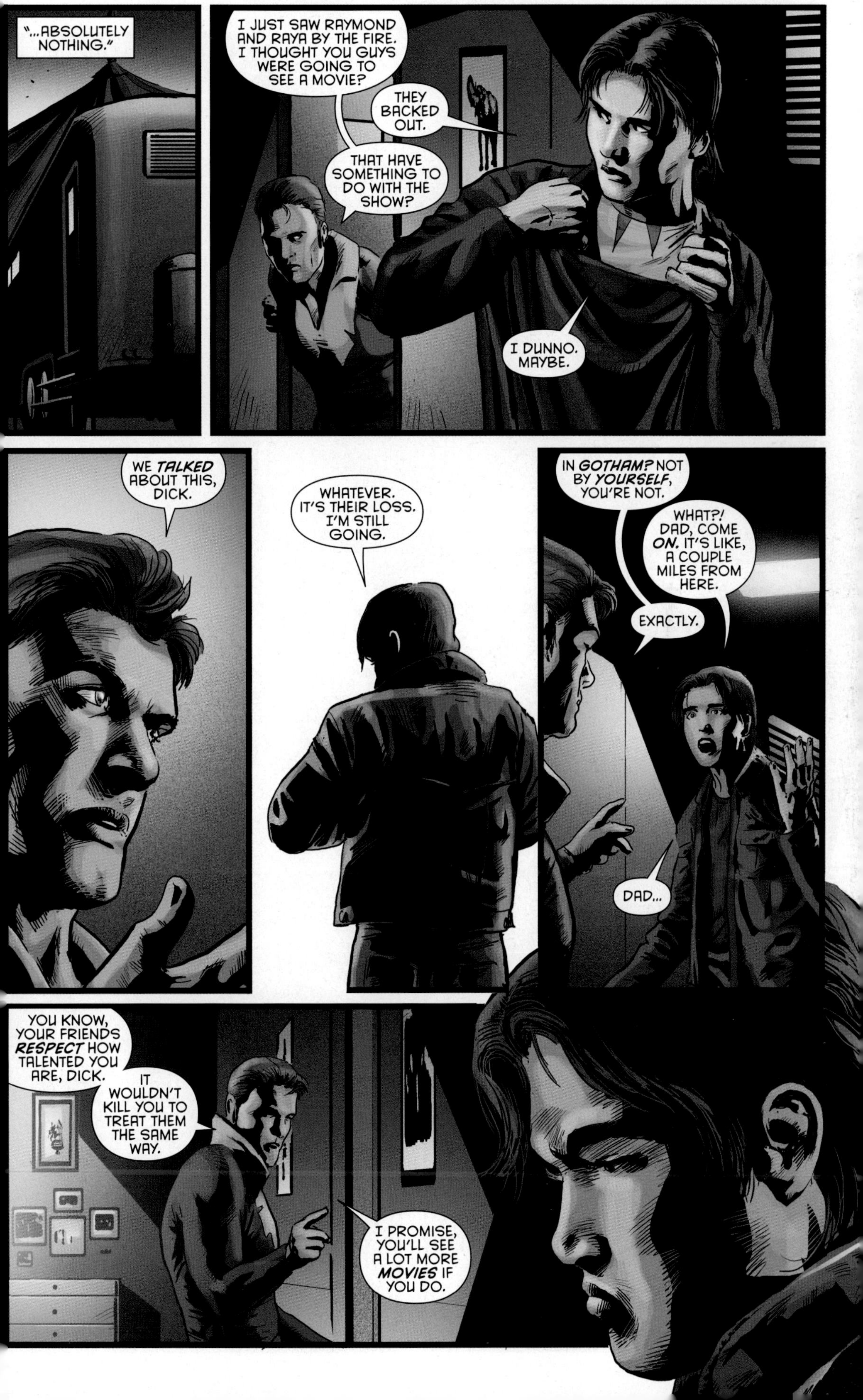
"...ABSOLUTELY NOTHING."
I JUST SAW RAYMOND AND RAYA BY THE FIRE. I THOUGHT YOU GUYS WERE GOING TO SEE A MOVIE?
THEY BACKED OUT.
THAT HAVE SOMETHING TO DO WITH THE SHOW?
I DUNNO. MAYBE.
WE *TALKED* ABOUT THIS, DICK.
WHATEVER. IT'S THEIR LOSS. I'M STILL GOING.
IN *GOTHAM?* NOT BY *YOURSELF*, YOU'RE NOT.
WHAT?! DAD, COME *ON*. IT'S LIKE, A COUPLE MILES FROM HERE.
EXACTLY.
DAD...
YOU KNOW, YOUR FRIENDS *RESPECT* HOW TALENTED YOU ARE, DICK.
IT WOULDN'T KILL YOU TO TREAT THEM THE SAME WAY.
I PROMISE, YOU'LL SEE A LOT MORE *MOVIES* IF YOU DO.

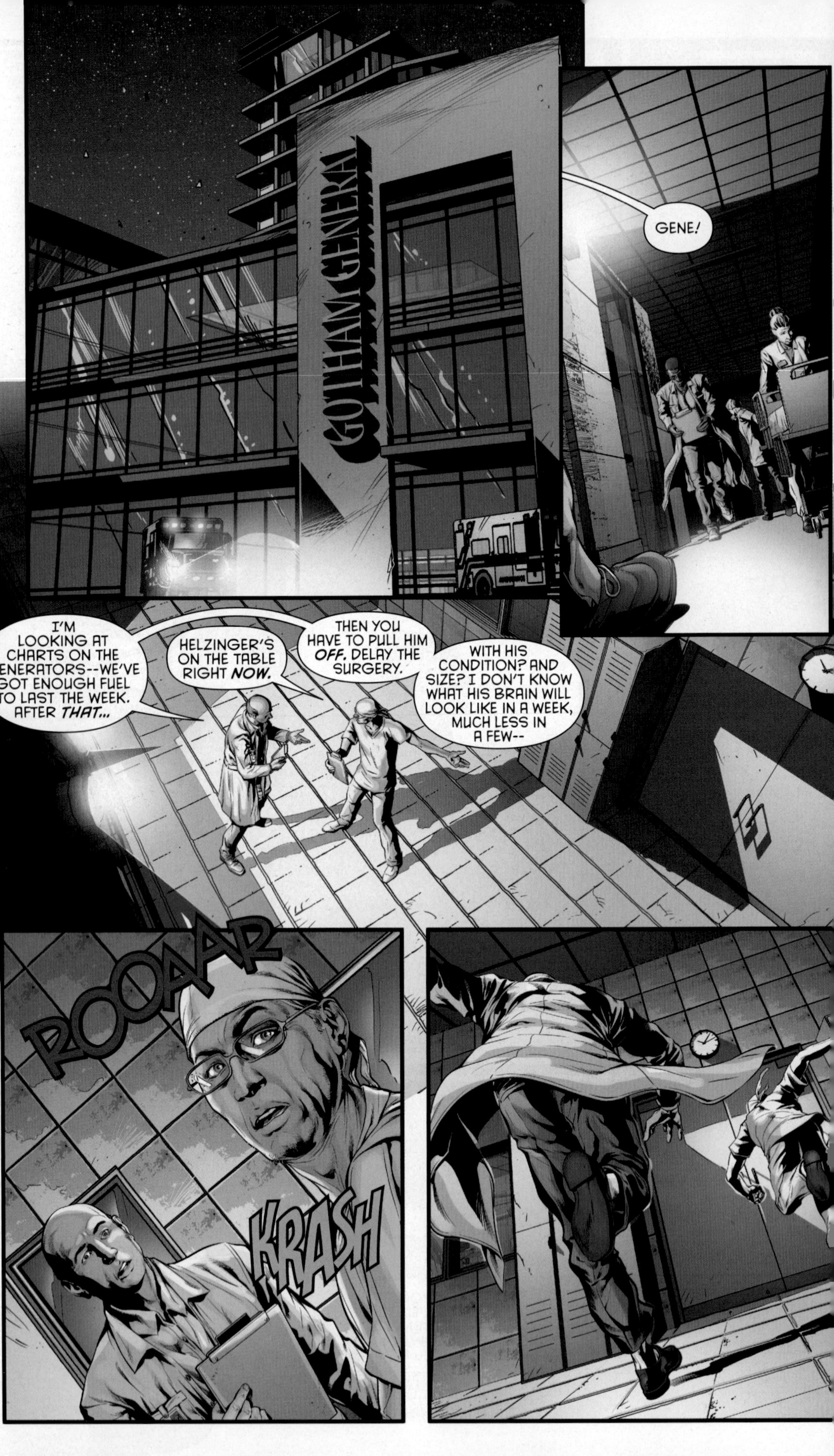
GOTHAM GENERAL
GENE!
I'M LOOKING AT CHARTS ON THE GENERATORS--WE'VE GOT ENOUGH FUEL TO LAST THE WEEK. AFTER *THAT*...
HELZINGER'S ON THE TABLE RIGHT *NOW.*
THEN YOU HAVE TO PULL HIM *OFF.* DELAY THE SURGERY.
WITH HIS CONDITION? AND SIZE? I DON'T KNOW WHAT HIS BRAIN WILL LOOK LIKE IN A WEEK, MUCH LESS IN A FEW--
ROOAAR
KRASH

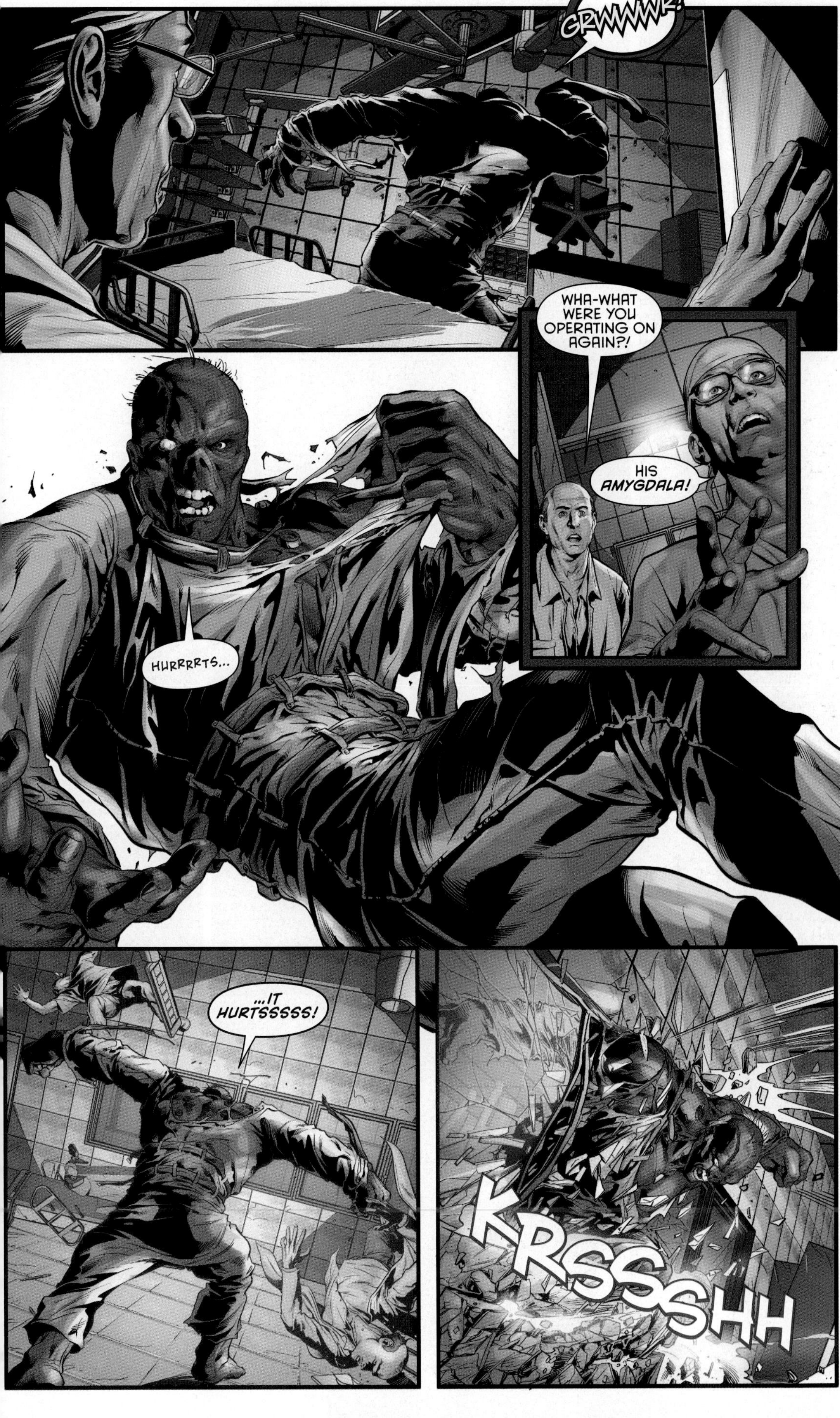
GRWWWR!
WHA-WHAT WERE YOU OPERATING ON AGAIN?!
HIS AMYGDALA!
HURRRRTS...
...IT HURTSSSSS!
KRSSSSHH

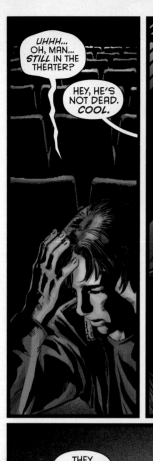

UHHH... OH, MAN... *STILL* IN THE THEATER?

HEY, HE'S NOT DEAD. *COOL.*

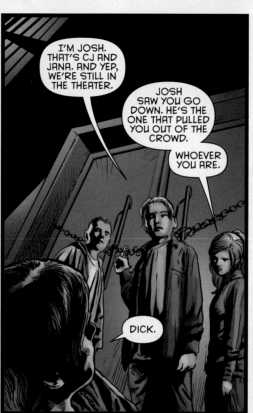

I'M JOSH. THAT'S CJ AND JANA. AND YEP, WE'RE STILL IN THE THEATER.

JOSH SAW YOU GO DOWN. HE'S THE ONE THAT PULLED YOU OUT OF THE CROWD.

WHOEVER YOU ARE.

DICK.

AND, *UH,* THANKS. I TOTALLY OWE YOU GUYS.

YOU LIVE NEARBY?

ACTUALLY, I'M IN TOWN WITH THE *CIRCUS.*

THEY STILL HAVE THOSE?

KAKLIK

DON'T BE AN IDIOT, JOSH. OF *COURSE* THEY HAVE THEM.

ALL RIGHT-- MY DAD'S PLACE ISN'T TOO FAR. YOU GUYS STAY TIGHT, I CAN GET US THERE.

THE CIRCUS IS SET UP ON THIRD STREET. I'LL POINT OUT THE ROUTE WHEN WE'RE CLOSE, DICK.

UNLESS YOU'D RATHER TAKE YOUR CHANCES ON THE *MAIN* STREETS WITH ALL THE RIOTERS AND STUFF.

WELL, WHEN YOU PUT IT LIKE *THAT...*

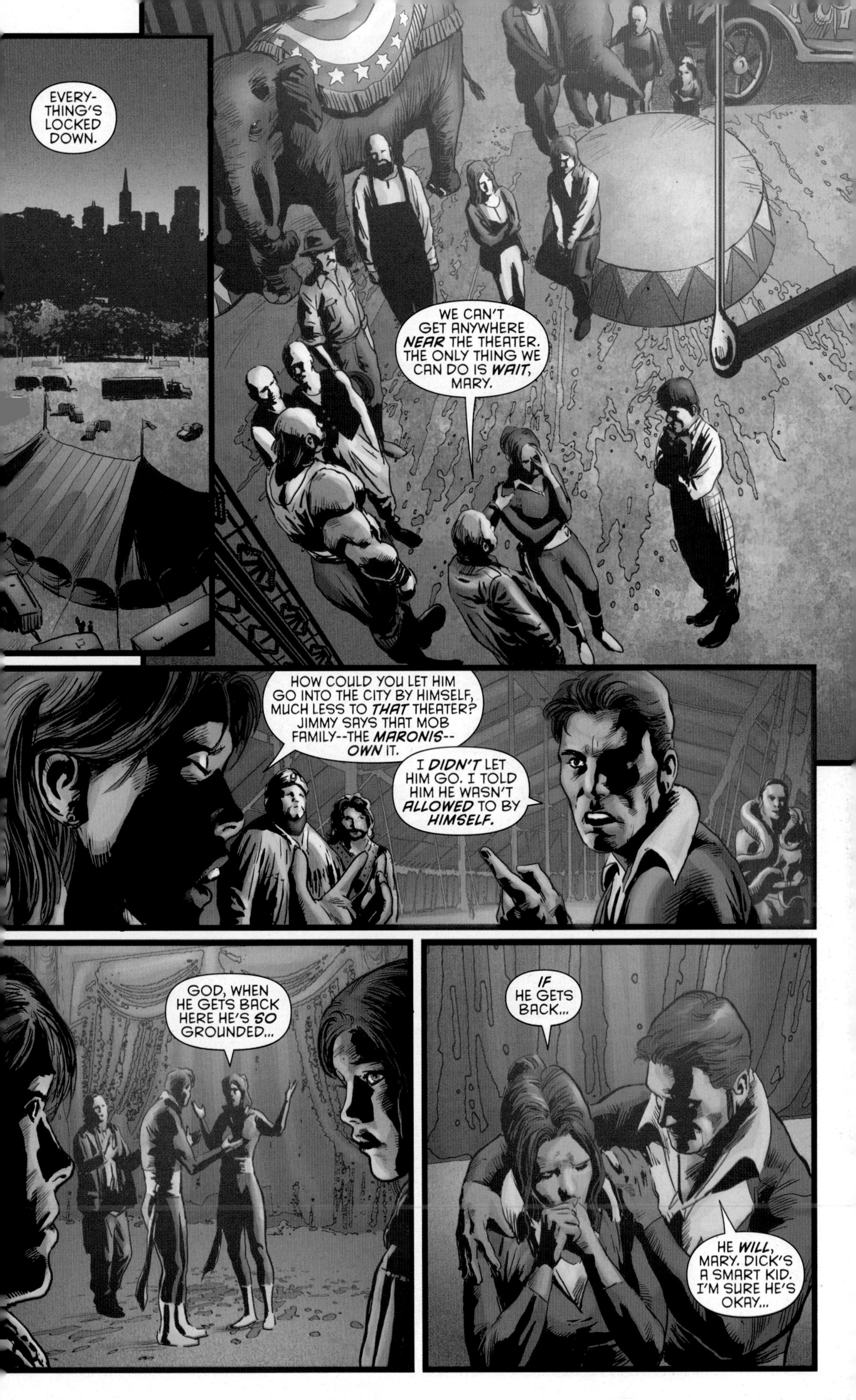
EVERY-THING'S LOCKED DOWN.
WE CAN'T GET ANYWHERE NEAR THE THEATER. THE ONLY THING WE CAN DO IS WAIT, MARY.
HOW COULD YOU LET HIM GO INTO THE CITY BY HIMSELF, MUCH LESS TO THAT THEATER? JIMMY SAYS THAT MOB FAMILY--THE MARONIS--OWN IT.
I DIDN'T LET HIM GO. I TOLD HIM HE WASN'T ALLOWED TO BY HIMSELF.
GOD, WHEN HE GETS BACK HERE HE'S SO GROUNDED...
IF HE GETS BACK...
HE WILL, MARY. DICK'S A SMART KID. I'M SURE HE'S OKAY...

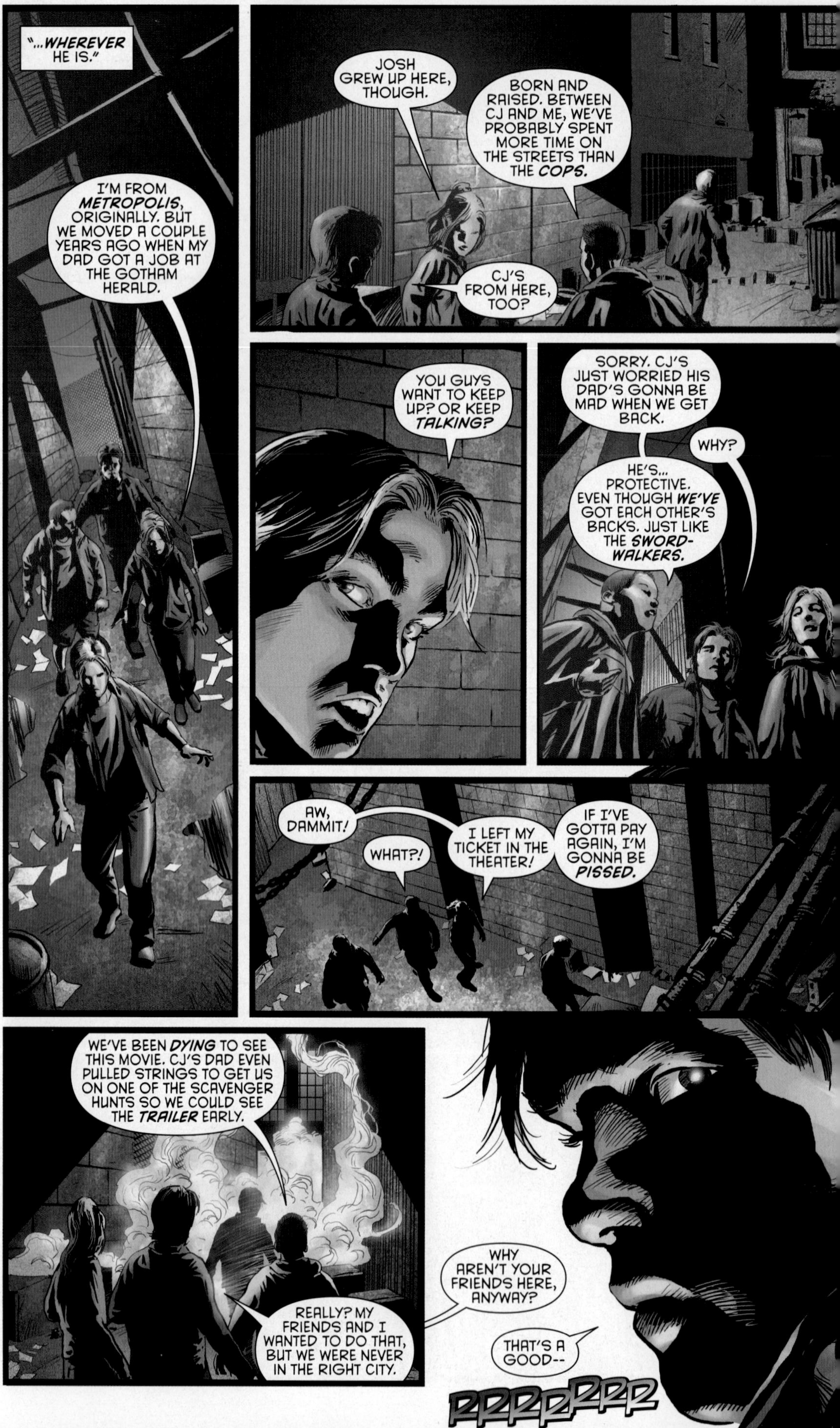
"...WHEREVER HE IS."
I'M FROM METROPOLIS, ORIGINALLY. BUT WE MOVED A COUPLE YEARS AGO WHEN MY DAD GOT A JOB AT THE GOTHAM HERALD.
JOSH GREW UP HERE, THOUGH.
BORN AND RAISED. BETWEEN CJ AND ME, WE'VE PROBABLY SPENT MORE TIME ON THE STREETS THAN THE COPS.
CJ'S FROM HERE, TOO?
YOU GUYS WANT TO KEEP UP? OR KEEP TALKING?
SORRY. CJ'S JUST WORRIED HIS DAD'S GONNA BE MAD WHEN WE GET BACK.
WHY?
HE'S... PROTECTIVE. EVEN THOUGH WE'VE GOT EACH OTHER'S BACKS. JUST LIKE THE SWORD-WALKERS.
AW, DAMMIT!
WHAT?!
I LEFT MY TICKET IN THE THEATER!
IF I'VE GOTTA PAY AGAIN, I'M GONNA BE PISSED.
WE'VE BEEN DYING TO SEE THIS MOVIE. CJ'S DAD EVEN PULLED STRINGS TO GET US ON ONE OF THE SCAVENGER HUNTS SO WE COULD SEE THE TRAILER EARLY.
REALLY? MY FRIENDS AND I WANTED TO DO THAT, BUT WE WERE NEVER IN THE RIGHT CITY.
WHY AREN'T YOUR FRIENDS HERE, ANYWAY?
THAT'S A GOOD--
RRRRRRRR

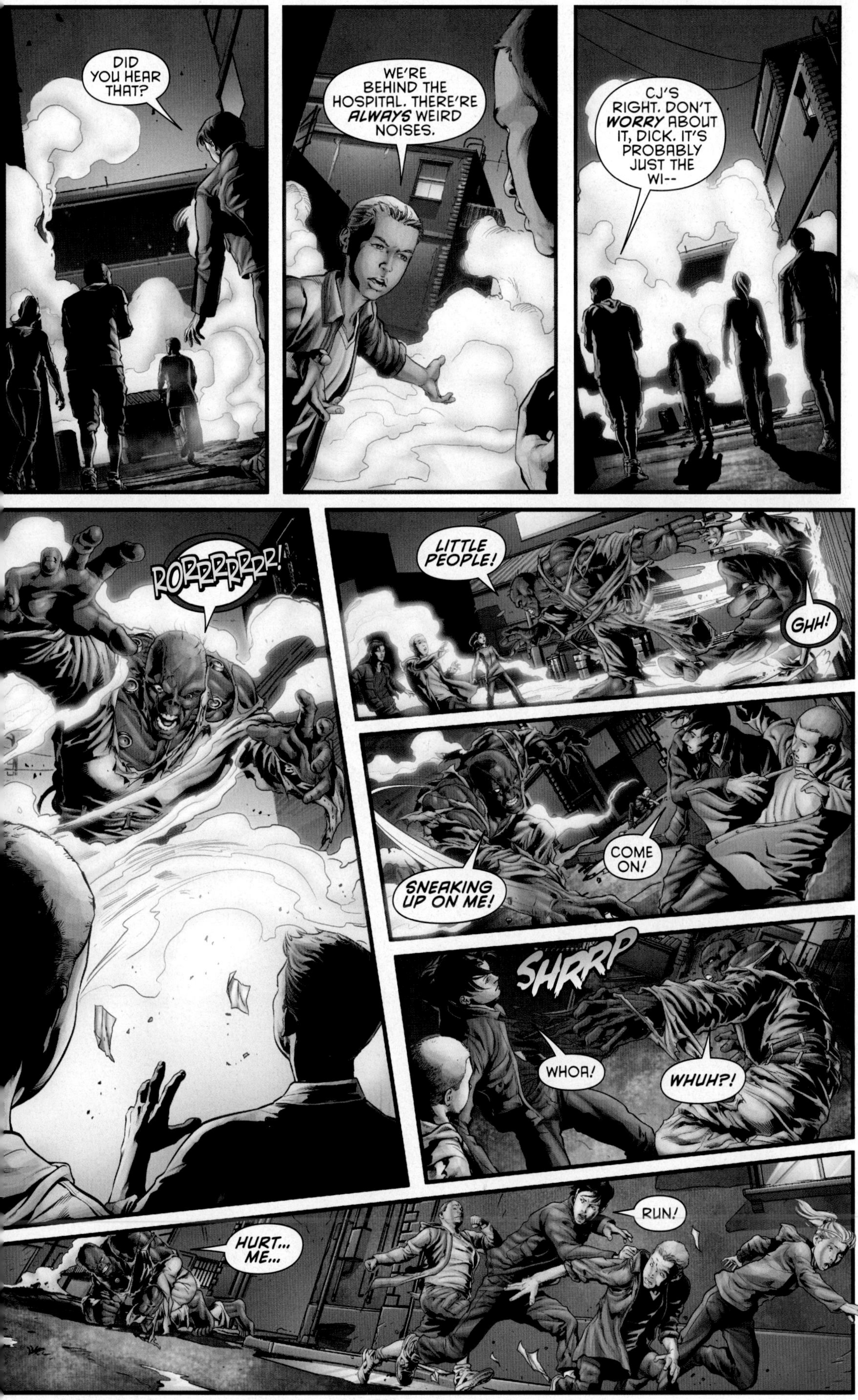
DID YOU HEAR THAT?
WE'RE BEHIND THE HOSPITAL. THERE'RE ALWAYS WEIRD NOISES.
CJ'S RIGHT. DON'T WORRY ABOUT IT, DICK. IT'S PROBABLY JUST THE WI--
RORRRRRRR!
LITTLE PEOPLE!
GHH!
SNEAKING UP ON ME!
COME ON!
SHRRP
WHOA!
WHUH?!
RUN!
HURT... ME...

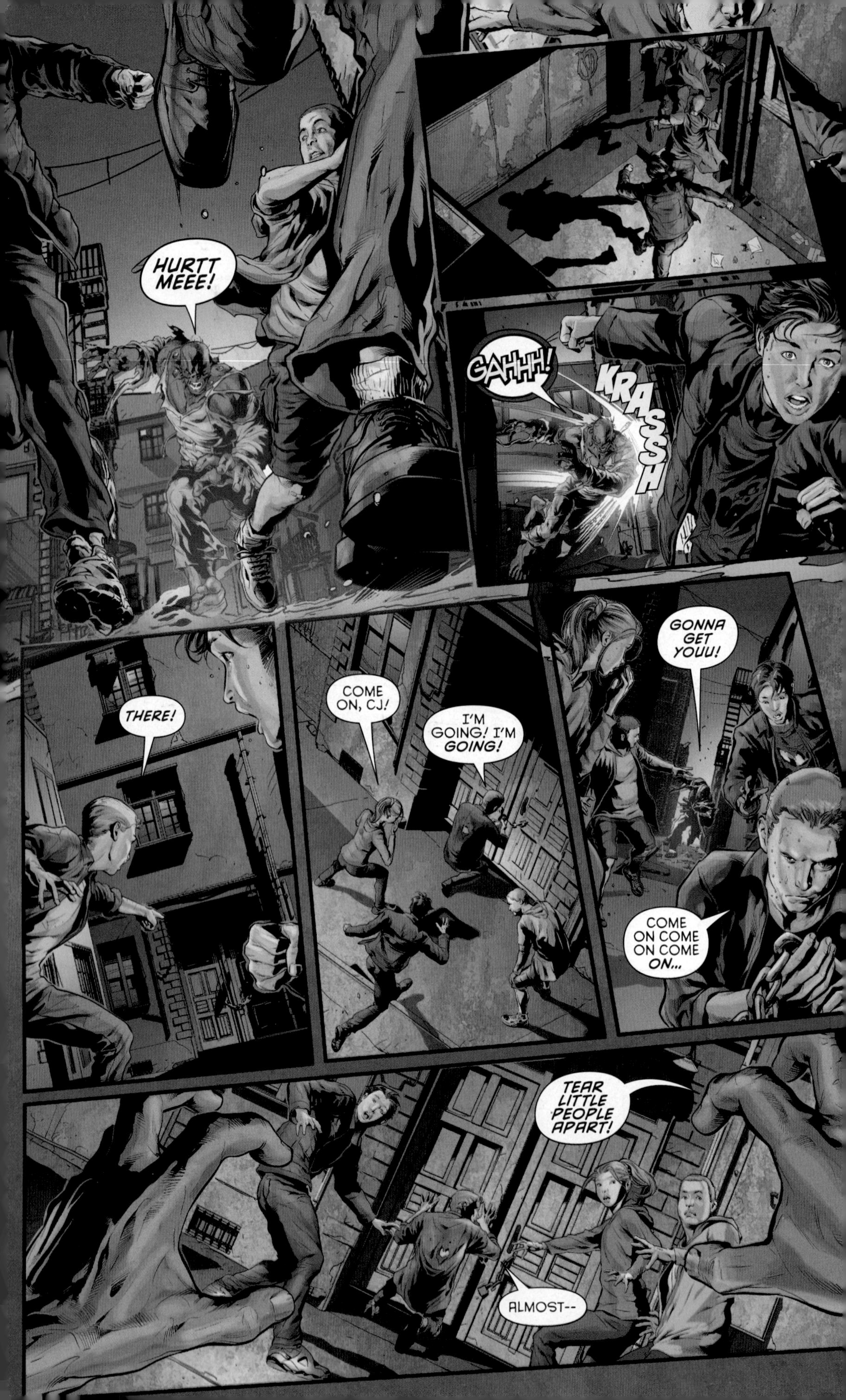
HURTT MEEE!
GAHHH!
KRASSH
THERE!
COME ON, CJ!
I'M GOING! I'M GOING!
GONNA GET YOUU!
COME ON COME ON COME ON...
TEAR LITTLE PEOPLE APART!
ALMOST--

--THERE!

RAAARRRR!

SLAM

EVERY →PANT← BODY →PANT← OKAY?

WHA- WHAT THE HELL *IS* THAT THING?!

NO...NO IDEA...

DID IT *GET* YOU?

JUST MY *SHIRT.* I'M *FINE.*

SLAM SLAM

RRRRR!

WHAT DO WE DO *NOW?*

SLAM KOOM SLAM

IS THERE ANOTHER WAY OUT?

THERE'S A SIDE DOOR--INTO THE OTHER ALLEY. IF WE HURRY, WE CAN GET TO IT BEFORE HE STARTS LOOKING FOR ANOTHER WAY IN!

UH, GUYS?

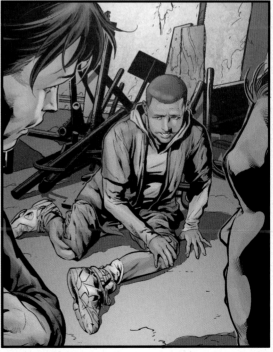

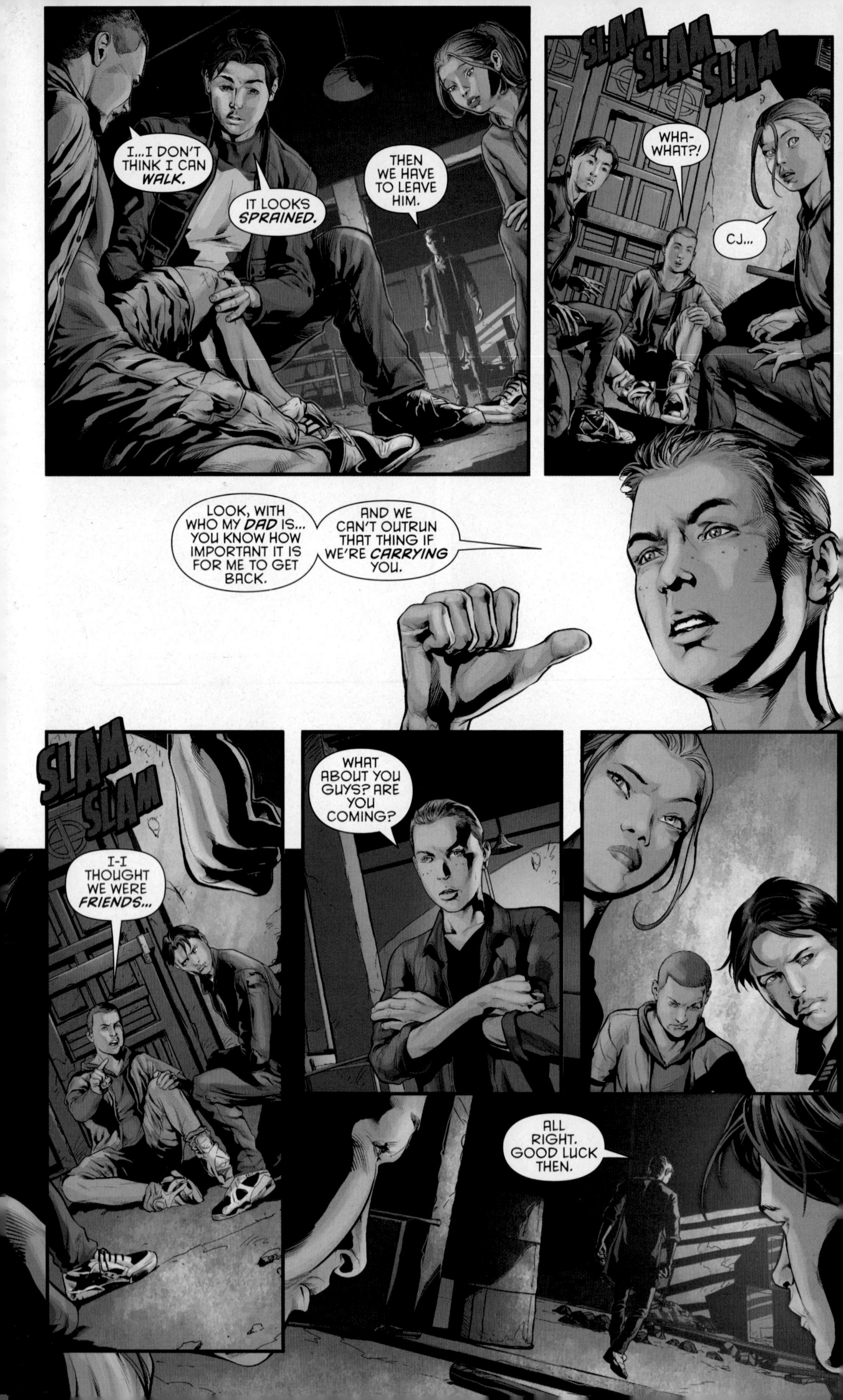
I...I DON'T THINK I CAN WALK.
IT LOOKS SPRAINED.
THEN WE HAVE TO LEAVE HIM.
SLAM SLAM SLAM
WHA-WHAT?!
CJ...
LOOK, WITH WHO MY DAD IS... YOU KNOW HOW IMPORTANT IT IS FOR ME TO GET BACK.
AND WE CAN'T OUTRUN THAT THING IF WE'RE CARRYING YOU.
SLAM SLAM
I-I THOUGHT WE WERE FRIENDS...
WHAT ABOUT YOU GUYS? ARE YOU COMING?
ALL RIGHT. GOOD LUCK THEN.

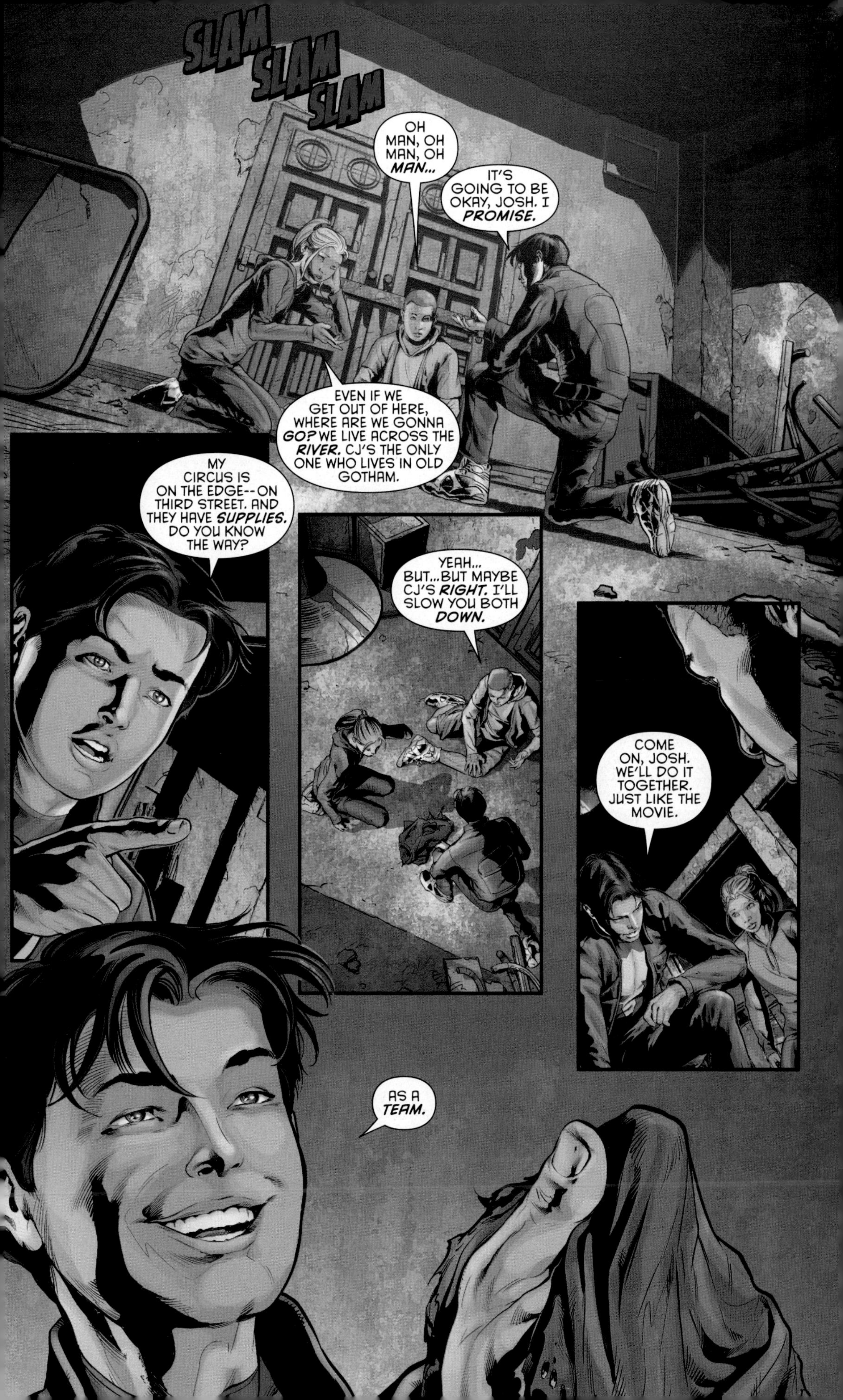
SLAM SLAM SLAM
OH MAN, OH MAN, OH MAN...
IT'S GOING TO BE OKAY, JOSH. I PROMISE.
EVEN IF WE GET OUT OF HERE, WHERE ARE WE GONNA GO? WE LIVE ACROSS THE RIVER. CJ'S THE ONLY ONE WHO LIVES IN OLD GOTHAM.
MY CIRCUS IS ON THE EDGE--ON THIRD STREET. AND THEY HAVE SUPPLIES. DO YOU KNOW THE WAY?
YEAH... BUT...BUT MAYBE CJ'S RIGHT. I'LL SLOW YOU BOTH DOWN.
COME ON, JOSH. WE'LL DO IT TOGETHER. JUST LIKE THE MOVIE.
AS A TEAM.

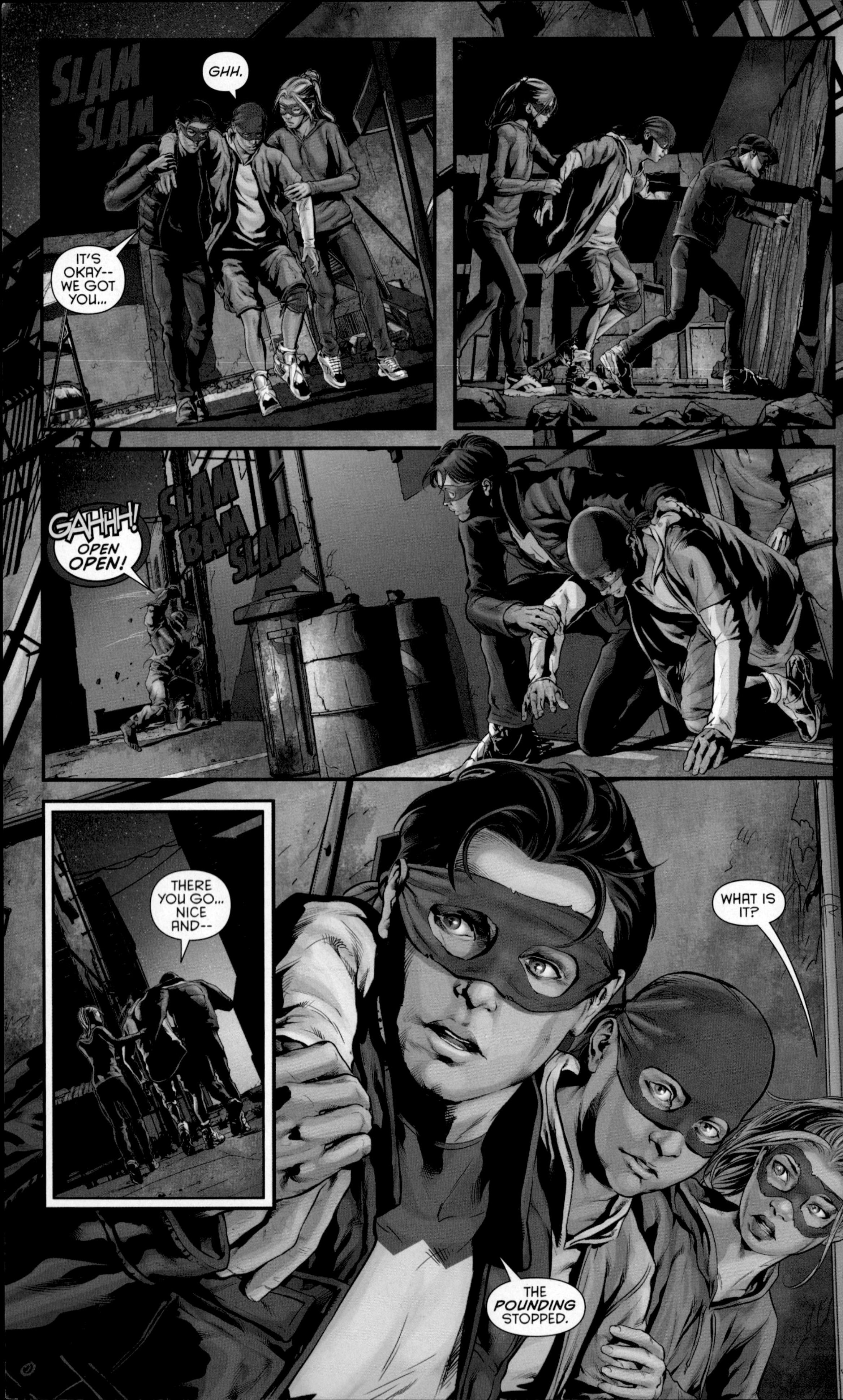
SLAM
SLAM
GHH.
IT'S OKAY-- WE GOT YOU...
GAHHH! OPEN OPEN!
SLAM
BAM
SLAM
THERE YOU GO... NICE AND--
WHAT IS IT?
THE POUNDING STOPPED.

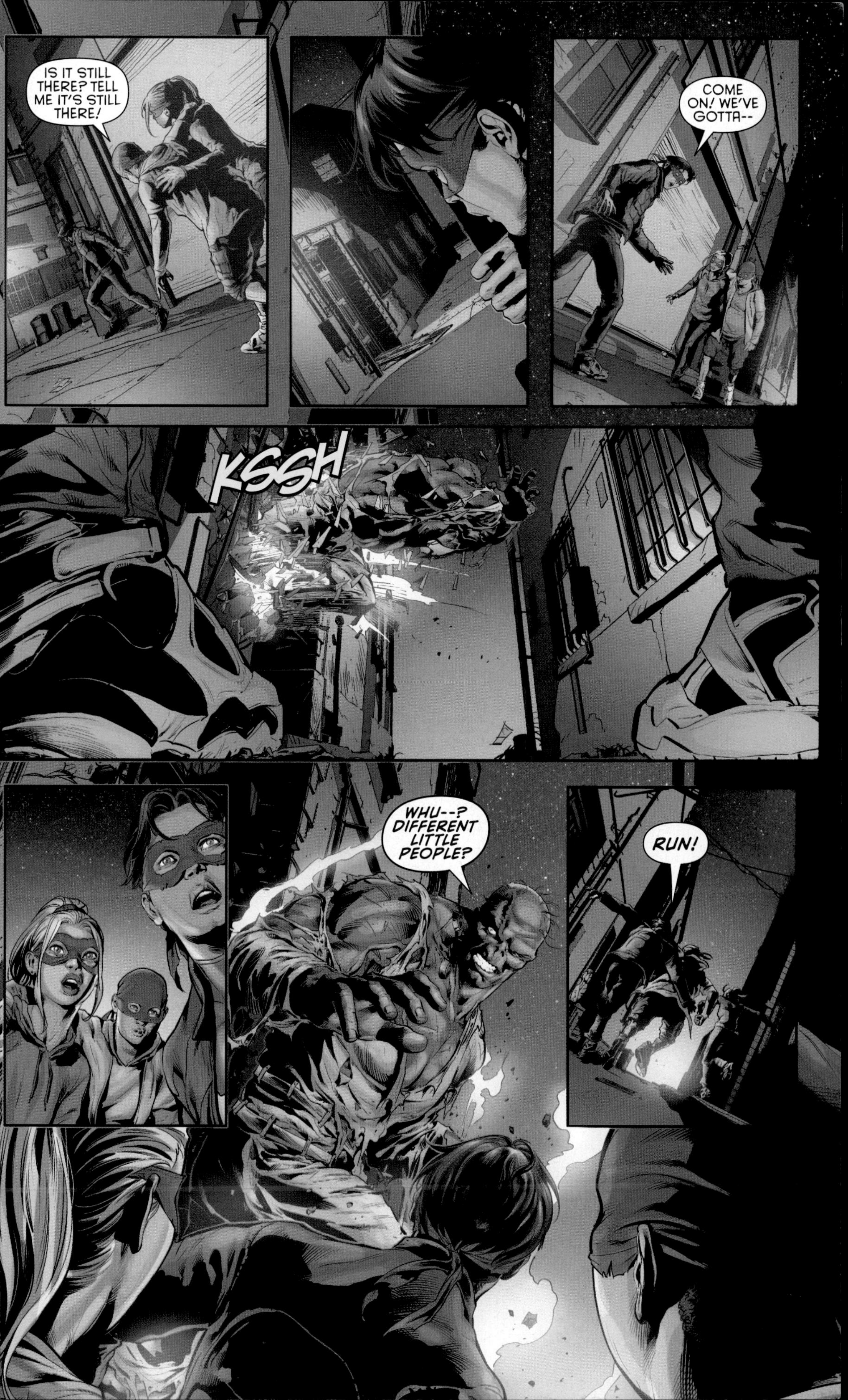
IS IT STILL THERE? TELL ME IT'S STILL THERE!
COME ON! WE'VE GOTTA--
KSSH
WHU--? DIFFERENT LITTLE PEOPLE?
RUN!

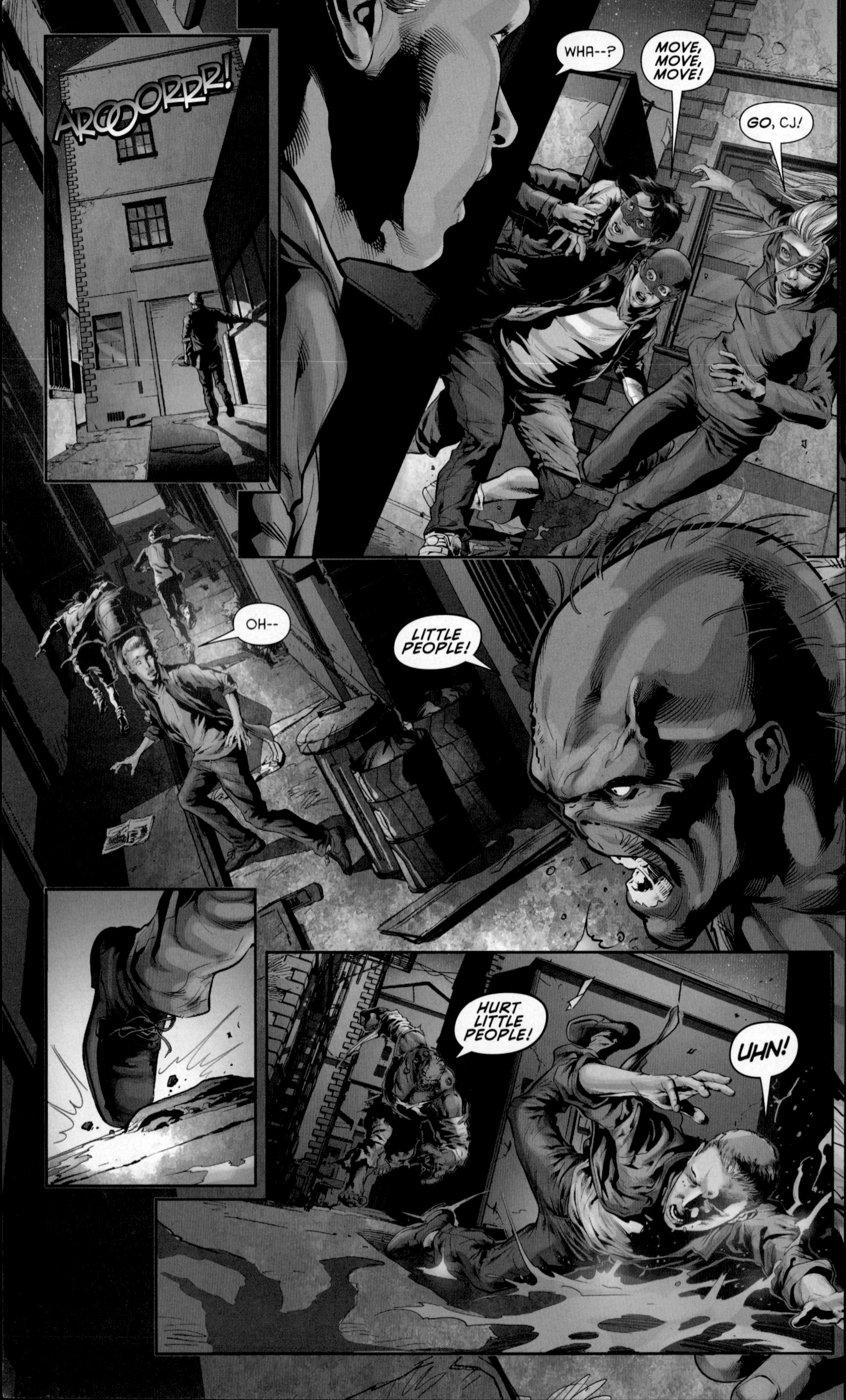
ARGOORRR!
WHA--?
MOVE, MOVE, MOVE!
GO, CJ!
OH--
LITTLE PEOPLE!
HURT LITTLE PEOPLE!
UHN!

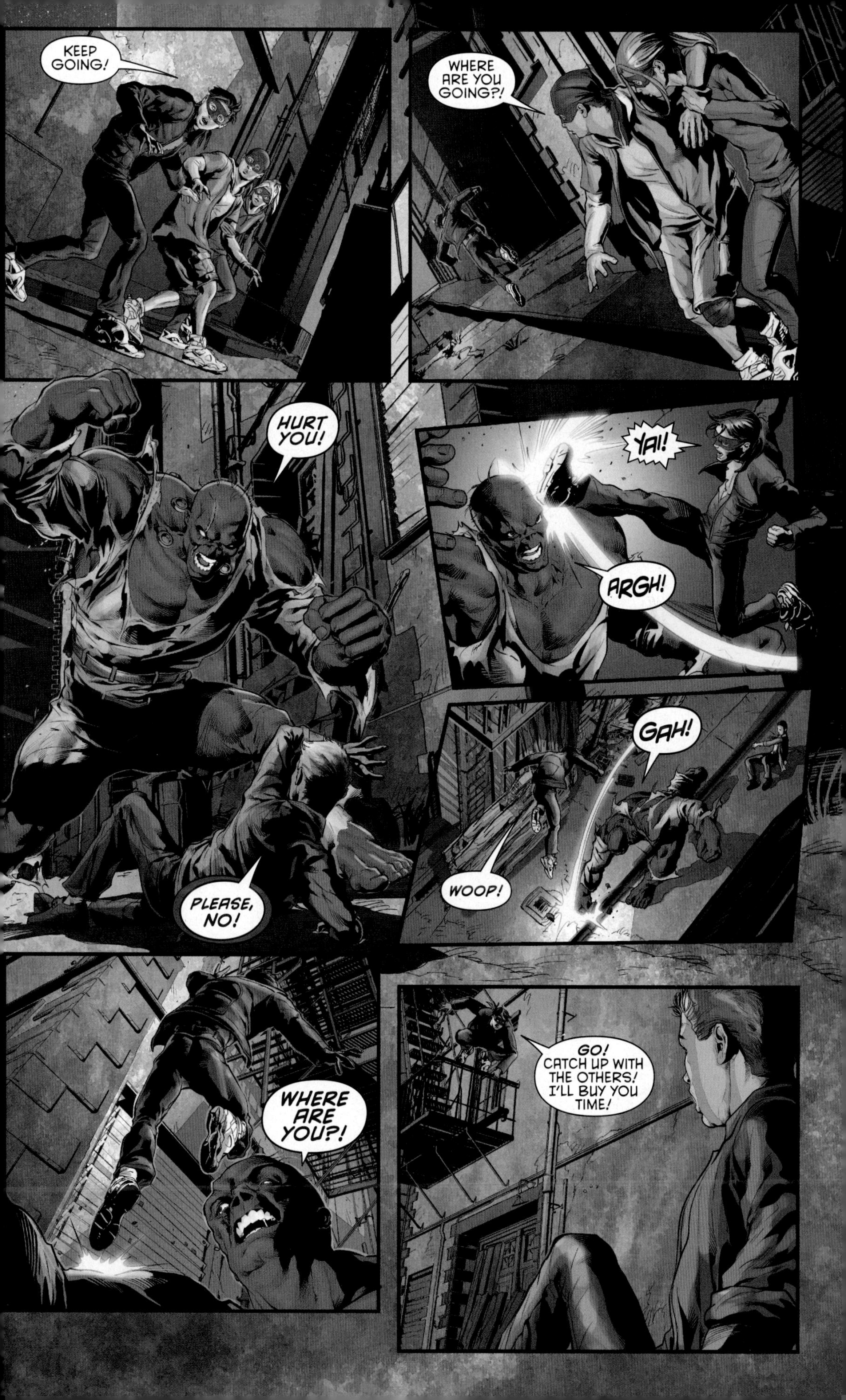
KEEP GOING!
WHERE ARE YOU GOING?!
HURT YOU!
PLEASE, NO!
YAI!
ARGH!
GAH!
WOOP!
WHERE ARE YOU?!
GO! CATCH UP WITH THE OTHERS! I'LL BUY YOU TIME!

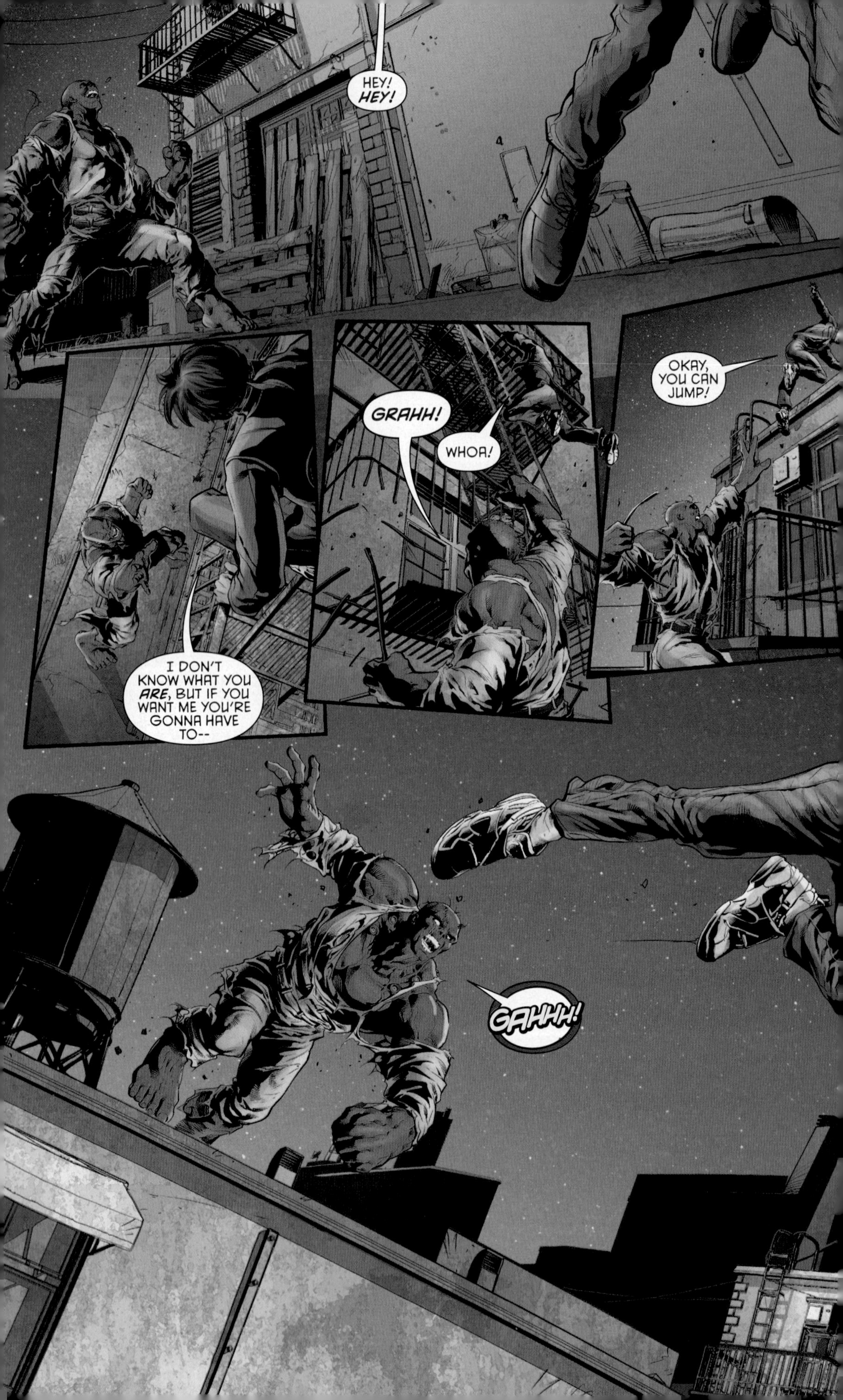
HEY! HEY!
I DON'T KNOW WHAT YOU ARE, BUT IF YOU WANT ME YOU'RE GONNA HAVE TO--
GRAHH!
WHOA!
OKAY, YOU CAN JUMP!
GAHHH!

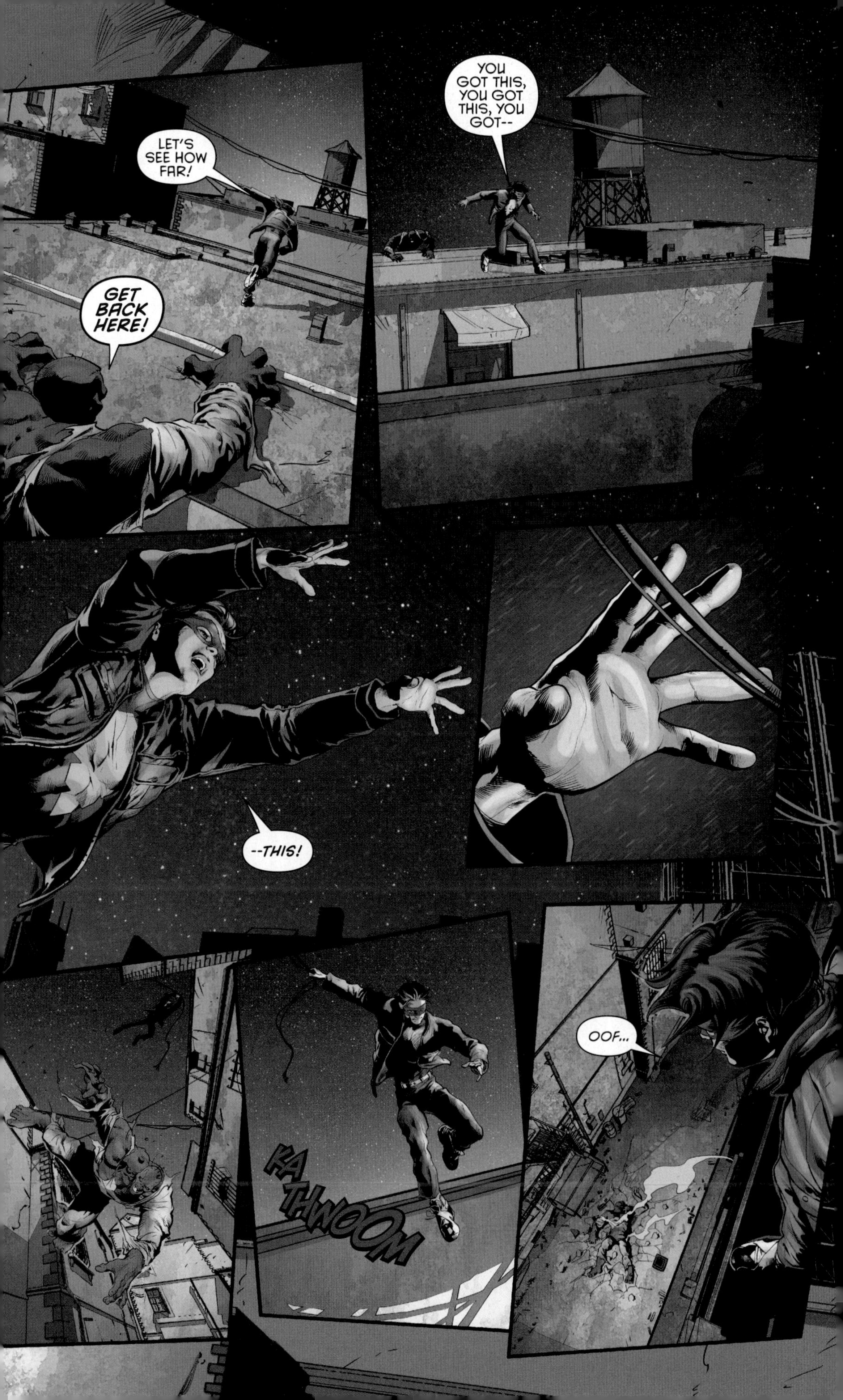
LET'S SEE HOW FAR!
GET BACK HERE!
YOU GOT THIS, YOU GOT THIS, YOU GOT--
--THIS!
KA THWOOM
OOF...

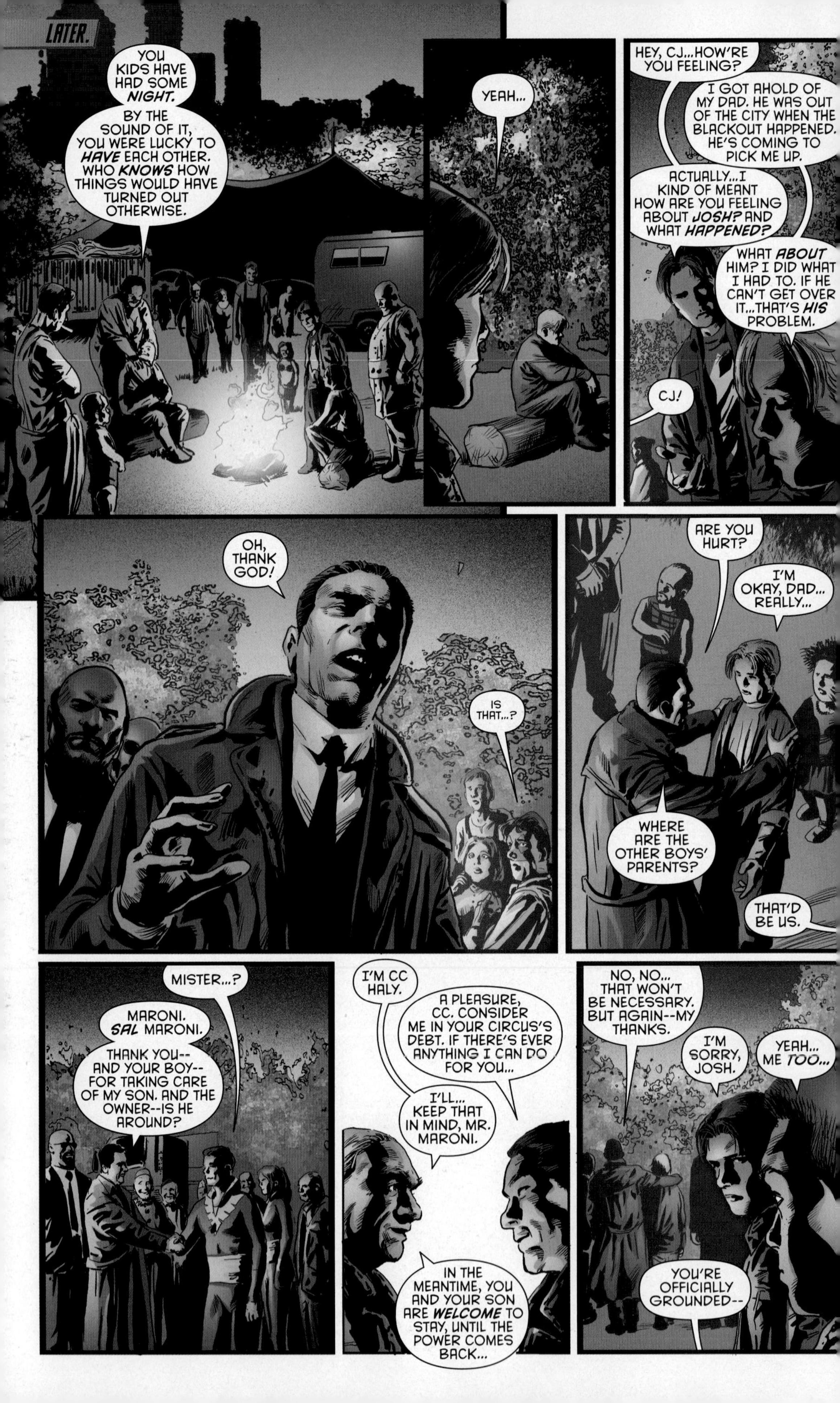
LATER.
YOU KIDS HAVE HAD SOME NIGHT.
BY THE SOUND OF IT, YOU WERE LUCKY TO HAVE EACH OTHER. WHO KNOWS HOW THINGS WOULD HAVE TURNED OUT OTHERWISE.
YEAH...
HEY, CJ...HOW'RE YOU FEELING?
I GOT AHOLD OF MY DAD. HE WAS OUT OF THE CITY WHEN THE BLACKOUT HAPPENED. HE'S COMING TO PICK ME UP.
ACTUALLY...I KIND OF MEANT HOW ARE YOU FEELING ABOUT JOSH? AND WHAT HAPPENED?
WHAT ABOUT HIM? I DID WHAT I HAD TO. IF HE CAN'T GET OVER IT...THAT'S HIS PROBLEM.
CJ!
OH, THANK GOD!
IS THAT...?
ARE YOU HURT?
I'M OKAY, DAD... REALLY...
WHERE ARE THE OTHER BOYS' PARENTS?
THAT'D BE US.
MISTER...?
MARONI. SAL MARONI.
THANK YOU-- AND YOUR BOY-- FOR TAKING CARE OF MY SON. AND THE OWNER--IS HE AROUND?
I'M CC HALY.
A PLEASURE, CC. CONSIDER ME IN YOUR CIRCUS'S DEBT. IF THERE'S EVER ANYTHING I CAN DO FOR YOU...
I'LL... KEEP THAT IN MIND, MR. MARONI.
IN THE MEANTIME, YOU AND YOUR SON ARE WELCOME TO STAY, UNTIL THE POWER COMES BACK...
NO, NO... THAT WON'T BE NECESSARY. BUT AGAIN--MY THANKS.
I'M SORRY, JOSH.
YEAH... ME TOO...
YOU'RE OFFICIALLY GROUNDED--

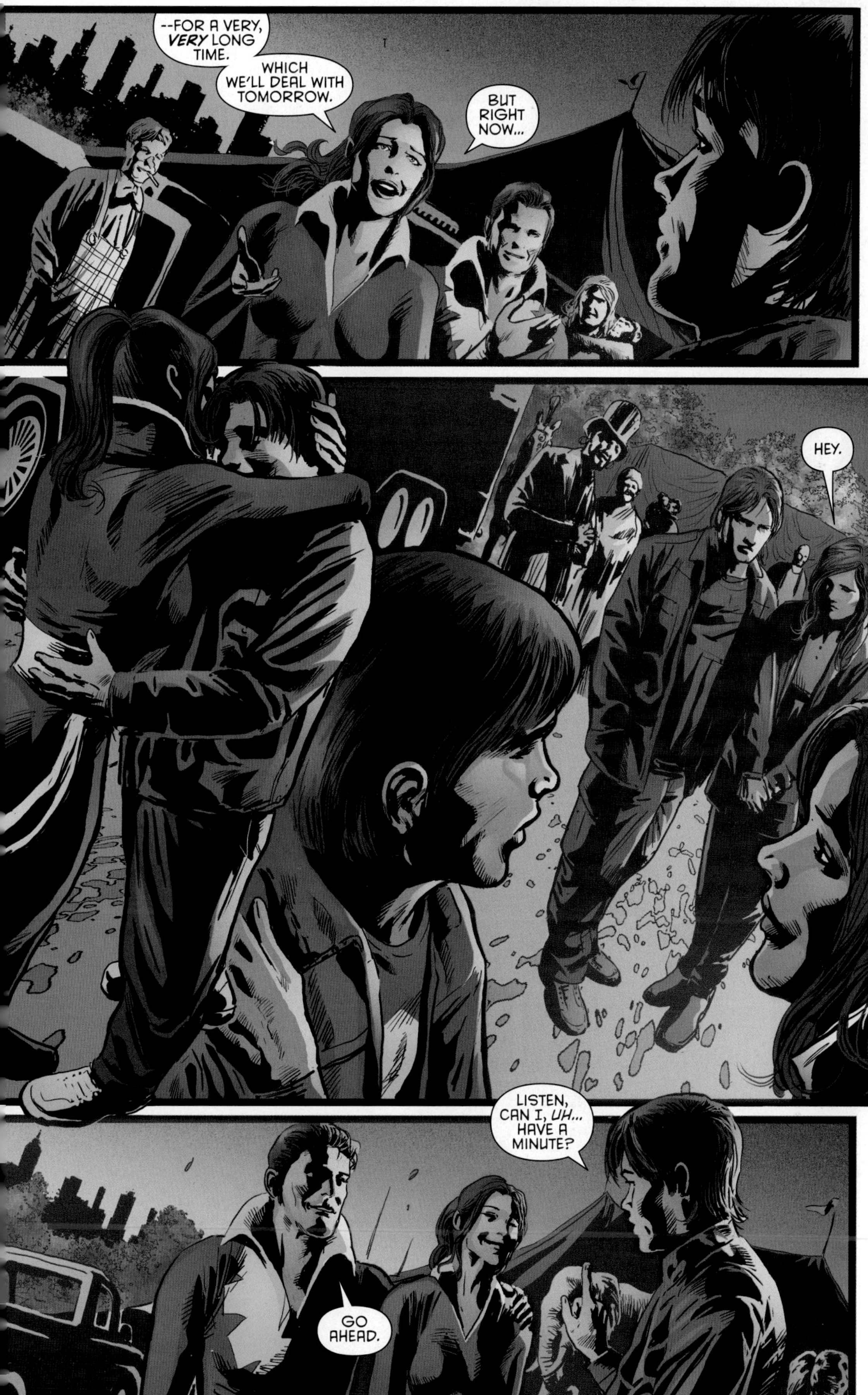
--FOR A VERY, VERY LONG TIME.
WHICH WE'LL DEAL WITH TOMORROW.
BUT RIGHT NOW...
HEY.
LISTEN, CAN I, UH... HAVE A MINUTE?
GO AHEAD.

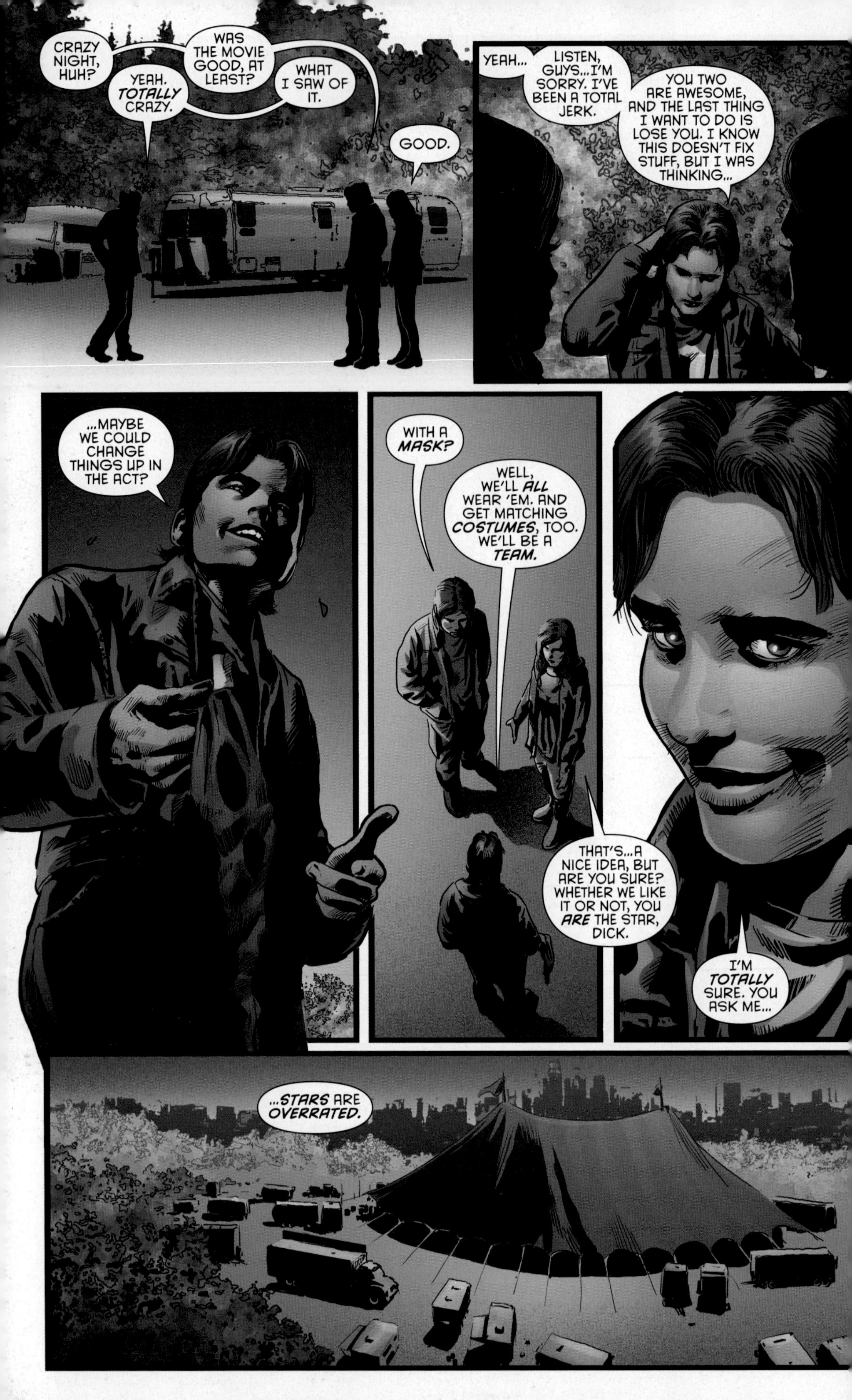
CRAZY NIGHT, HUH?
WAS THE MOVIE GOOD, AT LEAST?
YEAH. TOTALLY CRAZY.
WHAT I SAW OF IT.
GOOD.
YEAH...
LISTEN, GUYS...I'M SORRY. I'VE BEEN A TOTAL JERK.
YOU TWO ARE AWESOME, AND THE LAST THING I WANT TO DO IS LOSE YOU. I KNOW THIS DOESN'T FIX STUFF, BUT I WAS THINKING...
...MAYBE WE COULD CHANGE THINGS UP IN THE ACT?
WITH A MASK?
WELL, WE'LL ALL WEAR 'EM. AND GET MATCHING COSTUMES, TOO. WE'LL BE A TEAM.
THAT'S...A NICE IDEA, BUT ARE YOU SURE? WHETHER WE LIKE IT OR NOT, YOU ARE THE STAR, DICK.
I'M TOTALLY SURE. YOU ASK ME...
...STARS ARE OVERRATED.

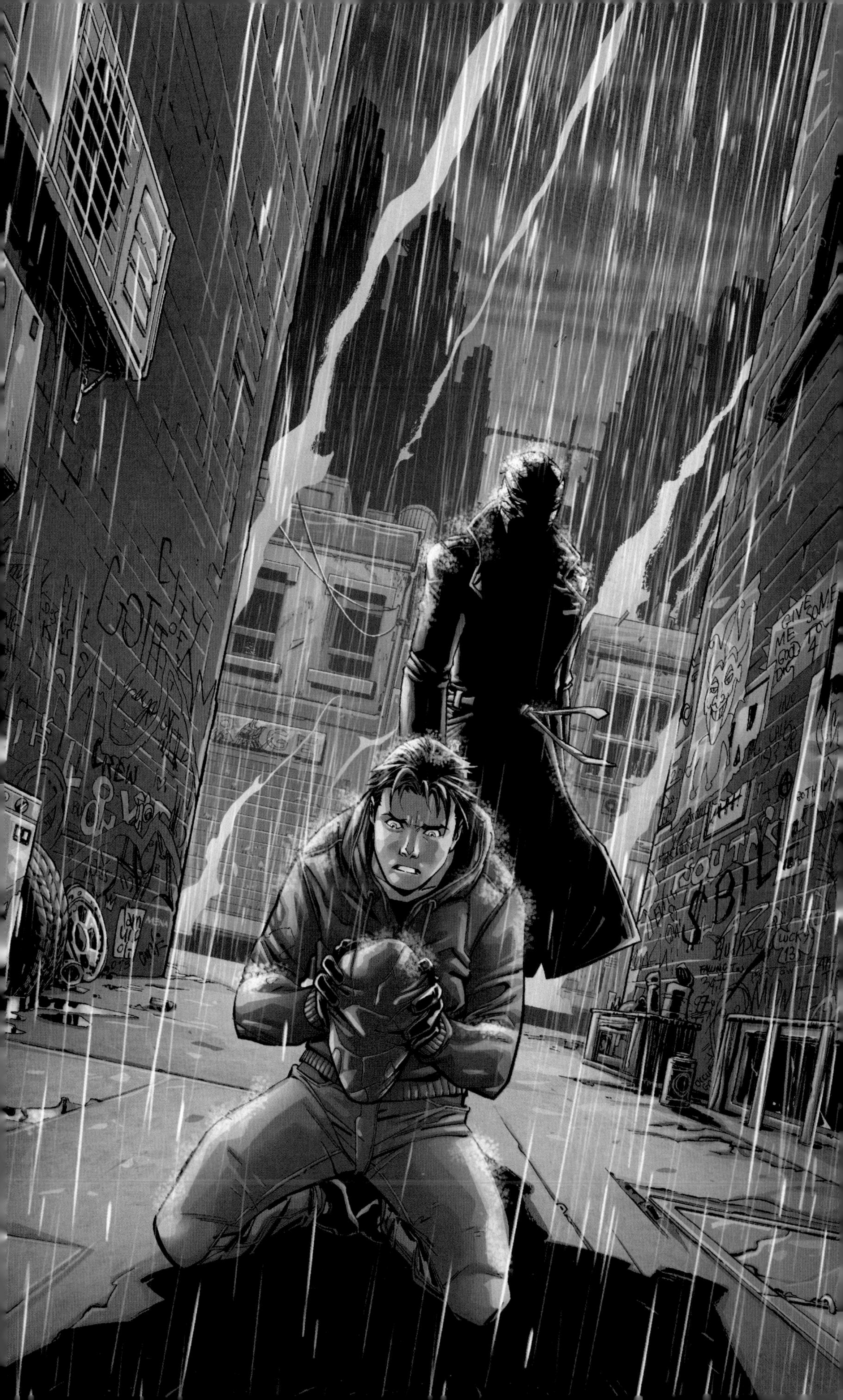
CITY OF GOTHAM
CREW
GIVE ME SOME GOOD DOG TO 4
SOUTH
LUCKY 13
FALLING

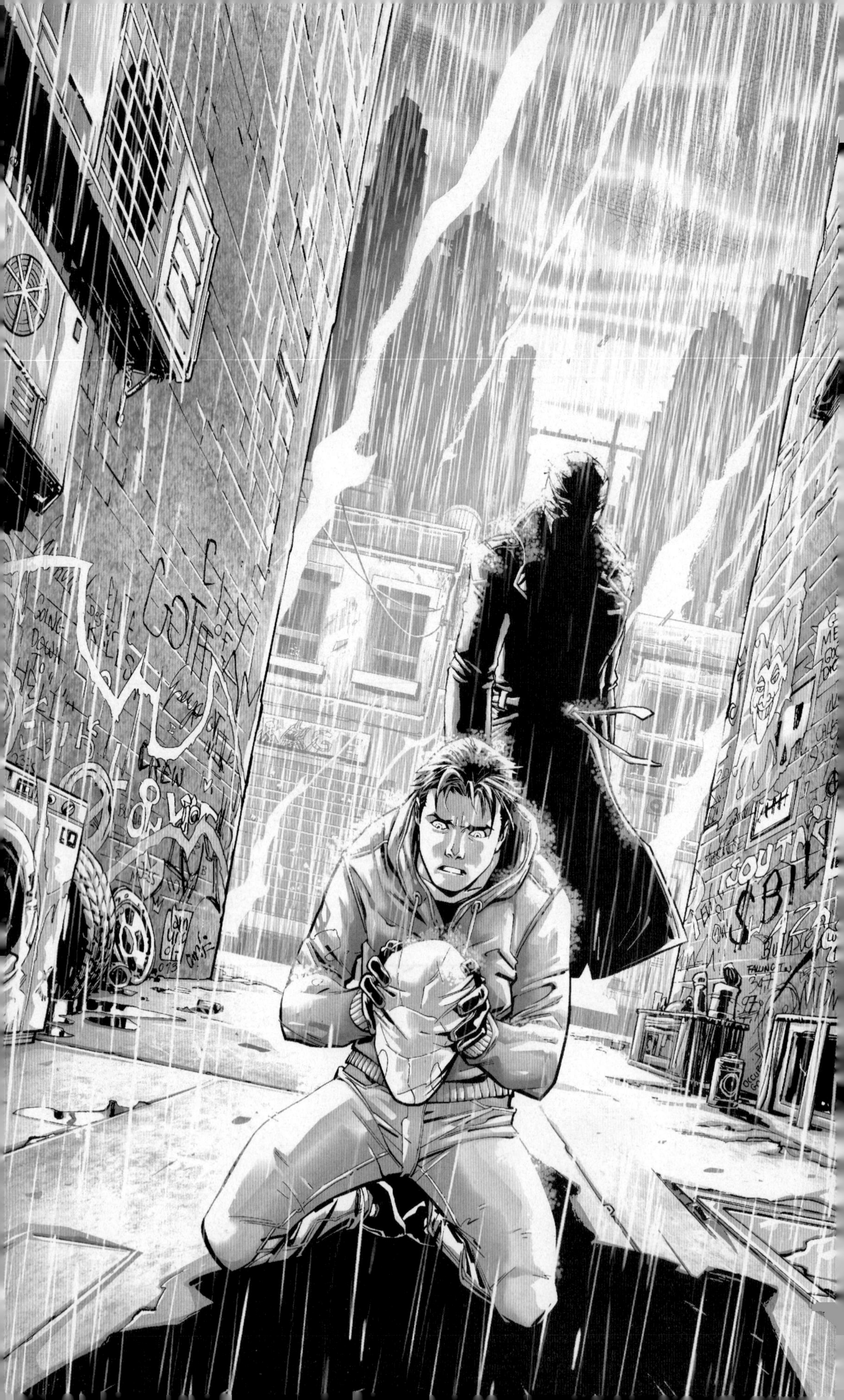

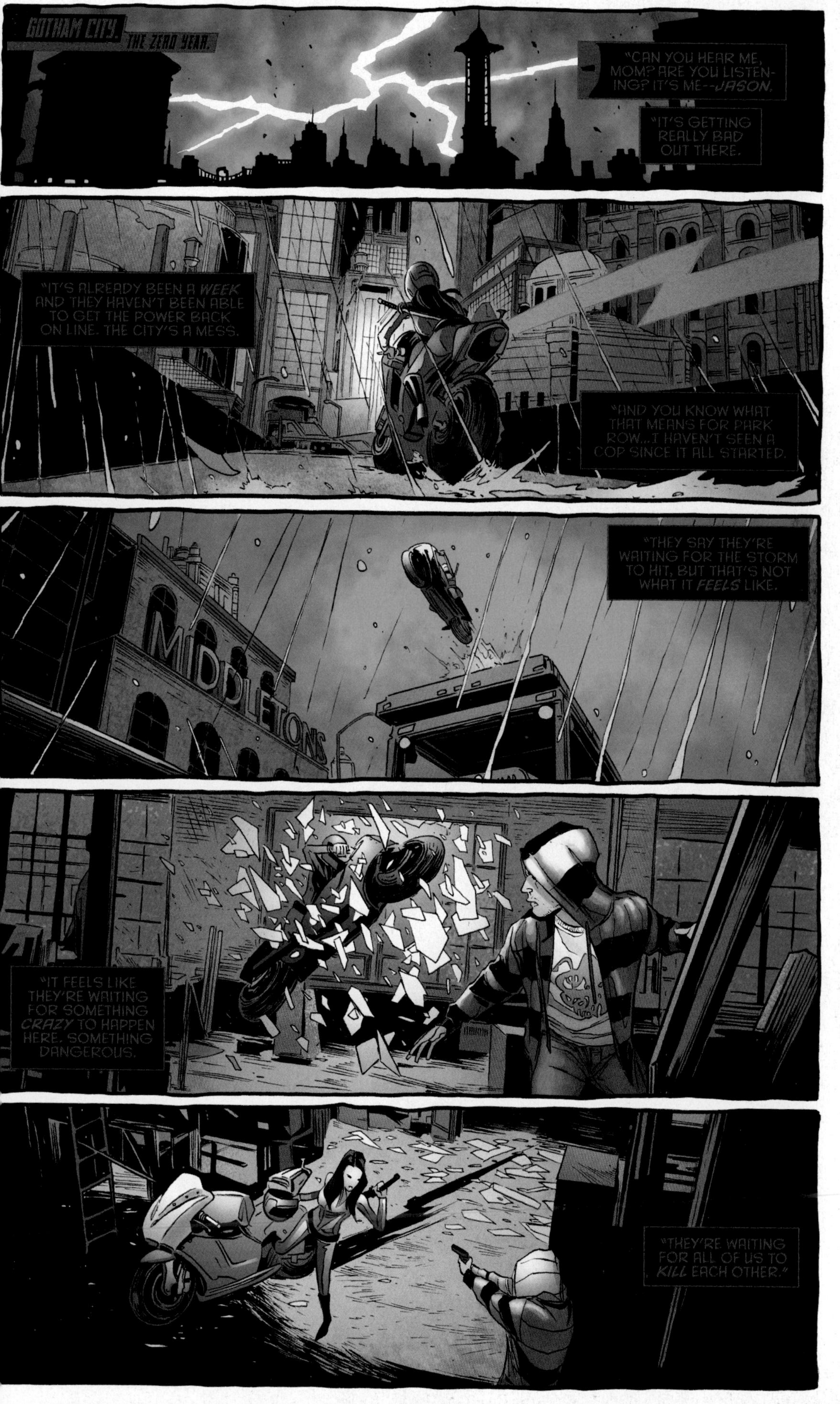
GOTHAM CITY.
THE ZERO YEAR.
"CAN YOU HEAR ME, MOM? ARE YOU LISTENING? IT'S ME--JASON.
"IT'S GETTING REALLY BAD OUT THERE.
"IT'S ALREADY BEEN A WEEK AND THEY HAVEN'T BEEN ABLE TO GET THE POWER BACK ON LINE. THE CITY'S A MESS.
"AND YOU KNOW WHAT THAT MEANS FOR PARK ROW...I HAVEN'T SEEN A COP SINCE IT ALL STARTED.
"THEY SAY THEY'RE WAITING FOR THE STORM TO HIT, BUT THAT'S NOT WHAT IT FEELS LIKE.
MIDDLETONS
"IT FEELS LIKE THEY'RE WAITING FOR SOMETHING CRAZY TO HAPPEN HERE. SOMETHING DANGEROUS.
"THEY'RE WAITING FOR ALL OF US TO KILL EACH OTHER."

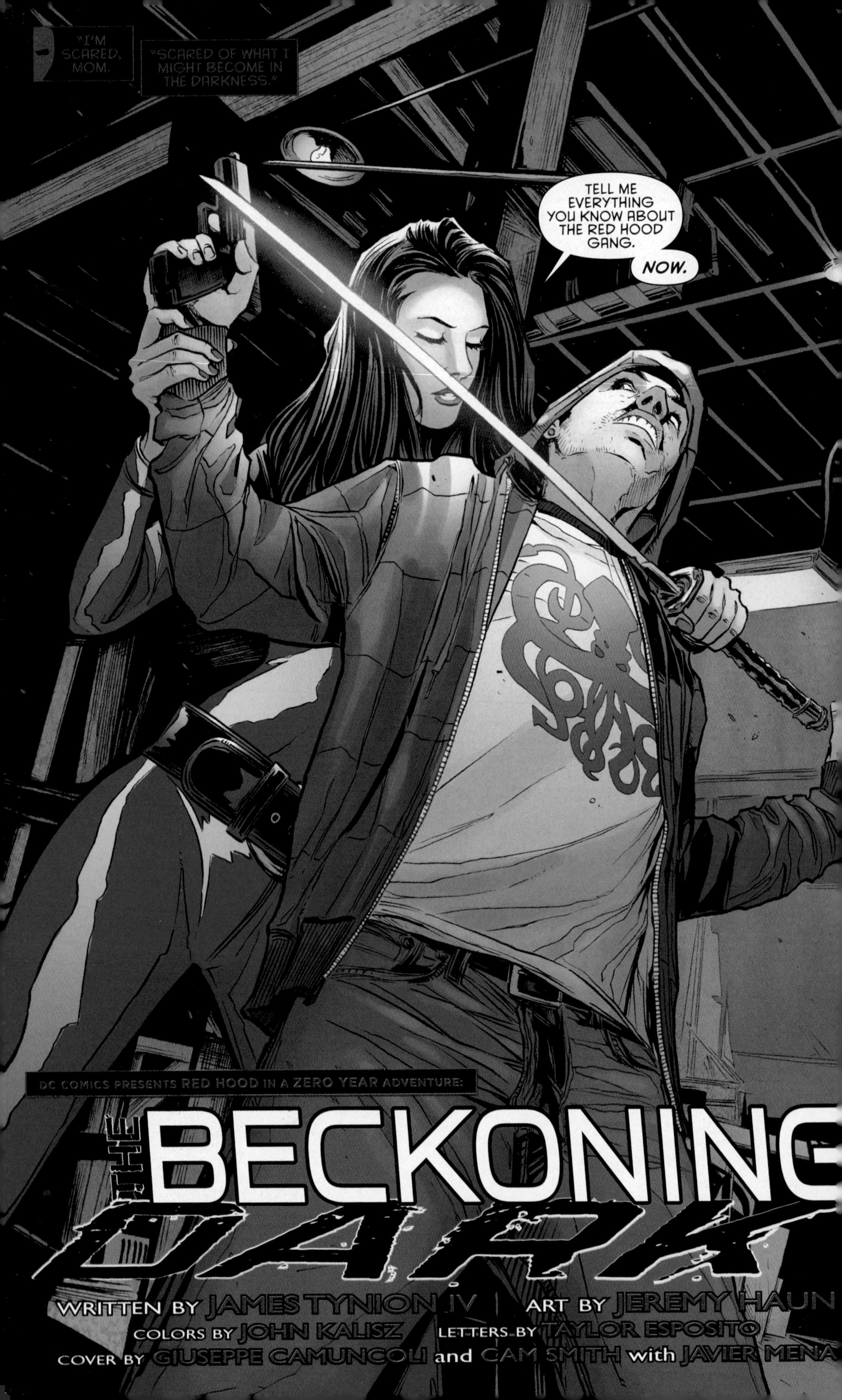

"I'M SCARED, MOM.
"SCARED OF WHAT I MIGHT BECOME IN THE DARKNESS."
TELL ME EVERYTHING YOU KNOW ABOUT THE RED HOOD GANG.
NOW.
DC COMICS PRESENTS RED HOOD IN A ZERO YEAR ADVENTURE:
THE BECKONING DARK
WRITTEN BY JAMES TYNION IV | ART BY JEREMY HAUN
COLORS BY JOHN KALISZ LETTERS BY TAYLOR ESPOSITO
COVER BY GIUSEPPE CAMUNCOLI and CAM SMITH with JAVIER MENA

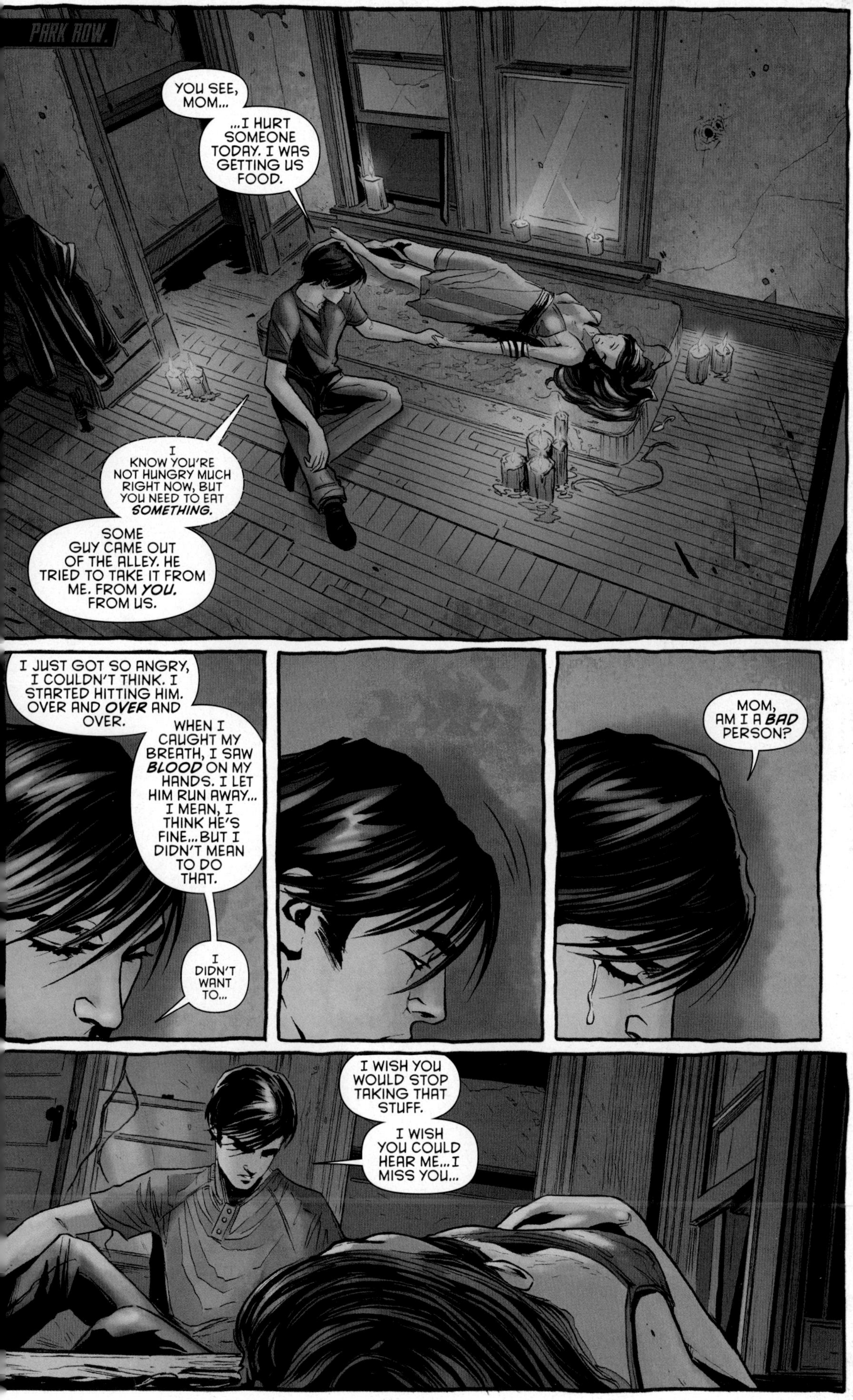
PARK ROW.
YOU SEE, MOM...
...I HURT SOMEONE TODAY. I WAS GETTING US FOOD.
I KNOW YOU'RE NOT HUNGRY MUCH RIGHT NOW, BUT YOU NEED TO EAT *SOMETHING.*
SOME GUY CAME OUT OF THE ALLEY. HE TRIED TO TAKE IT FROM ME. FROM *YOU.* FROM US.
I JUST GOT SO ANGRY, I COULDN'T THINK. I STARTED HITTING HIM. OVER AND *OVER* AND OVER.
WHEN I CAUGHT MY BREATH, I SAW *BLOOD* ON MY HANDS. I LET HIM RUN AWAY... I MEAN, I THINK HE'S FINE...BUT I DIDN'T MEAN TO DO THAT.
I DIDN'T WANT TO...
MOM, AM I A *BAD* PERSON?
I WISH YOU WOULD STOP TAKING THAT STUFF.
I WISH YOU COULD HEAR ME...I MISS YOU...

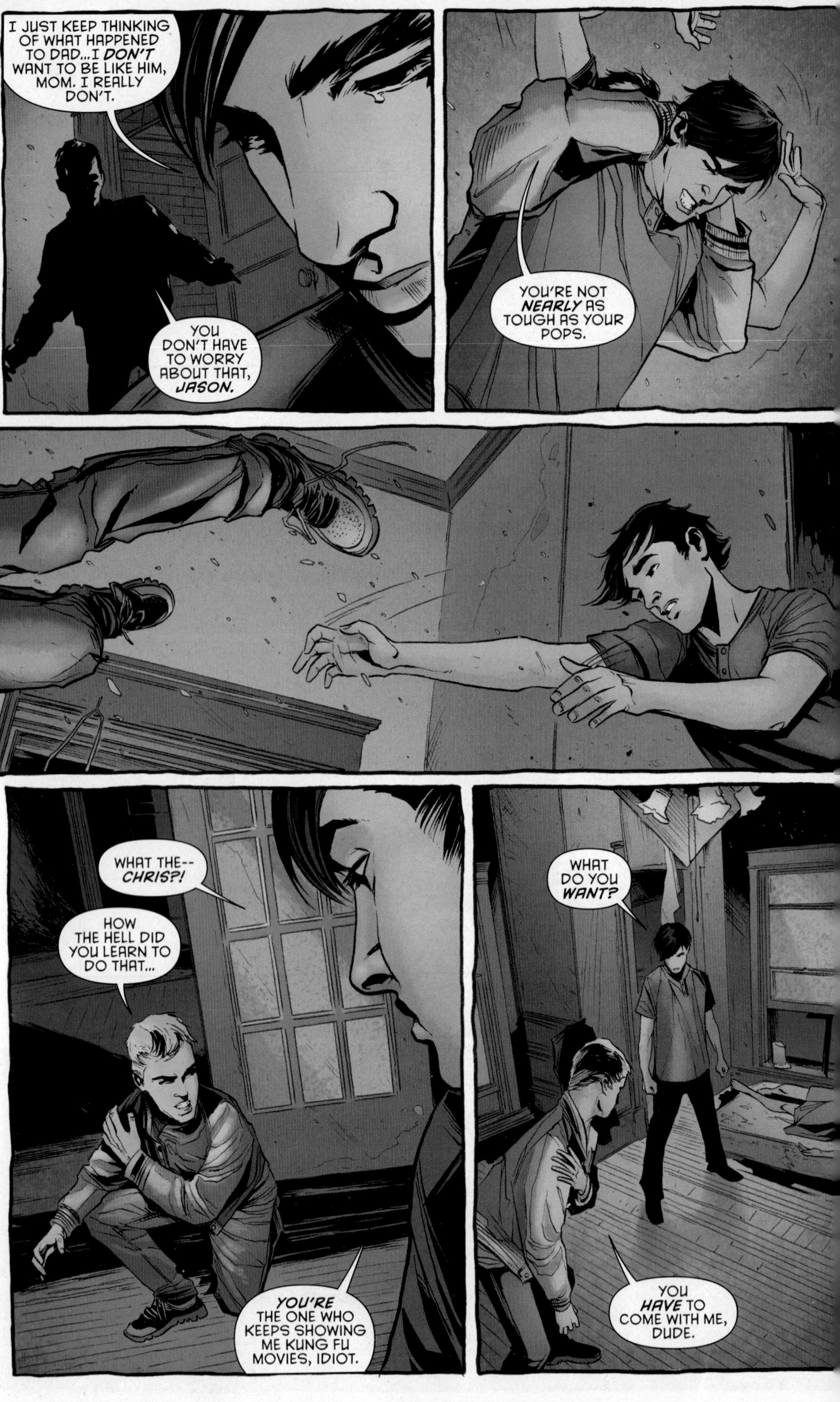
I JUST KEEP THINKING OF WHAT HAPPENED TO DAD...I DON'T WANT TO BE LIKE HIM, MOM. I REALLY DON'T.
YOU DON'T HAVE TO WORRY ABOUT THAT, JASON.
YOU'RE NOT NEARLY AS TOUGH AS YOUR POPS.
WHAT THE-- CHRIS?!
HOW THE HELL DID YOU LEARN TO DO THAT...
YOU'RE THE ONE WHO KEEPS SHOWING ME KUNG FU MOVIES, IDIOT.
WHAT DO YOU WANT?
YOU HAVE TO COME WITH ME, DUDE.

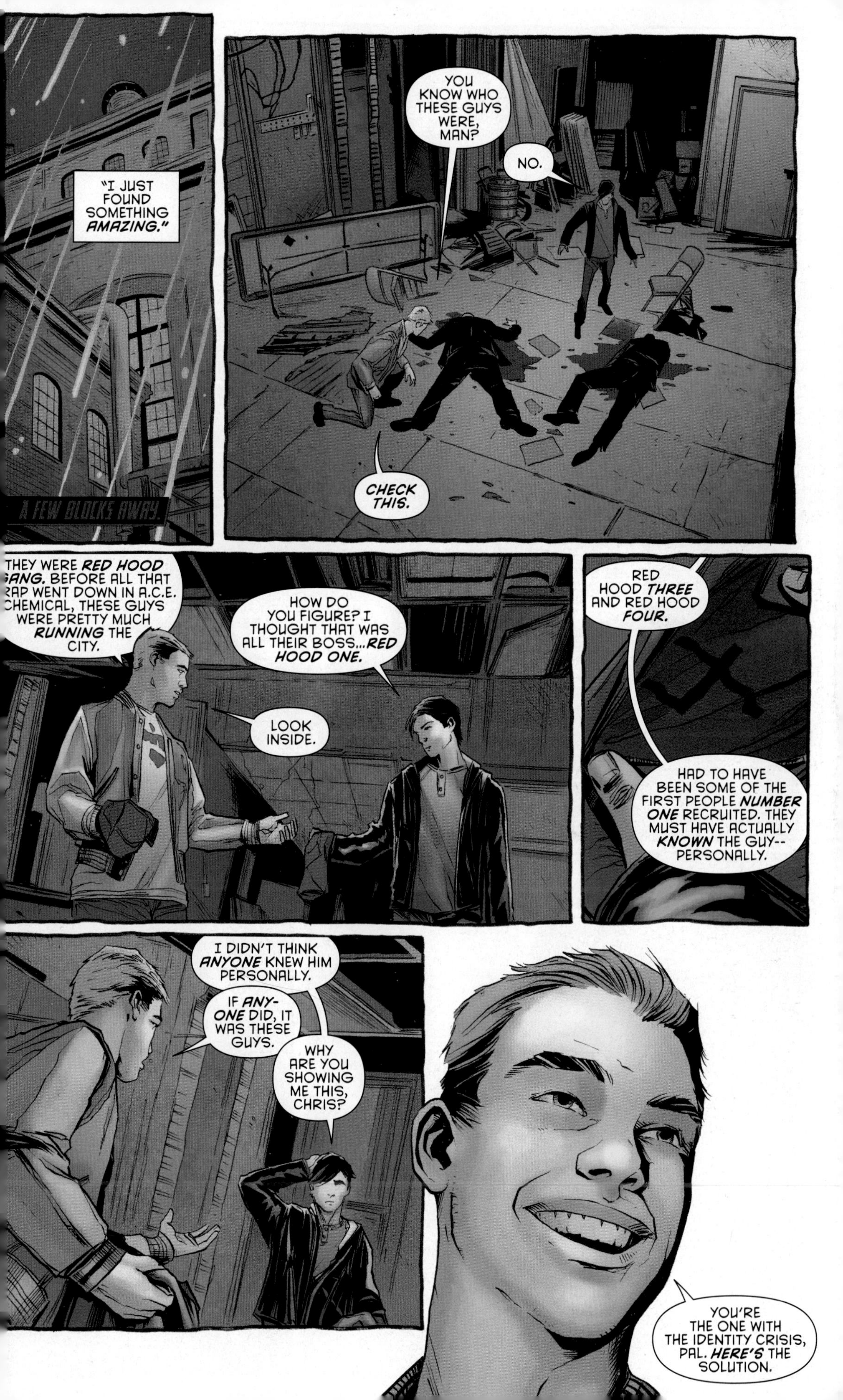
"I JUST FOUND SOMETHING *AMAZING.*"
A FEW BLOCKS AWAY.
YOU KNOW WHO THESE GUYS WERE, MAN?
NO.
CHECK THIS.
THEY WERE *RED HOOD GANG.* BEFORE ALL THAT RAP WENT DOWN IN A.C.E. CHEMICAL, THESE GUYS WERE PRETTY MUCH *RUNNING* THE CITY.
HOW DO YOU FIGURE? I THOUGHT THAT WAS ALL THEIR BOSS...*RED HOOD ONE.*
LOOK INSIDE.
RED HOOD *THREE* AND RED HOOD *FOUR.*
HAD TO HAVE BEEN SOME OF THE FIRST PEOPLE *NUMBER ONE* RECRUITED. THEY MUST HAVE ACTUALLY *KNOWN* THE GUY--PERSONALLY.
I DIDN'T THINK *ANYONE* KNEW HIM PERSONALLY.
IF *ANY-ONE* DID, IT WAS THESE GUYS.
WHY ARE YOU SHOWING ME THIS, CHRIS?
YOU'RE THE ONE WITH THE IDENTITY CRISIS, PAL. *HERE'S* THE SOLUTION.

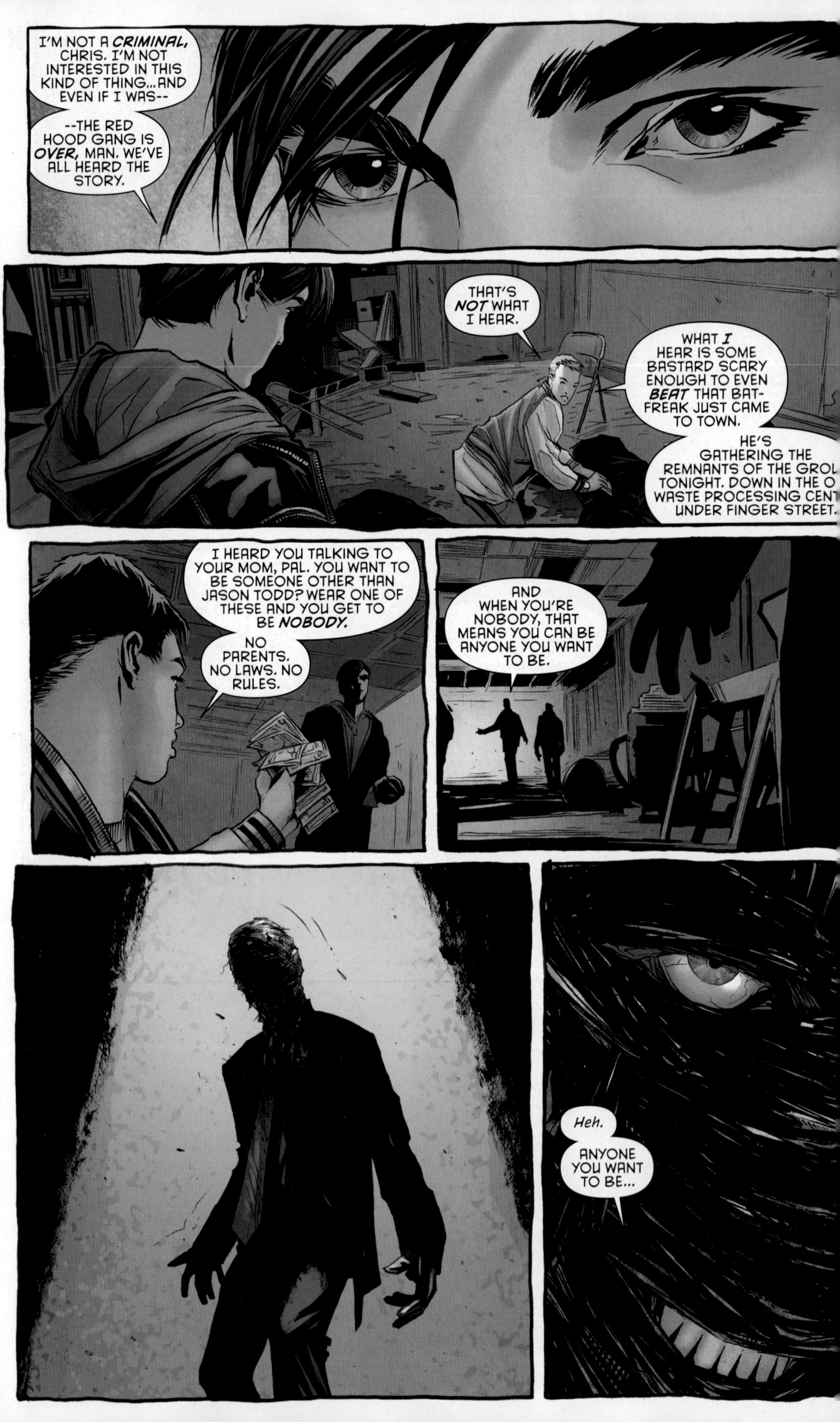

I'M NOT A *CRIMINAL,* CHRIS. I'M NOT INTERESTED IN THIS KIND OF THING...AND EVEN IF I WAS--
--THE RED HOOD GANG IS *OVER,* MAN. WE'VE ALL HEARD THE STORY.
THAT'S *NOT* WHAT I HEAR.
WHAT *I* HEAR IS SOME BASTARD SCARY ENOUGH TO EVEN *BEAT* THAT BAT-FREAK JUST CAME TO TOWN.
HE'S GATHERING THE REMNANTS OF THE GROU TONIGHT. DOWN IN THE O WASTE PROCESSING CENT UNDER FINGER STREET.
I HEARD YOU TALKING TO YOUR MOM, PAL. YOU WANT TO BE SOMEONE OTHER THAN JASON TODD? WEAR ONE OF THESE AND YOU GET TO BE *NOBODY.*
NO PARENTS. NO LAWS. NO RULES.
AND WHEN YOU'RE NOBODY, THAT MEANS YOU CAN BE ANYONE YOU WANT TO BE.
Heh.
ANYONE YOU WANT TO BE...

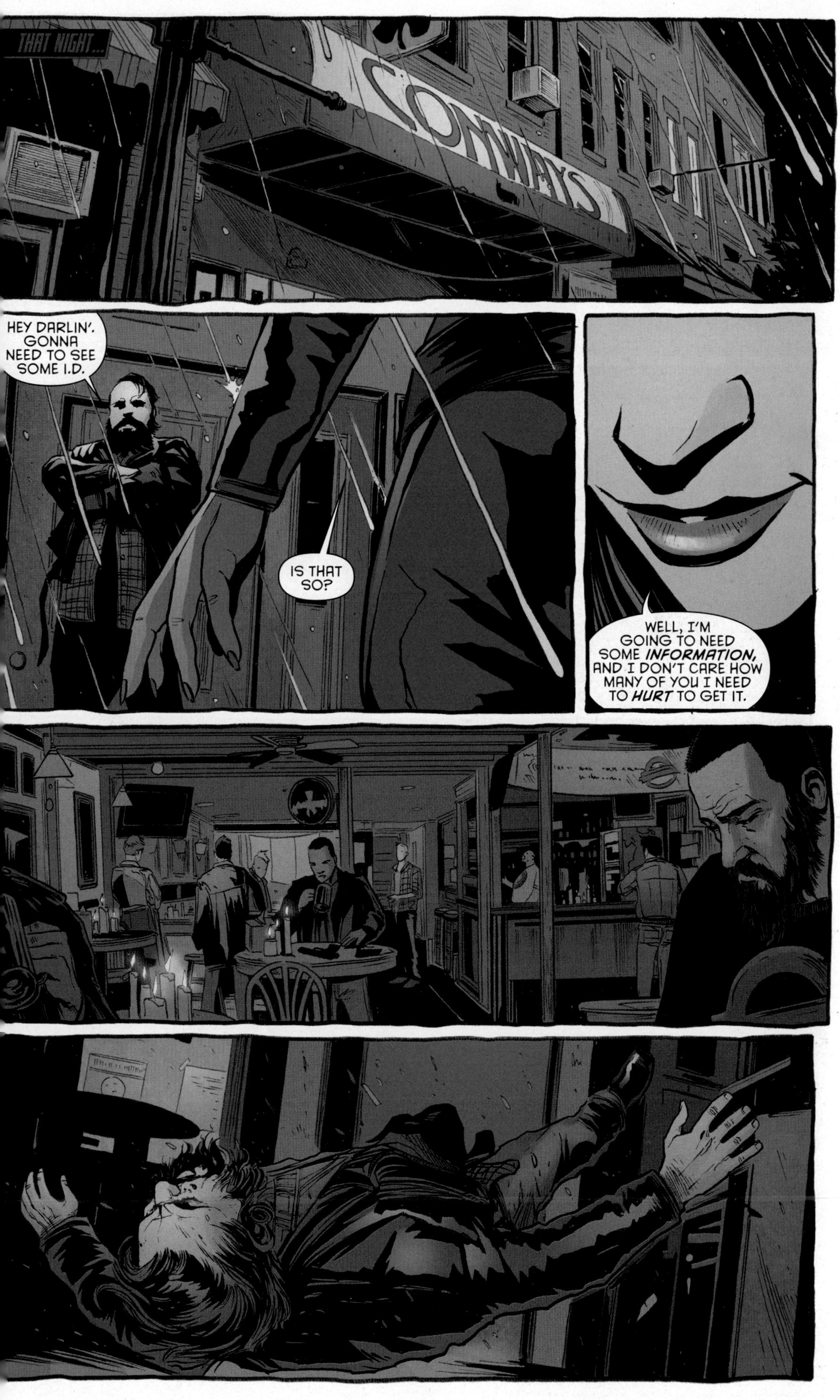
THAT NIGHT...
HEY DARLIN'. GONNA NEED TO SEE SOME I.D.
IS THAT SO?
WELL, I'M GOING TO NEED SOME INFORMATION, AND I DON'T CARE HOW MANY OF YOU I NEED TO HURT TO GET IT.

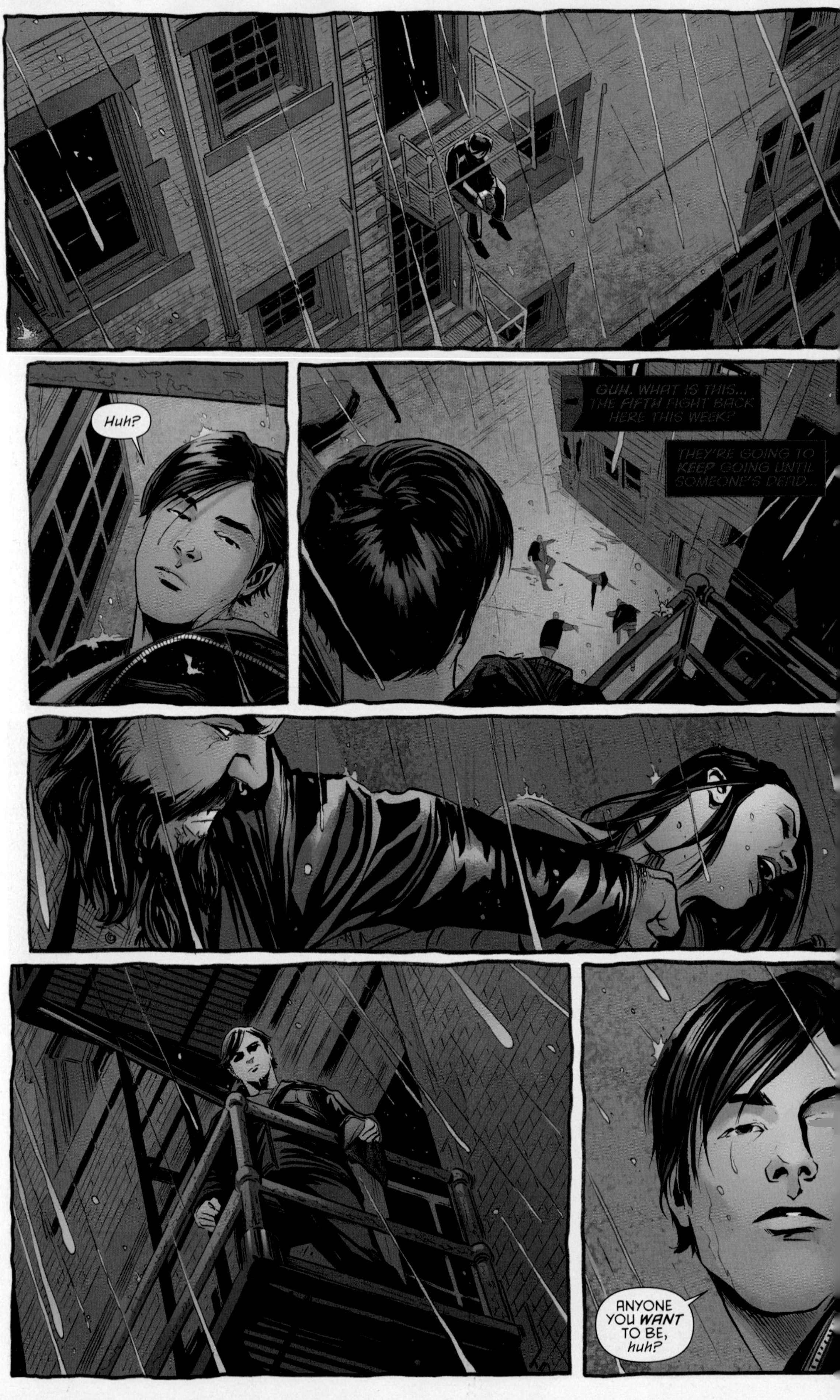
Huh?
GUH. WHAT IS THIS... THE FIFTH FIGHT BACK HERE THIS WEEK?
THEY'RE GOING TO KEEP GOING UNTIL SOMEONE'S DEAD...
ANYONE YOU *WANT* TO BE, *huh?*

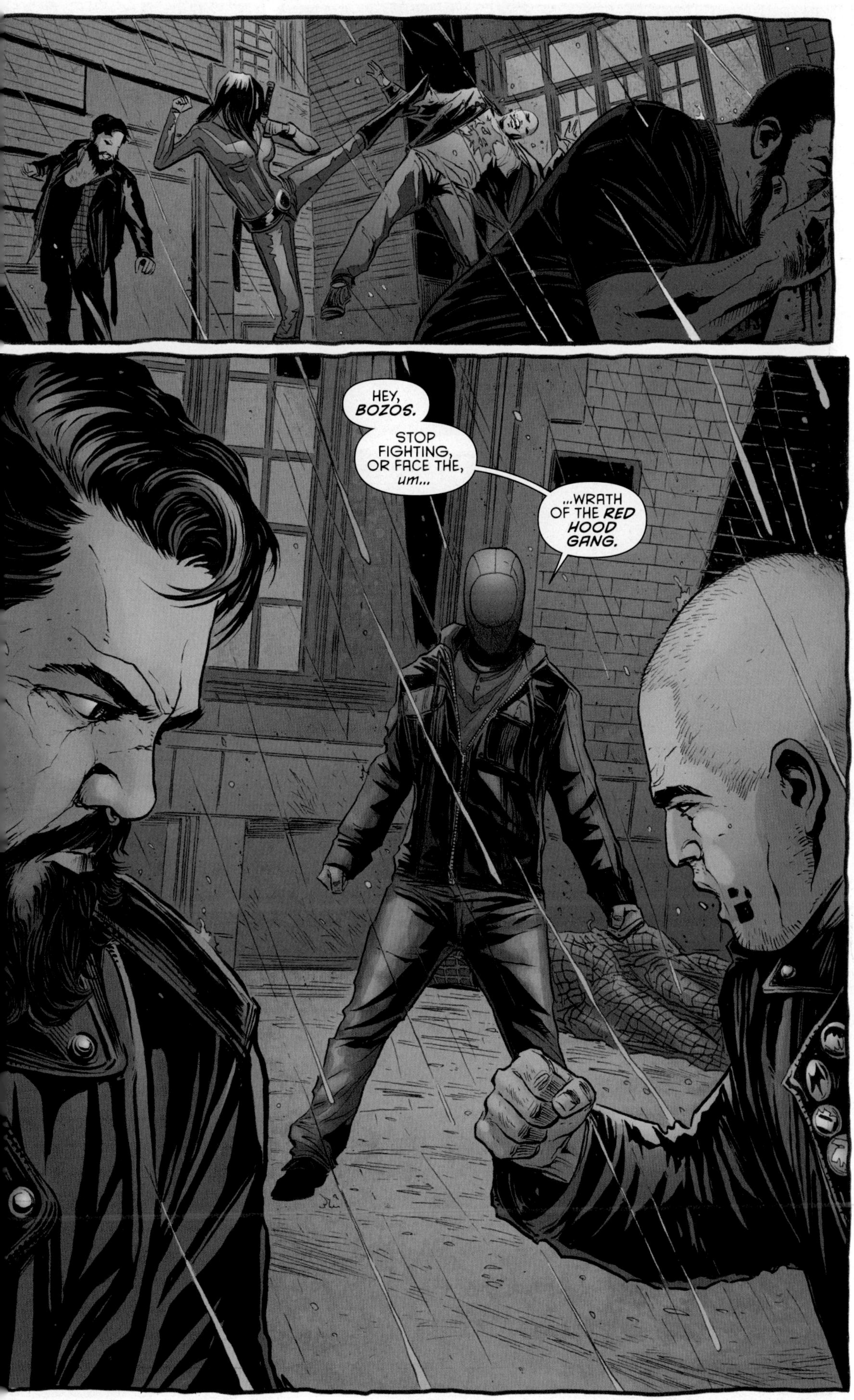
HEY, *BOZOS.*
STOP FIGHTING, OR FACE THE, *um...*
...WRATH OF THE *RED HOOD GANG.*

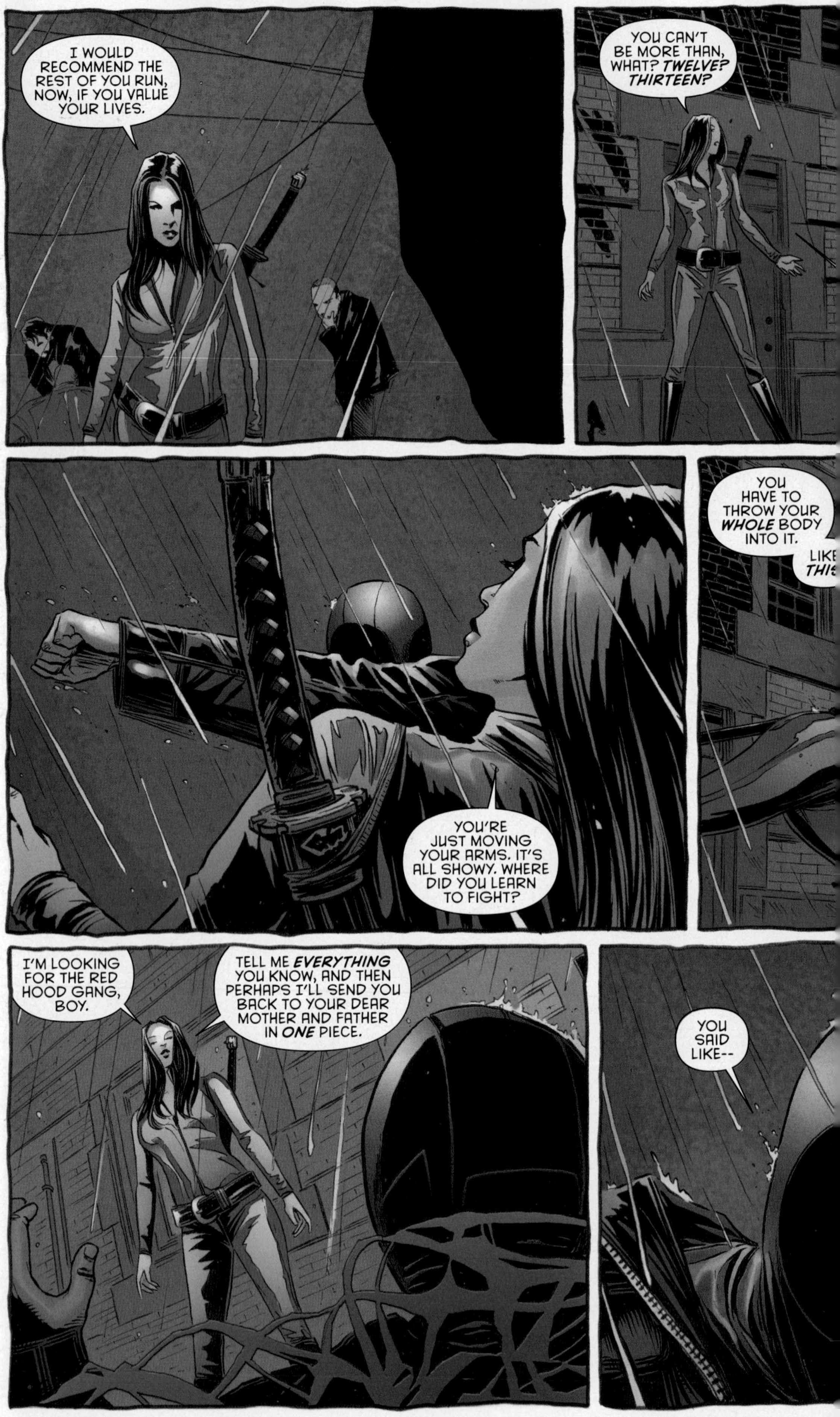
I WOULD RECOMMEND THE REST OF YOU RUN, NOW, IF YOU VALUE YOUR LIVES.
YOU CAN'T BE MORE THAN, WHAT? TWELVE? THIRTEEN?
YOU'RE JUST MOVING YOUR ARMS. IT'S ALL SHOWY. WHERE DID YOU LEARN TO FIGHT?
YOU HAVE TO THROW YOUR WHOLE BODY INTO IT.
LIKE
I'M LOOKING FOR THE RED HOOD GANG, BOY.
TELL ME EVERYTHING YOU KNOW, AND THEN PERHAPS I'LL SEND YOU BACK TO YOUR DEAR MOTHER AND FATHER IN ONE PIECE.
YOU SAID LIKE--

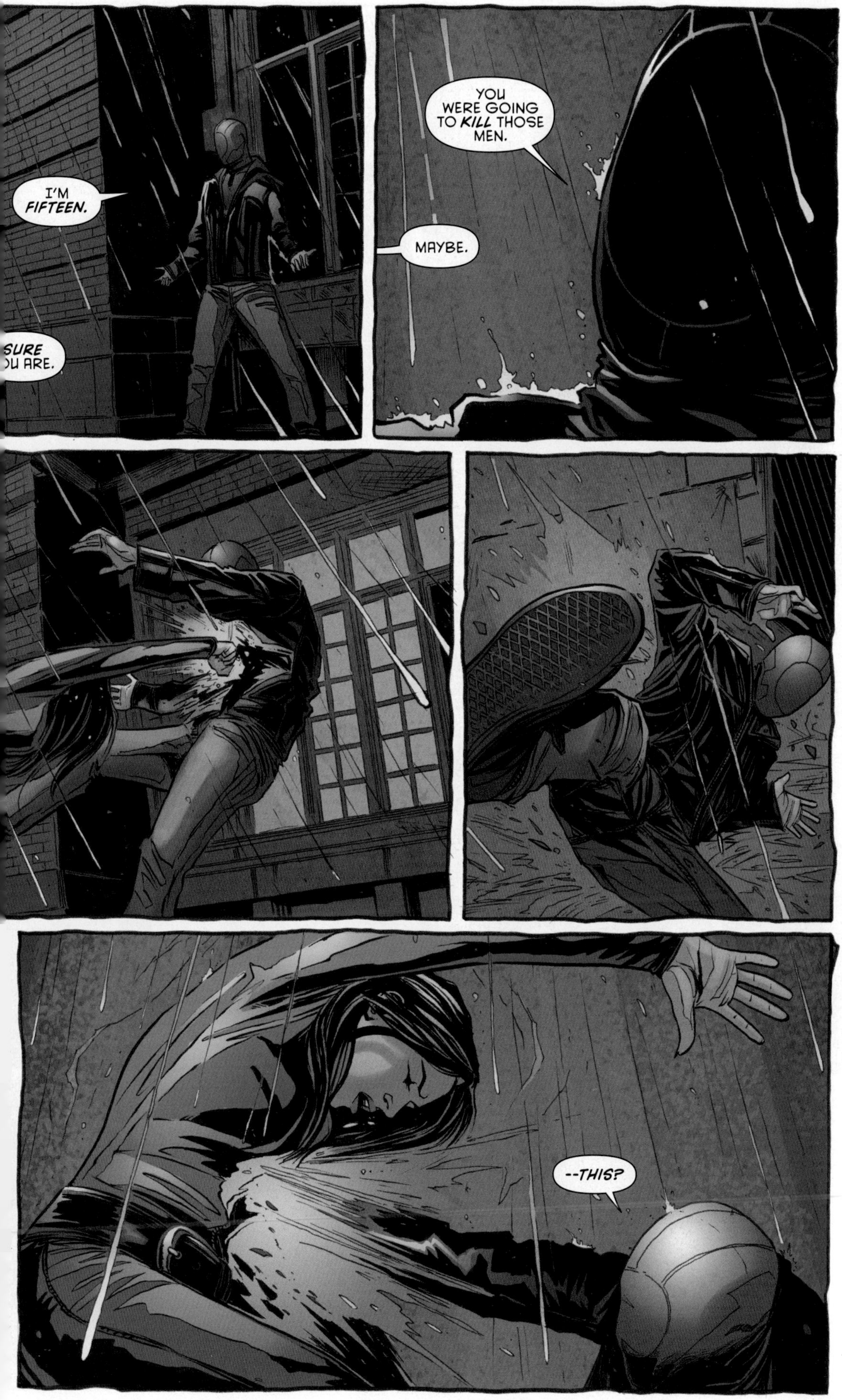
I'M FIFTEEN.
SURE OU ARE.
YOU WERE GOING TO KILL THOSE MEN.
MAYBE.
--THIS?

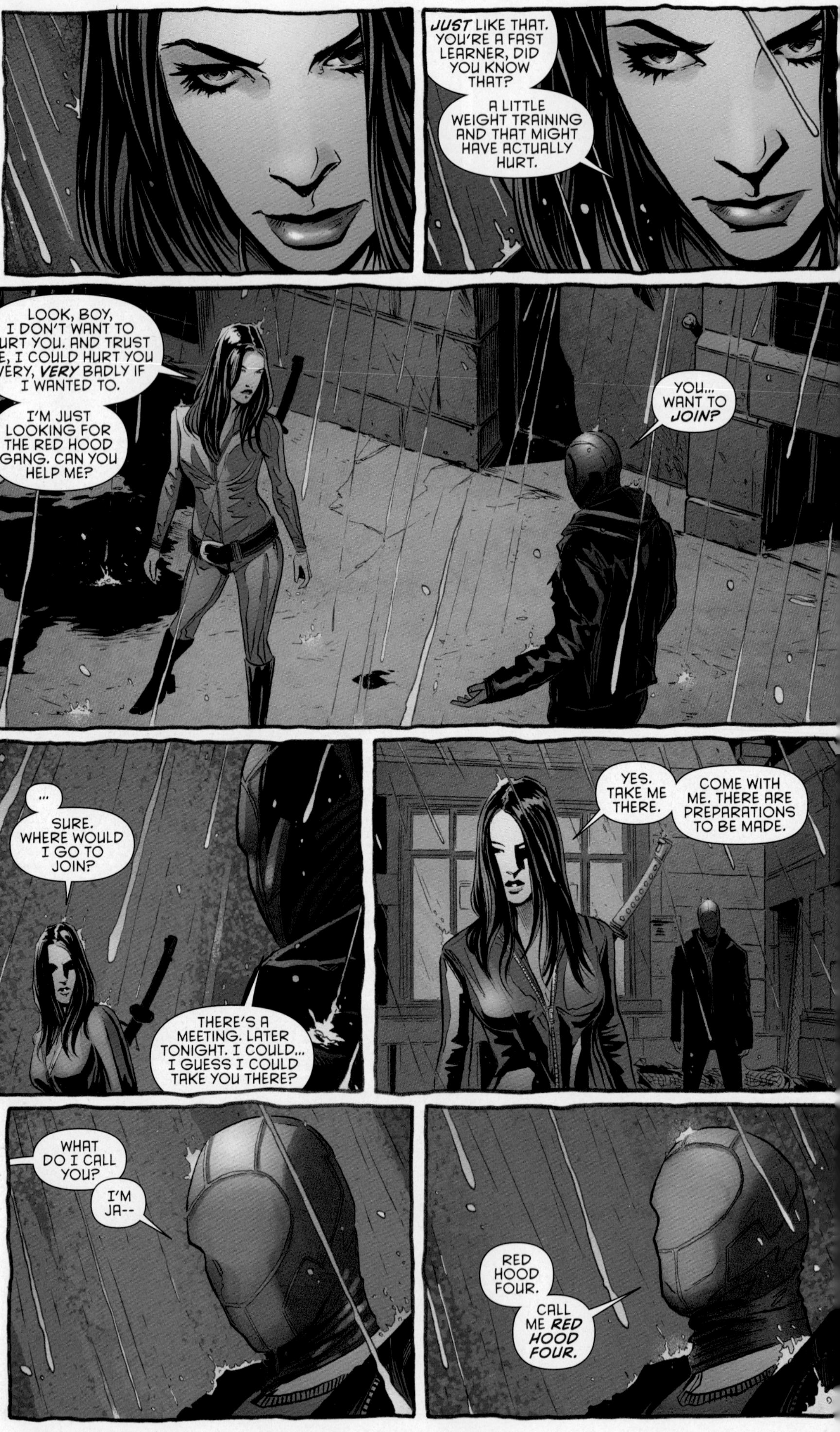
JUST LIKE THAT. YOU'RE A FAST LEARNER, DID YOU KNOW THAT?
A LITTLE WEIGHT TRAINING AND THAT MIGHT HAVE ACTUALLY HURT.
LOOK, BOY, I DON'T WANT TO HURT YOU. AND TRUST ME, I COULD HURT YOU VERY, VERY BADLY IF I WANTED TO.
I'M JUST LOOKING FOR THE RED HOOD GANG. CAN YOU HELP ME?
YOU... WANT TO JOIN?
...
SURE. WHERE WOULD I GO TO JOIN?
THERE'S A MEETING. LATER TONIGHT. I COULD... I GUESS I COULD TAKE YOU THERE?
YES. TAKE ME THERE.
COME WITH ME. THERE ARE PREPARATIONS TO BE MADE.
WHAT DO I CALL YOU?
I'M JA--
RED HOOD FOUR.
CALL ME RED HOOD FOUR.

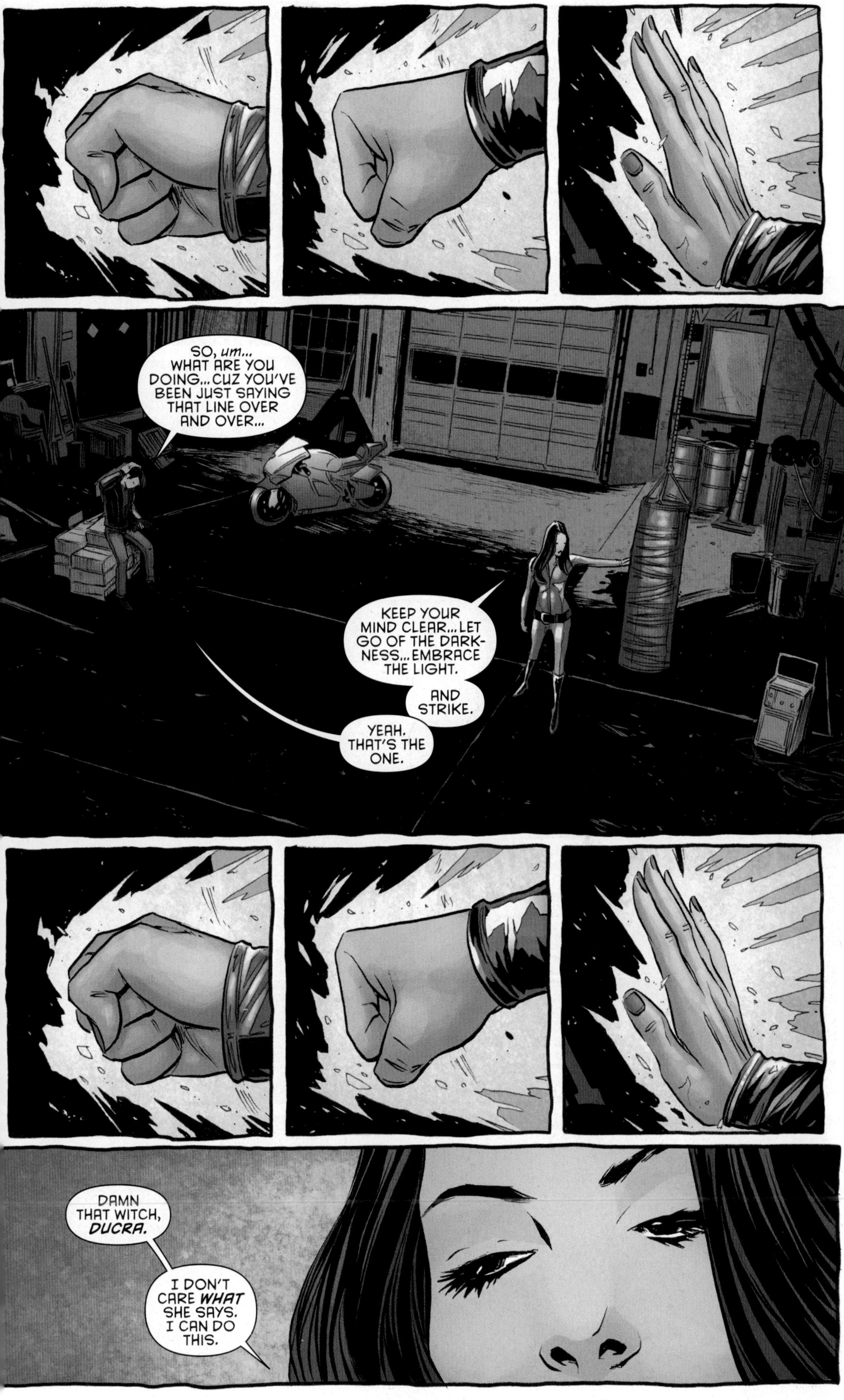

SO, *um*... WHAT ARE YOU DOING...CUZ YOU'VE BEEN JUST SAYING THAT LINE OVER AND OVER...
KEEP YOUR MIND CLEAR...LET GO OF THE DARK-NESS...EMBRACE THE LIGHT.
AND STRIKE.
YEAH. THAT'S THE ONE.
DAMN THAT WITCH, ***DUCRA.***
I DON'T CARE ***WHAT*** SHE SAYS. I CAN DO THIS.

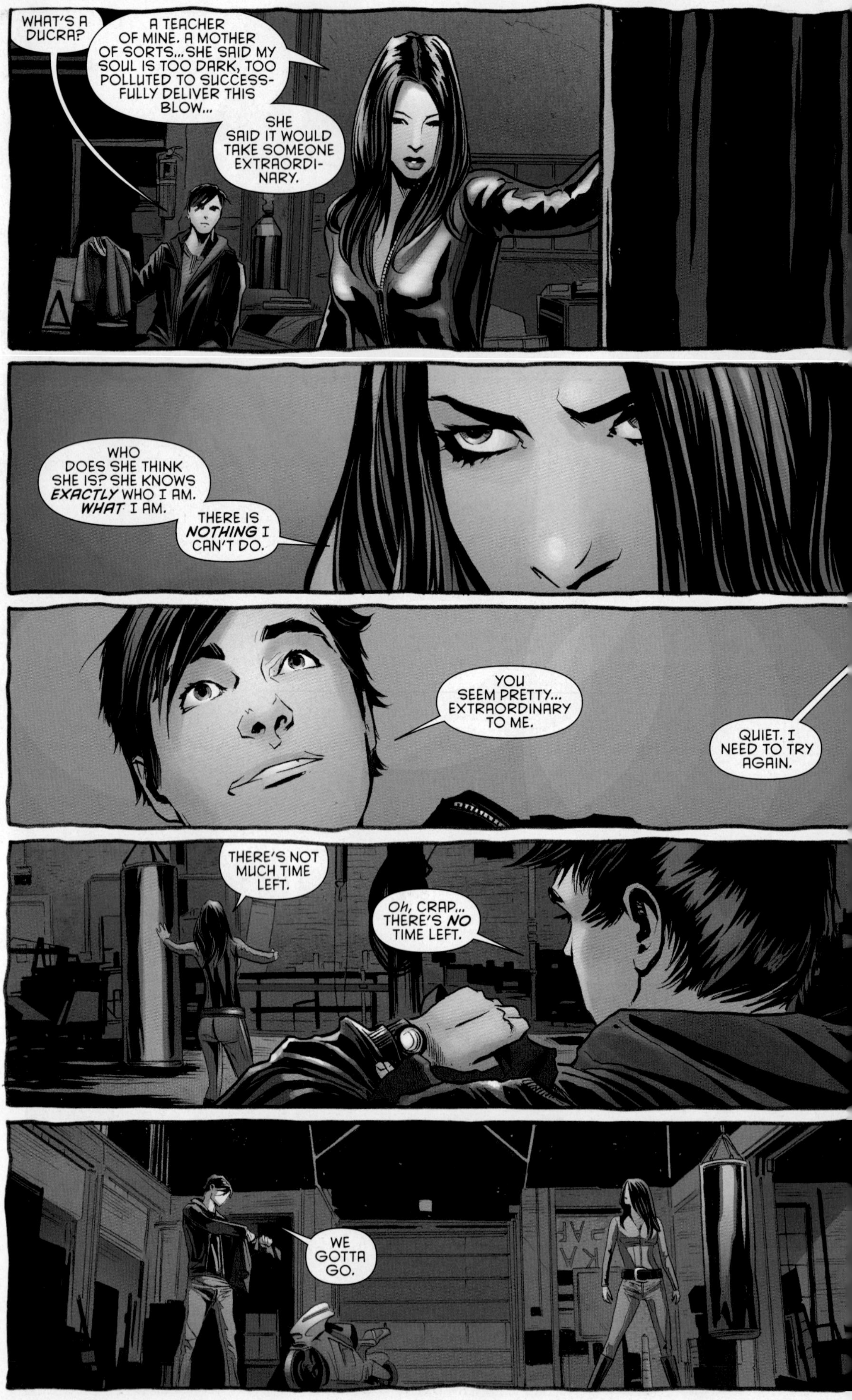
WHAT'S A DUCRA?
A TEACHER OF MINE. A MOTHER OF SORTS... SHE SAID MY SOUL IS TOO DARK, TOO POLLUTED TO SUCCESSFULLY DELIVER THIS BLOW...
SHE SAID IT WOULD TAKE SOMEONE EXTRAORDINARY.
WHO DOES SHE THINK SHE IS? SHE KNOWS *EXACTLY* WHO I AM. **WHAT** I AM.
THERE IS **NOTHING** I CAN'T DO.
YOU SEEM PRETTY... EXTRAORDINARY TO ME.
QUIET. I NEED TO TRY AGAIN.
THERE'S NOT MUCH TIME LEFT.
Oh, CRAP... THERE'S **NO** TIME LEFT.
WE GOTTA GO.

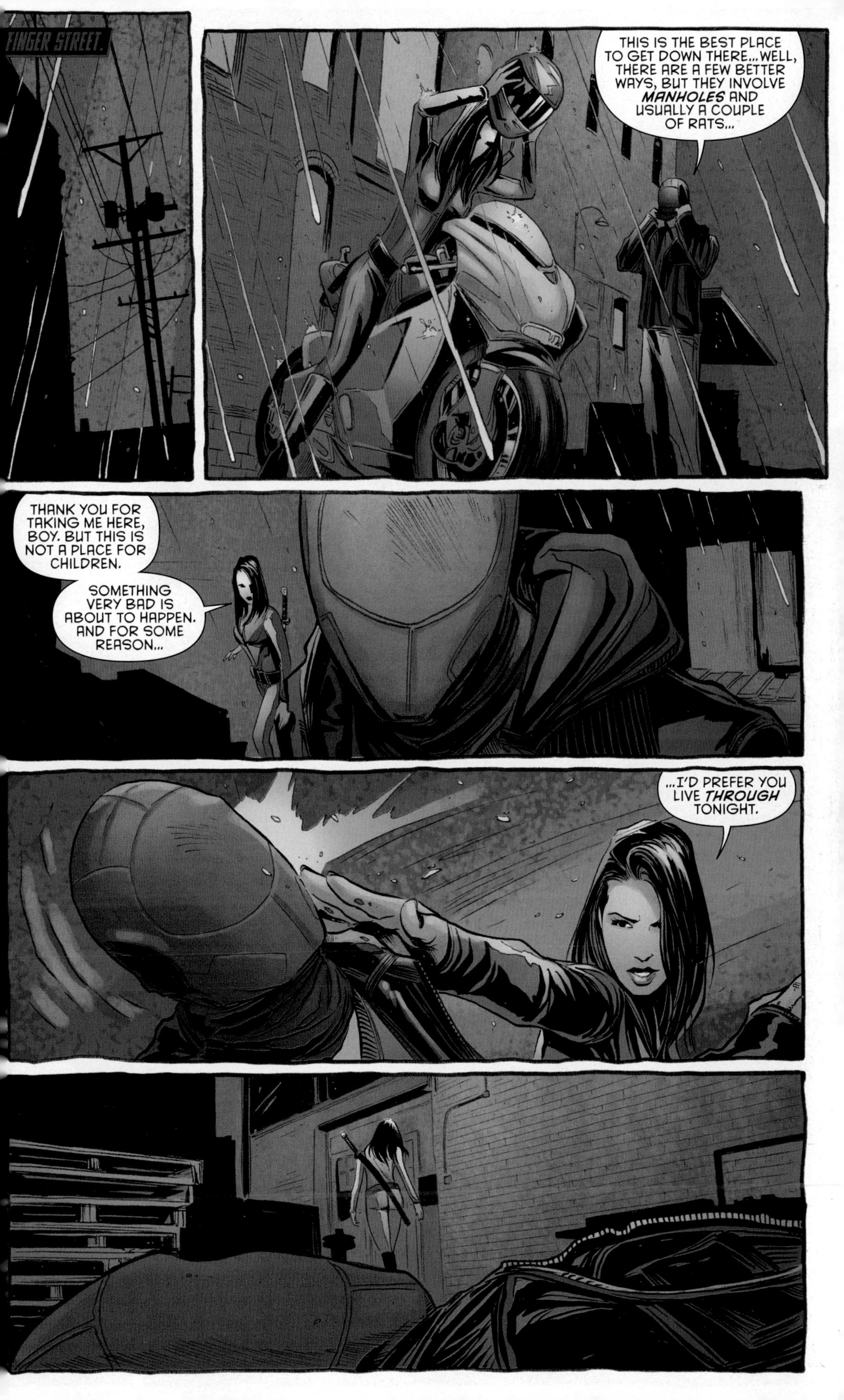
FINGER STREET.
THIS IS THE BEST PLACE TO GET DOWN THERE... WELL, THERE ARE A FEW BETTER WAYS, BUT THEY INVOLVE MANHOLES AND USUALLY A COUPLE OF RATS...
THANK YOU FOR TAKING ME HERE, BOY. BUT THIS IS NOT A PLACE FOR CHILDREN.
SOMETHING VERY BAD IS ABOUT TO HAPPEN. AND FOR SOME REASON...
...I'D PREFER YOU LIVE THROUGH TONIGHT.

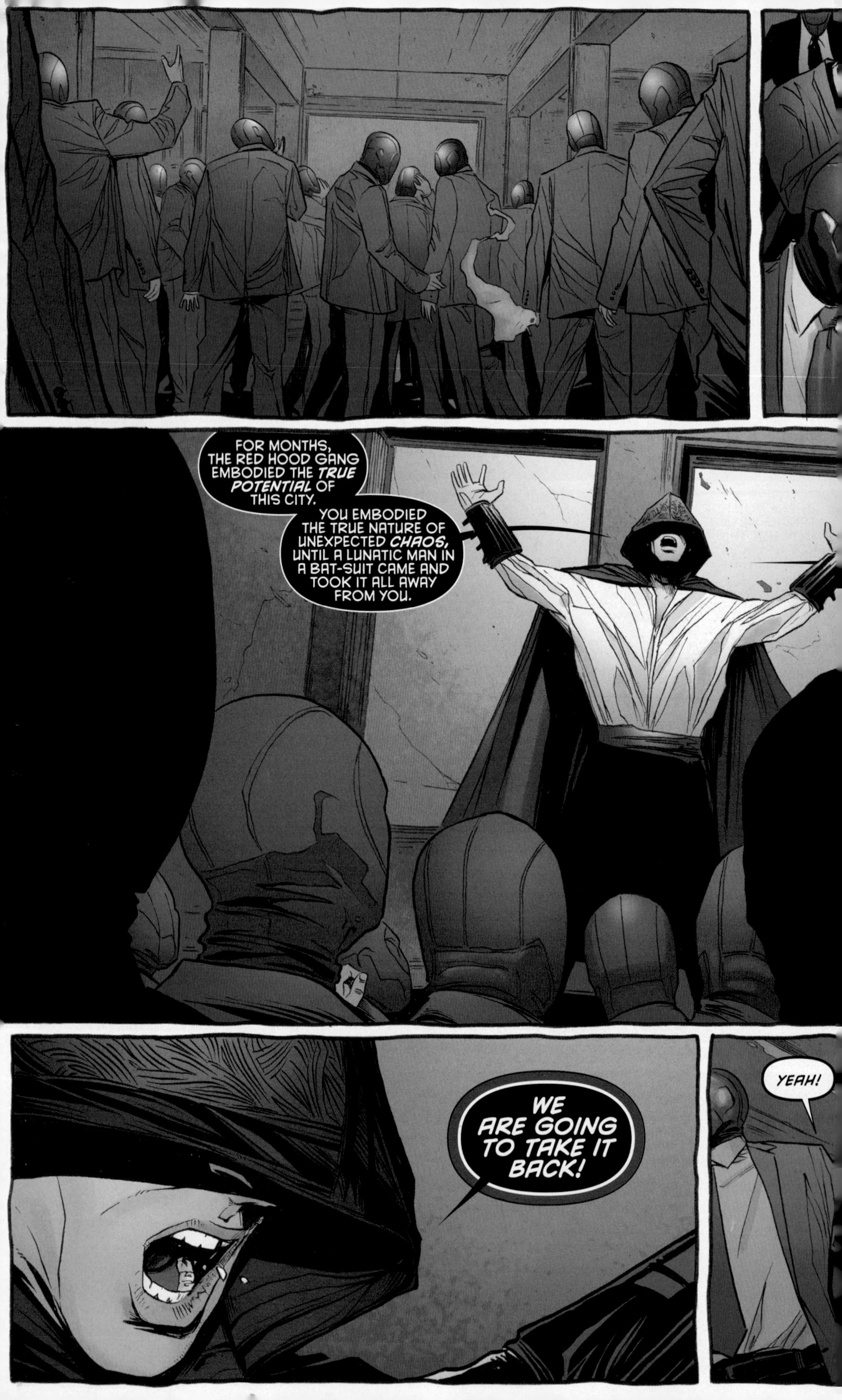
FOR MONTHS, THE RED HOOD GANG EMBODIED THE *TRUE POTENTIAL* OF THIS CITY.
YOU EMBODIED THE TRUE NATURE OF UNEXPECTED *CHAOS,* UNTIL A LUNATIC MAN IN A BAT-SUIT CAME AND TOOK IT ALL AWAY FROM YOU.
WE ARE GOING TO TAKE IT BACK!
YEAH!

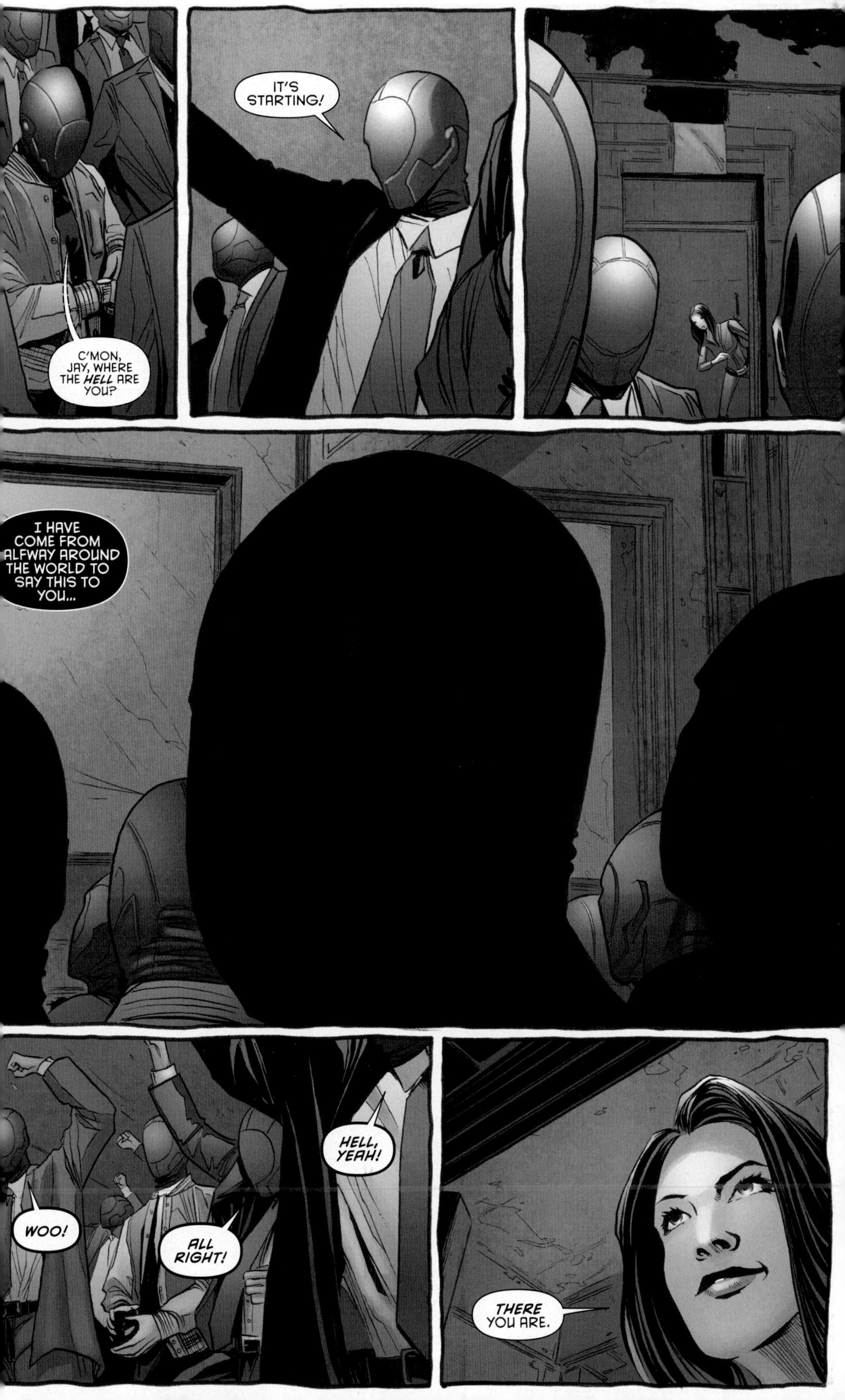
C'MON, JAY, WHERE THE *HELL* ARE YOU?
IT'S STARTING!
I HAVE COME FROM ALFWAY AROUND THE WORLD TO SAY THIS TO YOU...
WOO!
ALL RIGHT!
HELL, YEAH!
THERE YOU ARE.

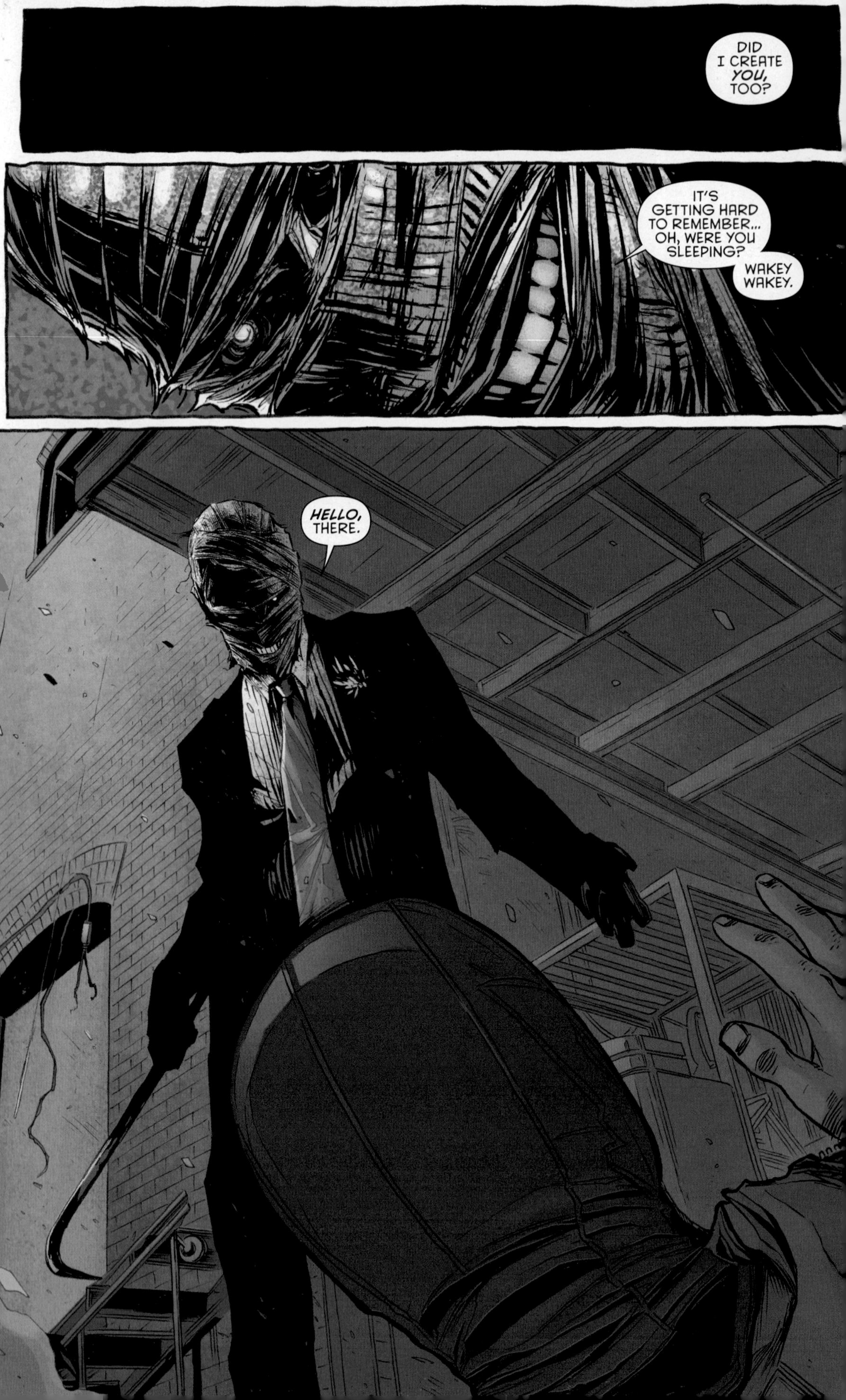
DID I CREATE *YOU,* TOO?
IT'S GETTING HARD TO REMEMBER... OH, WERE YOU SLEEPING?
WAKEY WAKEY.
HELLO, THERE.

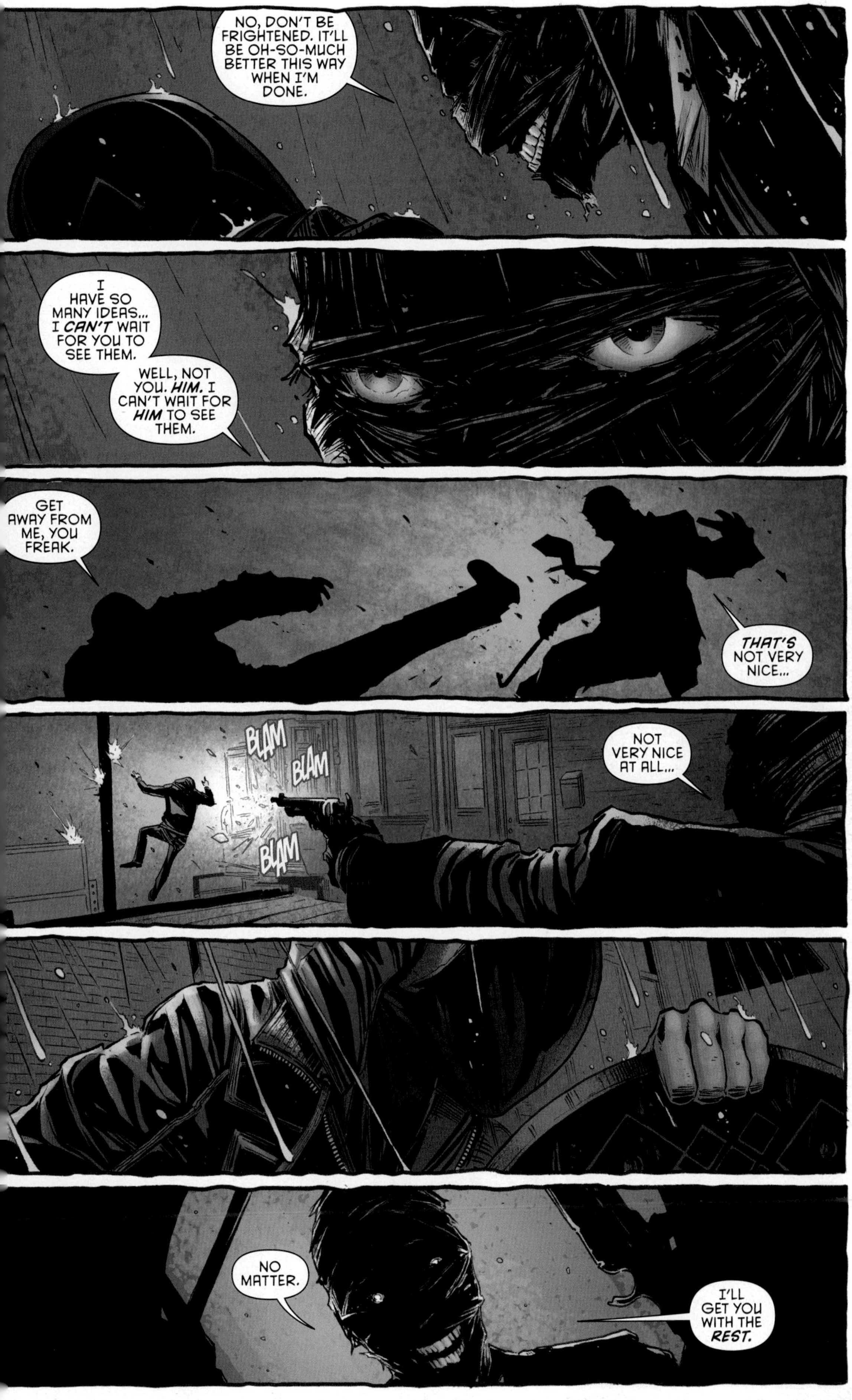
NO, DON'T BE FRIGHTENED. IT'LL BE OH-SO-MUCH BETTER THIS WAY WHEN I'M DONE.
I HAVE SO MANY IDEAS... I *CAN'T* WAIT FOR YOU TO SEE THEM.
WELL, NOT YOU. *HIM.* I CAN'T WAIT FOR *HIM* TO SEE THEM.
GET AWAY FROM ME, YOU FREAK.
THAT'S NOT VERY NICE...
BLAM
BLAM
BLAM
NOT VERY NICE AT ALL...
NO MATTER.
I'LL GET YOU WITH THE *REST.*

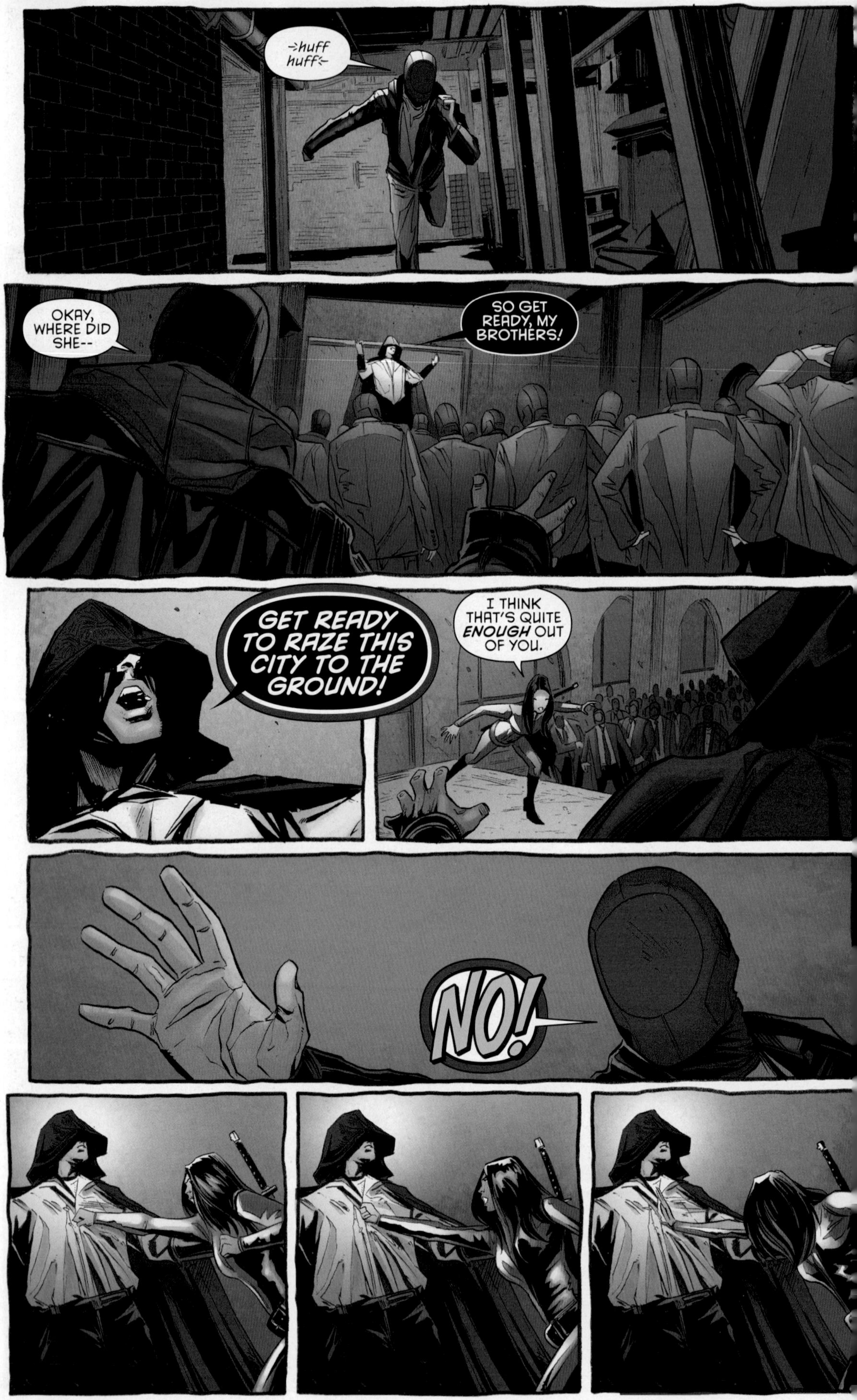

~huff huff~
OKAY, WHERE DID SHE--
SO GET READY, MY BROTHERS!
GET READY TO RAZE THIS CITY TO THE GROUND!
I THINK THAT'S QUITE ENOUGH OUT OF YOU.
NO!

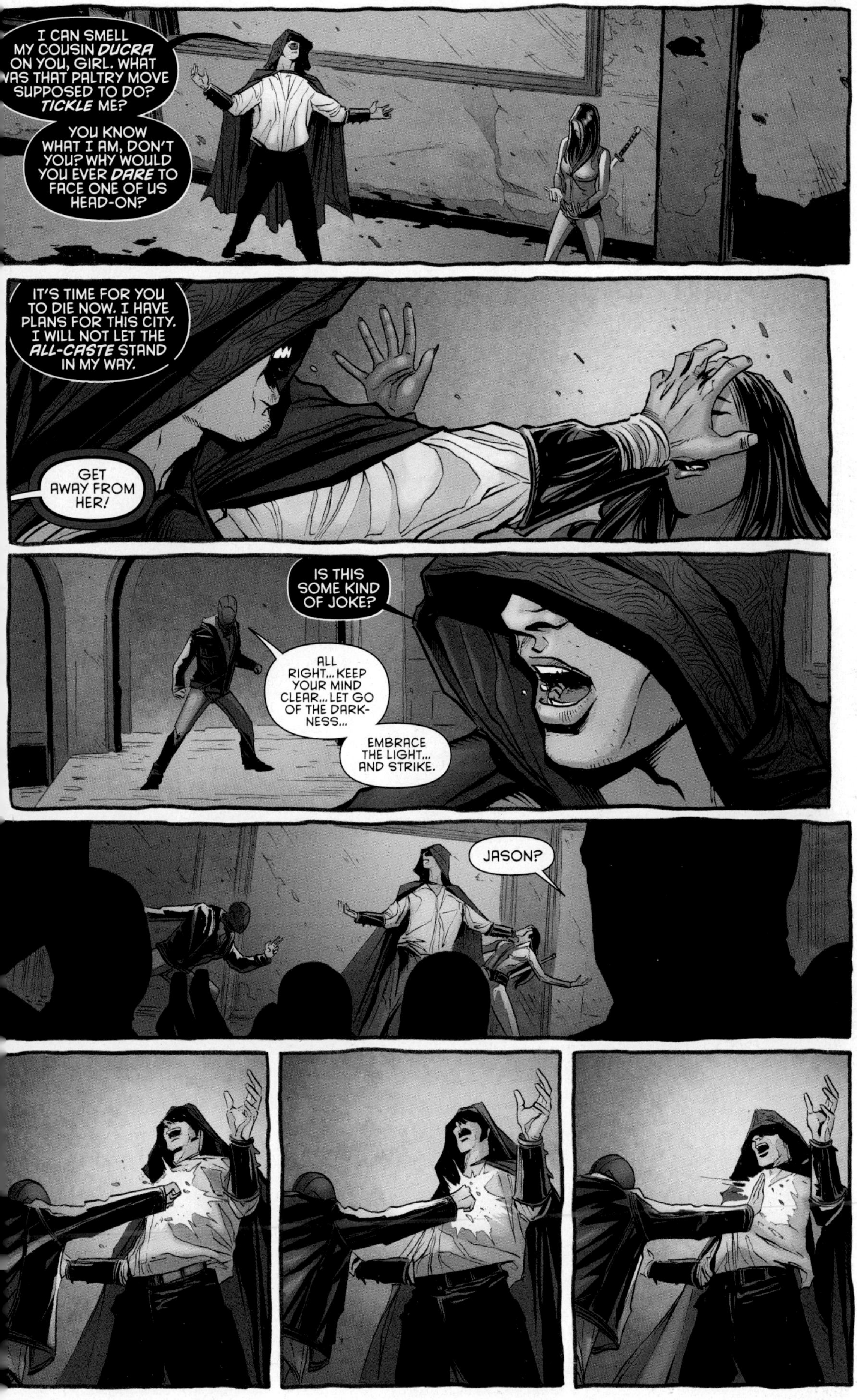
I CAN SMELL MY COUSIN DUCRA ON YOU, GIRL. WHAT WAS THAT PALTRY MOVE SUPPOSED TO DO? TICKLE ME?
YOU KNOW WHAT I AM, DON'T YOU? WHY WOULD YOU EVER DARE TO FACE ONE OF US HEAD-ON?
IT'S TIME FOR YOU TO DIE NOW. I HAVE PLANS FOR THIS CITY. I WILL NOT LET THE ALL-CASTE STAND IN MY WAY.
GET AWAY FROM HER!
IS THIS SOME KIND OF JOKE?
ALL RIGHT... KEEP YOUR MIND CLEAR... LET GO OF THE DARK-NESS...
EMBRACE THE LIGHT... AND STRIKE.
JASON?

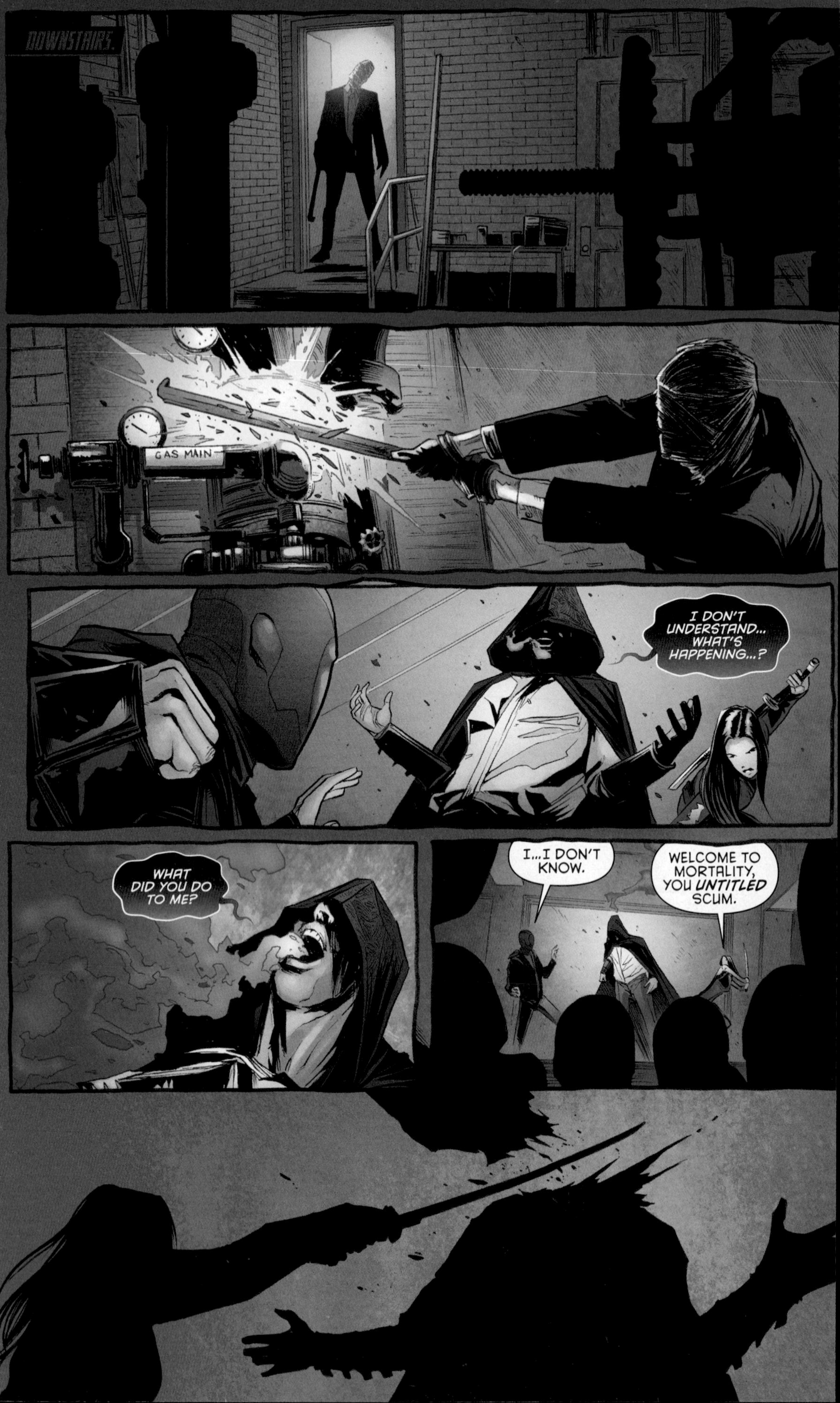
DOWNSTAIRS.
GAS MAIN
I DON'T UNDERSTAND... WHAT'S HAPPENING...?
WHAT DID YOU DO TO ME?
I...I DON'T KNOW.
WELCOME TO MORTALITY, YOU UNTITLED SCUM.

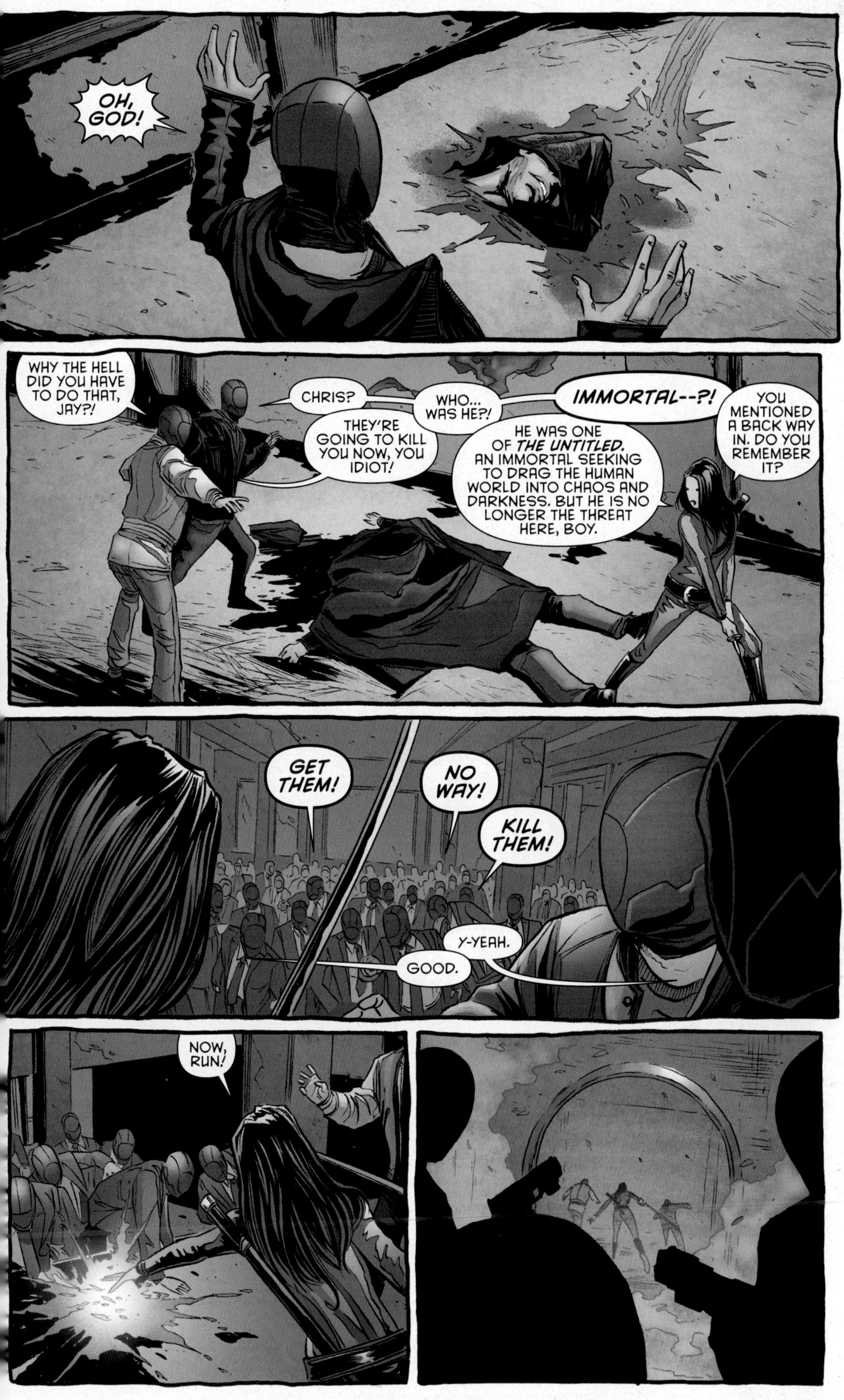
OH, GOD!
WHY THE HELL DID YOU HAVE TO DO THAT, JAY?!
CHRIS?
THEY'RE GOING TO KILL YOU NOW, YOU IDIOT!
WHO... WAS HE?!
IMMORTAL--?!
HE WAS ONE OF THE UNTITLED. AN IMMORTAL SEEKING TO DRAG THE HUMAN WORLD INTO CHAOS AND DARKNESS. BUT HE IS NO LONGER THE THREAT HERE, BOY.
YOU MENTIONED A BACK WAY IN. DO YOU REMEMBER IT?
GET THEM!
NO WAY!
KILL THEM!
Y-YEAH.
GOOD.
NOW, RUN!

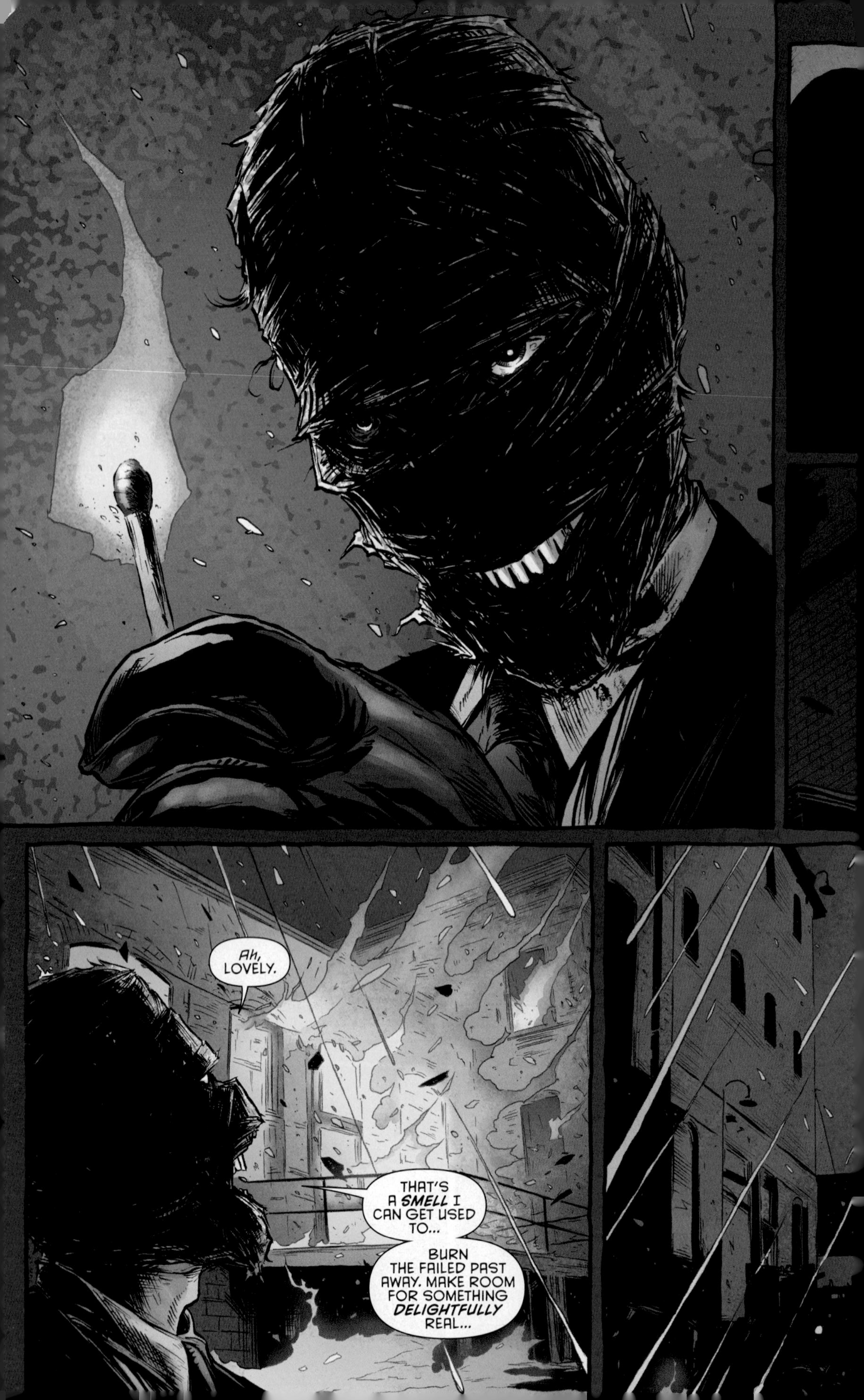

Ah, LOVELY.
THAT'S A SMELL I CAN GET USED TO...
BURN THE FAILED PAST AWAY. MAKE ROOM FOR SOMETHING DELIGHTFULLY REAL...

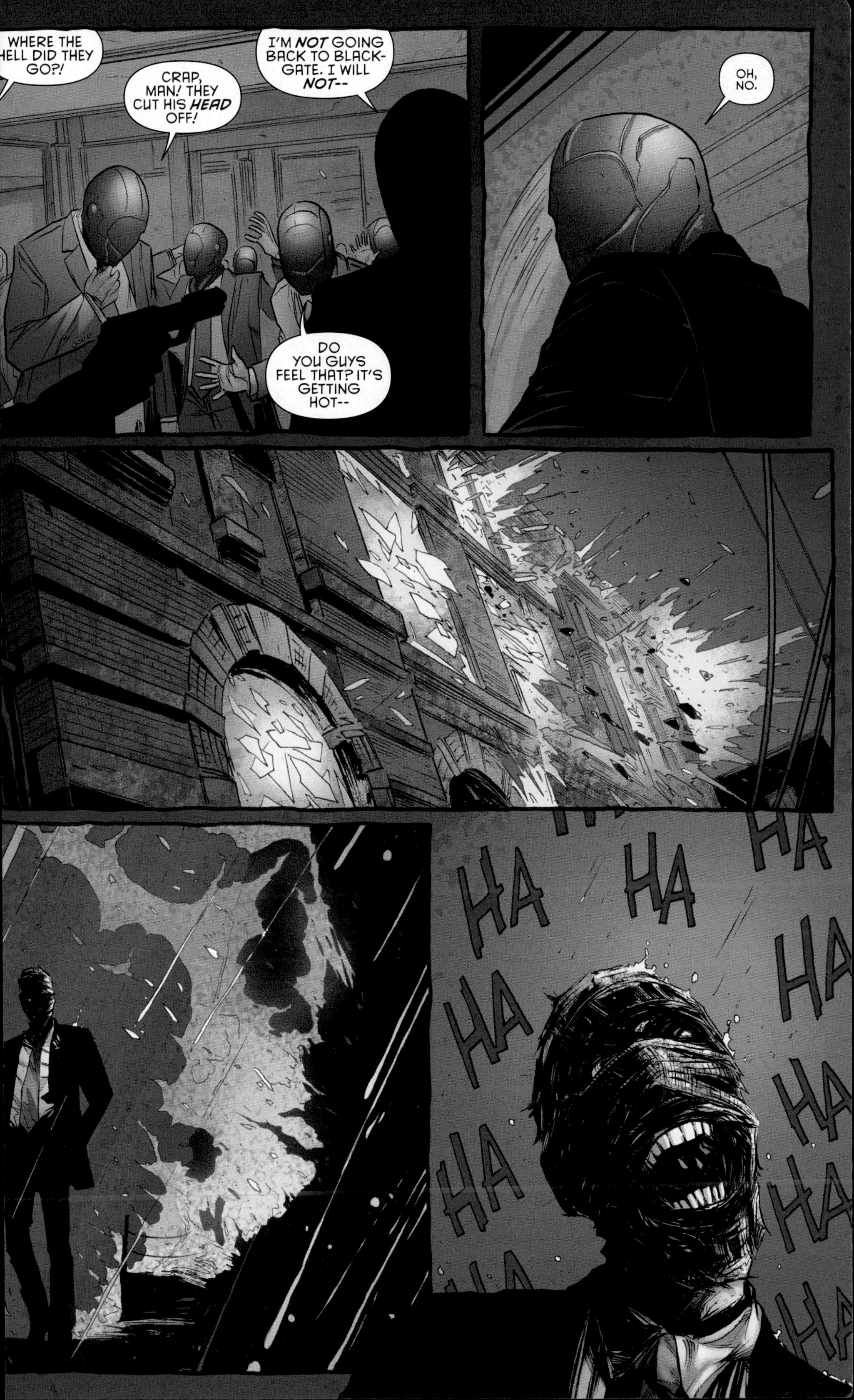
WHERE THE HELL DID THEY GO?!
CRAP, MAN! THEY CUT HIS *HEAD* OFF!
I'M *NOT* GOING BACK TO BLACKGATE. I WILL *NOT*--
DO YOU GUYS FEEL THAT? IT'S GETTING HOT--
OH, NO.
HA HA HA HA HA HA HA HA HA HA HA HA

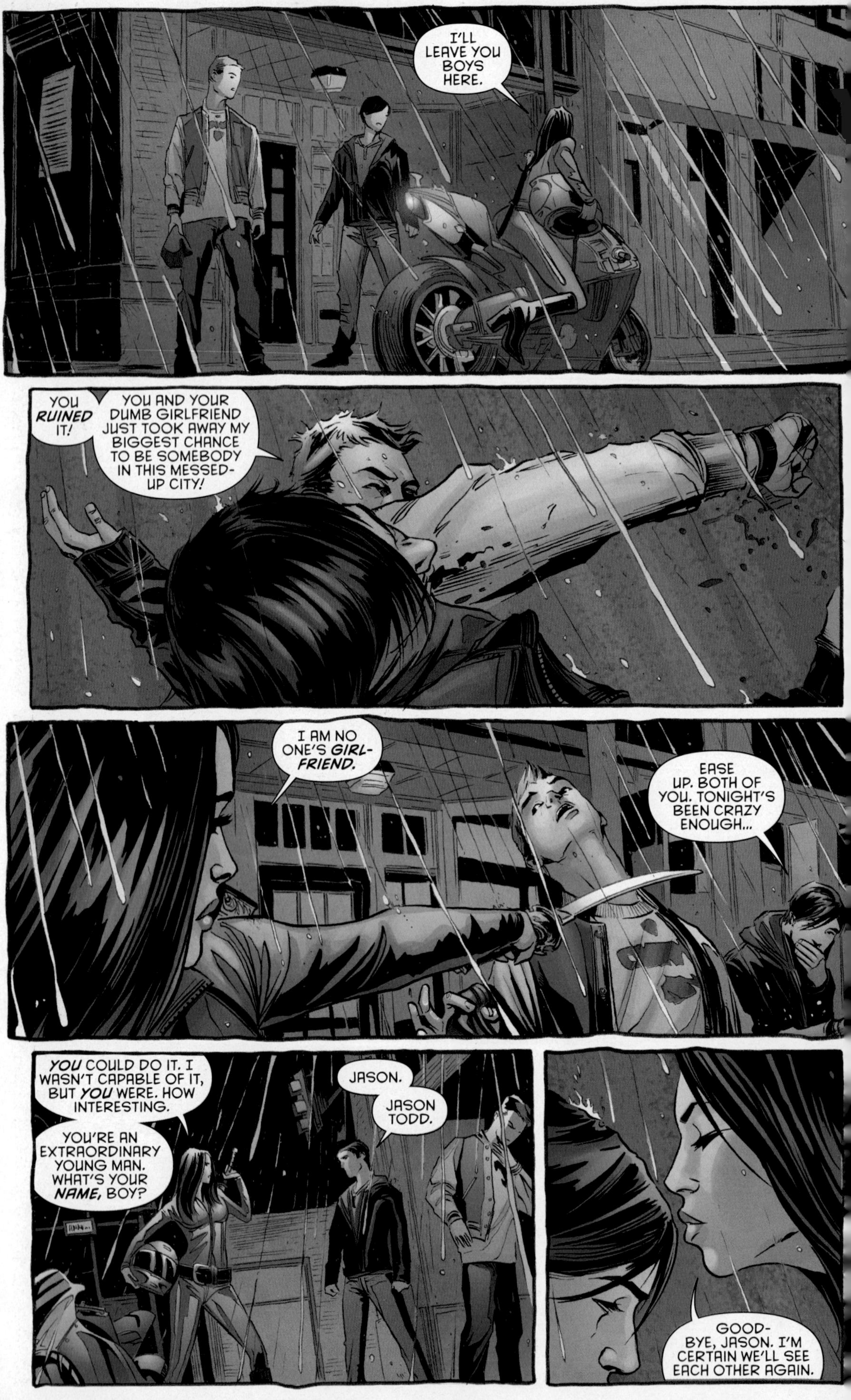
I'LL LEAVE YOU BOYS HERE.
YOU *RUINED* IT!
YOU AND YOUR DUMB GIRLFRIEND JUST TOOK AWAY MY BIGGEST CHANCE TO BE SOMEBODY IN THIS MESSED-UP CITY!
I AM NO ONE'S ***GIRL-FRIEND.***
EASE UP. BOTH OF YOU. TONIGHT'S BEEN CRAZY ENOUGH...
YOU COULD DO IT. I WASN'T CAPABLE OF IT, BUT ***YOU*** WERE. HOW INTERESTING.
YOU'RE AN EXTRAORDINARY YOUNG MAN. WHAT'S YOUR ***NAME,*** BOY?
JASON.
JASON TODD.
GOOD-BYE, JASON. I'M CERTAIN WE'LL SEE EACH OTHER AGAIN.

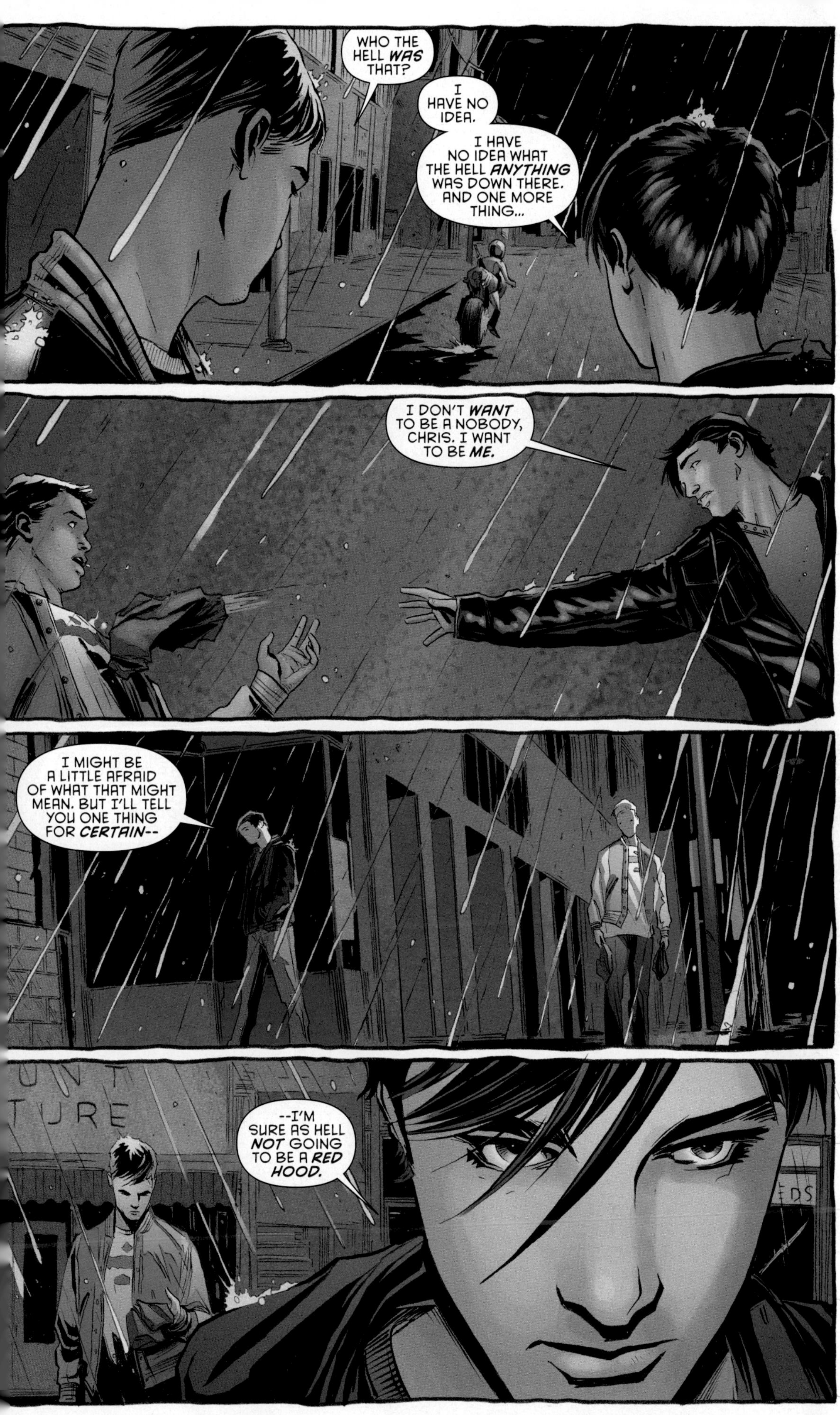

WHO THE HELL *WAS* THAT?
I HAVE NO IDEA.
I HAVE NO IDEA WHAT THE HELL *ANYTHING* WAS DOWN THERE. AND ONE MORE THING...
I DON'T *WANT* TO BE A NOBODY, CHRIS. I WANT TO BE *ME.*
I MIGHT BE A LITTLE AFRAID OF WHAT THAT MIGHT MEAN. BUT I'LL TELL YOU ONE THING FOR *CERTAIN*--
--I'M SURE AS HELL *NOT* GOING TO BE A *RED HOOD.*

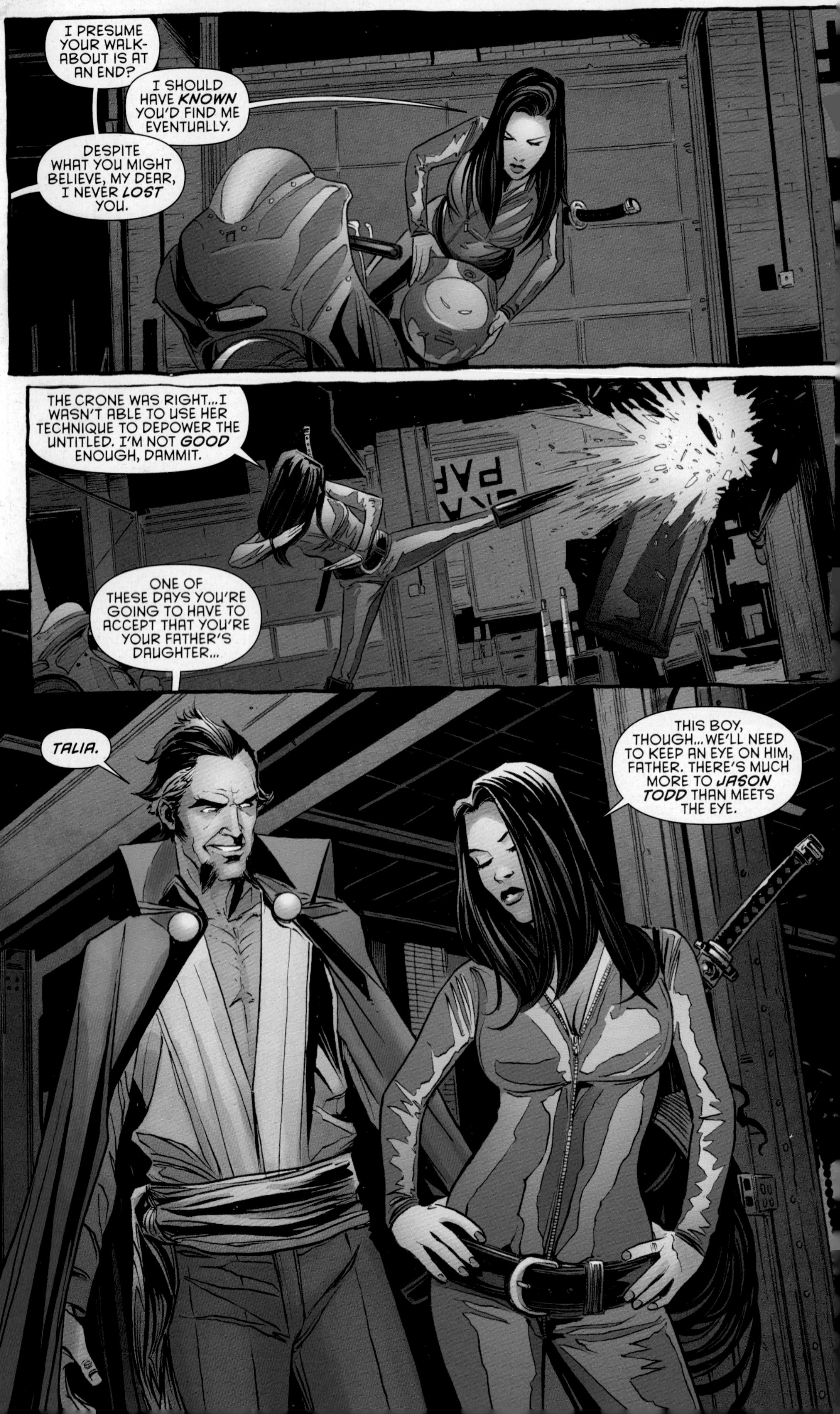
I PRESUME YOUR WALK-ABOUT IS AT AN END?
I SHOULD HAVE KNOWN YOU'D FIND ME EVENTUALLY.
DESPITE WHAT YOU MIGHT BELIEVE, MY DEAR, I NEVER LOST YOU.
THE CRONE WAS RIGHT...I WASN'T ABLE TO USE HER TECHNIQUE TO DEPOWER THE UNTITLED. I'M NOT GOOD ENOUGH, DAMMIT.
ONE OF THESE DAYS YOU'RE GOING TO HAVE TO ACCEPT THAT YOU'RE YOUR FATHER'S DAUGHTER...
TALIA.
THIS BOY, THOUGH...WE'LL NEED TO KEEP AN EYE ON HIM, FATHER. THERE'S MUCH MORE TO JASON TODD THAN MEETS THE EYE.

ZERO
YEAR

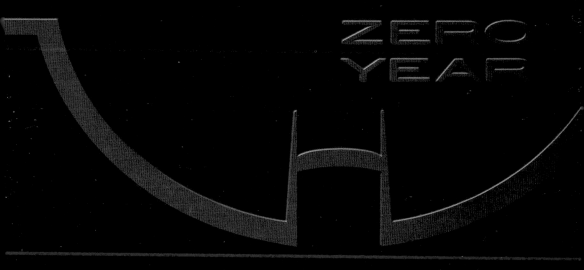

ZERO
YEAR

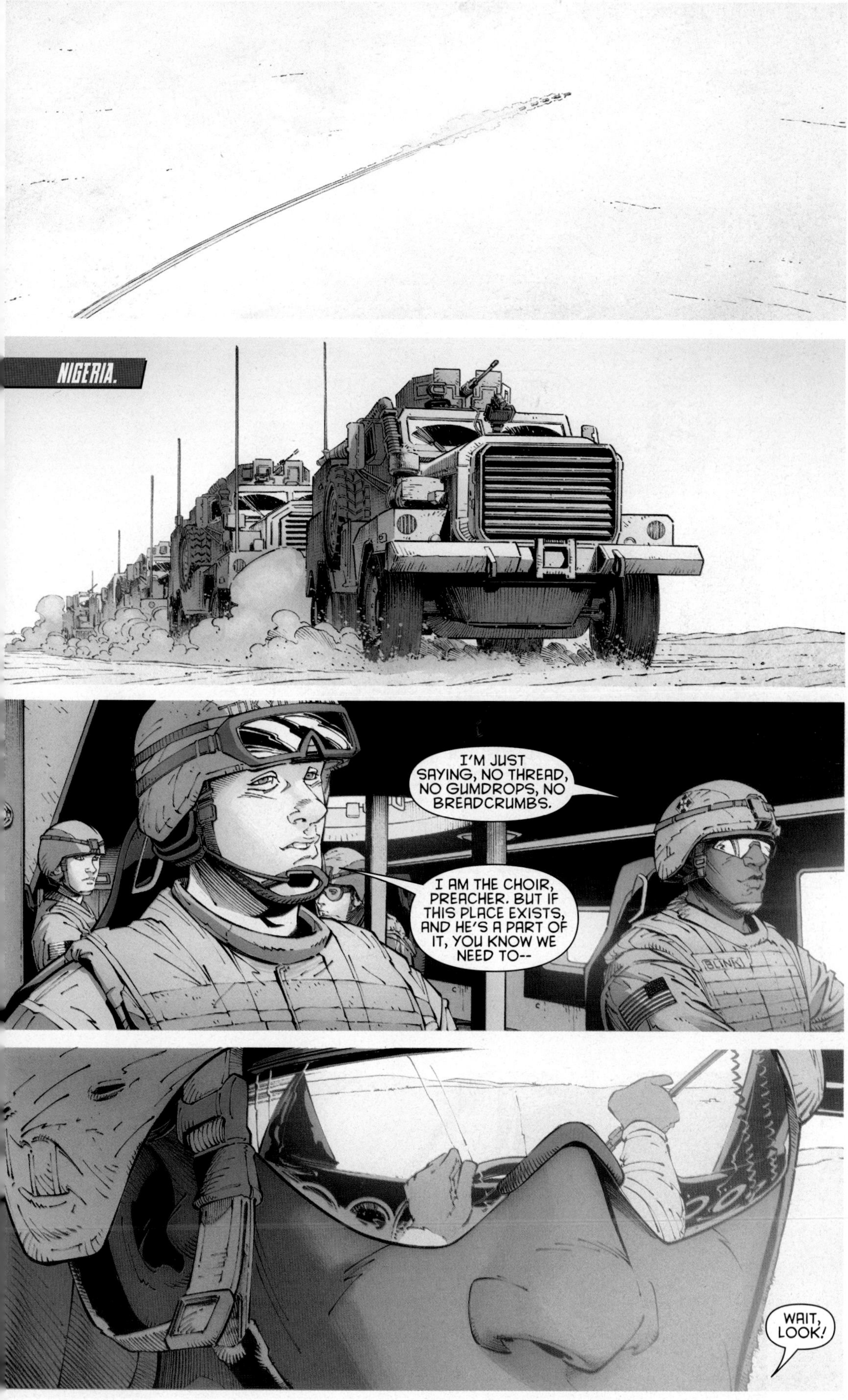
NIGERIA.
I'M JUST SAYING, NO THREAD, NO GUMDROPS, NO BREADCRUMBS.
I AM THE CHOIR, PREACHER. BUT IF THIS PLACE EXISTS, AND HE'S A PART OF IT, YOU KNOW WE NEED TO--
BLINK
WAIT, LOOK!

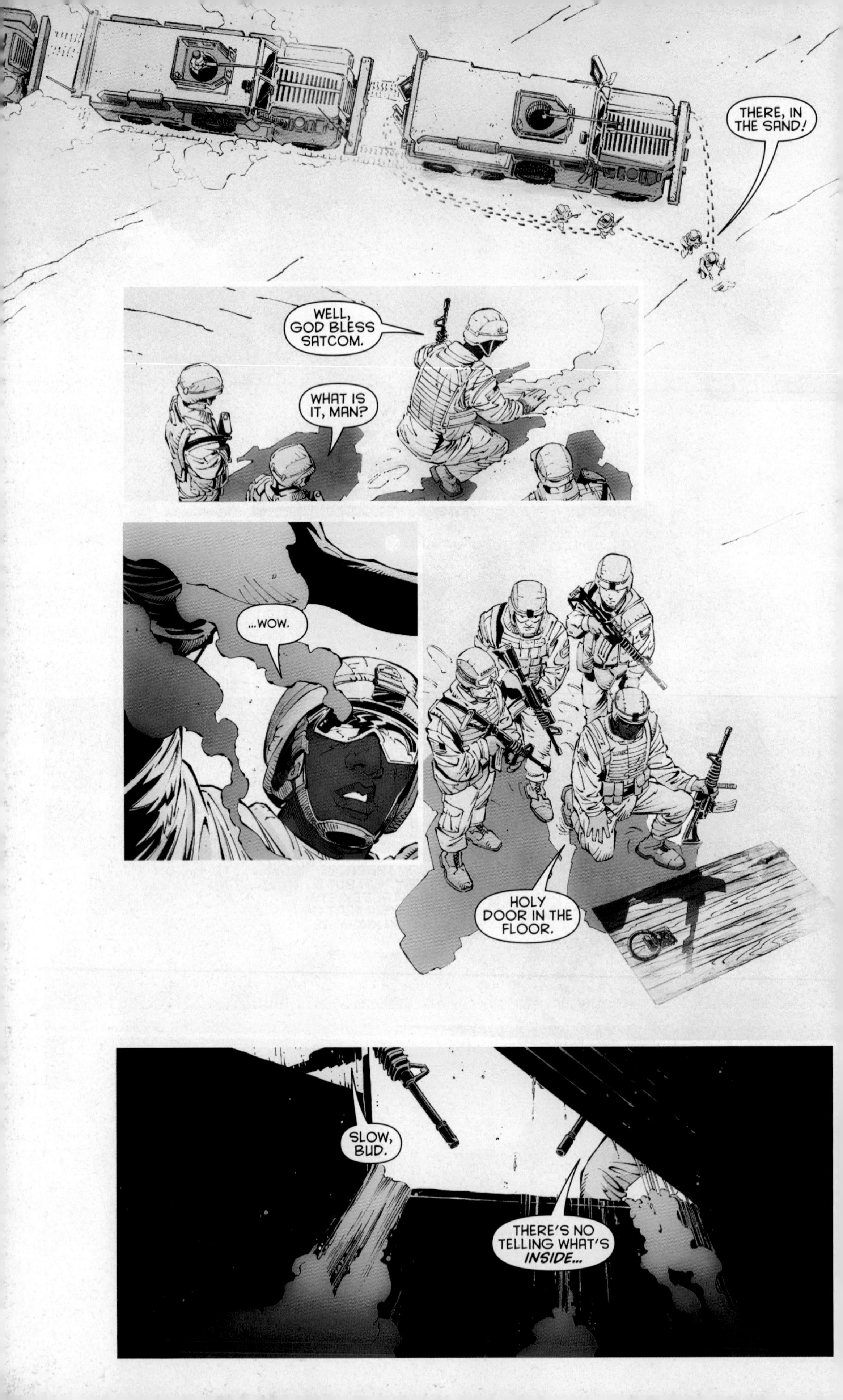

THERE, IN THE SAND!
WELL, GOD BLESS SATCOM.
WHAT IS IT, MAN?
...WOW.
HOLY DOOR IN THE FLOOR.
SLOW, BUD.
THERE'S NO TELLING WHAT'S *INSIDE...*

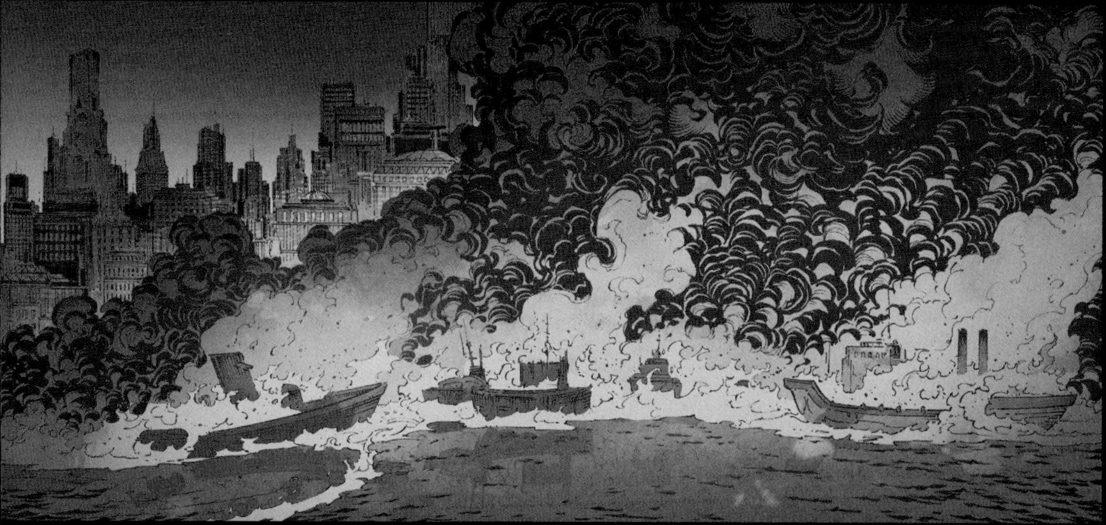

ZERO YEAR

DARK • CITY

SCOTT SNYDER WRITER **GREG CAPULLO** PENCILLER

DANNY MIKI - INKER

FCO PLASCENCIA - COLORIST • **NICK NAPOLITANO** - LETTERER

CAPULLO & PLASCENCIA - COVER

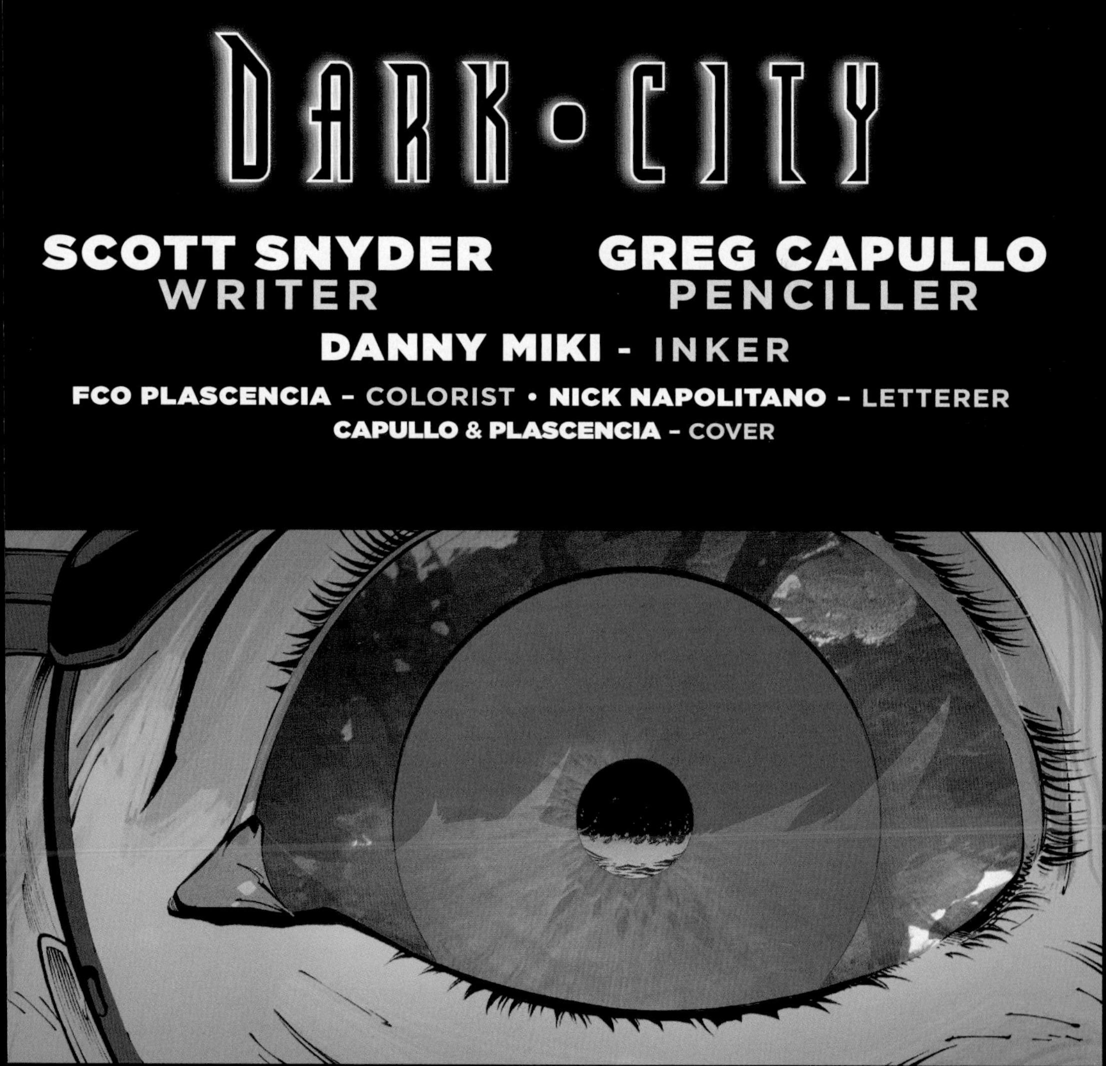

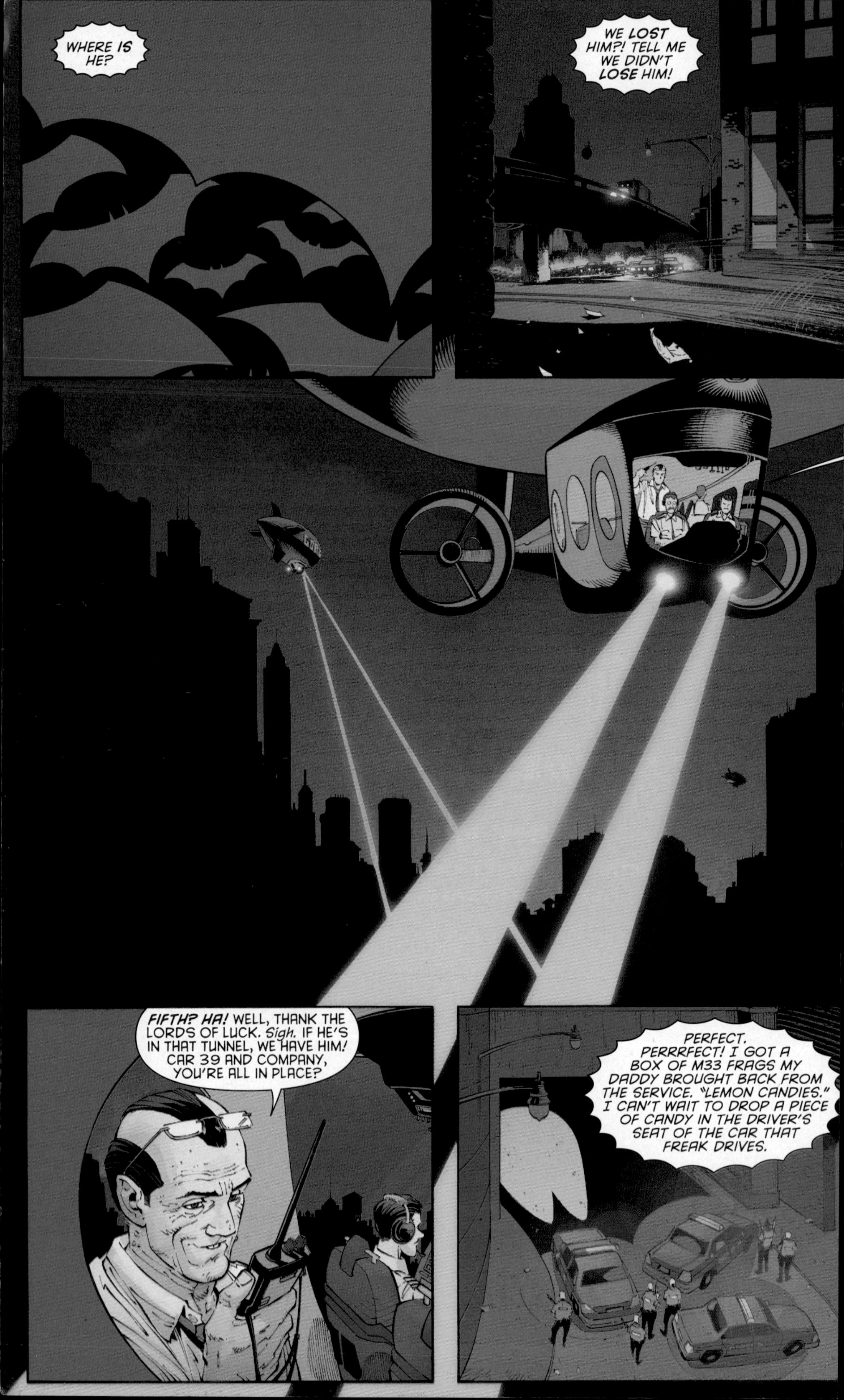
WHERE IS HE?
WE LOST HIM?! TELL ME WE DIDN'T LOSE HIM!
FIFTH? HA! WELL, THANK THE LORDS OF LUCK. Sigh. IF HE'S IN THAT TUNNEL, WE HAVE HIM! CAR 39 AND COMPANY, YOU'RE ALL IN PLACE?
PERFECT. PERRRFECT! I GOT A BOX OF M33 FRAGS MY DADDY BROUGHT BACK FROM THE SERVICE. "LEMON CANDIES." I CAN'T WAIT TO DROP A PIECE OF CANDY IN THE DRIVER'S SEAT OF THE CAR THAT FREAK DRIVES.

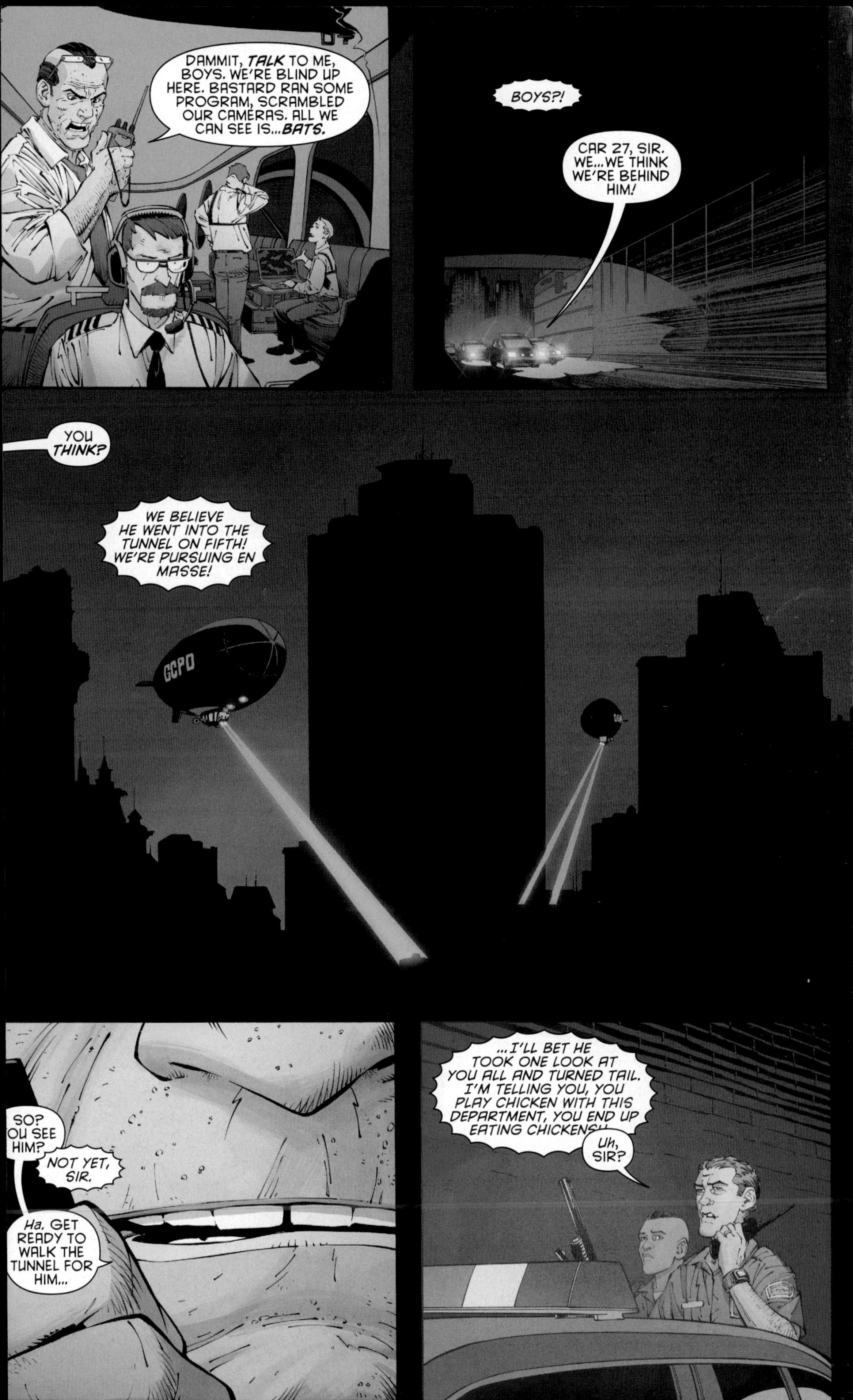
DAMMIT, TALK TO ME, BOYS. WE'RE BLIND UP HERE. BASTARD RAN SOME PROGRAM, SCRAMBLED OUR CAMERAS. ALL WE CAN SEE IS...BATS.
BOYS?!
CAR 27, SIR. WE...WE THINK WE'RE BEHIND HIM!
YOU THINK?
WE BELIEVE HE WENT INTO THE TUNNEL ON FIFTH! WE'RE PURSUING EN MASSE!
GCPD
SO? OU SEE HIM?
NOT YET, SIR.
Ha. GET READY TO WALK THE TUNNEL FOR HIM...
...I'LL BET HE TOOK ONE LOOK AT YOU ALL AND TURNED TAIL. I'M TELLING YOU, YOU PLAY CHICKEN WITH THIS DEPARTMENT, YOU END UP EATING CHICKENS
Uh, SIR?

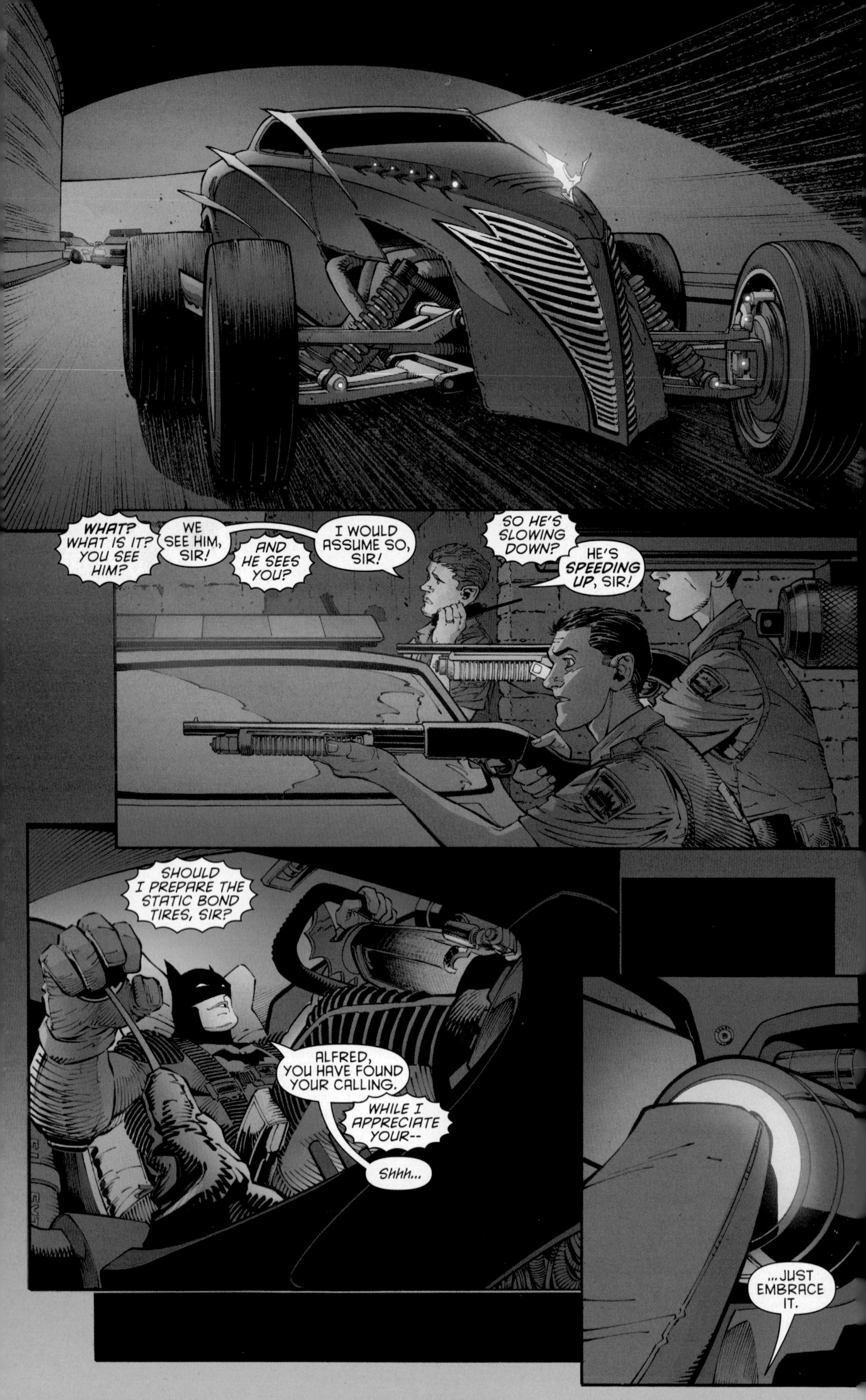

WHAT? WHAT IS IT? YOU SEE HIM?
WE SEE HIM, SIR!
AND HE SEES YOU?
I WOULD ASSUME SO, SIR!
SO HE'S SLOWING DOWN?
HE'S SPEEDING UP, SIR!
SHOULD I PREPARE THE STATIC BOND TIRES, SIR?
ALFRED, YOU HAVE FOUND YOUR CALLING.
WHILE I APPRECIATE YOUR--
Shhh...
...JUST EMBRACE IT.

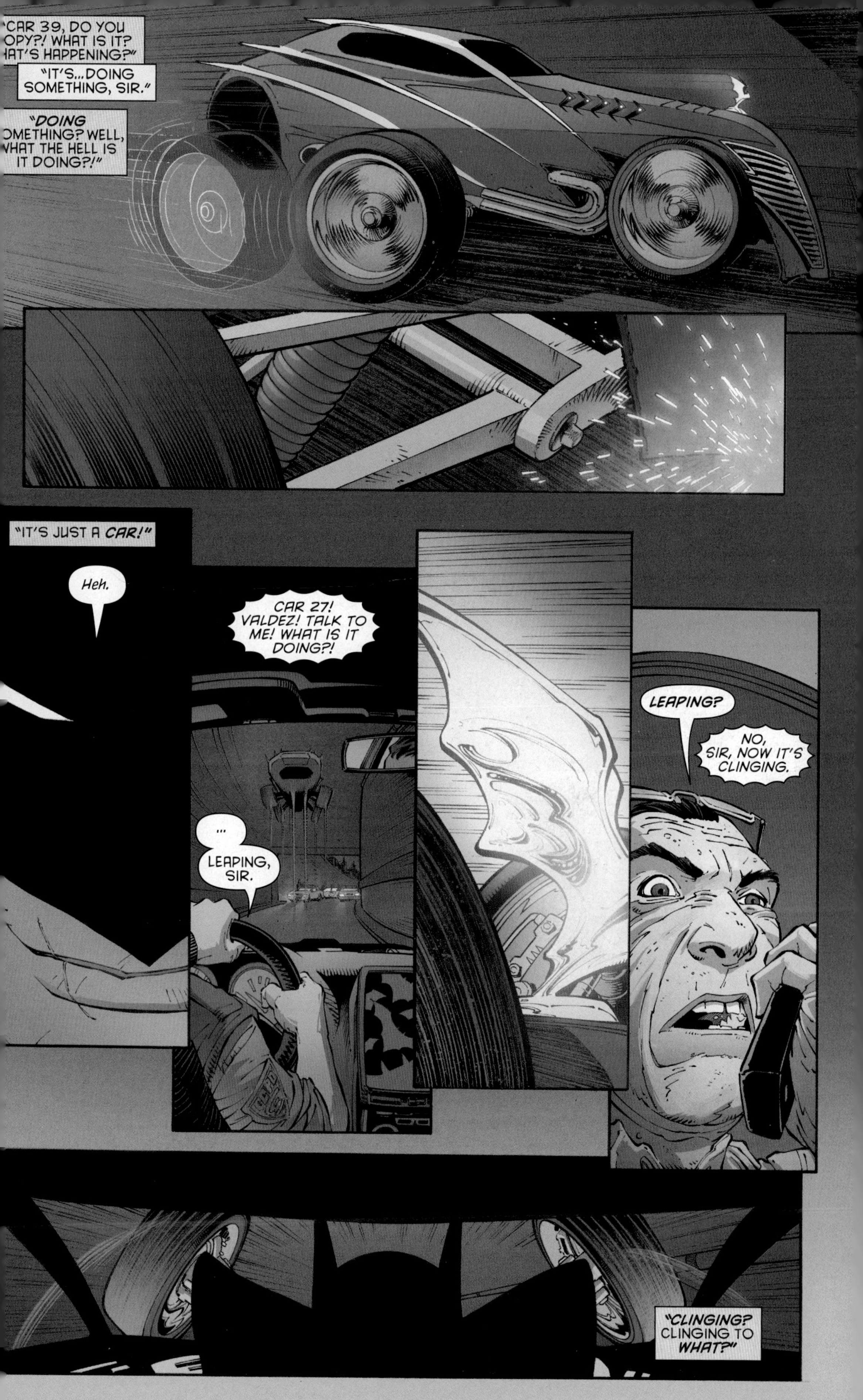

"CAR 39, DO YOU
OPY?! WHAT IS IT?
HAT'S HAPPENING?"
"IT'S...DOING SOMETHING, SIR."
"DOING
OMETHING? WELL,
HAT THE HELL IS
IT DOING?!"
"IT'S JUST A CAR!"
Heh.
CAR 27! VALDEZ! TALK TO ME! WHAT IS IT DOING?!
... LEAPING, SIR.
LEAPING?
NO, SIR, NOW IT'S CLINGING.
"CLINGING? CLINGING TO WHAT?"

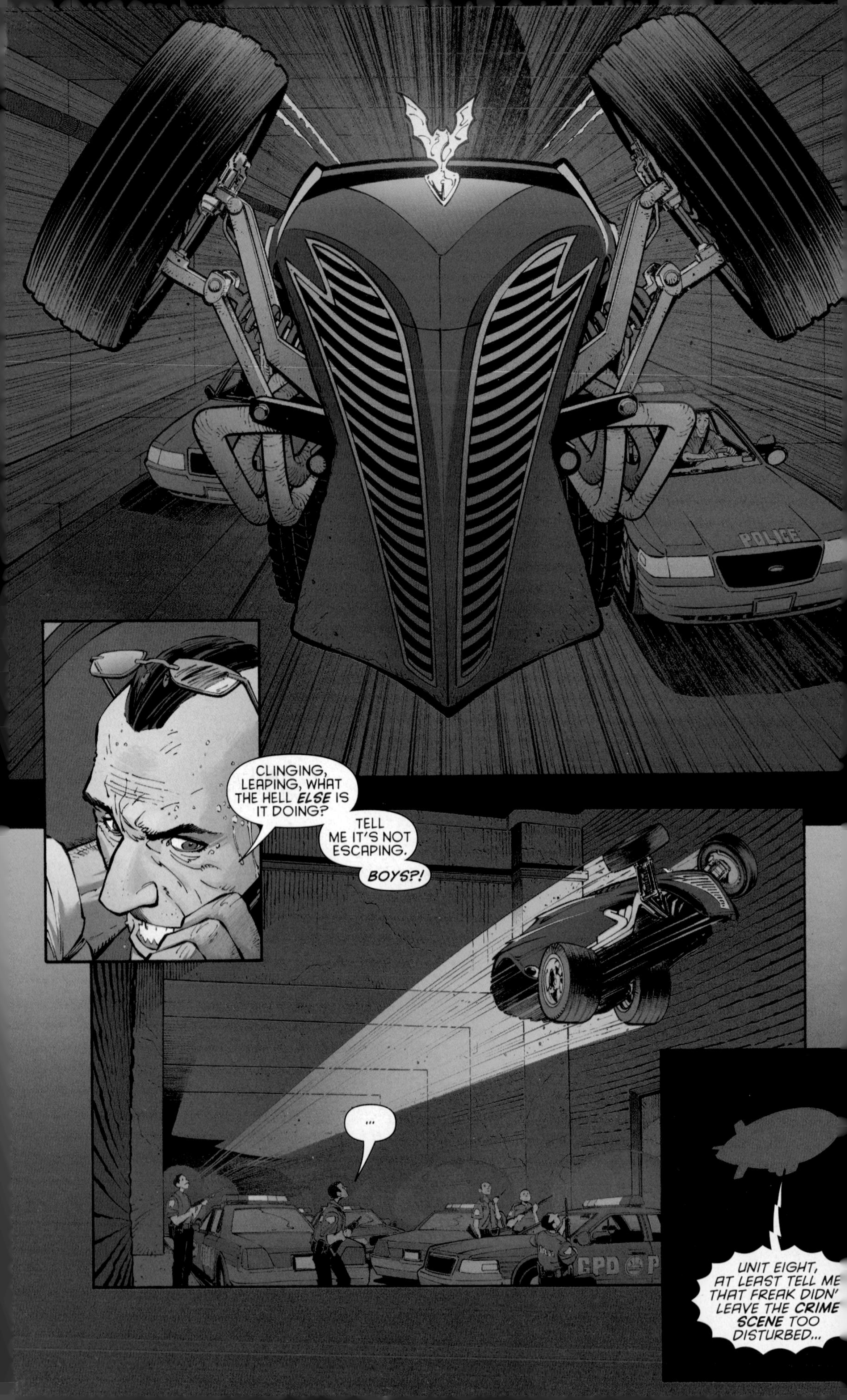

POLICE
CLINGING, LEAPING, WHAT THE HELL *ELSE* IS IT DOING?
TELL ME IT'S NOT ESCAPING.
BOYS?!
...
GPD
UNIT EIGHT, AT LEAST TELL ME THAT FREAK DIDN' LEAVE THE **CRIME SCENE** TOO DISTURBED...

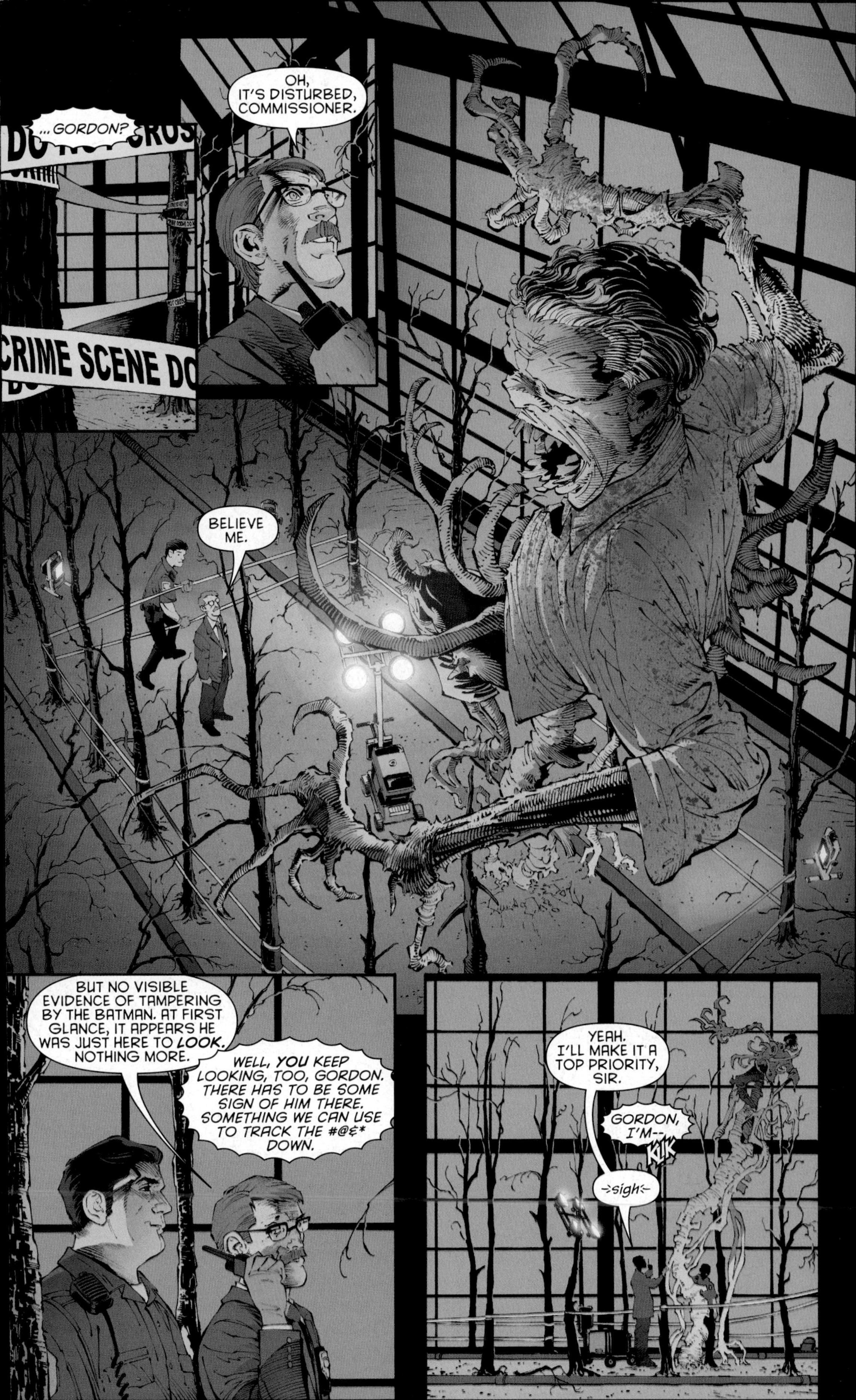
...GORDON?
OH, IT'S DISTURBED, COMMISSIONER.
CRIME SCENE DO
BELIEVE ME.
BUT NO VISIBLE EVIDENCE OF TAMPERING BY THE BATMAN. AT FIRST GLANCE, IT APPEARS HE WAS JUST HERE TO *LOOK*. NOTHING MORE.
WELL, YOU KEEP LOOKING, TOO, GORDON. THERE HAS TO BE SOME SIGN OF HIM THERE. SOMETHING WE CAN USE TO TRACK THE #@& DOWN.*
YEAH. I'LL MAKE IT A TOP PRIORITY, SIR.
GORDON, I'M--
KLIK
sigh

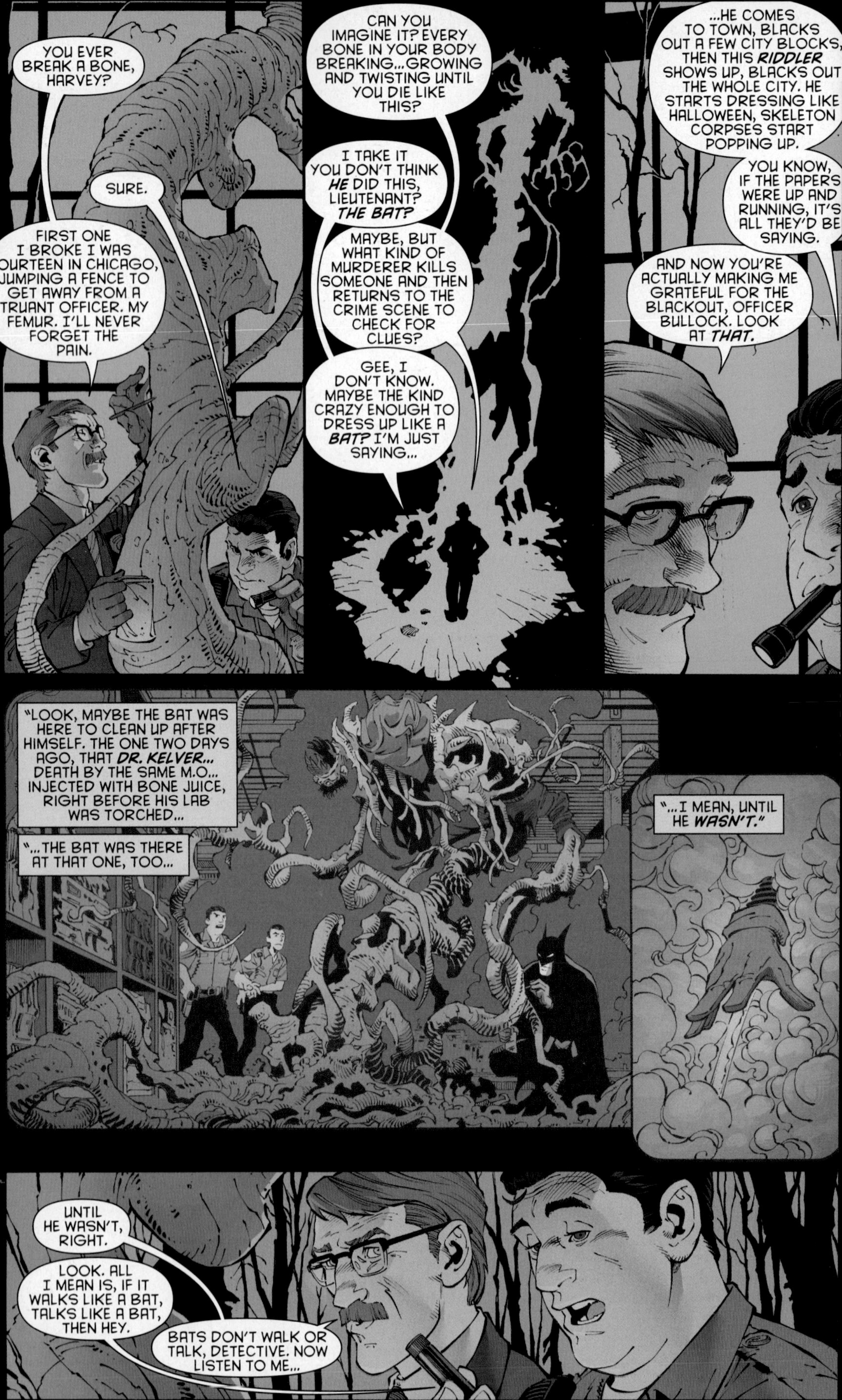
YOU EVER BREAK A BONE, HARVEY?
SURE.
FIRST ONE I BROKE I WAS FOURTEEN IN CHICAGO, JUMPING A FENCE TO GET AWAY FROM A TRUANT OFFICER. MY FEMUR. I'LL NEVER FORGET THE PAIN.
CAN YOU IMAGINE IT? EVERY BONE IN YOUR BODY BREAKING...GROWING AND TWISTING UNTIL YOU DIE LIKE THIS?
I TAKE IT YOU DON'T THINK HE DID THIS, LIEUTENANT? THE BAT?
MAYBE, BUT WHAT KIND OF MURDERER KILLS SOMEONE AND THEN RETURNS TO THE CRIME SCENE TO CHECK FOR CLUES?
GEE, I DON'T KNOW. MAYBE THE KIND CRAZY ENOUGH TO DRESS UP LIKE A BAT? I'M JUST SAYING...
...HE COMES TO TOWN, BLACKS OUT A FEW CITY BLOCKS, THEN THIS RIDDLER SHOWS UP, BLACKS OUT THE WHOLE CITY. HE STARTS DRESSING LIKE HALLOWEEN, SKELETON CORPSES START POPPING UP.
YOU KNOW, IF THE PAPERS WERE UP AND RUNNING, IT'S ALL THEY'D BE SAYING.
AND NOW YOU'RE ACTUALLY MAKING ME GRATEFUL FOR THE BLACKOUT, OFFICER BULLOCK. LOOK AT THAT.
"LOOK, MAYBE THE BAT WAS HERE TO CLEAN UP AFTER HIMSELF. THE ONE TWO DAYS AGO, THAT DR. KELVER... DEATH BY THE SAME M.O... INJECTED WITH BONE JUICE, RIGHT BEFORE HIS LAB WAS TORCHED...
"...THE BAT WAS THERE AT THAT ONE, TOO...
"...I MEAN, UNTIL HE WASN'T."
UNTIL HE WASN'T, RIGHT.
LOOK. ALL I MEAN IS, IF IT WALKS LIKE A BAT, TALKS LIKE A BAT, THEN HEY.
BATS DON'T WALK OR TALK, DETECTIVE. NOW LISTEN TO ME...

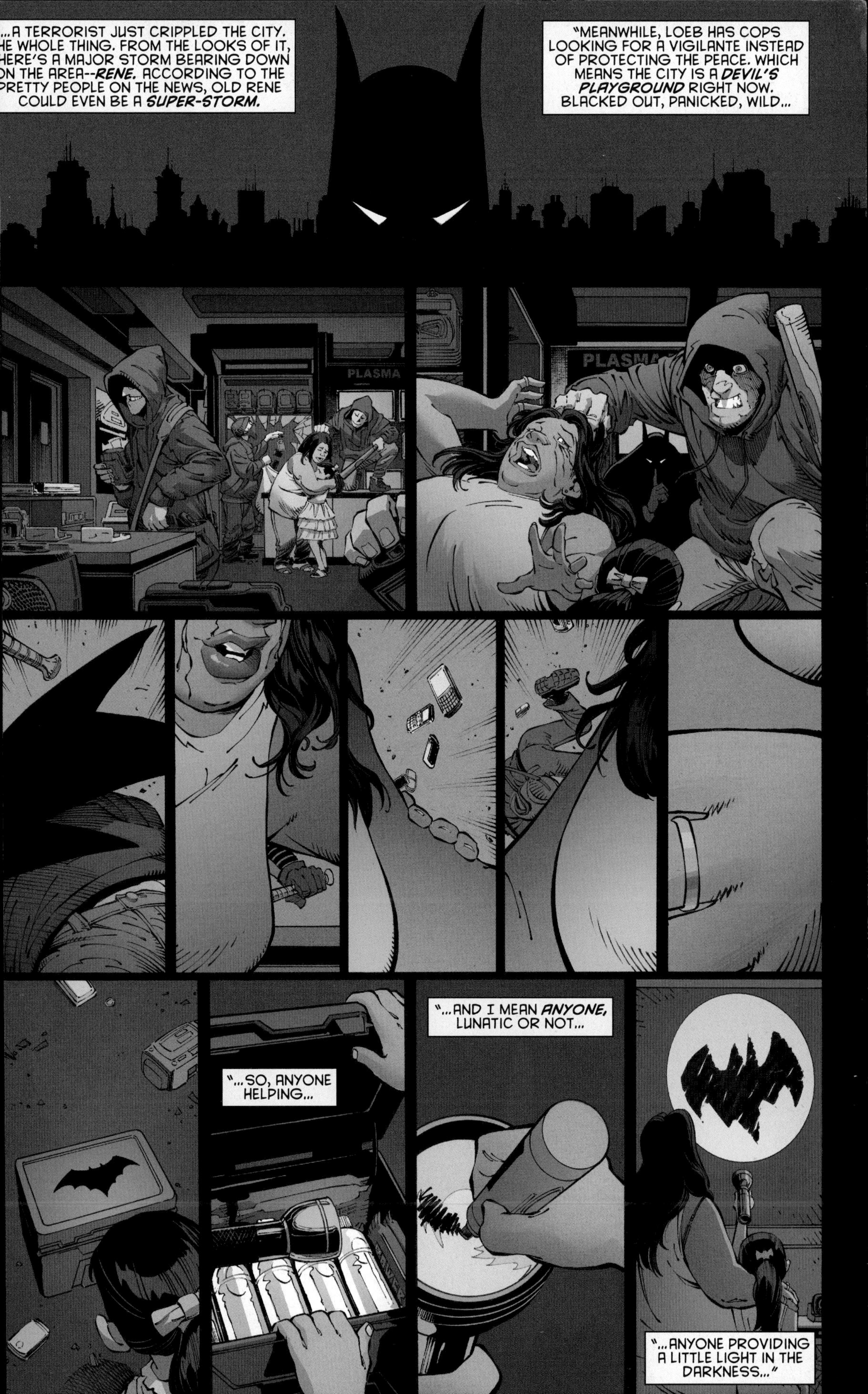
...A TERRORIST JUST CRIPPLED THE CITY. THE WHOLE THING. FROM THE LOOKS OF IT, THERE'S A MAJOR STORM BEARING DOWN ON THE AREA--RENE. ACCORDING TO THE PRETTY PEOPLE ON THE NEWS, OLD RENE COULD EVEN BE A SUPER-STORM.
"MEANWHILE, LOEB HAS COPS LOOKING FOR A VIGILANTE INSTEAD OF PROTECTING THE PEACE. WHICH MEANS THE CITY IS A DEVIL'S PLAYGROUND RIGHT NOW. BLACKED OUT, PANICKED, WILD...
PLASMA
PLASMA
"...SO, ANYONE HELPING...
"...AND I MEAN ANYONE, LUNATIC OR NOT...
"...ANYONE PROVIDING A LITTLE LIGHT IN THE DARKNESS..."

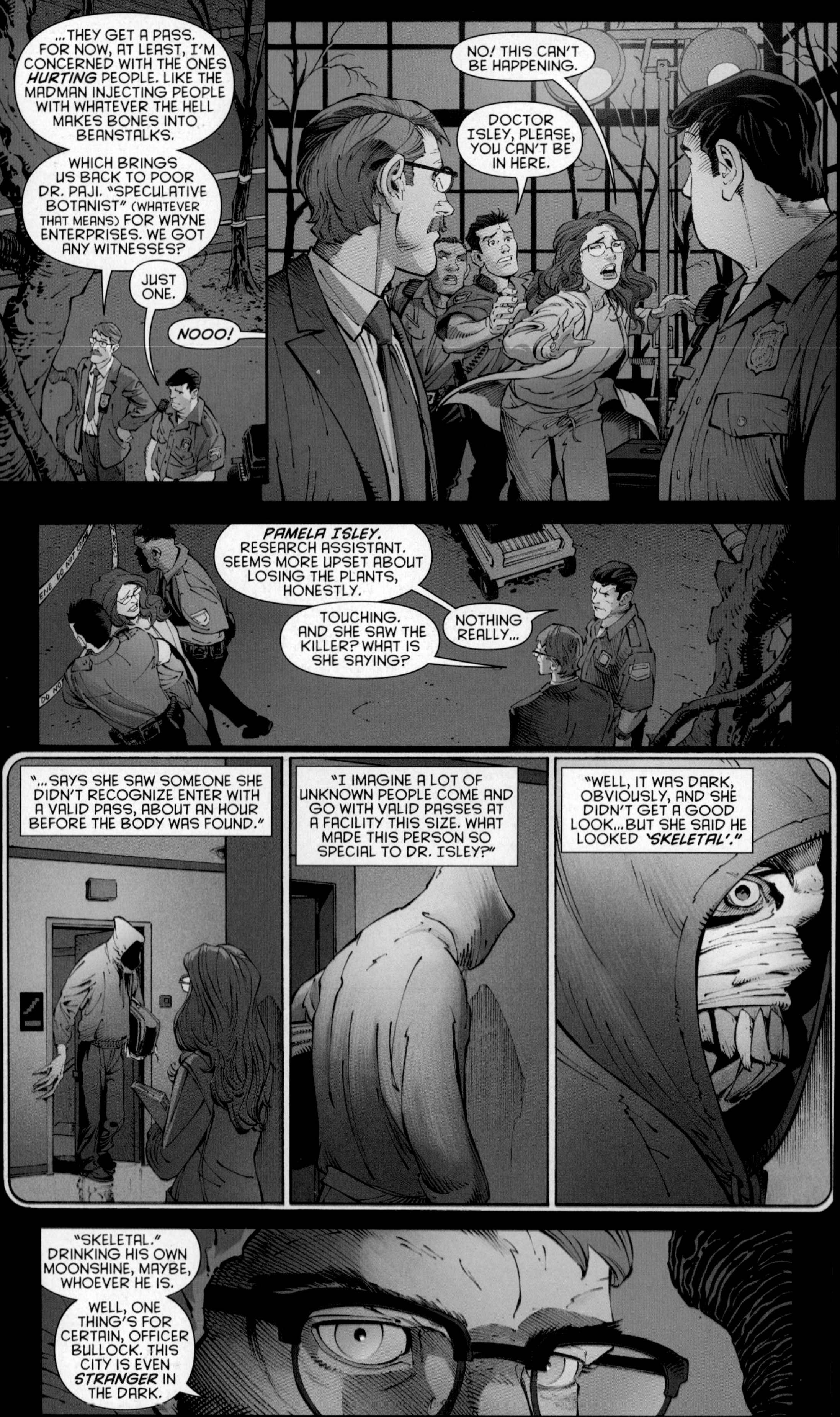

...THEY GET A PASS. FOR NOW, AT LEAST, I'M CONCERNED WITH THE ONES *HURTING* PEOPLE. LIKE THE MADMAN INJECTING PEOPLE WITH WHATEVER THE HELL MAKES BONES INTO BEANSTALKS.
WHICH BRINGS US BACK TO POOR DR. PAJI. "SPECULATIVE BOTANIST" (WHATEVER THAT MEANS) FOR WAYNE ENTERPRISES. WE GOT ANY WITNESSES?
JUST ONE.
NOOO!
NO! THIS CAN'T BE HAPPENING.
DOCTOR ISLEY, PLEASE, YOU CAN'T BE IN HERE.
PAMELA ISLEY. RESEARCH ASSISTANT. SEEMS MORE UPSET ABOUT LOSING THE PLANTS, HONESTLY.
TOUCHING. AND SHE SAW THE KILLER? WHAT IS SHE SAYING?
NOTHING REALLY...
"...SAYS SHE SAW SOMEONE SHE DIDN'T RECOGNIZE ENTER WITH A VALID PASS, ABOUT AN HOUR BEFORE THE BODY WAS FOUND."
"I IMAGINE A LOT OF UNKNOWN PEOPLE COME AND GO WITH VALID PASSES AT A FACILITY THIS SIZE. WHAT MADE THIS PERSON SO SPECIAL TO DR. ISLEY?"
"WELL, IT WAS DARK, OBVIOUSLY, AND SHE DIDN'T GET A GOOD LOOK...BUT SHE SAID HE LOOKED *'SKELETAL'*."
"SKELETAL." DRINKING HIS OWN MOONSHINE, MAYBE, WHOEVER HE IS.
WELL, ONE THING'S FOR CERTAIN, OFFICER BULLOCK. THIS CITY IS EVEN *STRANGER* IN THE DARK.

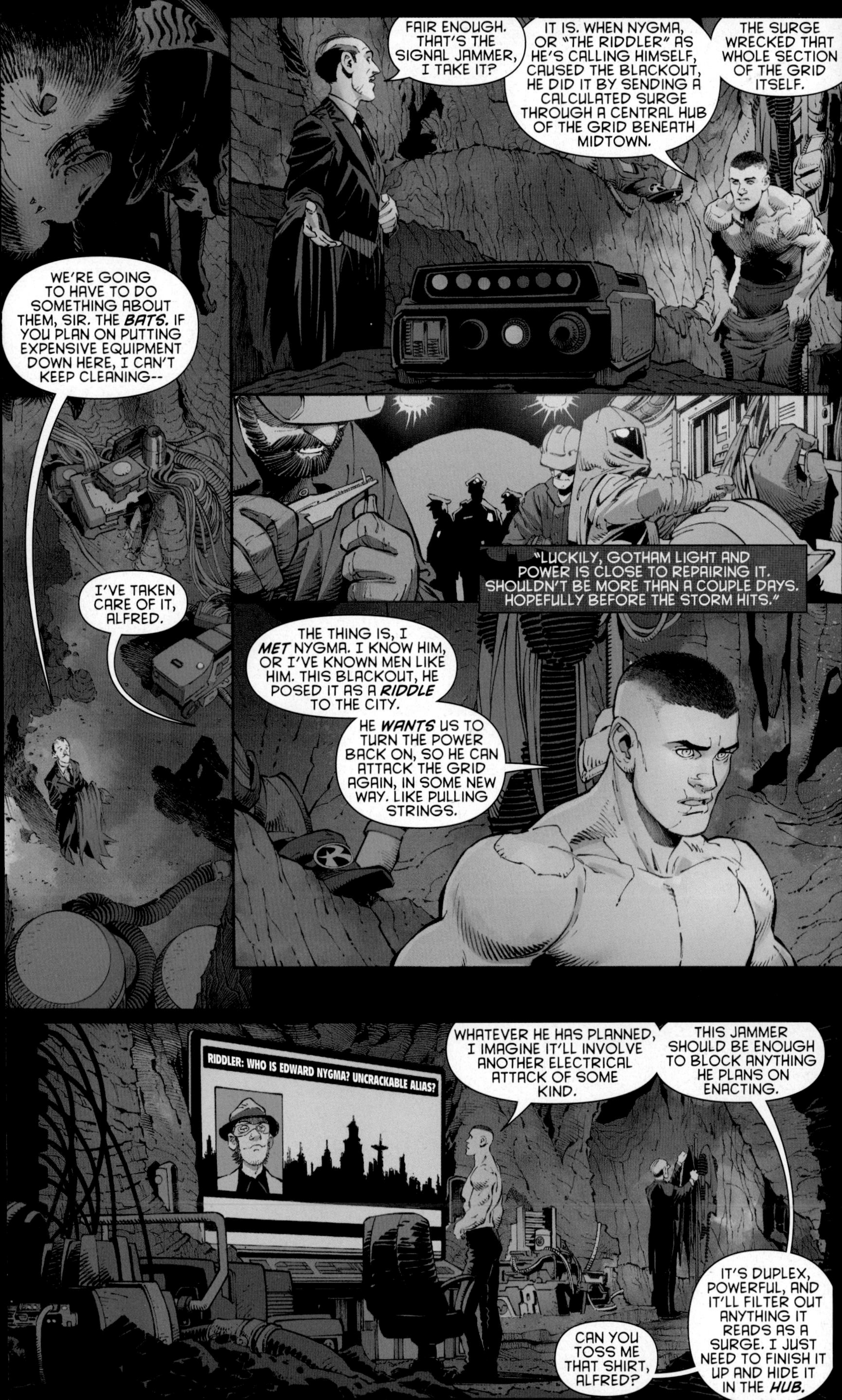

FAIR ENOUGH. THAT'S THE SIGNAL JAMMER, I TAKE IT?
IT IS. WHEN NYGMA, OR "THE RIDDLER" AS HE'S CALLING HIMSELF, CAUSED THE BLACKOUT, HE DID IT BY SENDING A CALCULATED SURGE THROUGH A CENTRAL HUB OF THE GRID BENEATH MIDTOWN.
THE SURGE WRECKED THAT WHOLE SECTION OF THE GRID ITSELF.
WE'RE GOING TO HAVE TO DO SOMETHING ABOUT THEM, SIR. THE BATS. IF YOU PLAN ON PUTTING EXPENSIVE EQUIPMENT DOWN HERE, I CAN'T KEEP CLEANING--
I'VE TAKEN CARE OF IT, ALFRED.
"LUCKILY, GOTHAM LIGHT AND POWER IS CLOSE TO REPAIRING IT. SHOULDN'T BE MORE THAN A COUPLE DAYS. HOPEFULLY BEFORE THE STORM HITS."
THE THING IS, I MET NYGMA. I KNOW HIM, OR I'VE KNOWN MEN LIKE HIM. THIS BLACKOUT, HE POSED IT AS A RIDDLE TO THE CITY.
HE WANTS US TO TURN THE POWER BACK ON, SO HE CAN ATTACK THE GRID AGAIN, IN SOME NEW WAY. LIKE PULLING STRINGS.
RIDDLER: WHO IS EDWARD NYGMA? UNCRACKABLE ALIAS?
WHATEVER HE HAS PLANNED, I IMAGINE IT'LL INVOLVE ANOTHER ELECTRICAL ATTACK OF SOME KIND.
THIS JAMMER SHOULD BE ENOUGH TO BLOCK ANYTHING HE PLANS ON ENACTING.
IT'S DUPLEX, POWERFUL, AND IT'LL FILTER OUT ANYTHING IT READS AS A SURGE. I JUST NEED TO FINISH IT UP AND HIDE IT IN THE HUB.
CAN YOU TOSS ME THAT SHIRT, ALFRED?

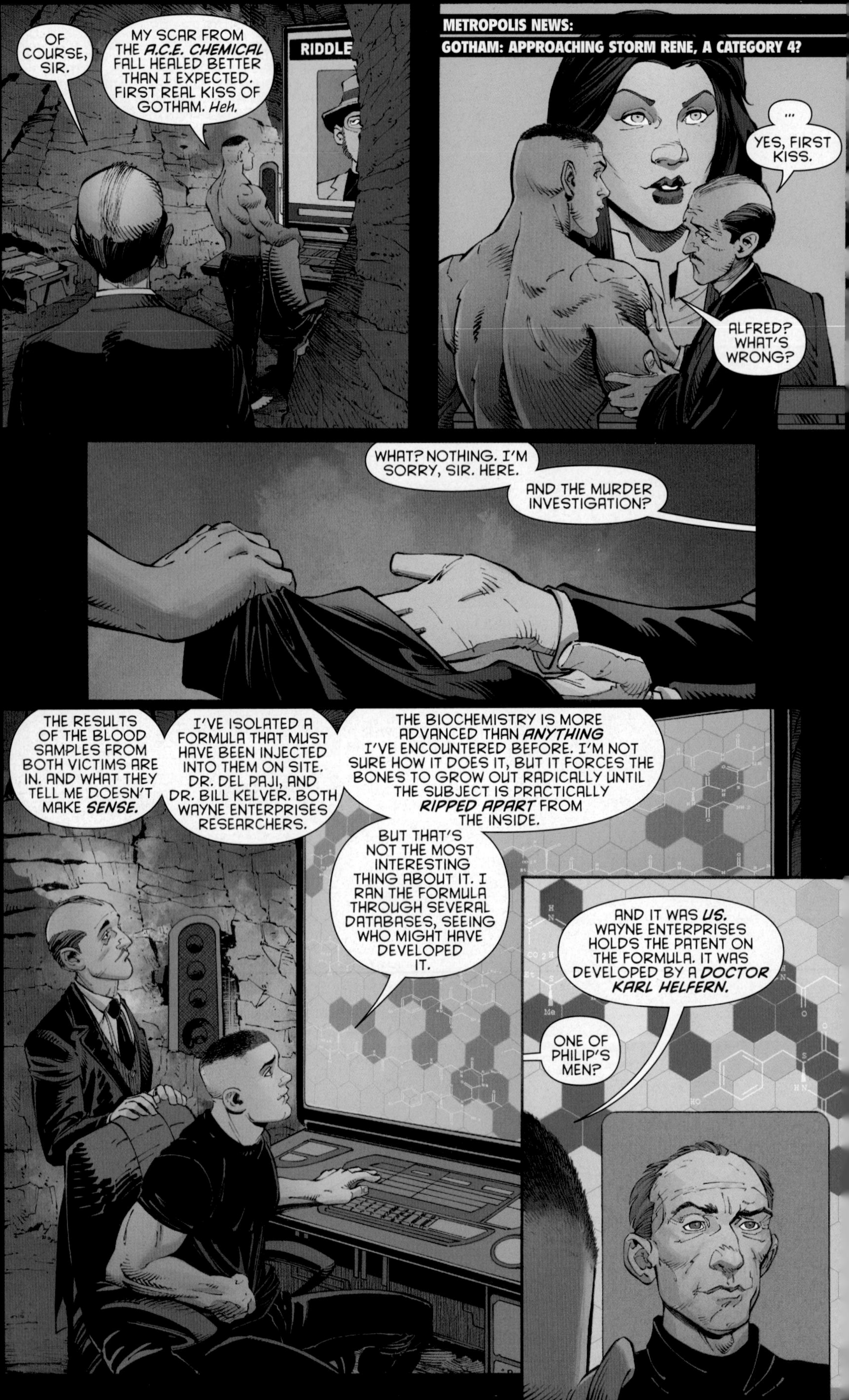
OF COURSE, SIR.
MY SCAR FROM THE A.C.E. CHEMICAL FALL HEALED BETTER THAN I EXPECTED. FIRST REAL KISS OF GOTHAM. Heh.
RIDDLE
METROPOLIS NEWS:
GOTHAM: APPROACHING STORM RENE, A CATEGORY 4?
...
YES, FIRST KISS.
ALFRED? WHAT'S WRONG?
WHAT? NOTHING. I'M SORRY, SIR. HERE.
AND THE MURDER INVESTIGATION?
THE RESULTS OF THE BLOOD SAMPLES FROM BOTH VICTIMS ARE IN. AND WHAT THEY TELL ME DOESN'T MAKE SENSE.
I'VE ISOLATED A FORMULA THAT MUST HAVE BEEN INJECTED INTO THEM ON SITE. DR. DEL PAJI, AND DR. BILL KELVER. BOTH WAYNE ENTERPRISES RESEARCHERS.
THE BIOCHEMISTRY IS MORE ADVANCED THAN ANYTHING I'VE ENCOUNTERED BEFORE. I'M NOT SURE HOW IT DOES IT, BUT IT FORCES THE BONES TO GROW OUT RADICALLY UNTIL THE SUBJECT IS PRACTICALLY RIPPED APART FROM THE INSIDE.
BUT THAT'S NOT THE MOST INTERESTING THING ABOUT IT. I RAN THE FORMULA THROUGH SEVERAL DATABASES, SEEING WHO MIGHT HAVE DEVELOPED IT.
AND IT WAS US. WAYNE ENTERPRISES HOLDS THE PATENT ON THE FORMULA. IT WAS DEVELOPED BY A DOCTOR KARL HELFERN.
ONE OF PHILIP'S MEN?

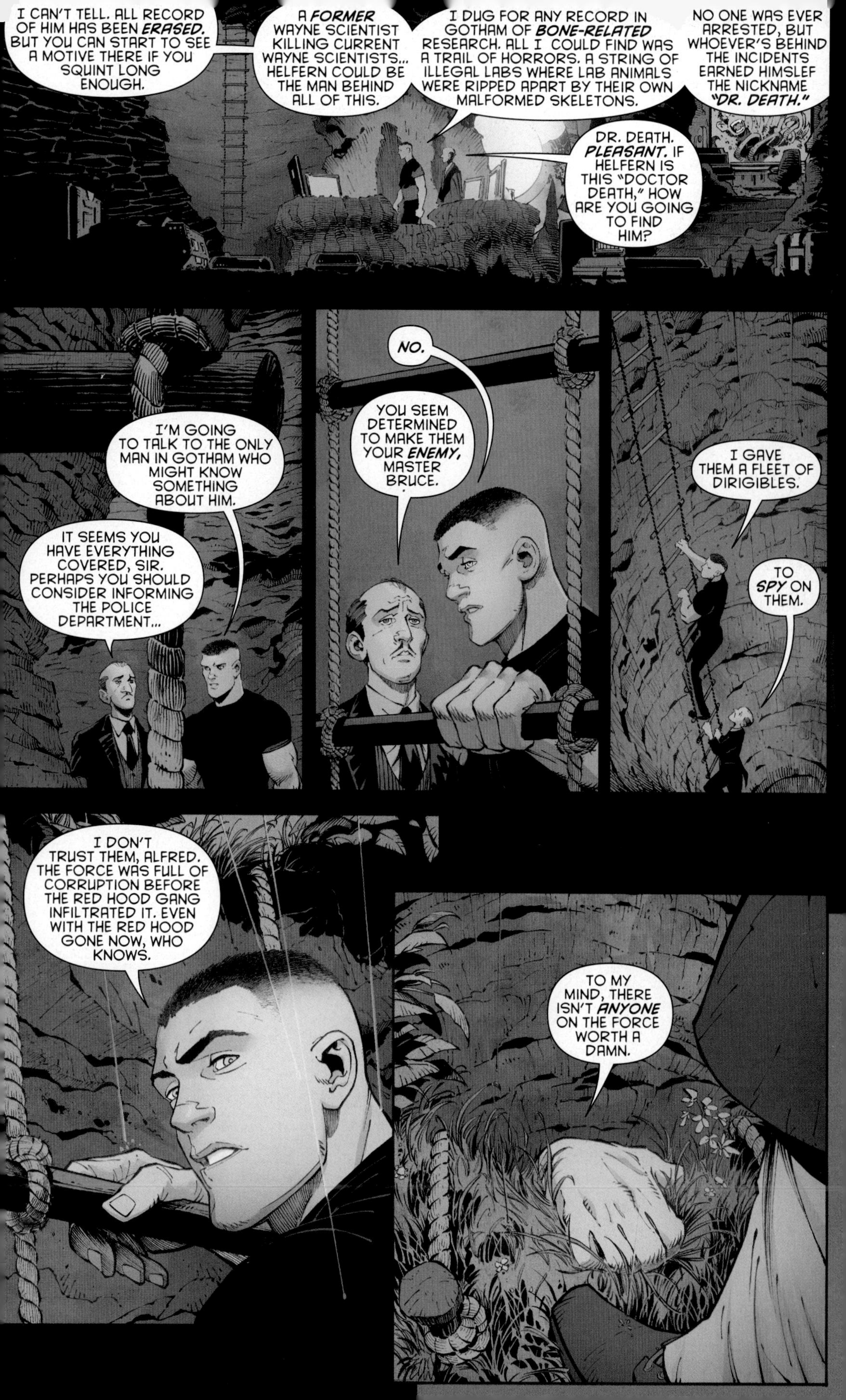
I CAN'T TELL. ALL RECORD OF HIM HAS BEEN ERASED. BUT YOU CAN START TO SEE A MOTIVE THERE IF YOU SQUINT LONG ENOUGH.
A FORMER WAYNE SCIENTIST KILLING CURRENT WAYNE SCIENTISTS... HELFERN COULD BE THE MAN BEHIND ALL OF THIS.
I DUG FOR ANY RECORD IN GOTHAM OF BONE-RELATED RESEARCH. ALL I COULD FIND WAS A TRAIL OF HORRORS. A STRING OF ILLEGAL LABS WHERE LAB ANIMALS WERE RIPPED APART BY THEIR OWN MALFORMED SKELETONS.
NO ONE WAS EVER ARRESTED, BUT WHOEVER'S BEHIND THE INCIDENTS EARNED HIMSLEF THE NICKNAME "DR. DEATH."
DR. DEATH. PLEASANT. IF HELFERN IS THIS "DOCTOR DEATH," HOW ARE YOU GOING TO FIND HIM?
I'M GOING TO TALK TO THE ONLY MAN IN GOTHAM WHO MIGHT KNOW SOMETHING ABOUT HIM.
IT SEEMS YOU HAVE EVERYTHING COVERED, SIR. PERHAPS YOU SHOULD CONSIDER INFORMING THE POLICE DEPARTMENT...
NO.
YOU SEEM DETERMINED TO MAKE THEM YOUR ENEMY, MASTER BRUCE.
I GAVE THEM A FLEET OF DIRIGIBLES.
TO SPY ON THEM.
I DON'T TRUST THEM, ALFRED. THE FORCE WAS FULL OF CORRUPTION BEFORE THE RED HOOD GANG INFILTRATED IT. EVEN WITH THE RED HOOD GONE NOW, WHO KNOWS.
TO MY MIND, THERE ISN'T ANYONE ON THE FORCE WORTH A DAMN.

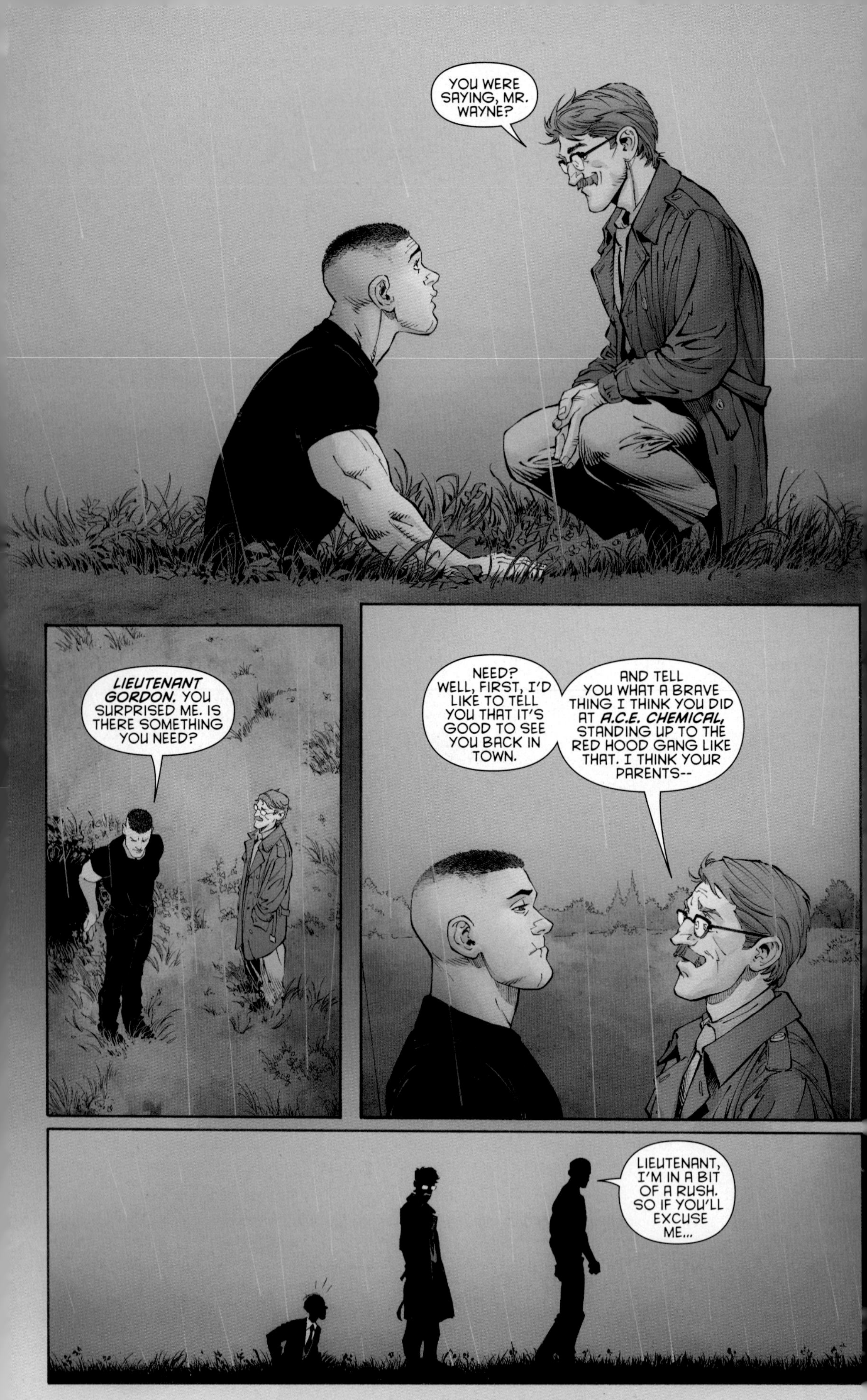
YOU WERE SAYING, MR. WAYNE?
LIEUTENANT GORDON. YOU SURPRISED ME. IS THERE SOMETHING YOU NEED?
NEED? WELL, FIRST, I'D LIKE TO TELL YOU THAT IT'S GOOD TO SEE YOU BACK IN TOWN.
AND TELL YOU WHAT A BRAVE THING I THINK YOU DID AT A.C.E. CHEMICAL, STANDING UP TO THE RED HOOD GANG LIKE THAT. I THINK YOUR PARENTS--
LIEUTENANT, I'M IN A BIT OF A RUSH. SO IF YOU'LL EXCUSE ME...

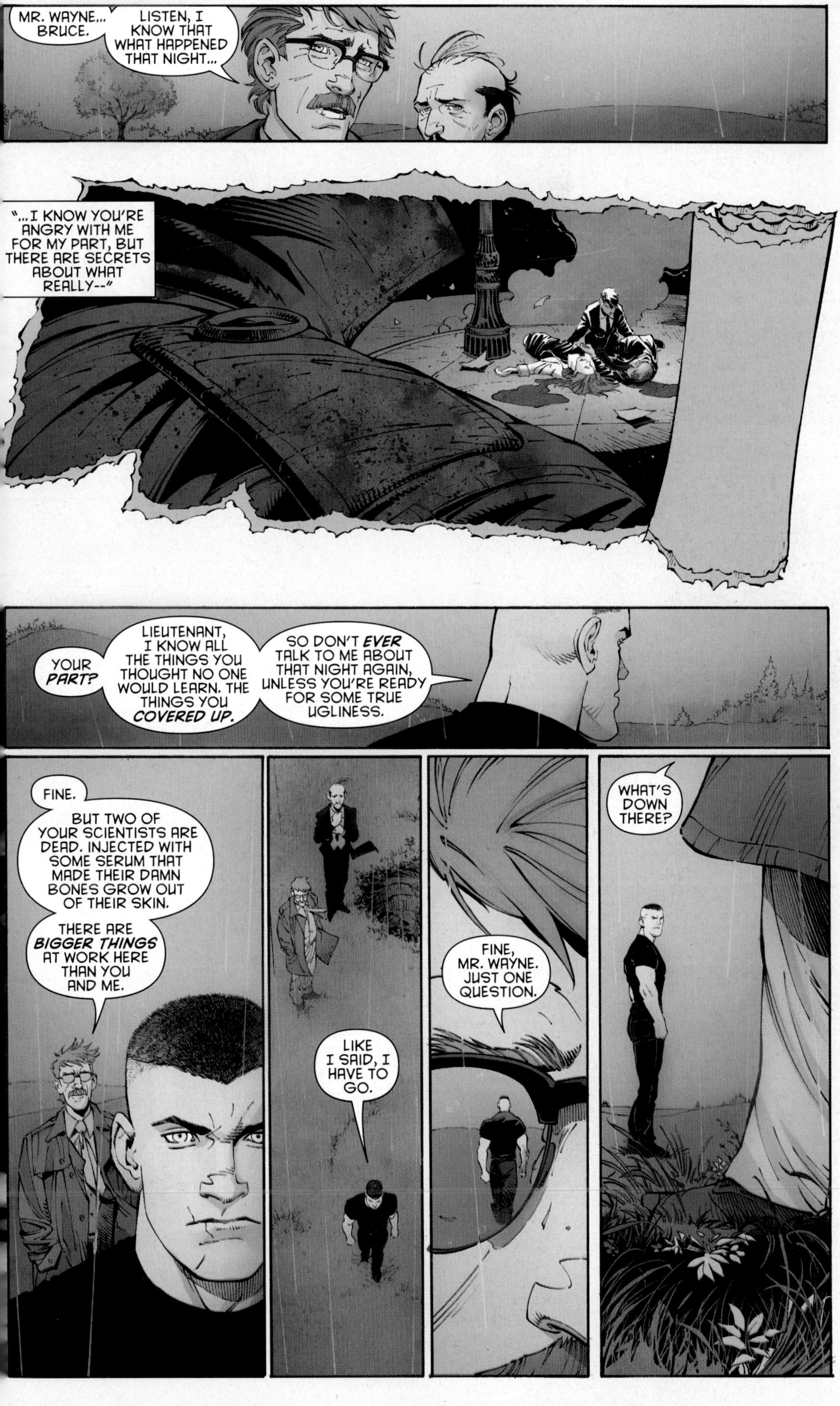

MR. WAYNE... BRUCE.
LISTEN, I KNOW THAT WHAT HAPPENED THAT NIGHT...
"...I KNOW YOU'RE ANGRY WITH ME FOR MY PART, BUT THERE ARE SECRETS ABOUT WHAT REALLY--"
YOUR *PART?*
LIEUTENANT, I KNOW ALL THE THINGS YOU THOUGHT NO ONE WOULD LEARN. THE THINGS YOU *COVERED UP.*
SO DON'T *EVER* TALK TO ME ABOUT THAT NIGHT AGAIN, UNLESS YOU'RE READY FOR SOME TRUE UGLINESS.
FINE.
BUT TWO OF YOUR SCIENTISTS ARE DEAD. INJECTED WITH SOME SERUM THAT MADE THEIR DAMN BONES GROW OUT OF THEIR SKIN.
THERE ARE *BIGGER THINGS* AT WORK HERE THAN YOU AND ME.
LIKE I SAID, I HAVE TO GO.
FINE, MR. WAYNE. JUST ONE QUESTION.
WHAT'S DOWN THERE?

WHY DO YOU ASK?

I'M JUST CURIOUS ABOUT OLD HOUSES.

I CAN HEAR THE GENERATORS... YOU KEEPING THE HOUSE RUNNING FROM THERE?

WE WERE JUST--

WHY DON'T YOU TAKE A LOOK?

...

GO ON.

SIR, I--

IT'S FINE, ALFRED. HE WANTS TO SEE. *LET* HIM.

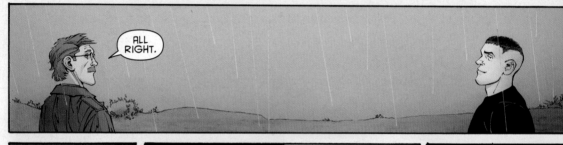

ALL RIGHT.

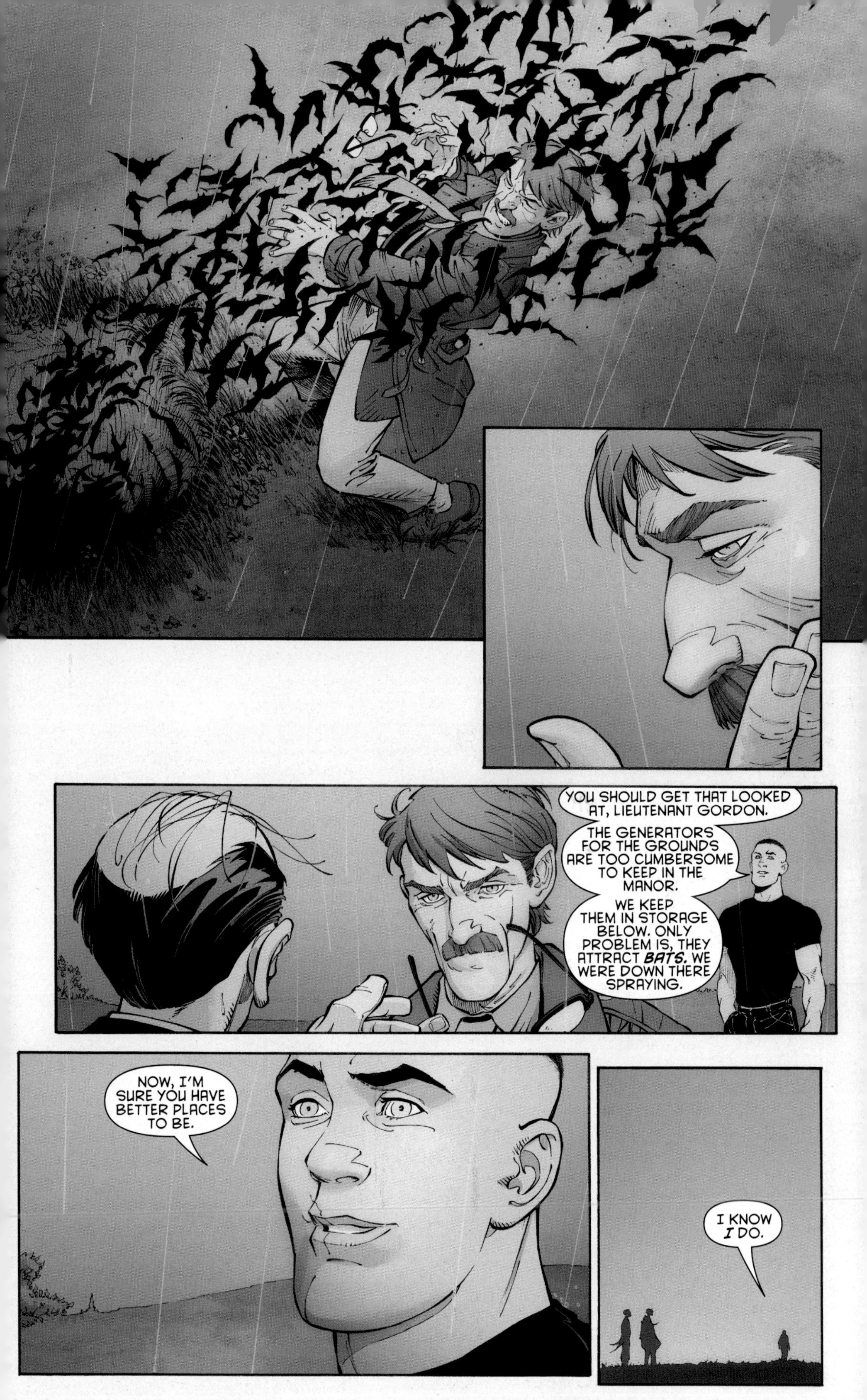
YOU SHOULD GET THAT LOOKED AT, LIEUTENANT GORDON.
THE GENERATORS FOR THE GROUNDS ARE TOO CUMBERSOME TO KEEP IN THE MANOR.
WE KEEP THEM IN STORAGE BELOW. ONLY PROBLEM IS, THEY ATTRACT **BATS.** WE WERE DOWN THERE SPRAYING.
NOW, I'M SURE YOU HAVE BETTER PLACES TO BE.
I KNOW ***I*** DO.

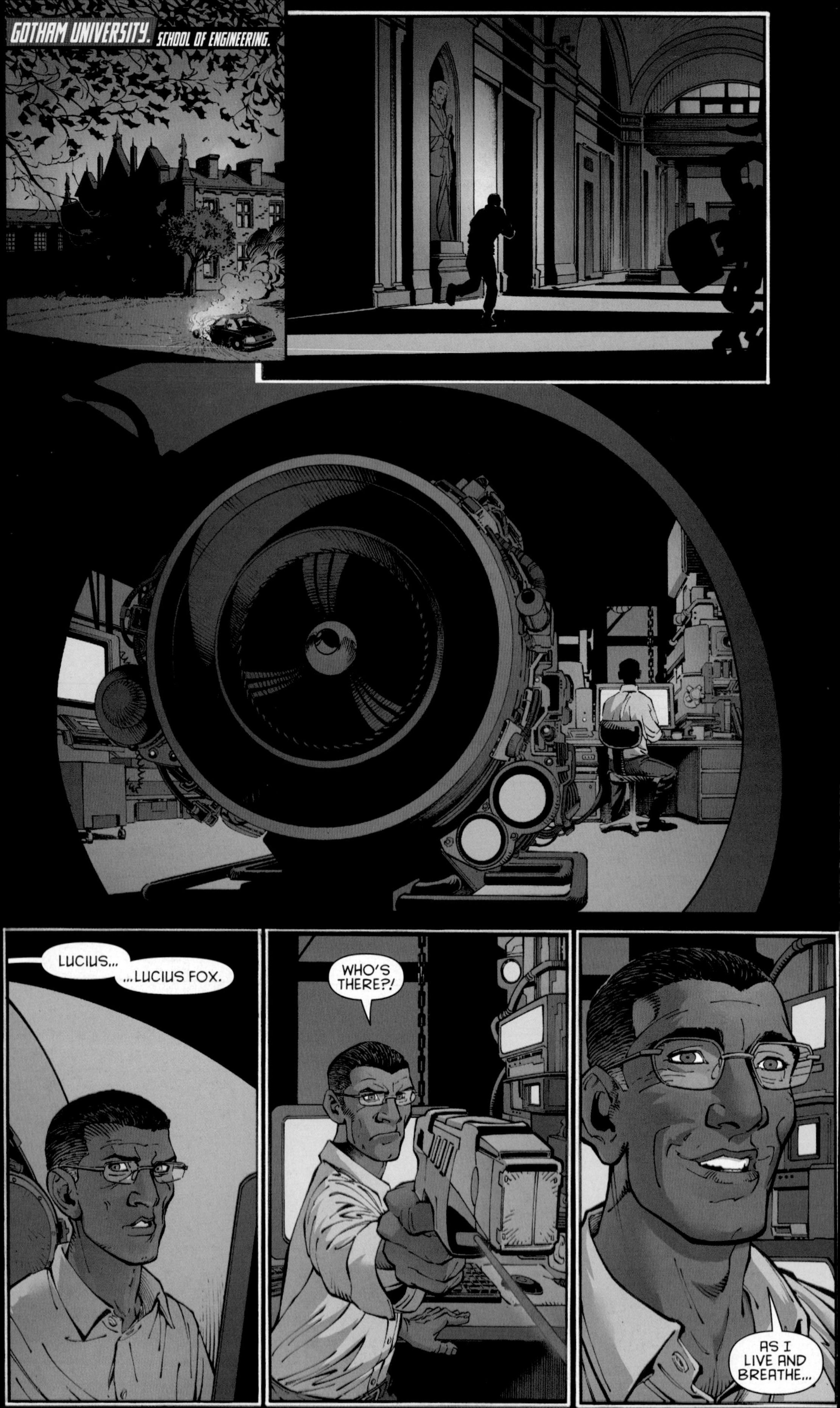
GOTHAM UNIVERSITY.
SCHOOL OF ENGINEERING.
LUCIUS...
...LUCIUS FOX.
WHO'S THERE?!
AS I LIVE AND BREATHE...

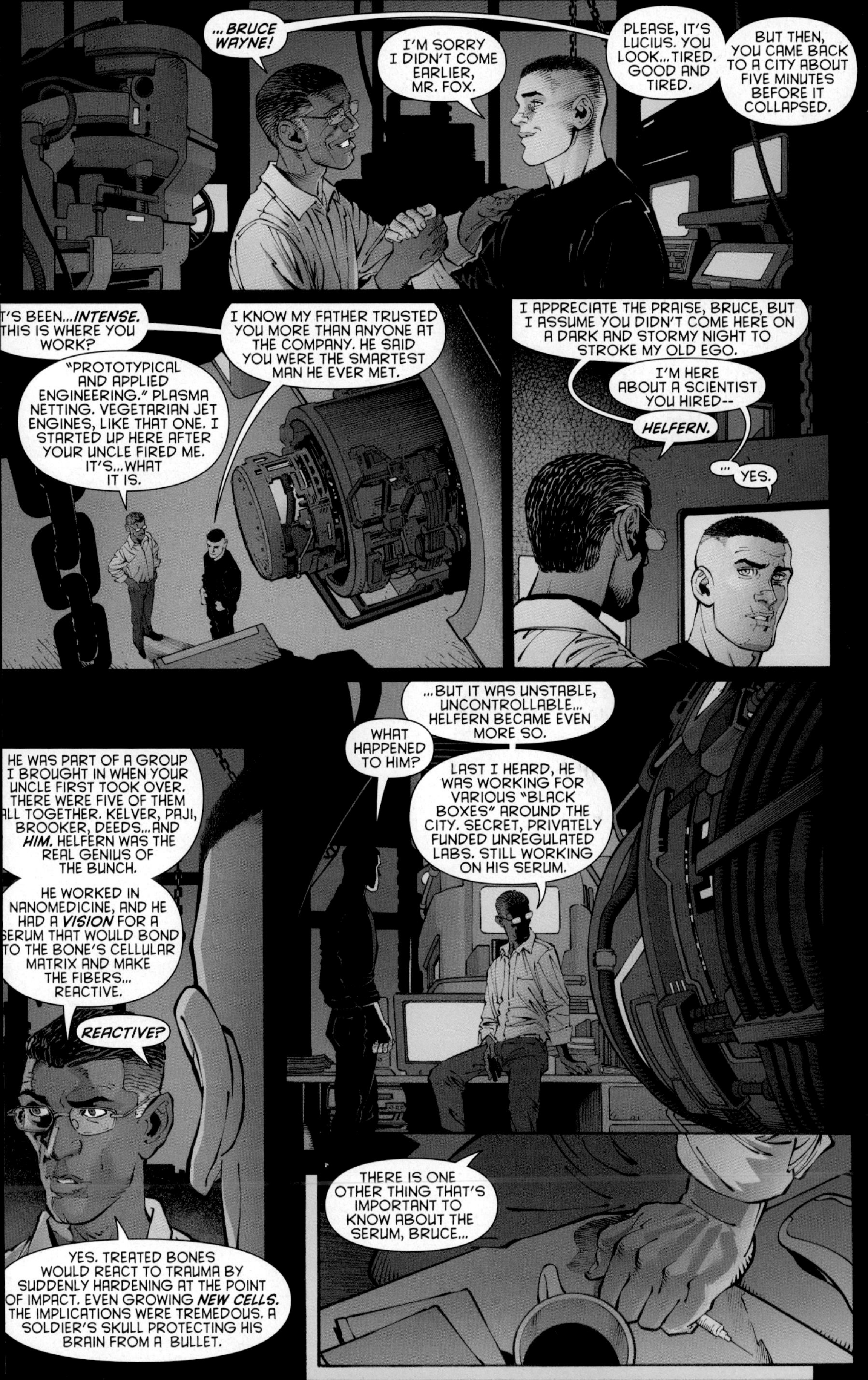
...BRUCE WAYNE!
I'M SORRY I DIDN'T COME EARLIER, MR. FOX.
PLEASE, IT'S LUCIUS. YOU LOOK...TIRED. GOOD AND TIRED.
BUT THEN, YOU CAME BACK TO A CITY ABOUT FIVE MINUTES BEFORE IT COLLAPSED.
T'S BEEN...INTENSE. THIS IS WHERE YOU WORK?
"PROTOTYPICAL AND APPLIED ENGINEERING." PLASMA NETTING. VEGETARIAN JET ENGINES, LIKE THAT ONE. I STARTED UP HERE AFTER YOUR UNCLE FIRED ME. IT'S...WHAT IT IS.
I KNOW MY FATHER TRUSTED YOU MORE THAN ANYONE AT THE COMPANY. HE SAID YOU WERE THE SMARTEST MAN HE EVER MET.
I APPRECIATE THE PRAISE, BRUCE, BUT I ASSUME YOU DIDN'T COME HERE ON A DARK AND STORMY NIGHT TO STROKE MY OLD EGO.
I'M HERE ABOUT A SCIENTIST YOU HIRED--
HELFERN.
... YES.
HE WAS PART OF A GROUP I BROUGHT IN WHEN YOUR UNCLE FIRST TOOK OVER. THERE WERE FIVE OF THEM ALL TOGETHER. KELVER, PAJI, BROOKER, DEEDS...AND HIM. HELFERN WAS THE REAL GENIUS OF THE BUNCH.
HE WORKED IN NANOMEDICINE, AND HE HAD A VISION FOR A SERUM THAT WOULD BOND TO THE BONE'S CELLULAR MATRIX AND MAKE THE FIBERS... REACTIVE.
REACTIVE?
YES. TREATED BONES WOULD REACT TO TRAUMA BY SUDDENLY HARDENING AT THE POINT OF IMPACT. EVEN GROWING NEW CELLS. THE IMPLICATIONS WERE TREMEDOUS. A SOLDIER'S SKULL PROTECTING HIS BRAIN FROM A BULLET.
WHAT HAPPENED TO HIM?
...BUT IT WAS UNSTABLE, UNCONTROLLABLE... HELFERN BECAME EVEN MORE SO.
LAST I HEARD, HE WAS WORKING FOR VARIOUS "BLACK BOXES" AROUND THE CITY. SECRET, PRIVATELY FUNDED UNREGULATED LABS. STILL WORKING ON HIS SERUM.
THERE IS ONE OTHER THING THAT'S IMPORTANT TO KNOW ABOUT THE SERUM, BRUCE...

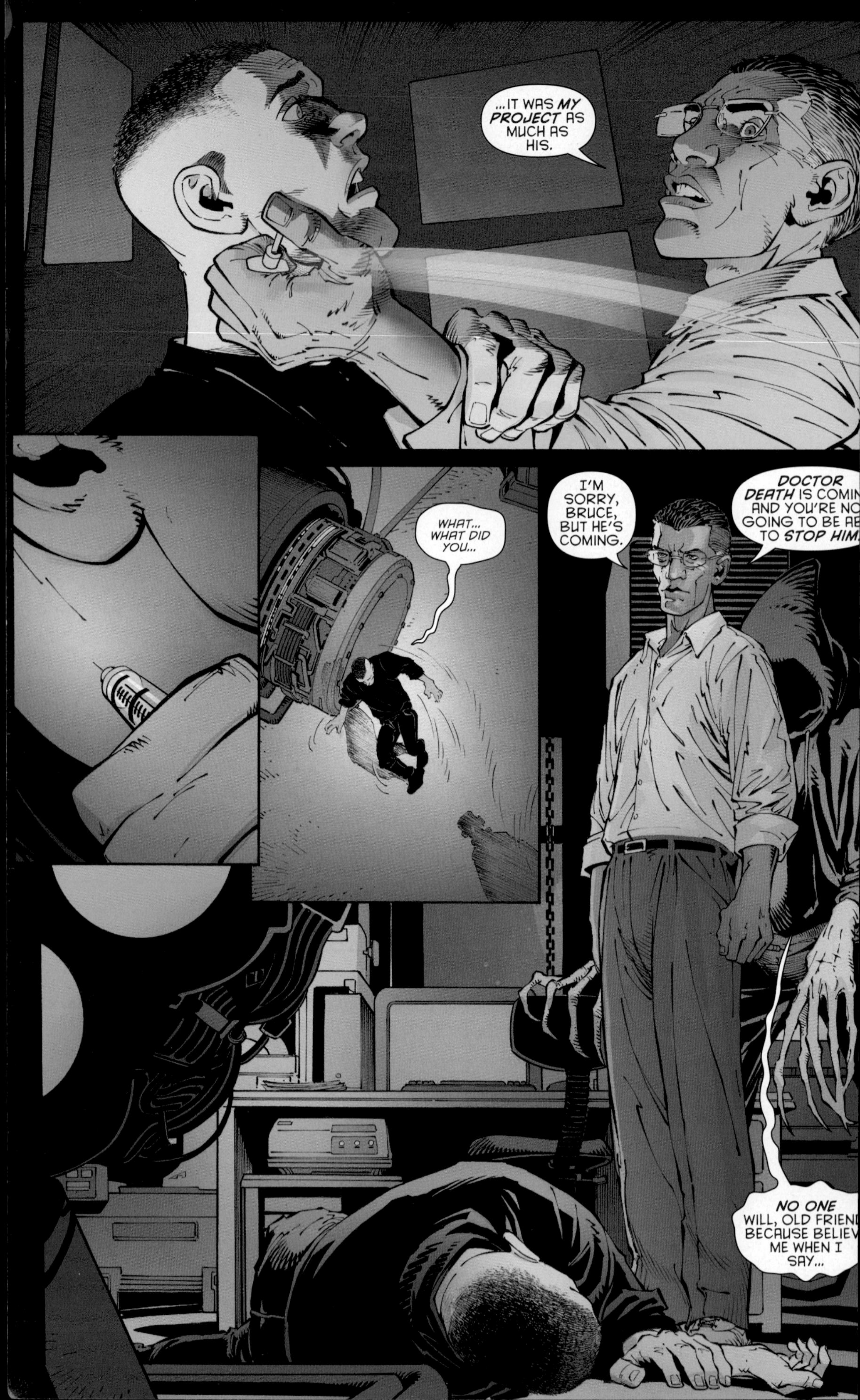
...IT WAS MY PROJECT AS MUCH AS HIS.
WHAT... WHAT DID YOU...
I'M SORRY, BRUCE, BUT HE'S COMING.
DOCTOR DEATH IS COMIN
AND YOU'RE NO
GOING TO BE AB
TO STOP HIM
NO ONE WILL, OLD FRIEND
BECAUSE BELIEV
ME WHEN I SAY...

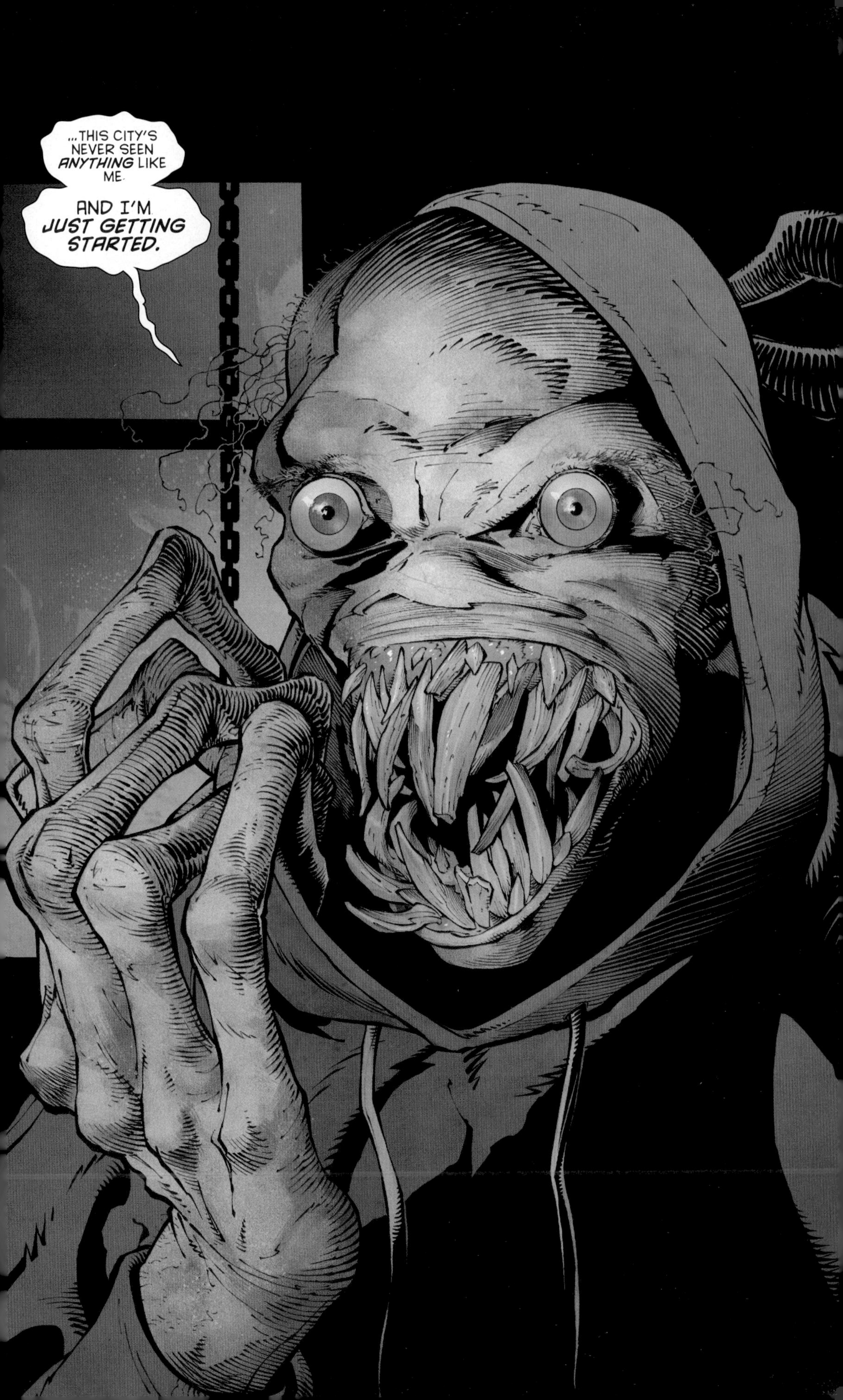
...THIS CITY'S NEVER SEEN *ANYTHING* LIKE ME.
AND I'M *JUST GETTING STARTED.*

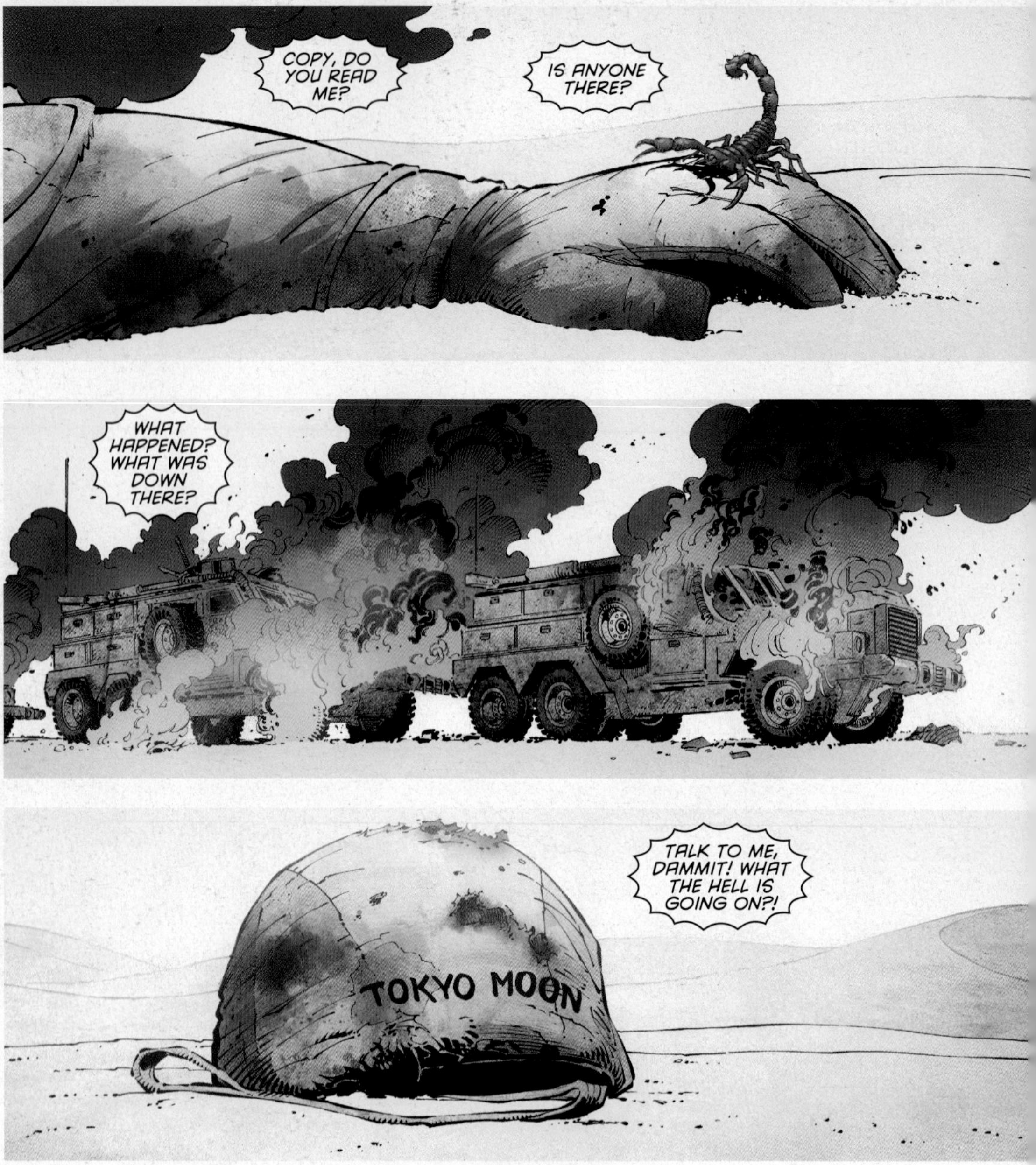
COPY, DO YOU READ ME?
IS ANYONE THERE?
WHAT HAPPENED? WHAT WAS DOWN THERE?
TALK TO ME, DAMMIT! WHAT THE HELL IS GOING ON?!
TOKYO MOON

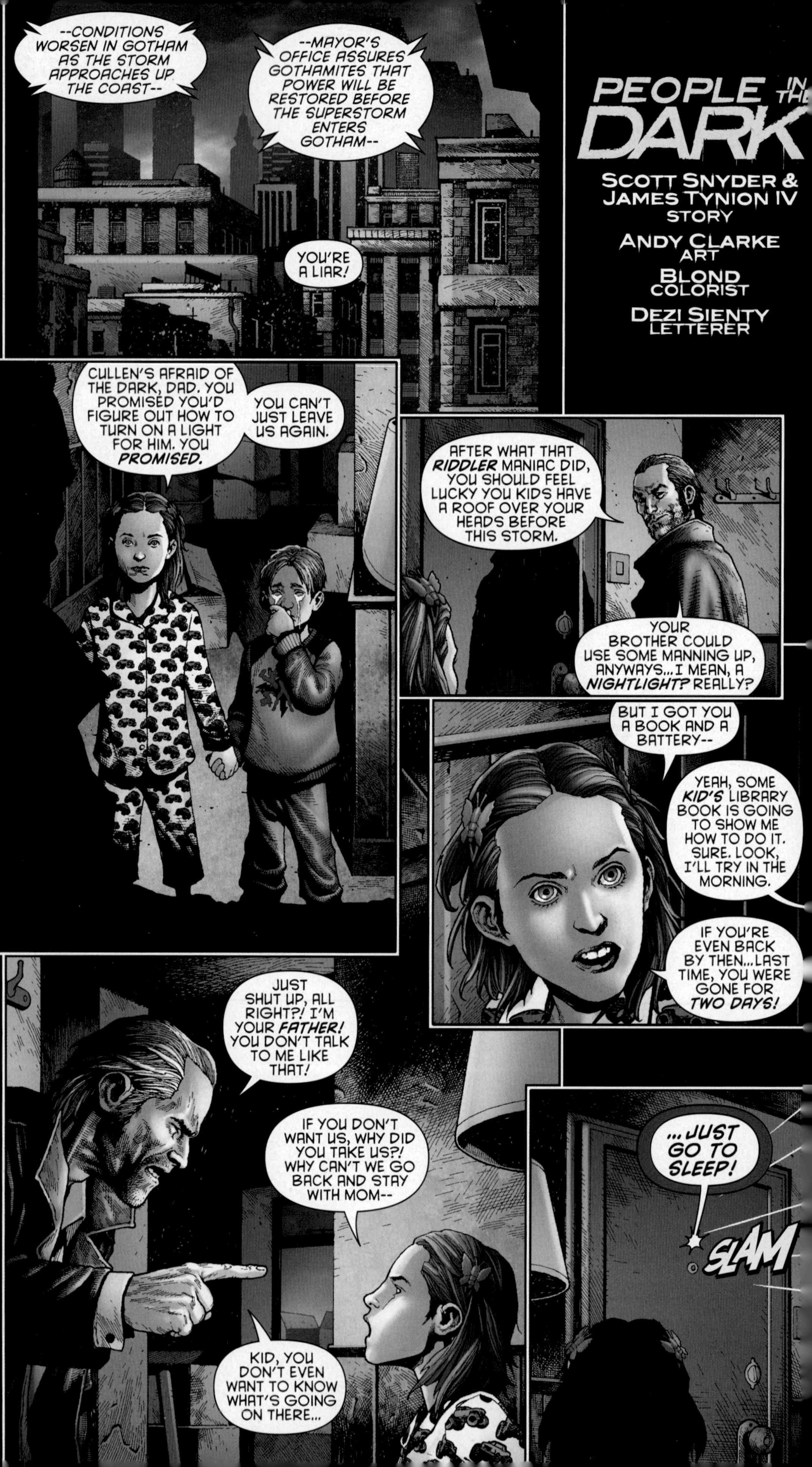

--CONDITIONS WORSEN IN GOTHAM AS THE STORM APPROACHES UP THE COAST--
--MAYOR'S OFFICE ASSURES GOTHAMITES THAT POWER WILL BE RESTORED BEFORE THE SUPERSTORM ENTERS GOTHAM--
YOU'RE A LIAR!
PEOPLE IN THE DARK
SCOTT SNYDER & JAMES TYNION IV STORY
ANDY CLARKE ART
BLOND COLORIST
DEZI SIENTY LETTERER
CULLEN'S AFRAID OF THE DARK, DAD. YOU PROMISED YOU'D FIGURE OUT HOW TO TURN ON A LIGHT FOR HIM. YOU PROMISED.
YOU CAN'T JUST LEAVE US AGAIN.
AFTER WHAT THAT RIDDLER MANIAC DID, YOU SHOULD FEEL LUCKY YOU KIDS HAVE A ROOF OVER YOUR HEADS BEFORE THIS STORM.
YOUR BROTHER COULD USE SOME MANNING UP, ANYWAYS...I MEAN, A NIGHTLIGHT? REALLY?
BUT I GOT YOU A BOOK AND A BATTERY--
YEAH, SOME KID'S LIBRARY BOOK IS GOING TO SHOW ME HOW TO DO IT. SURE. LOOK, I'LL TRY IN THE MORNING.
IF YOU'RE EVEN BACK BY THEN...LAST TIME, YOU WERE GONE FOR TWO DAYS!
JUST SHUT UP, ALL RIGHT?! I'M YOUR FATHER! YOU DON'T TALK TO ME LIKE THAT!
IF YOU DON'T WANT US, WHY DID YOU TAKE US?! WHY CAN'T WE GO BACK AND STAY WITH MOM--
KID, YOU DON'T EVEN WANT TO KNOW WHAT'S GOING ON THERE...
...JUST GO TO SLEEP!
SLAM

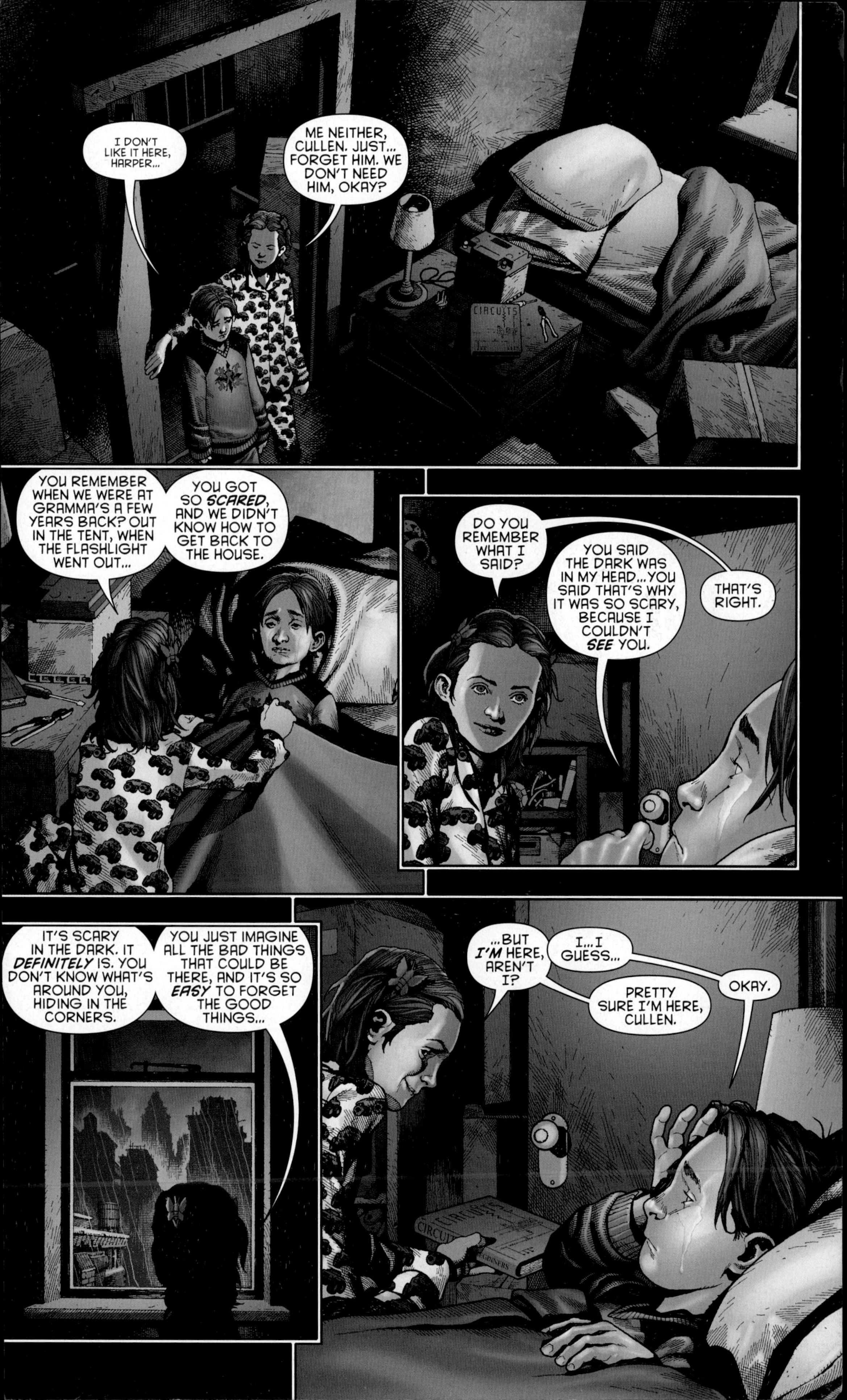
I DON'T LIKE IT HERE, HARPER...
ME NEITHER, CULLEN. JUST... FORGET HIM. WE DON'T NEED HIM, OKAY?
CIRCUITS
YOU REMEMBER WHEN WE WERE AT GRAMMA'S A FEW YEARS BACK? OUT IN THE TENT, WHEN THE FLASHLIGHT WENT OUT...
YOU GOT SO *SCARED*, AND WE DIDN'T KNOW HOW TO GET BACK TO THE HOUSE.
DO YOU REMEMBER WHAT I SAID?
YOU SAID THE DARK WAS IN MY HEAD...YOU SAID THAT'S WHY IT WAS SO SCARY, BECAUSE I COULDN'T *SEE* YOU.
THAT'S RIGHT.
IT'S SCARY IN THE DARK. IT *DEFINITELY* IS. YOU DON'T KNOW WHAT'S AROUND YOU, HIDING IN THE CORNERS.
YOU JUST IMAGINE ALL THE BAD THINGS THAT COULD BE THERE, AND IT'S SO *EASY* TO FORGET THE GOOD THINGS...
...BUT *I'M* HERE, AREN'T I?
I...I GUESS...
PRETTY SURE I'M HERE, CULLEN.
OKAY.
CIRCUITS
BEGINNERS

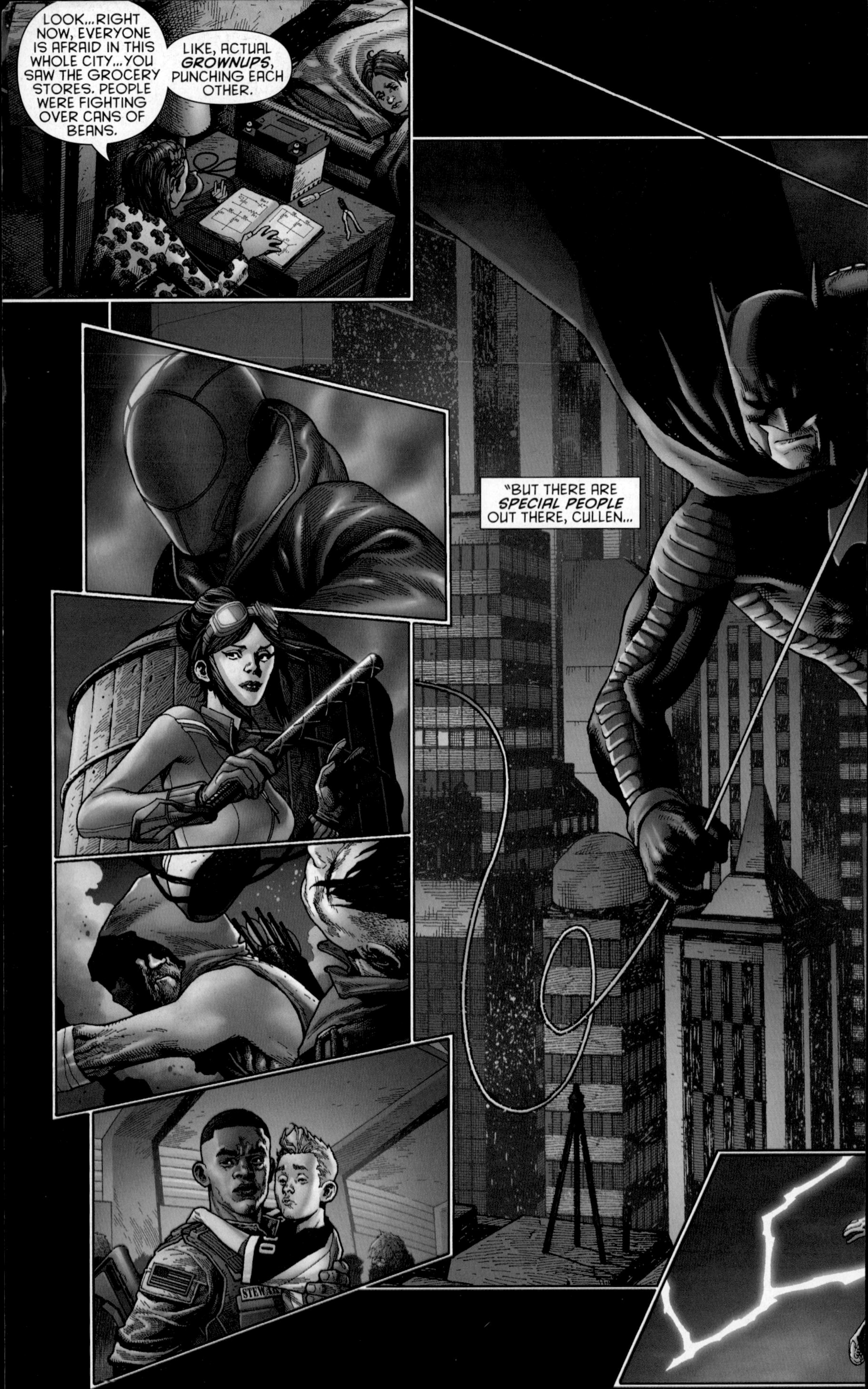
LOOK... RIGHT NOW, EVERYONE IS AFRAID IN THIS WHOLE CITY... YOU SAW THE GROCERY STORES. PEOPLE WERE FIGHTING OVER CANS OF BEANS.
LIKE, ACTUAL *GROWNUPS*, PUNCHING EACH OTHER.
"BUT THERE ARE *SPECIAL PEOPLE* OUT THERE, CULLEN...

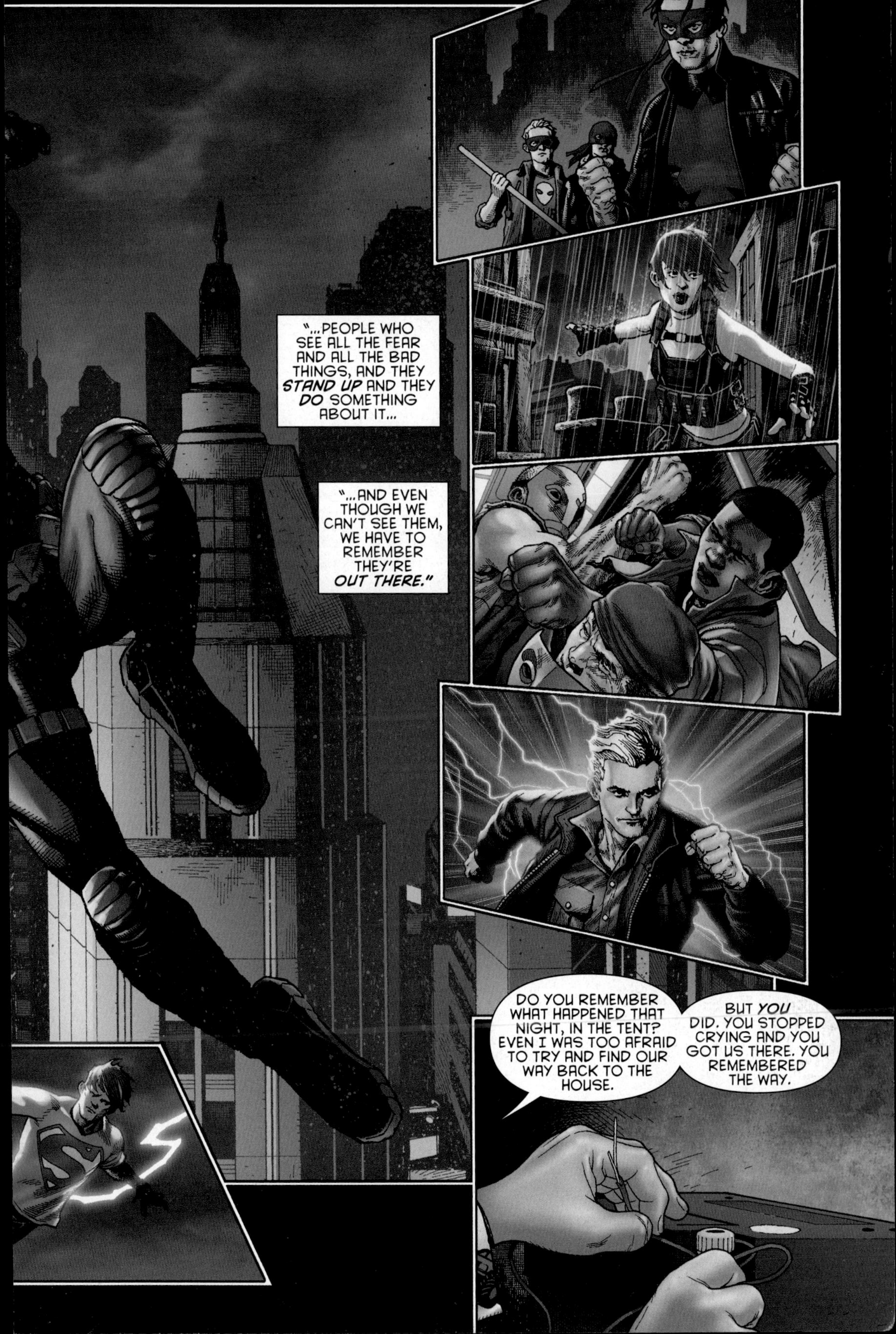
"...PEOPLE WHO SEE ALL THE FEAR AND ALL THE BAD THINGS, AND THEY STAND UP AND THEY DO SOMETHING ABOUT IT...
"...AND EVEN THOUGH WE CAN'T SEE THEM, WE HAVE TO REMEMBER THEY'RE OUT THERE."
DO YOU REMEMBER WHAT HAPPENED THAT NIGHT, IN THE TENT? EVEN I WAS TOO AFRAID TO TRY AND FIND OUR WAY BACK TO THE HOUSE.
BUT YOU DID. YOU STOPPED CRYING AND YOU GOT US THERE. YOU REMEMBERED THE WAY.

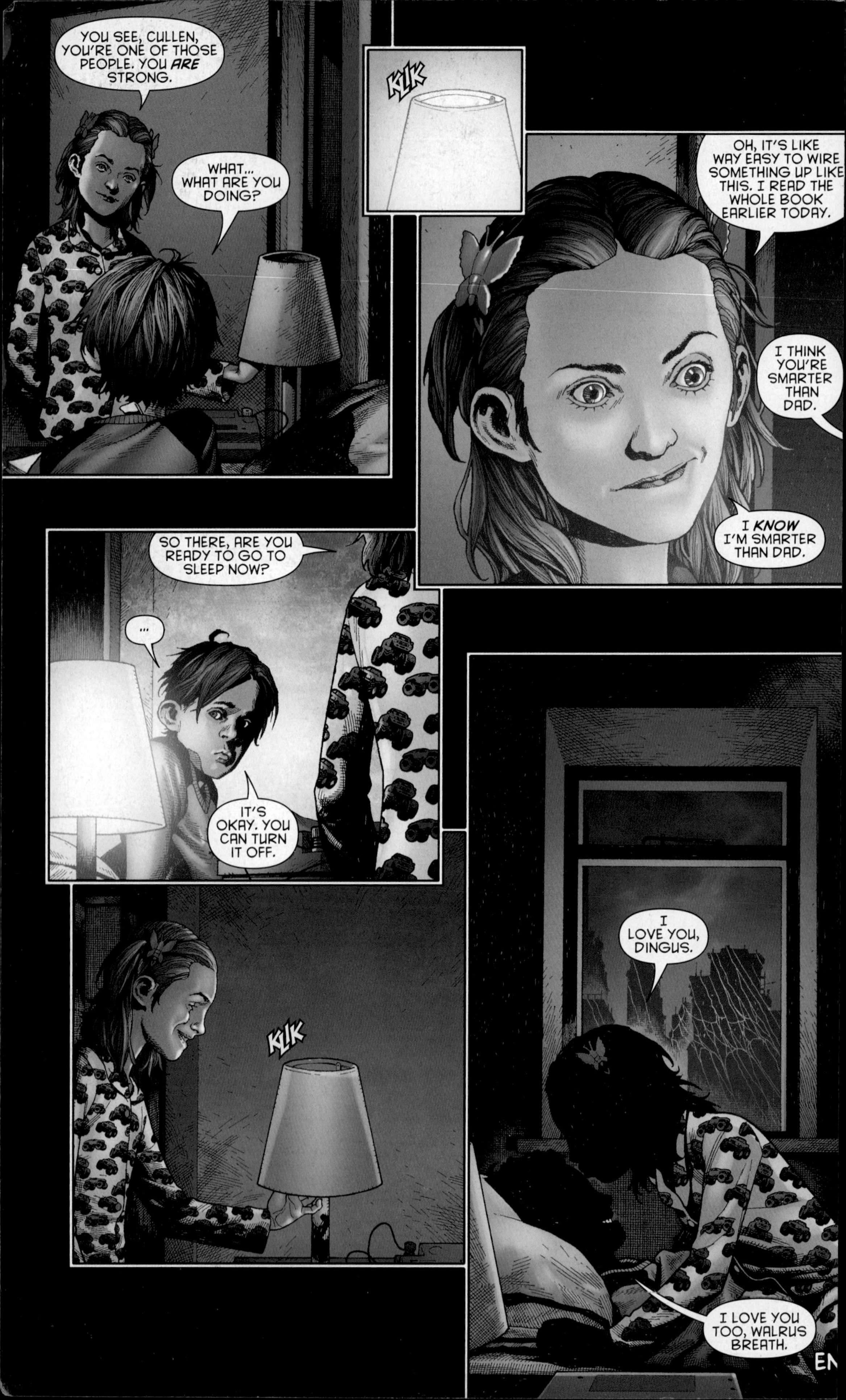
YOU SEE, CULLEN, YOU'RE ONE OF THOSE PEOPLE. YOU *ARE* STRONG.
WHAT... WHAT ARE YOU DOING?
KLIK
OH, IT'S LIKE WAY EASY TO WIRE SOMETHING UP LIKE THIS. I READ THE WHOLE BOOK EARLIER TODAY.
I THINK YOU'RE SMARTER THAN DAD.
I *KNOW* I'M SMARTER THAN DAD.
SO THERE, ARE YOU READY TO GO TO SLEEP NOW?
...
IT'S OKAY. YOU CAN TURN IT OFF.
KLIK
I LOVE YOU, DINGUS.
I LOVE YOU TOO, WALRUS BREATH.
EN

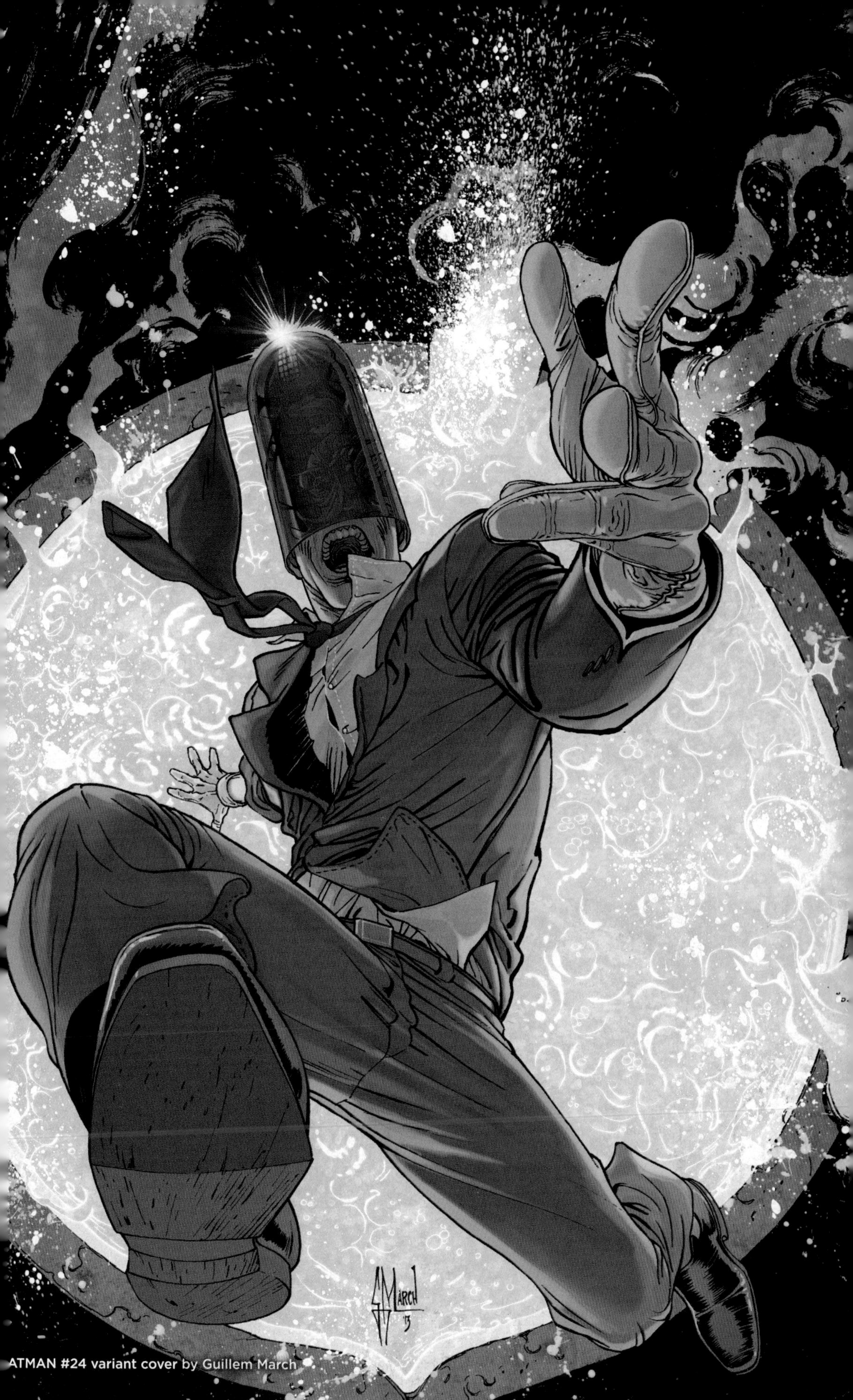

ATMAN #24 variant cover by Guillem March

BATMAN #25
variant cover
by Alex Garner

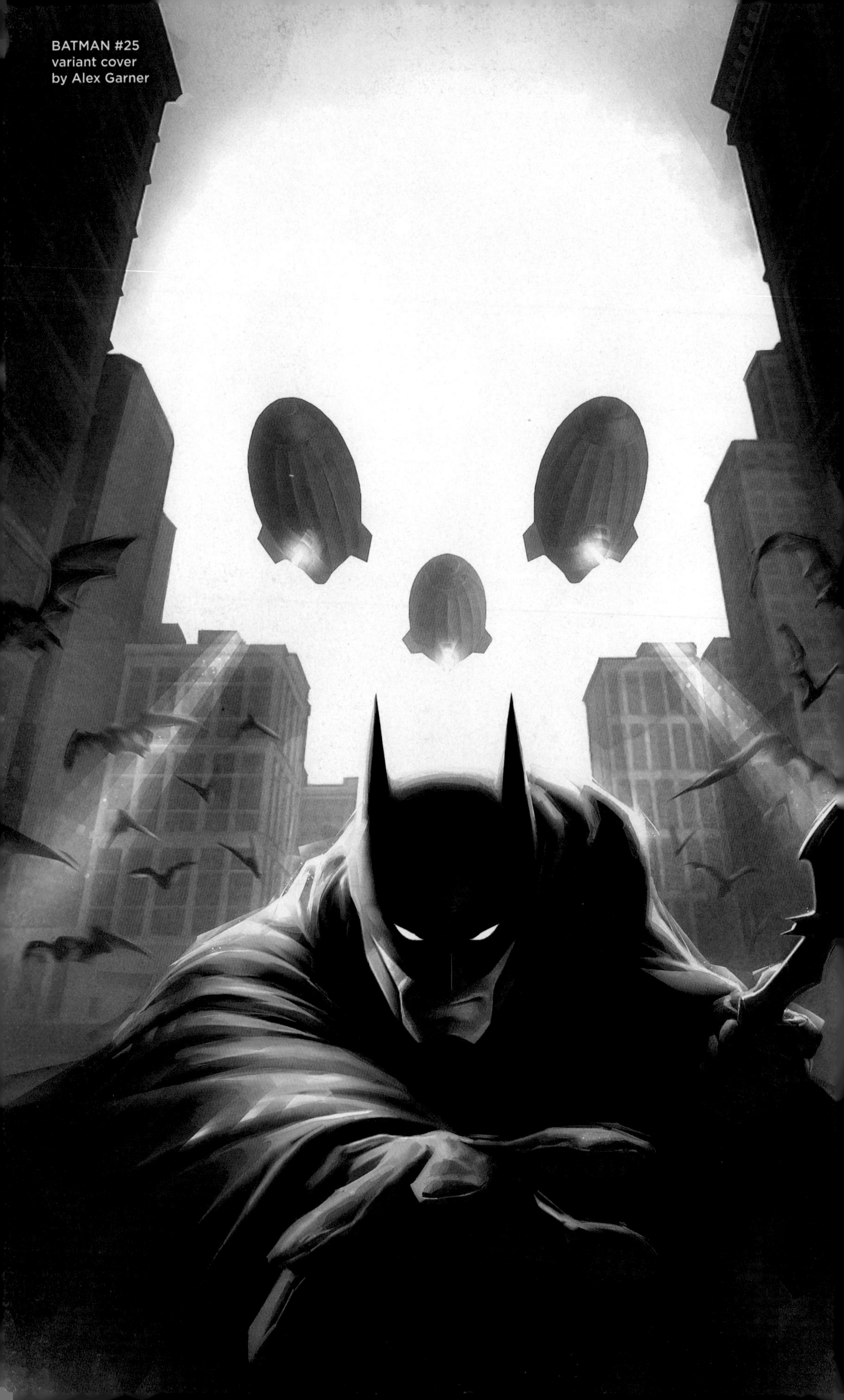

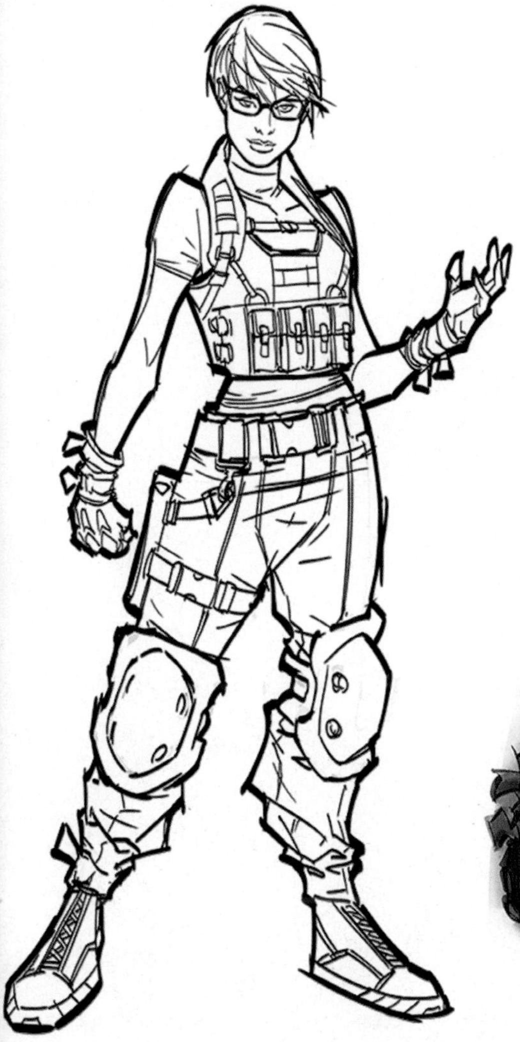

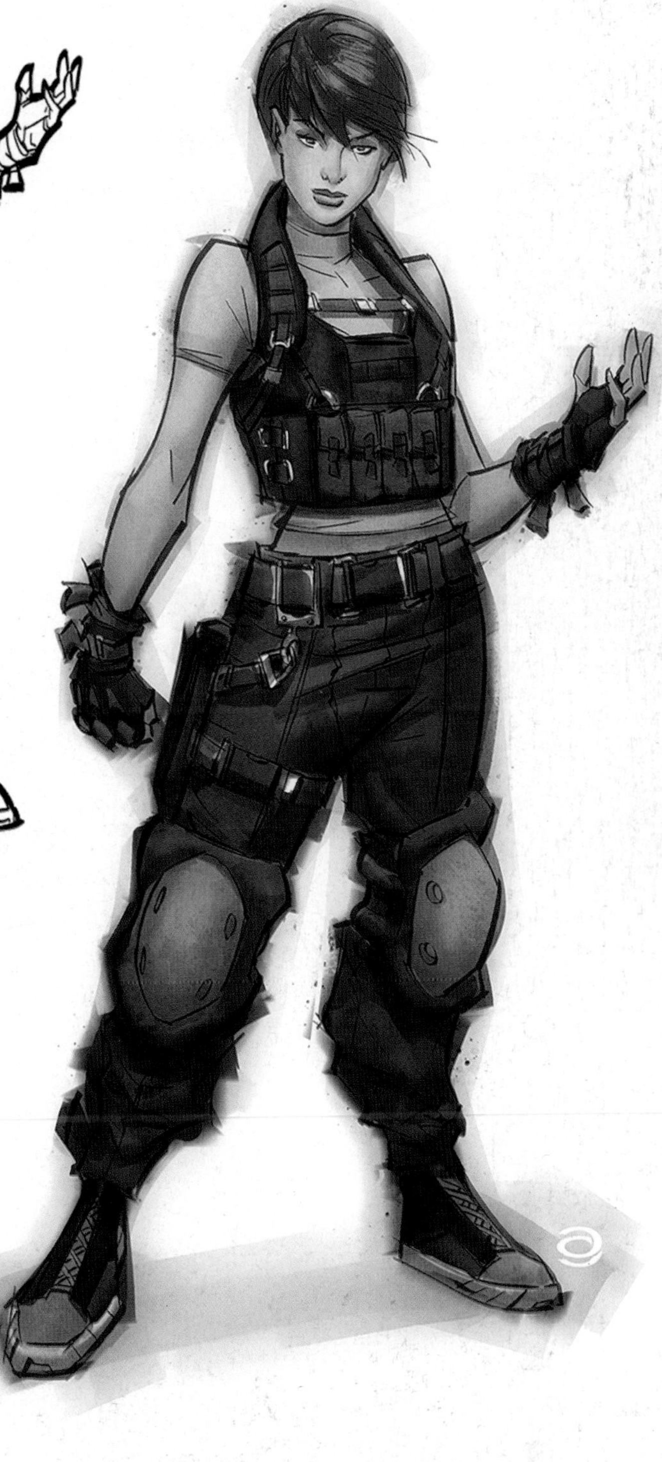

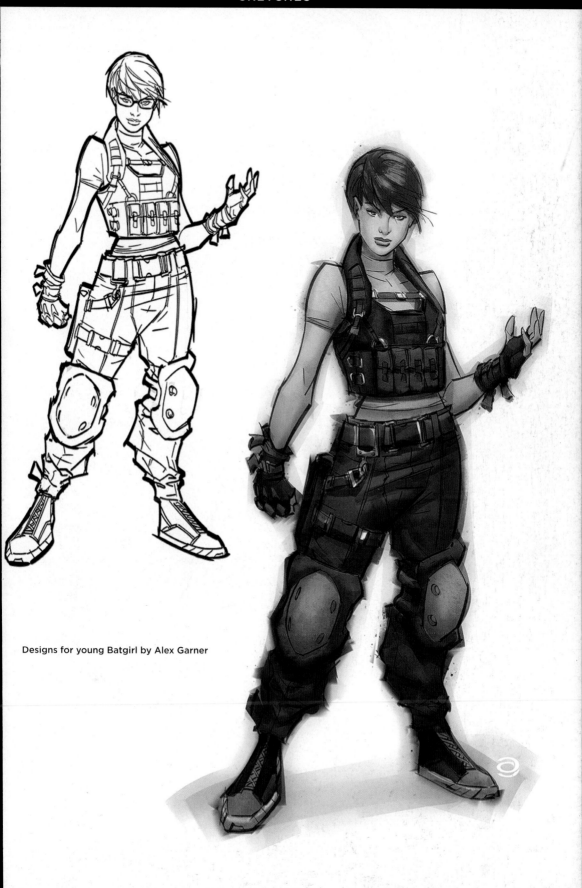

Designs for young Batgirl by Alex Garner

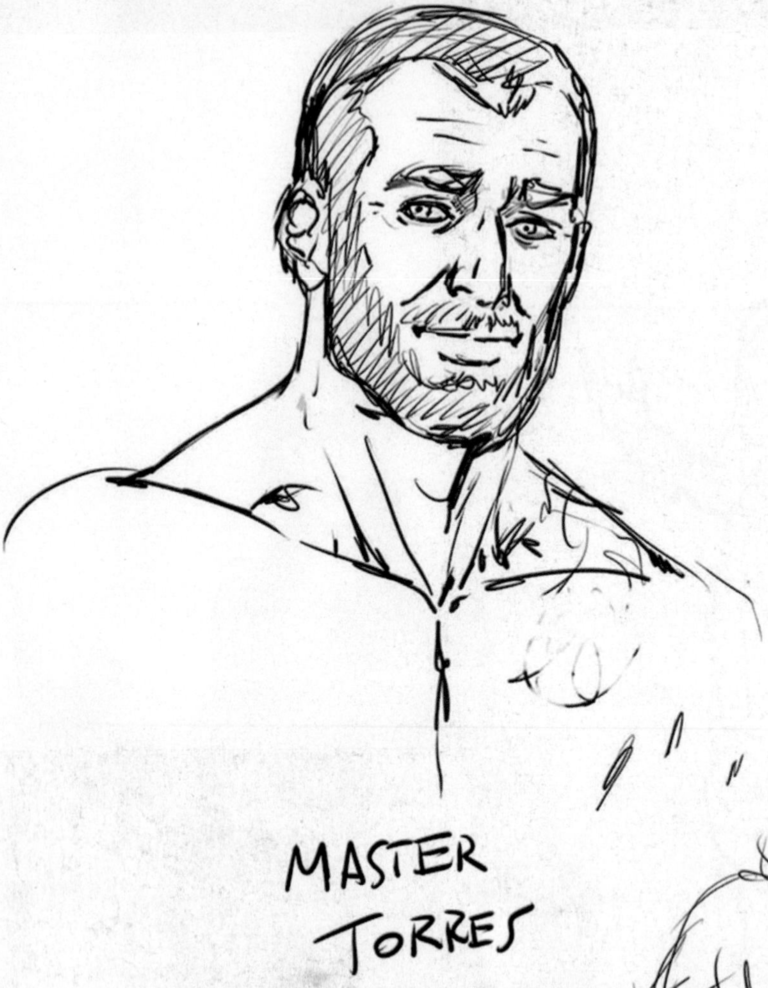
MASTER TORRES

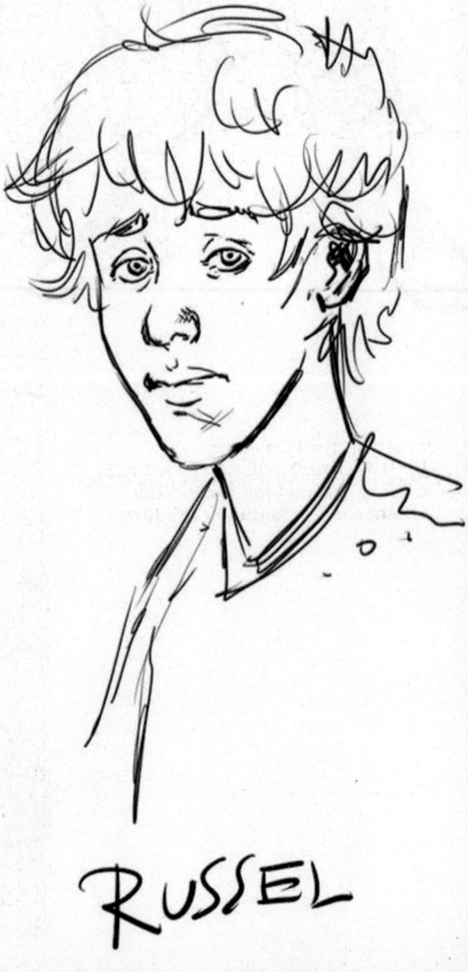
RUSSEL

Designs for Master Torres and Russell
from BATWING #25 by Eduardo Pansica

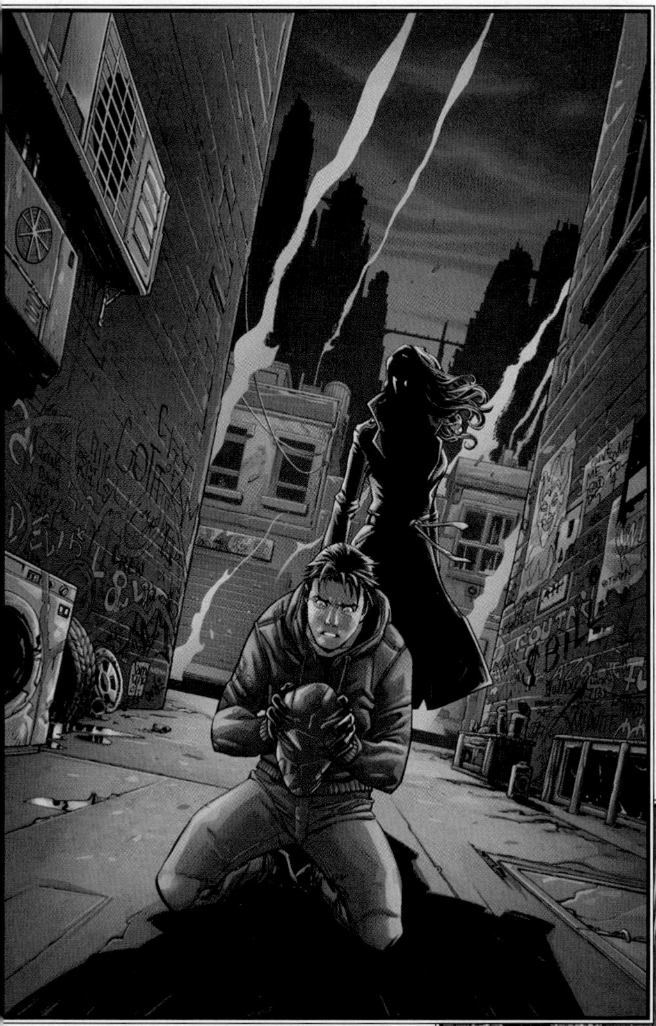

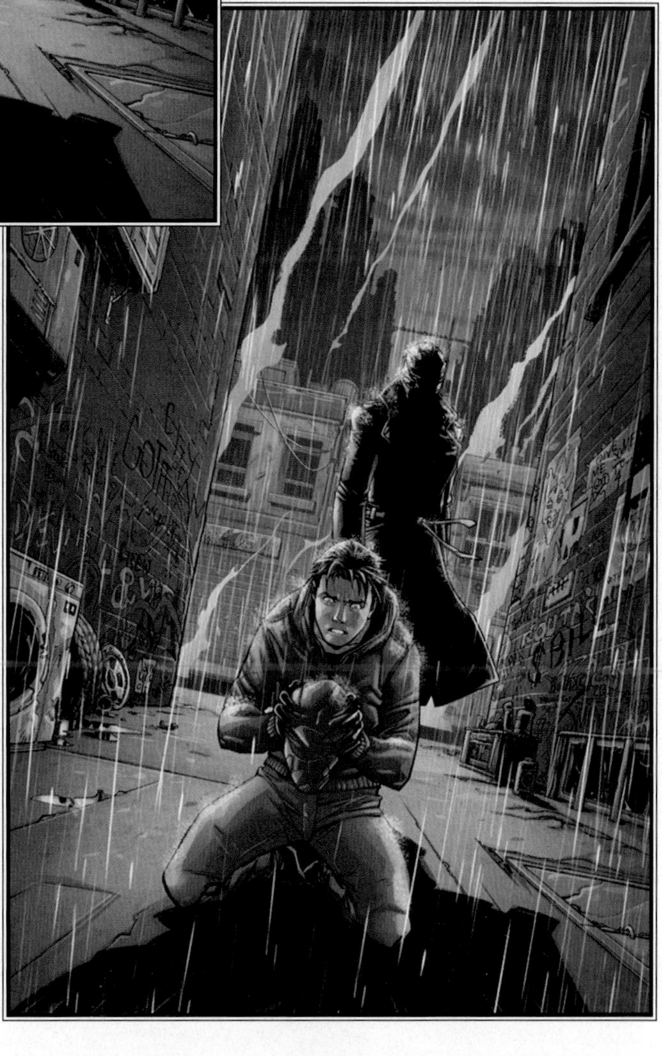

Unused original cover for
RED HOOD AND THE OUTLAWS #25,
featuring Talia al Ghul, next to the
published cover, featuring the Joker

DC COMICS™

START AT THE BEGINNING:

BATMAN VOLUME 1
THE COURT OF OWLS

**BATMAN VOL. 2:
THE CITY OF OWLS**

with SCOTT SNYDER and
GREG CAPULLO

**BATMAN VOL. 3:
DEATH OF THE FAMILY**

with SCOTT SNYDER and
GREG CAPULLO

**BATMAN: NIGHT OF
THE OWLS**

with SCOTT SNYDER and
GREG CAPULLO

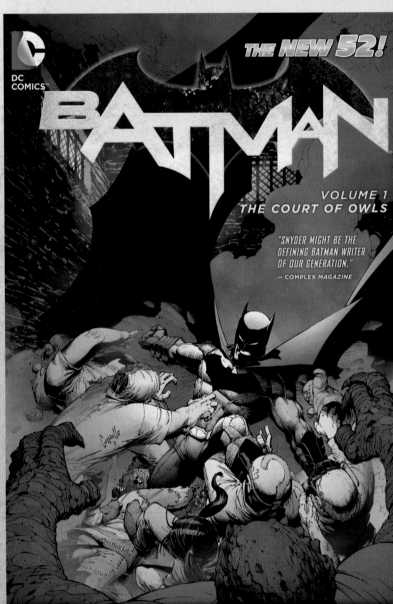

THE NEW 52!

DC COMICS™

BATMAN

VOLUME 1
THE COURT OF OWLS

"SNYDER MIGHT BE THE
DEFINING BATMAN WRITER
OF OUR GENERATION."
— COMPLEX MAGAZINE

SCOTT **SNYDER**   GREG **CAPULLO**   JONATHAN **GLAPION**

“Rock solid.”—IGN

“This is the kind of Batman story I like to read: an actual mystery with an emotional hook.”
—THE ONION/AV CLUB

START AT THE BEGINNING!

BATMAN & ROBIN
VOLUME 1: BORN TO KILL

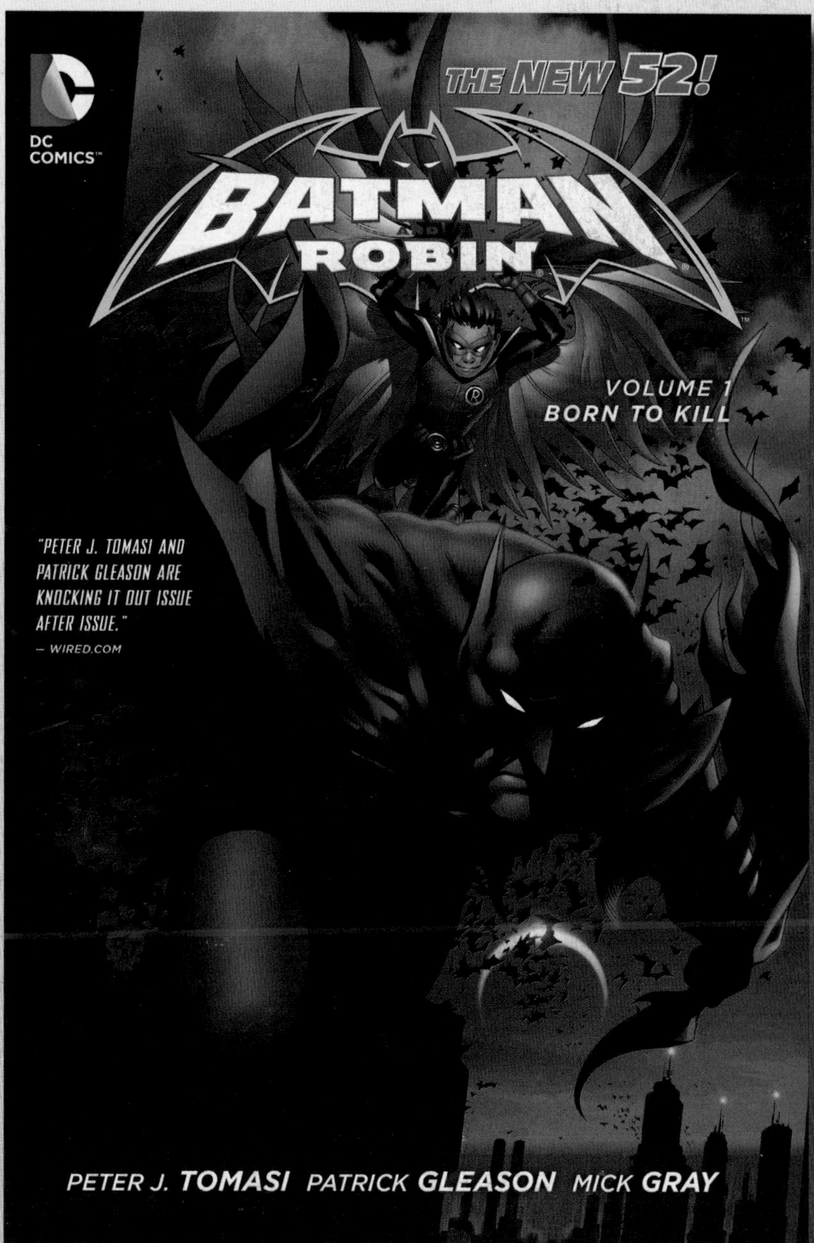
DC COMICS
THE NEW 52!
BATMAN
ROBIN
VOLUME 1
BORN TO KILL
"PETER J. TOMASI AND PATRICK GLEASON ARE KNOCKING IT OUT ISSUE AFTER ISSUE."
— WIRED.COM
PETER J. TOMASI PATRICK GLEASON MICK GRAY

BATMAN & ROBIN
VOL. 2: PEARL

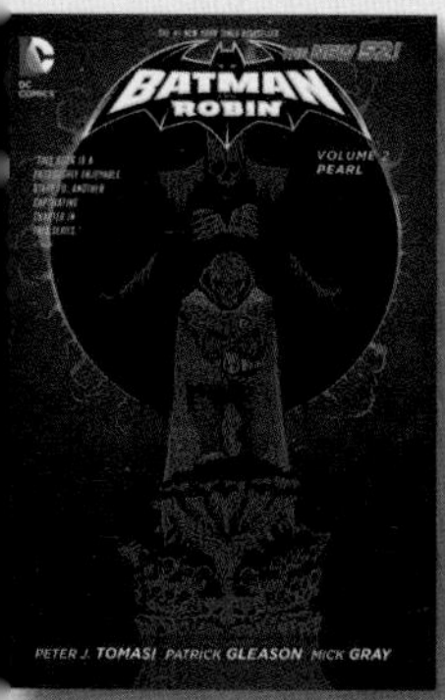
BATMAN
ROBIN
PETER J. TOMASI PATRICK GLEASON MICK GRAY

BATMAN & ROBIN
VOL. 3: DEATH OF THE FAMILY

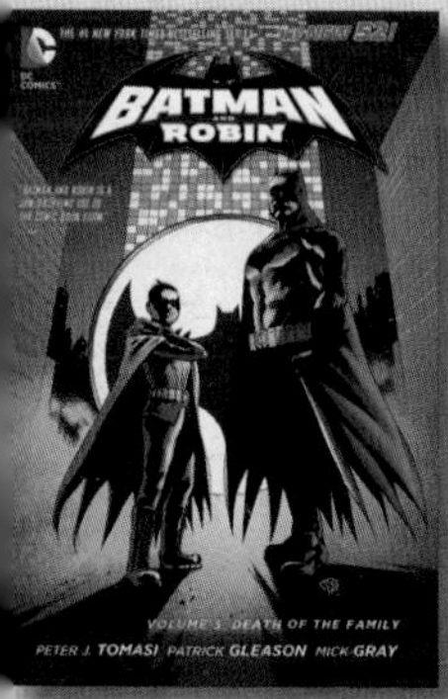
BATMAN
ROBIN
PETER J. TOMASI PATRICK GLEASON MICK GRAY

BATMAN INCORPORATED
VOL. 1: DEMON STAR

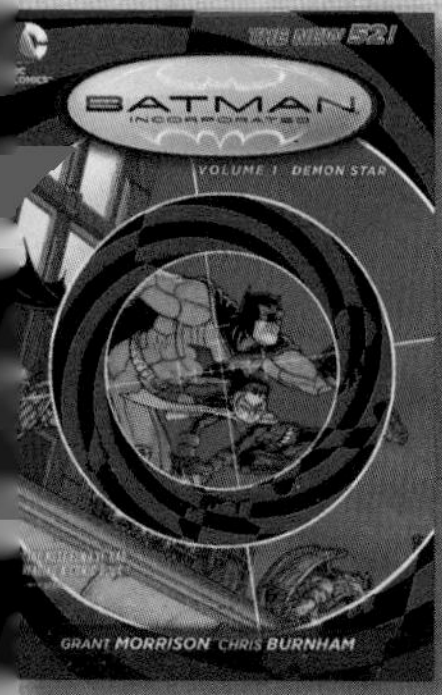
THE NEW 52!
BATMAN
VOLUME 1 DEMON STAR
GRANT MORRISON CHRIS BURNHAM

DC COMICS™

FROM THE *NEW YORK TIMES* BEST-SELLING WRITERS

ED BRUBAKER & GREG RUCKA

with MICHAEL LARK

GOTHAM CENTRAL BOOK TWO: JOKERS AND MADMEN

GOTHAM CENTRAL BOOK THREE: ON THE FREAK BEAT

GOTHAM CENTRAL BOOK FOUR: CORRIGAN

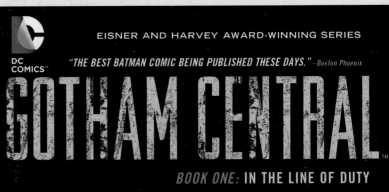

EISNER AND HARVEY AWARD-WINNING SERIES

"THE BEST BATMAN COMIC BEING PUBLISHED THESE DAYS." —*Boston Phoenix*

GOTHAM CENTRAL™

BOOK ONE: IN THE LINE OF DUTY

ED **BRUBAKER**
GREG **RUCKA**
MICHAEL LARK
INTRODUCTION BY **LAWRENCE BLOCK**